T0393476

The Palgrave Handbook of Comparative Economics

"A book full of insights on economic systems and how to transit from one to another. A good Reference Manual for academics and policy-oriented researchers, with many useful tools to understand our changing world."

—Claudia Senik, *Professor of Economics at Sorbonne University and Paris School of Economics*

"An invaluable guide to the post-communist economic transition and to the research it inspired, by a range of the leading experts from academia and policy circles."

—Daniel Treisman, *Professor of Political Science, University of California, Los Angeles*

"This volume is another proof, if you needed one, that the comparative perspective enormously enriches the social sciences. The volume thankfully brings together scholars with very different approaches allowing the reader to make up his or her own mind about their usefulness in explaining observations and helping us improve the world."

—Erik Berglof, *Professor and Director, Institute of Global Affairs, LSE School of Public Policy*

Elodie Douarin • Oleh Havrylyshyn
Editors

The Palgrave Handbook of Comparative Economics

palgrave
macmillan

Editors
Elodie Douarin
School of Slavonic and East European Studies
University College London
London, UK

Oleh Havrylyshyn
Carleton University
Ottawa, ON, Canada

ISBN 978-3-030-50887-6   ISBN 978-3-030-50888-3   (eBook)
https://doi.org/10.1007/978-3-030-50888-3

© The Editor(s) (if applicable) and The Author(s), under exclusive licence to Springer Nature Switzerland AG 2021
This work is subject to copyright. All rights are solely and exclusively licensed by the Publisher, whether the whole or part of the material is concerned, specifically the rights of translation, reprinting, reuse of illustrations, recitation, broadcasting, reproduction on microfilms or in any other physical way, and transmission or information storage and retrieval, electronic adaptation, computer software, or by similar or dissimilar methodology now known or hereafter developed.
The use of general descriptive names, registered names, trademarks, service marks, etc. in this publication does not imply, even in the absence of a specific statement, that such names are exempt from the relevant protective laws and regulations and therefore free for general use.
The publisher, the authors and the editors are safe to assume that the advice and information in this book are believed to be true and accurate at the date of publication. Neither the publisher nor the authors or the editors give a warranty, expressed or implied, with respect to the material contained herein or for any errors or omissions that may have been made. The publisher remains neutral with regard to jurisdictional claims in published maps and institutional affiliations.

Cover illustration: Brand X Pictures

This Palgrave Macmillan imprint is published by the registered company Springer Nature Switzerland AG.
The registered company address is: Gewerbestrasse 11, 6330 Cham, Switzerland

*This handbook is dedicated to Oleh Havrylyshyn,
who passed away on the 20th of September 2020,
and his wife Natalia.*

Foreword

The field of comparative economics was created primarily to understand the working of centralized planning in the Former Soviet Union (FSU). Broad questions included whether an economic system that relied on centrally set prices and material balances was sustainable, and could plausibly catch up with and even surpass the United States economy The first generation of comparative economists relied on sources that are opaque by current standards including official Soviet publications, surveys with emigres and field work in the FSU and Central and Eastern Europe (CEE) that was often secretive and even dangerous. Nevertheless, they successfully provided fundamental "stylized facts" about socialism that in fact have turned out to have very broad implications.[1] Joe Berliner's (1957) study of how managers in the FSU strategically under-preformed in order to avoid having their output quotas "ratcheted up" in future plans inspired Martin Weitzman (1980) to formally model the efficiency properties of the "ratchet" effect in socialist economies.[2] Years after the demise of the FSU, experimental, labour, organizational and personnel economists continue to study the operation and to mitigate the inefficiencies from the ratchet effect around the world. Janos Kornai's detailed studies (e.g., 1980) of how the socialist state persistently provides a large stream of subsidies and financial bailouts to inefficient state-owned companies inspired theoretical work on why it is so difficult to harden "soft budget" constraints in the FSU, CEE and China (e.g., Kornai et al. 2003; Lin and Tan 1999). And the theory of soft-budget constraints is used to understand how states interact

---

[1] For the importance of establishing stylized facts in economic research, see Smith (in Chap. 35).

[2] Gregory (in Chap. 3) discusses more broadly the insights gained from early Sovietologists and the extent to which they were later confirmed through archival work.

with politically connected firms and firms that are "too big to fail" around the world.[3]

During the 1980s and 1990s comparative economists continued to carefully document important stylized facts during the transition from a socialist to a market economy in China, CEE and the FSU. And their studies became more comparative because they could exploit sharp differences in initial conditions, institutions and reform strategies in formerly socialist economies in CEE, the FSU and Asia.[4] Some of the most important institutions emerged in China in the 1980s and include the household responsibility system, the entry of township village enterprises in the agricultural sector and the system of dual prices in urban enterprises. These institutions were responsible for China's rapid growth during a period of "reform without losers" (Lau et al. 2000)[5] and raised theoretical puzzles about incentives in a system where property rights were ill-defined. There was a sharp variation in the process of decentralization of tax and spending power in China, CEE and the FSU, which raised questions about why some local governments are supportive of market reforms and others are "grabbing hands" (Shleifer and Vishny 2002).[6] Even though there was a rapid price decontrol, privatization and opening up to world market in economies through the FSU and CEE, socialist institutions such as the soft-budget constraint and tacit political control of enterprises and financial institutions persisted, raising questions about the appropriate speed of reform and just what kinds of market institutions should be transplanted. Many of these studies have inspired a general theoretical debate about the importance of initial conditions, the appropriate sequencing and speed of reforms, the importance of establishing institutions to enforce property rights and contracts that have relevance for developing economics around the world.

In studies of socialism and the transition from socialism to markets, comparative economics has shown that fundamental market institutions such as soft budget constraints, township village enterprises, local governments that have strong control rights over enterprises under their jurisdiction, transplanted legal procedures that are unfamiliar to locals and that are easy to ignore are worthy of careful description because they can have profound

---

[3] This is also a key element of Lin's new structural economics, as discussed in Chap. 21.

[4] Similarly, chapters in Parts III and IV of the book show how our understanding of transition and economic development more broadly has greatly benefited from the availability of higher quality times series and micro-econometric data.

[5] A statement partly supported by Johnston's analysis of China's consideration for demographic issues (e.g., see Chap. 26), but which has since been nuanced by life satisfaction data as explained by Morgan and Wang in Chap. 25.

[6] A debate revisited in many different ways in Part III of the book, including studies by Åslund (Chap. 12), Guriev (Chap. 13), Campos (Chap. 14) and Douarin (Chap. 17).

effects on an economy.[7] The current comparative research agenda, as reflected in this book by many chapters on new issues and much broader development goals, builds on these findings and more generally considers the role of institutions in development. Institutions that shape markets are still carefully described whether they be in socialist or formerly socialist economies, or in economies operating centuries ago[8] (e.g., see Roland and Kung, Chaps. 6 and 7 respectively, in this volume) or, in developing economies that are not and never were socialist. The essays in this volume are at the cutting edge of the comparative economics agenda: they deal with the legacies of socialism, the transition from socialist to market economies and the fundamental importance of institutions around the world. Readers can learn about how history has shaped institutions and also understand the forces that enable these institutions to evolve and operate more effectively. This book is a must-read for scholars in all fields.

Pittsburgh, PA   Daniel Berkowitz

References

Berliner, J. S. (1957). *Factory and Manager in the Soviet Union*. Cambridge: Harvard University Press.

Kornai, J. (1980). *The Economics of Shortage*. Amsterdam: North Holland.

Kornai, J., Maskin, E., & Roland, G. (2003). Understanding the Soft Budget Constraint. *Journal of Economic Literature, 41*(4), 1095–1136.

Lau, L. J., Yingyi, Q., & Roland, G. (2000). Reform without Losers: An Interpretation of China's Dual-Track Approach to Transition. *Journal of Political Economy, 108*(1), 120–143.

Lin, J. Y., & Tan, G. (1999). Policy Burdens, Accountability, and the Soft Budget Constraint. *American Economic Review, 89*(2), 426–431.

Shleifer, A., & Vishny, R. (2002). *The Grabbing Hand: Government Pathologies and their Cures*. Cambridge: Harvard University Press.

Weitzman, M. L. (1980). The 'Ratchet Principle' and Performance Incentives. *The Bell Journal of Economics, 1*(1), 302–308.

---

[7] See, for example, the arguments presented by Guriev (Chap. 13) or Cojocaru (Chap. 27) on the importance of perception, and broken aspirations, for policy preferences, and support for further reforms. Or on a different tack, the discussion by Djankov (Chap. 10) regarding the weight of historical legacies.

[8] See Roland (Chap. 6) and Kung (Chap. 7).

Acknowledgements

A large project like a handbook cannot be the product of the work of one person alone—not even two—we thus feel we have too many people to thank to make it fit in a few paragraphs, but we will do our best…

We first need to express our extreme gratitude to all the authors who have contributed to the book. It would not exist without their efforts and patience with our editorial dunning. We felt privileged that so many of them agreed to contribute to the book. We also very much appreciated the discussions, suggestions and support: in many ways, it has been amazing to see our few-page-long proposal take shape in their hands. We have learned a lot from them, collectively and individually, and hope they will be as proud as we are of the final product. Among them all, we want to express special thanks to Sergei Guriev, Nauro Campos and Paul Wachtel, who through discussions and comments, both early and later in the process, have been particularly helpful in moving this project forward. We also want to thank everyone who attended our one-day discussion around comparative economics at SSEES in January 2020: the views expressed then, and the advice we received have had an important impact on the book too.

There are many other people who have helped the project evolve from just an idea to the book you are currently holding. Some of them may have helped unknowingly. This is a great opportunity for us to finally recognise their contributions. First, Yuemei Ji very kindly introduced us, and for that reason, she played a seminal role in this project for which we are both extremely grateful. Rachel Sangster (who was then at Palgrave) was the first to propose the idea of a handbook of comparative economics and her guidance in the early stages of the project was invaluable. Later on, the project was taken on by Wyndham Hacket Pain and Srishti Gupta, who have both provided perfect support.

Tomek Mickiewicz contributed enormously to developing Elodie's view of what comparative economics is, as a colleague and as a co-author, through countless discussions. She hopes he will recognise his influence in some aspects of the book. Slavo Radosevic and Nauro Campos both provided encouragement and support for the project overall, but also at "critical junctures": we hope you will both be pleased with the result.

It might be surprising to some, but we would like to thank our home institutions, Carleton University Centre for European Russian and Eurasia Studies, and the School of Slavonic and East European Studies (SSEES) at University College London, and in particular the Centre for the Comparative Study of Emerging Economies, as these very special places have played in important role in shaping the book. The latter in particular played a large logistical and financial role. Working in a multi-disciplinary area-study school has provided many opportunities to discuss what comparative economics, and comparative anything, means. As such, Elodie expresses special gratitude to colleagues across the disciplines, who have been willing to discuss and debate on transition, area studies, multi-disciplinarity, and beyond. Not to risk forgetting anyone, we would like to thank everyone at SSEES for helping, inspiring or contributing to the project in many different ways, with a special mention for Jan Kubik and Alena Ledeneva, whose comments and advice have been immensely useful. We also want to thank David Dalton, who has supported our work hands on, and always with great enthusiasm. SSEES also offers invaluable opportunities to hear the views from others on these issues, and the Centre for the Comparative Studies of Emerging Economies, in particular, has hosted seminars, workshops and conferences, which have greatly contributed to feed and broaden the relevant academic discussions. Many of the authors who have contributed to the book have visited SSEES to present their work on one occasion or another, starting to form the pieces that would later on click together to make this book what it is now. So, long live SSEES.

This is also a book that we have developed with our students in mind, and we hope that students beyond ours will find it useful and engaging. We are certainly looking forward to discussing it with future cohorts of students.

Finally, we cannot count how many hours have gone into this project, evening, nights, weekends. We are grateful to our spouses and families for their support and their understanding. This book really would not exist if they were not so super.

Last but not least, we are both grateful for the opportunity we have had to work together, and wanted to individually express our gratitude.

So Elodie wanted to thank Oleh: "When we both embarked on this project, we did not know each other very well and we had not worked together yet. Some would say it was a bit of a gamble, but we had a common vision from the start and working with Oleh has just been fantastic. I have learned a lot both in terms of academic knowledge and in terms of work ethic and organization. He has been patient, organized and excellent at gently keeping me on track. He has been a great role model: treating people with kindness and humility, but without compromising on the final objective. It has taken three years to transform our ideas into the book you are now holding: I would do it all over again, only on the condition that I could do it with Oleh."

While Oleh had the following to add about working with Elodie: "I need only say that the efforts and pleasures of working together have been mutual The reader should be aware how frequently I was amazed at the commonality of thinking, virtually full agreement on how to proceed. A unique experience in my career."

Contents

Notes on Contributors

Anders Åslund is a senior fellow at the Atlantic Council in Washington, D.C., and Adjunct Professor at Georgetown University. He has authored 15 books, including *Russia's Crony Capitalism: The Path from Market Economy to Kleptocracy* (2019). He has advised the Russian and Ukrainian governments and earned his D.Phil. from Oxford University.

Leszek Balcerowicz is Professor of Economics at Warsaw School of Economics. He was Chairman of the National Bank (2001—2007) and twice Deputy Prime Minister (1989—1991, 1997—2001) of Poland. He was also Minister of Finance in the first non-communist government in 1989. In 2007, he founded the Civil Development Forum think-tank.

Josef Brada Born in Czechoslovakia, Josef Brada emigrated to the United States in the early 1950s. He received his undergraduate education at Tufts University and a PhD in economics from the University of Minnesota. He has taught in the United States and abroad and served as consultant to international organizations and governments.

Randolph Luca Bruno is Associate Professor of Economics at University College London, SSEES. He is Research Fellow at IZA-Bonn and Senior Research Fellow at Fondazione Rodolfo DeBenedetti-Milan. His main research interests revolve around applied micro-econometrics, institutional/comparative economics, labour economics and innovation from both a macro and micro perspective.

Nauro F. Campos is Professor of Economics at University College London. His main research interests are political economy and European integration. He is the editor of *Comparative Economic Studies* (journal of the Association for Comparative Economic Studies) and of Cambridge University Press' series *Elements of Economics of European Integration*.

Sara Casagrande, Ph.D. is a postdoctoral research fellow in Comparative European Studies. Her research activity includes the European integration process, European institutions and institutional variety, and the economic, political and social prospects of the Eurozone. She is the author of scholarly studies and presentations at conferences.

Alexandru Cojocaru is a senior economist with the Poverty and Equity Global Practice of the World Bank. His research focuses primarily on issues related to poverty, economic inequality and subjective well-being. Alexandru holds a master's degree from Georgetown University and a PhD from the University of Maryland.

Bruno Dallago, Ph.D. is Professor of Economics at the University of Trento, Italy. He has been a visiting professor at various international universities, was President of the European Association for Comparative Economic Studies, and has been a consultant to international organizations. He is the author and editor of several scholarly books and journal articles.

Simeon Djankov is a Bulgarian economist, with a diverse career including academia, government (Deputy Prime Minister and Minister of Finance of Bulgaria) and international organizations (IMF, EBRD and World Bank).

Elodie Douarin joined the School of Slavonic and East European Studies at UCL in 2012, as a lecturer in Economics. Her main research interests relate to Institutional/Cultural Economics. She holds a PhD in Economics from Wye College (Imperial College), University of London.

Adnan Efendic is Professor of Economics at University of Sarajevo, School of Economics and Business, and affiliate fellow at CERGE-EI, Prague. He is an applied economist and his publications are mainly focused on formal and informal institutions and migration in transition and Western Balkans countries in particular.

Saul Estrin is Professor of Managerial Economics and Strategy at LSE and was formerly Adecco Professor of Business and Society at the London Business School. His research focuses on state-owned and labour-managed firms, privatization and recently on international economics issues and entrepreneurship.

Jan Fidrmuc obtained his PhD from the Center for Economic Research at Tilburg University (Netherlands) in 1999. He holds the Acceuil de talents

2020 chaire d'excellence at Lille Économie & Management (LEM), Université de Lille and is external advisor at the Institute for Strategy and Analysis at the Government Office of the Slovak Republic.

Francesca Gagliardi is a reader in Institutional Economics at the University of Hertfordshire (UK). Her research programme relies on the principles of comparative institutional analysis to study the creation and performance of SMEs, particularly cooperatives. Francesca is the treasurer of the World Interdisciplinary Network for Institutional Research.

Christopher J.Gerry joined the Oxford School of Global and Area Studies in 2017. He has held academic positions at HSE University in St Petersburg and UCL School of Slavonic and East European Studies. His research focuses on health behaviours and outcomes and public health policy in Russia and Eurasia.

Klarita Gërxhani is Professor of Economic Sociology at the European University Institute, Florence, Italy. Her interdisciplinary research combines economic-sociological theory with observational and experimental evidence. It has appeared in the *Journal of Political Economy*, *Annual Review of Sociology*, *Social Networks*, *Experimental Economics*, *Social Science Research* and the *Journal of Institutional Economics*, among others.

Paul R. Gregory is a research fellow at the Hoover Institution of Stanford University. He is Cullen Professor Emeritus, University of Houston. He has published broadly on Soviet economics, transition and economic history. His text *Soviet Economic Structure and Performance* was used for decades in courses on the subject.

Sergei Guriev joined Sciences Po as a tenured professor of Economics in 2013 after running the New Economic School in Moscow from 2004 to 2013. From 2016 to 2019, he was on leave from Sciences Po, serving as the Chief Economist of the European Bank for Reconstruction and Development.

Oleh Havrylyshyn is Adjunct Research Professor at Carleton University, and has a diverse career including in academia, in government (Deputy Minister of Finance, Ukraine), as an IMF senior official and an advisor in several countries. His numerous writings on transition are widely cited; the most recent book, *Present at the Transition* (2020), reflects personal insights on thirty years of post-communism.

Artjoms Ivlevs is Associate Professor of Economics at the Bristol Business School (UWE Bristol) and Research Fellow at the Institute of Labor Economics

(IZA, Bonn). His research interests include migration, subjective well-being, corruption and education, with a particular focus on the postsocialist economies of Central and Eastern Europe.

Lauren A. Johnston is Research Associate, China Institute, SOAS, University of London. She was previously a research fellow at University of Melbourne and a consultant with the World Bank and UNICEF. Lauren holds a PhD in International Economics (Peking), an MSc in Development Economics (SOAS) and a BA/B.Com (Melbourne). Her research focuses on China, economic demography and development.

Homi Kharas is a senior fellow in the Global Economy and Development programme at the Brookings Institution. His previous roles include executive secretary of the UN Secretary-General's High-Level Panel on the post-2015 development agenda and World Bank Chief Economist for the East Asia and Pacific region.

Carl Henrik Knutsen is Professor of Political Science at the University of Oslo. He has published extensively on different topics pertaining to the economic effects of political institutions and regimes, the determinants of regime change and survival, policy-making in autocratic regimes, and the measurement of democracy.

James Kai-Sing Kung is Sein and Isaac Souede Professor in Economic History at the University of Hong Kong. His research interests are steeped in the economic history of China, its institutions and its political economy of development. His recent papers appear in *The Quarterly Journal of Economics* and *The Economic Journal*.

Alena Ledeneva is Professor of Politics and Society at University College London. She has a PhD from Cambridge (Newnham, 1996) and is best known for her books *Russia's Economy of Favours* (1998), *How Russia Really Works* (2006) and *Can Russia Modernise?* (2013) She is a founder of *The Global Informality Project* (in-formality.com) and *Encyclopaedia of Informality*.

Justin Yifu Lin is a former World Bank Chief Economist and Dean of the Institute of New Structural Economics, Peking University. He has published more than 30 books. He has a PhD from the University of Chicago, is a corresponding fellow of the British Academy and a fellow of the Academy of Sciences for the Developing World.

Joaquim Oliveira-Martins is Deputy Director at the OECD Centre for Entrepreneurship, SMEs, Regions and Cities, and has held several senior positions at the OECD. He is also Associate Professor at the University of Paris-Dauphine and a fellow of the Academy of Social Sciences, UK (FAcSS).

John W. McArthur is a senior fellow in the Global Economy and Development programme at the Brookings Institution. He is also a senior adviser to the UN Foundation and a board governor for the International Development Research Centre. He previously managed the UN Millennium Project.

Tomasz Mickiewicz researches the role of formal and informal institutions (including social capital) as factors affecting entrepreneurship, foreign direct investment and performance. He publishes in comparative economics, regional economics, entrepreneurship and international business journals. He is one of the editors of *Entrepreneurship Theory and Practice*, covering economics of entrepreneurship.

Robson Morgan is Assistant Professor of Social Sciences, Minerva Schools at Keck Graduate Institute. He has a PhD in Economics from the University of Southern California.

Filip Novokmet is a postdoctoral researcher at the Institute for Macroeconomics and Econometrics, University of Bonn, and a researcher at the World Inequality Lab, Paris School of Economics. He obtained his PhD from the Paris School of Economics.

Slavo Radosevic is Professor of Industry and Innovation Studies at University College London. He previously worked at University of Sussex SPRU as a researcher (1993—1999) and before that as a researcher in Croatia. He was a special advisor to the EC Commissioner for Regional and Urban Policy.

Bruno T. da Rocha is a researcher at the Unit for Studies on Complexity and Economics of the Lisbon School of Economics and Management (ISEG, University of Lisbon). Previously, among other positions, he was a Robert Solow Postdoctoral Fellow at the University of Cambridge and worked as a consultant at the OECD.

Gérard Roland joined the Berkeley faculty as a professor in 2001. He received his PhD from Université libre de Bruxelles in 1988 and taught there from 1988 to 2001. He is a CEPR research fellow, where he was programme director from1995 to 2006. He serves as editor of the *Journal of Comparative Economics*.

Peter Sanfey is Deputy Director for Country Economics and Policy at the EBRD, where he has worked since 1997. He is also a senior visiting fellow at the European Institute, London School of Economics (2017—2020). He has published widely in refereed journals on transition, macroeconomics, labour economics and subjective well-being.

Ron P. Smith is Professor of Applied Economics at Birkbeck, where he has taught econometrics and statistics since 1976, after teaching at Cambridge. He has been a visiting professor at the London Business School and the University of Colorado and has published over 200 papers mainly on applied econometrics and defence economics.

Vito Tanzi received a PhD in economics from Harvard. He has been a professor of economics, Director of the Fiscal Affairs Department of the IMF, and Undersecretary for Economy and Finance in the Italian government. He has authored many books and articles on economics. The "Tanzi effect" is named after him.

Luca J. Uberti is Alexander Nash Fellow at the UCL Centre for Comparative Studies of Emerging Economies, University College London. His research, which has appeared in *Economic Systems* and *Economics of Transition* (amongst others), is on the consequences and determinants of institutional quality in developing and transition economies.

Paul Wachtel is Professor of Economics at the New York University Stern School of Business. Until recently he was the director of the Program in Business and Political Economy and editor of *Comparative Economic Studies*. He is the programme chair for the Dubrovnik Economic Conferences.

Fei Wang is Associate Professor of Economics at Renmin University of China and Research Fellow at China Institute for Employment Research, the National Academy of Development and Strategy of Renmin University of China, and the Global Labor Organization. Fei has a PhD in Economics from the University of Southern California. Fei's research areas include labour economics, population economics and subjective well-being.

Ronald Wintrobe is Professor Emeritus at Western University, Ontario, Canada. He has (co-)authored three books: *The Logic of Bureaucratic Conduct* (1982, with Albert Breton), *The Political Economy of Dictatorship* (1998) and *Rational Extremism: The Political Economy of Radicalism* (2006). His research has appeared in *The American Economic Review* and *The American Political Science Review*, among others.

Esin Yoruk is Senior Lecturer at Coventry Business School and Research Associate at CBiS–Centre for Business in Society–at Coventry University. She obtained her PhD from University of Sussex SPRU. Her research interests are technology and innovation management, and entrepreneurship from a systemic perspective.

List of Figures

List of Charts

List of Tables

1

Introduction to the Palgrave *Handbook of Comparative Economics*

Elodie Douarin and Oleh Havrylyshyn

1   What's in a Term?

With the fall of the Berlin Wall in 1989 and the expectation that soon the communist countries of Central Europe and the USSR would transition into capitalist market economies, most thought the field known as Comparative Economic Systems (CES) had lost its subject and indeed its very purpose—comparing capitalism and socialism. Such comparisons indeed became, if not obsolete altogether, far less important and interesting. Given the parallel renewal of emphasis on the critical role good-quality institutions play in determining economic performance, in a seminal article, Djankov, Laporta, Lopez-de-Silanes and Shleifer (2003) proclaimed CES was effectively dead and announced the birth of a New Comparative Economics (NCE), thus re-aligning the objective and definition of Comparative Economics (CE) with those of the "New Institutional Economics" (NIE). As Brada on the one hand, and Dallago and Casagrande on the other, in Chaps. 4 and 5 of this handbook show, not all analysts agreed CES was dead.

E. Douarin (✉)
School of Slavonic and East European Studies, University College London,
London, UK
e-mail: e.douarin@ucl.ac.uk

O. Havrylyshyn
Carleton University, Ottawa, ON, Canada
e-mail: olehhavrylyshyn@cunet.carleton.ca

© The Author(s) 2021
E. Douarin, O. Havrylyshyn (eds.), *The Palgrave Handbook of Comparative Economics*,
https://doi.org/10.1007/978-3-030-50888-3_1

1

Today, many still question just how new and different NCE is, and how much of relevance still remains from the old CES.

Explicitly recognising this origin, we propose here to explore what the broader umbrella field of *Comparative Economics (CE) is today? How can this term be defined?* Seeking an answer to this question was the central motivation behind the preparation of this handbook. To address this issue, we have compiled 36 chapters by established as well as younger scholars doing research in what they consider the field of Comparative Economics or neighbouring fields. We thus set out to depict CE through an organised presentation of a large set of views and personal take on the field today, what it is about, and how it relates to other cognate fields of enquiries. In Chap. 36, we return to the collective answer for the motivating question; it turns out to be neither straightforward nor singular, and in fact, one response might be that there is no precise definition of CE, yet another that there is no need for a definition; one might even say that the collective content of this handbook constitutes a definition of Comparative Economics today.

In this Introduction, we try to provide a "road-map" to the structure and contents of this handbook. The big picture may be summarised as follows. The book starts by discussing the evolution of the field from its origin to its new frontiers and goes on to illustrate how comparative analysis can be done even very far back in history. Then, it considers the important transition period from 1989 to the present when communist economies changed to market economies. The rest of the book then explores numerous new directions work in the field is taking: comparison of institutions; different and broader approaches to growth; new issues at the forefront of policy discussion, like inequality, populism and demographic decline; and novel methodologies for doing comparisons. The rest of the Introduction gives more details of our road-map. Section 2 elaborates on just what the old CES was, what it did, how it did this. Section 3 summarises the main lines of the evolutionary change of the old CES field into the NCE, in reaction to the end of communism and growing understanding of the importance of market-enhancing institutions. The fourth section introduces some of the more recent evolutions of the field, which can be broadly summarised as falling into one of two groups: (1) by proposing a more nuanced or sophisticated analysis of institutions than what was suggested in Djankov et al. (2003), or (2) by broadening the goals of development and the measures of success. These two perspectives are, for many, reminiscent of the ambitions of CES, but take full advantage of the new tools and terminologies developed since the early 1990s. Finally, the last section describes the structure of the book.

2 The "Old" Comparative Economics: The Origin of the Field

The fall of the Berlin Wall was a watershed moment for the field of Comparative Economics, and we made a deliberate choice to give a central place to this event in structuring the book: to explicitly recognise the origins and historical evolution of the field.

In the early 1990s, in one of the most influential textbooks in the field, Gregory and Stuart (1992, p. 14) emphasised a distinction between Comparative Economics (old-CE), which compares economic phenomena at different periods of time or across countries sharing a similar "setting", and Comparative Economic Systems (CES), which compare economic outcomes among countries with a different "setting". By "setting", they meant things like degree of private versus government ownership and market versus planning regimes. Taken literally such a view of CE (encompassing both old-CE and CES) could cover an almost boundless range of economic analysis, from a comparison of stabilisation policies of UK governments before a sterling crisis to those after, or a comparison of long-term performance in Soviet centrally planned regimes with that in market economies of Europe and North America. Perhaps because of the impossibly broad range the term opens up, in practice the field focused quite narrowly precisely on the comparison of plan versus market, of socialism versus capitalism. But such a focus was not merely a default option to help design separate university courses, textbooks and specialised journals—it had the additional appeal of being perhaps the only field which specifically addressed the central question put in the first chapters of all Introductory Economics textbooks: how does a society allocate its available labour, capital and natural resource wealth to achieve the optimal outcome.

Overall, CES did pretty much what it says on the tin: it compared economic systems in a horse race to establish their relative success measured through a number of different outcomes including but not limited to gross domestic product (GDP) growth.[1] "Economic systems" were often caricatured, especially in public discourse, to be of two diametrically opposed types: central planning versus market economy, though they were in fact defined with far more subtlety consisting of a spectrum in each of several dimensions. As explained in Gregory and Stuart (1992, p. 23 and 2004, p. 36), these dimensions included:

---

[1] However, some key practitioners insisted on a more limited "positive' rather than "normative" approach: Pryor (1985, p. 2) mostly describing "what is" and leaving it to societies to decide what they prefer.

1. "Organisation of decision-making arrangements: Structure"
2. "Mechanisms (rules) for the provision of information and for coordination: market and plan"
3. "Property rights: control and income"
4. "Mechanisms for setting goals and for inducing people to act: incentives"
5. "Procedures for making public choices: the role of government"

Presaging today's new approaches to development (as described, e.g. in Chap. 22 by Kharas and McArthur), CES indicators of success went beyond GDP growth to include macro stability, equity and broader measures of welfare, going beyond maximising aggregate income only (e.g. Koopmans and Montias 1971). For Gregory and Stuart, these "Performance Criteria" (1992, p. 33) of Comparative Economics were thus:

1. Economic growth
2. Efficiency
3. Income distribution (fairness)
4. Stability (cyclical stability, avoidance of inflation and unemployment)
5. Development objectives
6. National existence[2]

Including "development objectives" as the fifth goal, was already opening a connection to Development Economics and allowed for country-specific objectives to be added, such as reducing or eliminating poverty, changing the structure of the economy or increasing saving and investment shares. National existence reflected the need for a system to be viable, to perpetuate itself, to be sustainable.

However, in practice empirical works of the old CES rarely took into account specific measures of institutional variables, partly because the kind of indicators that exist today were not available but also because that was not the emphasis of these earlier economic studies. Outcomes were thus seen to be determined by the interplay of the type of economic system in place; environmental factors including "natural resource endowments, the level of economic development, the size of the economy, labour and capital inputs, random events, and so on"; and last but not least policies (Gregory and Stuart 1992, p. 28). "Environmental factors" are best understood as initial conditions and factor endowments. Thus institutions may have been less explicitly emphasised than they are today in the economics literature in general, but

---

[2] Performance criteria 5 and 6 however are not listed in the 2004 reincarnation of the book, its seventh edition (see Gregory and Stuart 2004, p. 46), and were replaced by: "viability of economic system".

importantly, they were not ignored in the CES framework. Indeed, Gregory and Stuart used the succinct definition of economic system provided by Assar Lindbeck (cited in Gregory and Stuart 1992, p. 16): "*An economic system is a set of mechanisms and institutions for decision making concerning production, income and consumption.*" They further cite Frederick Pryor who lists such institutions as "laws and rules, traditions, beliefs, values, behaviour patterns". In fact, Pryor's own writings (1985, pp. 405 and 14–15) follow closely today's conventional framework of separating environmental variables, policy variables and institutional variables, and the latter are clearly divided into formal and informal ones.

3 From "Old" to "New" Comparative Economics

With the nearly complete disappearance of planned economies after the fall of the Berlin Wall, Djankov et al. (2003) thus defined a "new" Comparative Economics, (NCE) explicitly assuming capitalism as the only viable economic system, with the focus now on institutions (property rights, rule of law). The objective of NCE was to identify the characteristics of the less-well-performing economies focusing on the shortcomings in their institutional set-up, and how this set-up impeded development. The central indicator of performance and the core focus of NCE (in early years at least) reverted to being economic growth or income per capita, and placing efficiency at the centre of the search for the optimal institutional arrangement. The political regime (democracy versus authoritarian regimes) was now also given a prominent place among the likely explanatory factors.

This new direction presented a key advantage: it aligned the objectives of Comparative Economics with those of the New Institutional Economics and provided a logical framework. However, this had two shortcomings. First, as contended by Brada (2009), this constituted an excessive narrowing down of the field, since growth and efficiency seemed to be the only criteria against which to judge the success of a given system. This reflected a more general move within economics at the time (Stewart 2009), whereby efficiency was seen as a key indicator, with growth and prosperity expected to trickle down to benefit all in society. The second shortcoming was that as some specific institutions were being dissected, others were being neglected (as we will discuss in the next section: both of these limits have progressively been corrected). The chapters in Part IV of this handbook illustrate the kind of research engendered by the new orientation of NCE.

4   Further Evolutions: More Institutions, More Outcomes

Addressing the shortcoming mentioned above, the frontier in comparative economics today is to explore further what comparing different contexts can bring in terms of:

1. Gaining a clearer sense and more detailed understanding of the role of institutions, with work being carried out towards investigating the impact of new types of institutions (e.g. culture or informal institutions), their complementarities (among formal institutions, or between formal and informal institutions), their persistence and change (legacies, windows of opportunity and critical junctures).
2. Broadening the set of indicators of success for an economic system to include inequality and redistribution, and measures of well-being going beyond material wealth to include education, health or life satisfaction.

First, this broadening of both the conceptualisation of the relevant institutional set-up to be investigated and the diversity of possible measures of success was to some extent already advocated by Hall and Soskice (2001). In their book on the "varieties of capitalism", they proposed a framework to investigate the comparative advantage of nations based on a typology of institutional arrangements, thus recognising that market economies (or capitalism) could differ significantly. Their emphasis on the "varieties of capitalism" was embedded in the political economy tradition and thus included not only political as well as economic arrangements, but also formal as well as informal institutions.

Second, and in line with a progressive evolution in the way "development" is conceived, researchers also slowly moved away from a focus on economic growth and individual incomes, towards a larger set of outcomes and social goals. Parts V and VI of this handbook provide examples of these developments.

Perhaps surprisingly, this shift in direction can be seen as a return to the "performance criteria" of the old CES. Indeed, in the old CES, equity and redistribution were seen as important performance criteria, something that has been increasingly recognised and strongly argued, for example, in the more general context of development economics by Ravallion (2001). Old-CES also recognised that development objectives could differ depending on local priorities and efforts to create a more sustainable economy, something that today is reflected in the perception of poverty and development as multi-dimensional concepts. The development of measures such as the Human

Development Index (HDI) at the macro level, or the Multidimensional Poverty Index (MPI) at the micro level, has crystallised the importance of human development, beyond pure economic outcomes, while in more recent years, the sustainable development goals (SDGs) propose multiple development objectives including health, education, human rights and environmental sustainability among other things.

5 Structure of the Book

Reflecting this evolution, this book aims to offer a comprehensive representation of what the field is today, including the newest form of comparative economic system. The book starts with a detailed presentation of how the field of "Comparative Economic Systems" has evolved partly due to the onset of transition—different chapters discussing the conceptual relations between different interpretations of comparative economics, or different evolutionary stages. Thus, Joseph Brada reflects in Chap. 2 on the evolution from CES to NCE, highlighting in particular what might have been lost in the process. Paul Gregory, in Chap. 3, draws the key lessons of CES and, in particular, what was learned from the opening of the Soviet archives after the fall of communism. Based on his practical experience as a key policy maker, Leszek Balcerowicz, in Chap. 4, discusses the importance of understanding the interplay of systems and institutions. Finally, Bruno Dallago and Sara Casagrande retrospectively provide a detailed reasoned critique of NCE, arguing it should continue to coexist with CES to enrich the debates underlying comparative economic studies. This section will set the scene for the broad academic debate around terminology and delineation of the different sub-fields relevant to comparative economics. We will return to some of the points raised in our Chap. 36, after a rigorous exploration of many interpretations of what comparative economics is today through the applied chapters of Parts II, III, IV, V and VI.

Part I: Evolution of the Field of Comparative Economic Systems

Chapter 2: A Historiography of Comparative Economics—Joseph Brada, Arizona State University
Chapter 3: The Soviet Economic System: An Archival Re-evaluation—Paul R. Gregory, Stanford University
Chapter 4: Institutions, Institutional Systems and Their Dynamics—Leszek Balcerowicz, Warsaw School of Economics
Chapter 5: The "New Comparative Economics": A Critical Review—Bruno Dallago and Sara Casagrande, University of Trento

Part II illustrates how the lessons from both CES and NIE are now used when economic historians assess past performance or investigate how past forces affect current outcomes. Thus, Gerard Roland in Chap. 6 and James Kung in Chap. 7 reinterpret the viability of past civilisations based on their institutional arrangements. Then, assessing economic performance in the past with the theoretical tools of today, Oleh Havrylyshyn in Chap. 8 applies concepts of NIE to show how good institutions explain the strong economic performance of Medieval Ragusa (Dubrovnik), while Filip Novokmet in Chap. 9 traces the century-long trends of income distribution, before during and after communism. Simeon Djankov in Chap. 10 demonstrates how economists can use historical developments to explain contemporary outcomes, in his case the achievements of economic liberalisation and democratisation of post-communist economies.

Part II: Comparative Economic Systems in Economic History

Chapter 6: Comparative Economic History—Gérard Roland, University of California, Berkeley
Chapter 7: The World's First Meritocracy Through the Lens of Institutions and Cultural Persistence—James Kai-sing Kung, University of Hong Kong
Chapter 8: Institutions Matter: But so Does History—A Comparison of Mediaeval Dubrovnik with Other Dalmatian Cities—Oleh Havrylyshyn, Carleton University
Chapter 9: Long-Run Inequality in Communist Countries: Before, During, and After—Filip Novokmet, University of Bonn
Chapter 10: Effect of Historical Forces on Liberalisation and Democratisation in Transition—Simeon Djankov, Peterson Institute for International Economics

---

Part III focuses on comparative studies of "transition" in post-communist Europe and the former Soviet Union, drawing on CES legacies and the embryonic lessons of the NCE on how to implement more efficient institutional arrangements. This was indeed a key catalytic period in the evolution of comparative economics, and in a sense, Part III comprises a focal point in the book, allowing the reader both to relate the experience of transition overall and to highlight the key lessons from that period for the field more generally. Chapter 11 by Oleh Havrylyshyn sets the stage by simply presenting the main statistical facts of the evolution over 30 years for the Soviet region, including measures of economic and social performance, distribution, institutional development and democratisation. The next two chapters complement each other: with Anders Åslund focusing narrowly on the importance of reform commitment by the leadership of a country, and Sergei Guriev giving a broader picture of how different political economy forces played out in different countries, impacting the reform process and key outcomes such as the rise of an oligarchy, corruption and popular attitudes towards reforms. Chapter 14 by Nauro Campos and Chap. 15 by Vito Tanzi pair up to give an insight into the role of international institutions such as the European Union (EU) and International Financial Institutions (IFIs), respectively. Paul Wachtel's Chap. 16 undertakes detailed comparative measurements of common variables to suggest that transition is virtually over as post-communist countries are no longer distinguishable from developing countries at a similar stage of development. Finally, Elodie Douarin in Chap. 17 ties in transition to the NIE, investigating in depth how the process of transition involved improvement of market-enhancing institutions, and how differing values and cultural traits resulted in different pace of implementation.

Part III: Post-Communist Transition

Chapter 11: Thirty Years of Transition: Eleven Stylized Facts—Oleh Havrylyshyn, Carleton University.
Chapter 12: The Importance of Domestic Commitment—Anders Åslund, Atlantic Council
Chapter 13: Political Economy of Transition Reforms—Sergei Guriev, Sciences Po Paris
Chapter 14: The EU Anchor Thesis: Transition from Socialism, Institutional Vacuum and Membership in the European Union—Nauro F. Campos, School of Slavonic and East European Studies, University College London
Chapter 15: Some Reflections on Transition: Its Roots, Complexity of the Process, and Role of IMF and Other Organisations—Vito Tanzi
Chapter 16: Are the Transition Economies Still in Transition?—Paul Wachtel, New York University
Chapter 17: Institutional Change in Transition: An Evolving Research Agenda—Elodie Douarin, SSEES UCL

Then, the fourth section of the book will focus on studies that reflect the emergence of NCE and a globalisation of the research agenda of comparative economics, but focusing on formal institutions and growth, reflecting the early conception of the field as spelt out in Djankov et al. (2003). In other words, Part IV groups together chapters looking beyond the transition region to bring broader lessons for development, but focusing on the central objective of growth and recognising the importance of policies but also institutions to achieve this objective. In Chap. 18, Luca Uberti and Carl Knutsen provide a detailed review of the literature on human capital and institution as primary drivers of growth. They then present new evidence, thanks to the use of a novel indicator of institutional quality. Chapter 19 brings policies back at the centre of the growth debate, as Joaquim Oliveira Martins and Bruno da Rocha argue for a more careful analysis of potential interactions between different policy areas. A detailed conceptual framework and their extensive review of the empirical literature support the notion that policies can be complementary and reforms thus sometimes need to progress on several fronts simultaneously to bear fruits. Jan Fidrmuc then questions the importance of economic and political liberalisation for growth in the post-communist world, including China and other Asian emerging economies. He concludes on the importance of democratic accumulation. Finally, Justin Yifu Lin presents in Chap. 21 the "New Structural Economics" perspective, an approach to promoting growth recognising the importance of initial conditions and proposing a framework for incremental change towards building an advanced and competitive market economy.

As already intended in Part I however, the narrowing of the scope of research into growth and institutions brought in by NCE was quickly contested and at the same time that the Washington consensus was coming into greater scrutiny, so too the comparative economic agenda was expanding to reflect some of the frustrations that were emerging. Notably, the goals of development had to be broadened, to accommodate concerns over health and life expectancy, for example, or increasing concerns over the lack of correlation between growth and perceived quality of life. Part V, thus, groups together chapters looking into broader goals of development. Chapter 22 explicitly tackles the need to broaden the goals of development, as Homi Kharas and John McArthur detail the frustration engendered by a narrow focus on efficiency and propose a new approach, while recognising the challenges it represents. Chris Gerry in Chap. 23 focuses our attention on health outcomes and their evolution in post-communist Europe in the past 30 years, detailing many of the possible factors that might explain this evolution, from economic, political to social and cultural factors. This chapter thus illustrates the impossibility to relate well-being and health to economic growth only. In Chap. 24, Peter

Sanfey discusses the happiness gap in transition and more generally the factors that are important in building a "good life", thus further demonstrating that well-being is built from many aspects of one's life, and concluding on the need to focus on a more sustainable agenda (in line with Chap. 22). The overall disconnect between growth and happiness also underlies Robson Morgan and Fei Wang's Chap. 25, as they investigate why economic growth in China has not led to a proportionate increase in life satisfaction, neither in urban, nor rural areas. Finally, Lauren Johnston argues, in Chap. 26, for an explicit consideration of demographic change in development policies, building from the experience of China and discussing lessons for other emerging or transition economies.

Part V: The "New" New Comparative Economics: Broadening the Goals

Chapter 22: Rethinking Development: Broadening the Goals and Altering the Approach—Homi Kharas and John W. McArthur, Brookings Institute
Chapter 23: Explaining the Heterogeneity of Health Outcomes in Post-Communist Europe—Christopher J. Gerry, University of Oxford
Chapter 24: Building the Good Life: Growth, Reforms and Happiness in Transition—Peter Sanfey, EBRD
Chapter 25: Growth and Subjective Well-Being in China—Robson Morgan, Keck Graduate Institute and Fei Wang, Renmin University of China
Chapter 26: Understanding Demographic Challenges of Transition Through the China Lens—Lauren A. Johnston, China Institute, SOAS

Moving beyond this broadening of the goals also led many to enquire into the "forgotten" drivers of institutional change in NCE, notably the "context", social norms and informal institutions that were implicitly important in CES but entirely missing from the early formulation of NIE and NCE. Thus Part VI starts by discussing some aspects of the political economy of reforms in Chap. 27, as Alexandru Cojocaru discusses the importance of inequality, real or perceived, in outcomes or opportunities, and their impact on policy preferences. In Chap. 28, Tomasz Mickiewicz analyses the rise of populism in Eastern Europe discussing some of the tools used to build broad-based support and highlighting key distinctive features of populism in this region compared to experience elsewhere in the world. Chapter 29 focuses on the diffusions of ideas and their impact on institutional change, as Tom Ivlevs reviews the empirical literature on "social remittances" or how migrants abroad can impact on institutional change back home by sending home new ideas and values. Chapters 30 and 31 introduce informal institutions and institutional trust. In Chap. 30, Klarita Gërxhani and Ron Wintrobe develop a theoretical model explaining the co-evolution of formal institutional quality and individual or societal tax evasion. Their model relies on the notion of "trust-based" political exchange, and emphasises the importance of social norms to explain behaviour. In a related effort, Alena Ledeneva and Adnan Efendic propose a detailed and critical literature review focusing on the ways the interplay between formal and informal institutions has been investigated so far. They argue for a new approach recognising the complexity of the relationship between formal and informal institutions, and test it empirically to explain the reliance on networks and trusted people in South East Europe. Finally, Chap. 32 presents entrepreneurship as a systemic product rather than the product of individual actions. Slavo Radosevic and Esin Yoruk present first a critical review of the entrepreneurship literature through an institutionalist lens, and more specifically building on insights from the Variety of Capitalism literature. They present three different concepts of entrepreneurship compatible with this perspective and discuss their advantages and drawbacks before discussing some empirical results illustrating an implementation of their preferred approach.

Our last section discusses some methodological aspects. Randolph Bruno and Saul Estrin, in Chap. 33, advocate a greater recognition of the potential benefits of investigating institutional systems, in their full diversity and through a potential clustering of associated institutions, based on their complementarities and relative advantages for achieving specific outcomes. In doing so, they argue for more empirical work to be conducted building on the logic of the Variety of Capitalism literature, and for more efforts to devise meaningful typologies of institutions to characterise specific institutional systems. Finally, they propose an empirical test focusing on the productivity of firms in understudied economies. In Chap. 34, Francesca Gagliardi presents a detailed review of the literature on institutional complementarities based on an extensive bibliometric review. In doing so, she both illustrates the evolution of her field of interest (in terms of research questions, disciplinary-expertise of authors, or journals in which they are published) and discusses some of the reasons behind this evolution. Her work emphasises the multi-disciplinary relevance of the comparative analysis of institutions, and the complementary skills and interests of researchers from different fields. Finally, Ron Smith in Chap. 35 presents a "tour de force", as he critically discusses approaches to establishing causality in econometrics, going through the logical steps any empirical analysis should take (from discussing the data needs and availability, establishing key stylised facts, demonstrating associations and finally establishing causality). His presentation discusses explicitly both micro- and macro-approaches and concludes on the need to learn from all steps of the analysis, recognising what can be learned from stylised facts and associations, as well as causal inference, to keep a richer and open interdisciplinary dialogue.

Part VII: Methodologies for Comparative Analysis

Chapter 33: Taxonomies and Typologies: Starting to Reframe Economic Systems—Randolph Luca Bruno, SSEES, UCL and Saul Estrin, London School of Economics
Chapter 34: Institutional Complementarities in Comparative Capitalism: A Bibliometric Account—Francesca Gagliardi, Hertfordshire Business School
Chapter 35: The Challenge of Identification and the Value of Descriptive Evidence—Ron P. Smith, Birkbeck Univesity

6   Some More Guidance on How to Read This Handbook

Here are some additional clues on how to use this handbook. The handbook was designed so that each chapter could be read independently—there is no need to read all chapters, or read them in the order they are presented, to understand the points being made by each chapter individually. However, the book as a whole makes a contribution of its own, by bringing these chapters together to tell a coherent story. That story is not only a story of change and evolution, but also a story of return to one's origins, of cross-disciplinary stimulation and, in places, of potentially contradictory assessments. If all questions were settled, we would probably not need a handbook of comparative economics!

If the detailed presentation of the book's outline above has not yet clarified to you which chapter you should read next, there are many ways to read it thematically, going beyond the structure we have chosen to give it. For example, if you are interested more specifically in how comparative economics relates to development economics, you might find some clues in Chaps. 2 and 17 (as they present some aspects of the evolution of CE, recognising some convergence towards development economics), Chap. 6 (as it presents an approach to studying economic development in antiquity relying on the notion of economic systems), Chap. 16 (as it explicitly discusses the distinction between transition economics and development economics and presents a detailed analysis of the dimensions in which an emerging economy can be investigated), Chaps. 21 and 26 (as they present specific approaches to development—Chap. 21 argues for the new structuralist approach to development, which pays closer attention to initial conditions and country-specific constraints, while Chap. 26 discusses the interplay between demographic change and economic development and draws some lessons from the Chinese experience) and finally Chap. 22 (a chapter entirely dedicated to detailing a new approach to development economics, recognising a diversity of outcomes of success and a departure from economic growth only, in a way reminiscent of old-CES).

For further suggestions, do make use of the index at the end of the volume, to identify which chapters to read if you are interested in economic growth more narrowly, or informal institutions or variety of capitalism. Health, demography, subjective well-being, productivity, property rights are other examples of key words to look for. Be guided by your curiosity!

References

Brada, J. (2009). The New Comparative Economics Versus the Old: Less Is More but Is It Enough? *The European Journal of Comparative Economics, 6*(1), 3–15.

Djankov, S., Laporta, R., Lopez-de-Silanes, F., & Shleifer, A. (2003). The New Comparative Economics. *Journal of Comparative Economics, 31*(4), 595–619.

Gregory, P., & Stuart, R. (1992). *Comparative Economic Systems* (4th ed.). Houghton Mifflin Company.

Gregory, P., & Stuart, R. (2004). *Comparing Economic Systems in the Twenty-First Century* (7th ed.). South-Western Cengage Learning.

Hall, P. A., & Soskice, D. (2001). *Varieties of Capitalism: The Institutional Foundations of Comparative Advantage*. Oxford University Press.

Koopmans, T. C., & Montias, J. M. (1971). On the Description and Comparison of Economic Systems. In A. Eckstein (Ed.), *Comparison of Economic Systems: Theoretical and Methodological Approaches* (pp. 27–78). Berkeley: University of California Press.

Pryor, F. (1985). *A Guidebook to the Comparative Study of Economic Systems.* Englewood Cliffs, NJ: Prentice-Hall Inc.

Ravallion, M. (2001). Growth, Inequality and Poverty: Looking Beyond Averages. *World Development, 29*(11), 1803–1815.

Stewart, F. (2009). Relaxing the Shackles: The Invisible Pendulum. *Journal of International Development, 21*, 765–771.

Part I

Evolution of the Field of Comparative Economics Systems

2

A Historiography of Comparative Economics

Josef Brada

1 Introduction

The central question of comparative economics is what makes for a good economic system. This age-old question has been studied by philosophers, religious authorities, and, when economics as a social science evolved, economists. In Sects. 2 and 3, I review some of the early writings on economic systems. These writings pose the central questions of comparative economics: what the goal of the economic system should be and what should be the criteria by which systems are judged. While these early writings stressed non-economic goals, the development of economic thinking about systems, described in Sect. 4, sets out a new line of thinking about systems, namely that peoples' wants were unlimited and that self-interested competitive behavior could lead to a system that maximized economic welfare without causing social strife. This notion was formalized by economists into the idea that a market economy would produce the most efficient allocation of resources, thus maximizing material welfare, as I describe in Sect. 5.

J. Brada (✉)
Arizona State University, Tempe, AZ, USA

CERGE-Economic Institute of the Czech Academy of Sciences,
Prague, Czech Republic
e-mail: josef.brada@asu.edu

© The Author(s) 2021
E. Douarin, O. Havrylyshyn (eds.), *The Palgrave Handbook of Comparative Economics*,
https://doi.org/10.1007/978-3-030-50888-3_2

Sections 6, 7, and 8 cover what is arguably the most striking example of the comparison of economic system, that of the capitalist market economy and the communist centrally planned economy that existed in the Soviet Union, China, and Eastern Europe. I describe how comparativists learned about the functioning of the planned economies, how they developed a "language" for describing the components of an economic system, and, finally, how the collapse of the planned economies shifted attention from market efficiency in allocating resources to the role of institutions in fostering high and ever-increasing living standards. These issues are described in Sects. 9 and 10, the section focusing on the intellectual challenges and opportunities raised by this new interest in institutions as an engine for economic progress. Section 11 concludes.

There has been considerable progress in defining what we mean by an economic system. It is a set of economic agents who interact through flows of information, through incentives, and through the production and exchanges of goods and services. These interactions are mediated by institutions, by policies and laws, as well as by custom and other aspects of the social system more broadly considered. Progress in comparing economic systems, which has received more attention from scholars over the centuries, has, on the other hand, reached something of an intellectual *cul de sac*, largely due to the inability to develop value-free ways of evaluating the performance of different economic systems.

2   Early Economic Comparisons

The study of economic systems dates to antiquity, or at least to that period of antiquity when options about the design of social and economic relations became feasible. While I do not, in this chapter, intend to analyze the extensive anthropological and historical literature on past civilizations, an eclectic survey of ancient thinking about economic systems is useful because, even in these earliest writings, penned by individuals who had no formal economic framework with which to tackle the comparison of economic systems, some of the key issues regarding the purpose and methodology of comparative economics were already evident.

A useful start is Plato's *Republic* (1950), an early attempt to envision an ideal state and an ideal economic system. Plato acknowledged the role that material and moral incentives play in economic life and noted the benefits of the division of labor. In his context, however, the division of labor aimed more to allow citizens to align their innate natures, that is, what Plato called the character of their souls, with their roles in society. Thus, some individuals would become the guardians of the state or "philosopher kings", others soldiers, artisans, farmers, and so on. Moreover, the objective of this ideal state was not to maximize output but rather to create a society and economy that would enable its citizens to achieve justice and social virtue.

In this brief description of *The Republic* lie two of the central issues of comparative economics. The first is that, as the reader may have noticed, there is nothing explicitly comparative about Plato's ideas, no other economic system to which he seems to compare his ideal state. However, comparative economics need not make an explicit comparison of two or more economic systems. Plato's readers knew to what system he was comparing his ideal state, namely the Athens of his time, in economic decline and facing growing social and political turmoil. Similarly, in the 1950s and 1960s, Western students of the Soviet economic system devoted the bulk of their efforts to analyzing the workings of the planned socialist economy with the expectation that this information would enable their readers to easily make the comparison with the capitalist market economy in which they lived. Thus, comparative economics can involve the study of a single economic system or subsystem yet contribute to our understanding of other systems by the use of such implicit comparisons. Of course, the absence of an explicit comparison of two or more systems raises a risk: relying exclusively on implicit comparisons makes comparative economics unmanageably broad, since describing any aspect of one economic system invites implicit comparisons with any number of other systems, impeding the systematization of the study of economic systems, and also because any such comparison of the explicit and implicit systems depends on each individual's own evaluation of the virtues of the implicit system.

The second issue is that of the criteria by which economic systems should be compared. Plato would not have argued for the desirability of his ideal state on the basis of the superiority of its allocation of resources or per capita income relative to other economic systems. His criterion for a good economic and political system was whether it created the conditions for achieving justice and virtue. In his economic system, changing individuals' behavior in favor of virtue was preferable to seeking higher levels of income to satisfy their material wants. But if an economic system has such explicit goals, can it be evaluated and compared to other systems solely on its ability to meet its own goals or should comparative economists seek to establish meta-criteria that can evaluate systems with differing goals in an objective fashion? Without such meta-criteria, comparative economics is constrained to be normative, valuing different systems according to the observer's or the system designer's criteria or preferences. This raises the question of whether comparative economics can be an objective undertaking, one that evaluates systems without relying on value judgments about their ability to meet arbitrary internally chosen or externally imposed criteria.

3   Economic Systems Based on Religion and Utopias

Much early writings on economic systems reflected the values of religious communities, and, as with Plato's *Republic*, in these writings, non-economic goals predominated. Heeding the words of Jesus that "…it is easier for a camel to go through the eye of a needle, than for a rich man to enter into the kingdom of God" (Matthew 19:24), early Christians showed little interest in seeking economic systems that would increase prosperity (Pryor 1993) and urged adherents to eschew efforts to improve their material situation. Buddhism also sought to encourage adherents to reduce their material wants in order to limit their earthly suffering and to enable them to reach a more enlightened state (Pieris 1963).

Nevertheless, not all religions frowned on success in economic activity. For example, Pryor (1985, pp. 216 and 220) concludes that "Islamic scholars see wealth as a useful means for living a virtuous life", although "(t)he search for a high standard of living is supposed to be a means, not a goal…". Similarly, the hostility toward seeking material success of the early Christian church was turned on its head by the Protestant Reformation, when material success achieved through thrift and rational economic activity came to be viewed as evidence of God's favor and an indication that individuals successful in earthly pursuits were predestined for salvation (Weber 2002).

While religions did not seek to give detailed explanations of how the economic systems they proposed would function, they did provide numerous rules about acceptable economic practices, including prohibitions on usury or interest, restrictions on various business dealings and on price and wage formation, promoting charitable behavior, and so on. Some of these strictures could be harmful to economic progress, although, of course, since the objective of religious thinkers was to encourage behavior pleasing to god rather than to maximize material welfare, this was not seen as a problem.[1]

---

[1] There has been considerable controversy regarding the relationship between such strictures, which we may view as institutions in the parlance of modern comparative economics, and their economic consequences. For example, although Islam is seen as pro-business, Kuran (2018) identifies a number of areas where its religious practices and injunctions hamper the economic progress of Islamic societies. Conversely, despite its seemingly ascetic views on consumption, some scholars have suggested that

Another genre of descriptions of ideal economic systems was works that described utopias. Plato's *Republic* is perhaps the first of such works, but, over the centuries, other notable descriptions of utopian societies can be found in More's early-sixteenth-century work, *Utopia* (2014), Bellamy's *Looking Backward* (1941), and in Marx's concept of full communism, in which such abundance is reached that it becomes feasible to apply his concept of "from each according to his ability, to each according to his needs" (https://www.marxists.org/archive/marx/works/1875/gotha/ch01.htm). Again, there is no systematic comparison of the utopian economic system with a rival, but readers are quite clearly expected to see the usually glaring differences between the utopian economy and the economy, and society, in which they lived. The above and other proposed secular utopias have a number of features in common. First, they assume high productivity so that people do not have to work long hours and can engage in a variety of occupations, property is often held in common, and individuals can obtain their material wants for free from communal supplies. The free availability of consumer goods is facilitated by people's willingness to promote the common good as well as by the less onerous nature of the labor required to maintain the economy. Similarly, the willingness to work depends less on individuals' need to earn a living and more on their public spiritedness. Equality was often, but not always, a component of utopian societies.

The systems proposed on religious grounds and secular utopias share several common elements, including the predominance of non-economic objectives, self-restraint in consumption and in material desires, and high levels of social solidarity. In this sense, both types of systems promote altruism over self-interestedness, and thus their viability depends in large part on the possibility of changing human nature from self-interest to self-restraint and social solidarity. Another characteristic of these writings is the mixing of an economic system with society more broadly considered so that the economy and society are seen as part and parcel of the same thing.

Buddhism does provide a basis for eco-friendly or sustainable economic development, and, in recent years, it has been touted as a pro-development religion, especially in the effort to measure the performance of economies by indices of human happiness rather than by measures such as gross domestic product (Pryor 1991; Daniels 1998). See Kharas and MacArthur for a discussion on sustainable economic development in this volume (Chap. 22).

4   Toward Systems Based on Self-Interest

Progress in the analysis of economic systems resulted from three changes in approach that foreshadowed the development of economics as we know it today. The first was the introduction of an explicitly economic criterion for evaluating economic systems, the ability of the system to satisfy people's unlimited material wants given technological and resource constraints. The second was the increased emphasis on how economic systems actually functioned rather than on how they should and on self-interest as a key motivator of human behavior. The third change, in part required by the first two, was the separation of the economic system from the social system, or the dominance of the economic system over the social system.[2] These changes in approach gave the study of economic systems both a clear economic criterion for comparing economic systems, and, as well, made human wants, from which religious and utopian systems had tried to free people, the centerpiece of explanations of human economic and social behavior.

Perhaps the first scholar to develop these changes in a systematic way was Ibn Khaldun (1969), a fourteenth-century scholar who viewed economic development as a cyclical process raising people from nomadic to urban or civilized societies. Khaldun postulated that human desires were unlimited (Haddad 1977) and that meeting those desires through increasing levels of what we would call per capita income, and what Khaldun equated with the term civilization, was the objective of the economic system. Achieving levels of income beyond the subsistence level required ever-increasing cooperation and the division of labor among people seeking their own self-interest (Irwin 2018) as well as strong central leadership, and these could only be achieved in large cities. Ibn Khaldun recognized the importance of capital accumulation, of technological improvements, and of the roles of a strong state and of religion in providing the basis for the social organization needed to sustain high productivity. Nevertheless, he warned against a ruler's direct participation in economic activities such as farming or trade as this would disincentivize private activity. He also believed that successful societies could eventually collapse as they exhausted their growth potential, but he argued that they would be replaced by new more vigorous ones that would use some of the economic legacies of the previous society as a springboard to achieve even higher levels of productivity.

---

[2] An obvious example of this tendency is Marx's concept of dialectical materialism, which viewed the social system as determined by the economic system. See Sabine (1937).

A more widely known exposition of these concepts is Adam Smith's (1976) *The Wealth of Nations*. Like Ibn Khaldun, Smith viewed the satisfaction of human wants as the goal of the economic system, and he stressed that achieving this end was consistent with individuals acting in their own self-interest, and, like Khaldun, he emphasized the importance of the division of labor and increasing productivity. Smith was neither a strict utilitarian, since he argued that sympathy made people sensitive to the condition of others and that such sympathy influenced their behavior, nor was he a staunch supporter of *laissez-faire* economics as witnessed, for example, by his strictures against business owners who colluded against the public interest. Rather, for the purposes of comparative economics, Smith's seminal contribution was the development of the possibility that an economy inhabited by self-interested and insatiable consumers could spontaneously result in an orderly society and in economic progress rather than in a brutish struggle of all against all.

5   General Equilibrium Theory and the Pareto Principle

The first step in turning Smith's insight into a deeper understanding of economic systems was left to the utilitarians, among whom Jeremy Bentham and John Stuart Mill were the most prominent. Utilitarians posited that people sought to maximize their own happiness or utility, which they derived from the goods they consumed, and, thus, individuals' choices should lead to the greatest happiness of the greatest number, as Bentham's famous turn of phrase had it. This formulation had two components. One was that individual behavior could be explained by individuals' utility maximization. The other was that, since individuals sought to satisfy their happiness, they should act so as to increase the general happiness of all. The former proposition led to the development of consumer theory as we now know it, the latter, promptly criticized when Mill proposed it, was the precursor of the notion of a social utility function, a measure of the aggregate utility or welfare that the economy produced. Thus cleansed of Smith's notions of empathy, the theory of the consumer based on utility maximization was formalized by a number of contributors and then codified by Alfred Marshall (1949) in his *Principles of Economics*.

Marshall, however, was mainly interested in models of individual markets, explaining how supply and demand interacted to set prices and created equilibrium in the market for a single good. It then remained to ask whether all markets in an economy could be brought to equilibrium through the price mechanism and, if so, what the consequences for the welfare of individuals and of society would be. This question was addressed by Walras (1954) and others in the nineteenth century and culminated with proofs by Arrow and Debreu (1954) and Debreu (1959) that broadly showed that competitive markets would lead to Pareto-efficient outcomes and that a Pareto-efficient outcome could be supported by market equilibrium prices. In a Pareto-efficient equilibrium, it is not possible to reallocate resources so as to make one individual better off without making others worse off or to produce more of one thing without reducing the production of something else. Consequently a (stylized) market system based on utility and profit maximization would result in equilibria that had desirable welfare properties in that it is not possible to find a more efficient allocation of resources. Thus, the case for a market economy rested on its efficiency properties, and other systems would be compared to the market economy based on such efficiency criteria.[3]

The establishment of the Pareto efficiency of a system based on markets meant that now the comparison of economic systems seemingly could be put on a scientific and objective basis. In simple terms, a(n) (idealized) market system was known to be Pareto optimal, and therefore alternative economic systems would have to demonstrate their ability to achieve Pareto optimality; if such proof could not be provided, they were inferior to the market economy in satisfying people's needs. Moreover, any Pareto-efficient outcome produced by a rival system could, in theory, be duplicated by a market economy, so other systems could at best only equal but not surpass the market economy in terms of the efficiency of resource allocation.

An early application of this efficiency characteristic of the market economy to the comparison of economic systems was the controversy over whether a socialist planned economy, such as was emerging in the Soviet Union, could be as efficient as a market economy. Ludwig von Mises (1920) sparked the controversy when he argued that insufficient information and the means of processing it would render a socialist economy allocationally inefficient and potentially unworkable. He was answered by Lange (1936, 1937) and Lerner

---

[3] The question of which Pareto-efficient equilibrium of the many that a system could produce was socially optimal or most desirable proved less tractable because it involved interpersonal comparisons of utility, as Robbins (1932), among others, had argued, and the idea of a social welfare function that could be used to select the socially most desirable Pareto optimum faded with the publication of Arrow's (1951) impossibility theorem. Thus, comparative economics had no means of choosing among the many possible Pareto-optimal equilibria that a system could produce, and, consequently, without adding additional criteria, a Pareto optimum that assigned most of the consumption to one individual while casting the remainder into poverty was not distinguishable in welfare terms from one that produced an egalitarian distribution of goods.

(1944), who proposed an economic system that combined social ownership of capital with consumer choice and a mechanism for price discovery that led to the equalization of commodity prices with their marginal costs, the necessary condition for efficient production. The Langer-Lerner model of a socialist market economy and the debate itself may seem rather artificial to modern readers, but it represents a breakthrough in comparative economics not only because of its use of developments in welfare economics to claim an objective criterion for judging economic systems, but also because, in contrast to most of the literature covered previously in this essay, it made an explicit comparison between two different systems both of which were explained in some detail.

The preoccupation with static efficiency retained a hold on comparative economics for some time. For example, considerable intellectual effort was devoted investigating whether a labor-managed firm, modeled on the economic system that emerged in Yugoslavia in the 1950s, could be as allocationally efficient as a capitalist firm (Ward 1958; Domar 1966; Vanek 1970). Likewise, the efficiency of the allocation of factors of production in the Soviet economy was studied by Thornton (1971), Danilin et al. (1985), Land et al. (1994), and others. Specific Soviet planning techniques such as materials balances (a rudimentary form of input–output) were subject to extensive analyses of their allocative inefficiencies (Levine 1959; Powel 1977). Abram Bergson summed up the then-prevailing Western view when he wrote:

> proponents and critics [of the Soviet economic system] agree that economic merit turns largely on economic efficiency…. (a)s exemplified by the Soviet experience, socialism must be less efficient economically than Western private enterprise. (Bergson 1964, pp. 354–355)

Despite the appeal of an objective criterion for judging economic systems that general equilibrium theory provided, comparisons of the static efficiency of economic systems proved not to be as fruitful as expected. There are several reasons for this. One is that the empirical work required to measure the efficiency with which productive resources were allocated in two economies was quite difficult, especially considering the dearth of data on firms in the Soviet Union and other communist countries. A second reason was the realization that static efficiency in resource allocation was only a partial criterion for evaluating economic systems. Since market and planned economies differed in other economic characteristics such as the distribution of income, growth, and so on, whether one or the other actually made individuals better off could not be determined. A third, and perhaps most compelling, reason for the failure to investigate the Pareto optimality of rival economic systems was the arrival of the Cold War, which turned the attention of comparative economists to the question of how the centrally planned economies of the Soviet Union, of Eastern Europe, and of China actually functioned, in large part to determine what their economic potential was in the struggle between the two systems.

6   Sovietology as Comparative Economics[4]

The rapid post-World War II growth of the Soviet economy made it a geopolitical rival to the United States and an attractive alternative economic model to policy makers in many developing countries as well as in some developed countries. Moreover, policy makers in the United States wanted to better understand the ability of the Soviet Union to support the economic burden of its growing military power. The first step in this process was to understand how planning in the Soviet economy functioned. Scholars in the United States, Europe, and Japan produced works that explained the planning process, the management of firms in the centrally planned economy, the allocation of labor, the roles of money and foreign trade, and so on. This was a difficult undertaking in light of the closed nature of Soviet society, language differences, and so on.

Despite these obstacles, by 1964 Abram Bergson was able to publish a book (Bergson 1964) that described in detail the institutions and functioning of the Soviet economy. His description was so accurate that it survived the analysis of the trove of "insider" information provided by emigres from the Soviet Union and compiled by the Soviet Interview Project as well as by the opening of Soviet archives after the collapse of the Soviet Union.[5] Bergson was able to supplement his own extensive research with the work of many other scholars. Monographs had appeared dealing in depth with various aspects of the Soviet economy, including managerial behavior, taxation, agriculture, and foreign trade. Moreover, there was also growing interest in the experience of other communist countries, at first those in Eastern Europe and then including China as well. Given Soviet hegemony over East Europe, it is rather surprising that these countries were able to implement economic systems that, while resembling the Soviet system, also differed from it in important ways. As Hewett (1983) noted, data on East European economies were more readily

---

[4] Some of the ideas in this section are drawn from Brada and Wachtel (2018), which deals in greater detail with the development of comparative economics during this period.

[5] See Chap. 3 by Paul Gregory in this volume for more on the opening of the Soviet archives.

available, Eastern European research institutes and colleagues were more open to foreigners, and the heterogeneity of their economic institutions and willingness to experiment with their economic system offered a variety that permitted a richer analysis than one based only on Soviet experience alone.[6] This was followed in due course by the study of the Chinese economy and particularly of the reforms that were being undertaken in China.

While comparative economics borrowed tools and insights, as well as intellectual fashions, from mainstream economics, the study of the planned economies also enriched mainstream economics, which had been based exclusively on the experience of market economies. Thus the so-called ratchet effect whereby managers limited plan over fulfillment so as not to receive higher output targets in the future, biases in index numbers in the face of rapid charges in the composition of final output, and the economics of pervasive shortage and of plan tautness were but a few of the insights developed as the result of the study of the planned economies.

Gradually, the study of the planned economies changed emphasis from concerns with the Pareto optimality of the planned economy to questions about the ability of planned economies to sustain economic growth. In part this was because the institutions of central planning had been adequately studied, but, more important, because output growth in the planned economies began to stagnate. Growth in most of them, with the exception of China, was slowing due to sluggish population growth, a declining impact of capital accumulation, and a lack of productivity improvements, and policy makers in these countries were undertaking reforms to try to restore the rapid growth that had characterized the immediate post-War period. However, most of the economic reforms introduced in the USSR and in Eastern Europe showed that introducing market elements into a system of central planning did not improve economic performance and that understanding the institutions into which new elements were to be introduced was critical for successful reform.[7] This created a paradox in that, in China, similar partial reforms did improve economic performance. Jefferson (2008) stresses the challenge posed by China's economic success with such reforms for both traditional Western

---

[6] This "varieties of communism" approach to the study of the Soviet Union and East Europe to some extent presaged the "variety of capitalisms" literature introduced by Hall and Soskice (2001).

[7] The inability of reforms to improve Soviet and East European economic performances may have been the result of poor implementation, of political interference or of the fact that reforms were mainly aimed at industry rather than agriculture, or it may have been an example of the workings of the theory of the second best (Lipsey and Lancaster 1956), which showed that removing one cause of inefficiency in the economy would likely worsen rather than improve performance if other causes of inefficiency were not addressed at the same time. See Chap. 19 in this volume by Da Rocha and Martins on the theory of second best and policy complementarities.

economics with its stress on maintaining macroeconomic equilibrium, and for the new institutional economics, which stresses the centrality of good institutions for economic prosperity. China was lacking in the rule of law, in the protection of private property, and in restraining corruption. Moreover, its financial system was weak and considerable government involvement in the economy persisted. All these shortcomings are seen by the traditional literature on institutions as barriers to economic success. Jefferson attempts to resolve this paradox, but it is clear that understanding when partial system changes can help or harm economic performance remains an elusive goal for comparative economics. This issue of how to approach the study of the behavior of complex systems resurfaces in the following section when we touch on the reductionist assumptions behind the Koopmans-Montias model of economic systems, and it also permeates much of the remainder of this essay.

7   The Economic System

The other, and perhaps more lasting, contribution to comparative economics during this time was the effort to construct a value-free way of describing and comparing economic systems. The effort was initially sparked by the need to provide students with some framework for comparing economic systems. Most textbooks on comparative economics such as Gregory and Stuart (1985) and Neuberger and Duffy (1976) used a relatively simple framework for comparisons. The economic performance of a country was determined by three factors: the environment, the economic system, and the policies followed by the country. The environment included the country's starting conditions, the preferences of the economic agents who made decisions in the economy, the resources and technology available to the country, the existing organizations and institutions, and the country's location. The system consisted of rules, both formal and informal, and institutions such as central banks and labor unions. According to Neuberger and Duffy (1976), the system functioned through various mechanisms including the delegation of decision-making authority, meaning who in the economy had the power to make decisions about the allocation of which resources; information, which included not only prices but also information about technology; and economic and social regulations. Economic agents could be motivated by a variety of incentive schemes, both moral and material, to make decisions and supply effort and other productive resources under their control. Finally, policies were seen as a special set of rules that were valid for relatively short periods of time and whose alteration would not change the essential nature of the system.[8]

Koopmans and Montias (1971) and extensions by Montias (1976) and Montias et al. (1994) sought to formalize this rather intuitive approach and to produce a rigorous, scientific, and value-free way to describe and evaluate economic systems. Thus, these authors took great pains to distinguish between institutions and policies, to explain the meaning of information and incentives, and so on. Their framework produced a useful and comprehensive set of concepts and principles that could describe and classify economic systems and their constituent parts and facilitate comparisons between, and analyses of, different economies and the outcomes they generate.

Despite the rich analytical and taxonomic structure of the Koopmans-Montias approach, its impact on the study of economic systems was less than expected for two reasons. The first is that it adopted the reductionist view that one could understand a complex social system by breaking it down into its constituent parts, studying how they worked, and then assembling the parts back into a whole. Since all economics had largely espoused this approach, Koopmans and Montias could hardly be blamed for following this path, although it is likely that complex systems cannot be analyzed in this way (Gleick 2008) and the interactions between economic system elements are discontinuous and not additive.[9] The second flaw of their approach to comparative economics as an intellectual enterprise was not due to their inability to lay out the fundamental links between system characteristics and outcomes but to their choice of criteria for evaluating systems, which were descriptive rather than prescriptive. Thus, Koopmans and Montias (1971) proposed to judge economic systems on the basis of at least six criteria, including high per capita consumption, its growth, equity in its distribution, the stability of employment and income, and so on.[10] This list of objectives, or criteria, by

---

[8] So, for example, a change in the corporate income tax from 20 to 25 percent would not involve a fundamental change in an economic system and would fall into the policy category; the abolition of the corporate income tax and its replacement by a value-added tax would be seen as a change in a formal rule, and thus a change in the system itself.

[9] This belief that getting into the details of economies, meaning the behavior of agents, institutions, laws, and so on, would lead to a better understanding of how they functioned was not limited to comparative economics. Traditional Keynesian macroeconomics was based on *ad hoc* descriptions of the behavior of macroeconomic aggregates using concepts such as the consumption function. At some point, economists decided that these *ad hoc* descriptions of macroeconomic behavior needed to have real micro-foundations derived from the utility-maximizing behavior of economic agents, and a vast effort was undertaken to base macroeconomics on explicitly modeled behavior of individuals, usually proxied by a "representative agent". Whether a better understanding of the macro-economy resulted is a matter of debate, but, in any case, no similar effort was made by comparative economists.

[10] The Koopmans-Montias criteria reflect the work of Balassa (1959, Ch 4), who proposed a more limited list, such as static efficiency, dynamic efficiency, and actual growth of output, as the criteria by which to evaluate economic systems.

which to judge economic systems has considerable descriptive value in that it gives a good approximation of the preferences that any observer would assign to the citizens or policy makers of a country, and so referring to these criteria should help explain the system's observed economic performance because these preferences would be reflected in the design of the system and the policies followed by decision makers. However, this greater precision in describing why systems achieved different outcomes made comparisons of these outcomes either impossible or of no real validity because each system would either have to be judged by its own criteria, rendering comparison with the outcomes produced by other systems that had different objectives meaningless, or requiring an evaluation of outcomes based on the observer's criteria, which might differ from the objectives espoused by the designers of either of the rival systems. Of course, both the single-criterion and the multiple-criteria approaches produced some useful insights about economic systems, and each approach dominated economic thinking at some period of time, but neither can or will completely dominate the analysis or evaluation of economic systems.[11]

8   The Economics of Transition

Before the shift in the way in which economic systems were to be compared from the single criterion of allocative efficiency to the multiple criteria proposed by Koopmans and Montias could be addressed by new research, the collapse of the communist countries of Eastern Europe and of the Soviet Union raised new questions and challenges for comparative economics. The knowledge of the planned economies and of their problems gave comparative economists an initial advantage in analyzing the situation and suggesting ways in which these economies could transition to market economies, but as transition progressed, economists with greater practical experience with the nuts and bolts of policy making and the functioning of market economy institutions came to the fore. The main area of contention was between those who advocated so-called "big-bang" reforms where prices would be freed and state-owned firms would be privatized as rapidly as possible. These policy prescriptions were countered by other economists, called gradualists, who argued for

---

[11] For example, as Sect. 9 shows, recently the new comparative economics has focused on per capita income as the main criterion for evaluating economic systems. However, as Chap. 22 by Kharas and MacArthur in this volume shows, multi-criteria development objectives are gaining ascendancy in evaluating outcomes and setting goals of economic development.

a slower approach. The essence of their argument for the more gradual introduction of free markets and for slower privatization of state-owned firms was that a market economy was more than just markets and privately owned firms. A market economy needed a wide variety of institutions, such as a central bank and functioning courts to enforce contracts and property rights, as well as new social attitudes toward risk-taking, the distribution of income, work, and so on, and, without these, neither markets nor private ownership alone could yield satisfactory economic performance. Since these new institutions and attitudes would take time to form, a big-bang approach would lead to economic chaos, public disappointment in the market economy, and backsliding in the process of transition.

Unfortunately, while the story of the political and bureaucratic creation of the Soviet economy had been covered in great detail by E. H. Carr's 12-volume *History of Soviet Russia*, which was extended by R. W. Davies' 7-volume series *The Industrialisation of Soviet Russia*, neither these books nor other studies of their time addressed how the Soviets abruptly transitioned from a market economy to a planned one by creating appropriate institutions to complement plans in the same way that capitalist institutions had been created to complement the workings of the market. Thus, there was little historical record to help economists' thinking about the transition from one economic system to another. The "big-bang" versus gradualism debate was further complicated by the fact that there was not much clarity about how good institutions arose. On the one hand, there was a line of thinking that institutions evolved spontaneously to reduce transaction costs, meaning economic agents' costs in undertaking transactions on the market, entering into long-term contracts, and so on. Thus, without the big-bang, there would be too few market transactions that could lead to the evolution of strong supporting institutions. On the other side, the argument was that economists knew what good institutions were and that they could be copied from well-performing market economies and put into place by the government.[12] Implicit in this argument was the reductionist idea that if an institution had economic value in the end state of transition, which was a functioning market economy, then its introduction at any time during the transition process had to improve the situation at the time of its introduction. Much of the advice provided by outsiders from both camps was probably correct, if at times contradictory, and useful to the process of transition. For the field of comparative economics, and for economics more generally, this period marked a change in emphasis from concerns

---

[12] There was a further debate about whether institutions that evolved in response to market needs were inherently superior to institutions designed and imposed by governments.

regarding the market mechanism and whether it produces optimal allocations of resources to questions of what institutions enable markets to function effectively and how institutions contribute to prosperity.

9   The New Comparative Economics[13]

Because comparative economists had concerned themselves with the study of the Soviet, East European, and Chinese planned economies from most of the post-World War II period, the demise of these economic systems seemed to portend a crisis for comparative economics. As Djankov et al. (2003) wrote:

> The traditional field of comparative economics dealt mostly with the comparison of socialism and capitalism…. Traditional comparative economics … studied under what circumstances either the plan or the market delivers greater economic efficiency…. By the time socialism collapsed in Eastern Europe and the Soviet Union, this question had lost much of its appeal…. If capitalism is triumphant, is comparative economics dead? (p. 595–6)

According to Djankov et al., comparative economics, meaning Sovietology, was dead, but they proposed a new comparative economics, one that involves comparisons among capitalist systems and that places primary emphasis on the role of institutions. This new comparative economics would focus on "…comparisons … of alternative capitalist models prevailing in different countries. Each capitalist country has many public and private institutions…. These differences [in institutions] and their consequences for economic performance are the subject of the new comparative economics" (p. 595–6).

The new comparative economics thus abandoned the emphasis on comparisons of market and planned economies, but it also implicitly de-emphasized the Koopmans-Montias approach of multiple criteria for evaluating system performance that was becoming evident in later versions of Sovietology, which had been coming to consider goals such as income distribution and growth as important system objectives. Rather, a single criterion, per capita income, became the dominant, if not the only, criterion by which economic systems would be judged. Just as important, the new comparative economics also copied early Sovietology's single explanation of economic performance, allocative efficiency, with a new single explanation, the quality of an economy's institutions. For example, Acemoglu and Robinson (2012)

---

[13] Parts of this section are based on Brada (2009).

compare the twin cities of Nogales, one located in the United States, the other just across the border in Mexico. They stress the similarities in geography and climate, in populations, and so on between the two cities and document the higher per capita income and better material standard of living in the Nogales that is located in the United States.

They argue that:

> there is a very simple explanation for the differences between the two halves of Nogales. [Citizens of the Nogales located in the United States] have access to the economic institutions of the United States, which enable them to choose their occupation freely, acquire schooling and skills, and encourage their employers to invest in the best technology ... These differences [between United States and Mexican institutions] ... are the main reason for the differences in prosperity on the two sides of the border. (p. 9)

This statement is, *mutatis mutandis*, a striking mirror image of the quote from Bergson in Sect. 5 of this chapter to the effect that it was the allocative efficiency of the market economy that made it better than the Soviet system. If we use a single criterion and accept only one explanation, then conclusions about economic systems are both more unequivocal and easier to reach.

Two streams of thought combined to bring per capita incomes and institutions to the fore. One was the work of economic historians such as Douglass C. North, who came to view institutions as central to economic progress.[14] The second was based on the insights gleaned from the study of modern economic growth. Solow (1957) estimated that, of the entire change in output per worker in the US economy in the first half of the twentieth century, about 13 percent was due to increases in capital per worker and the remaining 87 percent was due to an increase in total factor productivity (TFP). Using similar production function methodology, Hall and Jones (1999) demonstrated that TFP not only explains cross-country differences in the growth of per capita income but largely determines the international differences in the levels of per capita income as well. For example, they show that, of the 35-fold difference in per capita incomes between Niger and the United States, 12 percent is accounted for by differences in per capita endowments of capital, 25 percent is accounted for by differences in human capital, and the remaining 63 percent is accounted for by differences in TFP. They attribute these differences in TFP to differences in the quality of institutions in the two countries,

---

[14] North (1991) is a good concise exposition of this line of thinking.

a conclusion buttressed by the large sample of countries they use in their work as well as by other, similar, studies.

Thus, understanding the sources of inter-country TFP became the central focus of the new comparative economics. Before the nineteenth century, per capita incomes had been roughly the same in major civilizations around the world, and they grew only slowly. After 1800, European per capita income growth increased by 20-fold per century. Since the end of World War II, there has been an acceleration of per capita income growth elsewhere, principally in Asia (Prescott 1998). Because the main source of this growth is TFP improvements, any understanding of the link between economic systems and TFP would constitute an important contribution to the field of comparative economics.

In brief, the new comparative economics literature suggests that environmental factors such as natural resources are not important for explaining differences in per capita incomes, nor are starting conditions, because all countries started from more or less the same level, and location appears to play a mixed role. Policy does not appear much in this work, and thus the major explanatory factor is differences in institutions. While it is difficult to argue that good institutions that limit predation by governments or by individuals are not beneficial for economic performance, it had been just as difficult to argue that Pareto efficiency in the allocation of resources also was not important in determining economic performance. Thus, while the multiple criteria of the old comparative economics help explain why a system produces the outcomes that it does, the strength and the appeal of the new comparative economics is precisely that it is unicausal, emphasizing institutions as the main drivers of differences in economic outcomes, and it has only one performance criterion, per capita income. Thus, by limiting the complex causality between economic systems and their outcomes that characterized the old comparative economics, the new comparative economics is able to offer more in the way of concrete results on which economic system is better according to a single generally accepted criterion.

10   Institutions

While the effect of institutions on economic performance is now well accepted in cross-country comparisons, the emphasis on institutions raises a number of new research questions for comparative economists. The first of these is the difference between institutions and what might usefully be called culture. Some scholars see the former as formal constructs, usually underpinned by governments. These would include protection of property rights and the rule of law. Culture, on the other hand, represents behavior that is institutionalized or broadly accepted in a society but enforced mainly through social pressure rather than by government sanctions. The sources of culture insofar as it influences economic behavior are biological and technological. The technology part comes from the insights of Plato, Ibn Khaldun, and Smith that specialization and the division of labor lead to higher productivity. The biological component comes from evolutionary biology, which teaches that organisms seek to maximize the transmission of their genes into the future. An obvious way of doing this is through individual reproductive success, a selfish process. However, many species collaborate to improve the reproductive success of their kin because these kin also carry some of the same genes, so their reproductive success also helps spread (some of) these same genes. Such cooperative behavior among humans leads to the formation of clans, where members are all related to some degree and thus they cooperate with each other, improving everyone's reproductive success.

There are also examples of organisms that cooperate with non-kin, but the participants in such non-kin cooperation are faced by, and appear to closely monitor for, cheating or defecting from the cooperative relationship by the partner organism. This was already implicit in the work of Ibn Khaldun discussed above. Khaldun recognized that nomadic clans in North Africa consisted of related individuals, and, based on their kinship, they cooperated with each other to survive and reproduce. However, these clans were too small to sustain much of a division of labor, so there was no economic progress. Moreover, the rules for kin-based cooperation reflected the economic environment in which clans found themselves, so the type of cooperation, even within small groups, would be contingent on the available technology and on the environment, and this contingency applied to non-kin cooperation as well. In cities, much larger populations made possible a much greater degree of the division of labor and thus economic progress and higher living standards, but, because kin relations between cooperating individuals were weak or nonexistent, there was much greater risk of cheating and defection among cooperating individuals. In nature, defectors are shunned for their cheating, but shunning is not always a sufficiently effective deterrent, and thus Khaldun stressed the role of religion, which supplemented the punishment of shunning with the wrath of god, and of a vigorous ruler who would use the state's monopoly on violence to punish those who defected from reciprocal behavior. Thus cities, by supplementing kin-based reciprocity with man-made institutions, could achieve a greater division of labor and thus higher levels of prosperity.[15]

An open research question is how cultural institutions and formal or government-enforced institutions coexist. Studies show that cultural institutions, those enforced mainly by social pressure, persist for long periods of time (e.g. Alesina et al. 2013), and, as the economic and physical environment change, they may come to hinder rather than aid the functioning of the economic system or they may not be optimal from the outset (Kaplan and Hill 1992).[16] Thus, for example, as in the debate over the speed of transition, would the implanting of Western institutions into post-Communist societies have improved economic performance if citizens continued to have social attitudes inherited from the Communist era? If cultural institutions are relatively immutable, then how should more mutable man-made institutions be selected and implemented for best results? More broadly, whether there is a link between cultural norms—collectivist, individualistic, or gender based—and the efficacy of formal institutions remains under-researched.

Comparative economists also need to strive for a better understanding of the nature of institutions. For example, are institutions guided by some sort of social Darwinism in the sense that better institutions drive out less-effective ones, or do countries that fail to change their institutions appropriately simply fall behind permanently in the race for higher levels of per capita incomes? How easy is it to substitute for formal institutions that may be infeasible to implement due to cultural or political barriers? Gerschenkron (1962) showed that what were seen as institutional prerequisites for economic growth could, in relatively backward countries, be substituted for by new institutions that differed significantly from those used by countries that were early industrializers. Whether and in what way this experience can be generalized remains unclear.

A second challenge for the new comparative economics is the relationship between institutions and policies. Unless the new comparative economics chooses a definition of "institutions" that is so broad as to make the term questionable as an analytic concept, arguably the old comparative economics would continue to offer a richer and more realistic link between economic

---

[15] Greif and Tabellini (2017) provide an instructive example of the problems of scaling up clan-based cooperation in a different cultural and geographic setting from the one used by Khaldun.

[16] Some might even argue that, to the extent that characteristics such as differences in the propensity to cooperate are heritable and not just "taught", the economic characteristics of societies may have a genetic component.

As a further point of interest, it is noteworthy that these two studies, examining societies widely separated by geography and by their level of development, both identify gender-based differences in economic activity as being particularly long-lasting and resistant to changes in the environment.

outcomes and their causes: environment, system, which we may provisionally equate with institutions, and policies. The studies conducted in the framework of the new comparative economics described above take little or no account of policy differences. Outcomes are largely explained by institutional differences, themselves the products of relatively immutable cultural forces, an approach that leaves little or no room for policy as a determinant of economic outcomes. Such a stance might be acceptable either if institutions are defined so broadly as to include policies under the rubric of institutions or if policies were strongly determined by the institutional environment in which they are framed. The latter point of view has some validity; institutions do influence policies in explicit ways. For example, institutionalizing central bank independence improves the quality of monetary policy and results in lower inflation rates, and budgetary institutions do influence the quality of fiscal policy. Nevertheless, the proposition that all economic policy is endogenous and determined by economic institutions seems untenable. Moreover, it may well be the case that differences in policies also lead to changes in institutions in cases where the policy makes the institution function less efficiently.[17]

Part of the problem of discussing the relative role of institutions and policy is that the boundary between the two is not always clear. Montias (1976) defines "rules", which in his framework are analogous to institutions, as "stipulating or constraining the actions of a set of participants for an indefinite period and under specified states of these individuals' environment" (p. 18). Such a definition is quite consistent with the definition of institutions used by the new comparative economics. Montias also defines policy as "a class of contingent decisions, frequently announced … with a view to creating stable expectations about the future decisions of the policy maker" (p. 18). It is true that policies are generally contingent and that policy announcements are intended to convey information about future contingent acts. But, the economic purpose of policy is missing from this definition, because, after all, we

---

[17] The development of institutions to permit the efficient financing of sea-borne trade in the Mediterranean during the period of the Convivencia during which Jews and Muslims coexisted in Spain is an example of the importance of policy differences in the usefulness of institutions (Paine 2013). Jews and Muslims had their own rules or institutions that governed relations between those who financed voyages and the ship captains who undertook them, and each religious group administered and adjudicated disputes over the contracts signed under their respective institutions. There was, however, an important difference in the way the two institutions were parametrized. In the Muslim case profits were largely shared equally between the two parties. In the Jewish institution, the two parties were free to decide on how profits should be shared to reflect the relative risks or contributions of the two parties to the agreement. As a result, Muslim traders at times opted to use the Jewish institution, even though this involved placing themselves under the authority of Jewish adjudicators of disputes. Thus, the institution with less-efficient policies was to some extent replaced by the same institution that embodied better policies.

view policies as ways of obtaining certain economic outcomes. Montias' definition may thus not be entirely in tune with the common use of the term policy, which in everyday usage means the parameterization of institutional characteristics.

Somewhat incorrectly, institutions are viewed as system characteristics that are broader in their reach and effects. Frequently mentioned institutions such as the rule of law and private property map into good economic outcomes relatively uniquely, and lack of these institutions maps into bad economic performance. However, it is worth noting that other institutions have little effect on the functioning of the systems and yet others seemingly have none.[18] In contrast, the mapping from institutions to policies to outcomes is less rigid and less well studied, but it may be equally important in determining outcomes (Havrylyshyn and van Rooden 2003). The old comparative economics may have neglected institutions in favor of policy and allocative efficiency, but we should be careful not to have the pendulum swing too far the other way. Doubtless, institutions are an important driver of long-term economic progress, but policies matter also, and it behooves us to attempt to learn where policies come from and what effects they have in the long run.[19]

11   Conclusion

Comparative economics as conceived in this chapter is central to economics because what makes for a good economic system is, or should be, the most important question that economists ask. This question was first taken up by philosophers and religious authorities who, though not ignorant of the basic concept of economic systems such as prices, exchange, and the division of labor, tended to judge economic systems by their ability to achieve what were often non-economic ends, such as a more virtuous or cooperative society rather than merely a more productive one, and who believed that an economic system should be based on cooperation and reciprocal altruism rather than on competition.

---

[18] Hewett (1978) criticized Montias' claim that "only noblemen may bear swords" is an institution. By the definition of institutions, Montias was correct and Hewett was wrong; the non-effect of an institution on economic outcomes does not disqualify it from being an institution. There are also institutions with trivial economic effects. Tipping is thought to lead to better service and, in countries such as the United States, it is strongly supported as a cultural norm. Yet service in countries where it does not exist seems as good. Giving children an allowance may or may not encourage habits of thrift and the delaying of gratification, but, in some countries, it, too, is a widely accepted institution.

[19] See, for example, Uberti and Knutsen (Chap. 18 in this volume) for a discussion of institutions and human capital as drivers of growth.

A key step in thinking about economic systems was the works of Ibn Khaldun and, later, Adam Smith. Emphasis on thinking about how systems should function shifted from altruism to the maximization of individual welfare with the added insight that individual welfare maximization could lead to an orderly economic system that could benefit all citizens even if they only acted to maximize their own welfare. Thus, the criterion by which economic systems would be judged was their efficiency in meeting material wants by allocating resources efficiently. The market economy was thus seen as one, and perhaps the only, way to achieve this efficiency.

The rise of centrally planned economies in the communist countries was major impetus for thinking about economic systems, and scholars and policy makers began to address questions such as whether a planned economy could grow more rapidly than a market economy, whether central planning could avoid the business cycles that afflicted market economies, and whether the bureaucratic allocation of resources could match the efficiency of market allocations. At the same time, comparative economists made progress in explaining what the components of an economic system were and to some extent how they interact. Having a vocabulary and a clear understanding of the building blocks of economic systems was a prerequisite for further progress.

The collapse of the planned economies of Eastern Europe and the Soviet Union seemed to answer some of the questions regarding the relative merits of the market and the plan as a way of organizing economies, but it brought to the fore an interest in the role of institutions. This interest was fueled in part by the transition from plan to market in the former Soviet Bloc, in that it became evident that it was not only free markets and private firms that made a capitalist market economy function, but that institutions, meaning both formal ones such as the rule of law and central banks and informal ones such as social attitudes to work and the distribution of income that led to social acceptance of market-based outcomes were also necessary. With planned economies disappearing from the scene, emphasis turned to comparisons of market economies, both the ones existing now and those that existed in the past. The major element of comparison is now the quality of systems' institutions, where institutional quality is measured by the system's ability to achieve high levels of per capita income.

Despite considerable progress, the comparison of economic systems remains an unfinished task, one that may never be completed, because, despite numerous efforts, there seems no way to develop objective criteria by which two economic systems can be judged because different systems may, in fact, have different objectives. Moreover, when single criteria for evaluating systems are proposed, they tend to reflect the current intellectual fancy of economists, be it Pareto optimality and the market's ability to allocate resources efficiently or institutions with their ability to provide high and ever-increasing living standards. Thus, while the field has made progress in terms of descriptions and taxonomy, the value-free comparison of economic systems remains an impossible dream.

References

Acemoglu, D., & Robinson, J. A. (2012). *Why Nations Fail*. New York: Crown Business.

Alesina, A., Giuliano, P., & Nunn, N. (2013). On the Origins of Gender Roles: Women and the Plough. *Quarterly Journal of Economics, 28*(2), 469–530.

Arrow, K. J. (1951). *Social Choice and Individual Values*. New Haven: Yale University Press.

Arrow, K. J., & Debreu, G. (1954). The Existence of an Equilibrium for a Competitive Economy. *Econometrica, 22*(3), 265–290.

Balassa, B. A. (1959). *The Hungarian Experience in Central Planning: A Theoretical and Empirical Study*. New Haven: Yale University Press.

Bellamy, E. (1941). *Looking Backward*. Hollywood: A Armitage.

Bergson, A. (1964). *The Economics of Soviet Planning*. New Haven and London: Yale University Press.

Brada, J. C. (2009). The New Comparative Economics *Versus* the Old: Less Is More, but Is It Enough? *European Journal of Comparative Economics, 6*(1), 3–15.

Brada, J. C., & Wachtel, P. (2018). *Comparative Economic Studies* and Comparative Economics: Six Decades and Counting. *Comparative Economic Studies, 60*(4), 638–656.

Daniels, P. (1998). Economic Change, the Environment and Buddhism in Asia. *International Journal of Social Economics, 25*(6/7/8), 968–1004.

Danilin, I., Materov, I. S., Knox-Lovell, C. A., & Rosefielde, S. (1985). Measuring Enterprise Efficiency in the Soviet Union: A Stochastic Frontier Analysis. *Economica, 52*, 225–233.

Debreu, G. (1959). *Theory of Value: An Axiomatic Analysis of Economic Equilibrium*. New Haven: Yale University Press.

Djankov, E. L., Laporta, R., Lopez-de-Silanes, F., & Shleifer, A. (2003). The New Comparative Economics. *Journal of Comparative Economics, 31*(4), 595–619.

Domar, E. (1966). The Soviet Collective Farm as a Producer Co-operative. *American Economic Review, 56*(4), 734–757.

Gerschenkron, A. (1962). *Economic Backwardness in Historical Perspective*. Cambridge: Harvard University Press.

Gleick, J. (2008). *Chaos*. London: Penguin Books.

Gregory, P., & Stuart, R. (1985). *Comparative Economic Systems*. Boston: Houghton Mifflin.

Greif, A., & Tabellini, G. (2017). The Clan and the Corporation: Sustaining Cooperation in China and Europe. *Journal of Comparative Economics, 45*(1), 1–35.

Haddad, L. (1977). A Fourteenth-Century Theory of Economic Growth and Development. *Kyklos, 30*(2), 195–213.

Hall, R. E., & Jones, C. I. (1999). Why Do Some Countries Produce So Much More Output per Worker Than Others? *Quarterly Journal of Economics, 114*(1), 83–116.

Hall, P. A., & Soskice, D. (Eds.). (2001). *Varieties of Capitalism. The Institutional Foundations of Comparative Advantage*. Oxford: Oxford University Press.

Havrylyshyn, O., & van Rooden, R. (2003). Institutions Matter in Transition, but So Do Policies. *Comparative Economic Studies, 45*(1), 2–24.

Hewett, E. A. (1978). *The Structure of Economic Systems* by J. M. Montias (Book Review). *The ACES Bulletin, XX*(3–4), 101–105.

Hewett, E. A. (1983). Research on East European Economies: The Last Quarter Century. *The ACES Bulletin, XXV*(2), 1–21.

Ibn Khaldun. (1969). *The Muqaddimah: An Introduction to History*. Translated by F. Rosenthal; Abridged and Edited by N. J. Dawood. Princeton: Princeton University Press.

Irwin, R. (2018). *Ibn Khaldun: An Intellectual Biography*. Princeton: Princeton University Press.

Jefferson, G. H. (2008). How Has China's Economic Emergence Contributed to the Field of Economics? *Comparative Economic Studies, 50*(2), 167–209.

Kaplan, H., & Hill, K. (1992). The Evolutionary Ecology of Food Acquisition. In E. A. Smith & B. Winterhalder (Eds.), *Evolutionary Ecology and Human Behavior*. New York: Aldine de Gruyter.

Koopmans, T. C., & Montias, J. M. (1971). On the Description and Comparison of Economic Systems. In A. Eckstein (Ed.), *Comparison of Economic Systems: Theoretical and Methodological Approaches* (pp. 27–78). Berkeley: University of California Press.

Kuran, T. (2018). Islam and Economic Performance: Historical and Contemporary Links. *Journal of Economic Literature, 56*(4), 1292–1359.

Land, K. C., Knox Lovell, C. A., & Thore, S. (1994). Productive Efficiency Under Capitalism and State Socialism: An Empirical Inquiry Using Chance-Constrained Data Envelopment Analysis. *Technological Forecasting and Social Change, 46*(2), 139–152.

Lange, O. (1936). On the Economic Theory of Socialism: Part One. *Review of Economic Studies, 4*(1), 53–71.

Lange, O. (1937). On the Economic Theory of Socialism II. *Review of Economic Studies, 5*(2), 123–142.

Lerner, A. P. (1944). *The Economics of Control: Principles of Welfare Economics*. New York: Macmillan.

Levine, H. S. (1959). The Centralized Planning of Supply in Soviet Industry. In *Joint Economic Committee, U.S. Congress, Comparisons of the United States and Soviet Economies, Washington 1959*, pp. 151–176.

Lipsey, R. G., & Lancaster, K. (1956). The General Theory of Second Best. *Review of Economic Studies, 24*(1), 11–32.

Marshall, A. (1949). *Principles of Economics, An Introductory Volume* (8th ed.). New York: Macmillan.

von Mises, L. (1920). Economic Calculation in the Socialist Commonwealth. Retrieved from the Mises Institute at https://mises.org/library/economic-calculation-socialist-commonwealth.

Montias, J. M. (1976). *The Structure of Economic Systems*. New Haven: Yale University Press.

Montias, J. M., Ben-Ner, A., & Neuberger, E. (1994). *Comparative Economics*. Chur: Harwood Academic Publishers.

More, T. (2014). *Utopia* (2nd ed.). Miller, C. H., Harp, J., & Gibb, R. (Eds.). New Haven: Yale University Press.

Neuberger, E., & Duffy, E. (1976). *Comparative Economic Systems: A Decision-Making Approach*. Boston: Allyn and Bacon.

North, D. C. (1991). Institutions. *Journal of Economic Perspectives, 5*(1), 97–112.

Paine, L. (2013). *The Sea and Civilization: A Maritime History of the World*. New York: Vintage Books.

Pieris, R. (1963). Economic Development and Ultramundaneity. *Archives de sociologie des religions, 15*, 95–100.

Plato. (1950). *Dialogues of Plato*. New York: Pocket Books.

Powel, R. P. (1977). Plan Execution and the Workability of Soviet Planning. *Journal of Comparative Economics, 1*(1), 51–76.

Prescott, E. C. (1998). Needed: A Theory of Total Factor Productivity. *International Economic Review, 39*(3), 525–551.

Pryor, F. L. (1985). The Islamic Economic System: A Review Article. *Journal of Comparative Economics, 9*(2), 197–224.

Pryor, F. L. (1991). A Buddhist Economic System – In Practice. *The American Journal of Economics and Sociology, 50*(1), 17–33.

Pryor, F. L. (1993). The Roman Catholic Church and the Economic System: A Review Essay. *Journal of Comparative Economics, 17*(1), 129–151.

Robbins, L. (1932). *An Essay on the Nature and Significance of Economic Science*. London: Macmillan.

Sabine, G. H. (1937). *A History of Political Theory*. New York: Henry Holt & Co.

Smith, A. (1976). *An Inquiry into the Nature and Causes of the Wealth of Nations*. Oxford: Clarendon Press.

Solow, R. (1957). Technical Change and the Aggregate Production Function. *Review of Economics and Statistics, 39*(3), 312–320.

Thornton, J. (1971). Differential Capital Charges and Resource Allocation in Soviet Industry. *Journal of Political Economy, 79*(3), 545–561.

Vanek, J. (1970). *The General Theory of Labor-Managed Market Economies*. Ithaca: Cornell University Press.

Walras, L. (1954). *Elements of Pure Economics, or, The Theory of Social Wealth*. Homewood: R.D. Irwin.

Ward, B. (1958). The Firm in Illyria: Market Syndicalism. *American Economic Review, 48*(4), 566–589.

Weber, M. (2002). *The Protestant Ethic and the Spirit of Capitalism*. New York: Penguin.

3

The Soviet Economic System: An Archival Re-evaluation

Paul R. Gregory

The Soviet economic system has been a pillar in the study of comparative economic systems since its inception. Comparative systems began as a comparison of capitalism and socialism as represented by the Soviet economic system. This system was put in place in the late 1920s and early 1930s as Stalin's Communist Party promised breakneck industrialization, modernization, and exceptional growth.

Looking back from the end of the second decade of the new century, we know that the Soviet system appealed to many, but it collapsed. We know that the Soviet system imposed hardship and repression that cost millions of lives. It went into a "period of stagnation" beginning in the 1970s, which could not be reversed by the post-Stalin collective leadership. The economy experienced steep output declines in its last few years as the Soviet political system came to an ignominious end in December of 1991.

The Soviet planned economy was the most important experiment of the twentieth century. Its appeal of scientific planning, working-class rule, and economic growth persists. Post-Soviet admirers in the Western world insist that the experiment would have worked with a more enlightened leadership, especially one that would combine democracy and socialism. In a word: "Let's try it again. This time we'll get it right."

P. R. Gregory (✉)
The Hoover Institution of Stanford University, Stanford, CA, USA
e-mail: pgregory@stanford.edu

© The Author(s) 2021
E. Douarin, O. Havrylyshyn (eds.), *The Palgrave Handbook of Comparative Economics*,
https://doi.org/10.1007/978-3-030-50888-3_3

1   Western Historiography of the Soviet Economy

From the 1930s through to the 1950s, Maurice Dobb's *Soviet Economic Development Since 1917* (first published in 1929) served as the college text of choice (Dobb 1948). Dobb, a Marxist and party member (Dobb 1940), dished out Stalin's version of the necessity of collectivization, forced industrialization, and the superiority of planning over markets. Dobb conveniently failed to mention famines and repression, about which little was known at the time. It would not be until 1968 that Robert Conquest's *The Great Terror* (Conquest 1968) was published to the catcalls of cheer leaders for the Soviet regime. Dobb's pro-Soviet text taught two generations of university students.

The 1950s was a period of optimism for the Soviet system. Memories of the Great Depression still haunted the Western world. Soviet cosmonauts were the first in space. Soviet propaganda hailed the miraculous drive that supposedly transformed the USSR from a backward agricultural into a modern industrial state. The USSR's statistical department published astonishing figures for Soviet growth that showed the USSR would soon overtake the US economy.

The Austrians, F.A. Hayek (1940, 1944, 1945) and Ludwig von Mises (1935), picked apart the notion of viable central planning in their writings dating from the 1920s through to the 1940s. Hayek and Mises, writing from a theoretical point of view, doubted that a planned economy could function without a price system, private property, and market-driven incentives. They were correct in terms of the eventual collapse, but they would have been surprised by how long the Soviet system lasted.

The Russian-born British Sovietologist, Alex Nove, produced in 1961 the first widely used post-Dobb text, *The Soviet Economic System*. Nove's account was drawn mainly from Soviet publications on how the economy was supposed to work, not how it actually functioned. Nove's account largely avoided value judgments, although in later works Nove attempted to fashion a model of "feasible socialism" (Nove 1969). In 1969, Nove published his concise *Economic History of the USSR* (Nove 1969). Like his textbook, Nove's history again rested largely on Soviet sources.

The 1950s and 1960s saw major advances in research on the Soviet economy. The first fruits of Abram Bergson's calculations of real Soviet Gross Domestic Product (GDP) appeared in 1961 (Bergson 1961). The Bergson methodology would be ultimately taken over by the Central Intelligence Agency (CIA) (Joint Economic Committee 1982). It was the CIA growth figures that captured the "period of stagnation" that would plague the post-Khrushchev leadership.

Seminal studies of the inner workings of the Soviet economy began in the 1950s: In his first book entitled *Overcentralization in Economic Administration*, the then-obscure Hungarian economist, Janos Kornai (1994 [1959]) published his critique of the Hungarian planned economy. Kornai (2006, p. 85) studied the system's working arrangements by talking with those who actually ran the planned economy. Kornai warned against the use of official publications because: "Economic administration and planning texts are about how we would like the system to work not how it actually works" (Kornai 2006, p. 87).

Unbeknownst to Kornai, his findings were being corroborated by American scholars at about the same time. Joseph Berliner, *Factory and Manager in the USSR* (Berliner 1957), and David Granick, *Management of the Industrial Firm in the USSR: A Study in Soviet Economic Planning* (Granick 1954), agreed with Kornai's three basic findings.

First, only quarterly output plans mattered, and managers are driven by a fetish to fulfill their quarterly gross output orders by 100 percent, at any price. Plan targets other than gross output did not attract the attention of managers.

Second, managers were relatively uninterested in efficient use of resources. Authorities had to use norms to distribute inputs rather than to rely on managerial choice. As noted by Kornai: "If top management has to be forced by directives and disciplinary penalties to use resources efficiently, then this is evidence of the faulty character of the organizational forms of an economy" (Kornai 1994 [1959], p. 113).

Third, Berliner and Granick noted that, contrary to the myth of planning from the top down, managers engaged in unplanned transactions outside of the planning system, protected by local state and party officials. Gregory Grossman (1963) would later write that a "second economy" of transactions among firms provided the lubricant that made the supply system work.

In his monumental study of early Soviet planning, Eugene Zaleski (1980) found mounting evidence of the lack of firm plans. He relabeled the Soviet economy a "resource managed system." Plans other than quarterly or decadal (ten-day) gross output played at best a role of inspiration rather than of actual resource allocation.

The growing specialized literature on the Soviet economy of the 1950s and 1960s began to find its way into textbooks, the most durable of which was *Soviet Economic Structure and Performance* co-authored by me and the late Robert Stuart. This book, first published in 1974, went through seven editions, the last being 2001, a decade after the collapse of the USSR.

My book with Stuart proposed a teaching paradigm for the Soviet economic system: Start with economic history—the Russian economy, the 1920s, the industrialization debate, and founding the planned economy—turn to how the economy worked (planning, pricing, labor and capital, agriculture, and trade), and then focus on growth and performance. The working arrangements part relied heavily on Berliner, Granick, and Kornai. The performance part was based on the work inspired by Bergson.

Our book was largely a survey of the scholarly literature, which by the 1970s had become substantial. Higher editions of the text benefitted from the immigration of economists from the USSR in the 1970s. Of particular note, Igor Birman (1978) focused attention on the role of "planning from the achieved level" and budget deficits as a sign of system collapse.

Our text did not predict the collapse of the Soviet Union. Instead, it concluded that reform efforts had failed and there were no new ideas in sight. Instead, the Soviet economy had settled into a low-performance equilibrium, aptly called a "treadmill of reform" by noted analyst Gertrude Schroeder (1990). We felt that this state of affairs would continue for decades.

2   The Archival Revolution

The collapse of the Soviet economy preceded the political end of the USSR by several years. As attention turned to transition, few economic specialists remained behind to tap the Soviet state and party archives as they opened. In contrast, historians flocked to the archives to answer the "big questions" of war, peace, repression, modernization, and slave labor. Relatively few economists addressed the planned economy, the most notable exception being R.W. Davies and co-authors in their seven-volume series, *The Industrialization of Russia*, published by Macmillan, the last volume in 2018.

A coordinated effort in exploiting the opening of the Soviet Union's economic archives was conducted by the Hoover Institution Library and Archives, which not only acquired microfilms of the Soviet state and party archives but also supported research workshops, the early ones of which focused on the economy.

We are three decades into the Russian "archival revolution." For comparative economists, the most interesting question is the extent to which the archives changed our understanding of the Soviet planned economy? What "big questions" did we get right and which wrong?

The remainder of this essay is devoted to this question, starting with the nature of the Soviet dictatorship under the quarter-century Stalin rule.

3   Planners' Preference of the Dictator

We begin with the question raised decades ago by political scientist, Merle Fainsod, in the title to his *How Russia is Ruled* (Fainsod 1953). We reword Fainsod to ask how Stalin and his, to use the expression of Steve Wheatcroft (2004), "Team Stalin" managed the economy. In posing this question, we should recall Mises's and Hayek's proposition that the sheer size of the administrative task would make the planning of an entire economy impossible. To the contrary, Soviet texts boasted that dictators, planners, and technocrats, representing the masses, can scientifically guide society toward the eventual achievement of communism. They will free the economy from the "chaos" of the market. It will instead be guided by wise men steeped in the scientific principles of Marxism-Leninism.

Were Stalin and his Politburo such wise men who could produce superior performance to a market economy?

From approximately 1932 until his death in March 1953, Stalin was the dictator of the USSR. He was "not merely a symbol of the regime but the leading figure who made the principal decisions and initiated *all* state actions of *any* significance" (Khlevnyuk 2001, p. 325; my own italics).

At the very apex of Soviet administration stood the Politburo, headed by a General Secretary (Stalin). A much larger Central Committee met periodically to receive the directives of the Politburo. This elite was carefully chosen through a "nomenklatura" process to insure the best and most loyal guide society to communism.

Abram Bergson (1961, chap. 1) coined the term "planners' preference" to describe an economic system in which societal preferences are dictated by the highest political and state authorities of a communist state. Planners' preferences replace market demand for consumer goods, net exports, and investment demand as they scientifically guide society to a paradise of abundance and equity.

Mises and Hayek had argued that an entire economy would be too complex to manage administratively, that its managers would operate without rules, and they would not know what is scarce and what is abundant. The Polish economist, Oskar Lange (1938), to the contrary, argued that scientific planners could take an economy-wide approach. As such, they would internalize externalities, correct for monopoly power, avoid interest groups, and route out rent seeking. For these reasons, a socialist economy guided by planners' preferences could produce superior results to a market economy.

Let us examine how Stalin dictated and enforced planners' preferences.

4   The Stalin Dictatorship

Indeed, Stalin immersed himself deeply in economic matters, both minor and major. Reading his memos, telegrams, and letters reveal that he occupied himself with too many details and that he could not distinguish the important from the trivial. Stalin's correspondence is full of concern about "paper fulfilment" and angry calls for "implementation" committees and placing responsibility on wayward officials (Gregory 2004, pp. 165, 266). Stalin both gave orders and monitored their fulfillment. Stalin, to ensure collective responsibility, required each Politburo member to go on record by rubber-stamping his decisions with their signatures (Gorlitzki and Khlevnyuk 2004).

The archives show that economy-manager Stalin was beset by two types of dictator's curses: First, by holding subordinates responsible for results, he discouraged the flow of unfavorable information to his desk. Good news he got; he saw less of bad news (Wintrobe 1998). Second, subordinates did their best to avoid positions of responsibility (Gregory 2004, chap. 3); they pushed as many decisions as possible up to Stalin's desk. At times, an overwhelmed Stalin would erupt at his associates, "Decide this and decide soon" (Gregory 2004, p. 71), but he would then revert to form as his deputies pleaded: "Without you, we cannot decide."

As he tightened his grip, Stalin increasingly bypassed whatever formal procedures there were. The number of Politburo meetings declined with only one in the second half of 1937 (Rees and Watson 1997, p. 12). Instead of Politburo deliberations, Stalin reached decisions alone or through ad hoc subcommittees that he appointed. During the war years, Stalin ran the economy through the Committee of Defense (*Komitet oborony*). The literature has yet to establish the degree to which the Committee of Defense was run differently during the Second World War.

As to administrative complexity, the Politburo dealt with 200–1000 points per meeting in the mid-1930s. The decrees were prepared in advance by Central Committee branch departments or by delegated state bodies. The issues addressed varied from street names, to appointments, to the building of new industrial plants. In some cases, "in absentia" Politburo meetings were used to approve agenda items that were piling up unattended. The most important items were put in top secret "special folders" (*osobye papki*) for resolution.

Stalin used Politburo meetings to appoint ad hoc committees (*dvoikas, troikas*) to resolve specific issues. Stalin would appoint the chair (usually trusted deputies like Molotov or Kaganovich) and two or three other officials along with deadlines (often just a couple of days).

Such formalities were required because informal meetings of Politburo members were not allowed—to stave off coups. In handing out committee assignments, Stalin would appoint deputies who opposed each other. Such a practice meant that the opposing sides would have to reach a compromise before reporting back.

Stalin's deputies had to follow his frantic pace of work with little sleep. As they wore down physically and mentally, Stalin would order them to take vacation time but sometimes too late. One of his first ministers, Valerian Kuibyshev, literally worked himself to death. In the case of his industrial czar (Sergo Ordzhonikidze), overwork contributed to his death either by heart attack or, as was widely suspected, by suicide.

Team Stalin was beset by an array of principal–agent problems to Stalin chagrin. Stalin was appalled when "loyal" deputies began to fight for the interests of the agency to which he appointed them. Even the faithful Kaganovich began to fight for resources for railroads after he was appointed minister of transport.

Stalin railed against rent seeking within his narrow circle: "It is bad when we begin to deceive each other" (Khlevnyuk et al. 2001, p. 80). He complained bitterly about the "selfishness" of a minister and demanded that the "use of funds must be discussed in the interests of the state as a whole, not only in the interests of the ministry of heavy industry" (Khlevnyuk et al. 2001, pp. 72, 88). He particularly loathed the deputy minister of heavy industry (Pyatakov) for "turning our Bolshevik party into a conglomerate of branch groups" (Rees and Watson 1997, p. 16). When the time came, Stalin had him tortured and shot.

Stalin and the Politburo made the Soviet Union's highest-level decisions supported by some 375 employees of the Central Committee and 1000 employees of Gosplan and the state statistical agency. These numbers were far from enough. One Gosplan department head complained: "We cannot present and decide even one issue because of the complete lack of workers" (Gregory 2004, p. 128).

Duplicates of Politburo decrees (many joint with the Council of Ministers) were sent to the state administration for execution. Normally, the NKVD (People's commissariat for Internal Affairs) was included in the distribution list. Politburo decrees were subject to strict security. Recipients had to sign and return them within a specified period of time. Those who violated these rules, such as forgetting them in a hotel room, were punished.

Working at full speed with Stalin wielding the whip, the Politburo issued 2000–3000 decrees per year in the 1930s. The US Congress, during the same time period, passed an average of ten federal bills per year. These large differences reflect the complexity of management of an administrative-command system versus a democratic market economy.

Zaleski cites figures that underscore the limited coverage of central plans (Zaleski 1980, p. 188). As of 1953, there were some 10,000 indexes that were set by state agencies. The list of industrial products numbered some 20 million. The conclusion: The center planned only a miniscule portion of products that the economy produced. Presumably, this small number of products would be the most important (the so-called commanding heights), but that left the vast majority to be dealt with either "spontaneously" (*stikhino*) or by municipal or regional bodies.

5   The Planned Economy: Gosplan

The Gregory-Stuart and other texts place Gosplan, the State Planning Agency, at the core of the planned economy. Gosplan was the agency assigned to spelling out planners' preferences. Soviet planning texts explained that Gosplan compiled balances of planned outputs and the materials needed to produce these outputs. Imbalances were corrected by ad hoc administrative adjustments, guided by a system of implicit priorities. Once a balance was achieved, the output and input tables yielded a production plan and a delivery plan. Such planning by material balances, Soviet texts explain, was "scientific" and avoided the chaos of the market.

Soviet planning texts spoke of complex annual and quarterly enterprise *techpromfin* (technical industrial financial) plans of inputs, outputs, labor staffing, technology improvements, and profits. Real life was different: Both Kornai (1994 [1959]) and the ministerial archives (Gregory and Markevich 2002, pp. 787–814) reveal that enterprise managers paid attention only to the quarterly *val* (gross output) plan. Other parts of the plan were shunted to the side and prepared or calculated in retrospect.

The studies of Kornai, Berliner, and Granick already demonstrated in the 1950s that managers were judged by *val*. Failure to fulfill the *val* target was punished, sometimes severely. In the *Great Terror*, death or long Gulag sentences were common. Managers scrambled to meet their quarterly plans at any price (*lyuboi tzenoi*). Plan overfulfillment did not redound to the manager's benefit. Overfulfilling enterprises would simply get a tougher plan in the next period ("the ratchet effect"). The emphasis on *val* led to distortions—engine-less tractors, 20-pound nails, and the like. These distortions were the object of ridicule in Soviet satire publications, such as the plan being fulfilled with one huge nail.

The textbook account has Gosplan making the pivotal decisions for the economy through its material balances. Gosplan was crowned as the grand economic boss. What Gosplan decided was law, and plan fulfillment was a legal obligation of all producers (Belova 2001, pp. 131–158).

The logic of bureaucratic behavior therefore suggests that Gosplan should zealously protect its power from those under its tutelage. Gosplan was thought to be an empire builder based on its control of ministries and enterprises.

The archives tell a different story: Gosplan deliberately chose to work at high levels of aggregation. It did not plan actual transactions. Instead it planned generic products in tons, square meters, or numbers of trucks. The higher the level of aggregation, the more Gosplan was removed from actual transactions and hence from responsibility for results. Freedom from responsibility meant lesser chances of firing, prison, or even death sentences.

As originally intended, material balances were to be drawn up in physical terms, tons of this and square meters of that. It became immediately obvious that, with rare exceptions such as barrels of oil or tons of wheat, diverse products (such as types of steel or clothing) had to be added together (using administered prices). The balances were therefore of aggregated products, such as tons of rolled steel. When a plan calling for 10,000 tractors resulted in tractors being delivered without engines, authorities had to admonish tractor producers with special decrees condemning "unfinished production."

The formal planning procedures were complicated, contradictory, and confusing (Markevich 2003). The archives of ministries and enterprises are bereft of final "approved" plans. Plans were labeled "draft" or "preliminary." The draft plan was no more than an informal agreement which could be changed subsequently by virtually any superior. The "correcting" and "finalizing" of plans was a never-ending process; the "final" plan remained always on the horizon (Markevich 2003). Despite the lack of final plans, enterprises were obliged to fulfill the plan "by law" (Belova 2001, pp. 131–158).

For its part, Gosplan resisted planning actual transactions, calling them "syndicate work" (Belova and Gregory 2002, p. 271) and stating: "Gosplan is not a supply organization and cannot take responsibility either for centralized specification of orders by product type or by customer or the regional distribution of products" (Gregory 2004, p. 139). Gosplan also steered clear of inter-ministerial conflicts, arguing: "We are simply not equipped to deal with such matters (Belova and Gregory 2002, p. 271). In short, Gosplan limited its exposure by planning the economy from a height of 30,000 feet and avoiding responsibility for final results.

Stalin did appear, however, to want Gosplan to tell him the truth as a partial solution to his wider principal–agent problems (Belova and Gregory 2002, pp. 269–273). Not content to rely on Gosplan alone for truth telling, Stalin also assigned overlapping oversight to other agencies such as the NKVD or the control commissions.

Truth telling did not necessarily make an independent Gosplan leader such as Deputy Prime Minister, Voznesensky, popular with the other top party managers. Voznesensky was one of Stalin's favorites, but when others found an opportunity to sow distrust with the boss, Stalin had him shot (Gorlitzki and Khlevnyuk 2004, pp. 79–85).

6   Resource Managers Versus Planners

Few understood the workings of Zaleski's resource-managed economy, probably including its participants, but at its core the Stalinist system divided economic actors into "planners" and "resource managers" (Gregory 2004, chap. 6). The "planners," in effect, issued economic directives, while not being held responsible for their fulfillment. The "resource managers" were the subjects of the planners' directives and were held responsible for fulfilling them.

The "planners" included the Politburo, branch departments of the Central Committee, Gosplan and the state supply committee, the State Bank, state and local executive-branch officials, the planning departments of the ministries, and main administrations of ministries (called *glavki*).

Primary resource managers were enterprises and trusts. Ministries and main administrations could be both planners and resource managers. They issued directives to their subordinates as planners and received orders from their superiors as resources managers. Just about any superior—a local party boss, a mayor, or a Politburo member—could intervene in this jumbled mess of planning.

The resource-managed economy was one of arbitrary interventions from superiors of all sorts, some of which contradicted the others. These interventions received loose guidance from the implicit system of priorities.

Stalin (1937, p. 413) welcomed the freedom to adjust as the economy moved through its paces: "Only bureaucrats can think that planning work ends with the creation of the plan. *The creation of the plan is only the beginning* (my italics). The real direction of the plan develops only after the putting together of the plan."

Stalin and others valued "resource mobility." The future is uncertain. Bad and good things happen as we go along. We must be ready to move resources when the time comes. "Resource mobility" is akin to a fire department, ready to fight forest fires. Once they have controlled one fire, they move on to the next.

Resource mobility could not have been better designed for the exercise of political influence. Everything was tentative and subject to arbitrary change by someone higher up in the chain of command. Savvy politicians like Stalin and those below him would weigh the political benefits whenever an influential regional or industrial leader came in looking for resources.

Stalin's unwillingness to bind himself to plans cascaded down through the system, preventing the emergence of a formally rule-based or "law-governed" economy. There were few formal rules, and they were subject to override. Fresh guidelines were issued for each new plan. Ministries operated without charters (Gregory and Markevich 2002, pp. 793–794). The few accounting and loan administration rules were easily ignored with the tacit approval of higher ups (Gregory 2004, pp. 149–151).

The lament of the economic manager was against the bureaucratic planners who issued directives for which they were not responsible, no matter how stupid. As the minister of heavy industry complained: "They give us every day decree upon decree, each successive one is stronger and without foundation" (Gregory 2004, p. 153).

The producer's lament remained the same from 1930 to 1985. Industry czar Sergo Ordzhonikidze complained in 1930: "From the decrees that are being received I guess the impression is that we are idiots. They give us every day decree upon decree, each successive one is tougher than the previous and without foundation" (Khlevnyuk 1993, p. 32). A chief defense contractor (speaking more than 50 years later) echoed Ordzhonikidze: "They would stick their heads into every single issue. They would say: 'This must be so and so.' We told them they were wrong, but they would demand that things be done the way they said it should be done" (Ellman and Kontorovich 1998, p. 47).

Superiors gave orders but bore no responsibility. Ordzhonikidze (in an outburst in a Politburo meeting of August 1931) said: "You want to play the role of bureaucrat, but when my factories fall apart, it is I who must answer" (Khlevnyuk 1993, p. 55). The deputy manager of a military industrial plant echoed these sentiments 50 years later: "They [the defense branch department of the central committee] would inquire why the plan isn't being fulfilled, they acted like they were another Council of Ministers. But they had more authority and none of the responsibilities" (Ellman and Kontorovich 1998, p. 46).

The irritation of constant interventions came to be called "petty tutelage" (*melkaya opeka*) by resource managers. As early as the 1930s, industry czar Ordzhonikidze proposed what a half-century later would became the core of reform proposals: Give him firm production targets, and then let him fulfil these targets on his own without second-guessing by his superiors (Gregory 2004, pp. 245–246). Then, as later, his proposals for reform were ignored.

7   Money and Prices

Prior to the opening of the archives, we thought that money and prices were relatively unimportant in the Soviet command system. A "dictatorship of the seller" was supposed to turn the economy on its head. Instead of sellers seeking buyers, buyers sought sellers. Instead of allocation by price, a planners' "visible hand" was supposed to allocate goods (Nove 1961; Ellman 1979). Prices simply played the accounting role of adding things together.

The monopoly bank (Gosbank) was supposed to be a passive agent whereby the flow of money was dictated by the planned flow of goods. The finance ministry would give Gosbank credit plans for enterprises to settle anticipated transactions among enterprises. Separately, Gosbank allotted cash to enterprises to pay workers based upon their planned staffing. Gosbank was supposed to passively "follow" physical plans in a process called "ruble control" (Gregory and Tikhonov 2000, pp. 1021–1023). Insofar as all financial transactions were conducted by Gosbank, the central bank could supposedly monitor plan fulfillment by following credit and cash transactions among enterprises. Under ruble control, aberrations in financial plans (such as too much cash for the given number of workers) were supposed to signal deviations from physical directives.

The money stock was segregated into bank money for interfirm transactions and cash money for wage payments. Given that firms were supposed to use money only for planned purposes, there was supposed to be little incentive for them to acquire excess holdings of money.

Contrary to the purported passive role of money, the archives show that money played a much larger role than expected. "Ruble control" required very detailed physical plans to work. With enterprise plans subject to constant change, ruble control would have to keep up with revisions, but such was not the case. Allocation actually began not with physical plans, as ruble control requires, but with budgetary assignments to investment and other government uses such as military orders.

The Politburo allotted more time to how rubles would be spent than to "control figures" in physical units (Davies 2001; Gregory 2001; Davies et al. 2004). Financial outlays earned priority because broad-brush supply plans could not fix the detailed assortment of physical products or their final uses. Ministries liked this "money first" arrangement because it freed them to fulfill aggregate ministerial output in ruble form.

Plan targets were primarily fixed in rubles, not in physical units, because outputs were too heterogeneous to be planned in any other way. Supply quotas were also denominated in rubles (Harrison 1998). While the plan target for steel may have been in tons, the directive plan for the enterprise was in rubles. Markevich and Harrison (2004) report the case of an aircraft factory where managers, reprimanded for poor-quality work, were rewarded days later for fulfilling the plan—in rubles.

Actual allocations of resources were achieved through a "contract campaign" among ministries, ministry main administrations, and enterprises. The ministry's supply plan was only the first salvo in the "battle for the plan," in which factories bid with producers for the materials needed for their own plans (Harrison and Simonov 2000; Gregory and Markevich 2002).

The contract campaign bore some semblance to a market-like process, with decentralized contracting introducing a degree of price flexibility. By devising legal and illegal ways to bid up contract prices, suppliers could fulfill both plans and contracts with less effort and more financial gain.

The archives show that price setting was one of the most important activities of Soviet firms (Harrison 1998). Actual transaction prices were negotiated between buyers and sellers during contract campaigns loosely managed from above (Harrison and Simonov 2000; Gregory 2004, pp. 219–220).

Transactions were supposed to be carried out in official prices. Price handbooks, however, were often incomplete, out of date, lagged behind new products, or were ignored. The mammoth metals administration of the ministry of heavy industry employed only three persons in the pricing department (Gregory 2004, p. 280). Military buyers complained of prices based on "how much it costs whether the result of correct work or poor management" (Gregory 2004, p. 220). The "supply dictator" could demand higher prices in the process of negotiation.

Figure 3.1 illustrates the resulting bargain. Say, the plan calls for the transaction of output Q^* at the state price P^*. The supplier prefers to settle for a smaller real quantity, say Q', at the higher price P' along a unit-elastic curve through Q^*, P^*. The producer could justify the higher price by claiming higher costs or by asserting a quality improvement. The buyer, lacking alternative sources of supply, agrees to pay $Q' P'$.

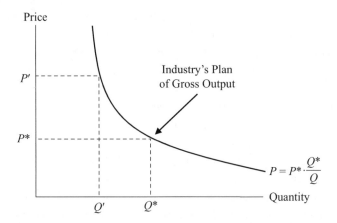

Fig. 3.1 Price setting

A powerful buyer like the military could perhaps complain to the Politburo about price gouging (Davies and Harrison 1997). Regular customers complained frequently to the state arbitration commission (Gregory 2004, p. 220). Complaints, however, meant the risk of disrupting relations with suppliers. A buyer refusing to pay an "illegal" high price would be reminded: "If you don't want to pay, we'll keep this in mind when we consider your next order" (Gregory 2004, p. 220).

Despite the supposed firewall between traceable bank money and anonymous cash, increases in official credits were in fact accompanied by increases in cash holdings (Gregory and Tikhonov 2000, p. 1030). The importance of cash money is underscored by numerous cases of fraud and embezzlement that resulted in the accumulation of large caches of illegal money (Belova 2001).

Unauthorized cash did not necessarily go to line private pockets. Harrison and Kim (2004) argue that the main purpose of siphoning of cash was to help fulfill the plan. Thus Soviet corruption differed from bribe-taking for personal enrichment: managers extracted side payments to recycle the funds into production.

8   Freezing the Economy at the Achieved Level

The Soviet term "from the achieved level" (*ot dostignutogo urovnya*) was made popular by émigré economist Igor Birman (1978). The term referred to the tendency of the Soviet economy to base the current plan on the previous plan plus/minus some small adjustments. Major changes in technology, input mix, and planners' preferences meant major changes in the already complex planning system described above. The archives show clearly that the system had a built-in bias against change. The system's directors opted to stick with existing resource allocations, thereby freezing the economy in place.

Indeed, administrative "balances" and contract campaigns were so difficult and time consuming to achieve that planners were loath to depart from the existing equilibrium. The archives offer illustrative examples: After the first distributions of Soviet-produced vehicles in the early 1930s, based on ad hoc and political considerations, vehicles were thereafter allocated "from the achieved level," whereby each year's plan was basically last year's plus some minor adjustments (Lazarev and Gregory 2003, pp. 1–16). Already in the 1930s, supply agencies were distributing materials "based on historical experience" (Khlevnyuk 1993, p. 32).

Bias against change continued into the 1980s. When a producer of welded materials wished to economize by using thinner metals, the official answer was: "I don't care about new technology. Just do it so that everything remains the same" (Ellman and Kontorovich 1998, p. 49). The leadership's only instrument to test the existing allocation was detailed engineering studies, such as of blast furnaces, which were applied rarely and proved of little use (Davies et al. 2003, p. 55).

An economy whose resource distribution patterns cannot change is doomed to poor performance. In the Soviet case, "campaigns" were required to change allocations and to introduce new technologies—poor substitutes for continuous change in market economies. Soviet industry produced the same lathes, vehicles, clothing, and so on for decades. The only exception was military production, which was singled out for priority and for which a quasi-competitive market existed (Harrison 2003).

"Campaigns" to alter the equilibrium could be double-edged swords as party officials blindly fulfilled the General Secretary's latest whim. Stalin ordered the White Sea canal built, whose shallow depth did not allow for commercial traffic. Ministers and regional party leaders rushed to fulfill Khrushchev's corn and chemical fertilizer programs irrespective of local conditions. Khrushchev's virgin land program turned parts of Siberia and Kazakhstan into dust bowls.

"From the achieved level" captures the main problem of the Soviet planned economy. It was not, as Hayek and Mises speculated, its ability to survive without prices, markets, and property rights. Instead the problem was its inability to adapt to changes in technology, knowledge, and resource availability.

9   Conclusions

The Soviet literature on economic planning pushed a fable of scientific planning in which an enlightened Politburo (representing the working class) sets the economy's major objectives. Planners in Gosplan then prepare material balances of key products, which translate into output and delivery plans. The plan is fulfilled in a "battle for the plan" as enterprises wage a "contract campaign" for deliveries and materials. Instead of chaotic markets, resources will be allocated according to scientific principles, so argued the scientific-planning myth.

The picture that emerges from the archives is of a leadership torn apart by vested interests to the dismay of Stalin. Stalin himself rails against subordinates who represent narrow interests. Rather than operate through established planning practices, Stalin prefers ad hoc committees. He seems to prefer "resource mobility" and "petty tutelage" to an orderly planning process, if such a thing exists.

The Soviet state and party archives paint an unflattering portrait of economic planning, as carried out by Gosplan and the state bank. Balances cannot be drawn up in physical terms. Enterprises operate on the basis of gross output targets which they must fulfill "at any price." Just about any superior can intervene with petty tutelage and change the plan which itself is never finalized. Because of the complexity and arbitrary nature of planning from material balances to contracting, the actors in this drama are loath to deviate from the "achieved level" irrespective of changes in tastes, technology, and resource availability. In effect "scientific planning" freezes the economy in place while market economies around it create new technologies, new products, and new ways of doing things—spurred on by the "anarchy of the market."

References

Belova, E. (2001). Economic Crime and Punishment. In P. R. Gregory (Ed.), *Behind the Façade of Stalin's Command Economy: Evidence from the State and Party Archives* (pp. 131–158). Stanford, CA: Hoover Institution Press.

Belova, E., & Gregory, P. R. (2002). Dictator, Loyal and Opportunistic Agents: The Soviet Archives on Creating the Soviet Economic System. *Public Choice, 113*(3–4), 265–286.

Bergson, A. (1961). *The Real National Income of Soviet Russia Since 1928*. Cambridge, MA: Harvard University Press.

Berliner, J. (1957). *Factory and Manager in the USSR*. Cambridge, MA: Harvard University Press.

Birman, I. (1978). From the Achieved Level. *Soviet Studies, 30*(2) April, 153–172.

Conquest, R. (1968). *The Great Terror*. Oxford: Oxford University Press, Conquest.

Davies, R. W. (2001). Making Economic Policy. In P. R. Gregory (Ed.), *Behind the Façade of Stalin's Command Economy: Evidence from the State and Party Archives* (pp. 61–80). Stanford, CA: Hoover Institution Press.

Davies, R. W., & Harrison, M. (1997). The Soviet Military-Economic Effort Under the Second Five-Year Plan 1933–1937. *Europe-Asia Studies, 49*(3), 369–406.

Davies, R. W., Khlevnyuk, O. V., Rees, E. A., Kosheleva, L. P., & Rogovaya, L. A. (Eds.). (2003). *The Stalin-Kaganovich Correspondence, 1931–36*. New Haven, CT: Yale University Press.

Davies, R. W. et. al. (2004). *The Industrialization of Soviet Russia*. London: MacMillan Palgrave.

Davies, R. W., et al. (Eds.). (2018). *The Soviet Economy and the Approach of War, 1937–1939* (The Industrialization of Soviet Russia) (Vol. 7). London: Palgrave Macmillan.

Dobb, M. (1940, August). What the Communist Party Has Meant to Me. *The Labour Monthly*, 445–446.

Dobb, M. (1948). *Soviet Economic Development Since 1917*. London: Routledge.

Ellman, M. (1979). *Socialist Planning*. Cambridge: Cambridge University Press.

Ellman, M., & Kontorovich, V. (1998). *Destruction of the Soviet Economic System*. White Plains, NJ: M.E Sharpe.

Fainsod, M. (1953). *How Russia Is Ruled*. Cambridge, MA: Harvard University Press.

Gorlitzki, Y., & Khlevnyuk, O. (2004). *Cold Peace: Stalin and the Soviet Ruling Circle, 1945–1953*. New York: Oxford University Press.

Granick, D. (1954). *Management of the Industrial Firm in the USSR: A Study in Soviet Economic Planning*. New York: Columbia University Press.

Gregory, P. R. (2001). The Dictator's Orders. In P. R. Gregory (Ed.), *Behind the Façade of Stalin's Command Economy: Evidence from the State and Party Archives* (pp. 11–33). Stanford, CA: Hoover Institution Press.

Gregory, P. R. (2004). *The Political Economy of Stalinism: Evidence from the Soviet Secret Archives*. New York: Cambridge.

Gregory, P. R., & Markevich, A. (2002). Creating Soviet Industry: The House That Stalin Built. *Slavic Review, 61*(4), 787–814.

Gregory, P., & Stuart, R. (1974). *Soviet Economic Structure and Performance*. New York: Harper and Row.

Gregory, P. R., & Tikhonov, A. (2000). Central Planning and Unintended Consequences: Creating the Soviet Financial System, 1930–1939. *Journal of Economic History, 60*(4), 1017–1040.

Grossman, G. (1963, October). The Second Economy of the USSR. *Problems of Communism, 26*(5), 525–540.

Harrison, M. (1998). Prices, Planners, and Producers: An Agency Problem in Soviet Industry, 1928–1950. *Journal of Economic History, 58*(4), 1032–1062.

Harrison, M. (2003). The Political Economy of a Soviet Military R&D Failure: Steam Power for Aviation, 1932 to 1939. *Journal of Economic History, 63*(1), 178–212.

Harrison, M., & Kim, B.-Y. (2004). *Plans, Prices, and Corruption: The Soviet Firm Under Partial Centralization, 1930 to 1990.* Working Paper. University of Warwick, Department of Economics. Retrieved from http://www.warwick.ac.uk/go/markharrison/papers.

Harrison, M., & Simonov, N. (2000). Voenpriemka: Prices, Costs, and Quality Assurance in Interwar Defence Industry. In J. Barber & M. Harrison (Eds.), *The Soviet Defence-Industry Complex from Stalin to Khrushchev* (pp. 223–245). Basingstoke: Macmillan.

Hayek, F. A. (1940). Socialist Calculation: The Competitive 'Solution'. *Economica, 7*(26), 125–149.

Hayek, F. A. (1944). *The Road to Serfdom.* Chicago: University of Chicago Press.

Hayek, F. A. (1945). The Use of Knowledge in Society. *American Economic Review, 35*(4), 519–530.

Joint Economic Committee of Congress. (1982, December 8). *USSR: Measures of Economic Growth and Development, 1950–1980.* Washington, DC: U.S. Government Printing Office.

Khlevnyuk, O. V. (1993). *Stalin i Ordzhonikidze: konflikty v Politburo v 30-e gody.* Moscow: Rossiia molodaia.

Khlevnyuk, O. V. (2001). Stalinism and the Stalin Period After the 'Archival Revolution'. *Kritika, 2*(2), 319–328.

Khlevnyuk, O. V., Davies, R. W., Kosheleva, L. P., Rees, E. A., & Rogovaia, L. A. (Eds.). (2001). *Stalin i Kaganovich. Perepiska. 1931–1936 gg.* Moscow: ROSSPEN.

Kornai, J. (1994 [1959]). *Overcentralization in Economic Administration.* Oxford: Oxford University Press.

Kornai, J. (2006). *By Force of Thought: Irregular Memoirs of an Intellectual Journey.* Cambridge, MA: MIT Press.

Lange, O. (1938). *On the Economic Theory of Socialism* (with Fred M. Taylor). B. E. Lippincott (Ed.). Minneapolis: University of Minnesota Press.

Lazarev, V., & Gregory, P. R. (2003). Commissars and Cars: A Case Study in the Political Economy of Dictatorship. *Journal of Comparative Economics, 31*(1), 1–19.

Markevich, A. (2003). *Was the Soviet Economy Planned? Planning in the People's Commissariats in the 1930s.* PERSA Working Paper No. 9. University of Warwick, Department of Economics. Retrieved from http://www.warwick.ac.uk/go/persa.

Markevich, A., & Harrison, M. (2004). *Quality, Experience, and Monopoly: Regulating the Soviet Seller's Market for Military Goods.* PERSA Working Paper No. 35. University of Warwick, Department of Economics. Retrieved from http://www.warwick.ac.uk/go/persa.

von Mises, L. (1935 [1920]). Die Wirtschaftsrechnung im Mises sozialistischen Gemeinwesen. Translated in *Collectivist Economic Planning: Critical Studies on the Possibility of Socialism*. F.A. Hayek (Ed.). London: Routledge, pp. 87–130.

Nove, A. (1961). *The Soviet Economy* (1st ed.). London: Allen & Unwin.

Nove, A. (1969). *An Economic History of the USSR*. London: Allen & Unwin.

Rees, A. E., & Watson, D. (1997). *The Nature of the Soviet Dictatorship: The Politburo*. Basingstoke: Palgrave MacMillan.

Schroeder, G. (1990, January). Economic Reform of Socialism: The Soviet Record. *The Annals of the American Academy of Political and Social Science, 507*, 35–43.

Stalin, I. V. (1937). *Voprosy Leninizma* (10th ed.). Moscow: Gospolitizdat.

Wheatcroft, S. G. (2004). From Team-Stalin to Degenerate Tyranny. In E. A. Rees (Ed.), *The Nature of Stalin's Dictatorship: The Politburo 1924–1953* (pp. 79–107). Basingstoke and London: Macmillan.

Wintrobe, R. (1998). *The Political Economy of Dictatorship*. Cambridge: Cambridge University Press.

Zaleski, E. (1980). *Stalinist Planning for Economic Growth 1933–1952*. Chapel Hill, NC: University of North Carolina Press.

4

Institutions, Institutional Systems and Their Dynamics

Leszek Balcerowicz

1   Introduction

Mainstream economics had for a long time neglected institutions either ignoring them completely by focusing on the proximate determinants of economic performance (consumption, investment, employment, productivity, etc.) or disregarding their variation by assuming an unrealistic set of market institutions (perfect competition), or an idealized conception of the state as a benevolent and omniscient entity. This was a sort of institutional "Daltonism" (color-blindness), which led mainstream economics to miss the most important issues of the real world or to formulate wrong conclusions, often with a statist bias recommending various government interventions as a cure for social ills. Against this background, it is important to recognize the impact of the analytical institutional economics of Hayek, Friedman, Buchanan, Tullock, Coase and most recently North. This literature has to some extent corrected the institutional Daltonism in economics, though much remains to be done precisely in the context of a New Comparative Economics orientation explored in this book.

I have focused on institutional issues both in my academic activity and as a policymaker in charge of Poland's economic reforms. The fusion of these two

L. Balcerowicz (✉)
Warsaw School of Economics, Warszawa, Poland
e-mail: lbalce@sgh.waw.pl

© The Author(s) 2021
E. Douarin, O. Havrylyshyn (eds.), *The Palgrave Handbook of Comparative Economics*,
https://doi.org/10.1007/978-3-030-50888-3_4

occupations has helped me to come to a view on four main tasks of institutional economics:

1. Clarifying and standardizing the definitions of the main institutional variables and improving their measurement.
2. Exploring what institutional arrangements in various spheres of social life can lastingly co-exist (i.e. form a system) and which cannot.
3. Expanding the enormously important research on the relationship between various institutional systems (stable or changing) and various dimensions of the people's standard of living, both economic and non-economic.
4. Explaining the political economy of institutional change including transitions from one system to another.

Perhaps not surprisingly given my own experience, this chapter focuses on the fourth problem, which, I think, is the most complex, but some discussion of the others is essential. For example, institutional dynamics depend on the institutional system, so some conceptual clarifications will be needed. Even though the relationship between the institutional system and country performance is not the main subject, I will also refer to the differences in systems' performance in order to explore a naïve but important question: why do regimes which perform very badly tend to persist, while those which perform much better are constantly under attack by some domestic forces?

The chapter is structured as follows: Sect. 2 aims to clarify the basic concepts: institutions, institutional systems, institutional systems versus policies, the political and economic systems. Section 3 contrasts the dynamics of the two best-known and polar-opposite systems: highly centralized and highly decentralized. Section 4 then extends the typology of institutional systems to a typology of major institutional transitions. Section 5 illustrates the latter with a brief discussion of two major institutional transformations in the twentieth century: toward socialism and away from it, while Section 6 parallels this with an analytical scheme for the determinants of liberal or statist economic transitions in democracy. Section 7 concludes.

2   Institutions and Institutional Systems

Institutions are best conceived as variables—factors that take various forms across countries and/or through time in a given location. They are usually defined as rules, which are not only enclosed in formal documents as written rules but also expressed or observed on a daily basis in their enforced practical form. One should thus distinguish two interdependent dimensions of institutional rules:

1. Their content
2. The mechanisms of their enforcement and the related degree of implementation

The degree of implementation of the rules can depend on their content, as easily illustrated by the story of the Prohibition in the US which shown that even a heavy application of police power could not stop certain behaviors—in this case consumption and consequent production of alcohol. Indeed the failure of preventing this behavior resulted in a wave of crime. This seems to be the case with the contemporary "war on drugs" too.

If rules in the form of prohibitions may be unenforceable (unless under terror), rules that seemingly describe individual liberties are sometimes a sham and are not taken seriously by their nominal beneficiaries: socialist history is full of such examples. Therefore, it has become useful to distinguish between *de jure* and *de facto* institutions; the former are stated by what is written and the latter are the results of the enforcement mechanisms. These mechanisms are usually divided into those that are part of the state and those which are "operated" by the smaller or larger groups in the society, for example, the caste system in India, the mafia in Italy, norms and public pressure to maintain them in all societies. In the literature rules enforced by the state are often called "formal", while those enforced by non-state mechanisms are called "informal". One of the most important issues in institutional economics is the relationship between formal and informal institutions, especially whether the latter strengthen the operation of the former, or—on the contrary—weaken it.

Rules are linked to organizations and networks. First, some rules prohibit certain organizations as, for example, under socialism, private firms were banned to ensure the monopoly of state ownership (and of central planning). Second, the more repressive are the rules, the stronger must be the enforcement apparatus, lest they remain on paper.

Let me now move from institutions to an institutional system (regime). I define it as a set of institutions that have a strong-enough internal cohesion that they can last a long time regardless of their performance. Obviously, depending on the system's performance, there will be different uses of force and intimidation toward those that oppose it, whether actively or potentially.

An institutional system should be conceived as consisting of rules and the related organizations (networks), which in turn consist of their own rules.

Institutional systems exist at various levels:

1. Localities (cities), provinces (regions) in federal states
2. Countries
3. The supra-national level (the most important example is the European Union)

The greatest variation in institutional systems exists among countries and it is this level I will focus on.

Important empirical questions are thus (a) which institutions, in various spheres of social life, can co-exist for a long time and form a stable institutional system, and (b) what are the "cohesion forces" or functional requirements (Balcerowicz 1995) behind this stability. For example, central planning, to replace market coordination, requires massive, multilevel bureaucracy to formulate the plan and distribute the commands and needed inputs. The existence of such a bureaucracy becomes a functional requirement of socialism since central planning cannot co-exist with decentralized organizational structures. This is, thus, an example of "institutional impossibility". Socialism, that is, a regime without private ownership and markets cannot lastingly co-exist, with democracy defined by an open and regular political competition as expressed by regular free elections. This is another "institutional impossibility".

Let me now distinguish between institutional systems and policies. There is much confusion on this point in the literature: some authors include certain factors into institutions, while other authors classify them as policies.[1] These conceptual differences often distort research on the relative role of institutions and policies in determining countries' performance.

I define policies as actions of policymakers which:

1. Result in a change in the institutions, for example, political or economic liberalization, switching from fixed rate to floating exchange rate regime, a change in electoral law. These policies are usually called reforms; or
2. Operate through other variables, for example, interest rates (monetary, policy), budgetary allocations (fiscal policy), changes of personnel.

---

[1] Rodrik et al. (2004, p. 156) for a similar point on policies as flow and institutions as stock.

Various institutional systems give rise to different sets of possible policies. The most important of institutional variables which differentiates these sets is concentration of political power, inversely related to the constrains on the executive and the level of the rule of law.

What policy is chosen from the set of policies allowed by a given institutional system depends mostly on the personality of the leader and on the country's economic and political situation. Despotic regimes allow psychopaths to gain and keep power and pursue the most destructive policies, terrible economic crises and even genocides (e.g. Mao, Stalin, Pol Pot). Contrary to the widespread anti-capitalist propaganda, the worst crises—in the sense of deep breakdowns in the economy—occur under the socialist dictatorship and not in market economies (for more, see Balcerowicz 2015).

A radical change of the institutional system, especially in its key dimension, the concentration of political power, affects a country's long-term growth performance through two channels:

1. It changes individuals' opportunity sets (the scope of freedom) and their incentives.
2. It changes the risk of very bad policies and the resulting risks of crises.

The first channel changes the speed of economic growth, and the second changes the frequency and severity of growth breakdowns.

It is useful to distinguish within a country's institutional system various functional subsystems, including the political and economic ones—though there can be no universal agreement on which institutions should be included in what system. Usually the political regime is defined as comprising the state organizations, the party system, the laws regulating the keeping and changing power in the state, and the extent of state power. A wide consensus exists that the economic system includes institutions which are most relevant for such economic outcomes as output, employment, saving investing, spending, and so on. Specifically, this includes things such as freedom of private ownership and enterprise, financial institutions accessible fairly to all, legal protection of these rights, and due process of commercial litigation without political influence.

Such a conceptual separation should not be confused with the separation between political and economic actors. One can argue that the degree of separation between them is one of the most important institutional variables distinguishing various institutional systems. At one extreme, there is socialism—a highly centralized system which involves enormous politization of economic life, resulting in a very limited autonomy of economic actors.[2] At the other extreme, there is the highly decentralized system of the free market, which, thanks to strong limitations and controls on political power (the checks and balances, the rule of law), enables extensive and well-protected private property rights. Examples of the latter type of system include historically liberal countries at the turn of the nineteenth and twentieth centuries such as Great Britain, Sweden or the US and in the contemporary world: Hong Kong, Ireland, Switzerland or Sweden (though the two last cases also have high taxes and some regulations).

Very different systems display very different performances. This issue is beyond the topic of this chapter, but it is broadly accepted that the systems closest to the highly decentralized model generally perform economically much better than the highly centralized ones—for the simple reason that an extended and well-protected economic freedom is widely superior to the politization of the economy.[3] As a result, the latter regimes have to rely on intimidation to keep the population in check, a policy not required, in the case of highly decentralized systems.

Also, very different institutional systems display very different dynamics which influences their long-term economic performance. It is this topic to which I now turn.

3   Different Institutional Systems Have Different Dynamics

The institutional dynamics, that is, the extent and direction of the change in institutions in a given country, depends on their initial institutional system. Let me discuss this issue by contrasting a highly centralized and highly decentralized regimes which I have characterized earlier.

In the former, with its heavy concentration of political power which rules out both economic and civil liberties, the decisions regarding the institutions are centralized too. At the same time a highly centralized regime with its ban on economic freedom produces increasingly worse economic results compared to the more liberal systems and over time. The naïve question is why

---

[2] Actual autonomy may be larger than the formal one because economic actors have better information about their own possibilities than their superiors. This information asymmetry cannot prevent the political rulers from taking very bad economic decisions.

[3] A recent confirmation of this superiority for post-communist countries is given by Havrylyshyn et al. (2016) which demonstrate that countries that have moved closest to a market regime performed much better than slow reformers.

socialist systems persist and are not abolished by those who suffer, that is, by the masses. The simple answer to this naïve question is that those who rule in such a bad regime are shielded from its economic consequences and those who suffer are intimidated and—in the worst cases—liquidated. Therefore, a radical change must come either from outside—see the occupations and reforms in Germany and Japan after World War II—or from within the "black box" of the ruling group. The external isolation of a country and the internal controls make the prediction of the regime change practically impossible.

A less naïve question is why a top ruler who concentrates so much power does not use it to change the regime via economic liberalization so that it performs economically better. Mancur Olson (1993) in his seminal article on democratization contrasted a "roving" bandit leader with a "stationary one". The time horizon of the former is short or uncertain; therefore, he (she) is not interested in making the subjected population more productive, because it would not increase his gains. However, the time horizon of the latter is long and reasonably certain. As a result, he should be interested in economic liberalization, as it would increase the population's output and, thus, the size of his share.

This concept is developed further by Clague et al. (1996), who suggested that, indeed, long-lasting autocracies have better economic systems than the unstable ones. However, there have also been many long-lasting despotic regimes which have displayed a terrible economic performance. The USSR existed for 70 years, Mao's China for 30 years, and North Korea and Cuba continue to exist to this day, and economically well-performing autocracies are very rare. Clearly, the economic incentives of a socialist autocrat to launch economic liberalization are either not present or are dominated by other factors. There are three possible explanations for this:

* An autocrat may be mostly interested in power and, therefore, in the preservation of highly centralized system. Stalin in the USSR is an example here.
* An autocrat may be blinded by the statist doctrine and isolated from sources of independent information. As a result, he/she may believe in the superiority of the existing regime. Gorbachev was a very intelligent man, but he was genuinely convinced that state ownership is a correct solution. Until his last days as a secretary of communist party of the USSR, he was very hesitant to accept private ownership (Taubman 2017).
* A dictator may be aware of the faults of the regime he governs. He thus may be interested in its economic liberalization. However, he may be afraid of how his "selectorate"—the group he depends on—will react to his

reforms or suspect they may try to sabotage them. This is a story of some tsars in Russia and some Popes in the Middle Ages.

In sum, bad economic performance of the socialist dictatorship is clearly not sufficient to engender changes and transition toward an economically more liberal system, because the ruling elite not only benefits from the *status quo* but is able to use force and intimidation to suppress any demands for change. Therefore, the link between the performance and the longevity of the system is weak, and inefficient systems can continue for a long time despite poor performance. However, in real life socialist regimes have differed in their duration and the mode and extent of transformation. A striking example of how much transformation can differ is found in the contrasting experiences of China, where the change started in the late 1970, and the USSR and the former Soviet bloc where it began only about 1989–1992. The comparison of these two cases is a fascinating subject for the comparative history and the political economy of institutional change. I return to this topic later.

Let me, for now, turn to the opposite case—that of the highly decentralized institutional system with the extensive individual liberties, both economic and non-economic, well protected by the rule of law. These features allow massive bottom-up institutional innovations in the way individuals cooperate and interact: in contracts, networks, business models and organizations. Also, economic liberties and the related competition produce a constant stream of technical innovation which, in turn, spur the institutional ones—consider how Internet search engines or mobile phones have transformed the ways in which people interact and cooperate.

In contrast to the highly centralized system, the highly decentralized one produces good economic and non-economic outcomes and allows a lot of individual freedom. The question why centralized regimes tend to persist despite their bad economic performance was explained above. The analogous question in the case of the highly decentralized systems is: why don't they automatically persist, despite their good performance in terms of prosperity and individual freedoms, that is, why are they often subjected to various statists attacks, which, if successful, worsen aggregate outcomes. In other words, what factors weaken the link between the good performance of the highly decentralized systems and their continued existence? This question is addressed in Sect. 4.

4 The Typology of Institutional Systems and of the Major Transitions

There can be various typologies of institutional systems. I present below one based on the several institutional variables which are nowadays measured by various indices—thanks to organizations like Freedom House, Fraser Institute, Heritage Foundation and so on. A cautionary note: I do not pretend that real-life regimes in history will fit neatly into this theoretical schema, the examples shown in the last column are only illustrative. In particular note that I do not here consider other dimensions that may affect both the choice of system and its performance, such as cultural norms, social values, trust levels, national identity and so on.[4] Nevertheless it is useful to have such a theoretical schema for a broad understanding of the interplay between various societal institutions and types of political regimes, as shown in Table 4.1.

Table 4.1 Types of institutional systems

	Dimensions				
Types	Mechanisms of succession	Civil rights	Rule of law	Economic rights (freedoms)	Examples of countries
Socialism	Non-democratic	Banned	Very low	Banned/command economy	North Korea, Cuba
Quasi-socialism	Non-D	Banned	Very low	Very limited	Belarus, Venezuela, many Arab countries
Liberal capitalism	Usually D	Extensive	High	Extensive, well and reasonably equally protected	Hong Kong, Ireland, Switzerland, Sweden, Estonia
Quasi-liberalism	Usually D	Extensive	High	More limited than under liberal capitalism due to more regulations. Protection similar to that under (3)	Most OECD countries
Crony (oligarchic) capitalisms	Non-D	Low	Low	Very unequal protection of private property rights	Russia, Kazakhstan

---

[4] I am grateful to Paul Wachtel for noting the importance of the other dimensions.

The organizations providing the indices referred to in the table offer detailed definitions for these institutional variables; but some clarification is useful. Every institutional system includes a mechanism for filling political (and other) positions, in other words—a mechanism of personal succession. Even in the most autocratic systems, there must be some mechanism to replace dictators after their death. One mechanism is democracy (D) a regular, open and legal competition for political positions through free elections (Schumpeter 1947), with extensive civil liberties (freedom of speech, freedom of association, etc.)—this is an example of functional necessity. Therefore, limiting these rights lowers the level of democracy, until it becomes a sham: for example, elections without choice that serve as an instrument to check the obedience of the ruled. Non-democratic mechanism (non-D) of filling in political positions includes dynastic succession, and the scheme whereby a head of the main organization which monopolizes power, such as a mono-party, or the army, succeeds to the ruler of the state.

Rule of law has many definitions. It is useful to define it as a variable, which has high values when the state rules through law (and not through enforcement by secret police). The law must meet certain formal requirements, for example, clarity, consistency, transparency and respect *de facto* the principle of due process. The larger are the deviations from these definitional requirements; the lower is the level of the rule of law.

Economic freedom is conceptually related to the type of property rights (private, communal, state) and to the extent of regulations limiting private rights. What is often overlooked is the distribution of economic rights across various groups in society. Historically, freedom differed across groups—both *de jure* and *de facto* (e.g. the rights of serfs versus those of aristocracy). Good governance is increasingly understood as equality before the law, and this equality has become a norm in modern democracies.[5] This is a great achievement, that is, there is no discrimination by the *de jure* institutions. But the protection of economic and other rights may differ across groups, difference is very important for the performance of a various economic systems.

Note that the definitions and measures of economic freedom often ignore differences in tax burden, which are strictly related to the size of fiscal spending. Whenever the latter is large, it is because of social expenditures—or in other words—of the welfare state. The more developed definitions of the economic freedom should include differences in tax burden broadly defined, perhaps including excess size and complexity of taxes.

I comment briefly on the types of the institutional systems sketched out based on the institutional variables discussed. Socialism overlaps with a highly

---

[5] As discussed in Rothstein and Teorell (2008).

centralized system; quasi-socialism, similarly to socialism, is generally non-democratic and also displays a very low level of rule of law. It is still dominated by the state sector but less so than under socialism, thus allowing a wider range of operations for private firms and for markets. This, however, has proven insufficient to allow quasi-socialism to perform much better than socialism. Poor economic outcomes in many Arab countries are ascribed by some observers to their religion: Islam. Kuran (2004) questions this long-standing thesis arguing in the context of the Ottoman regime that poor incentives for commercial activity—institutions in modern jargon—were an important causal factor. It is possible this applied as well to the second half of the twentieth-century period when "Arab socialism" prevailed (i.e. quasi-socialism in Table 4.1, as in Egypt under Nasser, Syria under the Assads, Iraq under Hussein).

Capitalism is usually defined as a system which allows private ownership of productive assets and a dominant role for markets; but this allows for a huge variation of capitalistic systems:

Liberal (entrepreneurial) capitalism overlaps with the category of the highly decentralized system. Its defining feature is a wide scope of economic freedom that is highly and reasonably equally protected within the framework of the rule of law. This produces a wide scope of free markets.

Quasi-liberal capitalism differs from the liberal one in that it suffers from substantially more regulations, which limit the economic freedom and the scope of free markets, especially with respect to labor markets. However, there are no sharp inter-group differences in the level of the protection of economic freedom. Quasi-liberal capitalism is a heterogeneous category: including, for example, France or Italy which suffer from more regulation than others, for example, Britain or the Netherlands.

Oligarchic (or crony) capitalism is distinguished by very unequal protection of nominally equal economic rights: the ruling politicians and/or people close to them enjoy privileges in the form of government contracts, licenses and—in the extreme cases like Russia—the possibility to use the state apparatus to grab the assets of other businesses or people.[6] Such situation exists because of unofficial politico-economic networks, that is, informal institutions, which penetrate the formal ones. Crony capitalism is obviously not only unjust but also inefficient because it sharply limits economic competition and—in its extreme form—exposes normal entrepreneurs to painful uncertainty. Russia today is a prime example of this category, as described in Aslund (2019).

---

[6] See Sonin (2003).

Typologies of institutional systems, based on clear and measurable criteria, can serve four analytical proposes:

First, they are indispensable for the comparative economics of stable institutional systems,[7] which aims at explaining differences in their performances (growth, employment, inflation, health, inequalities, etc.). Mainstream economics has been for far too long anti-institutional, that is, it either disregarded institutional factors or disregarded their variation. In the first case, it focused on the proximate factors of growth like investment rates; in the second, it implicitly assumed an idealized set of market institutions. In both cases, this institutional Daltonism led the most prominent representatives of mainstream economics to ignore the most important issues of the real world and sometimes to formulate deeply wrong conclusions (see the Samuelson-Nordhaus textbook where they seriously suggested that the USSR may overtake the US in the level of GDP) (Samuelson and Nordhaus 1985). The neo-institutionalism of Hayek, Friedman, Buchanan, Tullock, Coase, North and others has to some extent corrected the institutional Daltonism of mainstream economics. But much remains to be done.

Second, analytically based typologies define various types of institutional transitions, for example:

* toward liberal capitalism;
* toward socialism;
* from socialism to quasi-socialism, crony capitalism, quasi-liberal capitalism, liberal capitalism;
* from liberal capitalism to quasi-liberal or to crony capitalism;
* from quasi-liberal capitalism to liberal one;

By defining the institutional starting points and the direction of change, analytically based typologies may bring more order into a very broad and diffuse field of institutional change.

Third, a typology of institutional systems, and the related definition of the types of transitions, constitutes the necessary basis for the study of systems in transition and in particular for the study of countries undergoing institutional transitions. Indeed, this should be distinguished from the economics under stable institutional systems. The former deals with variables which are not present in the latter, for example, regarding the link between scope and pace of the economic liberalization and fiscal reform, on the one hand, and the

---

[7] Stability of the highly decentralized system is defined by the stability of their extensive freedoms which produces massive bottom-up institutional change.

country's economic performance, on the other. This issue was widely discussed in connection with the transition after socialism often with reference to a misleading and primitive juxtaposition of the "shock therapy" versus "gradualism" (for more on that, see Balcerowicz 2014).

Fourth, types of institutional transitions derived from a typology of institutional systems may be of help in the politics (political economy) of transitions which tries to explain—or even more ambitiously—to predict, the launching and the longevity of real-life reforms (or counter-reforms).

The comparative economics of institutional systems is enormously important from a practical point of view. Fortunately, we are here on relatively firm analytical grounds. One has to be blinded by the collectivist doctrines to deny the fundamental role of economic freedom and the rule of law for the economic and non-economic dimension of people's standard of living. Unfortunately, there is no lack of such people in academia, media and politics. But this is a fundamental political and communication problem, not an analytical one.

The economics of systems in transition can build on the comparative economics of stable systems in pointing out what is the best target system—the goal of transitions. There is still some confusion and some work to do regarding the modes of transitions and especially what is the optimal scope and pace of reforms under different initial conditions. I am speaking, of course, about the reforms, which aim at a lasting improvement in people's standard of living.

By far the more complex issue is the political economy (politics) of institutional transitions. The broader is the temporal and spatial scope of the history one deals with, the more tempting are sweeping generalizations (the "laws of history"), like the ones proposed by Hegel or Marx. They should be resisted as there are some fundamental reasons why such generalization (not to mention predictions) are bound to be misleading or highly superficial:

* As distinct from the physical objects people engage in strategic behavior.
* It is impossible to determine precisely what are the thresholds which, if surpassed, set in motion radical changes in group's behavior, for example, rebellions and civil wars.
* Social reality is not only shaped by some systematic forces (e.g. demography) but also by largely unpredictable shocks, for example, wars, fundamentally new technologies, the appearance and spread of doctrines (e.g. collectivism). And shocks interact in various ways. For example, the Great Depression has been interpreted by many intellectuals as the proof that the free market economy is fundamentally unstable, and this interpretation increased the popularity of the statist doctrine of Keynes.

In the following, I will briefly discuss selected cases of transitions.

5   Transition Toward Socialism and Away from It

Contrary to Marx's predictions, the socialist system first appeared in tsarist Russia and not in the most developed capitalistic countries. The Marxist ideology had infected a group of Bolsheviks: ruthless intellectual terrorists, headed by Lenin. They used the upheavals of World War I, in the Tsarist Empire, to capture the state and later perpetuated their power by terror. In this process, they had an unbelievable series of good fortunes (see Pipes 1990). The socialist system did not need to happen, but once it had happened in the USSR, it spread (after World War II) by invasion or military intimidation in the CEE. Therefore, there was nothing secret or complex about the diffusion of the Soviet model in Europe. It was also adopted by a number of domestic dictators—via imitation but also through professional and financial assistance from the USSR and other socialist countries—in Cuba and many African countries.

China in 1949 became another center of socialism after a destructive civil war and the war with Japan. It was then subjected until the late 1970s to the inhuman rule of Mao.

Therefore historically, socialism has always been introduced by internal or external force. Once introduced, it persisted despite its bad performance, because of the mechanisms I have described before: the ruling elite was shielded from its worse consequences, while the masses were intimated and to some extent indoctrinated.

The long existence of socialist systems despite their deplorable performance is not a puzzle. Much more puzzling and unexpected was their demise. This was—after the downfall of Nazism—the most liberating development in the twentieth century, analyzed in many books. However, no theory could have predicted what has happened in China in the late 1970s and in the Soviet bloc in 1989–1991.

In China, after the death of Mao, his successor Deng Xiaoping moved the country away from socialism, that is, from the dominance of state ownership in the economy and central planning. The share of the private and quasi-private sector in employment increased from close to zero in the late 1970s to above 80% in 2016. This massive privatization—mostly thanks to the setting up and developing of new private firms, has been the main driving force behind China's accelerated economic growth. And this happened under the rule of a monopolistic party which still calls itself "communist"! Chinese economic growth has been also helped by enormous private saving which, in turn, were possible thanks to keeping the welfare state in check. Fiscal spending indeed declined from 30% of GDP in the late 1970s to below 20% 15 years later.

The demise of socialism in the USSR was very different. Stalin, the Soviet despot, died in 1953 and his successor, Khrushchev, reduced the intensity of people's intimidation. However, neither he nor his successors attempted any serious liberalization of the economy—despite its growing inefficiency and massive shortages. This situation of growing economic problems and no market reforms continued during the 1980s—when Chinese rulers were liberalizing their economy. Only at the very end of the USSR, Gorbachev legalized the creation of private firms (but under the socialist name of the cooperatives). However the forces he had inadvertently set in motion under the heading of "glasnost" (freedom of the media, more open political competition) led to the dissolution of his party and the USSR. One wonders why the Soviet rulers were so much more orthodox in their economic polices compared to their Chinese colleagues. My guess is that this was largely due to differences in the personality of the rulers or the ruling groups in both countries. These factors matter in political developments, especially in systems with the heavy concentration of political power.

6   Economic Transitions Under Democracy

The economic transitions in democratic countries can be divided into liberal transition (deregulations, privatizations) and statist transition, that is, those which increase the degree of political control over the economy. There has been large variation in the frequency of both types of transition across democratic countries in the twentieth century. Also, when we look at single countries during this period, we notice that their economic system was not stable. The liberal capitalism from the turn of the nineteenth and twentieth centuries in countries like Britain or Sweden had been transformed—despite its good economic performance—into a quasi-liberal system. After World War II, some countries with a quasi-liberal system went further into the direction of statism, for example, Britain until Ms. Thatcher or France under Mitterrand. Some states displayed a sort of institutional fluctuations: Sweden went from liberal capitalism to a quasi-liberal system and in the early 1990s successfully launched liberal reforms. Britain shows a similar trajectory, thanks to Ms.

Thatcher's reforms. However, the later developments, especially in the energy sector, took a more statist direction. This is an example of reform reversal.

There are many studies of the economic transitions under democracy. Obviously, I cannot discuss them in this short paper. Instead, I will sketch an analytical scheme which describes some of the variables that influence the probability of liberal or statist transitions (for more see Balcerowicz 2015).

The future shape of an economic system can be conceived as resulting from two opposing forces: (1) the liberal one, those promoting market reforms and defending them (if achieved), and (2) the anti-liberal one, those opposing these reforms and defending the existing statist arrangements. Drawing on this analogy from physics, we can say that an economically inferior system will persist or even get worst if anti-liberal forces prevail. Market reforms (but not always in a necessary shape) will be launched when the balance changes to the benefit of liberal forces. Of course, this is just a simple analytical framework.

To move further one has to specify what determines the relative strength of the liberal and anti-liberal forces over time and across countries. I think that the main situational determinants are as follows:

1. The relative strength of various interest groups;
2. The relative strength of liberal and statist doctrines;
3. The economic situation;
4. The positive or negative linkages between market reforms and some widely shared ideas in the society.

These variables interact in the short run. In the longer run, they can influence each other. For example, an economic crisis, interpreted by influential intellectuals as a proof that free market capitalism is fundamentally fragile and thus demands more state intervention, is likely to strengthen the statist orientation n the society.

Speaking about interest groups, one must stress Olson's important contribution. First, he has shown in his path-breaking book (1965) that it is easier to create the narrowly based pressure groups (distributional coalitions) than larger ones, including pro-reform ones. As a result, the former accumulate various regulatory and fiscal privileges over time, which will increasingly harm economic growth—unless or until they are destroyed by some special circumstances like wars. Olson (1982) contrasted Japan and Germany after World War II in contrast to Britain. Olson's theory has spurred a substantial body of empirical research which—to some extent—supported his theory (e.g. Horgos and Zimmerman 2009).

While Olson tended to explain much with little, he never claimed that his theory of accumulation and discontinuity in the life of anti-reform pressure groups under democracy can explain all the variation in economic transitions under democracy. Indeed, there are some other factors at play:

First, some other forces than wars or revolutions can change the composition and the relative strength of various interest groups. For example, Internet-based technical change tends to reduce the role of trade unions.

Second, Olson's focus was on pressure groups and their financial incentives. However, there are also ideological pressure groups (e.g. radical ecologism) usually guided by statist preferences and led by anti-liberal intellectuals. One cannot help but be amazed that the economic freedom, so fundamental for economic prosperity and the existence of democracy, is so frequently attacked in the West.

Third, there are other situational factors than the pressure groups that influence the probability of liberal of statist transitions.

One of them is the *type of economic situation*. It is useful to contrast a visible economic improvement with an economic crisis.

The improving economic situation reduces the pressure for liberal reforms and may facilitate the anti-liberal policies. Market reforms under improving economic conditions are not ruled out but require a special leadership which is largely a chance factor.

An improvement in the economic situation of a country results from previous economic reforms or from other factors including external ones. In the first case, the question arises: will the economic improvement be sufficiently strongly linked in people's mind to the previous liberal reforms, thus protecting them, or will the anti-liberal forces use the ensuing economic slack and reverse at least some of those reforms? One can generally say that the improved economic performance due to market reforms is not a sufficient condition to protect them from reversal. There are various reasons for that: generational change, prevailing statist interpretation of economic crises by the gifted anti-liberal ideologies, the use of emotional issues like inequality against free markets and so on. Therefore, the liberal reforms need protection by liberal forces, that is, they have to win the communication battle with the anti-liberal ones.

Economic improvement due to non-policy factors (windfall gains) is not only likely to block liberal reforms but also to spur statist ones. The reason for that is the factor of the contribution of previous liberal reforms to the prosperity is absent. And the windfall gains, for example, discovery of new natural resources or improved terms of trade, mask structural problems in the economy and strengthen the voice of anti-liberal groups relative to the liberal ones.

The latter have to be especially skillful in communication to neutralize the harmful input of windfall gains upon the policies.

Let me now turn to the opposite economic situation: that of an economic crisis. It is usually thought that crises facilitate economic liberalization and (fiscal) reforms, as other options become much worse in the eyes of policy-makers. Many examples confirm this point: the reforms in Southeast Asia after 1988, radical liberal transitions in Poland and the Baltic countries in 1989–1991, reforms in Spain during the recent global financial crisis.

However, the link between the economic crisis and liberal reforms is far from perfect, as there are two intervening factors: the prevailing interpretation of the root causes of the crisis and the availability of windfall gains.

If like in Poland and some other post-socialist countries in 1989–1991, the interpretation prevails that the crisis was due to the inherited statist system, the liberal reforms are likely to be supported. If on the contrary most people think that it was the market system or market reforms that produced the crisis, statist transition is likely to follow, for example, New Deal Policies in 1930 in the US. The prevailing interpretation of the root causes of the crisis depends on the relative success of liberal and anti-liberal intellectuals in society. The communication battle about the root causes of the crisis is, therefore, a battle about future policies. The result of this battle depends not only on the engagement and the communication skills of the two opposing forces but also on situational factors which influence public opinion.

Argentina provides a striking example of the power of situational factors in shaping public opinion in conjunction with the appearance of windfall gains after a crisis. Under Menem and Cavallo, genuine market reforms had been introduced, liberalization and privatization, but they had left intact some basic weaknesses of Argentina's system: rigid labor markets and the mechanisms of fiscal irresponsibility of the provinces. Together with the negative shocks of the late 1990s and early 2000s, they undermined the economy and caused a deep crisis. A surge in anti-reform attitudes followed. However, even in such a situation, the increased anti-reform sentiment among voters did not need to lead to anti-reform policies. Another situational factor impacted on the policies chosen after the crisis, namely, the external conditions that followed the crisis. If they remain difficult or get worse, the best choice even for the anti-reform politicians could be to reform, as there would simply be no money to pursue populist policies, especially in the fiscal sphere. In contrast, if external forces provide a substantial relief, for example, the demand for and prices of countries' main exports improve, anti-reform policies pushed by the voters are likely to be pursued. This was the case of Argentina under the Kirchners—the increased demand for and prices of its main exports allowed them to go in a sharply anti-market direction (see Cavallo and Cavallo Runde 2017).

In general, it is bad for liberal reforms when bad (i.e. anti-reforms) guys in politics have good luck, or when good (i.e. pro-reform) guys have bad luck. It is good for the reforms when bad buys have bad luck or when good guys have good luck. What combination of situational variables and personality factors appears in reality is, to a large extent, a chance factor which introduces an element of unpredictability into economic transitions under democracy.

The last situational factors I will discuss here are positive or negative linkages perceived in people's minds based on past situations and because of developments that accompany market reforms. A positive linkage exists when market reforms can be linked to something highly valued by many people and negative linkages when market reforms can be linked to developments regarded as negative by many people. The liberalization from Soviet dominance was a highly positive factor for most people in CEE countries, and market reforms were seen as part of a departure from the Soviet system.[8] This was manifested in many ways and perhaps most succinctly captured in the famous phrase of Estonia's Marti Laar: "Goodbye Lenin, and just do it !" In contrast, in Russia there were many people for whom the dissolution of the Soviet Union had produced a disorientation and a loss of pride they derived from being citizens of a superpower. Gaidar (2006) discusses how these attitudes were mobilized by the nationalist and/or socialist politicians against market reforms and later enshrined in Putin's words: "The dissolution of the USSR was the greatest disaster of the 20th c."

The different transition after the collapse of socialism in the Soviet bloc provide an excellent "living laboratory" to test the analytical scheme I have outlined. The newly liberated countries have differed enormously in the speed and scope of their economic (and political) transitions. On the one hand, there were early radical reformers like Poland in 1990 and the Baltic counties two years later and, on the other hand, the laggards like Ukraine or countries which got stuck in quasi-socialism: Belarus and countries in Central Asia. (For more on the typology of economic transitions after socialism, see Balcerowicz 2015.) All the early radical reformers started under serious economic crisis that was widely and rightly blamed on the previous socialist, that is, anti-market regime. Neither of them obtained any windfall gains just after the collapse of socialism. Among the countries that had represented the

---

[8] The strength of the national identity, a product of the past, has influenced the power of the positive linkage. For example, it was very strong in Poland, Hungary, the Czech and Slovak republics and in the Baltic countries and to a lesser degree in Ukraine, but much less in Belarus and Central Asia.

largest deviations from a radical approach (Belarus, most of Central Asia), the positive linkages were much weaker than in the CEE (if they existed at all) because national aspirations—a product of history—were much weaker too. And in the case of Central Asia, the unpopularity of the Soviet regime was bound to be much weaker than in the CEE because in former countries, as in the former group, the feeling that the Soviet regime produced a relative decline was probably absent or much weaker given their inclusion in the USSR. This helps to explain why most of the presidents in the newly independent states were former communist rulers in the respective Soviet republics.

Russia deserves a special mention. Despite a negative linkage, in the beginning of 1992, it launched rather radical reforms under Yeltsin and Gaidar. This is a good illustration of the power of personality, that is, reform-committed leaders. The political conditions for radical reforms were, however, more difficult than in Poland and in the Baltics, and reformers were quickly replaced by non-reformers, whose anti-reformist position and loose fiscal policy produced an acute crisis in 1998. More recent developments under Putin illustrate the power of situational factors in conjunction with a personality not committed to reforms but power. Rising oil prices produced huge windfall gains, and negative linkages were activated against market reforms by statist politicians with nationalist, socialist or self-interested rent-seeking views. Market reforms stagnated and some were put into reverse (especially privatization).

In sum, the situational variables are very important in explaining the timing and direction of economic transitions. However, the personality factors are a necessary complement. On the one hand, favorable circumstances may be wasted because of the lack of a proper leader. On the other hand, despite less favorable conditions, gifted and reform-minded leaders may launch economic reforms.

7   Authoritarian Transitions After Free Elections

Bad political transitions were widespread in Europe in the interwar period. However, let me focus here on recent developments in some countries whereby an individual and his (her) group win genuinely free elections and then—by reducing the civil liberties and the rule of law—lower the level of legal political competition (democracy).

There have been many examples of such bad political transitions though they differ in degree. Some of them are already completed: the political system (both formal and informal) has been changed to such an extent that no opposition can—within the current framework—replace this ruling group. Elections usually continue to be organized, but they are a sham. This group includes Russia under Putin, Belarus under Lukashenka, Venezuela under Maduro, Nicaragua under Ortega, probably Turkey under Erdogan. According to Kornai (2016), Viktor Orban in Hungary has changed its political system so much that opposition can't win elections. In some other countries, author transitions are less advanced. Poland, since the elections in 2015 brought to power the Law and Justice Party headed by Jaroslaw Kaczynski, belongs to this group. There is also a category of democratically reversed authoritarian transitions, where a ruling group with autocratic inclinations has lost elections (Macedonia in 2016 and Sri Lanka in 2015 fit this category).

Once authoritarian transitions become more or less complete, the return to democracy would have to entail some splits in the ruling group because of personal conflicts, a catastrophic economic situation, or growing civic or external pressure.

There are not many comparative studies of recent authoritarian political transitions; hence, I propose to offer a few observations and to ask some questions with a view toward such an investigation.

To start with, one should distinguish two issues:

1. How to explain the electoral victory of a group, which tries to perpetuate itself in power by reducing the level of political competition?
2. What is the dynamics of authoritarian transition and its determinants?

With respect to the first question, one should avoid easy generalizations, like massive shifts in societies toward populism and nationalism. Behind each case of authoritarian transition lies a different combination of factors. For example, the victories of Law and Justice (PiS) in Poland happened under a fortuitous economic situation and mostly because of a very bad electoral campaign of the incumbents. As the economic situation begins to deteriorate due to the European recession, the power of PiS will probably decline.[9] In Hungary the economic situation was worse than in Poland, and Orban was helped by the scandals that plagued his competitors. Erdogan's authoritarian offensive was made possible by a failed coup against him. The start of a authoritarian

---

[9] This argument is elaborated in Balcerowicz and Laszek (2019).

transition depends on some chance factors but can have lasting consequences.

When considering the second issue, I start with the idea that authoritarian rulers have three instruments at their disposal:

1. Buying the support of some targeted groups by distributing money and jobs (clientelism);
2. Indoctrinating people by the captured media;
3. Changing laws to take full control over the state apparatus (political, police, prosecutors, tax administration and even the courts) in order to use it against opponents of the ruling group (intimidation).

The scope for clientelism depends on the economic situation. I noted in Sect. 6 that improving economic conditions help the rulers who push economic statism. Such conditions also help those who implement bad political transitions. As in every society, many people assess the ruling politicians through the prism of the current economic situation. Rulers with authoritarian inclinations are likely to use an improving economic situation as a guise to mask the taking over of the state apparatus, as Putin did in Russia when the price of oil was high, the economic situation was rapidly improving; hence, he was genuinely popular. When the price of oil collapsed and the economic situation deteriorated, he was already in full control of the apparatus of intimidation. The early phase of a bad political transition is thus crucial and this is when the democratic opposition should be especially vigilant regarding the developments in the state apparatus.

The probability that the winner of free elections would try to take over the state in order to eliminate political competition depends on a country's political culture: an important informal institution accumulated over a long time. Therefore, authoritarian transitions are much less likely in mature democracies, than in developing systems. Thus, it is not a surprise that virtually all recent cases of bad political transitions have happened in the latter group. The only major exception may be the US, though it is too early to conclude on this.

Finally, it is also striking that these transitions are not linked to economic liberalizations, which would improve societies' longer-term economic situation. Rather the opposite is true. Authoritarian rulers pursue—a statist agenda of increasing political control over the economy under the nationalistic or populist headings. This would suggest that when the economy gets worse due to these policies, the bad political transition will be under popular pressure, especially if the civil society manages to block the attempts of the autocrats to turn the state apparatus into a tool of repression. Preventing such a development is a decisive determinant of the duration of a bad political transition.

8   Concluding Comments

Analytical institutional economics has to a considerable extent already corrected the earlier statist bias of mainstream economics and directed attention of the profession to the important problems of the real world. However, much remains to be done in every one of the four fields I have listed in the beginning of this chapter, including especially the most complex one: understanding the driving forces of various institutional transitions. The analysis here does not provide a complete answer to all important issues societies face today, nor does it address all the complex institutional relations of politics and economics in post-communist societies.

However, the schema presented here should help throw some light on the broad choices and main challenges for those who believe in the institutional systems based on individual liberties and the critical importance of the rule of law. Bad systems can unfortunately persist because the power of the privileged elite which benefits from the existing system can be used to resist change, to the point of using force and intimidation. Good systems based on freedoms and the rule of law are subject to various collectivist attacks from the disaffected, despite their overall superior performance. Only if these attacks are pushed back and any legitimate concerns addressed, can the liberal transitions be preserved and the statist ones blocked. This is an unending challenge for liberal forces.

References

Aslund, A. (2019). *Russia's Crony Capitalism: The Path from Market Economy to Kleptocracy*. New Haven: Yale University Press.

Balcerowicz, L. (1995). *Socialism, Capitalism, Transformation*. Budapest: Central University Press.

Balcerowicz, L. (2014). Poland: Stabilization and Reform under Extraordinary and Normal Politics. In A. Aslund & S. Djankov (Eds.), *The Great Rebirth. Lessons from the Victory of Capitalism over Communism* (pp. 17–38). Washington: The Petersen Institute.

Balcerowicz, L. (2015). On the Economics and the Political Economy of Reforms. i *Decyzje*, nr 24.

Balcerowicz, L., & Laszek, A. (2019). Poland's Economic Miracle Won't Last. *Politico*, Opinion, October 10.

Cavallo, D. F., & Cavallo Runde, S. (2017). *Argentina's Economic Reforms of the 1990s in Contemporary and Historical Perspectives*. London and New York: Routledge.

Clague, C., Keefer, P., Knack, S., & Olson, M. (1996). Property and Contract Rights in Autocracies and Democracies. *Journal of Economic Growth, 1*(2), 243–276.

Gaidar, J. (2006). *Gibiel Imperii*. Moscow: ROSSPEN.

Havrylyshyn, O., Meng, X., & Tupy, M. (2016). *25 Years of Reforms in Ex-Communist Countries: Fast and Extensive Reforms Led to Higher Growth and More Political Freedom*. CATO Institute, Washington, Policy Analysis Number 795. [N.B.: updated in March 2018 in Polish version: "25 lat reform w krajach postsocjalisty-cznych—zaktualizowana". Warsaw: Forum Obywatelskiego Rozwoju].

Horgos, D., & Zimmerman, K. W. (2009). Interest Groups and Economic Performance: Some New Evidence. *Public Choice, 138*(3), 301–315.

Kornai, J. (2016). The System Paradigm Revisited. Clarification and Additions in the Light of Experiences in the Post-Socialist Region. *Acta Oeconomica, Akadémiai Kiadó, Hungary, 66*(4), 547–596.

Kuran, T. (2004). Why the Middle East is Economically Underdeveloped. *Journal of Economic Perspectives, 18*(3), 71–90.

Olson, M. (1965). *The Logic of Collective Action. Public Goods and the Theory of Groups*. Cambridge, MA: Harvard University Press.

Olson, M. (1982). *The Rise and Decline of Nations: Economic Growth, Stagflation, and Social Rigidities*. New Heaven, CT: Yale University Press.

Olson, M. (1993). Dictatorship, Democracy, and Development. *The American Political Science Review, 87*(3), 567–576.

Pipes, R. (1990). *The Russian Revolution*. New York: Random House.

Rodrik, D., Subramanian, A., & Trebbi, F. (2004). Institutions Rule: The Primacy of Institutions over Geography and Integration in Economic Development. *Journal of Economic Growth, 9*(2), 131–165.

Rothstein, B., & Teorell, J. (2008). What is Quality of Government? A Theory of Impartial Government Institutions. *Governance, 21*, 165–190.

Samuelson, P., & Nordhaus, W. (1985). *Economics*. New York: Mac Graw Hill.

Schumpeter, J. A. (1947). *Capitalism, Socialism and Democracy*. New York: Harper Torch Books.

Sonin, K. (2003). Why the Rich May Favor Poor Protection of Property Rights. *Journal of Comparative Economics, 31*(4), 718–731.

Taubman, W. (2017). *Gorbachev:His Life and Times*. New York: W.W.Norton and Company.

5

The "New Comparative Economics": A Critical Review

Bruno Dallago and Sara Casagrande

1 Introduction

The fundamental difference between the disciplines of comparative economic systems (CES) and the new comparative economics (NCE) lies in the different ways they treat the economic system and the comparative approach. Both CES and NCE are part of the broader field of comparative economic studies comparative economic studies (ces).[1] The discipline itself consists of the analysis of how human economic activities take place and are organized, and in the comparison of different ways of doing so and of related outcomes. Since this has to do with institutions, ces can be grouped with institutional economics and is similarly split on theoretical grounds, although this should not be so necessarily (Rutherford 1996).

The extremely popular concept of "economic system",[2] considered as a coordinated set of institutions, is central to CES, but much less so to NCE. CES often has a holistic approach and pursues fuller knowledge of how

---

[1] In the following, we use the term "comparative economic studies (ces)" in small initials to include the different versions of the discipline.

[2] The number of answers obtained when entering the term "economic system definition" in google.com is 200 million!

B. Dallago (✉) • S. Casagrande
Department of Economics and Management, University of Trento, Trento, Italy
e-mail: bruno.dallago@unitn.it; sara.casagrande@unitn.it

© The Author(s) 2021
E. Douarin, O. Havrylyshyn (eds.), *The Palgrave Handbook of Comparative Economics*,
https://doi.org/10.1007/978-3-030-50888-3_5

the system and institutions work, evolve and are embedded in the fundamental components of social life, and under the influence of politics. It also sees the system as shaping and constraining the choice of individuals and organizations, as well as conditioning the space for, and nature of, reforms in a path-dependent way. NCE sees the economic system as a kind of institutional menu for socially optimal choices, both public and private, in a constrained optimization process. In this perspective, normative goals are prominent.

The comparative approach is a powerful analytical instrument that promotes better comprehension and helps to highlight differences and similarities. In a very general sense, ces aims at describing, explaining, and choosing the different ways of organizing economic activity in different parts of the world. This perspective is common to CES and NCE, but in different ways.

The complexity of the world is sufficient in itself to justify the existence of many analytical approaches. Differences in theoretical background and in normative aims enhance analytical pluralism further. Our main aim in this chapter is to see whether CES and NCE offer incompatible analyses and perspectives, or whether they may be better considered as different but complementary approaches. Analytical pluralism may foster better understanding of complementarities and incompatibilities and act as insurance against analytical unilateralism. The chapter aims to assess the contribution of NCE to ces, by framing the NCE within the broad analytical goals of ces: the analysis and comparison of different economies and systems. Our aim is thus to highlight the goals and research program of NCE by comparing these to the more traditional CES perspective.

2   Comparative Economic Systems and Comparative Economics

The origin of ces in the West was due first to the rise and development of the Soviet Union. An interest in studying and comparing socialist and capitalist systems also developed in the Soviet Union, and later in Central and Eastern European countries (CEEC), mainly with the aim of showing the superiority of socialism. In the West, the main academic aim was to understand how an economic system works and to search for the best or a better system. Both aims led to a holistic approach, and to the social and political embeddedness of the discipline. The second originating factor was politically strategic and often plainly military, aimed at better measuring the geostrategic adversary. Studies originating in the USA during the Cold War and spreading to Western

Europe and Japan included efforts to recalculate Soviet statistics to make them comparable with Western statistics.

Differences notwithstanding, all ces studies refer to institutions, particularly formal ones, albeit in different ways, and this is central to the distinction between CES and NCE. In CES, institutions derive in great part from the culture and history of a country, and are under the influence of politics and social relations. Equally important is that institutions interact and that significant complementarities exist among them, so that alien institutions are rejected. Consequently, institutional choice and reforms are constrained and may be path dependent. The relation between institutions and economic efficiency goes generally from the former to the latter, although the search for efficiency, or at least economic sustainability, is also important. Particularly important in this perspective was the debate on economic reforms and transformation in Central and Eastern European Economies (CEECs.)

Actually CES started to focus on comparisons between socialist and capitalist countries from the 1940s. Different books were published in this period (e.g. Sikes 1940, 1951; Blodgett 1949; Oxenfeldt 1952; Loucks 1957; Loucks and Hoot 1948), usually showing a predominant historical–ideological approach, yet with interesting hints about the role of institutions.

A second important strand of literature saw institutions, and consequently the economic system, as following from economic rationality. The most prominent contribution was the debate on economic calculation in socialism between Austrian critics of socialism (von Mises and von Hayek) and neoclassical supporters of socialism (Lange and Lerner), which went directly to the institutional roots of the issue. The former maintained that socialism was economically inefficient due to the lack of competition and equilibrium prices and the superior cost of information coordination. The latter argued that planning can effectively and efficiently imitate the competitive market by determining equilibrium prices through trial and error, thus avoiding market distortions typical of capitalism.

Lavoie (1985) had perhaps the last word when he showed that the real advantage of capitalism lies in the rivalry among enterprises. Another important contribution came from Schumpeter (1942), who introduced an important evolutionary approach. Schumpeter considered the progressive bureaucratization of the entrepreneurial function as the main reason for the progressive fall in the profit rate and the main weakness of capitalism, leading to the prevalence of socialism. More recently, Reynolds (1966) criticized the typical CES procedure of dividing economic systems into different species with which a particular nation is associated (see also Mesa-Lago 1982), and maintained that the system should be a theoretical economic model (see also

Conn 1978). Reynolds also criticized CES for its lack of an evolutionary vision of economic organization and the scant consideration of different types of systems.

In an important book, Eckstein (1971) defined comparative economic systems as "a field in search of self-definition", and distinguished between the comparative systems approach (CSA) and the comparative economics approach (CEA). CSA aims at studying the economic system as a whole, with emphasis on the relationship among the parts, whereas CEA is a partial and sectoral approach aimed at focusing on some economic issues (such as labor markets or international trade). He argued these approaches should be considered as complements rather than alternatives, but admitted that the second has more possibilities for development.

The 1970s brought a new perspective, under the influence of political and military détente between East and West, growing openness and interaction among economies, and the rise of theories of convergence. Particularly important was the attempt to analyze and compare economic systems using the tools of economic theory, and to refine analytical methods.[3] Koopmans and Montias (1971, p. 1) moved to the micro-level and claimed that "the new circumstances invite approaches to the comparison of economic systems that altogether avoid prior classification according to the grand 'isms' and instead start from comparisons of organizational arrangements for specific economic functions". This new approach may be considered an anticipation of both the varieties of capitalism (VoC) and NCE. More recently, Montias et al. (1994) maintained that the new approach separates the economic system from social and political systems, and aims and applies the tools of economic theory. The ultimate objectives of comparative economic analysis should be "to isolate and measure the impact of the economic system—more precisely, the system's rules, laws, customs, and regular procedures—on basic economic outcomes" (Montias et al. 1994, p. 2; see also Rosefielde 2002). However, this initial change of paradigm had to proceed without the clarification of the role of institutions (Montias 1976). According to Bonin (1998), the fundamental reason is that for Montias (and Koopmans), institutions were not a primary concept allowing for precise description.

The three most popular CES textbooks between 1970 and 1980 were Neuberger and Duffy (1976—which we will refer to as ND from now on), Eidem and Viotti (1978) and Gregory and Stuart (1985). Of these, the first

---

[3] It is worth remembering that these contributions had wide appeal, thanks also to the important role of these authors. Eckstein was the president of the Association for Comparative Economic Studies (ACES) in 1974 and Montias was the founding editor of the *Journal of Comparative Economics* in 1977.

one (ND), based on the partial-equilibrium approach of neoclassical economic theory, "... goes farthest in trying to cleanse the field of the ideological virus" (Mesa-Lago 1982, p. 81). As Bonin (1998, p. 2) notes, ND "identified three structures of any economic system, namely, decision-making, information, and motivation. They used this framework to analyze hypothetical systems". The goal of removing ideology has often merged with that of removing social and political elements and replacing them with the supposedly objective tools of economic theory. This evolution, together with the collapse of the socialist system in Eastern Europe, led Greenwald (1994, p. 173) to foresee the passage from the old to what he defined as "new comparative economics".[4]

The move toward this position accelerated, particularly after 1989. The changes from one edition to the other of Gregory and Stuart (1999), perhaps the most popular textbook for decades and the first textbook to use the term "new comparative economics", show the way. Starting from the sixth edition in 1999, the book applied theories of institutional economics to the comparative analysis of conceptual models of capitalism and socialism, including theories of property rights, transaction cost, and principal–agent relations (Lo 2004, 2012). The orientation toward the analysis of the economic consequences of capitalist institutions in the economic, legal, political and cultural spheres became increasingly important. Brada summarized the new course as follows: "Economic systems consist of economic agents, institutions, incentives, information flows and policies. Comparative economics studies how these components come into being to form economic systems and how they influence the economic performance of systems" (https://spb.hse.ru/en/compecon/; see also Brada 2015).

This new approach, as often happens, strengthens the discipline in some sense and weakens it in another sense. According to Zimbalist (1984, p. 3), "it is only at significant peril that comparative economists can overlook noneconomic or 'political' factors. ...such abstraction should occur only with cognizance of the influences being suppressed". Similarly, Mesa-Lago (1982,

---

[4] "[T]he most complete, rigorous early treatment of the new approach to CES (new comparative economics) is provided by J. M. Montias (1976), while a less technical development of the paradigm is found in Neuberger and Duffy (1976) (ND) a text-book that attempts to provide a coherent decision-making theoretical framework, based on the Koopmans and Montias (1971) view of the place of the economic system in the total analysis of an economy's performance. David Conn (1977) formalized the ND framework and wrote a useful survey of the CES literature, distinguishing the contributions of theorists and comparativists in this endeavor." It is worth remembering that the first author to use the term new comparative economics was Collier Jr. (1989). Collier identified a shift in the old comparative economics not only as a consequence of its inclusion in modern economics and the more theoretical an analytical approach, but also for the topic change: from "unconventional" economies to "conventional" capitalist economies.

pp. 81–82) warns that scholars should "take ideology into account for reconciling their conclusions with reality".

For decades, the discipline dealt mainly with grand systems ("isms") and centered largely on Eastern Europe. This weakness risked limiting the discipline's influence to a particular historical period and geopolitical area. The merit of the debate was the successful effort to clarify that economic systems have an internal logic (coordination) and that fundamental complementarities exist among institutions. The issue of (systemic) efficiency had a role in these analyses, generally in explaining why the socialist system and CEECs were economically wasteful due to political interference.[5] The masterpiece of this approach is Kornai (1980, 1992), for its ability to render the construction and logic of the system, including the role of politics. CES textbooks are mostly in this line of analysis.

When economic reforms were implemented in Eastern Europe in the 1960s and the late 1970s in China, research highlighted the existence of "variants of socialism" and took an evolutionary flavor. A number of authors admitted that variants exist also in capitalism, including the Scandinavian social-democratic market economy and the German social market economy. Prominent in highlighting systemic variants, both socialist and capitalist, were the seven editions of Bornstein (1993).

With the appearance of variants in research, more sophisticated approaches considered also the merit of policies and reforms, as well as their institutional/systemic limits. Policy-makers and reformists should consider the internal logic of economic systems (coordination) and complementarities among its institutions. Although this remained an under-researched field, it played an important role in the debate on reforms under Gorbachev in the Soviet Union and Deng Xiaoping in China. Kornai (1986) authored a masterpiece on the 1968 Hungarian economic reform, highlighting the limits of the reform. Rodrik (1990, 1996) stressed that policies and reforms should be tailored to the features of the economic system.

The strength of CES lies primarily in its contribution to the knowledge and internal logic of different economic systems and the consequences for economies. Yet the ability of CES to predict the performance of those economies is limited, due primarily to the dominant role of the analysis of broader systemic level over the micro-level. As a result, the effect of existing institutions on systemic choice and social-engineering was overlooked. Transformation in

---

[5] The critics of capitalism provided a kind of symmetric analysis based on the supposed social and political unsustainability of the system. The theory of convergence between the two systems gave prominence to the commonality of problems to be managed, particularly technology and the increasing interaction among countries (Tinbergen 1962).

Central and Eastern Europe led to the rejection of CES as excessively linked to the study of socialism and socialist countries, a reaction similar to throwing out the baby with the bathwater: the powerful CES message on coordination and institutional complementarities was largely lost.

3   The New Comparative Economics

In the 2000s the institutional efficiency hypothesis took a new form in NCE (Djankov et al. 2003a; Shleifer 2002). Its central focus was institutions in capitalist economies. NCE applies an optimizing approach to society's choice of its institutions, based on its idiosyncratic institutional possibilities and under the constraint of social losses due to private expropriation (disorder) and to state expropriation (dictatorship). Thus, NCE can be considered as a part of New Institutional Economics (NIE), which aims at finding the conditions for, and assessing the comparative efficiency of, alternative institutions aimed at optimizing economic outcomes.

This approach has two main sources: the microeconomic perspective that part of CES had taken since the 1970s and neo-institutional economics. NCE represents both the continuation of a partial tradition of CES and a departure from it. NCE does not reject non-economic variables. In this sense, NCE looks like a more formalized continuation of the traditional CES approach.

With neo-institutional economics, NCE shares both the criticism of the neoclassical model of a pure free-market economy and the view that economic institutions have a fundamental role in determining performance, although NCE overlooks the importance of transaction costs (Williamson 1985). Similar to public choice theory, NCE emphasizes that fundamental institutional differences among countries derive from political and legal systems and the role of governments (Shleifer 2002). This brings NCE closer to, but not overlapping with, the political economy stance of such authors as Acemoglu and Robinson (2006). CES has a stronger tradition under this perspective (Wiles 1977; Aoki 2001) when it shows that institutional differences are often the consequence of pre-existing institutional differences and performance failure more than its direct cause.

NCE is grounded in four basic tenets. First, the fundamental problem for any economy is to keep disorder and dictatorship under control. As Lo (2004) correctly notes, this means generalizing market failures to "disorder" and government failures to "dictatorship". Disorder and dictatorship are thus defined by how far the real world is from the ideal state of an absence of transaction costs alongside perfectly enforced property rights.

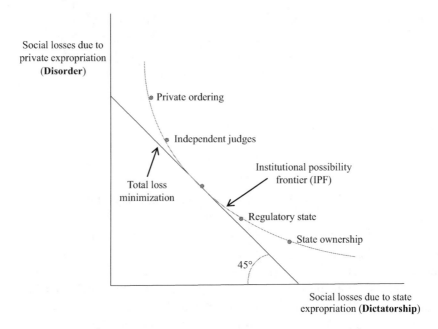

Fig. 5.1 The institutional possibilities frontier (IPF). (Source: Djankov et al. 2003a, p. 599)

Second, there is an institutional possibility frontier (IPF; Fig. 5.1) for any economy that reduces the problem of social choice to defining and enforcing property rights, thus excluding all other economic and non-economic variables. NCE aims at optimization for any given idiosyncratic situation, yet different IPFs for different societies remain unexplained—a major drawback for comparative studies.

Third, the IPF is convex and each point on it represents a different combination of disorder and dictatorship. Due to convexity, a society has diminishing marginal utility from the consumption of the two goods and is willing to sacrifice a growing amount of one good (say dictatorship) to obtain one more unit of another good (say disorder). Although standard in microeconomics, the diminishing marginal rate of substitution is problematic for analyzing equilibrium at the social level and opens serious problems for the aggregation of institutional preferences of individuals and the asymmetric power of decision-makers. It is hard to exclude non-economic factors from the core of the model, and the interaction among individuals, groups, and organizations. Political parties are just one example of these and governments play a preponderant role in defining social choice, particularly when the degree of dictatorship is important. If a society is not perfectly individualistic and competitive, which is the standard case, even the degree of disorder may be sticky. To solve these problems, NCE introduces civic capital.

Fourth, the efficient policy solution is to minimize losses. If the playing field is not perfectly level, however, some players have a greater say in the choice of the position of society on the IPF and may have an interest in keeping an advantageous position, even if this is undesirable for the rest of society. NCE introduces legal origin to deal with this problem.

4   A Reasoned Critique of NCE

NCE's rational choice of institutional architecture may provide important guidelines for institutional reforms, but it seems insufficient for really providing a convincing explanation, let alone a reliable normative guideline. NCE does not really explain the origin of institutions, nor their evolution or change, and gives little consideration to the interaction among, and coordination of, different institutions. Simplification of complex issues is useful if it allows greater analytical depth, but comes at the expense of explanatory power. What is missing in NCE is the broad and complex picture in which all relevant elements fit together.

First, it is not clear whether the IPF is continuous or not: for example, moving from state ownership ("socialism" in previous versions of the article) to private ordering may require much more than substituting dictatorship for disorder. It is also unclear how dictatorship and disorder can stay on the same convex isoquant and how countries can move freely along the IPF. Second, the same authors show elsewhere that the legal origin of a country locks the system into a particular area of the IPF. In particular, countries following common law are locked-into in the higher part of the IPF, with much disorder and little dictatorship. Conversely, countries following civic law have more dictatorship and less disorder. Yet in other studies, these same authors seem to credit the view that the overall amount of disorder plus dictatorship is lower in the former group of countries and higher in the latter, suggesting different positions of the respective IPFs. If so, this would mean that when a country moves along the IPF, the curve translates or rotates. What is unclear is whether moving along the rotating IPF (or moving to different IPFs) changes the economic performance of a country.

NCE's simplified and elegant representation in the economizing perspective of institutional social choice has difficulty in providing an explanation that is both theoretically strong and operationally useful. Moreover, the NCE comparative static representation is at odds with the nature of the issues it wants to explain. First, state ownership and private ordering are complex systems, including many and different institutions, as well as a peculiar interaction and coordination of these institutions. Conversely, the regulatory state and independent judges are particular bundles of institutions, or subsets of a system, that is, they are qualitatively and institutionally different from the former.

Second, the IPF representation suggests that moving from one position (e.g. state ownership) to another (e.g. private ordering) only implies trading less dictatorship for greater disorder. Yet each position identifies a *system*. A system is a coordinated and interacting complex of institutions—and behind them, powerful political, social and economic forces, alongside decision-making and coordination of activities—that allows no simple decision to move or to resist change. Third, the case of transformation in Central and Eastern Europe shows that the mover of systemic change may create the illusion of moving along the IPF: abandon dictatorship and move toward private orderings granting more individual freedom, which goes together with an increase in disorder. Yet being on the IPF implies the two situations are quantitatively equivalent, overlooking the need for institutional learning and organization, information problems, the need to acquire knowledge, or the stickiness of institutions (Dallago 1996; Rutherford 1996). Logically, until these processes mature, it makes more sense to consider that the IPF moves outward, that is, toward greater institutional inefficiency. This may have negative political consequences that could permanently worsen the institutional possibilities of a country.

These issues are not relevant when analyzing a pure theoretical model. Yet when this model is proposed to replace a discipline that pays attention to complexity, these weaknesses become serious (Dallago 2004). The authors try to regain realism by exogenously introducing civic capital, a concept that is broader than social capital. As a consequence, the shape and the location of the IPF "—and hence the efficient choice—varies across activities within a society, as well as across societies" (Djankov et al. 2003c, p. 5). It is civic capital, together with legal origins, that determines the shape and the location of a country's IPF: "Societies with more such capital, and an IPF closer to the origin, are more capable of achieving cooperation among their members" (Djankov et al. 2003a, p. 600). The determinants of civic capital include culture, endowments and technology. La Porta et al. (1997, 1998) identify historical legal origins, "broadly interpreted as highly persistent systems of social control of economic life" (La Porta et al. 2008, p. 326), as a crucial determinant of the legal system, and consequently economic and social outcomes (Djankov et al. 2003b). Civil law countries exhibit heavier government intervention in economic activity (La Porta et al. 1999), higher government ownership of banks (La Porta et al. 2002), and more burdensome regulation of new business entry (Djankov et al. 2002).

Unfortunately, the working of a system and changes to it involve fundamental qualitative and long-term issues that a basically quantitative and short-term representation as the IPF construction overlooks. A simple shift of the IPF would not reflect qualitative issues, such as the different behavior of actors and working and coordination of markets. NCE authors have considered important issues separately—such as the nature and working of courts, the features of bureaucracy, and various others. Qualitative differences explain why systemic change could move the economy to a lower equilibrium with both more disorder and dictatorship
. This outcome could be represented by a new IPF_2 farther from the origin. Yet this representation would transmit only the aggregate higher amount of losses, but would fail to reflect the qualitative fundamentals (such as the working of the economy, decision-making processes, quality of life) and the distribution of losses and gains.

The question of development is similarly challenging. Moving along the curve for a poor country is insufficient, since development requires moving the IPF inward to diminish losses for any given institutional system. However, development requires more: it requires not only less and lower losses, but also better allocation of resources, stronger incentives to investment and labor, access to sustainable technology, good management of natural resources, high returns to human capital (World Bank 2018) and, most importantly, more efficient and effective institutions. Indeed, each system on the IPF may actually include a bundle of positions. Also informal institutions are important, and there is no unique mapping between markets and the non-market institutions that underpin them (Rodrik 2000). The exogenous origin of institutions in developing countries is also important. As Acemoglu et al. (2001) show, in places where European colonists faced high mortality rates, they could not settle and set up extractive institutions, which persist to the present and have large effects on income (see also La Porta et al. 1998).

Among NCE critics, Rosser Jr. and Rosser (2008) emphasize the inability of NCE to consider properly cultural factors. They therefore support the new traditional economy (NTE) perspective as better suited to the study of comparative economics. According to NTE, income distribution and political systems co-evolve with cultural and socioeconomic characteristics. Disregard for the role of politics—which play a prominent role in Kornai (2016)—and income distribution are serious shortcomings of NCE. In the end, it is the nature and quality of institutions that matter. According to Acemoglu and

Robinson (2012), the fundamental question is whether institutions encourage inclusive growth or extractive activities, an issue that NCE disregards (see also Rosser Jr. and Rosser 2018). Baumol (1990) and Yano (2009) raise similar issues in their perspective. Baumol (1990) shows that the nature of entrepreneurship and its consequences for growth depend on the quality of institutions. For Yano (2009), the quality of markets, indispensable for healthy economic growth, depends on (competitive) fairness in dealing and pricing.

5   The Uneasy Coexistence of Complexity and Simplification

NCE may not provide an analysis of the economic system, but its comparative analysis of institutions is powerful and far reaching. According to Pryor (2005, p. 25), "the new comparative economics focuses on individual institutions rather than considering the economic system as an entity". On the plus side, NCE "draws the attention of economists and policy-makers to law and legal institutions…historical paths and past institutional choices thus seem to influence the trajectory for coevolution of legal institutions and markets in a long-term and persistent way" (Engelbrekt and Nergelius 2009).

The *comparative* approach of NCE lies in comparing the different positions on and of the IPF. Each position on the IPF distinguishes different combinations of disorder and dictatorship. Each location of the IPF is determined by the amount of civic capital available. Yet the latter is a largely undeveloped analysis and social capital can be interpreted as keeping the risk of disorder and dictatorship at bay in idiosyncratic ways. It is not clear whether this refers also to the IPF form and slope, or whether distinct economies differ only in the IPF location. If the latter, the rate of transformation of disorder and dictatorship along any IPF would be the same and reflect a constant feature of human nature.

Lo (2004, p. 7) correctly observes that the NCE effort to develop a general theory of efficient institutions "does allow for institutional diversity, but only within a tight limit". There are four main positions on the IPF—private orderings, independent judges, regulatory state and state ownership. Each depicts a kind of economic system defined along two dimensions, disorder and dictatorship. These positions are associated with progressively diminishing social costs of disorder and progressively rising social costs of dictatorship, that is, ranked in terms of increasing state power. Notice that each system refers to a world with perfect property rights and their enforcement. Thus all four positions on the IPF are possible and efficient.

Since each point on the IPF is equivalent, there is no efficiency reason to prefer one or the other system, except for society's relative preferences for disorder or dictatorship, as expressed by the existing legal regime, an exogenous factor. The position of a particular economy on its IPF, and the optimum combination of disorder and dictatorship, thus depends on the alternative legal systems of common law and civil law (Fig. 5.2). This means the complexity of economic systems is largely lost, as every legal system guarantees institutional stability on the IPF, but does not guarantee total loss minimization (Djankov et al. 2003a). To do so, the economy should be under a mixed legal regime, which recalls the theory of convergence popular in the 1960s and 1970s and a solution that would end comparative systemic analysis.[6]

NCE does not support the superiority of one particular legal regime over the others. While each regime has consequences for economic performance,

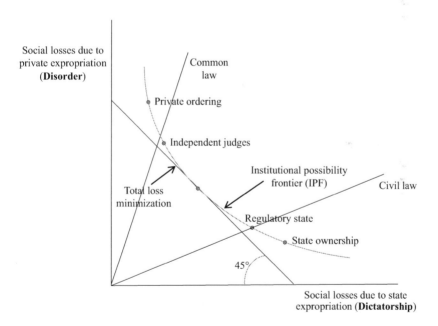

Fig. 5.2 The institutional possibilities frontier (IPF) and legal regimes. (Source: Own elaboration)

---

[6] According to La Porta et al. (2008, pp. 326–327), there are many arguments for convergence between common and civil law, and consequently for the different types of capitalism. Globalization is the most important such force, showing that the common law approach to social control of economic life performs better than the civil law approach. However, if the external context turns unstable and threatening, countries are likely to embrace civil law solutions.

the final effect depends on external circumstances (La Porta et al. 2008). This requires a further transformation of the IPF representation, as Lo (2004) observes: "for a given IPF, precisely which of the four strategies (and thus the associated institutional arrangements) is the most efficient depends on the slope of the [IPF]". The effect of modifications in the external context seems to suggest that the slope of the IPF may change as a consequence (Fig. 5.3).

In spite of the ingenuity of the solution, the dominance of the external context is problematic, since it implicitly denies the initial fundamental role of institutions and disregards the influence of the latter on the former. Other important factors—from culture through social relations to geography—are not considered. Moreover, not much is said about the costs and difficulties of change, let alone the cohesive forces of the existing economic system—that is, compatibilities and interaction among institutions. It also seems that NCE analysis of the nature and effect of globalization is rather simplistic.

The NCE interpretation contributed significantly to an appreciation of the importance of law for economics, as well as the trade-offs in any social construction. NCE concentrates on the fundamental trade-off between disorder

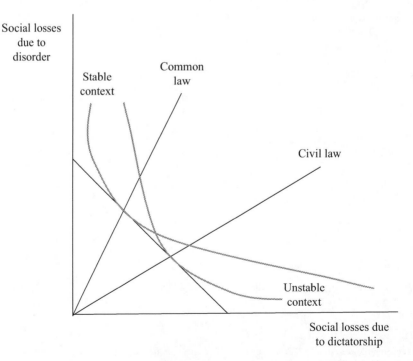

Fig. 5.3 The institutional possibilities frontier (IPF) and legal regimes in different external contexts. (Source: Own elaboration)

and dictatorship or, to put it another way, between market and state failures. In this, NCE supporters are more balanced than many economists and not alien to political economists such as Bardhan (2016) and Wolf Jr (1988). The NCE approach is at the basis of the influential Doing Business project of the World Bank (Djankov 2016). This application is a step forward from mainstream approaches in interpreting and explaining the rationality of differences among economies, and goes beyond CES in providing normative instruments. At the same time, the NCE interpretation is a step back from CES in explaining systemic complexity and resilience, as well as in predicting consequences in both positive and normative terms. In spite of its many merits, NCE is thin as an explanatory theory of the nature of economic systems, the differences between them, and as a predictive tool of their evolution. These issues highlight the limits and drawbacks of simplification.

6   The State of the Profession and Scientific Publications

It is useful to consider the self-imagine and self-classification of the discipline and the aims of authors before reaching at conclusions on the standing of ces within the domain of economics and the relation between CES and NCE. The most immediate, admittedly superficial observation is that NCE does not appear to have a clear place and standing in ces. There is no academic or scientific association directly linked to NCE, nor is there any scientific journal. Moreover, NCE is not included in the Journal of Economic Literature (JEL) classification. This classification covers a broad spectrum of nearly one million journal articles from 74 countries, most of which are in English or with English summaries, and published in 1999 journals indexed in EconLit as of fall 2019. Moreover, the classification covers books, collective volume articles, dissertations, working papers in economics, and book reviews from JEL.

The term "comparative" is used in 14 different groupings, either of two or three digits, in the JEL classification, from E63 (Comparative or Joint Analysis of Fiscal and Monetary Policy) to O57 (Comparative Studies of Countries). The term "system" is used twice: in E42 (Monetary Systems, Standards, Regimes, Government and the Monetary System, Payment Systems) and K4 (Legal Procedure, the Legal System, Illegal Behavior). The term "systems" is used twice: in the above mentioned E42 and in H61 (Budget, Budget Systems) and five times in the P category dedicated to "Economic systems".

Djankov et al. (2003a) classify their path-breaking article under the JEL codes of H1 (Structure and Scope of Government), K1 (Basic Areas of Law), P1 (Capitalist Systems), P14 (Property Rights), P16 (Political Economy), P37 (Legal Institutions, Illegal Behavior), P5 (Comparative Economic Systems), and P51 (Comparative Analysis of Economic Systems). The implicit message is twofold: NCE is part of CES, but looks toward important strands of neo-institutional economics—in particular, law and economics and property rights, but also political economy.

While the core contributions in ces are grouped in the P category (Economic systems) entirely or at least in great part, the names of academic associations and academic journals are less clear. There is a prevailing use of the term "studies" replacing "systems" or "economics" in the correct attempt not to discriminate against different approaches. Yet the term comparative economics has been gaining some ground.[7] It is interesting to read the description of the aim of associations and journals to find further examples of the lack of a unitary vision, the attempt to use different terms and to keep different approaches together (Appendix).

In recent years the number of topics analyzed by ces and the variety of approaches utilized have increased significantly, thanks to the progress of economic theories and analytical methods, as well as the transformation in Central and Eastern Europe and reforms in China. These events also attracted a significant number of new scholars, who brought new theoretical stances and observations, challenging traditional topics and approaches. Mainstream macroeconomists, who for a while dominated the analysis of transformation and policy-making, brought the first serious challenge. Their mixed performance and their approach, alien to CES tradition, created a kind of alien body in a traditional field of ces.

More challenging was NCE, because its approach is mainly in the domain of institutional economics, similar to CES. Moreover, NCE authors presented their views after years spent working on a substantial amount of data and

---

[7] Important examples include the American Association for Comparative Economic Studies (ACES), the European Association for Comparative Economic Studies (EACES), the Japanese Society for Comparative Economic Studies (JSCES), the Korean Association for Comparative Economic Studies (KACES) and the Italian Association for Comparative Economic Studies (AISSEC). Oddly enough, these and other associations have launched since 2015 a series of World Congress of Comparative Economics, although the change in the definition does not mean any change in the approach. More consistently, journals managed or coordinated with these associations keep the term "studies" or even "economic system" in their title, although "comparative economics" is also widespread. Noteworthy examples include *Economic Systems* of EACES, *The Journal of Comparative Economic Studies* of JSCES and *Comparative Economic Studies* of ACES. Yet both the US and the European associations have two journals in comparative economics: the *Journal of Comparative Economics* of ACES and *The European Journal of Comparative Economics* of EACES. The main differences between the two groups of journals are that the former is less formalized and more open to different scientific approaches.

subjects in a comparative way and with an interdisciplinary approach. Did the NCE challenge therefore bring real progress in its own merit and in CES? Was this new development helpful in clarifying issues and improving the knowledge and management of economies? Some hints may come from looking at the evolution of publications as reported by EconLit.[8] Data report the number of publications that authors self-classify under the code P (Economic systems) and relative sub-codes.[9] Chart 5.1 reports the findings for the years 1991 to 2018. Prior to 1991, the classification was not comparable.

The total number of publications grew steadily until 2011, then increased very rapidly, by 45%, between 2012 and 2014. One could have assumed this was due to an increased interest in the causes and consequences of the Global Recession, EU membership and in the return of autocratic regimes. In fact,

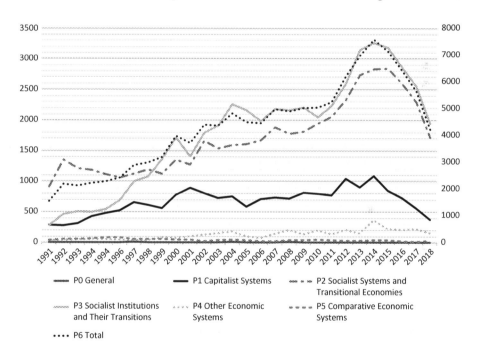

Chart 5.1 The number of publications in the EconLit database classified in category P and sub-categories. (Note: Total publications on the right-hand scale. The chart includes publications in the EconLit database under the category P, its sub-categories [such as P2 and P4] and sub-sub-categories [such as P23 and P42])

---

[8] The increase in the number of CES publications may in part be the outcome of the growing number of journals included in the database.

[9] The general P category covers studies in economic systems (previously comparative economics). P0 covers general issues; P1, studies about capitalist economic systems; P2, about the socialist and the transitional economic systems; P3, about socialist institutions and their transitions; P4, about other economic systems, such as the Islamic economic system; and P5, about comparative economic systems. NCE does not have any particular devoted category and most of its publications are listed under different categories.

this increase was largely due to publications on socialist systems (P2 and P3). Starting in 2015, the number collapsed and by 2018 it was at a lower level than in 2002 and at 55% of the 2014 level. Again, the collapse was mainly due to categories P2 and P3, where the number of publications in 2018 was at 60% of the 2014 level. Also P1 publications (capitalist systems) decreased considerably, so that by 2018 their number was barely more than one-third of the 2014 level. Publications in other sub-categories were much less numerous and their number more stable, with the partial exception of P4 publications (other economic systems) in the mid-2010s.

These figures suggest a number of considerations. First, socialist and post-transformation economies continue to dominate the field, perhaps due to increasing interest in China. Second, the international crisis strongly encouraged the interest of scholars, with particular concern for former socialist countries. Third, scholars publishing comparative studies on capitalist economies still prefer to classify their studies in different, more specialized categories. Fourth, the interest in general issues and comparative methods continues to cover a minimal part of the field, which apparently remains primarily a field of applied studies. Fifth, the field failed to take on a stronger position on the comparison of capitalist economies, which are showing important signs of differentiation and perhaps divergence, also within the EU. Sixth, NCE advent did not seem to change the above picture. Comparative scholars did not really devote much effort in taking on the theoretical challenge, at least in quantitative terms. However, it is possible that the new approach is hidden in applied studies, or that publications have been classified in other categories, possibilities that we did not explore.

7   To Conclude: Is Coexistence and Cooperation Possible?

Comparative economic studies are caught between Scylla and Charybdis. CES generates fine analyses of different systems, as well as important explanations of their nature and working, but its normative conclusions remain vague. NCE pushes the system into the background and concentrates on comparisons of key institutions, investigating important issues, such as the role of legal systems, but at the cost of excessive simplification and questionable normative significance.

Pryor (2005) highlights the fundamental issue, which is explaining "why particular institutions and organizations cluster together to form a distinct pattern or why certain economic institutions are complements, while others are not", and explaining why economic systems change. Economic systems "should be defined in terms of clusters of complementary or covarying institutions" (p. 26) and should be identified through empirical investigation by means of cluster analysis. Research from this perspective has proved that institutions cluster, forming distinct economic systems and leading to consistent patterns of economic outcomes (Kitschelt et al. 1999; Nicoletti et al. 1999; Pryor 2008; Soskice 1999; Visser 2001). These findings are in line with VoC results (Hall and Soskice 2001) and are central to CES, but more peripheral in NCE.

CES aims primarily at understanding, explaining and comparing institutional complementarities, interactions, lock-ins, path dependence and the effect on economic performance. CES has an evolutionary approach and is attentive to the link to politics and culture. These aspects also have a role in NCE, but the emphasis is on the role of legal systems and on comparing the efficiency properties of different capitalist systems. The approach is useful because it leads to important normative conclusions. However, the question is how sound these conclusions are without fuller understanding of all dimensions of a system.

The comparison of CES and NCE generates a trade-off between sound and detailed analysis (CES) and normative action based on restrictive analysis (NCE). Paraphrasing Brada (2009), CES is "more complete", but is it enough? In that regard, NCE's criticism of CES is not misplaced. CES provides a clear view of the fundamental importance of complementarity, coordination and lock-in among institutions and organizations that define different economic systems and the different outcomes they generate. However, CES has been unable to deliver a clear and useful theory to support reforms and policy-making. CES focuses on the right issues and poses the right questions, yet it is short on normative answers.

Important differences between the two approaches exist in the treatment of institutions, the concept of an economic system and the analytical method used. CES does not have a unified method, its interests are broad and varied, its approach holistic and its methodology eclectic. NCE has a more limited research program, but a more focused theoretical and applied approach. In short, CES is wider and more complete, whereas NCE is more selective and more operational.

Further differences concern the assumption about human nature underlying each approach. While CES does not have a defined view, NCE embraces opportunism. Analytical advantages notwithstanding, this view overlooks important aspects of economic life, such as altruism, fairness, cooperation and various supportive devices, including culture, ideology and religion, together with positive and negative incentives, alternative to opportunism. No mention is found on asymmetries of power and resources among individuals and organizations, from which so many cases of socially inefficient institutions and solutions derive. NCE sees (formal) institutions from the narrow functional perspective of controlling the twin dangers of dictatorship and disorder, but disregards informal institutions, except possibly through discussing civic capital. Similar observations could be made regarding the technocratic nature and role of the state.

It follows that the NCE reading of the economic system risks being deterministic. Nevertheless, the approach could still be important in a "as if" perspective—that is, if it were to lead, "as if" it were complete, complex and close to reality, to predictions on "what institutions are appropriate under what circumstances" (Glaeser and Shleifer 2003, p. 401). One strength of the NCE approach is the construction of large and coherent comparative databases. The World Bank's Doing Business database and related measurement program is built on the NCE approach and view by authors practicing NCE (Djankov 2016). This highly influential program has important consequences—for example on the flow of foreign direct investment (FDI). However, the program has been subject to severe criticism and the soundness of its results has been questioned (McCormack 2018; OECD 2019).

Institutions have a central role in NCE analysis, but explanatory variables are exogenous and NCE does not have a complete theory of institutional evolution.[10] In particular, NCE does not consider the possibility of inefficient solutions (Nelson 1995). It considers only the marginal adjustment of institutions, disregards any punctuated/revolutionary possibility and overlooks the chance that reforms might backfire, in the form of protectionist policies or populism, for instance. Although these are hardly cases for normative action, their disregard runs the danger that policy and reform recipes do not internalize these events and therefore may collide into them. Although less focused and normatively determined, the analysis and method of CES may be useful in warning NCE of such limitations and dangers. NCE is an important analytical approach for pursuing institutional efficiency in an "individualistic" world, in which individual actors are free to negotiate. Howsoever theoretically important these conditions are, they are partially met in only one part of

---

[10] "Efficient institutions could evolve from democratic pressures (…), from the influence of growth-seeking interest groups such as merchants (…), from a Coasian negotiation among the members of the elite, such as the Magna Carta or the American Constitutional bargain (…), or from a long term evolutionary process described by Hayek (…)" (Djankov et al. 2003a, p. 9).

the world. On this basis, NCE cannot be a general theory of economic systems.

NCE's ambition to place CES in the dustbin of science is misplaced. NCE has a lot to learn from CES, starting from its more complex analysis of the origin and nature of institutions. The rejection by CES of NCE is equally wrong, because NCE brings analytical strength in looking for normative conclusions from the perspective of institutional efficiency. This NCE perspective is important, particularly as a guideline for institutional reform. However, the restrictive analytical base raises the risk of excessive analytical simplification and may lead to problematic conclusions. The complexity of CES may be healthy for NCE.

We are then left with two incomplete research programs, different but methodologically complementary. This should push researchers following each of these research programs to consider the work of each other carefully and seriously. Cooperation is made difficult by deep methodological differences. So a healthy scientific competition is preferable to seek explanations, interpretations, and policy proposals. This competition recalls the distinction between classical/critical/old institutional theories and neo-institutional theories. Both NCE and CES have a useful role in improving our understanding of the working of economies and the management of change. They compete heuristically, but normatively may provide useful competitive contributions in different ways and cases.

NCE is analytically stronger than CES, but NCE is weak where CES is strong. The two approaches deal with similar problems and share similar aims. However, they use different theoretical approaches and see institutions and economic systems in different ways. Their convergence and merging are hardly possible and would be scientifically detrimental. Being different in both their theoretical stance and methods, they should continue to compete for improving our knowledge and analysis of different institutional constructions.

Appendix

ACES, the largest association in the field, uses the following self-definition of "the leading scholarly organization for the support of comparative economic studies. … The purpose of the Association is to provide scholarly exchange among persons interested in comparative studies of economic systems, institutions, and economic performance and development and to further the growth of research and instruction on these topics. … To promote development of the field of comparative economics, the Association awards, bi-annually, the Bergson Prize for the best paper published in *Comparative Economic Studies* and the Montias Prize for the best paper published in the *Journal of Comparative Economics*. The Association also provides funding for conferences that foster new avenues of research in comparative economics" (https://www.acesecon.org/ accessed on 17 June 2019). So ACES uses all terms (comparative economic studies, comparative studies of economic systems, comparative economics) as interchangeable terms.

EACES and JSCES don't show their aims or missions in their sites, but these can be obtained indirectly. In the latest announcement of the "EACES PhD Thesis Award 2018 for the best doctoral dissertation in comparative economic systems" (http://www.eaces.eu/news/eaces-award-2016/13), the association uses all the terms: the abovementioned comparative economic systems, comparative economic studies and comparative economics in the target: "EACES Award 2018 for the best doctoral dissertation in the fields of comparative economics. … The award will be given to the work that in the opinion of the jury has the greatest potential to impact the field of comparative economic studies in the future".

The *Journal of Comparative Economic Studies* of JSCES is "…Japan's first international journal of Comparative Economics", the heir of the academic journal "Comparative Economic Studies" previously published in Japanese. "The journal focuses on the comparative analysis of economic systems…" (http://www.ces.kier.kyoto-u.ac.jp/index_en.html).

The *European Journal of Comparative Economics*, funded and previously supported by EACES, aims at being "…an efficient disseminator of new comparative economic knowledge…" with particular reference for "…the importance of institutions in the economy and our deep need for additional research on their influence on the interaction of the units that play the economic game" and in particular "The study of economies that do not fit the paradigm of the competitive market…" (http://ejce.liuc.it/Default.asp?tipo=scope).

The clearest definition is offered by the *Journal of Comparative Economics* of ACES: "The mission of the *Journal of Comparative Economics* is to lead the new orientations of research in comparative economics. Before 1989, the core of comparative economics was the comparison of economic systems with in particular the economic analysis of socialism in its different forms. In the last fifteen years, the main focus of interest of comparative economists has been the transition from socialism to capitalism. In recent years, mostly as a result of the transition experience, a new orientation of comparative economics has emerged that focuses on the comparison of the economic effects of the various institutions of capitalism, be it in the legal sphere (common law versus civil law), in the political sphere (different types of democracies and electoral regimes) or in the sphere of culture, social norms, etc. This new orientation is a natural development following the very diverse experience of transitions from socialism to capitalism. The transition experience has indeed shown with a vengeance the importance of institutions in the process of economic development" (https://www.journals.elsevier.com/journal-of-comparative-economics).

This definition is clear and has the advantage of stressing the evolution of the field. Yet it raises more fundamental academic and scientific questions. First, which is the difference with institutional economics, which is itself largely comparative in its approach? Second, comparative economics apparently includes the comparison of economic systems, which means that economic systems are a subset of economics. Fair enough, the term economics tends to be used in the rather restrictive way of a science looking at technical and quantifiable interaction among variables, which does not leave much room for different economic systems. Third, this restrictive aspect appears in the "new orientation of comparative economics" that focuses on the "comparison of the economic effects of the various institutions of capitalism". This seems to go in the line of NCE, but leaves out of consideration the existence—actual or potential—of different and alternative economic systems, the interactions among different institutions and between institutions and other variables such as endowments or political relations. Fourth, since the analysis of the economic effects of institutions is the core of institutional theories of different brands, does such a mission imply that comparative economic studies are or should be a subset of institutional economics, only distinguished by the comparative approach? Is then the existence of a distinct comparative field justified?

References

Acemoglu, D., & Robinson, J. A. (2006). *Economic Origins of Dictatorship and Democracy*. Cambridge: Cambridge University Press.

Acemoglu, D., & Robinson, J. A. (2012). *Why Nations Fail: The Origins of Power, Prosperity, and Poverty*. New York: Crown Books.

Acemoglu, D., Johnson, S., & Robinson, J. A. (2001). Colonial Origins of Comparative Development: An Empirical Investigation. *American Economic Review, 91*(5), 1369–1401.

Aoki, M. (2001). *Toward a Comparative Institutional Analysis*. London: MIT Press.

Bardhan, P. (2016). State and Development: The Need for a Reappraisal of the Current Literature. *Journal of Economic Literature, 54*(3), 862–892.

Baumol, W. (1990). Entrepreneurship: Productive, Unproductive, and Destructive. *The Journal of Political Economy, 98*(5), 893–921.

Blodgett, R. H. (1949). *Comparative Economic Systems*. New York: Macmillan.

Bonin, J. P. (1998). The "Transition" in Comparative Economics. *Journal of Comparative Economics, 26*(1), 1–8.

Bornstein, M. (Ed.). (1993). *Comparative Economic Systems: Models and Cases* (7th ed.). Homewood, IL: Richard D. Irwin.

Brada, J. C. (2009). The New Comparative Economics Versus the Old: Less Is More but Is It Enough? *The European Journal of Comparative Economics, 6*(1), 3–15.

Brada, J. C. (2015). Comparative Economics. Definition of Comparative Economics. *Comparative Economic Studies*. Retrieved from www.palgrave-journals.com.

Collier, I. L., Jr. (1989, Fall). The New Comparative Economics. *Comparative Economic Studies, 31*(3), 23–32.

Conn, D. (1977). Toward a Theory of Optimal Economic Systems. *Journal of Comparative Economics, 1*(4), 325–350.

Conn, D. (1978). Economic Theory and Comparative Economic Systems: A Partial Literature Survey. *Journal of Comparative Economics, 2*(4), 355–381.

Dallago, B. (1996). Investment, Systemic Efficiency and Distribution. *Kyklos, 49*(4), 615–641.

Dallago, B. (2004). Comparative Economic Systems and the New Comparative Economics. *The European Journal of Comparative Economics, 1*(1), 59–86.

Djankov, S. (2016). The Doing Business Project: How It Started: Correspondence. *Journal of Economic Perspectives, 30*(1), 247–248.

Djankov, S., La Porta, R., Lopes-de-Silanes, F., & Shleifer, A. (2002). The Regulation of Entry. *Quarterly Journal of Economics, 117*(1), 1–37.

Djankov, S., Glaeser, E., La Porta, R., Lopez-de-Silanes, F., & Shleifer, A. (2003a). The New Comparative Economics. *Journal of Comparative Economics, 31*(4), 595–619.

Djankov, S., La Porta, R., Lopez-de-Silanes, F., & Shleifer, A. (2003b). Courts. *Quarterly Journal of Economics, 118*(2), 453–517.

Djankov, S., Glaeser, E., La Porta, R., de Silanes, F. L., & Shleifer, A. (2003c). *The New Comparative Economics*. Policy Research Working Paper Series No. WPS 3054. Washington, DC: World Bank. Retrieved from http://documents.world-bank.org/curated/en/755501468739478306/The-new-comparative-economics.

Eckstein, A. (Ed.). (1971). *Comparison of Economic Systems: Theoretical and Methodological Approaches*. Berkeley: University of California Press.

Eidem, R., & Viotti, S. (1978). *Economic Systems: How Resources Are Allocated*. New York: Wiley.

Engelbrekt, A. B., & Nergelius, J. (Eds.). (2009). *New Directions in Comparative Law*. Northampton: Edward Elgar Publishing.

Glaeser, E., & Shleifer, A. (2003). The Rise of the Regulatory State. *Journal of Economic Literature, 41*(2), 401–425.

Greenwald, D. (Ed.). (1994). *The McGraw-Hill Encyclopedia of Economics*. New York: McGraw-Hill Companies.

Gregory, P. R., & Stuart, R. C. (1985). *Comparative Economic Systems*. Boston, MA: Houghton Mifflin.

Gregory, P. R., & Stuart, R. C. (1999). *Comparative Economic Systems*. Boston, MA: Houghton Mifflin.

Hall, P. A., & Soskice, D. W. (2001). An Introduction to the Varieties of Capitalism. In P. A. Hall & D. W. Soskice (Eds.), *Varieties of Capitalism. The Institutional Foundations of Comparative Advantage* (pp. 1–68). Oxford: Oxford University Press.

Kitschelt, H., Lange, P., Marks, G., & Stephens, J. D. (1999). Convergence and Divergence in Advanced Capitalist Democracies. In H. Kitschelt, P. Lange, G. Marks, & J. D. Stephens (Eds.), *Continuity and Change in Contemporary Capitalism* (pp. 427–460). New York: Cambridge University Press.

Koopmans, T. C., & Montias, J. M. (1971). On the Description and Comparison of Economic Systems. In A. Eckstein (Ed.), *Comparison of Economic Systems: Theoretical and Methodological Approaches* (pp. 27–78). Berkeley: University of California Press.

Kornai, J. (1980). *Economics of Shortage*. Amsterdam: North-Holland.

Kornai, J. (1986). The Hungarian Reform Process: Visions, Hopes, and Reality. *Journal of Economic Literature, XXIV*(December), 1687–1737.

Kornai, J. (1992). *The Socialist System: The Political Economy of Communism*. Oxford: Oxford University Press.

Kornai, J. (2016). The System Paradigm Revisited: Clarifications and Additions in the Light of Experiences in the Post-Socialist Region. *Acta Oeconomica, 66*(4), 547–596.

La Porta, R., Lopez-de-Silanes, F., Shleifer, A., & Vishny, R. W. (1997). Legal Determinants of External Finance. *Journal of Finance, 52*(3), 1131–1150.

La Porta, R., Lopez-de-Silanes, F., Shleifer, A., & Vishny, R. W. (1998). Law and Finance. *Journal of Political Economy, 106*(6), 1113–1154.

La Porta, R., Lopez-de-Silanes, F., Shleifer, A., & Vishny, R. W. (1999). The Quality of Government. *Journal of Law, Economics and Organization, 15*(1), 222–279.

La Porta, R., Lopez-de-Silanes, F., & Shleifer, A. (2002). Government Ownership of Banks. *Journal of Finance, 57*(1), 265–301.

La Porta, R., Lopez-de-Silanes, F., & Shleifer, A. (2008). The Economic Consequences of Legal Origins. *Journal of Economic Literature, 46*(2), 285–332.

Lavoie, D. (1985). *Rivalry and Central Planning. The Socialist Calculation Debate Reconsidered*. Cambridge: Cambridge University Press.

Lo, D. (2004). *Globalisation and Comparative Economics: Of Efficiency, Efficient Institutions, and Late Development*. Working Paper No. 137. Department of Economics, School of Oriental and African Studies (SOAS), University of London.

Lo, D. (2012). *Alternatives to Neoliberal Globalization. Studies in the Political Economy of Institutions and Late Development*. Houndmills: Palgrave Macmillan.

Loucks, W. N. (1957). *Comparative Economic Systems*. New York: Harper.

Loucks, W. N., & Hoot, J. W. (1948). *Comparative Economic Systems: Capitalism, Socialism, Communism, Fascism, Co-operation.* New York: Harper Brothers.

McCormack, G. (2018). Why 'Doing Business' with the World Bank May Be Bad for You. *European Business Organization Law Review, 19*(3), 649–676.

Mesa-Lago, C. (1982). Comparative Economic Systems: A Review of Recent Textbooks. *Journal of Comparative Economics, 6*(1), 81–85.

Montias, J. M. (1976). *The Structure of Economic Systems.* New Haven: Yale University Press.

Montias, J. M., Ben-Ner, A., & Neuberger, E. (1994). *Comparative Economics.* Chur: Harwood Academic Publishers.

Nelson, R. R. (1995). Recent Evolutionary Theorizing About Economic Change. *Journal of Economic Literature, 33*(1), 48–90.

Neuberger, E., & Duffy, W. (1976). *Comparative Economic Systems: A Decision-Making Approach.* Boston: Allyn & Bacon.

Nicoletti, G., Scarpetta, S., & Boylaud, O. (1999). *Summary Indicators of Product Market Regulation with an Extension to Employment Protection Legislation.* Working Paper No. 237. Paris: OECD Economics Department.

OECD. (2019). How Much Difference Do the Doing Business Indicators Make? *OECD on the Level.* Retrieved from https://oecdonthelevel.com/2019/01/15/how-much-difference-do-the-doing-business-indicators-make/.

Oxenfeldt, R. A. (1952). *Economic Systems in Action: The United States, the Soviet Union and the United Kingdom.* New York: Rinehart.

Pryor, F. L. (2005). Market Economic Systems. *Journal of Comparative Economics, 33*(1), 25–46.

Pryor, F. L. (2008). System as a Causal Force. *Journal of Economic Behavior & Organization, 67*(3–4), 545–559.

Reynolds, L. G. (1966). *"Comparative Systems" or Comparative Economics.* Center Discussion Paper No. 11. Economic Growth Center, Yale University.

Rodrik, D. (1990). How Should Structural Adjustment Programs Be Designed? *World Development, 18*(7), 933–947.

Rodrik, D. (1996). Understanding Economic Policy Reform. *Journal of Economic Literature, 34*(1), 9–41.

Rodrik, D. (2000). Institutions for High-Quality Growth: What They Are and How to Acquire Them. *Studies in Comparative International Development, 35*(3), 3–31.

Rosefielde, S. (2002). *Comparative Economic Systems: Culture, Wealth, and Power in the 21st Century.* Massachusetts: Blackwell Publishers.

Rosser, J. B., Jr., & Rosser, M. V. (2008). A Critique of the New Comparative Economics. *Review of Austrian Economics, 21*(1), 81–97.

Rosser, J. B., Jr., & Rosser, M. V. (2018). *Comparative Economics in a Transforming World Economy.* Boston, MA: MIT Press.

Rutherford, M. (1996). *Institutions in Economics: The Old and the New Institutionalism.* Cambridge: Cambridge University Press.

Schumpeter, J. A. (1942). *Capitalism, Socialism and Democracy*. New York: Harper & Brothers.

Shleifer, A. (2002). The New Comparative Economics. *NBER Reporter*, Fall, 12–15. Retrieved from https://www.nber.org/reporter/fall02/newEconomics.html.

Sikes, E. R. (1940). *Contemporary Economic Systems—Their Analysis and Historical Background*. New York: H. Holt.

Sikes, E. R. (1951). *Contemporary Economic Systems*. New York: H. Holt.

Soskice, D. (1999). Divergent Production Regimes: Coordinated and Uncoordinated Market Economies in the 1980s and 1990s. In H. Kitschelt, P. Lange, G. Marks, & J. D. Stephens (Eds.), *Continuity and Change in Contemporary Capitalism* (pp. 101–134). New York: Cambridge University Press.

Tinbergen, J. (1962). *Shaping the World Economy: Suggestions for an International Trade Policy*. New York: Twentieth Century Fund Press.

Visser, J. (2001). Industrial Relations and Social Dialogue. In P. Auer (Ed.), *Changing Labour Markets in Europe: The Role of Institutions and Policies* (pp. 184–242). Geneva: International Labour Office.

Wiles, P. J. d. l. F. (1977). *Economic Institutions Compared*. Oxford: Blackwell.

Williamson, J. (1985). *The Economic Institutions of Capitalism*. New York: Free Press.

Wolf, C., Jr. (1988). *Markets or Governments*. In *Choosing Between Imperfect Alternatives*. Cambridge, MA: MIT Press.

World Bank. (2018). *The Changing Wealth of Nations 2018. Building a Sustainable Future* (G.-M. Lange, Q. Wodon, & K. Carey, Eds.). Washington, DC: The World Bank. Retrieved from http://documents.worldbank.org/curated/en/727941517825869310/The-changing-wealth-of-nations-2018-building-a-sustainable-future.

Yano, M. (2009). The Foundation of Market Quality Economics. *The Japanese Economic Review, 60*(1), 1–32.

Zimbalist, A. (Ed.). (1984). *Comparative Economic Systems: An Assessment of Knowledge, Theory and Method*. Netherlands: Springer.

Part II

Comparative Economic Systems in Economic History

6

Comparative Economic History

Gerard Roland

1 Introduction

Comparative economics has undergone many changes since it was created during the cold war in the twentieth century. The main focus of comparative economics then was the study of the socialist economic system, where allocation of resources was not done through the market but through central planning and where ownership of productive assets was public, not private. Comparative economics was then comparative only in the sense that the socialist economic system was compared to the capitalist economic system, but there was at the time little focus on trying to understand more deeply the workings of the capitalist economic system itself. Some scholars tried then to establish an abstract framework serving as a lens for comparing economic systems in general (see, e.g. Kornai 1971; Montias 1976; Neuberger and Duffy 1976).

With the collapse of the socialist economic system around the fall of the Berlin Wall in 1989, the focus of comparative economics immediately shifted to the study of the transition from the socialist economic system to the capitalist economic system (see, e.g. Roland 2000; Berglof and Roland 2007). There was little real comparative economics during this period, except for the fact that one needed to have some understanding of the capitalist economic

G. Roland (✉)
University of California, Berkeley, Berkeley, CA, USA
e-mail: groland@econ.berkeley.edu

© The Author(s) 2021
E. Douarin, O. Havrylyshyn (eds.), *The Palgrave Handbook of Comparative Economics*,
https://doi.org/10.1007/978-3-030-50888-3_6

system in order to be able to understand and evaluate transition strategies. Since the transition from socialism to capitalism had never happened before, there was little prior understanding of how to conduct the transition or what the effects of transition policies would be. As a consequence, there were many unexpected surprises in relation to the transition process, the output fall following price liberalization being only one of them (see Blanchard and Kremer 1997; Roland and Verdier 1999). The mistakes and surprises of the transition process led to a better understanding of the nature of the capitalist system and in particular the central role of institutions. The ideas of North (1990) and Williamson (1975), among others, that had for too long played a peripheral role in economics then became mainstream. The article by Acemoglu et al. (2001) analyzing the fundamental role of institutions in long-run growth, using modern instrumental variable techniques, became an instant classic.

The focus of comparative economics then shifted to the study of comparative institutional analysis, that is, the comparison of institutions focusing on differences in institutions in capitalist countries.[1] Djankov et al. (2003) called this the "new comparative economics", and Aoki (2001) proposed a rather abstract conceptual framework based on game theory to understand both institutions and institutional change. It is the only book to my knowledge that has attempted to provide a comprehensive comparative analysis of institutions. Other research in line with the new focus of comparative economics has been both quite prolific and visible.

One area has been the comparative analysis of legal systems, especially the differences between common law and civil law systems (see, e.g. La Porta et al. 1998), exploiting the fact that former British colonies had a common law system, whereas former Spanish and French colonies had a civil law system. Another line of research has to do with the comparative analysis of political systems. This research has so far been confined to the comparison of democratic political institutions and their economic effects. Persson et al. (1997, 2000) studied the differences between parliamentary and presidential democracies looking at the trade-off between separation of powers and legislative cohesion. Lizzeri and Persico (2001), Perotti and Rostagno (2002) and Persson et al. (2007) studied the economic effects of differences in electoral systems in parliamentary democracies (proportional versus majoritarian). Other research has focused on the differences in political regimes emerging from rural versus urban insurgencies (Wantchekon and Garcia-Ponse 2013).

A more recent line of research relates to the comparative analysis of culture. Sometimes scholars tend to oppose culture and institutions, but the

---

[1] In political science, the "varieties of capitalism literature" emerged in a somewhat parallel way.

institutionalist school considers that they are both institutions, the latter being formal and the former being informal institutions. Much of the comparative research on culture by economists has focused on differences in generalized trust, sometimes also interpreted as generalized morality or civic culture (see, e.g. surveys of this large literature by Guiso et al. 2006; Tabellini 2008) but also on differences between individualist and collectivist cultures (Gorodnichenko and Roland 2011, 2012, 2015, 2017; Gorodnichenko et al. 2015; Kyriacou 2016, Ahuja et al. 2017, Davis 2016, Davis and Williamson 2019, Hartinger et al. 2019 and many others). The economic effects of other cultural differences have been studied such as fertility norms or gender norms for labor supply (Fernandez et al. 2004; Fernandez and Fogli 2009).

As we can see, the new comparative economics has focused mostly on understanding the differences in institutions in the post-Cold War world. Because of the nature of this research, it gives a less polarized view of institutional systems compared to the early comparative economics of the Cold War.

However, there is no reason why the new comparative economics should focus only on contemporary institutions. What about comparative analysis of economic systems farther back in history? In the pre-industrial era, that is, in post-neolithic agrarian societies, there were important institutional and cultural differences, possibly as important as the differences studied by the early comparative economics. These differences have barely been studied, but they may affect developments in the twenty-first century and even beyond. China is the emerging power of the twenty-first century. The US-China trade war is already becoming one of the major issues of current international relations. To understand contemporary China, a market economy with a communist political regime, it is not enough to study communism as a political system.[2] One needs to understand Chinese culture and its history but also the long history of its specific institutions.[3]

Economic history has also done little to fill this gap as it has in the past focused too much on history in the Western world and the Mediterranean, and the focus has often been to try to understand the sources of economic success. The same cannot be said necessarily for political history (see, e.g. Fukuyama 2012, 2015) monumental historical work. The three volumes of Finer's *History of Government* provide a wealth of encyclopedic knowledge about institutions in all major civilizations of the world. They are an invaluable source of scholarship to understand institutions in the past. Finer's work

---

[2] In fact the emergence of a market economy under a communist political regime could not have been predicted, based only on understanding communist ideology or even the Leninist form of organization.

[3] On the nature of the current Chinese economic system, see Roland (2019).

is in my view one of the major achievements in social sciences in the twentieth century.

A broader geographical view of history gives scope for a broader research agenda, as it tends to show us that there is no unique way in which the evolution of technology led to pre-determined changes in institutions. There may be parallel historical paths or even bifurcations. The reason for diversity for institutional paths of pre-industrial societies has been neglected by researchers who have focused on other important questions such as why states formed earlier in some areas than in others (Bockstette et al. 2002; Carneiro 1970; Turchin 2016: Schönholzer 2017; Mayshar et al. 2015; Dal Bo et al. 2015).

Much of the literature on institutions takes the implicit or explicit view of "good" versus "bad" institutions, "inclusive" versus "predatory" (Acemoglu and Robinson 2012, see also Acemoglu and Robinson 2019). If we take a less normative approach (a positive approach), we realize that there has been in history a large diversity of institutions, not all easily classifiable in broad normative groups. The interest in the role of institutions in economic history has led to discovery of diversity of institutions in antiquity, in pre-industrial and pre-modern societies. This leads us thus to favor a comparative approach in the study of institutions in antiquity and in pre-industrial societies.

Overall, one can find at the time of formation of the first states differences between economic systems that could be as stark as those studied by early comparative economics focusing on the twentieth century. Thus, looking more closely at the ancient world, we find that some systems (Egypt, China, Peru under the Incas and others) were more like centrally planned economies. There was no private property of land (the land belonged to the Emperor or ruler); agricultural goods and craft goods were allocated by the government. Markets were hardly developed and foreign trade was under the control of government. Other economies, like ancient Mesopotamia, Athens, the Aztecs in Mexico, the Champa (covering roughly today's South Vietnam), were more clearly market economies with private property of land and developed markets, both domestically and internationally. Many other systems were in between both these systems. Nevertheless, as I will show, differences in institutions were not distributed randomly. In fact, we find two clear clusters with characteristics that are reminiscent of central planning on the one hand and market economies on the other hand. These two distinct institutional clusters that are comparable to the difference between socialism and capitalism in the twentieth century indicate that these were different systems with complementarities between their own institutions. These different systems operated in mostly rural societies where modern industrial technology was absent and where labor (in particular slave labor) and land were the major factors of production, and one can make the case for how these complementarities worked, that is, how partial institutions reinforced each other, thus creating clearly identifiable and distinct institutional systems that, following Roland (2017), I will call market versus statist systems.

Legal arrangements relative to land and labor were, for example, quite different. In market systems, there was private property of land but also of slaves. In statist systems, slaves were also used extensively, but they worked for the state. Households did not have the right to buy and sell slaves, and there were no private markets for slaves. In statist systems, land was owned by the state, and there was no market for land. In market systems, legal systems were designed to deal with horizontal conflicts between citizens, in particular over property right disputes. In statist systems, the law was essentially a tool for the ruler to oppress citizens, as in China's "legalist" doctrine developed during the Qin dynasty.

There were also marked differences in political institutions in market versus statist systems. Market systems were often organized in city-states, like in Mesopotamia, ancient Greece and Rome, the Champa Empire in South Vietnam or the Aztec city-states in Mexico. Statist systems, in contrast, were usually organized in territorial states like ancient Egypt, China or the Inca Empire. The latter were also much more centralized and had less developed cities, except for administrative centers.

Given these legal and political institutions, trade of private goods, within and across polities, was much more developed in market systems compared to statist systems. There were also important sociological differences, some a consequence of institutional differences, and others more a source of those differences. The role of merchants was much more recognized in market systems compared to statist systems. There was also more ethnic diversity and tolerance toward foreigners. Differences in kinship systems were also quite notable. Market systems were more present in places with bilineal kinship systems, whereas statist systems could be found more frequently in places with unilineal kinship systems. Strength of clan also affected the strength of market development. In societies with strong clans, a lot of economic activities were done inside the clan, on the basis of division of tasks within the clan. In societies with weaker clans, people needed to resort more to the market for their production and consumption.

The new research program laid out by the comparative analysis of institutions in the ancient past may help to revive comparative economics by improving our understanding of the diversity of institutions in the ancient past, the reasons for their emergence as well as their effects on economic trajectories in history, thereby substantially enriching economic history research on institutions. This would open many avenues such as understanding the diversity of institutions in today's world, understanding different cultural trajectories (such as the major difference between individualist and collectivist cultures) and understanding better economic systems understood as complementarities between various institutions (one example would be the link between the caste system, religious beliefs and marriage institutions in India).

The objective of this chapter is to present an overview of this nascent literature, from possible data sources to emerging research avenues. In Sect. 2, we thus survey some work on comparative archeology, an invaluable source to understand institutions in the ancient past. In Sect. 3, we survey some initial work from comparative psychology and biology on possible reasons for why specific cultures evolved in particular environments. In Sect. 4, we review the emerging literature on comparative institutions in history. In Sect. 5, we describe the comprehensive database we have been building on institutions in the ancient world. We also review some of the main questions raised in this new research program, including possible links between institutions in ancient times and modern cultures. Sect. 6 concludes.

2   Comparative Archeology

Archeology focuses generally on rigorous excavation and analysis of findings from ancient sites. It is rare that archeologists attempt to make broad theoretical syntheses from their observations. Bruce Trigger, a famous archeologist, but also anthropologist and ethno-historian, published a major work in comparative archeology in 2003 entitled *Understanding Early Civilizations: A Comparative Study*. Trigger compares seven important ancient civilizations (Egypt between 2700 and 1800 BC, Southern Mesopotamia between 2500 and 1600 BC, the Shang dynasty in China [1200–950 BC], the Mexico valley—where the Aztec ruled—between 1400 and 1500 CE, the Maya civilization between 250 and 800 CE, the Inca in Peru around 1500, the Yoruba kingdom in Benin between 170 and 1800 CE). The book reads a bit like an Excel file. In 27 distinct chapters, Trigger describes for each of these seven civilizations what he sees as important variables. I will list only the most important ones: kingship rules, whether states were territorial or city-states; the type of urban development (in particular administrative cities versus commercial cities); the characteristics of class systems and the degree of social mobility; patterns of family organization and gender roles, including kinship rules and inheritance rules; characteristics of government administration such as the degree of centralization and decentralization; characteristics of the legal system such as the legal code and legal procedures and relations between the law and the social hierarchy; military organization and reasons for going to war; geographical surroundings; types of implements; rules for land ownership; private or public nature of foreign trade; modes of transport; characteristics of craft production; ideal lifestyles and role models versus models not to follow; conceptions of the supernatural; religion; art; and architecture.

While Trigger does not theorize that much, the way he organizes his material makes it prone to quantification. His work has been a major source of inspiration for the data collection I report below.

While I know of no other comparative work as impressive as that of Trigger, there is more and more work by archeologists and historians trying to understand institutions in the past, and how they affect economic outcomes. A big topic is inequality. Following Piketty's (2013) monumental study on rising inequality under capitalism, there has been a lot of research on inequality in history. Scheidel (2017) documented that societies tend to have rising trends in inequality that only get reversed under the four following "horsemen" of apocalypse: (1) mass mobilization warfare, (2) transformative revolutions, (3) state collapse and (4) plagues. Kohler and Smith (2019) put together a volume where archeologists discuss what are the best ways to measure Gini coefficients of inequality using data from archeological excavations. Flannery and Marcus (2014) provide a tour de force by describing ancient societies at different stages in their development and showing through what mechanisms inequality appeared alongside with economic development.

3   Comparative Culture

Many studies have looked at the geographical reasons for the emergence of particular cultures. There is a well-known literature in economics giving geographical reasons for why some countries and regions have more trust than others (see, e.g. Buggle and Durante 2017). There is a less well-known literature in biology and psychology looking at geographical determinants of particular cultural systems, in particular determinants of the emergence of collectivist versus individualist cultures.

One strand of the latter literature refers to how different societies responded to the epidemiological environment. One such theory, put forward by a team of biologists and psychologists (Fincher et al. 2008), is the *parasite stress* theory, which states that the epidemiological environment, and in particular the types of infectious diseases faced by societies, affected social behavior, psychology and ultimately societies' culture. The main idea is that societies that evolved in an environment rich with infectious diseases tended to develop social norms that led them to be more closed toward foreigners and to impose stricter social rules and, more generally, norms that would minimize the spread of infectious diseases. In a nutshell, the idea is that collectivist culture developed as a means to protect societies from the disease environment they were facing. The authors collected data on historic pathogen prevalence for nine pathogens detrimental to human reproductive fitness (leishmanias, trypanosomes, malaria, schistosomes, filariae, leprosy, dengue, typhus and tuberculosis) for countries that also had an individualism/collectivism index from the well-known Hofstede (2001) database on culture.[4] Data on historic pathogen prevalence were based on old atlases, but they also separately collected data on current pathogen prevalence. They found a strong correlation, in particular between historic pathogen prevalence and measures of collectivism. In further work (Thornhill et al. 2010), they make the distinction between zoonotic and non-zoonotic parasite prevalence. Zoonotic diseases are not transmitted via human transmission, whereas non-zoonotic diseases are. According to the parasite stress theory, only the prevalence of non-zoonotic diseases should affect culture. This is indeed what they find, using the GIDEON database that records the presence of every human infectious disease across the world.

Other studies have examined the effect of differences in the distribution of particular variants of genes on cultural evolution. Chiao and Blizinsky (2010), two neuroscientists, found a link between collectivism and the frequency of the S allele of the serotonin transporter gene (5-HTTLPR). The latter is associated with increased negative emotion, including heightened anxiety, harm avoidance, fear conditioning, attentional bias to negative information as well as increased risk for depression in the presence of environmental risk factors. In particular, exposure to chronic life stress, such as interpersonal conflict, loss or threat, is considered a well-known risk factor for depression in S allele carriers of the 5-HTT. In typical East Asian samples, 70–80% of individuals are S-carriers, compared to 40–45% in European samples. East Asian populations nevertheless report less anxiety and mood disorders, despite their higher genetic propensity. This negative correlation is significant. They thus hypothesize that in countries with a higher frequency of the S allele, collectivist values evolved to protect individuals from stressful events that would trigger

---

[4] They also used other measures: (1) a measure developed by Suh et al. (1998) who combines Hofstede's index with other indicators by Harry Triandis, a pioneer in the cross-psychology study of individualism and collectivism, (2) a measure developed by Gelfand et al. (2004) on in-group collectivism practices within organizations, (3) Kashima and Kashima (1998) data on whether languages allow to drop first- and second-person pronouns in sentences.

depression and anxiety. They indeed find a robust association between the S allele and collectivism as measured by the Hofstede index and the Suh index. They state: "Emphasizing social norms that increase social harmony and encourage giving social support to others, collectivism serves an 'anti-psychopathology' function by creating an ecological niche that lowers the prevalence of chronic life stress, protecting genetically susceptible individuals from environmental pathogens known to trigger negative emotion and psychopathology. These findings complement notions that cultural values of individualism and collectivism are adaptive and by-products of evolution, more broadly".

A study in a similar spirit is that by Way and Liebermann that finds a positive correlation between collectivism and the frequency of the G allele in polymorphism A118G in the μ-opioid receptor gene, creating a stronger psychological pain from social exclusion. A similar positive correlation can be found between collectivism and the frequency of a variant of the MAOA enzyme (monoamine oxidase A) that breaks down neurochemicals such as serotonin and dopamine. The MAOA-uVNTR was also associated with greater pain from social exclusion. As in the Chiao and Blizinsky study, despite a higher propensity for depression implied by the higher frequency of these variants of genes, they also found a negative correlation between these gene variants and the occurrence of major depression in the population.

A further piece of evidence is provided by Luo and Han (2014), two psychologists from Peking University, who show that a particular variant of the oxytocin receptor gene polymorphism (OXTR rs53576), which has been linked to social cognition and behavior, is related to collectivism. The A allele of OXTR rs53576, which is more present in East Asian populations compared to European populations, is associated with deficits in empathy, positive affect, emotional support-seeking, self-esteem, maternal sensitivity, pro-social temperament and trust behavior, as well as higher reactivity to stress and propensity toward depression. As in the other studies, there is a negative correlation with depression.

While some of these studies do not have a very large sample of countries, they nevertheless show a clear pattern between the natural environment faced by collectivities (frequency of pathogens and frequency of particular versions of genes that are related to greater propensity of psychological suffering) and the evolution of cultures. They indicate that genes and cultural values can coevolve in the spirit of the pioneering work of Boyd and Richerson (1985) and provide important foundations for a comparative understanding of cultural systems. Whether they can be the whole story is another matter. Certainly, one can argue that there is also a coevolution between culture and institutions that may also be important. We now turn to survey some of the recent research on comparative institutions in history, most of which illustrates this coevolution.

4   Comparative Institutions

Research in economics on comparative institutions in history is relatively recent. A series of very interesting papers attempt to explain differences in institutions in antiquity. We only review in this article some of the most salient recent contributions. Mayshar et al. (2017) examine the role of differences in transparency of agricultural production in the formation of institutions. Their theory states that transparency in the conditions of agricultural production affects the government's ability to appropriate revenue from the farming sector. They contrast the case of ancient Egypt and Mesopotamia.

Ancient Egypt had high transparency of agricultural production. The Nile flooded regularly, bringing nutrients to the flooded soil that then delivered crops of cereals (mostly barley). The regular mild flooding of the Nile was thus the source of agricultural output that made it possible to develop the Egyptian civilization as early as seven millennia ago. There is a strong relation between the amount of flooding and the size of crops. So-called "Nilometers" measuring the extent of the flooding made it possible to predict quite accurately the future size of crops. As conditions of production were very homogenous along the Nile, it was thus also possible to predict sizes of crops locally based on the amount of flooding measured in different places. According to Mayshar et al., this helps explain the absence of private property of land in Egypt. Land was said to belong to the Emperor. Peasants were ordered to deliver a particular amount of grain every year, depending on the predictions for that particular year. This transparency assured a high level of revenues for the Egyptian government and thus a strong state capacity. Given the transparency, lower levels of government had few informational advantages, which led to a strong centralization in government power.

Mesopotamia, on the other hand, presented different natural conditions. Southern Mesopotamia had complex and varying farming conditions. Water was scarce and had to be rationed by the local elites. As in Egypt, owner-cultivated farming was also rare as water management assured high transparency to local elites. This informational advantage to local elites also explained why Southern Mesopotamia remained decentralized. In Northern Mesopotamia, agriculture was rainfed, creating uncertainty about the size of crops, with little transparency to local elites. This relative opacity explains the prevalence of private farming, according to Mayshar et al. (2017). Their model's explanation for the prevalence of private farming is the following: under strong transparency, the government can pay a farmer a fixed wage but dismiss him if he does not deliver the revenues demanded. On the other hand, with low transparency, dismissal does not work as it may be based on wrong information. In that case, it is optimal to let farmers own the land and never be dismissed from it while paying taxes to the government.

In another paper co-authored with Luigi Pascali, Mayshar et al. (2015) emphasize the role of storability of agricultural products on the emergence of states and a government hierarchy. They challenge the conventional wisdom, according to which increases in agricultural productivity led to a surplus that freed resources to fund a government apparatus. They emphasize instead the role of *appropriability*, which depends on storable surplus. They contrast the strong appropriability of grain, a high calorie food that can be stored for long periods and transported easily and can thus be taxed by a government, but also stolen by thieves, which creates demand for protection. In contrast, tubers do not last long when stored and can thus not be appropriated. All major states that emerged in history relied on cereals. They give different pieces of empirical evidence to support their theory. Note that the question addressed in this paper is quite different from the other one. The question here relates to the emergence of state structures, that is, why states appeared early in some areas and not in others. There is a large literature on that very important question (see, e.g. Dal Bo et al. 2015, Carneiro 1970; Turchin 2016; Schönholzer 2017 and others), but it is somewhat different from issues of comparative institutions in history, which is the topic of this paper.

Greif and Tabellini (2017) wrote an important paper comparing the role of clans and the organization of cities in China and in Western Europe. Clans have always played a very important role in the organization of Chinese society. Due to the prevailing patrilineal kinship system, Chinese people could always trace their ancestors only through the paternal side. Clan membership could thus always easily be defined by having a common male ancestor. Clans have always been paramount social organizations in China, and urban concentrations were mainly clan settlements. Non-clan members were allowed to live in urban clan settlements, but always at the margin. In contrast, clans never played a major role in Europe. Moreover, urban concentrations were not at all based on clan membership but were based on the notion of citizenship, implying rights and duties of the individual. European cities can be seen as places where individuals, regardless of their ancestry and family connections, share common interests in providing public goods. European cities were only one form of corporation, a mode of organization based on the participation of individuals with legally defined rights and responsibilities. Cities were indeed incorporated by a legal charter. European individualism was propagated by the Catholic Church, in particular with the notions of individual salvation of the soul and universal moral values, "generalized morality". In contrast, in China, collectivist values spread, mainly via Confucianism that emphasized ethical norms based on kinship and place within the family and the clan. In China, large migrations most often occurred within the clan structure, with whole clans moving, whereas in Europe, migrations were mostly individual, based on the nuclear family, possibly in its somewhat extended form. We lack the space to dwell further on this quite thorough and insightful comparative analysis.

The role of religion on comparative development has been studied by Grigoriadis (2019). He focuses more on Eastern and Western Europe as well as the Mediterranean. Among others, he analyzes differences between the institutional effects of Protestantism, Judaism, Catholicism, Orthodox Christianity and Islam in increasing order of collectivism. He analyzes in various chapters the effect of different religions on political regimes and the organization of government. While much of his analysis is at a granular level of comparison, and based partly on lab experiments, he finds that more collectivist religions are associated with more centralized, less democratic regimes and less representativeness, with democracy confined more to the local level. They provide public goods based on paternalistic ex post welfare guarantees instead of contractual public goods in more individualist religious environments. More collectivist countries have more accountability of local bureaucrats to the central government rather than the people. Values of solidarity, obedience and universal discipline permeate the organization of the state in societies where religion is more collectivist.

Acemoglu and Robinson (2019) have developed a comparative theory about the emergence of states. They find that in history three types of states emerged: (1) states with very little capacity that cannot impose order and are too weak to arbitrate conflicts between groups of subjects on its territory, (2) despotic states that dominate civil society and do not let it develop and (3) an intermediate case where civil society plays an important role and where the state is not strong enough to muzzle civil society but still strong enough to create the rule of law. In the latter case representing inclusive states, a competition evolves between a strong civil society and the state apparatus. Which one of those three systems emerges depends on a "narrow corridor" in terms of the relative power of the state and civil society. If the state is initially strong enough that it can muzzle civil society, then the state can become ever more despotic over time. If instead, it is initially too weak relative to civil society, then it leaves a space to various factions in civil society that make it impossible to build sufficient state capacity. It is not easy to fit analyses by Greif and Tabellini (2017) or Mayshar et al. (2017) in this framework, and it appears somewhat simplistic relative to these other types of comparative analysis.

5   A Comprehensive Database on Historical Institutions

I now report on recent work I did to gather data on institutions in antiquity. My motivation stemmed mostly from my interest on the effects of culture on long-run growth (Gorodnichenko and Roland 2011, 2017) and on political institutions (Gorodnichenko and Roland 2015). I thought the historical explanations for the emergence of collectivism versus individualism (e.g. those reviewed above in Sect. 3), while quite convincing and interesting, only gave a partial view of the possible explanations for the historical emergence of collectivist versus individualist culture. In line with recent work by Bisin and Verdier (2017), I thought it more fruitful to look at the coevolution of culture and institutions. Indeed, it is reasonable to hypothesize that particular early institutions may have affected cultural values and beliefs, which has in turn helped consolidate both these institutions and the underlying culture. Given the inertia of culture predicted by the Bisin-Verdier model (see also Roland 2004), institutions may have affected cultural values and beliefs that are still present in today's world. Reading Trigger (2003), I was strongly encouraged by his comparative findings on seven important ancient civilizations showing considerable variation in many institutions. In the spirit of earlier work on legal institutions (La Porta et al. 1998), I launched into a very time-consuming collection of data on institutions and institution-related variables in antiquity for 92 countries[5] (countries for which we have a score on the individualism-collectivism cultural cleavage). With the help of research assistants, data were collected on a number of variables listed in Table 6.1. A detailed description of the definition of those variables as well as the scoring rules used can be found in Roland (2018). It is nevertheless useful to say a few words about these variables.

Table 6.1 includes variables capturing institutional characteristics, grouped into legal, political and sociological institutions. These variables and their scores are described further in Appendix 1. Economic and geographical

---

[5] For a full list of countries including the time period covered and the societies investigated, see Table 6.1 in Roland (2018).

Table 6.1 Comparative economic history project

Legal institutions
- Strength of private property of land
- Index of importance of private property of slavery (4 variables)
- Horizontal versus vertical law composite index (3 variables)

Political institutions
- City-state versus territorial state
- Centralization of government (two variables)
- Importance of cities (two variables)

Sociological institutions
- Importance of merchants in societies
- Bilineal versus unilineal kinship of system
- Strength of clan in society (5 variables)
- Social stratification
- Ethnic diversity

Economic variables
- Intensity of private trade within the polity (domestic trade)
- Intensity of private trade across polities (international trade)
- Ease of transportation

Geographical variables
- Heterogeneity in conditions of production
- Distance to a hot trading zone outside the country
- Easiness of taxation
- Easiness of conquest
- Soil fractionalization

---

variables were also collected and are presented in more detail in Sects. 5.2 and 5.3, respectively.

Our starting point is that there was a very large difference in institutions in antiquity. As mentioned already above, some countries like ancient Egypt, ancient China and Peru functioned more like centrally planned economies. Private property of land was mostly non-existent and the land belonged to the Emperor. The same can be said of private property of slaves. Households could not buy and sell slaves, and the existing slaves were the property of the government.[6] This stands in stark contrast to market economies such as in ancient Greece or ancient Rome where private property of land and slaves played an important role. There were also marked differences between the legal systems. In China, but also in Egypt, and other countries, the nature of the legal system can best be characterized by China's "legalist" doctrine, which is still fully alive in China's communist regime. The essence of the legalist doctrine is that the law must be used as a tool of oppression of subjects by the government apparatus. In particular, it specifies punishments for violations of prohibitions, in particular relative to behavior with respect to government

---

[6] Contrary to received wisdom, the Egyptian pyramids were not built by slaves but by gangs of workers.

officials or government property. In that sense, it can be seen as regulating "vertical relations" between the state apparatus and the population. It can be characterized as "rule by law". This stands in stark contrast to "rule of law", where the law is established, as was the case for example in ancient Greece and ancient Rome to rule "horizontal conflicts" between citizens, in particular, conflicts over property or contract enforcement. In the former case, the law is there as an instrument of oppression; in the latter case, it exists to protect private property and private interests. Not surprisingly, in those countries where there was no private property over land and slaves, the organization of production and the allocation of resources were done via the state apparatus, not via the market. Mayshar et al. (2017) already emphasize this in their comparison between ancient Egypt and ancient Mesopotamia. It is therefore justified to say that some countries had a *statist institutional system*, whereas others had a *market institutional system*.

We did not want to satisfy ourselves simply with a narrative of the institutional differences between various states in antiquity, but wanted to collect data to see what kind of patterns would emerge in the distributions of data across countries, but also in the correlations between variables.

The title of some of the variables listed in Table 6.1 is mostly self-explanatory (we refer to Roland 2018, for an explanation of the exact scores), but it is worthwhile giving some explanations with respect to indicators built on the sum of different variables. Our index on the importance of private slavery is based on four sub-variables: (1) the prevalence of private slavery, that is, the importance of private slavery among the slave population, (2) the existence and extent of legal norms for private slavery, (3) the presence of slave trade and slave markets and (4) the importance of private slaves in the total population. Our index for "horizontal law" or rule of law is based on (1) the extent of property law, (2) the extent of contract law, (3) the extent of procedural law in public law. Our index of government centralization covers two variables: (1) the extent of centralization of government between the center and local government and (2) the extent of concentration of power in the hands of the executive. Our index on the importance of cities is based on two variables: (1) the degree of urbanization and (2) the importance of commercial cities relative to administrative cities. Finally, the strength of clan is measured by five sub-variables: (1) extent of family size (from nuclear to extended family), (2) the importance of unilineal kinship in society, (3) degree of geographical concentration of descent group, (4) degree of cooperation within the descent group and (5) power of clan structure in conflict resolution within descent group.

5.1   Are There Institutional Clusters?

We now present some figures showing the distribution of some of the institutional variables we collected. We computed synthetic indices to represent legal, political and social institutions. As shown in Table 6.1, our first index is a synthetic legal indicator, presented in Fig. 6.1, and is based on an average of scores for private land ownership, ownership of slaves and our horizontal law composite index. As one can see, the distribution is quite bimodal. Just to give an idea, the lowest scores (below 2) are for China, Egypt, Fiji, Ghana, Namibia, Nepal and Sierra Leone and the highest scores (above 9) are for ancient Greece and Rome, Anglo-Saxon and Scandinavian countries, Belgium and Spain.

There were thus presumably two clusters of countries: a first group with no or little private property of land and slaves and a legal system focused on imposing the power of the state on unfree subjects, and a second group with private property of land and slaves, and a legal system focused on protecting these property rights. We should expect the first group to have had very autocratic institutions. In that sense, there should be strong complementarity between legal and political institutions in early states. We do not have good measures of how autocratic they were, but it is useful to look at a synthetic index of political institutions, that is an average of government decentralization (including lack of concentration of executive powers), whether countries were city-states or territorial states and the importance of cities (including whether big cities were commercial rather than administrative centers). The distribution of this synthetic political index is presented in Fig. 6.2.

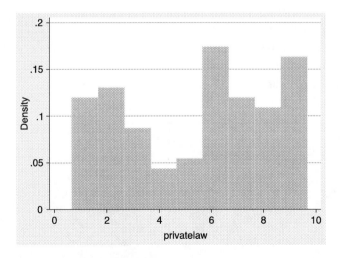

Fig. 6.1   Synthetic legal system indicator

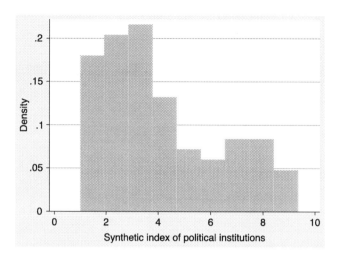

Fig. 6.2 Synthetic political institutions index

As we can see, this indicator is also quite bimodal. Among countries with the lowest scores, we have China, Bhutan, Chile, Japan, Korea and Nepal. Among countries with a high score, we have Greece, Italy, Belgium, the Netherlands, Malaysia, Nigeria and the United Arab Emirates. Note that Anglo-Saxon and Scandinavian countries do not have a high score on this synthetic political institutions index, because they had territorial states, albeit with checks on the executive, and not city-states. An important institution was the assembly of free citizens (*althing, althung, thing* in different Scandinavian or Germanic languages) that met at least annually to settle judicial conflicts between free citizens but also to make important political decisions. The king could not make important decisions without the support of that assembly. This presence of territorial states among these European countries is also the reason why the distribution of our political index is skewed to the right. This "Anglo-viking" exceptionalism is quite interesting, and worth of further research, especially since Trigger (2003) considered that the difference between city-states and territorial states was a fundamental one. This exceptionalism is something one needs to be aware of, especially given the often "Anglo-centric" nature of a lot of historical research.

Finally, we built a synthetic sociological index composed of (1) the role or merchants in society, (2) the weakness of the clan system (the opposite of the strength of clan indicator), (3) bilineal instead of unilineal kinship system, (4) social stratification and (5) ethnic diversity. As we can see below (Fig. 6.3), this indicator is only weakly bimodal with modes around 5 and 7. In particular,

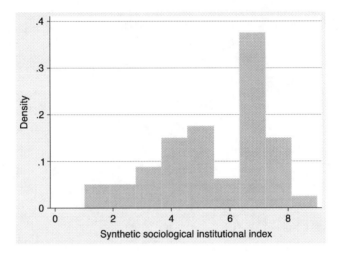

Fig. 6.3 Synthetic sociological index

the social stratification variable (not shown here) is more or less normally distributed.

Overall, there are good reasons to consider that there were two main clusters of institutions, especially considering the distribution of legal institutions, which is not only the most striking but also the most emblematic of these institutional differences.

5.2 Links Between Institutions and Markets

After having given an overview of the distribution of institutional variables we collected, the presumption is that there should be a link between institutions and market development. We should expect market development to be strong in countries having what we have labeled as "market institutions" and weaker in countries having statist institutions. This is indeed what we find. Obviously, we do not have precise measures for market development, but we collected data on the intensity of private trade within polities as well as across polities.

Here are the scoring rules.

Score for Trade Within a Polity

1–2: No private trade. Mainly distribution via the state apparatus. Some barter.

3–4: Very limited private trade. Distribution economy and subsistence production.

5–6: Trade limited in scope (goods traded), location and time.

7–8: Active trade with some limits and significant non-market activity.

9–10: Intensive internal trade an important engine of the economy, possibly in conjunction with intensive international trade.

Scores for Trade Across Polities

1–2: Mostly autarky or foreign trade conducted only by government emissaries.

3–4: Foreign trade controlled by the government, using some private merchants.

5–6: Substantial private foreign trade but overall limited relative to the size of the economy. Significant trade barriers and contraband.

7–8: Large foreign trade with trade barriers but quite widespread smuggling.

9–10: Intensive international trade conducted by private merchants playing a key role for the economy.

Note that the distribution of those variables is also quite bimodal (see Roland 2018). Countries with low scores for domestic trade are China and ancient Egypt, many Asian countries (Bhutan, Nepal, Korea, Japan) as well as some countries from Africa and Latin America. Among countries with the highest scores, we have the usual (ancient Greece and Rome, Northern European countries), but also Slovenia, Morocco and Libya, Saudi Arabia, Indonesia, Malaysia and Pakistan, Uruguay and Mexico. Scores for international trade are distributed quite similarly.

Figure 6.4 shows a regression where we create a combined institutional index, averaging our legal, political and sociological institutions and regress the intensity of private domestic trade on that index. As we can see, it is positive and highly significant.

In Fig. 6.5, we do the same thing for the intensity of private trade in international trade, and we see a similar result.

This clearly demonstrates that there is a strong correlation between institutions in antiquity and market development at the time. Statist systems had less market development, while market systems had more market development. This should obviously not come as a surprise, but the result further underlines the clusters we have identified, and shows a clear complementarity

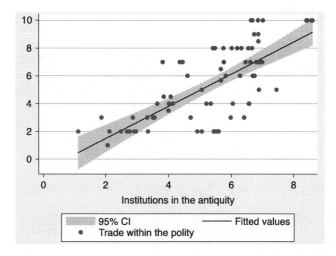

Fig. 6.4 Institutions in antiquity and intensity of domestic private trade

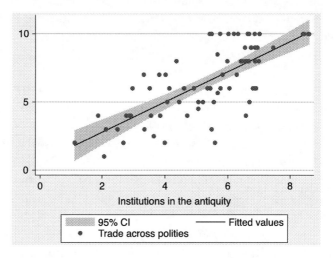

Fig. 6.5 Institutions in antiquity and intensity of private international trade

between institutions and the extent of the use of the state or the market as the main means of allocation of resources.

This of course raises the question of causality: were institutions the cause for market development, or was it instead market development that created a demand for institutions protecting private property? We are not in a position to answer that question. It is also not clear that that question is a crucial one, as there may have been a coevolution between both: better institutions fostered private trade which in turn led to more demand for institutions protecting property rights, and so forth. In any case, the complementarities evolved and possibly led to institutional divergence that is quite clear in the data.

5.3 What Explains the Differences in Systems?

The question then raised is why we see these differences, and what could have triggered a dynamic of divergence between market and statist systems.

Quite possibly, the answer can be found in differences in geographical conditions. In Table 6.2, we regress the combined synthetic institutional index on a number of geographical variables.

The first variable is a measure of heterogeneity in conditions of production. It measures the extent to which conditions of production differed in different parts of the territory.

Here is the scoring rule:

Heterogeneity in Conditions of Production

* 1–2: Very homogeneous geographical environment, one or only a few kinds of resources. Typically, barren land due to climate or other geographical constraints; alluvial plain only for grain production; plantation economy.

Table 6.2 Institutions in the antiquity and geography

	(1)	(2)	(3)	(4)	(5)	(6)
Heterogeneity production	0.334***					
	(0.104)					
Soil fractionalization		4.278**				
		(1.761)				
Ease of transportation			0.310***			
			(0.057)			
Log distance hot trading zone				−0.635***		
				(0.192)		
Distance to sea					−0.002*	
					(0.001)	
Log ruggedness (100 km)						−0.049
						(0.097)
Observations	75	75	75	66	75	72
R-squared	0.160	0.067	0.278	0.158	0.040	0.005

Robust standard errors in parentheses. ***$p<0.01$, **$p<0.05$, *$p<0.1$

3–4: A few kinds of resources/products, some differences of environment across the geographical surroundings.

5–7: Some diversity of notable resources, a differentiated environment across the geographical surroundings and closeness to places with different resources.

8–10: Very diverse geographical environment, many kinds of resources. Typically, vibrant interregional trade of natural resources.

The hypothesis is that strong heterogeneity of production would favor trade inside the polity, and thus the development of institutions protecting private property and trade. If instead, conditions of production were homogenous, there would be less advantages to trade across space, but instead more advantages to centralized allocation of resources by the government, possibly to take advantage economies of scale.

Soil fractionalization is another indicator of heterogeneity of conditions of production. It is based on data on the maximal potential production capacity in t/ha over 17 crops from the FAO's Global Agro-ecological Zones (GAEZ) database, scaled by historical calories per ton for each crop by the FAO.

Ease of transportation is based on the following scoring rule:

1: No access to water transportation (lakes, rivers or sea); land transportation has to overcome significant natural barriers (jungles, swamps or high mountains) typically lacked beasts of burden and wheeled carts.

2: Lacked navigable rivers, land transportation encounters significant natural barriers (jungles, swamps, high mountains).

3: Lacked water transportation, land has some natural barriers that block communication.

4–5: Lacked river transportation, but land routes are well-maintained and do not encounter much natural barriers.

6: Moderate river transportation, land transportation has some barriers (hills, trails, forests, deserts).

7: Moderate river transportation, easy land transportation (well-maintained roads or plains).

8: Fairly easy maritime and/or river transportation, difficult land transportation (e.g. jungles, mountains, bogs).

9: Easy maritime and/or riverine transportation, moderate difficulty of land transportation (e.g. forests, deserts, hills, trails).

10: Easy maritime and/or riverine transportation; easy land transportation (road systems; plains; etc.).

Distance to a hot trading zone is based on the number of km from the capital of a country at the time of the measurement and the closest hot trading zone where merchants used to gather to trade goods. Distance to the sea is the closest distance to the sea from the capital of the country at the time of the measurement (see Roland 2018, for details). Ruggedness is for 100 km distances (see Nunn and Puga 2012, for how to measure ruggedness).

The heterogeneity score and soil fractionalization are measures of the potential benefits from trade inside a country, whereas the other measures (easiness of transportation, distance to the sea, distance to a hot trading zone and ruggedness) are measures of the cost of transport. The latter would affect the benefit from trade as low costs of transport would make it possible to trade at a lower cost. As we can see from Table 6.2, the variables all have the right sign and are all significant, except for ruggedness. This does indicate that there is a correlation between geographical variables measuring potential benefits from trade and market institutions. This likely indicates a causal effect because geographical conditions do not change very much.

5.4 Comparative Economic History and Its Relevance for the Modern World

Why do these institutional differences from antiquity matter? I think they do for the following reason. As stated above, if there has been coevolution of institutions and culture in history, differences in institutions from antiquity may have affected cultural differences over time. Today's main cultural differences according to cross-cultural psychologists are between individualism and collectivism (see, e.g. Heine 2007). The difference between individualist and collectivist culture is explained in detail in Gorodnichenko and Roland (2012). The most common database measuring these cultural differences comes from Hofstede (2001). These cultural differences matter to understand the determinants of growth and innovation (Gorodnichenko and Roland 2011, 2017), the likelihood of adopting democracy (Gorodnichenko and Roland 2015) or differences in the organization of multinational firms (Miroshnik 2002; Gorodnichenko et al. 2015).

More broadly, tensions between China and the West are playing a central role in today's world. China has developed a collectivist culture in its millennial history. This culture has shaped China's institutions, and one can argue that collectivist culture plays a central role in China today. Understanding these cultural differences and the effects they have on the modern world is thus of crucial importance. If today's cultural differences date back to the ancient past, one cannot expect today's important cultural systems to change any time soon. We have no other choice than to try to learn to live peacefully, taking account these differences and understanding the role they play.

In Fig. 6.6, we show the result of a regression between our composite institutional index and Hofstede's individualism score. We see a significantly positive relation. This thus indicates a likely effect of institutions in the ancient past and modern culture. We are not in a position to identify the exact channels through which past institutions affected modern culture, but Fig. 6.6 is consistent with the Bisin-Verdier theory of coevolution of institutions and culture.

We also show in Table 6.3 reduced form regressions of Hofstede's individualism score with respect to geographical conditions that facilitated the emergence of market institutions. They have the expected sign and are all significant, except for the measure of heterogeneity of production. It would be difficult to argue that these geographical variables affected individualism directly. Most likely, they would be mediated via the joint development of market trade and market institutions. The development of private trade and protection of private property likely fostered the development of values of individualism, whereas embeddedness in statist institutions likely encouraged the development of collectivist values. These reduced form regressions thus confer plausibility to the idea that particular geographical conditions affected institutional systems in antiquity as well as the intensity of private trade in the ancient past.

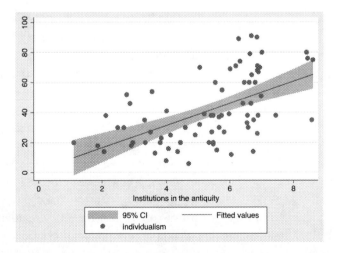

Fig. 6.6 Individualism in the modern world and institutions in antiquity

Table 6.3 Reduced form estimates: Individualism and geography

	(1)	(2)	(3)	(4)	(5)	(6)
Heterogeneity production	0.903					
	(0.987)					
Soil fractionalization		64.901***				
		(20.030)				
Ease of transportation			3.908***			
			(0.678)			
Log distance hot trading zone				−8.607***		
				(1.674)		
Distance to sea					−0.020**	
					(0.008)	
Log ruggedness (100 km)						−2.683***
						(0.865)
Observations	95	92	95	82	92	88

Robust standard errors in parentheses. ***$p<0.01$, **$p<0.05$, *$p<0.1$

6   Conclusion

In this chapter, we have argued that comparative economic history may be a fruitful avenue to do research in comparative economic analysis. We reviewed research on comparative archeology documenting patterns in institutional differences observed in early states. We reviewed the literature on the historical origins of cultural differences, based on pathogen prevalence and social adaptations to differences in the frequency of particular variants of genes. We also reviewed some recent work on comparative institutional analysis in ancient history. Finally, we presented research based on intensive data collection on institutions in antiquity for close to 100 countries. We do find institutional clusters that confirm that some ancient societies had statist systems, systems akin to centrally planned economies that existed for a few decades in the twentieth century. We also find that statist versus market systems in antiquity are strongly correlated with modern collectivist versus individualist cultural systems.

Reviewing the material discussed in this chapter, questions are raised about how to evaluate the differences between statist and market systems in the past, in some measurable dimensions. One measure might be economic performance. This is often done by population growth. Another might be stability. Egyptian and Chinese civilizations, which are prime examples of statist systems, lasted for millennia and were arguably very stable. Egyptian civilization, arguably the longest in human history, nevertheless disappeared and never recovered from the Roman conquest and subsequent domination by Copts and later Muslims. It seems also that statist systems could have been less territorially expansionist. Arguably, there are many other aspects of performance that could be compared with more data collection and analysis.

I would certainly in any case urge not to make too many comparisons between communist systems in the twentieth century and statist systems in antiquity. As devastating as they have been on the lives of hundreds of millions, communist systems only lasted a few decades, not much in historical perspective. The analysis of statist systems may, however, be fruitful in understanding better the current institutional system in China, as it emerged after the launch of economic reforms in 1978. That system has already lasted longer than Mao's communist system that lasted not more than 30 years. The current Chinese institutional system may still last for many more decades.

Appendix: Scoring Rules for Our Institutional Variables

(Numbers indicate the score)

Legal Institutions

Land Ownership

1: No evidence of private ownership, all land property belongs to the state or the ruler.
2: No evidence of private ownership in society, state ownership and institutional ownership.
3: No evidence of private ownership, communal ownership dominates. Land exchange is very limited (may only exist between tribes, villages or communities under very specific conditions).
4: Private ownership is limited and coexists with communal or institutional ownership. Land is inheritable within the family. Land transaction is rare.
5: Private ownership coexists with communal or institutional ownership. Land is conditionally inheritable. Land transaction (leasing, purchase and sale) is present but conditional, limited or restricted.

6: Private land ownership dominates. Land is conditionally inheritable. Land transaction is very rare.

7: Private land ownership dominates. Land is inheritable. Land transaction is rare.

8: Mostly private land ownership by individual. Land is inheritable. Some evidence of land transaction (leasing, purchase and sale).

9: Mostly private land ownership by individual. Land can be inherited, rent or sold and disposed at the owner's own will. Land transaction is common.

10: Mostly private land ownership by individual. Land can be inherited, rent or sold and disposed at the owner's own will. Land transaction is very common and land market exists.

Private Slavery

Four sub-variables: (A) prevalence of private slavery, (B) legal or social norm of slavery, (C) presence of slave trade and slave market and (D) (private) slave population

A: Prevalence of Private Slavery

1: Almost all unfree labors are owned as public slaves working for the ruler, the state or public institutions (temples, armies, etc.); no private slavery.

2: Most unfree labors are public slaves.

3: Private slaves and other types of unfree dependent labor such as serfs coexist.

4: Most unfree labor are private slaves.

5: Predominant most unfree labors are owned as private slaves.

B: Legal or Social Norm of Slavery

1: Slaves are not recognized as property but usually being regarded as servants or dependents of the ruler. Slaves cannot be mortgaged, bought or sold; or no slaves.

2: Slaves are not defined as property but usually being regarded as servants or dependents of the ruler or master. Slaves can rarely be transferred or mortgaged under special conditions.

3: Slaves are not defined as property but retain certain rights as person. Slaves are bounded to land or clans and generally cannot be bought, mortgaged or sold conditionally (debt bondage, limited service slavery, etc.).

4: Slaves are not defined as full private property but only partially or conditionally or they retain certain rights as person. Slaves can be mortgaged, bought or sold.

5: Slaves are defined in law or custom as full private property, and they can be mortgaged, bought or sold at the owner's will.

C: Presence of Slave Trade and Slave Market

1: Absence or near absence of slave market or slave trade.

2: Slave markets and slave trade exists but limited in scale.

3: Slave market and slave trade exist.

4: Active slave trade and slave market; a large number of slaves are traded.

5: Very active private slave trade and private slave market; very large number of slaves traded in markets.

D: Private Slave Population

1: No (private) slave population.

2: Private slaves constitute a very small portion of total population.

3: Private slaves constitute a portion of total population.

4: Private slaves constitute a large portion of total population.

5: Private slaves constitute a very large portion of total population.

Composite Law Index

Sum of three variables: property law, contract law and formal public law

A. Property Law

0: No mention of private property nor its protection or no concept of private property. Strong emphasis against transgression against state property.

1: No mention of private property nor its protection, or no concept of private property.

2: No explicit mention of protection of private property, but written codes on transfer of property, inheritance of property of individuals and how to solve disputes on property.

3: Written codes on transfer of property, inheritance of property of individuals and how to solve disputes on property, and the law also explicitly mentions protection of private property against potential expropriation.

B. Contract Law

0: No mention of contract in laws (the existence of commercial law usually suggests contract law).
1: Unwritten or customary law that has cases related to contract.
2: Written contract law mentioning cases of contract and enforcement.
3: Written contract law that has detailed conditions on regulation and enforcement of contract.

C. Comparison on Public Law

0: No procedural law, usually no specific procedure is followed.
1: Procedure but little protection.
2: Some formalized way of procedure.
4: Written procedural law.

Note. Customary law=0 or 1

Political Institutions

Government Centralization

Sum of two variables (concentration of power and degree of centralization)

Concentration of Power in Executive in the Central Government 1-5

1: The ruler's executive power is greatly limited by legislature and judiciary institutions. The ruler is subject to changes made by elections or assembly disapproval.
2: The ruler has large power in the executive realm but is limited in others.

3: The ruler has large power in legislature, executive and judiciary realms but his power constrained by other organizations or institutions (term limits, assembly consent, legal constraints, etc.).

4: The ruler has large power in legislature, executive and judiciary realms, but his power is potentially constrained.

5: The ruler has unlimited power in legislature, executive and judiciary realms. The ruler generally rules for life.

Relationship Between Central and Local Governments 1-5

1: Decentralized. The local government is independent from the center. The central government has no power in appointing local officials or intervening local administration.

2: Decentralized. The local government is de facto autonomous from the center. The central government has limited power in appointing local officials or intervening local administration.

3: Centralized delegational system. The local government is administered by hereditary local rulers, and the central government cannot replace local officials at will. No separation of different aspects of local administration.

4: Centralized bureaucracy. The local government is directly appointed by and responsible to the central government. The separation of powers and regular transfer of local officials are not institutionalized or not executed.

5: Centralized bureaucracy. The local government is administered by separate officials who are directly appointed by and responsible to the central government. Local officials cannot appoint lower-level officials at will, and they are transferred at regular intervals.

*A total score of 1 if no political authority beyond community (e.g. autonomous bands and villages)

Importance of Cities

Urbanization Rate:

0: Completely rural.

1: The polity has only a few settlements/towns, cities in the real sense do not exist; low urban population. =0%

2: The polity has a few towns or large settlements; relatively low urban population. <5%

3: The polity has a number of towns or cities, medium-level urban population. 5–10%

4: The polity has a notable number of towns and cities; urban population is relatively high. 10–15%

5: The polity is highly urbanized. Population is concentrated in urban centers and very high. >15%

Commercial Function of Cities:

1: Almost all cities are administrative/ceremonial/military centers; cities are not commercial centers.

2: Cities mostly are administrative/ceremonial/military centers; some commercial function.

3: Cities combined the function of administration and commerce.

4: Cities are primarily commercial and manufacturing centers.

5: Cities are commercial and manufacturing centers.

Sociological Institutions

Importance of Clan

Scores are based on the sum of scores of the following five variables.

A: Family Type (Nuclear Family vs. Extended Family) (2)

0: Nuclear family is the most common family type.

1: Mixed (stem families or mixed nuclear and extended family).

2: Extended large family/compound is the most common family type.

B: Importance of Unilineal Descent Group in Society (2)

0: No unilineal descent group.

1: Unilineal descent group only exists in particular social groups (e.g. only important in nobility).

2: Unilineal descent group is prevalent in all parts of social groups.

C: Localized vs. Non-Localized Descent Group (2)

0: The descent group is dispersed. Unilineally or bilaterally related individuals are not localized in one particular area.

1: Mixed.

2: The descent group is localized. Unilineally related individuals live in proximity (within a village, settlement, community, etc.).

D: Cooperation Within Descent Group (2)

0: The descent group is noncorporate. Individual relies more on kindreds, networks of relatives and friends.

1: The descent group is an economic or political corporation to some extent, but its role in sustaining cooperation is limited.

2: The descent group, acting as an economic and political corporation, sustains cooperation within the group by providing members public goods and social safety nets, including education, defense and protection, rituals, common economic activities, regulation of marriage, or mutual assistance and so on.

E: Conflict Resolution (2)

0: Authorities of the descent group has no formal power to resolve dispute between individuals.

1: Mixed.

2: Authorities of the descent group have supreme power to resolve disputes between individuals within the group. The whole descent group has collective responsibility while in conflict with outsiders.

Social Stratification

1: Society is not stratified. Status is not hereditary. Typically seen in pre-states or in tribes, clans based on kinship.

2: Few distinguishable social strata existed in society. Status is not hereditary for the most cases and widespread mobility between different social strata.

3: Society has a few social strata. Status is not strictly hereditary, and vertical mobility is possible through meritocracy, individual skill, valor, piety or wisdom.

4: Society has a few social strata. Some strata are hereditary, while there is mobility in the others. (Example: hereditary freemen and slaves. Lacked hereditary aristocracy within freemen. The vertical mobility within the group of freemen is possible and prevalent.)

5, 6: Society has many social strata. Some strata are hereditary while there is mobility in the others. (Example: Hereditary freemen and slaves. Weak hereditary aristocracy within freemen. The vertical mobility within the group of freemen is possible.)

7: Society has many social strata. Most strata are hereditary; limited vertical mobility between strata. Example: hereditary freemen and slaves. Within the freemen group, there were the distinctions between hereditary aristocratic groups and commoners/peasants/serfs.

8: Society is highly stratified. Caste exists in most social classes/groups. An individual's status is almost hereditary. Limited vertical mobility among different strata in the hierarchy.

9: Society is highly stratified. Caste exists in most social classes/groups. An individual's status is almost strictly hereditary. Limited vertical mobility among different strata in the hierarchy.

10: Society is highly stratified. Strong caste distinction in almost all classes/groups. An individual's status is strictly hereditary. Very limited vertical mobility among different strata in the hierarchy.

Ethnic Diversity

1: Perfectly homogeneous: single ethnic group sharing the same culture, ancestry, religion and language.

2: Two major ethnic groups roughly 10-20% to 80-90%.

3: Two major ethnic groups roughly 1/3-2/3.

4: Two major ethnic groups 50-50%.

5: Three major ethnic groups 5–20–75%.

6: Three major ethnic groups 20–30–50%.

7: Three major ethnic groups 1/3, 1/3, 1/3.

8: Four major ethnic groups.

9: Four or more ethnic groups.

10: Perfectly heterogeneous: many (more than four) ethnic groups with different culture, ancestry, religion and languages.

References

Acemoglu, D., & Robinson, J. (2012). *Why Nations Fail.* New York: Crown.

Acemoglu, D., & Robinson, J. (2019). *The Narrow Corridor. States, Societies and the Fate of Liberty.* London: Penguin Press.

Acemoglu, D., Johnson, S., & Robinson, J. (2001). The Colonial Origins of Comparative Economic Development. *American Economic Review, 91*(5), 1369–1401.

Ahuja, K., van der Schaar, M., & Zame, W. (2017). *Individualism, Collectivism and Economic Outcomes: A Theory and Some Evidence.* Discussion Paper UCLA.

Aoki, M. (2001). *Towards a Comparative Institutional Analysis.* Cambridge, MA: MIT Press.

Berglof, E., & Roland, G. (2007). *Economics of Transition. The Fifth Nobel Symposium in Economics.* London: Palgrave Macmillan.

Bisin, A., & Verdier, T. (2017). *On the Joint Evolution of Culture and Institutions.* NBER working paper No. 23375.

Blanchard, O., & Kremer, M. (1997). Disorganization. *Quarterly Journal of Economics, 112*(4), 1091–1126.

Bockstette, V., Chanda, A., & Putterman, L. (2002). States and Markets: The Advantage of an Early Start. *Journal of Economic Growth, 7*(4), 347–369.

Boyd, R., & Richerson, P. (1985). *Culture and the Evolutionary Process.* Chicago: University of Chicago Press.

Buggle, J., & Durante, R. (2017). *Climate Risk, Cooperation, and the Co-evolution of Culture and Institutions.* CEPR DP No 12380.

Carneiro, R. (1970). A Theory of the Origin of the State. *Science, 169*(3947), 733–738.

Chiao, J. Y., & Blizinsky, K. D. (2010). Culture-Gene Coevolution of Individualism-Collectivism and the Serotonin Transporter Gene. *Proceedings – Royal Society. Biological Sciences, 277*(1681), 529–537.

Dal Bo, E., Hernandez, P., & Mazzuca, S. (2015). *The Paradox of Civilization: Pre-industrial Sources of Security and Prosperity.* NBER working paper No 21829.

Davis, L. (2016). Individual Responsibility and Economic Development: Evidence from Rainfall Data. *Kyklos, 69*(3), 426–470.

Davis, L., & Williamson, C. (2019). Does Individualism Promote Gender Equality? *World Development, 123*, 104627.

Djankov, S., Glaeser, E., La Porta, R., Lopez de Silanes, F., & Shleifer, A. (2003). The New Comparative Economics. *Journal of Comparative Economics, 31*(4), 595–619.

Fernandez, R., & Fogli, A. (2009). Culture: An Empirical Investigation of Beliefs, Work and Fertility. *American Economic Journal: Macroeconomics, 1*(1), 146–177.

Fernandez, R., Fogli, A., & Olivetti, C. (2004). Mothers and Sons: Preference Formation and Female Labor Force Dynamics. *The Quarterly Journal of Economics, 119*(4), 1249–1299.

Fincher, C. L., Thornhill, R., Murray, D. R., & Schaller, M. (2008). Pathogen Prevalence Predicts Human Cross-Cultural Variability in Individualism/Collectivism. *Proceedings – Royal Society. Biological Sciences, 275*(1640), 1279–1285.

Flannery, K., & Marcus, J. (2014). *The Creation of Inequality: How Our Prehistoric Ancestors Set the Stage for Monarchy, Slavery and Empire*. Cambridge, MA: Harvard University Press.

Fukuyama, F. (2012). *The Origins of Political Order*. New York: Farrar, Strauss and Giroux.

Fukuyama, F. (2015). *Political Order and Political Decay*. New York: Farrar, Strauss and Giroux.

Gelfand, M. J., Bhawuk, D. P. S., Nishii, L. H., & Bechtold, D. J. (2004). Individualism and Collectivism. In R. J. House, P. J. Hanges, M. Javidan, P. W. Dorfman, & V. Gupta (Eds.), *Culture, Leadership, and Organizations: The GLOBE Study of 62 Societies* (pp. 437–512). Thousand Oaks, CA: Sage Publications.

Gorodnichenko, Y., & Roland, G. (2011). Individualism, Innovation and Long Run Growth. *Proceedings of the National Academy of Sciences, 108*(4), 21316–21319.

Gorodnichenko, Y., & Roland, G. (2012). Understanding the Individualism-Collectivism Cleavage and Its Effects: Lessons from Cross-Cultural Psychology. In M. Aoki, T. Kuran, & G. Roland (Eds.), *Institutions and Comparative Economic Development*. London: Palgrave.

Gorodnichenko, Y., & Roland, G. (2015). *Culture, Institutions and Democratization*. NBER Working Paper No 21117.

Gorodnichenko, Y., & Roland, G. (2017). Culture, Institutions and the Wealth of Nations. *Review of Economics and Statistics, 95*(3), 868–883.

Gorodnichenko, Y., Kukharskyy, B., & Roland, G. (2015). *Culture and Global Sourcing*. NBER Working Paper No. 21198.

Greif, A., & Tabellini, G. (2017). The Clan and the Corporation: Sustaining Cooperation in China and Europe. *Journal of Comparative Economics, 45*(1), 1–35.

Grigoriadis, T. (2019). *Religion and Comparative Development*. Cheltenham, UK: Edward Elgar.

Guiso, L., Sapienza, P., & Zingales, L. (2006). Does Culture Affect Economic Outcomes? *Journal of Economic Perspectives, 20*(2), 23–48.

Hartinger, K., Resnianski, S., & Wiederhold, S. (2019). *Individualism and Cognitive Skills: Evidence from a Large-Scale Skill Assessment*. Working Paper Ifo Institute, Munich.

Heine, S. J. (2007). *Cultural Psychology*. W. W. Norton & Company.

Hofstede, G. (2001). *Culture's Consequences: Comparing Values, Behaviors, and Organizations across Nations*. New York: Sage Publications.

Kashima, E., & Kashima, Y. (1998). Culture and Language: The Case of Cultural Dimensions and Personal Pronoun Use. *Journal of Cross-Cultural Psychology, 29*, 461–486.

Kohler, T., & Smith, M. (Eds.). (2019). *Ten Thousand Years of Inequality. The Archeology of Wealth Differences*. Tucson, AZ: University of Arizona Press.

Kornai, J. (1971). *Anti-equilibrium*. New York: North Holland.

Kyriacou, A. (2016). Individualism-Collectivism, Governance and Economic Development. *European Journal of Political Economy, 42*(C), 91–104.

La Porta, R., Lopez de Silanes, F., Shleifer, A., & Vishny, R. (1998). Law and Finance. *Journal of Political Economy, 106*(6), 1113–1155.

Lizzeri, A., & Persico, N. (2001). The Provision of Public Goods under Alternative Electoral Incentives. *American Economic Review, 91*(1), 225–239.

Luo, S., & Han, S. (2014). The Association between an Oxytocin Receptor Gene Polymorphism and Cultural Orientations. *Culture and Brain, 2*(1), 89–107.

Mayshar, J., Moav, O., Neeman, Z., & Pascali, L. (2015). *Cereals, Appropriability and Hierarchy*. CEPR Discussion Paper No 10742.

Mayshar, J., Moav, O., & Neeman, Z. (2017). Geography, Transparency and Institutions. *American Political Science Review, 111*, 622–636.

Miroshnik, V. (2002). Culture and International Management: A Review. *Journal of Management Development, 21*(7), 521–544.

Montias, J. M. (1976). *The Structure of Economic Systems*. Yale: Yale University Press.

Neuberger, E., & Duffy, W. (1976). *Comparative Economic Systems: A Decision-Making Approach*. Boston: Allyn and Bacon.

North, D. (1990). *Institutions, Institutional Change and Economic Performance*. Cambridge, UK: Cambridge University Press.

Nunn, N., & Puga, D. (2012). Ruggedness: The Blessing of Bad Geography in Africa. *Review of Economics and Statistics, 94*(1), 20–36.

Perotti, R., & Rostagno, M. (2002). Electoral Systems and Public Spending. *Quarterly Journal of Economics, 117*(2), 609–657.

Persson, T., Roland, G., & Tabellini, G. (1997). Separation of Powers and Accountability. *Quarterly Journal of Economics, 112*(4), 1163–1202.

Persson, T., Roland, G., & Tabellini, G. (2000). Comparative Politics and Public Finance. *Journal of Political Economy, 108*(6), 1121–1161.

Persson, T., Roland, G., & Tabellini, G. (2007). Electoral Rules and Government Spending in Parliamentary Democracies. *Quarterly Journal of Political Science, 2*(2), 155–188.

Piketty, T. (2013). *Capital in the Twenty First Century*. Cambridge, MA: Harvard University Press.

Roland, G. (2000). *Transition and Economics: Politics, Markets and Firms*. Cambridge, MA: MIT Press.

Roland, G. (2004). Understanding Institutional Change: Fast-moving and Slow-moving Institutions. *Studies in Comparative International Development, 38*, 109–131.

Roland, G. (2017). *The Deep Historical Roots of Modern Culture*. Based on the Keynote Lecture at the Second World Congress in Comparative Economics, St Petersburg.

Roland, G. (2018). Comparative Economics in Historical Perspective. *Comparative Economic Studies, 60*(4), 475–501.

Roland, G. (2019). Coexisting with China in the Twenty First Century. *Acta Oeconomica, 69*, 49–70.

Roland, G., & Verdier, T. (1999). Transition and the Output Fall. *The Economics of Transition, 7*(1), 1–28.

Scheidel, W. (2017). *The Great Leveler: Violence and the History of Inequality from the Stone Age to the Twenty First Century.* Princeton, NJ: Princeton University Press.

Schönholzer, D. (2017). *The Origin of the State: Extraction, Environmental Circumscription and Protection.* Working Paper UC Berkeley.

Suh, E., Diener, E., Oishi, S., & Triandis, H. C. (1998). The Shifting Basis of Life Satisfaction Judgments across Cultures: Emotions Versus Norms. *Journal of Personality and Social Psychology, 74*, 482–493.

Tabellini, G. (2008). Presidential Address: Institutions and Culture. *Journal of the European Economic Association, 6*, 255–294.

Thornhill, R., Fincher, C. L., Murray, D. R., & Schaller, M. (2010). Zoonotic and Non-Zoonotic Diseases in Relation to Human Personality and Societal Values: Support for the Parasite-Stress Model. *Evolutionary Psychology, 8*(2), 151–169.

Trigger, B. (2003). *Understanding Early Civilizations.* Cambridge, UK: Cambridge University Press.

Turchin, P. (2016). *Ultra-Society: How 10,000 Years of War Made Humans the Greatest Cooperators on Earth.* Chaplin, CT: Beresta Books.

Wantchekon, L., & Garcia-Ponse, O. (2013). *Critical Junctures: Independence Movements and Democracy in Africa.* Working Paper Princeton University.

Williamson, O. (1975). *Markets and Hierarchies: Analysis and Anti-trust Implications: A Study in the Economics of Internal Organization.* New York: Free Press.

7

The World's First Meritocracy Through the Lens of Institutions and Cultural Persistence

James Kai-Sing Kung

1 Introduction

Unlike the West, China had failed to undergo an industrial revolution, resulting in an "economic divergence" from Europe (Pomeranz 2000). Likewise, China had failed to experience a "political divergence"—Europe alone had planted the historical roots of the "constraints on the executive" and accordingly established a representative government as early as the fourteenth century (North and Thomas 1973; Greif et al. 1994; Levi 1988; Downing 1992; Ertman 1997; Acemoglu et al. 2005; Stasavage 2010; Becker et al. 2016). Nonetheless, China was the first in the world to have developed a meritocratic bureaucracy (Landes 1998; Stasavage 2011), and perhaps the only one of its kind originated in a preindustrial context long before the advent of the French Revolution and the Industrial Revolution (Hobsbawm 2010). Expanded and consolidated in the Song Dynasty (c. 960–1279), the civil exam system (*keju* in Chinese)—an epitome of meritocracy—became the first institution in the world by which top government officials were selected on a competitive basis. Moreover, unlike in an aristocracy or a caste-like system, the qualification and

I would like to thank Ting Chen for helpful suggestions and Sein and Isaac Souede for generous financial support. The remaining errors are mine.

J. K.-S. Kung (✉)
Faculty of Business and Economics, The University of Hong Kong, Pok Fu Lam, Hong Kong
e-mail: jameskung@hku.hk

© The Author(s) 2021
E. Douarin, O. Havrylyshyn (eds.), *The Palgrave Handbook of Comparative Economics*,
https://doi.org/10.1007/978-3-030-50888-3_7

honor, which promised a high-level job in the government and a generous remunerative package in the imperial Chinese context, could only be earned through one's own hard work but not bequeathed.

Why did China produce the world's first meritocratic institution nearly 800 years earlier than Europe? To what extent was it really meritocratic? What, for instance, is the yardstick with which we can measure meritocracy? Is there reasonable evidence to bear upon the determinants of success in the civil exam over generations? More broadly, what can history teach us about the long-run impact of meritocratic institutions and culture? For instance, does the presence of a meritocratic elite, as created by the civil exam system, permanently shape outcomes in a manner that generates long-lasting inequality, or, conversely, do the meritocratic institutions and culture serve to create a level playing field for the great majority to potentially narrow the inequality gap in terms of life chances and income? This chapter summarizes new evidence to shed light on these important issues and debates.

We will begin by revisiting an old debate sparked by the late Ping-ti Ho (1962), an eminent historian of late imperial China, who argued that many formerly commoner families were able to experience upward social mobility under the civil exam system. However, his argument is refuted by others on grounds that the civil exam was typically a long and arduous process entailing much financial and other resources, which thus put the rich and resourceful families and lineages at a distinct advantage over the humbler ones. In other words, the seemingly meritocratic institution amounts essentially to no more than a "reproduction of the status quo" (Hymes 1986; see also Elman 2000; Fairbank 1983). Indeed, recent evidence based on data spanning multiple generations find that both schools of thought are valid (e.g., Jiang and Kung 2020). While "family background" or specifically father's education did confer significant advantage on descendants in civil exam success, the system also allowed competent children from a commoner's background to successfully climb what Ho (1962) terms "the ladder of success". One school of thought emphasizes the mechanism of competition (as opposed to ascription) and as a corollary the possibility of mobility (both upward and downward). While recognizing such a possibility, the other school argues that resources are inevitably unevenly distributed, which would affect seemingly competitive outcomes.

Perhaps more interesting is the long-run impact of this meritocratic institution potentially transmitted through a culture of valuing learning and educational achievements that it unwittingly fostered. Viewed from the lens of cultural persistence, our research shows that, a strong *keju* culture as measured by the number of *jinshi*—the highest achievement in the civil exam—nurtured more than 500 years ago (the Ming and Qing dynasties combined) by an institution that was abolished in 1905 continues to exert a strong, positive impact on human capital outcomes even to this day as proxied by years of schooling (Chen et al. 2020). Going beyond human capital outcomes, we also examine whether historical prefectures with greater exam success might stifle entrepreneurship—premised on the intimate link between civil exam success and official appointment. By analyzing census survey data, we actually find more entrepreneurs and (to a lesser extent) professionals today in those locations where *jinshi* density was higher, suggesting that the best talent would be drawn to those sectors promising the greatest economic rewards. Conversely, the public sector—be it the government or state-owned enterprises—is not preferred by the elites of this generation, presumably because it is no longer as prestigious a sector to work in as it used to be in late dynastic or pre-reformed China. Specifically, after decades of economic suppression under communism, the elites have chosen to enter the private sector sanctioned by the reform-minded Chinese leaders—a sector where economic opportunities and rents have expanded by leaps and bounds. Regardless, our evidence consistently supports a story of persistence embedded in the cultural fabric of the *keju* institution woven in the distant past.

To confirm persistence, one must address the possible *channels* through which *keju* culture affects both human capital and similar outcomes such as occupational choice. What we have found, in this regard, suggests that local elite entrenchment was likely severe. Where there were more local elites (the *jinshi*), there were more schools (educational infrastructure), more social capital or institutions, and more political elites across dynasties or regimes, alongside more human capital. Moreover, except for the political elites, meritocratic status is transmitted persistently across generations even after a communist revolution (Chen et al. 2020). All of this points to a possible downside of meritocracy as it may produce or reproduce entrenched pockets of elites rather than levelling the playing field, over time, for those who were initially disadvantaged. Whether or not meritocracy indeed casts a "long shadow" as Daniel Markovits (2019) has recently argued in a different context or what Michael Young (1958) has presciently predicted would be an exciting research topic down the road.[1]

We organize the remainder of the chapter as follows. We begin in Sect. 2 by laying out the origins of China's civil exam system as it became vastly expanded

---

[1] Michael Young recently clarified in *The Guardian* (2001) that when he wrote *The Rise of the Meritocracy* nearly half a century ago (1958), it was meant to be a satire—"a warning against what might happen to Britain between 1958 and the imagined final revolt against the meritocracy in 2033" (June 29, 2001).

and consolidated in the Song Dynasty when the institution became more meritocratic both in terms of eligibility for taking the exam and the criteria for political selection. We then provide, in the same section, a brief introduction of the civil exam using the model adopted in the Ming and Qing dynasties as illustration, as it was in this post-Yuan dynasty (ruled by the Mongols) period that the system grew highly stable until it was abolished in the early twentieth century (c. 1905). In Sect. 3 we discuss the issue of social mobility and the related new findings. In Sect. 4 we go beyond the civil exam system to examine the persistence of a culture (*keju*) of valuing learning and educational achievements that was uniquely fostered by this institution, and in Sect. 5 we provide fresh evidence on the possible effect of this culture on entrepreneurship. Sect. 6 concludes the chapter.

2   Keju the Institution

2.1   Origins and Evolution

China's civil examination system, or *keju*, was designed to recruit learned individuals into the government, in a society where government service was considered the most honorable and prestigious occupation of all.[2] As talent rather than social or political connections was the sole criterion for selection into office, *keju* was thus intentionally meritocratic. But this was not always the case. Back in the Sui (c. 581–605) and the Tang (c. 618–907) dynasties, both of which were founded by aristocrats invariably seizing power from the incumbent emperor through a military coup, the emperors were patently aware of the danger of being surrounded by other aristocrats who might one day collude and turn their backs against them. Thus, while a centrally administered civil exam was implemented as early as during the Sui-Tang dynasties (c. 581–907) out of the emperors' intentions to select senior officials based on merit and avoid being surrounded by other aristocrats, it was not very successful. That is because, in the imperial dynasties prior to the Song, court politics was still very much dominated by the aristocrats, who, in addition to being economically resourceful (e.g., by owning vast tracts of land and many even their own independent army), also powerfully controlled the selection of officials through essentially a system of recommendation. These aristocrats were naturally against the emperors' preference for selecting bureaucrats from

---

[2] In the social hierarchy that existed back then, officials (*shi*) were ranked at the very top, followed by farmers (*nong*), craftsmen (*gong*), and merchants (*shang*) in that order.

a commoner background with arms-length relationships. With the civil exam a mere sideshow, the Tang Dynasty ended up with an overwhelming 80% of the prime ministers (*zaixiang*) from an aristocratic background. By monopolizing educational resources (e.g., teachers and texts), the aristocrats effectively blocked other social classes from competing with their children in the civil exam. This explains why, for well over three centuries since its inception, the Tang dynasty had produced a mere 6522 *jinshi*, averaging only 20 per year, and with close to 80% (76.4%) of them originating from the aristocratic families (Sun, 1980). By contrast, in a more or less comparable length of time the number of *jinshi* increased sevenfold to 42,509 during the Song dynasty (c. 960–1279), averaging 133 per annum. Moreover, the institution had become more "inclusive" in the parlance of Acemoglu and Robinson (2012), as the emperor now permitted even the merchants' children to take the civil exam—an important reason behind the enormous increase in *jinshi* numbers.

All of this was made possible by dint of a "commercial revolution" that occurred during the transition between the two dynasties, better known as the "Tang-Song transition" in Chinese history. In the earlier years of the Song Dynasty (c. 997), agricultural tax contributed the lion's share—roughly two-thirds—to state coffers. But with the gradual development of commerce, commercial tax eventually became the mainstay of Song's fiscal revenue, accounting for up to two-thirds of total tax revenue in 1085 (Bao 2001). As the main commercial tax contributors, the more than 10,000 Song merchants both large and small effectively exerted their political influence over the emperor and successfully lobbied for their children to be allowed to take part in the civil exam. From then on, *keju* became a more meritocratic institution (certainly in terms of eligibility), with an increasing share of *jinshi* scholars hailing from a "commoner" or non-aristocratic background. This fundamental change is illustrated in Fig. 7.1, which shows that, while the number of *jinshi* rose sharply from Tang to Song, the share of these scholars from an aristocratic background declined precipitously—a trend that had since led to the decline of aristocracy in imperial China (Chen and Kung 2020).

The civil exam system in China is indisputably the world's *earliest* meritocratic system. Using the Song Dynasty as benchmark, *keju* came into existence nearly 800 years before similar institutions were adopted in Europe, as Fig. 7.2 shows. Clearly, Song China was more sizeable than virtually all of the city-states in Europe combined at the time. Because collective action becomes a problem when merchants are numerous and scattered over a vast geographic area, the merchants in Song China lobbied hard for inclusion into the bureaucracy instead of sharing power with the emperor as their counterparts in Europe did, in a context where officials were held in the highest regard.

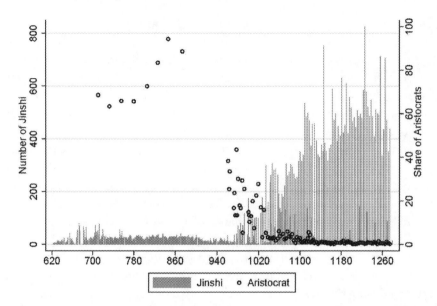

Fig. 7.1 Number of *Jinshi* and share of aristocrats in the *Jinshi* population from Tang to Qing. (Source: Chen and Kung 2020)

Whereas Europe sprouted the historical roots of the "constraints on the executive" and accordingly founded a representative government in the fourteenth century, China instead developed the meritocratic bureaucracy.

Indeed, after China's meritocracy finally grew stable in what turned out to be its last dynasty (the Qing Dynasty), the civil exam system began to draw deep admiration from such European intellectuals as Voltaire, Quesnay, and Christian Wolff, who all viewed it as a superior alternative to the traditional European aristocracy in terms of governance (Ford 1992). Quesnay made his admiration abundantly clear in *Despotism in China* (1767): "There is no hereditary nobility in China; a man's merit and capacity alone mark the rank he is to take, …, the Chinese constitution is founded upon wise and irrevocable laws". In *Essay sur les moeurs* Voltaire (1756) expressed a similar view: "The human mind may certainly not imagine a better government than that in which everything is decided by the great tribunals, subordinate to one another, whose members are admitted only after several stringent examinations. Everything in China is governed by these tribunals". Premised on the rationale that a solid-state administration should be built on merit and rational incentives for its civil servants, in a pioneering effort Prussia modeled its administrative reforms in 1770 after the Chinese "mandarin system" (Jacobsen 2015). The British colonial administrators also saw the potential virtues of the Chinese meritocratic system. Using the East Indian Company as experiment,

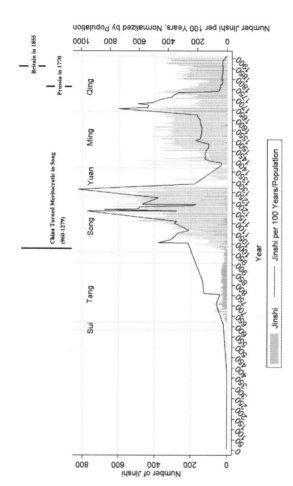

Fig. 7.2 Year of adopting a meritocratic selection system, China, Prussia, and Britain. (Source: Chen and Kung 2020)

the managers required their employees to pass the competitive examinations for both recruitment and promotion in an attempt to prevent corruption and favoritism. Its success soon led to the advocacy of adopting the Chinese mandarin system in Britain and the rest of the Commonwealth (Kazin et al. 2009).

Just when the Chinese civil exam system attracted wide praises elsewhere in the world for its meritocratic virtues, Qing China began to experience a prolonged period of being tormented by various Western powers. Beginning with Britain over the legality of selling opium to the Chinese, the unexpected defeat by the Japanese in the First Sino-Japanese War (c. 1894–1895) was the last straw that drove the Qing Chinese to resolutely carry out comprehensive reforms including one of the educational systems. The Late Qing Reforms were aimed at revitalizing an ailing regime that was not only weak in modern technology—military and otherwise, but also seriously deficient in a wide gamut of institutions underlying education, politics, and so forth. In education, the Qing decided to gradually replace the civil exam system in 1905 by a modern education system undergirded by a Western curriculum, effectively bringing the historical mission of the civil exam institution to a close after a millennium or so of existence.

2.2   Key Features and Characteristics

While the civil exam system underwent mostly continuous consolidation and expansion during the Song dynasty, it was nevertheless briefly interrupted by the Mongolian invasion (c. 1271–1368).[3] The key stylized features of the civil exam system that we describe below thus apply to that of the Ming (1368–1644) and Qing (1644–1911) dynasties, as it was during this time that the system had become firmly stabilized.

The county examination (*xianshi*) was the starting point of the three-tier civil exam system.[4] Success in this exam led to the qualification of a *shengyuan* or licentiate. To limit the number of qualified *shengyuan* candidates, however, the Qing government imposed a quota on each county and prefecture based on: (1) the size of the county or prefecture official school, (2) population, (3) tax obligations, and (4) past exam achievements (Chang 1955). For the most part the *shengyuan* quota had remained relatively stable throughout the two dynasties.[5]

---

[3] Only 1439 *jinshi* were qualified in the few civil exams that were held during the 97-year Mongolian invasion (Chen and Kung 2020).

[4] This section borrows heavily from Jiang and Kung (2020).

[5] After the 1850s, however, in an attempt to encourage the local (provincial) governments to help suppress the Taiping rebels (c. 1850–1864), Emperor Xianfeng increased the quota for those provinces that contributed (Chang 1955).

Provincial exam (*xiangshi*) was the next level up. Those who passed the exam became *juren*. The final stage of the civil exam leading to the highest degree, *jinshi*, consisted of two parts—the metropolitan exam (*huishi*) and, upon passing it, the palace exam (*dianshi*), which took place before the emperor.[6] Reproduced from Jiang and Kung (2020), Fig. 7.3 summarizes the various levels of the civil exam and the corresponding degrees in Qing China.

China's civil exam had three distinct characteristics.[7] Foremost was its *openness*. In principle, *keju* was open to all males regardless of social background. This means that a commoner—someone whose ancestors had never even passed the lowest level of the exam—was eligible to sit for the civil exam so long as he passed each level of the exam in the established sequence. The eminent historian of China, Ping-ti Ho, finds that in the Qing dynasty as many as 45.1% of *juren* and 37.2% of *jinshi* came from a commoner background (Ho 1962). However, others contend that those wealthy and powerful lineages or clans with sufficient linguistic and cultural resources enjoyed disproportionate advantages over the commoners in the civil exam (Elman 2000; Fairbank 1983). We defer taking on this debate until Sect. 3.

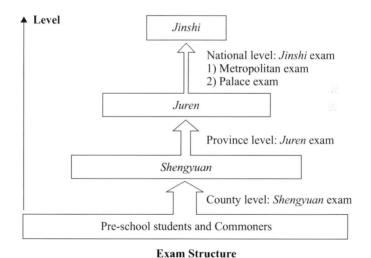

Fig. 7.3 Civil exam structure in Qing China. (Adapted from: Jiang and Kung 2020)

---

[6] As with *shengyuan*, both *juren* and *jinshi* were also regulated by a quota system but at the provincial level.
[7] This part is based on Chen et al. (2020).

Second, *keju* was relatively free of corruption. For instance, to prevent examiners from recognizing a particular candidate through his handwriting, all exam scripts were hand copied first and graded by as many as eight examiners who were oblivious to the identity of the candidates (as the candidates' names were concealed). Moreover, the examiners would be removed from office if they were found to have favored a particular candidate in their grading, or even faced a possible death penalty if they did so in the final stage of the exam (Shang 2004). The penalty was likely severe enough to deter corruption.

Last but not least, China's civil exam system was extremely competitive in itself, but made even more so by the regulation that one was also allowed to take the exam repeatedly. The passing rate for the *shengyuan*, for example, is estimated at only 1–1.5%, which comes as no surprise given the large number of men seeking fame and fortune through the qualification. This rate was much lower than the passing rates for the *juren* (6%) and *jinshi* (17.7%), respectively. By one estimate, the chances that someone starting from the *shengyuan* exam would eventually earn the titles of a *juren* and *jinshi* were a mere 0.09% (1.5% × 6%) and 0.016% (1.5% × 6% × 17.7%), respectively (Chen et al. 2020). The explosive growth in population since the mid-Qing only further intensified competition over time (Ho 1962; Jones and Kuhn 1978).

China's civil examination system was steeped in the Confucian classics based on the *Four Books* and the *Five Classics*, which formed at least two-thirds of the contents of both the *juren* and *jinshi* exams.[8] While the textbooks certainly represent a careful selection of the most distinguished Confucian scholars' works on moral philosophy as seen through the lens of history, literature, metaphysics, and statecraft (social science and politics), the exam system has come under heavy criticism for failing to equip the most talented scholars with "useful knowledge" essential for modern economic development (Mokyr 2002; Needham 1969). This criticism notwithstanding, others have credited this seemingly meritocratic institution for allowing social mobility before the advent of industrialization or a sharp increase in the returns to human capital investment.

---

[8] It was only at the final stage of the *jinshi* exam—the *palace* exam—that the candidates would be tested by the emperor himself on their knowledge beyond the Confucius classics, for example, with questions pertaining to statecraft.

3   Keju and Social Mobility

Whether *keju* promoted social mobility (Ho 1962; Kracke 1947) or served merely to reproduce the status quo (Hymes 1986) has long been debated by social historians of China. Premised on the stylized fact that passing the exams could be an arduous and lengthy process, so much so that continuous financial support from the family and/or lineage was absolutely crucial, its openness notwithstanding, the civil exam system is still seen as merely facilitating the transmission of social status between generations of the privileged (Elman 2013; Fairbank 1983). However, despite the importance of this debate, for decades it was left without a clear answer.

Recently, economists have begun tackling this question by exploiting data on family background and other characteristics to conduct multigenerational analysis of social mobility. For example, by employing selective genealogical records of central China of the Ming and Qing dynasties, Shiue (2017) finds that the transmission effect was strong for the father and the uncle but weak for the grandfather. Making use of a more representative sample and data involving four generations in late Qing China, Jiang and Kung (2020) find support for both sides of the argument concerning social mobility across generations. On the one hand, they show that family background indeed mattered—the chances of the successive generation ending up being a *juren* or *jinshi* were far greater among those whose fathers had attained comparable qualifications. But not every lineage that made it into the government managed to stay in the government. Some inevitably lost their places, presumably to those who moved up the social ladder through their own ability, thanks to the non-hereditary nature of these exam qualifications. Indeed, more than 60% of those with a *juren* or *jinshi* father failed to attain the same or higher status, suggestive of downward mobility. The validity of these descriptive findings is further supported by analysis that regresses the net odds of passing the *jinshi* (metropolitan) exam on "family background" (a categorical variable) and on father's education. *Juren* candidates from the "upper gentry" families (i.e., whose fathers had attained similar educational qualifications) enjoyed a distinct advantage in passing the *jinshi* exam over those from commoner families.

On the other hand, Jiang and Kung also find "ability"—proxied by "a candidate's ranking at the *juren* exam" and the "age upon passing the *juren* exam"—to be a significant determinant of success in passing the *jinshi* exam. Moreover, perhaps the *jinshi* was too high a threshold of the civil exam, wealth as proxied by the number of wives and concubines conferred no significant advantage.[9] Thus, while family background in general, and father's education in particular, made success in the civil exam more likely, certain measures of ability clearly also mattered. This finding undermines the claim that across generations, the civil exam institution was monopolized by the several hundred famous lineages who invariably were winners of the civil exam tournament—a claim also rendered unlikely by the fact that civil exam qualifications could not be retained by the successive generation but had to be earned by merit (through competition).

The question of social mobility arguably takes on even greater importance from a longer-term perspective. If it was indeed the case that legacies of the civil exam have a stronger effect for some (say the wealthier groups) than others, *keju* persistence may reinforce the existing inequality between these social groups, resulting in decreasing social mobility over time. However, to the extent that the civil exam has led to an increase in the years of schooling across the board, it may promote intergenerational mobility simply by increasing the accumulation of human capital and consequently income level of various social groups as time goes by. Which is a more likely outcome is an empirical question. Using the 1% mini census of 2005 for analysis, we find that, while parents' human capital has had a significant effect on the income and educational mobility of children such that those with parents of lesser educational attainment and income fared less well, this effect is significantly moderated in prefectures with a stronger *keju* culture, suggesting the equalizing effect *keju* persistence has had on social mobility in the long run (Chen et al. 2020). While compatible with the positive relationship identified in other contexts between education and social mobility (e.g., Lipset and Bendix 1959; Breen 2010; Chetty et al. 2014), this evidence should be taken as preliminary, as the underlying channels suggest a substantial amount of elite entrenchment (refer to Sect. 4.3 for details).

In reality perhaps it is *perceived* social mobility that matters more. The civil exam might just have favored the affluent families because anyone with lesser means would not have been able to compete, and even over the long term it might simply have been a thinly veiled reproduction of the status quo. The crux, however, remains whether the good majority continues to subscribe to its legitimacy (of promoting social mobility). The importance of perceived mobility for social stability is emphasized by Bai and Jia (2016). These authors argue that the probability that someone would participate in a revolution in 1911—the revolution that occurred after the abolition of the *keju* exam system in 1905 and ended 2000 years of imperial Chinese rule—was

---

[9] Data on landed wealth, which would have been more appropriate, are missing.

significantly higher in counties with higher quotas per capita on entry-level exam candidates (the *shengyuan*) across China. Put more simply, they argue that the odds of the would-be elites (those passing the higher level exams) participating in a revolution were positively correlated with the degree to which social mobility was blocked in a county—the larger the entry-level exam quota the greater the mobility.

4   Keju as Culture

4.1   Returns to the Civil Exam

Embedded in institutions are incentive properties that effectively impact behavior in a systematic manner. Over time, these incentives might produce a culture that persists over time even long after the institutions are abolished. Given that officials (*shi*) in imperial China were held in the highest regard, and that the civil exam was the only road to officialdom regardless of social background, *keju* has arguably produced a culture of valuing education and academic achievements over time. The eminent philosopher, Bertrand Russell, had made that insightful remark in *The Problem of China* nearly a century ago:

> at any rate, for good or evil, the examination system profoundly affected the civilization of China. Among its good effects were a widely-diffused respect for learning. (1922, p. 46)

Indeed, this culture of valuing learning and educational achievements is in turn reinforced by the success of becoming a *jinshi* scholar in imperial China. In his highly regarded book, *Income of the Gentry Class*, the eminent Chinese historian, Chung-li Chang (1962), points out that successful civil exam scholars, while making up a mere 2% of the population, earned a 16 times higher salaried income than a commoner or someone without any civil exam qualification, accounting for 24% of the nation's income. The difference would have been many times greater if the calculation included the income derived from a variety of businesses (such as real estate, banks, jewelry shops) which the *jinshi* scholars were allowed to operate. The promise of such handsome pecuniary rewards may explain why the literati flocked to take the *jinshi* exam despite the low success rate.

Moreover, a *jinshi's* success went far beyond his own personal success. Upon attaining this qualification a *jinshi* was also bestowed prestige and recognition by his lineage and local community (e.g., his name would be recorded in the books of family genealogy and local gazetteer; arches, gateways, and temples would be erected in his name), and even the nation at large (his name would be carved on the walls of the Confucian Temple in the national capital of Beijing) (Ho 1962). These various rewards—pecuniary and honorary—incentivized many to attempt to climb the ladder in late imperial Chinese society. The incentives were so powerful that even rich merchants would devote resources to help their sons succeed in the civil exam (Elman 2000; Needham 1969), with preparation for it beginning at the tender age of six to seven years old (Rawski 1979). This culture of valuing learning and educational success by the Chinese has had a history of nearly a century if we date the extraordinary strengths of these incentives all the way back to the Song Dynasty (or around 500 years if we take the Ming Dynasty as the starting point) before it was abolished in the early twentieth century.

4.2   Cultural Transmission

To test whether the civil exam system may have produced a legacy of valuing learning and educational achievements, in Chen et al. (2020), we relate civil exam success in the Ming-Qing period (a total of 543 years) to human capital outcomes as measured by years of schooling today. Premised on the notion that *jinshi* was the highest level of attainment under the civil exam system, we regard historical prefectures (today's municipalities) with the highest *jinshi* density (the absolute number normalized by population) as having produced the strongest *keju* culture for a period of more than 500 years and which may have nurtured and preserved a legacy of valuing learning and educational success to this day. After controlling for a gamut of variables—most notably those related to economic prosperity and geography—that might be correlated with years of schooling today, and identifying the exogenous variation in *jinshi* density across 278 Chinese prefectures,[10] we find that a doubling of *jinshi* per 10,000 people leads to an 8.5% increase in years of schooling in 2010, equivalent to a marginal effect of 0.74 years when evaluated at the mean of 8.712. This result is non-negligible. Figure 7.4 shows a simple correlation between the two key variables of interest without controlling for the confounders (Chen et al. 2020).

---

[10] We construct an instrumental variable using a prefecture's shortest river distance to its nearest sites of pine and bamboo—the two key ingredients required for producing ink and paper in woodblock printing at the time. Distance to these two raw ingredients is considered important because textbooks and exam aids (reference books) were crucial to *keju* exam success.

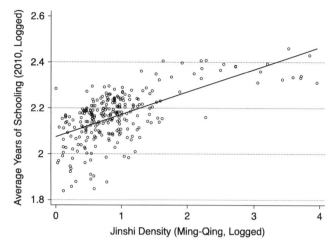

Fig. 7.4   Correlation between historical success in China's civil exam (*Keju*) and years of schooling today. (Source: Chen et al. 2020)

To verify this result, we further divide China's population into four distinct categories of educational achievement: "no education", "elementary and secondary school", "high school", and "university and above". Consistent with expectations, we find that the measure of historical *jinshi* density is positively and significantly correlated with only those having high school and above qualifications and its effect is strongest on university education.

A natural question arising from this finding pertains to how the cultural "trait" of valuing learning and educational achievements is transmitted across generations over time. In addressing this important question economists have devised a conceptual framework for understanding the "vertical transmission" of cultural traits across generations within the family through parental indoctrination and input (Becker, 1991; Doepke and Zilibotti 2014; Guryan et al. 2008). Empirically testing this kind of transmission poses a challenge, however. To circumvent this problem, we make use of specific questions asked in several survey instruments and link them to a uniquely constructed explanatory variable to perform the analysis.[11] Specifically, we construct a variable called ancestral *jinshi* density, which essentially is a measure of the achievements (if any) of the survey respondents' ancestors in a given population in a well-defined geographical area who had obtained a *jinshi* qualification back in Ming-Qing times using surname and hometown (prefecture) information as

---

[11] One of these survey instruments, for example, is the 2010 Chinese Family Panel Survey (CFPS), a nationally representative survey conducted by the Institute of Social Science Survey of Peking University covering 14,960 households in 25 provinces (refer to the center's website http://www.isss.edu.cn/cfps/ for further details).

the criteria for matching, assuming that people born in the same prefecture and sharing the same surname are likely to be related along the patrilineal line (Clark 2014).[12]

The analysis reveals that ancestral *jinshi* density does have a significantly positive effect on the respondents' attitude toward education. Specifically, those with more *jinshi* ancestors are more likely to view education as "the most important determinant of social status" and prefer their children "to receive more years of schooling". Moreover, these folks are also putting the money where their mouth is, by devoting more time and effort to supervising their children's homework. To ensure that what we are capturing is cultural transmission rather than inherited ability, we further control for the respondents' memory and logic test scores, their educational level and income, and a battery of other factors. Our story of cultural transmission remains intact (refer to panel A of Table 6 in Chen et al. 2020).

4.3   Other Possible Channels of Transmission

For a culture of learning and valuing education to become prevalent and deeply embedded in a society over time, the transmission probably has to rely on more than just the family channel to also involve a wider social context ranging from educational infrastructure to networks of social capital and perhaps also political elites. Educational infrastructure, for example, is widely recognized to be important for schooling outcomes (e.g., Duflo 2001), and evidence is available from the Song dynasty to show that prefectures having established more academies and printed more books exceled in the civil exam (Chen and Kung 2020). Similarly, a higher *jinshi* density in the Ming-Qing period is also correlated with significantly more primary and middle schools in the 1900s when a system of modern schools modelled upon the Western curriculum was established. More importantly, *jinshi* density has a more significant effect on modern universities than on primary and middle schools in both 1947 and 2010, suggesting that educational infrastructure in general, and higher education in particular, is an important channel through which *keju* culture has persistently transmitted.

For good or bad, social scientists have demonstrated the importance of social capital in facilitating collective action (e.g., Guiso et al. 2016; Putnam

---

[12] Let us give a simple example. Suppose there were 90 *jinshi* with the surname Kung in Suzhou prefecture in the Ming-Qing period. Given the population in this prefecture with the surname Kung today is 34,000, the normalized *jinshi* density for patrilineal ancestors having the surname Kung in Suzhou prefecture is thus 0.00264.

2000; Satyanath et al. 2017). Owing to the highly coveted title of the *jinshi*, these highly selective elites inevitably formed an exclusive network of the gentry class, who might have created abundant social capital via providing public goods and other philanthropic activities. In the case of imperial China, lineages and clans were the predominant social institutions through which social capital was accumulated. Likewise, by entering officialdom some of the *jinshi* scholars also became political elites, and to the extent that they helped boost educational resources back in their hometowns, they similarly fostered a culture of learning and enhanced the competitiveness of students in exams. Using a number of variables to proxy for social capital, we do find that *jinshi* density has a significantly positive effect on the strength of lineages (using the number of genealogies as proxy[13]) and the number of charitable organizations such as those engaged in relieving famine and running orphanages in the late Qing dynasty and beyond—evidence in harmony with the notion that social capital is also an important channel in fostering *keju* culture. Consistently we also find that *jinshi* density has a significantly positive effect on the number of high-ranking officials in both the late Qing and Republican eras, suggesting that *keju* culture also persists through the channel of political elites (Chen et al. 2020).

5   Beyond Human Capital Outcomes

If *keju* does have a persistent effect, it should arguably extend beyond human capital outcomes. One conjecture, for instance, is that historical prefectures with a strong *keju* culture might have nurtured a strong preference for government jobs, stifling entrepreneurship. To find out, once again we employ the 1% mini census of 2005 for empirical analysis. Specifically, we link the survey respondents to their ancestors who were a *jinshi* based on the information of surname and place of residence, and construct a measure called *jinshi* hometown density, under the assumption that the higher the density is the stronger the influence of *keju* culture on their descendants. One concern about this measure is that there are only a few thousand surnames in China with several dominant ones (e.g., Chen, Li, Zhang, Wang), such that they cover a disproportionate number of individuals who may not share a common ancestor along the patrilineal line. To mitigate this concern, we drop those

---

[13] Specifically, we use the number of genealogies compiled in a prefecture in the Ming-Qing period as measure. Genealogy is an appropriate proxy because resourceful clans tend to revise their genealogies more frequently in order to strengthen the sense of belonging and honor (Watson, 1982).

observations belonging to the top 10 surnames, which together account for approximately half of the sample. To make our estimates even more robust, we further control for prefectural and surname fixed effects.

Before we examine the effect of *keju* culture on entrepreneurship, we first check the socioeconomic status of survey respondents associated with varying historical *jinshi* hometown densities. To this end, we regress years of education, monthly income, and house value on *jinshi* hometown density, controlling for various individual characteristics (age, gender, and ethnicity) and whether or not they reside in an urban or rural area. Table 7.1 shows that those whose hometowns had a higher *jinshi* density back in the old days do enjoy more years of education, earn a higher monthly income, and own

Table **7.1** *Jinshi* ancestor density, socioeconomic status, and sectoral choice of descendants

	Year of education (logged)	Monthly income (logged)	House value (logged)	Private versus public sector	Farming versus private and public sector job
	(1)	(2)	(3)	(4)	(5)
Jinshi ancestor sensitive (hometown–surname)	0.053*	0.086*	1.227***	0.111***	−0.041*
	(0.025)	(0.035)	(0.153)	(0.030)	(0.017)
Age	−0.019***	−0.010***	0.030***	−0.003***	0.007***
	(0.000)	(0.000)	(0.000)	(0.000)	(0.000)
Male (=1)	0.225***	0.395***	−0.283***	−0.028***	−0.090***
	(0.002)	(0.002)	(0.009)	(0.002)	(0.001)
Han ethnicity (=1)	0.115***	0.113***	0.258***	0.046***	−0.048***
	(0.004)	(0.005)	(0.022)	(0.005)	(0.002)
Urban (=1)	0.427***	0.827***	0.164***	−0.307***	−0.588***
	(0.002)	(0.003)	(0.012)	(0.002)	(0.001)
Prefecture fixed effects	Yes	Yes	Yes	Yes	Yes
Surname fixed effects	Yes	Yes	Yes	Yes	Yes
Number of observations	502392	502392	502392	215135	502392
Adj. *R*-squared	0.324	0.368	0.143	0.157	0.465

Note: All regressions exclude: (1) observations of the top 10 surnames in the population in each prefecture, (2) prefectures without any *jinshi* in the Ming-Qing periods, (3) prefectures with fewer than 10 surnames in the 1% 2005 mini census, and (4) individuals not working at the time of the survey. Standard errors clustered at the prefecture-surname level are reported in parentheses. *$p < 0.05$; **$p < 0.01$; ***$p < 0.001$

housing property of a higher value, with level of significance ranging from 10% to 0.1% (columns (1)–(3)). As we have controlled for prefectural fixed effects, our comparisons are essentially restricted to observations within the same municipality.[14]

We then examine the effect of *keju* culture on entrepreneurship in column (4), using the dichotomous outcome of whether one works in the private or public sector as the only indicator. In sharp contrast to the conjecture that a strong *keju* culture may predispose one to choose public sector employment, we find that respondents whose hometowns had a higher *jinshi* density in imperial times tend to be concentrated in the private sector. Why are descendants of *jinshi* avoiding public sector work? Has the persistence finally run its course? Recall earlier that in imperial China, officials were held in the highest esteem, so much so that the civil exam attracted the best talent to compete. But by 2005, China was gradually opening up and moving away from its formerly planned economy—a development that had created rents in the private sector up for grabs. Just as their brilliant forefathers were enticed to compete in the civil exam for the extraordinary rewards it offered, the descendants of *jinshi* were now—and probably for the first time in their lives after living under radical communism for some time—able to seize unprecedented opportunities to increase the returns to their human capital. As a placebo test we check the likelihood of the *jinshi*'s descendants being a (humble) farmer, and confirm that it is highly unlikely—the two variables are negatively and significantly correlated (column (5)).

To further confirm our finding that *keju* culture does not necessarily stifle entrepreneurship, we subdivide the two major—public versus private—sectors into various occupations such as government officials, senior executives of the state-owned enterprises (SOEs) and of private firms, entrepreneurs, entrepreneurs including the self-employed, and not the least a number of professionals grouped together (including engineering, law, medical and healthcare, financial, education, and journalism professionals).

We report the results in Table 7.2. Most notable is that, while imprecisely estimated, *jinshi* hometown density is negatively correlated with employment in the state sector, irrespective of whether it was a government job or senior executive in an SOE (columns (1) and (2)). Conversely, *jinshi* hometown density is positively correlated with occupations in the private sector. For example, it is significantly correlated with employment in private firms (as a senior executive, at the 1% level of significance, column (3)), and even

---

[14] Interestingly the more expensive houses tend to be owned by females (column (3)), who back in imperial times were not even eligible for a formal education.

Table 7.2 *Jinshi* hometown density and occupational choice of descendants

	Occupation (=1)					
	Government officials	SOE senior executives	senior executives of private firms	Entrepreneurs (private firm owners)	Entrepreneurs (private firm owners + self-employed)	Professionals (engineering + law + medical + financial + education + journalism)
	(1)	(2)	(3)	(4)	(5)	(6)
Jinshi density (hometown–surname)	0.003	−0.001	0.011**	0.055***	0.100***	0.018+
	(0.003)	(0.002)	(0.004)	(0.006)	(0.015)	(0.009)
Age	0.000***	0.000***	0.000***	−0.000	−0.000***	−0.000***
	(0.000)	(0.000)	(0.000)	(0.000)	(0.000)	(0.000)
Male (=1)	0.004***	0.002***	0.006***	0.014***	0.061***	−0.026***
	(0.000)	(0.000)	(0.000)	(0.000)	(0.001)	(0.001)
Han ethnicity (=1)	−0.001**	−0.000	0.002**	0.007***	0.033***	−0.004**
	(0.000)	(0.000)	(0.001)	(0.001)	(0.002)	(0.001)
Urban (=1)	0.015***	0.010***	0.012***	0.021***	0.048***	0.189***
	(0.000)	(0.000)	(0.000)	(0.001)	(0.001)	(0.001)
Prefecture fixed effects	Yes	Yes	Yes	Yes	Yes	Yes
Surname fixed effects	Yes	Yes	Yes	Yes	Yes	Yes
Number of observations	502392	502392	502392	502392	502392	502392
Adj. R-squared	0.011	0.011	0.014	0.013	0.036	0.132

Note: All regressions exclude: (1) observations of the top 10 surnames in the population in each prefecture, (2) prefectures without any *jinshi* in the Ming-Qing periods, (3) prefectures with fewer than 10 surnames in the 1% 2005 mini census, and (4) individuals not working at the time of the survey. Standard errors clustered at the prefecture-surname level are reported in the parentheses. *$p < 0.05$; **$p < 0.01$; ***$p < 0.001$

more significantly correlated with respondents who are entrepreneurs (column (4)), including the self-employed (column (5)). Combined, these results provide more fine-grained evidence on the selection of the *jinshi* descendants into a variety of occupations in the private sector in general, and entrepreneurship in particular. Finally, we find that the *jinshi* descendants are also positively selected into a variety of professions, although the significance is only marginal (at the 10% level). To the extent that the professionals as a whole have attained the highest level of education among everyone (13.393 years of schooling, Table 7.3 in the Appendix), this finding is consistent with the positive relationship found between a strong *keju* culture and higher human capital outcomes. The lower-than-expected significance might be attributed to the possibility that many of the professional firms including law and engineering firms were still primarily state owned in 2005, and thus paid much less than opportunities in the rapidly expanding private sector that has drawn much talent. Overall our findings provide solid evidence to suggest that *keju* culture has positively impacted entrepreneurship in a context in which private initiatives had become increasingly sanctioned by the Communist Party alongside the predominance of a state-owned sector. A more conclusive verdict regarding the effects of *keju* culture on entrepreneurship and occupational choice, however, must await further research.

6 Conclusions

In this chapter we provide an analytical account of the world's first meritocratic institution—China's civil exam system—in terms of its origins, characteristics, and implications for social mobility. We show that the civil exam system was intentionally established by emperors of imperial China to circumvent the domination and influence of an aristocracy in political selection which throughout imperial Chinese history had overthrown many an incumbent. Our analysis reveals that the meritocracy in terms of exam eligibility was not actually realized until the arrival of a commercial revolution and accordingly the rise of a merchant class with their newly derived political power (from their tax contributions) when the barricade the aristocrats had set up to block everyone else from competing in the civil exam was finally torn down.

Of course, whether or not the civil exam was sufficiently meritocratic depends on more than just eligibility for participation. To the extent that exam success requires resources that families and lineages of a commoner background could ill afford, eligibility represented little more than empty promises. Premised on the upbeat assessment of some historians that upward social mobility existed in both the Song and Ming-and-Qing dynasties, we drew upon new analytical evidence to show that, while rich and resourceful families did enjoy advantages over their commoner counterparts in civil exam success, they far from monopolized it.

With regard to the culture of valuing learning and educational achievements bred by the *keju* institution, our research finds a strong causal relationship between historical success in the civil exam as measured by *jinshi* density in the old days and human capital outcomes measured by years of schooling today. New but still preliminary analysis further suggests that the same *keju* culture has not smothered entrepreneurship broadly defined. More specifically, the same *jinshi* density is significantly correlated with a strong propensity for private sector jobs in a context where the Chinese economy is moving away from central planning toward the market, and to a lesser extent a variety of professional jobs in the public sector. In short, a strong historical *jinshi* density is highly correlated with economic activities that either promise higher pecuniary returns (as in the private sector) or promote years of schooling (as entailed by professional training).

To the extent that merit is transmittable, we must also address the important questions regarding channels and persistence. We find that, while the family effectively serves as a primary channel through which certain "traits" (net of genetics) are transmitted, it is certainly not the only mechanism. Insofar as *jinshi* density is a good proxy for local elite entrenchment, we find that entrenchment of local elites is strongly correlated with more schools, more social capital, and more political elites across multiple regimes, not to mention higher human capital today. However, meritocratic the civil exam was originally intended to be, the outcome of an unwitting transmission of merits and accordingly entrenched pockets of elites poses a paramount challenge to social scientists and policymakers as to how to prevent today's society from obliviously falling into what Daniel Markovits (2019) terms a "meritocracy trap" through institutions and cultural persistence.

Appendix

Table 7.3 Sociodemographic characteristics of the surveyed individuals, by occupation

	Years of education	Annual income	House value	Age	Male (=1)	Han ethnicity (=1)	Urban (=1)
Government officials	12.498	1109.445	58764.950	43.678	0.789	0.926	0.676
SOE senior executives	12.490	1501.512	70579.470	43.833	0.791	0.958	0.792
Senior executives of private firms	10.841	2379.159	109590.000	40.149	0.780	0.969	0.532
Entrepreneurs (private firm owners)	9.705	1640.975	74981.810	39.845	0.730	0.966	0.400
Entrepreneurs (private firm owners + self-employed)	8.712	973.831	46074.980	40.062	0.678	0.955	0.284
Professionals (engineering + law + medical + financial + education + journalism)	13.393	1144.391	61968.340	37.937	0.433	0.945	0.839
Others	7.641	459.374	26945.040	40.751	0.519	0.916	0.139

References

Acemoglu, D., & Robinson, J. A. (2012). *Why Nations Fail: The Origins of Power, Prosperity, and Poverty*. Largo: Crown Books.

Acemoglu, D., Johnson, S., & Robinson, J. (2005). The Rise of Europe: Atlantic Trade, Institutional Change, and Economic Growth. *American Economic Review, 95*(3), 546–579.

Bai, Y., & Jia, R. (2016). Elite Recruitment and Political Stability: The Impact of the Abolition of China's Civil Service Exam. *Econometrica, 84*(2), 677–733.

Bao, W. (2001). *Study on Song's Local Fiscal History (Songdai Difang Caizhengshi Yanjiu)*. Shanghai: Shanghai Ancient Books Press (Shanghai Guji Chubanshe).

Becker, G. S. (1991). *A Treatise on the Family*. Cambridge, Mass.: Harvard University Press.

Becker, S. O., Boeckh, K., Hainz, C., & Woessmann, L. (2016). The Empire is Dead, Long Live the Empire! Long-Run Persistence of Trust and Corruption in the Bureaucracy. *The Economic Journal, 126*(590), 40–74.

Breen, R. (2010). Educational Expansion and Social Mobility in the 20th Century. *Social Forces, 89*(2), 365–388.

Chang, C.-l. (1955). *The Chinese Gentry: Studies on their Role in Nineteenth-Century Chinese Society* (Vol. 2). Seattle: University of Washington Press.

Chang, C.-l. (1962). *The Income of the Chinese Gentry: Studies on their Role in Nineteenth Century Chinese Society.* Seattle: University of Washington Press.

Chen, T., & Kung, J. K.-S. (2020). *Why Song China? The Rise of a Merchant Class and the Emergence of Meritocracy.* Working Paper.

Chen, Ting, Kung, J. K.-S., & Ma, C. (2020). Long Live Keju! The Persistent Effects of China's Civil Examination System. *The Economic Journal,* ueaa043. https://doi.org/10.1093/ej/ueaa043.

Chetty, R., Hendren, N., Kline, P., & Saez, E. (2014). Where is the Land of Opportunity? The Geography of Intergenerational Mobility in the United States. *The Quarterly Journal of Economics, 129*(4), 1553–1623.

Clark, G. (2014). *The Son also Rises: Surnames and the History of Social Mobility* (Vol. 49). New Jersey: Princeton University Press.

Doepke, M., & Zilibotti, F. (2014). Culture, Entrepreneurship, and Growth. In *Handbook of Economic Growth* (Vol. 2, pp. 1–48). Elsevier.

Downing, B. (1992). *The Military Revolution and Political Change.* Princeton, NJ: Princeton University Press.

Duflo, E. (2001). Schooling and Labor Market Consequences of School Construction in Indonesia: Evidence from an Unusual Policy Experiment. *American Economic Review, 91*(4), 795–813.

Elman, B. A. (2000). *A Cultural History of Civil Examinations in Late Imperial China.* Berkeley, CA: University of California Press.

Elman, B. A. (2013). *Civil Examinations and Meritocracy in Late Imperial China.* Cambridge, Mass.: Harvard University Press.

Ertman, T. (1997). *Birth of the Leviathan: Building States and Regimes in Medieval and Early Modern Europe.* Cambridge: Cambridge University Press.

Fairbank, J. K. (1983). *The United States and China.* Cambridge, Mass.: Harvard University Press.

Ford, B. (1992). *The Cambridge Cultural History of Britain.* London, UK: Cambridge University Press.

Greif, A., Milgrom, P., & Weingast, B. R. (1994). Coordination, Commitment, and Enforcement: The Case of the Merchant Guild. *Journal of Political Economy, 102*(4), 745–776.

Guiso, L., Sapienza, P., & Zingales, L. (2016). Long-Term Persistence. *Journal of the European Economic Association, 14*(6), 1401–1436.

Guryan, J., Hurst, E., & Kearney, M. (2008). Parental Education and Parental Time with Children. *Journal of Economic Perspectives, 22*(3), 23–46.

Ho, P.-T. (1962). *The Ladder of Success in Imperial China: Aspects of Social Mobility, 1368–1911.* New York: Columbia University Press.

Hobsbawm, E. (2010). *Age of Revolution: 1789–1848.* London: Hachette.

Hymes, R. (1986). *Statesmen and Gentlemen: The Elite of Fu-Chou Chiang-Hsi, in Northern and Southern Sung.* Cambridge: Cambridge University Press.

Jacobsen, S. G. (2015). Prussian Emulations of a Chinese Meritocratic Ideal? Early Modern Europe Debating How China Selected Civil Servants. *Journal for Eighteenth-Century Studies, 38*(3), 425–441.

Jiang, Q., & Kung, J. K.-S. (2020). *Social Mobility in Late Imperial China: Reconsidering the 'Ladder of Success' Hypothesis.* OnlineFirst, *Modern China*, https://doi.org/10.1177/0097700420914529.

Jones, S. M., & Kuhn, P. A. (1978). Dynastic Decline and the Roots of Rebellion in D. Twichett and J.K. Fairbank (Eds.). *The Cambridge History of China, 10*, part 1, 107–162. Cambridge: Cambridge Univerisity Press.

Kazin, M., Edwards, R., & Rothman, A. (Eds.). (2009). *On "Meritocracy" in The Princeton Encyclopedia of American Political History.* New Jersey: Princeton University Press.

Kracke, E. A. (1947). Family vs. Merit in Chinese Civil Service Examinations under the Empire. *Harvard Journal of Asiatic Studies, 10*(2), 103–123.

Landes, D. S. (1998). *The Wealth and Poverty of Nations.* New York: W.W. Norton & Company.

Levi, M. (1988). *Of Rule and Revenue.* Berkeley, CA: University of California Press.

Lipset, S. M., & Bendix, R. (1959). *Social Mobility in Industrial Society.* Berkeley, CA: University of California Press.

Markovits, D. (2019). *The Meritocracy Trap: Or, The Tyranny of Just Deserts.* London: Penguin.

Mokyr, J. (2002). *The Gifts of Athena: Historical Origins of the Knowledge Economy.* New Jersey: Princeton University Press.

Needham, J. (1969). *The Grand Titration: Science and Society in East and West.* Toronto: University of Toronto Press.

North, D. C., & Thomas, R. P. (1973). *The Rise of the Western World: A New Economic History.* Cambridge: Cambridge University Press.

Pomeranz, K. (2000). *The Great Divergence: China, Europe, and the Making of the Modern World Economy.* Princeton, NJ: Princeton University Press.

Putnam, R. D. (2000). *Bowling Alone: The Collapse and Revival of American Community.* New York: Simon and Schuster.

Quesnay, F. (1767). Despotism of China. *François Quesnay and Physiocracy*, 917–934.

Rawski, E. S. (1979). *Education and Popular Literacy in Ch'ing China* (Vol. 6). Ann Arbor: University of Michigan Press.

Russell, B. (1922). *The Problem of China.* London: Allen and Unwin.

Satyanath, S., Voigtländer, N., & Voth, H.-J. (2017). Bowling for Fascism: Social Capital and the Rise of the Nazi Party. *Journal of Political Economy, 125*(2), 478–526.

Shang, Y. 商衍鎏 (2004). 清代科舉考試述錄及有關著作 (Review of the Imperial Examination in the Qing Dynasty). Tianjin: 白話文藝出版社.

Shiue, C. H. (2017). *An Analysis with Five Linked Generations in China, 1300–1900.* Working Paper, University of Colorado.

Stasavage, D. (2010). When Distance Mattered: Geographic Scale and the Development of European Representative Assemblies. *American Political Science Review, 104*(4), 625–643.

Stasavage, D. (2011). *States of Credit: Size, Power, and the Development of European Polities*. Princeton, NJ: Princeton University Press.

Sun, Guodong 孫國棟. (1980). 唐宋史論叢 (*A Compendium on the History of the Tang and Song Dynasties*). Hong Kong: 商務出版社.

Young, M. D. (1958). *The Rise of the Meritocracy, 1870–2033: An Essay on Education and Quality*. London, UK: Thames and Hudson.

8

Institutions Matter: But So Does History—A Comparison of Mediaeval Dubrovnik with Other Dalmatian Cities

Oleh Havrylyshyn

1 Introduction

Ragusa, today's Dubrovnik has recently become well-known internationally, especially to all fans of The Game of Thrones, though few of them are likely to know why this magnificent mediaeval walled city became so prosperous that its historical monuments survived to become a stage for the TV series. Croatian historians and archeologists have written extensively on this source of local pride. Recently Havrylyshyn and Srzentic (2015) (henceforth HS) provided some quantification of Ragusa's economic evolution demonstrating first just how prosperous was this tiny city-state in the mediaeval period—rivaling mighty Venice in maritime trade, and second, giving some evidence that its great success is best explained by the high quality of its political, economic, and social institutions. However, HS were not able to explain convincingly why Ragusa was much more successful than other Dalmatian city-states, for lack of institutional information on the latter. The present chapter extends the analysis, based on some fragmentary data and qualitative evidence for the other Dalmatian states, in order to judge whether Ragusa's superior performance can be explained by its superior institutions. An immediate qualifier is in order: indicators of institutional quality like those recently

O. Havrylyshyn (✉)
Carleton University, Ottawa, ON, Canada
e-mail: olehhavrylyshyn@cunet.carleton.ca

© The Author(s) 2021
E. Douarin, O. Havrylyshyn (eds.), *The Palgrave Handbook of Comparative Economics*,
https://doi.org/10.1007/978-3-030-50888-3_8

185

developed by the World Bank[1] are nearly impossible to reproduce going back in history; hence, one must use proxies that are subject to uncertainty and are not precisely comparable for different economies of the time, a problem that is generally true for quantitative economic history research.

The analysis here is best situated in the context of the literature of the New Institutional Economics (NIE), which emphasizes the role good institutions play in economic development. Its prominence today may seem new, but as the pioneering work of North (1990) emphasized, institutions' relevance goes back in time a long way. In recent literature on institutions, works such as Acemoglu et al. (2005) (AJR), and Greif (2006), who investigated how institutional differences may explain different economic performance in places like the Spanish colonies of South America compared to English colonies in North America. Greif (2006: 1) motivates such studies by saying: "Studying institutions sheds light on why some countries are rich and others poor, why some enjoy a welfare enhancing political order and others do not". In this modern literature, one of the first to test the hypothesis in a very broad form were De Long and Shleifer (1993). Though their main explanatory variable is not institutions per se but the nature of the polity: they posit that in contrast to despotic or absolutist states with an autocratic ruler (Prince), non-absolutist governments are more likely to favor commerce, hence provide better institutions. This then leads to greater economic prosperity. Using city-growth as a proxy for economic growth their econometric analysis indeed shows non-despotic polities had much higher city growth.

Ragusa (now Dubrovnik) is much understudied in the economic literature perhaps because of its tiny size (about 50,000 population at the peak), but HS demonstrates it is an excellent historical example of the NIE thesis that good institutions lead to good performance. It had both of the key features noted in the literature: its institutions were very favorable to commerce, and while it was ruled by a hereditary aristocracy, it was by no means an absolutist Princely polity. Further, it was quite unique even among many non-absolutist states in the Mediterranean region in three ways. First, though ruled by a small patrician nobility, it always allowed essentially Smithian open entry to commercial activity by entrepreneurial commoners. Second, it was comparatively benevolent to the lowest strata of its society, and third, despite its size, its maritime commerce rivaled that of much larger and more famous Venice.

A methodological qualifier is in order. Like the earlier study of HS, the approach in this chapter for compiling quantitative information is not primary source archival search, rather it is based on secondary sources—that

---

[1] World Bank, (Annual) *World Governance Indicators*.

is, writings by others which contain some hard data, most commonly by historians who have pursued the laborious effort of archival search. In short, what I admittedly do here is best labeled as *gleaning*—gathering page-by-page any numbers of relevance. I am indebted to the numerous historians who have spent many years gathering such rich archival harvests, and this analysis stands on the shoulders of these giants.

Section 2 provides a brief background on the nature of Ragusa's polity, and its economic evolution using shipping tonnage as a proxy for output, which demonstrates the great economic success it achieved, largely through maritime trade, for a time rivaling 20 times larger Venice. Section 3 compares Ragusa with others polities for some institutional indicators in the legal sphere, while Sect. 4 focuses on issues of social fairness, and government policies on sanitation health, and low-income support. Section 4 ends by addressing the question: were Ragusa's institutions so much better than the others that one might conclude—as HS had done—this explains its great economic success—or is there different explanation? Section 5 draws some conclusions, indicating what can be firmly concluded, and what must remain tentative.

2 Ragusan Polity and Economy

2.1 How Did the Rulers Rule the Ruled?

Ragusa was an aristocracy and governing positions were almost entirely the monopoly of the hereditary nobility based on the "original" settler families who according to the founding myth came from Roman Epidaurus after it was invaded by Avars and Slavs in the late seventh century. But already in the first centuries, many rich merchants and Balkan "nobles" were often quietly "ennobled" in return for the benefits they could bring Ragusa.[2] This system was similar to Venice's, but an important difference for this chapter's thesis relates to the upward mobility of entrepreneurial commoners. In 1297, the *Serrata* closed the ranks of nobility to further expansion. This, in effect, also limited possible new entry into merchant activities by commoners as Acemoglu and Robinson (2012) emphasized. Cipolla (1976: 14) described the same phenomenon in sixteenth century. Northern Italy as an "oligarchic trend".

---

[2] Vekaric (2011), Vol. 1 shows in Table 7 the roots of the noble families; it is clear that a large proportion were not from Epidaurus. Illustratively, and indicatively of name roots is the case of one of the most powerful, the Sorgo (Sorgocevic). They were rich merchants from Cattaro in Albania, "rewarded by the Grand Council for bringing large amounts of sorghum and other victuals to Ragusa, at the time of the great shortages in the year 1292" (p. 68).

Ragusa closed its nobility in 1332, but evidence is clear that very rich and influential commoners continued to be "ennobled", and most important, in practice this only closed the door to high government office, but not to new economic endeavors, that is, open entry in Smith's sense remained. Furthermore, it is widely agreed by historians, contemporaneous and modern, that compared to most other states/nations in this period the nobility ruled with a relatively soft hand and even provided considerable support to meet the needs of the populace, which is explored further in Sects. 2 and 4. Perhaps thanks to this relatively more benevolent rule, Ragusa saw little of the social unrest that Pust (2011: 1) describes as "the long tradition of social uprisings in the Eastern Adriatic, especially towns under Venetian rule". Grubisa (2011) argues that Ragusa, though perhaps less open than early Florence's system of "democratic republicanism", was more attentive to the basic needs of all the population than was the case in most Eastern Mediterranean mediaeval polities. In sum, the Ragusan polity can be described as a relatively benevolent rather than a rapacious autocracy. Still, Pesorda-Vardic (2017) makes clear that the society was clearly hierarchical with three broad classes—nobles, citizens, plebeians, and peasants—and that the treatment of the last group which included rural dwellers, was far less benevolent than for the citizen category of commoners. The latter included both wealthy merchants—many wealthier than most nobles and what today one might consider an upper middle class of lawyers, notaries, physicians, teachers, small merchants, skilled craftsmen like shipbuilders, gold and silver smiths.[3]

The main governance activities such as membership in the legislative council, the executive council and courts were entirely the monopoly of the nobility, but many support activities like bookkeeping, formal recording, notarization, registration, and the like were done by commoner civil servants, as was the case for medical and teaching personnel in government hospitals and schools. A major difference with other Republican city-states was the extremely brief one-month term for the Head of State—the Rector, intended to ensure no one could dominate the top position and turn it into a de facto dynasty, as happened so often in Venice's history. The internal political instability and violent conflicts among groups or clans of nobles so common in the region were thus largely but not entirely avoided.

---

[3] A similar assessment is found in Janekovic Romer (1999), and by numerous earlier Croatian historians; see HS, chapter 3.

2.2 Growth of the Ragusan Economy

In the yet unpublished extensive background notes for his pioneering study of institutions in pre-industrial economies, Roland (2018) explicitly recognizes the large role of tiny Ragusa in antiquity, stating: "almost the entire trade on the Balkan peninsula was for centuries in the hands of the merchants from Dubrovnik".[4] It is notable that he adds: "activities of the Ragusan merchant fleet were supported by a well-developed financial system and promoted by a range of public institutions and interventions", a characterization consistent with the main conclusion of HS that Ragusa's economic success was largely due to its high-quality institutions. Many studies on Northern Italy point to the existence of market-friendly institutions as well (AJR 2005; Lane 1973), so Ragusa was not unique. Indeed, in Sects. 3 and 4, I present some fragmentary evidence that other polities in Dalmatia had institutions similar to Ragusa's. But first, this section briefly outlines Ragusa's undoubtedly superior performance in Late Middle Ages.

Unsurprisingly GDP estimates for this period are not available to show the evolution of output though some rough per capita estimates using the Maddisson approach by Stipetic (2004) put Ragusa's income well above Western Europe before 1600, and about two-thirds that of very rich Venice, confirming the qualitative consensus about its prosperity. Economic historians often rely on population growth as a proxy; estimates of city size in Italy by De Long and Shleifer (1993), extended by Bosker et al. (2008), for all Italian cities, show that after the decline due to the Plague in fourteenth century, most cities doubled in size in the fourteenth century; Ragusa more than tripled from about 20,000 to 70,000. Unlike the then-common process of gaining (or losing) territory by military force, Ragusa's expansion was done by purchase—itself a significant manifestation of its rapidly growing economic power.[5]

---

[4] These extensive notes, over 500 pages, were kindly provided to me by Gerard Roland; they summarize for over seventy countries/states the characteristics of institutions affecting economic activity. East Central Europe is discussed on pp. 366–369.

[5] The purchase of Konavle from a Bosnian King in 1425—without which an airport to bring in tourists today could not possibly exist anywhere near Dubrovnik—incidentally reflects the relatively high level of its financial sophistication: the purchase monies were immediately deposited back with the Ragusa Mint (effectively its only Bank then), with an interest of 5.5%. When the Bosnian rulers, years later needed the monies, they got a friendly reminder that this was a rotating term deposit and it could be withdrawn only with a penalty! (HS 2015).

Arguably, a better proxy for economic output in maritime republics such as Ragusa and Venice might be shipping tonnage[6]—a datum that happens to be available in Luetic (1969) with estimates from the start of the millennium. Using this and various other sources for Venice, the Netherlands and England, HS provide the estimates shown in Fig. 8.1. The Luetic estimates before 1400 are more uncertain, hence comparisons are shown only from 1375.

Perhaps the most striking fact in Fig. 8.1 is that in the late sixteenth century. Ragusan shipping capacity was not much less than that of Venice, a fact repeated numerous times by Croatian historians as a source of national pride. That it was a major rival to Venice is not in doubt, as recognized by more objective historians such as Fernand Braudel who called Ragusa "the pearl of the Adriatic (able) to snatch away goods from under the eyes of venetian merchants".[7] A less recognizable honorific was the then-common English term for the Ragusan Karak vessel: an "Argosy" as in Shakespeare's "Merchant of Venice" inter alia, clearly defined in dictionaries as "a ship of Ragusa". Equivalence with Venice is an exaggeration, but, given its tiny size of about 50,000 population and a mere 1100 km[2], being even close to Venice's shipping capacity was quite an achievement—however, this was only a measure of merchant vessels not war galleys of which Ragusa had at best a handful of very small ones. Nevertheless, it is clear that the fifteenth and sixteenth centuries were indeed the golden years of maritime prosperity, with shipping capacity increasing eightfold from 6000 tons in 1375 to 53,000 tons in 1575.[8]

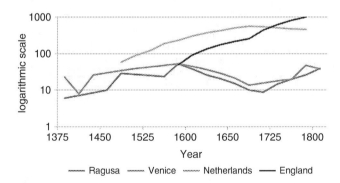

Fig. 8.1 Ship capacity (in 000 tons), 1375–1800. Ragusa, Venice, the Netherlands, and England. (Source: HS 2015)

---

[6] HS confirm this hypothesis for Ragusa showing that tonnage of shipping capacity correlates strongly with city growth.

[7] Cited in Stuard (1992: 31).

[8] See the HS compilation of shipping data in Appendix Table 4 (pp. 212–213) for these approximate values; even if the last is cut to half this is still more than quadrupling.

While no comparable data have been compiled for earlier periods, the strong growth of shipping tonnage from the late fourteenth century probably meant an equally strong growth of income. HS tentatively hypothesized that this strong economic success was attributable to better and more market-friendly institutions, more efficient governance, relatively fair rule-of-law (ROL), and a more socially equitable regime. In the rest of the chapter, this hypothesis is explored further and revised, based on new data comparing institutions in some other city-states of Dalmatia and Italy.

3   Good Institutions: Good Economic Performance

3.1   Fiscal Prudence

If there is one element on which all schools of thought in the NIE as well as in the debates on transition agree, it is that control of fiscal and monetary excesses is a sine-qua-non first step. Reinhartt and Rogoff (2009) emphasize how common were high debts and defaults in European economies of the late mediaeval period, due to borrowing for wars in particular and Pezzolo (2003) elaborates on Northern Italy. Thus for most polities a constant state of deficit budgets, defaults, and financial instability prevailed. In contrast, the extensive historical literature on Ragusa reviewed in HS (Ch. 7) paints a completely different picture of fiscal prudence and stability, with no reference to defaults to be found. Unfortunately, complete budget data for the relevant period are not available, but the status of its budget in the late eighteenth century is fully documented[9] and provides strong albeit implicit evidence of what happened in preceding centuries. The revenue and expenditure structures are reproduced in Fig. 8.2. The data certainly are quite consistent with long-standing fiscal prudence. The first notable feature is that expenditures were less than revenues by about 10% and second interest on debt is a mere 2% of expenditures—largely on domestic loans from local rich merchants. The last contrasts sharply with the situation in most European polities as documented in Koerner (1995): analyzing 25 kingdoms, principalities, and city-states from 1500 to 1800, he finds that service on the debt varied between 17% and 36% of total expenditures. Lane (1973) estimated that at this time Venice paid out a third—and even more in earlier years to service its debt. Note the 11% for

---

[9] Bjelovucic (1970: 44–45) based on the "Bara Bettera Memoirs" commissioned by the Austrian government just before it lost control of Dubrovnik to Napoleonic occupation in 1806.

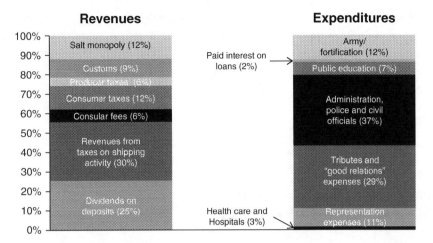

Fig. 8.2 Structure of Ragusa budget about 1800. (Sources: Shares are calculated using absolute ducat values in Bjelovucic (1970: 44–45)—see Table A7)

"representation expenses", paid mostly to the Ottomans, a euphemism for tribute.

Even more historically unique is the unheard of 25% of revenues earned from dividends (interest) on deposits of the state in various Italian banks. HS (2015: 16–17) compiled from various sources estimates of deposits in the Monti (Funds) of many major Italian banks over the period 1575–1790, showing considerable growth apart from a temporary decline in 1700–1725—most likely due to need for reconstruction funds after the severe earthquake of 1675. Overall, these data confirm that fiscal prudence had been a long-standing policy of the government, and not just a solitary episode around 1800.

To sum up, available statistics are consistent with the broad consensus of historians that Ragusa practiced very sensible prudent financial policy, and largely avoided the frequent crises in most other states.

3.2   Market-Friendly Policies and Institutions

Krekic (1980: 12) describes the Ragusan polity as "a government of the merchants, by the merchants, for the merchants", seemingly much like Venice, but this considerably understates the degree to which commoners were among the wealthiest merchants and the considerable numbers of nobles of modest means. On the first, Tadic (1948: 127) discusses at length how ship captains, who were generally commoners, parlayed their abilities into great wealth, noting that "one fourth of the Ragusan fleet was owned by merchants of Lopud", a nearby island where many ships were built and given the requirement that nobles live in the city, was by definition populated only by commoners. Unique data on lending activity over two centuries by Voje (1976) show commoners accounted for an increasing share, about 20% in 1300, 40% at the peak of Ragusan prosperity in 1450. HS (2015: 108–109) summarize the literature's findings on both the importance of commoners' wealth and the frequent cases of impoverishment of noble families. Arguably, this was attributable to two things: on the one hand, the considerable wealth of commoners must have meant that commercial activity was far more open to them than was the case in other aristocratic polities like Venice, and on the other hand, that the obligations of a very small "nobility" to perform the duties of governance as noted earlier diverted energy from commercial activity and perhaps even led some of them to bankruptcies. The wealthy commoner captain-merchant, Vice Skocibuha, was offered entry into the nobility and refused, apparently considering this burden inimical to his business rather than an opportunity to generate more wealth. Thus, one might, using today's NIE jargon, characterize the Ragusan business climate as generally open to small and big newcomers, and *not* oligarchic, for the privileged few.

Another piece of evidence on the ease of doing business and efficient ROL is quantifiable: how quickly bankruptcy cases were settled. HS (136–139) collected a small number of specific court cases described qualitatively by historians,[10] thus providing a crude but revealing comparison with the now-common statistics provided annually in the World Bank's *Doing Business Report*. In 2012, the average time to settle a bankruptcy or contract dispute in court was 1.7 years for the OECD countries, the worst was 3.4 for the Middle East and North Africa region, and 3.1 for Croatia. For Ragusa in the sixteenth century, the average is slightly over two years—even with a 100% margin of error, this still compares extremely well with modern "bests", especially given the much slower pace of document preparations, communication and travel of the time and some of these cases involved foreign claimants.

Palic (2006/7) in particular emphasizes the thoroughness and speediness of the process, the comprehensiveness of the underlying law and practices which contain many terms familiar even to the present day: sequester, liquidation, restructuring (*sanacija* in Croatian), rescheduling of term, and so on. He notes (p. 23) that "at that time, Dubrovnik was admired by Europe for its court procedures methods, being the exception from the middle ages

---

[10] Only a handful of these gave dates for the process, like start of court procedures, time limit for claims to be registered, date of final settlement; however, many other descriptions referred to relatively quick and efficient settlements, suggesting the quantified ones were not atypical.

Table 8.1 Year of first codified legal statutes: selected Dalmatian cities

City	Date: first statute	City	Date: first statute
Korcula	1265	Split	1240
Zadar	1305	Trogir	1322
Ragusa	1272	Brac	1305
Rab	Late 1260s	Hvar	1331
Sibenik	Late 1280s	Lastovo	1310

Sources: Karbic and Karbic (2013); for Split, Benyovsky-Latin (2019: 14)

darkness, showing justice and honorableness." Palic (2008: 83) further points to another informal institution favorable to doing business: the very limited use of debtor's prisons noting that unlike common practices elsewhere—"the ultimate aim of bankruptcy was not just settling (*with*) the lenders, but helping the debtor overcome inability of paying their debt, (*which*) created an atmosphere for further co-operation and doing business together". This tendency to encourage out-of-court settlement is also seen in other court actions—Table 8.1. Robe and Steiner (2015) similarly observe how much longer it took European and North American systems compared to the Renaissance states like Venice, to move way from frequent debt imprisonment and asset seizure toward greater leniency and flexibility allowing debtors to earn income that could resolve debts.

But while Ragusa appears to have been well ahead of west European polities in following sensible dispute resolution practice, it was not that unique in the region. I was unable to find comparable evidence on time to resolve disputes for other Dalmatian cities, but many writers on the issue describe the effectiveness, openness, and "reasonableness" of courts. The title of an article by Sander-Faes (2018), covering numerous cities within the Venetian Commonwealth makes this clear: "To Avoid The Costs Of Litigation The Parties Compromise: Extrajudicial Settlements In The Venetian Commonwealth".[11]

Some qualitative evidence of ease of doing business merits elaboration and it confirms the conclusions implied by the limited data. That well-functioning notary and registration procedures and records for business contracts were established at least as early as the thirteenth century are referenced by many writers, and according to Stipetic (2000: 18), existed from as early as 1200 with formalization in the 1272 Statute, with further details established in 1277 for economic rules in the Customs Book. That Ragusa was among the earliest states to formalize commercial registration and contract procedure is a common claim by Croatian historians. Dates for Western Europe given by

---

[11] Many other historians tell the same story, for example, Andric (2014), Benyovsky-Latin (2019).

Kuran (2011: 242) allow a broader comparison: "In Venice written contracts became mandatory on matters of importance (*in court cases*) in 1394, in France in 1566, in Scotland in 1579, and in Belgium in 1611. In England they became mandatory on all contracts with the Statute of Frauds of 1673". Kuran (p. 243) also mentions that the first agreement of Ottomans with western trading states imposing documentation requirements for court disputes involving foreign merchants was that with Dubrovnik in 1486, preceding the Mamluk-Florentine treaty of 1497 which did the same, and one of the most important "capitulations" was agreed with France in 1536.

Consider finally a much wider historical comparison taken from what may be the most extensive comparison of economic systems in the mediaeval period with the largest sample of countries, Roland (2018) includes a variable "Role of Merchants" corresponding to the concept of favorable business climate. In his Background Notes (fn. 4), Croatia, which includes other territories, is said to be "dominated by Ragusa". It scores 9 on a scale of 1–10 among the highest of nearly 50 European-North American territories. Only a handful (Belgium, the Netherlands) score 10, while the United Kingdom, the United States, and Canada of the time score a much lower 6. If the English colonies had institutions favorable to commerce as AJR (2005) argue, then Ragusa was even better: this may be a bit of an overstatement given the imprecision of all such measures in the literature, but as is often the case even with good data, relative comparisons tend to have greater reliability than absolutes.

3.3   The Quality of Judicial Procedures

3.3.1   Formal Laws

In assessing the quality of institutions, the NIE literature generally concurs on an important distinction between the existence of formal laws and regulations, and their informal implementation in practice—though it is extremely difficult if not impossible to measure the latter. The various modern indicators used in research try to do this by surveys asking affected agents about the quality of relevant institutions/processes—obviously not doable going back in history. Here I follow the procedure developed in HS—provide whatever quantitative evidence there is on formal laws, add any data on access, speed or other procedural events potentially reflective of informal implementation quality, and finally supplement with qualitative description from the historical literature. Several tables are presented below in this spirit.

On the formal level, it appears that Ragusa "scores" very well, but does not necessarily stand out as that much better than other Dalmatian cities. Benyovsky-Latin's (2019: 21) comprehensive review of writings describing Croatian cities in the Middle Ages makes clear that Dalmatian cities in particular saw "a more systematic functioning of urban administrations in the thirteenth century (which) resulted in a large number of notarial documents as well as those of fiscal and normative character". Table 8.1 showing for ten cities in Dalmatia the date of the first comprehensive legal code, or as it was often called "Statute", exemplifies this; the data are taken from Karbic and Karbic (2013). Significantly they qualify the dates noting many instances of extensive prior existence of less systematic and usually partial laws. The Statutes dated here are generally viewed as a systematic codification of all such preceding laws, covering comprehensively all sectors of judicial activity pertaining to all classes of society, including criminal, commercial activity and contacts, moveable and immovable property transactions, even operations of financial instruments such as loans, debentures, as well as all manner of personal and family matters.[12]

Given the dates shown in Table 8.1, the tentative conclusion of HS about Ragusa having the earliest comprehensive legal institutions must therefore be modified. Taken literally the evidence shows at least three cities, Korcula, Rab, and Split came slightly earlier. But this would be attributing more precision to these dates than they merit; all authors on this make very clear that some uncertainty exists because many of these statutes are not available in their original form, and in any event the dating of formal adoption by a legislative-ruling body is not necessarily reflective of preceding practice. That is to say, in most cases, the statute was a pulling together of prior existing laws covering different judicial areas, and in cities that had a long-standing history going back to Roman times, many good separate laws have existed not for decades but for centuries. Both of the works cited give numerous such examples, especially for Zadar,[13] Sibenik, Split, and Trogir. The most sensible conclusion is thus that Ragusa like other Dalmatian cities had comprehensive formal laws in place, not much later than the leading city-states of Northern Italy, and well before such legal consolidation took place in the rest of Europe. Brauneder (2012) implies this in an article entitled "The 'First' European Codification of Private Law" referring to Austria-Hungary's 1792 Galician Code, and the

---

[12] Benyovsky-Latin et al. (2018) also provide an extremely detailed account—310 footnotes!—with numerous examples of notarial, court, and informal settlement cases in the twelfth to fifteenth centuries, but only for the larger Dalmatian cities; their dating and descriptions are largely consistent with Karbic and Karbic.

[13] The old Zara, capital of the Illyrian autochthonous peoples predating Roman occupation.

All-Empire General Land Law of 1794. He bracketed "first" as a caveat to reflect the fact comprehensive codification was always preceded by earlier laws specific to a narrower category. Though he does not explicitly say Italians and Dalmatians came earlier, his conclusion adds credence to the thesis that in Dalmatia formal codification of civil law did come very early.

3.4   Efficiency of Court Procedures

As noted earlier, the actual, informal, implementation of laws is the real acid test of good institutions, but it is extremely difficult to assess this in retrospect. It has been possible so far to put together some limited indication of this in a few statistics of the nature of access to legal-notarial procedures, court decisions, and their speed, based largely on the extensive work of Lonza (1997, 2002).[14] Here and in Sect. 4, a number of tables are presented leading to the tentative broad conclusion that the actual practice of legal activities in Ragusa was on the whole quite efficient and speedy, and that the ROL was generally applicable to all segments of society with wide access and use thereof even by the lowest groups. But once again it seems that Dalmatian cities under Venetian rule were not a lot different.

I start with some evidence on speed in Table 8.2 showing the percent of cases completed by months; these data are gathered from an article of Lonza (1997) describing results of extensive primary research in the Dubrovnik Archives. She cautions that the sample is much smaller in the thirteenth and fifteenth centuries, nevertheless enough to conclude that courts seem to have

Table 8.2 Some quantitative evidence of efficiency and speed of Ragusa courts: thirteenth to eighteenth centuries—percent of cases completed, by months

Year	3–6 months	6–12 months	12+ months
1276	–	53	[47]
1418	–	61	[39]
1736–1737	–	75	[25]
1780–1783	–	64/78	[22–36/]
1750	7	64	29
1783	34	44	22

Source: Lonza (1997: 265–272)

---

[14] HS describe how the data in tables here were gleaned from the works of Lonza and others; briefly, the texts of such works frequently noted the number of cases of different varieties, the dates of beginning and end of court procedures, whether these were out-of-court settlements or court orders. Selected numbers of this sort were collected and compiled by HS in tabular form; here only a small selection of these is presented.

been quite quick, with well over half of cases (53%) being completed within one year, 47% requiring a year or more. Resolutions were also progressively reached faster: in the fifteenth century, cases beyond one year were down to 39%, and by the eighteenth century about 20–30% (sometimes with important year-on-year variations).

This limited quantitative evidence suggests Ragusan court procedures were generally efficient and well implemented. Later I present similar fragmentary evidence on a level-playing field with high accessibility to all classes. The non-quantitative history literature supplements this conclusion; it contains extensive qualitative descriptions of relatively efficient procedures in Ragusa, some cited here, many more referenced in HS.

It is also the case that this literature often says the same about other Dalmatian cities. Sander-Faes (2018: 128–129) gives an example from Zadar also suggestive of efficient and rapid resolution. In 1563, a Franciscan convent built a new *necessarium* (latrine) along a wall shared by its neighbor Francis Tubicina, who took legal action. Procedures continued into the summer of 1564, but by July, the courts encourage an extrajudicial settlement whereby the *necessarium* was moved to a different wall and the Convent was ordered to raise and extend the Tubicina wall.

A progressive increase in speed and in results friendly to commercial activity is also suggested by more frequent out-of-court settlement, often encouraged by the court. This was true not only for bankruptcy cases as already noted, but in general, as Table 8.3 demonstrates. The share of cases that did not go to formal hearing increased sharply from the start of fourteenth to the end of fifteenth century—and for formal hearings the share that reached final judgments fell sharply from about 40% to less than 20%.

Table 8.3 Trend of termination/final judgment proportions of cases, 1312–1499

Period	Complaint only	Final judgment
1312–1313	7.35	41.18
1348–1350	4.26	42.55
1372–1374	11.32	26.95
1401–1402	19.05	16.40
1423	25.73	16.40
1447	36.33	22.10
1466	48.59	2.1
1487	20.65	17.4
1499	17.02	13.8

Source: Lonza (2002), Table 3, p. 82 (total of 2142 cases studied)

4   Social Equity: Sufficiently Fair?

4.1   Wealth and Poverty

The most common starting point for modern analyses on social equity is some measure of income distribution. Enormous research efforts at Bocconi University's DONDENA project have recently provided historical income distribution trends for many city-states in Italy, Netherlands, Spain: see Alfani (2015), Ryksbosch (2014). These estimates show Gini coefficients generally well over 0.5 and up to 0.8 and more—a picture consistent with the Hobessian description of pre-industrial gaps between the wealthy and the poor. Then was Ragusa any better than this as the many encomiums by historians claim? Unfortunately, no direct comparison is possible—the immense archival work of the DONDENA projects is still to be done in the rich Dubrovnik Archives. Still, a lot of fragmentary evidence on social programs and support for low-income citizens, as well as data on provision of health, sanitation, urban infra-structure, is available.

In HS, we used the words "sufficiently fair" rather than "equitable" since there was no question about the monopoly role of the nobility in government, or the fact that most of the population had very low levels of income, particularly in the countryside. However, a consensus in the his-torical literature suggested the nobility paid sufficient attention to the well-being of those who must necessarily provide the work force on ships, shipyards, and trade-related activities, to ensure a degree of social stability unusual for the times. Quotes from Sisak (2011: 182) are typical of the literature:

The political monopoly of the nobility the normal state of affairs {but} the welfare which prevailed in the city and the possibilities to make profit and, to some extent to climb up the social scale were also important. The nobility [had] a privileged posi-tion, but they in turn had to ensure the well-being of the rest of the population. The government saw to it that there was no shortage of food or anything else, so it pro-cured grains and kept up the commodity reserves. Moreover the state was mindful of social welfare (assisting the poor who were directly sustained by the government), it secured the material life-conditions (waterworks, sewage, public fountains), it paid the doctors and apothecaries who treated everyone [without charge] from the Rector to the city's poor…it appointed teachers…{etc.}.

Tables below will illustrate quantitatively some of the infrastructural supports for all Ragusans. Sisak (2011) mentions one form of direct financial support that merits mention. As early as 1296, to minimize fire risk, new wooden buildings were limited, eventually prohibited, and by 1406, it was decided to destroy any remaining and replace them with stone structures. The law recognized: "simultaneous destruction of all (wooden houses) would harm very much the [poor] persons who own such houses," hence the program was to be implemented by having groups of only twenty-five demolished each year, and in addition "not to burden too much the poor men in demolishing the said houses" they would be reimbursed for one-third the value, allowed to keep the materials, and could build on the same spot a new stone or dry-wall house". Not overly generous, but perhaps "*sufficient*" to maintain social stability.

Sisak implies also there was at least some degree of opportunity, for social mobility, if not full equality. There is indeed evidence of this. HS cite many earlier writers discussing how commoners could become wealthier: skilled carpenters establishing a ship-building entity, sailors becoming captains; captains becoming rich merchants some wealthy enough to be invited to become part of the nobility. The comparative picture in the literature, however, once again makes clear that this limited sort of mobility was to be found throughout Dalmatia and Northern Italy.

4.2 Fair Rule-of-Law and Access to Legal System

For Ragusa, it is possible to illustrate how the lower classes were treated by the law, that is, to discuss how fair was the ROL, using the extensive archival work of Croatian scholars like Nella Lonza and Josip Lucic. However, comparable works for other cities do not seem to be available as Dubrovnik/Ragusa dominates such scholarship. The first such indicator, number of notary entries by category at the end of the thirteenth century (Table 8.4), does suggest a high usage of entries by lower classes, thus there was reasonable access. The category: "Service Employment" covers largely notarization of agreements/contracts between household heads [presumably from nobility or wealthier merchants and craftsmen] employees or servants—this single entry accounts for more than half (51.9) of the entire sample of entries, 1419 over three years. Selected examples are described, making it clear that one of the parties is from very low-income segment; even more indicative of a high degree of

Table 8.4 Ragusa 1299–1301: selected notary entries by category

Category	No. of entries	Percent
Testaments	149	10.4
Dowries	68	4.7
Service employment	741	51.9
Apprenticeship	39	2.7
Property transactions	171	12.0
Goods transactions	119	8.3
Ship/cargo transactions	19	1.3
Business/partner agreement	17	1.2
Collateral	40	2.8

Source: Authors' computations based on Lucic (1993)—the sample covered 1429 entries in 15 categories—not all are shown here

liberality is the presence of many household slaves, the agreement indicating some terms of the service and sometimes future manumission. But such open access was even slightly greater than this number, as apprenticeship was also large for lower groups, and even a few cases of testaments appear. A comparable systematic compilation is not available for later years, but related qualitative descriptions do not suggest this degree of access was reduced—if anything it may have increased.

To have some sense of the degree of access to the judicial system, HS calculated from these data the percentage of population using notary services. Summary values are in Table 8.5. Population estimates this early are imprecise hence these are given as a range. The Lucic (1993) study actually lists all the names shown in these documents, and it is clear some are repeated over the three years, hence these percentages overstate participation—no adjustment is possible, but I assume that the percentage is half that calculated. Thus, over three years, in the city, 15–25% availed themselves of a notary, and in the republic including rural areas, this was much lower, 10–15%. For a three-year period, this would seem to be quite high, as one would not expect most individuals or household to be notarizing documents regularly.

Table 8.5 Ragusa 1299–1301 notary entries relative to population

	No. of individuals named	Population range	% of population using notary
City	2000	4000–7000	30–50
Republic	3066	10,000–15,000	20–30

Source: Author's calculations based on Lucic (1993) and population summary tables in Havrylyshyn and Srzentic (2015)

4.3   Sanitation and Health Care Measures

Current public health literature suggests that effective measures on health are a good proxy for good governance.[15] Indeed actual implementation of measures on public health, sanitation, fire—safety may be a better indicator of institutional quality than formal laws—also true for notary access.[16] I turn to these next, culling from various sources the date of first introduction in different polities of specific measures or actions, starting with health in Table 8.6.

The most striking historical fact confirmed numerous times in books, academic articles, and a Google search, is the historical first introduction of

Table 8.6 Selective public health measures—approximate year first introduced

	Leprosarium	Quarantine	Public physicians	Public hospital[a]	Public health board	Bills of mortality
Constantinople	<1000			1136		
Damascus	1307			1307		
Ragusa	<1272	1377	1305	1346	Early 1400s	
Split	1332					
Trogir	1372			1357		
Zadar	~1350	1403		1254		
Venice	1423	1423			1348T 1486P	1504
Florence	<1300	1463			1348 T 1527P	
Genoa	1467	1467				
Milan		1488			1400T 1424P?	1452
Paris	<1300				1531T	
Marseilles	1476	1383				
Augsburg	1332	1397				
London	<1300	1518			1543	1603

Sources: Alembic and Markovic (2017), Borovecki and Lang (2001), Cipolla (1976), Fabijanec (2008), Nutton (2006), Porter (1997, 2006), Tognotti (2013), Tomic and Blazina (2015)
[a]Hospitals financed by state budget as opposed to charitable ones operated by religious orders

---

[15] See Greer et al. (2015). I am grateful to Adrianna Murphy of the London school of Hygiene for this reference.

[16] A nice example of this point is found in Zelic (2015: 503). The 1312 Statute of Split was translated into Italian in 1395 by a Friar Michael; it contained a provision about removing houses obstructing defensive walls, "he noted in the margin beside the aforementioned chapter, that the ordinance made no sense any more, because the task had been accomplished a long time before."

quarantine in 1377, attributed to Ragusa.[17] An article from the US Center for Disease Control, by Tognotti (2013: 2) "Lessons from the History of Quarantine", indeed unequivocally states: "quarantine was first introduced in 1377 in Dubrovnik". This was also frequently stated in many other sources ranging from the authoritative Cambridge History of Medicine (Porter 2006) to listings yielded by a Google search including of course Wikipedia.[18] As Table 8.6 shows Ragusa was indeed earlier than many others, only Augsburg in western Europe came about the same time (1332), and surprisingly Venice quite a bit later (1423). The only available datum for others in Dalmatia shows Zadar fairly soon after in 1403. Data on intended containment of perceived infectiousness of leprosy show special hospitals established in these cities later than Ragusa but again earlier than Venice.

On leprosy, still, according to Porter (2006: ch. 6) Western Europe and England established numerous hospitals already in twelfth and thirteenth centuries. Porter makes clear that for many centuries until recently most hospitals were charitable ones operated by religious organizations, and even this authoritative source provides no information on public hospitals in Late Middle Ages. That makes the Dalmatian—and Italian—record on such hospitals a significant marker. Consistent with the conventional wisdom that the Islamic world was ahead of Europe in sciences, Damascus had one of the first public hospitals—though Constantinople may have had one even earlier. However, the qualifier on imprecision and uncertainly in the literature merits repeating here.

The focus of the tables on public hospitals reflects the research question being asked: how early and effectively did a state government set up public health measures? Porter (2006: 183–184) discussing the extensive efforts of Italian cities to provide public health care notes that in the "fifteenth century there were thirty-three hospitals in Florence, roughly one for every 1000 inhabitants *(while) London had more than half a million people by 1700, and just two medical hospital of any consequence*".

Perhaps the most comprehensive indicator on public health policy is the establishment of Public Health Boards, as Cipolla (1976) translated into English the various different-named entities in Northern Italy. His thorough

---

[17] On October 22, 2019, the latter yielded many entries from a wide variety of writings, older, newer, by scholars from Croatia, Europe, the United States, etc.

[18] For "Quarantine" search, in the Wikipedia entry discussion of its early history, the first city mentioned as having quarantine is again Dubrovnik, in 1377, with a requirement of 30 days isolation, then called a *trentine*; over time, the period was extended to 40 days, hence *quarantine*. The Italian origin of the word should not mislead: Ragusa was a multilingual city (Latin for official business, Italian for commerce, and Croatian for everyday life).

analysis of such Boards was focused on Italy and intended to correct the prevailing views that the modernization of medicine started in Western Europe and England. In fact Northern Italy was far in advance of these countries in its efforts to take care of public health. As Cipolla states (p. 31): "The seventeenth century "Bills of Mortality" of London were derived from earlier Italian practice. If the Italian bills are not as famous as London's, it is simply because there has not been in Italy a John Graunt to study them".[19] This two- to three-century lead of Italy over Western Europe is also emphasized by Porter (1997: 120): "By 1300 public physicians were found in all large towns of Northern Italy—a century later the office was almost universal in Northern Italy and venetian territories (including Dalmatia)" but "only by 1500 were civic doctors being appointed in Northern France, Flanders, Germany, though Britain lagged behind". Cipolla (1976: 6) also notes: "when Linacre brought the idea of a college of physicians to England in early sixteenth century, institutions of this kind had been in existence in Italy for about three centuries". On p. 18, he adds: "there is no doubt that Italy was far ahead of other European countries in the field of public health". His dating of health boards is shown in Table 8.5.

For the purposes of this chapter, the other significant conclusion of the tables is how similar were the Dalmatian cities to the progressive Italian ones. The establishment of Health Boards is not specifically mentioned by the various sources writing on health measures, though Tomic and Blazina (2015) do discuss extensively "health officials" and their responsibilities, noting this for Dubrovnik for the early 1400s. Others like Alembic and Markovic (2017) in one of the most thorough analyses of health sanitation have no specific mention of health boards, but many references to health officials, regulations, oversight procedures. Nutton (2006: 67) is most explicit about Ragusa, listing the actions health boards could take: "they (*meaning health officials*) could impose quarantine (first in Dubrovnik in 1377), ban goods from entering, clean the streets, unblock waterways".

The admittedly fragmentary evidence in Tables 8.6 and 8.7 suggests Ragusa was indeed very early in implementing such good practices, about the same time as advanced Italian cities and often earlier than many major western European cities. The broader significance of this is implied in the conclusion of Porter (1997: 239): "Italy's hospitals remained the envy of Europe." Notably however, the other Dalmatian cities were not that far behind, indeed for some measures even earlier: Zadar's first public hospital may have been put in place

---

[19] Here, Cipolla seems to be sarcastically referring to the famous 1636 work of Graunt analyzing causes of death using the statistics of these bills.

Table 8.7 Urban hygiene and safety measures—approximate year introduced

	Waste regulations	Sewers	Street paving	Fire/building regulations
Ragusa	1272>>	1397 (center) 1407–1436 (all)	1389	1296 > 1370[a]
Split	1312			1312>>?
Trogir				
Zadar	1305			
Venice				
Genoa				
Marseilles				
Augsburg	1104			1104
Paris	1407	1370	1189	
Damascus				

Sources: Alembic and Markovic (2017), Borovecki and Lang (2001), Cipolla (1976), Fabijanec (2008), Nutton (2006), Porter (1997, 2006), Tognotti (2013), Tomic and Blazina (2015)

[a]The first regulations in 1296 did not prohibit wooden buildings but limited them to more substantial ones and provided some fire-fighting procedures; over time regulations were tightened, with no new wooden houses allowed, and eventually regulations and plans to destroy all wooden structures with some financial subsidy provided

in 1252, much earlier than that in Ragusa. Since all this dating in the various sources used is qualified and uncertain, precision is inappropriate—but the general sense of a broad similarity and timing in Dalmatia is clear. It may be best to put it as did Zelic (2015: 489) for Dalmatian communes: "the thirteenth century was indeed an epoch of spatial as well as legal consolidation".

4.4   Good Institutions: Necessary but Not Always Sufficient?

Andric and Birin (2019) emphasize that there is no doubt Ragusa was far more successful in competing with Venice in the Levant and Balkan trade, but other Dalmatian cities also did well even under Venetian dominance when, for example, the latter found it useful to let them become an intermediary for inland trade. They note how Split became such an entrepot, and recount numerous specific cases of very rich local merchants, most in fact commoners. According to Pust (2011: 11), Split under Venetian rule was designated as a merchant port and a special role in hinterland trade, thus for a time in seventeenth century, trade with Balkan territories of the Ottoman Empire "equaled or even topped the amount that went through Dubrovnik". Nevertheless, they did not do as well.

But the new comparisons of institutional quality, fragmentary as they are, suggest Ragusa's high-quality institutions and social programs for the bottom classes were not overwhelmingly superior or far more advanced compared to the rest of Dalmatia. Furthermore, most of them had at least equal geographically favorable conditions for trade to the Levant and access for inland trade. Thus, neither geography nor institutional quality alone can explain Ragusa's better performance.

An alternative explanation presents itself: Venetian occupation from the mid-fifteenth century of all Dalmatia except for Ragusa "imposed an entire system of restrictions of economic activities (of Dalmatian colonies), as a consequence of which economic development began to slow down in sixteenth century".[20] In a word, Venice protected its own monopoly of trade with the Ottoman Empire by imposing strict regulations on what each of these cities—Zadar, Split, Trogir, others—could or could not do. For example, Venice at a certain time decided to use Split as its major point of trade with the Balkan hinterland of various Slavic Kingdoms by then incorporated in the Ottoman Empire. But it restricted other cities from this and from most of the long-distance maritime trade. Ragusa was at least formally free from such Venetian restrictions. Furthermore, colonial status may have impeded development of health and social measures: Fabijanec (2008: 133) concludes: "Venetian authorities in Zadar did not take seriously the problem of contagion (*since*) Venice tended to adopt policies suitable to its own purposes (while) Dubrovnik (which had) a free hand could do so". Zelic (2015: 504), citing many earlier scholars confirms Venetian rule imposed itself harshly on Dalmatia as it was "immediately followed by purging municipal law-book". At the same time, he notes "the only law that were removed were those politically unacceptable" but since those "related to the physical aspects of urban environments were politically irrelevant", they were not necessarily purged.

Hence, it is possible that under Venetian rule, the health and safety dimensions analyzed here were not quite as developed as in Ragusa but the evidence shows this gap was minimal. More importantly, however, restrictions on trading that might compete with Venice were imposed. This suggests that no matter the quality of Dalmatian institutions, the military force of the imperial power could for a long time keep competitors down while the ruling polity could remain prosperous for centuries even with huge debt burdens. So to

---

[20] Pust (207): 1Pust (2011: 11).

summarize: Ragusa's institutions were probably just as good as in the rest of Dalmatia, and it had no geographic advantages (such as better coastal harbors or inland trade routes to Ottoman-occupied Balkan kingdoms); on the contrary, the much longer history of an established urban polity in Zadar, Split, or Korcula should have given them the advantage over neophyte Ragusa. The best explanation for their inability to compete with Ragusa may thus be that Venetian military power allowed it to impose economic restrictions and prevent them from "snatching away trade from under Venetian eyes" as relatively independent Ragusa did.

A short excursus is merited. It would be wrong to leave an impression of Venice having a negative influence on Dalmatian institutions. Not all local governance of benefit to populace were prohibited, only those that may have threatened Venice's trade. Furthermore, many researchers discuss the strong indirect influence of Venice's own high quality institutions; Alembic and Markovic (2017: 20) are very clear that Venetian and Italian achievements in culture, governance, and medicine were a model even for Ragusa which was freer to implement its own policies.

Nevertheless, Venice's direct rule of Dalmatia seems to have constrained their economic development compared to that of Ragusa, offsetting any positive effect of their good institutions on economic performance. This of course raises a new question: how could tiny Ragusa with virtually no military or naval power resist Venetian occupation? The most common answer given by historians is clever diplomacy—playing off Venice, The Papacy, The Porte against each other. The last two needed an intermediary conduit for minimizing conflict—Ragusa was useful to both as an open polity where they could communicate informally[21]—Ragusa provided the "Third Man" possibilities, much as Cold War Vienna in recent times. This clever diplomacy by Ragusa garners laudatory assessments from many historians, summarized in the phrase "Sette Bandieri" (Seven Banners) applied to Ragusa symbolizing its openness and tolerance to many foreigners, legations, religions. More skeptical even cynical assessments are implied in the title of an article by Kuncevic (2013): "Janus-faced Sovereignty", by which he means Ragusa was not really free, having to make many compromises with the big powers, and in fact paying the Porte substantial amounts for trading rights (as the last item on the revenue side of the Budget, Fig. 8.2 suggests).

---

[21] A similar assessment is made by Janekovic Romer (1999), and numerous earlier Croatian historians; writing, as reviewed in HS, Chapter 3.

5   Conclusions

To summarize the analysis of this chapter, consider the following syllogism:

* Historical consensus agrees: Italian Republics about the fourteenth to six-teenth centuries were well advanced on various legal, commercial, and public health institutions compared to Western Europe.
* Ragusa had good institutions similar to and generally as early as Italy and occasionally even earlier; but it was not unique as the rest of Dalmatia was about the same or at worst only slightly behind.
* However, independent Ragusa enjoyed a much stronger economic perfor-mance than the rest of Dalmatia.
* Therefore, better institutions alone cannot be the explanation of its supe-rior economic performance as had been hypothesized in Havrylyshyn and Srzentic (2015).
* One potential alternative explanation is geographical advantages—but in fact the others had as good allocation or even better harbors for maritime trade, and equivalent land routes for trade with Balkan Kingdoms.
* Another factor is more likely: all of Dalmatia except Ragusa was occupied by imperialist Venice from early fifteenth century, and faced restrictions on its economic activity and trading imposed to prevent competition with Venice.
* Thus, I conclude that Ragusa's high-quality institutions were important and indeed necessary to its economic success, they were not sufficient; Ragusa needed the good hand history dealt of being free from the trade restrictions Venice imposed on Dalmatian cities. These were dealt a bad hand by history in the form of restrictions analogous to English Navigation laws imposed on the 13 colonies four centuries later, but were far too small to resist the might of Venice.
* Put differently, institutions alone do not fully explain relative economic performance: in the mediaeval period, military, and especially naval power was effectively "a factor of production" in which powerful polities like Venice had a comparative advantage: they could for a long time keep com-petitors down by force and achieve economic prosperity with or without good institutions.[22] Carrying the huge debt burdens for centuries as did

---

[22] Acemoglu and Robinson (2012) argued that over time Venice was unable to remain a dominant eco-nomic power because after the closure of noble ranks in 1296 its institutions gradually deteriorated with concentration of both political and economic power in the elite—yet it remained prosperous and domi-nant for many centuries, perhaps thanks to naval power. In a word, "history" outweighed deteriorating institutions for a long time.

Venice (and some others) might only be explainable by use of military force. Thus, history mattered too.

* As a bottom line, let me "rescue" institutions as a critical ingredient of success. All of the above might best be summarized by saying that good institutions were a necessary but not sufficient condition for Ragusa to succeed. History in the form of imperial dominance by Venice on the Eastern Adriatic coast constrained other Dalmatian cities with perhaps equally good institutions from achieving economic success. Ragusa being free from such constraints thrived. If Ragusa had such freedom but did not develop quality institutions, could it have thrived?

References

Acemoglu, D., & Robinson, J. (2012). *Why Nations Fail: Origins of Power, Prosperity and Poverty*. New York: Crown Publishers.

Acemoglu, D., Johnson, S., & Robinson, J. (2005). Institutions as the Fundamental Causes of Long-Run Growth. In P. Aghion & S. Durlauf (Eds.), *Handbook of Economic Growth*. Amsterdam: Elsevier Publishers.

Alembic, T., & Markovic, H. (2017). Development of Health Care in Dubrovnik from 14th to 16th Century. *Collective Anthropology, 41*, 1–7.

Alfani, G. (2015). *Economic Inequality in northwestern Italy: A long-term view (14th to 18th.c.)*. Milano: Bocconi University, Dondena Working Papers No. 61.

Andric, T. (2014). *Life of the Split Popolani in the Middle Ages, the Example of Craftsmen in the Mid-Fifteenth Century*. Zagreb: Unpublished Doctoral Dissertation, University of Zagreb.

Andric, T., & Birin, A. (2019). The Middle Class Entrepreneurial Elite in Sibenik and Split (15th.c.). *Povijestni Prilozi, 56*, 109–130.

Benyovsky-Latin, I. (2019). *Towns and Cities of the Croatian Middle Ages*. Zagreb: Croatian Institute of History, Povijesni Prilozi.

Benyovsky-Latin, I., Begonja, S., & Jakus, Z. N. (2018). Immovable Property in Legal Actions as Documented in the Notarial Records: The Case of 13th Century Dalmatian Cities. *Mesto a Dejny, 7*(2), 6–54.

Bjelovucic, H. (1970). *The Ragusean Republic. Victim of Napoleon and Its Own Conservatism*. Leiden: E. J. Brill.

Borovecki, A., & Lang, S. (2001). Zdravstvene i socialjne institucije staroga Dubrovnika. *Revija Socialnije Politike, 3–4*, 301–308.

Bosker, M., Brakman, S., Garretsen, H., de Jong, H., & Schramm, M. (2008). Ports, Plagues and Politics: Explaining Italian City Growth 1300–1861. *Review of Economic History, 12*, 97–131.

Brauneder, W. (2012). The First European Codification of Private Law: The AGBG. *Zbornik PFZ, 63*(5–6), 1019–1026.

Cipolla, C. M. (1976). *Public Health and the Medical Profession in the Renaissance.* Cambridge: Cambridge University Press.

De Long, B., & Shleifer, A. (1993). Princes and Merchants: European City Growth Before the Industrial Revolution. *The Journal of Law and Economics, XXXVI,* 671–702.

Fabijanec, S. (2008). Hygiene and Commerce: The Example of Dalmatian Lazarettos Until the Sixteenth Century. *Ekonomska i Ekohistorija, 4*(3), 115–133.

Greer, S., Wismer, M., & Figueras, J. (Eds.). (2015). *Strengthening Health System Governance: Better Policies, Stronger Performance.* London: Open University Press.

Greif, A. (2006). *Institutions and the Path to a Modern Economy.* New York: Cambridge University Press.

Grubisa, D. (2011). Forms of Power in the Renaissance: Uniqueness of the Dubrovnik Mode. *Politicka Misao, 47*(5), 165–182.

Havrylyshyn, O., & Srzentic, N. (2015). *Institutions Always 'Mattered'. Explaining Prosperity in Mediaeval Ragusa (Dubrovnik).* Houndmills, Basingstoke: Palgrave.

Janekovic Romer, Z. (1999). Class and Power in the Republic of Dubrovnik in the Middle Ages. *Acta Historiae, 7,* 215–251.

Karbic, D., & Karbic, M. (2013). *The Laws and Customs of Medieval Croatia and Slavonia.* Studies in Russia and East Europe, No. 10 (M. Rady, Ed.). London: UCL School of Slavonic and East European Studies.

Koerner, M. (1995). Ch. 12: Expenditure. In R. Bonney (Ed.), *Economic Systems and State Finance.* Oxford: Oxford University Press and Clarendon Press, European Science Foundation.

Krekic, B. (1980). *Dubrovnik, Italy and the Balkans in the Late Middle Ages.* London: Variorum Reprints.

Kuncevic, L. (2013). Janus-Faced Sovereignty: The International Status of the Ragusan Republic in the Early Modern Period. In G. Karman & L. Kuncevic (Eds.), *The European Tributary States in the Sixteenth and Seventeenth Centuries* (pp. 91–122). Leiden, Boston: Brill.

Kuran, T. (2011). *The Long Divergence. How Islamic Law Held Back the Middle East.* Princeton: The Princeton University Press.

Lane, F. (1973). *Venice: A Maritime Republic.* Baltimore: The Johns Hopkins Press.

Lonza, N. (1997). *Pod Plaštem Pravde.* Dubrovnik: Zavod za Povijesne Znanosti, HAZU.

Lonza, N. (2002). Tuzba, Osveta, Nagodba: Modeli Reagiranja na Zlocin u Srednjovjekovnom Dubrovniku. *Anali Dubrovnik, 40,* 57–104.

Lucic, J. (1993). *Spis I Dubrovacke Kancelarije, Knjiga IV. Zapisi notara Andrije Benese 1295–1301. Precepta rectoris II (1299–1301). Testamenta II (1295–1301).* Zagreb: Monumenta Ragusina, Hrvatska Akademija Znanosti I Umjetnosti.

Luetic, J. (1969). *1000 Godina Dubrovackog Brodarstva.* Zagreb: Zora.

North, D. (1990). *Institutions, Institutional Change, and Economic Performance.* Cambridge: Cambridge University Press.

Nutton, V. (2006). Chapter 2: The Rise of Medicine. In R. Porter (Ed.), *The Cambridge History of Medicine* (pp. 46–70). Cambridge: Cambridge University Press.

Palic, V. (2006/7). Neki Primjere Sudovanja U Srednjovekovnom Dubrovniku: Povijesni Zbornik. Osijek: 2006/7. broj 1&2. 17–27.

Palic, V. (2008). Bankrot I Sekvestar Imovine Trgovca Nekih Dubrovackih Naseobina u XV i XVI Stoljecu. *Povijesni Zbornik. Godisnajk za Kulturu I Povijesno Naslijed, 2*(3), 73–83.

Pesorda-Vardic, Z. (2017). Orders of Society in Ragusan Narrative Sources: The Case of the Cittadini Ragusei. In I. Benyovsky-Latin & Z. P. Vardic (Eds.), *Towns and Cities of the Croatian Middle Ages. Image of the Town in Narrative Sources. Reality and/or Fiction?* (pp. 291–311). Zagreb: Croatian Institute of History.

Pezzolo, L. (2003). *Fiscal System and Finance in Northern Italy in the Early Modern Ages.* Venice: Nota di Lavorro 2003.09, Fomento di Scienze Economiche, Univerita Ca' Foscari.

Porter, R. (1997). *The Greatest Benefit to Mankind. A Medical History of Humanity.* New York: W.W. Norton & Company.

Porter, R. (Ed.). (2006). *The Cambridge History of Medicine.* Cambridge: Cambridge University Press.

Pust, K. (2011). The Popular Politics of the Mediterranean Periphery. Retrieved from https://wwww.academia.edu/1922717.

Reinhartt, C., & Rogoff, K. (2009). *This Time it's Different. Eight Centuries of Financial Folly.* Princeton: Princeton University Press.

Robe, M., & Steiner, E. (2015). *Insolvency and Its Consequences: A Historical Perspective.* CESifo DICE Report 4/2015.

Roland, G. (2018). *Comparative Economics in Historical Perspective. Comparative Economic Studies, 60*, 475–501.

Ryksbosch, W. (2014). *Economic Inequality and Growth Before the Industrial Revolution: A Case Study of the Low Countries (14th–19th c.).* Milan: Dondena Working Paper Series, No. 67.

Sander-Faes, S. (2018). *To Avoid the Costs of Litigation the Parties Compromise... Extra-Judicial Settlements in the Venetian Commonwealth circa 1550.* Proceedings of a Conference "Venice and its Stato di Mar", Venice 9–11 March 2017. Roma: Societa Dalmata di Storia Patria.

Sisak, M. (2011). Dubrovnik Republicanism and Its Ideologies. *Poloticka Misao, 47*(5), 179–200.

Stipetic, V. (2000). The Legacy of 15th Century Dubrovnik Scholars in Economic Thought. *International Review of Economics and Business, 3*(2), 17–38.

Stipetic, V. (2004). Population and Gross Domestic Product of Croatia (1500–1913) in the Light of Angus Maddison's Book "The World Economy: A Millennial Perspective". *Dubrovnik Annals, 8*, 109–176.

Stuard, S. (1992). *A State of Deference: Ragusa/Dubrovnik in the Medieaval Centuries.* Philadelphia: University of Pennsylvania Press.

Tadic, J. (1948). *Dubrovacki Portreti Beograd: Srpska Knjizevana Zadruga*. Kolo VLIV, Knjiga 305.

Tognotti, E. (2013). Lessons from the History of Quarantine, from Plague to Influenza. *Emerging Infectious Diseases, Historical Review, 19*(2).

Tomic, B. Z., & Blazina, V. (2015). *Expelling the Plague: The Health Office and Implementation of Quarantine in Dubrovnik 1377–1403*. Montreal: McGill-Queen's University Press.

Vekaric, N. (2011). *Vlastela Grada Dubrovnika (The Nobility of Dubrovnik)–3 Vols*. Zagreb-Dubrovnik: Zavod za Povijesne Znanosti, HAZU.

Voje, I. (1976). *Kreditna Trgovina u Srejdnovekovnom Dubrovniku: Djela LIX, Odeljenje Drustvenih nauka*, Vol. 29. sarajevo: Akademija Nauka Bosne i Hercegovine.

Wikipedia. *History of Water Supply and Sanitation*. Retrieved October 18, 2019, from https://en.wikipedia.org/wiki/History_of_water_supply_and_sanitation.

Wikipedia. *Quarantine*. Retrieved October 12, 2019, from https://en.wikipedia.org/wiki/Quarantine.

World Bank (Annual). *World Governance Indicators*. Retrieved from https://info.worldbank.org/governance/wgi/.

Zelic, D. (2015). Wooden Houses in the Statutes and Urban Landscapes of Medieval Dalmatian Communities. In Z. Radic et al. (Eds.), *Splitski Statut iz 1312* (pp. 498–507). Godine Split: Knjizevni Krug.

9

Long-Run Inequality in Communist Countries: Before, During and After

Filip Novokmet

1   Introduction

This chapter presents and analyses the long-term income inequality trends in post-communist countries in Eastern Europe, Russia and China in comparative perspective. The potential benefits of studying inequality in former communist countries are substantial, whether the goal is to better understand the role of economic forces, institutions, ideology or politics in shaping inequality, or to provide an important reference point for comparative analyses of the relationship between inequality and economic growth. The rise and fall of communism presents a "natural" experiment of historical significance, which can shed light on competing explanations of inequality determinants.

To study these issues, we have combined various methodological approaches to produce the first inequality estimates since the end of the nineteenth century up to the present. Our main long-run inequality indicators are top income shares, constructed from historical tax statistics. Fiscal data is a unique source for social scientists interested in studying inequality over the long run.

This chapter draws on Novokmet (2017, 2018), Bukowski and Novokmet (2019), Novokmet et al. (2018a, b), Kump and Novokmet (2018), Milanović et al. (2020)

F. Novokmet (✉)

Institute for Macroeconomics and Econometrics, University of Bonn, Bonn, Germany

e-mail: filip.novokmet@uni-bonn.de

© The Author(s) 2021

E. Douarin, O. Havrylyshyn (eds.), *The Palgrave Handbook of Comparative Economics*,

https://doi.org/10.1007/978-3-030-50888-3_9

It is their availability, often extending over the whole twentieth century and before, that makes them unique in comparison to other data sources.[1]

The analysis is further complemented by alternative historical evidence on the distribution, such as the distribution of wages, wealth and land owner-ship. For the recent decades, we have in addition combined household income survey and tax data to obtain more reliable estimates of the entire income distribution. We show that combining various methodological approaches is highly complementary and helps to deepen our understanding of the histori-cal inequality dynamics. A historical perspective is critical for understanding the evolution of income and wealth distribution, which is characteristically manifested in long-term structural processes.

The new series allow the analysis of long-term inequality trends before, during and after the communist period, creating a reference point for interna-tional comparison. This way, we can understand whether the inequality dynamics in ex-communist countries have been truly unique in comparison to the experience of non-communist countries, that is, whether we can iden-tify some common patterns in the evolution of inequality. A major finding is that income inequality in both ex-communist and non-communist countries followed the same U-shaped pattern: inequality was high at the beginning of the twentieth century, declined sharply in the first half of the twentieth cen-tury and increased at the roughly same time from the 1980s.

How can we explain this co-movement? Were there some common (sec-ular) forces which simultaneously affected income inequality in both world "blocks"? Relatedly, were these forces of economic or political character, or a mixture of both? The new long-run series allow us to shed a new light on the inequality determinants during the development process. Kuznets (1953) constructed the first top-income shares for the United States, which served as the empirical basis for his inverted-U curve hypothesis, according to which inequality rises in early phases of economic development but falls eventually as growth advances. Following Kuznets (1955), economists have generally applied the "demand and supply of skills" framework to explain changes in inequality: inequality rises as technological advances initially favour a smaller segment of skilled workers, but then falls as the rest of the workforce acquire new skills and enter high-productive sectors (the "race"

---

[1] Recently, research using income tax data to construct top incomes has provided a broad historical per-spective of income inequality in the international context (Kuznets 1953; Piketty 2001, 2003, 2014; Atkinson and Piketty 2007, 2010; Atkinson et al. 2011; Roine and Waldenström 2015).

between technology and education, Tinbergen 1974; Goldin and Katz 2008, etc.).

Piketty (2001, 2003, 2014) has however challenged this optimistic view. He has shown that in the case of France the secular decline in inequality in the first half of the twentieth century had little to do with the "Kuznets' process". Income inequality declined in France solely due to shocks to top capital incomes. On the other hand, inequality of labour income—supposed to reflect the mechanisms underlying the inverted U curve—remained remarkably stable in France. In other words, the secular fall of inequality in the first half of the twentieth century was "accidental", rather than the result of some "natural" economic forces innate to the development process.[2] In a similar vein, a recent surge of wage inequality in countries such as the United States has not been related to a "new industrial (technological) revolution" but is largely due to changes in policies and labour market institutions (e.g. see Piketty and Saez 2003).

Correspondingly, it will be shown that the secular fall of inequality in ex-communist countries also cannot be explained as an outcome of some natural processes. The development of inequality suggests even more straightforwardly the central role of policies and institutions in shaping inequality in the long run. Their critical role is manifested by unparalleled changes in the labour market and capital ownership arrangements which followed the rise and fall of communism. To a certain extent, the inequality experience in former communist countries can be seen as an extreme version of the inequality dynamic observed in Western countries, as suggested by a more pronounced U-curve pattern of top income shares. Political and institutional factors—such as steeply progressive taxation of income and inheritance, the rise of the welfare state, strong antitrust regulation and industrial de-concentration, or partial nationalisations—played a decisive role in reducing inequality in Western countries (Piketty 2014; Atkinson 2015). The communist governments went here to extremes by bringing to an end private property, and compressing income inequality to an extremely low level, "indeed a level that had probably never been experimented before in human history" (Novokmet

---

[2] Piketty has attributed the key role in shaping inequality to fiscal institutions and redistributive policies. For example, the introduction of steeply progressive taxation prevented the recovery of top wealth holdings after WWII. The recent rise of inequality has been explained by factors such as changing remuneration social norms, reduced income tax progressivity, stagnant minimum wage and the demise of trade unions. Piketty's finding has been confirmed in other developed countries (Atkinson and Piketty 2007, 2010; Atkinson et al. 2011; Roine and Waldenström 2015).

et al. 2018a, p. 217). Country-specific historical inequality patterns are further suggestive of this.[3]

Similarly, an increase of inequality worldwide since the 1980s could be partly explained by a marked policy turnaround. In Western countries, this "great reversal" is visible in the push against progressive taxation, reduced welfare state, de-unionisation, financial deregulation or the privatisation drive, among others. The reversal is even stronger in former communist countries, being a defining feature of the transition to a market economy. And it must be remembered that policy shifts in capitalist and former communist countries are closely interwoven. Thus, a threat of the communist "contagion" after the Bolshevik revolution contributed to the introduction of the pro-labour social legislation and various progressive policies in Western countries after WWI. According to some authors, the existence of communism as a viable political alternative kept inequality low in Western countries (Sant'Anna 2015; Milanović 2016).[4] By the same logic, the failure of communism in Eastern Europe contributed to the adoption of a pro-market agenda worldwide. A remark attributed to Vaclav Klaus, the chief architect of the Czech transition strategy, is telling of the perceived "common mission": "it took Margaret Thatcher one year to privatize three or four enterprises, while it took us one day to denationalize twice as many enterprises" (Zwass 1999).

While communism had the "homogenising" effect of compressing income inequality, the fall of communism resulted in a rise in inequality in all countries. This is not surprising, given very (and to some extent artificially) low income inequality during communism. And it was to a certain extent welcomed, given the adverse effect of too much equality on incentives. But it must be remembered that the transition process saw important variations across countries and resulted in markedly different inequality equilibria. A "Great Divide" in emerging legal and institutional frameworks between CE countries, on the one hand, and Russia and other FSU, on the other, has often been emphasised (Berglof and Bolton 2002, and Havrylyshyn's chapter in this Handbook). The different transition strategy taken in Russia compared to

---

[3] For example, Nikolić and Novokmet (2017) compare historical inequality trajectories in the former Czechoslovakia and Bulgaria, countries at markedly different levels of economic development before the Communist seizure of power after WWII (ibid., T.2). Accordingly, the two countries that had previously displayed notably different inequality levels all of a sudden became characterised by the most egalitarian income distribution in the post-WWII decades.

[4] Piketty and Saez (2014, p. 842) note in this respect that "the Kuznets' overly optimistic theory of a natural decline in income inequality in market economies largely owed its popularity to the Cold War context of the 1950s as a weapon in the ideological fight between the market economy and Socialism".

Central Europe or China reflects distinct political choices and beliefs and thus supports a claim that political "agency" is an important determinant of inequality. Russia is an example of extreme policy reversal in the 1990s.[5]

In the post-communist global order, economic forces have assumed a relatively larger importance in determining inequality. The advancement of globalisation and rapid technological change have generally been linked to productivity increases in former communist countries. In particular, Central European countries such as Poland or the Czech Republic, or notably China, have benefited from stronger integration into the world economy (Baldwin 2016). Yet, how these gains are distributed has become a critical aspect of the political economy in the twenty-first century (e.g. Milanović 2016, 2019). As mentioned, there is no basis to simply regard growing income inequalities as a temporary phenomenon, in line with the optimistic message of the Kuznets' curve. Hence, there is plenty of room for active policies promoting inclusive development. And while forces of international trade or automation have often exhibited inegalitarian tendencies, there is strong evidence that policies and institutions have played an important role both in moderating and in aggravating inequality across ex-communist countries. Their experience vividly suggests that there is no trade-off between inequality and growth, and moreover that mitigating a more substantial rise in inequality may be conducive to economic growth.

The rest of the chapter is organised as follows. Section 2 presents long-run trends in income inequality in former socialist countries. Section 3 documents the dramatic reduction in inequality in the first half of the twentieth century for Central European countries. Section 4 provides a detailed coverage of the communist period. Section 5 looks at the inequality development in the post-communist period. Section 6 concludes.

2 Secular Trends

We first present long-run trends in income inequality in former communist countries, primarily relying on top income shares series constructed from fiscal statistics.[6] Long-term top income shares series have been constructed for Russia, Poland, the Czech Republic, Hungary, Croatia and Slovenia

---

[5] For example, with the super-rapid ("voucher") privatisation or shrinking social state, evidenced in declining social transfers or minimum wage and so on.

[6] The top shares methodology is used in much of historical distributional research. The methodological approach consists in relating information in tax statistics to reference totals for population and income (Kuznets 1953; Piketty 2001; Atkinson 2007).

(Novokmet 2017, 2018; Bukowski and Novokmet 2019; Piketty et al. 2019; Kump and Novokmet 2018; Mavridis and Mosberger 2017).

Figure 9.1 shows that all countries for which we have historical inequality series since the end of the nineteenth century—Poland, Hungary, the Czech Republic and Russia—have displayed a marked U-shaped evolution of top income shares. The top 1% income share was around 15% in the late nineteenth and early twentieth centuries. Communism sharply reduced this to 5% or less. During the communist period, top shares remained at low levels. Although all countries are characterised by unusually low levels of monetary inequality, there are interesting variations: inequality appears to be particularly low in the Czech Republic and Hungary, with top 1% income shares below 3%, as opposed to 4–5% in Russia (and close to 6% at the end of the Stalinist period). However, the return to a market economy saw quite divergent developments: the top percentile share rose spectacularly in Russia to 20–25%, while in central Europe it stabilised at levels between 9 and 14%—with Poland at the upper end of the spectrum and the Czech Republic and Hungary at the lower end.

We analyse the transition from communism to the market economy by looking at the full income distribution from combined tax and household income survey data. More precisely, the tax data on high-income individuals has been used to correct the upper tail of the income distribution in surveys

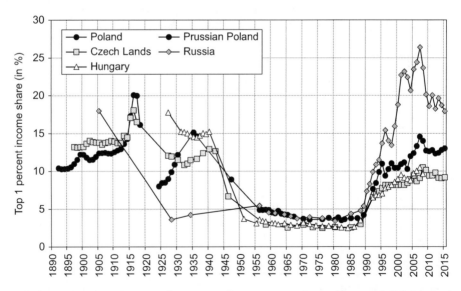

Fig. 9.1 Top 1% in former communist countries, 1890–2015. (Source: Bukowski and Novokmet 2019, Fig. 14)

(Novokmet et al. 2018; Piketty et al. 2019; Bukowski and Novokmet 2019).[7] In all cases, the new corrected series on the evolution of income inequality show that official survey-based measures strongly underestimate the level of income inequality in post-communist period. They also suggest a notably higher increase in income inequality since the end of communism until today. As a result, the new series on the entire income distribution in recent decades provides a richer and often new insight into the post-communist distributional dynamics in international comparison.

Figures 9.2a and b show the evolution of the bottom 50% and the top 10% income share, respectively, in Poland, Russia, China and France from 1980 until 2015. Income inequality has increased markedly in all countries since the beginning of their respective transitions towards market-oriented economies. However, it can be seen that the speed and magnitude of the change have been rather different across countries. In particular, it is important to note the strikingly fast increase in income inequality in Russia after the fall of the Soviet Union. The top 10% income share in Russia rose from less than 25% in 1990–1991 to more than 45% in 1996 and has remained around 45–50% ever since. This enormous rise came together with a sizable collapse of the bottom 50% share, which dropped from about 30% of total income in 1990–1991 to less than 10% in 1996, before gradually returning to about 18% by 2015.

In China, the rise in income inequality has been substantial between 1978 and 2015 (Piketty et al. 2019), but much more gradual than in Russia. The top 10% income share rose from 27% to 41% and the bottom 50% income share declined from 27% to 15%. While inequality was somewhat higher in

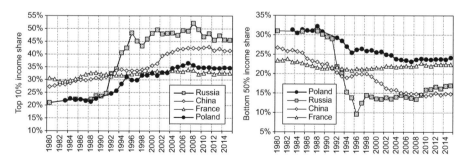

Fig. 9.2 Top 10% (2a) and bottom 50% (2b) in Poland, China, France and Russia, 1980–2015. (Source: Bukowski and Novokmet 2019, Fig. 15 and 16)

---

[7] For details on the Distributional National Accounts (DINA) methodology, see Alvaredo et al. (2016).

China than in Russia in 1978, it has now become substantially higher in Russia (Novokmet et al. 2018).

When we compare the evolution of income inequality in Russia to that of Poland, we also observe a marked divergence after 1991. Income inequality was broadly similar in both countries in the 1980s (Atkinson and Micklewright 1992; Flemming and Micklewright 2000)—slightly below 0.3 as measured by the Gini coefficient. But since the beginning of their transition towards market economies, the two countries have seen markedly divergent trajectories, and by 1995/6, the Gini index in Russia had surged to levels around 0.6, while in Poland it had "only" increased to 0.4. In Poland, between 1989 and 2015, the top 10% income share increased from 23% to 35% and the top 1% income share from 4% to 13%. In this respect, the contrasting development of the bottom 50% income shares in Russia and Poland is particularly striking (Fig. 9.2b). The bottom 50% share was around 30% of national income in both countries in the 1980s. But, while the bottom 50% share in Russia more than halved between 1991 and 1996, its Polish counterpart experienced a relatively moderate decline during the same period—from 30% to 25% of national income.

Finally, it is interesting to compare inequality in former communist countries to patterns in non-communist countries. Figure 9.3 shows top percentile shares in China, Russia, France and the United States. One observes a similar U-pattern in all countries in the long run. But concentration at the top is markedly higher in Russia than in China, and it has converged to the extreme

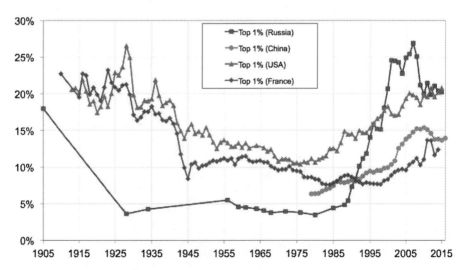

Fig. 9.3 Top 1% income share in Russia, China, the United States and France. (Source: Novokmet et al. 2018a, F.8a)

Table 9.1 Average annual growth rates in China, Russia and the United States, 1978–2015

Income group (distribution of per adult pretax national income)	China (1978–2015)	Russia (1980–2015)	United States (1978–2015)
Full population	6.2	1.1	1.3
Bottom 50	4.5	−0.5	0.0
Middle 40	6.0	0.5	0.9
Top 10	7.4	3.3	2.1
Including top 1	8.4	6.2	3.0
Including top 0.1	9.1	9.9	4.0
Including top 0.01	9.8	13.4	4.7
Including top 0.001	10.4	17.0	5.7

Source: Novokmet et al. (2018b), T. 1

levels observed in the United States. The top 1% income share in China is closer to the one observed in France, a country broadly representative of Western Europe (Novokmet et al. 2018b).

A complementary insight can be obtained by looking at the distributional impact of growth in Table 9.1. The economic transformation away from central planning has produced much higher growth in China than in Russia. Although in both countries, growth has not been equally shared, the outstanding growth experienced in China has substantially lifted the living standards of the poorest. In contrast the bulk of the post-communist growth in Russia has been captured by the richest. Over the 1989–2016 period, the top 1% captured more than two-thirds of the total growth in Russia, while the bottom 50% actually saw a decline in its living standards.

3 Decline in Capital Income Concentration

The long-run U-shaped evolution of income inequality during the twentieth century in former communist countries was not entirely different from the one documented in developed countries. The decline in the first half of the twentieth century was largely a "capital income phenomenon" (Piketty 2001; Atkinson et al. 2011). That is, the post-WWII downward trend worldwide was largely induced by the fall in capital income concentration. The introduction of communism meant a comparatively even greater shock to top capital incomes relative to other countries. The nationalisations and expropriations of the capital stock in a brief period after the communist seizure of power eliminated capital income as an important source of income dispersion at the top.

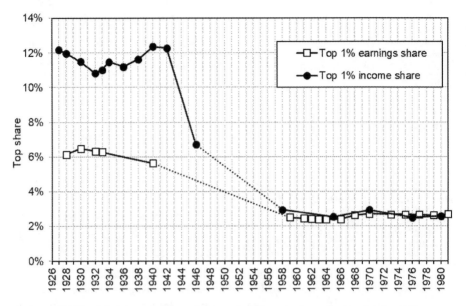

Fig. 9.4 Top 1% income share and the top 1% wage share in Czechoslovakia. (Source: Novokmet 2018, Fig. 26)

This can be vividly illustrated by comparing the development of the top 1% of the income distribution and the top 1% of the wage distribution in Czechoslovakia (see Piketty et al. 2006, Fig. 1). Figure 9.4 clearly conveys that the decline in concentration at the top, after the introduction of communism, was primarily caused by a decline in top capital incomes, which had accounted for a predominant share of top percentile's income during the interwar era. This seminal conclusion was first reached by Piketty (2001, 2003) for France, directly challenging the natural ("Kuznetsian") fall in inequality as an economy develops. The observed secular fall in inequality was anything but natural. It was caused instead by exceptional (political and military) shocks that decimated top capital incomes. As shown in Piketty (2001), wage inequality in France was largely unaffected. However, a wage compression did occur in countries that introduced communism (see Sect. 4), but as the figure indicates, it was of secondary importance for the evolution of top incomes when compared to shocks incurred by top capital incomes.[8]

---

[8] But shocks to capital income played an important role even before the arrival of communism, corresponding again to Western experience (Piketty 2001). This is suggested by the "structural" decline after WW1 in Central Europe (see Fig. 9.1 the Czech or Polish series; for Germany, see Dell 2007).The postwar situation worldwide opened a new page in the distributional history (e.g. Piketty 2014; Milanović 2016).

Next, we show that capital income—the return to the ownership of physical capital[9]—indeed made up the dominant income source at the top of the income distribution before the communist seizure of power in Central Eastern Europe. Figures 9.5a and b show a breakdown by income sources of the top 5% income group in Czechoslovakia and Poland in the late 1920s, on the eve of the Great Depression. In both countries capital income strongly dominated in groups constituting the top percentile and markedly increased its importance in higher-income groups. On the other hand, the importance of labour income is negatively related with the income rank at the top. Wage income thus makes the predominant income source for the top 5–1% group, and falls steadily for higher fractiles, to become practically irrelevant for the very top groups such as the top 0.01% and above.

The income source decomposition in Czechoslovakia provides a more detailed insight into top capital incomes. It can be seen that business profits and land income were the most important income sources in the late 1920s. The prime importance of business income suggests an "industrial character" of the top incomes in interwar Czechoslovakia.[10] This should not come as a surprise since the Czech Lands[11] had been the industrial powerhouse of the Habsburg Empire, comprising almost three-quarters of the Empire's industry. On the other hand, it is interesting to find that land income was an important income source at the very top of the income distribution in "industrialised" Czechoslovakia. Here equally, one needs to point to the historical patterns of industrialisation of the Czech Lands, which had also assumed a leading role in the emergence of intensive agriculture, with cultures such as sugar beet and hop being particularly important for the emergence of commercial agriculture. Coupled with the traditionally very high concentration of land ownership in Central Europe, a point to which we will return, this meant that the high land-income earners could still measure up to the new "entrepreneurial" bourgeoisie of big industrialists and financiers.

The importance of land income depended on the level of development, that is, the relative importance of the "traditional" agricultural land wealth compared to "modern" forms of wealth (e.g. manufacturing, industrial and financial capital). In this perspective, land incomes were more important for top incomes in Slovakia, then the "agrarian" part of Czechoslovakia (see

---

[9] Broadly covering dividends, interests, business profits, rents, land income and so on.

[10] This is revealed from the breakdown of the business income in top shares according to economic branches, which shows that bulk of high business incomes were earned in industry (Novokmet 2018, Fig. 15).

[11] The Czech Lands are Bohemia, Moravia and Silesia, and formed the Czech part of former Czechoslovakia and since 1993 the Czech Republic.

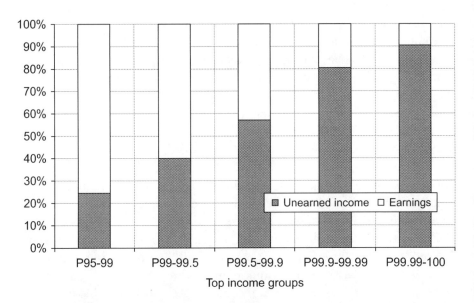

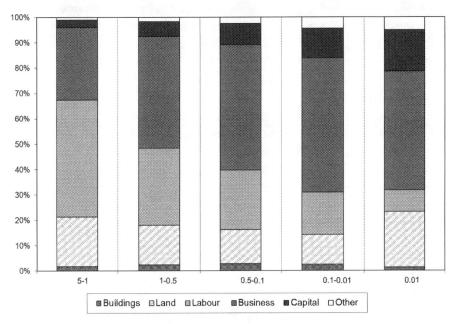

Fig. 9.5 (a) The decomposition of the top 5% by income source, Czechoslovakia 1927. (Source: Novokmet 2018, Fig. 14a.) (b) The decomposition of the top 5% by income source, Poland 1929. (Source: Bukowski and Novokmet 2019, Fig. 4)

Novokmet 2018, Fig. 20). Land inequality was equally pronounced in Slovakia (e.g. due to vast landholdings of the Hungarian nobility) and Hungary itself (Mavridis and Mosberger 2017, T.A4). Unfortunately, we do not have a detailed breakdown of top capital incomes for Poland, but it is reasonable to assume a similar—if not higher—importance of high land incomes.[12]

The Great Depression strongly affected top capital incomes. Thus, the contraction in international trade hit especially hard business profits in Czechoslovakia, where a large part of capital was tied to export-oriented industries. Further, the effects were devastating for top land incomes. As a result, the relative position of labour income at the top became more prominent. It may be argued that it was primarily due to a severe deflation that dominantly wage-composed top income groups were made better off relative to the very top (see Novokmet 2018, Fig. 14; Bukowski and Novokmet 2019, Fig. A7). Wage rigidity prevented a downward adjustment of their income relative to other income sources.[13] In Poland, although industrial and financial capital suffered even more in comparison to other countries, there was a rise in top shares during the Great Depression due to the deterioration of Polish farmers' income relative to top incomes built on non-agricultural sources. Almost two-thirds of the population of interwar Poland was made of small-holding peasants, and agriculture was also most adversely affected by the Great Depression particularly due to a strong fall in agricultural prices. In contrast, the fall in industrial prices was much less steep due to rapid cartelisation, which safeguarded industrial profits at the top.

The "price scissors" phenomenon is probably best known for the disastrous effects it had on the dominantly peasant economies of Eastern Europe during the Great Depression. In addition to its ruinous impact on the living standard of the Polish peasantry, we document it for Slovakia[14] in Central Eastern Europe. But deflation had an especially disastrous effect on peasants in South Eastern Europe. Nikolić and Novokmet (2017) attribute a sharp rise in

---

[12] First, Poland was still dominantly an agrarian economy before WWII and markedly less industrialised than Czechoslovakia, or even Hungary. Second, Poland was characterised by large land concentration in the hands of nobility, especially "Prussian Poland", which, like the Czech Lands, experienced a rapid development of commercial agriculture. Bukowski and Novokmet (2019) find that the "agricultural revolution" in Prussian Poland in the two decades preceding WW1 was accompanied by a notable increase in top incomes, which were almost exclusively concentrated in the countryside.

[13] For example, Czechoslovakia succumbed to the "gold orthodoxy" and adhered relatively longer to the French-led Gold bloc, while it managed to free itself from the consequent deflation by rather late devaluations in 1934 and 1936 (Eichengreen 1992).

[14] In contrast to Czech Lands, top incomes in Slovakia rose during the Great Depression, probably as a result of the rising urban-rural gap (see Novokmet 2018, T.21)

income inequality during the depression in Bulgaria to a surge in the urban-rural income gap. The sharp drop in agricultural prices relative to steady, but more moderate, fall in industrial prices—therefore "scissors"—disproportionally aggravated rural living standards. In the period of the sharpest increase in inequality, between 1929 and 1934, the income of peasants more than halved.

In general, developments in top income shares in Central Europe in the years immediately preceding WWII need to be understood in the light of increased state intervention in the economic sphere. As already hinted, a rapid industrial cartelisation in Poland played an important role in making the crisis less painful for top incomes. In Czechoslovakia, the recovery of top percentile was primarily due to a rise in top business incomes in top 0.1% group. As in Poland, an upturn of top business incomes probably occurred through the intense cartelisation of the economy (Teichova 1974).[15] An increased layering of the top percentile continued with the German occupation, when the Protectorate of Bohemia and Moravia became an integral part of the Third Reich's war economy. By 1942, the top 0.1% share surpassed its pre-depression levels. Big business thrived during the occupation and there was in parallel a strong increase in industrial concentration (see Olšovský 1961).[16]

Similarly, a growing state economy is visible in South Eastern Europe. In Bulgaria, for instance, this may be inferred from the rising concentration of top incomes in the capital city. In pre-communist South Eastern Europe, the over-centralisation and the large bureaucracy made capital cities exceedingly important in national life. But the Great Depression, in particular, was a major turning point, as the comprehensive interventionist measures of governments pushed traditional *étatisme* one step further. Figure 9.6b shows that while a third of the total income of the top 0.1% came from Sofia in the mid-1920s, the capital's share rises to 60% from the early 1930s. In general, the long-run trend of centralisation in the capital and stagnation of once thriving regional commercial centres was visible.[17]

---

[15] Rough estimates indicate that cartels controlled more than half of the industrial output in Poland in the 1930s (Landau 1978). The Czechoslovak industry had shown substantial cartelisation before, but only after the introduction of compulsory cartelisation in 1933, it became the dominant feature.

[16] There is rich historical evidence pointing to a marked enrichment of particular layers of society, in the first place of large industrialists who collaborated with the Nazi regime. In addition, wartime often offered various means for rapid and spectacular enrichment, for example, the infamous process of "Ariyanisation" through which Jewish property was confiscated Novokmet (2018, Table 2).

[17] Lampe and Jackson (1982, p. 240) comment that "previous economic centres suffered … for being far from the seat of political power".

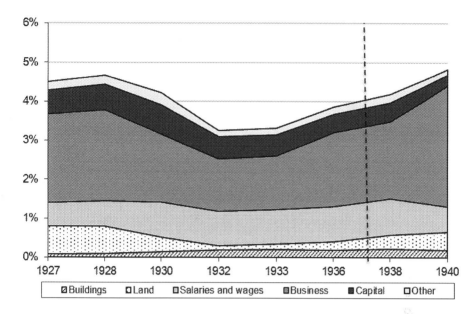

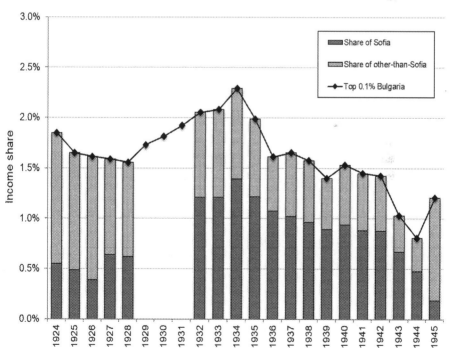

Fig. 9.6 (a) Top 0.1% in Czech Lands 1927–1936 and Protectorate of Bohemia 1938–1940. (Vertical intermittent line indicates that series refer to the Protectorate after 1938. Source: Novokmet 2018, Fig. 18). (b) Top 0.1% in Bulgaria, 1924–1945. (Source: Nikolić and Novokmet 2018, Fig. 11)

3.1   Wealth Inequality Before Communism

The strong concentration of capital income at the top of the income distribution is one defining feature of inequality in the first half of the twentieth century. This heavily concentrated "capitalist" tail of the distribution—typical at the time—suggests higher levels of wealth concentration. Historical evidence on wealth distribution in former communist countries is unfortunately scarce. However, it can be inferred from the limited available information that wealth inequality before communism was as high as in other European countries. As a consequence, the rapid nationalisation and expropriations of private capital at the onset of the communist era dramatically reduced wealth inequality and eliminated capital income, the most important source of income dispersion.

Thus, evidence for Czechoslovakia in 1919 shown in Fig. 9.7 clearly suggests high wealth inequality before communism, with the top 10% share around 70–80%, in line with levels documented in other European countries. Wealth inequality in countries that eventually introduced the communist system primarily depended on their specific historical context, such as the level of industrial development, patterns of industrial concentration or

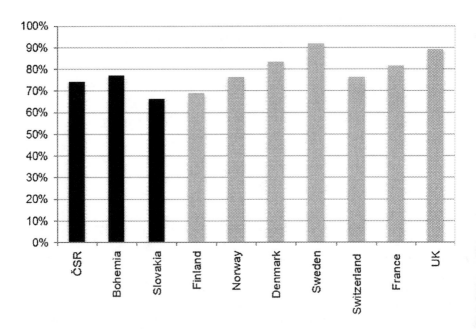

Fig. 9.7 Top 10% wealth share in 1919. (Source: Novokmet 2018, Fig. 23)

landownership, among others. Relatively more developed Central European countries had higher wealth concentration than those in SEE.

In this respect, corporate wealth had been traditionally concentrated in the Czech Lands (Teichova 1974), and the industrial structure characterised by larger units.[18] Evidence on the wealth distribution in 1943—when the wealth tax was introduced in the Protectorate of Bohemia and Moravia—suggest a still higher importance of business wealth for top wealth holders (Novokmet 2018, Fig. 25). The German occupation led to a stronger industrial concentration, benefiting (strategic) big businesses. It was also accompanied by the liquidations of medium and smaller businesses.

Similarly, a very high inequality in agricultural land ownership in Central Europe aggravated the overall wealth inequality. It is revealing in this respect that the very top of the tail of the wealth distribution in Czechoslovakia in 1919 was still dominated by landed wealth (ibid., Fig. 24). This is consistent with the relatively higher importance of landed incomes for top income groups, as shown above. The grand nobility was still after WW1 the most prominent wealth holder in the country. It may be said in this respect that the "persistence of the Old Regime", as noted by Arno Mayer (1981), probably nowhere manifested itself more than in Central Europe until WWI.[19]

Subsequently, post-WWII communist nationalisation policies reduced dramatically wealth inequality busting the large concentration of business wealth. The speed of the process was astonishing and its scope extreme. Most of large industry, trade and finance were nationalised immediately after WWII. By the end of the decade, even the majority of small shops and crafts were nationalised (e.g. through the *Battle for Trade* in Poland). Collectivisation of land ensued. Wealth holders further suffered from currency reforms, such as in 1950 in Poland or 1953 in Czechoslovakia, which virtually confiscated all personal savings.[20]

---

[18] This is a plausible feature of "industrial laggards". Namely, a relative backwardness of CEE in the nineteenth century entailed significant state intervention in promoting industrialisation (acting as Gerschenkron's "substitutes for prerequisites"), and here banks especially had a prominent role in pooling funds, thereby promoting cartelisation to minimise risk (Hilferding 1923; Rudolph 1976), which lead to oligopolistic structures in the heavy industry, engineering, banking and finance, and so on (Teichova 1974).

[19] Similarly, *Handbuch der Millionäre* suggests that most of the German millionaires before WWI were large landowners (Baten and Schulz 2005). Yet, it should be mentioned that big landed wealth had already been under the attack notably with the land reforms implemented after WW1 in the newly formed "nation" states of Central Eastern Europe.

[20] Other authors have pointed to similar trends elsewhere: for example, the abolishment of *zaibatsu* or the land reforms in Japan (Moriguchi and Saez 2008), nationalisations in France (e.g. of Renault in 1946, see Piketty 2001), etc.

4   Long-Term Labour Income Inequality

Top income shares measures are however silent on the dynamics within the remaining part of the distribution, such as within the bottom 90% (or often the bottom 99%). Therefore, our focus turns here to the developments in the distribution of labour income, which makes up a large share of total personal income. In socialist countries, in particular, with the expropriation of the private capital income, the earnings distribution became the main determinant of income inequality.

In a similar vein, assessing the long-run development of the earnings distribution is important for comparative purposes. Although the absence (existence) of private property income was frequently emphasised as the main distinguishing factor, the fact that earnings made up the dominant share of national income in both capitalist and communist countries suggests that the distribution of earnings might have had a decisive impact on overall income inequality.[21] It must also be remembered that it is not obvious that earnings should be necessarily more equally distributed under socialism. Namely, there is no reason to expect that inequality should disappear in socialist countries— at least during the "transition" stage to communism, to refer to the frequently used Marx's distinction from the *Critique of the Gotha Programme*. Bergson (1942, p. 227) notes in this respect that "it is a prevalent misconception that the persistence of inequality [in socialist economy] … in itself represents a departure from Marxist principles".

Over the twentieth century the distribution of earnings underwent dramatic changes in both East and West. The secular fall in wage inequality under communism corresponds to a period referred to as the "Great Levelling" in the United States (Goldin and Margo 1992; Goldin and Katz 2008). In general, the post-WWII decades saw a reduction in earnings dispersion internationally (e.g. Lydall 1968; Atkinson 2008). This resulted from a combination of market and non-market forces, including wartime wage compression, systematisation of wage scales, stronger trade unions and expansion of education. Technological changes were primarily biased towards manual workers (Baldwin and Forslid 2020, p. 3). At the same time, it is uncontroversial to say that non-market factors, in the first place political factors such as higher levels of state intervention in the economy, were relatively more important as

---

[21] Moreover because, as said above, there was an important reduction in capital income inequality in Western countries during the twentieth century.

determinants of earnings in socialist countries. The line between political and economic factors became still "fuzzier" in socialist economies.[22]

Broadly, state intervention in the distributional sphere in socialist countries was a result of constant tensions between efficiency and equity concerns.[23] Although the earnings distribution was largely administratively determined from the centre, it still depended to a large extent on economic considerations. The wage structure across occupations was used as a policy tool, for instance, to provide incentives for people to invest in particular skills, to attract them to particular industries or regions, or to stimulate the economy by widening earning differentials (Flakierski 1986; Atkinson and Micklewright 1992). McAuley (1979, p. 315) points to potential issues of inappropriate earning differentials, such as "shortages of particular skills, high rates of labour turnover, falling participation rates, and a general unwillingness to exercise initiative would all adversely affect economic performance and plan fulfilment".

The long-term trends in the earnings distribution can be assessed by looking at percentile ranks and occupational earnings ratios (e.g. Lindert and Williamson 2016).[24] Both indicators suggest a radical narrowing of the wage structure after the introduction of communism and a significant widening after the collapse of communism.

4.1   Wage Distribution by Percentile Ranks

4.1.1   Soviet Union/Russia

The century-long development of the decile ratio in Russia is presented in Fig. 9.8. It reveals the striking development after the fall of communism and the accompanying transition, which could be seen as major disruption in the history of inequality in Russia. The earnings distribution went through a spectacular roller coaster between 1991 and 2015. The decile ratio of slightly less than 4 in 1991 more than tripled by the end of the 1990s, to reach almost never-seen-before levels at above 10. There was a significant fall in the 2000s,

---

[22] For example, even the expansion of education, which is typically seen as one of the key economic mechanisms determining the wage distribution, could be seen as driven by the political domain.

[23] Flakierski (1992, p. 12) notes that "the socialist state had to reconcile the need for economic efficiency with ethical considerations of social justice in the field of distribution, which obviously was not easy".

[24] The long-term evidence on the wage distribution by percentile ranks is obtained from employer surveys. Comparable and exhaustive surveys were introduced in the Soviet Union in the 1920s and in CEE countries in the 1950s. Bergson (1942, 1944) is the seminal assessment of inequality of earnings in the Soviet Union in 1928 and 1934. Atkinson and Micklewright (1992) extensively analysed employer surveys in Czechoslovakia, Hungary, Poland and the Soviet Union since the 1950s until the late 1980s. Flakierski looked in detail at evidence for Poland and Hungary (1986), former Soviet Union and Yugoslavia (1989). We extend their analysis back to the pre-communist period.

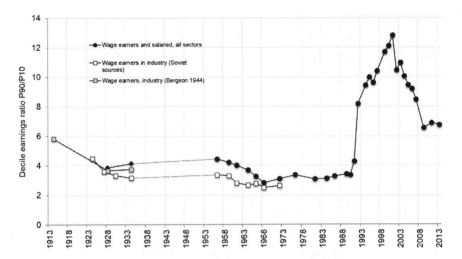

Fig. 9.8 Development of the decile earnings ratio, Russia 1913–2015. (Source: Bergson 1984; Atkinson and Micklewright 1992, own estimate from Rosstat survey on earnings (published in *Social'noye polozhenie i uroven' zhizni naseleniya*))

when the decile ratio almost halved, then seemingly stabilised at levels above 6 following the global crisis. Overall, the post-communist evolution of the distribution of earnings indeed stands out as unique in historical perspective—and as we shall see below in international perspective as well.[25]

Looking further back in time, we can discern a significant narrowing of the earnings distribution after the Revolution, thus confirming a previously established basic fact regarding income inequality in socialist countries. The chronological precedence of the Communist Revolution entailed that this "secular compression" was first visible in the Soviet Union. Bergson (1942, 1944), in a seminal assessment of inequality in the socialist economy, first identified this decline.[26] The communist period was characterised by relatively lower inequality, but we observe interesting variations. Bergson's work (1942, 1944) documented the moderate rise between 1928 and 1934. The dispersion widened during the Stalinist period. This was followed by a gradual decline between 1956 and 1970, a rise during the 1980s and during economic reforms.

---

[25] This striking development has been confirmed by Brainerd (1998), Flemming and Micklewright (2000) and so on.

[26] This decline is gauged from available data on the distribution among wage earners in industry, though these are a good predictor for all sectors. The comparison of decile ratios in periods when both estimates of the distribution for all workers and wage earners are available suggests that the distribution for industrial wage earners is representative of developments in the earnings distribution before WWII (Bergson 1984, p. 1077; evidence for Poland).

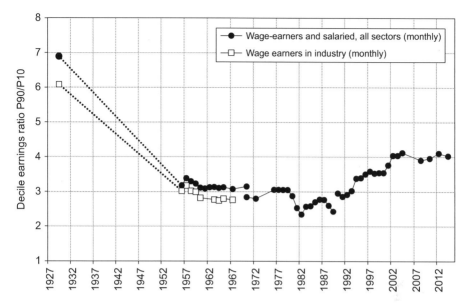

Fig. 9.9 Development of the decile earnings ratio, Poland 1929–2015. (Source: Bukowski and Novokmet 2019, Fig. A8)

4.1.2   Poland

Figure 9.9 shows the long-term evolution of the decile ratio in Poland. Just as income distribution, the earnings distribution is U-shaped through the course of the twentieth century. However, the U-pattern was less marked and has reached a considerably lower dispersion level, as the decile ratio (P90–P10) ratio fell from around 7 in 1929 to around 4 by 2015.

A dramatic decline in wage inequality took place between 1929 and 1956, when the decile ratio more than halved. The decline was so substantial in magnitude that the process could be indeed labelled, in the words of Kalecki (1964), as a "radical levelling". The decline is further corroborated by the newly collected evidence on the wage distribution of manual workers. Figure 9.10 shows a considerable inequality for manual workers in the inter-war period (suggesting at the same time a notable heterogeneity within this class, making it difficult to speak of the "proletariat" as a homogenous class) (Landau 1933). There was a sharp decline after WWII, and like in the Soviet Union, the decile ratio remained relatively stable during the socialist period.[27]

---

[27] It is true that a more significant reduction in earnings inequality occurred between 1980 and 1982—coinciding thus with the emergence of the Solidarity movement—yet it was short-lived, and earnings dispersion increased again after 1982. Moreover, there is considerable doubt about the data quality during the 1980s, given the prevalent economic turmoil (Flakierski 1986).

Earnings inequality significantly increased after 1989. A rising trend of earnings inequality after 1989 lasted until the early 2000s, with the decile ratio increasing over this period from 3 to 4. The significant widening of earnings distribution after 1989 occurred mostly in the upper part of the distribution, while the dispersion was more moderate at the bottom (there was no major disruption after 1989 at the bottom, especially when compared to Russia). Today, the decile ratio is significantly lower than it was in 1929.[28]

A more detailed insight is obtained by looking separately at the development of the upper and lower parts of the earnings distribution in Figs. 9.10a and b, as measured, respectively, by the P90/P50 and P10/P50 ratios (e.g. see Atkinson 2008). The figures show that the "radical levelling" was associated with a sharp compression of both the upper- and lower-tail inequalities. There was a sharp reduction in the upper-tail inequality, for all workers as for manual workers. The evidence on the distribution among manual workers provides additional insight into the development during the interwar era. It can be seen that the earnings dispersion sharply increased during the Great Depression. An indication of the same rising pattern is documented for manual workers in Warsaw[29] between 1921 and 1932, suggesting in addition a decline in dispersion during the second half of the 1930s.

The increase of earnings inequality during the Great Depression was related to the severe deflation, as higher-paid workers on longer contracts relatively benefited from wage rigidity.[30] A rise of earnings dispersion during the Great Depression is similarly observed internationally. The patterns regarding upper-tail inequality documented in Poland are confirmed in the case of the Czech Republic, which saw a momentous compression between the late 1930s and 1950s. In fact, the extent of levelling seems to have been even more radical than in the case of Poland.[31] By the late 1950s, the equalisation process had been completed (Večerník 1991).

---

[28] The difference between today and interwar Poland is more compressed upper- and lower-tail inequalities. Thus, while in 1929, P10 was barely 37% of median wage, in 2016 it is 54. On the other hand, P90 was 235% of median wage, while today is 205%.

[29] The data for Warsaw refers to the distribution of weekly wage among manual workers in medium-sized and large establishment.

[30] Landau (1933, p. 120) notes that a strong fall in wages had first occurred in small industry, while "in big industry the process was checked by collective contract". However, Landau adds that a major fall in wages eventually occurred in big industry after 1932. This plausibly contributed to a fall of upper-tail inequality, as indicated by the development of P90/P50 for manual workers in Warsaw.

[31] Evidence on the wage distribution for Czechoslovakia in the late 1920s/1930s and the late 1940s is based on insurance statistics. The evolution of the P90 ratio suggests that a significant narrowing of upper-tail inequality had already occurred before the communist coup of 1948. Maňák (1967) documented the first post-war wage regulation implemented in December 1945 (Večerník 1991), though the true "wage revolution" took place between 1948 and 1953, with a dramatic decline in wage inequality.

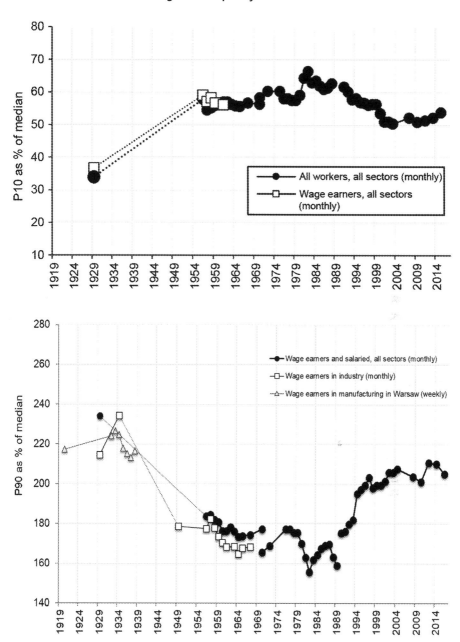

Fig. 9.10 Development of the upper part (a) and the lower part (b) of earnings distribution, Poland 1921–2015. (Source: Bukowski and Novokmet 2019, Fig. 8 and A9)

During the communist era, wage differentials were largely administratively determined. A moderate decline in upper-tail inequality in Poland is observed in the late 1950s/early 1960s, being slightly more pronounced for manual workers. This was followed, however, by a stronger rise in upper-tail dispersion during the 1970s. Yet, this rise came to an end in 1980 with the emergence of the Solidarity movement (Flakierski 1986, pp. 71–72), which gave a strong emphasis to egalitarian concerns in its demands. Flakierski (1991, p. 96) thus termed it as the most egalitarian movement in socialist countries.[32]

4.1.3   Gender Inequality

The only dimension of inequality which has not seen a widening dispersion since the 1990s is gender inequality. The earnings gap between male and female workers was significantly reduced following the fall of communism: while in the 1980s the median wage of women was around 70% of median for men, today the ratio is around 90% (Fig. 9.11). This is in line with the findings of Goldin and Katz (2008) and Kopczuk et al. (2010) for the United States, where the gender earnings gap contracted after the 1980s, amid a simultaneous and significant widening of earnings dispersion. Higher gender inequality during the socialist period was largely due to occupational segregation. Women accounted for a rather modest share of employment in sectors earning above-average wage, such as industry or construction. On the other hand, women made the bulk of the workforce in below-average wage sectors, such as services, and in administrative and clerical occupations (Atkinson and Micklewright 1992). Correspondingly, the rise in relative wage in the service sector contributed to the observed reduction of the gender gap (see, e.g. Fig. 9.13).

4.2   Occupational Earnings Gaps

Complementary evidence on the long-term changes in earnings distribution can be found by looking at the earnings skill ratio (Goldin and Katz 2008, p. 58), comparing average earnings gap between white-collar and manual workers.[33] A sharp reduction in earnings premium for skilled labour has been

---

[32] Although, as said, there are doubts about the reliability of data during this period of inflation and widespread shortages, a large part of the decline should be directly attributed to the demand of Solidarity from the Gdansk Agreement (Flakierski 1991).

[33] Phelps Brown (1977, p. 81) succinctly explains that "most of the white-collar occupations are distinguished from the manual by the level of education required by entrants, and the graduations of their pay

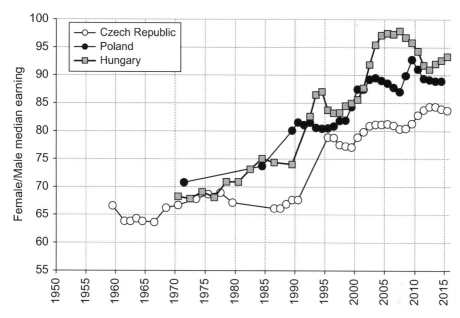

Fig. 9.11 Gender earnings gap in CR, Poland and Hungary. (Source: Before 1990: Atkinson and Micklewright 1992; after 1990: OECD)

documented worldwide between 1910 and 1970, as shown by Goldin and Katz (2008) for the United States. Lindert and Williamson (2016, p. 2002) further concluded that "it appears that the Great Levelling also squeezed most of the skilled and white-collar occupations in other industrial countries" (Morrisson 2000 shows this for Western Europe).

The reduction in skill premium was more dramatic in former socialist countries. The evidence on the long-term evolution of the "skill premium" is available for the industrial sector. Figure 9.12 shows a sharp reduction in the white-collar earning premium after WWII for Czechoslovakia, Poland and the USSR.[34] This reduction was followed by low and relatively stable differentials during the next four decades of the communist rule. Overall, the skill premium in industry during communism was very low in international comparison. Redor (1992) stresses low or non-existent skill premium as the most visible difference in wage distribution between capitalist and socialist countries.

---

are fairly closely associated with gradations of that level".

The white-collar premium has proved robust proxy for earnings inequality, but the two groups should not be assumed as uniform "classes". For example, historical evidence on the "labour aristocracy" suggests a heterogeneity within the class of manual workers, Hobsbawm or Gray). See also Fig. 9.11a.

[34] Arguably, the much sharper post-war reduction in skill gap in Czechoslovakia and Poland compared to the USSR should be related to the timing of the communist accession.

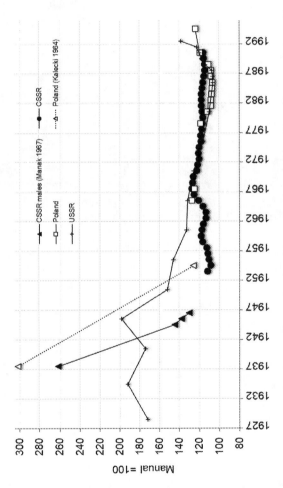

Fig. 9.12 White-collar skill premium in industry in Czechoslovakia, Poland and the USSR. (Source: Bukowski and Novokmet 2019, Fig. A13)

The figure further reveals a very high earnings premium for white-collar workers in interwar Poland and Czechoslovakia and interestingly a non-negligible premium in the Soviet Union until the 1950s. In Poland, according to Kalecki (1964), the average white-collar worker in industry earned in 1929 around three times more than the average manual worker. But, by 1950, the earnings gap between white-collar and manual workers had almost disappeared.[35] Similarly, according to Maňák (1967), the average male white-collar worker in industry earned two and a half times more than male manual worker in 1937 in Czechoslovakia, but the difference halved by 1948. By the mid-1950s, the premium had virtually vanished.

The very high skill premium in interwar Poland could be partly explained by economic forces: low literacy and educational attainments meant a limited supply of educated workforce, which could in turn explain a relatively larger premium in international comparison. White-collar workers were, to quote Paul Douglas, a "non-competing" group (Goldin and Katz 2008, pp. 63–64). Occupations with higher educational requirement were lavishly rewarded as a result. Note, for example, the very high premium obtained in sectors such as finance, traditionally dominated by white-collar clerical jobs (Fig. 9.13). However, the large majority of skilled jobs, irrespective of "collar denomination" (often difficult to differentiate), earned a considerable monetary premium. Bergson (1944) suggests this could also explain relatively higher premium in the Soviet Union before WWII.

On the other hand, the notion of "privileged class" mentioned by Kalecki (footnote 39) could imply that the large white-collar earnings premium before WWII included a "status" premium. And it may be said that Central Europe was a bastion of white-collar "privileges" before WWII.[36] For example, Kocka (1981, p. 462) sees a sharp "collar-line" (*Kragenlinie*) between wage earners and salaried employees (*Arbeiter* and *Angesttellte*) as "particularly sharp and socially relevant" in Germany in the late nineteenth and early twentieth centuries. He attributes this to clearly demarcated social consciousness of white-collar workers, primarily in their self-identification as private civil servants (*Privatbeamte*).[37] It could be conjectured that the self-ascribed "public role" of

---

[35] Kalecki (1964) summarised this development as follows: "a white-collar worker, who in pre-war Poland belonged to the privileged class compared to the manual worker, in 1960 earned on average little more than the manual worker".

[36] Although the white-collar premium had been lower in the interwar Czechoslovakia than in Poland, it was nonetheless substantial by international standards. In Czechoslovakia, skills were not in limited supply. Actually, the Czech Lands had one of the highest educational attainments in Europe at the time (Teichova 1988).

[37] According to Kocka, the collar division was finally "institutionalised" in Germany with a legal separation of insurance schemes for white-collar and manual workers. An equivalent development had taken

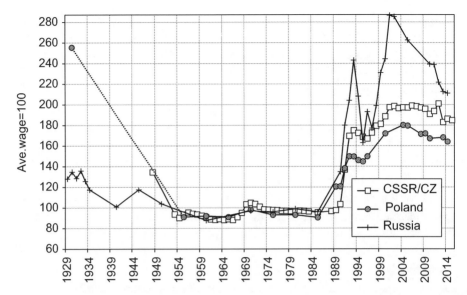

Fig. 9.13 Development of relative wage in finance. (Source: Bukowski and Novokmet 2019, Fig. A12)

white-collar workers became even more pronounced in interwar Poland, Czechoslovakia or Hungary, and it should not be considered in isolation from the newly gained national independence. Moreover, it may be said that the educated middle class, or the so-called *Bildungsbürgertum*, was a leading force in the national revival in Central Eastern Europe. Their political influence increased, epitomised, for example, by Tomas Masaryk, a professor-turned-president of interwar Czechoslovakia.[38]

If the interwar period might be termed as the "golden era" for white-collar workers in Czechoslovakia or Poland, the communist accession to power turned the situation on its head. Figure 9.13 shows that their premium disappeared rather quickly. Kalecki (1964) and Beskid (1964) argue that a decline in premium between white-collar and manual workers was the main cause underlying the overall earnings compression in Poland. They estimate that between 1937 and 1960 the real earnings of manual workers increased considerably, almost doubling for those employed, while white-collar workers experienced a 20% drop (Kalecki 1964, T.1.). In the words of Kalecki (1964, p. 231), "an important increase in the income of manual workers and a large fall in that of white-collar workers has led to a radical levelling of incomes".

---

place in Imperial Austria (ibid., p. 466), and the separate insurance schemes persisted into the new nation states in Central Eastern Europe that emerged from the German Empire and Austria-Hungary.

[38] The First Republic, in particular, is frequently seen as the golden age for salaried workers and civil servants, and often these are identified with the ascendant Czech bourgeoisie (Teichova 1988).

The sharp reduction in wage premium over a relatively short period suggests that non-economic factors played an important role in reducing the white-collar premium. The sharp narrowing of the differential should be attributed to public policies raising proportionally more incomes for the bulk of low-skilled manual workers. Manual workers made the political base of the communist rule and hence were strongly favoured. Intellectuals, on the other hand, were not seen as trustworthy (Milanović 1998, p. 20).[39,40]

Hence, it is not surprising that the Communist regime had been especially "merciless" towards the "status" premium of white-collar occupations. This corroborated with its ethical premise of eliminating perceived "unjust" inequalities from the pre-war period. Phelps Brown (1977) conjectures that communists were actually the "modernist" force that finally allowed economic forces to put an end to the traditional "status premium" in Eastern Europe.[41] At the same time, the wage compression attained a new pace under the central planning system. In part, placing a higher burden on high-wage workers provided communist governments with means to reconstruct and expand industry (Adam 1984, p. 195).

In sum, the "great levelling" in socialist countries should be primarily seen as an act of political agency. Bergson (1944, p. 193) explicitly attributes the narrowing of the wage distribution in the Soviet Union after the Revolution to the egalitarian ideology of the early Bolsheviks. This can explain a sharp narrowing of the skill differential amid general scarcity of skilled workers that had prevailed in the Soviet Union in the 1920s or Poland in the decades immediately following WWII, and especially when taken against the background of the pressing industrialisation needs (which accentuated the demand for skilled workers) and rapid urbanisation (which implied a rise in the supply of unskilled workers). Overall, the evidence for developing countries more

---

[39] Communists shared a suspicion of the "reliability" of intellectuals with the Nazis and saw the intelligentsia as natural enemies. During the occupation of Poland and Czech Lands, the Nazis pursued policies discriminating white-collar workers. Largely in consequence of the intelligentsia's pronounced role as the backbone of national consciousness—which had in part underlaid their higher social status during the interwar era—intelligentsia suffered the most during WWII (Gella 1989). Snyder (2011) argues that both the Nazi and Soviet occupational forces especially targeted the Polish intelligentsia during their respective invasions following the Molotov-Ribbentrop Pact. One mournful illustration is the fate of two brilliant interwar economists, the pioneers of the statistical investigation of economic and social inequality, Ludwyk Landau and Jan Wisniewski. The first was murdered by the Gestapo, while the second ended his life in Katyn.

[40] For example, the Czechoslovak Communist Party (KSČ) kept a strong anti-intellectual stance until the very end of its rule (Grzymala-Busse 2002, p. 31).

[41] Phelps Brown (1977, p. 66) writes: "As far back as the 1840s, John Stuart Mill thought that the spread of literacy would have brought down the relative pay of clerks had it not been for the traditional valuation of their status; and the effective reason for the comparatively low position of clerical pay in the Soviet structure may be that this tradition was destroyed by revolution, so that market forces could take the effect that continued to be denied them by customary attitudes in the West".

broadly after WWII suggests a narrowing of the differential despite the pronounced scarcity of skilled workers. Phelps Brown (1977, p. 70) attributes this to policy interventions, in particular to the minimum wage legislation.

The negative implications of "too much" egalitarianism on work incentives were recognised early on, and there were reoccurring attempts to increase skill premia—in the form of incentives to professionals such as engineers and technicians. Tensions were revealed early on, for example, in Lenin's pragmatic accessions to these "bourgeois specialists". They are also evident in the changing attitudes of Stalin towards specialists. Initially, Stalin had been one of their staunchest opponents, but the pressure of industrialisation led to a sharp turnaround in Stalin's attitude, leading to his famous critique of "petty-bourgeois" egalitarianism and the official abandonment of egalitarianism in 1931 (see Bergson 1944, p. 209).[42] Moreover, this "negative" connotation held until the end of the Soviet Union, as well as in other countries (Machonin 1969, etc.). But as Fig. 9.12 suggests, these attempts were of limited impact. Phelps Brown (1988, pp. 303-4) notes that any attempt at increasing the skill differential was offset by "giving priority to raising the standard of living of the main guard of manual workers".

5   Understanding the Post-Communist Inequality Patterns

The "return" to market economies may be seen as a reversal of process of communist equalisation, manifested in the rising wage dispersion and the rising concentration of private capital income. Income inequality significantly increased in the 1990s, driven primarily by the rising concentration at the top of the income distribution.

Rising earnings dispersion has been commonly identified as the main cause of rising income inequality in Central Eastern European countries during the first years of transition (Milanović 1998; Flemming and Micklewright 2000; Mitra and Yemtsov 2006, Milanović and Ersado 2012; Rutkowski 2001). Figures 9.14a and b piece together evidence on the upper and lower parts of the earnings distribution in ex-communist countries. As already indicated in the

---

[42]To quote Bergson (1944, p. 209): "in view of the pressure of the Soviet five-year program for industrial expansion, the abandonment of egalitarianism in 1931 is not difficult to explain on other grounds".

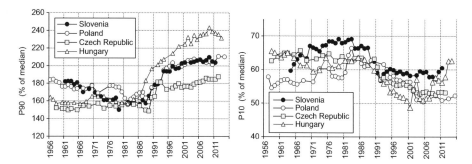

Fig. 9.14 The upper (a) and lower parts (b) of earnings distribution in CEE countries, 1956–2014. (Source: Kump and Novokmet 2018, Fig. 9a and 9b)

cases of Poland and the Czech Republic, there was a rise of earnings dispersion in all CEE countries after the fall of communism.[43] Figures show that the top earnings decile (relative to median) saw an immediate adjustment in Central European countries with the inception of the transition to the market economy. The top decile today in Poland and Slovenia takes an intermediary position, above the levels in the Czech Republic but below those in Hungary.

The common factor underlying the rise in earnings inequality was the relaxation of the government controls in wage determination, leading to the rising educational premium. A rise of earnings dispersion is seen both in countries that pursued the more "gradual" privatisation strategy, such as Poland or Slovenia, and the faster privatisation, such as the Czech Republic. This suggests that dispersion occurred both in the expanding private and shrinking public sector.[44] The lower part of the distribution saw a more moderate increase in dispersion. Differences across CEE countries are not large. Hungary had initially experienced a more material fall of the P10/50 ratio, but saw a stronger rise from the mid-2000s, practically reaching pre-1990 levels. The lower part of the distribution has been less dispersed in Slovenia than in other countries after the 1990s. On the other hand, the evolution of wage inequality in Russia

---

[43] As noted, comprehensive enterprise surveys carried out in socialist countries allow us to chart the wage distribution over the longer time span (Atkinson and Micklewright 1992; Atkinson 2008; Rutkowski 2001).

[44] Keane and Prasad (2006) find that earnings dispersion in Poland took place within both the public and private sectors, and thus within-sector inequalities were the dominant force behind the overall de-levelling trend.

underwent much more dramatic changes after 1991. The earnings inequality in Russia saw a striking rise in the 1990s (see also Fig. 9.8).[45]

Divergent post-communist inequality patterns in Russia and Poland have been often highlighted to emphasise the central role of policies and institutions in driving inequality during the transition process. Different transition strategies taken in Poland, on the one hand, and Russia, on the other, embody alternative political choices. For example, more extensive and better targeted social transfers and more generous minimum wage in Poland have been often seen as the most important mechanism "protecting" the bottom 50% of the distribution, thus precluding a sharp rise of inequality during the transition (Keane and Prasad 2002; Mitra and Yemtsov 2006; Bukowski and Novokmet 2019).[46] This stands in contrast to the Russian transition, where the bottom 50% share collapsed (Novokmet et al. 2018a).

Figure 9.15 illustrates the divergent evolution of minimum wage in Poland and Russia, by plotting the ratio of statutory minimum wage levels to the average wage. Although in both minimum wages fell in the second half of the 1980s, likely due to rising inflation, the transformation brought completely different developments. While in Poland, minimum wage rose abruptly from around 12% of the average in 1989 to nearly 35% in 1991 and stabilised at 35–40% level until 2009, in Russia it fell from 27% in 1989 to just 4% in 1995 and did not reach 10% until 2006 (e.g. Brainerd 1998).

On the other hand, market reforms marked the return of private capital income. It has often been argued that a higher share of capital income in total income should result in higher income inequality because capital income is generally more unequally distributed. Indeed, the literature has found that the rise of private capital income has aggravated income inequality in ex-communist countries (e.g. Mitra and Yemtsov 2006). In the case of Poland, Bukowski and Novokmet (2019) assess the relative importance of different income sources at the top of the distribution.[47] They find that the top 1%

---

[45] The P90/50 ratio jumped over 300% in 2001 and then saw a gradual decline attain levels around 250% in 2015. The P10/50 ratio fell to less than 15% in 1995 and then continually increased to 40% in 2015.

[46] Keane and Prasad (2002) have argued that this provided the general political support for market reforms and enterprise restructuring in Poland.

[47] Unfortunately, the tax data on high-income individuals used to correct the top of the income distribution in Russia and China do not allow us to distinguish different income sources at the top of the income distribution.

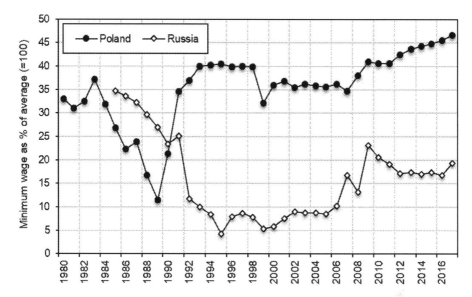

Fig. 9.15 Minimum wage to average wage ratio in Poland and Russia. (Source: Bukowski and Novokmet 2019, Fig. 17)

income share in Poland is today largely composed of business income,[48] which is rather unequally distributed. Although this confirms that capital incomes have also contributed to the rise of income inequality in Poland, access to more detailed income tax data (with breakdowns by income categories) would be necessary in order to evaluate the respective role of different income sources in the rise of inequality across ex-communist countries.

Perhaps a more robust way to look at this is to assess the importance of private wealth-income ratios (Piketty 2014; Piketty and Zucman 2014). The private wealth-income ratio has especially increased in ex-communist countries since the start of transition (rising from around 100% to 400–500% of national income; Fig. 9.16), with privatisation of state-owned assets as one of key factors underlying this increase. However, different privatisation strategies had a critical impact on inequality and wealth ownership. Again, it is useful to point to differences between countries. For example, the evolution of income and wealth inequality in China and Russia partly reflects the different

---

[48] However, it should be mentioned that business income includes both return to physical and human (entrepreneurial) capital.

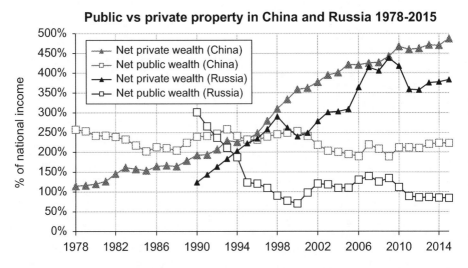

Fig. 9.16 Private versus public property in China and Russia. (Source: Novokmet et al. 2018b, Fig. 1)

privatisation strategies pursued in these two countries. The gradual privatisation process in China—where the government is still the majority owner of corporate assets—has limited the rise of income concentration. In Russia, on the other hand, the uncoordinated and rapid privatisation in the chaotic monetary and political context of the Russian transition (coupled with capital flight and the rise of offshore wealth) is likely to have led to the extreme levels of income and wealth concentration we see today. This finding is consistent with Forbes billionaire data, which show a much greater concentration of wealth in the hands of billionaires in Russia than in China and Western countries (Fig. 9.17a). We also observe a much higher increase in top income inequality in Russia than in ex-communist Eastern European countries that have followed more gradual privatisation strategies than Russia (Novokmet 2017). Here it should be added that the fact that a substantial part of the capital stock is owned by foreign wealth holders in CEE countries also contributes to lower inequality (Fig. 9.17b).[49]

Finally, a complementary insight is obtained by looking at the changing social structure since the beginning of transition. Milanović et al. (2020) argue that social class analysis provides a more comprehensive approach to study the distributional implications of China's movement towards capitalism. They find a dramatic change in the social composition of the Chinese

---

[49] In particular, the fact the holders of top capital incomes tend to be foreigners rather than domestic residents contributes to lower top income shares in countries like the Czech Republic or Hungary (Fig. 9.17b).

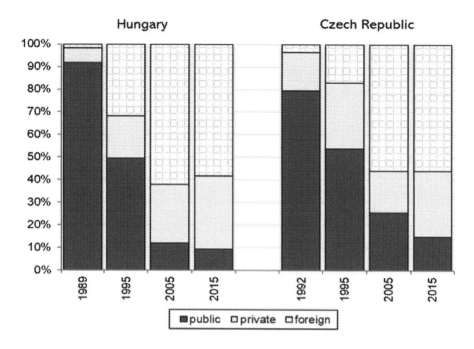

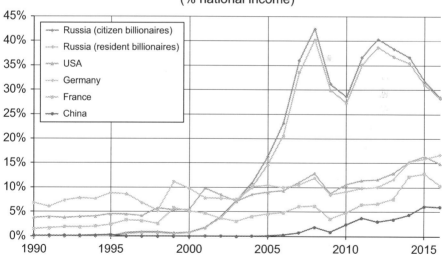

Fig. 9.17 (a) Total Forbes billionaire wealth: Russia vs. other countries (% of national income). (Source: Novokmet et al. 2018b, Fig. 5). (b) Corporate ownership by sector. (Source: National accounts of the Czech R. and Hungary)

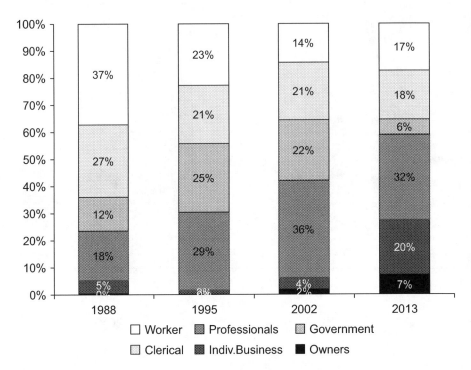

Fig. 9.18 Social composition of the top 5% income group in China. (Source: Milanović et al. 2020, Fig. 5)

elite (defined as the top 5% of the income distribution). While in 1988, three-quarters of the elite members were high government officials, clerical staff or workers, in 2013, professionals and small and large business owners accounted for over one-half of all elite members (Fig. 9.18).

6   Conclusion

In this chapter, we have provided comprehensive evidence on the long-run evolution of inequality in former communist countries. We document a marked U-shaped evolution of top income shares since the late nineteenth century. Top income shares were high at the beginning of the twentieth century due to strong concentration of capital income at the top of the distribution. The secular decline in inequality was largely caused by shocks to top capital incomes as communism eliminated private capital income with nationalisations and expropriations, and in addition it enforced strong wage compression. After the collapse of communism in 1989, income inequality has increased in all countries, however, with important variations across countries.

An important finding is that income inequality in both ex-communist and non-communist countries followed a U-shaped pattern in the long run. To a certain extent, the inequality experience in former communist countries can be seen as an extreme version of inequality developments in Western countries. Furthermore, the comparative historical account provides a unique perspective to assess the relative importance of economic versus non-economic factors in determining inequality. A broad synchronisation of top income shares in communist and non-communist countries presents a compelling argument against the "natural" decline of inequality along the development process. It rather points to the critical role of policies and institutions in shaping inequality in the long run. Their critical role is made clear by the unparalleled changes in the labour market and capital ownership arrangements which have accompanied the rise and fall of communism. We argue that institutional changes and policy interventions are an important driver of secular inequality trends, whether one looks at changes in the wealth distribution, earnings distribution, or the social structure.

Finally, history provides no basis to regard the recent rise of income inequalities as a temporary phenomenon—simply as an outcome of a renewed growth spur after the collapse of communism—and thus expect a spontaneous decline in line with the optimistic message of the Kuznets' curve (Piketty 2006). On the contrary, inequality is by no means predetermined to rise, as if an inevitable outcome of globalisation and technological progress. Inequality depends to a large extent on choices we make. This offers basis for optimism and encourages more active approach in promoting inclusive growth.

References

Adam, J. (1984). *Employment/Wage Policies in Poland, Czechoslovakia and Hungary Since 1950.* Springer.

Alvaredo, F., Atkinson, A., Chancel, L., Piketty, T., Saez, E., & Zucman, G. (2016). *Distributional National Accounts (DINA) Guidelines: Concepts and Methods Used in WID World.* WID.World Working Paper 2016/02.

Atkinson, A. B. (2007). Measuring Top Incomes: Methodological Issues. In A. B. Atkinson & T. Piketty (Eds.), *Top Incomes over the Twentieth Century: A*

Contrast between Continental European and English-Speaking Countries (pp. 18–42). Oxford: Oxford University Press.

Atkinson, A. B. (2008). *The Changing Distribution of Earnings in OECD Countries.* Oxford: Oxford University Press.

Atkinson, A. B. (2015). *Inequality.* Cambridge: Harvard University Press.

Atkinson, A. B., & Micklewright, J. (1992). *Economic Transformation in Eastern Europe and the Distribution of Income.* Cambridge: Cambridge University Press.

Atkinson, A. B., & Piketty, T. (2007). *Top Incomes over the Twentieth Century: A Contrast between Continental European and English-Speaking Countries* (Eds.). Oxford: Oxford University Press.

Atkinson, A. B., & Piketty, T. (2010). *Top Incomes: A Global Perspective* (Eds.). Oxford: Oxford University Press.

Atkinson, A. B., Piketty, T., & Saez, E. (2011). Top Incomes in the Long Run of History. *Journal of Economic Literature, 49*(1), 3–71.

Baldwin, R. E. (2016). *The Great Convergence: Information Technology and the New Globalization.* Cambridge: The Belknap Press of Harvard University Press.

Baldwin, R., & Forslid, R. (2020). Globotics and development: When manufacturing is jobless and services are tradable (No. w26731). *National Bureau of Economic Research.*

Baten, J., & Schulz, R. (2005). Making Profits in Wartime: Corporate Profits, Inequality, and GDP in Germany During the First World War I. *Economic History Review, LVIII, 1*, 34–56.

Berglof, E., & Bolton, P. (2002). The Great Divide and Beyond: Financial Architecture in Transition. *Journal of Economic Perspectives, 16*(1), 77–100.

Bergson, A. (1942). Distribution of the Earnings Bill Among Industrial Workers in the Soviet Union March, 1928, October, 1934. *Journal of Political Economy, 50*(2), 227–249.

Bergson, A. (1944). *The Structure of Soviet Wages–a Study in Socialist Economics.* Cambridge: Harvard University Press.

Bergson, A. (1984). Income Inequality under Soviet Socialism. *Journal of Economic Literature, 22*, 1052–1099.

Beskid, L. (1964). Płace realne na jednego zatrudnionego pracownika w 1960 r. w porównaniu z 1937 r. *Przegląd Statystyczny*, vol. 11/3.

Brainerd, E. (1998). Winners and Losers in Russia's Economic Transition. *American Economic Review, 88*, 1094–1116.

Bukowski, P., & Novokmet, F. (2019). *Between Communism and Capitalism: Long-Term Inequality in Poland, 1892–2015,* WID.World Working Paper 2019/08.

Dell, F. (2007). Top Income in Germany Throughout the Twentieth Century: 1891–1998. In A. B. Atkinson & T. Piketty (Eds.), *Top Incomes over the Twentieth Century: A Contrast between Continental European and English-Speaking Countries* (pp. 365–425). Oxford: Oxford University Press.

Eichengreen, B. J. (1992). *Golden Fetters: The Gold Standard and the Great Depression, 1919–1939.* New York: Oxford University Press.

Flakierski, H. (1986). *Economic Reform & Income Distribution: A Case Study of Hungary and Poland*. Armonk, New York/London: M.E Sharpe.

Flakierski, H. (1991). Social Policies in the 1980s in Poland: A Discussion of New Approaches. In *Economic Reforms and Welfare Systems in the USSR, Poland and Hungary* (pp. 85–109). London: Palgrave Macmillan.

Flakierski, H. (1992). Income Inequalities in the Former Soviet Union and Its Republics. *International Journal of Sociology, 22*(3), i–87.

Flemming, J. S., & Micklewright, J. (2000). Income Distribution, Economic Systems and Transition. In *Handbook of Income Distribution* (Vol. 1, pp. 843–918). New York: Elsevier.

Gella, A. (1989). *Development of Class Structure in Eastern Europe: Poland and her Southern Neighbors*. SUNY Press.

Goldin, C., & Katz, L. (2008). *The Race between Technology and Education*. Cambridge: Harvard University Press.

Goldin, C., & Margo, R. A. (1992). The Great Compression: The Wage Structure in the United States at Mid-century. *The Quarterly Journal of Economics, 107*(1), 1–34.

Grzymala-Busse, A. M. (2002). *Redeeming the Communist Past. The Regeneration of Communist Parties in East Central Europe*. Cambridge: Cambridge University Press.

Hilferding, R. (1923). *Das finanzkapital* (vol. 3). Verlag der Wiener Volksbuchhandlung.

Kalecki, M. (1964). A Comparison of Manual and White-Collar Worker Incomes with the Pre-War Period. In *Collected Works of Michal Kalecki: Volume IV: Socialism: Economic Growth and Efficiency of Investment (vol. 4)*. 1993. Oxford: Oxford University Press.

Keane, M. P., & Prasad, E. S. (2002). Inequality, Transfers, and Growth: New Evidence from the Economic Transition in Poland. *The Review of Economics and Statistics, 84*, 324–341.

Keane, M. P., & Prasad, E. S. (2006). Changes in the Structure of Earnings during the Polish Transition. *Journal of Development Economics, vol., 80*(2), 389–427.

Kocka, J. (1981). Capitalism and Bureaucracy in German Industrialization before 1914. *The Economic History Review, 34*(3), 453–468.

Kopczuk, W., Saez, E., & Song, J. (2010). Earnings Inequality and Mobility in the United States: Evidence from Social Security Data Since 1937. *The Quarterly Journal of Economics, 125*(1), 91–128.

Kump, N., & Novokmet, F. (2018). *After 'Self-management': Top Incomes in Croatia and Slovenia, 1960–2015*. WID.World Working Paper 2018/8.

Kuznets, S. (1953). *Shares of Upper Income Groups in Income and Savings*. New York: National Bureau of Economic Research.

Kuznets, S. (1955). Economic Growth and Income Inequality. *American Economic Review, 45*, 1–28.

Lampe, J., & Jackson, M. (1982). *Balkan Economic History, 1550–1950*. Bloomington: Indiana University Press.

Landau, L. (1933). *Płace w Polsce w związku z rozwojem gospodarczym.* Warszawa: Instytut Spraw Spolecznych.

Landau, Z. (1978). The Extent of Cartelization of Industries in Poland, 1918–1939. *Acta Poloniae Historica, 38,* 147–170.

Lindert, P. H., & Williamson, J. G. (2016). *Unequal Gains: American Growth and Inequality since 1700.* Princeton: Princeton University Press.

Lydall, H. (1968). *The structure of earnings.* Clarendon Press.

Machonin, P. (Ed.). (1969). *Československá společnost: Sociologická analýza sociální stratifikace.* Epocha.

Maňák, J. (1967). Problematika odměňování české inteligence v letech 1945—1948 (Příspěvek k objasnění počátků nivelizace). *Sociologický Časopis/Czech Sociological Review, 3,* 529–540.

Mavridis, D., & Mosberger, P. (2017). *Income Inequality and Incentives the Quasi-natural Experiment of Hungary, 1914–2008.* WID. World Working Paper Series, (2017/17).

Mayer, A. J. (1981). *The persistence of the old regime: Europe to the Great War.* Taylor & Francis.

McAuley, A. (1979). *Economic Welfare in the Soviet Union: Poverty, Living Standards, and Inequality.* University of Wisconsin Press.

Milanović, B. (1998). *Income, Inequality, and Poverty during the Transition from Planned to Market Economy.* Washington, DC: World Bank.

Milanović, B. (2016). *Global Inequality. A New Approach for the Age of Globalization.* Cambridge: The Belknap Press of Harvard University Press.

Milanović, B. (2019). *Capitalism, Alone: The Future of the System That Rules the World.* Harvard University Press.

Milanović, B., & Ersado, L. (2012). Reform and Inequality During the Transition: An Analysis Using Panel Household Survey Data, 1990–2005. In *Economies in Transition* (pp. 84–108). Palgrave Macmillan.

Milanović, B., Novokmet, F., & Yang, L. (2020). *From Workers to Capitalists in Less than Two Generations: A Study of Chinese Urban Elite Transformation between 1988 and 2013.* WID. world working paper 2019/10.

Mitra, P., & Yemtsov, R. (2006). *Increasing Inequality in Transition Economies: Is There More to Come?.* The World Bank. Policy Research Working Paper Series 4007.

Morrisson, C. (2000). Historical perspectives on income distribution: the case of Europe. In A. B. Atkinson & F. Bourguignon (Eds.). *Handbook of income distribution, 1,* 217–260.

Moriguchi, C., & Saez, E. (2008). The Evolution of Income Concentration in Japan, 1886–2005: Evidence from Income Tax Statistics. *The Review of Economics and Statistics, 90*(4), 713–734.

Nikolić, S., & Novokmet, F. (2018). Inequality in Eastern Europe, 1890–1950: Evidence from Dynamic Social Tables. *mimeo.*

Novokmet, F. (2017). *Between Communism and Capitalism: Essays on the Evolution of Income and Wealth Inequality in Eastern Europe 1890–2015 (Czech Republic,*

Poland, Bulgaria, Croatia, Slovenia, and Russia). PhDdiss. Paris School of Economics.

Novokmet, F. (2018). *The Long-run Evolution of Inequality in the Czech Lands, 1898–2015*. WID.World Working Paper Series No 2018/06.

Novokmet, F., Piketty, T., & Zucman, G. (2018a). From Soviets to Oligarchs: Inequality and Property in Russia 1905–2016. *The Journal of Economic Inequality, 16*(2), 189–223.

Novokmet, F., Piketty, T., Yang, L., & Zucman, G. (2018b). From Communism to Capitalism: Private versus Public Property and Inequality in China and Russia. *American Economic Review: Papers and Proceedings, 108*, 109–113.

Olšovský, R. (1961). *Přehled hospodářského vývoje Československa v letech 1918–1945*. Státní nakl. politické literatury.

Phelps Brown, H. (1977). *The Inequality of Pay*. Oxford: Oxford University Press.

Phelps Brown, H. (1988). *Egalitarianism and the Generation of Inequality*. Oxford University Press.

Piketty, T. (2001). *Les hauts revenus en France au XXe siècle*. Hachette.

Piketty, T. (2003). Income Inequality in France, 1901–1998. *Journal of Political Economy, 111*(5), 1004–1042.

Piketty, T. (2006). The Kuznets Curve: Yesterday and Tomorrow. In *Understanding Poverty* (pp. 63–72). Oxford University Press.

Piketty, T. (2014). *Capital in the 21st Century*. Cambridge: The Belknap Press of Harvard University Press.

Piketty, T., Postel-Vinay, G., & Rosenthal, J. L. (2006). Wealth Concentration in a Developing Economy: Paris and France, 1807–1994. *American Economic Review, 96*(1), 236–256.

Piketty, T., & Saez, E. (2003). Income Inequality in the United States, 1913–1998. *The Quarterly Journal of Economics, 118*(1), 1–41.

Piketty, T., & Saez, E. (2014). Inequality in the Long Run. *Science, 344*, 838–843.

Piketty, T., Yang, L., & Zucman, G. (2019). Capital Accumulation, Private Property and Rising Inequality in China, 1978–2015. *American Economic Review, 109*(7), 2469–96.

Piketty, T., & Zucman, G. (2014). Capital is Back: Wealth-Income Ratios in Rich Countries,1700–2010. *Quarterly Journal of Economics, 129*(3), 1255–1310.

Redor, D. (1992). *Wage Inequalities in East and West*. Cambridge University Press.

Roine, J., & Waldenström, D. (2015). Long-Run Trends in the Distribution of Income and Wealth. In A. B. Atkinson & F. Bourguignon (Eds.), *Handbook of Income Distribution* (Vol. 2). Amsterdam: North-Holland.

Rudolph, R. (1976). *Banking and Industrialization in Austria-Hungary. The Role of Banks in the Industrialization of the Czech Crownlands, 1873–1914*. Cambridge: Cambridge University Press.

Rutkowski, J. (2001). *Earnings Inequality in Transition Economies of Central Europe: Trends and Patterns During the 1990s*. World Bank Social Protection Discussion Paper No. 0117.

Sant'Anna, A. A. (2015). *A Spectre has Haunted the West: Did Socialism Discipline Income Inequality?* MPRA Paper

Snyder, T. (2011). *Bloodlands: Europe between Hitler and Stalin.* Random House.

Teichova, A. (1974). *An Economic Background to Munich: International Business and Czechoslovakia, 1918–1938.* London: Cambridge University Press.

Teichova, A. (1988). *The Czechoslovak Economy 1918–1980.* London: Routledge.

Tinbergen, J. (1974). Substitution of Graduate by Other Labour. *Kyklos, 27*(2), 217–226.

Večerník, J. (1991). Earning Distribution in Czechoslovakia: Intertemporal Changes and International Comparison. *European Sociological Review, 7*(3), 237–252.

Zwass, A. (1999). *Incomplete Revolutions: The Successes and Failures of Capitalist Transition Strategies in Post-Communist Economies.* ME Sharpe.

10

Effect of Historical Forces on Liberalization and Democratization in Transition

Simeon Djankov

1   Introduction

In the 30 years since the fall of communism, the 29 countries of the former Soviet bloc and Yugoslavia have undergone tremendous change. Nations that previously followed similar economic and political paths diverged rapidly. Income per capita at purchasing power parity more than quadrupled in Albania, Estonia, Kosovo, Poland, and Slovakia. All five outpaced such celebrated growth engines as Singapore and Korea at the same stage of their development. But in Tajikistan, Moldova, and Ukraine, the income increase since 1989 is modest. The divergence in political outcomes is even wider. Lithuania and Slovenia display the highest democratic development, with democracy scores identical to those of Germany and Sweden. Turkmenistan and Uzbekistan are the least free, on par with Iran.

1.1   Economic and Political Science Theories

In the first years of transition, economists had intense debate about the best policies for transforming centrally planned economies into dynamic market

---

The chapter is a shortened and revised version of the Discussion Paper Djankov (2016), where greater details on results and a fuller list of references can be found.

S. Djankov (✉)
Peterson Institute for International Economics, Washington, DC, USA
e-mail: SDjankov@PIIE.COM

© The Author(s) 2021
E. Douarin, O. Havrylyshyn (eds.), *The Palgrave Handbook of Comparative Economics*,
https://doi.org/10.1007/978-3-030-50888-3_10

economies. Broad consensus emerged on the basic economic model: liberalization of prices and markets, macroeconomic stabilization, and privatization of state-owned enterprises were deemed essential for achieving economic freedom and economic growth, but also developing new state institutions, capable of efficient and transparent support of markets. However, strong differences occurred concerning the speed and sequencing of these reforms.

Proponents of early economic reforms favored rapid liberalization and privatization to prevent asset stripping in state-owned enterprises given economic reforms would create a demand for more political freedom. Leszek Balcerowicz was among the most prominent proponent of this view (see, e.g., Balcerowicz 1995). Stanley Fischer added that reforms had to be fast because of the collapse of the previous nonmarket system (Fischer and Frenkel 1992). The rationale for rapid post-communist transformation was also illustrated in economic models first proposed by Shleifer and Vishny (1994).

Other prominent theorists argued that the creation of a market economy did not require enterprises to be privatized quickly. János Kornai, for example, favored gradual privatization and thought that the state should select responsible owners to run the economy (Kornai 1990). Murrell (1992), Roland (1994), and Stiglitz (1994) similarly argued that gradualism in privatization and the creation of market institutions would avoid a political backlash against the reformers. As Nobel Laureate Joseph Stiglitz (2002, p. 15) put it: "gradualist policies lead to less pain in the short run, greater social and political stability, and faster growth in the long [run]. In the race between the tortoise and the hare, it appears that the tortoise has won again." The debate on the speed and sequence of economic reforms continued among economists for over a decade. In the end both sides could claim some vindication with respect to privatization results. In the case of Russia, rapid privatization meant a lack of transparency and many negative consequences including evolution of an oligarchy and social resentment against reforms in general. But many other countries that privatized quickly (such as Czechoslovakia and then the Czech Republic, or Estonia) largely avoided these problems. Some countries that privatized more gradually (e.g., Slovenia) also achieved smooth transition and sustainable economic growth, while others slowly privatized countries such as Ukraine had much the same problems as in Russia. Arguably, the comparative results for economic and social performance (the last measured by indicators like poverty ratio and the Human Development Index) favor more the rapid reform position; countries that moved earliest and progressed farthest on the main elements of reform significantly outperformed those that delayed reforms.[1]

Political scientists were more united about the path to a successful democratic transition. Political evolution was predicated on multiparty elections (Huntington 1991), the banning of the former Communist Party in some countries (Treisman 2007), and the creation of parliamentary systems (Roberts 2010). Presidential systems were considered detrimental to subsequent democratic development (Frye 1997). Most countries liquidated the repressive institutions of the communist regime, like the secret police and the military draft (Nalepa 2010). Entry into the NATO and the European Union was considered in many post-communist countries a guarantee for achieving democracy (Gros 2014). With such measures, the path to democracy for post-communist nations seemed to be well-marked.

1.2 Data-Based Hypotheses

The actual post-communist experience surprised observers in some ways. The major question, and the one addressed in this paper, is why some countries moved faster to a market economy than to democracy. The divergence in political outcomes is 4–5 times larger than the divergence in economic outcomes. I test three explanations.

The first explanation is historical: I hypothesize that the fifth-century split of the Roman Empire into eastern (Byzantine) and western parts and the religious divide that followed was reflected in the fact that countries with Eastern Orthodox and Muslim religion reformed their politics less than countries where the population professes mostly Protestant and Catholic beliefs. Milan Kundera (1984, p. 1) wrote that "Geographic Europe (extending from the Atlantic to the Ural Mountains) was always divided into two halves which evolved separately: one tied to ancient Rome and the Catholic Church, the other anchored in Byzantium and the Orthodox Church. After 1945, the border between the two Europes shifted several hundred kilometers to the west, and several nations that had always considered themselves to be Western woke up to discover that they were now in the East."

This reasoning is consistent with Berdyaev's (1937) hypothesis that communism is a successor to Orthodoxy, with its insistence on respect for

---

[1] On the strong correlation between reform progress and performance, see, for example, Treisman (2014), though Roland (2014) in the same volume is less convinced of this correlation. Very detailed assessments concluding rapid reforms were superior and, providing many economic and social indicators, are to be found in the IMF (2014) and Havrylyshyn et al. (2016).

authority, disregard for legal rules, and repudiation of freedom of thought and expression. A separate literature on the effects of religion finds a similar negative association between Islam and political evolution toward democracy (e.g., March 2015). In contrast, the evidence on Islam and economic freedom is mixed: some studies show that the Muslim religion is inimical to economic growth (e.g., McCleary and Barro 2006); others (e.g., Noland 2005) find the opposite.

The second hypothesis for the uneven path to democracy is based on more recent (fourteenth to nineteenth centuries) imperial history. Countries that were part of the Austro-Hungarian Empire in the latter half of the nineteenth century maintained their European values (e.g., Dimitrova-Grajzl 2007) and were quickest to reintegrate into Europe after the fall of communism and to experience rapid political evolution. In contrast, countries that at the turn of the nineteenth century were part of either the Ottoman or Russian empires have rejected a path to democracy (Pop-Eleches 2007). In some cases, particularly in Belarus, the Caucasus, and Central Asia, an autocratic political model was established immediately after the fall of communism.

The third hypothesis is that post-1989 institutional choices, in particular the adoption of a strong parliamentarian system of government in the early transition, are associated with more economic freedom and democracy. This hypothesis, proposed by Timothy Frye (1997), is tested with data collected in this study. If supported by the evidence, the Frye hypothesis moves away from historical determinism and suggests practical steps to increase economic freedom and democratic opportunity.

Finally, to provide broader context, I note the results of econometric tests detailed in Djankov (2016) on role of other determinants such as dependence on natural resources, dominance by a major ethnic group, level of urbanization at the start of transition, and number of years under communism.[2]

There were three broad outcomes of the divergence in political evolution among post-communist countries: the remaining power of the old elite, the rise of rent seeking and corruption in countries with stunted political reform (Hellman 1998), and the opportunity for political reversals. Reforms to purge the old elite and to limit corruption largely won in Central Europe and the Baltics, whereas rent seeking and the rise of the oligarchy prevailed in the rest of the former Soviet Union and in Bulgaria, Romania, and most of the former Yugoslavia.

The rest of this chapter is structured as follows. Section 2 sets the stage by illustrating briefly the main features of three decades of transition, successes,

---

[2] The importance of greater or lesser time under communism is discussed by Pop-Eleches (2007).

and failures of post-communist transformation and the divergence among countries. Section 3 tests hypotheses on the reasons for the divergent paths toward economic freedom and democracy, and Sect. 4 concludes.

2   The Post-Communist Transformation in Figures[3]

The post-communist transformation started with an economic slump of 15–40 percent of GDP across countries due to the collapse of trade, the disorganization that ensued, and the reallocation of labor to the informal sector. With the exception of Czechoslovakia, where the immediate post-communist period was orderly, every country experienced years of economic destruction. The fact that the economic transition started with such a large output decline puzzled economists: because of myriad distortions under communism, they expected that removing them would result in some small decline as old factories were closed, but soon output would increase significantly. There is abroad consensus among experts that the decline was far beyond expectations, even after accounting for a likely overestimate due to an upward bias in official statistics of communist period.

One of the most visible signs of economic change was the shift to private property. By 2001, a dozen years after the fall of the Berlin Wall, the majority of productive assets in post-communist countries were in private hands; share of the private sector in GDP varied from 80 percent in the Czech Republic, Hungary, and Slovakia to 20 percent in Belarus and 15 percent in Turkmenistan (EBRD 2013). The effects of privatization on productivity were generally positive, especially in the manufacturing and service sectors, as were the economic effects, adding several percentage points to enterprise growth rates. Privatization to foreign investors was associated with 50 percent more restructuring than privatization to insiders (managers and workers). Domestic and international investment funds were associated with more than ten times as much restructuring as individual owners. State ownership of partially privatized firms was also surprisingly effective, producing more restructuring than enterprise insiders (Djankov and Murrell 2002).

Privatization and liberalization in the post-communist transition were part of broader reforms to achieve economic growth. Early reformers had to deal with pressing issues such as liberalization of prices and international trade,

---

[3] For more details on many of the variables used here, see Chap. 11 of this volume, where Havrylyshyn discusses the stylized facts of transition.

macroeconomic stabilization, restitution of property nationalized during the communist years, and—in the case of Czechoslovakia, the former Soviet Union, and the former Yugoslavia—the creation of many national institutions from scratch. Privatization and liberalization were seen, however, as critical for popular support for other reforms and for making political change irreversible. Anatoly Chubais (1999, p. 47), in evaluating Russia's reform path toward deregulation and privatization, remarked that "I really believe that now this historical problem is solved…even the communists have to accept the political reality in Russia. And the reality dictates that there's no room for those who want to take away private property. That's the result of the reform process, despite the mistakes that were made."

Thanks to such changes the precipitous fall in production was reversed and from 1995 on recovery began nearly everywhere. To show differences across the post-communist world, the 29 countries of the former Soviet bloc are organized into three groups, Balkans, former Soviet states, and Eastern Europe (see Note under Fig. 10.1).

2.1   Income

As seen in Fig. 10.1,[4] overall Eastern Europe and the oil-rich countries of Central Asia, the Caucasus, and Russia have grown faster than the world's average over the past quarter century. In the case of Russia and the other oil-rich countries, most of this growth was due to terms-of-trade effects as a result of rising commodity prices after 2000. Other former Soviet Union countries and the former Yugoslavia have grown more slowly than the world average. Incomes in Eastern Europe on average have shot up from around $10,650 per person in purchasing power parity to $23,730, and more for some like Slovakia. Slovenia started as one of the richest and now tops the group at a very high $30,600, not far behind the Western European average. The only dips in incomes took place in the early years of transition (1990–95) and less during the Eurozone crisis (2008–10).

However, the growth path of former Soviet Union and Balkan countries was uneven, with incomes rising by 58 percent in the first group (from $7045 to $11,160) and over 80 percent in the second (from $6185 to $11,310). Income per capita nearly tripled in Russia (from $8012 in 1990 to $22,990 in 2014), Kazakhstan (from $8,226 to $24,280), and Azerbaijan (from $8513 to $17,520) and doubled in Turkmenistan (from $8353 to $15,480). Oil wealth

---

[4] Unless otherwise indicated, data shown in this section is taken from World Bank, World Development Indicators.

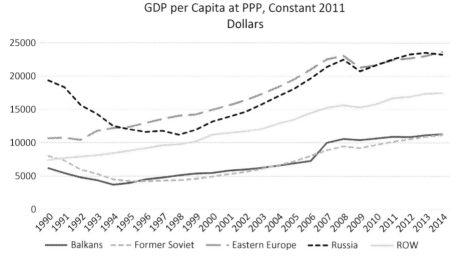

Fig. 10.1 GDP per capita in the Balkans, countries of the former Soviet Union, Eastern Europe, Russia, and the rest of the world (at purchasing power parity of 2011 dollars), 1990–2014. (Note: The 29 countries of the former Soviet bloc are organized in three groups: (i) The Balkans group comprises Albania, Bosnia and Herzegovina, Kosovo, North Macedonia, Montenegro, and Serbia. The Federal Republic of Yugoslavia is included in the Balkans group from 1989 to 2007, when it becomes Serbia and Montenegro. (ii) The former Soviet states include Armenia, Azerbaijan, Belarus, Georgia, Kazakhstan, the Kyrgyz Republic, Moldova, Russia, Tajikistan, Turkmenistan, Ukraine, and Uzbekistan. (iii) The countries in the Eastern Europe group are Bulgaria, Croatia, Czechoslovakia (1989–92), Estonia, Hungary, Latvia, Lithuania, Poland, Romania, Slovenia, and separately the Slovak Republic and Czech Republic from 1992. Russia, the largest country in the region, and a world average (ROW), is shown for comparison purposes. Source: World Bank, *World Development Indicators*)

contributed greatly to these increases, amounting to as much as 80 percent of government revenues. Some former Soviet Union countries experienced far smaller increases in incomes: for example, Moldova (19 percent) and Tajikistan (14 percent). Ukraine also is not much richer today than it was at the start of the transition, with income per capita in purchasing power parity of just $8,665, a 27 percent increase in comparison to 1990.

2.2 Living Standards and Life Expectancy

The upward bias in official Soviet income accounts implies the above assessment of increases in income understates the actual increase in living standards for most people over the last 30 years. Post-communist citizens have seen a vast jump in car purchases, travel abroad, and elite university education, among other gains.

From 1993 (the first year with comprehensive statistics) to 2015, for example, the average among the post-communist states went from one passenger car for every ten people to one car for every three, higher than the rate in Belgium. In Lithuania, Slovenia, and Poland, there are now more cars per person than in the United Kingdom or France (UNECE 2016). The number of phone lines per capita grew twice as fast as elsewhere, edging past Latin America. By 2015, cellphone subscriptions per person, at 1.37, had overtaken the West, and residents of post-communist countries who had rarely obtained exit permits made nearly 200 million international tourist trips (World Bank 2016).

Life expectancy increased by 5 years on average during the past quarter century in Eastern Europe, by 4 years in the Balkans, and by 3 years in the former Soviet Union (Fig. 10.2). Turkmenistan has the lowest life expectancy of the 29 countries, but that is still over 65 years; in Slovenia, part of the former Yugoslavia, the average life expectancy is 80 years, putting it ahead of the United States. But the advances are worse than average when compared to the global rise in life expectancy, which shot up by 5½ years in the past quarter century. When Eastern Europe is compared to other middle-income countries, the gap is even wider—life expectancy in the average middle-income

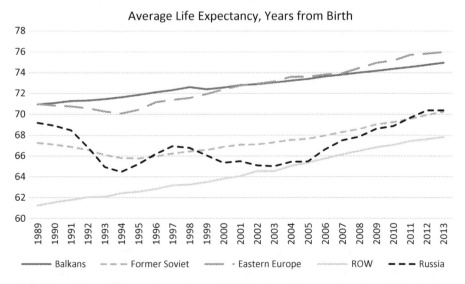

Fig. 10.2 Life expectancy (years from birth) in the Balkans, countries of the former Soviet Union, Eastern Europe, Russia, and the rest of the world, 1989–2013. (Note: Countries are grouped as in Fig. 10.1; see note for details. Source: World Bank, *World Development Indicators*)

country rose 7 years between 1989 and 2014. The stress of transition may be at least partly accountable for this disparity.

Poland, the Czech Republic, Slovakia, Hungary, and Slovenia experienced what medical researchers have described as "probably the most rapid decrease in coronary heart disease ever observed," because of the substitution of vegetable oils for animal fats (Zatonski et al. 2008, p. 4). Improvements in the former Soviet Union are less impressive. Russia's life expectancy rose by less than a year over the period, while registering steep declines in the mid-1990s and again in 1998–2000, during the Russian financial crisis. Still, in seven of the nine former Soviet republics that publish such statistics, consumption of fruits and vegetables shot up; Ukrainians, for instance, ate 58 percent more vegetables in 2011 than in 1991 and 47 percent more fruit (Shleifer and Treisman 2014).

The biggest gains were in reducing infant mortality, which fell by half throughout the region. By 2015 Slovenia had lower infant mortality than France. Even Turkmenistan, the worst performer, cut infant mortality from 90 deaths per 1000 births to fewer than 50. Russia and Ukraine reduced infant mortality in half, Bulgaria and Romania by 65 percent, and Hungary and Poland by 80 percent. This is by far the most successful measure of post-communist transformation. To put this success in perspective, communist countries made substantial progress in reducing infant mortality between 1970 and 1989 as well (Kelly 2016); but the actual number of infant deaths per thousand births in several of these countries—especially in Central Asia, Romania, and the former Yugoslavia—was significantly higher than in Western Europe. It is only in the post-communist period that the countries have matched Western standards.[5]

The evidence from direct consumption measures shows much greater improvements than official GDP numbers, confirming the concerns of many analysts about the upward bias of communist period income calculations.

2.3   Economic Reform

Governments have generally shrunk their presence in the economy, and by 2015 government consumption as a share of GDP was 10 percentage points less than in Western Europe, averaging about 17 percent of GDP. Exceptions are Azerbaijan and the Central Asian countries, where government revenues are fully dependent on oil and gas and government expenditures fluctuate

---

[5] Chapter 23 of this volume, by Chris Gerry, assesses the evolution of health outcomes in transition and beyond.

with the cycle of commodity prices. For example, government consumption in Turkmenistan was less than 10 percent of GDP in 2015, the lowest in the post-communist region.

Public debt fell correspondingly in the first decade of this century, with the trend particularly pronounced in the countries of the former Soviet Union. In the aftermath of the Eurozone crisis, debt increased somewhat, but to levels below those in Western Europe. Ukraine is the exception, where public debt has reached 90 percent of GDP. Uzbekistan had the lowest share of public debt to GDP in 2015, at 8.3 percent, followed by Estonia at 10.5 percent. Notably, Estonia maintained debt below 10 percent of GDP throughout the past 15 years and leads all of Europe in low public indebtedness (Åslund and Djankov 2014).

Economic reforms were implemented in all post-communist countries regardless of their achievements on democratization. Already in 1998 Eastern Europe matched and then surpassed the world's average in terms of economic freedom as measured by Heritage Foundation,[6] and by 2009, so did the former Yugoslavia. The former Soviet Union has also shown consistent evolution toward economic freedom, though Russia has shown considerable volatility, after a strong start in 1992.

In the World Bank's Ease of Doing Business index (Fig. 10.3), the countries of the former Soviet Union show a large dispersion in rankings for 2016, with Georgia at #24 and Tajikistan at #132, in contrast to the Eastern European countries, which are tightly grouped between Estonia at #16 and Hungary at number 42. Kazakhstan and Belarus, the only two countries with a single autocratic leader since the fall of the Berlin Wall, rank on par with Belgium and Italy, and even ahead of democracies such as Chile, Israel, and Greece, in reforming business regulation. The former Yugoslavia trails Eastern Europe substantially, with the recent exception of North Macedonia, which ranks #12.

2.4   Political Rights and Democracy

Unlike economic and social indicators, which have shown an upward trend throughout the past 30 years of post-communist experience, political rights and democracy have been more volatile, with recent reversals in both Eastern Europe and the former Soviet Union. In the Soviet Union, the authoritarian regime was all-encompassing, although this façade had cracked somewhat

---

[6] The Heritage Foundation comparisons are given in Djankov (2016); notably the general patterns are similar to those in the EBRD Index of Transition, as described in Chap. 11 of this volume. See also Chap. 17 for an update.

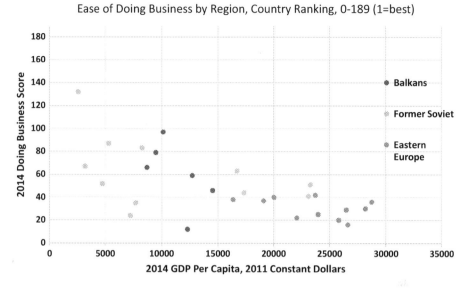

Fig. 10.3 Ease of Doing Business in the Balkans, countries of the former Soviet Union, and Eastern Europe, 2016. (Note: The 29 countries of the former Soviet bloc are organized in three groups, as in Figs. 10.1 and 10.2. See note for Fig. 10.1 for details. The x-axis is income per capita in constant 2014 dollars; the y-axis lists countries from top to bottom on the ease of doing business. Source: World Bank—*Doing Business Report 2016*)

during public protests against the Soviet intervention in Afghanistan in 1979, when anti-establishment leaders such as Andrei Sakharov became household names. Such leaders were exiled and put under house arrest. It took until the final years of Mikhail Gorbachev's perestroika, to ease the repressive apparatus.

The communist regimes in Eastern Europe ranged from Hungary's "softer" version (called "Goulash Communism") to the harshness of the Romanian regime under dictator Nicolae Ceaușescu. Each former Eastern Bloc country therefore had a slightly different experience of the late communist period and its own 1989 revolution. Some had stronger dissident movements—such as Czechoslovakia's Charter 77 initiative, whose leaders included Václav Havel—while others, such as Bulgaria, were less prepared for change. The events of 1989 were largely bloodless across the region; Romania was the exception, as over 1000 people were killed and 3000 wounded in the wake of the revolution, which also resulted in the execution of Ceaușescu and his wife.

Yugoslavia had an even milder version of communism than Hungary, with a market economy and political repression applied primarily with regard only to nationalist movements; in the 1960s and 1970s, thousands of university professors, writers, scientists, and priests from Belgrade, Zagreb, and Ljubljana lost their jobs because of their nationalist beliefs. In 1972, for example, Croatian politicians and intellectuals rebelled against the Serbian communist doctrine, and around 2000 students and intellectuals faced criminal charges. Similar dissident activity took place in Slovenia, also led by university professors and intellectuals. But the protesters' demands led in 1974 to the adoption of a new federal constitution giving greater autonomy to the individual republics.

These initial conditions belie the pattern of early political evolution: the Baltics and other Eastern European countries moved swiftly to democracy, while most of the former Yugoslav republics had a stunted drive toward democracy in the 1990s (see Fig. 10.4). Lithuania and Slovenia are the most democratic, Turkmenistan and Uzbekistan the most autocratic. Most countries of the former Soviet Union have not made steps toward democracy since the early 1990s, although this group pattern conceals some individual movements: Georgia has become more democratic reaching a level slightly superior to Ukraine's, making these two the best in the group. Russia became less democratic after 2006 and has plateaued after that. In contrast, the Balkans have seen a gradual but steady improvement in democracy, a process that continued until 2007 with the independence of Montenegro from Serbia. The biggest jump in democratization occurred in the former Yugoslavia following the ouster of Slobodan Milošević as Serbian president in 2000.

The political rights indicator of Freedom House illustrates this pattern (Fig. 10.4). The Baltics and Central Europe quickly embraced political rights. At the turn of the twenty-first century, the former Yugoslavia and former Soviet Union had similar levels of political rights and civil liberties. They have since diverged, with former Yugoslavia gaining freedoms and the former Soviet Union sliding back. Turkmenistan is at one end, with a complete absence of freedom, while Slovenia is at the other end, with full political rights and civil liberties, as in Western Europe.

The former Soviet Union countries initially pursued a democratic path, but the trend reversed in 1993–95 and most now stagnate as near-autocracies; political rights have gotten worse especially in Belarus and Russia. In the former Yugoslavia, the 1990s were a period of achieving greater freedoms, a trend that plateaued in the past decade. Scholars and policymakers from the region suggest that the biggest driver of reform for these countries—apart from Russia—is the prospect of entry in the European Union (e.g., Lukšić and Katnić 2016).

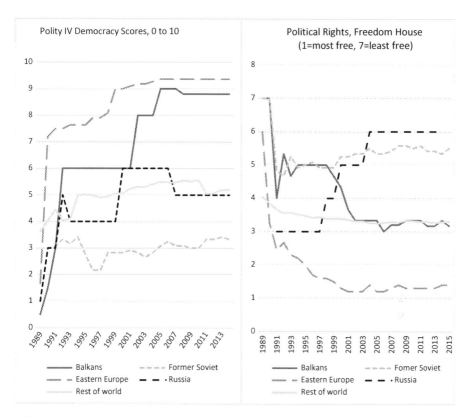

Fig. 10.4 Democracy (left) and political rights (right) in the Balkans, countries of the former Soviet Union, Eastern Europe, Russia, and the rest of the world (ROW), 1989–2015. (Note: The Democracy score ranges from 0 (complete autocracy) to 10 (full democracy). The political rights score ranges from 7 (least free) to 1 (most free). To show differences across the post-communist world, we organize the 29 countries of the former Soviet bloc into three groups, consistently with what we have done in Figs. 10.1, 10.2, and 10.3. See the note for Fig. 10.1 for details. Source: Center for Systemic Peace (2016), Polity IV Individual Country Regimes 1946–2013; Freedom House (2016))

Figure 10.4 illustrates well the main puzzle in the post-communist transformation: the stalled political evolution of a number of countries. In the Freedom House 2019 Report,[7] about a quarter of the post-communist countries—Azerbaijan, Belarus, Russia, and all of Central Asia except for the Kyrgyz Republic—are rated authoritarian. Armenia, the Kyrgyz Republic, Moldova, Georgia Nagorno-Karabakh, and Ukraine are rated as partly free.

Political scientists have explored the reasons for the survival of authoritarianism in the region. Brownlee (2007, p. 9) demonstrated that "the shift to authoritarianism with multiparty elections...does not represent an unwitting

---

[7] The 2019 scoring refers to 2018 status, hence does not reflect any changes in the last two years.

step toward full democratization." In other words, faking democracy has worked for authoritarian regimes. Krastev (2011, p. 13) suggests that, in contrast to the USSR before them, "The new authoritarian regimes' lack of any ideology also partly explains why the democratic world is reluctant to confront them. They do not seek to export their political models, and hence they are not threatening."

2.5   Divergence in the Transition

An overriding feature of transition since 1989 is the divergence in paths followed by different groups of countries on most dimensions of transformation. To illustrate the divergence across indicators of economic and political evolution, four measures—economic freedom (EcFree), ease of doing business (EDB), democracy (Democ), and political rights (Rights)—are normalized for the latest available year (in most cases 2015) and standard deviations calculated. The EDB variable is based on the normalization suggested by the World Bank, measuring distance to the regulatory frontier (World Bank 2016). The data, reported in Table 10.1., support the conclusion that divergence in economic indicators is significantly less than in political outcomes.

In particular, the standard deviation on the normalized index of economic freedom is 0.09 (mean value of 0.62) and on ease of doing business, 0.06 (mean value of 0.71). The high mean values (above the global averages of 0.58 and 0.54) suggest that post-communist countries have rapidly evolved toward greater economic freedom. In contrast, the standard deviations on democracy and political rights (0.35 and 0.31) are about half of the respective mean values (0.70 and 0.49), indicating wide divergence—about 4–5 times as much as in the economic evolution variables. The next section proposes an explanation of this difference using several sets of explanatory measures.

3   Divergence: Effects of History

I propose two historical hypotheses to explain the divergent paths to democracy in the post-communist world: the fifth-century religious divide between the eastern and western Roman Empire, and the more recent (fourteenth to nineteenth centuries) imperial history that split the region into three competing empires. These hypotheses take two separate stabs at a single issue: the long-term religious, cultural, and the geographic divide in Europe. In this regard, the Habsburg Empire can be thought of as a successor of the western

Table 10.1 Measure of economic and political evolution

Country	EcFree	EDB	Democ	PolRights
Albania	0.66	0.61	0.90	0.43
Armenia	0.67	0.74	0.50	0.71
Azerbaijan	0.61	0.68	0.00	1.00
Belarus	0.50	0.72	0.00	1.00
Bosnia and Herzegovina	0.59	0.64		0.57
Bulgaria	0.67	0.74	0.90	0.29
Croatia	0.62	0.73	0.90	0.14
Czech Republic	0.73	0.74	0.90	0.14
Estonia	0.77	0.79	0.90	0.14
Georgia	0.73	0.77	0.80	0.43
Hungary	0.70	0.73	1.00	0.29
Kazakhstan	0.67	0.73	0.80	0.86
Kosovo	0.63	0.66	0.80	0.43
Kyrgyz Republic	0.61	0.66	0.70	0.71
Latvia	0.70	0.78	0.80	0.29
Lithuania	0.75	0.79	1.00	0.14
Macedonia, FYR	0.67	0.80	0.90	0.57
Moldova	0.58	0.71	0.90	0.43
Montenegro	0.65	0.72	0.90	0.43
Poland	0.69	0.76	1.00	0.14
Romania	0.67	0.74	0.90	0.29
Russian Federation	0.52	0.71	0.50	0.86
Serbia	0.60	0.68	0.90	0.29
Slovak Republic	0.67	0.76	1.00	0.14
Slovenia	0.60	0.76	1.00	0.14
Tajikistan	0.53	0.54	0.10	1.00
Turkmenistan	0.41		0.00	1.00
Ukraine	0.47	0.63	0.50	0.43
Uzbekistan	0.47	0.63	0.00	1.00
Mean Balkans	0.63	0.68	0.73	0.45
Mean FSU	0.56	0.63	0.40	0.79
Mean Eastern Europe	0.69	0.76	0.94	0.19
Mean	0.62	0.71	0.70	0.49
Median	0.65	0.73	0.90	0.43
St dev	0.09	0.06	0.35	0.31
Skewness	−0.69	−0.86	−1.25	0.53

Note: The table summarizes the values for two measures capturing the state of the economy and two measures relative to democratization and political rights. These are economic freedom (EcFree) from the Heritage Foundation (2016), ease of doing business (EDB) from the World Bank (2016), democracy (Democ) from the Center for Systemic Peace (2016), and political rights (Rights) from Freedom House (2016). We note that political rights is constructed so that a higher score means *less* political rights. All values reported refer to the situation in 2015 and are normalized and standard deviations are calculated

Roman Empire, with the Ottoman and to a lesser degree the Russian empire as successors to the Byzantine empire. To tease out the effects of history, the importance of each is demonstrated, followed by a comparison to see which historical hypothesis is most effective in explaining economic and political evolution.

3.1   The Fifth-Century Religious Divide

That religion determines peoples' attitudes is by now a well-established fact in social science. Max Weber's (1905) pioneering analysis in The Protestant Ethic studied religion as an independent variable that influences economic outcomes. Religion can influence personal beliefs that reinforce particular social traits and values.

In the context of Eastern Europe, however, some scholars go even further to suggest that the spread of communism was made possible by the prevailing Eastern Orthodox religion. Nikolai Berdyaev, one of the premier Russian philosophers in the early twentieth century, argued that communism is a successor of Orthodoxy. As he explains, "The best type of communist, that is to say, the man who is completely in the grip of the service of an idea and capable of enormous sacrifices and disinterested enthusiasm, is a possibility only as the result of the Orthodox Christian training of the human spirit, of the remaking of the natural man by the Orthodox Christian spirit" (Berdyaev 1937, p. 170). Orthodoxy remains the prevalent religion in a number of post-communist countries: Armenia, Belarus, Bulgaria, Georgia, North Macedonia, Moldova, Montenegro, Romania, Russia, Serbia, and Ukraine.

Another literature links Islam, autocracy, and economic development arguing that political evolution is slower in countries where Islam dominates (e.g., Benhenda 2011). La Porta et al. (1999) find that countries with high proportions of Muslims exhibit inferior government performance. Kuran (2004) describes the possibility of an adverse effect on economic freedom from legal structures that restrict contracts, credit, insurance, and corporate ownership. McCleary and Barro (2006) establish that economic growth is inversely related to Muslim adherence. Noland (2005), however, refutes these findings. Nine post-communist countries profess Islam as their main religion: Albania, Azerbaijan, Bosnia and Herzegovina, Kazakhstan, Kosovo, the Kyrgyz Republic, Tajikistan, Turkmenistan, and Uzbekistan.

The former communist bloc can be divided into three groups: a Catholic-Protestant group in Central Europe and the Baltics (9 countries); an Orthodox group in Eastern Europe and the Caucasus (11 countries); and a Muslim group in parts of the former Yugoslavia, the Caucasus, and all of Central Asia (9 countries). The groups exhibit significant differences in the post-communist path to democracy (Fig. 10.5). Nearly all the progress occurs in the first years of transition. Among the nine countries in the Islam group, for example, democracy did not advance from 1990 to 2014. In contrast, there was gradual political evolution in the Orthodox countries, driven primarily by North Macedonia after 2002, Georgia after 2004, and Ukraine after 2014

The pattern of political evolution is not associated with divergent economic freedom and ease of doing business scores. In terms of economic freedom, the paths of the three groups are broadly similar until 2007, when progress toward economic freedom leveled off for the Orthodox and Muslim countries. In ease of doing business, Islamic countries show less progress toward business-friendly regulation.

3.2   The Nineteenth-Century Empires

The second possible explanation for the divergence in post-communist outcomes is the countries' more recent political history. Three large empires ruled over what is now the post-communist world between the fourteenth and nineteenth centuries: the Habsburg (Austro-Hungarian) Empire, the Russian Empire, and the Ottoman Empire. Each left an indelible mark on the structure of society.

The Habsburgs ruled over a federation of territories of the Holy Roman Empire. The capital was Vienna (except in 1583–1611, when it was moved to Prague). From 1804 to 1867, the Habsburg Monarchy was formally unified as the Austrian Empire and from 1867 to 1918 as the Austro-Hungarian Empire (Becker et al. 2016). Each Habsburg province was governed according to its own customs. Attempts at centralization began under Maria Theresa and her son Joseph II in the mid- to late eighteenth century but were soon abandoned. A greater attempt at centralization began in 1849 after the suppression of various nationalistic revolutions in 1848. The Kingdom of Hungary, in particular, ceased to exist as a separate entity, being divided into a series of districts. Following the Habsburg defeats in the wars of 1859 and 1866, this unification policy was abandoned, and after several years of experimentation in the early 1860s, the famous Austro-Hungarian Compromise of 1867 was effected, establishing the so-called Dual Monarchy of Austria-Hungary. In this system, the Kingdom of Hungary was given sovereignty and its own parliament.

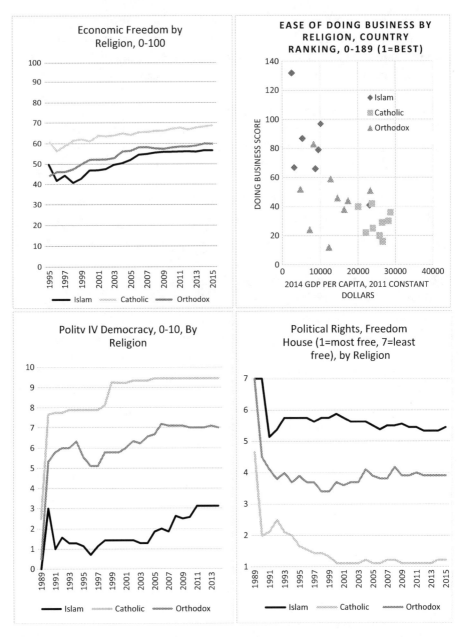

Fig. 10.5 Association between religious prevalence (Islam, Catholicism, Orthodoxy) and economic freedom, ease of doing business, democracy, and political rights, various years. (Note: The former communist bloc is divided into a Catholic-Protestant group in Central Europe (9 countries: Croatia, the Czech Republic, Estonia, Hungary, Latvia, Lithuania, Poland, the Slovak Republic, and Slovenia); an Orthodox group in Eastern Europe (11 countries: Armenia, Belarus, Bulgaria, Georgia, North Macedonia, Moldova, Montenegro, Romania, Russia, Serbia, and Ukraine); and an Islam group in parts of the

(*continued*)

Frantisek Palacky, the greatest Czech historian of the nineteenth century, wrote the 1848 *Psaní do Frankfurtu* ("A Letter to Frankfurt") in which he justified the continued existence of the Habsburg Empire as the only possible rampart against Russia's imperial ambitions: "A Russian universal monarchy would be an immense and indescribable disaster, an immeasurable and limitless disaster" (Baar 2010, pp. 29–34).

The Habsburg Empire collapsed under the weight of the various unsolved ethnic problems that came to a head with its defeat in World War I. In the peace settlement that followed, significant territories were ceded to Romania and Italy, new republics of Austria and Hungary were created, and the remainder of the monarchy's territory was parceled out among the new states of Poland; the Kingdom of Serbs, Croats, and Slovenes (later Yugoslavia); and Czechoslovakia. Central Europe lost its cultural and political ramparts, to be captured by the Soviet Union after World War II.

Six post-communist countries have distinct Habsburg lineage: Croatia, the Czech Republic, Hungary, Poland, Slovakia, and Slovenia. The pull toward Europe in these countries was clearly seen in the first wave of European Union entry, when the Central European countries joined as a group in 2004 (Lukšić 2015), followed by Croatia in 2013. EU accession for the rest of the former Yugoslavia is pending.

The Russian Empire existed from the sixteenth century until its overthrow by the February Revolution in 1917 (Bushkovitch 2011). Already in the fifteenth century, Tsar Ivan III (1462–1505) laid the groundwork for the empire, tripling the territory of his state, ending the dominance of the Mongol Golden Horde, and renovating the Moscow Kremlin. Peter the Great (1682–1725) fought numerous wars and built a huge empire that became a major European power. He moved the capital from Moscow to the new model city of St. Petersburg and led a cultural revolution that replaced some of the

---

former Yugoslavia, the Caucasus, and all of Central Asia (9 countries: Albania, Azerbaijan, Bosnia and Herzegovina, Kazakhstan, Kosovo, the Kyrgyz Republic, Tajikistan, Turkmenistan, and Uzbekistan). In the Czech Republic and Estonia, the majority of the population considers itself atheist, but the biggest religious groups are Catholic and Lutheran, respectively. The index of Economic Freedom ranges from 0 to 10, with higher values representing more freedom. The Ease of Doing Business index ranks countries from 1 to 189, with #1 being the most business-friendly environment and #189 the least business-friendly environment in the world. Democracy scores range from 0 to 10, with higher scores representing more democracy. The Political Rights index ranges from 7 to 1, with lower values representing more rights. Sources: Heritage Foundation (2016), World Bank (2016), Center for Systemic Peace (2016), Polity IV Individual Country Regime Trends, 1946–2013, World Religion Database, Freedom House (2016))

traditionalist and medieval social system with a Europe-oriented system. Catherine the Great (1761–96) presided over the Russian Empire's golden age. She expanded the empire rapidly by conquest, colonization, and diplomacy while continuing Peter the Great's policy of European integration. Tsar Alexander II (1855–81) promoted numerous reforms, most dramatically the emancipation of 23 million serfs in 1861. His policy in Eastern Europe was to protect the Orthodox Christians under the rule of the Ottoman Empire and eventually to liberate Serbia and Bulgaria in the war of 1878. Russia's involvement in the Balkans led to entry into World War I on the side of France, Britain, and Serbia against the German, Austrian, and Ottoman empires, but the war effort was hugely unsuccessful and the empire collapsed shortly thereafter. In its heyday, the USSR period, the Russian empire's borders encompassed 15 present-day countries: Armenia, Azerbaijan, Belarus, Estonia, Georgia, Kazakhstan, the Kyrgyz Republic, Latvia, Lithuania, Moldova, Russia, Tajikistan, Turkmenistan, Ukraine, and Uzbekistan.

The Ottoman Empire was founded in 1299 by Oghuz Turks under Osman I in north-western Anatolia. After conquests in the Balkans by Murad I in 1362–89, the Ottoman sultanate was transformed into a transcontinental empire and claimant to the caliphate (Shaw 1976). The Ottomans ended the Byzantine Empire with the 1453 conquest of Constantinople by Mehmed the Conqueror. During the sixteenth and seventeenth centuries, in particular at the height of its power under the reign of Suleiman the Magnificent, the Ottoman Empire was a multilingual empire controlling much of Southeastern Europe, Western Asia, the Caucasus, North Africa, and the Horn of Africa. At the beginning of the seventeenth century, the empire comprised 32 provinces and numerous vassal states.

Suleiman the Magnificent (1520–66) captured Belgrade in 1521, conquered the southern and central parts of the Kingdom of Hungary, and, after his victory in the Battle of Mohács in 1526, established Turkish rule in the territory of present-day Hungary. He laid siege to Vienna in 1529 but failed to take the city. Transylvania, Wallachia, and, intermittently, Moldavia in present-day Romania became tributary principalities of the Ottoman Empire. In 1555 the Caucasus was officially partitioned between Persia and the Ottomans, an arrangement that remained until the end of the second Russo-Turkish War (1768–74). The advancement of the Ottoman Empire in Europe was effectively stopped in 1593 on Croatian soil, at the Battle of Sisak, though later attempt to expand and even capture Vienna continued until 1683.

The collapse of the empire in Europe started with the Bulgarian uprising of 1876, when 100,000 people were massacred (Jelavich and Jelavich 1986). The fifth Russo-Turkish War (1877–78) resulted from the outcry against the massacre and ended with a decisive victory for Russia. In its aftermath, Ottoman holdings in Europe declined sharply. Bulgaria was initially established as an independent principality in the Ottoman Empire, while Romania achieved full independence, as did Serbia and Montenegro, albeit with smaller territories than they had before. In 1878 Austria- Hungary unilaterally occupied the Ottoman province of Bosnia and Herzegovina. Bulgaria declared full independence from the empire in 1908. Nine post-communist countries were under Ottoman yoke at various times: Albania, Armenia, Bosnia and Herzegovina, Bulgaria, Kosovo, North Macedonia, Montenegro, Romania, and Serbia.

Study of the patterns of movement toward economic freedom according to imperial lineage reveals that it is broadly similar across empires (Fig. 10.6). Countries formerly in the Ottoman Empire moved toward economic freedom almost as strongly as those of the former Austro-Hungarian Empire, while countries that belonged to the Russian Empire tended to open their economies more slowly after 2007, although they maintained an upward trend. In terms of the ease of doing business, variation within empire groups is insignificant, with few differences across the groups. This finding validates the view in Noland (2005) that the Ottomans were open to international trade and encouraged business activity as much as the Habsburgs.

In contrast, the three groups show pronounced differences in democracy and political rights. Countries that belonged to the Austro-Hungarian Empire are markedly more democratic and embrace more political rights for their citizens. Countries that were at one time part of the Ottoman Empire display little penchant for democracy and political rights, while countries that were once part of the Russian Empire seem most averse to democracy and political rights.

3.3 Main Conclusion on Historical Influences

In sum on divergence, the historical hypotheses work well to explain both economic and political evolution. The differences in the path to democratization are very large, while on economic freedom there is some divergence but it is far smaller. Religion is shown to be strongly associated with divergence in the political evolution to democracy, with Islam likely to lead to the least progress on democratization, while Orthodoxy is associated with more progress, and Catholicism appears as the most conducive to democratization. Religious legacy affects progress on economic freedom, with the same ordering but far less divergence—that is, a lesser effect. Notably the impact of religious legacy was in some cases offset if not fully negated by early reform-oriented institutional decisions.

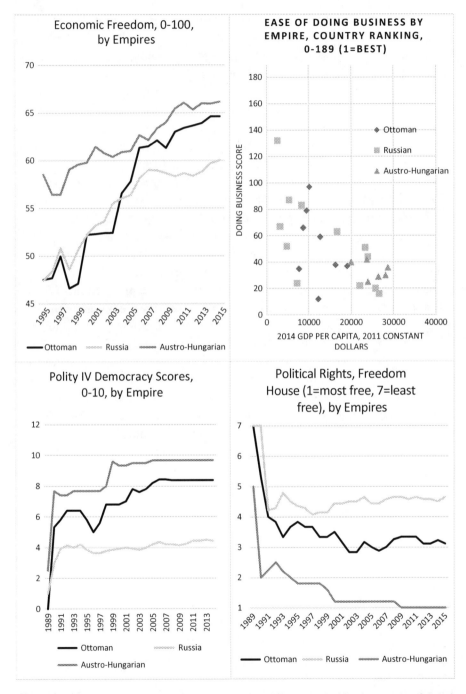

Fig. 10.6 Association between imperial lineage and economic freedom, ease of doing business, democracy, and political rights, various years. (Note: The Ottoman Empire group includes Albania, Armenia, Bosnia and Herzegovina, Bulgaria, Kosovo, North

3.4 Related Regression Analysis from Earlier Studies

The graphical evidence presented above has been put into a broader context by earlier studies, using simple regressions and dummying out the historical variables. This enables one to observe which country characteristics have the largest explanatory power.[8] The results of such an exercise carried out in Djankov (2016) are summarized here.

The regression analysis indicates that abundance of natural resources adversely affects economic freedom but has no effect on ease of doing business. Urbanization has a positive effect on economic freedom but negative on ease of doing business. Ethnic diversity plays no role in explaining either economic measure. Orthodoxy is associated with less economic freedom and wipes out the effect of urbanization as the coefficient becomes insignificant, probably because both Orthodox and Muslim countries are more rural; for example, there is a correlation of −0.71 between the Muslim dummy and urbanization. However, the statistical significance is weak, at 10 percent in the case of the Orthodox religion, and insignificant for economic freedom in the case of Islam. In contrast, the effect of both Orthodoxy and Islam on ease of doing business is positive and significant. Ethnicity also plays a role: ethnically homogeneous countries make it easier to run businesses. Study of the association between late empires and economic policy evolution yields no evidence in support of the hypotheses tested in this chapter. Having a dominant ethnic group is associated with ease of doing business. Both sets of historical variables are significant, confirming that the fifth-century religious divide is more relevant in explaining post-communist policy changes. However, the high correlation between Orthodoxy and the Ottoman Empire (coefficient of 0.45) creates multicollinearity that makes difficult the analysis of regression results. In sum, economic

---

Macedonia, Montenegro, Romania, and Serbia. The Russian group includes Azerbaijan, Belarus, Estonia, Georgia, Kazakhstan, the Kyrgyz Republic, Latvia, Lithuania, Moldova, the Russian Federation, Tajikistan, Turkmenistan, Ukraine and Uzbekistan. Finally, the Austro-Hungarian Empire comprises Croatia, Czech Republic, Hungary, Poland, Slovakia, and Slovenia. Sources: Becker et al. (2016), Bushkovitch (2011), Shaw (1976), Heritage Foundation (2016), World Bank (2016), Center for Systemic Peace (2016), Polity IV Individual Country Regime Trends, 1946–2013, Freedom House (2016))

---

[8] The analysis uses the last year of available data for each dependent variable, usually 2015. The rationale is that all sample countries started with a complete lack of democracy and political rights, as well as complete or near-complete lack of economic freedom. The most recent values are taken to represent the increase in both freedoms over the period.

policy evolution seems to be affected by Islamic legacy, but urbanization and natural resource abundance also play a role, while other explanatory variables perform poorly in explaining economic freedom and ease of doing business.

Evolution toward democracy and political rights is associated with less resource abundance and, in the case of political rights, higher urbanization. Once historical variables are added, however, these results become insignificant, as both Orthodoxy and Islam are shown to be negatively associated with political evolution. The coefficients on Islam are twice as large as those on Orthodoxy. In regressions excluding empire variables, one also sees a negative effect of natural resource abundance, a positive effect of urbanization, and, in the case of democracy, a positive effect of ethnic diversity. Once both sets of historical variables are included in the regressions, however, empires cease to be statistically significant and actually flip signs, perhaps due to multicollinearity. The fifth-century religious divide is the only consistently significant predictor of political evolution.

The inclusion in the regressions of presidential powers as a proxy for early institutional choice (see Frye 1997) in the regression doesn't change the results Presidential powers are not a good predictor of political evolution, and they only marginally weaken the explanatory power of history (in the case of the effect of Orthodoxy on democracy). This result may explain the wider divergence in political as opposed to economic evolution; present-day parliamentary systems negate the deleterious effects of history on economic but not political evolution.

The explanatory power of initial conditions like urbanization and ethnicity, history, and presidential powers is quite high, explaining about 70 percent of the variation across countries. Much of this explanatory power is derived from historical variables, while little is added by newer institutional choices. While countries have broadly converged toward greater economic freedom, they remain wide apart in political evolution.

3.5   Georgia: The Puzzle in Transition

Georgia is the most puzzling case for economic and political transformation. An Orthodox nation in the Caucasus and for much of its history part of the Russian then Soviet empire, it has surpassed expectations. Its economic freedom score in 2015 was 73, identical to Germany's. It ranks 24th on the 2016 Ease of Doing Business index, behind only North Macedonia and the Baltics in the post-communist region and on par with Austria and the Netherlands.

It scores 8 out of 10 on democracy, one notch below the Czech Republic. And its political rights score in 2015 was 3 out of 7 (where 1 is complete democracy), the same as Croatia's.

The initial post-communist years would not suggest such achievements. After the collapse of the Soviet Union in 1991, Georgia sank into a civil war, followed by a coup that brought the former communist leader Eduard Shevardnadze to power. Armed conflicts emerged in two of the country's regions. Georgia experienced the largest economic decline of any post-communist country in 1990–94, when nominal GDP fell 77 percent (UNECE 2000, p. 225). The economy continued its slide for the next decade as Shevardnadze's family took control of significant economic assets in banking, energy, telecommunications, construction, and the media. In this tight link between politics and business, Georgia was no different from its Caucasus neighbors Armenia and Azerbaijan.

The 2003 Rose Revolution reversed this as the population rose to expel Shevardnadze, though afterward Georgia faced a number of additional challenges. In 2006 Russia, its largest trading partner banned trade, quadrupled the price of Russian natural gas, and evicted tens of thousands of labor migrants. In August 2008 five days of full-fledged war with Russia killed 228 civilians, 160 soldiers, and increased the size of the occupied territories by 20 percent, displacing 110,000 people.

Nevertheless between 2004 and 2012 real annual economic growth averaged 7.2 percent and corruption decreased so dramatically that Georgia surpassed some developed countries on international governance indexes. In the World Bank's Control of Corruption index, for example, Georgia ranked second only to Estonia among all post-communist countries, and equal to Costa Rica and Portugal.

Georgia also provides some unique examples of policy reforms. After the Rose Revolution, the first step was to create new public security systems and reform the most corrupt institution, the police. The most visible and celebrated reform was the abolishment of the Soviet-style road police, which had nothing to do with law enforcement: its sole purpose was to extract bribes. In 2005 the government fired all 30,000 traffic police in Georgia. The goal was to transform the police from a punishing institution to a public agency that provided security and stability. The share of the Georgian people that had confidence in the police rose from 5 percent in 2004 to 87 percent in 2012 (Bendukidze and Saakhashvili 2014).

Georgia has staged the only successful post-communist restart of political transition. Both Ukraine in 2004 and the Kyrgyz Republic in 2010 tried with their Orange and Tulip Revolutions, respectively, but neither was successful at bringing in new political elites and charting a new economic path away from oligarchs. Georgia deserves further study to understand how countries can overcome their unfavorable history on the path to democracy.

4   Conclusions

In most of the post-communist states, life has improved, sometimes markedly as citizens enjoy higher living standards, the freedom to travel internationally, more secure property rights, and greater autonomy and personal dignity. Most countries have closed the income gap with the West, in some case considerably.

But strikingly economic progress has been more successful than political efforts. It appears that while post-communist reformers knew more or less how to do economic reform, few politicians had any idea how to build democracy. As a result, the citizens of a half-dozen post-communist countries still live in dictatorships. Georgia, Moldova, and Ukraine started on the path to democracy with a delay and now seek some form of integration with the European Union. Worse, several countries that started early on the path of democracy have since veered away.

In trying to identify the reasons for the disappointing results in democratic development, I show that history is a major determinant and that recent institutional choices only partially negate its effects. I also point to an outlier—Georgia—that perhaps can unlock the secret of successful political evolution.

The divergent paths of political evolution in the post-communist countries suggest that further study is needed to understand the combination of policies that bring about a thriving democracy in the face of strong countervailing forces (Kelejian et al. 2013). In some Central European countries, even successful economic reforms failed to bring legitimacy to liberal democracies. These insights have implications for the study of political evolution in other parts of the world, for example, among the Arab states, Cuba, North Korea, and much of Africa, which emulated the Soviet model in the 1950s and 1960s.

References

Åslund, A., & Djankov, S. (2014). *The Great Rebirth: The Victory of Capitalism over Communism*. Washington: Peterson Institute for International Economics.

Baar, M. (2010). *Historians and Nationalism: East-Central Europe in the Nineteenth Century*. New York: Oxford University Press.

Balcerowicz, L. (1995). *Socialism, Capitalism, Transformation*. Budapest: Central European University Press.

Becker, S., Boeckh, K., Hainz, C., & Woessmann, L. (2016). The Empire Is Dead, Long Live the Empire! Long-run Persistence of Trust and Corruption in the Bureaucracy. *Economic Journal, 126*(590), 40–74.

Bendukidze, K., & Saakhashvili, M. (2014). Georgia The Most Radical Catch-Up Reforms. Chapter 8, In A. Åslund & S. Djankov (Eds.).

Benhenda, M. (2011, February). Liberal Democracy and Political Islam: The Search for Common Ground. *Politics, Philosophy &Economics, 10*(1), 45.

Berdyaev, N. (1937). *The Origin of Russian Communism*. Glasgow: University Press.

Brownlee, J. (2007). *Authoritarianism in an Age of Democratization*. Cambridge: Cambridge University Press.

Bushkovitch, P. (2011). *A Concise History of Russia*. New York: Cambridge University Press.

Central Intelligence Agency (CIA). (2016). *Countries in the World*. Washington, DC.

Chubais, A.. (1999). *Privatizatsiya po-rossiiski* [Privatization in a Russian Way]. Moscow: Vagrius.

Dimitrova-Grajzl, V. (2007). The Great Divide Revisited: Ottoman and Habsburg Legacies on Transition. *Kyklos, 60*(4), 539–558.

Djankov, S. (2016). *The Divergent Postcommunist Paths to Democracy and Economic Freedom*. London School of Economics, Discussion Paper 758.

Djankov, S., & Murrell, P. (2002). Enterprise Restructuring in Transition: A Quantitative Survey. *Journal of Economic Literature, 40*(3), 739–792.

Djankov, S., Nkolova, E., & Zilinsky, J. (2016). The Happiness Gap in Eastern Europe. *Journal of Comparative Economics, 44*(1), 108–124.

EBRD (European Bank for Reconstruction and Development). (2013). *Transition Report 2013: Stuck in Transition?* London.

Fischer, S., & Frenkel, J. (1992). Macroeconomic Issues of Soviet Reform. *American Economic Review Papers and Proceedings, 82*(2), 36–42.

Freedom House. (2016). *Freedom of the World*. Washington DC.

Frye, T. (1997). A Politics of Institutional Choice: Post-Communist Presidencies. *Comparative Political Studies, 30*(5), 523–552.

Gros, D. (2014). From Transition to Integration: The Role of Trade and Investment. Chapter 12, In A. Åslund & S. Djankov (Eds.).

Havrylyshyn, O., Meng, M., & Tupy, M. (2016). *Twenty-five Years of Reforms in Post-Communist World: Rapid Reformers Outperformed the Gradualists*. Washington, DC: The CATO Institute. Policy Analysis Paper 795.

Hellman, J. (1998). Winners Take All: The Politics of Partial Reform in Post-communist Transitions. *World Politics, 50*(2), 203–234.

Heritage Foundation. (2016). *Index of Economic Freedom*. Washington.

Huntington, S. P. (1991). *The Third Wave Democratization in the Late Twentieth Century*. Norman: University of Oklahoma Press.

Jelavich, C., & Jelavich, B. (1986). *The Establishment of the Balkan National States, 1804–1920*. Seattle: University of Washington Press.

Kelejian, H., Murrell, P., & Shepotylo, O. (2013). Spatial Spillovers in the Development of Institutions. *Journal of Development Economics, 101*(C), 297–315.

Kelly, T. M. (2016). Infant Mortality: Eastern Europe: 1970–1989. In *Making the History of 1989*. Fairfax, VA: Roy Rosenzweig Center for History & New Media.

Kornai, J. (1990). *The Road to a Free Economy: Shifting from a Socialist System—The Example of Hungary*. New York: Norton.

Krastev, I. (2011). Paradoxes of the New Authoritarianism. *Journal of Democracy, 22*(2), 5–16.

Kundera, M. (1984). The Tragedy of Central Europe. *New York Review of Books,* 31 (7), April 26.

Kuran, T. (2004). Why the Middle East Is Economically Underdeveloped. *Journal of Economic Perspectives, 18*(3), 71–90.

La Porta, R., Lopez-de-Silanes, F., Shleifer, A., & Vishny, R. (1999). The Quality of Government. *Journal of Law, Economics, and Organization, 15*(1), 222–279.

Lukšić, I. (2015). *On the Lost Purpose of Transition*. University of Donja Gorica, Podgorica, Montenegro, Photocopy.

Lukšić, I., & Katnić, M. (2016). The Making of a State: Transition in Montenegro. *Cato Journal, 36*, 689–709.

March, A. (2015). Political Islam: Theory. *Annual Review of Political Science, 18*, 103–123.

McCleary, R., & Barro, R. (2006). Religion and Economy. *Journal of Economic Perspectives, 20*(2), 49–72.

Murrell, P. (1992). Evolution in Economics and in the Economic Reform of the Centrally Planned Economies. In C. Clague & G. Rausser (Eds.), *Emergence of Market Economies in Eastern Europe*. London and New York: Blackwell.

Nalepa, M. (2010). *Skeletons in the Closet: Transitional Justice in Post-Communist Europe*. New York: Cambridge University Press.

Noland, M. (2005). Religion and Economic Performance. *World Development, 33*(8), 1215–1232.

Pop-Eleches, G. (2007). Historical Legacies and Post-Communist Regime Change. *Journal of Politics, 69*(4), 908–926.

Roberts, A. (2010). *The Quality of Democracy in Eastern Europe: Public Preferences and Policy Reforms*. New York: Cambridge University Press.

Roland, G. (1994). On the Speed and Sequencing of Privatization and Restructuring. *Economic Journal, 104*(426), 1158–1168.

Roland, G. (2014). Transition in Historical Perspective. Chapter 13, In A. Aslund & S. Djankov (Eds.).

Shaw, S. (1976). *History of the Ottoman Empire and Modern Turkey*. Cambridge: Cambridge University Press.

Shleifer, A., & Treisman, D. (2014). Normal Countries: The East 25 Years after Communism. *Foreign Affairs*, Fall/Winter.

Shleifer, A., & Vishny, R. (1994). Politicians and Firms. *Quarterly Journal of Economics, 109*(4), 995–1025.

Stiglitz, J. (1994). *Whither Socialism*. MIT Press, Boston, MA.

Stiglitz, J. (2002). *Globalization and Its Discontents*. New York: Norton Publishing.

Treisman, D. (2014). The Political Economy of Change after Communism. Chapter 14, In A. Åslund & S. Djankov (Eds.).

Treisman, D. (2007). *The Architecture of Government: Rethinking Political Decentralization*. New York: Cambridge University Press.

UNECE (United Nations Economic Commission for Europe). (2000). *Economic Survey of Europe*, no. 1. New York: United Nations.

UNECE (United Nations Economic Commission for Europe). (2016). *Economic Survey of Europe*, no. 2. New York: United Nations.

Weber, M. (1905). *The Protestant Ethic and the "Spirit" of Capitalism—and Other Writings*. Berlin: Archiv für Sozialwissenschaft und Sozialpolitik.

World Bank. (2016). *World Development Indicators*. Washington.

Zatonski, W., Campos, H., & Willett, W. (2008). Rapid Declines in Coronary Heart Disease Mortality in Eastern Europe Are Associated with Increased Consumption of Oils Rich In Alpha-Linolenic Acid. *European Journal of Epidemiology, 23*(1), 3–10.

Part III

Post-Communist Transition

11

Thirty Years of Transition: Eleven Stylised Facts

Oleh Havrylyshyn

1 Introduction

In 2017 about 27 million trips abroad were recorded by Ukrainians and 40 million by Russians; in 2012 citizens of the entire region undertook 170 million foreign tourist trips, about 40% of the population.[1] Had these levels of travel been possible in Iron Curtain days the socialist worker's paradise would have been emptied of most workers within a decade. To state this in an academic work is mere hyperbole of course, but for citizens of post-communist countries these numbers and the enormous contrast with the pre-1989 reality symbolise dramatically what is perhaps the most important and hence our first *stylised fact of transition*:

SF1: The nearly thirty countries of the region have become widely integrated into the global community.

Not only did people begin to move about as freely as others around the globe, but so too did goods in trade, financial flows for investment or personal transfers, communications in all forms. Drabek and Benacek (2013) documented the enormous increase and shift in trade outside the former Soviet camp, most dramatically for former republics, as exports outside jumped from

---

[1] The World Bank's World Development Indicators.

O. Havrylyshyn (✉)
Carleton University, Ottawa, ON, Canada
e-mail: olehhavrylyshyn@cunet.carleton.ca

© The Author(s) 2021
E. Douarin, O. Havrylyshyn (eds.), *The Palgrave Handbook of Comparative Economics*,
https://doi.org/10.1007/978-3-030-50888-3_11

10% or less to more than 20%. Broadman (2005) earlier showed that many transition countries quickly achieved trade-to-GDP ratios higher than their size and level of development would predict in a global cross section. The four- to seven-decades-long forced isolation of the socialist camp is a thing of the past—a big achievement already.[2]

But there were many other achievements after thirty years that are worth noting—that is the main purpose of this chapter, which will review what has happened in three broad areas: economic and social well-being, transformation into a market economy with private ownership and transformation of the political regime into a more democratic system with greater personal freedoms. Indeed, one such freedom is precisely that first noted fact of travelling abroad. The guiding principle for this presentation is positivist, that is, "just the facts please", avoiding normative inferences and conclusions. In other words, the chapter will not discuss the many very important questions and debates such as the role of fast versus slow reforms in determining economic performance, the reasons for the sharp decline in output in the first years, the factors behind the initial widening of income distribution and its later closing, the interplay of democratisation and economic liberalisation, the reason for wide divergence in these trends across countries. These and other important issues are covered in great detail in the following chapters of Part 3 of the Handbook, and the intent of this chapter is only to provide a factual background for those discussions.

Having said that, transparency behoves me to disclose to the reader my general views on the main debates about transition, views which have been made clear in other writings in which I took part. I have argued early in the transition that a Big Bang strategy of early and fast reforms would be better than gradual movement, inter alia to avoid capture by anti-reform vested interests. Also, that attaching a country to an outside anchor such as the EU would help a great deal to keep the reform process from being subverted by opponents. And finally after the fact I have adduced empirical evidence that is consistent with the hypothesis: countries undertaking a rapid reform strategy have performed much better on many different measures.[3] I make this disclosure because there is always a risk that in presenting facts objectively, one is subject to erring on the side of choosing the facts that will best illustrate one' normative views, or, as McCloskey (1983) put it, all economics is

---

[2] A partial exception is Turkmenistan where it is still not easy to obtain an exit visa—though it is far better than earlier. However, its international l trade and investments have become substantial.

[3] Havrylyshyn (2006), Havrylyshyn et al. (2016) and Havrylyshyn (2020) are most representative.

rhetoric. The reader should keep my disclosure in mind and judge the objectivity of the facts presented below.

Section 2 of the chapter reviews several measures of performance since about 1990 in the area of economic and social well-being. Section 3 then describes the process of economic reforms, liberalisation, private sector evolution and the development of market-related institutions, and Section 4 discusses the trends in democratisation. Section 4 summarises, recapping the eleven stylised facts after thirty years of transition, assesses their significance, and, finally, compares them with the seven stylised facts Campos and Coricelli (2002) came to after a decade.

2   Outcomes for Economic and Social Well-Being

2.1   Income Per Capita: How Much Catching Up?

For citizens of communist countries the main objectives of the system's transition were, first and foremost, an increase in their standard of living to catch up with Western European levels, and, second, gaining the personal freedoms that were common in the West. Figure 11.1 shows that GDP per capita did indeed increase—and quite substantially in countries of Central Europe and the Baltics (CEB)—but only after a period of five to ten years of decline. Comparing official GDP calculations which started in the early nineties with the Net Material Product accounts in the communist period is known to underestimate the improvement for reasons noted later, the implication being that the improvements in standard of living are larger than Fig. 11.1 shows. Broadly, then, the second stylised fact can be stated thus:

SF2: Incomes declined initially in all countries, but much less in the CEB groups; in the late nineties and from 2000 growth became widespread so that after ten to twenty years, standard of living in almost all countries surpassed those of the communist period.

Some elaboration on this is useful. First, the variation across the region was substantial both in the period of the "transitional recession"[4] and in the recovery from 2000. In the CEB the decline was neither very long nor so deep, with recovery beginning as early as 1993–4. Once growth resumed, it was quite high for many years—ranging about 4–6% annually—at least until the

---

[4] Kornai (1994) discussed why this decline was inevitable to allow inefficient firms to either adjust or be replaced by new ones.

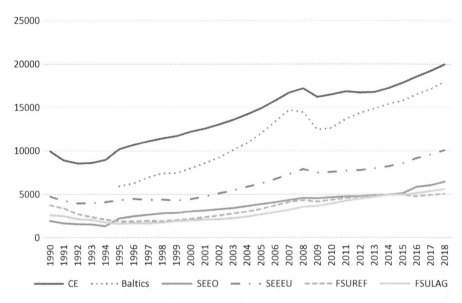

Fig. 11.1 GDP per capita by group: 1990–2018 constant $US 2010. Source: The World Bank, World Development Indicators; accessed April 20, 2020

Global Recession in 2007–8. In contrast, countries in the Former Soviet Union (FSU) endured negative growth for nearly a decade, and on average saw a less dynamic recovery afterwards. Belarus is the only exception, as it did not experience a recession from the nineties onwards, but also did not meaningfully reform, and in the long run did not do better than other FSU countries in catching up with Western incomes. True, later the impact of the Global Recession was much less severe in the FSU, but that may have been due to a fact discussed later: CEB countries had far more of their new export activities oriented towards the West.

For some countries in the very bottom groups in Fig. 11.1 official statistics suggest that incomes barely caught up to 1990 levels; two factors lead one to conclude that this understates considerably the actual improvements. First, NMP valuations were well-known by Sovietologists to overstate real values, and GDP in the transition period understates them, due to significant underground economic activity—estimated in some countries to be as high as one-third of official GDP. Second, we can also refer to direct consumption measures. United Nations statistics are available for the level of consumption of various goods and services, which allows a more direct comparison of standards of living in the Soviet period. And three decades later, Shleifer and

Treisman (2014: 8) conclude from these that "almost all statistics suggest a *dramatic* improvement in the quality of life since 1989 for citizens of the average post-communist country". Thus they observe that automobiles and telephones, which were sparsely available in Soviet times, saw ownership levels take a quantum leap as early as 2010 from an average of one automobile for every ten people to more than four per ten, and in the richer countries of Central Europe even higher. As anyone who travelled to the region around 1990 and also now can attest, the wide, empty boulevards of Soviet cities of yesterday are today the site of permanent traffic jams. Similarly, per person cell phone subscriptions of 1.2 per person exceed that of many Western countries, and the same is seen for internet connections. For a real sense of this, walk into the main department store of Bishkek in the poorest new country that emerged from the collapse of the Soviet Union, Kyrgyzstan, and you will see in what had been the old Soviet department store "TSUM" that a full third of the first floor consists of booths selling cell phones and SIM cards.

A major unfulfilled promise of the socialist paradise concerned lack of adequate housing space—not to speak of its quality. By 2011 housing space per capita had increased considerably in almost all countries ranging from a rise of 21% in Kyrgyzstan to 116% in Romania.[5] These numbers may even underestimate the improvement; in 2012, the median rate of ownership of housing in post-communist countries, which had essentially been zero in 1989, reached an extremely high 90%, far above that of Western European countries. And this general number does not account for the huge improvements in the quality of apartments, hinted at in the common term "Euro-Remont". "Remont" is the local word for home renovation, and it has become a source of personal pride for individuals to talk about doing not simply a "remont", but a "Euro-Remont", to imply much superior European quality of housing.

Perhaps the best summary answer to the question "how much catch-up was there?" is to compare over time a country's GDP per capita as a percentage of the average in the pre-enlargement EU15; these values are given in Table 11.1—but in keeping with the stylised nature of comparisons, as approximate values only.[6] On average, for all transition countries, there was a considerable catching up from about 30% of the EU15 average in 1990 to about 55% by 2016, though clearly still very distant from incomes of Western Europe. Two observations need to be made. Since EU countries were also growing—even if modestly—the change in this ratio is less than the absolute

---

[5] Only Tajikistan saw a slight decline perhaps due to the persistent civil conflict.

[6] Apart from the problem of GDP_NMP bias, such estimates vary among the literature sources used.

Table 11.1 Income catch-up trends. Approximate ratio of transition countries' GDP per capita to the EU15 average

	1990	1995	2005	2013	2016
[B] Balkans	34	28	30	–	40–
[I] All transition	~30	–	–	~50	55
[I] EU members	~40	–	–	~65	70
Selected Countries					
The Czech Republic	60	60+	75	–	80
Hungary	50	50+	60	–	70–
Poland	35	35+	50	–	70
Romania	35	30	40	–	55
Bulgaria	30	25	35	–	50

Source: Author's approximate compilations from [B] Berend (2009), Tables 8.1 and 8.2; N.B. Berend takes the data before 1990 from the well-known long-term historical estimates of Angus Maddison (2001). Central Europe: The Czech Republic, Hungary, Poland, Slovakia, Slovenia; Balkans: Bulgaria, Croatia, Macedonia, Romania; Central and Eastern Europe (CEE): all nine. [I] Roaf *et al.* (2014) p. 5: qualified as "about", hence marked in the table with ~ . [E] Economist (2018: 44) Notes: + or –: to avoid false precision values from [E] rounded to nearest 5, though other sources may consistently show slightly more (+) or less (–).

increase of income over the period. Furthermore, recall the bias in comparing 1990 national accounts with those in the market economy period, meaning the actual catch-up was likely somewhat higher than these ratios. For the non-member Balkan countries, the catch-up was more limited, perhaps due to the wars that resulted in a persistent decline until at least 2005; the wars also diverted the attention of governments from transition policies of any sort. At the top end, for the countries that became new members of the EU, this was substantial, particularly so for those farthest behind in 1990, Bulgaria and Romania; this last fact is consistent with conventional development theory, with convergence being strongest for the lowest income countries.

In sum, the third stylised fact is as follows:

SF3: Despite the transition recession of the nineties and a considerable diversity in economic performance, it is clear that after thirty years there has been a considerable catch-up with European standards of living for all transition countries; notably the largest catch-up is seen in the new EU members.

2.2   Income Distribution: First Worsens, then Gets Better but with Great Diversity

One of the most important issues of current debates and analysis by economists concerns the considerable widening of the income distribution gap between top incomes and those lower down, whether this is measured by the Gini coefficient or the top 10% share of income. In the transition literature, this stands out as perhaps the most important criticism raised in the late nineties of the apparent consequences of market reforms, by, for example, Milanovic (1998), UNDP (1998). I do not address in this chapter the debate on whether this was caused by too rapid reforms or on the contrary by too gradual reforms,[7] and keep to the intent of providing neutrally the background facts as best as they are known. The stylised representation of Fig. 11.2 shows the approximate nature of the different time paths of Gini values for two groups of transition countries: the solid line represents the FSU countries, and the dashed line the rest in CEB and South-East Europe (SEE).[8] Pertinent variations within these two groups are detailed in Table 11.2. It is widely agreed that in the first decade all post-communist countries experienced a substantial rise in the Gini from values in the low twenties typical of socialist countries; though the widening of the gap was far greater for most FSU countries (exceptions are noted later). Around 2000 the latter reached values of 0.40 and more , the highest being over 0.50 in Russia ; in comparison peaks in CEB/SEE countries were about 0.30–0.35. From 2000 on, roughly coinciding with the general trend of growing GDP for the entire region, Gini values gradually declined—but again with an important difference between the two groups, the FSU levels remaining well above 0.30 and about 0.40 for Russia. Data on distribution of income and wealth by deciles, as well as poverty ratios, exhibit the same trends.[9]

That the very low Gini values of about 0.22–0.23[10] in the socialist period would necessarily rise somewhat was neither a surprise nor the main concern of rapid reform critics like Branko Milanovic (2019)—rather, they argued that the extent of the widening went far beyond what might be considered appropriate in well-functioning market economies with private ownership producing profits for a new class of necessarily richer capitalists. Table 11.2 provides a relevant comparison of Gini values with other market economies, both developing and high income.[11] Central European (CEE) countries with Gini

---

[7] For those interested, Novokmet in this volume brushes on the subject.

[8] The values are not actual averages, just rough approximations to represent the pattern. "Actual" values and averages in Table 11.2 are based on one source only—The World Bank. Other sources tend to have higher values for FSU countries.

[9] The literature on this is reviewed in Havrylyshyn (2020, chap. 2).

[10] Though unofficial estimates for the Soviet Union were often higher in the mid-twenties, as shown in Havrylyshyn (2006, chap. 3).

[11] Most of the estimates shown are from the World Bank data base; it should be noted that for two cases, Russia and China, other estimates by individual scholars and the CIA typically show higher values, in the forties rather than the high thirties for the latest years.

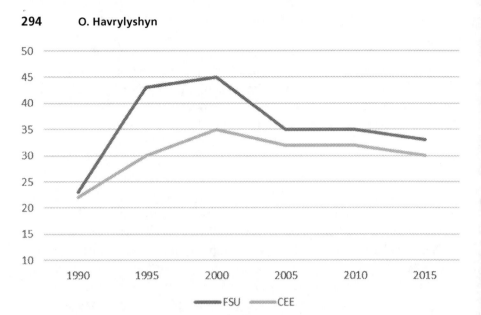

Fig. 11.2 Stylised picture of approximate trends in Gini values. Source: Approximate trends based on data from CIA and the World Bank as provided in https://wikipedia.org/List_of_countries_by_income_equality, 2020-02-17

values in the mid-twenties now appear to be comparable to Nordic countries like Denmark, which have always had the least unequal distribution among high-income economies. The Baltics score a little higher, but even they have Ginis lower than the highest among high-income countries like the US with a value over 0.40. Former Soviet Union countries which have seen the least progress towards a market economy (as shown in Fig. 11.4 later using the well-known European Bank for Reconstruction and Development [EBRD] indicator) labelled FSULAG in Table 11.2 have a score of around 0.35, distinctly lower than that for FSU countries with greater reform progress, labelled FSUREF, have Ginis of 0.40 and more and are comparable to the most unequal developing countries. Russia's latest is 0.38,[12] but reached a maximum of nearly 0.50 in the mid-nineties. Countries with the highest Ginis are known to suffer from dominance of new post-Soviet oligarchs, though there are some interesting exceptions: Ukraine and Kazakhstan, no less oligarchic than Russia, have Gini values of about 0.26–0.27. This raises an obvious research question: given the dominant oligarch presence (shown later) why is the Gini coefficient so much lower than in Russia and other FSU countries?

By comparing approximate values in other countries shown in Table 11.2, it becomes clear that after about two decades of widening trends, income

---

[12] The CIA factbook estimates a higher value of 0.41.

Table 11.2 Gini values over time—pre-tax selected countries and groups

	1988–90	1993	2002	2010	Latest
Central Europe (CE)	22	29	28	30	29
Baltics	25	35	36	36	35
SEE	21	27	33	33	34
FSUREF	27	42	36	38	32
[RUSSIA]	25	48	40	40	38
FSULAG	25	N/A	33	35	34
EU15	--	--	--	--	31
OECD	(Low)	Denmark	25	25	28
	(High)	USA	40	41	42
Developing	Lower	Indonesia	30	36	38
	Higher	Colombia	49	56	48
China	Rural		36	42	42
	Urban		32	40	37

Source: Values for first three columns from Havrylyshyn (2006, Table 3.5); 2010 and later: author calculations from World Bank, *World Development Indicators*

distribution in transition countries has fallen to levels well below those seen in most developing countries—including China—and generally slightly lower than in many rich economies like the US. The lower end of the range in developing economies is typified by Indonesia where the latest Gini is 0.38, about the same as for Russia; more typical countries like Colombia are in the high forties, with several over fifty. The average Gini in Western Europe, the pre-2004 EU of fifteen members, is 0.31. The Central European group of six countries defined in this chapter is thus seen to have a narrower income distribution pattern than the richer EU economies even before tax effects, more like that of Nordic countries which are all below 0.30.

To summarise on income distribution, one can posit the fourth stylised fact:

SF4: Income distribution and poverty measures deteriorated considerably in the nineties, in particular for FSU countries, but in all cases this reversed after 2000 with CEB and SEE groups stabilising at values of 0.30 or less, similar to the best market economies. Many FSU countries remained at much higher values, with some like Russia having values comparable to those in the worst developing country cases, at about 0.50.

2.3 Social Well-Being: A Comprehensive Measure

The widely used Human Development Index compiled annually by the UNDP is perhaps the single best statistical indicator of people's standard of living in different countries inasmuch as it incorporates GDP per capita values as well as other direct measures of social well-being like health (life

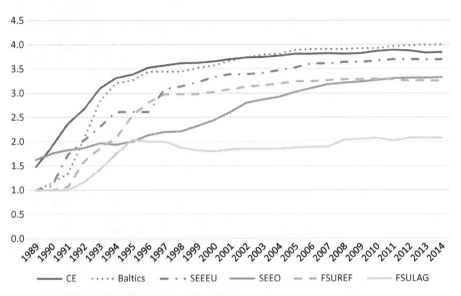

Fig. 11.3 Human Development Index by group, 1990–2019. Source: UNDP, Human Development Index. Data set: accessed April 20, 2020

expectancy), educational attainments, and so on. Its time path for transition countries is summarised for the same country groups as in charts in Fig. 11.3. The first conclusion to draw is that the change since 1990 was positive for all country groups, that is, Human Development Index (HDI) measuring overall social well-being has improved relative to that in the communist period. This is consistent with the preceding stylised facts on income. The second conclusion is in effect a caution about the statistical accuracy of any such synthetic indicators: in the first years till 1995 HDI shows rather opposite and puzzling movements for different groups: CE and the South-East Europe EU members (SEEEU, Bulgaria and Romania) appear to have experienced an increase during the time output declined significantly and unemployment rose; the Baltics also witnessed this but to a much lesser degree. In contrast, all others experienced a decline—which is more likely given the output fall. The explanation probably lies in changes to the definition and calculation of the HDI; in Havrylyshyn (2006) these puzzling results do not appear if earlier UNDP website values of HDI are used—there is a reduction in HDI in that decade but very minor, and the trend is reversed from 1995 in the CEB groups. Using 2013 website values, HMT (2016) finds much less of a decline for the FSULAG countries than seen in Fig. 11.3, but not the odd results for CE and SEE. Closer investigation suggests all the puzzles result from several retroactive changes in HDI values to reflect newer definitions, which results in some individual country values "jumping" up then down from one year to the next as can be seen on the UNDP data website. In a word, great caution is needed for the first decade, but the long-term trend is, nevertheless, clear. With this large grain of salt, I cautiously posit the fifth stylised fact:

SF5: Overall social well-being as measured by synthetic indicators covering broader aspects of personal living standards had definitely improved for transition countries by 2010 and kept on improving, but the improvement was probably smaller for the FSU.

3   Progress Towards a Market System

3.1   Overall Achievements in Systemic Transformation

I turn now to trace the progress of reforms aimed at transforming the economic regime from socialist central planning to a market economy with private ownership often—and unfortunately—shortened to just "socialism" and "capitalism".[13] The most commonly used measure of such progress has been the Transition Progress Indicators (TPI) compiled by the EBRD from 1990 until 2014 when this exercise ceased, including retrospective estimates back to 1989. Some specialists such as Campos and Horvath (2012) have criticised these estimates pointing out altogether valid shortcomings and possible errors in the subjective process of soliciting "independent expert" opinions. Despite the valid criticisms, I use the TPI as do many others for two reasons: there is no alternative as comprehensive and long-term; and as valid as the criticisms are for individual countries in specific years—for example, too generous for Russia in late nineties—they do not appear to affect the broader comparative picture which is what "stylised facts" by definition try to capture. What then do the indicators shown in Fig. 11.4 tell us?

The first striking trend is that with very few partial exceptions, most formerly socialist central plan countries (twenty-five in this sample) have progressed a very long way from the value of 1.0 designated for such regimes by the EBRD towards the complete transition to a competitive market capitalism value of 4.3—again arbitrarily designated. The exceptions are three FSU countries—Belarus, Turkmenistan and Uzbekistan , what I have labelled in this chapter as the laggard (FSULAG), which have reached a TPI value of

---

[13] In Havrylyshyn (2020) I discuss why these short-form labels are unfortunate because they mislead a great deal. This is not the place for an elaboration , but a brief explanation is worthwhile : capitalism , neo-liberalism , Smith's invisible hand principle are too often conflated without considering if the functioning of the market is competitive or dominated by oligopolists, oligarchs or other powerful vested interests. Even the best-known critics of neo-liberalism in their recent writings, for example, Stiglitz (2019) and Milanovic (2019), emphasise that properly competitive market economies can lead to a "good" capitalism different from what they judge the current form of capitalism to be in practice. I therefore prefer using the longer label: competitive market capitalism.

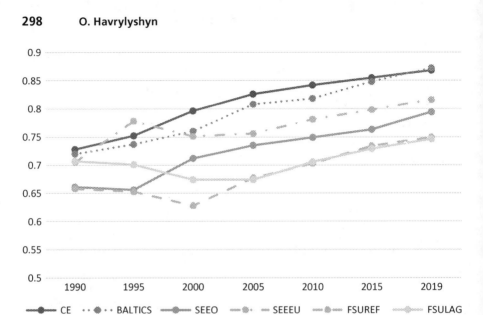

Fig. 11.4 Transition progress indicator, 1989–2014. Source: EBRD, Transition Reports, various years

merely 2.0, signifying some very limited role for private ownership and rudimentary market operations.[14] The share of the private sector in GDP is indicative of the limited transition there: while in all others this share ranges from 70% to 80%, not unlike that of many Western European countries, in Belarus it is less than 40%, less in Turkmenistan, perhaps a little more in Uzbekistan.[15]

The second notable point is the big difference in the early years between Central Europe and the Baltics on the one hand and most others on the other hand. The CEB countries moved very fast and very early to make the necessary policy changes transforming the economic system to a market economy with significant private ownership, in five years, that is, 1994, reaching TPI values of 3.0, which are defined as a reasonably functioning market economy . FSUREF countries needed ten years to get to this point, and then slowed their pace considerably, never reaching 3.5, while the CEB continued to progress steadily albeit attaining values of about 4.0, nearly the EBRD maximum scoring, more slowly.[16] Many observers have pointed to an apparent disappointing slowdown after these countries attained EU membership in 2004. Whether the lack of enforcement by Brussels once membership was attained is the reason behind

---

[14] Recent non-quantified reporting on Uzbekistan and to some extent Belarus does suggest some further progress since 2016.

[15] Havrylyshyn (2020).

[16] At least one country, Estonia, has exceeded the 4.0 value.

the slowdown is debated, but one should point out a simple mathematical reality: the maximum score of 4.3 sets an asymptote, and it is well-known that asymptotic phenomena generally mean the closer the curve is to the asymptote, the slower the further pace of approaching it. The specific reason for this slowdown may be that institutional reforms (defined in the literature as "second-generation") necessarily cannot be done as fast as simpler market liberalisation and macro stabilisation reforms (defined as first-generation).The differences between these two categories of transformational change are explored later.

Two more brief observations: The two SEE countries that have attained EU membership, Bulgaria and Romania (SEEEU in all figures), have move farther towards market economies than those still just potential candidates. In other words, new EU members have outdone other countries on this dimension much as they have in previous indicators. Also of interest, the other countries in SEE, which started in 1989 with the highest TPI score reflecting the much softer Yugoslav version of socialism with a considerable private sector and no formal central plan, moved very slowly until the late nineties, coinciding with the Yugoslav wars—but then accelerated to nearly catch up[17].

The above gives one considerable fodder for a stylised fact; hence I will break it into two:

SF6: Apart from three laggards in the FSU, twenty-five of the formerly communist countries have been enormously transformed into market economies with at least well-functioning markets with overwhelming private ownership, though a distinct gap between the FSU countries and the others is still evident.

SF7: The gap in transformation coincides very closely with EU membership—countries in the first waves of enlargement have gone farthest, those in the candidate category, or high prospects thereof, progressed less, but still farther than countries which had the lowest prospect of candidacy, that is, FSU countries.

3.2   Sequencing of Liberalisation and Institutional Development

One of the main reasons some analysts argued gradual reforms were better was that time was needed to put in place new market-enhancing institutions before fully liberalising markets (e.g. Roland and Verdier 1999). Kolodko (2000) was particularly critical of the Washington Consensus claiming its focus on liberalisation ignored institutions and lay behind the sharp fall in

---

[17] In the country groupings recall that Croatia and Slovenia have been included under Central Europe not SEE, for reasons described in analyses like Havrylyshyn (2006) and Tresiman (2014).

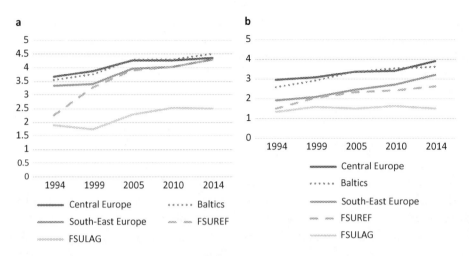

Fig. 11.5 TPI values by type: liberalisation and institutional development. Selected years: 1994–2014. Source: As in Fig. 11.4. Liberalisation and institutional elements defined in text

output in the first decade.[18] As noted, the aim of this chapter is not to assess these important transition debates, but rather to provide a broad picture of what actually happened. Therefore here I present some information on the time path of two types of reforms: those relating to market liberalising and those relating to institutional development.

The World Bank Governance Indicators in particular provide very detailed measures of institutional development, but the data generally start only in the late nineties. The TPI used above can be broken down into two separate components (LIB = liberalisation; INST = institutions), and has the advantage not only of being comparable in methodology, but of being available from the beginning of transition. Economic liberalisation (LIB) in Fig. 11.5a is the average of the sub-indicators of TPI covering small-scale privatisation, price liberalisation, and trade and foreign exchange liberalisations. Institutional development (INST) in Fig. 11.5b is the average of large-scale privatisation, enterprise restructuring and governance, competition policy, banking reform, and reform of securities markets and non-banking financial institutions. The EBRD and others have labelled these two sub-categories, respectively, as first- and second-generation reforms, a distinction widely used in the literature.

---

[18] Hartwell's (2013) book explores in detail the Kolodko thesis and concludes it was not the case that the International Financial Instituions (IFI) focus was solely on liberalising, nor did it have the consequence of delaying institutional development in the rapid reformers.

HMT (2016) has shown that despite the limited details of the TPI measures compared to others, they have a high degree of correlation.

The overarching conclusion to draw from Fig. 11.5 is that in all countries institutional development (right panel) lagged far behind liberalisation (left panel). Thus even the leaders in institutional development have not come close to achieving scores as impressive as they have achieved in terms of market liberalisation. However, for the countries of Central Europe, the gap was not very large with market liberalisation virtually completed at a score of 4.3, and institutions close behind at 3.9. The Baltic countries' liberalisation scores surpassed those of the CE by 2014, but lagged further behind on institutions, reaching only 3.5. Perhaps the most important observation is that the fastest institutional development took place in the same countries that moved early on market liberalisation.

Consider some individual countries (values not shown): all of the Baltic countries were close to each other from the beginning but Estonia was always in the lead. In the FSUREF group, Georgia lagged like the others until its 2003 Rose Revolution, INST rising from 2.1 to 3.0 in 2014.[19] Note as well that with the exception of the three laggards, FSULAG, the rest of the FSU eventually moved up quite high on the LIB scale, almost catching up , but on the INST scale remained very far behind. This includes perhaps the last to undertake a serious start on liberalisation, Ukraine, which until the mid-nineties was even less liberalised than the FSULAG group, but by 2010 was on par with the rest of the FSUREF, as well as the SEE group. But it remained very far behind the leaders on institutional development.

Related to the above trends are some of the developments one sees over time of much more detailed institutional indicators such as the Rule-of-Law (ROL) scores (measured by the World Bank's World Governance Indicators) and the Corruption Perception Index as measured by Transparency International in Berlin. I show only the latter in Fig. 11.6, which in effect measures not the degree of corruption but rather how well it is controlled; thus higher values signify less corruption. Arguably, good institutions are a policy input that should lead to good performance in various dimensions, including limited corruption. At the same time, formal laws/institutions that prohibit and punish corruption are widespread and equally seen in countries with high levels of corruption as in those with a low level. Therefore in practice many analysts suggest that the informal implementation of anti-corruption institutions is best measured by the results—that is, corruption levels.

---

[19] Its late catch-up is even more evident in the indicators for corruption discussed later—the Corruption Perceptions Index, moving from 134th position in 2004 to 51st in 2012, ahead of even some EU countries.

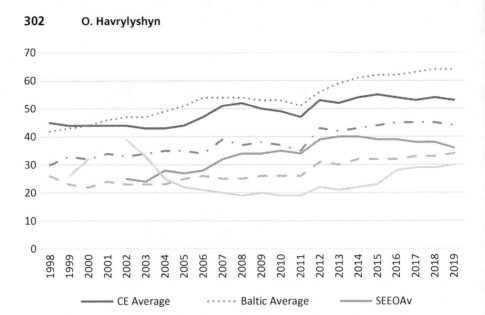

Fig. 11.6 Corruption Perception Index by group, 1998–2019. Source: Transparency International Website, Corruption Perception Index historical values: accessed April 22, 2020

This corruption indicator also shows that early liberalisers—CEB countries—scored best from the start and continued to improve. There is, however, an interesting difference between the Baltic and CE countries—while the latter saw greater achievements on institutional development, as Fig. 11.5 shows, in the case of the corruption indicator, the Baltics did far better throughout the period. Note also some difference between those that became EU members starting in 2004 for CE (except Croatia only in 2013) and Baltics , then in 2007 Bulgaria and Romania (SEEEEU). These three groups showed distinctly better achievements on controlling corruption than the other three.

The FSUREF countries achieved gradual but very limited improvement, though Russia and Ukraine, having reached scores of about 28.29 in the years 200–2005, stagnated afterwards, only recuperating these still low levels by the end of the period. Georgia was the exception after its 2004 Rose Revolution , moving steadily from similar levels to the high fifties by the end of the period. The FSULAG countries show strong improvement between 1998 and 2002, but this may have been due to a measurement problem.[20] Whatever the

---

[20] Until 2004, Transparency International did not have enough information to properly evaluate Turkmenistan—the FSULAG average was for the other two countries and both had better values.

explanation, after 2000, these lagging and very authoritarian countries continued to score very poorly on corruption.

The above data points to our next stylised facts:

SF8: Institutional development was clearly slower than liberalising reforms in all countries; however, it was not the gradual reformers who moved first on institutions—on the contrary, the countries that were fastest and went farthest on institutions are the very same that were early and rapid liberalisers.

SF9: While corruption levels in transition countries were from the beginning of the nineties much higher than in the market economies of Western Europe, they were much better in the CEB groups; over time the latter continually improved with the Baltics reaching levels comparable to European ones, while for the others significant improvement was observed only for EU membership candidates.

4   Trends in Democratisation

About 1990 both the Soviet camp countries and China set out on an analogous transformation, but there were two big differences. First, China was still a largely agrarian economy with a nascent industrial sector, while the Soviet area countries were for the most part quite industrialised—indeed, the consensus was they were over-industrialised. This is worth noting but will not be analysed further here. Second, China's transformation categorically excluded replacing the Communist Party monopoly by a more democratic system. In contrast, the countries that we focus on here all began a move towards more democracy—or at the least announced such an intention—of open elections and multi-party systems.

Many quantitative indices of democratisation have been compiled by political scientists even before the transition began, such as Polity Iv and the Freedom House Democracy Ratings. Both show broadly similar patterns, and I use the latter partly because in the early nineties Freedom House undertook a special effort to analyse the process of democratisation in the former communist region, scoring on several dimensions of the process (fairness of the election, freedom of the press, etc.). In Fig. 11.7, only the average overall score is shown, with 1.0 representing the fullest extent of democracy and 7.0 full authoritarian regimes or dictatorship.

The long-term trends are easy enough to distinguish. First, in the CEB, all countries saw significant early improvements in political freedoms reaching scores of about 2.0 by 2000, and continued to improve to values between 1.0

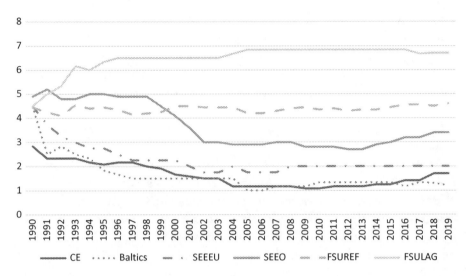

Fig. 11.7 Democracy scores by group, 1990–2019. Source: Freedom House, Democracy. Scores data: Accessed April 24, 2020

and 1.5 quite comparable to the leading democracies in the world. Second, at the opposite end are the three FSU laggard countries, with minimal democratisation to about 5.0 in the nineties, but then a reversal to near-authoritarian regimes.

Third, in the nineties the FSUREF and the SEEO region (South-East Europe EU candidates) were in between these two extremes—but after about 2000 their paths diverge—the former remaining in what one may characterise at best as a semi-democratic status, the latter slowly improving. Bulgaria and Romania (SEEEU) which began accession earlier show a much better record, starting at about the same level as the FSUREF, but steadily rising to catch up to the first wave of new members in the CEB. For the FSUREF group the flat line averaging the countries in the group hides a divergence between those like Russia, Kazakhstan, Armenia, Kyrgyzstan, Tajikistan, whose scores worsened after 2000 to levels of 5.0 to 6.0, and three cases with much better democracy scores between 3.0 and 4.0 : Georgia, Moldova and Ukraine. A sharp improvement came in Georgia with the Rose Revolution in 2004, and Ukraine in a more higgledy-piggledy path with its 2004 Orange and 2014 Euromaidan revolutions—and even more so its 2019 elections.

The reversal to more authoritarian regimes in the FSU countries other than the above three, not surprisingly, has led to doubts amongst political scientists about the perhaps premature declaration of "victory" of democracy over authoritarianism. Such doubts may have increased in recent years with the coming of so-called "illiberal democracy" in Hungary and Poland, reflected in the small but distinct upward tick in the CE trend line in Fig. 11.7 after 2017. This results from the change in scores of these two countries to values between 2.0 and 3.0—significant but still nowhere near the range of 6 to 7 for the authoritarian FSU regimes. This issue is beyond the remit of this chapter—though considered in other parts of the Handbook such as Chap. 27 on populism.

From the above scoring and time trends I draw the next stylised fact:

SF10: *The process of democratisation in post-communist countries has been quite varied; the strongest achievements of essentially democratic regimes have come to the new EU member countries, albeit some very recent slippage has occurred. In the FSU only a modest degree of democratisation was achieved in the nineties and with few exceptions there was a distinct reversal to authoritarian, but superficially electoral democracies. Georgia, Moldova and Ukraine have not fallen back, but are still far short of the standards in the CEB.*

A brief look at oligarchs and oligarchies.

The Greek term "oligarchy" forms part of the lexicon defining political regimes, and means rule by the few—as opposed to "democracy" meaning rule by the demos, that is, people. It is also widely known around the world that one outcome of the transition has been the creation of a group of oligarchs, or extremely rich capitalists. Giving some quantitative dimension to the extent of the oligarchy in transition is relevant because it affects both the economic trends and political evolution discussed earlier. A broad overview of the importance of oligarchs in different counties is provided by Fig. 11.8, which calculates a sort of "oligarch-intensity" ratio defined as a country's share of all "Forbes billionaires" in the world/country's share of world GDP. The values are readily available in the Forbes billionaire lists, and World Bank data bank, respectively. This measures not the wealth held in dollars, but just the number of billionaires; hence, it can only be considered a very broad-brush comparison. Further, it may underestimate the political power of the richest in small countries as surely having only a few hundred million in wealth can still make one powerful in Ukraine, and even more so Moldova, or the Kyrgyz Republic, or Slovenia. Such a fine analysis is beyond the scope of this chapter, but has been done by many analysts, for example, in the EBRD Transition Report for 2016, which concludes inter alia that in transition countries with a very high ratio, the main source of oligarch wealth is from resource exploitation, very different from the oligarch wealth basis in the rest of the world.

If all the world's billionaires were distributed in rough proportion to a country's economic size (GDP) the histogram of Fig. 11.8 would show all countries with a value of 1.0. This implies that countries where the value is

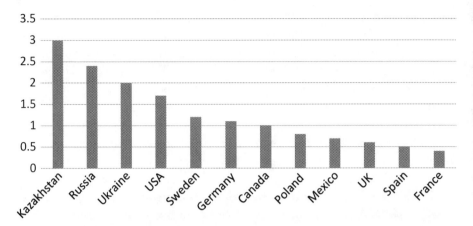

Fig. 11.8 Ratio: world share billionaires/share GDP, 2015. Source: Author's calculations based on Forbes Annual Report on Billionaires 2015 and World Bank data on GDP

above 1.0 have some special socio-political circumstances that allowed for a large concentration of wealth in a few hands and the higher the ratio the more one can say these circumstances are biased towards a privileged few. There is a widely known perception that in the FSU especially, insider favouritism and insider favouritism for privatisation of state assets has resulted in a high concentration of wealth and the rapid formation of very rich capitalists.

Broadly, the picture of Fig. 11.8 confirms this perception, with Kazakhstan, Russia and Ukraine showing ratios far above 1.0, even higher than that of the US. This also emphasises that in a global context the enormous formation of such concentrated wealth in such a short period is quite unique—other market economies have much lower ratios just above or just below 1.0—though the value of 1.2 for the pioneering welfare state Sweden may be a surprise. Perhaps these high ratios for FSU countries even underestimate concentration at the top; while all very wealthy individuals tend to hide some of this in safe havens, the huge values of capital flight estimated for the FSU suggest this tendency is even stronger among its rich.

The other important conclusion to draw is that transition countries in the Central European region are close to the notional "normal" of 1.0, and certainly far lower than the FSU cases. Havrylyshyn (2020, chap. 8) has calculated some numbers to compare the presence of billionaires as a proxy for oligarchy in CEB countries and the FSU in the period 2015–17. A few indicative numbers are given. While in Russia, Forbes counts eighty-three billionaires, Poland with GDP equalling 40% of Russia's shows four—if the intensity of oligarch formation in Poland had been as great as that in Russia, Poland should have not four but thirty-two billionaires. This is of course a synthetic counterfactual estimate, but is quite indicative of the very different nature of the capitalist environment of the two countries; Aslund (2018) thoroughly describes the non-competitive, insider-based crony "capitalism" of Russia, which the billionaire numbers seem to suggest did not prevail to the same degree in Poland and other CEB countries. Even Czechia with the largest number in CEB-six- is still proportinately far below Russia. However, one of them, President Andrej Babis, is a new political player there. In all the other countries of Central Europe, Baltics, South-East Europe no more than one Forbes billionaire is named.

From the above I posit the last stylised fact:

SF11: One outcome of transition has been the emergence of a new class of very rich capitalists—in itself not surprising as formerly communist societies now allowed private ownership, in effect, capitalism. However, in many countries of the FSU the extent of concentration of wealth into billionaire levels has been enormous and historically unique, earning these individuals a nefarious reputation as "oligarchs". Notably this tendency was far more muted in the countries to the west of the FSU.

5   Summary. Eleven Stylised Facts of Transition

This chapter has attempted to tell the story of thirty years of transition in an objective way with quantitative estimates of what happened in the form of conventional economic statistics like income per capita, but also many synthetic indicators like the state of democracy norms in a country. These have been summarised in eleven stylised facts, most of them with an elaboration of differences over time and across countries, giving us more than 500 words here just for such summaries. This may seem like a lot given the aim of stylisation is to give a succinct but still correct picture, but I proffer the thought that the process of post-communist transformation has been a momentous historical event occurring over a period of two to three decades in nearly thirty different countries, which should not be "Twitterised" into too few characters. Here I recap those stylised facts much more briefly.

1. *The nearly thirty countries of the region have become widely integrated into the global community.*
2. *Income declined in the nineties, recovered from 2000 surpassing Soviet levels. The duration and depth of decline was much less in the CEB groups, and the improvements much greater.*

3. *After thirty years there has been a considerable catch-up with European standards of living for all transition countries, but this is particularly strong for new EU members.*
4. *Income distribution deteriorated in the nineties reversing after 2000 CEB and SEE groups experienced less deterioration while in FSU countries Ginis reached values of .40 to .50, and in some remained high.*
5. *Social well-being as measured by HDI worsened initially especially in the FSU but again reversed and attained levels above those of Soviet years.*
6. *Twenty-five formerly communist countries have been effectively transformed into market economies, though FSU countries still lag behind.*
7. *The FSU lag in transformation coincides very closely with EU membership—new member countries have gone farthest, those with prospects of membership less so, but still farther than FSU countries.*
8. *Institutional development was slower than market-liberalising reforms in all countries; countries that were fastest and went farthest on institutions were the same that were early and rapid liberalisers.*
9. *Corruption levels were from the start much higher than in the market economies of Western Europe, but much better in the CEB groups; distinct improvement is visible from 2000 for those with EU membership or candidacy, but there has been little progress in the FSU.*
10. *Democratisation has been quite varied; new EU member countries have become effective democracies despite some recent slippage. In the FSU only a modest degree of democratisation was achieved in the nineties and with few exceptions—Georgia, Moldova, Ukraine—there has a strong reversal to authoritarian, but superficially electoral regimes.*
11. *An important parallel outcome of transition has been the emergence of a new class of very rich capitalists in FSU countries know widely as oligarchs. The extent of economic and political power these may have does not seem to occur as much in other countries of the West.*

If all this can be put in a nutshell even more succinctly, it might read as follows. There has been a tremendous amount of change in the entire region, lives are better for all citizens in many ways—materially, socially, politically, on personal freedoms. The degree of change is quite varied, however, being the greatest in the more western parts of the region. But even so, the aspirational motto so often uttered by people—"we want to live in a civilized country"—has been considerably fulfilled for all.

As a last word, let me point to some implications the transition event has for comparative economic analysis. Recall that at the outset many observers expressed the concern that there was an experience on how to move from capitalism to socialism, but none to guide us on how to reverse this—sometimes put into glib aphorisms like "you can make fish-soup from fish, but you can't make fish from fish soup", or no unscrambling of an omelette . In fact, it is now obvious you can—as the millions of "fish" citizens of the region now swimming in the civilised world would attest. This historical account of how different countries pursued transition provides clear examples of how it was done, what was done right, what was done wrong—a huge amount of well-described and well-quantified policy processes for comparative analysis. This provides rich material not only for comparative analysis of a historical nature, but for future needs of developing reform strategies. In a word, the three decades of reforms in nearly thirty countries with different histories and societies provide a treasure trove of expertise on how to do economic policy right.

Another useful perspective to summarise thirty years of transition is to compare the above stylised facts with those noted by Campos and Coricelli (2002), asking how an additional ten years changed things. They started by pointing to the sharp fall in output throughout the region. Here SF2 recognises this but adds two points: the initial decline was quite short-lived and far less severe in the countries of Central Europe and the Baltics; and in the next two decades GDP grew in all countries and in many quite substantially, resulting in considerable catch-up with Western Europe. Their second fact is that capital shrank—an aspect not addressed here. Their third and fourth facts refer to labour moving and trade being re-oriented; this is not only confirmed by the thirty-year evidence, but clearly this integration—or better re-integration—into the global community became even deeper after 2000, and comprised many dimensions of international flows, communications, migration, tourism and so on. Campos and Coricelli then note how the structure of output changed with manufacturing shares declining and those of services rising—again an aspect not covered here, but addressed in other Handbook chapters (e.g. Wachtel, 2020). Their sixth fact about the collapse of the Soviet regime institutions takes on a much more positive appearance as one looks more closely at the entire period: SF6, 7 and 8 emphasise that despite a slow start in the nineties on establishing market-based institutions, over the next twenty years this moved forward so that almost all countries can today be considered as effectively functioning albeit imperfect market regimes. Notably the greatest advances have been made in the non-FSU countries, in particular those that pursued EU membership requirements. One should add the point made in SF10: the latter group also achieved very high levels of democratisation—despite recent slippages, but in contrast most in the FSU reverted to more authoritarian regimes. This democratic reversion is one part of new facts after 2000 that are of a much more negative nature. SF9 and SF10 bring to the fore two important and related developments: a sharp increase in corruption in most FSU countries as well as a few others in the West, and the evolution of oligarchs as a powerful but negative force in the economics and politics of these countries. These last developments comprise the major challenges facing some post-communist countries in the future.

References

Berend, I. (2009). *From the Soviet Block to the European Union: The Economic and Social Transformation of Central and Eastern Europe Since 1973*. New York: Cambridge University Press.

Broadman, H. (2005). *From Disintegration to Reintegration: Eastern Europe and the Former Soviet Union in International Trade*. Washington, D.C.: World Bank.

Campos, N., & Coricelli, F. (2002). Growth in Transition: What We Know, What We Don't and What We Should. *Journal of Economic Literature, XI*, 793–836.

Campos, N., & Horvath, R. (2012). On the Irreversibility of Structural Reforms. *Economics Letters, 17.1*, 217–219.

Drabek, Z., & Benacek, V. (2013). Trade Reorientation and Global Integration, Chapter 13. In P. Hare & G. Turley (Eds.), *Handbook of the Economics and Political Economy of Transition* (pp. 167–180). London: Routledge.

Economist. (2018, April 21). Catching Up. 44.

Hartwell, C. (2013). *Institutional Barriers in the Transition to Market*. Houndmills, UK: Palgrave Macmillan.

Havrylyshyn, O., Meng, X., & Tupy, M. (2016). Twenty-five Years of Reforms in Post-Communist World: Rapid Reformers Outperformed the Gradualists. Washington D.C.: The CATO Institute. Policy Analysis Paper 795.

Havrylyshyn, O. (2006). *Divergent Paths in Post-Communist Transformation: Capitalism for All or Capitalism for the Few?* Houndmills, UK: Palgrave Macmillan.

Havrylyshyn, O. (2020). *Present at the Transition: An Inside Look at the Role of History, Politics and Personalities*. London: Cambridge University Press.

Kolodko, G. (2000). *Post Communist Transition. The Thorny Road*. Rochester: The University of Rochester Press.

Kornai, J. (1994). The Transformational Recession: The Main Causes. *Journal of Comparative Economics, 19*, 34–63.

Maddison, A. (2001). *The World Economy. A Millennial Perspective*. Paris: The OECD.

McCloskey, D. (1983). The Rhetoric of Economics. *The Journal of Economic Literature, 21*(2), 481–517.

Milanovic, B. (1998). *Income inequality and Poverty diring the Transition from Planned to Market Economy*. Washington, D.C.: The World Bank.

Milanovic, B. (2019). *Capitalism Alone. The Future of the System That Rules the World*. Cambridge, MA: The Belknap Press.

Roaf, J., Atoyan, R., Joshi, B., & Krogulski, K. (2014). *Twenty Five Years of Transition. Post-Communist Europe and the IMF.* Washington D.C.: The International Monetary Fund.

Roland, G., & Verdier, T. (1999). Transition and the Output Fall. *Economics of Transition, 7*(1), 1–28.

Shleifer, A., & Treisman, D. (2014). Normal Countries: The East 25 Years After Communism. *Foreign Affairs, 2014*, 25–41.

Stiglitz, J. (2019). *People, Power and Profits. Progressive Capitalism for an Age of Discontent.* New York: W.W. Norton and Company.

Treisman, D. (2014). Economic Reform After Communism: The Role of Politics, Ch.14. In A. Aslund & S. Djankov (Eds.), *The Great Rebirth: Lessons from the History of Capitalism Over Communism.* Washington, D.C.: The Peterson Institute.

UNDP. (1998). *Poverty In Transition.* New York: United Nations Development Program.

Wachtel, P. (2020). Are the Transition Economies Still in Transition? Chapter 16. In E. Douarin & O. Havrylyshyn (Eds.), *Palgrave Handbook of Comparative Economics.* Springer Nature.

12

The Importance of Domestic Commitment

Anders Åslund

1   Introduction

The outcomes of the economic transformations after communism have been remarkably different.[1] Almost all countries have become market economies with dominant private enterprise. There are only three exceptions—Belarus, Turkmenistan, and Uzbekistan, all three severe dictatorships. However, while the Central European and Baltic market economies are open and competitive, most of the post-Soviet countries can be characterized as crony capitalism, where the ruler distributes economic power and property to their relatives and friends. Some countries, such as Poland and Estonia, have more than doubled their GDP, while Ukraine, Moldova, Kyrgyzstan, and Tajikistan are about as poor as they were in 1989, according to World Bank statistics. In reality, however, many statistical flaws have understated the economic achievement substantially (Åslund 2002, 121–140).

These developments were not obvious, nor were their determinants. One of the most famous mistaken forecasts was a 1992 Deutsche Bank report that rated Ukraine as having by far the best prospects among the post-Soviet republics. It had so much going for it: large natural resources, good geographic

---

[1] I have discussed the political economy of postcommunist reform in numerous publications, notably in Åslund (1992, 2002, 2013).

A. Åslund (✉)
Georgetown University, Washington, DC, USA
e-mail: aaslund@atlanticcouncil.org

© The Author(s) 2021
E. Douarin, O. Havrylyshyn (eds.), *The Palgrave Handbook of Comparative Economics*,
https://doi.org/10.1007/978-3-030-50888-3_12

location, good infrastructure, and a well-educated labor force with many engineers (Havrylyshyn 2014, 165). None of these factors helped. This was a perfect example of misguided analysis.

The best contrary example is Estonia. It had minimal resources and suffered a massive terms of trade shock when it had to buy Russian oil and gas at world market prices. It experienced a major external shock in a complete geographical transformation of its foreign trade. Even so, Estonia did extremely well, because unlike Ukraine in the early transition it pursued very radical and sensible economic policies.

Many draw conclusions from history, culture, and religion, but no two countries could be more similar than Romania and Moldova, which essentially were the same ethnically and linguistically and both were predominantly orthodox Christians. Yet, Moldova has done far worse than Romania all along. Daron Acemoglu and James Robinson point to the differences between South and North Korea. North Korea had the resources; South Korea eventually opted for good policies (Acemoglu and Robinson 2012).

These examples show that the decisive factors especially in the early transition were not resources but policy and behind good policy lies political commitment to good policy. This chapter is devoted to policy commitment, which is closely related to the political economy of reform. The factors contributing to domestic commitment are many. Do people identify with their nation? How strong is civil society and the intelligentsia? Has a country experienced a real democratic breakthrough? What kind of political leader has emerged? How strong is the reform team? How good is the reform program? In order to reinforce the domestic commitment, timely and relevant international support is vital. Are founding parliamentary elections held in time? How are the political skills of the reformers?

2   Degree of National Cohesion

Often the most important factors are being neglected because they are taken for granted or they do not pertain to the standard political paradigm. Such a matter is national cohesion or identity. After World War II, Westerners have been shy in praising nationalism, while former colonies tend to see these matters more clearly.

But the population of a country in crisis needs to identify itself as a nation in order to bother about the development of that country. Few factors were as important for the success of economic reform as the degree of national cohesion. In previously independent countries, this might appear self-evident, but in the former Soviet Union and Yugoslavia the degree of success depended greatly on the sense of national cohesion.

Poland and Hungary were the two purest nation-states, and it was no surprise that they were early and successful reformers. As the Czech Republic and Slovakia parted company in early 1993 they also became successful reformers, admittedly Slovakia did so much later in 2003–2004. Bulgaria and Romania had other problems.

In the former Soviet Union, Estonia, Latvia, and Lithuania displayed the strongest national commitment, which carried over to become a strong commitment to economic reform. Estonia's prime minister Mart Laar noticed: "The strong national feeling among Estonians was vital. National pride helped us overcome the first difficult period of the reforms" (Laar 2014, 78). The other strong nation-states were Armenia and Georgia, though they were impeded by war. In Ukraine and Moldova, a substantial part of the population has strong nationalist sentiment, but they did not represent a majority, which led to confusion about policy aims.

Russia is difficult to classify because it has a strong sense of nation, but does it pertain to the Russian ethnic or linguistic nation or to the Russian empire? Many Russians also harbored old imperialist ambitions, and militant national minorities in Northern Caucasus, notably the Chechens, confused the Russian national idea (Clover 2016). The remaining post-Soviet countries had little sense of nationalism, which was not to their benefit in reforms. Their elites favored themselves rather than working for their nations.

3   Strength of Civil Society and Intelligentsia

Civil society and intelligentsia are difficult to measure but easy to feel. They are also difficult to separate. Civil society implies public engagement, while intelligentsia means independently thinking people of quality. Both were of great importance for the commitment and success of reform.

Any traveler to Eastern Europe under communism would agree that Hungarians and Poles were the freest and most outspoken people. Hungarians used to say: "We are the jolliest barrack in the camp." Unlike what Hungarians and Poles used to claim, this was not an inherited feature of theirs but a result of specific political events under communism. The bloody uprising in Budapest in November 1956 taught Moscow and the Hungarian communists to tread carefully with Hungarians. Multiple popular protests in Poland in

1956, 1968, 1970, 1976, and 1980 taught Moscow and the Polish communist party the same lesson. Thanks to impressive popular political resistance against strict communism, Poland and Hungary had good traditional universities and substantial exchange with the West. In the 1980s, millions of their citizens could visit the West, and often work or study there. These two countries benefited from their citizens' integration with the West.

By contrast, the easy subjugation of Czechoslovakia after the Prague Spring in 1968 taught Moscow and the Czechoslovak communists that Czechs and Slovaks could be repressed, allowing little civil society to develop. Bulgaria and Romania were strict communist dictatorships. Few intellectuals from these countries had studied in the West or had spent time there. The lesson was that obstinate opposition bred comparative personal and intellectual freedom and thus more civil society. That Czechoslovakia was comparatively wealthier and had remained a democracy throughout the interwar period turned out to be of less importance.

In the three Baltic states, nationalism, intellectual freedom, and civil society went together. They were strongest in Estonia, tightly followed by Lithuania and Latvia. Each of these three nations had lost about one-third of its population in and after World War II through war, repression, deportation, and emigration, but this did not kill but rather sustain their civil society, which was strong enough to support a substantial intelligentsia.

Within the former Soviet Union excluding the Baltics, Russia undoubtedly had the strongest civil society and intelligentsia. Being the center of an old and great imperial power, Russia actually allowed more intellectual freedom for its elite than it did in any of its dependencies.

4   Democratic Breakthrough or Regime Change

Reforms cannot be undertaken at will but only at an opportune time. Hardly any country carries out reforms in the absence of crisis, though many countries do not reform even in the worst of crisis. Nor do old establishments that have caused the problems carry out reforms. A major political breakthrough is a necessary but not sufficient precondition for serious reform. In the postcommunist world a democratic breakthrough was usually necessary before a serious reform attempt could be undertaken.

Governments change rather frequently, and it is difficult to assess what is a real regime change. As communism ended, countries did so in very different fashions. In Poland and Hungary, the old communist rulers agreed on a gradual democratization with the opposition at a roundtable, which appears the ideal change. In East Germany and Czechoslovakia, the old regimes were overthrown by peaceful mass protests. The three Baltic countries had reasonably democratic elections in 1990, which were won by the national people's front in each country. However, they gained national power only after Moscow recognized their independence in August 1991 after the failed communist coup in Moscow. All these countries experienced a clear democratic breakthrough.

In many countries, the situation was unclear. Bulgaria had a palace coup that unleashed gradual democratization; Romania saw a disorganized burst of violence; in most Soviet republics, democracy burgeoned but it did not quite flourish and debates persist whether any democratic breakthrough actually took place. Five republics saw no democratization, namely, Azerbaijan, Kazakhstan, Tajikistan, Turkmenistan, and Uzbekistan. The old regime persisted (Åslund 2013, 27–35).

The essence of a democratic breakthrough is that the nation as a whole gets a big say. It means a mobilization of the nation. At the same time, it forces the old establishment into submission, though only for a brief period, usually a few months. Poland's great reformer Leszek Balcerowicz has named this period a time of "extraordinary politics," when reformers can make many decisions that are otherwise blocked by vested interests (Balcerowicz 1994).

A democratic breakthrough needs to be followed by swift political reforms to provide a basis for the economic reforms. As the great Czech reform leader Vaclav Klaus put it: "We considered economic and political reforms interconnected and indivisible" (Klaus 2014, 57).

5   Why Speed Was So Important

Reforms succeed or fail depending on the speed of action. A democratic breakthrough opened up a brief window of action for the reformers. In that short time, they needed to act fast enough to establish the bases of a new political and economic system. If they failed to do so, the old elite would come back and it was set to transform its old political power into personal wealth.

In a seminal article, Joel Hellman formulated the essence of failed transition "The Winner Takes All" (Hellman 1998). The essential fight of the transition period was for or against rent seeking. The main source of rent seeking in the early transition was arbitrage between low state-controlled prices and several times higher market prices for commodities, computers, and hard currency. The early big fortunes in Russia were made on buying oil domestically for $1 per ton and selling it abroad for $100 per ton (Åslund 2013, 58). Such privileged trades required good connections in the old system, which the old elite possessed. With such profits the old powerful and newly wealthy could buy the state and avert the evolution of democracy and institutions expressing the popular will including a commitment to reform.

In the early transition, most reformers feared popular pressures rather than pressures from the old elite. Before the collapse of communism, Poland, Hungary, and Russia had experienced great wage pressures, strikes, and demands for far too great social expenditures financed with budget deficits. The old elite, on the contrary, was quiet and fearful.

Immediately after the collapse of communism, however, the popular pressures eased. The population at large was committed to postcommunist reform, calling for a "normal society" and a "return to Europe." Quicker than anybody anticipated, the old elite regrouped in state companies and the state apparatus, finding unanticipated sources of riches. They all had reasons to oppose reforms, but they were well advised to do so covertly in the name of reform. That was why the speed of reform was so important for the expression of domestic commitment for reform. In East Germany, the demonstrators formulated the essence with the slogan: "We are the people!" (Ash 1990).

The task of reform was to find people, institutions, and policies that could embody the popular endeavors. Much intellectual energy was being wasted on a discussion on fast or gradual reform. The obvious answer was that reform should be undertaken as fast as possible, if reform was to be successful. Mart Laar put it most succinctly: "To wait means to fail."

6   Political Leadership

Political leadership was of enormous importance, and the political leaders varied greatly. Some were strong but not focused. Others were traditionalist and concentrated on family enrichment. Some did not know what they were doing.

Both at the time and in hindsight, Polish prime minister Tadeusz Mazowiecki and Czech president Vaclav Havel looked like good democratic leaders. They did their jobs, leaving it to others to pursue economic reforms, while loyally offering the necessary political support. Estonia's prime minister Mart Laar and Georgia's president Mikheil Saakashvili were both political and reform leaders. Among the postcommunist leaders, none appeared weaker and more confused than Ukraine's president Leonid Kravchuk, who remains quite a nice man. Few have anything negative to say about him as a person, but he did not lead and embraced no idea. The strongest and most enigmatic leader was undoubtedly Russia's president Boris Yeltsin. He was fearless but wavered on policy focus. The presidents of half a dozen countries—Azerbaijan, Belarus, Kazakhstan, Tajikistan, Turkmenistan, and Uzbekistan—never aspired to much reform, and in many countries no political leader stood out.

The main task of a political leader is of course to lead. He or she needs to embody the domestic commitment to reform. This commitment should result in new political and economic institutions as well as sound economic policy, which is a tall order. If that is not the case, as in all of Central Asia apart from Kyrgyzstan, no reform can be forthcoming. The political leader also needs to appoint a strong reform team and commit to a credible reform program. In countries with not very successful reforms, the political leaders have tended to hesitate and wait, compromising with the old elite, when they should have pushed ahead.

The biggest flaw in political leadership has been outright corruption and it has been frightfully common. The sad judgment on many political leaders is that they entered office with the intention of enriching themselves while others arrived at that ambition eventually. The second problem has been weakness, while the third and less important has been limited understanding of what is needed.

7   Reform Team

Major reforms are usually carried out by a small group of top policymakers, typically professional economists around the minister of finance. Leszek Balcerowicz, Vaclav Klaus, Yegor Gaidar in Russia, and Ivan Miklos in Slovakia were all ministers of finance, though also deputy prime ministers at times.

In the early postcommunist transformation, will, competence, and insight were vital. In the Soviet Union, only Russia and the Baltic states had economists of sufficient understanding of market economies. The insightful policymakers did not have to be many, as the successes of Balcerowicz and Klaus show. All too often people talk about the need to build "capacity" for reform, while the truth is that only a handful of truly good people are needed for the actual decision-making. Education and training are vital, but if corruption prevails in top offices, good well-educated people will depart for the West because they do not want to work with the corrupt.

It is vital that the reform leaders have a strong commitment to reform. They are the ultimate bearers of that commitment, while they depend on support from the political leader. All the truly successful reform leaders, notably

Balcerowicz, Klaus, and Laar, were extremely stubborn. Moreover, they knew that statistics are poor in the transition between two systems. Therefore, they were guided by ideas rather than data (Balcerowicz 2014; Klaus 2014; Laar 2002).

Strong commitment to fundamental reforms is the opposite of compromise, because no compromise is possible in a fight between two systems, because it was a choice between two opposing systems. The state bureaucracy had many reasons to oppose a radical reform program, because it would deprive the old establishment of its power. Worse, even the human capital of the old elite would become obsolete. Bureaucrats easily colluded with secret service officers, state enterprise managers, and Communist Party officials. As Jeffrey Sachs put it: "Populist politicians will try to hook up with coalitions of workers, managers and bureaucrats in hard-hit sectors to slow or reverse the adjustment" (Sachs 1990).

For the sake of democracy, the reformers had to disarm the old elite through radical reform. The abortive coup in August 1991 in Moscow and the armed uprising by the predemocratic Russian parliament in October 1993 illustrated the threat of a bureaucratic counterrevolution. Jeffrey Sachs summarized the radicals' view of the politics of transition: "There is typically little consensus on what should be done, pessimism is rife, and the reformers' hold on power and on policy is tenuous." He refuted the idea that reformers succeed by constructing a "social consensus" and he underlined the degree of confusion, anxiety, and conflicting opinions at the time of any major reform (Sachs 1994, 504). In Poland in 1989, as in Germany in 1948, there was no consensus, and consensus was no precondition of successful reform. On the contrary, it arose out of successful reforms.

The reformers should not compromise with their sworn enemies but hold their own as long as they have a majority of the population behind them and deliver results. The most stubborn and eloquent were the winners.

Daniel Treisman has made an interesting attempt to rank the reform leaders by how much countries proceeded in reform as measured by the European Bank for Reconstruction and Development index during a certain period of intense early reforms. In this fashion, he establishes the three real reforms leaders as Russia's deputy prime minister Yegor Gaidar, Poland's Leszek Balcerowicz, and Bulgaria's prime minister Dimitar Popov, while the worst was Ukraine's president Leonid Kravchuk (Treisman 2014, 292). While neat, Laar and Klaus should clearly be among the top together with Balcerowicz, while Popov appeared more of a caretaker. The European Bank for Reconstruction and Development (EBRD) measures are not very precise, although we have no better measurement. The choice of time becomes inevitably spurious and the starting points vary greatly. Ultimately, many factors have an impact. That is the very point of this chapter, emphasizing how there are many aspects that determine a country's reform commitment rather than merely focusing on the leader.

Who were the most committed reform leaders? Two political leaders stand out: Mart Laar and Mikheil Saakashvili. In most countries, however, it was the minister of finance who was the real reform leader, though covered and supported by the top political leader. The two most obvious economic reformers were Leszek Balcerowicz and Vaclav Klaus. On the opposite side were the outright enemies of reform. The obvious cases are Turkmenistan's president Saparmurat Niyazov, Uzbekistan's president Islam Karimov, Tajikistan's president Emomali Rahmon, and Belarus's president Aleksandr Lukashenko. Needless to say, the anti-reformers lasted much longer because they were strict authoritarians. The real name of their game is kleptocracy, concentrating as much wealth as possible with the ruler, his family, and court.

8   Reform Program

Basically, all market-oriented economists had the same goal of a normal economy. All the reform programs are related to John Williamson's Washington Consensus (Williamson 1990). In the West, a debate erupted between gradualists and radical reformers. They by and large had the same goal, even if the degree of regulation and state ownership certainly varied, but those were not the issues discussed. Instead, the focus was on social cost. Would the social cost be greater or smaller if reforms were radical? Did any absolute limit exist to the degree of suffering people were prepared to take in terms of unemployment, output fall, or income fall?

Radical reformers such as Balcerowicz, Klaus, and Laar insisted that the key was that people saw the light at the end of the tunnel, that they saw that the transformation worked. Therefore, they wanted to move as fast and comprehensively as possible and rejected the very idea of the sequencing of reforms, which by definition meant that policymakers should hold back on some reforms that they were technically ready to implement. Their motto was that you do it as soon as you are able to do so, while accepting that not everything could be done at the same time.

Many Western thinkers of political economy, mainly political scientists but also theoretical economists, adopted a very different approach, wanting to minimize the social costs by moving slowly. The most prominent of them was probably Adam Przeworski, a leading scholar of comparative politics, who published an influential book *Democracy and the Market* in 1991. His ideas can be summarized in three postulates. *Przeworski's* first postulate was that democracy had to justify itself through material achievements: "To evoke compliance and participation, democracy must generate substantive outcomes: It must offer all the relevant political forces real opportunities to improve their material welfare" (Przeworski 1991, 32). Implicitly, he presumed that people opted for democracy for the sake of economic welfare, not for the sake of freedom.

Przeworski's second postulate was that people demanded quick results. "Can structural economic transformation be sustained under democratic conditions, or must either reforms or democracy be sacrificed?" (Przeworski 1991, 138). His underlying thought was, "Even if the post-reform system would be more efficient … a transient deterioration of material conditions may be sufficient to undermine either democracy or the reform process" (Przeworski 1991, 137).

His third postulate was that "the social cost is higher under the radical strategy, where social cost is defined as the cumulative decline in consumption during the period of transition" (Przeworski 1991, 163). "Inflation is likely to flare up again and again under inertial pressures. Unemployment, even if temporary, is difficult to tolerate. Increasing inequality stokes conflicts" (Przeworski 1991, 189).

Finally, he presumed that the threat to democracy came from a dissatisfied population. In his 1995 book, Przeworski returned with an even more devastating judgment: "We have been critical of the standard neoliberal recipes since we believe that they are faulty in three fundamental ways: They induce economic stagnation, they incur unnecessarily large social costs, and they weaken the nascent democratic institutions" (Przeworski 1995, 85). He assumed that "the continuing material deprivation, the technocratic style of policy making, and the ineffectiveness of the representative institutions undermine popular support for democracy" (Przeworski 1991, 189–190). Many political scientists shared his assumptions, but they do not appear to have had much relation to reality. By contrast, the outstanding political scientist Larry Diamond pointed out that people see democracy as a value in itself and do not judge it only by economic results (Diamond 1999).

9   International Support

It might appear contradictory to bring up international support when discussing domestic commitment, but it is vital. International support in the early part of a transformative reform consists of three parts—advise, financing of macroeconomic stabilization, and market access.

Advise is cheap but essential. A new reforming government encounters many problems that other countries have experienced before, notably how to control high inflation. Such knowledge should be imported. A few advisers at the top of a new government can do the job. The International Monetary Fund (IMF) possesses the knowledge, but each government needs its own trusted advisers who can work with the IMF. Any mistake deriving from ignorance can be very costly for reformers and can scare the public away from badly needed reforms.

In the early stage of reforms, the most important international action is macroeconomic financing. Without international financing covering the financing gap in the budget and the current account, any reform is doomed. Libertarians have long denigrated international financial institutions, claiming that free market solutions are preferable. However, in a serious financial crisis all forms of nongovernmental financing dry up. Only the IFIs (International Financial Institutions) and governments remain. Therefore, they have to stand up and deliver sufficient financing in time. One reason why Poland, Czechoslovakia, and the Baltic states succeeded was that they all received sufficient international financing just in time. Admittedly, the amounts needed were relatively humble, but they were necessary and arrived in time. The success of reform in these countries was never as secure as many representatives of Poland and the Czech Republic have claimed later on.

Russia stands out as the most tragic case: It had a decent reform plan at the end of 1991, a strong political leader, and an impressive reform team, but no international support for its macroeconomic stabilization was forthcoming in 1992 (Sachs 1994). As a consequence, the public respect for the reformers and the domestic commitment to reform faltered never to return.

In the longer term, market access is vital, but only after macroeconomic stabilization has been secured. In the early postcommunist transformation, the European Union divided the postcommunist world in two parts through its trade policy. Central and Eastern Europe, including the Baltic states, gained early great access to the vast EU market, while the former Soviet republics received minimal access. Thus, the Central Europeans could achieve their "return to Europe," which was immensely popular and greatly contributed to the commitment to reform. The former Soviet republics, by contrast, did not get anything that reinforced the anyhow weak commitment to reform (Åslund 2013, 318–323).

Jeffrey Sachs summarized the role of international assistance elegantly: "Of course, foreign aid is not the main factor in economic success. The reforms themselves are the key. My argument is that foreign aid is critical to helping the reforms themselves take hold" (Sachs 1994, 504). Most of these countries started from a position of depleted international reserves, excessive debt service, and, in the case of Poland and Bulgaria, excessive foreign debt. To give financial stabilization a chance, a country needed to replenish its currency reserves and be able to manage its foreign debt service. "The market cannot do it all by itself; international help is critical" (Sachs 1994, 504).

10   Founding Elections

Politics after a democratic breakthrough pursues a typical pattern. At the time of the democratic rupture, the dominant opposition forces have usually united in a popular front—Solidarity in Poland, the Civic Democratic Party in the Czech Republic, the National Fronts in the three Baltic states, and Democratic Russia in Russia. The aim of these anti-regime parties was to break the old regime to the benefit of freedom and democracy. In terms of ideology and economic policy, their members had very different views. As time passed and democracy was ascertained, these other elements came to play a greater role, and they split the National Fronts. Over time they all became fragmented by ideology and personalities.

Therefore, it was vital to hold early "founding elections" that provided a base for the newly formed political parties (McFaul 2001). Unfortunately, the importance of timing was poorly understood at the time. Several countries got it right, with parliamentary elections within a year or so after the democratic breakthrough notably in Hungary (March–April 1990), Czechoslovakia (June 1990), and Estonia (September 1992). Countries that held their first parliamentary elections more than two years after the democratic breakthrough were Poland (October 1991), Russia (December 1993), Latvia (June 1993), and Ukraine (March 1994) (Åslund 2002, 379). The reasons for the delayed founding elections varied. In Poland, Solidarity had agreed to keep the old establishment in government at a roundtable. In the former Soviet Union, old dysfunctional Soviet constitutions were given undue consideration.

With their early founding elections, Hungary, the Czech Republic, Slovakia, and Estonia established sizable political parties that were institutionalized and lasting, while their party fragmentation was and has remained limited. The worst example of party fragmentation was the Polish election of 1991, where Solidarity that had acted as one political party in the predemocratic elections in June 1989 split into a score of different parties. The eventual Polish coalition government consisted of no less than ten parties. Russia represented another danger of delayed elections, namely, the reaction of hard-core nationalists and communists, the red-brown coalition. Ukraine, finally, offered a third conundrum of late elections, namely, no order whatsoever, neither parties nor policies. The outcome was the most business-dominated parliament in any postcommunist party, which did not promote economic development but rent seeking.

For the population at large, early elections after a major political change is strongly demanded. It is a matter of legitimacy of the rulers, which is vital for the public commitment in the policies being pursued. After the public has expressed its view through an election, it is more likely to stay committed.

Many other electoral elements are also important, such as the electoral system, but these variables are not independent. The later elections have been held, the stronger the rent-seeking interests have grown, and they are prone to buy the politics. In 1994, many in Ukraine took pride in the many businessmen who had been elected to parliament, but soon they realized that the businessmen had entered parliament to make money on politics rather than trying to improve their nation.

11   Political Skills

One of the most evasive political factors is political skill, but we all know how important it is. It is one of these phenomena that you do not know how to measure, but you know it when you see it.

Most reform leaders identified themselves as economists and technocrats, being contemptuous of politics. Only after some time in government did they start seeing themselves as politicians. As a consequence, they focused on the substance of policies, while neglecting the public promotion of these policies. Therefore, most of them were not very successful as politicians. The Yegor Gaidar reform team came into office calling themselves a kamikaze team, which detracted from their credibility and tenacity.

Among the great reformers, Vaclav Klaus stands out as the most skillful politician. He started as minister of finance, and he went on to be a two-term prime minister and two-term president. Needless to say, he was an astute politician, and many of his tricks are worthy of attention. From the outset, he took Saturdays off and went out to one little town or the other, where he sat down talking to ordinary people, explaining his policies, and developing his popular pedagogic skills. He simplified. In his public advocacy he focused on ten theses and he repeated these ad nauseam. He emphasized that the "economy had to rid itself of its inefficient parts, which had become untenable under the new circumstances" and that the "transformation recession" was no normal recession but an inevitable consequence of communism. Therefore, output would first contract, but then it would rise faster than people dared to hope for. Before the price liberalization, he told people that prices would rise sharply but would soon level off and then fall gradually. He was always asked by how much, but unlike most other reformers, he avoided making any statement by indicating how much the prices would rise (Klaus 2014, 61–62). That was exactly what happened thanks to strict fiscal and monetary policy, so nobody could say that he had been wrong.

Klaus prepared the Czech people for hard times in the near future to achieve better welfare in the more distant future. He explained the mechanisms of the transformation in simple terms and he avoided making any forecasts with numbers. It helped that he had a good sense of humor. Thus, he maintained a strong Czech commitment to reform. The drawback was that Klaus for too long avoided necessary political adjustments, such as change of exchange rate policy, or greater details in policy, such as regulation of financial markets. But those problems arose much later.

12   Conclusions: Domestic Commitment for Economic Reform Is Vital for Success

The conventional wisdom of international economic assistance teaches that profound economic reform cannot be imposed from outside. The IMF or the World Bank cannot implement reforms in any country, however small or weak it may be. Reforms can only be carried out by the government in the country in question. The postcommunist period has offered us a wonderful set of countries with quite similar preconditions that developed in surprisingly different ways. Some countries have been highly successful, while others have failed. Some countries appear to have secured sound market economies, while others have got stuck in under-reform traps (Åslund 2013, 252–258).

In their captivating book *Why Nations Fail*, Daron Acemoglu and James Robinson have clarified why some countries succeed and other fail. They have captured the standard picture of a squirrel's wheel: Success breeds success, and failure breeds failure. The decisive factor is the political, legal, and economic institutions. The problem with their account, however, is that they do not explain how countries may change their track, and that is what successful postcommunist transformation is about.

A fundamental thesis of this chapter is that domestic commitment cannot be a matter of the old rulers. The ruling stratum in an authoritarian rent-seeking or captive state wants to maintain the status quo. Any reform will reduce their powers and wealth. Why would anybody want that? Singapore under Lee Kuan Yew is the only known example of a modern benevolent authoritarian, and that is a tiny city state. Singapore is an outlier best ignored. The Democratic Republic of Congo is a much more normal authoritarian state. A normal semi-developed state is an authoritarian kleptocracy, as Russia, Belarus, Kazakhstan, Azerbaijan, Tajikistan, Turkmenistan, and Uzbekistan are best described. Eventually, their dictators may die or lose power. That is the time they deserve our greater attention.

It is the other postcommunist countries that are of most interest today, those that have completed impressive reforms, most of Central Europe, or those whose doors are still open, such as Armenia, Georgia, Moldova, Ukraine, and most of the Balkans. This chapter has discussed the relative importance of the various factors that may impact their inclination to reform. Of critical importance is the domestic commitment to reform, which in turn depends on many factors of different weight. The starting point is that nothing can happen until a real democratic breakthrough or regime change takes place.

The direction of democratization is not obvious. Two prior elements need to exist, namely, a strong civil society, which can be understood as a broad popular education, and an intelligentsia, an intellectual elite. Both elements are required to create a society with a domestic commitment to reform.

Whatever happens, people usually blame or credit the political leader, while academic political scientists tend to play down the importance of a political leader. Having participated in numerous transitions, my main conclusion is that nothing is as important as the political leader. The problem is that in polite society we do not actually discuss whether or not the leader was honest. When history will eventually be written, after all the leaders have died, we shall finally receive an honest account of who was honest and worked for his country, and who was only interested in his personal wealth. If we try to do this today, we shall only be sued for libel because of the restrictive US and UK libel laws that minimize the freedom of speech.

After the quality of the political leader, timely and sufficient international financing is probably the most important factor for the maintenance of domestic commitment for reform. The amount of financing needed varies greatly, $1 billion for Poland or for all three Baltic states, but $25 billion for Russia. The point is that the needed amount needs to be given in time, otherwise reforms fail and with it domestic commitment for reform. Arguably, the third important element is founding elections.

The remaining elements appear more obvious. A competent reform team is needed. As John Williamson pointed out in 1994, it usually consists of nationals from the elite who have been educated abroad and have acquired sufficient distance from the national elite. Their strength is not connectivity but knowledge and integrity (Williamson 1994). Similarly, John Williamson summarized the obvious reform program of macroeconomic stability, deregulation, and privatization (Williamson 1990).

The ultimate question is what factor is most important. The general answer is that several of the factors need to be present to a certain extent. The least understood point is probably the need for a certain national cohesion, where the Baltic countries excelled. The need for a democratic or political breakthrough is clear and vital. Speed has also proven vital. Similarly, international financial assistance was vital and not well comprehended. Also, the need for early founding elections enjoys limited appreciation.

With regard to political leadership, reform leadership, and public commitment, however, one can see a certain balance. A peculiarity at the time was the very limited understanding of elementary economics in the Soviet Union. It was difficult to understand then how the old communists thought, and today it is virtually incomprehensible. Political leaders such as Prime Minister Tadeusz Mazowiecki and Lech Walesa in Poland and President Lennart Meri in Estonia did not take the lead for the reforms themselves, but they provided reliable coverage for their reformers. In the three Baltic countries the popular pressure for radical economic reforms was probably the greatest, because it was identified with national independence. If we could measure the public commitment to reform properly, Estonia would certainly come out on top, followed by Lithuania and Latvia in that order. An Estonian saying goes: "A national currency is the best border to Russia." Regardless of leaders, who were not bad, the Baltic countries could only go in one direction because of the strong popular commitment to reform. The same cannot be said about Central Europe, where the fear of Russia was no longer an organizing element. Curiously, in hindsight the reform program looks pretty obvious, while it consumed a lot of discussions at the time. After all, all successful market economies look pretty similar.

Thus, to sum up, the crucial factors appear to be some national cohesion, reasonable public understanding, a clear political break reinforced by early elections, reasonable political leader and preferably a strong reform leader, and international financial support, while the essence of the reform program and political skills appear just complementary.

References

Acemoglu, D., & Robinson, J. (2012). *Why Nations Fail: The Origins of Power, Prosperity and Poverty*. New York: Crown.

Ash, T. G. (1990). *We the People: The Revolution of '89 Witnessed in Warsaw, Budapest, Berlin & Prague*. Cambridge: Granta Books.

Åslund, A. (1992). *Post-Communist Economic Revolutions: How Big a Bang?* Washington, DC, and Westview: The Center for Strategic and International Studies.

Åslund, A. (2002). *Building Capitalism: The Transformation of the Former Soviet Bloc*. New York: Cambridge University Press.

Åslund, A. (2013). *How Capitalism Was Built: The Transformation of Central and Eastern Europe, Russia, and Central Asia* (2nd ed.). New York: Cambridge University Press.

Balcerowicz, L. (1994). Understanding Postcommunist Transitions. *Journal of Democracy, 5*(4), 75–89.

Balcerowicz, L. (2014). Poland: Stabilization SNF Reforms under Extraordinary and Normal Politics. In A. Åslund & S. Djankov (Eds.) The Great Rebirth: Lessons from the Victory of Capitalism over Communism. Washington, DC: Peterson Institute for International Economics. (pp. 17–38).

Clover, C. (2016). *Black Wind, White Snow: The Rise of Russia's New Nationalism*. New Haven: Yale University Press.

Diamond, L. (1999). *Developing Democracy: Towards Consolidation*. Baltimore, MD: John Hopkins University Press.

Havrylyshyn, O. (2014). Ukraine: Greatest Hopes, Greatest Disappointments. In A. Åslund & S. Djankov (Eds.) The Great Rebirth: Lessons from the Victory of Capitalism over Communism. Washington, DC: Peterson Institute for International Economics. (pp. 165–184).

Hellman, J. S. (1998). Winners Take All: The Politics of Partial Reform in Postcommunist Transitions. *World Politics, 50*(2), 203–234.

Klaus, V. (2014). Czechoslovakia and the Czech Republic: The Spirit and Main Contours of the Postcommunist Transformation. In A. Åslund & S. Djankov (Eds.) The Great Rebirth: Lessons from the Victory of Capitalism over Communism. Washington, DC: Peterson Institute for International Economics. (pp. 53–71).

Laar, M. (2002). *Little Country That Could.* London: Centre for Research into Post-Communist Economies.

Laar, M. (2014). Estonia: The Most Radical Reforms. In A. Åslund & S. Djankov (Eds.) *The Great Rebirth: Lessons from the Victory of Capitalism over Communism.* Washington, DC: Peterson Institute for International Economics. (pp. 73–87).

McFaul, M. (2001). *Russia's Unfinished Revolution: Political Change from Gorbachev to Putin.* Ithaca, NY: Cornell University Press.

Przeworski, A. (1991). *Democracy and the Market.* New York: Cambridge University Press.

Przeworski, A. (1995). *Sustainable Democracy.* New York: Cambridge University Press.

Sachs, J. D. (1990). What Is to Be Done? *The Economist, January, 13,* 19–24.

Sachs, J. D. (1994). Life in the Economic Emergency Room. In J. Williamson (Ed.), *The Political Economy of Policy Reform* (pp. 501–523). Washington, DC: Institute for International Economics.

Treisman, D. (2014). The Political Economy of Change after Communism. In A. Åslund & S. Djankov (Eds.) *The Great Rebirth: Lessons from the Victory of Capitalism over Communism.* Washington, DC: Peterson Institute for International Economics. (pp. 273–296).

Williamson, J. (1990). *Latin American Adjustment: How Much Has Happened?* Washington, DC: Institute for International Economics.

Williamson, J. (Ed.). (1994). *The Political Economy of Policy Reform.* Washington, DC: Institute for International Economics.

13

Political Economy of Transition Reforms

Sergei Guriev

1 Why Political Economy

Political economy is key to understanding the successes and the failures of post-communist transition. Interestingly, at the outset of transition, this was not a consensus view. Many economists would think of the reform agenda as the list of urgent changes that could have been implemented by a benevolent and omnipotent pro-market government.[1] Most of the debate was focused on the choice of the speed and sequencing of the reforms (e.g. Aghion and Blanchard 1994, see also a discussion in Roland 2000). This could be explained by several reasons. First, the political economy of reforms, as a field, was still developing. While Olson (1971) and Stigler (1971) had already described the major building blocks of modern political economy, it was only in 1994 when the first formal models of interest group politics emerged (see Grossman and Helpman 1994; Shleifer and Vishny 1994), and only in 2000 that the first

---

[1] Notable exceptions include Dewatripont and Roland (1992a, b) who argued that political economy constraints are critical for determining the speed and sequencing of reforms and Boycko et al. (1995) who argued that privatization was important not just to promote the efficiency of privatized firms but also in order to create a constituency of private owners who would have a stake in supporting pro-market reforms.

S. Guriev (✉)
Sciences Po, Paris, France
e-mail: sergei.guriev@sciencespo.fr

© The Author(s) 2021
E. Douarin, O. Havrylyshyn (eds.), *The Palgrave Handbook of Comparative Economics*,
https://doi.org/10.1007/978-3-030-50888-3_13

comprehensive textbook was published (Persson and Tabellini 2000).[2] The very important ideas of "winner takes all" and "why no political Coase theorem" emerged only later (Hellman 1998 and Acemoglu 2003, respectively); in many ways they were influenced by, more than they themselves drove, the transition reforms. In a sense, the transition experience has contributed not only to the revival of institutional economics as a mainstream field but also added to the urgency of developing the discipline of political economy of reforms (see a discussion in Acemoglu and Robinson 2013 and Sonin 2013).

Second, both the reformers within the post-communist countries and their supporters from the international financial institutions saw an urgent need to focus on the immediate challenges of introducing markets and of achieving macroeconomic stabilization. As I discuss below, the rigidity of the socialist regimes delayed the reforms until the moment when the old system simply stopped functioning. The last years of the socialist regimes, especially that of the Soviet Union, were characterized by major macroeconomic imbalances, galloping hidden inflation and shortages (Guriev 2019).[3]

Third, there was a general feeling that it was the "end of history" (Fukuyama 1989): as the Soviet system was so obviously bankrupt, it was hard to imagine that there could emerge a backlash against pro-market reforms.

Finally, in post-communist countries, there was a legacy of centralized control which suggested that a top-down approach would always prevail—whatever the resistance from the disgruntled citizens.

The reality was very different, especially in the countries which did not embark on the EU accession track. Indeed, EU accession provided an anchor to coordinate citizens' expectations and promote economic and political reforms towards the EU social model. While this model is not perfect, it does prevent substantial increases in inequality and state capture, two phenomena that were observed in many non-EU transition countries. The distributional

---

[2] The debate on political economy of reforms was already active: Fernandez and Rodrik (1991) showed how uncertainty about future distribution of reform gains would result in resistance to reform. Alesina and Drazen (1991) analyzed the political economy of macroeconomic stabilization. However, these academic papers were not yet fully integrated into the policy debate in transition countries.

[3] The severity of the imbalances implied that these economies would probably face major output decline without reforms. Angus Maddison's data show that Soviet per capita GDP started to fall already in 1990, before the beginning of the reforms; the average GDP per capita in Eastern Europe—Albania, Bulgaria, Czechoslovakia, Hungary, Poland, Romania,

—peaked in 1986, also before the reforms started. This consideration is very important for the interpretation of how much reforms were the cause of the decline in the early post-transition years, and the discussion on income comparisons over time later in this chapter. The right counterfactual of post-transition income levels is not the pre-transition level but the potential lower level due to the likely decline in the non-reform scenario (see Havrylyshyn 2006, ch. 3).

and institutional implications of the reforms had a major impact on political equilibrium—and therefore on the political economy of further reforms.

2   Political Economy Before Transition

It is instructive to start the discussion of political economy of transition with the analysis of political economy before the reforms. Albeit officially there were no public politics—and thus no interest groups—the reality was more complex. For example, Miller (2016) argues that Gorbachev's reforms could not succeed precisely because of the anti-reform stance of three powerful sectoral lobbies (agriculture, defense-industrial complex and energy industry). These lobbies would lose from dismantling the status quo. Yet, the reforms did take place—even though not by design but by virtue of the failure of the non-reform approach. Gorbachev promised higher living standards which he could not deliver without departing from the socialist economic model. As he kept prices fixed, raising incomes resulted in greater shortages and longer queues rather than in increased aggregate demand and productivity growth. Longer queues further undermined real output (Boycko 1992) and forced the government to borrow even more in order to pay for imported goods. Eventually, the Soviet Union, one of the two global superpowers, simply went bankrupt.

It is important that there were also strong interest groups that supported the reforms. Before the reforms, the wage distribution was compressed; the returns to human capital and effort were low. Therefore skilled and entrepreneurial individuals would be the natural beneficiaries of the forthcoming liberalization of wages and decriminalization of business activity.[4]

The other important pro-reform lobby comprised national elites in Central and Eastern Europe, as well as Soviet regional leaders who were interested in independence (or at least autonomy) from Moscow. Given the great heterogeneity of the "socialist camp", decentralization, federalization or even a breakup was also expected to raise efficiency and therefore bring economic benefits. This was especially important in Baltic republics and outside the Soviet Union where the reforms were part of a long-sought restoration of the nation state. The moment it became clear that Gorbachev would not send troops to Central

---

[4] The conventional wisdom is that Soviet mathematicians and theoretical physicists lost from reforms. This may be true in a sense that after the end of the Cold War, stable government funding for research and development was gone. However, the top notch scholars could move to the US universities or start their own businesses within Russia. As shown in EBRD (2016a), the skilled residents of the transition countries have benefitted from the reforms much more than the rest of the population.

and Eastern Europe, its communist regimes were doomed. In these countries, the transition from plan to market was also a liberation from occupation and the return to their European roots—a project supported by the vast majority of voters.

The heterogeneity of initial conditions, between countries and between subnational regions within countries, implied that the relative strength of different interest groups was different. Countries were also diverse in terms of incomes, human capital and capacity for implementing reforms. These two factors contributed to the very different reform choices that these countries made in the beginning of transition.

3   Political Economy After the First Round of Reforms

Given the heterogeneity of initial conditions—political, economic and social—it is not surprising that the speed and sequencing of reforms varied widely across the transition region. The view that post-communist countries immediately and fully implemented the one-size-fits-all "Washington Consensus" is factually incorrect. The Washington Consensus (Williamson 1990) consisted of ten items including not just liberalization and introduction of markets (price liberalization; liberalization of foreign trade and investment, of exchange rates and of interest rates; fiscal consolidation; privatization; and deregulation) but also protection of property rights, redirection of public spending from enterprise subsidies towards human capital and infrastructure, low tax rates and broad tax bases. Many countries picked and chose their favorite reform lists; in some countries, the Washington Consensus ten-item list has not been implemented to this day. Some countries have not fully removed sectoral subsidies; some have kept substantial state ownership; in many countries, there is still excessive red tape, and property rights are not protected well.

How did political economy change after the initial set of reforms? The pre-reform debate focused on the risk of anti-reform backlash, due to a large number of "losers" from the reform who would then vote for left-wing populists.[5] These were the years when the thinking of reformers was influenced by the experience of Latin American macroeconomic populism (Dornbusch and Edwards 1991; Edwards 2019).[6] In post-communist countries, these risks

---

[5] One of the earliest to argue this was the political scientist Adam Przeworski (1991).

[6] The Washington Consensus itself was a summary of reform recommendations for Latin America.

largely did not materialize. While in many countries the first post-transition elections did bring back socialists or even communists, these left-wing governments did not engage in irresponsible macroeconomic policies but instead continued and even accelerated the reforms (Treisman 2014). In Russia, where a macroeconomic meltdown did take place in 1998, it was not engineered by populists but was driven by reformers' inability to collect taxes and achieve macroeconomic stabilization.

However, there emerged a different major problem: the capture of the government and of political processes by beneficiaries of the first round of reforms. The transition economies needed to create both markets and political institutions. In the EU accession countries, the Acquis Communautaires anchored the forthcoming checks and balances early in the process. However, in other transition countries, the lack of an established legal system and the resulting increase in returns to rent-seeking produced "institutional economies of scale" (Guriev 2010): bigger businesses had a privileged access to the political and legal system and could leverage them against their competitors. This resulted in a "winner-takes-all" effect.[7] The business people who emerged richer from the first few transition years furthered their fortunes through political connections and capture of courts and of the state (Hellman et al. 2003).

In many countries, this capture was a consequence of the design of large-scale privatizations. Like trade liberalization, privatization is always a challenge from the point of view of political economy, because it promotes efficiency but creates both winners and losers. By definition, before privatization, most state-owned enterprises tend to hold excess employment (Boycko et al. 1995; Shleifer and Vishny 1994). Indeed, state-owned enterprises are controlled by politicians and used as a tool for securing political support. This means that privatization—which is supposed to lead to de-politicization of business decisions—usually results in layoffs. As the gains of privatization outweigh the losses, there should be sufficient resources for the government to compensate laid-off workers—by providing welfare benefits and retraining programs. However, this approach works only if the government captures a sufficient part of the gains of privatization and if it has the required capacity to carry out redistribution policies.

These conditions were not necessarily satisfied in the early transition economies (especially in non-EU accession countries). Indeed, neither targeted social support nor active labor market policies existed under communism (as

---

[7] Hellman (1998) analyzed the winner-takes-all effects in post-communist *politics*. Immature political systems did not have sufficient checks and balances to protect the opposition and minorities from the tyranny of the increasingly authoritarian governments in some transition countries.

poverty and unemployment were officially non-existent). The state capacity to deliver both had to be created from scratch—exactly at the time when privatization programs were already starting.

Further, in order to secure sufficient resources for redistribution, the government had to run privatization auctions in competitive and transparent ways. The key decision in this process was whether to open privatization to foreign investors. In some countries, governments referred to the public's nationalistic sentiment and banned foreigners from privatization. It is still not clear whether the anti-foreign bias was real or it was just a pretext for lowering the prices in privatization deals to benefit politically connected domestic bidders.

In the absence of competition from foreign buyers, state-owned assets were privatized at low prices. This was an implication of two factors. First, domestic investors were still relatively cash-poor (there could not be substantial legitimate private wealth before the reforms); financial markets were still underdeveloped; therefore, domestic buyers could not pay as much as foreigners. Second, with a smaller number of bidders, it was easy to rig privatization auctions, ensuring the state assets went to politically connected domestic buyers.[8]

The inability to sell state assets at market prices had catastrophic implications for the respective countries' political economy. The public considered the new owners illegitimate (Denisova et al. 2012). And the new owners understood that in order to protect their assets from expropriation, they had to further invest in political connections.[9] This has resulted in the emergence of oligarchs in Russia, Ukraine, Kazakhstan, Azerbaijan, Moldova and some other post-communist countries.

The situation in the EU accession countries of Central and Eastern Europe was different. In these countries, foreigners were allowed to participate in privatizations. This helped raising substantial revenues from privatization but also led to a foreign control over whole industries. In particular, in many countries, foreigners took over the majority of the banking system. Initially, this was a popular outcome (as foreign-owned banks offered better services

---

[8] The most blatant example of large-scale rigging was Russia's loans-for-shares auctions. Freeland (2000) provides accounts of Russian winners of those auctions who explicitly bragged about designing these auctions in a way to keep foreigners away from bidding. More recently, during the 2011 London court case between Boris Berezovsky and Roman Abramovich, influential Russian businessmen and policymakers testified under oath that at least certain auctions were rigged to limit competition.

[9] The threat of re-nationalization and re-privatization was not theoretical. For example, in privatization, Kryvyi Rih Stal was privatized to two Ukrainian oligarchs for 0.8 billion dollars. After the 2004 Orange Revolution, the new government re-nationalized and privatized this company to Mittal for 4.8 billion dollars.

and rates). However, after the global financial crisis, foreign banks—especially those which provided foreign currency-denominated mortgages—became a convenient scapegoat. Still, EU accession has certainly helped promoting fairer competition for assets and therefore prevented creating an oligarchic system. The prospective membership provided incentives to proceed early and consistently on institutional reforms, which impeded non-competitive activities and oligarchization.

Figure 13.1 shows the progress in reforms in different parts of post-communist regions in terms of EBRD's Transition Indicators (EBRD 2013). These indicators range from 1 to 4, where 1 stands for an unreformed command economy and 4 stands for a functioning market economy (with a possibility of a "4+"). Central European countries reached the level of 3.5 by the mid-1990s and continued increasing their scores getting almost to 4 by 2013. The progress was much slower in South-Eastern Europe (late accession countries such as Romania and Bulgaria and the West Balkan countries with uncertain accession opportunities) which only reach 3.3 by 2013. The reform progress in post-Soviet countries was less impressive. These countries' reform scores have been plateauing since the mid-1990s and are now at the levels of 2.7 (Central Asia), 3.3 (Russia) and 3 (others).

4   The Anti-reform Backlash: Inequality and Unfairness

In many post-communist countries, the first round of reform has drastically reduced support for market economy and democracy (EBRD 2016b). The conventional explanation—that market reforms resulted in a substantial increase in inequality—is correct. EBRD (2016a) tracked the evolution of income distribution in 1989–2016. Figure 13.2 shows that the rich benefitted from the reforms the most. The top 10 percent's incomes have almost doubled. The bottom 10 percent's incomes have increased only by 17 percent.

EBRD (2016a) has also reconstructed Milanovic's "Elephant Curve" (Milanovic 2016) for each post-communist country and for the region as a whole. The "elephant curve" analysis allows to identify which parts of income distribution benefitted and lost from the reforms.

The original Milanovic's chart (see Fig. 13.3) describes the evolution of global income distribution in 1988–2008 and is referred to as an "elephant curve" because it visually resembles an elephant. It shows that the main beneficiaries of the 20 years of globalization and technological change were the

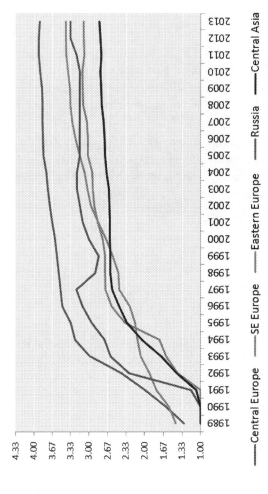

Fig. 13.1 Average transition indicators, on a 1 to 4+ scale, since 1989. (Source: EBRD (2013). For each geographical region, the figure shows the simple average of the scores for six EBRD Transition Indicators across all countries in the region. The six country-level transition indicators for each country include large-scale privatization, small-scale privatization, governance and enterprise restructuring, price liberalization, trade and foreign exchange systems, and competition policy. Central Europe includes Croatia, Estonia, Hungary, Latvia, Lithuania, the Slovak Republic, Slovenia, Poland; Southern-Eastern Europe includes Albania, Bosnia and Herzegovina, Bulgaria, Kosovo, Montenegro, Northern Macedonia, Romania, Serbia; Eastern Europe includes Armenia, Azerbaijan, Belarus, Georgia, Moldova, Ukraine; Central Asia includes Kazakhstan, the Kyrgyz Republic, Mongolia, Tajikistan, Turkmenistan, Uzbekistan)

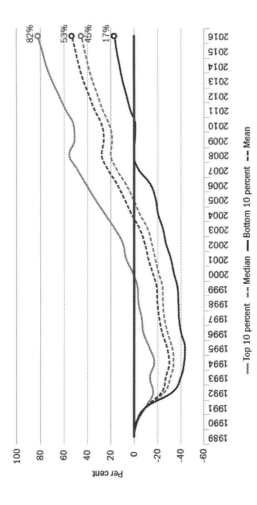

Fig. 13.2 Cumulative income growth in post-communist countries since 1989. (Source: EBRD (2016a))

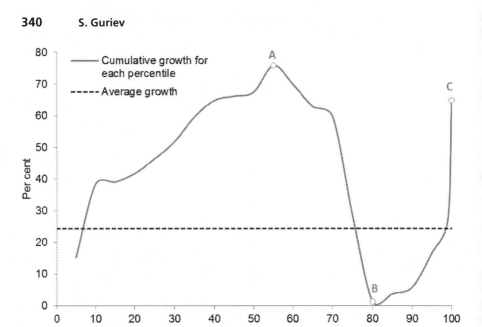

Fig. 13.3 Relative gain in real per capita income by global income distribution's position, 1988–2008. (Source: Milanovic 2016, EBRD (2016a))

global top 1 percent (point C on the chart, the tip of the elephant's trunk) and the global middle class (point A on the chart, the top of the elephant's head—upper-middle class in emerging markets, especially China and India). However, the lower half of the top decile and the second decile of the global income distribution (point B, the bottom of the elephant's trunk, lower-middle class in the advanced economies) have seen virtually no increase in their real incomes over these 20 years.

The typical post-communist elephant curve does not look like an elephant at all (Fig. 13.4).[10] Unlike the global elephant curve's highly non-linear relationship between the initial position in the income distribution and the income growth, the shape of the respective relationship for the post-communist countries is monotonically increasing: those who were rich to start with grew even richer and the initially poor's growth fell further behind the rich's.

The main takeaways from this "post-communist elephant curve" analysis (EBRD 2016a) are as follows. First, while within most countries transition increased incomes substantially *on average*,[11] the main gains were

---

[10] These patterns are especially salient in the "elephant curves" of individual countries; see Fig. 13.5 for Russia.

[11] That standards of living have improved substantially in most countries should not be in doubt. Official income comparisons may show that several countries have not yet returned to socialist period levels or barely so. However, comparisons between post-reform and Soviet-era output measures overstate the pre-

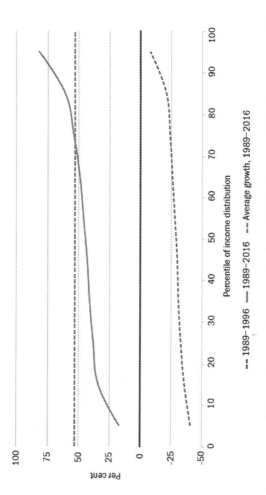

Fig. 13.4 Cumulative income growth in post-communist countries since 1989 by income decile. (Source: EBRD (2016a))

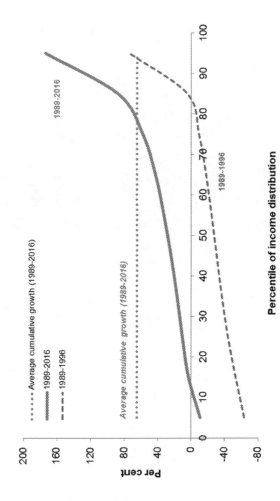

Fig. 13.5 Cumulative income growth in Russia since 1989 by income decile. (Source: EBRD (2016a))

concentrated in the upper 20–30 percent of households. Those likely to be the households with originally higher skills (especially with generic rather than specific skills), those with higher initial wealth (however limited) and those living in large cities. The bottom 70 percent of households experienced income growth below country average.

Second, while on average the region as a whole, and most countries within it, has experienced partial convergence with the West, this was not the experience of the majority of households—but only of the top 44 percent. For the bottom 56 percent, their incomes in 2016 were farther behind those in the West than in the beginning of transition.

Third, these patterns were especially salient after the first few years of reforms. By the mid-1990s, the vast majority of households saw a decline in their incomes relative to pre-transition levels, while the only ones with positive income growth were those from the top decile of income distribution. However, starting about 2000, incomes recovered throughout the region, and in most countries the distribution gap narrowed again, especially in Central European countries where the Gini and poverty ratios returned close to their socialist period level. Even in post-Soviet countries where inequality remained high, there has been virtually no increase in inequality since the mid-1990s.[12]

While the increase in inequality is an important explanation behind the reduced support for reforms, there is growing evidence that not only the distributional *outcomes* of the reforms matters; the fairness of the *process* plays a major role as well. In particular, it is the growth in *unfair inequality*, or inequality of opportunity, that undermines the support for reforms.

Inequality and unfairness are certainly related but are not the same thing—especially in countries with a communist past. As discussed above, most of the increase of inequality actually took place immediately after price liberalization—that is, even before privatization and the emergence of the new super-rich. As shown in Milanovic (1999), this immediate increase in income inequality was driven by the decompression of wages—which was at least partly a desirable outcome of the reforms. In a command economy, wages were compressed, thus undermining incentives to work hard. The command economy thus exemplified a situation of "unfair equality" (Starmans et al. 2017) where additional effort was not rewarded. In the post-communist

---

reform living standards (Havrylyshyn 2006). The evidence on increases in physical consumption measures (Guriev and Zhuravskaya 2009, Table 13.1) points in the same direction. Also, see footnote 4 for the discussion of an additional source of bias against the positive impact of reforms.

[12] Ukraine is an important exception where official estimates of inequality have remained low throughout the three decades of transition. This is probably because the main beneficiaries of reforms are those who have emigrated and the superrich who are not covered by the regular household surveys.

context, replacing unfair equality with fair inequality (where inequality was supposed to be driven by hard work and talent rather than by circumstances of birth) would thus be a positive development.

Unfortunately, in many transition countries, there is now substantial *unfair* inequality, or "inequality of opportunity". Inequality of opportunity is usually measured as a share of inequality of outcomes (in particular, of incomes) that can be explained by exogenous circumstances (parental background, place of birth, gender, ethnicity or race). In some transition countries, these factors account for half of the total income inequality (EBRD 2016a).

Inequality of opportunity is not only inacceptable on ethical grounds—it is also inefficient. Indeed, if success is driven by circumstances of birth rather than by talent and effort, this directly reduces productivity of talented workers born in disadvantaged families and places (and those of disadvantaged gender, ethnicity and race).

Inequality of opportunity is especially important in post-communist countries as communist ideology emphasized equality of opportunity as its key distinguishing feature relative to a capitalist model. This is why the failure of reformers to carry out the transition to market in a way perceived to be fair had the potential to re-activate the deeply entrenched suspicion that market economy promotes inequality of opportunity.

Unfortunately, in many cases reforms provided ample support for these beliefs. The leading example is Russia's "loans for shares" privatization. In economic terms, handing over the crown jewels of Soviet industry to newly emerging oligarchs did promote efficiency (Guriev and Rachinsky 2005). However, the very fact that the loans for shares auctions were not carried out in a fair and competitive way led to an outright rejection of oligarchs' property rights by the general public.[13] This undermined the trust in Russian reformers and resulted in illegitimacy of private property in Russia, and eventually, contributed to the rise of Putin.[14]

In order to test the importance of (real or perceived) unfairness of transition for reduced support for market reforms, EBRD (2016a) decomposed income inequality into fair and unfair inequality (the "fair inequality" is the part of income inequality that is not related to exogenous circumstances). As

---

[13] In a July 2003 poll, 88 percent Russians said that all large fortunes were amassed in an illegal way, 77 percent said that privatization results should be partially or fully reconsidered, and 57 percent agreed that government should launch criminal investigations against the wealthy (Guriev and Rachinsky 2005, 140).

[14] The Russian example was not unique. Lukashenko in Belarus, Orban in Hungary and PiS party in Poland used the "corrupt elites" narratives to come to power and then consolidate their regimes. In Georgia, the Georgian Dream party won the 2012 election against the successful pro-reform Saakashvili government campaigning on the agenda of the incumbents' abuse of law-and-order agencies.

shown in Table 13.1, residents of transition countries were less likely to support reforms if unfair inequality was high—but were *more* likely to support reforms if inequality was fair, even if it was high. Furthermore, the rejection of unfair inequality was a significant factor behind a reduced support for reforms, even controlling for the respondent's living standards: that is, the impact of perceived unfairness was not driven by his/her own socio-economic status, objective or perceived.

5   Political Economy of Oligarchic Capture

Given the prominence of oligarchs in many transition economies,[15] it is worth discussing how this system works and why it may be detrimental for transition to market. Initially, the reformers saw privatization as a necessary condition for maintaining the demand for further reforms. Without private

Table 13.1 Support for markets as a function of "fair" and "unfair" income inequality

	Support for market reforms	
Unfair income inequality	−1.093*	−1.012*
	(0.480)	(0.473)
Fair income inequality	1.046**	1.064**
	(0.354)	(0.356)
Subjective perception of relative economic wellbeing		0.017**
		(0.005)
Objective income decile	0.010***	0.008**
	(0.003)	(0.002)
Observations	12,258	12,185

Sources: Guriev (2018), Table 2A.2.
Notes: Linear probability model. Dependent variable: dummy for the support for market economy. Subjective perception of economic wellbeing is the self-perceived income decile (1 corresponds to the poorest decile). Objective income decile is the objective decile in the income distribution based on respondent's income. Additional controls include gender, education level, age and life satisfaction, region dummies, inequality of opportunity with respect to jobs and education, country inflation, unemployment and per capita GDP. Standard errors are clustered at the country level and are shown in parentheses
*, ** and *** indicate statistical significance at the 10, 5 and 1 percent levels, respectively

---

[15] EBRD (2016a) shows that the post-communist region is unique among emerging markets in having disproportionately high billionaire wealth relative to its share in global GDP. This region is also distinct in having most billionaire wealth coming from natural resources and from regulated industries—both sectors with highest dependence on rents and on political connections.

ownership, there are no stakeholders interested in institutions protecting private property rights and other market institutions (Boycko et al. 1995). This logic presumed that the privatization process was unimportant; what mattered was the emergence of a class of private owners who would lobby for institutional reforms enshrining property rights and would also improve corporate governance at the firm level.

In practice, it turned out that the illegitimacy of the privatization *process* was more important than its *outcomes*. The lack of political support for the emerging property rights increased political risks for the new owners. This is why they preferred to invest in political connections to protect their property rather than to create rule of law (that would be unlikely to clear them of their "original sin"). The resulting underdevelopment of political and legal institutions respectively raised the relative returns to rent-seeking, so instead of lobbying for institutional reforms, oligarchs engaged in rent-seeking against each other and against other private owners (Sonin 2003). Even though private owners (collectively) would benefit from building modern political and economic institutions, the oligarchs (individually and as a group) continued to benefit from institutions of crony capitalism. As Acemoglu (2008) shows, this system cannot deliver long-term economic growth.

It is important that the emergence of oligarchs—in addition to undermining rule of law and promoting corruption—also slowed down or reversed democratic reforms. This was not a coincidence: the political illegitimacy of oligarchs' property rights implied that their wealth would be harder to defend if policies reflected the preferences of the majority.

In addition to acquiring political connections and influence over courts, oligarchs have also tried to capture the media. In many transition countries today, non-state media are owned by large business groups with substantial interests in non-media industries. This creates a "circular" business model: an oligarch uses his media outlets to influence laws and regulations, which provide his non-media business with preferential treatment and protect it from competition; then he uses the rents from his non-media business to subsidize the media business.[16] In addition to distorting competition in the non-media business, this business model also undermines the business model of independent media. Stand-alone media companies cannot compete in such an environment as they lack the rents from non-media business and cannot afford the best talent.

---

[16] This business model was not pioneered in transition region: Silvio Berlusconi used it extensively and effectively (see Durante and Knight 2012; DellaVigna et al. 2016).

Is there a case for the oligarchic media ownership model—as at least there is a competition *between* oligarchic media? There is no reason to be optimistic. First, in most small countries (or subnational regions of Russia), there is only one oligarch—who also happens to be linked to the government. Second, even in large countries, the number of oligarchs is sufficiently small so that they can still collude—and collude they do whenever the issues are of common interest.

Can the oligarchic equilibrium be checked by a strong leader or by the EU institutions? Anti-corruption and anti-oligarchic agenda is a natural platform for any populist leader (be it Lukashenko, Putin or Orban). The main question is to what extent this leader—once in power—would be accountable to the people and constrained by democratic institutions. As Guriev and Sonin (2009) show, an unconstrained strong ruler can effectively divide and rule the oligarchs, by appropriating their rents. There is no reason to believe that he is interested in deconstructing the system, while he can just redirect the gains from corruption.

On the other hand, if democratic institutions are sufficiently strong, then the popularity of an anti-oligarch agenda should help cleaning up the system whatever the "strong leader" would like to do. However, in such countries, oligarchs are unlikely to emerge in the first place.

6 Political Economy Today

Nowadays, the post-communist region includes a great diversity of political and economic outcomes. There are consolidated democracies and consolidated dictatorships; there are crony capitalist societies and polities transitioning from autocracy to democracy—and those moving away from democracy. There are healthy economies and there are those with stagnating investment and growth. What is striking is that, in the transition region, there is a very strong correlation between democracy and prosperity (Roland 2014; Treisman 2014). This correlation directly follows from the analysis above. The backlash against inequalities and unfairness of initial reforms helped fuel the appeal of anti-reform politicians. In those countries where democratic institutions were sufficiently strong (these were mostly the EU accession countries), the anti-reform politicians who could not deliver on their promises were voted out; reforms and growth continued. In those countries, where the anti-reform politicians managed to subvert democratic checks and balances, they built crony capitalism which led to stagnation rather than growth.

The initial view that the EU accession safeguards both economic and political reforms was generally vindicated. However, EU membership brought new tensions as well. First, the influx of foreign direct investment resulted in the rise of "colonization" fears and the backlash against foreign owners especially after the global financial crisis. Second, as the Western European labor markets were opened up to the workers from the East, this created both huge benefits for those East European citizens who moved to the West—but also a disillusionment for their compatriots who stayed behind. This exodus of (mostly young and skilled) workers has been one of the largest labor reallocations in history (EBRD 2018, Chapter 2). It has affected the political economy in both the East and the West. In the West, especially in the UK, the arrival of the "Polish plumbers" created competition for the low-skilled British workers and contributed to the Brexit vote (Viskanic 2017). In the East, the fear that emigration (coupled with aging) undermines both economic development and social/cultural relevance may have fueled the anti-European and nativist backlash observed in some parts of the region.[17]

The non-EU post-communist countries have mostly converged to non-democratic politics,[18] either in the form of repressive dictatorships or "informational autocracies" (Guriev and Treisman 2019). The latter pretend to be democracies, holding multi-party elections and avoiding mass repressions. However, they rely on propaganda, censorship and co-optation of the elites that helps staying in power without resorting to violence.

Post-communist non-democracies have not been exemplary *economic* reformers. In order to maintain their hold on power, these countries' rulers have eliminated political checks and balances, which in turn has led to higher corruption. A growth-promoting reform agenda includes re-instating rule of law, but this would undermine the regime's political control. Institutional reforms that can deliver investment and growth reduce the probability of the incumbents' staying in power; hence the rulers in these countries prefer stagnation.

---

[17] EBRD (2018, chapter 2) shows that the exodus cost transition countries' firms about 20 percentage points of TFP growth.

[18] There are some exceptions in the EU Eastern Partnership countries and in the Western Balkans, where the prospect of EU membership/integration/approximation did play a positive role similar to what was observed in early transition in the EU accession region. On the other hand, there are exceptions among the EU members as well: there are many similarities between modern Hungary and the informational autocracies of the East.

7   Implications

Looking back at the political economy of successes and failures of transition to market, can we conclude on what should have been done differently? As argued in Guriev (2019), the three key mistakes of the reformers were related to inclusion, governance and communication. First, the reformers have not done a good job explaining their strategy to the public and have not anchored expectations correctly (this was especially hard in non-accession countries). Second, they have also not paid sufficient attention to mitigating the stark distributional implications of the reforms. In most transition countries, the reforms have raised income of an average citizen but not that of the median citizen. The benefits of the reforms were mostly appropriated by the better-off, skilled and politically connected elites, while the majority of households—including the most vulnerable ones—have benefitted less or even lost out. Finally, the reforms have created a perception of unfairness. Insufficient attention to governance and anti-corruption policies led to excess returns to rent-seeking, lobbying and political connections. In many countries even those individuals who have materially benefitted from reforms now believe that the new system is unfair—and thus do not support markets and democracy.

Could these mistakes have been avoided? The reformers would retort that they did not have enough capacity to carry out reforms and invest time and effort in communicating their strategy to the public.[19] They would also say that generous social safety nets would not have been affordable in the post-communist economies emerging from the bankruptcy of the previous regimes and in many cases even saddled with substantial debt. This, of course, would imply that the new governments would have been better off restructuring or even writing off debts and attracting more support from the West. The reforms should have also moved fast in removing price controls, trade barriers and subsidies to firms—to free up resources to support the most vulnerable households (in line with the Washington Consensus!). This would also have helped fighting corruption, as price controls and subsidies created rents, thus leading to the emergence of oligarchs. The reformers should have also paid special attention to carrying out privatization auctions in a free and fair way—allowing foreign investors to help raise prices and thus increasing the political legitimacy of privatization.

---

[19] In Czech Republic and in Poland, the reformers have paid a special attention to explaining the reforms to the people (Klaus 2014; Balzerowicz 2014); these are examples of two countries where a broad public support for reforms was created. In this sense, these exceptions confirm the rule.

Most importantly, the reformers themselves needed to make sure to maintain their own integrity. Confidence in reforms is based on confidence in reformers. If the public believes that the reforms are carried out with the intention to benefit the reformers themselves, rather than to promote social welfare, the backlash is imminent.

These lessons are certainly not limited to the post-communist region. Structural reforms in other countries also generate winners and losers, and commitment to inclusion, fairness and communication helps maintaining support for reforms.

References

Acemoglu, D. (2003). Why Not a Political Coase Theorem? Social Conflict, Commitment, and Politics. *Journal of Comparative Economics, 31*(4), 620–652.

Acemoglu, D. (2008). Oligarchic Versus Democratic Societies. *Journal of European Economic Association, 6*(11), 1–44.

Acemoglu, D., & Robinson, J. (2013). Economics versus Politics: Pitfalls of Policy Advice. *Journal of Economic Perspectives, 27*(2), 173–192.

Aghion, P., & Blanchard, O. (1994). On the Speed of Transition in Central Europe. In S. Fischer & J. Rotemberg (Eds.), *NBER Macroeconomics Annual 1994.* Cambridge: MIT Press.

Alesina, A., & Drazen, A. (1991). Why Are Stabilizations Delayed? *American Economic Review, American Economic Association, 81*(5), 1170–1188.

Balzerowicz, L. (2014). Poland: Stabilization and Reforms under Extraordinary and Normal Politics. In A. Aslund & S. Djankov (Eds.), *The Great Rebirth: Lessons from the Victory of Capitalism over Communism.* Washington, DC: Peterson Institute for International Economics.

Boycko, M. (1992). When Higher Incomes Reduce Welfare: Queues, Labor Supply, and Macro Equilibrium in Socialist Economies. *Quarterly Journal of Economics, 107*(3), 907–920.

Boycko, M., Shleifer, A., & Vishny, R. (1995). *Privatizing Russia.* Cambridge, MA: MIT Press.

DellaVigna, S., Durante, R., Knight, B., & La Ferrara, E. (2016). Market-Based Lobbying: Evidence From Advertising Spending In Italy. *American Economic Journal: Applied Economics, 8*(1), 224–256.

Denisova, I., Eller, M., Frye, T., & Zhuravskaya, E. (2012). Everyone Hates Privatization, But Why? Survey Evidence from 28 Post-Communist Countries. *Journal of Comparative Economics, 40,* 44–61.

Dewatripont, M., & Roland, G. (1992a). Economic Reform and Dynamic Political Constraints. *Review of Economic Studies, 59*(4), 703–730.

Dewatripont, M., & Roland, G. (1992b). The Virtues of Gradualism and Legitimacy in the Transition to a Market Economy. *Economic Journal, 102*(411), 291–300.

Dornbusch, R., & Edwards, S. (1991). *The Macroeconomics of Populism in Latin America*. Chicago, IL: University of Chicago Press.

Durante, R., & Knight, B. (2012). Partisan Control, Media Bias And Viewer Responses: Evidence From Berlusconi's Italy. *Journal of the European Economic Association, 10*(3), 451–481.

EBRD. (2013). *Stuck in Transition*. Transition Report 2013, European Bank for Reconstruction and Development, London.

EBRD. (2016a). *Transition for All: Promoting Equal Opportunity in an Unequal World*. Transition Report 2016–17, European Bank for Reconstruction and Development, London.

EBRD. (2016b). *Life in Transition: A Decade of Measuring Transition*. London: European Bank for Reconstruction and Development.

EBRD. (2018). *Work in Transition*. Transition Report 2018–19, European Bank for Reconstruction and Development, London.

Edwards, S. (2019). On Latin American Populism, and Its Echoes around the World. *Journal of Economic Perspectives, 33*(4), 76–99.

Fernandez, R., & Rodrik, D. (1991). Resistance to Reform: Status Quo Bias in the Presence of Individual-Specific Uncertainty. *American Economic Review, 81*(5), 1146–1155.

Freeland, C. (2000). *Sale of the Century: Russia's Wild Ride from Communism to Capitalism*. New York: Crown Business.

Fukuyama, F. (1989). The End of History? *The National Interest, 16*, 3–18.

Grossman, G., & Helpman, E. (1994). Protection for Sale. *American Economic Review, 84*, 833–850.

Guriev, S. (2010). Business Groups in Russia. In A. Colpan, T. Hikino, & J. Lincoln (Eds.), *Oxford Handbook of Business Groups*. New York: Oxford University Press.

Guriev, S. (2018). Revisiting Transition Reform. In E. Novotny, D. Ritzberger-Grunwald, & H. Shuberth (Eds.), *Structural Reforms for Growth and Cohesion*. Northampton, MA: Edward Elgar.

Guriev, S. (2019). Gorbachev vs. Deng: A Review of Chris Miller's The Struggle to Save the Soviet Economy. *Journal of Economic Literature, 57*(1), 120–146.

Guriev, S., & Rachinsky, A. (2005). The Role of Oligarchs in Russian Capitalism. *Journal of Economic Perspectives, 19*(1), 131–150.

Guriev, S., & Sonin, K. (2009). Dictators and Oligarchs: A Dynamic Theory of Contested Property Rights. *Journal of Public Economics, 93*(2009), 1–13.

Guriev, S., & Treisman, D. (2019). Informational Autocrats. *Journal of Economic Perspectives, 33*(4), 100–127.

Guriev, S., & Zhuravskaya, E. (2009). (Un)Happiness in Transition. *Journal of Economic Perspectives, 23*(2), 143–168.

Havrylyshyn, O. (2006). *Divergent Paths in Post-Communist Transformation. Capitalism for All or Capitalism for the Few?* New York: Palgrave Macmillan.

Hellman, J. (1998). Winners Take All: The Politics of Partial Reform in Postcommunist Transitions. *World Politics, 50*, 203–234.

Hellman, J., Jones, G., & Kaufmann, D. (2003). Seize the State, Seize the Day: State Capture and Influence in Transition Economies. *Journal of Comparative Economics, 31*(4), 751–773.

Klaus, V. (2014). Czechoslovakia and the Czech Republic: The Spirit and Main Contours of the Postcommunist Transformation. In A. Aslund & S. Djankov (Eds.), *The Great Rebirth: Lessons from the Victory of Capitalism over Communism*. Washington, DC: Peterson Institute for International Economics.

Milanovic, B. (1999). Explaining the Increase in Inequality During Transition. *Economics of Transition, 7*(2), 299–341.

Milanovic, B. (2016). *Global Inequality: A New Approach for the Age of Globalization*. Cambridge, MA: Harvard University Press.

Miller, C. (2016). *The Struggle to Save the Soviet Economy: Mikhail Gorbachev and the Collapse of the USSR*. Chapel Hill, NC: University of North Carolina Press.

Olson, M. (1971). *The Logic of Collective Action: Public Goods and the Theory of Groups*. Cambridge, MA: Harvard University Press.

Persson, T., & Tabellini, G. (2000). *Political Economics: Explaining Economic Policy*. Cambridge, MA: MIT Press.

Przeworski, A. (1991). *Democracy and the Market: Political and Economic Reforms in Eastern Europe and Latin America*. Cambridge: Cambridge University Press.

Roland, G. (2000). *Transition and Economics: Politics, Markets, and Firms*. Cambridge and London: MIT Press.

Roland, G. (2014). Transition in Historical Perspective. In A. Aslund & S. Djankov (Eds.), *The Great Rebirth: Lessons from the Victory of Capitalism over Communism*. Washington, DC: Peterson Institute for International Economics.

Shleifer, A., & Vishny, R. (1994). Politicians and Firms. *Quarterly Journal of Economics, 109*(4), 995–1025.

Sonin, K. (2003). Why the Rich May Favor Poor Protection of Property Rights? *Journal of Comparative Economics, 31*, 715–731.

Sonin, K. (2013). The End of Economic Transition. *Economics of Transition, 21*(1), 1–10.

Starmans, C., Sheskin, M., & Bloom, P. (2017). Why People Prefer Unequal Societies. *Nature Human Behavior, 1*(4), 0082.

Stigler, G. (1971). The Theory of Economic Regulation. *Bell Journal of Economics and Management Science, 2*(1), 3–21.

Treisman, D. (2014). The Political Economic of Change After Communism. In A. Aslund & S. Djankov (Eds.), *The Great Rebirth: Lessons from the Victory of Capitalism over Communism*. Washington, DC: Peterson Institute for International Economics.

Viskanic, M. (2017). *Fear and Loathing on the Campaign Trail: Did Immigration Cause Brexit?* Mimeo: Sciences Po. Retrieved from SSRN: https://ssrn.com/abstract=2941611 or https://doi.org/10.2139/ssrn.2941611.

Williamson, J. (1990). What Washington Means by Policy Reform. In J. Williamson (Ed.), *Latin American Adjustment: How Much has Happened?* (pp. 5–20). Institute for International Economics: Washington, DC.

14

The EU Anchor Thesis: Transition from Socialism, Institutional Vacuum and Membership in the European Union

Nauro F. Campos

1   Introduction

The biggest enlargement in the history of the European Union (EU) took place less than 20 years ago. Few anticipated it would so clearly mark the end of the transition from socialism as well as so fundamentally transform the European economy and the European Union.

The fall of the Berlin Wall is one the defining moments of the twentieth century. It signposts the beginning of the end of the socialist experiment in Eastern Europe. This collapse was a process that took almost two years to complete. It ended with the implosion of the Soviet Union in 1991. This collapse marks the beginning of a fundamental transition from state socialism to market capitalism, from authoritarian centrally planned economies to democratic regimes supported by market-oriented economies (Roland 2000).

I would like to thank, Erik Berglöf, Elodie Douarin, Sergei Guriev, Oleh Havrylyshyn, Paul Wachtel, and seminar participants at the UCL Palgrave Handbook of Comparative Economics Workshop in January 2020 (London) for valuable comments and suggestions on previous versions. The usual disclaimer applies.

N. F. Campos (✉)
School of Slavonic and East European Studies, University College London, London, UK

ETH Zürich, Zürich, Switzerland

IZA Institute of Labor Economics, Bonn, Germany
e-mail: n.campos@ucl.ac.uk

© The Author(s) 2021
E. Douarin, O. Havrylyshyn (eds.), *The Palgrave Handbook of Comparative Economics*,
https://doi.org/10.1007/978-3-030-50888-3_14

The Eastern Enlargement, when eight former Soviet Bloc countries became full-fledged EU members in May 2004, brings the transition from socialism that started in 1989–1991 to a close. Why? Because a wedge opened between Central and Eastern European (CEE) and former Soviet Union countries (FSU). This great divide became perhaps the most robust stylised fact of the transition despite being among the least expected at the beginning of the process (Berglöf and Bolton 2002). Central and Eastern European starkly diverged from former Soviet Union countries despite being broadly comparable across many dimensions, including per capita incomes. In the CEE, the fall in per capita output was substantially smaller than in the countries that emerged from the Soviet Union, reform programmes went deeper, privatisation programmes were more extensive, labour markets adjusted earlier, financial sectors emerged faster, international trade re-orientation was swifter, democracies matured quicker and the happiness gap closed up first. Institutions provide one of the key explanations for this divergence.

What were the key stylised facts that characterised the period from the fall of the Berlin Wall to the 2004 Enlargement? Campos and Coricelli (2002) identify seven key stylised facts. There was a large output contraction accompanied by massive capital depreciation and huge changes in the labour force. There was substantial structural change and re-orientation of international trade. There was a rise in poverty and inequality; both were practically inexistent before 1989. They also tried to call attention, early on, to the fact that a defining stylised fact of transition in its first decade was the emergence of what they called an "institutional vacuum."

Although it was clear that a wedge was developing, few would have imagined the role EU membership would end up playing in its creation. We now know that for those countries that did not join the EU, the institutional vacuum remains. Because of EU accession, the wedge developed. On the one side, economic dynamism and institutional renewal; on the other side, economic stagnation (chiefly for those countries without natural resources) and institutional vacuum. While at the start of their transition FSU countries had, for instance, incomes per capita marginally lower than those in CEE that eventually joined the EU, the gap that opened since is yet to close.

The EU anchor thesis posits that the prospect of membership in the European Union played a key role in filling in the institutional vacuum that followed the collapse of socialism (Berglöf and Roland 1997, 2000; Roland and Verdier 2003). Because such a prospect was higher in Central and Eastern European countries than in the former Soviet Union countries, the gap between the two groups of countries grew.

What was the impact of the 2004 EU Enlargement on the new member states? Accession was instrumental: it meant better institutions, more labour mobility, more trade, better integration in global value chains, greater levels of technological development. The negotiations for EU membership helped not just to anchor but also to fine-tune institutional change. Financial integration fuelled this exceptionality by facilitating capital and people flows (Friedrich et al. 2013).

In turn because of the 2004 Enlargement the EU also changed enormously. Diversity across member countries increased sharply: the lowest GDP per capita was 67% of the EU average before enlargement and decreased to 48% afterwards. Labour mobility increased and Europe witnessed an unprecedented rise in cross-border banking acquisitions in new members. Deeper integration of both capital and labour, together with a push for more democracy and efficiency of EU institutions, created huge opportunities for the EU. Unfortunately, potential longer-run positive effect of enlargement were neutralised by the lingering effects of the Great Recession and the difficulties at the EU level in providing a coherent policy response. Many European countries became the target of populist parties and politicians—in new and old member states alike (Guiso et al. 2019)—and a commensurate response is yet to come forward.

This chapter is organised as follows. Section 2 examines the EU anchor thesis. Based on a textual analysis of the *Conclusions of the Presidency of the European Council* before 2004, we document that the enlargement process was characterised by huge uncertainty, and, although, in hindsight, it may seem carefully planned and executed, this was not the case. There was still considerable uncertainty about the process until the Treaty of Amsterdam was signed in 1997 and there was uncertainty (until even later) about which countries would join when. Moreover, although the accession process affected many areas and early attention focused on the effects of the continued reform efforts regarding stabilisation, liberalisation and privatisation, it has since become clear that the longer-lasting and most consequential effect has been mostly in terms of building up key institutions (such as the judiciary, bureaucracy and competition authority) in the candidate countries. Section 3 focuses on whether the prospect of EU membership did accelerate institutional development. It documents the initial institutional gap and how the EU anchor was instrumental in closing it. Section 4 investigates whether these new institutions fostered by the prospect of EU membership can be linked to better economic outcomes. Section 5 concludes.

2   An Enlargement Like No Other

The European integration project that started out in 1957 with the signing of the Treaty of Rome has experienced four main enlargement episodes. New members were admitted in 1973 (UK, Ireland and Denmark), in the 1980s (Greece in 1981 and Portugal and Spain in 1986) and in 1995 (Austria, Finland and Sweden). As can be seen, in each of these three enlargements only three countries became full-fledged members. This is a relatively small number and accession was managed without much need for bureaucratic machinery. Incumbent member states took a leading role in the first and second enlargements, while European institutions like the European Commission took a somewhat larger role in the third enlargement. This was not because the countries of the third wave were unprepared to join, but instead because this enlargement occurred at the same time of the single market and the fall of the Berlin Wall, which complicated the process (Tatham 2009).

The Eastern Enlargement, the fourth one, was unique in at least three fundamental ways. Firstly, this enlargement had a much larger number of candidate countries compared to all previous enlargements (this is true even accounting for the fact that Norway was also a candidate in 1973 and 1995, as was Switzerland in 1995). Despite the relatively large numbers, there was broad consensus that the benefits of the Eastern Enlargement would be larger than its estimated costs and that these benefits would accrue to both Eastern and Western Europe (Baldwin et al. 1997).

The second reason the 2004 Enlargement was unique is that the number of policy areas that the transition economies had to negotiate was considerably larger and more detailed than had been the case in previous rounds. The 1973 Enlargement followed the completion of the Customs Union and the 1995 Enlargement occurred once the single market was in place, yet when the transition economies started their accession process, the *acquis communautaire* already had about 30 chapters, each one covering a different policy area.

The third aspect that makes the Eastern Enlargement unique is partly a natural consequence of the larger number of candidates: the accession process became more formalised and managed more explicitly by the European institutions (European Council 1994, p. 12), while member states took on a much smaller role.

However, it is important to stress that a more structured accession process does not mean that it was all clearly defined and designed from the outset. The opposite would perhaps not be a bad characterisation. Based on an analysis of all the *Conclusions of the Presidency of the European Council* before 2004, we document that the enlargement process was characterised by huge uncertainty.

In the early and mid-1990s there was still uncertainty surrounding the accession process. There was still considerable uncertainty about the process until the Treaty of Amsterdam was signed in 1997 (European Council 1997) and there was also uncertainty about which countries would join when, until even after Amsterdam. There was not much clarity at the start, to put it mildly, about the timing, about the process itself and even about the identity of future members.

In the early 1990s, a much optimistic forecast was that some Visegrád countries would be able to join the EU before the turn of the century (European Council 1993). By 1997, the educated expectation was that the first candidates would join by 2002. It is only later that 2004 was chosen as the official year for the first wave of enlargement (Tatham 2009).

The uncertainty about the timing was also associated with much uncertainty about the process itself. The early 1990s were ambitious times at the European Community: let's not forget the concurrent deepening (single market) and broadening (Sweden, Finland and Austria as incoming members) that were already burdening the European institutions, stretching their capacity to design, manage and implement policies. On top of this, the external environment was also rather eventful with the reunification of Germany, the collapse of the USSR and the violent large-scale conflicts first in the Gulf and then in the Balkans.

By the middle of the decade, the Commission took full charge of the accession process and agreed, designed and put in place a system of monitoring the accession of an unprecedentedly large set of candidates.

In addition to when and how, uncertainty about who also lingered. A hypothetical experiment may conveniently sum this up. Imagine what would be the answer if someone had in 1997 asked the following question in Prague, Budapest, Tallinn and Sofia: "what do you think are the chances that your country will be a full member of the EU by 2004?" We can speculate that the average response from Wenceslas Square would have been 70%, while that from Erzsebet Ter would have been 65%. In late 1998, the average response in Sofia would perhaps not have been too far away from that in Tallinn, with both surely indicating probabilities well below that in Visegrad countries.

Uncertainty about which countries would join when was difficult to dissipate. Indeed, as late as December 1999, the official view was that "Cyprus, Hungary, Poland, Estonia, the Czech Republic and Slovenia" had made satisfactory progress with the negotiations, but that the "European Council ha[d] decided to convene bilateral intergovernmental conferences in February 2000 to begin negotiations with Romania, Slovakia, Latvia, Lithuania, Bulgaria and Malta on the conditions for their entry into the Union and the ensuing Treaty adjustments" (European Council 1999, pp. 1–2). Clarity about the more precise composition of what later became known as the "two waves," that is, regarding the decision to have ten members joining in 2004 and Bulgaria and Romania joining at a slightly later date, only came in late 2001 (European Council 2001).

The Copenhagen Criteria and the Commission managing and monitoring the accession process were effective in utilising this triple uncertainty (how, when, who) as leverage to accelerate the pace of transformation in Central and Eastern Europe. This strategy, in large part, reflects some key characteristics of the EU, in particular its weak enforcement powers but powerful incentives for outsiders to join (Berglöf and Roland 2000).

The prospect of EU membership (as well as the risk of delayed membership or even the threat of exclusion) was instrumental because it prompted rapid institutional transformation. Many have argued that the prospect of EU membership and membership itself is a major source of benefits in terms of productivity, technology, trade, labour mobility and capital flows. However, the longer-lasting benefits of accession have stemmed from the extraordinarily rapid institutional transformation we witnessed in the run-up to 2004.

Various studies compare the EU anchor thesis with other plausible alternative explanations (such as initial conditions, democracy, civil society, structural reforms, culture, etc.). Many authors initially expected that the prospect of EU membership would have a substantial effect on the design and implementation of structural reforms by relaxing political constraints. We must clarify that we are here distinguishing between key structural reforms such as privatisation, internal (price) and external (trade) liberalisation from others that were earlier on usually referred to as "second-generation reforms," and which could be better described as institutional change (Babecký and Campos 2011). Taking this into account, we start by noting that Beck and Laeven (2006) provide one of the first systematic attempts to understand institutional development in the former socialist economies. Their econometric evidence highlights that countries' historical experience under socialism (more entrenched socialist elites and more years under socialism) as well as those countries with larger endowments of natural resources were less likely to show a consistent build-up of what they term market-compatible institutions. They also show evidence that the prospect of EU membership is associated with countries developing market-based institutions at a faster rate (2006, p. 162). The econometric evidence offered by Di Tommaso et al. (2007) supports these findings, highlighting the role of liberalisation and of economic and political legacies in fostering institutional development in the transition economies. They also report robust evidence that the "signing of a partnership or association agreement with the EU" raises the level of institutional development (2007, p. 875). Schweickert et al. (2011) study the impact of incentives related to potential EU and NATO membership on institutional change in twenty-five transition countries up to 2008. They show evidence that EU membership is a key driver of institutional development even when accounting for economic liberalisation. Schönfelder and Wagner (2016) investigate whether being a member of the euro area or an EU member state or a candidate country of the European Union drives institutional development. They find a differential impact: although there is evidence that the prospect of EU membership is indeed associated with rising institutional development, being an EU member state is not. In more recent work, Schönfelder and Wagner (2019) examine the impact of membership status but instead of investigating the absolute level of institutional development, they look at the effect in terms of convergence in institutional development. They find that the prospect of EU membership is a powerful driver of both beta and sigma convergence in institutional development.

3   The Institutional Channel

Does the prospect of EU membership foster institutional development? Here the three key institutional dimensions we will discuss are the capacity and independence of the public administration (bureaucracy) and of the judiciary (rule of law.) Furthermore, we also analyse competition policy capacity and independence, issues that have not received due attention in the past but have come to the fore recently (Gutierrez and Philippon 2019).

We have seen how the EU anchor thesis postulates that the prospect of membership in the European Union played a key role in filling in the institutional vacuum that followed the collapse of socialism, with highly differentiated effects in Central and Eastern European and the former Soviet Union countries.

The prospect of EU membership turned out to be a major driver of institutional change. But can this be gauged? From 1997 onwards, the EU implemented a system of regular standardised monitoring in a range of institutional areas which corresponded, to a considerable extent, to the individual chapters of the *acquis communautaire*. The *Progress Towards Accession* reports that the European Commission published every year for every candidate country offers a unique vantage point. Quantifying these annual reports yields a longitudinal dataset that captures changes in the nature, direction and speed of convergence of these key institutional areas. These reports provide invaluable details allowing us to trace the national paths in meeting the institutional requirements of EU membership—from the transplantation of laws and regulations to the creation of regulatory organisations endowed with necessary powers, resources and personnel.

By quantifying all progress towards accession, Bruszt and Campos (2019) constructed a panel of new de jure (independence) and de facto (capacity) institutional measures for 17 EU candidate countries yearly since 1997.[1] The analysis concentrates on three key institutional areas—the judiciary, bureaucracy and competition policy—and includes measures of potential inputs and outputs into each of these three areas.

Figure 14.1 summarises these measures. It displays the yearly averages of six key outcome measures, namely, the capacity and independence of the judiciary, of the bureaucracy and of competition policy for all (post-1995) 17 EU candidate countries. For instance, judiciary capacity refers to access to the necessary resources and expertise, while independence is defined in terms of appointment and promotion of judges. EU norms establish basic parameters for the functioning of the judiciary, emphasising workload and bottlenecks of the judicial system.

These are categorical variables taking values between 1 and 4, with 4 indicating levels of institutional development comparable to those of established EU member states and 1 reflecting severe deficiencies in moving towards EU norms. We divide the countries between those that joined the EU (new member states, NMS) and those that did not (candidates). For most of the former, data are available yearly between 1997 and 2005, while for the latter between 2005 and 2013. In the figure, we overlap these nine-year windows.

This rich data provides detailed empirical evidence of a powerful EU anchor in terms of institutional development. The prospect of EU membership seems to have been a formidable driver of institutional change among candidate countries, for those joining both early and late. Moreover, the prospect of EU membership fostered a narrowing of the gap between these countries' levels of institutional development and that of EU existing members.

The EU anchor seems to have been especially powerful regarding the independence of competition policy authorities and judiciary capacity, both increasing dramatically in a relatively short period of time. There also seems

---

[1] The 17 candidate countries are divided into new members states (NMS) and candidate countries. NMS are Bulgaria, Croatia, the Czech Republic, Estonia, Hungary, Latvia, Lithuania, Poland, Romania, Slovakia and Slovenia. Candidate countries in the sample are Albania, Bosnia, Kosovo, Macedonia, Montenegro, Serbia and Turkey.

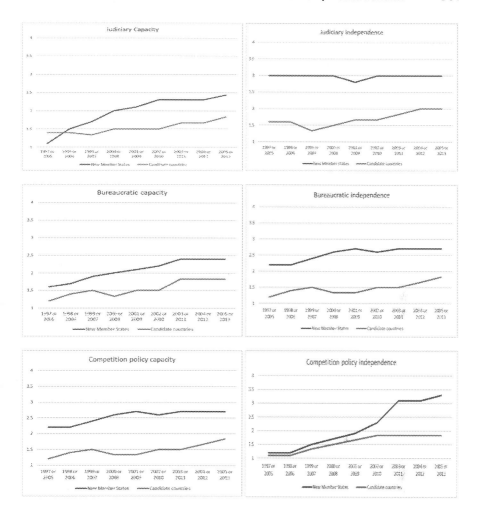

Fig. 14.1 The institutional lift from the prospect of EU membership: yearly averages for new member states (1997–2005) and candidate countries (2005–2013) of six key de jure (independence) and de facto (capacity) institutional dimensions. (Source: Bruszt and Campos 2019)

to be strong evidence of the effects that the prospect of EU membership has had in terms of the capacity and independence of the civil service (bureaucracy) as well as regarding competition policy capacity. Out of six key dimensions, in only one case (namely, judiciary independence) we see weak evidence of institutional development in the run-up to EU membership. This is interesting: it can be either because most of the relevant changes took place at the very beginning of the transition (and hence before 1997; notice that such a caveat needs also be considered for all institutional dimensions) or because this was indeed lagging (as students of populism in Central Europe may nowadays fear).

It really cannot be stressed enough that the institutional change documented above happened over nine years, not nine decades, and it was not preceded by a violent or long international war. This makes it a truly extraordinary evolution.

There are at least four other aspects worth mentioning because they raise interesting questions for future research. Firstly, the levels at the end of the time-windows for the new member states and for candidates tend to be higher for de jure (independence) than for de facto (capacity) dimensions. It would be nice to have similarly detailed institutional data for earlier members so as to compare entrants' progress with the situations within the EU.

Secondly, neither new member states nor candidate groups seem to have reached, at the end of the period of analysis, average EU levels (a score of 4) in any of these six institutional dimensions. On the one hand, this attests to the quality of the data and to the political nature of the accession decision. On the other, it highlights the need for a fuller political-economy understanding of the accession process.

Thirdly, although there is surprisingly little difference between new member states and candidates at the outset, the speed of convergence of the latter group has been much slower. This may point towards variation in the credibility of the prospect of EU membership to act as an anchor over time, something we still know little about.

Last, but not the least, these reports stop once a country joins the EU. Yet the impression one gets is that progress has slowed after accession or, put differently, once a country is part of the EU, the impact of this anchor fades or even disappears.

4   Effects of EU Membership

The previous section has shown that across a variety of institutional domains one can observe much bigger improvements among countries on their way to join the EU compared to those for which the prospect of joining is more remote. The next natural question is whether the effects of these institutional improvements prompted by the possibility of EU membership are indirect or direct (i.e., whether they can be identified directly in terms of growth and productivity.)

There is a disappointingly small literature presenting econometric estimates of the benefits from EU membership. More precisely, there are very few papers or books that answer questions such as "what would be the level of per capita income in a given country had it not joined the EU?" Many believe, incorrectly, that this literature is vast because of the many papers on the benefits from trade liberalisation, from the single market and from the euro (see, among others, Baldwin and Seghezza (1996), Baldwin (1989), and Frankel (2010), respectively). Yet, papers on the benefits of membership itself are few and far between.

There are at least two main reasons for this paucity. Badinger and Breuss (2011) note that "[g]enerally it is easier to conduct ex ante studies on economic integration than to analyse the outcome ex post. This is also documented by the much larger number of ex ante studies. Some of the rare ex post studies, in particular those on the single market, are somewhat disillusioning. The expected pro-competitive effects and the implied growth bonus from the single market appear to have not been fully realised so far. To some extent this also applies to the Economic and Monetary Union of the European Union" (2011, p. 308). On the other hand, Sapir (2011) argues that while the literature on the static benefits of integration is vast, that on the dynamic benefits is scarce.

Moreover, the majority of these studies are quite candid about the fragility of their estimates. Henrekson et al. (1997) estimate that membership may increase growth rates by about 0.6% to 0.8% per year but note that such estimates are "not completely robust" (1997, p. 1551). Badinger (2005) estimates that "GDP per capita of the EU would be approximately one-fifth lower today if no integration had taken place since 1950" but cautions that these are "not completely robust" (p. 50). Crespo Cuaresma et al. (2008) find large growth effects from EU membership, but warn that country heterogeneity remains a real concern. Indeed, country heterogeneity is one of the most common reasons invoked for the lack of robustness of these effects.

Campos et al. (2019) use the synthetic control method (SCM) to estimate EU membership benefits—on a country-by-country basis—in terms of economic growth and productivity. SCM is used to estimate what would have been the levels of per capita GDP and productivity if such country had not become a full-fledged EU member. Notice that although EU membership is ultimately binary (membership is yes/no), economic integration is a continuum. There are many areas over which economies integrate (finance, goods, services, policies, etc.) and it is plausible that this process varies across areas and over time.

The synthetic control method estimates the effect of a given intervention (in this case, joining the EU in 2004) by comparing the evolution of an aggregate outcome variable (growth and productivity) for a country affected by the intervention vis-à-vis that for an "artificial control group." The latter is a weighted combination of other units (countries) chosen so as to match the treated country, before intervention, for a set of predictors of the outcome variable.

Because accession implies lengthy negotiations, it means that the prospect of membership is announced in advance. Therefore, anticipation effects are potentially a very important issue. In particular, they may lessen the relevance of the official date of EU accession as a "treatment." This is particularly important for the 2004 Enlargement. For this reason, Campos et al. (2019) present results not only for both growth and productivity, but also for both the actual date of enlargement (2004) and also for a date that marks the start of the officially monitored accession period (i.e., after 1998).

Figure 14.2 shows estimates of the benefits of joining the EU for the eight former transition economies that did so in 2004. What is the magnitude of these economic benefits? Campos et al. (2019) compute the difference between actual and synthetic counterfactuals in per capita GDP for the whole period, using the first ten and the first five years after accession. This allows them to compare the results from the 2004 Enlargement to those from previous enlargements.

There is considerable heterogeneity across countries. Estimates of the net benefits of joining the EU are clearly much larger in, for instance, Lithuania and Latvia than in Slovakia and Slovenia. Yet they are all positive across the board. For the first ten years post-accession, these estimates suggest that if these eight countries had not joined the EU, their per capita incomes would have been approximately 15% lower. These range from 31% for Latvia to a mere 0.3% for Slovakia and are particularly significant for the Baltics and Hungary.

This exercise answers another interesting question: are these 15% net benefits from the 2004 Enlargement different (larger or smaller) than the benefits from previous enlargements? A key caveat in this case is that because enlargements were spread over time, the set of incumbent countries, the "accession criteria" and the economic and political context all changed substantially between 1973 and 2013. With these in mind, Campos et al. (2019) estimate that smaller benefits accrue to the Scandinavian enlargement (about 4%), while the estimated benefit for the 1973 Enlargement and for Spain is smaller but comparable (12%) to that of the 2004 Enlargement, and that of Portugal is larger (20%). They find negative returns for only one country: Greece.

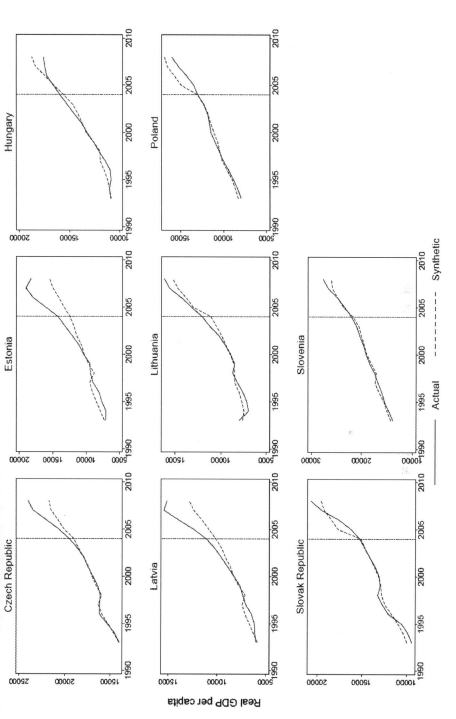

Fig 14.2 The effects of the prospect of EU membership on per capita income: synthetic counterfactual estimates for the eight Central and Eastern European former communist countries that joined the European Union in 2004. (Source: Campos et al. 2019)

5   Conclusions

The sharp dividing line which opened up during the transition between the CEE and FSU countries was among the least expected developments that followed the fall of the Berlin Wall. The differences that emerged over a large range of issues but also how long they persisted are both remarkable. It is a huge challenge to explain this divide because it is surely a product of various and complex reasons.

However, one reason that we believe played a large role is the prospect of joining the EU, which influenced differentially the countries of CEE compared to those of the FSU, with the notable exception of the Baltic states. The institutional vacuum that appeared early in transition was successfully filled in some countries (CEE and the Baltics) but not in others (rest of the FSU) and this has had political as well as economic implications (EU membership for the former, and faster growth and greater productivity for the latter).

This chapter has shown evidence that not only did the prospect of EU membership foster institutional development in the CEE (but not in FSU countries), but it also had significant effects on economic growth and productivity. The chapter documented the initial institutional gap and how the EU anchor was instrumental in closing it in the countries that actually joined the EU (even when compared to other candidate countries that have not yet joined). We showed that institutional development prompted by the prospect of EU membership is clearly documented for the judiciary, bureaucracy and competition policy. Further evidence is now available that shows that CEE countries experienced deeper institutional development, which translated into faster GDP and productivity growth. These results strongly suggest that the EU anchor thesis is a credible explanation for an important part of the starkly contrasting transition experiences observed following the collapse of communism, especially when comparing the CEE and the Baltic states versus the rest of the FSU.

A number of suggestions for future research emerge from this analysis. Firstly, it is important to promote the construction of more granular measures of institutional change, covering a broader range of institutional aspects, as well as more countries and years. Secondly, and once better measures are available, it will be important to try to establish more solidly the relative roles of EU membership, on the one hand, and liberalisation and initial economic, political and social conditions, on the other, as main drivers of institutional development. Thirdly, further theoretical work should be carried out to provide a clear conceptual as well as empirical understanding of the direct and indirect (via institutions) effects of EU membership on productivity.

References

Babecký, J., & Campos, N. F. (2011). Does Reform Work? An Econometric Survey of the Reform–growth Puzzle. *Journal of Comparative Economics, 39*(2), 140–158.

Badinger, H. (2005). Growth Effects of Economic Integration: Evidence from the EU Member States. *Review of World Economics, 141*, 50–78.

Badinger, H., & Breuss, F. (2011). The Quantitative Effects of European Post-war Economic Integration. In M. Jovanovic (Ed.), *International Handbook on the Economics of Integration*. London: Palgrave Macmillan.

Baldwin, R. (1989). The Growth Effects of 1992. *Economic Policy, 9*, 247–281.

Baldwin, R., François, J., & Portes, R. (1997). The Costs and Benefits of the Eastern Enlargement: The Impact on the EU and Central Europe. *Economic Policy, 12*, 125–176.

Baldwin, R., & Seghezza, E. (1996). Growth and European Integration: Towards an Empirical Assessment. *CEPR Discussion Paper No. 1393*.

Beck, T., & Laeven, L. (2006). Institution Building and Growth in Transition Economies. *Journal of Economic Growth, 11*(2), 157–186.

Berglöf, E., & Bolton, P. (2002). The Great Divide and Beyond: Financial Architecture in Transition. *Journal of Economic Perspectives, 16*(1), 77–100.

Berglöf, E., & Roland, G. (1997). *The EU as an 'Outside Anchor' for Transition Reforms*. Stockholm: Östekonomiska Institutet.

Berglöf, E., & Roland, G. (2000). From 'Regatta' to 'Big Bang'? The Impact of the EU Accession Strategy on Reforms in Central and Eastern Europe. IMF, mimeo.

Bruszt, L., & Campos, N. F. (2019). Economic Integration and State Capacity. *Journal of Institutional Economics, 15*(3), 449–468.

Campos, N. F., & Coricelli, F. (2002). Growth in Transition: What We Know, What We Don't, and What We Should. *Journal of Economic Literature, 40*(3), 793–836.

Campos, N. F., Coricelli, F., & Moretti, L. (2019). Institutional Integration and Economic Growth in Europe. *Journal of Monetary Economics, 103*, 88–104.

Crespo Cuaresma, J., Ritzberger-Grünwald, D., & Silgoner, M. A. (2008). Growth, Convergence and EU Membership. *Applied Economics, 40*, 643–656.

Di Tommaso, M., Raiser, M., & Weeks, M. (2007). Home Grown or Imported? Initial Conditions, External Anchors and the Determinants of Institutional Reform in the Transition Economies. *Economic Journal, 117*(520), 858–881.

European Council. (1993). *Copenhagen European Council: Conclusions of the Presidency*. Reproduced from the Bulletin of the European Communities 6/1993.

European Council. (1994). *Essen European Council: Conclusions of the Presidency*. Reproduced from the Bulletin of the European Communities 12/1994.

European Council. (1997). *Amsterdam European Council: Conclusions of the Presidency.* Reproduced from the Bulletin of the European Communities 6/1997.

European Council. (1999). *Helsinki European Council: Conclusions of the Presidency.* Reproduced from the Bulletin of the European Communities 12/1999.

European Council. (2001). *Laeken European Council: Conclusions of the Presidency.* Reproduced from the Bulletin of the European Communities 12/2001.

Frankel, J. (2010). The Estimated Trade Effects of the Euro. In A. Alesina & F. Giavazzi (Eds.), *Europe and the Euro.* Chicago: University of Chicago Press.

Friedrich, C., Schnabel, I., & Zettelmeyer, J. (2013). Financial Integration and Growth: Why is Emerging Europe Different? *Journal of International Economics, 89*(2), 522–538.

Guiso, L., Herrera, H., Morelli, M., & Sonno, T. (2019). Global Crises and Populism: The Role of Eurozone Institutions. *Economic Policy, 34,* 95–139.

Gutierrez, G., & Philippon, T. (2019). How EU Markets Became More Competitive Than US Markets: A Study of Institutional Drift. NYU, mimeo.

Henrekson, M., Torstensson, J., & Torstensson, R. (1997). Growth Effects of European Integration. *European Economic Review, 41,* 1537–1557.

Roland, G. (2000). *Transition and Economics: Politics, Markets, and Firms.* MIT Press.

Roland, G., & Verdier, T. (2003). Law Enforcement and Transition. *European Economic Review, 47*(4), 669–685.

Sapir, A. (2011). European Integration at the Crossroads: A Review Essay on the 50th Anniversary of Bela Balassa's Theory of Economic Integration. *Journal of Economic Literature, 49*(4), 1200–1229.

Schönfelder, N., & Wagner, H. (2016). Impact of European Integration on Institutional Development. *Journal of Economic Integration, 31*(3), 472–530.

Schönfelder, N., & Wagner, H. (2019). Institutional Convergence in Europe. *Economics, 13*(2019-3), 1–23.

Schweickert, R., Melnykovska, I., Belke, A., & Bordon, I. (2011). Prospective NATO or EU Membership and Institutional Change in Transition Countries. *Economics of Transition, 19*(4), 667–692.

Tatham, A. F. (2009). *Enlargement of the European Union.* Kluwer Law.

15

Some Reflections on Transition: Its Roots, Complexity of the Process, and Role of the IMF and Other Organizations

Vito Tanzi

1 Historical Background on Central Planning

At the end of the nineteenth century when the Marxist branch of socialism—the version that would nationalize the means of production and eliminate free markets replacing them with decisions made by central planners representing the Communist Party—started attracting large followings among workers and intellectuals, the reaction of orthodox and, predominantly, laissez-faire economists was highly skeptical. They doubted that such a system could be feasible in the real world. Economic systems need a market, and a market needs prices, for determining the use and the exchange of capital and consumer goods. It was also realized that markets need some essential public and private institutions to protect property rights, insure the sanctity of contracts, and prevent abuses.

In those years, two important Italian economists, Vilfredo Pareto, in 1896, and Enrico Barone, in 1908, were among the very few economists who thought that the system proposed by Marx, while difficult, might be possible, at least in theory. Barone provided an elaborate, mathematical proof to that

Conversations with John Odling-Smee were particularly helpful. Oleh Havrylyshyn and George Iden, at the IMF; Salvatore Schiavo-Campo, at the World Bank; Piroska Nagy, at the EBRD; and Istvan Szekely, at the European Commission, also provided useful information. Of course, all of the above are not responsible for the views expressed in this chapter or for any errors that it may contain.

V. Tanzi (✉)
Honoraty President, International Institute of Public Finance, Munich, Germany

© The Author(s) 2021
E. Douarin, O. Havrylyshyn (eds.), *The Palgrave Handbook of Comparative Economics*,
https://doi.org/10.1007/978-3-030-50888-3_15

effect. The debate about the feasibility of central planning continued and became more intense after the Bolshevik Revolution, in 1917, the confiscation of private property, and the introduction of central planning, in Lenin's and Stalin's Russia. Russia provided the first real life test of Marx' ideas. In later years, other countries would provide additional tests.

In a book first published in Germany, in 1922, Ludwig von Mises reaffirmed the view that a collectivist system would need a system of prices, for allocating consumer and capital goods. While in a market economy the needed prices were determined by the market, he rhetorically asked: how would they be determined in an economy without a market? His conclusion was a negative one: in such an economy, it would not be possible to organize, rationally and efficiently, the system of production. Therefore, the system would generate large inefficiency and much waste.

A couple years later, after a visit to Russia, during his honeymoon with his Russian-born wife, where he could observe directly ongoing developments, John Maynard Keynes (1925) wrote that he had not been impressed by what he had seen in the USSR economy. What had impressed him, however, was the almost religious spirit and dedication that he had observed among the revolutionaries and the workers.

In spite of the above concerns, by major, non-socialist economists, the economy of the USSR did survive. Furthermore, in the decade of the 1930s, while much of the rest of the world was in a deep state of depression, it was carrying out a major process of industrialization that, in the 1940s, would make possible for it to defeat the powerful military forces of Nazi Germany, and in the preceding years had also produced some impressive infrastructural works, including the Moscow Metro.

During the late 1920s and the decade of the 1930s, the feasibility of a (Marxist) planned economy continued to be debated by economists, and the debate became progressively more intense, especially during the Great Depression. The feasibility and efficiency of a collectivist economic system continued to be questioned, especially by economists of the Austrian School, including F. Hayek, von Mises, and others (for example: see von Hayek, 1988). The planned system was defended by a small but growing number of prominent economists, who had some sympathies for the socialist ideology. These economists included Lord Robbins, Abba Lerner, and Fred Taylor, who was the then president of the American Economic Association, Oscar Lange, and some others at the University of Cambridge in England (e.g. Lange and Taylor, 1938).

The Great Depression had raised fundamental questions, in the mind of many economists and citizens, about the claimed superiority of the market system and even about the survivability of economies that depended on it. The impact that the Depression was having on the quality of life and on the standards of living of many unemployed workers in capitalistic countries had made the debate highly, and inevitably, topical. It had become more difficult to defend a system that was leaving a fourth of all workers without jobs and many families without income.

The nationalization of the means of production and the introduction of central planning in Russia had put a small group of bureaucrats, who claimed to represent all workers on behalf of the Communist Party, in charge of most of the important economic decisions. These decisions included what to produce; where to invest the available, scarce capital resources; how to use the available workers; how much to save for the country; how and also to whom to distribute what was produced; what part of the consumer goods that were produced would be offered free to the citizens, and what part would be sold; what money wages would workers get, and how different should wages be across occupations, in a society that aimed at equality in the standards of living; how would the output of collective farms and the products of public enterprises be sold; how to insure that demands for the goods sold were met by sufficient supplies; what pensions would workers receive when they retired; and so on. These questions point to the difficulties that the planners faced. They also explain the skepticism expressed by orthodox economists about central planning.

Although the above decisions were undoubtedly difficult to make and they challenged the skills of the planners, and mistakes occurred, they were being made. The Soviet economy was surviving and was surviving without the 25–30 percent unemployment rates, and the large collapse in outputs, that many market economies were experiencing in the 1930s. As a consequence, the debate moved from whether the Marxist form of socialism was feasible, to whether it was efficient, compared with market economies.

As applied in the USSR, central planning had rendered unnecessary the existence of many institutions, both public and private, and also of many individual skills, that exist in market economies. Therefore, the USSR and, later, other planned economies had existed, some for decades, without these institutions and skills. In later years, when they initiated their transition to become market economies, these countries would need these institutions and skills. The missing institutions would have to be created, and the missing skills would need to be reacquired, to make the transition feasible, efficient, and durable. This could not be achieved overnight, by simply changing some laws and some policies. Their creation would require years and much effort. This would be an area that would create difficulties during the transition.

On the government side, institutions such as tax systems, tax administrations, budget offices, treasuries, pension systems, regulatory commissions, genuine central banks and other financial institutions, that had not been necessary in a centrally-planned economy, and that in market economies had developed over centuries, would again become necessary and would have to be created In a short time.

On the private side, commercial, saving, and investment banks, financial markets, stock markets, privately owned enterprises, limited liabilities enterprises and other legal forms of enterprises, realistic depreciation rules, payment systems, various kinds of legal services, bankruptcy procedures, liability rules for shareholders, ownership rules, real estate agencies, and so on would be needed. See Djankov et al. (2003). These institutions, skills, and rules would be needed before the centrally planned economies could reconvert into viable, market economies. The countries would also need some long-term financial assistance during the period of reconversion.

No existing international organization had all the needed resources and knowledge to provide guidance and assistance in all the above areas. Therefore, a cooperative effort, one that would include various International Financial Institutions (IFIs), some foreign banks and governments, and others, would have to be involved. This would create some initial, obvious problems of coordination, cooperation, and, at times, leadership. The main international institutions that would be involved, besides the International Monetary Fund (IMF) and the World Bank, were the European Bank for Reconstruction and Development (EBRD) and the European Commission, although the Economic for Organisation Co-operation and Development (OECD) and the Asian Development Bank (ADB) would also play some roles.

The USSR had been the first country to introduce central planning, and it had almost completely abolished private property and the free market. Furthermore it had lived with the centrally planned system for some seven decades, until at least the end of the 1980s. Therefore, by the time of the transition, no living Russian had any useful memory of how a market economy, even an imperfect one, operated. Contacts with market economies had been limited, so that even economics books and theoretical knowledge had not been easily available to most Russians. This meant that very few, if any, Russians, had a clear idea on what to do—a problem that may have been even greater in some of the other newly independent states.

Other transition countries had introduced central planning decades later, after World War II, or in the case of China even later. Furthermore, some of those countries had introduced lighter versions of central planning (Hungary, Poland, Yugoslavia, and some others). The lighter version had retained some market features and had left some space for small private activities and to individual incentives and initiatives. Hungary had joined the IMF in 1982 and in the 1980s had already received some technical assistance from the IMF. Poland had joined the IMF in 1986 and had continued to allow some private activities and some private ownership of land during the years of central planning.

Some economists from these countries had been allowed to participate in the annual congresses of international academic associations, such as the International Institute of Public Finance, IIPF. Hungarian and Polish members had even been part of the Boards of the IIPF. One of these individuals would become prime minister of Hungary. See chapter on Hungary, in Tanzi (2010). China had applied for membership in the IMF in the mid-1980s. See Tanzi (2008). These countries would find somewhat easier to make the transition back to markets, or, in the case of China, a transition to a mixture of market and state control. These countries had still some living individuals who had memories of how markets had operated. Some of them, such as Hungary and Poland, had important economists, such as Kornai and Balcerowics who understood markets. For these countries, the transition would be less traumatic and more successful.

2   From the 1940s to the 1980s

When World War II ended, the USSR emerged as one of the winners of the war. In the years that had preceded the war, and during the war, its centrally planned economy had proven to be sufficiently robust, and it had focused its resources toward the production of *essential, basic* goods, the creation of major infrastructures, and the production of war materials (tanks, planes, and ammunitions) that had made it possible for it to win the war, even though at great costs.

It ought to be noted that, during wars, market economies tend to resemble, in various aspects, centrally controlled economies. The reason is that they have to promote a limited objective with their limited resources, that of *winning the war*. During wars, government spending goes sharply up, many prices are controlled, *rationing* of various goods is introduced, many private enterprises shift their activities toward producing war material, tax rates go up, and *conscription* in the armed forces becomes acceptable, even in democratic economies. These changes make market economies resemble, in some important ways, those of collective systems, while the war lasts.

By the end of World War II, the Soviet Union had become one of the two world's super powers. It had acquired both military might and, for many people, ideological, or soft, power. It had also brought under its control a large number of East European and Asian countries that had chosen, or, more often, had been forced, to adopt some version of the same economic system and of the same political ideology as Russia's. Many of these countries had become closely linked in a large political and economic structure that had become the Soviet Union, or in other looser political and economic aggregates.

Within that Soviet Union there was regional specialization. Some countries specialized in producing particular goods, which they exchanged for other goods with the other members of the Union. There was far less economic exchange with the rest of the world. The exchanges between Soviet countries were conducted either through barter or using artificial and bureaucratically set prices. No genuine market prices were used because such prices did not exist, and there was no use of financial instruments. Money was just a convenient means of keeping accounts.

In the 1950s, the USSR was widely considered a successful and powerful country, both economically and militarily. It had definitely become a great power. By the end of the 1950s, it was considered so powerful and so successful that questions were being raised, both in the USA and in other countries, as which economic system, market or centrally planned, would end up winning the long-run competition for the minds and souls of the world populations. In the late 1950s, there was even a study, commissioned by the Joint Economic Committee of the US Congress, which addressed the above issue. The study was directed by Professor Otto Eckstein, a refugee from Germany, who was then the youngest, full professor in the economics department at Harvard. Many leading economists of that period contributed to that study. The group produced a report (the "Eckstein Report") that, according to some Kennedy biographers, influenced significantly the thinking of the Kennedy Administration and its response to the challenges that were coming from the Soviet Union in those years. See Tanzi (2019).

As time passed and as the war years became a distant memory, the economy started facing some of the difficulties that von Mises, Hayek, and others had anticipated in the 1920s and 1930. As the number of goods (and, increasingly, of services) produced became more numerous, more diverse, and more sophisticated, and as the initial and almost religious, socialist enthusiasm, that both Pareto and Keynes had recognized in earlier decades, started to be replaced by growing cynicism and corruption, the economies of Russia and of other socialist countries started facing growing difficulties, and they started lagging behind the fast growing economies of Western European and other advanced countries.

These problems intensified in later years and became significantly damaging in the 1980s, when the USSR had to increase its military spending, to keep up with that of the USA, during the Reagan Administration, and had to deal with growing corruption. See David Remnick's Pulitzer Prize winning book, 1993. In later years, the economic difficulties would intensify and would bring the collapse of the Soviet System, and the realization, by many economists, that the criticisms that had been advanced in past decades, by von Mises, Hayek, and others, had had validity.

Janos Kornai had reported, in his 1992 book, data on the larger amounts of energy and capital needed to produce a given amount of GDP in several centrally planned economies, compared with market economies. And Wassily Leontief, the Russian-born Nobel Prize winner and the creator of the "input-output system", had referred to the centrally planned system as an "input-input system", because large inputs went in, but little valuable output came out of it.

A basic conclusion would be that central planning works better in economies which are producing few basic goods for everyone. It works progressively less well as the economies become richer and they need to produce more, and more differentiated, goods and services. When the incentives of *individuals* became more important than those of the whole *community*, and when the quality and the number of goods and services to be produced increased, the collective system lost much of its attraction, and it proved to be inefficient. By that time the centrally planned economies had produced their own class structures, the "new class", that was based on different privileges for different members. It had become a less egalitarian society.

In the 1980s, the time had come to begin to think about abandoning a ship that was having difficulties and had started to sink, and about initiating a transition to a new system. By a trick of history, the 1980s and the 1990s were years when, after many years of "Keynesian Revolution" and the growth of welfare states in advanced countries, the free market and a limited government role had come to being glorified, again, by many Western economists, as they had been in the distant past, during the laissez-faire years. Those were the years when the "Washington Consensus" and "market fundamentalism" had become popular and the pursuit of efficiency was being glorified over that of equity.

These pro-market ideologies would urge, or often push, several centrally planned countries to undertake regulatory and tax policies that would move their economies toward significantly free markets, with relatively little government interventions. They would influence the final destination that several (but not all) transition countries would aim for and would reach. If the transition had taken place two decades earlier, the final destinations might have been a little different. It would have had a little less market and a little more government and more concern for equity. The outcomes would have been more equitable, which might have reduced future problems, such as populist mistrust of democracies and of markets.

Between 1987–1988 and 1993–1995, while the transition was under way, the Gini coefficients of many transition countries (Russia, Ukraine, Kyrgyzstan, Lithuania, Moldova, Turkmenistan, Estonia, and some others) increased a great deal. In several cases they increased by more than 20 points, reaching the level of the Gini coefficient in the USA. In only a few countries (Slovak, Hungary, Slovenia, Poland) were the changes small. See Tanzi and Tsibouris (2000, Table 3, p. 181) and Kolodko (2000, Table 4.3, p. 127); both tables were based on data from Milanovic (1998). During the years of central planning, the income distribution had been relatively even, broadly similar to that of Denmark.

3   The Start of the Transition

By the second half of the 1980s, disenchantment with central planning and growing macroeconomic problems reached a zenith. The possibility of giving more freedom to the Russian and to other economies started with attempts, by Gorbachev, in the 1985–1990 years, to bring some changes to the system but without abandoning it. That attempt would create macroeconomic difficulties, because it weakened the existing, controlled economic system without replacing it with a viable alternative. The attempt started to create a kind of institutional vacuum, with damaging consequences for the economy. Some, initially timid, movement toward creating a new system started in the early 1990s, in Russia, and in other centrally planned countries, including China. It lasted for about a decade. That decade included some very difficult years, for both the Russian population, for that of other Soviet republics and for other centrally planned economies, with the exception of China that had started growing at a high rate. See Tanzi (2008).

In the 1990–1997 period the average *annual* rate of growth of many transition economies became negative. In some of them it became as negative as 10 or more percent. Declines of this magnitude had not even been seen during the Great Depression. Only a few countries (Poland, Slovenia, Czech Republic, and Hungary) escaped these deep depressions, which in several countries reduced the estimated GDPs by more than half and in some by up to 80 percent. In Russia the annual, negative rate of growth over that period had been almost 8 percent, and the GDP had fallen by about half. See Table 2.1, p. 58, in Kolodko (2000).

In those years Russia and all the newly independent countries became members of the IMF and of other global institutions. Experts from the IMF, the World Bank, the OECD, and the EBRD, in close collaboration with the European Commission, made a first joint visit to Russia in 1990 and produced a report (IMF, the World Bank, OECD and EBRD, 1990) that set out the assistance that these institutions could provide in future years, in stabilization and in structural policies. There would be frequent visits to Moscow and to other transition countries in the years that followed. See also IMF, the World Bank, OECD and EBRD (1991).

In 1992 a training center was opened in Vienna by three IFIs (IMF, World Bank, and EBRD) with the aim of training personnel from Russia and from other former Soviet Union countries on how market economies operated. The teaching was done by staff sent from the IMF, the World Bank, and the EBRD. The courses were often attended by high officials from the transition economies. Some of them would assume ministerial positions in later years.

The transition to market would require major changes, first in the minds of many individuals, who had lived under central planning and, in the case of Russian individuals, had continued to believe that Russia was still a world power, undergoing temporary and correctable difficulties. See Tanzi (2010). They were facing a new world, one alien to them. They needed to adjust to the reduced standing that their country had on the world stage. This would prove to be difficult. In some ways the experience of the Russians resembled that of individuals sent to another planet, one with different physical laws and ecology. This attitude would make it harder for them to accept the technical advice that they would receive, compared with officials from other countries that did not have these mental blocks.

Perhaps a comment could be made about the reaction of Chinese officials to the advice that they were receiving, and that proved to be very productive to China. See Ahmad et al. (1995). I shall cite from p. 34 of my 2008 book on China.

The form of collaboration [the technical assistance to China] had a distinct Chinese flavor that made it different from [that of] Russia. In short, in other cases, a country would request a Fund mission that would visit the country for two-three weeks and would write a lengthy [confidential] report, making specific recommendations. If the country liked the recommendations, it might either implement them, or occasionally ask for the temporary stationing in the country of [highly qualified] experts, hired by the IMF. These experts would assist the country's authorities in the daily process of implementation of the Fund's recommendations. In some cases, as for example in the reform of treasures, the creation of budget offices, the reform of customs, or the introduction of value added taxes, this implementation required a lot of nuts-and- bolt knowledge and daily decisions that only experts who had been through this process in their own countries had the knowledge to make. The Chinese were not interested in this form of assistance. With them we would agree on a program of assistance that involved seminars in China with IMF experts, visits in Washington by large number of Chinese, additional seminars, discussions of particular topics and reports that did not tell them what to do but that described in some detail, what other countries—countries chosen by the Chinese authorities—had done in a particular area adding our own observation on the practice. (p. 34)

During these exchanges, we found the Chinese participants extremely serious and involved listeners. They specifically discouraged us from choosing a specific option. After these discussions, it would be they, rather than the IMF, who would select the preferred course of action. (pp. 34–35)

The transition would require long-term financial assistance, human resources, and much adaptation. The simple and quick transplanting of the policies and the institutions of market economies to the transition countries would be neither wise nor possible. But a too slow transition risked placing those who continued to believe in the old system in charge of the new, after some cosmetic changes.

The needed assistance was expected to come mainly from the IMF, the World Bank, the newly created EBRD, and to a much lesser extent the OECD and the European Commission. It was also expected to come from a few foreign governments and especially from the US government, and a few foreign private institutions.

Because of its financial resources and its capacity to act quickly, the IMF found itself often in a leading position. Gaidar, who for a crucial period was the Russian prime minister, once commented to the author of this chapter that the central role of the IMF was a mistake, because the comparative advantage and the focus of the IMF were macroeconomic stability, and short-run financial assistance, while the transition countries and Russia in particular needed structural and institutional changes and long-term financial assistance. There was some truth in Gaidar's view, even though the IMF had several departments capable of providing assistance in the creation of the missing institutions. However, a slow process of change would have created its own difficulties, because insiders would have found it easier to maintain power.

Free agents and *private* financial institutions from some foreign countries, especially from the USA, hoping to make large financial gains from the ongoing chaos in all of the former Soviet countries would play a significant and not always a positive role, especially during the process of privatization of state assets, a process that required large funds to purchase the assets, and during the creation of financial markets, when public bonds, which, because of the high risks, paid high nominal interest rates, became available, in the second half of the 1990s. These developments attracted foreign speculators and, in turn, may have put some indirect pressures on the IMF to keep the Russian market liquid with its stabilization programs. This may have happened with the 1998 financial program to Russia by the IMF.

Some minor problems of coordination among the activities of the various actors, assisting with the transition, would inevitably develop, especially at the personal level, but they did not become significant. For the most part the different institutions focused on their specific areas of responsibilities and cooperated. The missions that visited the countries often had staff members from more than one institution. However, the fact that the time horizon of the IMF was shorter than that of other IFIs, and also, at the beginning, that the managers of three of the most involved international institutions (the IMF, the EBRD, and the OECD) happened to be French civil servants did create some minor irritants. See Tanzi (2010, pp. 31–32).

Some more fundamental problems and some less important ones arose during the early years of the transition. See Tanzi (2010). The individuals who had to make some of the economic decisions, within the centrally planned economies (especially in Russia), had only vague notions of how market economies operated and had to be convinced of the need for some reforms. For example, they could not conceive that in market economies there was no government office that set the prices of goods and services, and they could not understand who would set the prices.

The precise meanings of some economic terms were, at times, not conveyed by the literary translations of Russian words into English words, and vice versa. Words such as "income", "profit", "ruble zone", and similar had different meanings or connotations in English and Russian at that time. And the concept of interest rate was a total abstraction. In early meetings, this problem made some conversations difficult, in spite of the use of good interpreters. The words could be translated more easily than their meanings could be conveyed.

The problems were not just on the Russian side. On the side of those assisting with the transition (who, for the most part, were economists trained in good American or British universities), it was not always fully appreciated that the economic relations between some dependent and some independent variables (between the supply of a product, the trade balance, or tax revenue, and changes in the prices of products, in the exchange rate, or in a tax rate) depended on the underlying economic structures. It was naïve to expect that the reactions, to changes in these variables, would be the same in Russia at that time as they were assumed to be in well-working market economies.

This problem would have an impact on the results of financial programs. This problem was not always understood, or fully appreciated, by all the economists sent to advise and to assist the transition countries. Some of them continued to put high trust on the impact that some short-run policy changes could have. Especially in the early years, changes in *policies* tended to receive far more attention than changes in *institutions*.

There was a tendency to consider *stabilizing* the economies, whatever that meant, as more important than drastically *transforming* them. For this reason, great importance was given, even by some individuals in higher IMF positions, to the expected (positive) impact that rapidly freeing prices and privatizing state enterprises would have on the economy. *Freeing prices* and *privatizing public enterprise*s were expected to go a long way toward establishing market economies and were considered keys to successful transitions. Unfortunately, in many countries, only freeing prices without developing good market institution and simultaneously expanding money supply led to very high inflations; and privatizing assets led to large changes in the income distributions of many countries. These would create some immediate and some longer-run problems.

There was not enough appreciation that the performance of market economies depends on the existence and the well-functioning of some basic institutions, such as tax systems, tax administrations, treasuries, budget offices, central banks, financial markets, and others. These institutions had been missing in the centrally planned countries, and their creation would require years and much patient work. In the meantime second best alternatives would have to be used and some countries used them. These less optimal alternatives might prove more effective in the short run than in the long run.

In the earlier years, the liberalization of prices could have been limited to particular services and to some products, and the privatization of public enterprises and assets could have been limited to *new* activities, to small enterprises, and possibly to some agricultural land, and small apartments. Large state enterprises, especially those that controlled valuable and exportable natural resources and that could have provided badly needed public revenue and foreign exchanges, could have been kept public, until later times. For the larger public enterprises, the alternative would have been to gradually and progressively promote their commercial behavior and their integration with domestic and world markets.

Some studies have argued that state enterprises, especially in some sectors, may prove to be as productive and efficient as private enterprises. See Estrin et al. (2018). Evidence from some countries, including France, Italy, and some others, provide concrete examples of the existence of economically efficient public enterprises. This was the choice made by China and by a few other centrally planned countries. These countries kept some of the large enterprises public and created some forms of "state capitalism", that combined some central planning with markets and that allowed these countries to grow rapidly, thus avoiding the deep "transition depressions" that Russia and other countries experienced.

Some problems were caused by sequencing, during the1990s. The creation of some essential institutions should have preceded the adopting of some policies, such as the total freeing of prices and the privatizing of public assets, but that approach would have required time and the view was that time was not on the side of a good transition because it would have allowed insiders opposed to the transition to strengthen even more their positions.

That the above problem did not receive the attention that it deserved, within the IMF, becomes clear from a close reading of Boughton's (2012), thousand pages long account of the IMF activities in the 1990s. That book includes hundreds of pages connected with the transition in the Soviet System and the role that the IMF played in Russia and in other transition countries. It focuses mostly on "policies" and on the work of the Fund's area departments. The effort by functional departments to create fiscal and monetary institutions and good statistics, and the difficulties encountered in these essential activities, receives few and superficial mentions in the thousand pages, perhaps because many of the technical assistance reports were "confidential". See pp. 162–164 and 319–336.

A successful move to a market economy would have required significant and longer-run financial assistance, changes in various policies, and *especially* the creation of missing institutions. The policies introduced and the institutional reforms should not have been considered as separate and independent processes but all ingredients that were needed to achieve the final objective, the creation of well-functioning and equitable market economies. Different timing needs, and concerns that insiders would highjack the transition, made this difficult.

The IMF did not have funds for *long-run* financing, and the Western governments, especially the USA, were not willing to provide them, while there were pressures to change these countries and especially Russia in a short time. Furthermore, within both the transition countries, and also within the IFIs, there were few if any individuals who had detailed and intimate knowledge of how centrally planned economies operated *and*, at the same time, deep knowledge of market institutions. The truth was that nobody knew with any precision how to conduct a successful transition, one that would have needed long-run financing, profound policy changes, and institution building. Nobody had a clear idea of what the proper sequencing should be: first institution building or liberalization? The problem faced was totally new, and no previous experience existed to provide an example.[1]

The changes introduced in the early years of the transition had been aimed at destroying the existing, centrally planned economic system that in spite of its obvious and major shortcomings had provided some economic stability and a low level of subsistence to the countries' populations. The changes had also upended the incentive structure that had existed, thus reducing the importance of some positions held by influential bureaucrats and policymakers. This change was certain to stimulate strong oppositions to the reforms from the losers or, in the case of the managers of some potentially valuable public enterprises, to encourage behavior and actions (by insiders, some with contacts and connections in advanced countries), that would make it possible for them to benefit greatly from the privatization programs, as it did.

Some of these insiders would become the future oligarchs who, within the space of a few years, and at still young ages, joined the lists of the world's richest individuals. This would happen in countries that, at that time, were being encouraged to introduce flat taxes and other elements of market fundamentalism, including the elimination of many regulations. See Klebnikov (2000) and Nagy (2000).

For obvious reasons, at the beginning of the transition, there was significant and unavoidable uncertainty on what to do. The departure point (let us call it point A, the centrally planned, economic environment) was broadly known, even though it was somewhat different between the countries that were part of the Soviet Republic and the other centrally planned countries, and so was, within some range, the final destination point (say point B, a free market environment) on which there was little discussion at the time. What was not known was how to get from point A to point B, and there was no available map to show the road.

---

[1] Douarin and Mickiewicz (2017) in Chaps. 3 and 11 discuss the complexity of institution building but also note that during the transition all countries followed a sequence of liberalization then institutions—there is no example of countries doing institutions first.

The above ignorance or uncertainty guaranteed that mistakes would be made and that the transition would require more time and would encounter more difficulties than the "big bang" optimists had expected and that some insiders would take advantage of the changes. The transition would be messy. For many countries, it would include economic depressions deeper than those during the Great Depression of the 1930s, and rates of inflation as high as had been experienced by Latin American countries in the last century.

Unfortunately, for several of the countries, the final destination might be considered less optimal than had been hoped. The transition did not raise the standards of living for the majority of the populations to the levels of the Western European democracies and left many disillusioned with the work of markets, as recent surveys have indicated (EBRD 2011). On the other hand, for a few lucky individuals, the transition brought fabulous riches.

It should be repeated that the ideological climate that prevailed in the Western countries in 1980s and the 1990s, especially in the USA and the UK, and that influenced the policies during the transition ("market fundamentalism" and "Washington Consensus") in indirect ways determined some of the policy choices that were made. Flat taxes, low tax levels, conservative social programs, and deregulation were chosen at a time when the income distributions of several of the countries were becoming, or were expected to become, significantly less even. Also the deep trust in the magic of the market affected some of the choices. Putting it differently, point B had different possible stops, and the one that was chosen by many countries, and the specific road taken to get there, was influenced by the market fundamentalism that was then prevailing in the USA and in some other Western countries in those years.

4   Concluding Comments

Several foreign institutions, governments, and foreign private interests provided assistance to the formerly centrally planned countries during the years of transition. Because of this, and because of the complexity of the task, minor frictions, mistakes, and other difficulties were inevitable, both between different IFIs and even between different parts of some of the IFIs.

Among the IFIs, some different views were held on what to do, how quickly to do it, and who should do it. These differences existed between the International Monetary Fund, on one hand, and the World Bank and the EBRD on the other. The role of the OECD was minimal. The World Bank and the EBRD were involved in specific structural areas and provided some financial assistance to enterprises. But given the circumstances, it can be concluded that collaboration worked better than it might have worked.

Within the IMF, the *functional* departments that dealt mainly with Technical Assistance activities (the Fiscal Affairs Department, the Monetary and Central Banking Department, and the Statistical Department) generally had a better appreciation of the difficulties and the time that would be needed to create institutions, such as tax systems, tax administrations, financial markets and capable central banks, and the development of reliable statistics. Some high level and competent fiscal experts were hired from several countries and worked hard to make the needed changes.

Some of the statistics available and used by the IMF missions, on inflation, GDP levels and changes, and on personal incomes inevitably suffered from shortcomings. As market economies, the countries would need reliable statistics. Pension systems would need major reforms to be sustainable, as would existing health systems. The experts in the regular Fund missions that negotiated the financial programs may not have always fully appreciated the difficulties and the time needed to make the needed institutional reforms.

The Monetary and Central Banking Department made use of experts from at least 23 countries and provided more than 100 man-year of assistance. The assistance from that department dealt with (a) monetary operations and the creation of securities markets for government securities, (b) achieving a market-based determination of interest rates and exchange rates, (c) foreign exchange operations, (d) supervision of banks and of bank restructuring, (e) developing payment systems, (f) central bank accounting and audit, and (g) assistance in legislative framework. See Knight et al. (1999).

The World Bank focused on the legal framework of private property, including the creation and the operations of new forms of private enterprises, and with the many issues arising out of the processes of privatization, in addition to providing loans to enterprises. In some cases the World Bank entered areas of interest and main responsibilities of the IMF, such as tax reform, requiring the occasional need to clarify responsibilities. However in many areas there was close collaboration between the IMF and the World Bank.

The remit of the EBRD was largely that of providing loans to private enterprises while promoting the broad objective of creating private activities within democratic countries. Its activities were broad and, for the most part, they were complementary to those of the IMF. Therefore there were little or no frictions except at the very beginning. The responsibilities of the EBRD were progressively adjusted over the years of its involvement with transition countries.

The area departments of the IMF, which were staffed mainly by economists with a macroeconomic orientation, and whose main function was that of dealing with relatively short-run developments, and with assessing the countries' macroeconomic situations, did not always appreciate the difficulties and the importance of creating new institutions in countries that had not had them. There were times when the area departments engaged in policy advice that could not be successfully implemented because of the absence, or the low efficiency of the existing institutions, including tax administrations. This would create occasional problems.

There would also be differences in the interpretations of some economic terms such as the meaning of "tax evasion" and "fiscal deficits" in the prevailing circumstances. See Tanzi (1993, 2010). These issues occasionally led to some problems, as happened in the 1998 large, IMF financial program with Russia. That program had been based on revenues' estimates that the Fiscal Affairs Department (FAD) had considered highly unrealistic and had challenged. The estimates had been based on the unrealistic assumption that high tax evasion by public enterprises could be quickly reduced. The staff of FAD was not surprised when the program failed within a short time, because of the fiscal difficulties.

Jacques de Larosière, who had been the Managing Director of the IMF in the 1980s and became the second head of the EBRD in 1992, in one of his first acts in his new position, got rid of macroeconomists at the EBRD and replaced them with experts in loans to new enterprises. He rightly saw the role of the EBRD as that of assisting the transition countries in creating democratic countries with market-oriented economies, and not that of short-run stabilization. He had wanted to minimize duplication of functions and possibility of conflict with the IMF. See de Larosière (2018).

The transition by former Soviet countries and many in Central Europe, away from central planning systems, with little or no political and economic liberty for the populations, and from low standards of living, toward market economies with democratic institutions, and toward higher standards of living, was a momentous, extraordinary, and historic event. It was also a highly necessary and desirable one.

The transition accomplished a significant part of the needed change. Because of it, the world is today a safer and much better place than it was before, and that it would have been if the transition had never happened. The IFIs, the many governments, and the individuals that, through their work, contributed to the transition deserve much credit for the results achieved.

Unfortunately, because of (a) the great complexity of the task; (b) the resistance that came from many of those who would lose power in the reformed countries; (c) some errors made during the transition; and, (d) perhaps, the market fundamentalism that prevailed in important countries during the transition years, and that paid little attention to the goal of inequality in the distribution of incomes and to the need to create adequate safety nets for many of the citizens who would lose the low level, but real, protection that the governments had offered them, in many countries, the destination point may have been less good as hoped, or anticipated.

The destination has been associated with significant income inequality and with less social protection, making some or many citizens think nostalgically about the time when many of their financial risks were taken care of by the governments. In many of the transition countries, recent surveys have indicated that (a) respect for democracy is now low; (b) respect for the market economy is also low; (c) populism has become a growing concern; and (d) some of these economies have started to reverse the pro-market and pro-democracy policies that they had introduced in earlier years. See the introduction chapter in Szekely (2019) and EBRD (2011).

Hopefully, this may be just a passing phase, but it is one that is raising worries and that raises questions as to whether a better job could not have been done during the transition years.

References

Ahmad, E., Gao, Q., & Tanzi, V. (1995). *Reforming China's Public Finances*. Washington, DC: IMF.

Barone, E. (1908). Il ministero della produzione nello stato collettivista. Giornale degli Economisti, September, 267–294, October, 391–414. Republished in English, with the Title of "The Ministry of Production in the Collective State", as an Appendix to von Hayek, F. A. (Editor) (1935). Collective Economic Planning: Critical Studies on the Possibility of Socialism (London: George Routledge &Sons).

Boughton, J. M. (2012). *Tearing Down Walls: The International Monetary Fund 1990–1999*. Washington, DC: The International Monetary Fund.

Djankov, S., Gleaser, E., La Porta, R., Lopez-de-Silanes, F., & Shleifer, A. (2003). The New Comparative Economics. *Journal of Comparative Economics, 31*(4), 595–619.

Douarin, E., & Mickiewicz, T. (2017). *Economics of Institutional Change – Central and Eastern Europe Revisited*. London: Palgrave Macmillan.

Estrin, S., Liang, Z., Shapiro, D., & Carney, M. (2018). State Capitalism, Economic Systems and the Performance of State Owned Firms. *Acta Oeconomica, 69*(Special Issue 1), 175–194.

European Bank for Reconstruction and Development. (2011). *Transition Report Chapter 3*. London: EBRD.

Hayek, F. A. von (Ed.). (1988). *The Fatal Conceit: The Errors of Socialism* (W.W. Bartley III, Ed.). The Economics of Chicago Press.

IMF, The World Bank, OECD, and EBRD. (1991). *A Study of the Soviet Economy, Three Volumes*. Washington, DC: World Bank.

IMF, The World Bank, OECD, EBRD. (1990). *The Economy of the USSR*. The World Bank.

Keynes, J. M. (1925). *A Short View of Russia*. London: The Hogarth Press.

Klebnikov, P. (2000). *Godfather of the Kremlin: Boris Berezovsky and the Looting of Russia*. New York, San Diego and London: Harcourt.

Knight, M., Peterson, A. B., & Price, R. T. (1999). *Transforming Financial Systems in the Baltics, Russia, and Other Countries of the Former Soviet Union*. Washington, DC: The International Monetary Fund.

Kolodko, G. W. (2000). *Post-Communist Transition: The Thorny Road*. University of Rochester Press.

Kornai, J. (1992). *The Socialist System: The Political Economy of Communism*. Princeton, NJ: Princeton University Press.

De Larosière, J. (2018). *50 Years of Financial Crises*. Paris: Odile Jacob.

Milanovic, B. (1998). Income. Inequality, and Poverty During the Transition from Planned to Market Economies. World Bank Regional and Sectoral Study, 1998–2002. Washington, DC.

Nagy, P. M. (2000). *The Meltdown of the Russian State*. Cheltenham, UK: Edward Elgar Publishing Limited.

Lange, O. & Taylor, F. M. (1938). *On the Economic Theory of Socialism*. New York, Toronto, London: McGraw-Hill Book Company.

Pareto, V. (1896). *Cours d'Economie Politique* (Vol. II). Lausanne: F. Rouge.

Remnick, D. (1993). *Lenin Tomb: The Last Days of the Soviet Empire*. New York: Random House.

Szekely, I. (Ed.). (2019). *Faces of Convergence*. The Vienna Institute of International Economic Studies.

Tanzi, V. (Ed.). (1992b). *Fiscal Policies in Economies in Transition*. Washington, DC: IMF. Russian and Chinese Editions Available.

Tanzi, V. (1993). Financial Markets and Public Finance in the Transformation Process. Chapter 1 in Tanzi, V. (Editor) Transition to Market: Studies in Fiscal reforms. Washington, DC: IMF. Russian and Chinese editions available.

Tanzi, V. (2008). *Peoples, Places and Policies: China, Japan and Southeast Asia*. New York: Jorge Pinto Books.

Tanzi, V. (2010). *Russian Bears and Somali Sharks: Transition and Other Passages*. New York: Jorge Pinto Books.

Tanzi, V. (2019). Observing Russia's Transition. In *The World of Transformation*. Moscow.

Tanzi, V., & Tsibouris, G. (2000). Fiscal Reform Over Ten Years of Transition. *IMF Working Paper*, 1–32.

Von Mises, L. (1922, English Edition in 1936). *Socialism: An Economic and Sociological Analysis*. London: Jonathan Cape.

16

Are the Transition Economies Still in Transition?

Paul Wachtel

There is no doubt that the fall of the Berlin wall in 1989 and the dissolution of the Soviet Union two years later were dramatic and significant historical watersheds. The cold war that defined international relations in the post-World War II era came to an end and with it the idea that central planning and state ownership were viable approaches to economic organization. In the course of a few years, about 30 countries were thrust into a transition from one economic system to another. In many respects the transition experience was unprecedented and many expected that it would take a long time. Some countries chose a radical approach—termed shock therapy, or big bang—and others a more gradual approach to change. Proponents of the big bang often thought that it would quickly bring improvement. In fact, it quickly brought a sharp decline in activity followed by a gradual return to growth. All told, most transition economies returned to growth within a few years, and the unique elements of transition began to disappear.[1]

Our hypothesis here is that the approximately 30 transition countries may now look very much like other low- and middle-income countries. They seem to have similar economic structures and share many similar economic and

---

[1] That is not meant to imply that all transitions experiences have been successful. Some economies are stagnating and only a few exhibit strong evidence of convergence.

P. Wachtel (✉)
New York University Stern School of Business, New York, NY, USA
e-mail: pwachtel@stern.nyu.edu

© The Author(s) 2021
E. Douarin, O. Havrylyshyn (eds.), *The Palgrave Handbook of Comparative Economics*,
https://doi.org/10.1007/978-3-030-50888-3_16

political problems as well as a common problem which is that convergence to developed country income levels is very slow. If true, it is now no longer necessary to think of these countries as transition economies. Instead, the transition countries are emerging market economies that look very much like their peers without the same central planning legacy.[2]

The chapter is organized in two sections, the first one discusses transition and the transition literature ("Was transition special?"), and the second presents data on a variety of economic indicators to see whether the transition countries differ from their peers ("Are transition countries still different?"). A discussion of the results and a conclusion follow.

1   Was Transition Special?

Before we begin to look at the transition experience, it is worth noting that in at least some instances the differences between transition economies and "normal" economies were smaller than originally thought. Perhaps, the differences between developing economies with extensive government intervention and direction of market outcomes and ones where communist ideas—government control of all resources and the absence of market mechanisms to determine prices—prevailed were over-emphasized because of political realities more than economics. In the Cold War the entire Soviet bloc was veiled in mystery behind the Iron Curtain which gave emphasis to the differences between communist countries and the rest of the world. But the fact was that many third-world economies (as they were then called) were highly controlled statist economies and many communist countries had some market mechanisms or were starting to introduce market-oriented reforms.[3] In the post-war period prior to transition, both developing and communist countries emphasized capital accumulation. They differed with respect to the strength of the planning mechanism—whether it was centralized control or centralized nudging. The objective—invest for import substitution—was shared by communist countries and many former colonies that gained independence in the post-war period. Banks in many developing countries were largely state owned, and the financial system was used to channel credit in support of government

---

[2] My first thoughts on these issues were expressed in Olofsgård et al. (2018). The discussion here builds on Wachtel (2019).

[3] Yugoslavia was always "reformed"; some Central European economies had moderately large amounts of private sector activity and ownership and had begun to reform; even Russia introduced reforms by the 1980s. Without any political reforms, China turned to private entrepreneurship in the quest for economic growth.

objectives; further, major industries were often state owned resulting in state control of a large share of output.

It would be an exaggeration to suggest that the communist countries were not different. First, there was the greater preponderance of state ownership and the efforts to abolish private ownership of property altogether. With some exceptions, there were no limited liability corporations or access to finance which prevented the development of private enterprise. Second, there was the use of planning mechanisms to determine output and prices without much regard for market forces.

Many will dispute the idea that planned economies were not so different, and it surely was not the standard view at the time transition began. Most observers thought at the time that transition would take a very long time and involve enormous economic shocks. The dissolution of communist regimes was rightfully viewed as a unique happenstance. As *The Economist* opined (March 24–30, 1990, p. 22):

> Hundreds of books have been written on the transition from capitalism to communism but not the other way. There is no known recipe for unmaking an omelet.

Since this process was thought to be lengthy and unprecedented, many institutions were developed to study the unfolding phenomenon: SITE at the Stockholm School of Economics started in 1989, the Bank of Finland's *Review of Economies in Transition* began publishing in 1991 and became part of BOFIT, and the European Bank for Reconstruction and Development started operation in 1991 and established the academic journal, *Economics of Transition*, in 1993.

In the introduction to the first issue of *Economics of Transition* (1(1), p. 2), Jacques Attali, president of the EBRD, wrote:

> Immediately after the overthrow of totalitarianism, the consensus approach was to favour a simple and immediate implementation of *laissez-faire* doctrines.....
> Today there is growing awareness of that those countries face structural and institutional obstacles never before experienced...

He went on to cite examples of institutions that were weak or non-existent in these countries such as means for tax collections or methods for transferring securities or property ownership or a banking system based on lending. He concluded:

it is impossible to divorce economic questions from the wider institutional background against which they arise....it is not just a question of putting in place market economies: it is a question in many cases of rebuilding the entire fabric of a nation.

His brief comments suggest a realization that the essence of transition from the very start was institutional development. Perhaps what made transition seem so different was the fact that economists at that time were just beginning to think about the importance of institutions.

The new institutional economics (NIE) which emphasizes the role of political structures and public institutions was gaining prominence just as transition was occurring (see Williamson 2000).[4] In a survey, Murrell (2008) shows how studies of transition through the 1990s slowly began to appreciate the importance of NIE. In addition, empirical work demonstrating the importance of institutions in economic outcomes generally did not begin to appear until the 1990s. For example, empirical work on the finance-growth nexus that associates credit deepening and the quality of financial intermediation with economic growth begins with Barro (1991) and King and Levine (1993) among others with cross-country panel data sets and Rousseau and Wachtel (1998) with historical time series data. Similarly, the cross-country empirical literature on legal institutions starts with the La Porta et al. (1998) research on law and finance which focused on the protections for investors in different legal systems. Research on the role of both social and political institutions on economic outcomes, such as the influential book by Acemoglu and Robinson (2012), is even more recent.

The lessons of transition for NIE were observed by Ronald Coase in his 1992 Nobel address (quoted by Murrell 2008, p. 672):

The value of including institutional factors in the corpus of mainstream economics is made clear by recent events in Eastern Europe...without appropriate institutions no market economy of any significance is possible.

Murrell suggests that the early failures of transition reforms (e.g. the privatization and banking debacles) made economists generally more aware of NIE. The intellectual influences between NIE and transition ran in both directions.[5]

---

[4] NIE has origins in economic theory that go back many years. The importance of institutions was more broadly recognized when Douglas North and Robert Fogel shared the 1993 Nobel Prize "for having renewed research in economic history by applying economic theory and quantitative methods in order to explain economic and institutional change."

[5] Olofsgård et al. (2018) discuss the influence of transition on the economics literature.

Measurement of institutional development and quality only begin in the 1990s. Among the first such efforts was the EBRD's Transition Indicators introduced in 1994 which are very popular and widely used in the research community.[6] Havrlyshyn and van Rooden (2003) discuss a number of other institutional indicators, most of which started about the same time. The very popular global data from the World Bank's Doing Business project were only introduced in 2002.

The political and economic shock of transition immediately brought about surprisingly deep declines in output and hyperinflation in virtually all transition countries. The declines in output, in some cases as much as 50%, were surprisingly large. Such shocks occurred both in countries that adopted "shock therapy" policies and those that chose a more gradualist approach. These transition recessions were deep, and the dislocation of resources, individuals and institutions was extensive (Campos and Coricelli 2002). Although they might have been deeper than expected, the transition recessions were probably shorter than expected. Within a few years, efforts to measure transition progress began to appear. An early retrospective by the Task Force on Economies in Transition (National Research Council 1998) stated that (pp. 1–2):

> Current reforms will alter fundamentally the way post-communist societies, political systems, and economies function and interact. More than 5 years into the process, what do we know about social change at this pace and scale?
>
> From its inception, the task force doubted that present versions of any existing theories—including various theories preferred by its own members—could adequately encompass these extraordinarily complex processes and explain the very different rates and patterns of transformation across the post-communist world.
>
> Moreover, many people thought that road was plainly marked: stabilization, liberalization, and privatization would transform highly bureaucratized, statist economic systems into dynamic, competitive capitalist economies.

Anders Aslund (National Research Council 1998, chapter 18) suggested three criteria for transition progress: stabilization (particularly of inflation), liberalization and private sector development. By 1997, transition, according to these criteria, was accomplished in most countries with the exception of five failures: Azerbaijan, Belarus, Bulgaria, Tajikistan and Turkmenistan. In Bulgaria failure was due to the inability to stabilize the macroeconomy and

---

[6] See https://www.ebrd.com/what-we-do/economic-research-and-data/data.html and Myant and Drahokoupil (2012) for a critical evaluation.

lower inflation. In the others, there was little effort to embark on deregulation or liberalization; a market economy had not been established.[7]

The ten-year mark led to several retrospectives on transition progress including academic studies such as Blejer and Skreb (2001) and studies from the IMF (Fischer and Sahay 2000), the World Bank (2002) and the EBRD (Gros and Suhrcke 2000). Table 16.1 summarizes the differences across the region in the initial transition shock.

By 1998, only three countries had recovered sufficiently to match the level of GDP prior to transition (1989): Poland, Slovakia and Slovenia.[8] Further, monetary stabilization had brought inflation rates to single digits in most countries by 1998. The reports emphasize the differences emerging at the ten-year mark in transition progress between CEE and the FSU countries.

Along similar lines, Gros and Suhrcke (2000) ask whether we can distinguish transition economies from the other 130 countries of the world, holding the level of GNP per capita constant. The answer is yes but it is not a very strong yes. The transition economies have more employment in industry, more energy use and a higher fraction of the population in secondary and tertiary education, all legacies of the structure of planned economies. There is a split among the transition countries when measures of financial and institutional framework are examined; the Central European countries which were candidates for EU membership were indistinguishable from other countries with their level of GNP but the CIS and SEE countries lagged.

A symposium in the *Journal of Economic Perspectives* in 2002 provided a comprehensive evaluation of the transition economies. Svejnar (2002) made a distinction between type I reforms (macroeconomic stabilization, price liberalization, small-scale privatization and breakup of state-owned enterprises) and type II reforms (large-scale privatization and development of banking and legal systems). This typology is useful today to distinguish between transition and development. Transition is characterized by the first type of reforms,

Table 16.1 The transition recessions

	GDP decline	End of decline
Central and Eastern Europe	28%	1992
Baltics	43	1994
Other former Soviet Union	54	1995

Source: Fischer and Sahay (2000)

---

[7] Another early retrospective on transition, Fischer et al. (1996) focused on macroeconomic performance in the early years.

[8] GDP is an imperfect measure of economic wellbeing for countries undergoing structural upheaval, and it is subject to measurement error during the transition. The GDP declines overstate the fall in consumption and wellbeing. Nevertheless, income inequality, measured by Gini coefficients, increased in most countries during the 1990s.

macroeconomic stabilization and the establishment of a market economy. In that sense transition had been completed by the late 1990s.[9] The virtually unique historical experience called transition did not last as long as anticipated. Even with transition in this narrow sense complete, many countries were still very poor and vulnerable to crony capitalism and structural rigidities that could inhibit growth.

If transition to a market economy with the end of the communist era took place so quickly, why is it still the object of study? One answer is that observers often fail to distinguish between transition (to a market economy) and convergence (to a Western level of development). The creation of the institutions that make Western economies successful engines of growth is quite something else. Thus, convergence to living standards found in developed countries takes a long time. Many non-communist societies are bureaucratized and statist because institutions to foster competition and increased productivity do not exist. A second answer is that transition has taught the economics profession a great deal about the importance of institutions and how to address institutional change. Poor institutions have made the pace of convergence very slow though large parts of the non-communist world (e.g. much of Latin America, Africa, the Middle East, South Asia) although these countries did not have to go through a transition. The slow pace of convergence is a global issue and not a problem specific to transition.

The transition countries differ among themselves in the way that they undertook the reform process. In the early years of transition, economists debated the merits of big bang vs. gradualism. In a 15-year retrospective on transition, Havrylyshyn (2007) examines the difference between rapid and gradual reformers, and Table 16.2 shows his grouping of countries by their

Table 16.2 Transition countries grouped by early reform strategies

Sustained big bang	Advance start/ steady progress	Aborted big bang	Gradual reforms	Limited reforms
Estonia	Croatia	Albania	Azerbaijan	Belarus
Latvia	Hungary	Bulgaria	Armenia	Uzbekistan
Lithuania	Slovenia	Macedonia	Georgia	Turkmenistan
Czech Republic		Kyrgyzstan	Kazakhstan	
Poland		Russia	Ukraine	
Slovakia			Tajikistan	
			Romania	

Source: Havrylyshyn (2007, p. 6)
Note: Slovakia underwent rapid economic reforms between 1990 and 1992, when it was a part of the Czechoslovak federation

[9] With the exception of Aslund's five failures noted above.

early reform strategies. It goes without saying that the big bang countries (in the first column) have out-performed the gradual reformers (in the next to last column). In a 25-year retrospective, Havrylyshyn et al. (2016, p. 23) conclude that the "main debate between rapid and gradual reformers seems to be settled in favor of the former." However, a quick glance suggests that the distinguishing factors might not have been the choice of reform strategy. The rapid reformers had initial institutions and cultural attitudes that enabled them to succeed.

Countries with a greater willingness and ability to undertake reforms were able to stabilize their economies and create market institutions that put them on the road from transition to convergence. This conclusion is echoed in the IMF's (2014) history of the first 25 years of transition; the report's executive summary says (p. v):

> To revitalize the convergence process [after the financial crisis,]… stronger commitment to market-based policies is needed. Two broad priorities stand out. First, a renewed focus on macroeconomic and financial stability in some countries, to rein in persistent deficits and increasing debt, and to address rising levels of bad loans in banks. Second, to raise the pace and depth of structural reforms in areas such as the business and investment climate, access to credit, public expenditure prioritization and tax administration, and labor markets.

It is interesting that this conclusion says nothing about the communist era legacy; it could be applied as a prescription for convergence to any emerging market or developing economy around the world. Transition is complete in the sense that the formerly planned economies might be indistinguishable from other countries around the world. In the next section we demonstrate this by comparing transition countries to others at similar income levels.

2   Are Transition Countries Still Different?

The question addressed here is whether the 30 or so countries we call transition economies because they began a transition to a market economy 30 years ago are still different.[10] There are many papers, some already cited, that have chronicled transition progress. Instead, the focus here is on the present and

---

[10] China looms as the elephant in the room in any discussion of transition. Although not really part of the Soviet bloc, it did adhere to communist ideas of economic organization and has clearly transitioned to a market economy. Its experiences are very different and it remains an anomaly in many respects. We will ignore the elephant in the room.

asks two related questions: (a) do these countries differ from peers at similar income levels, and (b) are the differences becoming smaller?

The large differences among the transition countries, which existed before transition started and continue to this day, cannot be overlooked. So, we will group them as the World Bank does according to the level of income. Among the transition countries with reasonably available data, there are seven lower middle-income, twelve upper middle-income and eight high-income transition countries. The high-income (HI) countries are the Baltics and the Central European countries, many of which have been members of the EU for over a decade and some of which have adopted the Euro. The upper middle-income (UMI) countries are former republics of the CIS and the countries in Southeastern Europe. The lower middle-income (LMI) countries are all former CIS republics.[11] Our data comes from the World Bank World Development Indicators database unless otherwise noted. Table 16.3 provides a summary of some of the main indicators, and complete tables with all the measures discussed here are shown in the Appendix with data for each country and the average for all countries in the income group shown at five-year intervals from 2005 onwards.

We start with a measure of economic progress—the level of real GDP per person employed (in PPP $) in Appendix Table 16.6. For the high-income transition countries, worker productivity in 1995 was between one-quarter and one-half the level in all HI countries. By 2005, it ranged from about one-half to two-thirds, and by 2018 it was over two-thirds in all the countries and as high as 80% in some. The Central European countries and the small Baltic states have converged steadily. Of course, the HI average includes the world's richest economies, and the future pace of convergence to their productivity levels is likely to be slow.

The 11 transition countries in the EU can be compared to the EU-28. In 2005, labor productivity per person and hour in these transition countries averaged 59.8% of the EU-28 average. A decade later, in 2018, the average was 70.4%, and all the transition countries exhibited significant convergence with the exceptions of Slovenia and Hungary. Half of the transition countries had higher productivity in 2018 than Portugal. The only EU transition country that was still less than half of the EU-28 productivity level was Bulgaria.[12]

---

[11] Lower middle-income transition economies: Armenia, Georgia, Kyrgyzstan, Moldova, Tajikistan, Ukraine, Uzbekistan.

Upper middle-income transition economies: Albania, Azerbaijan, Belarus, Bosnia, and Herzegovina, Bulgaria, Croatia, Kazakhstan, North Macedonia, Romania, Russia, Serbia, Turkmenistan. High-income transition economies: Czech Republic, Estonia, Hungary, Latvia, Lithuania, Poland, Slovakia, Slovenia.

Several countries for which data were often missing are not included. In all tables, entries are blank when data are missing.

[12] Data downloaded from Eurostat https://ec.europa.eu/eurostat/web/products-datasets/-/tesem160.

Table 16.3 Summary of indicators, 2018 except as noted

	GDP per person employed (constant 2011 PPP $)	Manufacturing value added (% of GDP), *2017*	Gross capital formation (% of GDP), *2017*	Labor force participation rate—male (% of male population ages 15+)	Domestic credit to the private sector (% of GDP)
Czech Republic	$67,719	24.1	25.9	68.4	52.1
Estonia	$61,343	13.6	26.1	70.9	62.6
Hungary	$60,702	19.6	22.7	65.0	33.4
Latvia	$55,844	10.7	22.2	67.9	36.1
Lithuania	$61,553	17.2	17.9	66.7	40.7
Poland	$60,538	17.6 (2015)	19.8	65.5	52.7
Slovak Republic	$65,991	20.3	22.5	67.3	61.5
Slovenia	$70,005	20.6	20.2	62.7	43.2
All high income	**$94,489**	**14.1**	**21.8**	**68.3**	**144.0**
Albania	$29,958	6.1	25.0	64.9	33.1
Azerbaijan	$33,307	4.7	24.4	69.7	20.8
Belarus	$35,758	21.6	28.0	70.3	27.8
Bosnia and Herzegovina	$37,965	13.1	21.0	58.6	58.6
Bulgaria	$42,994	14.7	20.1	61.6	51.3
Croatia	$57,463	12.5	20.9	58.2	55.9
Kazakhstan	$50,619	11.2	26.6	77.1	27.3
North Macedonia	$37,711	12.7	33.0	67.5	50.3
Romania	$55,054	20.1	23.4	64.2	25.9
Russian Federation	$53,012	12.2	24.1	70.5	76.0
Serbia	$29,481		19.6	62.1	41.5
Turkmenistan	$39,540			78.2	
All upper middle income	**$34,748**	**20.5**	**31.4**	**74.9**	**122.6**
Armenia	$23,777	10.60	19.3	69.9	55.6
Georgia	$20,733	10.70	32.4	78.7	68.0
Kyrgyz Republic	$9167	15.00	32.9	75.8	23.9
Moldova	$13,898	11.60	22.8	45.6	23.5
Tajikistan	$11,936	10.00	27.2	59.7	12.3
Ukraine	$19,095	12.10	19.9	62.8	34.1
Uzbekistan	$14,817		29.5	78.0	
All lower middle income	**$17,854**	**15.30**	**27.2**	**77.2**	**44.4**

Source: See Appendix Tables

GDP per person employed provides a broader look at all the transition countries. Only three of the seven transition LMI countries grew more rapidly from 1995 to 2005 or from 2005 to 2018 than the average of all LMI countries. There was significant catch-up in Armenia, Georgia and Ukraine (until the Russian incursions). For the UMI countries, 10 of 12 grew more rapidly than the typical UMI country from 1995 to 2005, but then convergence took a pause. From 2005 to 2018, only one of these countries grew more rapidly than the typical UMI country.

The picture is different for the HI transition countries. All these countries have consistently experienced convergence with the average for all HI countries since 1995. The 8 HI transition countries had GDP per person that was 45% of the HI average in 1995, 58% in 2005 and 67% in 2018.

We turn next to the structure of the economies. Specifically, the proportion of GDP that comes from value added in manufacturing (Appendix Table 16.7). The HI transition countries are more heavily engaged in manufacturing than other HI countries. In 2017, the proportion was highest in the Czech Republic (24.1%), 10 percentage points higher than the average for all HI countries. It was also above 20% in the Slovak Republic and Slovenia. While the share of value added in manufacturing has declined somewhat in HI countries overall (from about 17% to 14%), the share in the HI transition countries has hardly changed.

The global average value added in manufacturing has been constant around 20% of GDP in UMI countries and a bit lower in LMI countries. In the transition countries, it is generally lower because natural resource sectors (e.g. Russia) or agriculture dominate. In Belarus and Romania, the manufacturing shares have declined but are still about 20%. Manufacturing sectors contracted in the initial decade of transition, but the manufacturing share in GDP stabilized after the early transition experience.

The share of value added in the service sector in GDP (Appendix Table 16.8) has increased in LMI and UMI transition countries. Although there are large differences among the countries, on average the service sector share in 2017 is about the same as in other LMI and UMI countries. For the HI transition countries, the service sector share is lower than it is elsewhere, and there has been little change in the last 20 years.

The World Bank data—starting in 1995—does not show some of the dramatic changes that occurred in the first years of transition.[13] However, the data does suggest that for the last 20 years or so the structure of these

---

[13] Havrylyshyn (2013) indicates that in the first few years of transition, the share of manufacturing in GDP dropped, the share of consumption increases, and the trade patterns shifted to the EU.

economies as indicated by the shares of manufacturing and services in GDP are similar to those found in comparator countries. Also striking is that with few exceptions, the structures of these economies have not changed a great deal since 2000. The deep change and structural upheaval that we might associate with transition does not seem to be going on any more.

Of course, discussion of structural change in transition economies often focuses on privatization (see Estrin et al. 2009) particularly on the different approaches used in the 1990s to privatize. Our issue is whether the process is over or whether these economies are still different. Until 2010, the EBRD kept track of estimates of the private sector share of GDP in transition countries.[14] In 1994, a few Central European transition countries reported figures around 50% (Czech Republic was higher), and many countries (particularly in central Asia) reported figures no higher than 20%. By 2010, virtually all the transition countries reported that the private sector share was between 70 and 80%. The exceptions were Central Asia and Belarus. By that time, the private sectors were about the same size as they would be elsewhere.

More specific comparative data is available in the OECD's PMR (Product Market Regulation) indicators. PMR provides indices of public ownership and the scope of SOEs (i.e. the extent to which dominant firms in industries are government controlled); the index values range from 0 to 6, most to least competition friendly. Although only advanced transition countries that are OECD member (plus Kazakhstan) are surveyed, the data shown in Table 16.4 are revealing. On these two measures of the private sector, the advanced OECD countries are mostly within one standard deviation and always within two standard deviations of the OECD average. The advanced transition countries do not stand out. Further data on employment in SOEs (including minority ownership) indicates that the share of non-agricultural employees in

Table 16.4 PMR indicators, 2018

	Public ownership	Scope of SOEs
Czech Republic	1.60	1.98
Hungary	2.07	3.46
Latvia	2.40	3.38
Lithuania	3.20	4.41
Poland	2.98	4.75
Slovak Republic	2.19	2.65
Slovenia	1.91	3.50
Kazakhstan	4.01	4.54
OECD average (Std Dev)	2.15 (0.57)	3.01 (1.01)

[14] See EBRD Structural Change Indicators https://www.ebrd.com/what-we-do/economic-research-and-data/data/forecasts-macro-data-transition-indicators.html.

SOEs is higher in Norway, Finland and France than in any OECD transition country. The only indication in the OECD data that the transition countries are different is that there are still (2017) large numbers of majority state-owned enterprises in a few places—270 in Hungary and a bit more than 100 in Lithuania, Poland and the Slovak Republic.

The share of capital formation in output is both an important structural element for a growing economy and a distinguishing characteristic of Soviet era economies with very high levels of investment. In all of the transition countries, investment rates are usually over 20% (Appendix Table 16.9). Investment rates in these countries and globally rose before the financial crisis and then declined slightly. The share of gross capital formation in GDP for the transition LMI countries varies but is around the average for all LMI countries. For UMI transition countries, the ratio is a bit lower than in other UMI countries where on average the ratio is high, over 30% of GDP. The investment rates in the high-income transition countries are mostly higher than in other HI countries, but by only a few percentage points. The rate of capital formation in HI transition countries has declined, and by 2017 it was within 2 percentage points of the average for all HI countries (21.8%) except in the Czech Republic and Estonia where it was about 26%.

Foreign direct investment is an important catalyst for economic development. It brings innovative ventures and new technology, encourages exports and demonstrates investor confidence in an economy. FDI flows can be variable over time and from country to country as investor interests vary in often unpredictable and idiosyncratic ways (Appendix Table 16.10). Worldwide, average FDI flows have been about 1–2% of GDP in LMI countries and 2–3% in UMI countries. Since the mid-2000s, FDI flows in LMI and UMI transition countries have been mostly above the averages for the respective country groups. The HI transition countries attracted FDI flows from the onset of transition. FDI inflows were above the HI country average until the mid-2000s. Since that time, FDI flows to HI transition countries have varied from country to country with some above and some below the overall HI country average.

The share of exports in GDP in the transition countries is high when compared to other countries in the same income group (Appendix Table 16.11). Since 1995, the export shares have risen significantly for the HI transition countries, many of which are now thoroughly integrated into the EU and have export shares well over 50% of GDP. The export shares rose modestly for the UMI transition countries. The share data does not show the shift in trade patterns away from trade within the old Soviet bloc. Some of the less successful LMI transition countries have lost their traditional trading partners and have not replaced them, so the export shares in some instances have fallen since 1995.

The size of the government sector (revenue as a share of GDP, Appendix Table 16.12) is generally higher than the average for all countries in the respective income groups. For the HI countries the share has not changed noticeably in 20 years. In 2017 the government share in all the HI transition countries was above the average for all HI countries. Specifically, the overall average was 24.9%, and the average for eight HI transition countries was 36.2%.

Next, we turn to indicators of human capital development—tertiary school enrollment rates (Appendix Table 16.13) and R&D researchers per million (Appendix Table 16.14). There is considerable variation in enrollment rates among transition countries. Gross tertiary school enrollment rates are higher than in other LMI and UMI countries. Enrollment rates were relatively high in the late 1990s and have increased slightly since then. For HI transition countries, enrollment rates vary around the average for all HI countries. Among the HI transition countries, tertiary enrollment rates are much lower in Hungary and Slovakia than elsewhere.

The number of researchers per million has been fairly high in some of the UMI and LMI transition countries with a strong education tradition—Bulgaria, Croatia, Georgia, Russia, Serbia. The numbers of researchers are much higher among the HI transition countries. However, the number of researchers in all of these HI transition countries is below the average for all HI countries.

A broad measure of labor activity—labor force participation rates (LFPR)—indicates that many transition countries differ from other countries in the same income group (Appendix Tables 16.15 for men and 16.16 for women). Labor force participation rates in the transition countries are frequently less than elsewhere. In some instances, the differences are large: 2018 adult male LFPR is 58.2% in Croatia and 62.8% in Ukraine, about 15 percentage points lower than in all UMI and LMI countries, respectively. Male LFPRs have trended down over the last 15 years, but this has not been the case in many transition countries. Among the HI transition countries, LFPRs have declined for men and remained largely unchanged for women. Overall, the data suggests that transition and traditional mores continue to influence labor force participation in UMI and LMI countries.

The last sector that we will look at is the financial sector where, perhaps, the changes brought about by transition have been most profound. To a greater extent than elsewhere, banking and financial sector transition was more dramatic because these sectors were largely non-existent in the pre-transition era. Domestic credit to the private sector as a % of GDP was below 15% in all of the LMI transition countries in 2000 (Appendix Table 16.17). There was considerable credit deepening in the next two decades, particularly in Armenia, Georgia and Ukraine. Ukraine experienced a credit boom in the 2000s when the ratio ballooned and subsequently crashed to among the lowest levels in

2018. Among the larger UMI transition countries, only Bulgaria and Croatia have had significant credit deepening since 2000. The credit to GDP ratio in all the UMI transition countries in 2018 is substantially below the average for all UMI countries. In the HI transition countries, the credit ratio goes up and down as some countries with considerable deepening subsequently suffered financial crises (Hungary, Slovenia and the Baltics) that reversed the progress made. None of the HI transition countries have—at any time in the last 20 years—come within 50 percentage points of the average credit depth ratio in HI countries around the world (about 150%).

Further evidence regarding financial sector development comes from the IMF Financial Development Index Database that provides indexes that measure the depth, access and efficiency of financial institutions (banks and others) and financial markets. The Financial Institutions Index (FI), which is an aggregate of Financial Institutions Depth Index, Access Index and Efficiency Index and the Financial Markets Index (FM), calculated similarly, is shown in (Appendix Tables 16.18 and 16.19 respectively).

Financial institutions (largely bank) development in 2017 in LMI and UMI transition countries is above the average for all countries in the income group. Bulgaria, Croatia and Georgia stand out while Albania, Azerbaijan, Belarus and the Central Asian countries lag. For HI transition countries, although there was rapid improvement prior to 2005, the indexes in 2017 are all slightly less than the average for all HI countries.

Financial market development is much less advanced. There are only a few instances where the 2017 index value comes close to the average for all countries in the income group. The average among HI transition countries is 0.16, while the overall HI average is 0.43; only Hungary and Poland come close both with an index value of 0.34. Financial market development is weak in UMI and LMI countries, and the transition countries are no exception. Further there has been little improvement on the Financial Market Index since 2000, and in a few instances (e.g. Russia, Hungary), earlier progress has been reversed.

Looking specifically at the sub-indexes (not shown in the Appendix) for financial institution and financial market depth, we find that the transition countries lag their income group peers in virtually all instances. The only exceptions are among some LMI countries where the bar (the average for all LMI countries) is very low. All in all, the financial sectors of the transition countries, particularly the more developed ones, are different.

A related issue is whether the business environment in transition countries is different than elsewhere; indicators from several sources are shown in Table 16.5.[15] The corruption perceptions index values vary a great deal from country to country, but in most places, they are close to the average for all

---

[15] Only the most recent data are shown since these indicators are all fairy recent.

Table 16.5 Measures of the business environment

Business environment				
	Corruption perceptions index, 2018	Index of economic freedom, 2019	Time required to start a business (days), 2018	Time required to enforce a contract
Czech Republic	59	73.7	24.50	678
Estonia	73	76.6	3.50	455
Hungary	46	65.0	7.00	605
Latvia	58	70.4	5.50	469
Lithuania	59	74.2	5.50	370
Poland	60	67.8	37.00	685
Slovak Republic	50	65.0	26.50	775
Slovenia	60	65.5	8.00	1160
High income	**66**	**71.4**	**11.80**	621
Albania	36.0	66.5	4.50	525
Azerbaijan	25.0	65.4	3.50	277
Belarus	44.0	57.9	9.00	275
Bosnia and Herzegovina	38.0	61.9	80.00	595
Bulgaria	42.0	69.0	23.00	564
Croatia	48.0	61.4	22.50	650
Kazakhstan	31.0	65.4	5.00	370
North Macedonia	37.0	71.1	15.00	634
Romania	47.0	68.6	35.00	512
Russian Federation	28.0	58.9	10.10	337
Serbia	39.0	63.9	5.50	635
Turkmenistan	20.0	48.4		
Upper middle income	**38.0**	**59.7**	**24.90**	634
Armenia	35.0	67.7	4.00	570.00
Georgia	58.0	75.9	2.00	285.00
Kyrgyz Republic	29.0	62.3	10.00	410.00
Moldova	33.0	59.1	4.00	585.00
Tajikistan	25.0	55.6	10.00	430.00
Ukraine	32.0	52.3	6.50	378.00
Uzbekistan	23.0	53.3	3.00	225.00
Lower middle income	**33.2**	**55.4**	**24.00**	**687.50**

Sources: The Heritage Foundation, 2019 Index of Economic Freedom; Transparency International, Corruption Perceptions Index; World Bank, World Development Indicators, 5.3 Business Environment

countries in the respective income group. Exceptions are Hungary and the Slovak Republic among HI transition countries and Azerbaijan, Russia and the Central Asian republics, among the others. The transition countries all score within striking distance of the country group averages on the index of economic freedom.

Two measures from the World Bank's Doing Business Indicators are also shown in Table 16.5: the time required to start a business and the time required to enforce a contract. Here again there is large variation among countries with the LMI countries doing the best relative to the group averages. Most countries have reduced bureaucratic delays and improved the efficiency of legal procedures so that they are in line with their peer countries.

Does our data examination provide enough information to answer the question posed as the title of this section—are transition countries still different? For the most part the answer appears to be no. That is not to say that all the transition countries are economic success stories. Nor does it imply that there is not a lot of variation from country to country. Our data examination only suggests that the economic structures of these countries are similar to those found in other countries at the same income level. If anything, the HI transition countries, despite their integration into the European community, still lag other rich countries in many respects, and the middle-income transition countries might be more advanced than other countries at that level of income.

3   The Anomaly of the Financial Sector

There is one noticeable structural difference that sets the transition countries, at all levels of income, aside. Financial institutions and markets are significantly less developed than elsewhere. Although, most countries have the institutions needed to provide a business-friendly environment, the financial institutions remain weakly developed, and financial depth is below levels found in the peer countries. This anomaly poses two questions. First, why are financial institutions underdeveloped, and second, why have the transition countries fared so well in their absence?

The lagging development of financial institutions is not surprising because the sector was largely non-existent in virtually all of these countries prior to transition (Bonin and Wachtel 2003). Nevertheless, as soon as transition began, there was significant institution building including the establishment of many new banks, privatization of existing state-owned banks and considerable foreign direct investment in banking (Bonin et al. 2015). Financial services for consumers—deposit services, mortgage and consumer lending—grew rapidly, but lending to business enterprises lags. Haselmann and Wachtel (2010) use survey information to demonstrate the factors, such as the absence of credit registries and collateral laws, that inhibit bank lending to business. Non-bank institutional development has also been slow for two reasons. First, small countries often do not have the critical mass of activity to sustain stock, bond and money markets. Second, larger enterprises in transition countries have access to European financial markets, particularly in those countries that have joined the EU.

Studies of transition banking usually emphasize the role of foreign ownership and foreign funding of banks (Bonin et al. 2015; IMF 2013). However, foreign ownership and funding made credit availability in transition vulnerable to external shocks, particularly the financial crisis. During the crisis the Vienna Initiative led to steps to insulate the transition banking sectors from the shock; nevertheless, lending growth slowed down. An IMF (2013) evaluation of financing in transition points out that there are other significant sources of financing. Cross-border funding by BIS reporting banks exceeds 20% of GDP in most transition countries. It is much higher than in Asia or Latin America (where foreign bank ownership is also very high). Perhaps, the more advanced transition countries have succeeded despite the fact that financial sector development, measured by the domestic credit to GDP ratio, lags because financing and financial services are obtained from abroad. Close relationships to foreign, largely European, financial sources and institutions provide substantial FDI and loans (often to subsidiaries in the transition countries) although portfolio investment is not large compared to similar countries in Asia and elsewhere with more developed capital markets (Mileva 2008).[16]

4   Normalcy and Convergence

The question posed by our title—are the transition countries still in transition?—has been asked before. Alan Gelb writing in Brown (1999) suggested that the question came up when the World Bank prepared the *1996 World Development Report: From Plan to Market*. Their answer was that transition is over when the problems confronted by transition economies resemble those faced by other countries at similar levels of development which is exactly what

---

[16] These observations will be controversial. The benefits of foreign loans and capital flows that were apparent before the crisis are offset by the fact that foreign funding transmitted the crisis shock to the region. Moreover, the post-crisis weakness of European banks has meant that lending continues to lag.

we have shown to be the case now. Other authors in Brown (1999) had more specific definitions of the end of transition which usually involved the end of central planning, private ownership of capital and a functioning market system. In their view transition was still underway at the end of the twentieth century.

But, even as transition was getting underway, some observers noted that many of the issues faced by these formerly communist countries were no different than those found in middle-income countries around the world. In particular, Shleifer and Treisman (2005) pronounced Russia to be a normal middle-income country. They argued that the transition collapse in output was less serious than it appeared in the official statistics and that Russian consumers were better off in the 2000s than a decade earlier. Further, pervasive corruption, weakness of democratic institutions and a dominant role of oligarchs or politically connected families that control a large part of the economy were all characteristics of many middle-income countries without a communist past. The authors did not change their views a decade later despite Russia's political back sliding which they view as normal for a middle-income country albeit disappointing. Shleifer and Treisman (2014) argue that all of the transition countries resemble their peers at similar income levels.

Normalcy however might not be a very satisfactory situation. The transition countries share some normal characteristics with other similar countries that are caught in what is sometimes termed a middle-income trap. The term is a misnomer; a better term would be middle-income challenge. Middle-income countries often face a growth slowdown which makes the rate of convergence to high income difficult and slow. Once structural transformations occur and there are robust levels of physical and human capital, maintaining growth is a challenge. Further productivity growth requires an economy where sophisticated technology is diffused and innovation is common.

Most of the transition countries face this middle-income challenge. The richer countries of Central Europe (e.g. Czech and Slovak Republics, Slovenia) are squeezed between increasing real wages and diffusing technological advances throughout the economy. Further many of these countries are relatively small, so economies of scale are limited in domestic markets. Of course, the EU member companies do have the advantage of a wider market area. Slovakia, for example, has successfully exploited its position and now produces more automobiles per capita than any other country in the world. However, increasing wages; the difficulty in applying the advanced technologies used in the auto industry, where robots are common, to other sectors of the economy; and the reliance on a highly cyclical and perhaps shrinking global industry make the Slovak economy vulnerable.[17] Convergence with the major economies of Western Europe is a steep path.

The World Bank's categorization of middle-income countries is broad. Among the transition countries output per worker in the best off UMI countries (Croatia and Romania) is at least four times larger than in the poorest LMI countries (the difference in real GDP per capita is even larger). So while some countries might be facing a slow convergence path, others (e.g. Moldova and the Central Asian countries) are still undergoing the structural changes needed to make them modern middle-income countries. Our data examination suggests that most of the transition countries are on a middle-income plateau. At the upper level they are challenged by a very steep convergence path. At the lower level they need to complete the structural and institutional changes to facilitate more rapid growth. In many of these countries, including Russia, a retrograde political structure and reform reversals has eroded some of the institutional developments that would facilitate rapid growth.

The 11 Central and Eastern European transition countries that are members of the EU continue to converge with the EU averages but at a pace which has slowed down in the last decade. Aslund (2018) provides a number of reasons for this including incomplete reforms to public pension systems, a still large fiscal burden, the poor quality of tertiary education and lagging R&D expenditure. Székely and Ward-Warmedinger (2018) attribute the slowdown to reform reversals and cite explicit examples of legislative changes or politically motivated actions. In any event, some of the progress made in the 1990s in anticipation of joining the EU has been reversed in a changed political and global economic environment in the 2010s. Similarly, Mihaljek (2018) emphasizes that convergence is a slow process that requires sustained reforms.

In conclusion, we should reiterate that normalcy and convergence are two different things. The transition countries are normal in the sense that the challenges that they face are not specific to or caused by their transition status. There is a myriad of political and economic reasons why convergence is a slow and slowing process, but none of the literature cited seems to relate this specifically to their status as formerly planned or transition countries.

One caveat is worth mentioning—the role of path dependence. Some institutions, once put in place, are very difficult to change. For example, Aslund (2018) points to the poor quality of higher educational institutions with little

---

[17] See Automobile Woes Cast Cloud Over Eastern Europe, *Wall Street Journal*, Nov. 24, 2019 https://www.wsj.com/articles/automobile-woes-cast-cloud-over-eastern-europe-11574607781?mod=searchresults&page=1&pos=2.

R&D and an inability to react to the needs of a modern economy. This is ironic because these Central European institutions were distinguished in the pre-communist era. In this instance the influence of the communist era is long-lasting and transition might still be to come. However, there other examples where path dependence might have served these economies well. Path dependence in Central European central banks and commercial law systems were important to facilitate change at the outset of transition.

5   Conclusion

When transition sprang into view almost 30 years ago, we thought that it would be very important because of the unique nature of the transition from a planned to a market economy. To the surprise of many, the changes occurred very quickly, and the transition countries—though sometimes unstable and struggling—do not look all that different than emerging market economies around the world.

Many of the distinguishing characteristics of the formerly planned economies have disappeared without a trace. The elaborate planning and allocation mechanisms of the Soviet Union are completely gone. Business enterprises with limited liability and the freedom to produce, market and engage in foreign trade as they wish were absent in the communist era but taken for granted today.

Our examination of the characteristics of these countries found only one area where transition stands out as different. The financial sectors of the transition economies are smaller and less well functioning than those in other countries.

It is perhaps unfair to generalize too much because the transition economies—running from Central Europe to Central Asia and from the Baltic to the Balkans—are hardly a homogenous group. Income levels among these countries differ enormously as do levels of industrialization and economic development. Further there are differences in the prevalence of functioning market mechanisms for resource allocation and in the quality of public and private institutions. Whereas some transition countries, such as those in the EU, might be hard to distinguish from other developed countries, there are clear laggards. FSU countries such as Moldova and the Central Asian states are far behind. But, even there transition may be over since these countries resemble other poor countries, such as those in Central America or sub-Saharan Africa, with barely functioning markets and institutions, without having the same planned economy legacy. Moreover, political structures in transition vary from democracy to autocracy with concomitant variation in the rule of law. As a result, the transition economies are facing serious problems. But our argument is that these problems are not due to the transition experience. Countries around the world at all levels of income are struggling to preserve democratic norms and provide a growth-friendly and equitable economic environment.

The enormous emphasis on transition might reflect the politics and political thought of the twentieth century as much as it reflects a set of unique economic issues. Marxist political thinking was at one time an important part of political theory, and the Cold War was the dominant political issue after World War II. Thus, transition which brought an end to both Marxist ideology and the Cold War received enormous attention. However, from an economic perspective, the transition economies might not have been so dramatically different. It is true that planning mechanisms, state ownership and non-market allocations were pervasive prior to transition, but similar institutions existed elsewhere. Statist, controlled economies with non-market allocations were to be found in other parts of the world. Once transition began, these countries joined many others in what we termed the middle-income challenge. The transition countries, along with many others, are experiencing a slow pace of convergence; it is a global problem that is not unique to transition.

If anything, transition was important because it became a laboratory that taught economists and policy makers a great deal about economic growth and development, particularly the role of institutions. The transition experience turned attention to institutions and away from traditional development ideas that emphasized capital accumulation. Nevertheless, the puzzle about the next stage remains. In both transition and other emerging market economies, convergence is very slow, and maintaining a just democratic society is a challenge everywhere.

Acknowledgment Able research assistance from Aparajitha Suresh and thoughtful comments on an earlier version from Barbara Katz are much appreciated. Suggestions from the editors, Elodie Douarin and Oleh Havrylyshyn, were of an enormous help in sharpening the arguments.

Appendix

Table 16.6a GDP per person employed

	1995	2000	2005	2010	2015	2018
GDP per Person Employed (Constant 2011 PPP $) High Income Countries						
Czech Republic	$40,072.90	$46,071.70	$54,939.80	$60,750.50	$63,353.40	$67,718.90
Estonia	$25,716.40	$37,216.20	$49,829.00	$53,124.40	$56,299.30	$61,342.60
Hungary	$42,025.80	$47,106.40	$57,106.80	$59,087.90	$57,630.80	$60,702.30
Latvia	$21,223.20	$28,093.90	$39,631.30	$44,283.80	$49,575.20	$55,844.20
Lithuania	$23,517.10	$30,141.60	$42,939.10	$52,355.10	$58,256.60	$61,552.90
Poland	$29,045.20	$38,594.10	$45,276.20	$50,445.80	$56,279.70	$60,538.30
Slovak Republic	$32,707.90	$40,113.50	$48,019.70	$58,897.00	$63,156.90	$65,990.70
Slovenia	$41,988.40	$50,540.70	$56,754.70	$60,826.00	$64,836.10	$70,005.40
All High Income	**$70,734.10**	**$78,858.00**	**$84,947.60**	**$87,872.90**	**$91,881.20**	**$94,489.20**
GDP per Person Employed (Constant 2011 PPP $) Upper Middle Income Countries						
Albania	$12,466.20	$15,587.00	$21,368.80	$27,203.60	$28,173.70	$29,957.80
Azerbaijan	$8344.90	$11,524.50	$18,423.00	$34,437.40	$34,904.50	$33,306.70
Belarus	$14,372.70	$17,929.20	$23,975.30	$32,264.70	$33,987.10	$35,758.00
Bosnia and Herzegovina	$5903.60	$21,874.80	$29,733.60	$32,937.20	$37,802.20	$37,964.80
Bulgaria	$21,691.40	$25,602.60	$31,625.00	$36,726.60	$40,162.90	$42,994.00
Croatia	$31,366.60	$42,266.10	$50,507.60	$52,299.80	$55,145.30	$57,463.00
Kazakhstan	$18,260.80	$21,937.30	$32,378.10	$39,733.00	$47,094.50	$50,619.10
North Macedonia	$29,083.50	$30,923.60	$34,761.90	$36,577.80	$37,384.10	$37,710.50
Romania	$20,817.40	$21,805.50	$34,752.70	$40,367.90	$47,864.00	$55,053.90
Russian Federation	$29,255.10	$31,399.80	$40,208.30	$46,807.50	$50,663.30	$53,011.70
Serbia	$14,849.20	$16,201.80	$25,027.00	$30,143.50	$29,920.60	$29,481.40
Turkmenistan	$13,251.40	$15,017.90	$16,433.70	$22,970.10	$34,381.40	$39,540.40

(continued)

Table 16.6a (continued)

	1995	2000	2005	2010	2015	2018
All Upper Middle Income	**$13,112.50**	**$15,228.20**	**$19,100.30**	**$25,170.70**	**$30,793.40**	**$34,748.00**
GDP per Person Employed (Constant 2011 PPP $) Lower Middle Income Countries						
Armenia	$5564.70	$7874.00	$13,688.40	$17,257.70	$20,921.70	$23,777.00
Georgia	$4573.70	$6967.30	$10,406.10	$14,228.50	$17,844.80	$20,733.10
Kyrgyz Republic	$4443.00	$5339.90	$5860.00	$6830.40	$8271.80	$9166.70
Moldova	$6171.40	$5606.90	$7821.60	$10,577.60	$11,592.00	$13,897.80
Tajikistan	$6011.00	$5681.40	$7452.50	$8578.60	$10,550.00	$11,936.20
Ukraine	$11,325.20	$11,585.60	$16,668.30	$18,056.80	$17,000.90	$19,095.30
Uzbekistan	$6464.50	$7156.50	$7641.30	$9863.40	$12,949.70	$14,817.10
All Lower Middle Income	**$7876.40**	**$8573.50**	**$10,270.50**	**$13,086.60**	**$15,933.50**	**$17,853.80**

Source: **World Bank**—*World Development Indicators*: People—2.4 Decent Work and Productivity

Table 16.6b GDP per person employed as % of average for country group

	1995	2000	2005	2010	2015	2018
GDP Per Person Employed as % of High Income Group Average						
Czech Republic	57%	58%	65%	69%	69%	72%
Estonia	36%	47%	59%	60%	61%	65%
Hungary	59%	60%	67%	67%	63%	64%
Latvia	30%	36%	47%	50%	54%	59%
Lithuania	33%	38%	51%	60%	63%	65%
Poland	41%	49%	53%	57%	61%	64%
Slovak Republic	46%	51%	57%	67%	69%	70%
Slovenia	59%	64%	67%	69%	71%	74%
GDP Per Person Employed as % of Upper Middle Income Group Average						
Albania	95%	102%	112%	108%	91%	86%
Azerbaijan	64%	76%	96%	137%	113%	96%
Belarus	110%	118%	126%	128%	110%	103%
Bosnia and Herzegovina	45%	144%	156%	131%	123%	109%
Bulgaria	165%	168%	166%	146%	130%	124%
Croatia	239%	278%	264%	208%	179%	165%
Kazakhstan	139%	144%	170%	158%	153%	146%
North Macedonia	222%	203%	182%	145%	121%	109%
Romania	159%	143%	182%	160%	155%	158%
Russian Federation	223%	206%	211%	186%	165%	153%
Serbia	113%	106%	131%	120%	97%	85%
Turkmenistan	101%	99%	86%	91%	112%	114%
GDP Per Person Employed as % of Lower Middle Income Group Average						
Armenia	72%	92%	133%	132%	131%	133%
Georgia	58%	81%	101%	109%	112%	116%
Kyrgyz Republic	56%	62%	57%	52%	52%	51%
Moldova	78%	65%	76%	81%	73%	78%
Tajikistan	76%	66%	73%	66%	66%	67%
Ukraine	144%	135%	162%	138%	107%	107%
Uzbekistan	82%	83%	74%	75%	81%	83%

Table 16.7 Manufacturing value added as % of GDP

	1995	2000	2005	2010	2015	2017
Manufacturing, Value Added (% of GDP) High Income Countries						
Czech Republic	21.50	23.60	23.00	21.20	24.10	24.10
Estonia	17.40	15.50	14.70	13.70	13.90	13.60
Hungary	18.10	19.10	18.90	18.20	20.50	19.60
Latvia	17.70	13.70	11.50	12.00	10.50	10.70
Lithuania	16.70	16.80	18.20	16.90	17.40	17.20
Poland	19.40	16.10	16.10	15.60	17.60	
Slovak Republic	23.10	21.40	20.90	18.90	20.10	20.30
Slovenia	21.70	21.80	20.70	17.60	20.00	20.60
All High Income		**17.10**	**15.30**	**14.20**	**14.20**	**14.10**
Manufacturing, Value Added (% of GDP) Upper Middle Income Countries						
Albania		4.30	4.40	5.50	5.70	6.10
Azerbaijan	11.50	5.30	6.50	4.80	5.00	4.70
Belarus	28.00	27.00	25.30	22.00	20.60	21.60
Bosnia and Herzegovina	11.40	8.50	9.90	10.90	11.70	13.10
Bulgaria	9.80	12.10	13.60	11.70	13.60	14.70
Croatia	17.10	14.80	13.20	12.00	12.50	12.50
Kazakhstan	14.60	16.50	12.00	11.30	10.30	11.20
North Macedonia	18.70	9.00	9.70	9.90	11.80	12.70
Romania	23.90	19.80	21.30	22.90	19.60	20.10
Russian Federation			15.70	12.80	12.50	12.20
Serbia	23.40	23.60				
Turkmenistan	38.20	9.80				
All Upper Middle Income			**22.80**	**21.60**	**20.40**	**20.50**
Manufacturing, Value Added (% of GDP) Lower Middle Income Countries						
Armenia					9.20	10.60
Georgia		12.20	12.10	10.60	10.90	10.70
Kyrgyz Republic	8.60	18.10	12.90	16.90	14.10	15.00
Moldova	22.30	14.00	13.10	10.00	12.00	11.60
Tajikistan	26.80				8.70	10.00
Ukraine	31.00	16.30	17.40	13.20	11.90	12.10
Uzbekistan						
All Lower Middle Income	**18.60**	**16.80**	**17.50**	**16.10**	**15.70**	**15.30**

Source: **World Bank**—*World Development Indicators*: Economy—4.2 Structure of Output

Table 16.8 Service value added as % of GDP

	1995	2000	2005	2010	2015	2017
Services, Value Added (% of GDP) High Income Countries						
Czech Republic	51.50	54.10	54.10	55.60	53.80	54.50
Estonia	55.00	60.20	59.10	60.20	60.10	60.00
Hungary	51.90	53.50	55.50	56.40	53.70	55.20
Latvia	54.10	61.20	64.70	64.20	64.60	64.50
Lithuania	51.30	57.00	56.60	60.80	60.00	60.70
Poland	49.10	56.80	56.10	56.20	56.30	
Slovak Republic	51.70	53.20	53.50	56.30	55.50	55.60
Slovenia	52.40	53.90	55.60	58.70	56.30	56.70
All High Income		**65.80**	**67.30**	**69.10**	**69.60**	**69.80**
Services, Value Added (% of GDP) Upper Middle Income Countries						
Albania	22.00	44.30	43.60	44.00	46.30	48.00
Azerbaijan	37.90	35.80	25.10	28.20	40.70	38.10
Belarus	41.20	39.90	39.60	42.40	47.70	47.60
Bosnia and Herzegovina	53.60	55.90	54.70	55.60	56.30	55.80
Bulgaria	65.40	54.10	53.60	59.00	58.20	58.00
Croatia	50.40	53.20	55.40	58.30	57.80	57.80
Kazakhstan	54.00	48.40	52.00	51.70	59.30	57.40
North Macedonia	45.60	52.80	55.80	55.10	53.70	54.60
Romania	40.30	49.20	47.90	46.40	53.80	56.80
Russian Federation	52.20	49.70	48.80	53.10	56.10	56.30
Serbia	41.10	42.90	47.20	51.70	50.90	50.90
Turkmenistan	19.10	28.90	42.90	28.10		
All Upper Middle Income		**47.60**	**50.00**	**54.80**	**55.40**	
Services, Value Added (% of GDP) High Income Counties						
Armenia					48.20	50.80
Georgia		53.20	51.10	61.40	58.80	57.60
Kyrgyz Republic	35.60	30.00	42.40	49.30	52.10	49.90
Moldova	33.10	45.30	50.40	54.50	53.00	53.20
Tajikistan	21.20	31.50	40.60	45.10	42.50	41.40
Ukraine	37.50	39.50	50.20	55.10	51.20	50.90
Uzbekistan	34.70	37.20	37.00	42.60	35.90	33.70
All Lower Middle Income	**40.70**	**42.20**	**45.20**	**46.50**	**48.90**	**49.10**

Source: **World Bank**—*World Development Indicators*: Economy—4.2 Structure of Output

Table 16.9 Gross capital formation as % of GDP

	1995	2000	2005	2010	2015	2017
Gross Capital Formation (% of GDP) High Income Countries						
Czech Republic	33.70	31.40	29.10	27.10	28.00	25.90
Estonia	28.70	28.80	33.20	21.30	24.90	26.10
Hungary	23.10	28.30	25.40	20.70	22.60	22.70
Latvia	15.90	24.70	35.10	19.30	22.20	22.20
Lithuania	22.70	18.80	24.10	18.00	20.60	17.90
Poland	19.70	24.60	19.90	21.30	20.50	19.80
Slovak Republic	26.40	27.60	29.70	24.00	24.50	22.50
Slovenia	25.10	28.50	28.40	22.20	19.30	20.20
All High Income	**23.20**	**24.00**	**23.10**	**20.80**	**21.80**	**21.80**
Gross Capital Formation (% of GDP) Upper Middle Income Countries						
Albania	21.30	30.80	36.90	30.30	25.80	25.00
Azerbaijan	23.80	20.70	41.50	18.10	27.90	24.40
Belarus	24.70	25.40	28.50	39.70	29.00	28.00
Bosnia and Herzegovina	20.00	20.60	27.20	16.30	18.70	21.00
Bulgaria	17.20	19.20	27.90	22.60	21.20	20.10
Croatia	16.80	20.20	27.80	21.40	20.00	20.90
Kazakhstan	19.90	18.10	31.00	25.40	27.90	26.60
North Macedonia	19.70	21.90	19.80	24.50	30.40	33.00
Romania	23.30	19.70	22.90	27.10	25.10	23.40
Russian Federation	25.40	18.70	20.10	22.60	22.40	24.10
Serbia	14.40	10.50	22.70	17.60	18.60	19.60
Turkmenistan		34.70	22.90	51.90		
All Upper Middle Income	**29.70**	**26.40**	**29.80**	**33.30**	**32.10**	**31.40**
Gross Capital Formation (% of GDP) Lower Middle Income Countries						
Armenia	20.80	18.20	28.40	26.00	20.70	19.30
Georgia	4.00	26.60	33.50	21.60	31.50	32.40
Kyrgyz Republic	18.30	20.00	16.40	27.40	34.70	32.90
Moldova	24.90	23.90	30.80	23.90	23.60	22.80
Tajikistan	28.70	9.40	11.60	23.80	28.90	27.20
Ukraine	26.70	19.60	26.30	20.90	15.90	19.90
Uzbekistan	24.20	19.60	28.00	20.20	26.10	29.50
All Lower Middle Income	**26.20**	**24.10**	**29.40**	**30.60**	**27.60**	**27.20**

Source: **World Bank**—*World Development Indicators*: Economy—4.8 Structure of Demand

Table 16.10 FDI net inflow as % of GDP

	1995	2000	2005	2010	2015	2017
Foreign Direct Investment, Net Inflows (% of GDP), High Income Countries						
Czech Republic	4.30	8.10	10.10	4.90	0.90	5.20
Estonia	4.60	7.30	22.30	13.30	−3.10	5.80
Hungary	10.30	5.80	7.50	−16.00	−4.50	−9.30
Latvia	3.10	4.10	4.80	1.80	3.10	3.70
Lithuania	0.90	3.30	3.20	2.30	2.30	2.50
Poland	2.60	5.40	3.60	3.80	3.20	2.00
Slovak Republic	0.90	7.50	6.30	2.40	1.70	6.20
Slovenia	0.70	0.70	2.70	0.70	4.00	2.50
All High Income	**0.90**	**4.80**	**3.30**	**2.70**	**4.00**	**2.60**
Foreign Direct Investment, Net Inflows (% of GDP), Upper Middle Income Counties						
Albania	2.90	4.10	3.30	9.10	8.70	7.90
Azerbaijan	10.80	2.50	33.80	6.30	7.60	7.00
Belarus	0.10	0.90	1.00	2.40	2.90	2.30
Bosnia and Herzegovina		2.70	5.60	2.60	2.40	2.60
Bulgaria	0.50	7.60	13.80	3.60	5.20	4.90
Croatia	0.50	4.90	4.00	2.40	0.30	3.70
Kazakhstan	4.70	7.50	4.50	5.00	3.60	2.90
North Macedonia	0.20	5.80	2.30	3.20	2.90	3.40
Romania	1.10	2.80	6.60	1.90	2.40	2.80
Russian Federation	0.50	1.00	2.00	2.80	0.50	1.80
Serbia	0.30	0.80	5.70	4.00	5.90	6.60
Turkmenistan	9.40	4.50	5.20	16.10	8.50	5.50
All Upper Middle Income	**2.00**	**3.00**	**3.30**	**3.20**	**2.30**	**1.80**
Foreign Direct Investment, Net Inflows (% of GDP), Lower Middle Income Countries						
Armenia	1.70	5.50	6.00	5.70	1.70	2.20
Georgia		4.30	7.10	7.70	11.90	12.10
Kyrgyz Republic	5.80	−0.20	1.70	9.90	17.10	−1.40
Moldova	1.50	9.90	6.40	4.10	2.80	1.70
Tajikistan	0.80	2.70	2.40	1.70	5.80	2.60
Ukraine	0.60	1.90	9.10	4.70	3.40	2.50
Uzbekistan	−0.20	0.50	1.30	4.20	0.10	3.00
All Lower Middle Income	**1.40**	**0.90**	**2.20**	**2.10**	**2.40**	**2.00**

Source: **International Monetary Fund**—*International Financial Statistics and data files, World Bank and OECD GDP estimates*

Table 16.11 Exports as % of GDP

	1995	2000	2005	2010	2015	2017
Exports of Goods and Services (% of GDP) High Income Countries						
Czech Republic	40.40	48.20	62.20	66.00	81.00	79.70
Estonia	67.80	61.60	65.90	75.10	77.30	76.50
Hungary	39.10	66.70	62.50	81.80	89.00	88.20
Latvia	34.60	36.90	43.20	53.70	60.40	61.10
Lithuania	37.10	38.50	53.80	65.30	75.80	80.90
Poland	23.00	27.20	34.60	40.10	49.50	54.30
Slovak Republic	56.70	54.10	72.00	76.30	92.30	96.90
Slovenia	45.60	50.00	59.60	64.30	76.90	82.90
All High Income	**22.20**	**25.80**	**27.30**	**29.50**	**31.20**	**31.50**
Exports of Goods and Services (% of GDP) Upper Middle Income Countries						
Albania	12.60	20.10	23.00	28.00	27.30	31.60
Azerbaijan	32.50	40.20	62.90	54.30	37.80	48.50
Belarus	49.70	69.20	59.80	50.10	58.00	66.80
Bosnia and Herzegovina	20.40	28.70	31.60	29.70	34.90	40.10
Bulgaria	32.50	36.50	42.90	50.20	64.10	67.40
Croatia	27.60	36.50	39.40	37.60	48.10	51.10
Kazakhstan	39.00	56.60	53.20	44.20	28.50	34.40
North Macedonia	31.40	32.90	34.80	39.80	48.70	55.40
Romania	25.60	21.60	24.50	32.40	41.00	41.50
Russian Federation	29.30	44.10	35.20	29.20	28.70	26.10
Serbia	8.10	9.90	28.00	32.30	45.30	50.50
Turkmenistan	84.00	55.20	30.70	45.90	35.70	22.50
All Upper Middle Income	**20.90**	**26.20**	**32.60**	**27.20**	**24.80**	**24.50**
Exports of Goods and Services (% of GDP) Lower Middle Income Countries						
Armenia	23.90	23.40	28.80	20.80	29.70	37.30
Georgia	25.50	23.00	33.70	35.00	44.70	50.30
Kyrgyz Republic	29.50	41.80	38.30	51.60	35.20	34.30
Moldova	60.10	49.60	51.20	27.80	31.90	31.10
Tajikistan	65.60	86.80	54.20	14.90	10.50	15.70
Ukraine	47.10	62.40	48.70	47.10	52.60	48.00
Uzbekistan		24.70	37.80	31.30	15.30	21.80
All Lower Middle Income	**20.80**	**27.60**	**28.60**	**27.20**	**23.70**	**23.70**

Source: **World Bank**—*World Development Indicators*: Economy—4.8 Structure of Demand

Table 16.12 Government revenue as % of GDP

	1995	2000	2005	2010	2015	2016
Revenue, Excluding Grants (% of GDP) High Income Countries						
Czech Republic	33.20	30.80	31.20	30.40	31.20	31.70
Estonia	39.20	33.60	32.40	36.00	35.60	35.50
Hungary	41.30	37.80	34.80	38.40	40.00	40.70
Latvia	38.70	39.20	37.00	38.30	39.80	41.30
Lithuania	31.80	34.50	31.40	30.10	31.20	31.80
Poland	39.10	34.20	33.30	31.90	32.50	33.00
Slovak Republic	42.10	37.70	34.90	33.00	40.20	37.20
Slovenia			39.20	37.80	39.70	38.30
All High Income	**24.80**	**25.60**	**24.40**	**23.70**	**25.10**	**24.90**
Revenue, Excluding Grants (% of GDP) Upper Middle Income Countries						
Albania	21.50				24.70	24.30
Azerbaijan	18.00			46.80	34.20	34.90
Belarus	30.00	28.70	33.80	29.60	29.70	28.90
Bosnia and Herzegovina			35.50	38.40	38.60	38.10
Bulgaria			34.80	30.40	34.20	32.40
Croatia	36.20	35.30	37.70	35.50	38.10	39.70
Kazakhstan		11.30		21.40	13.70	13.70
North Macedonia			32.40	28.90	27.00	26.40
Romania	27.30	31.10	30.90	30.70	32.40	29.60
Russian Federation	21.30	24.60	30.30	26.10	24.50	24.20
Serbia				34.50		
Turkmenistan						
All Upper Middle Income			**17.30**	**19.10**	**21.30**	**21.10**
Revenue, Excluding Grants (% of GDP) Lower Middle Income Countries						
Armenia			19.30	22.60	23.10	22.80
Georgia		10.40	18.10	23.90	24.70	24.30
Kyrgyz Republic					30.10	28.10
Moldova	28.40	24.50	31.70	26.30	26.40	25.40
Tajikistan		10.60				
Ukraine		26.80	35.10	34.40	35.80	31.20
Uzbekistan					20.70	20.80
All Lower Middle Income	**16.00**		**15.80**	**16.30**	**15.40**	**14.80**

Source: **World Bank**—*World Development Indicators*: Economy—4.12 Central Government Finances

Table 16.13 Tertiary school enrollment rate

	1995	2000	2005	2010	2015	2017
School Enrollment—Tertiary (% Gross) High Income Countries						
Czech Republic	20.60	28.30	48.30	63.90	64.50	63.70
Estonia	25.40	54.50	67.90	68.20	72.20	71.40
Hungary	22.20	35.90	65.00	63.70	49.00	48.00
Latvia	22.80	56.20	75.40	69.10	74.30	80.60
Lithuania	26.30	50.90	79.70	86.60	69.70	71.10
Poland	31.20	49.70	63.60	74.80	66.90	67.00
Slovak Republic	18.60	28.40	40.40	57.10	50.70	47.80
Slovenia	30.40	55.20	79.20	89.20	80.30	77.80
All High Income	**51.80**	**56.00**	**66.00**	**73.20**	**75.50**	**76.50**
School Enrollment—Tertiary (% Gross) Upper Middle Income Countries						
Albania	10.20	15.50	23.20	44.50	62.00	58.40
Azerbaijan	18.40			19.30	25.50	25.90
Belarus	40.70	55.10	67.60	79.60	89.60	88.20
Bosnia and Herzegovina		21.00				
Bulgaria	36.40	44.10	45.40	57.80	70.30	71.20
Croatia	26.20	32.40	44.80	54.00	66.50	66.50
Kazakhstan	35.60	31.80		46.20	46.40	46.60
North Macedonia	18.60	22.70	29.20	37.50	41.10	
Romania	13.40	23.90	46.40	64.00	46.70	48.20
Russian Federation	43.10	55.80	72.60	..	79.90	80.60
Serbia			44.20	49.10	58.30	62.10
Turkmenistan						
All Upper Middle Income	**11.70**	**17.30**	**27.10**	**33.40**	**49.20**	**51.10**
School Enrollment—Tertiary (% Gross) Lower Middle Income Countries						
Armenia	19.10	35.50	39.50	53.00	46.50	51.10
Georgia	43.50	39.10	51.40	32.60	46.50	51.80
Kyrgyz Republic	21.10	35.40	42.60	42.20	46.70	45.10
Moldova	30.20	32.50	36.10	38.10	41.20	41.10
Tajikistan	20.90	17.90	20.50	22.90	26.60	29.20
Ukraine	42.30	48.80	70.30	80.20		
Uzbekistan		13.10	10.10	9.40	8.20	8.50
All Lower Middle Income	**8.00**	**11.10**	**12.90**	**18.00**	**23.70**	**23.90**

Source: **World Bank**—*World Development Indicators*: People—2.8 Participation in Education

Table 16.14 Researchers in R&D per million

	2000	2005	2010	2015	2017
Researchers in R&D (per million people)					
Czech Republic	1346.20	2356.10	2774.00	3591.30	3689.90
Estonia	1905.50	2457.10	3060.60	3183.30	3568.90
Hungary	1409.40	1574.20	2149.70	2587.50	2924.00
Latvia	1599.70	1457.40	1838.70	1813.20	1785.90
Lithuania	2220.80	2283.60	2752.70	2785.50	3013.20
Poland	1431.20	1620.40	1683.30	2158.50	2528.00
Slovak Republic	1843.80	2022.70	2809.40	2648.40	2795.00
Slovenia	2180.50	2631.40	3766.40	3807.60	4467.80
All High Income	3080.40	3532.90	3829.60	4157.70	
Researchers in R&D (per million people)					
Albania					
Azerbaijan					
Belarus					
Bosnia and Herzegovina		66.90		354.20	463.90
Bulgaria	1185.20	1308.30	1482.70	1983.40	2130.50
Croatia	1529.30	1308.10	1641.30	1503.10	1865.40
Kazakhstan			367.20	769.40	661.60
North Macedonia	651.20	540.20	532.10	858.50	729.00
Romania	925.30	1071.30	967.70	878.40	890.20
Russian Federation	3459.20	3234.80	3088.10	3121.70	2851.70
Serbia			1514.80	2071.20	2079.20
Turkmenistan					
All Upper Middle Income	**732.20**	**895.40**	**945.20**	**1201.20**	**1332.00**
Researchers in R&D (per million people) Lower Middle Income Countries					
Armenia					
Georgia				1304.00	1339.70
Kyrgyz Republic					
Moldova		719.50	760.90	758.20	723.90
Tajikistan					
Ukraine			1328.00	1006.00	994.10
Uzbekistan	660.10	630.80	543.20	496.70	496.30
All Lower Middle Income					

Source: **World Bank**—*World Development Indicators*: States and Markets—5.13 Science and Technology

Table 16.15 Labor force participation rate—Adult men

	1995	2000	2005	2010	2015	2018
Labor Force Participation Rate—Male (% of Male Population Ages 15+), Modeled ILO Estimate,						
Czech Republic	71.30	69.30	68.90	68.00	68.20	68.40
Estonia	71.70	66.60	64.70	67.10	69.50	70.90
Hungary	59.40	57.90	58.40	58.20	63.40	65.00
Latvia	70.20	64.90	65.60	65.30	67.60	67.90
Lithuania	71.10	66.50	62.90	62.30	65.00	66.70
Poland	66.60	63.60	63.00	64.30	65.10	65.50
Slovak Republic	69.00	67.80	68.60	67.60	67.80	67.30
Slovenia	64.60	63.90	66.00	65.50	62.80	62.70
All High Income	**71.50**	**70.90**	**69.80**	**69.00**	**68.40**	**68.30**
Labor Force Participation Rate—Male (% of Male Population Ages 15+), Modeled ILO Estimate,						
Albania	73.90	73.60	67.90	63.00	65.20	64.90
Azerbaijan	72.00	70.70	68.40	67.50	68.70	69.70
Belarus	66.80	65.80	67.30	69.60	71.00	70.30
Bosnia and Herzegovina	61.90	60.80	60.50	59.90	58.40	58.60
Bulgaria	59.20	55.90	56.40	59.50	60.10	61.60
Croatia	66.00	62.90	61.10	59.80	59.40	58.20
Kazakhstan	78.30	77.10	75.20	75.80	77.00	77.10
North Macedonia	67.00	65.50	66.00	68.60	67.60	67.50
Romania	75.20	71.10	61.20	64.30	64.20	64.20
Russian Federation	70.80	69.10	67.80	70.30	71.20	70.50
Serbia	66.70	66.10	64.50	59.40	60.50	62.10
Turkmenistan	75.00	75.30	75.20	76.20	78.10	78.20
All Upper Middle Income	**81.30**	**79.80**	**77.50**	**76.20**	**75.60**	**74.90**
Labor Force Participation Rate—Male (% of Male Population Ages 15+), Modeled ILO Estimate						
Armenia	69.20	66.60	65.90	71.60	70.20	69.90
Georgia	76.00	73.80	72.90	75.10	78.70	78.70
Kyrgyz Republic	73.80	73.90	76.10	76.60	75.60	75.80
Moldova	53.10	52.30	50.80	45.20	47.30	45.60
Tajikistan	55.40	54.80	54.90	57.00	58.90	59.70
Ukraine	66.70	64.40	62.90	63.00	63.30	62.80
Uzbekistan	74.70	74.60	74.60	75.60	77.40	78.00
All Lower Middle Income	**81.60**	**80.70**	**80.30**	**78.70**	**77.70**	**77.20**

Source: **World Bank**—*World Development Indicators*: People—2.2 Labor Force Structure

Table 16.16 Labor force participation rate—Adult women

	1995	2000	2005	2010	2015	2018
Labor Force Participation Rate—Female (% of Female Population Ages 15+), Modeled ILO Estimate,						
Czech Republic	52.3	51.6	50.8	49.2	51.4	52.4
Estonia	53.7	52.6	53.5	55.0	56.0	57.0
Hungary	40.6	41.1	42.9	43.8	47.3	48.3
Latvia	52.2	48.9	50.4	53.9	54.3	55.4
Lithuania	53.7	54.8	50.6	52.5	54.5	56.4
Poland	51.2	49.6	47.8	48.3	49.0	48.9
Slovak Republic	51.6	52.3	51.3	50.6	52.0	52.7
Slovenia	51.5	51.2	52.8	53.2	52.0	53.3
All High Income	**49.6**	**50.7**	**51.4**	**52.0**	**52.4**	**52.9**
Labor Force Participation Rate—Female (% of Female Population Ages 15+), Modeled ILO Estimate						
Albania	53.70	51.80	48.10	45.70	47.70	47.20
Azerbaijan	56.30	56.30	57.70	60.20	62.50	63.10
Belarus	52.60	53.30	55.40	57.50	58.60	58.10
Bosnia and Herzegovina	39.50	38.60	37.80	37.10	35.70	35.60
Bulgaria	50.90	44.30	44.70	47.70	48.60	49.50
Croatia	45.90	45.30	46.20	46.20	47.00	45.70
Kazakhstan	65.40	65.60	64.40	65.40	65.40	65.10
North Macedonia	42.60	40.90	42.00	42.80	43.50	42.70
Romania	61.80	57.90	46.30	46.30	45.20	45.60
Russian Federation	53.70	54.70	55.20	55.90	55.60	54.90
Serbia	47.60	46.90	45.40	42.90	44.10	46.80
Turkmenistan	50.90	51.80	52.10	52.40	53.00	52.80
All Upper Middle Income	**60.10**	**59.40**	**57.40**	**55.70**	**55.00**	**54.30**
Labor Force Participation Rate—Female (% of Female Population Ages 15+), Modeled ILO Estimate,						
Armenia	48.70	48.00	47.50	49.60	51.20	49.60
Georgia	60.70	54.60	55.20	56.00	58.90	57.80
Kyrgyz Republic	56.10	55.20	54.10	52.20	49.80	48.00
Moldova	50.00	50.20	46.30	38.60	41.30	38.90
Tajikistan	29.50	30.00	30.20	29.50	28.30	27.80
Ukraine	54.00	50.80	48.60	48.40	47.40	46.70
Uzbekistan	51.20	51.80	52.30	52.70	53.30	53.40
All Lower Middle Income	**38.20**	**38.30**	**38.40**	**36.30**	**35.40**	**35.60**

Source: **World Bank**—*World Development Indicators*: People—2.2 Labor Force Structure

Table 16.17 Domestic credit to the private sector % GDP

	1995	2000	2005	2010	2015	2018
Domestic Credit to the Private Sector (% of GDP), High Income Countries						
Czech Republic	65.40	45.10	29.40	46.70	49.90	52.10
Estonia			57.00	93.00	68.90	62.60
Hungary	21.70	31.80	43.30	60.80	35.70	33.40
Latvia				95.50	48.80	36.10
Lithuania				58.60	41.50	40.70
Poland	16.50	26.50	27.10	48.70	53.60	52.70
Slovak Republic				45.10	53.20	61.50
Slovenia			52.10	85.30	49.90	43.20
All High Income	**136.00**	**155.10**	**143.60**	**146.20**	**144.10**	**144.00**
Domestic Credit to the Private Sector (% of GDP), Upper Middle Income Countries						
Albania	3.80	4.90	15.50	39.10	37.20	33.10
Azerbaijan	1.20	5.90	9.50	17.90	38.50	20.80
Belarus	6.10	8.90	15.90	41.80	27.90	27.80
Bosnia and Herzegovina		37.40	42.10	61.80	58.70	58.60
Bulgaria	27.70	12.00	39.40	68.30	55.40	51.30
Croatia	26.20	31.70	52.00	68.20	64.40	55.90
Kazakhstan	7.10	11.20	35.70	39.30	37.70	27.30
North Macedonia	22.00	17.00	23.30	44.90	52.00	50.30
Romania		7.10	20.10	39.20	29.90	25.90
Russian Federation					57.30	76.00
Serbia		45.70	26.40	47.20	40.70	41.50
Turkmenistan		..				
All Upper Middle Income	**53.60**	**56.00**	**61.80**	**82.00**	**110.20**	**122.60**
Domestic Credit to the Private Sector (% of GDP), Lower Middle Income Countries						
Armenia	7.30	9.90	8.00	28.40	45.60	55.60
Georgia	6.10	8.70	14.70	34.00	54.60	68.00
Kyrgyz Republic	12.50	4.20	7.90	13.60	22.80	23.90
Moldova	6.70	12.70	23.60	29.50	29.10	23.50
Tajikistan		13.80	9.10	14.20	22.70	12.30
Ukraine	1.50	11.20	32.20	78.60	56.70	34.10
Uzbekistan						
All Lower Middle Income	**28.60**	**27.90**	**32.60**	**40.40**	**42.50**	**44.40**

Source: **International Monetary Fund**—*International Financial Statistics and data files, World Bank and OECD GDP estimates*

Table 16.18 Financial Institutions Index

	1995	2000	2005	2010	2015	2017
Financial Institutions Index (FI), High Income Countries						
Czech Republic	0.49	0.43	0.48	0.53	0.55	0.56
Estonia	0.38	0.49	0.56	0.59	0.54	0.53
Hungary	0.32	0.40	0.47	0.54	0.46	0.51
Latvia	0.18	0.38	0.53	0.61	0.51	0.48
Lithuania	0.21	0.34	0.48	0.53	0.47	0.46
Poland	0.31	0.37	0.48	0.59	0.61	0.60
Slovak Republic	0.36	0.39	0.50	0.54	0.59	0.59
Slovenia	0.41	0.52	0.67	0.74	0.66	0.65
All High Income	**0.56**	**0.60**	**0.64**	**0.66**	**0.66**	**0.66**
Financial Institutions Index (FI), Upper Middle Income Counties						
Albania	0.27	0.21	0.28	0.41	0.41	0.41
Azerbaijan	0.16	0.15	0.22	0.27	0.32	0.32
Belarus	0.12	0.15	0.28	0.30	0.34	0.34
Bosnia and Herzegovina	0.37	0.29	0.42	0.47	0.51	0.52
Bulgaria	0.40	0.43	0.54	0.66	0.67	0.68
Croatia	0.31	0.40	0.55	0.67	0.67	0.69
Kazakhstan	0.21	0.14	0.27	0.32	0.38	0.35
North Macedonia	0.25	0.32	0.32	0.48	0.51	0.51
Romania	0.30	0.19	0.32	0.52	0.53	0.51
Russian Federation	0.19	0.25	0.37	0.49	0.52	0.58
Serbia	0.26	0.35	0.29	0.43	0.46	0.46
Turkmenistan	0.00	0.22	0.22	0.18	0.20	0.22
All Upper middle income	**0.29**	**0.31**	**0.36**	**0.41**	**0.45**	**0.45**
Financial Institutions Index (FI), Lower Middle Income Countries						
Armenia	0.14	0.20	0.20	0.34	0.45	0.47
Georgia	0.10	0.13	0.18	0.31	0.46	0.53
Kyrgyz Republic	0.09	0.09	0.18	0.17	0.24	0.23
Moldova	0.22	0.25	0.38	0.43	0.44	0.43
Tajikistan	0.00	0.09	0.11	0.15	0.15	0.22
Ukraine	0.16	0.23	0.31	0.39	0.38	0.37
Uzbekistan	0.37	0.29	0.32	0.37	0.36	0.43
All Lower middle income	**0.21**	**0.22**	**0.24**	**0.28**	**0.31**	**0.32**

Financial Institutions Index: Aggregate of Fin. Institutions Depth Index, Fin. Institutions Access Index & Fin. Institutions Efficiency Index

Source: **IMF Financial Development Index Database.** (IMF sources this data from World Bank FinStats, IMF's Financial Access Survey)

Table 16.19 Financial Markets Index

	1995	2000	2005	2010	2015	2017
Financial Markets Index (FM), High Income Countries						
Czech Republic	0.19	0.30	0.39	0.17	0.19	0.19
Estonia	0.39	0.13	0.25	0.13	0.11	0.11
Hungary	0.24	0.53	0.50	0.58	0.37	0.34
Latvia	0.07	0.18	0.06	0.08	0.05	0.07
Lithuania	0.05	0.09	0.10	0.06	0.05	0.05
Poland	0.32	0.42	0.31	0.34	0.34	0.34
Slovak Republic	0.03	0.09	0.02	0.06	0.05	0.05
Slovenia	0.46	0.36	0.39	0.32	0.11	0.10
All High Income	**0.28**	**0.43**	**0.45**	**0.45**	**0.43**	**0.43**
Financial Markets Index (FM), Upper Middle Income Countries						
Albania	0.01	0.01	0.00	0.00	0.01	0.00
Azerbaijan	0.02	0.02	0.05	0.03	0.06	0.07
Belarus	0.00	0.01	0.01	0.09	0.01	0.01
Bosnia and Herzegovina	0.01	0.01	0.02	0.02	0.01	0.01
Bulgaria	0.04	0.03	0.09	0.07	0.06	0.06
Croatia	0.13	0.08	0.09	0.12	0.12	0.10
Kazakhstan	0.12	0.12	0.32	0.30	0.27	0.28
North Macedonia	0.14	0.31	0.08	0.03	0.03	0.04
Romania	0.01	0.06	0.06	0.05	0.08	0.09
Russian Federation	0.11	0.23	0.39	0.52	0.38	0.37
Serbia	0.10	0.11	0.06	0.04	0.05	0.05
Turkmenistan	0.00	0.03	0.03	0.04	0.03	0.03
All Upper middle income	**0.10**	**0.12**	**0.14**	**0.15**	**0.14**	**0.15**
Financial Markets Index (FM), Lower Middle Income Countries						
Armenia	0.04	0.06	0.03	0.02	0.03	0.03
Georgia	0.02	0.04	0.06	0.03	0.05	0.05
Kyrgyz Republic	0.34	0.34	0.13	0.05	0.02	0.02
Moldova	0.24	0.27	0.27	0.27	0.27	0.27
Tajikistan	0.00	0.00	0.00	0.00	0.00	0.00
Ukraine	0.02	0.08	0.09	0.09	0.07	0.04
Uzbekistan	0.07	0.10	0.32	0.04	0.07	0.09
All Lower middle income	**0.06**	**0.10**	**0.10**	**0.09**	**0.09**	**0.08**

Financial Markets Index (FM): Aggregate of Financial Markets Depth Index, Financial Markets Access Index and Financial Markets Efficiency Index

Source: **IMF Financial Development Index Database** (IMF sources this data from World Bank FinStats, Dealogic Corporate Debt Database, Bank For International Settlement (BIS) debt securities database)

References

Acemoglu, D., & Robinson, J. (2012). *Why Nations Fail*. Crown Publishing.

Aslund, A. (2018). What Happened to the Economic Convergence of Central and Eastern Europe After the Global Financial Crisis? *Comparative Economic Studies, 60*(2), 254–270.

Barro, R. J. (1991). Economic Growth in a Cross Section of Countries. *Quarterly Journal of Economics, 106*(2), 407–443.

Blejer, M., & Skreb, M. (Eds.). (2001). *Transition: The First Decade*. Cambridge, MA: The MIT Press.

Bonin, J., & Wachtel, P. (2003). Financial Sector Development in Transition Economies: Lessons from the First Decade. *Financial Markets, Institutions and Instruments, 12*, 1–66.

Bonin, J., Hasan, I., & Wachtel, P. (2015). Banking in Transition Economies. In A. Berger, P. Molyneux, & J. Wilson, eds., *The Oxford Handbook of Banking* (2nd ed., Chapter 39, pp. 963–983). Oxford University Press.

Brown, A. N. (Ed.). (1999). *When Is Transition Over?* Kalamazoo, MI: W.E. Upjohn Institute for Employment Research.

Campos, N. F., & Coricelli, F. (2002). Growth in Transition: What We Know, What We Don't, and What We Should. *Journal of Economic Literature, 40*(3), 793–836.

Estrin, S., Hanousek, J., Kocenda, E., & Svejnar, J. (2009). The Effects of Privatization and Ownership in Transition Economies. *Journal of Economic Literature, 47*(3), 699–728.

Fischer, S., & Sahay, R. (2000). *The Transition Economies After Ten Years*. IMF Working Paper 00/30.

Fischer, S., Sahay, R., & Vegh, C. A. (1996). Stabilization and Growth in Transition Economies: The Early Experience. *Journal of Economic Perspectives, 10*(2), 45–66.

Gros, D., & Suhrcke, M. (2000). *Ten Years After: What Is Special About Transition Countries?* EBRD.

Haselmann, R., & Wachtel, P. (2010). Bankers Perception of the Legal Environment and the Composition of Bank Lending. *Journal of Money, Credit and Banking, 42*(5), 965–984.

Havrylyshyn, O. (2007). *Fifteen Years of Transformation in the Post-Communist World*. Development Policy Analysis No. 4. Washington, DC: Cato Institute.

Havrylyshyn, O. (2013). Is the Transition Over? A Definition and Some Measurements. In P. Hare & G. Turley (Eds.), *Handbook of the Economics and Political Economy of Transition*. Routledge.

Havrylyshyn, O., & Van Rooden, R. (2003). Institutions Matter in Transition, But So Do Policies. *Comparative Economic Studies, 45*, 2–24.

Havrylyshyn, O., Meng, X., & Tupy, M. (2016). *25 Years of Reforms in Ex-Communist Countries: Fast and Extensive Reforms Led to Higher Growth and More Political Freedom*. Policy Analysis Number 795. Washington, DC: CATO Institute.

International Monetary Fund. (2013). *Financing Future Growth: The Evolving Role of the Banking Systems in CESEE.* Central, Eastern and Southeastern Europe – Regional Economic Issues.

International Monetary Fund. (2014, October). *25 Years of Transition: Post-communist Europe and the IMF.* Regional Economic Issues Special Report Prepared by James Roaf, Ruben Atoyan, Bikas Joshi, Krzysztof Krogulski and an IMF Staff Team.

King, R., & Levine, R. (1993). Finance and Growth: Schumpeter Might Be Right. *Quarterly Journal of Economics, 153*(3), 717–738.

La Porta, R., Lopez-de-Silanes, F., Shleifer, A., & Vishny, R. W. (1998). Law and Finance. *Journal of Political Economy, 106*, 1113–1155.

Mihaljek, D. (2018). Convergence in Central and Easter Europe: Can All Get to EU Average? *Comparative Economic Studies, 60*, 217–229.

Mileva, E. (2008). *The Impact of Capital Flows on Domestic Investment in Transition Economies.* Working Paper Series No. 871. European Central Bank.

Murrell, P. (2008). Institutions and Firms in Transition Economies. In C. Menard & M. M. Shirley (Eds.), *Handbook of New Institutional Economics, chapter 26* (pp. 667–699). Dordrecht, The Netherlands: Springer.

Myant, M., & Drahokoupil, J. (2012). Transition Indicators of European Bank for Reconstruction and Development: A Doubtful Guide to Economic Success. *Competition and Change, 16*(1), 69–75.

National Research Council. (1998). *Transforming Post-Communist Political Economies.* Washington, DC: The National Academies Press.

Olofsgård, A., Wachtel, P., & Becker, C. M. (2018). The Economics of Transition Literature. *Economics of Transition, 26*(4), 827–840.

Rousseau, P. L., & Wachtel, P. (1998). Financial Intermediation and Economic Performance: Historical Evidence from Five Industrialized Countries. *Journal of Money, Credit and Banking, 30*(3, Part 2), 657–678.

Shleifer, A., & Treisman, D. (2005). A Normal Country: Russia After Communism. *Journal of Economic Perspectives, 19*(1, Winter), 151–174.

Shleifer, A., & Treisman, D. (2014). Normal Countries: The East 25 Years After Communism. *Foreign Affairs, 93*(6), 92–103.

Svejnar, J. (2002). Transition Economies: Performance and Challenges. *Journal of Economic Perspectives, 16*(1), 3–28.

Székely, I. P., & Ward-Warmedinger, M. (2018). Reform Reversals: Areas, Circumstances and Motivations. *Comparative Economic Studies, 60*, 559–582.

Wachtel, P. (2019). Reflections on Transition After 30 Years: Transition vs. Convergence. *Ifo DICE Report, 17*(III, Autumn), 3–8.

Williamson, O. (2000). The New Institutional Economics: Taking Stock, Looking Ahead. *Journal of Economic Literature, 38*, 595–613.

World Bank. (2002). *Transition – The First Ten Years: Analysis and Lessons for Eastern Europe and the Former Soviet Union.* Washington, DC.

17

Institutional Change in Transition: An Evolving Research Agenda

From Natural **Experiment** *to Sequencing of Reforms, to Cultural Legacies*

Elodie Douarin

This chapter discusses some of the lessons from "transition economics", that is, the field of research focusing on the transformation away from central planning towards market economies in Eastern Europe and Central Asia since the early 1990s, focusing on the role of "institutional change". We discuss the emergence of institutions as an important issue in the transition literature, and what has been learned from the process of economic and political liberalisation in the region. At first, transition was seen as a natural experiment taking place across all former communist countries, which simply involved replacing the failed communist regime and central planning by a democratic market economy. As strong divergence soon appeared in the paths followed by different countries, it seemed that a "natural sequence" emerged—democratisation, economic stabilisation and liberalisation, then completion of the process through further institutional change. Simultaneously historical legacies appeared as a credible determinant of how successfully this sequence was followed, opening the way for a new agenda of research into the exact nature of these legacies, and the role of culture, beliefs and values in institutional change.

The chapter thus starts by discussing briefly the evolution of transition economics away from the "natural experiment" paradigm towards a focus on

E. Douarin (✉)
School of Slavonic and East European Studies, University College London,
London, UK
e-mail: e.douarin@ucl.ac.uk

© The Author(s) 2021
E. Douarin, O. Havrylyshyn (eds.), *The Palgrave Handbook of Comparative Economics*,
https://doi.org/10.1007/978-3-030-50888-3_17

institutional change (Sect. 1). We then review key stylised facts, pertaining to institutional change in transition, by summarising the trajectories of economic and political liberalisation in the region in Sect. 2. We discuss in particular the role of policies, historical legacies and path dependency in explaining these trajectories. In Sect. 3, we argue that a deeper understanding of these trajectories calls for a better understanding of people's preferences, as more needs to be learned about the factors that facilitate the emergence of broad support for change, especially towards more democratic political institutions. Finally, in Sect. 4, we discuss a few examples of studies looking back in time or using cross-sectional heterogeneity to explain changes in support for democracy, policy preferences or behaviours, before discussing studies trying to zoom in on individual preferences to explain the mechanics of change at the micro level. We conclude on a cultural turn in transition studies, opening the way for transition as development and calling for further (pluridisciplinary) research on values and beliefs, or culture, as important factors shaping the de facto impact of formal institutions, and institutional change.

1   Growth and Reforms: From Natural Experiment to Institutional Analysis

The early debates regarding transition focused on how best to implement a complex set of reforms. Many academics at the time saw it as a natural experiment, where different recipes could be tested to identify the best way to create efficient markets. It was the "end of history", and soon we would know everything. Many thought that, as "the market" was triumphing as the only viable economic system, the fall of the Berlin Wall was creating an "institutional vacuum" or a "tabula rasa", in countries that were broadly similar as to their level of economic development, mid-level incomes, educational achievements, and so on. The best policy choices would thus lead to the best outcomes.

This view was soon understood to be too simplistic, if not actually naïve. For example, the countries of the region were not identical and the legacies of the past had to be accounted for. Maybe tellingly, to this day there is no established consensus on how best to control for initial conditions. The problem is broader, however, and becomes clear when looking at evidence published to date on the growth impact of reforms. Meta-analysis is particularly useful in these situations, as it can help analyse the heterogeneity in the effect measured and its possible causes, in a large set of sources. A few meta-analyses have indeed been conducted recently to take stock of what has been learned so far from this early literature focusing on reforms and growth, and all discuss at length the fact that specifications differed widely, and, thus, so did conclusions (see, for example, Babecký and Campos 2011). Notably, the same conclusion had been reached a decade earlier in the meta-analysis conducted by Havrylyshyn (2001)—the continuity and confirmation of this problem underlines how difficult it is to identify the determinants of growth.

One rare early consensus exists, however, and it is that the most important reforms to start with were to stabilise, liberalise (internal and external exchanges) and privatise (at least small-scale enterprises). These constitute jointly the "first stage of institutional reforms", as explained by Balcerowicz (1995), for example, reflecting on his experience of leading Poland through transition, or as stated in Svejnar (2002). More reforms were needed, but the rest, the "second stage institutional reforms", could wait a little, and generally followed on from the first-stage reforms, in the sense that good progress in first-stage reforms subsequently explained continued progress in reforms. The short-term costs of reforms were recognised, but the longer-run benefit would soon outweigh these costs (i.e. patterns described as the J-curve of reforms as discussed, for example, in Hellman 1998).

In addition to this, a number of examples can be found in the literature of "eureka moments", where researchers identified an additional control that proved important for our understanding of the trajectory of change but was too long overlooked. One such example can be found in a paper published by Christoffersen and Doyle, in as late as 2000, demonstrating that controlling for export market growth impacted strongly on the estimated impact of liberalisation. Indeed, this variable captures an important aspect of transition: the fact that a large set of previously relatively integrated countries were going through a similarly difficult transformation. Thus trade had to be reoriented away from former communist trade partners, some of which were also implementing broad reforms and experiencing economic contraction, while themselves reorienting trade towards new economic partners. Controlling for this reduced significantly the size of the negative shocks associated, in the short run, with liberalisation.[1] Similarly, Babecký and Campos (2011) discuss the important role of external liberalisation, a factor not always controlled for in early empirical studies. More generally, their meta-analysis highlights the high diversity of controls used and large variations in the results obtained, even if the average results reveals a positive effect of reforms on growth in the long run.

Maybe of special interest in this area is the fact that a debate even existed over the best way to measure reforms or policies. The early efforts of De Melo

---

[1] Havrylyshyn (2001) identified four early studies using export variables; three found it to be significant.

et al. (1996) and their liberalisation index were replaced by the European Bank for Reconstruction and Development (EBRD) transition indicators, which the Bank continued to produce yearly until 2016. These indicators have been extensively used, but have also been criticised mostly for lacking transparency and reflecting outcomes as much as inputs of reforms (see Campos and Horvath 2012). They remain, however, the longest time series of consistently constructed indicators of reforms in transition, and thus remain a highly useful tool to analyse progress in reforms—quantitatively and relatively objectively.

We thus use them in Fig. 17.1 to illustrate how reforms progressed in the region. The reforms are grouped into first-stage and second-stage reforms, with first-stage reforms including liberalisation (internal and external) and small-scale privatisation. These constituted the first steps to be taken to create functioning markets. The second-stage reforms include governance, competitions and large-scale privatisation, reforms that were expected to be more challenging. This last set of reforms is often described as capturing something closer to "institutional change" (as opposed to policy change) as these reforms require more than the stroke of a pen. Progress in this dimension also correlates with property rights protection and other indicators of higher-order institutional quality. The paths followed by post-communist economies show that progress in first-stage reforms was mixed, but nearly all countries in the region (with the exception of non-reformist Belarus, Turkmenistan and Uzbekistan, labelled as laggards in Fig. 17.1) had rapidly completed these reforms. As the EBRD indicators are coded from 1 to 4+ (with 4+ reflecting the situation in a "typical" advanced market economy), we can see that the faster reformers (the countries of Central and Eastern Europe and the Baltics or CEB) had reached a score of 12 (or 12/3=4 on average for each of 3 components of first-stage reforms) by 1994 (i.e. nearly completed these first-stage reforms), demonstrating how quickly they had been able to implement the reforms needed to create bare-bone market economies. The countries in South East Europe (SEE) progressed slowly in the first decade of transition due to internal conflicts; however, by the early 2000s, they had caught up with the slower reformers of the Former Soviet Union (FSU). Second-stage reforms took longer, and marked differences are still observed today, but there has been progress everywhere (albeit very small in the laggards group), with only few and limited reversals. In CEB, the average score capturing progress in second-stage reforms is just under 11 today (or 3.5 on average for each of the 3 components of second-stage reforms). Further reforms would thus be needed to complete the process of transformation towards "typical market economies", and even more reforms would be required in the SEE and FSU region to close the gap. However, very little has happened since 2008.

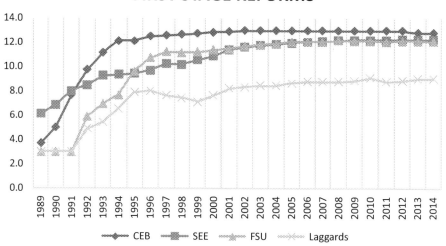

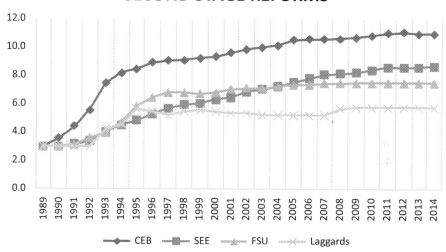

Fig. 17.1 First- and second-stage reforms—average EBRD transition indicators by category and region. (Note: First-stage reforms are the average of the country scores for liberalisation, exchange and small-scale privatisation, while second-stage reforms are the average of large-scale privatisation, competition and governance. The CEB includes the Czech Republic, Estonia, Hungary, Latvia, Lithuania, Poland and Slovakia. The SEE includes Albania, Bulgaria, Bosnia and Herzegovina, Croatia, Macedonia, Montenegro, Romania, Serbia and Slovenia. The FSU includes Armenia, Azerbaijan, Georgia, Kyrgyzstan, Kazakhstan, Moldova, Russia, Tajikistan and Ukraine. The laggards are Belarus, Uzbekistan and Turkmenistan. Source: Author's calculations based on EBRD transition indicators)

The key findings of this literature are thus simple: early comprehensive reforms covering the basics of stabilisation, liberalisation and small-scale privatisation have helped both returning to growth faster and then following up with faster completion of second-stage reforms. Contrary to the arguments sometimes presented that reforms had to go slowly to ease the social pain of transition, it is now known that the pain experienced in the countries where these first-stage reforms were delayed or only partially implemented was greater (e.g. see discussion in Havrylyshyn et al. 2016). The trajectories of economic liberalisation were more varied than expected, but the simultaneous political liberalisation of the region revealed an even greater divergence. Arguably, the end of the "natural experiment" myth had thus come. Within a decade, it had been replaced by the realisation that what we needed to understand was much more complex than investigating the impact of specific policies. Transition was about institutional change, and what made it feasible.

2   Transition as Institutional Change: Key Stylised Facts About Economic and Political Institutions in the Region

Thirty years after the fall of the Berlin Wall, institutional quality is widely recognised as a central driver of growth and economic development, and institutions are thus widely studied. The launch of the new comparative economics (Djankov et al. 2003) clearly crystallised a turning point in transition economics and contributed to making institutions a particularly salient field of enquiry for scholars interested in the economies emerging from communism. As already stated, that was the end of "the natural experiment" view of transition, arguably the start of a recognition that it was in fact "a transformation" away from central planning, and experiences were bound to differ.

The transformation away from communism that started in the early 1990s was all about the intertwined process of economic and political liberalisation. And thirty years later, indicators capturing economic and political freedom in the region clearly demonstrate an impressive, but uneven, progress. Key trends can be illustrated using indicators of political and economic freedom, as is done in Figs. 17.2 and 17.3. As before, we group countries by relatively homogenous transition reform paths. Here, we have chosen to use the Index of Economic Freedom (or EF) to capture the institutional development in the economic sphere in the region. It is an indicator produced by the Heritage Foundation to provide a comparable measure of institutional quality across

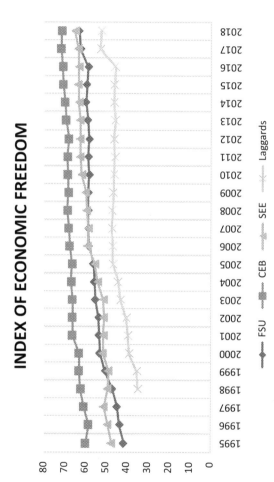

Fig. 17.2 Index of Economic Freedom, 1995–2018: average by region. (Note: The CEB comprises the Czech Republic, Estonia, Hungary, Latvia (from 1996), Lithuania (from 1996), Poland and Slovakia for 1995–2018. The FSU includes Armenia (from 1996), Azerbaijan (from 1996), Georgia (from 1996), Kazakhstan (from 1998), Kyrgyzstan (from 1998), Moldova (from 1995), Russia (from 1995), Tajikistan (from 1998) and Ukraine (from 1995). Finally, the SEE comprises Albania (from 1995), Bulgaria (from 1995), Bosnia and Herzegovina (from 1998), Croatia (from 1996), North Macedonia (from 2002), Montenegro (from 2002), Romania (from 1995), Serbia (from 2002) and Slovenia (from 1996). Countries have entered the dataset sequentially, as reflected in the grouping description. Source: Author's own calculation based on Index of Economic Freedom Panel Dataset 2018 (Heritage Foundation 2019))

POLITICAL FREEDOM AND CIVIL LIBERTIES

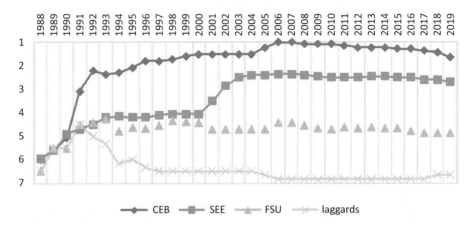

Fig. 17.3 Political freedom and civil liberties, 1988–2018. (Note: The countries are grouped as in Fig. 17.1. The score presented is the average of the political freedom score and the civil liberties score produced by Freedom House. The scores range from 1 for completely free to 7 for completely unfree; a higher score thus means less free-dom—the vertical axis is thus presented in reverse order. Source: Author's calculations based on Freedom House, various years)

the world. The index measures on a scale from 0 to 100 (with a higher score meaning a higher level of economic freedom) the degree of economic freedom present in four major areas: (1) size of government; (2) legal system and secu-rity of property rights (i.e. Rule of Law); (3) regulatory efficiency; (4) open markets. It explicitly focuses on the quality of de facto economic institutions, and it allows for global comparisons, thus usefully complementing, while remaining consistent, the picture provided by the transition indicators of the EBRD in Fig. 17.1. Indeed, Fig. 17.2 shows that early differences in reform paths persisted; in other words, early starters maintained their advance as the CEB group became "moderately free" (i.e. score of 60 and above) in 1997, the SEE group in 2009 and the FSU only in 2017. Since then the CEB region has become "mostly free" (i.e. scores of 70 and above) and the other regions are yet to catch up. The laggards remain to date "mostly unfree", reflecting their reluctant approach to reforms.

Thus, overall, by 2017, all the countries in the region (except the laggards) had functional markets and medium-high levels of economic freedom.[2] Rank

---

[2] For comparison, the average index of Economic Freedom in 2018 in the world (reported in 2019) was 60.8.

ordering by country groups has mostly persisted, although differences have slowly reduced over time. A final push in reforms would be needed for complete convergence, but even the freer economies in the group could reform towards further economic liberalisation. However, since the economic crisis of 2008 the average Index of Economic Freedom for each of the countries considered has been nearly stable, or at least the pace of change has reduced markedly.

To capture political liberalisation, we rely on the indicators created by Freedom House. Their indicator of political freedom across the world ranges from 1 to 7 with scores of 1 to 3 given to politically "free" countries, scores above 3 and up to 5 to "partially free" countries and finally scores of 5 and above to countries labelled as "non-free". This overall indicator is the simple average of two underlying indicators: one measuring political freedom per se, and the other focusing on civil liberties (each of these also range from 1 to 7, with 1 indicating a more democratic context). Their evolution is presented in Fig. 17.3, and it illustrates marked differences by region. It shows clearly that early progress in democratisation stalled very quickly in the FSU, while it was reverted in the group of laggards. Countries in the CEB region experienced rapid democratisation from the early 1990s, as did SEE countries but only from the early 2000s.

These general trends have led many to conclude that the economic transformation of these countries had to some extent been more successful than their political transformation. As indicated in Djankov (2016), it seemed that reformers had a recipe for economic transformation that was much more effective than the recipe for political transformation.

Beyond this simple description of trends, the empirical literature focusing on explaining the evolution of these indicators (or other related indicators, also aiming at capturing the evolution of political and economic institutions in the region) simply confirms the intuitive explanations underlying our description. To discuss this, we can refer to the work of Djankov (2016) as an example of the research published to date on the long-term drivers of institutional quality. Djankov (2016) focuses on the importance of historical legacies in the institutional evolution (using the same indicators as those we have used to construct Figs. 17.2 and 17.3) of the transition region. His regressions are cross-sectional, aiming to explain current institutional quality over the region with historical legacies; specifically he aims to test potential long-run effects of religion and empires in the region. His argument is that both capture important differences inherited from the past. He also controls for resource-rich countries (variable labelled "resource") and the percentage of the population living in cities in 1990 (variable labelled "urban"). These variables capture initial economic conditions, while the political context is captured through a measure of ethnic fractionalisation in 1989 (ethnic) as well as presidential powers, a variable created by Frye (1997) and capturing early institutional choices in the early years of transition. Overall, the variables in his specification accounts for about 70% and 80% of the variation in economic and political liberalisation achieved by 2015, respectively, while religion appears as the most reliable explanatory factor, as at least one religious dummy is significant in each of his models. From his analysis, Djankov thus concludes (Djankov 2016, 11):

> The explanatory power of initial conditions like urbanization and ethnicity, history, and presidential powers is quite high, explaining about 70 percent of the variation across countries. Much of this explanatory power is derived from historical variables, while little is added by newer institutional choices. While countries have broadly converged along economic freedom dimensions, they remain wide apart in political evolution.

However, we note that he does not control for policy choices in his regressions, even though these have been recognised to be important to our understanding of the trajectories of economic liberalisation in the region. In Table 17.1, we thus replicate the analyses in Djankov (2016) for the index of EF with two notable differences: (1) we use the raw values of the indicators produced by the Heritage Foundation for 2018 instead of rescaled values for 2015 and (2) we include an indicator of relative commitment to reforms (labelled as "nine" in Tables 17.2 and 17.3), which reports the year in which a score of 9 (i.e. an average score of 3) was reached for the three indicators capturing progress in first-stage reforms.[3] We present results (see Tables 17.2 and 17.3) for overall economic freedom (presented in columns 1 and 2) but also for indicators of economic freedom pertaining to international trade (columns 3 and 4), investment (columns 5 and 6) and financial liberalisation (columns 7 and 8). Our results confirm the importance of reforms in explaining economic liberalisation, as our indicator of relative commitment to reforms is systematically significant and improves the regressions' fit, especially for financial liberalisation. However, this addition does not alter Djankov's conclusions, as religion and empire significantly explain differences

---

[3] The lower the commitment to reform, the later this score of 9 can be reached: a later year means less commitment. Thus the negative sign of the estimated coefficient for this variable indicates that low commitment was bad for long-term institutional development. Early reformers developed better institutions. We note that this variable correlates with the indicator of presidential powers developed by Frye (1997) and used by Djankov (2016) to capture early institutional choices: indeed, nearly all the countries where reforms were implemented fast also had low presidential powers. The two variables are thus entered in turn, rather than jointly.

Table 17.1 Economic and political change: policies versus legacies

VARIABLES	(1) Overall1	(2) Overall2	(3) Trade1	(4) Trade2	(5) Invest1	(6) Invest2	(7) Financial1	(8) Financial2
Resource	1.762	−0.267	3.284	1.694	1.543	−1.028	6.042	−0.373
	(2.388)	(2.001)	(1.939)	(1.675)	(6.385)	(4.581)	(6.958)	(4.596)
Urban	0.114	0.101	−0.143	−0.153	−0.080	−0.129	−0.060	−0.118
	(0.169)	(0.155)	(0.138)	(0.129)	(0.453)	(0.354)	(0.494)	(0.355)
Ethnic	−0.029	0.040	−0.058	−0.008	−0.203	−0.008	−0.118	0.157
	(0.087)	(0.082)	(0.070)	(0.069)	(0.232)	(0.188)	(0.253)	(0.189)
Islam	−6.656	−8.681	−12.347*	−14.270**	−47.501**	−38.430**	−19.032	−19.066
	(7.990)	(6.527)	(6.488)	(5.466)	(21.367)	(14.946)	(23.286)	(14.994)
Orthodox	−5.977	−9.609*	−5.127	−8.251**	−36.879**	−31.847***	−12.984	−19.192*
	(6.500)	(4.659)	(5.279)	(3.902)	(17.383)	(10.667)	(18.944)	(10.702)
Ottoman	8.831	11.925**	3.561	6.135	32.021*	30.764**	8.117	15.065
	(6.292)	(5.161)	(5.109)	(4.322)	(16.826)	(11.818)	(18.337)	(11.856)
Russian	3.506	7.832*	−1.472	1.866	3.760	11.005	−7.913	6.731
	(5.050)	(4.419)	(4.101)	(3.701)	(13.505)	(10.118)	(14.717)	(10.150)
Presidential	−0.663		−0.534		−0.340		−1.822	
	(0.444)		(0.360)		(1.187)		(1.294)	
Nine		−0.274**		−0.199**		−0.869***		−1.151***
		(0.106)		(0.088)		(0.242)		(0.242)
Constant	67.045***	601.566***	103.719***	492.517**	101.471***	1815.604***	94.562**	2352.216***
	(12.789)	(208.887)	(10.386)	(174.936)	(34.203)	(478.289)	(37.274)	(479.837)
Observations	29	29	29	29	29	29	29	29
R-squared	0.514	0.595	0.588	0.635	0.655	0.790	0.490	0.736

Own calculations using the Index of Economic Freedom 2018 (Heritage Foundation), Djankov's data (2016) downloaded from https://www.piie.com/publications/working-papers/divergent-postcommunist-paths-democracy-and-economic-freedom and the transition indicators produced by the EBRD (several years)

Standard errors in parentheses. Significance: ***$p < 0.01$; **$p < 0.05$; *$p < 0.1$

Table 17.2 Preferences for political authoritarianism

	1989–1993	1994–1998	1999–2004	2005–2009	2010–2014
1. Belarus		5.09			4.97
2. Russia		5.52		5.25	5.74
3. Slovenia		4.66		4.42	4.86
4. Hungary		4.53		4.68	
5. Poland				5.08	4.86
6. Spain		4.14	3.63	3.66	4.2
7. Switzerland		3.93		3.43	
8. US		3.39	4.04	4.06	4.13

Table 17.3 Preferences for economic intervention

	1989–1993	1994–1998	1999–2004	2005–2009	2010–2014
1. Belarus	4.3	4.86			4.89
2. Russia	4.38	5.06			5.64
3. Slovenia		4.72		4.57	4.95
4. Hungary		5.4		5.21	
5. Poland		5.32		5.41	5.16
6. Spain	5.37	4.92		4.47	4.48
7. Switzerland		4.54		5.16	
8. US		4.12		4.22	4.2

Average scores for preferences for political authoritarianism and economics intervention, defined following Roland (2014, 265). "Economic interventionism" is based on the average of seven indicators rescaled to be scored on a scale from 1 to 10. The seven indicators capture (1) views on preferences between private and public ownership (with a high score translating as support for public ownership), (2) views on whether competition is harmful or desirable (with a high score translating as a belief that competition is harmful), (3) an indicator of discrimination against foreigners (with a high score meaning that respondents think it is best to give priority to nationals when jobs are scarce), (4) an indicator of discrimination against women (with a high score meaning that respondents think it is best to give priority to men when jobs are scarce), (5) views regarding the link between hard work and success (with a high score translating that hard work doesn't bring success, as it is more a matter of luck), (6) an indicator of whether imagination is an important quality for a child (with a high score meaning that imagination is not important) and finally (7) an indicator of attitudes towards inequality (with a high score translating a belief that equality is good). Roland (2014) had also included an indicator related to attitudes towards older workers, but we could not include it here, as it was missing too often. Then "political authoritarianism" is the average of three indicators scored on a scale from 1 to 10. These three indicators are (1) support for the notion that experts should take decisions rather than the government, (2) support from strong leaders and finally (3) lack of support for democracy. See Fig. 17.4 in appendix for details.

Sources: Author's calculations based on the World Value Survey, harmonised dataset 1989–2014

in economic institutions in the region, even when policy choices are accounted for.[4]

Roland (2014) also presents regressions looking into the short- and long-run determinants of institutional quality. However, he uses indicators of institutional quality, which differ from those we have discussed so far, namely, Rule of Law, Government Effectiveness and Control of Corruption, all from the World Bank. These indicators reflect de facto institutional quality, and arguably reflect economic institutions. In his estimations, he focuses on (1) geographical controls (ruggedness, landlocked and distance to equator, as well as resource rents), (2) trust and ethnic fractionalisation as translating to long-run cultural values and factors believed to facilitate cooperation, respectively, (3) state antiquity as long-term institutional legacies and finally (4) democratisation and EU membership, as shorter-run drivers. His long-run regressions are complemented by shorter-run panels focusing on yearly changes in institutional quality, using the same set of determinants. Overall Roland (2014) concludes that democratisation and EU membership are the strongest drivers explaining current institutional quality in the region, in both sets of regression. Trust is the main control in his specification capturing historical legacies, as it measures a cultural trait, something that is passed down the generations, learned from past exchange and relevant to economic behaviour. However, it does not appear as a relevant driver.

That said, based on a larger review of the literature, Douarin and Mickiewicz (2017) concluded that, focusing on economic institutions, three types of drivers were generally considered as relevant. Firstly, early progress in reforms, especially the key reforms of stabilisation, liberalisation and small-scale privatisation (or "first-stage institutional reforms") was key to continued progress in reforms and a rapid return to growth. Secondly, political institutions have had an impact too, as countries that became democratic in the early years of transition also progressed faster in their reforms in the economic sphere. Finally, cultural factors also played a role with specific cultural legacies facilitating or impeding reforms. The fact that early progress in reforms is generally found to explain institutional development above and beyond political institutions and cultural factors (see, for example, Di Tommaso et al. 2007) is especially relevant. Indeed, it strongly indicates that (1) early comprehensive reforms were desirable and (2) their implementation reflects a critical juncture that sent some countries on a new institutional development path. At the

---

[4] In fact, controlling for policy commitment, as we have done, generally increases both the magnitude and significance of the effects estimated for religion and empire, implying that they explain even better the residual differences in economic institutions.

same time, this literature very much underscores the importance of historical legacies, because of its strong relevance to political liberalisation, and because it also explains progress in economic liberalisation, beyond the role of policy choices. In summary, institutions matter indeed, but institutional evolution seems to be at least partly driven by history—hence, history matters too.

We could stop there and be content with these stylised facts, but the natural inclination for any academic is to query findings further. Here two fundamental questions come to mind: (1) if political institutions show so much persistence, can we explain when divergence happens? And (2) if reforms were so important, which factors facilitated their implementation? Overall, these two questions are related and get to the essence of institutional change and persistence, by focusing our attention on underlying factors, which means that a similar shock can translate into a "critical juncture", sending countries on a new development trajectory, or not. This is moving beyond the recognition that history matters, to ask how?

3   Going Deeper Into the Causes of Institutional Change: Understanding Support for Reforms

What were the factors that facilitated democratisation and early reforms? The pull factor of the EU, when it came to accelerating institutional change with the prospect of enlargement, has been well evidenced (see, for example, the findings of Di Tommaso et al. 2007, or Campos in this volume). The importance of a good leader or reform team has also been well documented. This is discussed by Åslund in this volume. Consistently, Treisman (2014) attempted to identify the leaders who had been able to push reforms forward beyond what could have been predicted by initial conditions. However, here we propose to look instead into a related issue: that of popular support for reforms, an issue that we believe is fundamental and still less well understood.

Indeed, we can note that all the factors we have mentioned (institutional pull of the EU, good leaders, supportive population) seemed to be credible ingredients that facilitated early reform implementation and continued progress in reforms. All these factors are linked, as they are about the political economy of reforms—committed leaders were more likely to be found in countries where the population had fought for a break away from communism (rather than obtained it due to the collapse of the USSR, for example), and they were more likely to be successful where the population was supportive of reforms, where the aspiration to reclaim a European identity was stronger and where the prospect of EU integration was credible. This general pattern has been described in detail in Havrylyshyn (2006) and worked out as a vicious versus a virtuous circle. Indeed, reforms were more likely in more democratic countries and they generated a faster return to growth, then leading to more support for markets and democracies, a greater likelihood of continued reforms, and so on. On the contrary, tepid reforms led to a protracted economic downturn and sceptical attitudes towards markets and democracy, which then led to more resistance towards reforms (see also Denisova et al. 2012).

In earlier work, Lipset (1959) had claimed that economic development was a necessary prerequisite for democratic consolidation, but the post-communist experience turned that proposition on its head. Indeed, countries that started transition at relatively similar levels of economic development (e.g. Poland and Ukraine) had strikingly different experiences, overall illustrating a scenario of democracy leading to growth, rather than growth leading to democracy. While Poland went through rapid economic and political liberalisation in the early 1990s, economic reforms stagnated in Ukraine and the country experienced a prolonged and deep economic crisis following the collapse of the USSR. While it has not reverted to an authoritarian regime, as have many in the FSU, Ukraine continues to struggle with democratisation, and remains even today much behind Poland in democratic terms (even accounting for Poland's recent democratic backsliding[5]). Investigating exactly the divergent paths of Poland and Ukraine, Hartwell (2016) emphasises early decisions regarding economic reforms and democratisation; he does talk about good leaders and the prospect of EU membership. But looking deeper, he recognises the crucial role played by history. For example, Poland benefitted from a vibrant civil society prior to 1989, which continued to be effectively mobilised after the collapse of communism; as a result accountability and appropriate levels of executive constraints were successfully negotiated in the early days of transition. Empirical evidence suggests that Ukraine would potentially have done much better. Historical path-dependency effects were the reason for slower reforms than in Poland, but one needs to look beyond the less-than-complete democratisation in Ukraine (which as noted was still among the more democratised countries of the FSU). An important part of the story was a long-standing desire for independence, which led the Rukh opposition to compromise with the old guard in a sort of Faustian bargain: if they agreed

---

[5] The recent populist backlash in Poland is discussed by Mickiewicz in this volume (Chap. 28).

to independence, Rukh would not push for rapid economic reforms, and leave this dimension to the old guard, whose interests were to delay reforms.[6]

Overall, this brings to the fore the question of support for reforms and how change is negotiated within a social and political group; it is about human agency in shaping institutions, the fact that institutional change happens in a specific social group, with its beliefs, values and expectations, and its power structure. This can be related to two broad strands of literature. The first one is the political economy literature, which tend to focus on a micro approach and to emphasise the incentives, preferences and relative power of different groups in the population (see Guriev in this handbook, for example). The second one relates to "institutional stickiness", which implies that "likely success, of any proposed institutional change is a function of that institution's status in relationship to indigenous agents in the previous time period" (Boettke et al. 2008), by which they mean that if formal institutional change is to "stick", it needs to be supported by compatible informal institutions or cultural values in the sense of values and practices adhered to by the population.

Thus the importance of support for reforms, support for markets and democracy, has in particular been emphasised by a number of authors in the context of transition. The proposed wholesale change in institutions in the economic and political spheres that transition entailed indeed required some underlying support for both markets and democracy. Focusing on change, Grosjean and Senik (2011) note that democracy has increased support for markets in the transition region, while economic liberalisation has not led to an increase in support for democratisation. They thus conclude that political liberalisation may have been a necessary condition for a broadening of the public support for large economic reforms. Focusing on stability instead, Roland (2010, 2014) argues that preferences for democracy and market have evolved little in the region since the beginning of transition, and differences between specific groups of countries have remained surprisingly stable. In the evidence he presents, the differences in support for authoritarian versus democratic leaders, as well as the differences in support for government intervention, between the countries of the transition region (as a group) and EU countries or the US are particularly striking and the differences are remarkably stable in time (Roland 2010, 12, 2014, 266). This appears to reflect strongly held values that are transmitted and are specific to a group, and can constitute constraints or barriers to further reforms—it is what some would

---

[6] The details of the process are developed by Havrylyshyn (2017), with a brief summary of the Faustian Bargain on pp. 310–311.

thus call culture, but more broadly can be defined as social values, in effect historical legacies.

Tables 17.2 and 17.3 present average scores for "political authoritarianism" and "economic interventions" created following Roland's definitions (2014, 265) but by country rather than country group. Averaging over country group can indeed potentially hide variations between countries and in time, especially as the group of countries included in each round of the World Value Survey changes. Here we present average scores for a selection of countries, selected for being included in the 1981–1985 or 1989–1993 waves—so prior to or around the time of transition,[7] and then at least twice from 1994 onwards. Tables 17.2 and 17.3 bring some interesting nuances on Roland's conclusions. Table 17.3 shows that differences regarding preferences for economic intervention are only clear when comparing the US to the rest of the countries presented. Transition and European countries (represented by Belarus, Russia, Slovenia, Hungary and Poland on the one hand and by Spain as an EU member and Switzerland as a close neighbour on the other hand) show much variations waves on waves, and overall comparable scores. For support for political authoritarianism, however, depicted in Table 17.2, differences are much more marked, with the transition countries overall showing much stronger preferences for authoritarianism, with average scores for the indicator roughly 1 point (on a scale of 1 to 10) above that of the Western European countries for which scores are reported, and the US.[8]

4   Institutional Change as Stepping Back in Time—Values and Beliefs and the Persistence of Political Institutions— Or Zooming in on the Mechanisms of Change

Thus recognising that history matters lead us to emphasise the importance of human values and beliefs, and their evolution, as important possible explanatory factors for institutional change, we propose to review a few examples of

---

[7] However, due to missing values or questions, it turned out to be impossible to compute some of the indicators of interest in these two first waves.

[8] The average scores for the variables used to construct the two indexes in Tables 17.2 and 17.3, before rescaling, are presented in Fig. 17.4 in appendix. They show marked differences between transition and non-transition countries for all the constitutive variables of "preferences for authoritarianism", while for "preferences for economic intervention", differences are most notable for importance of imagination for a child and views on private versus public ownership.

studies adopting this approach and considering explicitly factors relating to people's mindset, cultural views, social norms, and so on. The deeper drivers of institutional change discussed here are thus calling for an improvement on our understanding of how the preferences and values that can contribute to shape democratic evolution, or political liberalisation, are shaped, or changed. We review here some of the evidence accumulated on the subject, focusing on investigation using historical case study or long-term effects of earlier changes to explain observed differences in Sect. 4.1. We will discuss in Sect. 4.2 studies which are instead trying to describe change as it occurs. Section 4 overall thus discusses the investigation of institutional change as the result of two processes: looking back or zooming in.

4.1   Stepping Back in Time

Thus answering the question of how best to implement reforms and enquiring on the factors that facilitated progress in reforms generated new questions, regarding the key factors able to explain the democratisation trajectories in the region.

We have already mentioned studies that have demonstrated the role of specific values on persistence of political institutions in particular. These included, for example, Roland (2010) focusing on average values in different groups of countries, as explaining limited support for reforms over an extended period of time, or investigating the role of trust (which was shown to not consistently matter—Roland 2014). In both cases, the driver investigated was a measure of average value held in society, an average societal view that was assumed to be stable in time, and relevant to people's behaviours, and thus to institutional change. Others studies adopting this approach could be added, including Gorodnichenko and Roland (2011, 2012), who discuss how "individualism" (a national cultural trait, measuring preferences for group versus individual reward/incentives) matters for development and growth, or Williamson and Kerekes (2011), who discuss the long-term impact of a range of cultural values on property rights protection. All these studies represent efforts to understand differences in performances at a given point in time through differences in long-held values. They generally assume that individual values can be aggregated into cultural traits and that culture is stable. They thus rely on measures collected at one point in time and assumed to be continuously valid in time, and relevant to the national population. However, these studies are mostly useful to explain stability, or to demonstrate the effect of an event in the past that might have shaped these values, with the benefit of hindsight.

They are also highly dependent on the quality of the measures used (for a discussion see Taras et al. 2009). Going forward, they are, however, unlikely to help to forecast change or to provide clear insights into how change might come.

Similarly, studies in the spirit of Djankov (2016) are a useful illustration of where cultural changes can come from: specific experiences in the past, but the notion that religions or empires have shaped institutional change in the long run remains a bit of a "black-box" finding—why exactly and how did it matter for long-term change? Narrowing down the focus can thus potentially bring new insights into some of the mechanisms explaining stability of change, and why specific events may have had longer-run impacts.

For example, Bruszt et al. (2012) explain that those countries where democratic institutions developed faster after the fall of communism were also characterised by a greater level of civic engagement during the communist period, with the existence of a political opposition and the level of state repression both contributing to explain reform progress and institutional change in transition. To some extent, the argument thus raised echoes the work of Ekiert and Kubik (2001) linking popular protest to democratic consolidation in Poland. In addition to this, Pop-Eleches and Tucker (2017) present a detailed analysis of the legacies of communism over the whole region, and argue that the communist experience had a deep impact on the attitudes and beliefs of the population who lived through it. With regard to the present discussion in particular, they conclude that preferences for markets and democratisation were greatly affected by the lived experience of communism. In particular, their model specification emphasises the importance of communist socialisation and exposure to repression on political attitudes (see also Pop-Eleches and Tucker 2014). Overall, this suggests that democratisation was in fact facilitated by a cumulated experience of political and civic engagement through time, thus potentially explaining that those countries which had been under communism the longest and where the political repression had been the strongest were also those where the democratic transition was the most difficult, and where reforms progressed the least or at the slowest pace.

Of course, it is possible to continue to push the origin of the divergence in path further in the past, and we can indeed find in the literature some interesting examples of earlier legacies that can further explain the institutional path followed by different countries. Relevant examples here include an analysis presented by Darden and Grzymala-Busse (2006), who noted that the emergence of democratic institutions and the implementation of market reforms were more likely if the new leaders in the early years of transition were not communists and thus if the values and beliefs of the local population were compatible with a rejection of communism.[9] They thus posited that school curricula in the early years of mass education should have had a deep impact on the beliefs communicated to the population at the time, and then passed on from generation to generation afterwards. They thus argued in particular that a pre-communist nationalist curricular content subsequently led to a more pronounced anti-communist sentiment, and thus a faster move towards both democracy and markets.

Overall this lends credibility to the argument put forward by Shleifer and Treisman (2014) that as time passes and we are better able to appreciate the longer-run path of development of the transition countries, it becomes clearer that they have simply moved closer to the institutional profile typical in their immediate neighbourhood. By some indicators, Tajikistan has become more similar to Afghanistan, Estonia to Sweden, reflecting the argument stated in Kopstein and Reilly (2000, 1) regarding the "spatially dependent nature of the diffusion of norms, resources, and institutions that are necessary to the construction of political democracies and market economies in the post-communist era". In other words, economic reforms and, more strongly, democratisation have progressively returned, after the fall of communism, to a relatively predictable path reflecting earlier history and norms. This has also been described as "institutional stickiness" (Boettke et al. 2008), as already mentioned—which implies that if formal institutional change is to "stick", it needs to be supported "bottom-up" by compatible values.[10] According to Ekiert and Ziblatt (2013), the evolution of political institutions in Central and Eastern Europe since transition strongly correlates with the patterns of the past, and this relevance of the "deep past" (to use their terminology) might even be stronger because of the frequent "disjunctures" that have characterised the region. For Ekiert and Ziblatt (2013), formal and informal institutions are more likely to become incompatible when large changes are repeatedly experienced, preventing the progressive co-evolution expected in less hectic contexts, prompting a stronger adherence to values and norms from an earlier time.

Overall, this literature does highlight continuity, and change, and has sometimes identified clear mechanisms to explain change, but it seems to still fall short of offering a grand theoretical frame to understand future changes.

---

[9] In an earlier statement of the underlying argument, Bunce (1999, pp. 784–785) had noted: "Where there was significant protest (sometimes repeatedly, sometimes not, and sometimes early and sometimes late during the socialist era), where this protest was at once anticommunist, nationalist, and liberal, and where opposition leaders were in place, the collapse of Communist Party hegemony and the subsequent holding of free elections *allowed mass publics to reveal their true preferences*, the opposition to take power, and democratization and economic reform to be implemented" (italics added).

[10] An argument put forward by Ledeneva and Efendic too in this volume.

This would require looking at individual values, and policy preferences, how they might change and how they can translate into policy choice. This requires looking into the political economy and the sociology of reforms.

4.2 Institutional Change as Zooming In

In recent years, the focus on democratisation and its potential drivers has intensified, and researchers have looked into cross-sectional heterogeneity in (often) national samples, to try and identify more contemporary drivers of change. The focus on national samples allows to keep constant a lot of the macro-conditions experienced by the population. Regional or local sources of variations in access to information, for example, or past experiences, can then be used to explain differences in attitudes.

For example, Guriev et al. (2019) have recently exploited differences in 3G coverage as an exogenous variation in sources of information to assess its impact on political trust and support for specific parties. Using a large sample of individuals in 116 countries, they find that internet access reduces public approval of government, especially in countries where the internet is not censored and where traditional media are censored. They further indicate that in Western Europe, internet access can then be related to increase populist voting shares. This constitutes an example of a broader range of studies trying to shed lights on how individuals' views are shaped. Other studies have made use of differences in mobile network coverage or access to foreign channels to similarly explain divergence in political attitudes (e.g. Peisakhin and Rozenas 2018).

In this volume, Ivlevs reviews the literature linking migration and democratisation in sending countries. He discusses the possibility that through their communications, migrants send "social remittances" back to their family and friends left behind—where social remittances are ideas and information which can then change the values and beliefs held by friends and relatives back home. This literature tends to show that migration indeed can be associated with changes in political institutions in sending countries, and that the effect is probably causal, as it is also found in studies dealing with issues relating to reverse causality or self-selection into migration. This effect has also been more frequently identified in the context of migration towards more politically free countries, which resulted in improvement in political liberalisation at home (see, for example, Docquier et al. 2016). For example, in a study focusing on Moldova, Barsbai et al. (2017) concludes that municipal-level westward migration (i.e. towards more democratic countries) is associated with lower voting shares for the communist party back home.

Other complementary efforts, however, add an important dimension—that of the interaction between an individual's preferences or values on the one hand and social norms on the other. For example, also in this volume, Gërxhani and Wintrobe propose a simple theoretical model linking general trust, government trust and tax morale. To them, the views of the public on the government and their general perception of political institutions quality emerge from the repeated interactions they have with them, through information (in particular on corruption), taxation and public good delivery, and through individuals' perception of how the rest of the population will behave. They are building on the notion of "trust-based political exchange", which can lead to either a high equilibrium of mutual trust (trust in government and good levels of public good delivery) or a low equilibrium of low institutional quality (high corruption, low public good delivery, and low tax morale/high tax evasion, low trust in government). They further test the predictions of their model on a reduced form equation using Albanian data. One of the key interests of their approach for our argument here is that it considers explicitly that national level outcomes (e.g. the degree of tax evasion) do not depend only on individual preferences, but also on perception of institutional quality, and on social norms.

Other approaches bringing in this social dimension can be added. For example, Shayo (2020) presents a review of the literature on social identity and its links to a large range of economic policies. In his paper, he reviews evidence compatible with the idea that people cultivate multiple social identities (be it ethnic, religious or professional identities) which influence their choices, as they give preferential treatment to in-group members and conform to the norms of the group, even if these actions can seem detrimental to them, individually, in the short run. To the extent that the values translated through identities shape individual preferences for policies, they will also be relevant to institutional change. Gennaioli and Tabellini (2019) similarly consider how specific economic shocks can result in people adopting new identities that then lead them to change their behaviours and the policies they perceive as desirable.

These are only a few examples of ways the impact of individuals' values and beliefs on institutional quality and institutional change can be investigated. In all cases, the risk of reverse causality is explicit, either in the use of instrumental approaches or in the recognition of possible interrelations. The model suggested by Gërxhani and Wintrobe assumes an endogenous change or co-evolution of taxpayers' values and institutional quality. These studies are typical of the "behavioural/sociological/cultural turn" in the study of institutional change in recent years—values, beliefs and preferences are now key variables to be investigated to sharpen our understanding of the individual and social constructs underlying institutions and institutional change.

In some literature, these will be described as being part of the "informal institutions" of a given country/region/society, or as "cultural" factors. The key distinguishing feature for these values and beliefs to be labelled as informal institutions or culture is that they are relatively slow-moving (Roland 2004; Tabellini 2008) or transmitted to the next generation (Guiso et al. 2006; Alesina and Giuliano 2015). The distinction between culture and informal institutions, if there is any, is less clear. For Alesina and Giuliano (2015), there is no distinction but they prefer the term culture, over concerns that informal institutions will always be seen as subdued to, or determined by, formal ones (p. 902). For Voigt (2018), culture is a broader concept including informal institutions among other things. He also contends that "internal institutions", that is, institutions that are maintained without relying on an (external) formal rule, can be divided into immutable (and thus self-enforced) social conventions (such as language rules), ethical rules (or personal belief about what is right or wrong, enforced through self-commitment), social norms (i.e. behaviours sanctioned by societal control) and formal private rules (enforced through organised private rules). He thus advocates for opening the relative black-box of "informal institutions" further. However, Voigt (2018) himself concedes that measurements that are typically used currently in the empirical literature do not easily map into his concepts. And the wealth of evidence accumulated with established measures is probably too large and compelling to be ignored. Here we want to argue instead for a need to understand values in their social context, to be able to identify which values matter for change. Indeed, understanding this would imply, for example, (1) having a better understanding of how individual values are aggregated into social norms (this would include being able to answer questions relating to whose values matter, does the distribution of views over the population matter, and how, etc.) or relatedly (2) being able to explain if individual values and social norms differ, in which context social norms will mute individual values and in which context values will reshape social norms, and so on. These very much remain open questions.

5 Conclusions

The macro literature on political and economic liberalisation after communism is relatively easy to summarise. First, early reforms facilitated further reforms and continue to be associated with greater economic liberalisation. Countries where the "first-stage institutional reforms" were implemented early and comprehensively completed their reforms faster and today have good-quality economic institutions. Democratisation was an important driver of reforms, but reforms explained institutional progress over and beyond democratisation. Second, political liberalisation instead appeared to reflect some longer-run persistence as it translated factors specific to the communist or pre-communist era. The question of why the communist experience and in particular the fall of the Berlin Wall had only a limited impact on political liberalisation, as countries seem to have returned to earlier paths, is however central to our understanding of, for example, why Ukraine did not turn out as well as Poland.

Initial attempts to account for culture through legacies (of religious affiliation or of empire), often focusing on cross-country analysis, and aggregate measure of culture, while informative, have only limited policy relevance. However, they bring into focus the importance of values and beliefs held in the population, as relevant factors for political liberalisation. It is important to document the elements of culture that "stick" and those which do not, but more remains to be learned, especially from more micro-level investigation, of the values and beliefs potentially supportive of political liberalisation, their emergence, their transmission and their aggregation into social values or national cultural traits.

The literature on culture is bound to be harder to summarise because the patterns of change will be more diverse and the values and beliefs investigated may also be more diverse and complex. However, it is an agenda that has been investigated for a long time by other social scientists (as in: non-economists) and an agenda that will benefit from (1) further enquiry and (2) more inter-disciplinary exchange. For example, as argued by Ivlevs in this volume, "social remittances" had long been established in other social science communities before economists took an interest. It is often hard to identify the appropriate instrument and fully establish causality—and in the early literature on social remittances, co-evolution or correlations were more frequently reported than fully robust causal link. However, the evidence accumulated was sufficiently large and well-established to warrant more investigation into the direction of causality.[11]

The way ahead is thus to continue to promote a pluri-disciplinary research agenda into the values and beliefs that shape people's behaviours, especially as far as support for market reforms and democratisation is concerned. This may mean, in particular, more open mindedness to approach institutional change at the micro level, using the perspective of sociologists or psychologists, who rely less on causal inference, but have been studying value change for a long time. Economists may have much to learn from the work of sociologists and

---

[11] See also Smith in this volume for a discussion of causality and pluri-disciplinarity in comparative economics.

anthropologists who have argued that institutional change and value change in particular would be better understood using "contextual holism", an approach recognising the role of individuals, social structures and balance of power in negotiating meaning and interpretation and thus in generating and aggregating values within a specific society (see Kubik 2013). This would thus also lead to a greater understanding of the importance of context and diversity, requiring a narrowing down of the area of study into a meaningful case study and allowing a better understanding of the micro-mechanisms of change, as well as more reflection of the adjustments needed to translate these micro-foundations meaningfully into macro-processes in cross-country investigation for example.

Overall, this chapter has highlighted two important "turns" in the transition economics literature, first an "institutional turn" marking the end of the "natural experiment myth" and leading a greater focus on institutional change. In particular, this meant acknowledging the relevance of initial conditions to the subsequent liberalisation paths, and recognising the longer-run legacies at play. However, the findings of this literature led to new questions, regarding why certain legacies matter and how. This gave rise to a second turn in the transition literature, which can be labelled as a behavioural, social or cultural turn (according to the reader's preferences) to reflect a narrower focus on the emergence and transmission of values and beliefs that can influence and explain specific behaviours. While the behavioural literature will arguably focus on micro-level interactions, the cultural literature is generally associated with more macro-level processes (e.g. focusing on national culture à la Hofstede, or a broad concept such as social trust) or relative black-box indicators reflecting past experiences (e.g. legacies of religion and empires), while the social literature might focus more on interactions between actors and structures, as well as the balance of power. However, all propose to establish how values and beliefs explain different outcomes, and have thus something to contribute to improve our understanding of institutional change.

Acknowledgements Research assistance from Nancy Baez is gratefully acknowledged. I am also very grateful for the comments received from the participants to the workshop on "Frontiers of Comparative Economics: Towards a Handbook of Comparative Economics" held on the 17th of January 2020 at SSEES, UCL, in particular Sergei Guriev, Jan Kubik and Alena Ledeneva. I want to thank Nauro Campos for useful discussions. Finally, I am greatly indebted to Oleh Havrylyshyn for his encouragements, comments and suggestions. All the remaining errors are mine.

Appendix

Fig. 17.4 Average raw score per country and waves for the indicators used to construct our indicators of "preference for authoritarianism" and "preference for economic intervention"—see Tables 17.2 and 17.3

References

Alesina, A., & Giuliano, P. (2015). Culture and Institutions. *Journal of Economic Literature, 53*(4), 898–944.

Babecký, J., & Campos, N. (2011). Does Reform Work? An Econometric Survey of the Reform–Growth Puzzle. *Journal of Comparative Economics, 39*(2), 140–158.

Balcerowicz, L. (1995). *Socialism, Capitalism, Transformation.* Budapest: Central European University Press.

Barsbai, T., Rapoport, H., Steinmayr, A., & Trebesch, C. (2017). The Effect of Labour Migration on the Diffusion of Democracy: Evidence from a Former Soviet Republic. *American Economic Journal: Applied Economics, 9*(3), 36–69.

Boettke, P., Coyne, C., & Leeson, P. (2008). Institutional Stickiness and the New Development Economics. *American Journal of Economics and Sociology, 67*(2), 331–358.

Bruszt, L., Campos, N., Fidrmuc, J., & Roland, G. (2012). Civil Society, Institutional Change and the Politics of Reform: The Great Transition. In G. Roland (Ed.), *Economies of Transition the Long-Run View, Studies in Development Economics and Policy* (pp. 194–221). London: Palgrave Macmillan.

Bunce, V. (1999). The Political Economy of Postsocialism. *Slavic Review, 58*(4), 756–793, Special Issue: Ten Years after 1989: What Have We Learned?

Campos, N., & Horvath, R. (2012). Reform Redux: Measurement, Determinants and Growth Implications. *European Journal Political Economy, 28*, 227–237.

Christoffersen, P., & Doyle, P. (2000). From Inflation to Growth. *Economics of Transition, 8*, 421–451.

Darden, K., & Grzymala-Busse, A. (2006). The Great Divide: Literacy, Nationalism, and the Communist Collapse. *World Politics, 59*(1), 83–115.

de Melo, M., Denizer, C., & Gelb, A. (1996). *From Plan to Market: Patterns of Transition.* Policy Research Working Paper no. 1564, The World Bank, Policy Research Department, Transition Economics Division.

Denisova, I., Eller, M., Frye, T., & Zhuravskaya, E. (2012). Everyone Hates Privatization, But Why? Survey Evidence from 28 Post-Communist Countries. *Journal of Comparative Economics, 40*, 44–61.

Di Tommaso, M., Raiser, M., & Weeks, M. (2007). Home Grown or Imported? Initial Conditions, External Anchors and the Determinants of Institutional Reform in the Transition Economies. *The Economic Journal, 117*, 858–881.

Djankov, S. (2016). *The Divergent Postcommunist Paths to Democracy and Economic Freedom.* Peterson Institute for International Economics. Working paper 16-10.

Djankov, S., Glaeser, E., La Porta, R., Lopez-de-Silanes, F., & Shleifer, A. (2003). The New Comparative Economics. *Journal of Comparative Economics, 31*(4), 595–619.

Docquier, F., Lodigiani, E., Rapoport, H., & Schiff, M. (2016). Emigration and Democracy. *Journal of Development Economics, 120*, 209–223.

Douarin, E., & Mickiewicz, T. (2017). *Economics of Institutional Change—Central and Eastern Europe Revisited* (3rd ed.). New York: Palgrave MacMillan.

Ekiert, G., & Kubik, J. (2001). *Rebellious Civil Society: Popular Protest and Democratic Consolidation in Poland, 1989–1993*. Ann Arbor: University of Michigan Press.

Ekiert, G., & Ziblatt, D. (2013). Democracy in Central and Eastern Europe One Hundred Years On. *East European Politics and Societies., 27*(1), 90–107.

Frye, T. (1997). A Politics of Institutional Choice: Post-Communist Presidencies. *Comparative Political Studies, 30*(5), 523–552.

Gennaioli, N., & Tabellini, G. (2019). *Identity, Beliefs, and Political Conflict*. Working Paper, Bocconi University.

Gorodnichenko, Y., & Roland, G. (2011). Which Dimensions of Culture Matter for Long-run Growth? *American Economic Review Papers and Proceedings, 101*(3), 492–498.

Gorodnichenko, Y., & Roland, G. (2012). Understanding the Individualism-Collectivism Cleavage and Its Effects: Lessons from Cultural Psychology. In M. Aoki, T. Kuran, & G. Roland (Eds.), *Institutions and Comparative Economic Development* (International Economic Association Series). London: Palgrave Macmillan.

Grosjean, P., & Senik, C. (2011). Democracy, Market Liberalisation and Political Preferences. *The Review of Economics and Statistics, 93*(1), 365–381.

Guiso, L., Sapienza, P., & Zingales, L. (2006). Does Culture Affect Economic Outcomes? *Journal of Economic Perspectives, 20*(2), 23–48.

Guriev, S., Melnikov, N., & Zhuravskaya, E. (2019, June 30). 3G Internet and Confidence in Government. Retrieved from SSRN https://ssrn.com/abstract=3456747 or https://doi.org/10.2139/ssrn.3456747.

Hartwell, C. (2016). *Two Roads Diverge: The Transition Experience of Poland and Ukraine*. Cambridge: Cambridge University Press.

Havrylyshyn, O. (2001). Recovery and Growth in Transition: A Decade of Evidence. *IMF Staff Papers, 48*, 53–87.

Havrylyshyn, O. (2006). *Divergent Paths in Post-Communist Transformation—Capitalism for All or Capitalism for the Few?* London: Studies in Economic Transition, Palgrave Macmillan.

Havrylyshyn, O. (2017). *The Political Economy of Independent Ukraine. Slow Starts, False starts, and a Last Chance?* London: Palgrave MacMillan.

Havrylyshyn, O., Meng, X., & Tupy, M. (2016). *25 Years of Reforms in Ex-Communist Countries: Fast and Extensive Reforms Led to Higher Growth and More Political Freedom*. Washington, DC: Cato Institute.

Hellman, J. (1998). Winners Take All: The Politics of Partial Reform in Post-Communist Transitions. *World Politics, 50*(2), 203–234.

Heritage Foundation. (2019). *Index of Economic Freedom*. Washington.

Kopstein, J., & Reilly, D. (2000). Geographic Diffusion and the Transformation of the Post-Communist World. *World Politics, 53*(1), 1–37.

Kubik, J. (2013). From Transitology to Contextual Holism: A theoretical Trajectory of Post-Communist Studies. In J. Kubik & A. Lynch (Eds.), *Post-Communism from Within—Social Justice, Mobilization and Hegemony*. University Press Scholarship Online.

Lipset, S. M. (1959). Some Social Requisites of Democracy: Economic Development and Political Legitimacy. *American Political Science Review, 53*(1), 69–105.

Peisakhin, L., & Rozenas, A. (2018). Electoral Effects of Biased Media: Russian Television in Ukraine. *American Journal of Political Science, 62*, 535–550.

Pop-Eleches, G., & Tucker, J. A. (2014). Communist Socialization and Post-Communist Economic and Political Attitudes. *Electoral Studies, 33*, 77–89.

Pop-Eleches, G., & Tucker, J. A. (2017). *Communism's Shadow: Historical Legacies and Contemporary Political Attitudes*. Princeton, NJ: Princeton University Press.

Roland, G. (2004). Understanding Institutional Change: Fast-Moving and Slow-Moving Institutions. *Studies in Comparative International Development, 38*(4), 109–131.

Roland, G. (2010). *The Long-Run Weight of Communism or the Weight of Long-Run History?* WIDER Working Paper 2010/083. Helsinki: UNU-WIDER.

Roland, G. (2014). Transition in Historical Perspective. In A. Åslund & S. Djankov (Eds.), *The Great Rebirth—Lessons from the Victory of Capitalism over Communism*. Washington, DC: Peterson Institute for International Economics.

Shayo, M. (2020). Social Identity and Economic Policy. *Annual Review of Economics, 12*(1), 355–389.

Shleifer, A., & Treisman, D. (2014). Normal Countries: the East 25 Years After Communism. *Foreign Affairs, 93*(6), 92–103.

Svejnar, J. (2002). Transition Economies: Performance and Challenges. *Journal of Economic Perspectives, 16*(1), 3–28.

Tabellini, G. (2008). Institutions and Culture. *Journal of the European Economic Association, 6*(2–3), 255–294.

Taras, V., Rowney, J., & Steel, P. (2009). Half a Century of Measuring Culture: Review of Approaches, Challenges, and Limitations Based on the Analysis of 121 Instruments for Quantifying Culture. *Journal of International Management., 15*, 357–373.

Treisman, D. (2014). The Political Economy of Change After Communism. In A. Aslund & S. Djankov (Eds.), *The Great Rebirth: Lessons from the Victory of Capitalism Over Communism*. Washington, DC: Peterson Institute for International Economics.

Voigt, S. (2018). How to Measure Informal Institutions. *Journal of Institutional Economics, 14*(1), 1–22.

Williamson, C., & Kerekes, C. (2011). Securing Private Property: Formal Versus Informal Institutions. *Journal of Law and Economics, 54*(3), 537–572.

Part IV

New Comparative Economics: Growth and Formal Institutions in a Globalised World

18

Institutions, Human Capital and Economic Growth

Luca J. Uberti and Carl Henrik Knutsen

1   Introduction

Economists and social scientists have long debated the relative importance of institutions and human capital (and, relatedly, geography and culture) as fundamental determinants of economic growth. Although the importance of education is hardly ever denied, a dominant position, both in academic and policy circles, asserts the primacy of institutions. In an influential paper, Acemoglu et al. (2014: 880) conclude that the "evidence provides support for the view that institutions are the fundamental cause of long-run development, working not only through physical capital and TFP, but also through human capital". Given the paucity of (especially, time series) data on institutional quality, however, the issue is far from settled. In a meta-regression analysis (MRA), for instance, Efendic et al. (2011: 598) find that, "although the positive effect of [good] institutions on economic performance is on its way to

L. J. Uberti (✉)
University College London, London, UK
e-mail: l.uberti@ucl.ac.uk

C. H. Knutsen
University of Oslo, Oslo, Norway
e-mail: c.h.knutsen@stv.uio.no

© The Author(s) 2021
E. Douarin, O. Havrylyshyn (eds.), *The Palgrave Handbook of Comparative Economics*,
https://doi.org/10.1007/978-3-030-50888-3_18

becoming conventional wisdom, […] the evidence base is not as robust as it should be".

In this chapter, we re-open this debate by reviewing the empirical literature on the relative importance of institutions and human capital for growth. We identify two fundamental limitations in existing work. First, the lack of long time series indicators measuring "institutional quality" has made it difficult to use panel data techniques to account for unobserved country-level heterogeneities. Thus, any number of country-specific confounders could be driving the cross-country relationship between institutions, human capital and growth. Unobserved cultural characteristics, for example, might co-determine these three outcomes: countries with a "good" culture may simultaneously invest in education (Papagapitos and Riley 2009), establish well-functioning institutions (Tabellini 2008) and generate economic prosperity (Gorodnichenko and Roland 2017). Second, the empirical literature has insufficiently investigated the potentially heterogeneous effects of institutions. Recent thinking suggests that different institutions may be more or less appropriate at different levels of development (Acemoglu et al. 2006). "Good" property rights institutions, in particular, may become *more* of a binding constraint on growth as a country transitions from an "extensive" growth strategy based on investment and technological imitation to an "intensive" strategy based on productivity growth and, later, innovation (Che and Shen 2013).

We employ a novel, expert-coded indicator of institutional quality from the Varieties of Democracy (V-Dem) dataset, which measures the share of a country's population enjoying effective property rights protection. The V-Dem measure has unrivalled historical coverage and the methodology behind it was carefully developed to ensure over-time and cross-country comparability (Pemstein et al. 2017). The aim of this chapter is twofold: (1) replicate and validate important existing results, identified from our literature review, using this new data; (2) extend the literature by addressing the limitations identified—that is, the paucity of evidence based on long panels, and the implicit assumption that the effect of institutions is independent of the stage of development.

We find that, in countries with intermediate levels of development, both property rights institutions and human capital matter for economic growth. Human capital, however, is found to be relatively *more* consequential than institutions when unobserved country-level heterogeneities are accounted for in a panel data framework. Second, holding human capital constant, we allow the growth effects of institutions to depend on the level of development. We replicate existing cross-sectional results suggesting that "good" institutions may be particularly important in *developing* economies (Knack and Keefer

1995; Lee and Kim 2009). Once we control for country fixed effects, however, this finding is reversed: broad-based protection of property rights clearly enhances growth, but only in relatively *advanced* economies. These findings provide evidence of substantial non-linearities in the relationship between institutional quality and growth.

The chapter proceeds as follows: First, we discuss the theoretical arguments and empirical evidence linking property rights institutions to growth. Next, we review studies on how human capital relates to growth and institutions. In both cases, we focus on empirical studies that rely on observational data, although some of these questions are now also being examined using experimental methods (e.g. Cassar et al. 2014). We then describe the data, and present our empirical analysis. We conclude by identifying a set of relevant questions for future research.

2 Institutions and Human Capital: A Review of the Literature

2.1 Property Rights and Growth: Theory

Institutions are conventionally defined as the formal and informal rules that guide economic, social and political interaction, and their enforcement characteristics (North 1990). Here, we focus specifically on a dimension of institutional quality that has received particular attention in the literature—protection of property rights—and, in particular, the degree to which property rules are enforced. How the substantive content of those rules affects economic performance is the topic of parallel literatures (e.g. on economic freedom and legal origin), and beyond the scope of this chapter.

The economic theory of property rights is well-known, and discussed in several prominent contributions (Besley 1995; Knack and Keefer 1995; North 1990; Clague et al. 2003). Effective property rights protect the fruits of investment, and the underlying capital, from the risk of expropriation by the state or private organizations. As such, they reduce transaction costs and increase the expected profitability of investment in physical and human capital.[1] Besides promoting factor accumulation, secure property rights enhance the efficient *allocation* of factor inputs. When asset-holders face the risk of

---

[1] Contract enforcement, in addition, reduces transaction costs, clearing the way for the financial and commercial arrangements that are necessary to carry out investments. Yet, we focus here on the breadth of effective property rights enforcement.

expropriation, they invest in less specialized, but more mobile, forms of capital that may be relocated across sectors or jurisdictions, leading to a static efficiency loss. In addition, high expropriation risk may discourage productivity-enhancing specialization, technical learning and innovation (Kremer 1993; Nelson 2005). This dynamic consequence of bad institutions is critical, as technological change is considered the most consequential (proximate) determinant of economic growth (Barro and Sala-i-Martin 2004; Helpman 2006; Acemoglu 2009).

Albeit plausible, these arguments have recently attracted criticism, especially for their empirical relevance in developing and emerging economies. Some authors have argued that a universal enforcement of property rights may be neither *feasible* nor *necessary* for growth in the early stages of development (North et al. 2009; Khan 2010; Chang 2011).[2] Let us consider these two arguments in turn, starting from considerations of feasibility.

As noted by Khan (2007: 160), "the enforcement of property rights and the rule of law is closely correlated with the average productivity of assets since it is the income generated by assets that ultimately has to pay for the enforcement of formal institutions". Enforcing property rights (and contracts) involves high fixed costs to finance the police, courts of law, lawyers, notaries and so on. Thus, on the *supply* side, resource constraints can make it difficult for states to establish and maintain a universal rule of law. In developing countries, moreover, competitive firms are typically few in number, and display low levels of organizational and technological sophistication. Firms can thus rely on corruption and special relationships with politicians to protect their assets (and enforce contracts), and thus have no incentives to *demand* a system of universal enforcement. Past a certain level of economic sophistication, however, it becomes impossible to protect property rights by means of special relationships, and demand for a universal rule of law will increase.

Even if they cannot establish a well-functioning rule of law, however, low-income countries are not necessarily condemned to economic stagnation. Under some conditions, even a selective enforcement of property rights may be sufficient to stimulate economic dynamism—for instance, when protection is not granted unconditionally to politically connected firms, but only to firms that fulfill performance targets (on exports, investment, technology; see, e.g. Chang 1993; Khan and Sundaram 2000). North et al. (2012: 10) note that "there is still a lot of room for most developing nations to grow economically", even if their economies are anchored on institutional

---

[2] Similarly, when the productive sector is small and, typically, connected through informal political or familial relations, Pareto-improving market exchanges could be sustained by personal relations of trust.

arrangements—"limited access orders"—that exclude non-elites from key economic and political organizations (see also North et al. 2009). Acemoglu et al. (2006) present a formal model in which "anticompetitive policies which increase the amount […] that monopolists can appropriate […] may increase the equilibrium growth rate" in countries far from the world technology frontier.

As an economy approaches the frontier, however, expanding the protection of property rights becomes a binding constraint on further growth (Khan 2010; Hanson 2014). Here, learning and innovation are more complex, risky undertakings. Effectively protecting the formal rights of an increasing share of asset-holders is thus necessary to sustain investment and ensure that "good, new ideas" emerge and are acted upon, irrespective of who comes up with them. In a similar model to Acemoglu et al.'s (2006), Che and Shen (2013) endogenize institutional transitions, showing that at low levels of income "general protection strategies" (universal property rights protection) are more costly and generate fewer social benefits than "partial protection strategies" (or "industrial policies"). Only "when the economy passes certain threshold values" does it become optimal for a government to allocate effort towards supplying a universal rule of law (2013: 245).

While the traditional view of North (1990) implies that "good" property rights institutions enhance growth in both rich and poor economies, this alternative view predicts that the positive effect of "good" institutions may be small or even negligible in very poor countries, and should become larger as an economy develops (Khan 2007). To adjudicate between these two theories empirically, the relationship between property rights and economic growth should be allowed to depend on level of development. Furthermore, if universal enforcement becomes a binding constraint only past a certain threshold, the moderating influence of development should be expected to be non-linear—zero at first, and positive (and potentially increasing) once the threshold has been crossed.

2.2   Property Rights and Growth: The Evidence

The empirical literature on institutions and growth gained momentum in the early 1990s. Some early studies conjectured that the failure to observe evidence of convergence in income levels—a key prediction of neo-classical growth theory—may be due to unobserved cross-country differences in institutional endowments. Mankiw et al. (1992: 431), for instance, speculated that in low-income countries the "economic agents who could make the productive investments do not do so [...] because they fear future expropria-tion". Islam (1995: 1149) suggested that "the process of convergence is thwarted to a great extent by persistent differences in [...] institutions".

This possibility was first examined explicitly by Knack and Keefer (1995), who created multi-dimensional indices of property (and contractual) rights based on data from two international consulting firms: Political Risk Services (PRS) and Business Environmental Risk Intelligence (BERI).[3] They found that omitting these measures of institutional quality from a cross-country growth regression biases downwards the estimated neo-classical convergence rate.[4] By interacting their institutional index with initial income, Keefer and Knack (1997) also found that a country's speed of convergence to its steady state depends on the institutional environment, with faster conver-gence achieved by countries with better institutions.[5] These results also imply that the effect of institutions on economic growth is higher in countries with *lower* initial incomes.

Subsequent cross-country evidence, however, cast some doubt on these findings. Glaeser et al. (2004), for instance, criticize the validity of the PRS (*International Country Risk Guide*) and other "outcome-based" measures of institutional quality, and find that more "objective", "rule-based" measures of judicial independence and constitutional review (the "input" to good institu-tions) enter with insignificant coefficients in cross-country regressions for the period 1960–2000. Moreover, even an "outcome-based" index of executive constraints (from Polity IV) enters insignificant if the initial-year value is used instead of the mid-period or average value. "At least in the OLS regressions", Glaeser et al. (2004: 285) conclude, "the evidence that institutions cause eco-nomic growth, as opposed to growth improving institutions, is non-existent". Using a first-difference estimator with instrumental variables, Dollar and Kray (2003) also find that the PRS index is an insignificant predictor of growth. Still, the use of a short panel of decadal growth averages for 1970–2000 suggests that Dollar and Kray's tests may suffer from low statistical power.

The use of empirical growth regressions was soon complemented by stud-ies that relied on plausibly exogenous historical shocks to identify the causal impact of institutions. Since the focus is on long-run effects, these studies

---

[3] See, respectively, https://www.prsgroup.com/ and http://www.beri.com/.

[4] To control for the quality of property rights, earlier contributions (Barro 1991; Dawson 1998) used indices of economic and political freedom, or the number of coups, revolutions and political assassina-tions (for criticism of these proxies, see Knack and Keefer 1995).

[5] Their results are robust to using alternative indicators of institutional quality, such as Polity's (Marshall et al. 2013) index of constraints on the chief executive from the Polity dataset, which has been a widely used proxy for the risk of expropriation.

often specify the dependent variable differently. This may matter for the results. In a meta-analysis, Efendic et al. (2011) find evidence that model specifications in which output *level* is the dependent variable generally yield *higher* estimated institutional effects than specifications with output growth as dependent variable, whether or not the institutional variable is treated as endogenous and instrumented for.

This "long-run literature" was spearheaded by a string of seminal papers using colonial history as a "natural experiment" (Acemoglu et al. 2001, 2002; Sokoloff and Engerman 2000).[6] The basic identification argument is well-known. The institutional endowments of former colonies are largely the product of colonial history. Where population density (and urbanization rates) were high before European contact (and/or in regions where settlers faced an unfamiliar disease environment), European colonizers elected to establish "extractive" institutions that exploited the local population. In more sparsely populated (and/or more salubrious), regions where Europeans could feasibly settle in large numbers, the colonizers had incentives to set up "inclusive" institutions that protected the property rights of a broader cross-section of the population. Supposedly, these institutional differences persisted over time and continue to shape comparative performance of institutions, and thereby economies, across former colonies today. Hence, colonial-era mortality rates and pre-colonial population densities may be used as instruments for present-day institutions, overcoming the critical issues of reverse causation from income to institutional quality.

One objection is that instruments drawn from colonial history are likely to violate the exclusion restriction of instrumental variable models (Sachs 2003). Colonial history may affect economic development through other channels unrelated to institutions. Supporters of the "geography hypothesis", for instance, have noted that settler mortality is related to climatic and ecological conditions, which directly affect agricultural productivity, transport costs and the disease environment—all of which may directly influence economic performance (Sachs and Warner 1997).

Khan (2012) questions the validity of the settler mortality instrument on historical and conceptual grounds. The institutions brought by European settlers to the likes of South Africa, the United States and Australia, he argues, were far from "inclusive" in any meaningful sense. To the extent that European colonizers protected property rights, they only did so *for the white settler class*, typically a small share of the population (e.g. in Algeria or Zimbabwe). In

---

[6] These key findings have been re-affirmed in several later studies (Easterly and Levine 2003; Rodrik et al. 2004; Acemoglu and Johnson 2005; Fielding and Torres 2008; Bennett et al. 2017).

highly racialized settler societies, maintaining a functioning colonial economy required violent and intrusive exertions of state power to seize and redistribute land, confine and discipline native labour and stamp out pre-colonial economic activities (and the associated property rights) that jeopardized the interests of the settler class (Austin 2008; Mkandawire 2010). Thus, it is far from clear whether we should attribute the superior performance of settler colonies (relative to their non-settler counterparts) to their supposedly "inclusive" institutions or to other (far from "inclusive") characteristics.

One reason why this controversy has persisted is the paucity of long time series data on institutional quality. This data limitation has prevented tracking the institutional evolution of countries over time, and the use of panel data techniques to control for potential joint determinants of institutions and prosperity—notably, culture. One exception is Siddiqui and Ahmet (2013). Using a panel data framework, they report a positive growth effect of "institutions that reduce the cost of protecting property rights" (a principal component from a factor analysis of 31 institutional indicators), conditional on human capital endowments and country fixed effects. Their Generalized Method of Moments (GMM) regressions, however, cover just 84 countries from 2002 to 2006.

Another limitation is that existing empirical studies focus on testing the "average" relationship between institutional quality and economic performance, leaving open the possibility that there may be non-linear patterns. In particular, the literature has not systematically tested whether the relationship depends on the level of economic development. One partial exception is Lee and Kim (2009). Using panel data for 63 countries during 1965–2002, the authors conclude that political institutions (proxied by Polity's measure of executive constraints) and secondary education are more important drivers of growth in *lower-* than in higher-income economies. This finding is broadly consistent with the cross-sectional results reported by Keefer and Knack (1997). Lee and Kim's (2009) analysis, however, has limitations. First, the heterogeneous effect of executive constraints is tested by splitting the sample into income groups, instead of allowing the coefficient on institutions to depend on GDP per capita by means of interaction terms. Second, Lee and Kim's (2009: 544) panel regressions do not include initial GDP per capita on the right-hand side, effectively (and unrealistically) assuming that countries are in their steady states.

2.3   Human Capital, Institutions and Growth: Theory and Evidence

If other determinants of economic growth are correlated with institutions, the estimated relationship between institutions and growth may be subject to omitted variable bias. A key potential confounder is human capital. For the former colonies examined by Acemoglu et al. (2001), Glaeser et al. (2004) have suggested a particular historical trajectory that may lead to a spurious relationship: in their account, the main import of European settlers to the territories they colonized was their superior human capital (see also Bolt and Bezemer 2009).[7] The underlying assumption is that, when people migrate, they bring along various "internal institutions" (their culture, beliefs and know-how), but leave behind the "external institutions" (laws and governance practices) of their homeland (Fernández and Fogli 2009).

This view is vigorously resisted by Acemoglu et al. (2014: 883–4), who report historical evidence suggesting that the early settlers of British North America (a region that developed "inclusive" institutions and experienced fast growth), were actually *less* literate than the Spanish settlers of the South American colonies (which were subject to "extractive" institutions and never developed into advanced market economies). Yet, it is at least plausible that the literacy rates of *all* European settlers were higher than those of indigenous people. If so, the overall literacy rates of North America's "settler" colonies (where the indigenous population was relatively small) should have been higher than the rates found in many of their "non-settler" counterparts in South America (which had a large indigenous population and fewer European settlers). Thus, it remains possible that colonial settlement, as proxied by settler mortality, may have influenced subsequent economic performance through *both* institutions and human capital, undermining Acemoglu et al.'s (2001) instrumentation strategy.

This point can be made more generally. If both institutions and human capital matter for economic performance, and if human capital systematically improves the quality of institutions (or vice versa), the estimated direct effect of institutions on growth (arrow a in Fig. 18.1) may be inflated, unless the effect of human capital is also accounted for. Yet, if institutions primarily affect growth indirectly by promoting human capital formation (arrows c and b in Fig. 18.1), accounting for human capital would simply control away an

---

[7] A different objection, which Acemoglu et al. (2001: 1390) resist, is that instead of capturing the effect of the *institutions* brought by European settlers, the mortality instrument captures the effect of having "more Europeans", who might have brought along a particularly developmental European *culture* .

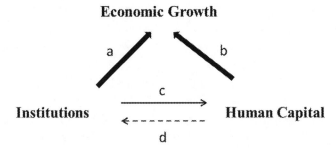

Fig. 18.1 Causal relations between growth, institutions and human capital

important component of the total effect of institutions on growth. We first discuss the plausible assumption that human capital exerts a direct effect on economic growth (arrow b in Fig. 18.1), before turning to the more contentious assumptions as to how and why human capital and institutions are related (arrows c and d in Fig. 18.1).

Human capital can be defined as the knowledge and skills possessed by the country's workforce (Barro and Sala-i-Martin 2004; Helpman 2006; Acemoglu 2009). One way to conceptualize the contribution of human capital to the growth process is as another form of capital entering the production function directly in a labour-augmenting form.[8] The standard formulation, which extends the neo-classical Solow (1956) model, is presented by Mankiw et al. (1992). Their accompanying empirical estimates indicate that human capital is an important source of variation in cross-country income levels, alongside physical capital.[9]

Human capital may also influence long-term growth through other, more indirect, channels. Education constitutes a key input to the research sector, thus affecting aggregate productivity (Lucas 1988). Based on historical data from mid-eighteenth-century France, Squicciarini and Voigtlander (2015) show that "upper-tail entrepreneurial skills"[10] promote the uptake of more complex technologies from the frontier, shifting the production function and raising total-factor productivity (see also Kremer 1993). In several endogenous growth models, output, investment (Romer 1990) and fertility (Becker et al. 1990) are co-determined by human capital. In the literature on the "fundamental" determinants of development (Glaeser et al. 2004; Bolt and Bezemer 2009), human capital is assumed to influence growth through all of

---

[8] Workers equipped with human capital are more productive, leading to a multiplicative relationship between labour (L) and human capital (H).

[9] Some, though not all, growth accounting exercises have corroborated this pattern (see Helpman 2006).

[10] As compared to the literacy and schooling rates of the average worker.

its "proximate" determinants—including technology (total factor productivity), fertility preferences and savings decisions. Consistent with this view, panel data evidence for the period 1965–1995 suggests that both the quantity (e.g. average number of years of school attainment) and quality of education (as measured by scores on internationally comparable examinations) matter for economic growth (Barro 2001). The quality of schooling, however, is found to be economically more significant (see also, e.g. Cohen and Soto 2007; Hanushek and Woessman 2013).

Although human capital may exert a direct effect on economic growth, the omission of human capital from the regression only influences the estimated coefficient on institutions if human capital is *correlated* with institutions. Such a correlation could emerge, for example, if human capital promotes institutional development (arrow d, in Fig. 18.1). Notably, education may shape the norms and values of citizens, promote the rise of a middle-class, and enhance citizens' ability and propensity to organize politically to challenge their rulers (Lipset 1959; Welzel 2012). Democratic consolidation, in turn, provides a system of checks and balances on executive power, creating strong incentives for rulers seeking re-election to refrain from expropriation (Knutsen 2011; Ansell and Samuels 2015). Education may thus enhance the security of property rights by promoting democracy.

However plausible, this argument is not unequivocally supported by the evidence. Stringent studies accounting for country fixed effects and the endogeneity of human capital to institutional outcomes find no clear evidence of a causal link running from education to institutions (Acemoglu et al. 2005; Acemoglu et al. 2014: 903–905; Dahlum 2017). Thus, the relationship between institutions and human capital may result from a causal effect running in the opposite direction—"good" institutions creating incentives for individuals and governments to invest in education (arrow c, Fig. 18.1).[11] If so, human capital would be *more* "fundamental" than preferences and technology as a determinant of growth, but still *less* "fundamental" than institutions. Thus, including human capital in growth regressions would not correct for omitted variable bias, but actually introduce (post-treatment) bias by controlling away a part of the mechanism through which institutions influence prosperity.

Yet, even if we focus narrowly on the relative size of the *direct* effects of institutions and human capital, conditional on each other, the empirical evidence is still mixed. Using a rich subnational dataset from 110 countries, for

---

[11] Alternatively, the correlation between human capital and institutions may result from joint determination by a third, more «fundamental» factor, such as culture (Bjornskov and Meon 2013).

instance, Gennaioli et al. (2013) find that education attainment, but not (regional) institutions, play an important role in explaining regional income differences within countries. Their findings, however, are far from conclusive. Estimates of the growth effects of human capital may be plagued by reverse causality problems, as the provision of (quality) education could be affected by income levels and economic growth (Bils and Klenow 2000). Controlling for country fixed effects, therefore, may be insufficient to fully account for the endogeneity of institutions, as reverse causality and measurement error persist as threats to inference.

To address this problem, Acemoglu et al. (2014) use historical information on Protestant missions and school enrollment rates (prior to the expansion of Protestant missionary activity in the early twentieth century) as instruments for contemporary human capital. To instrument for contemporary institutions, they use settler mortality rates and pre-colonial (1500) population density, as in Acemoglu et al. (2001, 2002). In simple Two Stage Least Squares (2SLS) models that treat both human capital and institutions as endogenous, both variables enter as significant. Human capital, however, loses significance when standard controls are included in the regression, leading the authors to infer that human capital is not a fundamental determinant of economic development. Yet, none of Acemoglu et al.'s (2014) instrumental variable models pass the standard identification tests,[12] suggesting that they may suffer from weak instrument problems. In other models (reported in their Table 6), their measure of property rights institutions (a Rule of Law index from the World Bank's *Worldwide Governance Indicators*) also enters as insignificant when control variables are included, along with human capital.

Indeed, the panel analyses conducted by Lee and Kim (2009) and Siddiqui and Ahmet (2013) indicate that, even after controlling for country fixed effects and the endogeneity of human capital in a GMM framework, *both* property rights institutions and human capital enter as significant. In sum, we regard it as very plausible that education policies may exert a substantial independent effect on economic performance even after the impact of property rights institutions is accounted for. In the next sections, we further investigate this possibility using panel data.

---

[12] These tests include the Kleibergen-Paap under-identification and weak identification tests.

3 Empirical Analysis

3.1 Data

We employ a balanced panel with information covering 118 countries during 1955–2010, for a total of 1298 (=118 × 11) observations. Our GDP data come from Fariss et al. (2017), who employ a dynamic latent-trait model to produce GDP and population estimates that are less error-prone than other existing data sources (e.g. the Maddison project data). Furthermore, Fariss et al. (2017) use imputation techniques to reduce the incidence of missing values, which allows us to mitigate potential sample selection problems (e.g. countries with low growth and poor protection of property rights are more often missing data). We use their time series benchmarked to the Purchasing Power Parity (PPP)-adjusted, 2011 US Dollars, Maddison times series.

To proxy for human capital, we use the number of years spent in education by the average worker, available from 1950 on a 5-year basis (Barro and Lee 2013).

To measure property rights institutions, we draw on new and extensive data from the Varieties of Democracy (V-Dem) project (Coppedge et al. 2018a, b). In particular, we focus on V-Dem's Property Rights Index (*PRI*, tagged *v2xcl_prpty* by V-Dem). Similar to most other V-Dem indicators, *PRI* is coded from 1900 onwards and, as of Version 8 of V-Dem, from as early as 1789 for several polities (Knutsen et al. 2018).

The *PRI* indicator is coded by country experts based on the following question: "Do men/women enjoy the right to private property?" The six response categories range from "virtually no one enjoys private property rights of any kind" to "virtually all citizens enjoy all, or almost all, property rights". The documentation accompanying the question indicates that "private property includes the right to acquire, possess, inherit, and sell private property, including land. Limits on property rights may come from the state (which may legally curtail individual rights or fail to enforce them); customary laws and practices; or religious or social norms" (Coppedge et al. 2018a: 162).

Thus, *PRI* captures a broad set of potential threats to secure property ownership. By focusing on *de facto* protection of property rights—and not just on whether *de jure* conditions protecting private property, which may or may not be followed, are in place[13]—*PRI* captures the extent to which the enforcement of property rights is broad-based, as opposed to limited to a more or less

---

[13] The measures also aggregate across various kinds of property, such as land, financial investments and personal belongings.

narrow subset of asset-holders (e.g. land-owners, politically connected firms). As such, it captures the influence of both formal and informal institutions in determining enforcement outcomes (see also Williamson and Kerekes 2011).

The V-Dem questions used for *PRI* are posed to multiple country experts per country—typically political scientists, historians and academics who have conducted research on the country in question. The experts' ordinal scores are processed through V-Dem's "measurement model", a Bayesian item-response model designed to recover a latent, cardinal dimension (Pemstein et al. 2017). The model addresses issues of "differential item-functioning" (i.e. different experts interpreting the ordinal categories differently) and weighs more reliable experts more strongly in the aggregation of final scores.

Theoretically, *PRI* ranges from 0 to 1, but the empirical minimum and maximum values across the 1298 (country—5-year) observations in our sample are, respectively, 0.003 (Mozambique, early 1980s) and 0.95 (Germany, 1990s and 2000s). The sample mean of *PRI* is 0.58 (close to Iran, 2000s) and the median is 0.65 (close to Iraq, 1950s). Within-country variance accounts for about 23% of total sample variance, allowing us to make within-country comparisons over time without a too substantial loss of efficiency.

The face validity of *PRI*, with its substantial within-country variation, is illustrated in Fig. 18.2, which documents the evolution of property rights institutions in four large countries—China, India, the Democratic Republic of the Congo and the United States. China, India and the United States have property rights scores going back to 1789. The exception is Congo, which has a time series extending back to 1900, when King Leopold's personal rule over the colony was about to end. In 1908, Congo was handed over to the Belgian state. Accordingly, we see a slight uptick in the quality of property rights protection. While property rights scores saw a further improvement with decolonization in 1960, the score remained relatively low for as long as the country was under Mobutu's kleptocratic rule (Wrong 2000).

For the United States, there is also substantial variation over time. For the most part, the property rights score shows an improving trend, with a steep increase around the end of the Civil War (1865) and another one around the late 1960s reflecting the achievements of the civil rights movement. Also, India mainly experienced step-wise increases, both during British colonial rule and after. The Chinese time series, by contrast, displays a non-monotonic pattern. While property rights improved slightly in the period following the end of the Qing Imperial regime, there was a marked downturn in property rights protection under Mao (1949–1976), followed by a gradual improvement during the more recent decades of Communist Party rule.

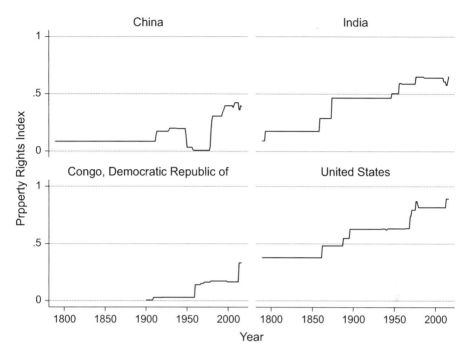

Fig. 18.2   Property Rights Index (*PRI*) score for four selected countries (1789–2016)

PRI correlates positively (though not perfectly) with other relevant measures of property rights enforcement, such as Henisz's (2000) Polcon III index, often used as a measure of business risk (coeff. = 0.59, obs. = 2842), the Rule of Law index from the World Bank's *Worldwide Governance Indicator* (coeff. = 0.62, obs. = 507) and with the Law and Order index from Political Risk Services' (PRS) *International Country Risk Guide* (coeff. = 0.39, obs. = 3451). For illustrative purposes, Fig. 18.3 shows a scatter-plot of *PRI* versus an index of Protection against Expropriation from PRS, as used by Acemoglu et al. (2001), for 116 countries during 1985–1995. The correlation is moderate (coeff. = 0.49), either because the measures are picking up slightly different concepts (this is hard to evaluate, given the lack of clarity about the PRS methodology and what their measures actually capture), or because of measurement error in one or both measures. Nonetheless, in our estimation sample, *PRI* also correlates positively with the log of GDP per capita (coeff. = 0.60) and with GDP per capita growth (coeff. = 0.13).

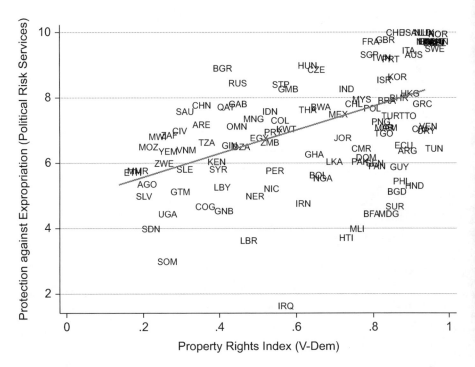

Fig. 18.3 Property Rights Index (V-Dem) and Protection against Expropriation (PRS) for 1985–1995 (averages)

3.2 Model Specification and Estimation Issues

We use V-Dem's *PRI* indicator to investigate: (1) whether human capital exerts a direct effect on growth independently of institutions; (2) whether the effect of inclusive property rights institutions on growth depends on the level of development. In answering *both* questions, we compare cross-section with panel results. For these two sets of results to be comparable, we only include the countries for which information on GDP per capita, institutions and human capital is available as early as 1950.

To address point (1), we estimate the following models:

$$\Delta \ln Y_{i,1955-2010} = \rho \ln Y_{i,1955} + \omega H_{i,1955-2010} + \varphi PRI_{i,1955-2010} + \varepsilon_i \quad (1a)$$

$$\Delta \ln Y_{i,t} = \rho \ln Y_{i,t-1} + \omega H_{i,t-1} + \varphi PRI_{i,t-1} + \sigma \Delta \ln Y_{i,t-1} + \tau_t + \mu_i + v_{i,t}, \quad (1b)$$

where $1955 < t < 2010$. Equation (1a) replicates standard cross-country growth regressions à la Barro (1991); equation (1b) is the corresponding panel model à la Islam (1995).

To mitigate the influence of business cycle fluctuations, and reduce serial correlation in the panel regression disturbances (v_{it}), we divide the dataset in 5-year intervals—a standard approach in the empirical growth literature (e.g. Islam 1995). Thus, $\Delta \ln Y_{it}$ denotes the average 5-year (percentage) growth rate of GDP per capita, while $\Delta \ln Y_{i, 1955 - 2010}$ is the average of these eleven 5-year rates during 1955–2010. For the cross-section, $\ln Y_{i, 1955}$ denotes initial levels of GDP per capita; for the panel regression, $\ln Y_{i, t - 1}$ denotes the initial GDP per capita level for each 5-year period. $\ln Y_{i, 1955}$ and $\ln Y_{i, t - 1}$ control for the neo-classical convergence effect, allowing countries to experience out-of-steady-state dynamics (Barro 1991; Mankiw et al. 1992).

H denotes the Barro-Lee measure of human capital, while PRI is the property rights index from V-Dem. We do not include measures of the "proximate" determinants of GDP per capita growth (investment, Total Factor Productivity (TFP), fertility preferences, etc.), as we are interested in estimating the *total* effect of institutions and human capital on economic performance, conditional on each other (for a similar discussion on democracy and growth estimates, see Knutsen 2012). All the proximate determinants may act as channels of influence for both institutions and human capital. As such, equations (1a) and (1b) may be thought of as reduced-form specifications.

In panel regressions, institutions and human capital are less likely to be endogenous to GDP per capita *growth* than to GDP per capita *levels*. Still, in equation (1b), both H and PRI are lagged by one 5-year period to mitigate the risk that estimates may partly reflect the causal effect of economic growth on, respectively, educational attainment and institutional quality. Moreover, as an additional control for reverse causality, all our panel models include lagged growth ($\Delta \ln Y_{i, t - 1}$), as suggested by Acemoglu et al. (2019). μ_i and τ_t denote country- and time-period fixed effects, respectively. μ_i accounts for potential unobserved joint (country-specific) determinants of institutions, human capital, and economic development. These include not only all (slow-moving or time-invariant) cultural characteristics of countries, but also geography, history, and so on. τ_t captures global trends and shocks affecting all countries simultaneously - for instance, trends in technical change at the frontier and as well as global shocks on economic growth (e.g. global economic crises, both of which may also correlate with institutions and human capital.

Next, to investigate the relative importance of property rights institutions as engines of growth at different levels of development, we allow φ, the coefficient on PRI, to depend linearly on per capita income, leading to a specification with an interaction term ($PRI \times \ln Y$). To allow this dependence to be non-linear, and approximate the threshold effects discussed above, we also consider a specification with a squared income term ($\ln Y)^2$ and an interaction between *PRI* and $(\ln Y)^2$, in line with existing theories of non-linear economic growth (e.g. Fiaschi and Lavezzi 2007). Thus, our cross-section and panel equations become:

$$\Delta \ln Y_{i,1955-2010} = \rho \sum_{j=1}^{2} \left(\ln Y_{i,1955} \right)^j + \omega H_{i,1955} + \varphi_0 PRI_{i,1955-2010}$$

$$+ \sum_{j=1}^{2} \varphi_j \left(\ln Y_{i,1955} \right)^j \times PRI_{i,1955-2010} + \varepsilon_i \tag{2a}$$

$$\Delta \ln Y_{i,t} = \rho \sum_{j=1}^{2} \left(\ln Y_{i,t-1} \right)^j + \omega H_{i,t-1} + \varphi_0 PRI_{i,t-1}$$

$$+ \sum_{j=1}^{2} \varphi_j \left(\ln Y_{i,t-1} \right)^j \times PRI_{i,t-1} + \sigma \, \Delta \ln Y_{i,t-1} + \tau_t + \mu_i + v_{i,t} \tag{2b}$$

Equations (1a) and (2b) are estimated by simple Ordinary Least Squares (OLS), while equations (1b) and (2b) are estimated by using a Prais-Winsten Generalized Least Squares (GLS) estimator with panel-corrected standard errors (PCSEs). In panel data models, this estimator is often preferable to OLS as it corrects for AR(1) serial correlation within panels, panel-level heteroskedasticity and cross-sectional correlation across panels, producing more reliable estimates of slope coefficients and standard errors (Beck and Katz 1995).[14]

3.3 Empirical Results

Panel A, Table 18.1 displays the cross-section results. Model 3 is the full specification given in Equation (1a), while models 1 and 2 are reduced specifications that enter institutions and human capital separately. While the coefficient on human capital is only slightly attenuated (from 0.019 to 0.017) when both institutions and human capital are included in the regression, the coefficient on institutions drops by 48% (from 0.109 to 0.057). These findings are consistent with those of simple cross-country regressions (with output levels on the left-hand side) that treat both human capital and institutions as exogenous (Acemoglu et al. 2014, see their Table 18.2).[15] In model 3, a

---

[14] Our panel results, however, are qualitatively consistent if we use OLS with heteroskedasticity-robust standard errors clustered at the country level. The results are available upon request.

[15] In addition, we note that the rate of conditional convergence to the steady state, measured by the coefficient on $\ln Y$, increases when important determinants of the steady state (e.g. human capital, institutions) are included in the regression (as noted by Knack and Keefer 1995).

Table 18.1 Institutions, human capital and growth: Cross-section versus panel estimates

	(1)	(2)	(3)
Panel A: Cross-section Results (Dependent variable: average GDP per capita growth, 1955–2010), OLS			
Ln Y (1955)	−0.004	−0.027***	−0.031***
	(0.008)	(0.008)	(0.009)
PRI (1955–2010)	0.109***		0.057**
	(0.031)		(0.027)
H (1955–2010)		0.019***	0.017***
		(0.003)	(0.003)
Adjusted R-squared	0.12	0.30	0.32
Number of observations (countries)	118	118	118
Panel B: Panel Data Results (Dependent variable: 5-year GDP per capita growth, 1955–2010), PCSE			
ln $Y_{(t-1)}$	−0.280***	−0.314***	−0.313***
	(0.071)	(0.076)	(0.080)
$PRI_{(t-1)}$	0.080*		0.071
	(0.044)		(0.046)
$H_{(t-1)}$		0.045***	0.045***
		(0.015)	(0.015)
Country fixed effects	Yes	Yes	Yes
Time-period fixed effects	Yes	Yes	Yes
Lagged GDP per capita growth	Yes	Yes	Yes
Adjusted R-squared (overall)	0.21	0.22	0.22
Number of observations	1298	1298	1298
Groups (countries)	118	118	118

Notes: ***, ** and * indicate that the coefficients are significant at the 1%, 5% and 10% levels, respectively. Panel A reports OLS regressions with heteroskedasticity-robust standard errors in parenthesis. Panel B reports Prais-Winsten regressions with panel-corrected standard errors (PCSE) in parenthesis.

standard-deviation increase in institutional quality (human capital endowments) is associated with a 0.08 (0.28) standard-deviation increase in rate of economic growth.

The cross-sectional relations displayed in Panel A might be biased if country-specific factors omitted from the regression (geography, culture, etc.) influence human capital, institutions and economic performance simultaneously. Yet, the panel data estimates presented in Panel B—with Model 3 corresponding to the fixed-effects specification in equation (1b)—suggest that the impact of institutional quality on growth, as estimated in cross-sectional regressions, may not be severely biased by the omission of country-level unobservables. While the coefficient on *PRI* in model 3 is not statistically significant at conventional levels (p-value = 0.12), the magnitude of the panel estimates does

Table 18.2   GMM models (DV: 5-year GDP per capita growth, 1955–2010)

	Diff-GMM	Sys-GMM
	(1)	(2)
ln $Y_{(t-1)}$	−0.305***	−0.056***
	(0.117)	(0.021)
$PRI_{(t-1)}$	0.181*	0.213***
	(0.098)	(0.070)
$H_{(t-1)}$	0.049*	0.025***
	(0.027)	(0.007)
Country fixed effects	Yes	Yes
Time-period fixed effects	Yes	Yes
Lagged GDP per capita growth	No	No
Number of observations	1180	1180
Groups (countries)	118	118
Number of instruments	111	103
Instrument lags (for ln Y)	(1 9)	(1 6), collapse
Instrument lags (for PRI and H)	(1 11), collapse	(1 3)
Arellano-Bond AR(2) test [p-value]	[0.509]	[0.525]
Hansen test of overid. restrictions [p-value]	[0.098]	[0.157]

Notes: ***, ** and * indicate that the coefficients are significant at the 1%, 5% and 10% levels, respectively. Column (1)/(2) reports the estimated parameters of a two-step "difference GMM"/"system GMM" model with Windmejer-corrected standard errors. Both estimators employ the "orthogonal deviations" transform. All the regressors are treated as predetermined and instrumented for. Whenever necessary for the model to be diagnostically sound, the instrument matrix was collapsed

not change *systematically* relative to the corresponding cross-sectional estimates. By contrast, the estimated effect of human capital on economic growth more than *doubles* in size when going from cross-section (0.017) to equivalent panel specifications (0.045), suggesting that the omission of country-specific factors may introduce a downward bias in the cross-sectional estimates of H.[16]

As in panel A, entering both institutions and human capital simultaneously in the regression attenuates the estimated impact of institutional quality (from 0.080 to 0.071), while the estimated effect of human capital endowments remains unchanged. In model 3 (panel B), a standard-deviation increase in institutional quality (human capital endowments) is associated with a 0.10 (0.71) standard-deviation increase in growth.[17]

---

[16] We also estimated pooled models without country fixed effects (μ_i). The results, available upon request, are qualitatively consistent with those of the cross-sectional regressions reported in Panel A (Table 18.1).

[17] In addition, the results in panel B reproduce another important result from the empirical growth literature. When controlling for unobservable determinants of the steady state in fixed-effects panel models, the rate of conditional convergence to the steady state increases roughly by a factor of 10 (from 0.031 to 0.313), in line with the findings of Islam (1995).

While the inclusion of μ_i flexibly controls for omitted variable bias, the inclusion of lagged GDP per capita growth (as in Acemoglu et al. 2019) may be insufficient to fully purge the reverse causal influence of economic growth on institutional reforms (education policies) from the estimated coefficient on *PRI (H)*. To address this concern, we also present GMM models—both "difference" and "system" specifications—that treat $PRI_{i,t-1}$ and $H_{i,t-1}$ as predetermined (i.e. correlated with the error term in the previous time-period) and instrument for them in GMM style.[18]

The results, displayed in Table 18.2, also suggest a positive effect of both human capital and property rights institutions on growth. In both models 1 and 2 (Table 18.2), the GMM estimate on *PRI* is substantially higher than the corresponding PCSE (GLS) estimate, while the GMM estimate of *H* is substantially smaller in model 2 (Table 18.2). Yet, our results are qualitatively unaltered. In model 2, one standard-deviation increase in institutional quality (human capital endowments) is associated with a 0.30 (0.41) standard-deviation increase in the rate of economic growth. Our findings do not provide support for theories that stress the primacy of either human capital or institutions only. Rather, we find that *both* institutions and human capital have a direct, independent influence on economic performance.

Theoretical models (Acemoglu et al. 2006; Che and Shen 2013) and historical accounts (Khan and Sundaram 2000; North et al. 2012) suggest that property rights institutions may be more important for growth in already rich economies. By contrast, other empirical findings, based on both cross-section (Keefer and Knack 1997) and panel data (Lee and Kim 2009) suggest that property rights protection may be more important for poor economies seeking to catch up.

To address this controversy, we estimate equations (2a) and (2b), comparing the cross-section to the fixed-effects panel results (Table 18.3). The models in column 1 include a simple interaction term between *PRI* and $\ln Y$, while those in column 2 correspond to the specification with quadratic interaction terms given by equations (2a) and (2b). Since the inclusion of higher-order terms may lead to multicollinearity, columns 3 and 4 experiment with more parsimonious specifications that exclude potentially multicollinear terms. Based on adjusted R-squared, the best fit to the data is achieved by the models in column 2. For the cross-sectional regressions, however, Ramsey's RESET test cannot reject the null that model 1 has no omitted non-linear terms

---

[18] We also instrument for $\ln Y_{t-1}$ to correct for dynamic panel ("Nickel") bias. Standard tests (Arellano-Bond's AR(2) test, and Hansen's J-test) suggest that the instrument matrix satisfies the overidentifying restrictions.

Table 18.3 Models with interaction terms

	Linear	Quadratic	Parsimonious spec. A	Parsimonious spec. B
	(1)	(2)	(3)	(4)
Panel A: Cross-section Results (Dependent variable: average GDP per capita growth 1955–2010), OLS				
Ln Y (1955)	−0.001	−0.340**	−0.130*	−0.090
	(0.015)	(0.167)	(0.077)	(0.074)
$(\text{Ln } Y)^2$ (1955)		0.022**	0.009*	0.006
		(0.011)	(0.005)	(0.005)
PRI (1955–2010)	0.496***	−1.787		0.305***
	(0.189)	(1.438)		(0.099)
PRI × Ln Y	−0.059**	0.544	0.081***	
	(0.024)	(0.366)	(0.025)	
PRI × $(\text{Ln } Y)^2$		−0.039*	−0.010***	−0.004***
		(0.023)	(0.003)	(0.001)
H (1955–2010)	0.019***	0.020***	0.020***	0.020***
	(0.003)	(0.003)	(0.003)	(0.003)
Adjusted R-squared	0.346	0.352	0.350	0.347
Observations (countries)	118	118	118	118
Panel B: Panel Data Results (Dependent variable: 5-year GDP per capita growth, 1955–2010), PCSE				
Ln $Y_{(t-1)}$	−0.324***	1.776***	1.330***	1.157***
	(0.091)	(0.485)	(0.297)	(0.263)
$(\text{Ln } Y_{(t-1)})^2$		−0.140***	−0.112***	−0.100***
		(0.033)	(0.021)	(0.019)
$PRI_{(t-1)}$	−0.065	3.353		−1.058***
	(0.358)	(2.081)		(0.274)
$PRI_{(t-1)}$ × Ln $Y_{(t-1)}$	0.018	−1.111**	−0.277***	
	(0.046)	(0.553)	(0.071)	
$PRI_{(t-1)}$ × $(\text{Ln } Y_{(t-1)})^2$		0.087**	0.035***	0.017***
		(0.036)	(0.009)	(0.004)
$H_{(t-1)}$	0.044***	0.037***	0.035**	0.034**
	(0.014)	(0.014)	(0.014)	(0.014)
Country fixed effects	Yes	Yes	Yes	Yes
Time-period fixed effects	Yes	Yes	Yes	Yes
Lagged GDP per capita growth	Yes	Yes	Yes	Yes
Adjusted R-squared (overall)	0.220	0.286	0.285	0.284
Observations	1298	1298	1298	1298
Groups (countries)	118	118	118	118

Notes: ***, ** and * indicate that the coefficients are significant at the 1%, 5% and 10% levels, respectively. Panel A reports OLS regressions with heteroskedasticity-robust standard errors in parenthesis. Panel B reports Prais-Winsten regressions with panel-corrected standard errors (PCSE) in parenthesis

(*p*-value = 0.205). Based on these tests, we consider model 1 (panel A) as our preferred cross-sectional specification, and model 2 (panel B) as our preferred panel specification.

The results in Table 18.3 show that including interaction terms does not substantially alter the estimated relationship between human capital and growth. The panel data estimates of the human capital effect are still nearly twice as large in magnitude as the corresponding cross-sectional estimates, consistent with the findings reported in Table 18.1.

To interpret the estimated impact of institutional quality, Fig. 18.4 displays the marginal effect of *PRI* on growth, as function of initial level of development, for the different cross-country specifications. Figure 18.5 shows the same plots for the corresponding panel specifications. The cross-sectional specifications (Fig. 18.4) replicate the patterns reported by Keefer and Knack (1997) and Lee and Kim (2009). Property rights institutions have a positive effect on growth in low-income countries. The estimated effect, however, decreases in magnitude as a country develops, becoming statistically indistinguishable from zero at 2200 (PPP-adjusted 2011) USD, roughly equivalent

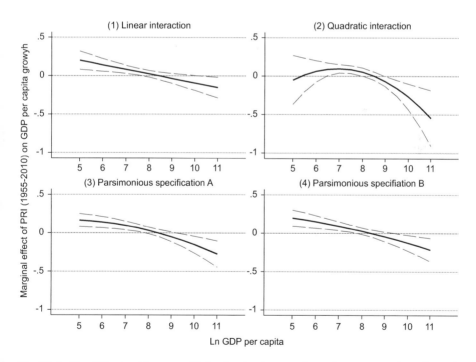

Fig. 18.4   The Effects of Property Rights Institutions on Growth, as a Function of Initial Income Levels (with 90% confidence intervals). Cross-Section Specifications (from panel A, Table 18.2)

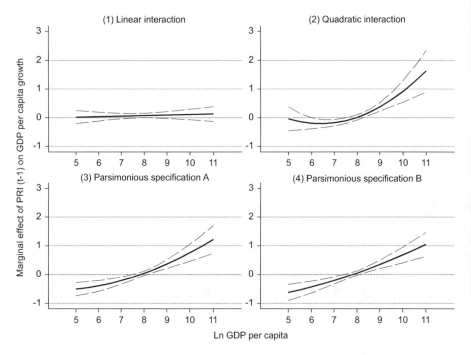

Fig. 18.5 The Effects of Property Rights Institution on Growth, as Function of Initial Income Level (with 90% confidence intervals). Fixed-Effects, Panel Specifications (from Panel B, Table 18.2)

to the income level of Brazil in 1965 or Pakistan in 2010. Specifications (2)–(4) even suggest a negative impact of property rights institutions at high income levels, when holding human capital constant. Yet, this negative relationship is not statistically significant at 5% in our preferred specification (model 1).

The estimated sign and magnitude of the interaction term coefficients may also be subject to omitted variable bias.[19] This expectation is corroborated by the data. When unobserved heterogeneities are accounted for in a fixed-effects panel data framework, the interaction term coefficients change signs throughout (compare panels A and B in Table 18.3). Accordingly, the shape of the relationships displayed in Fig. 18.5 is inverted. The effects of property rights institutions are close to zero (or even negative in the parsimonious models 3

---

[19] The joint influence of omitted country characteristics (e.g. culture, history, geography) might *itself* be subject to the moderating influence of income levels. For instance, at low levels of income, the high estimated effect of institutions might possibly be biased *upwards* by the omission of country-specific characteristics that are beneficial for both institutional quality and growth at low income. The *same* omitted factors, however, may bias the institutional effect *downwards* at high income if they become growth-reducing, but still contribute to promoting institutional quality.

Table 18.4 Effects of institutional change in Post-Mao China

year	GDP pc (US$ PPP)	M.E. of PRI	(s.e.)	PRI	$\Delta \ln Y / 5$[a]
1980	947	−0.188***	(0.070)	0.25	4.9
1985	1331	−0.152**	(0.064)	0.30	6.8
1990	1524	−0.132**	(0.062)	0.30	2.7
1995	2204	−0.062	(0.057)	0.36	7.4
2000	2934	0.009	(0.054)	0.38	5.7
2005	4592	0.149**	(0.057)	0.38	9.0
2010	6365	0.273***	(0.072)	0.42	6.5

Notes: ***, ** and * indicate that the coefficients are significant at the 1%, 5% and 10% levels, respectively. Delta-method standard errors in parenthesis. M.E. stands for marginal effects, which are based on model 2, Panel B in Table 18.3
[a]Average annualized rate of GDP per capita growth over the following 5-year period

and 4) in poor countries. Yet, the gains from widening access to property rights protection increase substantially as a country develops, becoming positive and statistically distinguishable from zero when income levels cross a threshold of around 3800 USD, about the level of Greece in 1960 or Romania in 1995. Thereafter, the magnitude of the effect increases sharply, reaching 0.290 (p-value = 0.000), or twice the average marginal effect (0.140, p-value = 0.003), in countries with an income level of 6600 USD (e.g. Colombia in 2010 or Turkey in 2000).

Insofar as the panel results are more reliable, we find support for the notion that property rights protection is key for growth in upper-middle income and advanced economies; yet, we find no evidence to suggest that broad-based property rights enforcement enhances growth in low and low-middle income economies.

These findings are consistent with the case of post-Mao China.[20] Here, a spectacular growth acceleration was achieved with only modest and gradual changes in the system of property rights (Oi and Walder 1999). Table 18.4 reports the estimated effects of property rights institutions for a country at China's income levels during 1980–2010. Throughout the 1980s and 1990s, the effects of broadening enforcement would have been null, or even negative. By 2005, however, 25 years of sustained growth had pushed China past the income threshold after which "good" institutions bring substantial economic benefits. In 2010, had China improved the quality of its institutions (0.42) to the level of Italy (0.84), its average *annual* rate of economic growth during

---

[20] However, our findings are not *driven* by the case of China. Dropping China from the sample does not substantially alter the results reported in Table 18.3 (model 2, panel B). The results are available upon request.

2010–2015 would have increased by 2.3 percentage points, from 6.5% to 8.8%.[21]

4   Conclusion

This chapter has argued that the existing literature on the fundamental determinants of economic development may be overly polarized between proponents of the view that "institutions rule" (Rodrik et al. 2004) and advocates of the primacy of human capital (Glaeser et al. 2004).[22] Our results suggest that both human capital and property rights institutions may play roles in shaping economic growth. The proponents of the institutionalist thesis have often been too sanguine about the validity of instrumental variable strategies intended to address the endogeneity of institutions. Accordingly, they often overstate the conclusion that "inclusive" property rights protection is the most important precondition for economic growth. The detractors of the institutionalist thesis, by contrast, have sometimes made selective use of the evidence to make their case for the primacy of human capital (or geography).

Part of the reason why this highly polarized controversy has persisted, we propose, is the paucity of long time series data on institutional quality, so far preventing the use of panel data estimation techniques to account for endogeneity. Another limitation of the empirical literature is its failure so far to take seriously the possibility that "inclusive" institutions may matter differently at different stages of economic development.

Using a new indicator of institutional quality with extensive coverage over time, our empirical analysis addresses these two limitations. Conditional on country fixed effects, we find that *both* institutions and human capital have an independent, direct relationship with economic performance. Yet, conditional on human capital, the "inclusiveness" of property rights institutions is found to clearly enhance growth only as a country achieves middle-income status.

Our analysis points forward to at least four fruitful avenues of research. *First*, future work could draw on even more extensive time series, with V-Dem variables extending back to 1789, to assess potential temporal heterogeneities in the relationship between institutions and economic performance across modern history. Relatedly, more research is needed to shed light on *which* particular institutions matter. So far, very few studies (Acemoglu and Johnson

---

[21] =(0.84 − 0.42) × 0.273/5.

[22] Or geography (Sachs 2003).

2005; Siddiqui and Ahmet 2013) have investigated the *relative* importance of different institutions—for instance, property rights versus contract enforcement—for economic prosperity. Are different aspects of institutional quality more important at different levels of development, or for different economic outcomes (e.g. inequality, employment, etc.), or in countries with different socio-economic structures and political systems? While "good" property rights institutions may not matter in low-income countries, other dimensions of institutional quality may be important for growth in such contexts.

Second, future studies should also pursue similar research questions for human capital. Only recently have studies begun to differentiate between different types of human capital—for instance, basic literacy versus higher-level technical or entrepreneurial skills (e.g. Lee and Kim 2009; Squicciarini and Voigtlander 2015). Do different types of human capital matter differently at different stages of development? Answering this question could help developing countries craft more tailored, growth-oriented education policies. At least, future work could extend our models by also conditioning the influence of human capital on the level of development.

Third, our analysis has largely focused on estimating the *independent, direct* effects of institutions and human capital on performance. Human capital exerts a quantitatively larger *direct* effect on economic growth, conditional on institutions, than institutions do, conditional on human capital. Yet, this finding cannot rule out the possibility that institutions may also influence economic performance via human capital. The large drop in the estimated effect of PRI when H is included in the regression (see Table 18.2) is consistent with this view. Human capital may also influence performance via institutions, although the robustness of the estimated coefficient on H to including PRI runs counter to this possibility, as does the balance of evidence reviewed in this chapter. That said, more research is needed to properly disentangle the various indirect causal pathways by examining whether "good" institutions promote human capital accumulation, and whether the overall level of education facilitates the emergence of "inclusive" institutions.

Fourth, future studies should further investigate empirically *how* human capital and, especially, institutions, affect the aggregate production function. The effect of both these "fundamental" determinants of economic growth (provided human capital may be viewed as "fundamental") should be expected to work through the "proximate" determinants (as in Becker et al. 1990). Yet, we still do not know whether, for instance, institutions influence economic performance primarily by promoting investment, by reducing transaction costs and increasing aggregate productivity, or by modifying the fertility preferences of the population. Despite its long life and large expansion from the early 1990s, the research programme on comparative institutions is far from over. These, and other, core questions of development should preoccupy social scientists in the years to come.

References

Acemoglu, D. (2009). *Introduction to Modern Economic Growth*. Princeton: Princeton University Press.

Acemoglu, D., & Johnson, S. (2005). Unbundling Institutions. *Journal of Political Economy, 113*(5), 949–995.

Acemoglu, D., Johnson, S., & Robinson, J. A. (2001). The Colonial Origins of Comparative Development. *American Economic Review, 91*(5), 1369–1401.

Acemoglu, D., Johnson, S., & Robinson, J. A. (2002). Reversal of Fortune: Geography and Institutions in the Making of the Modern World Income Distribution. *Quarterly Journal of Economics, 117*(4), 1231–1294.

Acemoglu, D., Johnson, S., Robinson, J. A., & Yared, P. (2005). From Education to Democracy. *American Economic Review, 95*(2), 44–49.

Acemoglu, D., Zilibotti, F., & Aghion, P. (2006). Distance to Frontier, Selection and Economic Growth. *Journal of the European Economic Association, 4*(1), 37–74.

Acemoglu, D., Gallego, F. A., & Robinson, J. A. (2014). Institutions, Human Capital and Development. *Annual Review of Economics, 6*, 875–912.

Acemoglu, D., Naidu, S., Restrepo, P., & Robinson, J. A. (2019). Democracy Does Cause Growth. *Journal of Political Economy, 127*(1), 47–100.

Ansell, B. W., & Samuels, D. J. (2015). *Inequality and Democratization*. Cambridge: Cambridge University Press.

Austin, G. (2008). The 'Reversal of Fortune' Thesis and the Compression of History: Perspectives from African and Comparative Economic History. *Journal of International Development, 20*(8), 996–1027.

Barro, R. J. (1991). Economic Growth in a Cross Section of Countries. *Quarterly Journal of Economics, 106*(2), 407–433.

Barro, R. (2001). Human Capital and Growth. *American Economic Review, 91*(2), 12–17.

Barro, R., & Lee, J.-W. (2013). A New Data Set of Educational Attainment in the World, 1950–2010. *Journal of Development Economics, 104*, 184–198.

Barro, R. J., & Sala-i-Martin, X. (2004). *Economic Growth*. Cambridge, MA: MIT Press.

Beck, N., & Katz, J. N. (1995). What to Do (and Not to Do) with Time-Series Cross-Section Data. *American Political Science Review, 89*(3), 634–647.

Becker, G., Murphy, K., & Tamura, R. (1990). Human Capital, Fertility, and Economic Growth. *Journal of Political Economy, 98*(5), S12–S37.

Bennett, D. L., Faria, H. J., Gwartney, J. D., & Morales, D. R. (2017). Economic Institutions and Comparative Economic Development: A Post-Colonial Perspective. *World Development, 96*, 503–519.

Besley, T. (1995). Property Rights and Investment Incentives: Theory and Evidence from Ghana. *Journal of Political Economy, 103*(5), 903–937.

Bils, M., & Klenow, P. J. (2000). Does Schooling Cause Growth? *American Economic Review, 90*(5), 1160–1183.

Bjornskov, C., & Meon, P.-G. (2013). Is Trust the Missing Root of Institutions, Education and Development? *Public Choice, 157*, 641–669.

Bolt, J., & Bezemer, D. (2009). Understanding Long-Run African Growth: Colonial institutions or Colonial Education? *Journal of Development Studies, 45*(1), 24–54.

Cassar, A., d'Adda, G., & Grosjean, P. (2014). Institutional Quality, Culture, and Norms of Cooperation: Evidence from Behavioral Field Experiments. *The Journal of Law and Economics, 57*(3), 821–864.

Chang, H.-J. (1993). *The Political Economy of Industrial Policy*. Palgrave Macmillan.

Chang, H.-J. (2011). Institutions and Economic Development: Theory, Policy and History. *Journal of Institutional Economics, 7*(4), 473–498.

Che, D., & Shen, L. (2013). The Co-Development of Economies and Institutions. *The Economics of Transition, 21*(2), 37–74.

Clague, C., Keefer, P., Knack, S., & Olson, M. (2003). Property and Contract Rights in Autocracies and Democracies. In S. Knack (Ed.), *Democracy, Governance and Growth* (pp. 78–109). Ann Arbor: University of Michigan Press.

Cohen, D., & Soto, M. (2007). Growth and Human Capital: Good Data, Good Results. *Journal of Economic Growth, 12*, 51–76.

Coppedge, M., Gerring, J., Knutsen, C. H., Lindberg, S. I., Skaaning, S.-E., Teorell, J., Altman, D., Bernhard, M., Steven Fish, M., Cornell, A., Ðahlum, S., Gjerløw, H., Glynn, A., Hicken, A., Krusell, J., Lührmann, A., Marquardt, K. L., McMann, K., Mechkova, V., Medzihorsky, J., Olin, M., Paxton, P., Pemstein, D., Pernes, J., von Römer, J., Seim, B., Sigman, R., Staton, J., Stepanova, N., Sundström, A., Tzelgov, E., Wang, Y.-T., Wig, T., Wilson, S., & Ziblatt, D. (2018a). V-Dem Dataset v8.

Coppedge, M., Gerring, J., Knutsen, C. H., Lindberg, S. I., Skaaning, S.-E., Teorell, J., Altman, D., Bernhard, M., Cornell, A., Steven Fish, M., Gjerløw, H., Glynn, A., Hicken, A., Krusell, J., Lührmann, A., Marquardt, K. L., McMann, K., Mechkova, V., Olin, M., Paxton, P., Pemstein, D., Seim, B., Sigman, R., Staton, J., Sundtröm, A., Tzelgov, E., Uberti, L., Wang, Y.-T., Wig, T., & Ziblatt, D. (2018b). V-Dem Codebook v8.

Dahlum, S. (2017). *Schooling for Dissent? Education, Autocratic Regime Instability and Transitions to Democracy*. Oslo: University of Oslo.

Dawson, J. (1998). Institutions, Investment, and Growth: New Cross-Country and Panel Data Evidence. *Economic Inquiry, 36*, 603–619.

Dollar, D., & Kray, A. (2003). Institutions, Trade and Growth. *Journal of Monetary Economics, 50*(1), 133–162.

Easterly, W., & Levine, R. (2003). Tropics, Germs, and Crops: How Endowments Influence Economic Development. *Journal of Monetary Economics, 50*(1), 3–39.

Efendic, A., Pugh, G., & Adnett, N. (2011). Institutions and Economic Performance: A Meta-Regression Analysis. *European Journal of Political Economy, 27*, 586–599.

Fariss, C. J., Crabtree, C. D., Anders, T., Jones, Z. M., Linder, F. J., & Markowitz, J. N. (2017). *Latent Estimation of GDP, GDP Per Capita, and Population from Historic and Contemporary Sources.* Working Paper.

Fernández, R., & Fogli, A. (2009). Culture: An Empirical Investigation of Beliefs, Work, and Fertility. *American Economic Journal: Macroeconomics, 1*(1), 146–177.

Fiaschi, D., & Lavezzi, A. M. (2007). Nonlinear Economic Growth: Some Theory and Cross-Country Evidence. *Journal of Development Economics, 84*(1), 271–290.

Fielding, D., & Torres, S. (2008). Cows and Conquistadors: A Contribution on the Colonial Origins of Comparative Development. *Journal of Development Studies, 44*(8), 1081–1099.

Gennaioli, N., La Porta, R., Lopez-de-Silanes, F., & Shleifer, A. (2013). Human Capital and Regional Development. *Quarterly Journal of Economics, 128*, 105–164.

Glaeser, E. L., La Porta, R., Silanes, F. L.-d., & Shleifer, A. (2004). Do Institutions Cause Growth? *Journal of Economic Growth, 9*(3), 271–303.

Gorodnichenko, Y., & Roland, G. (2017). Culture, Institutions, and the Wealth of Nations. *Review of Economics and Statistics, 99*(3), 402–416.

Hanson, J. K. (2014). Forging then Taming Leviathan: State Capacity, Constraints on Rulers, and Development. *International Studies Quarterly, 58*(2), 380–392.

Hanushek, E. A., & Woessman, L. (2013). Do Better Schools Lead to More Growth? Cognitive Skills, Economic Outcomes, and Causation. *Journal of Economic Growth, 17*, 267–321.

Helpman, E. (2006). *The Mystery of Economic Growth.* Cambridge, MA: Belknapp Press.

Henisz, W. J. (2000). The Institutional Environment for Economic Growth. *Economics and Politics, 12*(1), 1–31.

Islam, N. (1995). Growth Empirical: A Panel Data Approach. *Quarterly Journal of Economics, 110*(4), 1127–1170.

Keefer, P., & Knack, S. (1997). Why Don't Poor Countries Catch Up? A Cross-Country Test of an Institutional Explanation. *Economic Inquiry, 35*(3), 590–602.

Khan, M. H. (2007). Beyond Good Governance: An Agenda for Developmental Governance. In J. K. Sundaram & A. Chowdhury (Eds.), *Is Good Governance Good for Development?* New York, NY: Bloomsbury Academic Publishing.

Khan, M. H. (2010). *Political Settlements and the Governance of Growth-Enhancing Institutions.* SOAS University of London.

Khan, M. H. (2012). Governance and Growth: History, Ideology, and Methods of Proof. In A. Noman, K. Botchwey, H. Stein, & J. E. Stiglitz (Eds.), *Good Growth and Governance in Africa: Rethinking Development Strategies.* Oxford: Oxford University Press.

Khan, M. H., & Sundaram, J. K. (2000). *Rents, Rent-Seeking and Economic Development: Theory and Evidence in Asia*. Cambridge: Cambridge University Press.

Knack, S., & Keefer, P. (1995). Institutions and Economic Performance: Cross-Country Tests Using Alternative Measures. *Economics and Politics, 7*(3), 207–227.

Knutsen, C. H. (2011). Democracy, Dictatorship and Protection of Property Rights. *Journal of Development Studies, 47*(1), 164–182.

Knutsen, C. H. (2012). Democracy and Economic Growth: A Review of Arguments and Results. *International Area Studies Review, 15*(4), 393–415.

Knutsen, C. H., Teorell, J., Wig, T., Cornell, A., Gerring, J., Gjerløw, H., Skaaning, S.-E., Ziblatt, D., Marquardt, K., Pemstein, D., & Seim, B. (2018). Introducing the Historical Varieties of Democracy Dataset: Patterns and Determinants of Democratization in the Long 19th Century. *Journal of Peace Research, 56*(3), 440–451.

Kremer, M. (1993). The O-Ring Theory of Economic Development. *Quarterly Journal of Economics, 108*(3), 551–575.

Lee, K., & Kim, B.-Y. (2009). Both Institutions and Policies Matter but Differently for Different Income Groups of Countries: Determinants of Long-Run Economic Growth Revisited. *World Development, 37*(3), 533–549.

Lipset, S. M. (1959). Some Social Requisites of Democracy: Economic Development and Political Legitimacy. *American Political Science Review, 53*(1), 69–105.

Lucas, R. E. (1988). On the Mechanisms of Economic Development. *Journal of Monetary Economics, 22*(1), 3–42.

Mankiw, G. N., Romer, D., & Weil, D. N. (1992). A Contribution to the Empirics of Economic Growth. *Quarterly Journal of Economics, 107*(2), 407–437.

Marshall, M. G., Gurr, T. R., & Jaggers, K. (2013). *Polity IV Project: Political Regime Characteristics and Transitions, 1800–2013*. Center for Systemic Peace.

Mkandawire, T. (2010). On Tax Efforts and Colonial Heritage in Africa. *Journal of Development Studies, 46*(10), 1647–1669.

Nelson, R. R. (2005). *Technology, Institutions, and Economic Growth*. Cambridge, MA: Harvard University Press.

North, D. C. (1990). *Institutions, Institutional Change and Economic Performance*. Cambridge: Cambridge University Press.

North, D. C., Wallis, J. J., & Weingast, B. R. (2009). *Violence and Social Orders: A Conceptual Framework for Interpreting Recorded Human History*. Cambridge: Cambridge University Press.

North, D. C., Wallis, J. J., Webb, S. B., & Weingast, B. R. (Eds.). (2012). *In the Shadow of Violence: Politics, Economics and the Problems of Development*. Cambridge: Cambridge University Press.

Oi, J., & Walder, A. (Eds.). (1999). *Property Rights and Economic Reform in China*. Stanford, CA: Stanford University Press.

Papagapitos, A., & Riley, R. (2009). Social Trust and Human Capital Formation. *Economics Letters, 102*, 158–160.

Pemstein, D., Marquardt, K. L., Tzelgov, E., Wang, Y.-T., Krussel, J., & Miri, F. (2017). *The V-Dem Measurement Model: Latent Variable Analysis for Cross-National and Cross-Temporal Expert-Coded Data*. Gothenburg: V-Dem Working Paper 21.

Rodrik, D., Subramanian, A., & Trebbi, F. (2004). Institutions Rule: The Primacy of Institutions over Geography and Integration in Economic Development. *Journal of Economic Growth, 9*(2), 131–165.

Romer, P. (1990). Endogenous Technological Change. *Journal of Political Economy, 98*(5), 71–102.

Sachs, J. (2003). *Institutions Don't Rule: Direct Effects of Geography on Per Capita Income*. NBER Working Paper No. 9490.

Sachs, J., & Warner, A. M. (1997). Fundamental Sources of Long-run Growth. *American Economic Review, 87*(2), 184–188.

Siddiqui, D. A., & Ahmet, Q. M. (2013). The Effect of Institutions on Economic Growth: A Global Analysis based on GMM Dynamic Panel Estimation. *Structural Change and Economic Dynamics, 24*, 18–33.

Sokoloff, K., & Engerman, S. (2000). Institutions, Factor Endowments, and Paths of Development in the New World. *Journal of Economic Perspectives, 14*(3), 217–232.

Squicciarini, M. P., & Voigtlander, N. (2015). Human Capital and Industrialization: Evidence from the Age of Enlightenment. *Quarterly Journal of Economics, 130*(4), 1825–1883.

Tabellini, G. (2008). Institutions and Culture. *Journal of the European Economic Association, 6*, 905–950.

Welzel, C. (2012). *Freedom Rising: Human Empowerment and the Quest for Emancipation*. Cambridge: Cambridge University Press.

Williamson, C., & Kerekes, C. (2011). Securing Private Property: Formal Versus Informal Institutions. *Journal of Law and Economics, 54*(3), 537–572.

Wrong, M. (2000). *In the Footsteps of Mr Kurtz*. London: Fourth Estate.

19

Reform Design Matters: The Role of Structural Policy Complementarities

Joaquim Oliveira-Martins and Bruno T. da Rocha

1   Introduction

The study of the conditions under which structural reforms lead to economic growth remains an active area of research. An under-researched aspect is the fact that the impact of a given reform on economic growth may depend, to a significant extent, on how advanced reforms are in complementary areas. That is, reforms interact. It is likely, therefore, that piecemeal reforms will not generate all the expected returns. For an intuitive example consider a country that opens its economy to international trade. This will induce a need to reallocate resources across sectors; such reallocation will be more achievable if, for example, firm entry regulations and exit mechanisms are sufficiently flexible.

The authors would like to thank Elodie Douarin and Oleh Havrylyshyn for very useful comments on the first draft of this paper. The views expressed in this paper are those of the authors and do not necessarily reflect those of the OECD and its Member countries. Rocha acknowledges financial support from Fundação para a Ciência e Tecnologia (Portugal) through research grant UIDB/05069/2020.

J. Oliveira-Martins
OECD Centre for Entrepreneurship, SMEs, Regions and Cities, Paris, France

PSL - University of Paris Dauphine, Paris, France
e-mail: joaquim.oliveira@oecd.org

B. T. da Rocha (✉)
UECE/REM and CEsA, ISEG, University of Lisbon, Lisbon, Portugal
e-mail: brunorocha@iseg.ulisboa.pt

© The Author(s) 2021

493

E. Douarin, O. Havrylyshyn (eds.), *The Palgrave Handbook of Comparative Economics*,
https://doi.org/10.1007/978-3-030-50888-3_19

The bulk of this chapter is dedicated to taking stock of the already sizeable but relatively sparse work on this issue. We start by describing the basic theoretical foundations of policy complementarities, triggered by the problem of the Second Best (Lipsey and Lancaster 1956). Next, our focus is to map existing results on structural reforms, with an emphasis on empirical studies and, in particular, on different approaches to identify policy complementarities and test their significance for economic growth. We discuss the specific experience of post-communism transition in a separate section, as a significant part of existing work on reform complementarities has emerged in the context of the literature devoted to better understand the recession of the early transition phase and the ensuing—and very diverse—growth trajectories in formerly planned economies. We then focus on structural reforms more generally, noticing that many of the findings are related to openness to international trade and capital flows; this suggests, importantly, that the process of integrating developing and emerging economies in the world economy can benefit greatly from a design of reform packages that takes into consideration the significance of reform synergies. We also discuss in a brief way some findings on the adjacent topics of complementarities in labour market policies and in innovation policies.

At the end of the chapter, we reflect on how developing this perspective can help improve our current understanding of economic growth dynamics, namely in low- and middle-income economies. However, more research is necessary to consolidate the apparently emerging picture that structural reforms constitute a set of interacting components, that is, a policy package that nests a web of pair-wise interactions. Possible topics for future research are thus discussed and include the precise channels through which reform complementarities affect economic growth, the challenges associated with the identification of causal effects of different reform combinations, and, finally, the implications of incorporating reform complementarities in political economy analyses.

2   Theoretical Elements

The theory of structural reform has been traditionally associated with the removal of market distortions to reach, as far as possible, a first best situation where economic mechanisms can deliver both a market equilibrium and a welfare optimum. In this context, Lipsey and Lancaster (1956) provided a rather gloomy conclusion. In the presence of many initial distortions, they showed that typically there is no possibility to remove them in such a manner that an increase in welfare is ensured in a non-ambiguous way. The only approach is to remove *all* distortions simultaneously. However, in practice removing all distortions simultaneously is nearly impossible because of imperfect knowledge and implementation costs and constraints. Often, a long and uncompressible time is needed to undertake certain reforms; for example, sequencing reforms over time implies that only some distortions are removed at once. Governments may also lack political capital: political cycles are typically much shorter than the time needed to reap the benefits from reforms. There are actually few examples of countries (e.g. Chile, Czech Republic, or Estonia) that attempted to implement what could be regarded as an approximation to a *radical* reform programme, that is, a rapid removal of a large number of distortions. Most countries have typically adopted more gradual reform paths.

After the seminal paper of Lipsey and Lancaster, economic theory remained somewhat muted on how to overcome the Second Best problem. In some sense, the initial point (many distortions) and the endpoint (First Best) were known, but there was little indication on how to manage transition between these two states of the economic system. Against this background, Foster and Sonnenschein (1970) proposed a *radial* reform approach. They proved that the following result holds in single equilibrium theory (i.e. one single equilibrium per price vector):

Theorem (Foster and Sonnenschein 1970): *with a flat production function and if no commodity is inferior in the production function, then a radial increase in distortion is associated with a reduction in utility.*

A radial increase in distortion derives from the comparison between two Second Best d-equilibria, associated each with a vector of distortions, d_1 and d_2. The d-equilibria differ by a proportional shift in all distortions simultaneously, say $d_2 = k.d_1$ where $k > 1$. This isomorphic shift is required in order to ensure that the mapping between d-equilibria and distortion is unique. The theorem implies that, if a radial increase in distortions decreases utility, then a radial reduction in distortions (a radial reform) unambiguously increases welfare.

While the intuition for a radial reform strategy is appealing, note that these authors focused specifically on price distortions and associated tax reforms. Their theoretical framework is of difficult application in more general contexts; indeed, this would imply the construction of a general metric of structural reforms that would be necessary to define equiproportional shifts across all types of distortions. For the purposes of reform design and policy implementation, one needs a more flexible framework leading to a reform strategy, which can be shown to increase welfare while being tractable from a policy point of view. This framework can be based on the concept of *super-modularity* (Topkis 1998; Milgrom and Roberts 1995) and can be applied to a reform package where pairs of individual reforms exhibit complementarity, that is, policies reinforce each other.

The notion of complementarity goes back to the neoclassical concept of Edgeworth-complements. It was developed to characterise the case where having more of a given product increases the marginal utility of having more of another product. The two products are then said to be complements. The concept of policy complementarity can be defined as follows. Assume a given pay-off function depending from two reforms R_1 and R_2: $U(R_1, R_2)$. To simplify, let us assume here that the reform metric has only two values: 0 for no-reform and 1 when the reform is implemented. The two reforms are said to be complementary when the following relation holds:

$$U(1,1) - U(0,1) \geq U(1,0) - U(0,0).$$

The increase in U when a given reform is implemented is bigger when the other reform has already been implemented. The return from moving from the minimum (0,0) to (0,1) (or to (1,0)) is less than the return from moving from (0,1) (or from (1,0)) to the maximum (1,1). In other words, doing both reforms has a higher return than doing each reform separately. This definition can be generalised to a case of n reforms. When these relations hold for every pair of reforms, $U(.)$ is said to be *supermodular* (Topkis 1998). Optimising in such a system can be achieved by increasing all reforms in parallel, but not necessarily in the same proportion. As shown by Milgrom and Roberts (1995) this achieves at least half of the potential gains of an unrestricted optimisation.[1]

If structural reforms are linked by a web of complementarities, a more "balanced" reform strategy is preferable. Suppose a package of five structural reforms measured by a reform indicator in the scale 0–4, with 0 meaning no reform. In the presence of policy complementarities, moving from (0,0,0,0,0) to (2,2,2,2,2) should provide a higher increase in the pay-off function than, say, moving to (4,4,2,0,0). Both packages have the same (unweighted) average, but the second package is clearly unbalanced: the first two reforms were fully implemented, the third one only partially, and for the other policy areas there was no reform. Using an indicator that measures the degree of policy

---

[1] A simple demonstration of this result is provided in Macedo and Oliveira Martins (2008).

coordination, the effect of policy complementarities can be assessed with econometric techniques (see below).

3 Results on Reform Complementarities

3.1 The Post-Communist Transition

The abandonment of central planning and transition to market was a massive-scale event. Nearly 30 economies implemented an extensive set of market-oriented reforms—the largest "natural experiment" in economics ever (Sonin 2013). There is now, of course, a large accumulated literature on the link between structural reforms and the recession of the early transition phase and the subsequent, and very diverse, growth trajectories in these economies; we refer the reader to, for example, the recent volume edited by Åslund and Djankov (2014), the meta-analyses in Iwasaki and Kumo (2019) and Babecký and Havránek (2014), and the earlier literature surveys of Havrylyshyn (2006) and Campos and Coricelli (2002).

More specifically, the dimensions of speed, sequencing, and complementarity in reform packages were the object of many discussions in academic and policy circles in the first 10–15 years of the transition process, between economists advocating a "big-bang" or "shock therapies", and those in favour of more gradual implementation of structural reforms. This debate was often reduced to the sole issue of the pace of reforms and, thus, can be deemed to have been somewhat misfocused (Sonin 2013). Policy linkages appear to be a more fundamental aspect than reform speed per se;[2] these do not imply necessarily the implementation of "big-bang" reforms, as they can be built through gradual advancements in a breadth of interacting areas (conversely, a government may proceed to complete very rapidly a number of reforms but leave important complementary areas unreformed). This focus on reform complementarities was at the core of the OECD approach towards transition economies. For example, a comparative study of the three Baltic States (OECD 2000) concluded that it was more important to get the reform links right rather than pushing reform in any single area.[3]

Planned economies were based on an integrated system of (large) state-owned firms, who had to follow their part of the plan, in a context where

---

[2] Staehr (2005) and Wolf (1999) discuss the difference between reform *levels* and reform *speed*. In their econometric analyses reform speed is not associated to economic growth in transition economies. See also Iwasaki and Kumo (2019).

[3] See also OECD (2002) on Romania.

prices were fixed by the state. With privatisation came a decentralised quest for profit. There were, as noted by Roland (2000, p. 12), evident complementarities between privatisation and price liberalisation. On the one hand, profit incentives in distorted markets lead to resource misallocation, as prices do not reflect economic scarcity; on the other hand, free prices alone do not deliver optimal allocative resources if firms do not face incentives for value maximisation. It is likely, hence, that piecemeal reforms will generate negative outcomes. For example, privatisation without price liberalisation generates opportunities for agents interested in extracting rents from arbitrage, for example, acquiring a firm to buy under-priced inputs just to export these to economies where they are rightly priced. As observed inter alia by Rocha (2015), distortions of this type may discourage prospective investors with the "right" market skills—those necessary to improve productivity and innovate—,[4] who in principle will be less interested in operating in sectors where prices are still the object of arbitrary regulations. The uncertainty associated to not knowing the "true" prices in the economy, that is, those that would have been formed by market forces is an important obstacle to identifying a firm's true value.

The model in Qian (1994) investigates what happens when prices are liberalised without hardening the firms' budget constraints. In this analysis, state-owned firms benefit from a softer budget constraint, as the state-owned bank refinances their bad projects. This leads to welfare losses. Soft budget constraints inflict a double loss on consumers: first, household demand is crowded out by the firm demand for inputs for poor projects; and second, prices, which are now flexible, increase (in the model the same goods are demanded by households for consumption and by firms as an input: textiles, grain, gasoline, electricity, cars, etc.). Note that soft budget constraints were pervasive during transition; the refinancing and bailouts of bad projects happened frequently (Kornai 1994, 2001). Hence, insofar as privatisation leads, in principle, to an increase in the hardness of a firm's budget constraint, Qian's model can be regarded as capturing a form of interplay between privatisation and price liberalisation. A related work is Gates et al. (1996), which shows that, due to a complementarity in incentives faced by firm managers, privatisation and input price rationalisation (i.e. setting the input price equal to economy-wide shadow price) are complementary reforms, that is, the joint implementation of these reforms will lead to increases in welfare.

---

[4] Namely foreign owners; the literature finds that privatisation to foreign owners has better effects on firm performance than privatisation to domestic owners. See Iwasaki and Mizobata (2018), Estrin et al. (2009), and also section 5.2 in Bloom et al. (2012) regarding differences in management practices.

The empirical evidence in Rocha (2015) suggests, indeed, the existence of a nexus of interplay between price liberalisation and privatisation in the early transition period (the author focuses on 1990–1997 and carries out a 27-country panel data analysis). This initial phase, marked by a massive collapse of output in which these economies moved, dramatically, from the pre-transition situation of being dominated by supply constraints to experiencing widespread demand constraints, is often called the *transformational recession* (Kornai 1994). In this regard, the literature has emphasised the initial negative effect of privatisation associated to defensive restructuring through labour shedding and/or reduction of real wages,[5] with a significant negative impact on aggregate demand; see, for example, the model in Katz and Owen (1993), in which it is never optimal to privatise all firms immediately due to the effect this would have on the level of unemployment. What the results in Rocha (2015) seem to imply is that this immediate negative macroeconomic impact of privatisation may have been counterweighted, to a large extent, in those countries that implemented privatisation in an environment where prices were essentially free. In other words, exploiting this form of reform interaction probably contributed to mitigate the effects of the early transformational recession.

Conceivably, price liberalisation and competition policy constitute another pair of interacting reforms. More specifically, since in planned economies the production structure was based on a network of highly specialised vertically integrated monopolies, price liberalisation led to the exercise of market power, that is, monopolies charging monopoly prices to downstream industries (Li 1999). The expected negative impact on output of firms exerting a monopolistic or cartelistic behaviour can be mitigated, however, by the implementation of competition-promoting policies, for example, the break-up of large firms.[6]

Zinnes et al. (2001) analyse how the effect of privatisation on output depends on a set of slower-moving agency-related policy reforms directed at prudential regulation, corporate governance, the hardening of enterprise budget constraints, and management objectives. The authors consider a 24-country sample for the period 1990–1998. The main result is that there is a certain threshold level of these complementary policies for the transfer of ownership

---

[5] Defensive or *reactive* restructuring is based on shedding labour, cutting obsolete production lines, getting rid of non-productive assets, and so on, while *strategic* restructuring involves new investments and often requires financial intermediation.

[6] Table 3 in Rocha (2015) provides some empirical evidence of such a complementarity link, in that the coefficient of the interaction term between price liberalisation and competition policy is positive and statistically significant.

to generate a positive economic performance response. The authors' analysis suggests that countries in the western Former Soviet Union did not meet this condition, while the Caucasus and Central Asia were borderline.

3.1.1   A Broader View: Peering Beyond Pair-Wise Interactions

The discussion above has identified theoretical and empirical results that point to the existence of three interactions between specific pairs of reforms: privatisation and price liberalisation, price liberalisation and competition policy, and privatisation and agency-related institutional reforms. This suggests, for example, that the effect of privatisation on output was dependent on the existence of, at least, both a system of free prices and a good (agency-related) institutional framework.

Could reform interdependence be, then, a more general pattern in post-communist transition, in the sense that most if not all main reform areas were linked by an intricate web of complementarities? This hypothesis seems to be supported by analyses that look at reforms from this angle. Oliveira Martins and Price (2000), for example analyse policy interdependence in Slovakia by identifying four broad policy blocks related to liberalisation, stabilisation, exit, and entry. According to the authors, the success of the transition process depends on benefiting from the positive feedback between all four areas, while avoiding the negative impact that results from lack of progress in any given area. For instance, if exit mechanisms are enforced and induce enterprise liquidations but the conditions for entry of new firms are not in place, the pace of restructuring may become politically unsustainable as unemployment rises.

Macedo and Oliveira Martins (2008) take this intuition to data by proposing a *complementarity index*: the inverse of the Hirschmann-Herfindahl concentration index applied to the European Bank for Reconstruction and Development (EBRD) reform indicators.[7] A reform strategy that exploits policy synergies is reflected in an even distribution of individual reform indicators. The index is used in a panel analysis for 27 countries for the period 1989–2004, in which it is found that both the general level of reforms (the simple average of reform indicators) and *changes in their complementarity* have

---

[7] The nine covered policy areas are price liberalisation, large-scale privatisation, small-scale privatisation, governance and enterprise restructuring, trade and foreign exchange system, competition policy, banking reform and interest rate liberalisation, securities markets and non-bank financial institutions, and infrastructure. The authors also present a 9 × 9 matrix with 36 potential bilateral policy interactions. For instance, large-scale privatisation can generate more returns if securities exchanges are developed, as this eases financing mechanisms (see column 1 line 8 in their Table 1); also, competition policy will benefit from banking sector reform, as this enhances entry mechanisms (column 6 line 7).

a positive impact on economic growth. Their interpretation is that the former effect provides a long-run target for reforms, while the latter provides guidance on the conduct of the transition process.[8] Punthakey (2014) builds closely on this work, extending the analysis to 1989–2012 and 30 countries and using instead the negative of the standard deviation of reform indicators as a measure of reform complementarity. He confirms the main result in Macedo and Oliveira Martins (2008); in addition, his simulation applying estimated coefficients to the case of Kazakhstan shows that a partial reform scenario results in a negative impact on GDP growth. Finally, Banalieva (2014) provides a rare piece of micro evidence on the existence of reform complementarities by employing an adaptation of the Macedo and Oliveira Martins index (2008) in a panel of 211 firms of 14 transition economies from 1991 to 2009. Results appear to be robust: the implementation of synchronised reforms improved firm performance in transition economies.

This strand of work is based on the idea of constructing a variable that aims at capturing reform complementarities, or general *reform coordination*, and using it as a regressor in econometric analyses (in most cases growth regressions). Staehr (2005) takes a different route. He applies principal component analysis on the EBRD reform indices to identify "reform clusters" in a panel of 25 transition economies from 1989 to 2001; the principal components are then used as explanatory variables in growth regressions. The first principal component, which corresponds essentially to the sum of the eight reform indices and is taken as representing "a cluster of synchronised, broad-based reforms", appears to have a positive effect on growth. According to the author, that suggests a mutually reinforcing effect of various reform elements. The second principal component has positive factor loadings for price liberalisation, international market opening, and small-scale privatisation (with negative loadings for the rest of the EBRD indices), capturing what are generally called "early reforms" or "first-stage reforms". These also appear to have a positive effect on growth.[9] While the economic interpretation of the principal

---

[8] The *level* of complementarity displays a negative sign in the Macedo and Oliveira Martins (2008) growth regressions. As noted by the authors, in the context of transition high complementarity by itself does not necessarily lead to higher output growth. Indeed, transition is about shifting from a socialist system that, in some sense, had its own coherence but was totally rigid and distorted, towards a flexible market system (that also has a high complementarity). To make this structural change, not all reforms can be implemented at the same time. Reformers had to accept a less coherent system during the initial phase of the transition and the second-best costs associated with it. As the transition progresses and the average level of reforms continues to increase, at some point the complementarity index begins to increase.

[9] The transition literature has emphasised the difference between first-stage ("liberalisation") and second-stage (i.e. more "institutional") reforms, sometimes noting that implementing the former stimulated the development of the latter. See, for example, Douarin and Mickiewicz (2017), Di Tommaso et al. (2007), and Havrylyshyn and van Rooden (2003).

components that were computed is not completely straightforward, the presented evidence seems to indicate that some unsynchronised reform combinations were detrimental to growth, for example, bank liberalisation without enterprise restructuring. The Czech experience in the mid-1990s, when excessive bank lending to non-restructured firms contributed to banking sector problems and unsatisfactory economic growth, may be an example of such a reform mismatch.

3.2   Beyond Transition: Reform Complementarities in Opening the Economy

The results summarised so far offer an interesting view on the relation between structural reforms and economic growth in post-communist transition; yet, the existing evidence on the importance of policy complementarities goes beyond this specific period and group of countries. For example, the notion that opening the economy to international trade is contingent on other structural factors to generate gains in economic growth has been explored by a number of authors. Indeed, trade openness is a force that induces a reallocation of resources to sectors in which the economy has a comparative advantage, but, in theory, this requires factor movement not to be hampered. As observed by Rodrik (2006), trade liberalisation will not work if capital markets do not allocate finance to expanding sectors, labour market institutions do not work properly to reduce transitional unemployment, and so on. This is formalised in Chang et al. (2009), which derive an open-economy extension of the classic two-sector Harris-Todaro model to show that trade liberalisation leads to increases in income per capita only when labour market distortions are sufficiently small. Because of labour market distortions, trade reform may result in flows of workers to the "wrong" sector. Related to this, Dennis (2006) produced GTAP (Global Trade Analysis Project) simulations for Morocco and Tunisia where it is shown that the welfare gains of trade reforms under conditions of flexible factor markets can be as much as six times the gains compared to a rigid factor market scenario.

In addition, econometric evidence appears to corroborate the notion that trade opening should be accompanied by a variety of complementary policies. Chang et al. (2009), for example, estimate a comprehensive set of growth regression models and find positive interaction terms between a proxy of trade openness and proxies of educational investment, financial depth, inflation stabilisation, public infrastructure, governance quality, labour market flexibility, ease of firm entry, and ease of firm exit. Freund and Bolaky (2008) give particular emphasis to the interplay between trade openness and firm entry regulations, while Calderón and Fuentes (2006) conclude that the effect of trade openness on growth depends on institutional quality (measured through the combination of four governance indicators—rule of law, bureaucratic quality, corruption, and democratic accountability).

An important aspect is that not all the variables considered in studies of this type can be seen as a direct measure of a given policy. To be sure, outcome-based variables, like the financial depth (the ratio of private domestic credit to GDP), may reflect prevailing policies in a certain domain, for example, the banking sector. Yet, such variables may also depend on other factors, notably *other policies*, economic growth (i.e. there could be reverse causality problems), business cycles, or expectations.[10] This implies that the interpretation of estimated pair-wise interactions as evidence in favour of policy complementarities has to be taken with caution, not only due to the relatively imprecise link between outcome and policy that characterises certain variables, but also to the fact that, in principle, these variables are likely to be more endogenous in growth regressions.

Another major dimension of international integration is, of course, opening the economy to capital flows—in fact, the literature has investigated cases that point to the existence of instances of interplay between trade openness and financial openness, often with a focus on the idea that the latter should not precede the former. As observed inter alia by Eichengreen (2001), if the capital account is liberalised while import-competing industries are still protected, capital inflows could be directed to sectors in which the country does not have a comparative advantage. Martin and Rey (2006) show in a general equilibrium model that emerging markets are less prone to financial crashes if they start opening their financial account after they open up to trade in goods. The point is discussed by Prasad and Rajan (2008), who, based on existing empirical studies, argue that economies that are open to trade will be in a better position to service external obligations through export revenues and hence face less risk from sudden stops or reversals of capital inflows. Neary (2009) explores a different angle by highlighting the interactions between falling trade costs and lifting restrictions on cross-border mergers and acquisitions. In his model, the latter reinforces the effects of trade liberalisation, as the pattern of international specialisation moves closer to what would prevail under

---

[10] In Chang et al. (2009) trade openness is measured as the ratio of trade to GDP *adjusted for structural country characteristics*; more specifically, this is the residual of a regression of the log of the ratio of exports and imports to GDP on the logs of area and population, and dummies for oil exporting and for land-locked countries. The authors use this variable as an attempt to strengthen the outcome-policy connection, as the volume of trade is an outcome measure related to trade policy, but not exclusively so.

perfect competition. A related contribution is the much-studied "Bhagwati hypothesis", according to which the beneficial effect of foreign direct investment on economic growth is stronger in countries that pursue an outwardly oriented trade policy. These economies will attract a greater volume of FDI and the efficiency gains originating from productivity spillovers will be larger, as resources will be allocated in a less-distorted environment, that is, more based on the comparative advantage of a given country. The abundant empirical evidence—Kohpaiboon (2006), Makki and Somwaru (2004), Balasubramanyam et al. (1996), and so on—formed a base from which a policy implication can be derived: foreign investment regimes should not be liberalised before opening the economy to trade.

Nonetheless, it should be noted that the link between capital account liberalisation and economic growth remains unclear (Bumann et al. 2013), especially in emerging and developing economies, where its effects appear not to be positive (Ahmed 2013; Klein and Olivei 2008). Several studies have examined the link between financial development and the benefits of opening the economy to capital flows (e.g. Gu and Dong 2011; Eichengreen et al. 2011; Alfaro et al. 2004). An especially interesting example is the Alfaro et al. (2010) model, in which local financial markets enable FDI to promote growth through backward linkages. The way the concept of financial development is interpreted is based on a policy argument. In the model the domestic financial system intermediates resources at a cost—lower levels of development are associated with a cost wedge that could reflect taxes, interest ceilings, required reserve policies, regulations, and so on. Hence, reforms in these areas will lead to more financial development and then increase the effect of FDI on growth.

There is also an extensive body of literature showing that foreign bank presence tends to improve the efficiency of the domestic banking system (Giannetti and Ongena 2012; Manlagnit 2011; Claessens et al. 2001, etc.). Results in Taboada (2011), in particular, show that foreign presence in the banking sector leads to improvements in capital allocation mostly in common law countries; the author argues that this can be the result of increased competition, as in these countries banks are typically less constrained in their activities. In general, under the assumption that foreign banks will be more interested in entering a given country if banking activity is not constrained by interest rate controls floors or ceilings, directed credit schemes, entry barriers, or limits on branches or the range of activities that banks can take, these references can be regarded as suggesting, even if indirectly, an important interaction between opening the economy to capital flows and domestic reforms in the banking sector.

3.2.1 *Structural reforms as a system?*

In a similar way to the literature on post-communist transition, some empirical studies have attempted to identify complementarities across an extended number of policy areas in less specific samples of economies. The early contribution of Aziz and Westcott (1997) captures "the dispersion across policy stances" through the standard deviation of standardised measures of de facto trade openness, macroeconomic stability (less variance of inflation), and size of government (smaller share of government expenditure in GDP). Gallego and Loayza (2002) use a dummy variable as proxy for the "joint progress in policy-related growth determinants", which takes the value of 1 if a country is above the world median in de facto trade openness, domestic credit to the private sector, schooling, life expectancy, and below the world median in the black-market premium on foreign exchange and government consumption. In both cases the evidence is in favour of a positive association between policy complementarities and economic growth—but, as discussed above, the extensive usage of outcome-based variables is problematic. Macedo et al. (2014) consider the standard deviation among six policy indicators: openness to trade, openness to international flows of capital, banking and financial system, business regulations, protection of private property rights (all from the Heritage index of Economic Freedom), and an index for network infrastructure. The reported regressions cover between 70 and 116 countries in the period 1994–2006; policy dispersion appears to have a negative effect on growth, in particular in samples that exclude higher-income economies.

Coricelli and Maurel (2011) apply the Macedo and Oliveira Martins (2008) complementarity index to policy indicators covering trade openness, capital account liberalisation, the banking sector, and securities markets. They consider a panel of 91 countries in the period 1989–2005 and focus specifically on recession periods, showing that reform complementarity has a negative impact on the depth and length of recessions. That is, piecemeal reforms seem to expose countries to more severe contractions in economic activity. Rocha (2019) looks at annual growth rates in 1973–2005 in the same group of countries (minus Taiwan) and considers a system of three major policies—trade openness, capital account liberalisation, and banking sector reforms—, based on the fact that the literature suggests the existence of pair-wise interactions between these reforms (as also seen in this chapter). More formally, he posits for country j, year t, and a set of n policies P_i that:

$$\text{Growth in } GDPpc_{j,t} = \beta \left(\frac{1}{n} \sum_i^n P_i^\eta \right)^{\frac{1}{\eta}}_{j,t-1} + X_{j,t-1}\gamma + \alpha_j + \mu_t + \varepsilon_{jt},$$

with $0 \le P_i \le 1$ and $n = 3$ in this case; X contains control variables, α and μ are respectively country and year fixed effects, and ε is the error term. The equation is estimated by nonlinear least squares. The "policy technology" is mod-

elled as a power mean. We have, therefore, that $\dfrac{\partial}{\partial P_1 \partial P_{\neq 1}} \left(\beta \left(\dfrac{1}{n} \sum P_i^\eta \right)^{\frac{1}{\eta}} \right) > 0$

(the condition for the existence of reform complementarities) requires necessarily that η is smaller than 1 when β is larger than 0.[11] The estimates presented by the author confirm these conditions: estimated η and β are around 0.4 and 0.042 respectively, with Wald tests rejecting the $\eta = 1$ hypothesis (which would correspond to a zero-complementarities point or, in other words, to structural reforms having purely additive effects). According to these results, the effect on economic growth of any one of the considered three reforms depends simultaneously *on the other two areas*. Less "policy dispersion" is beneficial for economic growth: moving from $(P_1, P_2, P_3) = (0,0,0)$ to a "balanced" policy package of $(1/3,1/3,1/3)$ generates 1.4 percent of additional economic growth (with a t-statistic of 3.81). If the policy package is instead an unbalanced $(1,0,0)$, the point estimate for additional growth will be of only 0.3 percent with a p-value of 0.518, that is, statistically indistinguishable from 0.

3.3   Reform Complementarities Within Specific Policy Areas

The relevance of reform complementarities has been discussed in the context of labour market policies in developed economies, often focusing on the link between high unemployment and rigidities in European labour markets. Orszag and Snower (1998) and Coe and Snower (1997) provide theoretical arguments in favour of broad labour market reforms, involving simultaneous reforms on a variety of policy dimensions, such as unemployment benefits, job security legislation, payroll taxes, and active labour market policies.

---

[11] Indeed, for $n = 3$, we have that $\dfrac{\partial}{\partial P_1 \partial P_2} \left(\left(\dfrac{1}{3} \sum P_i^\eta \right)^{\frac{1}{\eta}} \right) = (1-\eta) \left(\dfrac{1}{3} \right)^{1/\eta} (P_1 P_2)^{\eta-1} (P_1^\eta + P_2^\eta + P_3^\eta)^{\frac{1-2\eta}{\eta}}$; all terms after $(1 - \eta)$ are positive.

Bassanini and Duval (2009) examine the issue empirically for a panel of 20 OECD economies, finding that the effect of a given policy reform on unemployment appears to be greater the more employment-friendly the overall institutional framework (which includes not only all the considered labour market policies but also an indicator of the stringency of anti-competitive product market regulations). However, the magnitude of such reform complementarities appears to be moderate for the average OECD country. Note, in addition, that the sign of the interaction between the deregulation of labour and product markets in OECD economies is a theme that remains unclear. Regarding employment effects, the empirical evidence in Berger and Danninger (2007) suggests that they are complements, whilst Fiori et al. (2012) and Amable et al. (2011) conclude they are substitutes. The Dynamic Stochastic General Equilibrium analysis in Cacciatore et al. (2016) supports the latter, also in terms of aggregate output dynamics. Égert (2018) concentrates instead on the effects of reforms on aggregate investment and finds that these two domains of market deregulation are complements.

Finally, Mohnen and Röller (2005) focus on innovation policies—or, to be more precise, obstacles to innovation that are in principle affected by policies, for example, regulations or lack of finance. This study forms part of a wider literature on complementarities in innovation activities at the firm level, for example, Hagedoorn and Wang (2012). The authors propose a discrete test of supermodularity in innovation policies leading to a number of inequality constraints, which they test using data on four EU countries (Ireland, Denmark, Germany, and Italy). Their evidence regarding propensity to innovate suggest the existence of a number of complementary relationships in innovation policies, whereas, in the case of intensity of innovation, results often point to the substitutability among policies.

4   Identifying Policy Complementarities: A Way Forward

As the mapping of pair-wise reform complementarities evolves to become more complete, the hypothesis that many policy areas constitute, in reality, a *system*, and are thus linked by an intricate web of complementarities emerges as increasingly plausible. This more comprehensive perspective is already at the basis of some of the studies that were discussed in this chapter (see Table 19.1). However, more evidence is needed. Indeed, furthering this type of approach has the potential to offer valuable insights on the effects on

Table 19.1 Identifying policy complementarities in empirical studies

Identification method	Example
Interaction term between two specific policy variables (most common approach).	Chang et al. (2009)
Interaction term between a specific policy variable and a measure of the overall policy stance.	Bassanini and Duval (2009)
Discrete supermodularity tests leading to a number of inequality constraints; test all possible pair-wise policy combinations.	Mohnen and Röller (2005)
Dummy variable that takes value 1 if all reforms are above a certain level and 0 otherwise (i.e. test if joint progress carries a premium over the sum of individual effects).	Gallego and Loayza (2002)
Construction of a complementarities index regressor, that is, test if policy "dispersion" or "fragmentation" has a negative effect on economic growth.	Macedo and Oliveira Martins (2008)
Estimation of a general policy function, that is, a power mean of policy indicators, which nests the hypothesis that the effect of a policy on, for example, economic growth depends on all other policies.	Rocha (2019)

economic growth of different reform dynamics, that is, piecemeal reforms vis-à-vis reform strategies that are more balanced across different policy areas.

4.1   *Policy complementarities as central in economic development processes*

According to Sect. 3.2, reform interactions seem to be especially important for the type of essential "first-generation" structural policies that are more relevant for developing and emerging economies (in the sense of being largely completed in developed countries), in particular regarding their integration in the global economy through openness to trade and to capital flows. For example, as noted by Eichengreen (2001), "limits on capital movements are a distortion. It is an implication of the theory of the second best that removing one distortion need not be welfare enhancing when other distortions are present. There are any number of constellations of distortions, especially in developing countries, for which this is plausibly the case" (p. 341). Policy complementarities could also be a key ingredient to overcome the so-called "middle-income trap". Indeed, certain countries may have periods of fast catching-up, but afterwards the convergence process slows down and they seem to be stuck at an intermediate level of income. This can be due to certain reform gaps that hinder the potential positive effect of the structural reforms already implemented. In this context, Hausmann et al. (2008) developed an approach based on "growth diagnostics" that aims at identifying the main country-specific growth bottlenecks. Addressing these reform gaps provides a reform strategy that increases policy complementarity.

Related to this, there is now a sizeable literature showing that misallocation of resources explains a large part of the difference in income per capita between rich and poor economies (Restuccia and Rogerson 2017). This research, if combined with the discussion in this chapter, suggests indirectly that an important channel through which reform interactions operate on growth is through generating important gains in terms of allocation of resources in the economy (as the massive reallocation "experiment" of the post-communist transition already seemed to imply). Investigating this link constitutes clearly an interesting topic for future research. The systematic assembly of empirical regularities could, eventually, motivate the venture of constructing a tractable general theory on the link between, on the one hand, the way many structural policies interact to shape the gamut of incentives that economic agents face in the markets they operate in (the micro-level), and, on the other hand, the observed long-run variation in average income levels (the macro-level).

4.2   Growth channels and causality Links: tentative elements for a research agenda

The hypothesis according to which the effect of a given policy on growth depends on given economic conditions or variables (e.g. financial development, human capital levels, or even business cycle conditions) is naturally different from the hypothesis that such an effect could depend *on another policy or a set of policies*. While both angles are relevant and may be more or less intertwined, the former is less directly connected to the specific issue under analysis here—the existence of interaction links between structural reforms. Note, however, that even if the econometric evidence of an association between reform complementarities and aggregate economic growth becomes more solid in the future, such association will not be informative *per se* of the specific *channels* through which reform complementarities affect growth. Indeed, one could ask: is this complementarity equally present in the reform determinants of productivity, employment, and investment, including foreign direct investment? Does the effect on aggregate productivity operate mainly through growth in within-firm productivity, or through improving resource allocation between firms and sectors in the economy? Addressing these questions is a complex task, but attempting to do so is likely to provide valuable insights on the relationship between structural reforms and economic growth. It is certain that this will entail the need for more studies with industry- and firm-level data.

We see the development of ways of portraying *reforms as a system* as a promising avenue for future research. As seen in the text, this may include the construction of variables that measure policy "fragmentation" or "variance"—an obstacle to the realisation of reform complementarities—or the usage of iterative nonlinear techniques to directly estimate nonlinear functional forms. While the robust identification of this type of relationships has the potential to improve our understanding of how structural reforms influence long-run growth dynamics, it should be noted that this poses additional challenges in terms of identifying causality patterns. Indeed, establishing causality between policies and expected outcomes is often difficult even for simpler linear specifications;[12] these difficulties are amplified when combinations between two or more explanatory variables are considered.

To be sure, as said above, variables that represent a measure of structural policy choices (in many cases *de jure* indicators) represent a more obvious link between theory and empirics (in the sense of being more directly connected to the incentives that govern microeconomic decisions) and are arguably less endogenous to economic growth than *de facto* variables. However, it is clear that further work is needed on this front. This may include, in a first phase, the narrative identification of plausibly exogenous episodes of joint implementation of reforms vs. piecemeal reforms; the causal effect of these different "reform shocks" could then be estimated using, for example, Local Projections (Jordà 2005) or Synthetic Control methods (Abadie et al. 2010). Another necessary endeavour is to peer more into the "black box" of policymaking processes, both in theoretical and in empirical terms, and, in particular, to investigate under which conditions discoordination among policy areas can emerge and persist over long periods of time. This work can provide guidance on whether "policy dispersion" indicators are to be regarded as essentially exogenous to economic growth or, if not, how to identify variables that could serve as plausible instrumental variables for this class of variables.

What is more, the explicit integration of reform complementarities in political economy analyses may contribute to shed light on the determinants of the implementation of structural reforms and the existence of bidirectional links between reforms and economic growth. We believe that, given the evidence discussed in this chapter, exploring the political economy implications

---

[12] Notice however that a reverse causality argument is not totally clear-cut. High growth, actual or expected, can either generate pressure for reforms in some areas or generate circumstances where reforms are perceived as being not very necessary.

of reform interactions across broad policy areas—trade openness, capital account liberalisation, banking sector reform, business entry regulations, business exit mechanisms, and so on—may prove especially useful to uncover underlying reforms-growth dynamics in observed long-run growth trajectories in developing and emerging economies.

As a simple speculative example, one can think of a negative case in which a government starts by implementing piecemeal reforms, as a way to avoid deepening policies with larger political costs. The government does so ignoring the true functional form of the "policy technology", in which complementarities play a key role. Hence the implemented piecemeal reforms will have a small or even negative impact on economic growth. This in turn will generate frustration over reforms in the electorate and therefore may prevent the implementation of more reforms and even lead to political instability or policy reversals, effectively locking in the country in a "no reforms, no growth" cycle. Possibly this represents part of what happened in Brazil, Argentina, or Russia over the past decades, where reforms have been quite sluggish or erratic and growth performance in general has been disappointing. South Korea may well illustrate the opposite case. The polity-policies-growth triangle can be better understood by investigating mechanisms of this type and how they depend on differences across political systems and the very quality of public governance and policymaking processes—namely the ways government structures are organised and departments communicate between themselves, as this may facilitate, or obstruct, the coordination among different policy areas.

5   Concluding Remarks

In this chapter, we have put together and discussed contributions from different literature strands on the theme of structural policy interactions. We hope to have articulated a coherent mosaic that contributes to build a more structured view of this topic. Given the available empirical evidence and theoretical analyses, there are reasons to believe that structural policy complementarities were not only important in the post-communist transition period but may also generate substantial growth gains in developing and emerging economies in the future. Therefore, in our view, exploring in a more exhaustive way the notion that the effect of a given reform on economic growth depends on other reforms should be a priority point for future research. As argued in this chapter, this may entail both the study of the specific channels through which reform complementarities affect economic growth (e.g. their effect on the allocation of resources in the economy) as well as aiming at identifying the causal effects of different reform combinations (something that we regard as particularly challenging). In addition, the integration of reform complementarities in political economy analyses could offer a new angle to study the determinants of the implementation of structural reforms, including how better governance systems could generate the systematic identification and effective implementation of important policy complementarities.

References

Abadie, A., Diamond, A., & Hainmueller, J. (2010). Synthetic Control Methods for Comparative Case Studies: Estimating the Effect of California's Tobacco Control Program. *Journal of the American Statistical Association, 105*(490), 493–505.

Ahmed, A. D. (2013). Effects of Financial Liberalization on Financial Market Development and Economic Performance of the SSA Region: An Empirical Assessment. *Economic Modelling, 30*, 261–273.

Alfaro, L., Chanda, A., Kalemli-Ozcan, S., & Sayek, S. (2004). FDI and Economic Growth: The Role of Local Financial Markets. *Journal of International Economics, 64*(1), 89–112.

Alfaro, L., Chanda, A., Kalemli-Ozcan, S., & Sayek, S. (2010). Does Foreign Direct Investment Promote Growth? Exploring the Role of Financial Markets on Linkages. *Journal of Development Economics, 91*(2), 242–256.

Amable, B., Demmou, L., & Gatti, D. (2011). The Effect of Employment Protection and Product Market Regulation on Labour Market Performance: Substitution or Complementarity? *Applied Economics, 43*(4), 449–464.

Åslund, A., & Djankov, S. (Eds.). (2014). *The Great Rebirth: Lessons from the Victory of Capitalism over Communism*. Washington, DC: Peterson Institute for International Economics.

Aziz, J., & Westcott, R. F. (1997). Policy Complementarities and the Washington Consensus. *International Monetary Fund Working Paper 97-118*.

Babecký, J., & Havránek, T. (2014). Structural Reforms and Growth in Transition: A Meta-analysis. *Economics of Transition, 22*(1), 13–42.

Balasubramanyam, V. N., Salisu, M., & Sapsford, D. (1996). Foreign Direct Investment and Growth in EP and IS Countries. *Economic Journal, 106*(434), 92–105.

Banalieva, E. R. (2014). Embracing the Second Best? Synchronization of Reform Speeds, Excess High Discretion Slack, and Performance of Transition Economy Firms. *Global Strategy Journal, 4*(2), 104–126.

Bassanini, A., & Duval, R. (2009). Unemployment, Institutions, and Reform Complementarities: Re-assessing the Aggregate Evidence for OECD Countries. *Oxford Review of Economic Policy, 25*(1), 40–59.

Berger, H., & Danninger, S. (2007). The Employment Effects of Labor and Product Market Deregulation and Their Implications for Structural Reform. *IMF Staff Papers, 54*(3), 591–619.

Bloom, N., Schweiger, H., & Van Reenen, J. (2012). The Land That Lean Manufacturing Forgot? Management Practices in Transition Countries. *Economics of Transition, 20*(4), 593–635.

Bumann, S., Hermes, N., & Lensink, R. (2013). Financial liberalization and Economic Growth: A Meta-analysis. *Journal of International Money and Finance, 33*, 255–281.

Cacciatore, M., Duval, R., Fiori, G., & Ghironi, F. (2016). Short-term Pain for Long-Term Gain: Market Deregulation and Monetary Policy in Small Open Economies. *Journal of International Money and Finance, 68*, 358–385.

Calderón, C., & Fuentes, R. (2006). Complementarities between Institutions and Openness in Economic Development: Evidence for a Panel of Countries. *Cuadernos de Economía, 43*(127), 49–80.

Campos, N. F., & Coricelli, A. (2002). Growth in Transition: What We Know, What We Don't, and What We Should. *Journal of Economic Literature, 40*(3), 793–836.

Chang, R., Kaltani, L., & Loayza, N. V. (2009). Openness can be Good for Growth: The Role of Policy Complementarities. *Journal of Development Economics, 90*(1), 33–49.

Claessens, S., Demirgüç-Kunt, A., & Huizinga, H. (2001). How Does Foreign Entry Affect Domestic Banking Markets? *Journal of Banking and Finance, 25*(5), 891–911.

Coe, D. T., & Snower, D. J. (1997). Policy Complementarities: The Case for Fundamental Labor Market Reform. *IMF Staff Papers, 44*(1), 1–35.

Coricelli, F., & Maurel, M. (2011). Growth and Crisis in Transition: A Comparative Perspective. *Review of International Economics, 19*(1), 49–64.

Dennis, A. (2006). Trade Liberalization, Factor Market Flexibility, and Growth: The Case of Morocco and Tunisia. *World Bank Policy Research Working Paper 3857.*

Di Tommaso, M. L., Raiser, M., & Weeks, M. (2007). Home Grown or Imported? Initial Conditions, External Anchors and the Determinants of Institutional Reform in the Transition Economies. *Economic Journal, 117*(520), 858–881.

Douarin, E., & Mickiewicz, T. (2017). Transition as Institutional Change. In *Economics of Institutional Change: Central and Eastern Europe Revisited* (pp. 279–296). Cham: Palgrave Macmillan.

Égert, B. (2018). Regulation, Institutions and Aggregate Investment: New Evidence from OECD Countries. *Open Economies Review, 29*(2), 415–449.

Eichengreen, B. (2001). Capital Account Liberalization: What do Cross-Country Studies Tell Us? *World Bank Economic Review, 15*(3), 341–365.

Eichengreen, B., Gullapalli, R., & Panizza, U. (2011). Capital Account Liberalization, Financial Development and Industry Growth: A Synthetic View. *Journal of International Money and Finance, 30*(6), 1090–1106.

Estrin, S., Hanousek, J., Kocenda, E., & Svejnar, J. (2009). The Effects of Privatization and Ownership in Transition Economies. *Journal of Economic Literature, 47*(3), 699–728.

Fiori, G., Nicoletti, G., Scarpetta, S., & Schiantarelli, F. (2012). Employment Outcomes and the Interaction between Product and Labor Market Deregulation: Are They Substitutes or Complements?'. *Economic Journal, 122*(558), 79–104.

Foster, E., & Sonnenschein, H. (1970). Price Distortion and Economic Welfare. *Econometrica, 38*(2), 281–297.

Freund, C., & Bolaky, B. (2008). Trade, Regulations, and Income. *Journal of Development Economics, 87*(2), 309–321.

Gallego, F., & Loayza, N. (2002). The Golden Period for Growth in Chile: Explanations and Forecasts. In N. Loayza & R. Soto (Eds.), *Economic Growth: Sources, Trends, and Cycles* (pp. 417–463). Santiago, Chile: Central Bank of Chile.

Gates, S., Milgrom, P., & Roberts, J. (1996). Complementarities in the Transition from Socialism: A Firm-Level Analysis. In J. McMillan & B. Naughton (Eds.), *Reforming Asian Socialism: The Growth of Market Institutions* (pp. 17–37). Ann Arbor: University of Michigan Press.

Giannetti, M., & Ongena, S. (2012). Lending by Example: Direct and Indirect Effects of Foreign Banks in Emerging Markets. *Journal of International Economics, 86*(1), 167–180.

Gu, X., & Dong, B. (2011). A Theory of Financial Liberalisation: Why Are Developing Countries So Reluctant? *The World Economy, 34*(7), 1106–1123.

Hagedoorn, J., & Wang, N. (2012). Is There Complementarity or Substitutability between Internal and External R&D Strategies? *Research Policy, 41*(6), 1072–1083.

Hausmann, R., Rodrik, D., & Velasco, A. (2008). Growth Diagnostics. In J. Stiglitz & N. Serra (Eds.), *The Washington Consensus Reconsidered: Towards a New Global Governance*. New York: Oxford University Press.

Havrylyshyn, O. (2006). *Divergent Paths in Post Communist Transformation: Capitalism for All or Capitalism for the Few?* Houndsmills, UK: Palgrave Macmillan.

Havrylyshyn, O., & van Rooden, R. (2003). Institutions Matter in Transition, But So Do Policies. *Comparative Economic Studies, 45*(1), 2–24.

Iwasaki, I., & Kumo, K. (2019). J-curve in Transition Economies: A Large Meta-analysis of the Determinants of Output Changes. *Comparative Economic Studies, 61*(1), 149–191.

Iwasaki, I., & Mizobata, S. (2018). Post-privatization Ownership and Firm Performance: A Large Meta-analysis of the Transition Literature. *Annals of Public and Cooperative Economics, 89*(2), 263–322.

Jordà, Ò. (2005). Estimation and Inference of Impulse Responses by Local Projections. *American Economic Review, 95*(1), 161–182.

Katz, B., & Owen, J. (1993). Privatization: Choosing the Optimal Time Path. *Journal of Comparative Economics, 17*(4), 715–736.

Klein, M. W., & Olivei, G. P. (2008). Capital Account Liberalization, Financial Depth, and Economic Growth. *Journal of International Money and Finance, 27*(6), 861–875.

Kohpaiboon, A. (2006). Foreign Direct Investment and Technology Spillover: A Cross-industry Analysis of Thai Manufacturing. *World Development, 34*(3), 541–556.

Kornai, J. (1994). Transformational Recession: The Main Causes. *Journal of Comparative Economics, 19*(1), 39–63.

Kornai, J. (2001). Hardening the Budget Constraint: The Experience of the Post-socialist Countries. *European Economic Review, 45*(9), 1573–1599.

Li, W. (1999). A Tale of Two Reforms. *RAND Journal of Economics, 30*(1), 120–136.

Lipsey, R. G., & Lancaster, K. (1956). The General Theory of Second Best. *Review of Economic Studies, 24*(1), 11–32.

Macedo, J. B. de, & Oliveira Martins, J. (2008). Growth, Reform Indicators and Policy Complementarities. *Economics of Transition, 16*(2), 141–164.

Macedo, J. B., Oliveira Martins, J., & da Rocha, B. T. (2014). Are Complementary Reforms a "Luxury" for Developing Countries? *Journal of Comparative Economics, 42*(2), 417–435.

Makki, S. S., & Somwaru, A. (2004). Impact of Foreign Direct Investment and Trade on Economic Growth: Evidence from Developing Countries. *American Journal of Agricultural Economics, 86*(3), 795–801.

Manlagnit, M. (2011). The Economic Effects of Foreign Bank Presence: Evidence from the Philippines. *Journal of International Money and Finance, 30*(6), 1180–1194.

Martin, P., & Rey, H. (2006). Globalization and Emerging Markets: With or Without Crash? *American Economic Review, 96*(5), 1631–1651.

Milgrom, P., & Roberts, J. (1995). Complementarities and Fit Strategy, Structure, and Organizational Change in Manufacturing. *Journal of Accounting and Economics, 19*(2–3), 179–208.

Mohnen, P., & Röller, L. H. (2005). Complementarities in Innovation Policy. *European Economic Review, 49*(6), 1431–1450.

Neary, J. P. (2009). Trade Costs and Foreign Direct Investment. *International Review of Economics and Finance, 18*(2), 207–218.

OECD. (2000). *OECD Economic Surveys: Baltic States, a Regional Economic Assessment*. Paris.

OECD. (2002). *OECD Economic Surveys: Romania*. Paris.

Oliveira Martins, J., & Price, T. (2000). Policy Interdependence during Economic Transition: The Case of Slovakia 1999–2000. *OECD Economics Department Working Papers 253*.

Orszag, M., & Snower, D. (1998). Anatomy of Policy Complementarities. *Swedish Economic Policy Review, 5*(2), 303–343.

Prasad, E., & Rajan, R. G. (2008). A Pragmatic Approach to Capital Account Liberalization. *Journal of Economic Perspectives, 22*(3), 149–172.

Punthakey, J. (2014). Exploring Policy Complementarities in Transition Economies: The Case of Kazakhstan. *OECD Regional Development Working Papers, 2014/09.*

Qian, Y. (1994). A Theory of Shortage in Socialist Economies Based on the Soft Budget Constraint. *American Economic Review, 84*(1), 145–156.

Restuccia, D., & Rogerson, R. (2017). The Causes and Costs of Misallocation. *Journal of Economic Perspectives, 31*(3), 151–174.

Rocha, B. T. da. (2015). Let the Markets Begin: The Interplay between Free Prices and Privatisation in Early Transition. *Journal of Comparative Economics, 43*(2), 350–370.

Rocha, B. T. da. (2019). *Structural Reforms as a System: Complementarities between Trade Openness, Capital Account Liberalisation, and Banking Sector Reform.* Paper presented at the Annual Development Economics and Policy Conference (Research Group on Development Economics, German Economic Association), June 2019, Berlin.

Rodrik, D. (2006). Goodbye Washington Consensus, Hello Washington Confusion? A Review of the World Bank's Economic Growth in the 1990s: Learning from a Decade of Reform. *Journal of Economic Literature, 44*(4), 973–987.

Roland, G. (2000). *Transition and Economics: Politics, Markets, and Firms.* Cambridge and London: MIT Press.

Sonin, K. (2013). The End of Economic Transition. *Economics of Transition, 21*(1), 1–10.

Staehr, K. (2005). Reforms and Economic Growth in Transition Economies: Complementarity, Sequencing and Speed. *European Journal of Comparative Economics, 2*(2), 177–202.

Taboada, A. G. (2011). The Impact of Changes in Bank Ownership Structure on the Allocation of Capital: International Evidence. *Journal of Banking and Finance, 35*(10), 2528–2543.

Topkis, D. M. (1998). *Supermodularity and Complementarity.* Princeton, NJ: Princeton University Press.

Wolf, H. (1999). Transition Strategies: Choices and Outcomes. *Princeton Studies in International Finance 85.* Princeton, NJ: Princeton University Press.

Zinnes, C., Eilat, Y., & Sachs, J. (2001). The Gains from Privatization in Transition Economies: Is "Change of Ownership" Enough? *IMF Staff Papers, 48*(1), 146–170.

20

Democracy as a Driver of Post-Communist Economic Development

Jan Fidrmuc

1   Introduction

Formerly communist countries pursued a variety of reform paths. The political changes they went through were precipitated by economic stagnation throughout the Eastern Bloc countries during the 1980s, and made possible by the *perestroika* and *glasnost* initiatives introduced by Mikhail Gorbachev in the Soviet Union in the second half of the 1980s. This has led to (largely) peaceful protests in Central and Eastern Europe (the only exception to the peaceful nature of the protests being Romania), similarly peaceful pro-independence movements in the Baltics, as well as interethnic strife in the

J. Fidrmuc (✉)
Lille Économie & Management (L.E.M), Université de Lille, Lille, France

PRIGO University, Havířov, Czechia

Institute for Strategy and Analysis (ISA), Government Office of the Slovak Republic, Bratislava, Slovakia

CESifo, Munich, Germany

Rimini Centre for Economic Analysis (RCEA), Rimini, Italy

Global Labor Organization (GLO), Geneva, Switzerland
e-mail: jan.fidrmuc@gmail.com

© The Author(s) 2021
E. Douarin, O. Havrylyshyn (eds.), *The Palgrave Handbook of Comparative Economics*,
https://doi.org/10.1007/978-3-030-50888-3_20

former Yugoslavia and parts of the Soviet Union (such as the secessionist conflicts in Azerbaijan, Georgia and Moldova). Initially, most communist countries seemed to embrace political liberalization. In the course of 1989, Hungarian and Polish governments entered into negotiations with the opposition, the Soviet Union and Poland held partially free elections, the Berlin Wall fell, and Communist-led governments from the Baltic states and Poland in the North to Bulgaria and Albania in the South agreed to relinquish power in free and fair elections. In the next two years, political liberalization continued, with free elections and transfers of power in a number of countries. In 1991, the Soviet Union kicked the bucket, followed by Yugoslavia in 1992. The main exceptions were the communist countries outside of the broader European space: China, Vietnam, Cuba and North Korea. These continue to subscribe to the Communist ideology and have remained under the formal and unchallenged rule of their Communist Parties.

Alongside political liberalization, formerly communist countries also undertook wide-ranging economic reforms. They abandoned central planning, price controls and exclusive public ownership of productive assets and introduced elements of the market economy (in some cases gradually and slowly, in other instances in rapid and big-bang fashion). Even the countries that shied away from political liberalization did embrace economic reforms: China started to liberalize its economy as early as 1978, shortly after the death of Mao Zedong. Cuba and North Korea eventually also introduced limited elements of market exchange and allowed some private enterprise.

The simultaneous implementation of political and economic reforms in most formerly communist countries was unprecedented: in the previous instances of successful economic transitions, pro-reform governments maintained a high degree of autocratic control while the reforms were being implemented. Indeed, Przeworski (2005) argues that no low-income country has succeeded in introducing and maintaining democracy, with the sole exception of India. All other instances of successful democratizations were countries that first brought their economies on a path toward prosperity and attained a moderate level of economic development, and only introduced political changes later. Examples of such successful economic-reform-first-democracy-later transitions are Chile, Taiwan and Singapore. The economic performance of China also seems to fit this pattern: since the onset of economic reforms in 1978, it has experienced four decades of almost uninterrupted growth. This relationship between economic development and the ability to sustain democracy has been generalized in the so-called *Lipset Hypothesis*: countries need to become sufficiently well-off before they are able to successfully introduce and sustain democracy (Lipset 1959).

The experience of the post-communist countries seems to be in line with the Lipset Hypothesis: a number of countries, especially those with low- or moderate-income levels at the outset of transition, experienced setbacks and reversals in their political development. Following the first (fully or partially) free elections in the early 1990s, post-communist governments from Belarus to Kazakhstan re-introduced elements of autocracy and authoritarian rule. In some countries, the head of state has stayed the same since the early or mid 1990s (Belarus), is a direct descendant of the first post-Soviet ruler (Azerbaijan), or a hand-picked successor (Kazakhstan, Turkmenistan and Uzbekistan). Even in Russia, which outwardly subscribes to the notion of holding free elections and has an active civic society and opposition, Vladimir Putin has held the reins of power firmly for the last two decades. Other countries maintained largely free elections but political developments were strongly influenced by newly emerged interest groups or members of the former elites: Ukraine, Moldova, Armenia, Georgia and Serbia could be placed in this group.

In contrast, the countries in Central and South-Eastern Europe, which were more developed at the outset of reforms, have largely maintained their commitment to democracy, despite some setbacks (such the conflicts that followed the break-up of Yugoslavia in the early and mid 1990s) and deviations (such as Slovakia in the mid 1990s and Poland and Hungary in the late 2010s). Most of these countries went on to become middle-income or high-income economies and are currently either members of the EU or candidates for membership. Three decades after the post-communist changes began, 11 out of 27 EU member states are former communist countries.

This raises the question whether economic development of the post-communist countries was helped or hindered by the adoption of democracy. Figures 20.1 and 20.2 depict the evolution of output per person in the 35 countries that have a legacy of being ruled by a communist regime in the past (regardless of whether they are still ruled by a Communist Party at present). The countries are divided into two groups based on output per person (in 2010 prices) in 2018. Figure 20.1 presents the 18 countries in the lower (approximately) half of the distribution of output per person in 2018 (or the latest year for which data are available). Figure 20.2 presents the 17 countries forming the upper half of the distribution. Both groups share the same basic patterns. The early 1990s were marked by falling in output per person.[1] This output fall at the beginning of the post-communist transition was labeled

---

[1] The East Asian countries—China, Vietnam, Laos and Cambodia—show different pattern, with no output fall. Economic reforms in these countries started earlier (1978 in the case of China), and were much more gradual (see Roland 2000).

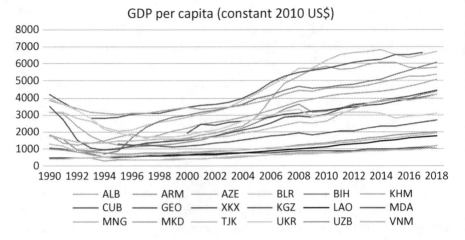

Fig. 20.1 Evolution of output per person, low-output group. (Notes: Level of output per person, in constant 2010 US$. Countries included here are those in the lower half of the distribution of output per person in 2018 (of in the latest year for which data are available))

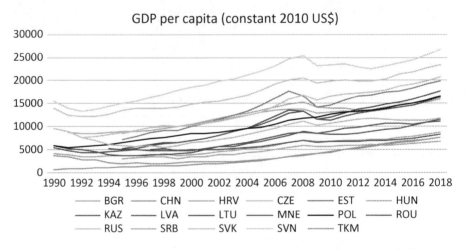

Fig. 20.2 Evolution of output per person, high-output group. (Notes: Level of output per person, in constant 2010 US$. Countries included here are those in the upper half of the distribution of output per person in 2018 (of in the latest year for which data are available))

transformational recession (Kornai 2004). It was caused by the disorganization associated with changes in the economic system, end of central planning and price controls, transfer of ownership, and the fall in demand (including, most notably, fall in investment) that these profound changes precipitated. In some cases, the period of output fall was relatively short-lived (e.g. Poland, Hungary,

Czech Republic), though in some cases it was rather steep (Albania). The output fall was followed by a recovery. Some countries saw their output increase several fold (note however that data for the early 1990s are missing for several countries so that the starting points are not always the same). Some of the most impressive results have been reported by countries that started from a relatively low point: China saw its output per person increase more than tenfold, and Vietnam and Laos approximately 4 times. Bosnia, whose economy was particularly adversely affected by the civil conflict in the 1990s, made up for the war-inflicted loss by increasing its level of economic development more than 8 times. Nevertheless, impressive growth performance was not limited only to countries with a low starting point or those afflicted by conflict: Albania, Estonia, Latvia, Lithuania, Poland and Slovakia all saw their output per person rising approximately threefold. In contrast, according to official statistics, the level of economic development in Kyrgystan, Tajikistan and Ukraine in 2018 is below the starting point from 1990, while Russia, despite its vast mineral wealth, has only increased its output per person by about a quarter.[2]

Figures 20.3 and 20.4 present the evolution of democracy for the same two groups of countries. Democracy is measured by the average Freedom House Index (see next section for detailed explanation) which ranges from 1 (no democracy) to 7 (full democracy). For comparison, Figs. 20.5 and 20.6 show the evolution in the Index of Economic Freedom (compiled by the Heritage Foundation, see next section). Both groups of countries show evidence of substantial political and economic liberalization,[3] but both subsamples also include countries that largely shied away from substantial political and economic reforms. The overall pattern is summarized in Fig. 20.7, which shows the ratio in output per person in 2018 (or the latest year for which data are available) and 1990 (or the earliest available year) on the vertical axis, and the ratio of the levels of democracy in 2017 and 1989 (the year that preceded the beginning of fundamental political and economic reforms in most countries). The relationship between democratic improvement and economic development is almost flat, with a hint of hump-shaped curvature. In other words,

---

[2] Estimates of economic performance based on the official statistics can be misleading (this is also mentioned by Havrylyshyn, in Chap.10 of this volume). This is because Soviet era national accounts were based on Net Material Product, whereas the subsequent statistics measure GDP. Because of the differences between these two measures, the official statistics may considerably understate the increase in income and wellbeing. More direct measures of consumption generally show much greater improvements in living standards than the official statistics.

[3] In the graphs of political and economic freedom, the extent of freedom is depicted by the width of the band corresponding to each country.

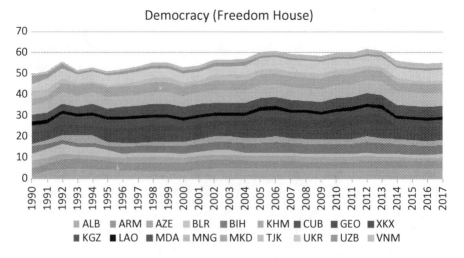

Fig. 20.3 Evolution of democracy (Freedom House Index), low-output group. (Notes: The graph depicts the level of the democracy index (Freedom House) in each country and each year. The width of each country's band reflects the index value (wider band means more democracy). The bands are stacked up for better readability, to avoid overlapping lines for countries with similar levels of democracy. The countries included are the same as those in Fig. 20.1)

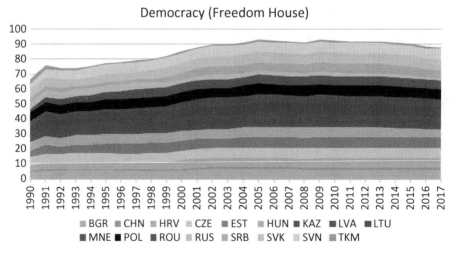

Fig. 20.4 Evolution of democracy (Freedom House Index), high-output group. (Notes: The graph depicts the level of the democracy index (Freedom House) in each country and each year. The width of each country's band reflects the index value (wider band means more democracy). The bands are stacked up for better readability, to avoid overlapping lines for countries with similar levels of democracy. The countries included are the same as those in Fig. 20.2)

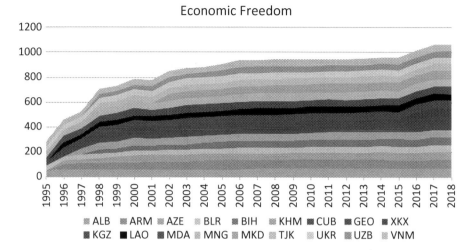

Fig. 20.5 Evolution of economic freedom, low-output group. (Notes: The graph depicts the level of the economic freedom index (Heritage Foundation) in each country and each year. The width of each country's band reflects the index value (wider band means more economic freedom). The bands are stacked up for better readability, to avoid overlapping lines for countries with similar levels of economic freedom. The countries included are the same as those in Fig. 20.1)

countries that implemented the most dramatic changes in terms of political liberalization were not rewarded by greatest gains in economic development. Rather, their performance is overshadowed by countries that were reluctant to embrace democratic reforms, such as the South-East Asian countries. This seems to give support to those advocating pursuing economic reforms first and leaving off democratization until a later stage (or not undertaking it at all).

The weak relationship between democracy and economic prosperity mirrors earlier findings in the literature: Barro (1996), Helliwell (1994), Przeworski and Limongi (1993), de Haan and Siermann (1995), Baum and Lake (2003), Doucouliagos and Ulubasoglu (2008), among others, find that this relationship is insignificant, hump-shaped or even negative (the latter implying that democratization should lower growth performance). Tavares and Wacziarg (2001) conclude that this is because democracy improves some factors that boost growth (such as human capital) but causes a deterioration in others (such as lowering the accumulation of physical capital and raising the size of government). Similarly, Giavazzi and Tabellini (2005) conclude that it is economic liberalization rather than political reforms that bring about better economic performance. In contrast, Fidrmuc (2003) argues that among post-communist countries, democratization served as catalyst of economic

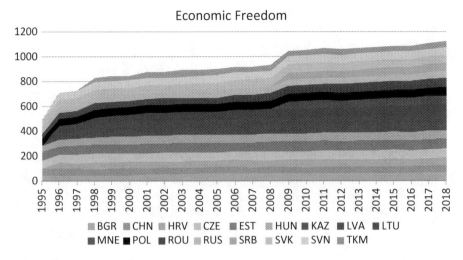

Fig. 20.6 Evolution of economic freedom, high-output group. (Notes: The graph depicts the level of the economic freedom index (Heritage Foundation) in each country and each year. The width of each country's band reflects the index value (wider band means more economic freedom). The bands are stacked up for better readability, to avoid overlapping lines for countries with similar levels of economic freedom. The countries included are the same as those in Fig. 20.2)

reforms, so that countries that progressed further in terms of political liberalization benefitted through faster growth. This finding is also confirmed by Doucouliagos and Ulubasoglu (2008), whose meta-analysis finds that democracy lead to both higher economic freedom and lower political instability.

In this chapter, I revisit the question of the impact of democracy on growth. Although the analysis is motivated by the specific experience of the post-communist countries, I also present results obtained with a global sample encompassing all countries for which relevant data are available. In the next section, I introduce the data and methodology used in the analysis. Section 3 discusses the results on the relationship between democracy and economic growth. However, growth is not the only outcome of interest that can be influenced by the level of democracy. Democracy increases transparency and reduces economic uncertainty. Therefore, it can also lead to increases in investment in physical and/or human capital. Higher investment should, in turn, lead to faster economic growth. Democracy can thus raise living standards either directly, by raising growth, or indirectly, through its impact on capital (which then raises growth). This possibility is considered in Section 4. The final section summarizes the findings and offers a few concluding lessons.

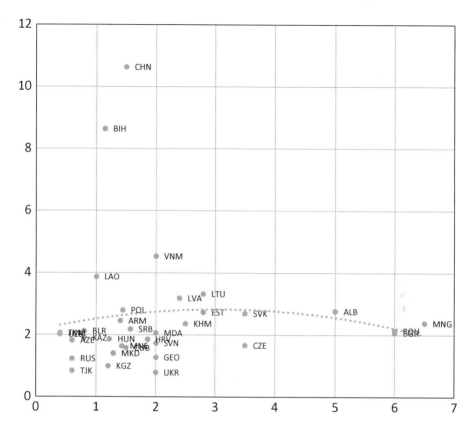

Fig. 20.7 Relative Changes of Output per Person and Democracy since 1990. (Notes: Change of output per person between 2018 (2017 for Cuba) and 1990 (or the earliest available year) is on the vertical axis, while change in the Freedom House Index 2017/1989 is on the horizontal axis. Both changes are computed as ratios. Output series starts in 1990, except for Bosnia (1994), Cambodia (1993), Croatia (1995), Estonia (1995), Latvia (1994), Lithuania (1995), Moldova (1995), Montenegro (1997), Serbia (1995) and Slovakia (1992))

2   Data and Methodology

The analysis is based on a standard model of growth estimated with annual data (see Mankiw et al. 1992; Islam 1995). The analysis draws on data from four main sources. First, economic statistics are from the 2019 version of the World Bank's World Development Indicators;[4] Gross Domestic Product (GDP) per capita (in constant 2010 US$), gross fixed capital formation (as percentage of GDP), and population growth. The main outcome variable is

---

[4] See http://datatopics.worldbank.org/world-development-indicators/.

the growth rate of GDP per capita. As an additional measure of economic success, I also use the life expectancy at birth (for both genders).

Two indexes of democracy are commonly used in the literature, the one constructed by the Polity IV Project,[5] and the Freedom House Index.[6] Polity IV constructs two basic indexes, of democracy and autocracy, each of which ranges from 0 to 10. These two are combined into a summary measure, referred to as Polity 2, which subtracts autocracy from democracy. The resulting measure thus ranges from a minimum of –10 (for the most autocratic and least democratic political regimes) to 10 (fully democratic regime free of autocracy). The Polity 2 measure is available from 1800 (or from the time the country acquired independence if it only emerged later), with missing values for periods of major disruptions, foreign occupations and the like.

Freedom House is a non-governmental organization that monitors and evaluates the state of political rights and civil liberties across the globe. The resulting indexes range in value from 1 (fully free) to 7 (not free at all). I use the average of both indexes with a reversed scale for the sake of intuitiveness (so that higher values correspond to more democracy). The Freedom House Index is available annually from 1972.

Economic freedom is measured using the Index of Economic Freedom compiled by the Heritage Foundation.[7] I use the overall index, which summarizes progress in the various areas for which the Heritage Foundation measures the extent of economic freedom. This overall index is constructed to range from 1 to 100. The downside of this index is that it is only available from 1995 onwards. Crucially, this results in the early part of the post-communist transition being left out of the analyses entailing economic freedom. There are alternative indexes of economic freedom, such as the Progress in Transition indicators published by the European Bank for Reconstruction and Development (EBRD), but those are not available for a sufficiently broad sample of countries.

Both democracy indexes are available only for countries in their contemporaneous definitions. Therefore, the values for the Soviet Union, Yugoslavia and Czechoslovakia are used for the successor countries of these unions for the period before independence. Although there may have been some local differences, the same political and economic system applied throughout these three multinational unions. West German values are used for all of Germany for the period before unification because East Germany adopted the West

---

[5] https://www.systemicpeace.org/polity/polity4.htm.

[6] https://freedomhouse.org/.

[7] https://www.heritage.org/index/.

German political and legal system when the two countries merged. Since the Heritage Foundation only publishes its index from 1995 onwards, this problem does not arise with respect to the Index of Economic Freedom. Finally, pre-independence economic data are only used when such data are reported in the World Development Indicators.

For the sake of comparability, political and economic freedom indexes are rescaled so that they range from 0 (not free) to 1 (completely free). The various indexes of political and economic freedoms display rather high correlation with each other. This makes including all of them in the same regression potentially problematic: the estimated coefficients could change depending on which other variables are included. A possible solution to this is to use principal component analysis (PCA) to combine the Polity 2 Index, average Freedom House Index and Index of Economic Freedom. PCA is a statistical technique that transforms mutually correlated variables into a set of uncorrelated *principal components*, each of which is a linear combination of the original variables. With n original variables, the PCA yields n uncorrelated principal components. Each successive component, however, explains a lower share of the variation in the original variables. A commonly used rule of thumb on deciding which principal component to use is based on each principal component's eigenvalue: if the eigenvalue is greater than unity, then the principal component is retained. The first eigenvalue is 2.337, followed by 0.565 and 0.098. The first principal component explains 78% of the variation in the data, and is positively correlated with all three indexes: the component loadings for Polity 2, Heritage Index and Freedom House Index (all rescaled to vary between 0 and 1) are 0.597, 0.502 and 0.626, respectively. The PCA thus yields one principal component, which is henceforth referred to as Principal Component 1. The advantage is that this approach collapses all three indexes into one weighted index. The downside, however, is the limited availability of the Heritage Index, so that the Principal Component 1 can only be constructed for the period from 1995 onwards.

If democracy has an effect on economic growth and economic outcomes in general, this effect should occur by altering people's behavior. Democratic countries tend to have effective law and order systems, offer better protection of property rights and contract enforcement, and have fair and unbiased court systems. Corruption and nepotism tend to be less rife too. All of this encourages people to invest their time and resources in value creation and wealth accumulation rather than in rent seeking and in protecting their wealth from rent seeking and predation by others. This has several implications. First, democracy encourages individuals and firms to engage in economic exchange: outcomes of such exchanges are less uncertain in a democratic regime with a fair and independent judiciary and effective law and order system. This decrease in economic uncertainty should foster economic growth directly. Second, democracy encourages investment in physical capital: in the absence of democracy, investment is associated with greater risk that the future returns will be captured by predatory governments or rent seekers. This also helps boost growth, but indirectly: greater investment in physical capital translates into higher growth in the future. Finally, once democracy is introduced, the effects may not occur straight away: people may need some time to accept the changes in the political and institutional environment and learn how to behave in the new regime. Therefore, the duration of democracy may be even more important than its current level.

To account for the role played by the tradition of democracy, I create a variable that I denote *democratic capital*. This is a measure reflecting democracy accumulated and sustained over a period of time. Specifically, I treat the annual level of democracy as investments in democratic capital. In this way, democratic capital in country j at time t can be expressed as

$$DK_{jt} = DK_{jt-1}(1-\theta) + I_{jt-1} \tag{20.1}$$

where DK_{jt} stands for the stock of democratic capital, I_{jt} is the annual investment (i.e. the value of the index) and θ is the annual depreciation rate of democratic capital, reflecting how quickly it would dissipate without further investments.[8] Then, applying the perpetual inventory method, a country with a stable value of the democracy index, $\overline{I}$, will converge to a steady-state value of democratic capital:

$$DK_{j\infty} = \overline{I}\Big/\theta. \tag{20.2}$$

Furthermore, the higher is the depreciation rate, the less past realizations of democracy matter and hence convergence to this steady-state value is correspondingly faster. I use $\theta = 0.2$ (i.e. 20% depreciation rate). This means that a country that experiences any change in its level of democracy will approach the new steady-state level of democratic capital in approximately one generation (around 25 years, faster if the change is relatively modest).

The same formula could in principle be used also to estimate the initial value of democratic capital for each country for the years not covered by the

---

[8] Persson and Tabellini (2009) follow a similar approach but choose a lower depreciation value and include also spatial effects in their measure.

data. However, that would assume that the level of democracy in preceding years was stable. The Freedom House Index is available from 1972 and the Polity 2 from 1800. As the analysis only concerns the period from 1990 onwards, my estimate of democratic capital should be close to the *steady-state* value for any country for which data are available at least from the 1970s. I therefore omit countries with data starting in 1980 or later, or those that have breaks in the series of democracy. Given that the Index of Economic Freedom is only available from 1995, no similar stock variable can be constructed for economic freedom.

The empirical model takes the following form:

$$\Delta \ln y_{jt} = \beta_0 + \beta_1 \ln y_{jt-1} + \beta_2 \ln s_{jt} + \beta_3 \ln\left(\delta + n_{jt} + g\right)$$
$$+ \beta_4 \omega_{jt-1} + \mu_j + \varepsilon_{jt} \tag{20.3}$$

where y_{jt-1} stands for output per person, s_{jt} is the ratio of investment in physical capital to output, $\delta + n_{jt} + g$ is the sum of depreciation rate of physical capital, population growth rate and the rate of technological progress (since depreciation and technological progress are not observed, I follow Mankiw et al. 1992, and assume that together they are equal to 0.05), and ω_{jt-1} is a measure of political or economic freedom or democratic capital. The political/economic freedom and democratic capital measures are lagged. This is because political/economic reforms may take some time to affect economic performance, and also to diminish the possibility of endogeneity bias due to reverse causality from economic development to institutional quality. All equations are estimated with country-specific fixed effects and robust standard errors.

Table 20.1 presents the descriptive values for all countries included in the data set, for the period from 1990 to 2018. Table 20.2 shows corresponding figures only for the post-communist countries. Tables 20.3 and 20.4 show correlation matrixes for the same two sets of countries. The indexes of political and economic freedoms, and also both democratic capital variables, are strongly correlated with output per person, which is in line with the Lipset Hypothesis. In contrast, the correlation with economic growth is close to 0: if political or economic freedom have an impact on growth, this is not readily apparent from correlation coefficients.[9] The two democracy indexes are strongly correlated with each other, and both are also robustly correlated with economic freedom; the correlations between democracy and economic

---

[9] Note that the empirical analysis below utilizes growth of per capita output computed as log-difference of output rather than percentage growth.

Table 20.1 Descriptive statistics: all countries

Variable	N	Mean	Std. Dev.	Min	Max
GDP pc growth (log difference)	5679	0.018	0.061	−1.050	0.877
GDP pc growth (annual %)	5679	0.021	0.062	−0.650	1.404
GDP pc (constant 2010 US$)	5726	13,429	20,434	164	193,746
Investment (GFCF, % of GDP)	4707	0.223	0.075	−0.024	0.680
Population growth (annual %)	6485	0.015	0.016	−0.110	0.175
Life expectancy at birth, total (years)	5775	68.267	9.749	26.172	85.417
Polity 2	4850	3.013	6.651	−10.000	10.000
Index of Economic Freedom (heritage)	4058	59.361	11.739	1.000	90.500
Freedom House Index (reversed scale)	5567	4.519	2.004	1.000	7.000
Polity 2 (rescaled)	4850	0.651	0.333	0.000	1.000
Economic freedom (rescaled)	4058	0.594	0.117	0.010	0.905
Freedom House (rescaled)	5567	0.586	0.334	0.000	1.000
Principal component 1	3418	0.000	1.529	−4.878	2.471
Democratic capital (polity)	4858	3.017	1.658	0.000	5.000
Democratic capital (Freedom House)	5310	2.693	1.603	0.000	5.000

Notes: Data refer to period 1990–2018. All countries for which data are available. Principal component 1 (PC 1) is the first principal component of Polity 2, Freedom House Index and Economic Freedom. GFCF refers to Gross Fixed Capital Formation

Table 20.2 Descriptive statistics: post-communist countries

Variable	N	Mean	Std. Dev.	Min	Max
GDP pc growth (log difference)	892	0.028	0.076	−0.604	0.653
GDP pc growth (annual %)	892	0.032	0.075	−0.453	0.922
GDP pc (constant 2010 US$)	913	5951	5443	321	26,759
Investment (GFCF, % of GDP)	860	0.237	0.074	0.026	0.577
Population growth (annual %)	1019	0.003	0.012	−0.110	0.078
Life expectancy at birth, total (years)	977	70.620	4.729	52.935	81.176
Polity 2	977	2.131	7.211	−10.000	10.000
Index of Economic Freedom (heritage)	773	55.234	13.698	1.000	79.100
Freedom House Index (reversed scale)	986	3.907	2.045	1.000	7.000
Polity 2 (rescaled)	977	0.607	0.361	0.000	1.000
Economic freedom (rescaled)	773	0.552	0.137	0.010	0.791
Freedom House (rescaled)	986	0.484	0.341	0.000	1.000
Principal component 1	685	−0.365	1.813	−4.878	2.181
Democratic capital (polity)	968	2.631	1.684	0.001	4.995
Democratic capital (Freedom House)	1020	2.091	1.552	0.000	4.980

Notes: Data refer to period 1990–2018. Only post-communist countries. Principal component 1 (PC 1) is the first principal component of Polity 2, Freedom House Index and Economic Freedom

Table 20.3 Correlation matrix: all countries

	Grow	GDP	Inv	Popgr	Lifep	P2	IEW	FH	P1	DKP2
Growth (Δlog)	1									
GDP pc	−0.12	1								
Investment	0.243	−0.01	1							
Pop growth	−0.22	−0.14	−0.03	1						
Life exp	0.026	0.591	0.177	−0.43	1					
Polity 2	−0.02	0.329	−0.04	−0.4	0.378	1				
IEW	−0.06	0.605	0.106	−0.14	0.551	0.463	1			
FH	−0.02	0.508	−0.01	−0.4	0.489	0.887	0.611	1		
PC 1	−0.03	0.532	0.016	−0.37	0.527	0.913	0.752	0.962	1	
DK p2	−0.03	0.389	−0.03	−0.4	0.45	0.951	0.502	0.883	0.904	1
DK fh	−0.05	0.552	−0.01	−0.39	0.528	0.867	0.641	0.965	0.949	0.917

Notes: Data refer to period 1990–2018. All countries for which data are available. Principal component 1 (PC 1) is the first principal component of Polity 2, Freedom House Index and Economic Freedom

Table 20.4 Correlation matrix: post-communist countries

	Grow	GDP	Inv	Popgr	Lifep	P2	IEW	FH	P1	DKP2
Growth (Δlog)	1									
GDP pc	−0.173	1								
Investment	0.259	−0.035	1							
Pop growth	0.020	−0.266	0.176	1						
Life exp	−0.164	0.598	−0.096	−0.279	1					
Polity 2	−0.203	0.503	−0.137	−0.481	0.339	1				
IEW	−0.058	0.526	0.181	−0.241	0.354	0.661	1			
FH	−0.182	0.645	−0.105	−0.477	0.399	0.922	0.679	1		
PC 1	−0.172	0.609	−0.049	−0.454	0.395	0.958	0.815	0.964	1	
DK P2	−0.201	0.545	−0.126	−0.474	0.376	0.968	0.690	0.913	0.949	1
DK fh	−0.190	0.690	−0.106	−0.454	0.435	0.907	0.730	0.970	0.960	0.940

Notes: Data refer to period 1990–2018. Only post-communist countries. Principal component 1 (PC 1) is the first principal component of Polity 2, Freedom House Index and Economic Freedom

freedom are somewhat stronger in the subsample of post-communist countries than in the full sample. Similarly, the two democratic capital variables are also strongly correlated with each other, and both are robustly correlated with economic freedom.

3   Democracy and Growth

As I am mainly interested in the relationship between democracy and economic development in post-communist countries, the analysis is limited to the period from 1990 onwards. However, for the sake of comparability, I present results for all countries and then for post-communist countries separately. When constructing the post-communist subsample, any country with substantial history of communist rule in the past is counted as post-communist, even if it remains formally ruled by a communist party.[10] This is because they were all, at least initially, motivated by the desire to replicate the Soviet economic system based on central planning and tight central regulation (even if their subsequent paths diverged). All regressions are estimated with country-specific fixed effects and with robust standard errors.

Table 20.5 presents the first set of results, with data for all countries (global sample). The first column features the baseline Solow model, that is, without political or economic freedom (ω_{jt-1}). All variables have the expected signs and are significant: economic growth is higher in poorer countries than in richer ones, and depends positively on investment in physical capital and negatively on population growth. In the next three columns, I add the Polity 2, economic freedom and Freedom House indexes (rescaled so that they range between 0 and 1), respectively. Both indexes of democracy (Polity 2 and Freedom House) are positively and significantly associated with economic growth. Both have similarly sized coefficients, suggesting that they indeed measure largely the same underlying concept of political freedom (as is already implied by their high correlation coefficient). In contrast, economic freedom appears to have little impact in the global sample. This last finding is somewhat surprising, given the large literature finding positive association between economic freedom and growth (see Doucouliagos and Ulubasoglu 2006; Williamson and Mathers 2011; Hall and Lawson 2014, among others). This

---

[10] The following countries are considered post-communist: Albania, Armenia, Azerbaijan, Belarus, Bosnia and Herzegovina, Bulgaria, Cambodia, China, Croatia, Cuba, Czech Republic, Estonia, Georgia, Hungary, Kazakhstan, Kosovo, Kyrgyzstan, Laos, Latvia, Lithuania, Moldova, Montenegro, Mongolia, North Macedonia, Poland, Romania, Russia, Serbia, Slovakia, Slovenia, Tajikistan, Turkmenistan, Ukraine, Uzbekistan and Vietnam.

Table 20.5 Economic growth, democracy and economic freedom: all countries

	(1)	(2)	(3)	(4)	(5)	(6)	(7)
	$\Delta \ln y_{jt}$	$\Delta \ln y_{jt}$	$\Delta \ln y_{jt}$	$\Delta \ln y_{jt}$	$\Delta \ln y_{jt}$	$\Delta \ln y_{jt}$	$\Delta \ln y_{jt}$
$\ln y_{jt-1}$	-0.029***	-0.025***	-0.032***	-0.034***	-0.033***	-0.033***	-0.035***
	(0.007)	(0.005)	(0.005)	(0.007)	(0.005)	(0.005)	(0.005)
$\ln s_{jt}$	0.033***	0.032***	0.032***	0.033***	0.032***	0.033***	0.032***
	(0.008)	(0.008)	(0.006)	(0.008)	(0.006)	(0.006)	(0.006)
$\ln(n_{jt} + 0.05)$	-0.047***	-0.054***	-0.058***	-0.054***	-0.066***	-0.059***	-0.066***
	(0.015)	(0.017)	(0.013)	(0.016)	(0.014)	(0.013)	(0.014)
$P2_{jt-1}$		0.036***			0.025**		
		(0.012)			(0.009)		
EFW_{jt-1}			-0.006		-0.008	-0.014	
			(0.026)		(0.026)	(0.026)	
FH_{jt-1}				0.042**		0.029***	
				(0.016)		(0.011)	
$PC1_{jt-1}$							0.007**
							(0.003)
Constant	0.187***	0.106*	0.191***	0.179***	0.152***	0.179***	0.187***
	(0.063)	(0.055)	(0.059)	(0.067)	(0.062)	(0.059)	(0.064)
N	4492	3994	3237	4357	3047	3205	3047
R-squared	0.014	0.025	0.051	0.020	0.060	0.062	0.060
F	9.68***	10.12***	30.07***	9.18***	25.13***	26.57***	32.86***

Notes: Estimated over 1990–2018. All countries for which data are available. P2: Polity 2 Index. EFW: Economic freedom in the world. FH: Freedom House index. All three indexes are rescaled to range between 0 and 1. Estimated with country fixed effects and robust standard errors (in parentheses). Significance: 1% ***, 5% ** and 10% *

pattern is also obtained when either democracy index is entered alongside economic freedom (columns 5–6): the democracy indexes are significant and positive while the economic freedom index remains insignificant. A possible explanation rests in the fact that economic freedom is also robustly associated with investment (Doucouliagos and Ulubasoglu 2006). It is therefore possible that the positive coefficient of investment also picks up the positive effect of economic freedom. Another possibility is that the insignificant coefficient reflects heterogeneity among countries or broader regions: it is possible that economic freedom boosts growth only in some countries (such as the post-communist subsample, discussed below). The final column features the first principal component obtained in principal component analysis on the Polity 2, economic freedom and Freedom House indexes: again, its coefficient is positive and significant (note that the scale of the principal component is different so that the size of this effect cannot be immediately compared with those of the two democracy indexes).

Table 20.6 presents analogous regression results for the post-communist countries only. There are a few differences: investment in physical capital has a stronger association with growth while population growth is only borderline significant. The impact of political freedom is positive but not significant, but economic freedom significantly boosts economic growth, and its impact is approximately double that of democracy in the sample with all countries. The first principal component of political and economic freedoms is again significantly positive, and its effect is also approximately double that obtained in the global sample. It appears therefore that for the economic development of post-communist countries, economic freedom has been more important than political freedom. This would lend support to the approach of countries such as China and Vietnam that liberalized their economies without simultaneously introducing wide-ranging political freedoms.

Next, I replace political freedom by democratic capital, a stock rather than flow variable (Tables 20.7, 20.8). Both democratic capital variables (based on the Polity 2 and Freedom House indexes) are strongly positively associated with economic growth. Note that as democratic capital is accumulated over time, this positive relationship is unlikely to be driven by reverse causality: democratic capital does not reflect the current level of democracy but its history and duration. The positive relationship is robust to introducing economic freedom into the regression (columns 3–4). In the last two columns, I explore the possibility that the effect of democratic capital is non-linear (inverted U-shaped), as suggested by Fig. 20.7. The quadratic term is indeed negative but it is only significant for democratic capital based on the Freedom House Index. However, the turning point, beyond which the effect of higher values

Table 20.6 Economic growth, democracy and economic freedom: post-communist countries

	(1)	(2)	(3)	(4)	(5)	(6)	(7)
	$\Delta \ln y_{jt}$	$\Delta \ln y_{jt}$	$\Delta \ln y_{jt}$	$\Delta \ln y_{jt}$	$\Delta \ln y_{jt}$	$\Delta \ln y_{jt}$	$\Delta \ln y_{jt}$
$\ln y_{jt-1}$	-0.023	-0.0112	-0.043***	-0.026	-0.044***	-0.043***	-0.040***
	(0.014)	(0.009)	(0.009)	(0.015)	(0.009)	(0.008)	(0.007)
$\ln s_{jt}$	0.078***	0.065***	0.041***	0.077***	0.039***	0.041***	0.039***
	(0.021)	(0.018)	(0.011)	(0.021)	(0.011)	(0.010)	(0.011)
$\ln(n_{jt}+0.05)$	-0.073*	-0.066*	-0.033*	-0.071**	-0.040*	-0.033*	-0.038*
	(0.038)	(0.041)	(0.019)	(0.039)	(0.021)	(0.019)	(0.021)
$P2_{jt-1}$		0.031			0.019		
		(0.051)			(0.022)		
EFW_{jt-1}			0.090**		0.104**	0.085*	
			(0.046)		(0.047)	(0.047)	
FH_{jt-1}				0.044		0.014	
				(0.057)		(0.031)	
$PC1_{jt-1}$							0.014**
							(0.006)
Constant	0.117	0.006	0.312***	0.125	0.278***	0.309***	0.328***
	(0.162)	(0.135)	(0.091)	(0.168)	(0.099)	(0.089)	(0.099)
N	893	863	710	893	690	710	690
R-squared	0.073	0.057	0.071	0.070	0.059	0.065	0.040
F	4.88***	3.35**	16.78***	4.00**	13.80***	14.37***	19.35***

Notes: Estimated over 1990–2018. Post-communist countries only. P2: Polity 2 Index. EFW: Economic freedom in the world. FH: Freedom House Index. PC1: first principal component based on P2, EFW and FH. All three indexes are rescaled to range between 0 and 1. Estimated with country fixed effects and robust standard errors (in parentheses). Significance: 1% ***, 5% ** and 10% *

Table 20.7 Economic growth and democratic capital: all countries

	(1)	(2)	(3)	(4)	(5)	(6)
	$\Delta \ln y_{jt}$	$\Delta \ln y_{jt}$	$\Delta \ln y_{jt}$	$\Delta \ln y_{jt}$	$\Delta \ln y_{jt}$	$\Delta \ln y_{jt}$
$\ln y_{jt-1}$	−0.035***	−0.040***	−0.036***	−0.034***	−0.034***	−0.036***
	(0.007)	(0.008)	(0.005)	(0.005)	(0.007)	(0.009)
$\ln s_{jt}$	0.033***	0.038***	0.031***	0.033***	0.033***	0.036***
	(0.006)	(0.007)	(0.006)	(0.006)	(0.006)	(0.007)
$\ln(n_{jt}+0.05)$	−0.045***	−0.053***	−0.063***	−0.059***	−0.046***	−0.054***
	(0.018)	(0.016)	(0.014)	(0.013)	(0.018)	(0.016)
$DKP2_{jt-1}$	0.014***		0.008***		0.017***	
	(0.003)		(0.002)		(0.007)	
$DKP2^2_{jt-1}$					−0.001	
					(0.001)	
$DKFH_{jt-1}$		0.014***		0.006**		0.031***
		(0.003)		(0.003)		(0.010)
$DKFH^2_{jt-1}$						−0.003**
						(0.002)
EFW_{jt-1}			−0.016	−0.021		
			(0.027)	(0.026)		
Constant	0.191***	0.227***	0.183***	0.197***	0.182***	0.178
	(0.065)	(0.074)	(0.064)	(0.059)	(0.061)	(0.082)
N	3893	3893	2980	3143	3893	4176
R-squared	0.023	0.023	0.051	0.058	0.023	0.024
F	10.82***	10.73***	26.05***	26.93***	8.79***	9.01***
Turning point					13.93	4.49

Notes: Estimated over 1990-2018. All countries. DKP2: Democratic capital based on Polity 2 Index. DKFH: Democratic capital based on Freedom House Index. Turning point: value of democratic capital at which the relationship reaches its maximum. Estimated with country fixed effects and robust standard errors (in parentheses). Significance: 1% ***, 5% ** and 10% *

of democratic capital becomes negative, is relatively high: 4.5, which is a value attained by countries where almost perfect democracy has been sustained.[11]

A very similar pattern appears also for the post-communist countries: growth is always strongly boosted by democratic capital, regardless of whether it appears in the regressions alone (columns 1–2) or alongside economic freedom (columns 3–4). When considering non-linear effects of democratic capital, the quadratic term is again only significant for democratic capital based on the Freedom House Index and the turning point is again relatively high at 4.35. Hence, sustained democracy is robustly and positively associated with economic growth: countries with higher democratic capital tend to grow

---

[11] The steady-state value of democratic capital is given by equation (20.2). A country with perfect democracy (i.e. democracy index of 1) would thus converge to a steady state value of 5 (1/0.2, where 0.2 is the depreciation rate). Within the sample, value of 4.5 was attained, for example, by Spain in 1991 and Slovenia in 2004.

Table 20.8 Economic growth and democratic capital: post-communist countries

	(1)	(2)	(3)	(4)	(5)	(6)
	$\Delta \ln y_{jt}$	$\Delta \ln y_{jt}$	$\Delta \ln y_{jt}$	$\Delta \ln y_{jt}$	$\Delta \ln y_{jt}$	$\Delta \ln y_{jt}$
$\ln y_{jt-1}$	−0.032**	−0.044**	−0.046***	−0.045***	−0.019*	−0.036*
	(0.015)	(0.018)	(0.010)	(0.008)	(0.011)	(0.021)
$\ln s_{jt}$	0.053***	0.072***	0.038***	0.042***	0.048***	0.064***
	(0.017)	(0.020)	(0.011)	(0.011)	(0.017)	(0.021)
$\ln(n_{jt}+0.05)$	−0.049	−0.063	−0.040*	−0.031*	−0.051	−0.064
	(0.044)	(0.040)	(0.021)	(0.018)	(0.042)	(0.039)
$DKP2_{jt-1}$	0.025***		0.005	0.008	0.062**	
	(0.008)		(0.005)	(0.005)	(0.029)	
$DKP2^2_{jt-1}$					−0.007	
					(0.004)	
$DKFH_{jt-1}$		0.024***				0.057**
		(0.006)				(0.023)
$DKFH^2_{jt-1}$						−0.007*
						(0.004)
EFW_{jt-1}			0.097*	0.062		
			(0.051)	(0.050)		
Constant	0.159	0.263	0.296***	0.335***	−0.001	0.154
	(0.181)	(0.201)	(0.105)	(0.089)	(0.149)	(0.223)
N	829	893	667	710	829	893
R-squared	0.053	0.069	0.054	0.059	0.037	0.058
F	5.49***	5.57***	12.85***	14.09	4.29***	4.73***
Turning point					4.70	4.35

Notes: Estimated over 1990–2018. Post-communist countries only. DKP2: Democratic capital based on Polity 2 Index. DKFH: Democratic capital based on Freedom House Index. Turning point: value of democratic capital at which the relationship reaches its maximum. Estimated with country fixed effects and robust standard errors (in parentheses). Significance: 1% ***, 5% ** and 10% *

faster than those with low stocks. The relationship may become flatter as countries accumulate and maintain democratic capital but only at rather high levels.

4 Democracy and Investment

Besides boosting growth, democracy—whether its contemporaneous level or accumulated democracy embodied in democratic capital—can also affect investment in physical and human capital. Since physical and human capital are determinants of growth, any impact that political or economic freedom has on investment in either would indirectly affect also economic development. Therefore, I use the same variables measuring political/economic freedoms and democratic capital to explain investment in physical and human capital. Measuring investment in the former is rather straightforward: I use the investment to GDP ratio used in the regressions reported in the previous section as the dependent variable. Quantifying investment in human capital is more challenging. School enrollment is often used but this measure can be prone to mismeasurement. Furthermore, in the global sample, using school enrollment results in a large number of omitted observations because of missing data. Therefore, I use life expectancy at birth as a proxy for investment in human capital. This is a forward looking measure: it reflects how long an infant could expect to live if the prevailing patterns of mortality at the time of his/her birth stay the same throughout his/her life. The longer an individual expects to live, the more it pays to invest in human capital (see, e.g. Jayachandran and Lleras-Muney 2009; and Hansen 2013). Therefore, life expectancy at time t should be closely correlated with human capital investments at t and in the years immediately following t.[12]

I estimate the following relationships:

$$\ln s_{jt} = \gamma_0 + \gamma_1 \ln y_{jt-1} + \gamma_2 \omega_{jt-1} + \mu_j + \varepsilon_{jt} \tag{20.4}$$

$$\ln LE_{jt} = \gamma_0 + \gamma_1 \ln y_{jt-1} + \gamma_2 \omega_{jt-1} + \mu_j + \varepsilon_{jt} \tag{20.5}$$

where s_{jt} is again the ratio of investment in physical capital to GDP, LE_{jt} is the life expectancy at birth (for both genders), and ω_{jt-1}, as before, stands for political/economic freedom or democratic capital. Both models control for the lagged level of output per person: this is to keep the level of economic development constant.

Tables 20.9 and 20.10 present the results for investment in physical capital in all countries and in post-communist countries, respectively. Political freedom—but not economic freedom—translates into more investment in physical capital, in the global sample. This is confirmed also when the indexes are replaced with the principal component, and when using democratic capital. Economic freedom also has a positive effect but is not significant. Similar pattern also appears for post-communist countries, but the significance levels are lower: all measures of economic and political freedoms and democratic capital appear with positive signs but only the Polity 2 Index, and the democratic capital variables based on this index, are statistically significant.

Finally, Tables 20.11 and 20.12 show analogous regression results for investment in human capital, proxied by life expectancy. The estimates mirror

---

[12] I did not include life expectancy in the models of growth presented in the preceding sections, as it is closely correlated not only with human capital but also with output per person.

Table 20.9 Institutional determinants of investment: all countries

	(1)	(2)	(3)	(4)	(5)	(6)
	lns_{jt}	lns_{jt}	lns_{jt}	lns_{jt}	lns_{jt}	lns_{jt}
lny_{jt-1}	0.171***	0.206***	0.180***	0.150***	0.169***	0.161***
	(0.056)	(0.044)	(0.043)	(0.055)	(0.048)	(0.046)
EFW_{jt-1}	0.198					
	(0.225)					
$P2_{jt-1}$		0.164*				
		(0.086)				
FH_{jt-1}			0.240***			
			(0.086)			
$PC1_{jt-1}$				0.085**		
				(0.034)		
$DKP2_{jt-1}$					0.043*	
					(0.023)	
$DKFH_{jt-1}$						0.054**
						(0.026)
Constant	−3.112***	−3.391***	−3.208***	−2.815***	−3.102***	−3.058***
	(0.468)	(0.367)	(0.365)	(0.467)	(0.380)	(0.370)
N	3238	3999	4362	3048	3898	4181
R-squared	0.029	0.044	0.042	0.028	0.043	0.041
F	5.87***	13.04***	11.84***	7.66***	12.00***	12.00***

Notes: Estimated over 1990–2018. All countries. Estimated with country fixed effects and robust standard errors (in parentheses). Significance: 1% ***, 5% ** and 10% *

Table 20.10 Institutional determinants of investment: post-communist countries

	(1)	(2)	(3)	(4)	(5)	(6)
	lns_{jt}	lns_{jt}	lns_{jt}	lns_{jt}	lns_{jt}	lns_{jt}
lny_{jt-1}	0.077	0.199***	0.187***	0.077	0.158**	0.164**
	(0.085)	(0.061)	(0.060)	(0.090)	(0.063)	(0.061)
EFW_{jt-1}	0.220					
	(0.385)					
$P2_{jt-1}$		0.257**				
		(0.122)				
FH_{jt-1}			0.081			
			(0.142)			
$PC1_{jt-1}$				0.048		
				(0.066)		
$DKP2_{jt-1}$					0.055**	
					(0.023)	
$DKFH_{jt-1}$						0.032
						(0.026)
Constant	−2.227***	−3.304***	−3.081***	−2.089***	−2.957***	−2.920***
	(0.621)	(0.518)	(0.515)	(0.755)	(0.513)	(0.500)
N	711	864	894	691	830	894
R-squared	0.010	0.008	0.011	0.004	0.006	0.012
F	1.21	7.08***	4.84**	1.57	7.42***	4.90**

Notes: Estimated over 1990–2018. Post-communist countries only. Estimated with country fixed effects and robust standard errors (in parentheses). Significance: 1% ***, 5% ** and 10% *

Table 20.11 Institutional determinants of life expectancy: all countries

	(1)	(2)	(3)	(4)	(5)	(6)
	$\ln LE_{jt}$	$\ln LE_{jt}$	$\ln LE_{jt}$	$\ln LE_{jt}$	$\ln LE_{jt}$	$\ln LE_{jt}$
$\ln y_{jt-1}$	0.127***	0.098***	0.101***	0.118***	0.084***	0.093
	(0.013)	(0.014)	(0.015)	(0.013)	(0.014)	(0.015)
EFW_{jt-1}	−0.018					
	(0.062)					
$P2_{jt-1}$		0.077***				
		(0.020)				
FH_{jt-1}			0.031			
			(0.022)			
$PC1_{jt-1}$				0.014**		
				(0.006)		
$DKP2_{jt-1}$					0.025***	
					(0.005)	
$DKFH_{jt-1}$						0.015***
						(0.005)
Constant	3.165***	3.340***	3.352***	3.226***	3.431***	3.392***
	−0.1029	(0.119)	(0.118)	(0.105)	(0.109)	(0.117)
N	3444	4286	4855	3190	4162	4611
R-squared	0.565	0.590	0.583	0.566	0.599	0.590
F	53.42***	32.86***	29.21***	52.41***	42.70***	40.60***

Notes: Estimated over 1990–2018. All countries. Estimated with country fixed effects and robust standard errors (in parentheses). Significance: 1% ***, 5% ** and 10% *

Table 20.12 Institutional determinants of life expectancy: post-communist countries

	(1)	(2)	(3)	(4)	(5)	(6)
	$\ln LE_{jt}$	$\ln LE_{jt}$	$\ln LE_{jt}$	$\ln LE_{jt}$	$\ln LE_{jt}$	$\ln LE_{jt}$
$\ln y_{jt-1}$	0.074***	0.073***	0.071***	0.072***	0.063***	0.064***
	(0.010)	(0.008)	(0.008)	(0.009)	(0.008)	(0.009)
EFW_{jt-1}	0.012					
	(0.047)					
$P2_{jt-1}$		0.026***				
		(0.009)				
FH_{jt-1}			0.012			
			(0.014)			
$PC1_{jt-1}$				0.005		
				(0.005)		
$DKP2_{jt-1}$					0.009***	
					(0.002)	
$DKFH_{jt-1}$						0.010***
						(0.003)
Constant	3.649***	3.642***	3.668***	3.667***	3.720***	3.711***
	(0.071)	(0.069)	(0.067)	(0.073)	(0.060)	(0.068)
N	690	870	900	671	838	900
R-squared	0.418	0.426	0.416	0.427	0.395	0.421
F	54.52***	43.44***	40.48***	53.17***	85.43***	65.41***

Notes: Estimated over 1990–2018. Post-communist countries only. Estimated with country fixed effects and robust standard errors (in parentheses). Significance: 1% ***, 5% ** and 10% *

those obtained for physical capital: economic freedom does not affect life expectancy, whereas political freedom and democratic capital boost life expectancy, and therefore should help stimulate investment in human capital. As with investment in physical capital, the regression results are stronger with the Polity 2 Index than with the Freedom House Index; the democratic capital variables, nevertheless, are strongly significant regardless of which index was used to construct them. Similar patterns appear in the global sample and in the post-communist subsample; the estimated effects, however, are somewhat larger in the global sample.

In summary, improvement in democracy, especially lasting improvement, encourages greater acquisition of physical and human capital. In this way, democracy boosts economic development not only directly but also indirectly by fostering investment, which in turn translates into faster economic growth.

5   Conclusions

This study revisits the potential effect of democracy on economic development in a broad global sample of countries, and also separately in a subsample of post-communist countries. During the 1980s and 1990s, scores of Latin-American, South-East Asian, post-communist and African countries embraced democratization alongside (and often at the same time as) economic reform. This so-called third wave of democratization (Huntington 1991), and the associated wide-ranging improvements in human rights and civil liberties across the world, has been seen as an extraordinary and glorious achievement (*end of history* according to Fukuyama 1989) that deserves to be praised and celebrated. However, do better human rights and civil liberties translate also into greater wellbeing? Is the key to economic development and prosperity in implemented political or economic reforms? The present paper seeks to shed light on these questions.

The formerly communist countries offer a unique opportunity to analyze this relationship because, in the early 1990s, they attempted to (re)introduce democracy after several decades of authoritarian rule. There was substantial heterogeneity in the strength and duration of their commitment to democratization, however. With the benefit of 30 years of hindsight, this diversity of approaches and outcomes allows a detailed analysis of whether democracy fosters or improves economic development. Therefore, besides approaching this question in a broad global sample including all countries for which the required data are available, I also consider a separate subsample of post-communist countries only.

The results are reassuring: democracy has a robustly positive impact on economic growth, and also on key factors of economic growth—investment in physical and human capital. This is true both for the contemporaneous level of democracy—measured either using the Polity 2 Index or the Freedom House Index—and for related measures of accumulated democracy (democratic capital), which reflect not only the level but also the duration of the democratic regime. Hence, improvements in the level of democracy have translated not only into greater respect for human rights and civil liberties—they have also brought about gains in the material level of wellbeing.

Somewhat surprisingly, when comparing the roles of democracy and economic freedom, democracy takes primacy. This finding, which stands in contrast with a vast body of literature confirming a positive relationship between economic freedom and growth, can be rationalized with recourse to several observations. First, the global sample, in which economic freedom does not correlate with growth, may be too heterogenous to obtain a significant estimate. Indeed, economic freedom is robustly correlated with economic growth in the subsample of post-communist countries. Second, inasmuch as economic freedom encourages investment in physical capital (as the literature suggests), then its positive effects can be picked up by the coefficient of that variable instead. Finally, the data for political freedom covers a longer period, which may also help explain why the effect of economic freedom is not precisely estimated.

Hence, the results of my analysis give support to embracing democratization early on, and especially to sustaining democracy in the longer term: the gains from democratization appear especially strong when considering democratic capital, which measures sustained rather than current democracy. Importantly, it appears that little can be gained by postponing democracy and focusing merely on economic liberalization. Suppressing democracy for the sake of maintaining political stability and reform momentum may occasionally work, but it is far from a universal recipe on how to attain prosperity. Rather, postponing democracy is likely to help entrench authoritarianism, benefitting primarily the ruling elite, not the populace at large.

References

Barro, R. J. (1996). Democracy and Growth. *Journal of Economic Growth, 1*(1), 1–27.

Baum, M. A., & Lake, D. A. (2003). The Political Economy of Growth: Democracy and Human Capital. *American Journal of Political Science, 47*(2), 333–347.

de Haan, J., & Siermann, C. L. J. (1995). New Evidence on the Relationship Between Democracy and Economic Growth. *Public Choice, 86*, 175–198.

Doucouliagos, C., & Ulubasoglu, M. A. (2006). Economic Freedom and Economic Growth: Does Specification Make a Difference? *European Journal of Political Economy, 22*(1), 60–81.

Doucouliagos, C., & Ulubasoglu, M. A. (2008). Democracy and Economic Growth: A Meta-Analysis. *American Journal of Political Science, 52*(1), 61–83.

Fidrmuc, J. (2003). Economic Reform, Democracy and Growth During Post-Communist Transition. *European Journal of Political Economy, 19*(3), 583–604.

Fukuyama, F. (1989). The End of History? *The National Interest, 16*, 3–18.

Giavazzi, F., & Tabellini, G. (2005). Economic and Political Liberalizations. *Journal of Monetary Economics, 52*(7), 1297–1330.

Hall, J. C., & Lawson, R. A. (2014). Economic Freedom of the World: An Accounting of the Literature. *Contemporary Economic Policy, 32*(1), 1–19.

Hansen, C. W. (2013). Life Expectancy and Human Capital: Evidence from the International Epidemiological Transition. *Journal of Health Economics, 32*(6), 1142–1152.

Helliwell, J. F. (1994). Empirical Linkages Between Democracy and Economic Growth. *British Journal of Political Science, 24*, 225–248.

Huntington, S. P. (1991). Democracy's Third Wave. *Journal of democracy, 2*(2), 12–34.

Islam, N. (1995). Growth Empirics: A Panel Data Approach. *The Quarterly Journal of Economics, 110*(4), 1127–1170.

Jayachandran, S., & Lleras-Muney, A. (2009). Life Expectancy and Human Capital Investments: Evidence from Maternal Mortality Declines. *The Quarterly Journal of Economics, 124*(1), 349–397.

Kornai, J. (2004). Transformational Recession: The Main Causes. *Journal of Comparative Economics, 19*, 39–63.

Lipset, S. M. (1959). Some Social Requisites of Democracy: Economic Development and Political Legitimacy. *American Political Science Review, 53*(1), 69–105.

Mankiw, N. G., Romer, D., & Weil, D. N. (1992). A Contribution to the Empirics of Economic Growth. *The Quarterly Journal of Economics, 107*(2), 407–437.

Persson, T., & Tabellini, G. (2009). Democratic Capital: The Nexus of Political and Economic Change. *American Economic Journal: Macroeconomics, 1*(2), 88–126.

Przeworski, A. (2005). Democracy as an Equilibrium. *Public Choice, 123*, 253–273.

Przeworski, A., & Limongi, F. (1993). Political Regimes and Economic Growth. *Journal of Economic Perspectives, 7*(3), 51–69.

Roland, G. (2000). *Transition and Economics: Politics, Markets and Firms*. London: The MIT Press.

Tavares, J., & Wacziarg, R. (2001). How Democracy Affects Growth. *European Economic Review, 45*(8), 1341–1378.

Williamson, C. R., & Mathers, R. L. (2011). Economic Freedom, Culture, and Growth. *Public Choice, 148*(3–4), 313–335.

21

Economic Development, Transition, and New Structural Economics

Justin Yifu Lin

After the Second World War, many former colonies and semi-colonies in the world obtained political independence from colonial powers and started their industrialization and modernization drives with the goal of quickly catching up with developed countries. In response to the need for guidance, Structuralism emerged as the first generation of development economics, aiming to advise developing countries on how to use government intervention to overcome market failures, and to achieve industrialization and modernization. However, with widespread development failures, Neoliberalism replaced this early Structuralism in the 1980s as the dominant mode of policy thinking, focusing on eliminating government failures in developing countries though shock therapy so as to establish properly functioning market systems. For most neoliberal economists, economic theories, and the policy advice derived from them, can be applied in the same way to developed and developing countries. However, so far on this precept, among the nearly 200 developing economies that existed in the aftermath of the Second World War, only 13 have been able to catch up or substantially close the income gap with advanced countries. This chapter therefore reviews the ideas and disappointing results of Structuralism and Neoliberalism, before introducing the main ideas of "New Structural Economics". Additionally, it discusses how to apply New Structural

J. Y. Lin (✉)
Institute of New Structural Economics, Peking University, Beijing, China
e-mail: justinlin@nsd.pku.edu.cn

© The Author(s) 2021
E. Douarin, O. Havrylyshyn (eds.), *The Palgrave Handbook of Comparative Economics*,
https://doi.org/10.1007/978-3-030-50888-3_21

Economics to formulate industrial policy for accelerating economic development and to achieve the industrialization and modernization dream of developing nations, and calls for a structural revolution in modern economics.

1   The Failures of Structuralism and Neoliberalism

Before modern times, all countries in the world lived mainly on agriculture and were poor, measured by today's standard (Kuznets 1966; Maddison 1995). After the eighteenth century, some countries in Western Europe became industrialized and "advanced", while most countries in other parts of the world stayed agrarian and became "backward" (Pomeranz 2000). Most of the poorer developing countries also became colonies of the Western powers. After the Second World War, in response to the need for guiding the industrialization and modernization efforts of newly independent developing countries, development economics emerged as a new sub-discipline in modern economics. The first generation of development economics was "Structuralism" (Prebisch 1950; Rosenstein-Rodan 1943). The understanding of development economists at the time was that if a developing country wants to be as rich as a high-income country, it has to have the same high level of productivity as a high-income country. In turn, this requires the country to develop the same advanced capital-intensive industries as those seen in a high-income country. Similarly, if a developing country wants to be as strong as a high-income country, it has to have the same advanced military industries, which are also capital-intensive industries, as in a high-income country. However, those advanced industries could not develop spontaneously in the market in a developing country. Structuralists believed that the failure for advanced capital-intensive industries to develop spontaneously in a developing country was due to market failures caused by various structural rigidities, such as households' low propensity to save and irresponsiveness to price signals in a developing country (Arndt 1985). Hence, Structuralism advocates that the state overcome market failures by adopting an import-substitution strategy in order to develop advanced capital-intensive industries with direct, administrative resource mobilization and allocation, similar to the practices of the Stalinist planning model in socialist countries. This policy thinking was in line with the Keynesianism then prevailing in macroeconomics, which emphasized market failures and advocated a proactive state role. Most developing countries, socialist and non-socialist alike, followed this strategy after the

Second World War. Such a strategy ushered in a period of rapid investment-led growth, but in general, firms in those advanced industries were nonviable in an open, competitive market (Lin and Tan 1999), suffered from the problems of x-inefficiency and became white elephants[1] after they were established (Leibenstein 1966). Their survival relied on government subsidies and protections, giving rise to rents and rent-seeking (Krueger 1997). Subsequently, this resulted in stagnation, and crises broke out frequently, causing some further divergence between the developed and developing countries during the twentieth century (Pritchett 1997). As shown in Fig. 21.1, the income gap between developing and developed countries on average widened in the 1960s and 1970s, in spite of various development efforts by the developing countries themselves, with support from multilateral and bilateral development institutions (Lin and Wang 2017).

Due to the failure of these structuralist policies, Neoliberalism had replaced Structuralism as the dominant approach to policy by the 1980s. According to Neoliberalism, the main reason for the failure of developing countries to catch up with developed ones was excessive state intervention in the market, causing misallocation of resources, rent-seeking, and so forth (Lal 1983). With Neoliberalism, developing countries were advised to overcome "government failures" by adopting the "Washington Consensus"—a set of policies advocating privatization, marketization, and stabilization with a "big bang", so as to

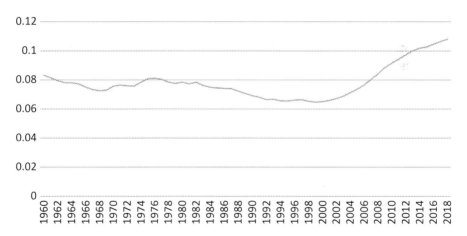

Fig. 21.1 Per capita GDP of developing countries as a share of per capita GDP of high-income countries. (Data source: World Bank, World Development Indicators, 2020)

---

[1] "White elephants" refers to assets or firms which are very costly to maintain but generate output of low value, so that they fail to make a profit.

quickly build up the institutions required for a well-functioning market economy, as in advanced countries (Williamson 1990). Most developing countries, both socialist and non-socialist, followed this recipe in the 1980s and 1990s. However, the results were again disappointing again. As shown in Fig. 21.1, the gap between per capita gross domestic product (GDP) in developing and developed countries widened further. In fact, the frequency of crises in developing countries in the 1980s and 1990s was even higher than in the 1960s and 1970s. This is why some economists refer to the 1980s and 1990s as "lost decades" for developing countries (Easterly 2001).[2]

A few developing economies such as China, Hong Kong SAR, South Korea, and Singapore were able to achieve great success in their development efforts and to narrow the gap with, or even overtake, developed countries in terms of per capita income, as shown in Fig. 21.2. These high-performing economies have one thing in common. This is that they did not follow the mainstream policy recommendations in their development from low- to middle- or high-income countries, and/or in their transition from a planned to a market economy. Hong Kong, South Korea, and Singapore all adopted an export-oriented development strategy, initially cultivating small-scale, labor-intensive industries, instead of the import-substitution strategy to develop large-scale, capital-intensive industries, as advocated by Structuralism. As a result, they moved up the industrial ladder to more capital-intensive industries (similar to those

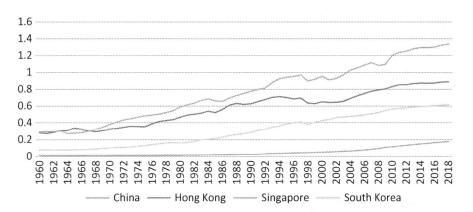

Fig. 21.2 Per capita GDP of high-performing economies as a share of per capita GDP of high-income countries. (Data Source: World Bank, World Development Indicators, 2020)

---

[2] The widening of income gap between developed and developing countries after the Second World War does not mean that there has been no improvement of income and living standards in developing countries. Rather, it means that the average annual per capita GDP growth rate in developing countries was less than the average annual per capita GDP growth rate of 2% per year in high-income countries over last 100 years (Maddison 1995).

found in advanced countries) only step by step, in a market economy, but with active government facilitation. China achieved dynamic growth in its transition from a planned economy to a market economy by adopting a dual-track, gradualist approach. Indeed, the state provided transitory subsidies to firms in the old capital-intensive priority industries, while liberalizing the entry for, and actively facilitating the growth of, new labor-intensive industries by establishing special economic zones or industrial parks to overcome infrastructure bottlenecks. This strategy stands in contrast to the shock therapy advocated by Neoliberalism (Lin 2013a). Incidentally, mainstream economists of the 1980s and 1990s considered this gradual approach to be the wrong transition strategy, warning that it would worsen rent-seeking, corruption, misallocation, and income disparity (e.g. Murphy et al. 1992). Against this backdrop, it is natural to ask why those economies that followed the dominant policy approach in their development and transition failed, while those that succeeded adopted the wrong policies from the perspective of mainstream Structuralism or Neoliberalism.

2 New Structural Economics

In coming up with New Structural Economics as a response to the puzzles in the above section, I propose to go back to Adam Smith. What I mean by this is not a return to the ideas popularized by *The Wealth of Nations*—which reflected Adam Smith's findings from his reflections on the economic experiences of the eighteenth century—but to go back to his methodology, as exemplified in the full title of his book, *An Inquiry into the Nature and Causes of the Wealth of Nations*. First, we need to understand the nature of modern economic growth. According to Kuznets (1966), rapid, sustained income growth is a modern phenomenon, which occurred only after the industrial revolution of the eighteenth century. Before that, the size of an economy might have risen, but per capita income in the economy did not increase. The nature of modern economic growth, with its ever-increasing per capita income, is a process of continuous structural transformation. This process involves continuous technological innovation in existing industries; the emergence of new, high value-added industries; and improvements of hard infrastructure, such as power supply and road networks, as well as institutions (soft infrastructure). As Rodrik (2011) explains "… developing countries are qualitatively different from developed ones. They are not just radially shrunk versions of rich countries. In order to understand the challenges of under-development, you have to understand how the structure of employment and production—in particular the large gaps between the social marginal products of labor in traditional versus modern activities—is determined and how the obstacles that block structural transformation can be overcome."

New Structural Economics proposes to use the neoclassical economic approach to study the determinants and impacts of economic structure and its evolution, which are the essence of modern economic growth, in an economy's development (Lin 2011). By convention, I should refer to this type of research and findings as Structural Economics, with the word "new" added to distinguish it from the "old" Structuralism.[3] In a similar way, "new" is added to new institutional economics to distinguish it from the institutional school which prevailed in the United States in the early twentieth century.

The main idea of New Structural Economics is that the economic structures in an economy, including the structure of technology and industry, which determine labor productivity, and hard infrastructure, such as power supply, road network, and port facilities, and soft infrastructure, such as financial and legal institutions, which determines transaction costs, are endogenous to the economy's endowment structure, which is given at any specific time, but changeable over time.

Endowments—and the endowment structure—determine the economy's total budget and relative factor prices at any specific time. These, in turn, determine the industries in which the economy has comparative advantages at that time. If all the industries in the economy are consistent with the economy's comparative advantages, the economy has the optimal industrial structure at that time. Such a structure enables an economy to have the lowest possible factor costs of production in its domestic and international markets. From this perspective, a high-income country's industries, especially those producing tradable goods and services, are mostly capital-intensive because their factor endowment is one of relative abundance in capital, whereas low-income countries' industries are mostly resource-intensive or labor-intensive because their factor endowment is one of relative abundance in natural resources and/or labor. Therefore, the optimal industrial structure of an economy at any one time is endogenous to the structure of its given factor endowments. As an economy's structure of factor endowments evolves from one level of development to another, the optimal industrial structure of that economy will evolve accordingly and endogenously. When the industries in an economy evolve from traditional, natural resource-intensive or labor-intensive industries to modern capital-intensive industries, a continuous improvement in hard infrastructure (such as power supply, road networks, and port

---

[3] Old Structuralism, or early development economics, has been described in the previous section.

facilities) and soft infrastructure (such as financial institution and legal system) is required to reduce transaction costs. This is because of the increasing economies of scale in production, expanding market scope, and rising risks in production and market exchanges. The latter improvements are required to turn the industries of an economy's comparative advantages into the economy's competitive advantages.

Income growth in an economy depends on increasing labor productivity by upgrading the industrial structure from natural resource- or labor-intensive industries to capital-intensive industries, which in turn depends on the upgrading of the endowment structure so that it is relatively abundant, rather than relatively scarce, in capital. With the upgrading of industrial structure, improvements in hard and soft infrastructure are also required to reduce transaction costs and so realize the industries' production potential.

From the above analysis, the best way to achieve dynamic growth in an economy is to develop its industries by following the comparative advantages determined by its endowment structure. With such industries, and appropriate hard and soft infrastructure, the economy will be more competitive, produce the largest surplus, have the highest possible returns to capital and so the largest possible savings. This will ensure the fastest upgrade of the endowment structure, and achieve the most rapid industrial upgrade and income growth (Ju et al. 2015). In this process, a developing country can have latecomer advantages, and thus have faster technological innovation and industrial upgrading than high-income countries, which leads to convergence with high-income countries (Lin 2009; Gerschenkron 1962).

The question then is how to ensure that the economy will grow in a manner that is consistent with its comparative advantages. The goal of firms is profit maximization, which is, all things equal, a function of the relative prices of factor inputs. The criterion for a firm's industrial selection is typically the relative prices of capital, labor, and natural resources. Therefore, the precondition for a firm to follow the comparative advantage of a given economy in its decision to stay in or to enter an industry is to have a market system that provides the price signals that reflect the relative scarcities of factors of production in the endowment structure. Such a system exists only in a competitive market. In a developing country, where a competitive market does not usually exist, the state must take steps to improve market institutions so as to create and protect effective competition in the product and factor markets. In the process of industrial upgrading, firms need to have information about production technologies and product markets. If that information is inadequate, each firm will need to invest resources to collect and analyze it. First movers attempting to enter a new industry may either succeed (because the industry is consistent with the country's new comparative advantage) or fail (because they have targeted the wrong industry). In case of success, their experience offers valuable and free information to other prospective entrants. They will not have monopoly rents because of competition from newly entering firms. Moreover, these first movers often need to devote resources to train workers in the new business processes and techniques, but competitors may hire those experienced workers by offering higher wages. In case of failure, the experience of failing firms still provides useful information to other firms, advising them not to enter the sector or what mistakes to avoid. However, first movers must bear the costs of failure. In other words, the social value of their investments is usually much larger than their private value, and there is an asymmetry between the first movers' gains from success and the cost of failure. In addition, successful industrial upgrading in an economy also requires new types of financial, legal, and other "soft" and "hard" infrastructure, to facilitate production and market transactions so as to allow the economy to reach its production-possibility frontier by reducing transaction costs. Improving hard and soft infrastructure requires coordination beyond individual firms' own capability. Economic development is therefore a dynamic process marked with externalities and that requires coordination. While a competitive market is a basic requirement for effective resource allocation at each stage of development, the state must play a proactive, enabling role to help an economy to move from one stage to another.

The development recipe of New Structural Economics is consistent with the findings of the World Bank's *Growth Report by the Commission on Growth and Development* (2008). After the Second World War, only 13 economies among about 200 economies in the world were able to achieve an outstanding economic growth performance of 7% or more, on average annually, for 25 years or more. High-income countries on average grew at a rate of 3–3.5% annually. Therefore, these 13 economies were able to achieve substantial convergence in their income level, closing the gap with high-income countries. The Commission of Growth and Development found that these successful economies had the following five characteristics: (1) they were open economies; (2) they maintained macroeconomic stability; (3) they had high savings and high investment rates; (4) they had a largely well-functioning market or were moving toward a market economy; and (5) they all had a credible, committed, and proactive state.

The first four characteristics are compatible with the recommendations of Neoliberalism, drawn on the insights of neoclassical economics, but the last characteristic is not. Probably because of this, Michael Spence, chairman of the Commission, points out that these five characteristics are ingredients for success, but not a recipe for success (Brady and Spence 2010). However, without a recipe, how can the state in a developing country formulate its development policy? In fact, the New Structural Economics' principle of following a country's comparative advantages, as determined by its factor endowments, in order to develop its industries is the recipe for success.

According to New Structural Economics, an efficient market and a facilitating state—characteristics 4 and 5 in the Growth Commission's findings—are the two institutional preconditions for a country to develop according to its comparative advantages, as determined by its endowment structure. If a country follows its comparative advantages in their development strategy, it will be an open economy, specializing in the export of whatever it has comparative advantage in and importing goods and services in which it has no comparative advantages (characteristic 1). Due to its competitiveness, the economy will not experience domestically generated macroeconomic crises and will be better able to withstand external shocks and so it will sustain macroeconomic stability (characteristic 2). Moreover, as argued earlier, an economy following its comparative advantages in industrial development will generate the largest economic surplus and have greater incentives for saving and investment (characteristics 3). Therefore, following one's comparative advantage is a recipe for development success.[4]

3   The Failure of Structuralism and Washington Consensus: A New Structural Economics Perspective

From the perspective of New Structural Economics, Structuralism failed because it ignored the endogeneity of the economic structure to a country's endowment structure, and because it recommended an import-substitution strategy to develop industries that were too capital-intensive for the country's

---

[4] One of the major differences between New Structural Economics (NSE) and Neoclassical Economics is the role of the state in industrial upgrading. NSE advocates the adoption by the state of a facilitating role to compensate for the first mover's externality and to coordinate/provide necessary improvements in hard and soft infrastructure for the industries of new comparative advantages determined by the changing endowment structure. In contrast, Neoclassical Economics shies away from the state's proactive role in facilitating structural transformation because of concerns about rent-seeking and state capacity. NSE develops a Growth Identification and Facilitation Framework (GIFF) to identify industries of latent comparative advantages and infrastructure bottlenecks and advises governments on how to turn latent comparative advantages into competitive advantages in a pragmatic way, which can be followed by a state with any capacity and does not generate distortions and rent-seeking (Lin 2017; Lin and Monga 2011). See also the discussion in Sect. 4.

level of development, going against the comparative advantages determined by its factor endowments. As a result, the firms in the priority sectors of such a strategy were nonviable in open competitive markets, the state's strategy was mostly a policy burden to them, and they required state subsidies and protection to help with their initial investment and continuous operation (Lin and Tan 1999). The state's protection and subsidies led to interventions and various distortions in the market, causing misallocation of resources, rent-seeking, corruption, soft budget constraints, and political capture.

The successful East Asian economies instead adopted an export-oriented development strategy. Initially, this focused on developing labor-intensive manufacturing, so exploiting the comparative advantages determined by their abundant labor supplies in the 1950s and 1960s. Step by step, they then moved up the industrial ladder to more capital-intensive industries with gradual accumulation of capital and changes in comparative advantages in the development process (Lin 2009).

In contrast, Neoliberalism, and the reforms recommended by the Washington Consensus, failed because it neglected the fact that government intervention and distortions of the market before the transition were endogenous to the needs of protecting nonviable firms in existing industries established by the previous comparative-advantage-defying strategy. Consequently, Neoliberalism advised the state to eliminate all government protections and distortions immediately in the transition in order to establish a well-functioning market economy, causing the collapse of old priority industries and deindustrialization (Rodrik 2016). Moreover, Neoliberalism opposed the adoption of sector-targeted policies to compensate first movers and to provide location-specific improvements in hard and soft infrastructure, needed for industrial upgrading in accordance with changes in the country's comparative advantages. This was due to concerns that the state lacked the information required for the location and industry selection, as well as over the possibility of capture. However, governments tend to have limited fiscal resources and are thus unable to improve infrastructure and institutions for the whole nation simultaneously.

The transition economies that have achieved stability and dynamic growth during their journey toward higher income levels—including China, Vietnam, and Cambodia in the 1980s and Mauritius in the 1970s—typically adopted a pragmatic dual-track approach. In each case, the state provided transitional supports to nonviable firms in the old priority industries and eliminated support only when firms in those sectors became viable because of a change in comparative advantage, following a period of growth and accumulation of capital. At the same time, the state liberalized private firms' entry into previously repressed labor-intensive industries in which they enjoyed comparative advantages. The state also typically played a facilitating role by setting up special economic zones or industrial parks to overcome infrastructure bottlenecks, providing a one-stop service to improve the business environment and engaging in active investment promotion to attract foreign investment (Lin 2013a). Such a transition strategy contributed to economic stability and dynamic growth, and was also favorable to domestic capital mobilization and Foreign Direct Investment (FDI). Ironically, the mainstream transition thinking in the 1980s and 1990s regarded this dual-track approach as the worst one possible (Murphy et al. 1992).

4   Industrial Policy and a Facilitation State

New Structural Economics argues that the state has an essential role in facilitating industrial upgrading in the process of economic development because of the need to address externalities and to solve coordination problems in the improvement of infrastructure and institutions. Industrial policy is a useful instrument for the state to use in this facilitating role. This is because the coordination required for improvements in infrastructure and institutions may differ across industries and locations, and the state's resources and capacity are limited, so that the state needs to deploy them strategically.

For advanced countries, industrial upgrading requires indigenous invention of new technology through research and development (R&D). Firms have incentives for the development of new technology because the government will grant a patent to a new breakthrough. Firms may not be interested in research if its findings become public information. However, without findings from research, the potential to achieve breakthroughs in technological development is limited. State support for research is essential for economic development in an advanced country. However, the state needs to allocate its limited budget for research strategically, according to the potential that the research findings may bring to the country's economic development. In fact, in an advanced country the allocation of research budget is an industrial policy that determines the direction of technological and industrial development (Mazzucato 2011; Gruber and Johnson 2019).

A developing country has the advantage of backwardness in industrial upgrading as its industries are within the global frontier (Gerschenkron 1962). For an industrial policy in a developing country to be successful, it should target industries that conform to the economy's latent comparative advantage (Lin 2016). Latent comparative advantage refers to an industry that, while enjoying low factor costs of production in an international comparison (i.e. consistent with the country's comparative advantage determined by its factor endowments), the transaction costs are nevertheless too high to be competitive in domestic and international markets because of inadequate hard and soft infrastructure.

Firms in an industry with latent comparative advantages will be viable and the industry can be competitive once the state helps to reduce transaction costs by improving hard and soft infrastructure.[5] How can the state pick the industries that are in line with the economy's latent comparative advantages and play a facilitating role? Depending on the targeted industry's distance to the global technology frontier and the length of the innovation cycle, New Structural Economics classifies industries in a developing country into five categories and recommends state facilitation according to their respective bottlenecks for growth (Lin 2017).

1. For an existing industry still below the global technology frontier, the state should identify the binding constraints in infrastructure, financing and human capital, and remove them in order to help firms to catch up. The state may also follow the procedures in the Growth Identification and Facilitation Framework to help firms enter a new industry (as described in Lin and Monga 2011).

2. For an industry that is already on the global technological frontier, the state should support firms' R&D activities, especially the basic research needed for product and technology development, so as to maintain the industry's technological leadership globally, as many advanced countries do.

3. For an industry that has already lost comparative advantage due to rising wages, the state should help firms either to shift to high value-added activities, such as branding, product design, and marketing management, or to relocate to countries with low wages.

4. For an industry with a short innovation cycle, which relies more on human than on physical capital, in a country with abundant human capital, and especially one like China with a large domestic market, the state can set up incubation parks, encourage venture capital, and protect intellectual property to facilitate innovation and help start-up companies.

5. For an industry with a long innovation cycle, necessary for national defense or economic security even though the industry is not in line with the country's comparative advantage, the state should subsidize its R&D with

---

[5] The state's removal of bottlenecks in hard and soft infrastructure to reduce transaction costs for the new industries will not cause distortions and generate rents, so that rent-seeking can be avoided.

direct fiscal support instead of price distortions and other market interventions.

A developing country has typically poor infrastructure and weak institutions nationwide. Instead of trying to improve infrastructure and strengthen institutions for the whole country, without any industry- or location-specific focus, as Neoliberalism advocates, the state may use the above pragmatic approach to support technological innovation and industrial upgrading in specific industries and locations, so generating quick wins for competitiveness, job growth, export diversification, capital accumulation, and fiscal revenue expansion. These quick wins will set off a virtuous cycle of development that may well spread to the whole country.

5   New Structural Economics and a Call for Structural Revolution in Modern Economics

Most existing economic theories are generated from the economic phenomena and experiences of advanced countries and are inevitably embedded in the economic structures, including industries, infrastructure, and institutions, of those countries. Due to the structural differences across countries at different levels of development, theories generated from advanced countries may not be applicable in developing countries. In particular, with their focus on one-sector or even one-production factor, most theories assume only quantitative but not qualitative differences between a developing country and a developed one. These theories also often implicitly take the industrial and institutional structure of advanced countries as optimal, with any deviation perceived as a distortion and suboptimal. Neglecting the endogeneity of structure and structural difference has prevented Structuralism and Neoliberalism acting as a useful guide to development and transition in developing countries.

Structural difference and its endogeneity have implications for other sub-disciplines in modern economics, alongside development and transition economics. This is because the scale of production, the scope of the market, the source of risk and the binding constraints on choices in other sub-disciplines are likely to be different for countries at different levels of development. For example, technological innovation for a developed country on the global technological frontier means invention, as described by the endogenous growth literature (Romer 1990), but for a developing country within the global technological frontier, it may mean imitation and technological borrowing (Lin 2009). Similarly, the financial arrangements suitable for an advanced country dominated by capital-intensive large firms—such as a stock market, venture capital, big bank, and corporate bonds—may not be appropriate for a developing country with firms in services, manufacturing, and agricultural sectors being predominantly small in scale (Lin et al. 2013). For a developed country, fiscal stimulus may encounter the constraint of Ricardian equivalence, whereas a developing country may use the stimulus to invest in bottleneck-releasing, growth-enhancing infrastructure and thus overcome the constraint (Lin 2013b). New Structural Economics attempts to endogenize structural differences for countries at differential levels of development and to explore the implications of this in every subfield of modern economics. Such efforts are not only a gold mine for original research but are also necessary for making modern economics relevant for guiding the choices of governments, firms, and households in countries at different stages of development. The result of such research will make theories in modern economics more applicable, better able to address economic issues and to guide policies in developing countries.

6   Concluding Remarks

It is the dream of every developing country to become a prosperous high-income country. To bring prosperity to a nation is consistent with a political leader's personal goal of staying in power and leaving a memorable legacy (Lin 2009). After the Second World War, most developing countries, having gained political independence from colonial powers, started to pursue industrialization and modernization following the ideas first of Structuralism and then Neoliberalism, but most failed. Only a few developing countries were able to narrow substantially their income gap with high-income countries, or even to overtake them. Their policies were considered to be wrong from the perspectives of mainstream Structuralism and Neoliberalism. As Keynes (1935, p. 384) said, "It is ideas, not vested interests, which are dangerous for good or evil." Many policies, such as the import-substitution strategy of the 1960s and 1970s, and the shock therapy of the 1980s and 1990s, brought harmful or even disastrous consequences: despite being formulated with good intentions, they were guided by the wrong ideas. A bad policy may create its own vested interests, such as the protected industrialists in Latin America's import-substitution strategy, even though it was a strategy that was initiated when Latin American countries were governed by the landed classes in the 1930s (Lin 2009).

This chapter has reviewed Structuralism and Neoliberalism, introduced the basic ideas of New Structural Economics, and called for a structural revolution in modern economics. I believe the studies of endogeneity, as well as the impact of structure and structural transformation on countries at different levels of development, should be the focus of comparative economics. Such studies will produce new, relevant policy insights and assist developing countries—which still consist of 85% of the world's population—to realize their dream of becoming prosperous, modern, advanced industrialized, high-income countries.

References

Arndt, H. W. (1985). The Origin of Structuralism. *World Development, 13*(2), 151–159.

Brady, D. H., & Spence, M. (2010). The Ingredients of Growth. *Stanford Social Innovation Review, 8*(2), 34–39.

Commission on Growth and Development. (2008). *Growth Report: Strategies for Sustained Growth and Inclusive Development*. Washington, DC: World Bank.

Easterly, W. (2001). The Lost Decades: Developing Countries' Stagnation in Spite of Policy Reform 1980–1998. *Journal of Economic Growth, 6*, 135–157.

Gerschenkron, A. (1962). *Economic Backwardness in Historical Perspective, a Book of Essays*. Cambridge, MA: Belknap Press of Harvard University Press.

Gruber, J., & Johnson, S. (2019). *How Breakthrough Science Can Revive Economic Growth and the American Dream*. New York: PublicAffairs.

Ju, J., Lin, J. Y., & Wang, Y. (2015). Endowment Structures, Industrial Dynamics, and Economic Growth. *Journal of Monetary Economics, 76*, 244–263.

Keynes, J. M. (1935 [1964]). *The General Theory of Employment, Interest, and Money*. New York: Harcourt, Brace and World.

Krueger, A. O. (1997). Trade Policy and Economic Development: How We Learn. *American Economic Review, 87*(1), 1–22.

Kuznets, S. (1966). *Modern Economic Growth: Rate, Structure and Speed*. New Haven, CT: Yale University Press.

Lal, D. (1983). *The Poverty of 'Development Economics'*. Cambridge, MA: Harvard University Press.

Leibenstein, H. (1966). Allocative Efficiency vs. X-Efficiency. *American Economic Review, 56*(3), 392–415.

Lin, J. Y. (2009). *Economic Development and Transition: Thought, Strategy, and Viability*. Cambridge, UK: Cambridge University Press.

Lin, J. Y. (2011). New Structural Economics: A Framework for Rethinking Economic Development. *The World Bank Observer, 26*, 193–221.

Lin, J. Y. (2013a). Demystifying the Chinese Economy. *The Australian Economic Review, 46*, 259–268.

Lin, J. Y. (2013b). Global Infrastructure Initiative and Global Recovery. *Journal of Policy Modeling, 35*(3), 400–411.

Lin, J. Y. (2016). The Latecomer Advantages and Disadvantages: A New Structural Economics Perspective. In M. Andersson & T. Axelsson (Eds.), *Diverse Development Paths and Structural Transformation in Escape from Poverty* (pp. 43–67). Cambridge: Cambridge University Press.

Lin, J. Y. (2017). Industrial Policies for Avoiding the Middle-income Trap: A New Structural Economics Perspective. *Journal of Chinese Economic and Business Studies, 15*(1), 5–18.

Lin, J. Y., & Monga, C. (2011). Growth Identification and Facilitation: The Role of State in the Process of Dynamic Growth. *Development Policy Review, 29*(3), 264–290; "Rejoinder": 304–309.

Lin, J. Y., Sun, X., & Jiang, Y. (2013). Endowment, Industrial Structure and Appropriate Financial Structure: A New Structural Economics Perspective. *Journal of Economic Policy Reform, 16*(2), 1–14.

Lin, J. Y., & Tan, G. (1999). Policy Burdens, Accountability, and the Soft Budget Constraint. *American Economic Review: Papers and Proceedings, 89*(2), 426–431.

Lin, J. Y., & Wang, Y. (2017). *Going Beyond Aid: Development Cooperation for Structural Transformation*. Cambridge, UK: Cambridge University Press.

Maddison, A. (1995). *Monitoring the World Economy, 1820–1992*. Paris: Organisation for Economic Cooperation and Development.

Mazzucato, M. (2011). *The Entrepreneurial State*. London: Demos.

Murphy, K., Schleifer, A., & Vishny, R. (1992). The Tradition to a Market Economy: Pitfall of Partial Reform. *Quarterly Journal of Economics, 107*, 889–906.

Pomeranz, K. (2000). *The Great Divergence: China, Europe and the Making of Modern World*. Princeton University Press.

Prebisch, R. (1950). *The Economic Development of Latin America and Its Principal Problems*. New York: United Nations.

Pritchett, L. (1997). Divergence, Big Time. *Journal of Economic Perspective, 11*(3), 3–17.

Rodrik, D. (2011). *The Future of Economic Convergence*. NBER Working Paper #17400.

Rodrik, D. (2016). Premature Deindustrialization. *Journal of Economic Growth, 21*(1), 1–33.

Romer, P. (1990). Endogenous Technological Change. *Journal of Political Economy, 98*(5), S71–S102.

Rosenstein-Rodan, P. N. (1943). Problems of Industrialisation of Eastern and South-Eastern Europe. *Economic Journal, 53*, 202–211.

Williamson, J. (1990). What Washington Means by Policy Reform. In J. Williamson (Ed.), *Latin American Adjustment: How Much Has Happened?* Washington, DC: Institute for International Economics.

Part V

The "New" New Comparative Economics: Broadening the Goals

22

Rethinking Development: Broadening the Goals and Altering the Approach

Homi Kharas and John W. McArthur

1   Introduction

How do economic systems affect outcomes? This is the central question asked by students of comparative economics. To answer it, at least two things are needed: prioritized outcomes of interest and a definition of economic systems that affect those outcomes. Because economics considers itself a science, each element must in turn be subject to testable hypotheses and empirical analysis. This is a fundamental logic of neoclassical economics and its offshoot, economic development growth theory.

In "traditional development think," the most common outcome of interest is income or change in income. The economic system is defined as the set of factors generating labor, physical capital, and technologies, including ideas. Other relevant and much debated factors include potentially exogenous drivers like geography (Bloom and Sachs 1998; Nunn and Puga 2012), colonial history (Acemoglu et al. 2001), constraints to agricultural productivity

H. Kharas
Brookings Institution, Washington, DC, USA

J. W. McArthur (✉)
Brookings Institution, Washington, DC, USA

United Nations Foundation, Washington, DC, USA
e-mail: jmcarthur@brookings.edu

© The Author(s) 2021   **563**
E. Douarin, O. Havrylyshyn (eds.), *The Palgrave Handbook of Comparative Economics*,
https://doi.org/10.1007/978-3-030-50888-3_22

(McArthur and McCord 2017), susceptibility to malaria (Sachs and Malaney 2002), ethnolinguistic fractionalization (Alesina et al. 2003), legacies of the slave trade (Nunn 2008; Nunn and Wantchekon 2011), and, increasingly, susceptibility to climate change (Fankhauser and Tol 2005; Dell et al. 2012).

Notions of both outcomes and systems have evolved over time. Ever since its inception as a concept, gross domestic product (GDP) and its growth have been understood as much narrower than social welfare (Kuznets 1934). Over time, new measurement approaches and indices have been constructed to assess these broader outcomes, such as the Human Development Index since 1990 and the Organisation for Economic Co-operation and Development's Better Life Index since 2011. Meanwhile, institutions are now considered to be a major part of economic systems (World Bank 2002) and metrics like governance, democracy, and the ease of doing business have been developed and evaluated through mainstream empirical analyses of economic growth.[1] Concurrently, overarching theories of growth have had to confront challenges of parameter heterogeneity, model uncertainty, and endogeneity of explanatory factors (e.g., Rodrik 2012), leading to new econometric techniques (e.g., Durlauf et al. 2005). Nonetheless, the fundamental logic in development economics of comparing the characteristics of countries with seemingly good economic performance against those of countries with apparently bad economic performance remained unchanged for decades. This logic tied development economics to comparative economics and new institutional economics.

That frame of reference is now changing. A new strand of economic thinking is moving the field away from ordinal judgments about one country's economic performance versus another's. The starting point for this is that no country has yet found a sufficient pathway to satisfy the criteria of "sustainable development," defined as "development that meets the needs of the present without compromising the ability of future generations to meet their own needs" (World Commission on Environment and Development 1987, para. 1). A new approach of sustainable development economics (SDE) is taking shape to encompass economic, social, and environmental outcomes at the same time, supported by systems of governance across society. It is a framework incorporating multiple actors, including governments, but also firms, universities, civil society organizations, and others.

The idea that GDP is not a good measure of human well-being is not new. In a 1968 speech, Robert F. Kennedy famously quipped that "[GDP] measures neither our wit nor our courage, neither our wisdom nor our learning,

---

[1] Research projects like the Worldwide Governance Indicators, Polity IV, and the Ease of Doing Business have helped to prompt and advance respective elements of institutions-focused academic debate.

neither our compassion nor our devotion to our country; it measures everything, in short, except that which makes life worthwhile." But it is only recently that the mainstream global economics community has begun to take the issue more seriously.[2]

With involvement from the pinnacle of the economics profession, in 2008 the French government created the Stiglitz-Sen-Fitoussi Commission (Stiglitz et al. 2009) on the measurement of economic performance and social progress, just as a global financial crisis was exploding. The 2009 final Commission report is explicit in saying "the whole Commission is convinced that the crisis is teaching us a very important lesson: those attempting to guide the economy and our societies are like pilots trying to steer a course without a reliable compass" (p. 9). The Commission recommended a dual emphasis on both measures of current well-being and measures of sustainability. Since then, a number of countries have widened the aperture of their official metrics. For example, the British Office of National Statistics has regularly reported on personal well-being, India has developed an Ease of Living Index to measure the quality of life of urban citizens, and New Zealand has introduced a well-being budget as a way of guiding the allocation of public investments and spending. A series of World Happiness Reports (e.g., Helliwell et al. 2019) have also drawn attention to the underlying cross-country challenges of promoting human well-being.

The new metrics of sustainable development have common underpinnings. They look beyond GDP to other measures of life satisfaction and opportunity. They address issues of inequality by looking in more granular fashion at what is happening to different groups of people, not just to the average in a country. And they take a broad perspective on environmental issues and other global public goods, considering externalities or spillovers across time and space.[3] Together, these threads mirror the familiar critique of utilitarianism and the rise of capability theory en route to SDE. They have implications for comparative analysis that this chapter aims to consider.

At an overarching level, the framing of sustainable development has occasioned a transition from a conception of "the" developing world to "a" developing world.[4] This is partly because, as noted earlier, no country has completely

---

[2] Noting the exception of early movers like Bhutan, where the concept of Gross National Happiness was introduced in 1972.

[3] Editor footnote: Several chapters in the Handbook discuss some aspects of the relationship between income distribution and life satisfaction. See, for example, Chap. 27 by Cojocaru for an in-depth discussion of the links between inequality, life satisfaction, and preferences for redistribution, Chap. 13 by Guriev on the link between inequality and policies in transition, or Chap. 25 by Morgan and Wang on China.

[4] See Kharas (2015).

succeeded in generating outcomes that succeed fully across economic, social, and environmental fronts. Economic systems cannot be considered sustainable if they violate planetary boundaries, if they do not improve core living standards like life expectancy, or if they promote crony capitalism or state capture (see Rockström et al. 2009; Diwan et al. 2019; Åslund 2019; and Pei 2017).

It is also because there is no single view on how different types of outcomes should be weighted or prioritized. Similar to Arrow's (1950) impossibility theorem, a citizenry's diversity of rank preferences among economic, environmental, and social issues impede a "fair" prioritization, posing a central challenge to societal systems of governance. Moreover, there is no single view on how to prioritize outcomes across individual people. In many societies, norms have evolved away from pursuing objective functions that focus, implicitly or otherwise, on average population outcomes. Emphasis has commonly shifted toward maximin-type objective functions focused on mitigating exclusion, especially for identifiable groups within a population.

Conceptually, SDE frames a universal agenda that does not readily lend itself to a rank ordering of country performance.[5] Each country frames its own reference point and needs to ensure its future multi-variate measures of performance are better than current ones. In some dimensions, particularly linked to natural capital, there are global binding constraints.[6]

Instead of ranking countries, what SDE seeks to do is to help countries identify, each for itself, the strengths and weaknesses of their sustainable development approaches, often through comparative benchmarking with other countries, but along a wide range of indicators. In one sense, this redefines conceptions of ends and means, because the ends now include a broader range of material and non-material elements that might previously have been considered only "means."

Another implication of SDE is that the institutional approaches necessary to attain the ends might differ considerably from one dimension to another. Institutions are not inherently judged as "good" or "bad," but are assessed relative to the different outcomes they generate. This holds both for national and international institutions. For example, in the realm of global health and disease control, new institutions have been created precisely to tackle the problems of global public goods in a way that traditional development

---

[5] Notwithstanding attempts to consolidate individual measures of absolute progress across countries (e.g., Sachs et al. 2019), as discussed further below.

[6] For example, the carbon budget of greenhouse gas emissions associated with a 2 °C average global warming will be depleted within a short period if recent trajectories continue, and all countries will share the trajectory through the pooled nature of the world's atmosphere.

organizations could not do. The assessment of any country, therefore, rests not just with outcomes in its own domain, but in its interactions with global cooperation mechanisms.

2   Three Frames to the Challenge of Sustainable Development

Sustainable development economics has roots in classical economics. Just as the basic problem of classical economics is often described as how to allocate scarce resources to fill as many needs as possible, SDE can also be described as having a foundation in navigating scarcity across multiple concurrent domains.[7] But the analytical terrain extends beyond the traditional—and important—concerns around income and income inequality. Instead it incorporates both a broader set of outcome measures of interest and a broader conception of interests.

The problems SDE aims to solve can be distilled to three core frames. The first is a re-coupling of economic growth with higher levels of well-being for regular families. The second is a de-coupling of economic growth and environmental degradation. The third is a "we-coupling" to ensure all people perceive equitable access to their society's forward progress. This "Re-De-We" conception represents problems to be solved concurrently, rather than in sequence. In that respect it also offers a shorthand test for assessing the effectiveness of public policy.[8]

2.1   Re-coupling Economic Growth and Household Well-Being

The essence of the re-coupling frame is a shift from a traditional focus on incomes, especially average incomes, to a focus on what really matters to people. In part, this links to traditional concerns over inequality and perceptions of fairness within any society's social contract. But it also links directly to concerns about which outcomes are most important to people. Empirically, there are both objective and subjective elements.

---

[7] Scarcity of individual capabilities can inhibit life satisfaction (Mullainathan and Shafir 2013). Scarcity of natural capital can inhibit both human and planetary outcomes (Rockström et al. 2009). Scarcity of social capital can impede accumulation of other forms of capital (Glaeser et al. 2002).

[8] This frame was initially presented in McArthur (2018) in similar spirit but slightly different detail.

Among fast-growing developing economies, Botswana provides one case study of objective issues. The country is oft-cited as having been a huge economic success, with strong public institutions that had managed to avoid the "resource curse" even after a major diamond discovery that helped propel an average per capita economic growth rate of 7 percent between 1966 and 1999 (Lewin 2011). Yet by 2000, more than 35 percent of adults were estimated to be infected with HIV/AIDS, and life expectancy at birth had fallen to just 52 years, down from 61 years in the late 1980s (World Bank 2020). The same societal processes that were generating economic growth were also contributing to a rapid decline in life expectancy. In 1996, a dramatic scientific breakthrough in antiretroviral treatment shifted HIV from being a *de facto* death sentence to a treatable disease (Science 1996). But in Botswana and other countries with high HIV prevalence, it was only after an innovative multisectoral international response to make antiretrovirals available that AIDS-related mortality began to fall. Life expectancy then climbed back up quickly, reaching 69 years by 2017.

The United States, meanwhile, provides an important case at the higher end of the income scale. The country recently saw declines in average life expectancy three years in a row—2015, 2016, and 2017, linked considerably to opioids—even while experiencing consistent economic growth per capita (CDC 2020).[9] Other objective measures of well-being have been worsening in the United States too. Suicide rates have risen by roughly a third since 2000 (NIMH 2020) and the share of the population measured as obese has increased from 30.9 percent in 2000 to 40 percent in 2017 (OECD 2020).

These objective declines in measures of well-being can be linked to subjective assessments of well-being. A growing literature on "happiness" indicates that individual perceptions of utility hinge on much more than material factors.[10] Personal security, the ability to fulfill one's aspirations, agency, voice, and community are all part of the non-strictly economic dimensions of well-being. The classic depiction is captured in Fig. 22.1, mimicking Layard's (2006) chart showing a lack of connection between income and happiness in the United States. While real gross national income (GNI) per capita has more than doubled since 1975, there has been no increase—if anything a decrease—in the share of the population feeling "very happy."

Easterlin and others (2010) have confirmed this relationship in the long-term for a larger sample of developed and developing countries. Carol Graham

---

[9] Note that the United States did register a small uptick in overall life expectancy in 2018, even while suicide rates continued to climb.

[10] See, for example, the 2019 World Happiness Report (Helliwell et al. 2019) and preceding editions; also Graham (2008) in *The New Palgrave: A Dictionary of Economics (2nd edition)*.

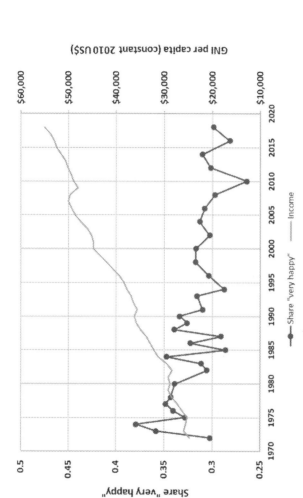

Fig. 22.1 GNI per capita and share of population feeling "very happy" in the USA, 1972–2018. (Sources: NORC at the University of Chicago (2019), World Bank (2020))

(2010) found that rapid economic growth can actually be bad for happiness (the "paradox of unhappy growth"), perhaps because of the uncertainty and instability typically associated with high growth ("will it continue"), or because of the change in relative socio-economic status that growth can bring about if one group gains more than another. Among the most prominent recent global examples of traditional economic success, China registered dramatic declines in life satisfaction concurrent with its unprecedented economic growth and poverty reduction over the 1990s and early 2000s (Graham et al. 2017). India also saw a considerable drop in life satisfaction at the same time as its major gains in economic growth and poverty reduction from 2006 to 2017 (Graham et al. 2018).

Several arguments have been put forward to explain the frequent disconnect between income and well-being, all involving an understanding that people do not always behave in the way that *homo economicus* would. These differences in behavior can have both macroeconomic effects and socio-political effects. For example, Stutzer (2003) found that higher income aspirations reduced life satisfaction, even as actual income gains improve it. Well-being depends on the relative movement of these two, not just on the absolute levels of income growth. Wooden et al. (2009) find that the combination of long hours and overworking has the greatest impact on reduced life satisfaction, because long hours detract from leisure time, family, and community commitments. Similarly, Bell et al. (2012) find that overemployment (i.e., working more hours than desired) has negative effects on different measures of self-perceived health, which in turn can negatively impact earnings, leading to an apparent contradiction between hours worked and labor earnings.

Non-material components of well-being may be important as ends unto themselves and as instruments for achieving other ends. For example, Mullainathan and Shafir (2013) map the cyclical path through which a scarcity-driven focus on immediate goals can crowd out the ability to think about the longer term. They note that low-income individuals are less able to plan for the future or handle shocks. This perpetuates a cycle of low non-economic well-being feeding into income poverty, which can further diminish non-economic well-being, generating a particularly adverse form of sustainable development challenge.

2.2   De-coupling Growth and Environmental Degradation

The essence of the de-coupling frame is a shift from focusing on what matters for human well-being to what matters for the planet. In geological terms, humanity's recent dominating nature on the Earth's physical environment has led some scientists to describe the world as now living in the "Anthropocene" epoch. Carbon emissions and climate change dominate the public discourse, but other nature-linked phenomena like species extinction, collapse of fisheries and mangroves, plastic pollution in oceans, and nitrogen and phosphorous overuse are further examples of the deteriorating state of the planet.

In an ideal world, richer societies, with access to greater levels of resources, technology and stronger institutions would put in place systems to minimize the extent of environmental degradation. In reality, this is far from the case. Figure 22.2 below shows a cross-country scatter plot, as of 2018, of economic output per ton of carbon dioxide emissions on the vertical axis and GNI per capita on the horizontal axis (expressed in purchasing power parity terms). A sustainable global economy would show a strong positive slope in the graph, with increasing economic output per unit of environmental input as incomes rise. Rich countries would be natural leaders in de-carbonizing their economies. Instead, there is no clear relationship across income levels. Many of the countries with the highest levels of economic output per ton of carbon dioxide emissions also have very low incomes, such as the Democratic Republic of Congo, Chad, and Rwanda at the top-left section of the figure.

By contrast, Australia, Canada, and the United States have relatively high average incomes but very low economic output per unit of carbon emissions. This compares to France, Great Britain, and Norway, which have similar average incomes but produce more than twice as much income per unit of emissions. Among the large and fast-growing emerging economies, China is amongst the least efficient in terms of the value of economic product per unit of emissions. India has considerably lower GNI per capita than China but a higher level of greenhouse gas efficiency. Among smaller economies, Estonia is a small economy well known for its highly successful deployment of digital technology, but still registers as highly inefficient in terms of climate-relevant technology. Trinidad and Tobago registers the lowest ratio of income generated per ton of emissions.

It is possible that the "true" version of the graph is U-shaped, whereby developing countries first grow by relying on more carbon-intensive techniques and then later turn toward decarbonization. This kind of

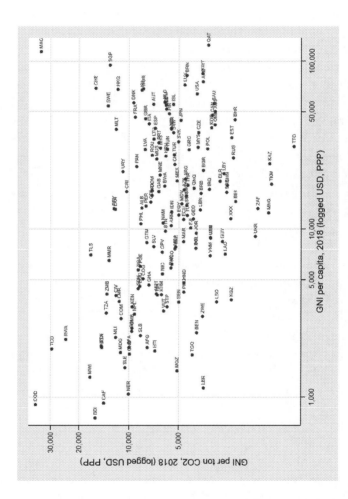

Fig. 22.2 GNI per ton of Carbon Dioxide Emissions and GNI per capita in 2018. (Note: Includes countries with populations of at least 200,000 people in 2018. Sources: Global Carbon Atlas (2019) and World Bank (2020))

environmental Kuznets curve has been suggested before (e.g. World Bank 1992) but fell out of fashion when rigorous econometric techniques were used to assess trends (Stern 2004). In any case, if current economic growth trajectories are going to continue, the amount of carbon dioxide generated per unit of GNI will need to drop by at least 90 percent by 2050, in order to remain within 2 degrees of average warming. For that reason, economic growth needs to decouple itself from greenhouse gas emissions nearly entirely, suggesting the need for widespread breakthroughs in low-carbon energy technologies. More broadly, the same de-coupling challenge pertains to many forms of environmental capital, ranging from clean air to oceanic assets to food and land systems.

2.3 We-Coupling to Leave No One Behind

The essence of the we-coupling frame is a shift in focus from national averages toward recognition that every individual person matters and identities can also matter. In terms of ethical ambition, it can be described as a requirement of leaving no one behind and identifying whether particular groups of people are being systematically excluded from life opportunities. In more technical terms, it can be considered a maximin approach to assessing progress, in that a society's overall average success is hugely discounted by the extent to which some groups of people are excluded from that success.

The most universal aspect of this challenge is unequal opportunity for women and girls. Again, the problem is not necessarily mitigated by increased incomes. On the World Economic Forum's gender equality index for 2020, arguably the best available synthesis assessment across economic, educational, health, and political empowerment measures, no country in the world registers full parity (World Economic Forum 2019). The largest gaps tend to be driven by unequal outcomes under categories of political empowerment and of economic participation and opportunity. Even the top-ranked country, Iceland, still has an average 12 percent gap for half its population across the index's indicators. Many countries also rank very differently than one might predict based solely on GNI per capita. Japan, for example, has among the world's highest average per capita incomes, but ranks 121st on the gender equality index. Meanwhile, Rwanda ranks 9th on the index, even though it is still classified as a low-income country. The Philippines ranks higher (16th) than the United Kingdom (21st) and Bangladesh ranks higher (50th) than both Luxembourg (51st) and the United States (53rd). The point here is not to interpret index rankings with false precision, but only to highlight the danger in presuming that gender parity is a simple product of higher incomes.

Problems of identity-linked exclusion and inequality are common across countries, although the mix of factors driving exclusion differs in each country. For example, race, ethnicity, geography, religion, class, sexual orientation, and indigenous status are all common drivers. The challenges are pervasive even in high-income advanced economies. In the United States, for example, Chetty et al. (2019) have shown that Black and American Indian children have considerably lower rates of upward income mobility than other groups, leading to persistent intergenerational gaps.

Being part of a majority ethnicity or identity group does not necessarily prevent negative outcomes. Case and Deaton (2017) have documented the uniquely stark increase, since the late 1990s, in all-cause mortality for white non-Hispanic adult Americans, especially those with high school education or less. The main drivers of these "deaths of despair" include increases in suicide, drug overdose, and alcohol poisoning. The trend suggests that if income growth is not accompanied by reasonable distributional outcomes, functioning healthcare institutions and an appropriate regulatory environment for prescription drugs, the usual mediating variables between income growth and mortality, the relationship between the two can weaken or even reverse.

Across the border to the north, a large share of Canada's indigenous communities have not benefitted from the same economic and social outcomes as the rest of the society (Biggs and McArthur 2018). Estimated rates of child poverty, food insecurity, and infant mortality are at least twice as high for indigenous compared to non-indigenous people (McArthur and Rasmussen 2017; Sheppard et al. 2017). As of January 2020, 58 indigenous communities still do not have access to safe drinking water through their local public systems (Indigenous Services Canada 2020). The patterns of discrimination and injustice toward Canada's indigenous people have a long and sordid history, prompting widespread public acknowledgment of the need for more proactive societal efforts to promote reconciliation (Truth and Reconciliation Commission of Canada 2015).[11]

---

[11] Recent polling indicates that nearly two-thirds of Canadians believe individual citizens have a role to play in bringing about reconciliation between indigenous and non-indigenous people (Environics et al. 2019).

3 New Thinking About Economic Systems

The proliferation of outcome variables of interest has driven a proliferation of lines of inquiry regarding drivers of causality and functional form. In theory, this need not be the case. If all key societal outcomes of interest were commonly generated through the same processes that lead to growth in output or income per capita, then research would reasonably focus on identifying the singular functional form driving progress. But since trends have varied substantially enough across enough key variables of interest, there is a strong rationale for exploring the variations in causal mechanisms that might explain the relevant ranges of outcomes.

Amid the breadth of outcomes of inquiry, SDE requires broadening the consideration of pertinent actors and means of organizing them. Parsimonious conceptions of governments interacting with firms are inadequate for capturing the drivers of progress. There might be multiple and varied complements of production for any key variable of interest. The mix of agents driving an economy to excel on health outcomes might be very different from the mix of agents that drive performance on gender equality or environmental outcomes or any other key measure of sustainable development.

Consider the example of health outcomes. Independent of traditional questions of public versus private responsibilities for health service financing and provision, health outcomes are likely to be affected by a collective assortment of health professionals participating in a globalized labor market, plus academic researchers that generate bench science and patient-based evidence, firms that develop new medical technologies and methods of service delivery, and civil society organizations that provide a challenge function to other actors. The success of public sector agents might be defined by their ability not simply to regulate market actors but also to align incentives and contributions from a full complement of scientific and civil society actors.

Moreover, health outcomes like mortality and morbidity are affected by actions and decisions made outside the health sector, such as how transport design and urban planning might affect habits of movement and diet, and in turn measures of obesity and overweightness. So, the vector of agents that might affect a single variable of interest might intersect with functional forms driving outcomes across different domains of expertise. In some respects, the conceptual overlays are similar to the traditions of economic general equilibrium modeling. However, the intersectional aspects of implied modeling across disparate domains of specialist expertise typifies the new SDE approaches.

Across SDE's dimensions of interest, the mix of pertinent actors is likely to differ by the degree of "public good-ness" embedded in the relevant issue. Infectious disease control, for example, has a high degree of public good-ness and has heavier weight of responsibility on public sector actors, including the provision of incentives for market actors to generate research, such as on vaccines with little direct commercial return. Education has a mixed degree of public good-ness, since individuals garner direct benefits from marginal investments in learning at the same time as there are economy-wide returns to labor market skills that can drive both technical and technological progress. Agriculture, meanwhile, tends to be driven by private returns to enterprise, while benefitting from a mix of public investments and interventions, ranging from roads providing market access to research that improves farm-wide productivity and insurance instruments that limit risks of bankruptcy or interrupted food supply for the non-agricultural labor force. The place-specific nature of plant technology—in that some plants can only grow in some places—defines the boundaries for technology diffusion, and hence affects the social returns to investments in plant-specific technologies and yields, which might have first-order effects on overall patterns of urbanization and structural transformation (McArthur and McCord 2017).

Another layer of complexity embedded within the new SDE is a debate over the appropriate scale of analysis. An entire new field of development economics research (e.g., Banerjee and Duflo 2011) explicitly eschews "big" questions of optimal policy approach and instead focuses on incremental pragmatism, exploring the merits of one intervention at a time, one location at a time. Part of this movement was in response to changing fashions in global conventional wisdom, particularly as advanced by international financial institutions (IFIs) that played highly influential global economic roles during the second half of the twentieth century.

For example, the IFIs shifted their orientation over time from an initial emphasis on investment in infrastructure to human capital formation, then to getting incentives right, then to public institutions, and now to resilience as the priority for economic growth. As each major cycle of prevailing policy ideas was discarded by the next one, the empirical basis for evaluating what actions might or might not actually be working on the ground became less clear. This challenge of defining country-scale counterfactuals prompted attention to smaller-scale interventions, ideally tested through randomized control trials, as had previously become common in the field of medicine and public health.

Within economics, the proliferation of RCTs has generated a wide body of field-level empirical results, often with uncomfortable implications for policymakers and policy advocates whose favored approaches hinged on less evidence than presumed. A considerable amount of research has focused on testing specific interventions and on improved understanding of household-level decision making in specific contexts. A significant element has also focused on the psychology of poverty, and the unique constraints imposed by conditions of deprivation (e.g., Mani et al. 2013). In select cases, RCTs have been implemented at a country scale (e.g., Romero et al. 2020).

The ultimate merits of RCTs and micro-empiricism have been subject to critique. Scholars like Pritchett and Sandefur (2015) assess tradeoffs between internal and external validity, finding that non-experimental evidence can outperform experimental evidence from a separate context. Deaton and Cartwright (2018) argue that RCTs can be useful in generating knowledge but need to be applied as one of many methods of understanding. Measurement of very specific interventions within very specific contexts might provide information on "what worked better" but does not necessarily provide helpful information on "what works in general" or, more importantly, "why things work."

Altogether, these debates pose deep questions around even the appropriate framing of arguments over functional form. Should empirical specifications be framed as cross-country comparative questions, as economy-specific intrinsic questions, or as hyper-targeted individual questions? Such choices affect not only the nature of research results but also the ability to compare and learn from results across frames. Different arguments might prevail for different issues. For example, the dynamics of infectious disease control might be similar enough across economies to merit cross-country comparison of systems and actors, while the incentives for fertilizer use might need to be tested in a place-specific manner, based on biophysical yield response potential, average farm size, marginal input-output cost ratios, and community-specific sociology. At the same time, the incentives promoting low-carbon energy technologies might naturally be tested at an economy-wide scale but will be of limited benefit absent complementary breakthroughs in energy storage technology, which might require highly targeted public incentives for basic science and market-based innovation.

4   Representative Institutional Shifts

At the level of international institutions, the transition to SDE is reflected in an evolution from the World Bank to the Global Fund to Fight AIDS, TB, and Malaria. During the second half of the twentieth century, the World

Bank was the world's preeminent development finance institution, with a primary focus on investments and policy actions to promote economic growth in developing countries. The shifting tides of the comparative economics debate were reflected in the shifting tides of World Bank lending practices—and corresponding debates between Bretton Woods institutions and UN organizations—but generally with an aim of optimizing economic outcomes.

By 2000, the so-called "Washington Consensus" had been driving an emphasis on macroeconomic fundamentals and market-friendly institutions as the key to long-term development success. But the emphasis on economic fundamentals provided no effective policy response to the HIV/AIDS pandemic that had by that point infected 25 million people in low- and middle-income countries, and was driving stark declines in life expectancy in many countries, such as the Botswana example described earlier. The World Bank did provide financing for health sectors in many countries, but never at a scale adequate to finance the antiretroviral treatment that was needed to keep people alive. As a result, there were no international institutions to make treatment available, and as of 2000 only around 10,000 HIV-infected people in developing countries were able to self-finance the life-saving medicine.

In that context, then-UN Secretary-General Kofi Annan, with technical support from economist Jeffrey Sachs and other leading health figures, launched the Global Fund to Fight AIDS, TB, and Malaria. The idea was to create a new form of multilateral institution outside the normative confines of Bretton Woods and UN organizations. Importantly, the Global Fund was funded primarily by advanced economy governments but had a multi-stakeholder governance structure comprised of developed country governments, developing country governments, private sector representatives, and civil society representatives from both developed and developing countries, including those representing ultimate beneficiaries of Global Fund programs. Financing was also guided by a foundation-type model, with countries needing to develop their own multi-stakeholder applications for funding vetted by technical peer review, rather than government-laden political review. The organization's unique governance model and focus on delivery targets helped to drive evidence-based decision-making that might not have been possible amid more typical intergovernmental pressures affecting a multilateral entity (Schmidt-Traub 2018).

Alongside the bilateral US President's Emergency Program for AIDS Relief, launched in 2003, the Global Fund became the primary multilateral institution for tackling the problem of access to AIDS treatment, which some policymakers, including then-Administrator of the U.S. Agency for International Development Andrew Natsios (Donnelly 2001), and some economists (e.g., Easterly 2006) considered misguided. Over time, a constellation of private, public, and civil society actors took mutually reinforcing decisions to expand public sector-type pooled procurement of antiretroviral therapy, produced by market actors, which in turn facilitated ongoing declines in the cost of treatment. This in turn enabled further expansion of treatment programs.

This new form of governance made a difference. The development community was initially skeptical—the 2008 Accra Agenda for Action recommended that "existing channels for aid delivery [be] used and, if necessary, strengthened, before creating separate new channels…" But within a few years it became clear that newly created vertical funds were doing well on resource mobilization, learning and innovation, and tracking impact and results (Gartner and Kharas 2013).

The virtuous cycle of lower cost treatment and expanded treatment generated iterative learning-by-doing in health treatment protocols. In the early 2000s, when treatment was estimated to cost $10,000 per patient per year, or even $1000 per year, the limited scale of treatment programs informed the definition of global treatment protocols, defined by CD4 counts of immune system strength in blood tests. In simplified terms, when medicine was expensive the WHO suggested a high illness threshold for when HIV-infected people should receive treatment. But as the cost of treatment declined to roughly $100 per patient per year, treatment protocols evolved such that, by 2015, WHO guidelines recommended that any person infected with the virus should be on treatment, both to limit the harm of the infection and to reduce the risk of transmission to others (see World Health Organization 2015). As of mid-2019, an estimated 24.5 million people were on antiretroviral therapy, out of an estimated 37.9 million infected people. In countries with high HIV prevalence—like Botswana, Malawi, Zambia, and Zimbabwe—life expectancy has shot up accordingly (UNAIDS 2019).

5   The Policy Interaction: Agenda 2030 and the Sustainable Development Goals

In the policy domain, the most complete expression to date of SDE is found in Agenda 2030, a 2015 agreement among all 193 member states of the United Nations to pursue 17 sustainable development goals (SDGs), accompanied by dozens of targets and indicators to be met by 2030.[12] The SDGs incorporate all three of the "Re-De-We" frames discussed above, to varying

---

[12] See United Nations (2015).

degrees. They include non-material aspects of well-being, with a clear emphasis on basic needs as well as voice and agency. There is a strong focus on gender equality. Multiple goals consider planetary health, covering land, water, and air. The agenda gives weight to both inequality and exclusion, summarized in the pledge of "no one left behind."

Unlike much of comparative economics that focuses on long-run or steady-state outcomes, the SDGs represent a growing emphasis on quantitative, time-bound goal setting across issues. The SDGs are presented as an integrated group of goals, rather than 17 separate goals. Some targets are set in absolute terms, such as the elimination of extreme poverty, and others are set in relative terms, such as a one-third reduction in non-communicable disease mortality relative to each country's baseline.

Analytically, the goals raise inherent general equilibrium-type questions around entry points and optimal sequencing (UN-IGS 2019). There can be a temptation to assess progress on each goal independently and additively ("Country A is achieving this much on poverty and this much on education, while Country B is achieving that much on poverty and that much on education"), to permit an aggregated ranking of countries across indicators. Policymakers often want to be able to compare and learn from such easy-to-understand performance metrics across countries.

The Sustainable Development Solutions Network has conducted such a ranking exercise (Sachs et al. 2019). In admirably aiming to promote rigorous benchmarking of the SDGs, a worthwhile exercise unto itself, the "SDG Index" also makes a number of analytical assumptions contrary to SDE, including that an appropriate set of weights can be agreed upon across outcome variables, despite the Arrow-type ranking paradox described earlier. In theory, a country with extraordinary success on 16 of the 17 goals could rate at the top of the synthesized index ranking. But what if the lagging goal is due to extremely high greenhouse gas emissions, and the country remains the world's top emitter? Is the country still succeeding on the challenges of sustainable development?

In order to facilitate cross-country comparisons, the index also converts relative domestic targets into absolute global benchmarks. In some cases, this leads to poor countries being judged relative to the global technological frontier, rather than to their rate of progress on local challenges. In others, it leads to modified interpretations of success in terms of ensuring universal access to basic services. For example, is a country with 99.5% access to basic services "successful" on a global standard if the 0.5% without access are all members of a group facing a long history of discrimination, such as indigenous people lacking access to clean drinking water in Canada? These are the types of conceptual challenges that emerge amid a transition from thinking about "the" to "a" developing world.

It is probably the case that the intersectionality of the goals implies that the metric of success of each should reflect the co-integration of the target indicators across goals. Similarly, there is a challenge in the maximin nature of results across outcomes of interest. For example, it is questionable to describe poverty as being sustainably reduced if hunger, or unemployment, or gender equality are not being reduced at the same time. Moreover, the current state of poverty may reflect current conditions, but not the resilience of that achievement and other issues that could also affect poverty in the long-term.

For policymakers, the operative question is how to ensure an acceleration of progress on business-as-usual trends where needed to achieve the goals. The agenda also contains indicators of progress, but differences in approaches, models, and tools available to each country will dictate how progress could be advanced in different national circumstances. The one exception is the common theme that the health of the planet is a shared responsibility across all countries, a principle bedeviled by difficulties in identifying the common but differentiated responsibilities of each.

A focus on the outcome-oriented dynamics reverses standard assessments. It is not enough to assess an intervention in terms of what has been achieved in the past tense. The question must also be asked in the future tense: is the intervention (together with others) part of a concerted package that will move the agenda forwards at the requisite speed? There is some evidence to suggest this type of goal-oriented mindset resonates more naturally with outcome-oriented disciplines like health sciences or natural sciences than with economics, which historically focuses more on marginal effects and tradeoffs (McArthur and Zhang 2018).

Although the SDGs are an intergovernmental commitment, their strength lies in the inclusive process through which they were developed. This process brought in views of business, academia, local governments, civil society, and many other voices, generating a sense of diffused conceptual ownership and partnership that is quite new. Notably, the business community has increasingly embraced the SDGs as a common reference point for its own thinking on how to incorporate environmental, social, and governance indicators into operating strategies. The Business and Sustainable Development Commission (2017) argued that the SDGs present a $12 trillion global market opportunity, flipping the conventional emphasis on corporate responsibilities.

More recently, in August 2019, 181 CEO members of the US Business Roundtable released a new statement on the purpose of the corporation that shifted away from the primacy of shareholder interests toward principles that serve the interests of all stakeholders—customers, employees, suppliers, communities, and shareholders.[13] Easy to say, a skeptic might rightly argue, but in this case there are potential indications of real change afoot. Pacific Investment Management Company (PIMCO), for instance, is one of the world's largest investment firms and has been explicitly championing SDG bonds (Mary et al. 2019). BlackRock, the world's largest asset manager, is putting sustainability at the heart of its strategy going forward and will stop investing in firms that present a high "sustainability risk."

Dynamic pathways, interrelationships, joint distributions of outcomes, global spillovers, and broad dimensions of well-being—these terms provide a sense of a new understanding of pertinent outcomes compared to steady-state economics with distributional weights. Agenda 2030 has created a growing consensus on what outcomes should be pursued, in returning to first principles, to meet the needs of the present without compromising the ability of future generations to meet their own needs. It permits the generalized ambition of sustainable development to be disaggregated into specific problems, faced by specific people, in specific places (Kharas et al. 2019).

6   Future Areas of Inquiry

Why were intergovernmental institutions governed by the conceptual debates of twentieth-century comparative economics era unable to address the AIDS pandemic, despite its horrendous human and societal consequences? Why was a new form of multilateral enterprise able to galvanize different forms of societal agents around a common set of life-and-death metrics at a relatively—in historical if not absolute human terms—rapid pace? Why have other pressing challenges, ranging from greenhouse gas emissions to billions of women facing unequal life opportunities to hundreds of millions of people lacking basic literacy skills, still not seen much progress? These are the types of questions that the new SDE seeks to address.

If SDE is defined by concurrent proliferations of outcome variables of interest, functional forms to investigate, and agents to be considered, one upshot for the new comparative economics is an expansion of the dimensions for actual comparison. In practical terms, the twentieth century norm of comparing "policy technology" across countries is now complemented by comparing policy technology across outcome domains. A post-2000 ecosystem of advances in global health policy and institutions has framed something of a

---

[13] See Business Roundtable (2019).

new global policy production function from which other expert communities are learning. For example, leaders in international education policy will not simply ask what countries can learn from each others' efforts to promote education; they now also ask what they can learn from progress in global health policy (e.g., Gillard 2019). Leaders in agriculture and food policy increasingly ask the same questions (Chatham House 2019). It is for SDE to define and debate the elements of the relevant production functions for relevant outcome variables of interest across the full range of scales of action. It is an eclectic approach, not belonging to any single school of thought, but borrowing ideas from many.

The field of SDE faces one other crucial form of frontier challenge. The accelerating pace of technological change in select industries, especially biomedical and digital communications technologies, might have consequences for the questions of how societies even manage technological change. Collison and Cowen (2019) argue that an explicit study of identifying progress-increasing interventions should be a key next step for societies, both to accelerate technological discoveries and diffusion and to manage the downsides of technological change. In past periods of technological revolution, advances in technology have been presumed to be overall welfare enhancing for society. The foremost analytical questions hinged on a search for Pareto optimality, managing tradeoffs between implementing the benefits of the new technology and limiting the costs of those adversely affected. Although we do not yet know what future technologies will offer, there is a chance that some (for example, deep fake news) will diffuse at an extremely rapid pace and will be Pareto minimizing, meaning they make everyone—or at least all but a very few—worse off. Questions of instantaneous diffusion of technological advance across globally interconnected "learning" machines could enhance monopolistic powers in forms that have never been anticipated.

We have argued that SDE must take into account a complex set of dimensions—on outcomes, technologies, institutions, partnerships, and timeframes, to name a few. It is a wide-ranging and evolving field, hopefully based in empirics, and seeking to address not just the problems that are visible today, but also the problems that may arise in the future. It differs from traditional comparative economics in that institutions are not assessed on a single scale, nor judged along only one dimension. Instead, they are tested against their contribution to solving the pressing problems of the day and may be fine-tuned, replaced, or discarded as economies, societies, technologies, politics, and the natural environment evolve. SDE does not always look for the best among existing institutions, as is the case with traditional comparative economics. It also looks toward the creation of new institutions. And it does not look at countries simply on their own terms, but also as components of a larger global partnership to achieve sustainable development.

Acknowledgments We thank Carol Graham and the editors for extremely helpful feedback on earlier drafts and we thank Helena Hlavaty for invaluable research assistance.

References

Acemoglu, D., Johnson, S., & Robinson, J. A. (2001). The Colonial Origins of Comparative Development: An Empirical Investigation. *American Economic Review, 91*(5), 1369–1401.

Alesina, A., Devleeschauwer, A., Easterly, W., Kurlat, S., & Wacziarg, R. (2003). Fractionalization. *Journal of Economic Growth, 8,* 155–194.

Arrow, K. (1950). A Difficulty in the Concept of Social Welfare. *Journal of Political Economy, 58*(4), 328–346.

Åslund, A. (2019). *Russia's Crony Capitalism: The Path from Market Economy to Kleptocracy.* Oxford University Press.

Banerjee, A. V., & Duflo, E. (2011). *Poor Economics: A Radical Rethinking of the Way to Fight Global Poverty.* Public Affairs.

Bell, D., Otterbach, S., & Sousa-Poza, A. (2012). Work Hours Constraints and Health. *Annals of Economics and Statistics, 105/106,* 35–54.

Biggs, M., & McArthur, J. (2018). A Canadian North Star: Crafting an Advanced Economy Approach to the Sustainable Development Goals. In R. Desai et al. (Eds.), *From Summits to Solutions: Innovations in Implementing the Sustainable Development Goals* (pp. 265–301). Washington: Brookings Press.

Bloom, D. E., & Sachs, J. D. (1998). Geography, Demography, and Economic Growth in Africa. *Brookings Papers on Economic Activity, 1998*(2), 207–295.

Business and Sustainable Development Commission. (2017). *Better Business, Better World.* Report of the Business and Sustainable Development Commission.

Business Roundtable. (2019). Business Roundtable Redefines the Purpose of a Corporation to Promote 'An Economy that Serves All Americans'. Retrieved February 5, 2020, from https://www.businessroundtable.org/business-roundtable-redefines-the-purpose-of-a-corporation-to-promote-an-economy-that-serves-all-americans.

Case, A., & Deaton, A. (2017, Spring). Mortality and Morbidity in the 21st Century. *Brookings Papers on Economic Activity, 2017,* 376–443.

Centers for Disease Control and Prevention (CDC). (2020). Mortality in the United States, 2018. Retrieved from https://www.cdc.gov/nchs/products/databriefs/db355.htm.

Chatham House. (2019). Towards an Outcome-oriented Food & Agricultural Aid and Development System: What is Needed to Achieve SDG 2.3 and 2.4? Centre on Global Health Security Meeting Summary.

Chetty, R., Hendren, N., Jones, M. R., & Porter, S. R. (2019). Race and Economic Opportunity in the United States: An Intergenerational Perspective. *The Quarterly Journal of Economics* (qjz042). https://doi.org/10.1093/qje/qjz042.

Collison, P., & Cowen, T. (2019, July 30). We Need a New Science of Progress. *The Atlantic*.

Deaton, A., & Cartwright, N. (2018). Understanding and Misunderstanding Randomized Controlled Trials. *Social Science & Medicine, 210*, 2–21.

Dell, M., Jones, B. F., & Olken, B. A. (2012). Temperature Shocks and Economic Growth: Evidence from the Last Half Century. *American Economic Journal: Macroeconomics, 4*(3), 66–95.

Diwan, I., Malik, A., & Atiyas, I. (Eds.). (2019). *Crony Capitalism in the Middle East: Business and Politics from Liberalization to the Arab Spring.* Oxford University Press.

Donnelly, J. (2001, June 7). Prevention Urged in AIDS Fight. *Boston Globe*.

Durlauf, S. N., Johnson, P. A., & Temple, J. R. W. (2005). Growth Econometrics (Chapter 8). In *Handbook of Economic Growth, Volume 1A* (pp. 555–677). Elsevier.

Easterlin, R. A., McVey, L. A., Switek, M., Sawangfa, O., & Zweig, J. S. (2010, December 28). The Happiness-Income Paradox Revisited. *Proceedings of the National Academy of Sciences of the United States of America, 107*(52), 22463–22468.

Easterly, W. (2006). *The White Man's Burden: Why the West's Efforts to Aid the Rest Have Done So Much Ill and So Little Good.* New York: Penguin Press.

Environics Institute, The Mowat Center, The Canada West Foundation, Le Centre d'Analyse Politique—Constitution et Fédéralisme (CAP-CF), Institute for Research on Public Policy, and The Brian Mulroney Institute of Government. (2019, October). *2019 Survey of Canadians—Toward Reconciliation: Indigenous and Non-Indigenous Perspectives.* Final Report.

Fankhauser, S., & Tol, R. S. J. (2005). On Climate Change and Economic Growth. *Resource and Energy Economics, 27*(1), 1–17.

Gartner, D., & Kharas, H. (2013). Scaling Up Impact: Vertical Funds and Innovative Governance. In L. Chandy, A. Hosono, H. Kharas, & J. Linn (Eds.), *Getting to Scale: How to Bring Development Solutions to Millions of Poor People* (pp. 103–137). Washington: Brookings Institution Press.

Gillard, J. (2019, December 3). Global Education: Ideas for the Way Forward. Global Partnership for Education, Education for All blog. https://www.globalpartnership.org/blog/global-education-ideas-way-forward. Retrieved February 5, 2020.

Glaeser, E. L., Laibson, D., & Sacerdote, B. (2002). An Economic Approach to Social Capital. *The Economic Journal, 112*(483), F437–F458.

Global Carbon Atlas. (2019). Territorial Emissions Data. Retrieved from http://www.globalcarbonatlas.org/en/CO2-emissions. Downloaded December 23, 2019.

Graham, C. (2008). Economics of Happiness. In S. N. Durlauf & L. E. Blume (Eds.), *The New Palgrave Dictionary of Economics*. London: Palgrave Macmillan.

Graham, C. (2010). Happy Talk: The Economics of Happiness. The Brookings Institution. Retrieved February 5, 2020, from https://www.brookings.edu/articles/happy-talk-the-economics-of-happiness/.

Graham, C., Laffan, K., & Pinto, S. (2018). Well-being in Metrics and Policy. *Science, 362*(6412), 287–288.

Graham, C., Zhou, S., & Zhang, J. (2017). Happiness and Health in China: The Paradox of Progress. *World Development, 96*(C), 231–244.

Helliwell, J., Layard, R., & Sachs, J. (2019). *World Happiness Report 2019*. New York: Sustainable Development Solutions Network.

Independent Group of Scientists Appointed by the UN Secretary-General (UN-IGS). (2019). *Global Sustainable Development Report 2019. The Future is Now: Science for Achieving Sustainable Development*. New York: United Nations.

Indigenous Services Canada. (2020). Ending Long-term Drinking Water Advisories. Retrieved February 5, 2020, from https://www.sac-isc.gc.ca/eng/1506514143353/1533317130660.

Kennedy, R. F. (1968). Remarks at the University of Kansas (Speech, Lawrence, Kansas, March 18). The John F. Kennedy Presidential Library and Museum.

Kharas, H. (2015, January 9). The Transition from 'The Developing World' to 'A Developing World'. *Kapuscinski Development Lecture*, Riga, Latvia.

Kharas, H., McArthur, J. W., & Ohno, I. (Eds.). (2019). *Leave No One Behind: Time for Specifics on the Sustainable Development Goals*. Brookings Institution Press.

Kuznets, S. (1934). *National Income 1929–1932*. A report to the U.S. Senate, 73rd Congress, 2nd Session. Washington, DC: US Government Printing Office.

Layard, R. (2006). Happiness and Public Policy: A Challenge to the Profession. *The Economic Journal, 116*(510), C24–C33.

Lewin, M. (2011). Botswana's Success: Good Governance, Good Policies, and Good Luck. In P. Chuhan-Pole & M. Angwafo (Eds.), *Yes, Africa Can: Success Stories from a Dynamic Continent*. Washington, DC: World Bank Publications.

Mani, A., Mullainathan, S., Shafir, E., & Zhao, J. (2013). Poverty Impedes Cognitive Function. *Science, 341*, 976–980.

Mary, S., Schuetz, C., & Albrecht, O. A. (2019, October). SDG Bonds: Their Time Has Come. PIMCO Viewpoint.

McArthur, J. (2018, December 10). These are 3 Major Challenges for the World in 2019. World Economic Forum, Agenda. Retrieved from https://www.weforum.org/agenda/2018/12/3-tasks-for-the-year-ahead-to-fix-society.

McArthur, J., & McCord, G. C. (2017). Fertilizing Growth: Agricultural Inputs and Their Effects in Economic Development. *Journal of Development Economics, 127*(July), 133–152.

McArthur, J., & Rasmussen, K. (2017). Who and What Gets Left Behind? Assessing Canada's Domestic Status on the Sustainable Development Goals. *Global Economy and Development Working Paper 108*.

McArthur, J. W., & Zhang, C. (2018). Measuring the Diffusion of the Millennium Development Goals across Major Print Media and Academic Outlets. *Global Policy, 9*(3), 313–326.

Mullainathan, S., & Shafir, E. (2013). *Scarcity: Why Having Too Little Means So Much*. Palgrave Macmillan.

National Institute of Mental Health (NIMH). (2020). Suicide. Retrieved February 5, 2020, from https://www.nimh.nih.gov/health/statistics/suicide.shtml.

NORC at the University of Chicago. (2019). GSS 1972–2018 Cross-Sectional Cumulative Data (Release 2, December 20, 2019). Retrieved from https://gss. norc.org/get-the-data/stata. Downloaded December 30, 2009.

Nunn, N. (2008). The Long Term Effects of Africa's Slave Trades. *Quarterly Journal of Economics, 123*(1), 139–176.

Nunn, N., & Puga, D. (2012). Ruggedness: The Blessing of Bad Geography in Africa. *The Review of Economics and Statistics, 94*(1), 20–36.

Nunn, N., & Wantchekon, L. (2011). The Slave Trade and the Origins of Mistrust in Africa. *American Economic Review, 101*(7), 3221–3252.

Organisation for Economic Cooperation and Development (OECD). (2020). OECD. Stat Online Database. Non-Medical Determinants of Health. https://stats.oecd.org/Index.aspx?DataSetCode=HEALTH_LVNG. Retrieved February 5, 2020.

Pei, M. (2017). *China's Crony Capitalism: The Dynamics of Regime Decay*. Harvard University Press.

Pritchett, L., & Sandefur, J. (2015). Learning from Experiments When Context Matters. *American Economic Review: Papers & Proceedings, 105*(5), 471–475.

Rockström, J., Steffen, W. L., Noone, K., Åsa, P., Stuart Chapin, F., III, Lambin, E., Lenton, T. M., et al. (2009). Planetary Boundaries: Exploring the Safe Operating Space for Humanity. *Ecology and Society, 14*(2), 32.

Rodrik, D. (2012). Why We Learn Nothing from Regressing Economic Growth on Policies. *Seoul Journal of Economics, 25*(2), 137–151.

Romero, M., Sandefur, J., & Sandholtz, W. A. (2020). Outsourcing Education: Experimental Evidence from Liberia. *American Economic Review, 110*(2), 364–400.

Sachs, J., & Malaney, P. (2002). The Economic and Social Burden of Malaria. *Nature, 415*, 680–685.

Sachs, J., Schmidt-Traub, G., Kroll, C., Lafortune, G., & Fuller, G. (2019). *Sustainable Development Report 2019*. New York: Bertelsmann Stiftung and Sustainable Development Solutions Network (SDSN).

Schmidt-Traub, G. (2018). The Role of the Technical Review Panel of the Global Fund to Fight HIV/AIDS, Tuberculosis and Malaria: An Analysis of Grant Recommendations. *Health Policy and Planning, 33*(3), 335–344.

Science. (1996, December 19). Breakthrough of the Year: New Weapons Against HIV. Retrieved February 6, 2020, from https://www.sciencemag.org/news/1996/12/breakthrough-year-new-weapons-against-hiv.

Sheppard, A., Shapiro, G. D., Bushnik, T., Wilkins, R., Perry, S., Kaufman, J. S., Kramer, M. S., & Yang, S. (2017). Birth Outcomes Among First Nations, Inuit, and Metis Populations. *Statistics Canada Health Reports, 28*(11), 11–16.

Stern, D. I. (2004). The Rise and Fall of the Environmental Kuznets Curve. *World Development, 32*(8), 1419–1439.

Stiglitz, J. E., Sen, A., & Fitoussi, J.-P. (2009). *Report by the Commission on the Measurement of Economic Performance and Social Progress*. Commission on the Measurement of Economic Performance and Social Progress.

Stutzer, A. (2003). The Role of Income Aspirations in Individual Happiness. *Zurich IEER Working Paper No. 124.*

Truth and Reconciliation Commission of Canada. (2015). *Honouring the Truth, Reconciling for the Future: Summary of the Final Report of the Truth and Reconciliation Commission of Canada.*

UNAIDS. (2019, December 1). Fact Sheet—World AIDS Day 2019.

United Nations. (2015). Transforming Our World: The 2030 Agenda for Sustainable Development. General Assembly Resolution 70/1.

Wooden, M., Warren, D., & Drago, R. (2009). Working Time Mismatch and Subjective Well-being. *British Journal of Industrial Relations, 47*(1), 147–179.

World Bank. (1992). *World Development Report 1992: Development and the Environment*. New York: Oxford University Press.

World Bank. (2002). *World Development Report 2002: Building Institutions for Markets*. New York: Oxford University Press.

World Bank. (2020). World Development Indicators Database. Retrieved January 31, 2020, from https://datacatalog.worldbank.org/dataset/world-development-indicators.

World Commission on Environment and Development (Brundtland Commission). (1987). *Our Common Future*. Oxford: Oxford University Press.

World Economic Forum. (2019). *Global Gender Gap Report 2020*. Geneva: World Economic Forum.

World Health Organization. (2015, September 30). Treat All People Living with HIV, Offer Antiretrovirals as Additional Prevention Choice for People at "substantial" risk. News Release. Retrieved February 5, 2020, from https://www.who.int/mediacentre/news/releases/2015/hiv-treat-all-recommendation/en/.

23

Explaining the Heterogeneity of Health Outcomes in Post-Communist Europe

Christopher J. Gerry

1 Introduction

Over the past half century, an East–West health divide emerged as a complex product of historical, social and economic forces. The failure of the Former Soviet Union (FSU) and Central and East European (CEE) countries to improve the health of their populations from the 1960s and the subsequent sharp falls in life expectancy in the 1990s demonstrate how socio-economic, socio-psychological and socio-cultural circumstances can combine to deliver sustained periods of declining or stagnating health even when the technologies, medicines, knowledge and policies are available to deliver improved population health. Similarly, the divergence experienced within the combined FSU and CEE region since 2000 suggests the ongoing importance of the institutional context in shaping social policies, as well as the long run impact of historical legacies on the culture and norms which shape human behaviour. In this chapter, with the historical context of the late Soviet period in mind, we focus on seeking to describe and understand the remarkable population health dynamics which characterise the former command economies.

C. J. Gerry (✉)
Oxford School of Global and Area Studies, University of Oxford, Oxford, UK

International Centre for Health Economics, Management, and Policy, National Research University Higher School of Economics, St. Petersburg, Russia
e-mail: christopher.gerry@sant.ox.ac.uk

© The Author(s) 2021
E. Douarin, O. Havrylyshyn (eds.), *The Palgrave Handbook of Comparative Economics*,
https://doi.org/10.1007/978-3-030-50888-3_23

2   Part 1: From Stagnation to Collapse

As the economies and societies of a war-ravaged Europe were rebuilt in the two decades following the Second World War, there were, as should be expected, significant advances in population health outcomes. Across Europe, life expectancy steadily increased, mortality declined and health in the poorer countries, including in the FSU and CEE, was converging on that of the richer parts of the industrialised world. Shared technological advances, in the form of new medicines and treatments, were rapidly transforming the capacity both to prevent and to treat disease. Infectious and respiratory diseases, particularly those responsible for infant and child mortality, were in decline, as knowledge of how to prevent such disease was shared and implemented across political and social divides (Vallin and Meslé 2001, 2004; Meslé and Vallin 2011).

While at the start of the twentieth century life expectancy in the countries of the FSU and CEE lagged behind Western European (WE) levels by around ten years, by the mid-1960s, a clear convergence in health trends was in evidence. Indeed, as Fig. 23.1 shows, just three years separated the life expectancies experienced in Western Europe (WE), Japan, Australia, North America, CEE, the Baltics, Belarus, Russia and Ukraine. To some extent, this period of 'catching-up' reflected the high priority that the communist system placed on universal access to basic health care and to the eradication of infectious disease in particular. During the 1950s, boosted by high rates of economic growth, the countries of the FSU and CEE established primary care facilities, adopted new medical protocols and acted swiftly to reduce the negative effects of vaccine-preventable diseases. The rapid reductions in infant and child mortality that followed, and the associated increase in life expectancy, provided ample evidence of the benefits of these policies and completed the industrialised world's so-called 'epidemiologic transition' (Omran 1971).

In the years that followed the countries of the industrialised world, other than those of the FSU and CEE, continued to experience steady rises in life expectancy for men and women as they began to address the new population health challenges linked with cardiovascular disease (CVD) and the health behaviours giving rise to it. Unfortunately, the countries of CEE and the FSU did not engage with this 'cardiovascular revolution' and so, just as CVD mortality began to recede in Western Europe, it correspondingly increased rapidly across Eastern Europe and the FSU, although it was in the latter that health deteriorated most consistently through the 1970s and 1980s.

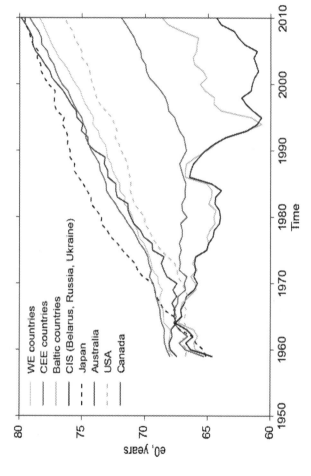

Fig. 23.1 Life expectancy at birth in selected countries, 1950–2010. *Source*: Gerry et al. (2017)

From the late 1960s therefore, a prolonged period of stagnating and declining health in CEE and the FSU began and a new East–West health gap took hold. Developments were particularly bad in the FSU, where health outcomes not only stagnated, but the post-war health gains themselves were actually overturned, in what Shkolnikov et al. (2004) termed the 'mortality reversal'. Remarkably therefore, from the late 1960s, these countries not only bucked the global trend of convergence towards a low-mortality regime but gave back some of the gains they had made through the epidemiologic transition. Worse was to come though as, following the fall of the Berlin Wall and the subsequent collapse of the Soviet Union, many parts of the region entered a new and acute stage of epidemiological crisis characterised by steep rises in mortality due to cardiovascular disease, injuries and violence, and infections and respiratory diseases. As Fig. 23.1 shows, these trends were starkest in the countries of the FSU but, among these, Russia was the most extreme example and so merits separate examination. Figure 23.2 shows the remarkable collapse in life expectancy for Russian males from 64.2 in 1989 to 57.6 in 1994. Overall though, the aggregated observed divergence in East–West health that emerged in the second half of the last century was a product of the long-run stagnation in public health outcomes and the extraordinary increases in mortality during the early 1990s.

Before moving on, we should address an obvious concern relating to the reliability and consistency of mortality data during the Soviet period, which might lead one to question whether the unprecedented fluctuations of the 1990s were, at least in part, statistical artefacts. In this regard, the noteworthy contributions of several distinguished epidemiologists and demographers (Meslé et al. 1992; Shkolnikov et al. 1995; Leon et al. 1997; Shkolnikov and Meslé 1996; Meslé et al. 2003; Meslé and Vallin 2011; Leon 2011; Grigoriev et al. 2014) have proved decisive in forensically interrogating—and reconstructing where necessary—Soviet era mortality statistics. Through examining standardised death rates by cause, it has been established beyond doubt that the post-Soviet mortality crisis is not an artefact stemming from unreliable data or inconsistent classifications. On the contrary, while mortality rates in less responsive mortality categories (e.g. neoplasms) remained stable, the observed increases in those categories that can respond over shorter time periods (e.g. external cause deaths, infectious deaths and circulatory deaths) demonstrate a clear shift from an undisputed long-term—sustained but gradual—deterioration of public health to a new, acute stage of epidemiological crisis at the start of the 1990s.

While, as documented elsewhere in this book, the late-Soviet decline in communist economic performance and the economic and political disruption

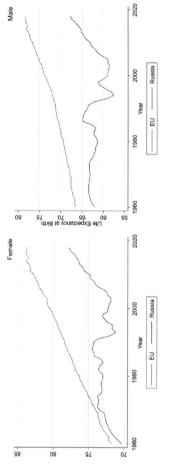

Fig. 23.2   Life expectancy in Russia and the European Union, 1950–2010. *Source*: Leon (2011)

of the early 1990s had commonalities across the region, population health patterns have exhibited long-run and short-run heterogeneity which does not correlate with the corresponding map of economic performance. In very broad-brush terms, in the countries of what became known as the 'mortality belt'—the countries of the Former Soviet Union with western European borders (Belarus, Estonia, Latvia, Lithuania, Moldova, Russian Federation and Ukraine)—life expectancy for both males and females had reversed from the 1960s and then fluctuated considerably during both the 1980s and the 1990s. In contrast, the countries which border the mortality belt (Czech Republic, Poland, Slovakia, Hungary, Romania and Slovenia) and that also underwent substantial economic shocks during the early 1990s experienced only minor increases in mortality during the initial transitional shock. Finally, somewhat paradoxically perhaps, the Central Asian Republics, despite being poorer and experiencing deeper and more prolonged economic crises, suffered less steep increases in mortality during the 1990s and from lower initial levels of crisis-related mortality (Guillot et al. 2011). We comment further on this in part 3, but for now simply observe that the East–West health gap that had emerged in the 1960s was becoming more complex over time, as new mortality gaps between parts of the FSU and CEE started to take shape.

3   Part 2: From Collapse to Recovery

The 1990s was a decade of turmoil for the former command economies of CEE and FSU. Besides the political, economic and social transitions imposed on their populations, many of these countries also experienced major health and demographic shocks in the form of sharply rising mortality rates. As noted earlier, male (female) life expectancy at birth in Russia declined by an astonishing 6.6 (3.3) years in a period of just 5 years, from 1989. To put this decline in perspective, since the beginning of the 1990s, it has taken 30 years of steadily improving health outcomes in the Western industrialised countries to accumulate a 5-year increase in life expectancy. In contrast, by the early 2000s, Russian life expectancy, which had been in the top 40 during the 1960s, was ranked 136 in the world, just below Bangladesh, North Korea and Iraq, and alongside Ukraine, Azerbaijan, Kyrgyzstan, Kazakhstan and Turkmenistan (United Nations Population Division 2019). There were similar collapses in ranking for Belarus, Ukraine and the Baltic States, while the CEE countries experienced smaller but nonetheless significant declines (e.g. Poland fell from 40th to 58th during the same period).

In one sense, it is easy to comprehend these dramatic developments. The collapse of the command economy system resulted in a new era of profound economic and social instability, somewhat euphemistically referred to as the 'transition'. The introduction of market economic reforms in countries with few public or private financial or legal institutions, unsatisfied consumer demand, a monetary overhang and a dysfunctional labour market gave rise to growing official and unofficial unemployment, the spread of unpaid wages and payment-in-kind, hyperinflation that wiped out people's savings, the growth of inequalities to levels comparable to Latin America and the pervasive rise of poverty (Mickiewicz 2005). In this context, fostering, as it did, increased levels of crime, family breakdown, poor nutrition, deteriorating work conditions, weakening adherence to already loose health and safety guidance, and the abuse of alcohol and drugs, it is no surprise that population health suffered and that, in many parts of the region, male life expectancy plummeted to just 60 years of age (Fig. 23.3(a)) and similarly, for females, there were widespread falls by multiple years in the space of a short period of time at the start of the 1990s (Fig. 23.3(b)).

As Fig. 23.3 makes it clear, the population health decline was experienced across the region but not in equal measure. Accordingly, in the Baltic States, Russia, Ukraine, and Belarus, the decline was much steeper than that in CEE, South-Eastern Europe, the Caucasus, and Central Asia. For the entire region however, following the initial decline as transition began, health began to improve in the mid-1990s and for CEE, South-Eastern Europe, the Caucasus and Central Asia this set-in train what would become a steady and continual increase in their life expectancies so that, by 2000, life expectancy was above its 1990 level in all of these sub-regions. It was these rapid gains in life expectancy in Czech Republic, Hungary, Poland, Slovakia and Slovenia that drove the emergence of a new mortality gap in Europe, between the countries of the mortality belt on the one hand and the CEE and South-Eastern European countries on the other.

This new mortality gap was exacerbated by the 1998 currency crisis, which gave rise to renewed episodes of poverty and economic vulnerability that became associated with a further period of deteriorating health in Russia, Ukraine, Belarus and the Baltic States. For these countries it was only during the buoyant years of economic growth in the early 2000s that they progressed beyond their 1990 (and hence also their 1960) level of life expectancy. However, this process itself has propagated further regional heterogeneity as part (the Baltic countries) of what we referred to earlier as the mortality belt are now progressing towards the trend set by the CEE countries, while other

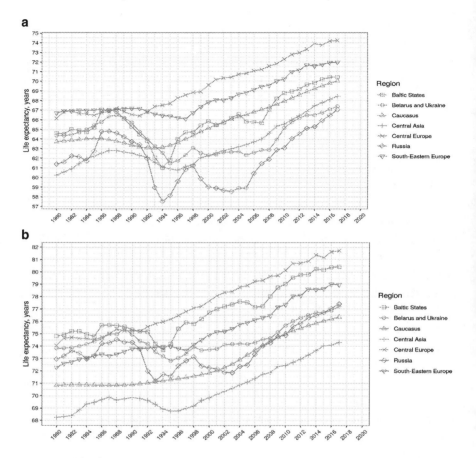

Fig. 23.3 **(a)** Life expectancy at birth (25 transition countries), males 1980–2020. **(b)** Life expectancy at birth (25 transition countries), females 1980–2020

parts (e.g. Russia, Ukraine and Belarus) remain serious laggards (Gerry et al. 2017).

The rapid economic recovery from the 1998 financial crisis, driven by a global boom that prompted steeply rising oil prices, was impressive and sustained and gave rise to reductions in poverty, greater scope for public investment and progressive social policy, renewed private sector investment and, for the countries of CEE and South-Eastern Europe, the prospect and reform incentives of EU membership. Correspondingly, the entire transition region has benefitted from increases in life expectancy which have taken all countries well beyond their initial transition conditions but still well below those of the industrialised Western OECD countries. Reassuringly, the more recent global financial crisis, beginning in 2007–2008, and subsequent economic stagnation have had little identifiable empirical impact on health outcomes in the region, bar a relatively mild slowdown in the rate of growth of life expectancy.

Surveying the data, we don't have to look far for evidence of the proximate drivers either of the 1990s collapse in life expectancy or of the recovery in the 2000s. As political, economic and social disorder set in during the 1990s and the mortality rate rose, it soon became clear that the excess mortality was due principally to what are known as 'external cause' deaths—including those resulting from accidents and violence, poisoning and other adverse effects— and, as for much of the rest of the world, cardiovascular related deaths. Figure 23.4 plots the extraordinary story of external cause mortality during the transition period. Taking 1988 as the point of departure, there is relatively little difference between the regions, with external cause mortality rates ranging from 75 per 100,000 to 115 per 100,000, albeit with the higher rates observed for the countries of the mortality belt.[1] Through the first half of the 1990s, the rate increases in all parts of the region, but the rate of increase in the Baltics and in Russia, and to a lesser extent, Ukraine and Belarus, is phenomenal. In Russia, for example, the rate increased from 110 in 1988 to almost 250 in 1994 (the highest in the world at that time). To put this in perspective, the corresponding rate for western European countries typically lay below 50 per 100,000 during the 1990s. Mirroring overall mortality rates in the FSU countries, the rate fell sharply in the mid-1990s, before beginning a sustained decline from 2002 in Russia and 2005 in the Baltics, interrupted only by a brief upturn at the time of the 1998 financial crisis.

While the most recent data are not yet comprehensively available, what the evidence does show is that the mortality belt countries have experienced extraordinary fluctuations and spikes in mortality due to injuries, accidents and poisonings and that only by 2014–2015, rates had approximately returned to the already high levels seen in 1988. Meanwhile, the other post-communist countries of CEE, South-Eastern Europe, and Central Asia had all experienced only modest increases in this category of mortality, followed by sustained falls from mid-way through the 1990s, which has seen their external mortality rates fall well below that observed in the mortality belt countries and converging slowly towards those observed in western European countries.

Turning to the other major cause of death in the transition region—cardiovascular and heart-related diseases—we see a different but no less important set of trends. As explained earlier, the Communist region did not follow the

---

[1] The sharp rise recorded for the Caucasus in 1988 relates to the devastating earthquake of 1988 in the Armenian town of Spitak, causing more than 25,000 deaths.

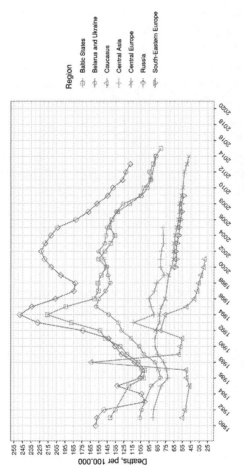

Fig. 23.4 Age-standardised deaths due to external causes, all ages, per 100,000

West into the cardiovascular revolution from the 1960s and so the initial conditions for transition included exceptionally high rates of ischaemic heart disease mortality for most of the region, though it was historically lower in the CEE region.[2] During the early part of the 1990s, the mortality rate rose noticeably in the mortality belt region as well as in the rest of the Former Soviet Union. For Belarus and Ukraine, the rate continued to rise through to 2004, while in Russia—mirroring all-cause mortality—it fell through to 1998, increased through to 2004, before beginning a steady decline. The Baltic States experienced their peak in 1994 and have subsequently enjoyed a rate which is now converging towards western European levels. For the Caucasus and Central Asia, with less reliable data available, it would appear that the rate of deaths due to ischaemic heart disease is now roughly what it was at the start of transition.

There are two key take-aways from Fig. 23.5. First, deaths due to heart disease were and are still very high, relative to OECD countries, as well as to many emerging economy countries. By way of comparison, the equivalent age-standardised death rates for Japan, Germany, Italy, Norway, Spain, Brazil and Mexico are all below 100 (Nowbar et al. 2019). There are a number of reasons why cardiovascular disease mortality has been higher in the FSU and CEE than in other industrialised countries. The quality of primary health care and of secondary preventative health care, characterised by low levels of treatment and relatively poor adherence to medication is a prime reason, but region-distinct health behaviours also play a role too. Smoking, particularly among males, has been at levels consistently above 50% for several decades, while there is strong evidence that the pattern of alcohol consumption (i.e. drinking to intoxication) is also linked to high levels of cardiovascular-related mortality and, though less systematically clear, that diet and exercise are also important factors (Ezzati et al. 2015). All of these factors weigh more heavily in the FSU than they do in Central or South-Eastern Europe.

The second takeaway of Fig. 23.5 is that, with the exception of CEE, at the start of transition there was little difference, within the region, in the rate of mortality due to heart disease, whereas by 2014–2015, there was a remarkable divergence emerging that saw Ukraine and Belarus with some of the highest mortality rates in the world, Russia with high but rapidly declining death rates, the Baltic States (particularly Estonia) leading Russia in this decline,

---

[2] There is some consensus, notwithstanding the earlier comments regarding the reliability of data, that deaths due to cardiovascular disease in the Soviet era may have been over-recorded as physicians faced pressure to record well-defined diagnoses even in cases where the cause of death was not absolutely evident. This implies that the observed increase in these deaths in the 1990s is a lower bound estimate of the actual increase (Meslé et al. 1992).

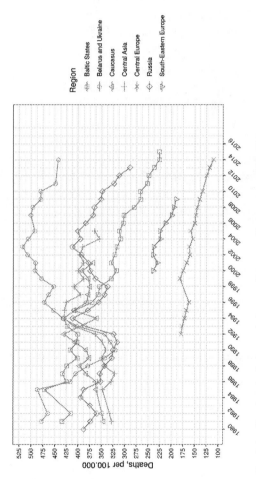

Fig. 23.5 Age-standardised deaths due to ischaemic heart disease, all ages, per 100,000

while the CEE region was converging on those parts of the world with mortality rates below 100. In sum, a combined look at the trends and patterns in deaths due to external causes and heart (and cardiovascular) disease sheds light not only on the overall East–West European health divide but also upon how the 'East' part of that divide is itself fracturing into distinct sub-regions— some of which are converging on the West and some of which remain as laggards.

There have inevitably been many studies digging deeper into these data. In particularly, there are forensic seams of demographic (Shkolnikov and Cornia 2000; Vishnevsky 2003; World Bank 2005), epidemiological (Leon et al. 1997; McKee et al. 1998; McKee and Shkolnikov 2001; Leon et al. 2007; Zaridze et al. 2009) and social science (Shapiro 1995; Cockerham 2000; Cornia and Paniccia 2000; Brainerd and Cutler 2005; Gerry 2012) literature examining the unique patterns of fluctuation in health outcomes that came to dominate the public health narrative across this region in the 1990s and early 2000s. Indeed, it is no surprise that the literature has focused on the unprecedented fluctuations of the 1990s more than the differential rates of recovery in the subsequent two decades.

Although there is some disagreement and much nuance emerging within this literature, there are perhaps four important stylised facts which can be agreed upon. First, there was more similarity in the economic and political disruption within the transition region than there was in the health outcomes associated with the disruption (i.e. the diversity in health outcomes is not a straightforward reflection of the diversity of income per capita outcomes). Second, a mortality belt comprising Russia, Ukraine, Belarus, Moldova, and the Baltic States, with worse population health outcomes, pre-existed the period of economic and political transition but was impacted systematically differently by it during the 1990s. Third, no matter the historical context and legacy of the Soviet period, there were uniquely steep fluctuations in life expectancy (and related health indicators) during the 1990s. Fourth, since the 1990s, a further divergence has emerged, with parts of the mortality belt (e.g. the Baltic countries) now converging on the dynamics of Western OECD countries, and parts remaining in relative stagnation, while the CEE region makes rapid progress in catching up with the West (EBRD 2016).

Before moving on, it is instructive to situate this emerging heterogeneity within a more global context. The most recent data (United Nations Population Division 2019) confirm that Belarus, (113), Moldova (120), Russia (126) and Ukraine (119) remain ranked alongside the FSU Central Asian countries, and the developing countries of South Asia (e.g. Bangladesh) and North Africa. In contrast, the CEE countries and Estonia have had a stronger relative performance. Czech Republic (46), Estonia (54), Poland (52), Slovakia (61) and Slovenia (31) now find themselves among or ahead of the rapid developers of South East Asia (e.g. China, Vietnam), the traditionally healthier countries of South Eastern Europe and the emerging markets of Central and South America. Indeed, the absolute gap between these CEE countries and the rich OECD countries is narrowing progressively. This is broadly consistent with the technical study of Gerry et al. (2017), which, in statistically examining convergence among different health indicators, and decomposing by age and gender, concluded that 'some countries in the transition region are stuck in low level equilibria, while others are beginning to converge on the health dynamics of western advanced economies'. Interestingly, both that study and the UN Population data suggest that the Baltic States themselves are now diverging internally, with Estonia joining the more advanced CEE countries and Lithuania and Latvia remaining closer to the other under-performing FSU countries.

4   Part 3: Explaining Comparative Health Outcomes in Transition Economies

A compelling multidisciplinary literature has helped to establish the proximate causes of the unique empirical developments outlined in the previous two sections. While much remains disputed on the margins, the powerful role of external cause death and cardiovascular related deaths provide the necessary clues for beginning to understand these health patterns. The literature also broadly concurs that while the underlying stagnation in health was caused by the long-run failure to address the rise of cardiovascular disease, the fluctuations of the 1990s, and their later echoes in parts of the region, were caused by the stress associated with the political, social and economic turmoil of the 1990s. The stress placed by the transitional process on individuals is associated with an increased risk of circulatory disease and is, in turn, exacerbated by the increased dangerous use of alcohol (and alcohol surrogates) consumed as a behavioural response to the stress (e.g. Shkolnikov et al. 2004; Zaridze et al. 2009). Yet these behavioural responses differed greatly across the region.

From a development perspective, one may have expected ex ante that economic and social turmoil would impact the health of infants and the elderly—as the potentially most vulnerable population groups—most severely. Yet, beyond a very brief initial shock at the start of transition, this is not the pattern observed in the countries of the mortality belt. Alongside declining maternal and neonatal deaths, mortality rates soon started to fall for the elderly and for children, even as overall life expectancy was in decline. On reflection, this is not the paradox it might at first seem, as the Soviet system bestowed acute care systems which had already demonstrated success in reducing deaths from communicable disease and those occurring in infancy, including through establishing comprehensive childhood vaccination programmes, and was beginning to improve the treatment of chronic conditions among elderly patients. A development perspective is therefore not the appropriate one for understanding health patterns in the FSU and CEE countries. In actuality, for the countries of the mortality belt, it was working-age adults, and particularly males, who suffered the largest and most striking increases in mortality and who continue to be most vulnerable in the laggard countries of the FSU today.

Having established that health was deteriorating in the region over the long run, that the social and economic collapse had differential health effects across the region and that, where health deteriorated most starkly, it was the working age—males in particular—that bore the brunt, more recent literature has attempted to explain these patterns with reference to the implementation and effects of economic and political reform policies carried out during the 1990s. Mackenbach (2013) and Mackenbach et al. (2013) explored the importance of political determinants, in particular democratisation, along with other social and economic factors, on population health. Their findings that democratic stock is positively related with health outcomes are in line with a tentative consensus in the literature (e.g. Baum and Lake 2001; Besley and Kudamatsu 2006), although neither the precise mechanism through which this effect operates nor its empirical grounding in CEE and the FSU is yet established.

On the more economic side, attention fell on the causal pathways from privatisation and liberalisation strategies through to individual health experiences. Stuckler et al. (2009) argued that the rapid implementation of mass privatisation was a crucial determinant of differences in adult mortality trends. While these claims were forcefully undermined by Earle and Gehlbach (2010), Gerry (2012) and others, they were important insofar as they raised the question of how economic policies and strategies implemented at the macro level can influence and shape micro-level outcomes and how this relationship is conditioned by institutional factors. Subsequent work (Idram et al. 2016) has allowed for a preliminary examination of some of the pathways (e.g. unemployment, low wages, social capital) linking macroeconomic strategies (e.g. mode of privatisation, pace of liberalisation) with individual-level outcomes (e.g. life satisfaction, health).

While the important debates in the aforementioned literature were intel-
lectually lively, the continued focus on the causal effects of specific decisions
taken in the early part of the 1990s on health outcomes that have continued
to respond in similar ways to subsequent social and economic turmoil (e.g. in
1998, 2008, 2014) is surely misplaced. The Baltic States provide a useful
reminder of why. From the mid-1990s (Fig. 23.3) life expectancy recovered
rapidly in all three countries, while Russia and, to a lesser extent, Ukraine and
Belarus continued to be affected by political, social, and economic disturbances, such as the economic crisis of 1998. Figure 23.3 also shows a downturn in life expectancy in the Baltic States during 2004–2005 and, although
not shown in that figure, this is precisely the period where, despite experiencing similar economic booms, Lithuania fell behind Estonia and Latvia in
reducing adult working-age deaths. From this point, the Baltics themselves
began to diverge from one another in ways that it is difficult to imagine are
linked to policy decisions taken in 1991–1992 (Jasilionis et al. 2011).

To further illustrate this, Fig. 23.6 presents the mortality rates for Russian
men and women of working age and draws our attention to the consistent

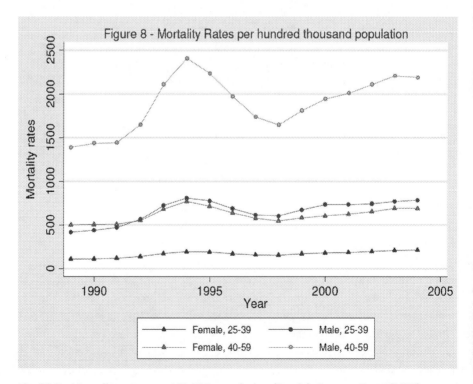

Fig. 23.6 Mortality rates per 100,000 population (Russia). *Source*: Gerry (2007)

pattern of excess mortality among elderly cohorts of working-age males. The figure also demonstrates that this mortality differential pre-dates the collapse of the Soviet Union and continued well beyond the initial period of economic and social dislocation and into the decade of economic recovery and growth (1998–2008). As we have seen, beyond the period of this figure, Russian life expectancy increased fairly rapidly, but the contribution to total mortality of these age groups remains unusual.

Figure 23.7 plots the mortality rate by age for the 12 FSU countries for various years, according to data availability, since the global financial crisis. To put this in perspective, consider that, if we were to plot this graph for advanced OECD economies, it would appear as a series of largely flat lines situated

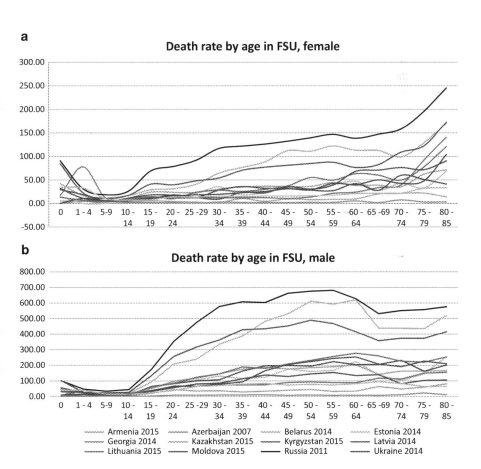

Fig. 23.7 (a) Female mortality rates per 100,000 population in 12 FSU countries (various years). (b) Male mortality rates per 100,000 population in 12 FSU countries (various years)

close to the *x*-axis before starting to turn upwards around the 65–70 years marker and then rising sharply through to age 85–90. In other words, mortality rates would be low across the life course and then would be dominated by those dying at old age. This, in essence, captures the health challenges facing advanced economies. No longer are they fighting to come to terms with CVD or man-made diseases threatening the working-age population but are instead developing their capacity to cope with increasing levels of morbidity and multimorbidity among the growing elderly population.

For females, Fig. 23.7 shows that, compared to advanced economies, there are excess deaths in most FSU countries as they approach age 50 approximately and thereafter there are relatively steep increases in the mortality rate from around age 70. However, Russia, Belarus and Ukraine stand out among these countries as they each have many more excess deaths across the adult life span. In Russia, for example, the death rate for 50-year-old females is three times the average of the main group of FSU countries.

For males, the picture is starker still, with Russia, Belarus, and Ukraine contrasting even more sharply with the other nine FSU countries. The latter group experiences excess deaths progressively across the life course, before flattening out at around age 60, and therefore not experiencing the sharp rise in mortality among the oldest age groups, typically seen in advanced economies. In contrast, Russia, Ukraine and Belarus all follow a pattern with sharply rising mortality rates from around age 15, all the way up to around about age 50–55, before then declining and flattening out through the older age groups. In other words, in each case, mortality rates for middle-aged males are higher than the rates for elderly males. This is not the case for advanced economies, is increasingly not the case for the CEE economies and is also much less of a concern for the other FSU countries. And this has been a sustained pattern across more than two decades.

These figures provide compelling evidence that Russia, Belarus and Ukraine are indeed very special cases with regard to their population health outcomes. In each case, the burden of ill-health for males has been and remains greater than that for females and, as discussed earlier, this is particularly the case for mortality due to alcohol (CVD, liver cirrhosis, external causes) and tobacco (lung cancer, CVD)-related causes. In each of these countries therefore behavioural risk factors such as alcohol use and smoking, and metabolic risk factors, including high systolic blood pressure, high total cholesterol, and high body mass index, continue to contribute strongly to the burden of disease, in ways that are different to elsewhere. The inability of the health system to respond quickly enough to CVD-related and behavioural health challenges and the low level of health system finance probably also interacted with specific cultural and economic factors to magnify the effects of socio-economic transition on mortality.

This is not to dismiss some impressive and largely successful public health policies that have introduced strict controls on alcohol and tobacco sales and related advertising and that have begun to increase duties on these products in all three countries. These policies have delivered success, and tobacco and alcohol use has fallen precipitously and contributed to the observed growth in life expectancy in these countries as well as elsewhere. Rather, it is to note that in Belarus, Ukraine and Russia there have been particular patterns in age- and gender-related population health that deserve our attention, even as there have been substantive improvements in population health generally and, particularly from 2005 to 2011 in Russia, rapid growth in life expectancy for both men and women.

Before concluding therefore, and with strong evidence of both the burden of ill-health and the proximate drivers of it, let us pause to reflect upon the fundamental social and cultural drivers which interact with social and economic circumstances and characteristics to have the extraordinary impacts we observe on successive cohorts of middle-aged males. Put differently, it seems that, no matter the cohort, middle-aged males have been consistently drinking, smoking, committing suicide, succumbing to work place and road traffic accidents and neglecting diet and exercise in far greater numbers and at far greater cost than any other population groups in these, or indeed in most other, countries. To make sense of this, we must briefly revisit the story of economic transition through the lens of the economic, social, geographical and cultural specificities of Russia.[3]

5   Part 4: Focus on Russia

By the time of the 1998 financial crisis, Russian industrial production had fallen by 60% as the outdated industrial structures of the Soviet Union were exposed to market forces. Even following a period of rapid economic growth and industrial restructuring after 1998, by 2015, industrial production stood at just 85% of its 1990 level and only the gas sector has regularly surpassed 1990 levels of production (Illarionov 2013). This industrial 'decline' has transformed the labour market, the suitability of human capital, and the lives

---

[3] In the interests of brevity, we focus this part of the discussion specifically on Russia, although most of what is said can equally well be applied to Belarus and Ukraine, subject to the caveat that Russia is of course the natural resource powerhouse of the region.

of the workers employed in these sectors. Between 1992 and 2015, the proportion of the labour force recorded as 'industrial' declined from 34 to 19% while the percentage of labour employed in wholesale/retail trade and catering increased from 7 to 21% and the total number employed in the private sector from single digits to 62% (Russia in Figures 2016).

These changes left middle-aged males, with occupational and training backgrounds in the industrial sector, facing competition for fewer and lower paid jobs, often outside their region of residence. Many were faced with the option of seeking employment in alternative sectors, requiring different or lower skills, retraining for the new economic and industrial landscape or, as has been the case with large numbers, relying on the formal and informal institutional support of the Russian labour market in the form of wage arrears, payments-in-kind, unpaid leave and the shifting of workers into part-time employment (Gimpelson and Kapeliushnikov 2014). Indeed, these same institutional responses have echoed once again during recent economic stresses, with significant increases in unpaid wages and part-time employment being recorded in Samara, Tver, Ivanovo and Ulyanovsk—regions with high concentrations of workers in the transport sector (Operational Monitoring 2016).

Understanding how these unusual institutional forms took root is important for understanding the lives of Russian workers during the last three decades. In the Soviet Union, work–life balance was largely mediated through the enterprise, particularly in 'single company' towns. A typical worker might live in housing stock owned by the enterprise, receive medical care from an enterprise polyclinic, leave children at an enterprise kindergarten and utilise leisure facilities owned by the enterprise. Accordingly, the life trajectories of the people of these enterprises and towns have been inextricably linked to the fortunes of the firms themselves. Where the firms have stagnated or failed, the lives of the workforce have mirrored them not only because of the labour market effects but also because of the impact on the housing stock, health care, child care and other forms of welfare provision. That is, it is not only job loss per se that results in stress and vulnerability, but persistent downward socioeconomic mobility linked to deteriorating labour market conditions, lack of renewal of enterprise-level social welfare provision (and housing) and the accompanying gradual erosion of prestige and self-esteem.

These experiences have inevitably come up against the sense of self-worth and identity of the typical Russian male, for whom the capacity to support his family is integral. In the Soviet period, male wages were also typically insufficient to provide full support for the household independently and therefore most women worked outside of the home. To supplement this dual-wage earner household structure, the model of the enterprise, elaborated earlier, provided for many of the household resources that the male wage alone could not provide for in the form of childcare, subsidised food and household assets and enterprise health care. In this environment, the male breadwinner identity was asserted through the expectation that they earn more and provide their earnings to the household budget. Women would combine waged work with their domestic responsibilities and make a more modest 'top-up' contribution to the household budget. The resulting tripartite model—male earnings, female earnings, enterprise support—shaped the emergent roles and responsibilities of the man, preserving the 'breadwinner' stereotype through higher earnings and the female 'caregiver' stereotype through the expectation that women earn less, do less paid work and combine work with their domestic responsibilities (Kiblitskaya 2000)—the so-called 'double burden'.

However, across much of Russia, this tripartite model has essentially collapsed and the responsibility for supporting the family has been increasingly returned to its individual members, as the welfare state and the enterprises providing it have progressively failed. At the same time, the emergent labour market institutions with their downwardly flexible wages, have undermined the capacity for Russian males to maintain a significant provider role, particularly middle-aged males with increasingly obsolete skills. In consequence, the cultural norms that defined the Soviet model are extended into the modern era but without the safety nets and social support mechanisms that were embodied in the Soviet enterprise.

Outside of the labour market, at home, the traditional cross-generational matrifocal model of sharing has taken on renewed importance in the context of economic instability and the changing nature of welfare provision. The powerful mother–grandmother nexus serves to facilitate continued female labour force participation while also compensating for the withdrawal of enterprise and state provided welfare. Yet, where this occurs, it furthers the marginalisation of males. Specifically, those unable to fulfil the perceived primary breadwinner role find little scope for defining new roles within a domestic sphere in which the cross-generational combination of women dominates. Ashwin and Lytkina (2004) characterise this process through which the labour market difficulties of middle-aged males have been further compounded by a domestic marginalisation, as a new kind of 'double-burden'. While versions of this are also found in other developed and transition societies (e.g. the Baltics), in Russia there are at least two additional factors that have served to normalise it. First, the extended nature of industrial decline and stagnation is a particular by-product of Russia's economic geography. Second, in Russian urban areas especially, there is a limited tradition of (healthy) 'masculine' activities outside of the home and workplace through which to build a meaningful sense of self.

On this basis, Ashwin and Lytkina (2004) argue that men in Russia were especially vulnerable to the rapid changes in the labour market and in social life that took place in the early transition period and that became normalised across much of the stagnating industrial landscape of Russia. Unemployed, underemployed or under earning males, cede their main household-based identity as the breadwinner. Confronted by this loss of status, large numbers of males turn to alcohol—their (male specific) primary means of stress relief (Abbott et al. 2006). As we have seen, the crisis in male mortality that characterises population health patterns in Russia, Ukraine and Belarus has been principally driven by excessive death rates among working-age men, due to external causes (accident, suicide, violence, and alcohol poisoning) as well as the eight disease categories closely linked with alcohol abuse. Indeed, the evidence is overwhelming (Zaridze et al. 2009) that male use (and misuse) of alcohol has played a crucial role in the evolution of population health that we have observed. Not only is consumption high (among those that drink) but it involves hazardous consumption patterns in the form of binge drinking. It, of course, also follows that the misuse and abuse of alcohol are most common among those suffering unemployment, downward wage flexibility, and marital breakdown.

In sum, the evidence is clear that, as well as being most common among those with lower educational status and employment in manual occupations, alcohol abuse is closely associated with family breakdown, and with unemployment and labour market 'failure' often acting as the link (Stickley et al. 2015). That is, among middle-aged men, lacking the social workplace-oriented bonds of their earlier years, further instability in employment and its consequent impact on family life and masculine identity is the most likely explanation for social isolation and the escalating alcohol abuse associated with it during this period of the life course. For the current cohort of middle-aged Russian males, growing up as they did in the Soviet Union, experiencing their early labour market years during the turbulent upheavals of the 1990s and finding, as they entered middle age, the economic, industrial and social landscape transformed, the strains and stresses have been acute and, just as in the 1990s, many still struggle to survive.

6 Conclusion

This chapter has sketched out a half century long population health narrative for the former command economies of CEE and the FSU. The narrative has established a pattern of stagnation and decline from the 1960s to the 1980s, which gave rise to an East–West health divide in Europe. After a long period of convergence caused by reductions in child mortality, the east of the continent incrementally fell behind once the iron curtain descended. Then, as the curtain was raised, in the early 1990s, the entire Eastern European and Former Soviet region experienced major public health shocks as their command economies collapsed, although these shocks to health differed greatly in their depth and breadth across the region. As the nineties unfolded, a further mortality gap emerged in the Eastern part of Europe itself, defined by the so-called mortality belt. This and the rapid recoveries that have taken hold across the region since then have heralded a period of growing, post-Communist heterogeneity in health outcomes. Some countries are now converging on Western health standards, while others remain closer to those of the less developed world, despite their more advanced industrial and social welfare heritage.

Digging deeper into the data, we demonstrated that the mortality belt countries are those with higher levels of external cause and cardiovascular related deaths and that these, in turn, have responded rapidly to fluctuations in economic performance, which have raised population stress levels and given power to behavioural traits and practices, such as alcohol misuse, that underpin the extreme health patterns witnessed, in particular, in Russia, Ukraine and Belarus. In these countries, it is successive cohorts of middle-aged men who have found themselves in environments in which they have succumbed to these unhealthy behaviours. But uncovering the fundamental reasons for this is complex. Money and prosperity are important, but they are not at the root of the problem: male health outcomes are generally better in the poorer Central Asian countries than they are in Russia, Ukraine and Belarus, yet the same is not true for females, subject to the same economic, social and political contexts. This suggests that, while investment in the health system and progressive social policies are important, these—and economic development more generally—also interact with specific cultural, historical and institutional factors that shape the outcomes we observe.

In the case of Russia, we examined how industrial and labour market change have combined with the domestic household sector, traditions of social welfare provision, gender identity and behaviours in ways which appear to have persistently disenfranchised middle-aged males. Yet, the FSU countries of Central Asia experienced more persistent economic and industrial declines, and are characterised by not dissimilar expectations and norms around gender roles, but exhibit more favourable adult mortality patterns. The evidence and data are less reliable for the Central Asian region, but in Kyrgyzstan and Kazakhstan, it has been established that fluctuations in mortality in the 1990s were, as in Russia, linked to changes in deaths due to cardiovascular disease and external causes. There is evidence too that alcohol plays a key role in those deaths. However, compared with Russia, the rate of death in these categories is lower and the degree of fluctuation is smaller, and so the mortality advantage that these Central Asian countries developed over Russia in the 1990s and 2000s was largely due to differences in patterns and amounts of alcohol consumption. Moreover, the patterns of mortality in Central Asia are divided over ethnic lines, with the mortality patterns of those with Russian ethnicity aligning much more closely with those observed in Russia (Guillot et al. 2011). This observation not only re-emphasises the importance of cultural norms in determining health patterns but also reminds us of the folly of over-reliance on purely economic and social frameworks for understanding differences in mortality levels and trends within the CEE and FSU region.

So, where does this leave us? The empirical stylised facts of European population health make gloomy reading for the countries of CEE and the FSU as they still seek to bridge the health gap with the West that emerged during the 1960s and 1970s. Their progress in doing so has been diverse. The best performing countries (e.g. Czech Republic—now Czechia—and Slovenia) are beginning to close that gap, while others (e.g. Russia, Ukraine and Belarus) are left a long way behind. These developments draw attention to at least four newer population health phenomena which underscore the population health outcomes that countries can achieve and which all merit further research. First, for a given level of economic development, the capacity of society to achieve health improvements through effective health policies, enhanced social conditions or favourable behavioural changes varies greatly. Second, the factors that drive health behaviours are a complex product of country-specific industrial and labour market dynamics, socio-economic change, norms and behaviours. Third, population health responds to reforms of political and economic institutions and, likely, the interaction between them. Finally, as societies become more successful at extending lives, the sources of future health divides may well lie in their capacity to make further life expectancy gains at old age. All four areas provide rich possibilities for Comparative Area Studies research.

References

Abbott, P. A., Turmov, S., & Wallace, C. (2006). Health World Views of Post-Soviet Citizens. *Social Science & Medicine, 62*, 228–238.

Ashwin, S., & Lytkina, T. (2004). Men in Crisis in Russia: The Role of Domestic Marginalisation. *Gender & Society, 18*(2), 189–206.

Baum, M. A., & Lake, D. A. (2001). The Invisible Hand of Democracy: Political Control and the Provision of Public Services. *Comparative Political Studies, 34*(6), 587–621.

Besley, T. J., & Kudamatsu, M. (2006). Health and Democracy. *American Economic Review, 96*(2), 313–318.

Brainerd, E., & Cutler, D. (2005). Autopsy on an Empire: Understanding Mortality in Russia and the Former Soviet Union. *Journal of Economic Perspectives, 19*(1, Winter), 107–130.

Cockerham, W. (2000). Health Lifestyles in Russia. *Social Science and Medicine, 51*, 1313–1324.

Cornia, G. A., & Paniccia, R. (Eds.). (2000). *The Mortality Crisis in Transitional Economies*. Oxford: Oxford University Press.

Earle, J., & Gehlbach, S. (2010). Mass Privatisation and the Post-communist Mortality Crisis: Is there Really a Relationship? *The Lancet, 375*(9712), 372.

European Bank for Reconstruction and Development. (2016). *Transition for All: Equal Opportunities in and Unequal World*. Transition Report, 2016–2017. Chapter 2.

Ezzati, M., Obermeyer, Z., Tzoulaki, I., et al. (2015). Contributions of Risk Factors and Medical Care to Cardiovascular Mortality Trends. *Nature Reviews Cardiology, 12*, 508–530. https://doi.org/10.1038/nrcardio.2015.82.

Gerry, C. J. (2007). 'The Most Acute Problem': Russia's Vanishing Men. In P. Duncan (Ed.), *Convergence and Divergence: Russia and Eastern Europe Into the Twenty-First Century* (Studies in Russia and Eastern Europe series 2). London: UCL SSEES.

Gerry, C. J. (2012). The Journals are Full of Great Studies but can We Believe the Statistics? Revisiting the Mass Privatisation-Mortality Debate. *Social Science and Medicine, 75*(1), 14–22.

Gerry, C. J., Raskina, Y., & Tsyplakova, D. (2017). Convergence or Divergence? Life Expectancy Patterns in Post-communist Countries, 1959–2010. *Social Indicators Research, 140*, 309–332.

Gimpelson, V., & Kapeliushnikov, R. (2014). *Between Light and Shadow: Informality in the Russian Labour Market*. IZA Discussion Paper, No. 8279. Bonn.

Grigoriev, P., Meslé, F., Shkolnikov, V., Andreev, E., Fihel, A., Pechholdova, M., & Vallin, J. (2014). The Recent Mortality Decline in Russia: Beginning of the Cardiovascular Revolution? *Population and Development Review, 40*(1), 107–129.

Guillot, M., Gavrilova, N., & Pudrovska, T. (2011). Understanding the "Russian Mortality Paradox" in Central Asia: Evidence from Kyrgyzstan. *Demography, 48*(3), 1081–1104.

Idram, D., King, L., Gugushvili, A., et al. (2016). Mortality in Transition: Study Protocol of the PrivMort Project, a Multilevel Convenience Cohort Study. *BMC Public Health, 16*, 672.

Illarionov, A. (2013). "Industrial Catastrophe in Post-Soviet Russia," Cato at Liberty. Retrieved from http://www.cato.org/blog/industrial-catastrophe-post-soviet-russia

Jasilionis, D., Meslé, F., Shkolnikov, V., & Vallin, J. (2011). Recent Life Expectancy Divergence in Baltic Countries. *European Journal of Population, 27*(4), 403–431.

Kiblitskaya, M. (2000). Once We Were Kings: Male Experiences of Loss of Status at Work in Post-communist Russia. In S. Ashwin (Ed.), *Gender, State and Society in Soviet and Post-Soviet Russia* (pp. 90–104). London: Routledge.

Leon, D. (2011). Trends in European Life Expectancy: A Salutary View. *International Journal of Epidemiology, 40*, 271–277.

Leon, D., Chenet, L., Shkolnikov, V., Zakharov, S., Shapiro, J., Rakhmanova, S., et al. (1997). Huge Variation in Russian mortality Rates 1984–1994: Artefact, Alcohol or What? *The Lancet, 350*, 383–388.

Leon, D., Saburovo, L., Tomkins, S., Andreev, E., McKee, M., & Shkolnikov, V. (2007). Hazardous Alcohol Drinking and Premature Mortality in Russia: A Population based Control Study. *The Lancet, 369*(9578), 2001–2009.

Mackenbach, J. P. (2013). Political Conditions and Life Expectancy in Europe, 1900–2008. *Social Science & Medicine, 82*, 134–146.

Mackenbach, J. P., Hu, Y., & Looman, C. W. N. (2013). Democratization and Life Expectancy in Europe, 1960–2008. *Social Science & Medicine, 93*, 166–175.

McKee, M., Sanderson, C., Chenet, L., Vassin, S., & Shkolnikov, V. (1998). Seasonal Variation in Mortality in Moscow. *Journal of Public Health, 20*(3), 268–274.

McKee, M., & Shkolnikov, V. (2001). Understanding the Toll of Premature Death Among Men in Eastern Europe. *British Medical Journal, 323*, 1051–1055.

Meslé, F., Shkolnikov, V., & Vallin, J. (1992). Mortality by Cause in the USSR in 1970–1987: The Reconstruction of Time Series. *European Journal of Population, 8*, 281–308.

Meslé, F., & Vallin, J. (2011). Historical Trends in Mortality. In *International Handbook of Adult Mortality* (pp. 9–47). New York: Springer.

Meslé, F., Vallin, J., Véronique, H., Andreev, E., & Shkolnikov, V. (2003). Causes of Death in Russia: Assessing Trends since the 1950s. In I. E. Kotowska & J. Józwiak (Eds.), *Population of Central and Eastern Europe. Challenges and Opportunities* (p. 389). Warsaw: Statistical Publishing Establishment.

Mickiewicz, T. (2005). *Economic Transition in Central Europe and the Commonwealth of Independent States* (Studies in Economic Transition). Palgrave Macmillan.

Nowbar, A. N., Gitto, M., Howard, J. P., Francis, D. P., & Al-Lamee, R. (2019). Mortality From Ischemic Heart Disease: Analysis of Data from the World Health Organization and Coronary Artery Disease Risk Factors from NCD Risk Factor Collaboration. *Cardiovascular Quality and Outcomes, 12*(6), 1–11.

Omran, A. R. (1971). The Epidemiological Transition: A Theory of the Epidemiology of Population Change. *The Milbank Memorial Fund Quarterly, 49*(4), 509–538.

Operational Monitoring of the Economic Situation in Russia: Trends and Challenges to Socio-Economic Development. (2016). No. 9(27).

Russia in Figures. (2016). Federal'naya sluzhba gosudarstvennoi statistiki. Retrieved from www.gks.ru

Shapiro, J. (1995). The Russian Mortality Crisis and Its Causes. In A. Anders (Ed.), *Russian Economic Reform in Jeopardy?* (pp. 149–178). London and New York: Pinter Publishers.

Shkolnikov, V., & Meslé, F. (1996). The Russian Epidemiological Crisis as Mirrored by Mortality Trends. In J. Da Vanzo (Ed.), *Russia's Demographic "Crisis"* (pp. 113–161). Santa Monica: RAND Center for Russian and Eurasian Studies.

Shkolnikov, V., Meslé, F., & Vallin, J. (1995). La Crise Sanitaire en Russie, 1970–1993. *Population, 50*(4–5), 907–982.

Shkolnikov, V. M., Andreev, E. M., Leon, D. A., McKee, M., Meslé, F., & Vallin, J. (2004). Mortality Reversal in Russia: The Story So Far. *Hygiea Internationalis, 4*(4), 429–480.

Shkolnikov, V. M., & Cornia, G. A. (2000). The Population Crisis and Rising Mortality in Transitional Russia. In G. A. Cornia & R. Paniccia (Eds.), *The Mortality Crisis in Transition Economies* (pp. 179–253). New York: Oxford University Press.

Stickley, A., Koyangi, A., Roberts, B., Murphy, A., Kizilovaf, K., & McKee, M. (2015). Male Solitary Drinking and Hazardous Alcohol Use in Nine Countries of the Former Soviet Union. *Drug and Alcohol Dependence, 150*, 105–111.

Stuckler, D., King, L., & McKee, M. (2009). Mass Privatisation and the Post-communist Mortality Crisis. *The Lancet, 373*, 399–407.

United Nations Population Division. (2019). Retrieved November 14, 2019, from https://www.un.org/en/development/desa/population/index.asp

Vallin, J., & Meslé, F. (2001). Trends in Mortality in Europe since 1950: Age-, Sex- and Cause Specific Mortality. In *Trends in Mortality and Differential Mortality* (pp. 31–186). Strasbourg: Council of Europe.

Vallin, J., & Meslé, F. (2004). Convergences and Divergences in Mortality: A New Approach of Health Transitions. *Demographic Research, Special Collection 2, 23*, 11–44.

Vishnevsky, A. (2003). *The Depopulated Superpower*. Russia in Global Affairs, No. 3. Retrieved from http://eng.globalaffairs.ru/numbers/4/488.html

World Bank. (2005). *Dying Too Young: Addressing Premature Mortality and Ill Health Due to Non-communicable Diseases and Injuries in the Russian Federation.* Washington, DC: World Bank.

Zaridze, D., Maximovitch, D., Lazarev, A., Igitov, V., Boroda, A., Boreham, J., et al. (2009). Alcohol Poisoning is a Main Determinant of Recent Mortality Trends in Russia: Evidence from a Detailed Analysis of Mortality Statistics and Autopsies. *International Journal of Epidemiology, 38*(1), 143–153.

24

Building the Good Life: Growth, Reforms and Happiness in Transition

Peter Sanfey

1   Introduction

In the past four decades, behavioural economics has taken off as a major area of research. Nobel Prizes in economics have been awarded to some of the leading contributors to this field, such as Daniel Kahneman (in 2002), Robert Shiller (in 2013) and Richard Thaler (in 2017). In his entertaining memoir, Thaler (2015), noting his own appointment as President of the American Economic Association and that of Shiller the following year, joked that "[T]he lunatics are running the asylum!"[1] But many of the findings and implications of behavioural economics, far from being treated as jokes or curiosities, are now taken very seriously by academics and policy-makers. The establishment

---

The author is Deputy Director for Country Economics and Policy, EBRD, and a Senior Visiting Fellow at the European Institute, London School of Economics. I thank Paul Frijters, Jakov Milatović, Jelena Nenadić, and the editors of the Handbook, Elodie Douarin and Oleh Havrylyshyn, for helpful comments and suggestions. The views in this chapter are those of the author only and not of the EBRD.

[1] Thaler (2015, p. 347).

P. Sanfey (✉)
European Bank for Reconstruction and Development, London, UK
e-mail: sanfeyp@ebrd.com

© The Author(s) 2021
E. Douarin, O. Havrylyshyn (eds.), *The Palgrave Handbook of Comparative Economics*,
https://doi.org/10.1007/978-3-030-50888-3_24

of the "nudge" unit at the heart of the UK government is just one example of policies being driven by the insights of this fast-growing field.[2]

One of the main areas of interest for behavioural economists has been that of individual well-being—how it is determined and what the implications of how people feel about life are for their behaviour and decision making. Many different terms are used to capture the concept, with "subjective well-being", "life satisfaction" and "happiness" being the most popular. Research in this field has exploded in recent decades; Easterlin (2019) even draws a parallel between the "Happiness Revolution" of the late-twentieth century and the industrial and demographic revolutions of previous centuries. Economists in particular have exploited large data sets to gain new insights into what makes people happy and why some people and nations are more satisfied than others. The cross-country focus has been especially relevant from a comparative economics perspective, because it raises fundamental questions about the influence of different systems and institutions on well-being.

My focus in this chapter is on the evolution of life satisfaction in former communist or socialist countries of central and eastern Europe and the former Soviet Union (FSU) during the transition period, which for most of these countries began in the early years of the 1990s. The first part of this process was traumatic, typically featuring deep recessions, growing unemployment and poverty, and large-scale emigration of many younger educated people in search of a better life.[3] Once transition countries started to appear in cross-country league tables of life satisfaction, they were usually clustered near the bottom. Has this "happiness gap" persisted over time? And what can be done to ensure that any remaining gaps are narrowed or closed in the long term? These are the main questions I will attempt to answer below.

Recent life satisfaction trends in the transition region have been encouraging. In this chapter I will argue that there is clear evidence that the conditional happiness gap has been closing steadily during the transition to the point where it no longer exists. By "conditional", I mean the difference in the level of happiness or satisfaction after controlling for differences across countries in other variables, particularly average income per capita. A raw (unadjusted) happiness gap still remains, however, between transition countries and advanced OECD members. Whether this can be fully closed over time depends on the extent to which transition countries can build robust market economies and the institutions needed to sustain high levels of material

---

[2] More details on the nudge unit, or Behavioural Insights Team (to use the more formal name), are available here: https://www.gov.uk/government/organisations/behavioural-insights-team.

[3] Prior to transition, emigration opportunities had been very limited except in certain countries such as those of former Yugoslavia.

well-being. In this chapter I will point to recent research that draws a link between life satisfaction and some of the qualities that are needed for successful economies, such as good governance, environmentally friendly policies and measures to promote the inclusion of disadvantaged groups.

2   The Economics of Happiness: A (Very) Short Overview

What makes people happy? This age-old question has preoccupied philosophers, politicians, social scientists and ordinary people for thousands of years. As the historian Darrin McMahon remarks, "[T]he search for happiness is as old as history itself" (McMahon 2006, p. 1). But for one branch of social science—economics—this search was neglected for many years. Economists like to measure things, and happiness or satisfaction, by its very nature, is inherently difficult to quantify. One can simply ask people how happy they are and then compute and analyse the results, but economists have traditionally been wary of such an approach, preferring to examine the "revealed preference" of what people do, rather than what they say.[4]

All of this has changed in recent decades. Easterlin's (1974) study of the cross-country link between income and satisfaction was an early example of economists taking an interest in subjective well-being. His paper was little noticed at the time but is now widely cited. Labour economists such as Hamermesh (1977), Freeman (1978) and Borjas (1979) used subjective data to analyse job satisfaction and its importance for behaviour in the workplace. But, as Clark (2018) notes, it was not until the 1990s that the literature really began to take off. Why this was so may be explained by a combination of factors, including the following.

First, the past few decades have seen an enormous growth in comprehensive and high-quality data sets that include questions on subjective well-being. National surveys such as the British Household Panel Survey (BHPS) or the German Socio-Economic Panel (GSOEP) provide a wealth of information on large, random samples of individuals, following many of them over time and thus allowing panel data analysis. Global surveys such as the World Values Survey (WVS) and the Gallup polls, while not panels, are highly informative about the differences across countries and regions in how people perceive their well-being. And for the transition region, the three waves of the EBRD-World Bank Life in Transition Survey (LiTS) (discussed in more detail below)

---

[4] The notion of revealed preference was first introduced by Samuelson (1938).

give an unrivalled overview of how the transition has affected people's lives, attitudes and well-being.

Second, economists have increasingly recognised that using economic reasoning and econometric techniques can give new insights on the correlates of life satisfaction and the size of these relationships. Economists have brought a rigour to the analysis of subjective data that complements and extends the work of other social sciences in this field. To illustrate this point, consider the following generic equation:

$$Y = \alpha + \beta X + \gamma C + \varepsilon, \tag{24.1}$$

where Y is a measure of subjective well-being, X is a set of control variables, including individual characteristics as well as aggregate variables, C is a set of country (or regional) dummies, and α and ε are the constant and error terms, respectively. The vectors β and γ can be estimated using appropriate econometric techniques, for example, by taking into account the ordinal nature of the dependent variable (and hence using ordered probit or logit rather than ordinary least squares), by adjusting standard errors (clustering) for differences in level of aggregation on the right-hand side, and so on. Once the βs are obtained (and subject to the normal caveats and confidence levels), they can tell us whether, and by how much, happiness is related to personal variables such as income or employment status. They can also enable calculations on the monetary costs and benefits of different levels of satisfaction. For example, the estimates can tell us how much extra income would be needed to compensate for being unemployed rather than employed. The γ estimates allow us to see which countries/regions have an unexplained gap (either positive or negative) in satisfaction, namely, a level of satisfaction that differs from other countries/regions in ways not fully explained by other control variables.

Third, subjective data are now trusted by economists and policy-makers to an extent that was unimaginable several decades ago. Partly this reflects the fact that the literature has revealed a number of findings that occur repeatedly across different surveys, countries and time.[5] Robust results in the literature include the "U-shaped" relationship between life satisfaction and age (satisfaction declines with age up to a point, usually around the mid- to late-40s, and rises thereafter), the negative impact of unemployment on happiness, and

---

[5] Authoritative overviews of the economics of happiness literature include books by Layard (2005), Frey (2008), Powdthavee (2011), Weimann et al. (2015) and Clark et al. (2018), and survey articles by Frey and Stutzer (2002) and Clark (2018). The annual *World Happiness Report* (started in 2010—Helliwell et al. 2019 is the latest edition) is also an excellent guide to the literature and the latest research and findings on global levels of happiness.

the fact that richer countries tend to report higher levels of well-being on average than poorer ones.

Lastly, the increasing use of satisfaction data may also be due to the fact that efforts to corroborate these data by other means, such as time use data, show a significant correlation. But subjective data are inevitably prone to fluctuations and mis-measurement to a greater extent than objective data on variables such as income, education level and so on. People's happiness or mood can be influenced by the framing and location of the question within the survey, changing reference points and random events.[6] On balance, however, a broad consensus has been reached that the advantages and usefulness of subjective data on well-being outweigh the methodological concerns. Reviewing the literature in this area, Kahneman and Krueger (2006, p. 7) conclude that "[G]lobal life satisfaction questions have been found to correlate well with a variety of relevant measures". And a comprehensive set of guidelines prepared by the OECD (2013) argues convincingly that subjective well-being data contain valid information, though it cautions that "affect" data, which are related to feelings or emotional states, are less reliable than measures of life satisfaction.

3 Life Satisfaction in Transition: The Early Years

At the time of writing (late-2019), it is just over 30 years since the fall of the Berlin wall, the symbolic event that launched the transition to market economies in central and eastern Europe, and soon after in the Soviet Union, which collapsed at the end of 1991. In the west, these developments were almost universally seen as a good thing. Optimism abounded in academic and policy circles. Phrases such as the "end of history", the "Washington consensus" and the "coming Russian boom" entered the popular discourse.[7] Many believed that the transition to market forces would soon bring strong growth and unalloyed benefits to people who had endured decades of stagnation, shortages and relative decline.

As we now know, the reality proved much more complicated and difficult than most had foreseen. All transition countries, virtually without exception, entered deep recessions, and some took many years to return to pre-transition

---

[6] See, for example, Deaton (2012).

[7] The origins of these phrases are usually attributed to, respectively, Fukuyama (1989), Williamson (1990) and Layard and Parker (1996).

levels of GDP. Inequality rose sharply, with some people—mainly the younger, urban and better educated, as well as the politically connected—doing well while many others suffered badly. The harsh impact of transition was seen not just in economic measures but also in other socio-economic variables. For example, research by Adserà et al. (2019), building on findings first presented in EBRD (2016), shows that there was a dip of more than one centimetre (in some specifications of the model) in the height of people born around the start of transition. They attribute this phenomenon to a combination of the falling economies, deteriorating health systems and food scarcity prevalent in the first years of transition. For many other people, the upheaval to their lives caused by transition was undoubtedly a major cause of stress and unhappiness.

The early years of transition—the first half of the 1990s—coincided with a surge of interest globally, as noted, in research on subjective well-being. But relatively few studies were carried out at this time on happiness or life satisfaction in the former communist region. There was a growing awareness that transition was making many people unhappy, but the data to confirm this were scarce.[8] Once the first decade of transition was over, however, researchers began to document the extent of the happiness gap in the transition region.

Several authors used the World Values Survey to measure well-being across countries and over time. The key question in the WVS is the following: "All things considered, how satisfied are you with your life as a whole these days?" with answers being on a numerical scale from 1 (most dissatisfied) to 10 (most satisfied). Helliwell (2002) carries out an analysis of the first three waves, in 1980–1982, 1990–1991 and 1995–1997, respectively. This paper combines individual and aggregate data and includes a range of OECD and non-OECD countries, with the latter including several transition countries in wave 2 and even more in wave 3. A limitation of the paper is that transition countries are grouped into regions in order to save degrees of freedom. There are two transition groups: one for eastern Europe and the other for the former Soviet Union (FSU). The econometric results suggest that life satisfaction was particularly low in both regions in wave 2, but a difference emerged by wave 3, with levels of satisfaction recovering somewhat in eastern Europe but not in the FSU.

Sanfey and Teksoz (2007) also use the WVS, focusing on waves 2–4, with wave 4 having been carried out in the period 1999–2002. For those transition countries included in all three waves, a V-shaped pattern is evident in most cases, with wave 3 (mid-1990s) being the low point. The econometric results bring out the positive association between life satisfaction and levels of education and income, in line with patterns observed from studies in non-transition countries. The U-shape age pattern is also apparent, though the recovery in happiness in later years is more sluggish than typically found in western studies, highlighting the difficulties transition was causing for older people. And life satisfaction was higher in countries with better standards of governance, a finding to which I return below.

Another paper that uses the WVS is Guriev and Zhuravskaya (2009). Their paper replicates some of the above results but goes further than previous research in exploring why people are unhappy in this region. Their results show that the happiness gap can be explained by a range of individual and aggregate variables. The gap is no longer statistically significant once one takes into account the decline in the quality and quantity of public services, the rise in inequality, the increase in income volatility and the unanticipated drop in human capital (because skills acquired under the old regime were often no longer useful in the new circumstances).

By the mid-2000s, therefore, we had a clearer idea of how people in much of the transition region had been affected by the changes of the previous 15 years. But we were missing a comprehensive picture of the whole region—from central Europe to central Asia—of the attitudes, values and experiences of individuals in different countries. This is the gap that the Life in Transition Survey (LiTS), designed and implemented jointly by the EBRD and World Bank, was designed to fill. The LiTS is a household survey, carried out periodically in virtually all transition countries, as well as some non-transition comparator countries, with a sample of at least 1000 individuals per country. Three waves have been completed: in 2006, 2010 and 2016.[9]

In LiTS I, interviewees were asked whether they agreed/strongly agreed or disagreed/strongly disagreed with the following question: "All things considered, I am satisfied with my life now." The option "neither agree nor disagree" was also allowed, giving a five-point scale. For the region as a whole, the positive responses outweigh the negative by 44 per cent to 33 per cent, with 23 per cent neither agreeing nor disagreeing.[10] This was seen at the time as mildly encouraging.[11] But, as EBRD (2007b) noted, similarly worded questions in western Europe or North America typically yielded satisfaction rates of 80–90 per cent. Such a difference highlights how far, as of the mid-2000s, the

---

[9] Further information about the LiTS and the data from all three rounds of the survey are available from the EBRD website: https://www.ebrd.com/what-we-do/economic-research-and-data/data/lits.html. See also Sanfey (2013).

[10] Those who replied "don't know" or who did not answer the question are excluded from this calculation.

[11] See EBRD (2007a).

transition region still had to go to deliver levels of well-being comparable to those of advanced market economies.

4   The Global Crisis and Its Impact on Well-Being

The global crisis in 2007–2009 hit the transition region somewhat later than in the most advanced countries, but with an impact that was severe and sustained, with reverberations that are still being felt more than a decade later. The crisis originated in the US mortgage sector in summer 2007, spilling over soon after into other financial instruments and institutions, and across borders to other advanced market economies in Europe and elsewhere. The effect on the transition region was apparent in just a few countries by the first quarter of 2008, but it spread gradually to other countries throughout that year and, by the first quarter of 2009, it was affecting virtually the whole region (EBRD 2009). The impact on aggregate GDP was dramatic: average (weighted) growth in the transition region dropped from 4.1 per cent in 2008 to -5.5 per cent in 2009, according to EBRD (2013), with few countries managing to escape a recession.

How did the crisis affect levels of subjective well-being? To answer this, we can turn to the second round of the LiTS, which was rolled out in mid-2010. This round repeated the first wave's life satisfaction question discussed earlier. It also added a similar question at the end of the survey, namely: "All things considered, how satisfied or dissatisfied are you with your life as a whole these days? Please answer on a scale of 1 to 10, where 1 means completely dissatisfied and 10 means completely satisfied." It turns out that the responses to the two life satisfaction questions are broadly consistent although they differ significantly among some groups, and the answers to the later question are influenced to a degree by previous questions on social capital (see Nikolova and Sanfey 2016). For ease of comparison with the first wave, I will focus here on responses to the earlier question (on a five-point scale).

Several interesting findings emerged from the survey (see EBRD 2011a). First, levels of satisfaction overall dropped on average only slightly relative to 2006. The percentage of those who agreed (or strongly agreed) in 2010 that they were satisfied with life was 42.7 per cent, versus 44.2 per cent in the previous round. Out of 29 transition countries, life satisfaction rose between 2006 and 2010 in 13 cases and fell in 16. Second, there was a clear link between movements in satisfaction scores and in GDP. Those countries that suffered severe recessions in the crisis such as Romania, Slovenia and the three Baltic states (Estonia, Latvia and Lithuania) also witnessed steep drops in average life satisfaction. In contrast, there was a large increase in the percentage of those satisfied with life in Azerbaijan and Mongolia, both of which emerged relatively unscathed from the crisis. A simple cross-country regression confirmed the significant positive correlation between changes in average life satisfaction and the GDP growth rate in 2009 (see EBRD 2011b). And third, the data also showed a positive correlation between satisfaction and optimism, with the latter being measured by those who agree that children born now will have a better life than the current generation.

These results point to a certain level of resilience in the transition region. But the second round of the LiTS also brought home the persistence of the raw happiness gap between these countries and those in western Europe. Five non-transition comparator countries were included in this wave: France, Germany, Italy, Sweden and the UK. When all countries in the sample are ranked by life satisfaction, the comparators occupy four of the top five places, ranging from 71 per cent satisfied in France to nearly 90 per cent in Sweden.[12] (The exception is Italy, where barely 50 per cent of people were satisfied.) As the transition region entered the second decade of the twenty-first century, therefore, it still had a lot of catching up to do in terms of bringing subjective well-being to advanced western standards.

5   The Post-Crisis Years: Is the Happiness Gap Closing?

Since 2010, the transition region has entered a period of gradual economic recovery, hesitant at first but accelerating in more recent years. The impact of rising growth has been seen in labour markets in particular, with a number of EU member states in the region reporting labour shortages and record low unemployment rates in recent years. Further south and east, countries in the Western Balkans have been growing relatively robustly in the past few years, the Ukrainian economy seems to be on the mend after a series of crises and political turbulence, and central Asian economies continue to record strong growth, albeit from low starting points and subject to concerns about data

---

[12] Tajikistan was ranked third in life satisfaction, an odd result given that the country was, and remains, the poorest in the transition region.

quality and reliability.[13] Naturally, this leads one to ask whether good GDP growth rates are delivering happiness gains for their citizens.

To examine the happiness gap, Djankov et al. (2016) pool data from four different surveys: the Pew Global Attitudes Survey, Eurobarometer, the European Values Survey, and the EBRD-World Bank Life in Transition Survey. The advantage of this approach is the large number of observations from complementary sources. The data stretch from the early 1990s to 2014. Their cross-country econometric results yield a clear conclusion: people in transition countries are significantly less happy than those in other countries, even after controlling for differences in income and other variables. This result is derived from a cross-country panel equation in which the dependent variable is binary (satisfied/not satisfied), derived from the four surveys mentioned earlier, and the independent variables include GDP per capita (in logs and adjusted for purchasing power parity), the share of the population of orthodox faith, and other survey controls and year fixed effects. Interestingly, however, the dummy variable representing eastern European economies becomes smaller and not statistically significantly different from zero when a measure of corruption perceptions is added to the equation.[14]

The arrival of the third wave of the LiTS in 2016 enabled researchers to look anew at the happiness gap. LiTS III included once again the agree/disagree life satisfaction question (the other life satisfaction question [on the 1–10 scale] included in wave 2 was dropped from wave 3). It also included several non-transition comparator countries: Germany, Italy and Turkey were retained from wave 2, and Cyprus and Greece were added.

The good news is that, based on the evidence of LiTS III, the happiness gap between transition and non-transition countries appears to have been closed once we control for differences in income per capita and other variables. This result was first unveiled in the EBRD *Transition Report 2016–2017* (EBRD 2016) and explored further in Guriev and Melnikov (2018). The EBRD report presents the findings of a conventional satisfaction equation which includes the usual personal controls found in many other studies. A dummy for resident of a post-communist country is included; in all specifications the coefficient on this dummy is insignificantly different from zero.

One weakness of these LiTS results is that the number of non-transition comparator countries is very small. Guriev and Melnikov (2018) extend the

---

[13] The latest macro data and short-term forecasts are available in the EBRD's biannual publication: *Regional Economic Prospects*, available here: https://www.ebrd.com/what-we-do/economic-research-and-data/data/forecasts-macro-data-transition-indicators.html.

[14] Amini and Douarin (2019) also find a strong role for corruption perceptions in explaining the happiness gap.

analysis by including also results from the 2010–2016 waves of the annual Gallup World Poll. The advantage of this survey is the large number of non-transition countries; some specifications of their model include more than 100 countries (transition and non-transition combined). The regressions, which are carried out year by year, identify a significant happiness gap in the transition region in 2010 and (in some specifications) in 2011, but insignificant thereafter (2012–2016). The authors find that the convergence in transition is driven mainly by the growing importance of younger, educated, middle-income cohorts.

Further cheering evidence of improved subjective well-being in transition countries emerges from the *2019 World Happiness Report* (Helliwell et al. 2019). The report presents a happiness ranking for 2016–2018, covering 156 countries. It is still the case that the top 10 is dominated by rich western European countries, as well as New Zealand (eighth) and Canada (ninth). Only three post-communist countries are in the top 40: the Czech Republic (20th), the Slovak Republic (38th) and Poland (40th). But a different picture emerges when the rankings are presented for the *change* in happiness between 2005–2008 and 2016–2018. Now ten transition countries feature in the top 20, headed by Bulgaria in the third place. The report notes that central and eastern Europe is the only region where the actual increase in happiness over this time period exceeded predicted levels (where the predictions were derived from a standard happiness regression with controls for income, corruption and other variables).

6   Building the Good Life—How to Make Rising Life Satisfaction Sustainable?

From the perspective of late-2019, one can view the life satisfaction glass in the transition region as being half-full or half-empty. On the positive side, there is now convincing evidence, discussed in the previous section, to suggest that life satisfaction in the region is on an upward trend and that the conditional happiness gap has been eliminated. A sense of national pride has also been restored in many countries, particularly in those that suffered most in the early years. But for many people who live in these countries, this will not be enough. Being told to know your place and be happy with your lot may not go down well among those who aspire to do better and achieve greater levels of well-being. The issue is whether transition countries can converge towards the most advanced comparator countries in terms of both objective and subjective measures of satisfaction, including raw happiness scores. If they can, how will that be achieved and how long will it take?

In this section I will draw on an EBRD framework, developed in 2016, for evaluating the strength and sustainability of a market economy. The essence of this revised way of thinking about transition is the view that successful economies are based on certain "qualities", namely: competitive, well-governed, green, inclusive, resilient and integrated.[15] The EBRD has developed a methodology, described in EBRD (2017) and updated in subsequent Transition Reports, to measure each quality, by country, on a 1–10 scale. In brief, the methodology is as follows. First, the key components of each quality are identified. For example, the well-governed quality is divided into governance at the national level and at the corporate level. Second, relevant indicators and data sources are gathered for all countries, where available. And third, scores are derived from these indicators, benchmarked against a best-practice frontier. The whole process is therefore very much data-driven and can be applied to non-transition countries as well.

Chart 24.1 shows the 2019 results for each economy where the EBRD currently invests.[16] In most transition countries, the scores are typically well

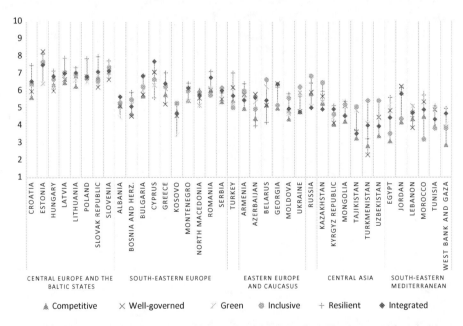

Chart 24.1 Average transition qualities, 2019. Note: The assessment of transition quality scores are also on a 1–10 scale and are prepared by the EBRD according to a methodology described here: https://2019.tr-ebrd.com/reform/. Source: EBRD (2019)

---

[15] See EBRD (2017) for an explanation of this approach and a methodology for measuring and scoring countries (on a scale of 1 to 10) on each quality.

[16] As of December 2019, the EBRD is investing in 37 countries, as well as the West Bank and Gaza.

below those in a group of advanced OECD comparator countries where the EBRD has also carried out the calculations. This suggests that a comprehensive reform agenda is needed to bring the standards in each quality close to those in best practice countries. Such an agenda may take many years to achieve but, if delivered, could be expected to help the region reach the living standards of rich countries in western Europe and elsewhere.

Are the transition qualities linked to life satisfaction measures as well? There is plenty of indirect evidence to suggest that that is the case. Chart 24.2 shows the close correlation between happiness, as presented in the 2019 *World Happiness Report*, and a simple average of the six transition qualities, as measured by the EBRD. The chart includes all countries where the EBRD is operating, as well as a group of high-income OECD countries as comparators. The chart shows the latter group clustered in the upper right-hand corner of the chart. These countries typically are among the happiest group in global cross-country surveys, and they consistently outperform the transition region in terms of the EBRD's measurement of desirable qualities of a sustainable market economy. Next best on both measures, on average, are the central European and Baltic states, followed by other regions, with those in central Asia performing worst on transition qualities and those in the southern and

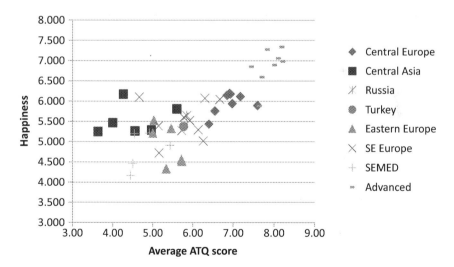

Chart 24.2 Happiness and transition qualities. Note: Happiness is measured on a 1–10 scale and the data are taken from the *World Happiness Report 2019*. The assessment of transition quality scores is also on a 1–10 scale and is prepared by the EBRD. The latest scores for the 37 countries where the EBRD operates are published in EBRD (2019). The advanced comparator countries include the following: Canada, Czech Republic, France, Germany, Japan, Sweden, the UK and the US. Source: Helliwell et al. (2019) and EBRD

eastern Mediterranean (SEMED) region scoring lowest in terms of happiness (hence the U-shaped appearance of the scatter plot).

A strong correlation proves nothing, of course.[17] But there is a growing body of research that suggests that improving transition quality scores could have a causal impact on happiness independently of the effect on income or other variables. One quality for which there is evidence in the literature of a positive and possibly causal relationship with life satisfaction is governance. The earlier papers by Helliwell and Huang (2006) and Sanfey and Teksoz (2007) found a positive and significant relationship between governance measures and life satisfaction in at least some regression specifications. More recently, Helliwell et al. (2019), reviewing and replicating previous work in this area, point to the importance of policy delivery and control of corruption in determining well-being. And recent research by the EBRD (2019), using data from the Gallup World Poll, identifies a significant impact of governance perceptions on satisfaction with life. As an illustration, taking Ukraine as an example, the EBRD estimates that closing half of the gap in governance between Ukraine and the G7 country average would be associated with narrowing the gap in life satisfaction (between Ukraine and the G7) by 15 per cent.

The relationship between happiness and other qualities is relatively unexplored, but an important step in this direction is Sachs (2016). He runs a simple cross-country regression, using the standard (Cantril ladder) measure of happiness (one observation per country) from the World Happiness Report as the dependent variable. On the right-hand side he includes the World Economic Forum's Global Competitive Index, the Index of Economic Freedom produced jointly by the *Wall Street Journal* and the Heritage Foundation, and a Sustainable Development Goal (SDG) index, produced by the UN Sustainable Development Solutions Network and combining 17 Sustainable Development Goals (SDGs) into one overall index. GDP per capita (in logs) and the unemployment rate are also added to the model. When each index is included by itself (without unemployment and GDP per capita), the coefficients are positive and significant. When the three indexes are included jointly, the index of economic freedom is no longer statistically significant. Lastly, when all five variables are added, unemployment, income

---

[17] The pairwise correlation coefficient between the two variables in Chart 24.2 is 0.73. When pairwise correlations are calculated between happiness and individual transition qualities, the highest correlation is with competitiveness (0.77) and the lowest is with resilience (0.59). A simple multiple regression (not reported here) of happiness on the six qualities also points to a closer link between happiness and competitiveness than with other qualities, but the small number of observations and strong multicollinearity among the regressors obviously prevent any firm conclusions being drawn at this point.

per capita and the SDG index are significant with the right signs (positive for the SDG index and income and negative for unemployment) while the other two indexes are insignificant.

The robustness of the SDG index, which includes strong inclusion and green elements, is tentative evidence that improving these qualities can have a direct effect on people's well-being. Clark (2018) also discusses some of the literature linking green policies with happiness, which shows that reducing pollution and providing green spaces increase well-being. The negative effect of aggregate unemployment on satisfaction has been found too in other studies. Di Tella et al. (2003), for example, estimate that a one percentage point increase in the unemployment rate has twice the (negative) impact on subjective well-being as a one point increase in the inflation rate. To the extent that high unemployment may be a proxy for low competitiveness, it suggests that efforts to bring about a more competitive economy may improve people's level of happiness directly, in addition to the presumed indirect benefits of higher growth, more jobs and so on.

7 Conclusion

Three decades after the fall of the Berlin wall, it is fair to say that life has improved on average for people in post-communist countries. Not only are most countries much richer than they were 30 years ago, but people seem more content too. Transition countries no longer cluster together at the bottom of global happiness tables. Research in the past five years has shown fairly convincingly that the happiness gap between transition and non-transition regions at similar levels of income and development has closed. At the same time, however, the transition itself is far from complete. There are still sizeable gaps vis-à-vis advanced OECD countries in terms of the qualities needed to deliver a successful and sustainable market economy. Closing these gaps will require patience and long-term vision, and a combination of profit-driven private sector activity and socially oriented government-led policies. Countries that perform best in terms of strengthening their governance, becoming more competitive and resilient, enhancing links with other economies, and delivering green and inclusive policies can also expect to see their citizens reporting even better levels of life satisfaction, comparable to those in the world's richest countries. When that happens, we may then be able to say that the transition is truly complete.

References

Adserà, A., Dalla Pozza, F., Guriev, S., Kleine-Rueschkamp, L., & Nikolova, E. (2019). *Transition, Height and Well-being*. EBRD Working Paper No. 234.

Amini, C., & Douarin, E. (2019). Corruption and Life Satisfaction in Transition: Is Corruption a Social Norm in Eastern Europe? *mimeo*. SSEES, UCL.

Borjas, G. J. (1979). Job Satisfaction, Wages and Unions. *Journal of Human Resources, 14*, 21–40.

Clark, A. E. (2018). Four Decades of the Economics of Happiness: Where Next? *The Review of Income and Wealth, 64*(2), 245–269.

Clark, A. E., Flèche, S., Layard, R., Powdthavee, N., & Ward, G. (2018). *The Origins of Happiness: The Science of Well-being Over the Life Course*. Princeton University Press.

Deaton, A. (2012). "The Financial Crisis and the Well-being of Americans", 2011 OEP Hicks Lecture. *Oxford Economic Papers, 64*(1), 1–26.

Di Tella, R., MacCulloch, R. J., & Oswald, A. J. (2003). The Macroeconomics of Happiness. *Review of Economics and Statistics, 85*(4), 809–827.

Djankov, S., Nikolova, E., & Zilinsky, J. (2016). The Happiness Gap in Eastern Europe. *Journal of Comparative Economics, 44*(1), 108–124.

Easterlin, R. (1974). Does Economic Growth Improve the Human Lot? In P. A. David & W. B. Melvin (Eds.), *Nations and Households in Economic Growth* (pp. 89–125). Stanford University Press.

Easterlin, R. (2019). Three Revolutions of the Modern Era. *Comparative Economic Studies, 61*, 521–530.

EBRD. (2007a). *Life in Transition: A Survey of People's Experiences and Attitudes*. London: EBRD.

EBRD. (2007b). *Transition Report 2007: People in Transition*. London: EBRD.

EBRD. (2009). *Transition Report 2009: Transition in Crisis?* London: EBRD.

EBRD. (2011a). *Life in Transition: After the Crisis*. London: EBRD.

EBRD. (2011b). *Transition Report 2011: Crisis and Transition—The People's Perspective*. London: EBRD.

EBRD. (2013). *Transition Report 2013: Stuck in Transition?* London: EBRD.

EBRD. (2016). *Transition Report 2016–17: Transition for All: Equal Opportunities in an Unequal World*. London: EBRD.

EBRD. (2017). *Transition Report 2017–18: Sustaining Growth*. London: EBRD.

EBRD. (2019). *Transition Report 2019–20: Better Governance, Better Economies*. London: EBRD.

Freeman, R. B. (1978). Job Satisfaction as an Economic Variable. *American Economic Review, 68*, 135–141.

Frey, B. S. (2008). *Happiness: A Revolution in Economics*. MIT Press.

Frey, B. S., & Stutzer, A. (2002). What can Economists Learn from Happiness Research? *Journal of Economic Literature, 40*, 402–435.

Fukuyama, F. (1989). The End of History? *The National Interest, 16*, 3–18.

Guriev, S., & Melnikov, N. (2018). Happiness Convergence in Transition Countries. *Journal of Comparative Economics, 46*(3), 683–707.

Guriev, S., & Zhuravskaya, E. (2009). (Un)happiness in Transition. *Journal of Economic Perspectives, 23*(2), 143–168.

Hamermesh, D. S. (1977). Economic Aspects of Job Satisfaction. In O. C. Ashenfelter & W. E. Oates (Eds.), *Essays in Labor Market Analysis* (pp. 53–72). John Wiley.

Helliwell, J., & Huang, H. (2006). *How's Your Government? International Evidence Linking Good Government and Well-being.* NBER Working Paper 11988.

Helliwell, J. F. (2002). *How's Life? Combining Individual and National Variables to Explain Subjective Well-being.* NBER Working Paper 9065.

Helliwell, J. F., Layard, R., & Sachs, J. D. (Eds.). (2019). *World Happiness Report 2019.* New York: Sustainable Development Solutions Network.

Kahneman, D., & Krueger, A. B. (2006). Developments in the Measurement of Subjective Well-being. *Journal of Economic Perspectives, 20*, 3–24.

Layard, R. (2005). *Happiness: Lessons from a New Science.* Allen Lane.

Layard, R., & Parker, J. (1996). *The Coming Russian Boom: A Guide to New Markets and Politics.* The Free Press.

McMahon, D. M. (2006). *Happiness: A History.* Grove Press.

Nikolova, E., & Sanfey, P. (2016). How Much Should We Trust Life Satisfaction Data? Evidence from the Life in Transition Survey. *Journal of Comparative Economics, 44*(3), 720–731.

OECD. (2013). *OECD Guidelines on Measuring Subjective Well-being.* Paris: OECD.

Powdthavee, N. (2011). *The Happiness Equation: The Surprising Economics of Our Most Valuable Asset.* Icon Books.

Sachs, J. D. (2016). Happiness and Sustainable Development: Concepts and Evidence. In *World Happiness Report 2016.* Sustainable Development Solutions Network, Chap. 4.

Samuelson, P. A. (1938). A Note on the Pure Theory of Consumers' Behaviour. *Economica, 5*(17), 61–71.

Sanfey, P. (2013). People and Transition: Life in Transition Survey. In G. Turley & P. Hare (Eds.), *Handbook of the Economics and Political Economy of Transition* (pp. 313–320). Routledge International Handbooks, Chap. 25.

Sanfey, P., & Teksoz, U. (2007). Does Transition Make You Happy? *Economics of Transition, 15*(4), 707–731.

Thaler, R. H. (2015). *Misbehaving: The Making of Behavioural Economics.* Allen Lane.

Weimann, J., Knabe, A., & Schöb, R. (2015). *Measuring Happiness: The Economics of Well-being.* MIT Press.

Williamson, J. (1990). What Washington Means by Policy Reform. In J. Williamson (Ed.), *Latin American Adjustment: How Much Has Happened?* Institute for International Economics, Chap. 2.

25

Growth and Subjective Well-Being in China

Robson Morgan and Fei Wang

Over the past few decades, China has experienced an economic growth period that is unparalleled in modern history. If one assumes that increasing access to material goods improves well-being, then by observing the trends in almost all of the frequently used objective measures of material wealth during this time, one can easily conclude that this period has resulted in massive improvements in well-being. However, if subjective measures are used to assess the trajectory of well-being in China during this time, a different picture emerges. Based on subjective well-being data from both urban and rural China stretching back to 1990, there is very little evidence that well-being has been determined by the improving trends of material wealth.

This chapter summarizes and expands on a few prior studies of subjective well-being trends in China since 1990. The chapter starts by reviewing objective measures of growth in China since 1990 to show that nearly all Chinese people have seen an improvement in material well-being over this time period. The trends in material well-being are then compared to those for subjective well-being in urban China. We first show that urban subjective well-being follows a different pattern than the objective measures of growth and then

R. Morgan
Keck Graduate Institute, Claremont, CA, USA

F. Wang (✉)
Renmin University of China, Beijing, China
e-mail: fwang@ruc.edu.cn

© The Author(s) 2021
E. Douarin, O. Havrylyshyn (eds.), *The Palgrave Handbook of Comparative Economics*,
https://doi.org/10.1007/978-3-030-50888-3_25

consider some explanations using macro- and micro-level data. Rural subjective well-being trends for the years in which data are available are then compared and some potential determinants are discussed.

The chapter concludes that simply observing trends in material wealth and assuming that trends in well-being follow a similar path are not supported by evidence from subjective well-being studies. Our analysis of China supports findings from the subjective well-being literature as a whole—that is, that factors such as labor market strength, social safety net generosity, and social comparisons are more important in determining subjective well-being than material living standards. While these determinants of subjective well-being have been found to be important in many other countries, it is particularly interesting that these factors still shape well-being in China. This is because if there were ever a period in a country where one might expect raising material wealth to be the primary driver of subjective well-being, it would be that of China's rapid rise from a relatively poor country to a middle-income country in just over two decades.

The authors use the term subjective well-being in this chapter to refer to subjective measures of either life satisfaction or happiness. Both measures reflect a survey respondent's evaluative judgment of their life as a whole and are considered comparable because they correlate with the same explanatory variables (Helliwell et al. 2012).[1] For an introduction to these measures, see Sanfey (Chap. 24) in this volume.

1   Background and Motivation: China's Economic Growth

In less than three decades, China has been transformed from a poor communist country into the world's second-largest economy by embracing the free market. Between 1990 and 2015, China's gross domestic product (GDP) per capita doubled, then doubled again, and then grew even more. In total, GDP per capita went up fivefold (Penn World Table 2016). This transformed material living conditions in China. Bicycles were replaced by cars; fans by air-conditioning units; and color televisions, washing machines, and other

---

[1] As claimed by Helliwell et al. (2012), happiness and life satisfaction are not the same because happiness is more of a fleeting emotional state, while life satisfaction is a longer-term evaluative assessment. In Mandarin, happiness represents a temporary mood only when it is translated to *Kuaile*. If the translation is *Xingfu*, a word used by most questionnaires, happiness would refer to a general long-term feeling of life and could be considered as a similar concept to life satisfaction.

modern comforts became commonplace in urban centers, and not uncommon in rural areas (NBSC 2016).

Urban centers were where economic growth was most prominent. While income inequality, which was virtually non-existent in 1990, did increase substantially, the very high economic growth rates were not just pushed by the skyrocketing incomes of the newly rich. Almost everyone in urban China saw an increase in personal income and consumption during this period (Cai et al. 2010a, b).

It is typically assumed in economics that increasing consumption boosts well-being. If this assumption is taken as true, the implications for well-being in China are straightforward: with almost everyone in China experiencing increased consumption, and the average level of consumption increasing at a never-before-seen pace, well-being must have followed the same trajectory. Yet, when people were asked how they felt about their lives during this time, the trend did not follow economic growth. In fact, subjective well-being data show a decline (Easterlin et al. 2012, 2017; Bartolini and Sarracino 2015).

2 Subjective Well-Being in Urban China: The Pattern from 1990 to 2015

Subjective well-being data in China are more complete in urban centers compared to rural areas. Additionally, the development paths of rural and urban China differed in both timing of reforms and economic development. For example, rural China started moving away from central planning in 1978, whereas this transition occurred in urban areas starting just after 1990. Furthermore, economic growth has disproportionally benefited urban areas. For these reasons, this chapter separates rural and urban subjective well-being analysis.

How has subjective well-being changed in urban China since 1990? Figure 25.1 illustrates patterns that four datasets have picked up between 1990 and 2015 (Easterlin et al. 2017).[2] Notice that, although none of the datasets span the entire 25-year period, the strength of this figure is that it illustrates that all four independent datasets are picking up the same trends in subjective well-being during different periods. Before 2000, all four datasets show a decline in subjective well-being. After 2005, all show a recovery in

---

[2] WVS, Gallup 1, and Horizon record life satisfaction; Gallup 2 measures ladder of life; and CGSS shows the measure of happiness. Other than the type of measures, the range of scales is also different. Please refer to Technical Box 3.1 of Easterlin et al. (2017) for detailed definitions of the measures.

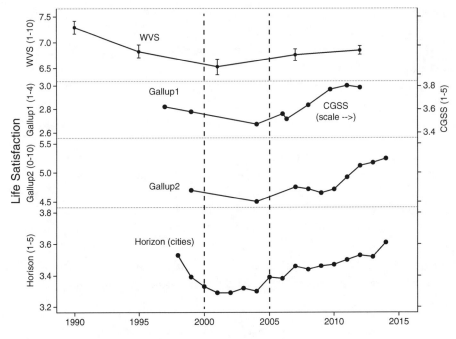

Fig. 25.1 Mean subjective well-being, five series, 1990–2015. (Source: Easterlin et al. 2017)

subjective well-being. The overall pattern that emerges is an initial decline in subjective well-being from 1990 to around 2000, a trough somewhere between 2000 and 2005, and then a recovery from 2005 onward.

These four datasets show that subjective well-being followed a U-shaped pattern from 1990 to 2015. But what about the overall trend in subjective well-being? That is, are Chinese people in urban areas happier in 2015 than in 1990? The survey with the longest timespan, the World Values Survey (WVS), shows that the highest level of subjective well-being was measured in 1990. This is statistically significantly higher than the level recorded in 2012, the final year of available data. From 2012 onward, both the Gallup 2 and Horizon data show the recovery trend in subjective well-being continued until 2015 at about the same rate it had been recovering since 2005. Comparing the dramatic drop in subjective well-being found in the WVS data between 1990 and 2000 with the modest increase between 2005 and 2012, it seems unlikely that this continued recovery rate would have resulted in higher subjective well-being in 2015 compared to 1990.

To summarize, the data on subjective well-being in urban China since 1990 show that subjective well-being followed a U-shaped pattern that bottomed out between 2000 and 2005. The size of the decline between 1990 and 2000 appears to outweigh the size of the recovery from 2005 to 2015. Neither observation supports the idea that an increase in subjective well-being followed the massive increase in material well-being seen in urban China during this time. The disparate trends in GDP per capita and subjective well-being imply that there must be other life circumstances that are dominating any effect increasing material wealth has on subjective well-being.

3 Determinants of Subjective Well-Being in Urban China

The pattern of subjective well-being in urban China over this period is largely determined by conditions in the labor market, changes in the level of the social safety net, and income comparison and habituation effects. This statement is supported by comparing the experience of urban China to the transition countries of Eastern Europe, by observing macroeconomic trends and by micro-level regression analysis.

3.1 Comparison to the Transition Countries of Eastern Europe

To explain why the pattern of subjective well-being in urban China does not follow the rising trend in incomes in recent decades, we must consider how other events have affected the lives of urban residents. In 1990, the year with the highest recorded level of subjective well-being in the WVS, urban China was still a Soviet-style, centrally planned economy. While incomes were low, urban China enjoyed the stability that a centrally planned economy can provide. The majority of the urban population were employed by state-owned enterprises, where jobs came with a number of benefits. This was referred to as an "iron rice bowl" because it was thought that these jobs and their associated benefits were guaranteed for life (World Bank 2007). Interestingly, the level of subjective well-being recorded in pre-transition urban China, at 7.29, is almost exactly identical to pre-transition Russia, at 7.26 (Easterlin 2014).

From 1990, the urban Chinese economy started to move away from central planning in a process that resembled what occurred in the East European transition countries. The state-owned enterprises that employed a large number of urban residents were greatly downsized (Knight and Song 2005). The social safety net was essentially dismantled and what was previously handled by the state—finding a job, securing income, ensuring access to healthcare and housing—was now left to individuals.

In addition to the loss of the "iron rice bowl", the move away from state-owned enterprise employment meant that many workers were released into a newly created job market that was struggling to allocate labor. This resulted in high levels of urban unemployment, while workers struggled to adjust to this new economic system (Gustafsson and Ding 2013). The primary difference between China's experience and that of the East European transition countries was that GDP per capita in China was continually rising during the entire transition.

Despite the differing GDP trends, the pattern of subjective well-being during the transitions for these countries is strikingly similar. An initial precipitous drop, similar in magnitude across all transition countries, followed by a recovery that does not seem to fully reach pre-transition levels (Easterlin et al. 2012). The similar experiences provide evidence that the generosity of the social safety net and labor market conditions are important determinants of subjective well-being.

3.2   Macro-Level Evidence

Given that subjective well-being during the period of interest here follows a U-shaped path, any indicator that is a primary determinant of subjective well-being is also likely to have either a U-shaped or a hill-shaped pattern. This is because if the relationship between an indicator and subjective well-being were positive, we would expect that the initial drop and recovery in subjective well-being was being pushed by a drop and recovery in the indicator that is the primary determinant. Alternatively, if the relationship between an indicator and subjective well-being were an inverse relationship, the drop and recovery in subjective well-being would be pushed by an increase and then decrease in that indicator. The similar patterns shared by China and the transition countries motivate further examination of macroeconomic trends in the unemployment rate and in the generosity of the social safety net.

Examining the trends of the urban unemployment rate provides evidence that labor market conditions were an important determinant of subjective well-being in urban China over the time period in question. Figure 25.2 illustrates that multiple datasets show the unemployment rate following a hill-shaped pattern which inversely mirrors the U-shape trend in subjective well-being (Easterlin et al. 2017). The fact that the rate of unemployment peaked between 2000 and 2005, the same window of time in which subjective well-being reached a minimum, supports the argument that labor market conditions are important.

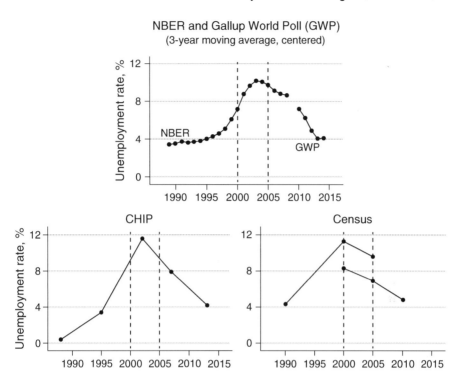

Fig. 25.2 Urban Unemployment Rate, Four Series, 1988–2015 (percent of labor force). (Source: Easterlin et al. 2017)

Additional evidence that the strength of the social safety net was an important determinant of subjective well-being can be seen by comparing the patterns of subjective well-being with changes in measures of social safety net generosity during this transition period. As can be seen in Fig. 25.3, the measures of pension and healthcare generosity follow the pattern of subjective well-being (Easterlin et al. 2017). In this case, because the relationship between the social safety net and subjective well-being is positive, we see the lowest levels of safety net generosity coinciding with the lowest levels of subjective well-being.

3.3   Micro-Level Evidence

Findings from micro-level data analysis complement the macro-level evidence. The yearly coverage of micro-level data, however, does not span the entire period from 1990. The data instead cover just the recovery part of the transition, from 2002 to 2012. Therefore, the analysis cannot directly inform us about the causes of decline in subjective well-being, but rather about the

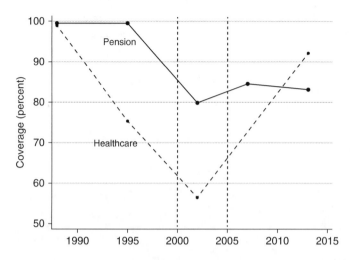

Fig. 25.3 Safety Net Indicators: Pension and Healthcare Coverage, 1988–2013 (urban households). (Source: Easterlin et al. 2017)

factors that lead to the recovery. The analysis finds that the improving quality of the labor market is chiefly responsible for the increase in subjective well-being in 2002–2012. Furthermore, although individual income increases do contribute to higher levels of subjective well-being, these contributions are cancelled out by income comparison and adaptation. The net result is that income changes during the recovery period are not statistically significantly related to changes in subjective well-being (Morgan and Wang 2019).

Data for the micro-analysis come from the Horizon Research Consultancy Group. The data that were analyzed are representative of urban populations in China with the following characteristics: people aged 18–60 in Beijing, Shanghai, Guangzhou, Wuhan, Shenyang, Xi'an, and Chengdu. A modified version of an Oaxaca decomposition is developed to estimate the contribution (in percentage) of changes in variables or groups of variables to the overall change in subjective well-being that occurred between 2002 and 2012. In short, the decomposition is a two-step process. The first step pools data from all years and regresses subjective well-being on explanatory variables. This establishes the relationship between subjective well-being and the explanatory variables. The second step uses the established relationships and the changes in explanatory variables between 2002 and 2012 to compute the relative contribution to change in subjective well-being or each variable or group of variables.

The explanatory variables of specific interest for this chapter are employment status and income variables. We are specifically interested in whether a person is unemployed, because the quality of the labor market is a focus of this analysis. Someone is defined as unemployed if they are not formally or informally working, or are retired. This is broader than the traditional definition of employment and includes discouraged workers. There are three variables that measure income levels—personal income, income level of a comparison group, and approximated previous period personal income level. Together, these variables are used to identify the relationship between subjective well-being and income level, income comparisons, and habituation to income.[3]

The main findings from the analysis are presented in Table 25.1. The right-hand column reports the percentage contribution of changes in a variable or

Table 25.1 Contribution of the change in variable values to the increase in life satisfaction between 2002 and 2012

Variables	$\Delta \overline{LS} = 0.292$	
	Δx	Contribution (%)
Male	0.03	**−0.6**** ($p = 0.0345$)
Education		**4.5**** ($p = 0.0277$)
Middle school	−0.05	−0.4
High school	0.01	0.5
College	0.05	4.4
Employment status		**29.0***** ($p = 0.0000$)
Unemployed	−0.20	31.5
Retired	−0.09	−2.5
Income		**−55.4** ($p = 0.4695$)
Own income		
3001–5000	0.12	8.4
5001–8000	0.40	44.4
> 8000	0.18	20.4
Previous income		
3001–5000	0.21	−1.9
5001–8000	0.39	−86.5
> 8000	0.15	14.0
Reference income		
3001–5000	0.24	−9.0
5001–8000	0.74	−44.9
> 8000	0.02	−0.4
Age		**−10.5** ($p = 0.1586$)
Cohort		**66.4** ($p = 0.1570$)
City		**9.4**** ($p = 0.0478$)
Year		**57.0** ($p = 0.4501$)

Source: Morgan and Wang (2019)
Bolded numbers indicate whole contribution of variable categories *$p < 0.10$, **$p < 0.05$, ***$p < 0.01$

---

[3] For a more thorough description of the methodology, see Morgan and Wang (2019).

group of variables to the change in subjective well-being between 2002 and 2012. Differences in gender, city, educational attainment, and employment status all significantly contribute to the change in subjective well-being. Of the variables or groups of variables that are statistically significant, employment status is by far the largest contributor, supporting the macro-analysis in the previous section. All income variables grouped together—so as to represent the overall contribution of change in income to change in subjective well-being—are not statistically significant. This finding helps to explain why trends in income are not followed by trends in subjective well-being during this transition period.

3.4   Urban China: Conclusion

The evidence presented here—a comparison to transition countries, with observations of macroeconomic trends and micro-level regression analysis—points to the same conclusion. This is that, rather than income, it is the strength of the labor market and the generosity of the social safety net that defines the U-shape in subjective well-being between 1990 and 2015 in urban China.

While some of these findings might be surprising, it is worth noting that they are in line with findings from the subjective well-being literature as a whole. The conclusion that income did not shape the pattern of subjective well-being in modern urban China is consistent with the finding that long-run income changes are not related to long-run changes in subjective well-being (Easterlin et al. 2010). Unemployment is commonly found to be a strong predictor of subjective well-being, not only for people who are unemployed, but there also appears to be spillover effects for those who remain employed (Di Tella et al. 2003; Wolfers 2003; Arampatzi et al. 2015). Furthermore, a handful of studies highlight the positive relationship between subjective well-being and the degree of generosity of the social safety net (Di Tella et al. 2003; O'Connor 2017; Pacek and Radcliff 2008; Radcliff 2013).

4   Subjective Well-Being in Rural China and Its Determinants

Although the share of rural population in the total is declining, residents with agricultural *Hukou*[4] (the rural population) still make up 56.6% of all Chinese in 2018 (NBSC 2018). An analysis of China's subjective well-being that omits

---

[4] The *Hukou* system is China's household registration system. A household member owns either agricultural *Hukou* or non-agricultural *Hukou* according to the location of their residence and the nature of their work. China's urban-rural duality is largely shaped by the differentiation of non-agricultural and agricultural hukou.

the agricultural *Hukou* holders is therefore far from comprehensive. During China's rapid development, some studies have found that the subjective well-being of the rural population is lower than for urban residents (Easterlin et al. 2017; Asadullah et al. 2018); some indicate that rural happiness is not as low as usually thought when compared to urban or more-developed regions (Davey et al. 2009; Knight et al. 2009); and some argue that rural subjective well-being is higher than in urban areas (Knight and Gunatilaka 2010b; Graham et al. 2017; Cai and Wang 2018). More research is therefore needed to determine subjective well-being in rural China. Even within the rural population, subjective well-being inequalities could be present among different subgroups, such as between rural local residents and rural-to-urban migrants, between rural people in wealthier regions and those in less developed provinces, or among members of the rural population with a different socioeconomic status.

The literature usually examines subjective well-being in rural China based on cross-sectional data (e.g., Davey et al. 2009; Knight et al. 2009). Some studies examine trends of rural subjective well-being over time, but have not included analyses of the factors behind the trends in subjective well-being (e.g., Easterlin et al. 2017; Clark et al. 2019). This section extends the literature by illustrating the subjective well-being trends of China's rural population as a whole, along with the trajectories of various subgroups. Once the trends in subjective well-being have been established, some potential determinants of the trends are explored.

4.1   Subjective Well-Being in Rural China: Overall Trends and Heterogeneity

The rural population in this section is defined as those holding an agricultural *Hukou*. We use two popular individual-level datasets to present an analysis of subjective well-being in rural China: the Chinese General Social Survey (CGSS) and the China Family Panel Studies (CFPS).

The CGSS is one of the earliest nationally representative and long-term surveys in China, starting in 2003. The CGSS project is implemented every one or two years, and primarily focuses on social structure and the quality of life in both urban and rural China. Because the first wave in 2003 excludes the rural population, our analysis will be based on eight waves collected between 2005 and 2015—specifically, the waves of 2005, 2006, 2008, 2010, 2011, 2012, 2013, and 2015.

The CFPS is a nationwide, large-scale, multidisciplinary tracking survey project mainly focusing on the economic and non-economic welfare of Chinese residents, as well as topics including economic activities, educational achievements, family relationships and dynamics, population migration, and health. The first national survey was conducted in 2010, followed by biennial surveys in 2012, 2014, 2016, and 2018. For our analysis, we use the first four waves, from 2010 to 2016.

The subjective well-being measure in CGSS is "happiness". The question posed in the 2005 and 2006 surveys is: "overall, what do you feel about your life?", with five options to answer, of very unhappy, unhappy, average, happy, and very happy. The question was changed to "overall, do you think you are happy?" in 2008 and was adjusted again to "overall, do you think your life is happy?" in 2010. The options are slightly different, too. In the 2008 data, the five options are very unhappy, not too happy, average, happy, and very happy, while the 2010 options are very unhappy, relatively unhappy, average, relatively happy, and very happy. The questions and options in 2011–2015 are identical to those in 2010. The five options, regardless of the survey year, are coded as 1, 2, 3, 4, and 5, representing least happy to most happy. Despite the differences in questions and options among waves, the happiness measure is essentially comparable over time.[5] The subjective well-being measure in CFPS is "life satisfaction". The question posed, "how satisfied are you with your life?", is uniform through all waves. The options range from "very dissatisfied" to "very satisfied", and are coded as 1, 2, 3, 4, and 5. The use of different datasets and measures of subjective well-being is a useful "double check" on any phenomena that are discovered in a single dataset. Conclusions will be made only when different measures produce similar results, so that concerns arising from the use of various measures can be largely mitigated.

Figure 25.4a presents the average subjective well-being of rural dwellers over time for both CGSS and CFPS.[6] Despite fluctuations in the middle, both sets of data confirm that the subjective well-being in the ending year is significantly higher than that in the beginning year. Figure 25.4b, a three-year moving average of Fig. 25.4a, shows a clearer pattern. Both datasets imply a yearly increase of 0.04 in the level of subjective well-being on a scale of 1–5, or average annual growth of 1%.

---

[5] The Mandarin translation of happiness is *Kuaile* in 2008 and is *Xingfu* in other waves. As discussed before, *Kuaile* may be associated with temporary mood, while *Xingfu*, similar to life satisfaction, may refer to long-term feeling of life. Except for CGSS 2008, happiness measures are essentially comparable along CGSS waves and with CFPS measures of life satisfaction.

[6] The average life satisfaction from CFPS is a weighted average, where the individual national panel weights, provided by the CFPS team, are used. Weights are not available for CGSS before the wave of 2011, and the average happiness from the data is unweighted.

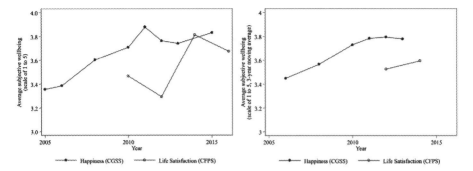

Fig. 25.4 Average subjective well-being in rural China by year, CGSS (2005–2015) and CFPS (2010–2016)

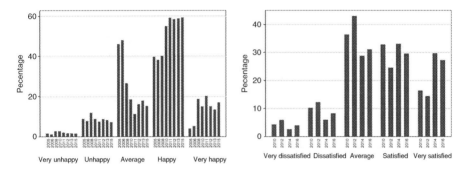

Fig. 25.5 Distributions of subjective well-being, CGSS (2005–2015) and CFPS (2010–2016)

Figure 25.5 further shows changes in the distribution of subjective well-being, for both CGSS (Fig. 25.5a) and CFPS (Fig. 25.5b). Both figures confirm that the shares of those choosing codes 1–3 for subjective well-being (i.e., from very unhappy to average) decline over time, while the share of respondents reporting being "happy" or "satisfied" rises.

Does this increase in subjective well-being hold for different subgroups? Our analysis finds that subjective well-being trends are broadly similar for most subgroups in rural China, but there are differences in the level of subjective well-being and the growth rate for some groups. All curves are three-year moving averages. Figure 25.6 shows average subjective well-being trends for males and females. Both sets of data reveal that males and females share similar growing paths of subjective well-being. Females are found to be more satisfied with their lives in CFPS, while CGSS does not show such a disparity.

Figure 25.7 exhibits the average subjective well-being by age group (Fig. 25.7a) and birth cohort group (Fig. 25.7b). Age is divided into a young

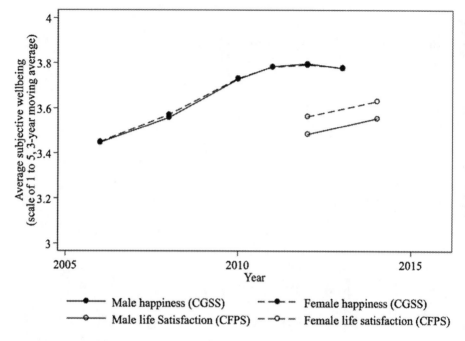

Fig. 25.6 Average subjective well-being by gender and year, three-year moving average from CGSS and CFPS

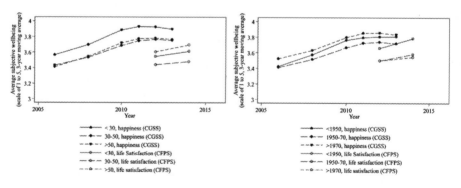

Fig. 25.7 Average subjective well-being over time, by age group and birth cohort group, three-year moving average from CGSS and CFPS

group (below 30 years of age), a middle-aged group (30–50), and an elderly group (above 50). The subjective well-being of all age groups grows over time and no differences are present in the trends.

The birth cohort is grouped to three categories, the cohorts born before 1950, in 1950–1970, and after 1970. Figure 25.7b shows that the subjective well-being of the oldest birth cohort group rises slightly more swiftly than for the other two cohort groups. The relative magnitudes of subjective well-being among the three groups, however, do not show consistent patterns between the CGSS and CFPS.

People with agricultural *Hukou* may live in rural or urban areas. The rural-urban migrants have been exposed to a more economically and socially developed urban China and thus may have a different subjective well-being from those still living in rural areas. Figure 25.8 displays subjective well-being by place of residence. Evidence shows that the subjective well-being of migrants is higher than for rural residents, but both CGSS and CFPS show that the gap between them has narrowed, becoming negligible after 2011. Although some research (e.g., Nielsen et al. 2010) concludes that rural-urban migrants have similar levels of subjective well-being, more studies have found that migrants are unhappier than their urban counterparts. Easterlin et al. (2017), and Liu et al. (2017), show that migrants have lower subjective well-being than urban residents. Knight and Gunatilaka (2010a), and Cai and Wang (2018), find that rural-urban migrants are even unhappier than the population that

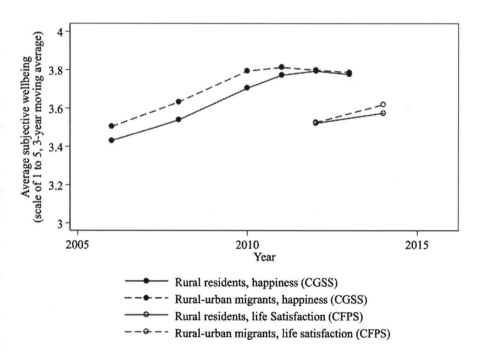

Fig. 25.8 Average subjective well-being over time, by place of residence, three-year moving average from CGSS and CFPS

remained in rural areas. Based on the data used in this chapter, featured in Fig. 25.8, rural-urban migrants are happier than rural residents in earlier years.

Figure 25.9 shows how subjective well-being evolves differently for those living in eastern provinces compared to other provinces of China. The eastern provinces include, from north to south, Hebei, Beijing, Tianjin, Shandong, Jiangsu, Shanghai, Zhejiang, Fujian, Guangdong, and Hainan, ten coastal and more developed provinces. The figure indicates that residents in all provinces have experienced growing levels of subjective well-being, and that the less-developed, non-coastal regions have subjective well-being levels that are slowly catching up with the more developed regions.

Lastly, Fig. 25.10 shows how subjective well-being grows for groups of people with different educational levels. Education has three categories: primary school or below, junior high school, and senior high school or above. The figure shows that all groups have had growing levels of subjective well-being, and that the least-educated group, primary school or below, has seen a slightly faster growth rate than the groups with more education.

Figures 25.6, 25.7, 25.8, 25.9, and 25.10 show evidence that there has been an increase in subjective well-being for almost all groups of people in

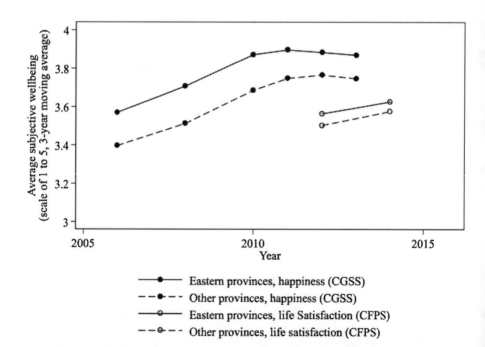

Fig. 25.9 Average subjective well-being over time, eastern and other provinces, three-year moving average from CGSS and CFPS

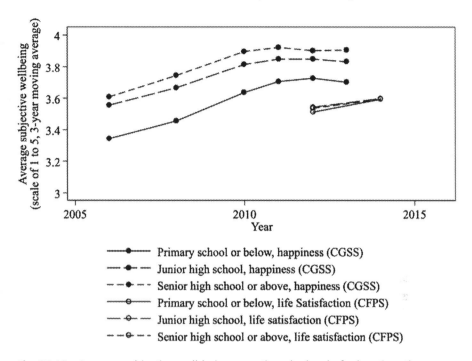

Fig. 25.10 Average subjective well-being over time, by level of education, three-year moving average from CGSS and CFPS

rural China. Furthermore, vulnerable groups, such as the less-educated, those remaining in rural areas and those living in poorer provinces, are catching up with the advantaged groups in terms of subjective well-being. In other words, subjective well-being inequalities in rural China have diminished. Figure 25.11 further shows the coefficient of variation (the standard deviation divided by the mean) of subjective well-being over time. The curve from the CGSS data confirms that the variation of subjective well-being within the rural population has reduced to a lower level, particularly after 2010.

4.2   Potential Determinants of the Subjective Well-Being Trends in Rural China

One potential determinant of the trends shown in the previous section is the change in population composition. Table 25.2 shows how some key average respondent characteristics vary by survey year, for both CGSS (Panel A) and CFPS (Panel B).

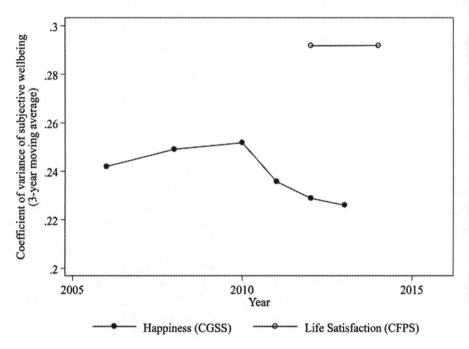

Fig. 25.11 Coefficient of variation of subjective well-being over time, three-year moving average from CGSS and CFPS

Table 25.2 also confirms variation in the population composition over time. The average age, share of migrants, and the percentage of better-educated population all rise over time. As Figs. 25.8 and 25.10 have implied, a population with a higher fraction of migrants or a better level of education tends to have a greater subjective well-being. Therefore, the change in population composition could be a potential reason for the growth of subjective well-being. Nevertheless, the varying composition cannot be the only determinant, as subjective well-being grows consistently regardless of population characteristics.

Easterlin (2010) suggests a theoretical framework for analyzing the determinants of personal happiness, where life satisfaction is the outcome of satisfaction with various life domains. The domains Easterlin specifically mentions are material living conditions, family life, health, and work. The four life domains highlighted by Easterlin were previously found to be the most influential factors affecting happiness in different cultures around the world (Cantril 1965).

Table 25.2 Descriptive statistics of selected individual characteristics by wave

Year	2005	2006	2008	2010	2011	2012	2013	2015
Panel A. CGSS								
Male (%)	47.2	46.2	47.0	47.4	44.1	50.6	49.2	46.1
Age (years)	44.0	41.8	43.0	46.9	47.9	48.8	48.5	50.0
Year of birth	1961	1964	1965	1963	1963	1963	1964	1965
Migrants (%)	11.4	21.2	29.9	28.9	32.6	34.4	38.4	37.9
Eastern provinces (%)	34.2	35.3	24.4	24.0	23.1	25.8	26.0	27.5
Junior high school or above (%)	41.5	50.2	46.3	46.3	48.5	47.5	51.0	50.3

Year	2010	2012	2014	2016
Panel B. CFPS				
Male (%)	50.1	47.7	49.3	50.2
Age (years)	42.3	43.8	46.2	45.1
Year of birth	1968	1968	1968	1971
Migrants (%)	33.9	35.7	42.4	44.2
Eastern provinces (%)	34.7	36.9	37.5	35.6
Junior high school or above (%)	41.8	43.1	41.6	46.9

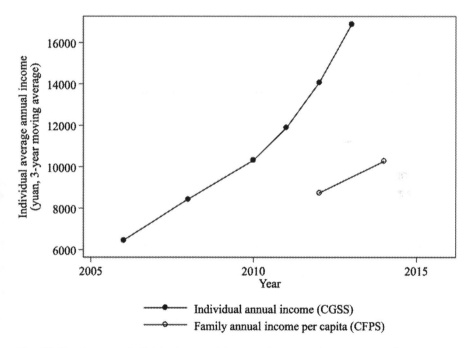

Fig. 25.12 Average individual annual income by year, three-year moving average from CGSS and CFPS

Figure 25.12 shows how individual income, a typical indicator of material living conditions, changes over time. The income variable of CGSS is measured by the individual annual overall income, and that from CFPS by family annual income per capita. Unsurprisingly, both income variables increase substantially over time. However, based on the analysis in urban China, the trend of subjective well-being is unlikely to be primarily determined by the increase in income. Knight et al. (2009) have shown that social comparison and aspirations or expectations for the future could greatly affect subjective well-being in rural China, even when the sampled individuals live in poverty. Gao and Smyth (2011) find that, for rural-urban migrants, high expectations of future income partially offset increases in subjective well-being driven by rising income. In contrast, satisfaction with family life, health, and work is determined by actual life circumstances rather than aspirations or expectations.

As Easterlin (2010) points out, the formation and dissolution of unions are key determinants of satisfaction with family life. Liu and Guo (2008) find that marital status is crucial to the happiness of the rural elderly whose children have left home. Zhou et al. (2015) show that being married and having family support are positively associated with the subjective well-being of rural residents. Figure 25.13 shows how the rate of marriage varies by year of survey. Being in a marriage or in cohabitation is coded as "married", while being single, divorced, and widowed are captured by the opposite category. The figure shows a declining marriage rate over the time period. Therefore,

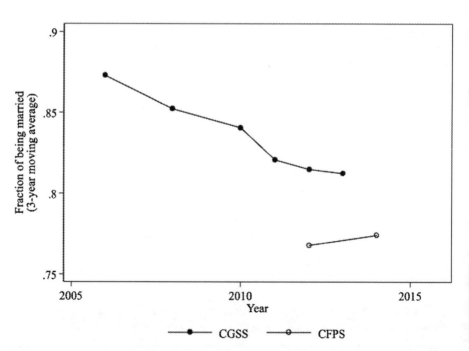

Fig. 25.13 Rate of marriage by year, three-year moving average from CGSS and CFPS

satisfaction with family life is unlikely to be a driving force behind trends in subjective well-being in rural China.

We use self-rated health to measure individual satisfaction with health in both datasets. The original response options are inconsistent between the two datasets, as well as between survey waves within each dataset. All response options are thus regrouped into three categories: unhealthy, average, and healthy, coded 1, 2, and 3. We additionally use the percentage of population reporting chronic disease in CFPS to measure average health status. Liu and Guo (2008), Zhou et al. (2015), and Fang and Sakellariou (2016) find that good health or the absence of chronic disease is positively correlated with subjective well-being in rural China. Figure 25.14 shows the trends of the two self-rated health variables and the chronic disease measure. There is no consistent evidence to support improving health status in explaining subjective well-being trends. First, there is no clear trend for self-rated health in CGSS. Second, although the indicator of self-rated health improves over time in CFPS, the rate of chronic disease also rises. Therefore, health is unlikely to be the cause of rising subjective well-being in rural China.

Easterlin et al. (2012), Easterlin et al. (2017), and Morgan and Wang (2019) have shown that unemployment rates and the deterioration of the

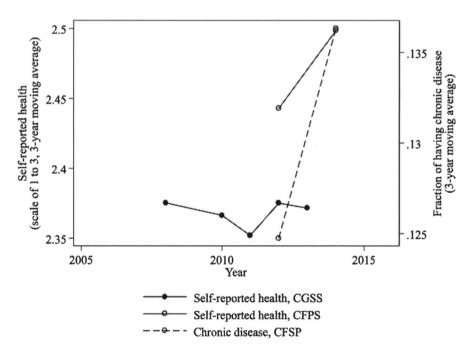

Fig. 25.14 Health measures by year, three-year moving average from CGSS and CFPS

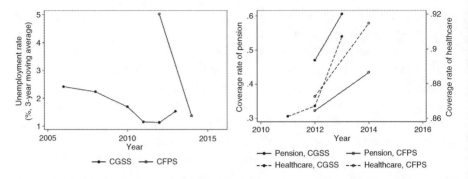

Fig. 25.15 Unemployment rate and coverage of social safety net by year, three-year moving average from CGSS and CFPS

social safety net are key determinants of subjective well-being trajectory in urban China. The two factors reflect the importance of work-related satisfaction in shaping subjective well-being. The social safety net is also found to be a crucial determinant of subjective well-being in rural China. Liang and Zhu (2015) show that an incomplete social security system leads to low life satisfaction among landless peasants. Fang and Sakellariou (2016) find that access to pension is positively associated with subjective well-being in rural areas. Han and Gao (2019) find that the participation in *Dibao*, a minimum livelihood guarantee scheme in China, has positive effects on the subjective well-being of rural residents. Figure 25.15 displays unemployment rates (Fig. 25.15a) and the coverage of pension and healthcare (Fig. 25.15b) by year to see whether the two factors help to explain the rising subjective well-being of rural China. Both datasets show decreasing unemployment rates and growing coverage of the social safety net, implying that the two factors may be crucial determinants of the subjective well-being trend in rural China.

4.3 Summary of Rural Analysis

This section shows that subjective well-being in rural China has been rising since 2005, and an improvement in well-being has been enjoyed by all subgroups of the rural population we analyze here. Suggestive evidence is presented that supports the idea that rural trends in subjective well-being are determined by the same factors as urban trends. A falling unemployment rate and improving coverage of work-related social safety net, particularly pension coverage, can account for the overall increase in the subjective well-being of China's rural population.

The analyses are still premature. First, more data are needed to outline the whole picture of the subjective well-being in rural China. Second, analyses using micro-econometric approaches, such as Morgan and Wang (2019), are necessary to quantify the contribution of each potential determinant to the trend of subjective well-being in rural China. This section, hopefully, has provided basic evidence and motivation for further studies.

5 Conclusion

China's experience in the past three decades provides a unique context in which to study subjective well-being. China has experienced changes on an unprecedented scale and at an unprecedented rate since 1990. Despite the unique context, we find that determinants of subjective well-being in China are largely consistent with those in other countries of the world. The strength of the labor market and the social safety net are of paramount importance. Furthermore, even in urban China, where economic growth has been concentrated, we find no evidence that increasing incomes are sufficient to improve subjective well-being. The experience in China since 1990 is another reminder that simply chasing higher incomes and economic growth is unlikely to improve the well-being of a society.

References

Arampatzi, E., Burger, M. J., & Veenhoven, R. (2015). Financial Distress and Happiness of Employees in Times of Economic Crisis. *Applied Economics Letters, 22*(3), 173–179.

Asadullah, M. N., Xiao, S., & Yeoh, E. (2018). Subjective Well-Being in China, 2005–2010: The Role of Relative Income, Gender, and Location. *China Economic Review, 48*, 83–101.

Bartolini, S., & Sarracino, F. (2015). The Dark Side of Chinese Growth: Declining Social Capital and Wellbeing in Times of Economic Boom. *World Development, 74*, 333–351.

Cai, S., & Wang, J. (2018). Less Advantaged, more Optimistic? Subjective Well-Being among Rural, Migrant and Urban Populations in Contemporary China. *China Economic Review, 52*, 95–110.

Cai, H., Chen, Y., & Zhou, L. A. (2010a). Income and Consumption Inequality in Urban China: 1992–2003. *Economic Development and Cultural Change, 58*(3), 385–413.

Cai, F., Wang, M. Y., & Wang, D. W. (Eds.). (2010b). *The China Population and Labor Yearbook: The Sustainability of Economic Growth from the Perspective of Human Resources* (Vol. 2). Leiden: Brill.

Cantril, H. (1965). *The Pattern of Human Concerns*. New Brunswick, NJ: Rutgers University Press.

Clark, W. A. V., Yi, D., & Huang, Y. (2019). Subjective Well-Being in China's Changing Society. *Proceedings of the National Academy of Sciences, 116*(34), 16799–16804.

Davey, G., Chen, Z., & Lau, A. (2009). "Peace in a Thatched hut—that is Happiness": Subjective Wellbeing among Peasants in Rural China. *Journal of Happiness Studies, 10*(2), 239–252.

Di Tella, R., MacCulloch, R. J., & Oswald, A. J. (2003). The Macroeconomics of Happiness. *The Review of Economics and Statistics, 85*(4), 809–827.

Easterlin, R. A. (2010). *Happiness, Growth, and the Life Cycle*. New York: Oxford University Press.

Easterlin, R. A. (2014). Life Satisfaction in the Transition from Socialism to Capitalism: Europe and China. In A. Clark & C. Senik (Eds.), *Happiness and Economic Growth: Lessons from Developing Countries* (pp. 6–31). Oxford: Oxford University Press.

Easterlin, R. A., McVey, L. A., Switek, M., Sawangfa, O., & Zweig, J. S. (2010). The Happiness-Income Paradox Revisited. *Proceedings of the National Academy of Sciences, 107*(52), 22463–22468.

Easterlin, R. A., Morgan, R., Switek, M., & Wang, F. (2012). China's Life Satisfaction, 1990–2010. *Proceedings of the National Academy of Sciences, 109*(25), 9775–9780.

Easterlin, R. A., Wang, F., & Wang, S. (2017). Growth and Happiness in China, 1990–2015. Chapter 3. In J. F. Helliwell, R. Layard, & J. Sachs (Eds.), *World Happiness Report 2017* (pp. 48–83). New York: Sustainable Development Solutions Network.

Fang, Z., & Sakellariou, C. (2016). Social Insurance, Income and Subjective Well-Being of Rural Migrants in China—An Application of Unconditional Quantile Regression. *Journal of Happiness Studies, 17*(4), 1635–1657.

Gao, W., & Smyth, R. (2011). What Keeps China's Migrant Workers Going? Expectations and Happiness among China's Floating Population. *Journal of the Asia Pacific Economy, 16*(2), 163–182.

Graham, C., Zhou, S., & Zhang, J. (2017). Happiness and Health in China: The Paradox of Progress. *World Development, 96*, 231–244.

Gustafsson, B., & Ding, S. (2013). Unemployment and the Rising Number of Non-Workers in Urban China: Causes and Distributional Consequences. In S. Li, H. Sato, & T. Sicular (Eds.), *Rising Inequality in China: Challenges to a Harmonious Society* (pp. 289–331). Cambridge: Cambridge University Press.

Han, H., & Gao, Q. (2019). Does Welfare Participation Improve Life Satisfaction? Evidence from Panel Data in Rural China. *Journal of Happiness Studies*. https://doi.org/10.1007/s10902-019-00157-z.

Helliwell, J. F., Layard, R., & Sachs, J. (2012). *World Happiness Report 2012*. New York: Sustainable Development Solutions Network.

Knight, J., & Gunatilaka, R. (2010a). Great Expectations? The Subjective Well-Being of Rural–Urban Migrants in China. *World Development, 38*(1), 113–124.

Knight, J., & Gunatilaka, R. (2010b). The Rural–Urban Divide in China: Income but not Happiness? *The Journal of Development Studies, 46*(3), 506–534.

Knight, J. B., & Song, L. (2005). *Towards a Labour Market in China*. Oxford: Oxford University Press.

Knight, J., Song, L., & Gunatilaka, R. (2009). Subjective Well-Being and Its Determinants in Rural China. *China Economic Review, 20*(4), 635–649.

Liang, Y., & Zhu, D. (2015). Subjective Well-Being of Chinese Landless Peasants in Relatively Developed Regions: Measurement using PANAS and SWLS. *Social Indicators Research, 123*(3), 817–835.

Liu, L. J., & Guo, Q. (2008). Life Satisfaction in a Sample of Empty-Nest Elderly: A Survey in the Rural Area of a Mountainous County in China. *Quality of Life Research, 17*(6), 823.

Liu, Y., Zhang, F., Wu, F., Liu, Y., & Li, Z. (2017). The Subjective Wellbeing of Migrants in Guangzhou, China: The Impacts of the Social and Physical Environment. *Cities, 60*, 333–342.

Morgan, R., & Wang, F. (2019). Well-Being in Transition: Life Satisfaction in Urban China from 2002 to 2012. *Journal of Happiness Studies, 20*(8), 2609–2629.

National Bureau of Statistics of China. (2016). Statistical Communiqué of the People's Republic of China on the 2015 National Economic and Social Development. Released on February 29, 2016. Retrieved from http://www.stats.gov.cn/english/PressRelease/201602/t20160229_1324019.html.

National Bureau of Statistics of China. (2018). Statistical Bulletin of National Economic and Social Development in 2018. Retrieved from http://www.stats.gov.cn/tjsj/zxfb/201902/t20190228_1651265.html.

Nielsen, I., Smyth, R., & Zhai, Q. (2010). Subjective Well-Being of China's Off-Farm Migrants. *Journal of Happiness Studies, 11*(3), 315–333.

O'Connor, K. J. (2017). Happiness and welfare state policy around the world. *Review of Behavioral Economics, 4*(4), 397–420.

Pacek, A., & Radcliff, B. (2008). Assessing the Welfare State. *Perspectives on Politics, 6*(2), 267–277.

Penn World Table 9.0. (2016). Released on June 9, 2016. Retrieved from http://www.rug.nl/research/ggdc/data/pwt/pwt-9.0. https://doi.org/10.15141/S5J01T.

Radcliff, B. (2013). *The Political Economy of Human Happiness: How Voters' Choices Determine the Quality of Life*. Cambridge: Cambridge University Press.

Wolfers, J. (2003). Is Business Cycle Volatility Costly? Evidence from Surveys of Subjective Well-Being. *International Finance, 6*(1), 1–26.

World Bank. (2007). *China's Modernizing Labor Market: Trends and Emerging Challenges.* Washington, DC: World Bank.

Zhou, Y., Zhou, L., Fu, C., Wang, Y., Liu, Q., Wu, H., et al. (2015). Socio-Economic Factors Related with the Subjective Well-Being of the Rural Elderly People Living Independently in China. *International Journal for Equity in Health, 14*(1), 5.

26

Understanding Demographic Challenges of Transition Through the China Lens

Lauren A. Johnston

1   Introduction

In 2018, for the first time, the world was home to more people aged over 64 than under 5 (World Bank 2019). This shift is disproportionately reflected in global gross domestic product (GDP), more than 80% of which is now generated in countries with ageing populations (World Bank 2019). The underlying ageing trend, moreover, is accelerating (Lutz et al. 2008). Within demography, a population is described as "ageing" when one of three standard thresholds is crossed. The first threshold is a senior population share (those aged above 64 years) of 7% or higher; the second, a child population share (aged below 15 years) of 14% or lower; the third, a ratio of senior to child population share of more than 30%. By child share, the indicator of the three that is typically first to cross the "ageing" threshold, already some three-quarters of countries are now "ageing" (see Johnston 2019a, Appendix 1).

The older a population, the longer their average person's lifespan. The longer the average person's lifespan, the earlier a technological reference point the average person has. For example, a large share of Japan's famously aged population has memory of life without the Internet, where in "younger" India a much higher share of today's population has been raised in the Internet age.

L. A. Johnston (✉)
China Institute, School of Oriental and African Studies, University of London, London, UK
e-mail: lj11@soas.ac.uk

© The Author(s) 2021   **661**
E. Douarin, O. Havrylyshyn (eds.), *The Palgrave Handbook of Comparative Economics*,
https://doi.org/10.1007/978-3-030-50888-3_26

Hence, it is argued, "Old Japan, with its old thinking and old way of doing things, is the crux of Japan's political crisis" (Hewitt 2003, 1). In countries and sub-regions where the older part of the population is disproportionately dominant politically and economically—which includes Japan's post-war generation—ageing effects on the economy and society risk being magnified. With this in mind, a new and unprecedented international economic demography has developed only relatively recently (see Bloom et al. 2015).

Transition economies, understood as those moving from a centrally planned to a market-based economy, are no exception, and the majority of them now classify as "ageing" (see Table 26.3).[1] On average, however, compared with established market economies, population ageing in transition economies has taken place at low per capita incomes (see Johnston et al. 2016). Despite that potential additional development hurdle, among transition economies only in the Chinese case has there been a consistent and sustained level of policy attention paid to the potential ramifications for economic development of being "first old, not rich" (see Johnston 2019a). This has produced a uniquely vibrant literature and policy discourse on the interaction of economics and demography (e.g. Wu 1980, 1986; Cai 2004; Cai and Wang 2006; Cai et al. 2018; Jiang et al. 2018). It would be useful if this literature were better understood by transition economy policymakers.

This chapter elaborates China's unique, and uniquely relevant, set of economic demography circumstances, and the related literature, as a reference for the demographic challenge faced by other transition economies. It begins by elaborating China's unique population and economic planning from 1980. It then outlines the policy-relevant frameworks of the economic demography matrix (EDM) and economic demography transition (EDT), both of which have been extrapolated from China's approach. These concepts are then applied to the transition economies of Central and Eastern Europe. Finally, policy suggestions for navigating the potential problems linked to population ageing are offered. The contribution of this chapter is therefore to the literature on transition economies and on EDT.

---

[1] In this chapter, transition economies at the national level include the following countries: Albania, Armenia, Azerbaijan, Belarus, Bosnia and Herzegovina, Bulgaria, Croatia, Czech Republic, Estonia, Georgia, Hungary, Kazakhstan, Kosovo, Kyrgyzstan, Lithuania, Macedonia, Moldova, Mongolia, Montenegro, Poland, Romania, Russia, Serbia, Slovakia, Slovenia, Tajikistan, Turkmenistan, Ukraine and Uzbekistan. China is also considered a transition economy, but is a special case in terms of reform process.

2 China's One-Child Policy and Demographic Dividend Plan, and Associated Concerns

In the late 1970s China found itself emerging from some decades of political instability and autarky, as well as two centuries of "national humiliation". The "reform and opening" agenda that was launched in December 1978 by Deng Xiaoping was intended to realise lasting national social and economic modernisation. Two important "centennial" goals formed a broader political backdrop to this. According to the first, set for by 2021, the hundredth anniversary of the founding of the Chinese Communist Party, all Chinese were to enjoy at least moderate prosperity. By the second, with a target date of 2045, the hundredth anniversary of the founding of the People's Republic of China, China was to be an all-round modern state. In this way, it would reclaim its earlier position in the world economy.

In late 1978, China was not only poor in terms of income per capita, but also demographically "young": the median age was around 21.9 years (UN estimates 2019). From a peak of more than six children per woman in the mid-1960s, in 1980 the total fertility rate (TFR) had fallen to 2.65 per woman (Fig. 26.1). China's TFR was, however, still above the replacement level of 2.1 children per woman. Consequently, China would need to generate high rates of growth to achieve the intended per capita increases in income and welfare that would help to realise its longer-term modernisation aims.[2]

Renmin University demographer Wu (1980) noted that "the greatest obstacle to production and income per capita growth is population growth" (Wu 1980, 38), a logic consistent with the Solow growth model. In 1980 the *Open Letter to All Members of the Communist Party and Communist Youth League—on the Issue of Controlling the Population Growth* marked the start of the incremental implementation of a "One-Child-Per-Couple" policy (see Jiang et al. 2013). The aim was not only to reduce population-related pressures, but also to utilise the ensuing process of demographic transition to facilitate modernisation.

By making China's population trends more predictable, the One-Child Policy to some extent also fixed China's demographic dividend period.[3] The demographic dividend is a transitory elevation of growth potential that results from a rise in the share of the working-age population. This rising share of working-age population (Fig. 26.2) itself follows falling fertility (Fig. 26.1)

---

[2] Given skewed birth rates in favour of males, the replacement rate may be slightly higher in China's case.

[3] See Feng, W., Cai, Y., & Gu, B. (2013) for debate on the legacy of the One-China Policy.

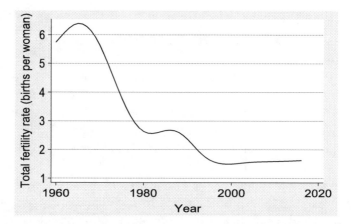

Fig. 26.1 Total fertility rate (births/woman). The TFR is the average number of children a hypothetical cohort of women would have at the end of their reproductive period if they were subject throughout their lives to the fertility rates of a given period and were not subject to mortality. It is expressed as children per woman (World Health Organisation (WHO) 2019). China's TFR has now stabilised at around 1.6, which is below the replacement level of 2.1. (Source: World Bank, *World Development Indicators* (2019a))

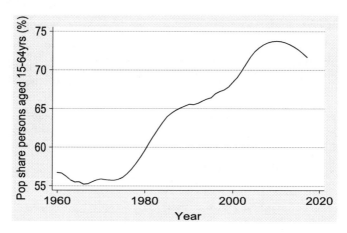

Fig. 26.2 Workforce-aged population share (%). For implicit international comparability, World Bank data is presented. In China, however, the retirement age is 60 years for men and lower for women, inferring that China's actual workforce population share may be lower than presented

and morbidity rates of the demographic transition process that these endogenously define. However, the demographic dividend lies specifically in the potential of the temporary increase in working-age population share to itself increase total productivity and national output. China experienced a 42-year demographic dividend, from 1972 to 2014. This is estimated to have boosted growth by as much as 1.4% annually (see Mason et al. (2017) and Cai et al. (2018)).

A working-age population boom eventually fades, however, as the larger population cohort moves into retirement and is replaced by a proportionately smaller working-age cohort. The underlying demographic transformation in China's case is captured visually in the contrast between the population pyramids in the early phase in 1980 (Fig. 26.3) and in late phase in 2015 (Fig. 26.4). Between these years, China's workforce as a share of the population peaked around 2011 (Fig. 26.2). China's median population age rose from 21.9 years when the modernisation agenda began in 1980, to some 38.4 years in 2020 (UN estimates 2019). That is to say, instead of being rich in low-wage, prime-age workers as it was four decades ago, China now has a shrinking workforce and a rapidly rising pensioner population.

For countries that are both poor and young, like China in the late 1970s, the demographic dividend period offers added potential for rapid development. If the dividend coincides with circumstances enabling waves of low-wage, largely rural workers to transfer to the industrial sector, this can produce sustained and rapid gains in productivity and income through the period of dividend, a process captured by the Nobel Prize-winning Lewis Model (Lewis 1954). Capturing the dividend for development is not automatic, however.

China's policymakers understood the transitory potential of its hundreds of millions of low-wage workers to power national modernisation, implementing a policy agenda to capture that potential (see Cai (2010) for associated

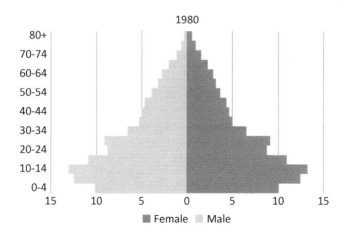

Fig. 26.3 Population pyramid of China, 1980

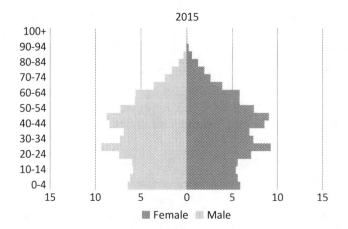

Fig. 26.4 Population pyramid of China, 2015

policies). One example is the incentive offered to foreign investors for labour-intensive export-oriented manufacturing investments in economic zones along China's coast from the mid-1980s. In turn, this opened the door for millions of rural labourers to relocate to cities and coastal regions to work in the resulting factories (see Cai 2010). Given China's demographic scale, this explains how and why the country became the world's factory from the 1990s onward.

Following a period of demographic dividend, however, comes a period of intensifying population ageing. If new sources of growth are not identified, the resulting relatively high share of elderly dependents dampens the economic growth rate directly by reducing the per capita labour supply and production growth. This goes some way to explaining an element of China's recent growth deceleration, from some 30 years of growth around 10% per year to about 6% more recently, alongside sluggish growth in many high-income countries—most famously, Japan, which has seen its workforce population share falling since the mid-1990s.

In China's case, since demographic transition was officially induced by the One-Child Policy, which formed part of a much broader national development agenda, Chinese planners were attuned from the 1980s to the fact that they should be ready for the onset of population ageing. In an important contribution to China's economic demography literature, Wu (1986) reached the conclusion that unusually rapid declines in the fertility rate at low per capita income levels meant that China would ultimately "get old before it became rich". In economics, this can also be understood via a more static economic demography combination of "not rich, (first) old" (未富先老) (Johnston 2019).

A fear at that time in China was that for given total fertility rate projections there was no feasible growth rate at which China could become a high per capita income country before reaching the more advanced phase of demographic transition, population ageing. Hence, China's fate was to be "not rich, first old". Fear that this might also mean that China would never become rich opened a door to a vibrant economic demography literature that is especially relevant to transition economies.

Like China, today's relatively developed transition economies were a frontier of population ageing at relatively low per capita incomes (see Jiang et al. 2018). Indeed, when Slovenia joined the high per capita income group in 1997, it became the world's first country to get rich after getting old. In its footsteps, since 2006, the Czech Republic, Estonia, Hungary, Slovak Republic, Latvia, Poland and Croatia have also joined the high-income per capita group. Conversely, Bulgaria, Romania, Serbia, Bosnia and Herzegovina, Macedonia, Montenegro, Albania, Kosovo, Ukraine, Georgia, Belarus, Russia, Moldova, Armenia and Kazakhstan are among the transition economies studied here that are demographically old, but not rich (Table 26.3).[4]

In other words, within and across transition economies, demographic change and economic growth are taking place at different speeds. It may be useful, even important, not only that the region's policymakers become more aware of these developments and their consequences, but also that they learn from them. Moreover, from this could be drawn lessons for "younger" developing countries that are likely in future to be "not rich, first old" themselves. Section 3 below explores the economic logic underpinning China's fear of "premature ageing", which sheds light on some of the issues that may be affecting transition economies that are "poor-old" today, alongside those that are presently "poor-young" in a probable "poor-old" future.

3   The Economic Logic of China's "Getting Old Before Getting Rich" Concern

Chinese policymakers' concern from the mid-1980s about becoming "not rich, first old" is more commonly understood as "getting old before getting rich". From an economic point of view, it can be understood as the prospect of a fall in labour supply and production growth eliminating the demographic

---

[4] Bulgaria and Romania are the only two members of the EU that have per capita income levels below the high-income threshold (EU Observer 2018).

dividend element of China's growth rate, implying lower rates of new resource generation for realising the goal of modernisation. Moreover, the transition to new advanced sources of growth itself would be challenging.

Further, an enlarged elderly population share would re-direct financial and human resources towards caring responsibilities—and so away from the (not yet completed) process of national development. In addition, the rapid speed with which China would eventually age (see Fig. 26.4) might also mean that China would not be able to prepare adequately to provide for the needs of its elderly. Lastly, a falling working-age population would instigate a shortage of labour that would put upward pressure on wages. In a development context, it was feared that China would experience disproportionate wage inflation without having reached a parallel technological competitiveness at the international level in more capital-intensive industries.

Drawing such challenges together led to fears that China would ultimately never reach the economic frontier. As Wu (1986, 37) put it, China would suffer an "advanced country disease" (population ageing) as a developing country. This might hinder or even halt its modernisation prospects. Worse, it was thought that China's experience of premature ageing was unique, since other East Asian countries, such as Japan, South Korea, Taiwan, Hong Kong and Singapore, had become advanced economies while their demography was still youthful. Although China used these economies as developmental reference points, the country was alone on its economic demography trajectory and would have to find its own path.

By definition, if Japan, South Korea, Taiwan, Hong Kong and Singapore all went straight from being "poor and young" to "rich and young" (and only more recently to "rich and old"), this implies four fundamental economic demography categories: poor-young, poor-old, rich-young and rich-old. Together these form the economic demography matrix (EDM; Table 26.1). Movement of a country within and between these quadrants reflects change in that country's economic demography transition (EDT). The EDT embodies concurrent and interrelated change in the demographic transition (movement between the "young" and "old" EDM quadrants) and from economic development (movement between the "poor" and "rich" quadrants). In this framework, the relative speed and direction of demographic and economic change help to determine whether a country becomes old before or after becoming rich. This in turn shapes the ways in which the older cohort itself shapes the economy (see for example Johnson and Zimmermann 2008; Johnston 2012).

In this context, thanks to a number of changes, including the wider and more affordable access to birth-control technologies, in the later years of the

Table 26.1   The economic demography matrix

	Demographic transition	
	Early	Late[b]
Economic transition		
High income per capita[a]	*Rich and young*	*Rich and old*
Low and middle income per capita	*Poor and young*	*Poor and old*

Sources: Johnston et al. (2016), Johnston (2018)

[a]The World Bank considers a nation with a per capita income exceeding US$12,055 (2017, Atlas method) as a high per capita income country (World Bank 2018)

[b]In demography, when a nation's population share of people aged 65 rises above 7%, it is considered to have entered a population ageing phase

twentieth century the process of demographic transition across countries began to happen at relatively low per capita incomes, in some low-income countries but not others. Mostly this took place without receiving explicit attention in the literature. The country in which policymakers were unusually aware of the onset of demographic transition at lower per capita incomes, however, was China. This was because the almost universal imposition of the One-Child Policy was itself linked to more rapid demographic transition—at low per capita incomes, and the ensuing literature and policies (see Sects. 2, 3 and 4).

In the language of Table 26.1, what 1980s policymakers in China realised was that China, starting from the poor-young quadrant, would first move right to the poor-old quadrant. Given the absence of regional precedent for moving to a "rich" quadrant from the poor-old quadrant, Chinese policymakers took earnestly China's "first old, not rich" fear.[5] In retrospect, it may be argued that this fear and foresight about China's unique EDT circumstances around the One-Child Policy was responsible for instigating a unique approach to development—the EDT strategy approach (see Johnston 2019a). This approach is the topic of Sect. 4.

4   China's EDT Approach to National Development

In response to their "old before rich" fears, China's policymakers appear to have devised an economic strategy that is broadly complementary to rapid demographic transition. This dual strategy started in the early 1980s and can

---

[5] South Korea later would get old about as it got rich (see Johnston 2018).

itself be simplified into two tiers (see Johnston 2019c). The first tier required the development and implementation of policies to capture for national development the opportunities offered by China's expected multi-decade demographic dividend. The second tier required advanced preparation for the inevitable onset on rapid population ageing, including by achieving success in the first tier.

4.1   The First Tier: Expeditious Capture of the Demographic Dividend

In the first tier, policymakers offered incentives for investors in labour-intensive and industrial value-chain production to set up along China's coast, while allowing waves of migrant rural labour to move to these emerging industrial and export-oriented hot spots. This began in earnest from the start of the "reform and opening" era. The groundbreaking "Law on Chinese-Foreign Equity Joint Ventures" of 1979 committed the state to greater protection of foreign property rights. This helped to attract early foreign investors. The same year, the State Council issued the "Trial Measures on Using Imports to Support Exports", which introduced a programme of favourable trade and exchange terms for imports needed to build China's export base (Yang 1991).

By May 1980 the State Council had also approved the "Meetings of the Guangdong and Fujian Provinces", following which "export special zones" were renamed "special economic zones" (SEZs). By August 1980 the "Guangdong Special Economic Zones Regulations" were approved, leading to SEZs in Shenzhen, Zhuhai, Shantou and Xiamen, and marking the official start of China's export-powerhouse coastal SEZs (gov.cn 2009; Liang 1999). The tax-incentivised factories that were set up thereafter, in many cases relocated from capital-rich, high-income countries to labour-rich China, instigated several decades of migration of rural workers to China's coastal regions in pursuit of higher incomes (see Tung and Cho 2000). Reflecting a virtuous Lewisian circle, the income gains of those workers and the remittances to their home villages increased urban and rural consumption, and further incentivised such rural-urban migration.

The role of the SEZs was formalised under the China's Coastal Development Strategy (CDS), which was approved by the State Council in February 1988 (see Yang 1991). The official title of the strategy was the "Outward-oriented development strategy in the coastal areas". The initiative included 12 provinces—Beijing, Fujian, Guangdong, Guangxi, Hainan, Hebei, Jiangsu, Liaoning, Shandong, Shanghai, Tianjin and Zhejiang—which today account for a very large share of China's GDP. In sum, the CDS was intended to allow China's more prosperous coastal provinces to fully participate in international trade and, via a Lewisian process of transfer of low-wage agricultural labour to the industrial sector, capture the potential of China's low-wage demographic dividend.

Export orientation highlights the "opening" half of China's "reform and opening" agenda. China was also lucky with its timing, as the era of its low-wage demographic dividend and opening up broadly coincided with the high-wage demographic dividend era of Japan, Hong Kong, Singapore, the United States, Canada and West European economies. This provided the conditions for "poor-young" China to produce seemingly limitless volumes of low-cost manufactured goods, and mostly "rich-young" high-income countries to provide the related high-technology goods, and services—until around the beginning in 2008—when both low-wage and high-wage demographic dividends broadly came to a halt.

4.2 The Second Tier: Advanced Post-Low-Wage Demographic Dividend Preparations

The success of the first tier generated the resources that would support the second tier of the strategy. That is, rising national and household incomes would permit the investment in education needed to achieve the second-tier goals of raising productivity and minimising dependency risks. In other words, resources would incrementally and explicitly be invested in the education of the next generation. In the tradition of Becker and Lewis (1973), fewer children per household meant that per capita spending on the children's education was substantially higher than in the earlier period. In theory, this smaller, more educated cohort would then be sufficiently productive so as to provide for the larger older generation.

Concurrently, retirement promises made to the larger and older cohort in their prime earning years have consistently been modest. This ensures that these retirement costs do not become unsustainable and thus will not stall China's modernisation agenda in the case of an early onset of population ageing in terms of national development Thanks to its long-run EDT strategy, China is arguably at least comparatively well-positioned to continue its development (see Johnston et al. 2016; Johnston 2019a, b). In recent years, more information has emerged on China's strategy for moving from the "poor-old" to the "rich-old" quadrant of the EDM.

4.3   China's Next-Phase Strategy for the Goal of Transition from "Poor-Old" to "Rich-Old"

Ageing populations pose many economic challenges, increasing strains on the labour supply, and on fiscal and corporate resources, as a smaller share of the population are net productivity contributors. At the same time, an increasing share of resources, including human capital, must be directed towards the care of the old. In other words, there is a simultaneous challenge of managing falling output per head alongside a rising dependency per head.

Thanks to continuous research and policy thinking following the implementation of the One-Child Policy, China's economic planning system has been preparing for the onset of population ageing for decades. More recently there has been increasing emphasis on a shift of the growth model away from low-cost and labour-intensive sectors towards more capital- and innovation-intensive sectors. Although success is not guaranteed and the path ahead will be difficult, China is expected gradually to move out of sectors that it has dominated in recent decades (see Garnaut et al. (2017), as well as). Such trends are likely to be accentuated by the China-US trade war that began in 2018, and also the likely effects of the coronavirus outbreak that began in December 2019, which could incentivise a reduction in dependency on China as an industrial supplier globally.

In 2013, a few years before China's outward investment first exceeded inward foreign investment, China launched a flagship international political economy strategy, the Belt and Road Initiative (BRI) (see Huang 2016; Johnston 2019c). Under the BRI, China has allocated significant sums to supporting its outward investors, as well as to supporting growth in developing countries through concessional project financing and other incentives. In the post-COVID-19 era, developing countries well-positioned to attract international industrial investment may find themselves, for the first time in decades, in the right place at the right time.

Transition economies are fundamental to the BRI, with the intended economic corridor across Eurasia (see Fig. 26.5) traversing the territory of several of them. While the BRI will improve the links of China's poorer and younger Western provinces to international markets and open up a second, non-maritime trade corridor with European and Middle Eastern markets, Eastern and Central European economies may also become new production hubs, by way of Chinese and other investment, for these markets.

Complementing that outward agenda to help its poorer provinces to integrate with international markets while also investing in "poor-young"

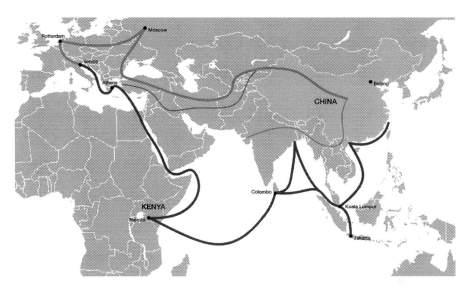

Fig. 26.5 Belt and Road Initiative map. (Note: Land-based routes are part of the concept of a "Silk Road economic belt", as launched in Kazakhstan. Ocean-based routes are part of the "Maritime Silk Road", as launched in Indonesia. Source: adapted from Johnston (2019b))

countries (i.e. those that can expect a demographic dividend in the future), China has also recently begun to address more directly the fact that its rate of population ageing is gathering pace. A series of directives linked to ageing and the economy, and to the challenge of pension sustainability, have been initiated. For example, the 2019 Work Report, the annual report on the work of the Government of China, promised to reform the management of age-care insurance funds and guaranteed the payment of pensions on time and in full (Zhou 2019). In March, the Ministry of Finance transferred into the state pension fund a stake of almost 7% in the People's Insurance Company of China (He 2019). This was a first step in what is expected to be a relatively standard pattern in the future, as China sets aside assets to cover its emerging pension-related liabilities.

New opportunities in financial services for foreign investors are also emerging. For example, in April 2019 China's State Council released a set of "Opinions on promoting the development of pension services" (gov.cn 2019a). This set out 28 policy proposals for addressing a range of issues presently or imminently expected to affect ageing China. Throughout China's "reform and opening" period, in general the financial sector remained state-owned and closed to foreign investors. More recently, however, the authorities have begun to court the private sector and foreign investors to help provide innovative services to meet China's pension obligations which, despite being kept relatively low, have been driven up by recent rapid population ageing.

With broader application across economic sectors, in November 2019 the "National Medium and Long-Term Plan to Actively Cope with Population Ageing" was issued by the State Council (gov.cn 2019b). Described as a "programmatic document for China to meet the challenges of population ageing", it captures key issues and proposes targeted policies and solutions, for dealing with an ageing population while continuing with economic development. In January 2020 five central departments issued a notice on "Guiding Opinions on Promoting the Development of Industry Producing Products for Seniors" (gov.cn 2020). The Opinions encourage all economics actors to be innovative and productive in sectors of importance to older populations, from mobility-related products to communication-facilitating technologies that are especially useful for elderly users.

The flurry of related directives highlights not only the accelerating rate of population ageing, but also that China remains a middle-income country. That is, it is "first old, not rich", while still wanting to become rich in per capita terms. Is it reasonable to be hopeful that China will succeed? The next section explores China's 1980s-based "old, not rich" fears for getting rich in a cross-country context using recent data on countries entering the high-income group.

5   Updating China's 1980s-Derived "Old Not Rich" Fears

After arriving at the worrying concept of "getting old before rich" in the mid-1980s, few researchers then re-evaluated the dynamic relevance of the concept. In turn, China's point of comparison remained the earlier economic demography characteristics of East Asia, and not the demographic characteristics of more recent entrants to the high-income group. Moreover, in the absence of an extrapolation of the concept into what is now understood as the EDM, there was little by way of comparative study of China with other "poor-old" economies. The story was similar for the comparative study of how ageing itself may bring different economic and social impacts in each of "poor-old" and "rich-old" contexts (see Johnston et al. 2016 for related discussion).

That is, China consistently saw itself as a static old-before-rich exception, and not as a country case upon the dynamic economic demographic transition spectrum (see Johnston 2019). In this section, we review those points, and in Sect. 6 draw on the discussion of China's economic demography to look at the case of East and Central European transition economies.

5.1 Countries Now Tend to Get Old Before—If Ever— Getting Rich

One reason to be hopeful that China and other ageing developing countries—many of which are transition economies—can still become rich is the fact that the pattern of becoming rich while remaining old demographically does not appear to be an exception. It may even now be a "new normal" stage of a successful development process.

Table 26.2 sets out the demographic characteristics of countries entering the high-income group from the late 1980s, according to three different demographic indicators of population ageing. The first, Ageing 1, distinguishes between countries where the share of the population aged 65 and over makes up above or below 7% of the total. Ageing 2 looks at the share of children in the population, with 14% as the threshold between "young" and "old" populations. Ageing 3 is a ratio of Ageing 1 and Ageing 2, with the threshold between "old" and "young" population set above 30%, or 0.3.

Perhaps the most striking feature of Table 26.2 is that only two countries (Equatorial Guinea and Oman) entering the high-income group in recent decades were "young" by share of child population. Moreover, they both entered the per capita rich income group owing to oil-based commodity wealth. On this measure, even South Korea, one of China's own reference points for having become economically rich before demographically old was in fact "old" by child population share at the time of entering the high-income group.

Variation across countries in terms of demographics and the growth of per capita income—reflected in Table 26.2 both directly and indirectly—contrasts China's earlier assumptions around high-income country group entrance and demography. It is not true, that is, that most countries, at least contemporarily, get 'rich' when 'young'. They also underpin the need to endogenise an EDT approach to economics in general. Given the high propensity for transition economies to be "poor-old" economies, and the challenges of getting rich from that position, nowhere is this EDT approach more relevant than for the transition economies of Eastern and Central Europe. Better understanding links between economics and demography across countries and time, in general, would provide useful comparative reference points.

Table 26.2 Demographic profile of countries upon entering the high-income group (1988–2017, %)

Year became rich	Country	Ageing 1		Ageing 2		Ageing 3	
1988	Cyprus	9.9	Old	25.2	Old	39.1	Old
1994	Macao SAR, China	7.2	Old	25.8	Old	27.9	Young
1994	Portugal	14.7	Old	18.2	Old	80.7	Old
1995	South Korea	5.9	Young	23.0	Old	25.7	Young
1996	Greece	15.1	Old	16.4	Old	95.5	Old
1997	Slovenia	13.1	Old	17.1	Old	76.3	Old
2002	Antigua & Barbuda	7.0	Old	28.8	Old	24.3	Young
2006	Czech Republic	14.2	Old	14.6	Old	96.9	Old
2006	Estonia	17.0	Old	15.0	Old	113.2	Old
2006	Trinidad & Tobago	7.4	Old	21.5	Old	34.6	Old
2007	Equatorial Guinea	3.2	Young	40.7	Young	7.9	Young
2007	Hungary	16.1	Old	15.1	Old	106.4	Old
2007	Oman	2.7	Young	30.2	Young	8.9	Young
2007	Slovak Republic	11.9	Old	16.0	Old	74.4	Old
2009	Latvia	18.2	Old	14.1	Old	129.0	Old
2009	Poland	13.4	Old	15.1	Old	88.3	Old
2012	Chile	10.2	Old	21.1	Old	48.1	Old
2012	Lithuania	18.1	Old	14.5	Old	125.4	Old
2012	Russian Federation[a]	13.1	Old	15.4	Old	85.0	Old
2012	Uruguay	14.1	Old	22.0	Old	64.1	Old
2014	Argentina[a]	10.8	Old	25.3	Old	42.6	Old
2014	Seychelles	6.8	Young	23.2	Old	29.4	Young
2014	Venezuela, RB[a]	6.1	Young	28.4	Old	21.5	Young
2017	Croatia	20.0	Old	14.4	Old	138.9	Old
2017	Panama	7.9	Old	27.3	Old	28.9	Young

Palau entered the high-income group in 2018, but recent demographic data is not available in the source database
Sources: Johnston (2019a); World Bank, *World Development Indicators* (2020)
[a]Countries with volatile per capita incomes that see their high-income group classification fluctuate with upper-middle income classification

5.2   Prospective Differences Between "Poor-Old" and "Rich-Old" Economies

An additional potential benefit of greater endogenisation of the EDT to mainstream economics derives from comparative economics in terms of economic demography. Returning to Table 26.1, which presents the EDM, there may be relatively consistent structural characteristics of countries in each corner of the matrix.

For example, all else constant, when compared with "rich-old" economies, "poor-old" ones retain convergence growth potential. While China's economy has been growing at a rate of some 5% in recent years, "rich-old" Japan, which is at the same stage of ageing but with a higher income level, had a lower rate of economic growth, as is typical for a more mature industrialised phase. This means more new resources are being generated in China than in Japan, which may relatively provide for China's ongoing development needs.

Similarly, in old-after-rich Japan the older cohort dominated the economic agenda through their adulthood. In old-before-rich China, conversely, today's older (and larger) generation has never been an important driver of consumption, even in their prime earning years. This means that China is relatively well-placed because, just as it puts greater emphasis on consumption as a growth engine, it has developed a newly enriched, higher-spending younger consumer class for whom higher levels of consumption have been relatively normal from the start. In Japan, by contrast, the younger and middle-aged cohort of the "lost decades" feels less economically prosperous than the larger, older population whose retirements they are responsible for providing.

In China's case, when today's older generation leaves the workforce, the impact will be different. Whereas in "rich-old" Japan the education gap between generations is narrow and the human capital embodied in the older cohort is deep, in China human capital is dramatically skewed in favour of the young. As China's population share of workers falls, just maintaining output per capita requires improved productivity per capita. In theory at least, China's younger cohort are well-positioned to utilise their relatively better skills to maintain, if not increase, productivity levels.

China's human capital investment in its smaller, younger population share is the result of the explicit focus of its longer-term EDT national development strategy. This, however, is not necessarily the path that has been taken by all "poor-old" economies. In fact, it is challenging to draw strict conclusions about the relationship between ageing and the economy across countries. With that caveat, the next section studies the economic demography characteristics of Central and East European countries in the context of the EDM, China and some broader issues, including emigration.

6 Eastern and Central Europe Within the Economic Demography Transition (EDT) Framework

6.1 Survey of Eastern and Central European Economies

Table 26.3 presents demographic characteristics related to ageing for transition economies in 2018. It uses the same ageing indicators as Table 26.2, but adds income per capita data. This provides an implicit EDM map of transition economies which can be summarised as follows: Central and Eastern Europe, and the Baltics, like the OECD, qualifies as "rich-old"; South-eastern Europe, like China, is upper-middle income and old (poor-old); transition economies not otherwise classified are a mix of poor-old and poor-young. But even the "Stans", which in 2018 were consistently "young" by Ageing 1 and Ageing 3 indicators, are already categorised as "old" by the criterion of Ageing 2, which is the share of children in the population. This implies that a process of demographic transition has begun in these countries. The data in Table 26.3 implies that, where countries of the region have not been as active in planning for their EDT as China, it might be timely to do so.

We know from Tables 26.1, 26.2, and 26.3 that Central and Eastern Europe, and the Baltics, are not only "rich-old", but that they all entered the high-income group after getting old. Factors contributed to that per capita income growth, including the role of EU membership, are not explored herein.[6] However, in a context of China's "old before rich" fears, this provides several precedents for getting rich after getting old (see Johnston et al. 2016; Jiang et al. 2018). Johnston (2019) finds that, since 1996, countries have a much higher chance of entering the high-income group from being demographically "old" rather than young, as was the earlier precedent from North-East Asia. Planning a process of development in transition economies that continuously accounts for economic and demographic transition in parallel, as China has done for years, appears logical.

The approach more generically and extrapolated across different demography transition stages is elaborated next using the total fertility rate (TFR). The TFR is the number of children who would be born per woman (or per 1000 women) if each were to pass through their childbearing years having children according to the current schedule of age-specific fertility rates. Table 26.4 uses demographic-transition-related cut-off points from the World Bank's *World Development Indicators*, Johnston (forthcoming, Johnston 2020) for the TFR, and population share of children (0–14 years) and the old (65 years and over) to classify societies by their stage of demographic transition. Table 26.5 presents transition economies according to the categories set out in Table 26.4.

The countries listed in Table 26.5 are the demographic transition indicator corollary of Table 26.3. From this it is clear that most transition economies in Eastern and Central Europe are "low fertility rate societies"—that is, they have already passed the demographic dividend period. At the other extreme, there are no transition economies in the high-fertility-rate society category,

---

[6] For a discussion of this, see Campos (2020)—Chap. 14 in this volume.

Table 26.3 Transition economies by selected demographic and income per capita indicators (2018)

	Ageing 1		Ageing 2		Ageing 3		Per capita income		EDM Group
	Value	Category	Value	Category	Value	Category	Level	Category	
Central and Eastern Europe, and the Baltics									
Latvia	20.0	Old	16.0	Old	1.3	Old	16,510	Rich	Rich-old
Lithuania	19.7	Old	14.9	Old	1.3	Old	17,430	Rich	Rich-old
Slovenia	19.6	Old	15	Old	1.3	Old	24,580	Rich	Rich-old
Estonia	19.6	Old	16.4	Old	1.2	Old	21,140	Rich	Rich-old
Czech Republic	19.4	Old	15.6	Old	1.3	Old	20,240	Rich	Rich-old
Hungary	19.2	Old	14.4	Old	1.3	Old	14,780	Rich	Rich-old
Poland	17.5	Old	15.1	Old	1.1	Old	14,100	Rich	Rich-old
Slovakia	15.6	Old	15.5	Old	1.0	Old	18,260	Rich	Rich-old
South-East Europe									
Bulgaria	21.0	Old	14.6	Old	1.4	Old	8860	Upper-middle (UM)	Poor-old
Romania	18.3	Old	15.5	Old	1.2	Old	11,290	UM	Poor-old
Serbia	18.3	Old	15.7	Old	1.1	Old	6390	UM	Poor-old
Bosnia & Herzegovina	16.5	Old	14.8	Old	1.1	Old	5740	UM	Poor-old
Macedonia	13.7	Old	16.5	Old	0.8	Old	5450	UM	Poor-old
Montenegro	15.0	Old	19.2	Old	0.8	Old	8430	UM	Poor-old
Albania	13.7	Old	17.7	Old	0.8	Old	4860	UM	Poor-old
Kosovo	n.a.		n.a.		n.a.		4220	UM	n.a.
Former Soviet Union/transition economy not elsewhere classified									
Ukraine	16.4	Old	15.8	Old	1	Old	2660	Lower-middle (LM)	Poor-old
Georgia	14.9	Old	19.8	Old	8	Old	4440	UM	Poor-old
Belarus	14.9	Old	16.9	Old	0.9	Old	5670	UM	Poor-old
Russia	14.7	Old	17.9	Old	0.8	Old	10,230	UM	Poor-old

(continued)

Table 26.3 (continued)

	Ageing 1		Ageing 2		Ageing 3		Per capita income		EDM Group
	Value	Category	Value	Category	Value	Category	Level	Category	
Moldova	11.5	Old	15.9	Old	0.7	Old	2980	LM	Poor-old
Armenia	11.3	Old	20.6	Old	0.6	Old	4230	UM	Poor-old
Kazakhstan	7.4	Old	28.5	Old	0.3	Young	8070	UM	Poor-old
Azerbaijan	6.1	Young	23.4	Old	0.3	Young	4050	UM	Poor-young
Kyrgyzstan	4.5	Young	32.4	Old	0.1	Young	1220	LM	Poor-young
Turkmenistan	4.4	Young	30.8	Old	0.1	Young	6740	UM	Poor-young
Uzbekistan	4.4	Young	28.7	Old	0.2	Young	2020	UM	Poor-young
Mongolia	4.1	Young	30	Old	0.1	Young	3660	UM	Poor-young
Tajikistan	3	Young	36.8	Old	0.1	Young	1010	Low-income	Poor-young

As of July 1, 2019, low-income economies are defined as those with a GNI per capita, calculated using the World Bank Atlas method, of US$1025 or less in 2018; lower middle-income economies are those with a GNI per capita between US$1026 and US$3995; upper middle-income economies are those between US$3996 and US$12,375; high-income economies are those with a GNI per capita of US$12,376 or more. (World Bank 2018)

Source: Data from World Bank, World Development Indicators (2019a)

Note: Data in Table 26.2 offers background in that all "rich-old" transition economies were "old" upon entering the high-income group. That is, and in EDM language, they were first poor-young, then poor-old and then rich-old

Table 26.4   Demographic transition phases

	TFR (no. children)	Child share (% pop.)	Elder share (% pop.)
Low fertility rate society[a]	<1.7	<19.0	>10.7
Demographic dividend era	1.7–2.4	19.0–28.9	5.8–10.7
Pre-demographic dividend	2.4–5.0	28.9–43.5	2.8–5.8
High fertility rate society[b]	>5.0	>43.5	<2.8

Source: Johnston (2020, forthcoming)
Note: Phase classifications identified using the thresholds presented in Table 26.2
[a]Post-demographic dividend
[b]"Malthusian"

Table 26.5   Transition economies by Demographic Dividend Phase (based on TFR, 2017)

Demographic circumstance	TFR range	Countries
Low fertility rate society[a]	<1.75	Albania (1.64), Bulgaria (1.54), Bosnia & Herzegovina (1.28), Belarus (1.54), Czech Republic (1.63), Estonia (1.60), Croatia (1.42), Hungary (1.53), Lithuania (1.69), Latvia (1.74), Moldova (1.26), North Macedonia (1.50), Montenegro (1.74), Poland (1.39), Romania (1.64), Slovak Republic (1.48), Slovenia (1.58), Ukraine (1.37).
Demographic dividend	1.75–2.51	Armenia (1.75), Azerbaijan (1.90), Georgia (2.06), Russian Federation (1.76), Uzbekistan (2.46)
Pre-demographic dividend	2.51–5.02	Kazakhstan (2.73), Kyrgyz Republic (3.0), Tajikistan (3.61), Turkmenistan (2.84)
High-fertility-rate society	>5.02	None

Source: World Bank, *World Development Indicators* (2019a)
[a]See Table 26.4 for societal structure (demographic) definitions

and just four countries—Kazakhstan, the Kyrgyz Republic, Tajikistan and Turkmenistan—in the pre-demographic dividend category.

At the youthful extremum, a high-fertility-rate society can be caught in the Malthusian Trap, whereby population growth overrides per capita economic gains, so inducing economic stagnation. From the older end of the dependency spectrum, a country faces a similar prospect. In this case, however, it is the needs of older dependents directly exhausting or inhibiting, per capita productivity gains and innovation. This old-age dependency stagnation risk scenario is known as the Johnston Trap (Johnston 2019).

Between these extremes of stagnation, different demographic transition phases also imply different factor endowment comparative advantages. For example, a rich-old country has a high probability of having relatively high-cost and richly endowed human capital. This means that a rich-old country is likely to specialise in highly capital-intensive sectors. In contrast, a poor-young country may be in the early or middle phase of a demographic dividend growth period, and so might be creating investor and education incentives to reap from a process of development.

An approach to managing the economy that takes into account these two respective underpinning rates of change over time, and their interaction, is probably the most powerful long-run approach to development. China's contemporary economic development agenda is a case in point. Table 26.6 presents a basic guide to economic policy priorities through the different demographic transition phases, which link also to the phases of economic demography transition.

As noted, China has had a long-run economic demography transition approach since the 1980s, following the imposition of a One-Child Policy. From an early phase in demographic transition, preparations were hence also being made for later EDT requirements. This includes the fiscal burden of pensions and the need for future human capital to be more richly endowed than earlier in order to push the production possibility frontier, despite a falling workforce population share and consequent adverse dependency ratio shifts.

6.2   A Global EDT Approach

From a global perspective, it is important for transition economy policymakers and entrepreneurs to understand the demographic difference of their own prospective development era, whether demographic dividend-related or post-demographic dividend, compared with the era of East Asian development. An export-oriented development strategy played a major role in East Asia's rapid industrialisation in the second half of the twentieth century. The strategy worked by each country successively joining the region's global value chain and exporting to the higher-income world, mainly Europe and North America. Usefully, over the second half of last century, those high-income countries were also in a demographic dividend period. As a result, there were rapid productivity gains and a large working-age population offering demand for East Asia's lower-cost exported goods.

Circumstances will be different for later developers over the next several decades, including transition economies and those trying to raise their per capita incomes to higher per capita income levels again. Instead of a demographic dividend, those established high-income countries are now

Table 26.6 Policy priorities through EDT phases

Demographic society	Policy priorities
"Older" population countries (poor-old and rich-old countries)	
Low fertility rate	Adapting to ageing
	Maintaining and improving welfare in the context of declining workforce population share and a growing old-age share. At this stage, attitudes to the elderly and their productive engagement of the economy—while also ensuring that the "weight" of the old does not dampen the next generations' productivity—is fundamental
Late demographic dividend	Sustaining productivity growth
	Creating conditions necessary to reap the second demographic dividend and beginning to prepare for ageing. Countries typically need to begin reshaping retirement policies and concurrently ensure that the smaller share of youth is not disadvantaged, but instead able to be extremely productive, given the need to provide for the old. Incentives to direct the savings of the elderly into the most productive areas need to be crafted
"Younger" population countries (poor-young and rich-young)	
Early demographic dividend	Accelerate job creation
	Creating increasingly productive jobs for the growing share of the population in working ages to reap the demographic dividend. This requires appropriate macro-fiscal and labour frameworks, including making it easier for parents to work formally
High fertility rate	Sparking the demographic transition (if sought by population)
	Improving human development (health and education) outcomes to accelerate the fertility decline and create a population age structure with fewer child dependents as well as a larger working-age share of the population

Source: Johnston (2020, forthcoming), World Bank (2019b)
Note: Rich-young countries have a different set of challenges to the more classic poor-young countries in terms of reaping the potential of a demographic dividend. These countries typically encounter challenges in resource-rent management and distribution. With the exception of Equatorial Guinea, most such countries are in the Middle East and Southeast Asia, not Africa. See Johnston et al. (2016). See Table 26.2 for empirical definitions of each society (demographic) type

undergoing rapid old-after-rich population ageing (see Johnston 2019 for prospective relative rich-old and poor-old challenge differences). The demand and broader economic structure should be expected to shift too.

On the one hand, high-income coastal provinces in China may enter global consumer markets so as to offer new demand (see Lin and Wang 2014). Technology shifts, political economy factors and other changes may also shift the environment again. This serves to highlight the need for each country, China included, not to seek to cut-and-paste from yesterday's development success story, but rather to set up a suitable economic policy environment in line with their own EDT, and the global circumstance around it.

6.3   Emigration

This chapter is insufficiently long to systematically analyse the impact of emigration on the economic demography challenges of transition countries. Nevertheless, this factor is endogenous and central to the demographic challenges facing the East and Central European transition economies, so that it is not a new topic to the literature (see for example Rosenstein-Rodan 1943). Moreover, in era of population ageing across most major economies, emigration may become more fractious and sensitive an issue within and between countries, driven by competition for labour and taxpayers.

The last point may be especially true in countries where the population is generally against high levels of emigration to fill labour market needs (see Szczepanikova and Van Criekinge 2018). Similarly, the different approaches of members of the EU in response to both labour shortages and third-country crises producing high numbers of refugee arrivals may also induce heightened political frictions within the EU.

In response to falling birth rates, rapid population ageing and emigration to other EU states, some transition economies in the region have recently begun to offer incentives for births and for migrants to return home. In 2015, under it hard-line populist Prime Minister, Victor Orbán, Hungary began running a scheme to encourage young expatriates to return to Hungary. The "Come home, young person" scheme offered free flights home to Hungary for young nationals living abroad and offered them 100,000 forints (about €250) every month for a year after their return (Szakacs 2019).

In 2019 Orbán noted: "There are fewer and fewer children born in Europe. For the West, the answer (to that challenge) is immigration. For every missing child there should be one coming in and then the numbers will be fine". In a speech announcing new related incentives, he went on to say that "we do not need numbers. We need Hungarian children". New measures included the expansion of a loan programme for families with at least two children to help them buy homes, subsidies for car purchases and waiving personal income tax for women raising at least four children (Szakacs 2019).

For all countries in the region, population ageing presents a multitude of economic and political challenges. Even in Germany, there is perhaps increasing divergence of consensus around "first old, not rich" East German political economy and "old-after-rich" West German political economy and EDT conditions. For example, it is probable that retirees in West Germany are, on average, richer than retirees in former East Germany, and hence may be more likely to respond adversely to greater direct and visible pressures upon the public purse. Similarly, the East German region has experienced large-scale emigration, leaving it one of the "oldest" areas in the world (Rankin 2020), which may also affect the sub-region's political economy. It therefore may be useful for the political classes there to better understand the endogenous differences between the EDT of the two historically separated regions in order to find greater consensus within and between them.

6.4 A Different Approach Going Forward

Given the political risks to the EU of such deviation on immigration and political consensus more generally, it appears to be timely that governments with ageing populations across the world might cooperate to incentivise innovation in a number of areas. Table 26.7 summarises some suggestions for cooperation, with the aim of fostering debate.

Table 26.7 Potential policy responses to population ageing in transition economies

Area	Prospective policy response details
Elderly care costs	Incentivise entrepreneurs to develop initiatives and innovations that reduce the fiscal and private burden, in terms of the labour and monetary cost, of caring. Promote rapid adoption across countries of such useful initiatives and ideas, including technologies and living arrangements
	Foster accommodation ownership and allocation so as to maximise allocation of housing resources across generations and minimise caring needs, for example, by encouraging independent co-living among older citizens in place of living alone in family homes that they are otherwise disincentivised (logistically and financially) to leave
Fiscal and pension-related matters	For transition economies that are part of a broader economic union involving free movement of labour, it may be important to develop tax- and pension-related cost sharing. If young labour from some member countries contributes to pension systems in one country, but this adversely affects pension sustainability in their home country, it may be a source of intra-union and intra-generational friction, as well as alongside economic inefficiencies
	Similarly, the fall in a country's working-age population share should trigger a review of the national tax structure across all countries, if this has not already begun beforehand. As income tax payers become rarer, rather than increasing per-worker income taxes, it may be necessary to shift the tax burden—towards taxation of consumption or rent-based wealth, for example. This will depend on each country's economic demography transition and national characteristics. Fiscal change may need to be continuous with economic demography itself. The drop in the working-age population share may nonetheless offer a useful and politically efficient point at which to begin a national review

(continued)

Table 26.7 (continued)

Area	Prospective policy response details
Foster intra-generational communication and support	In transition economies especially, the older cohort have had a different lifespan to the younger cohort (a fact that may receive insufficient attention across EU countries and within reunified Germany). Fostering communication and understanding of this difference, and encouraging inter-generational communication, including between retirement homes and schools, may support community and so economic cohesion
	This would also implicitly recognise that in non-transition "old" (high-income) economies, the old have had relatively comfortable lives, a fact that itself may inspire political divergence between transition and non-transition members of economic and political unions
	In the Netherlands, there are programmes for university students to live for free in the homes of the elderly in return for basic support and company. Such programmes, if not already in place, may be established across transition economies with rapid population ageing, alongside other creative house-sharing arrangements
Foster a positive "population decline" debate and policy approach	Persons in child-bearing age may or may not respond to calls for them to reproduce at higher rates. It is highly probable that, without migration, many transition economies will experience rapid population decline over the coming decades, if this has not started already. Since attracting migrants will become increasingly competitive, and it might in the end be impossible as all countries to reach a more advanced stage of demographic transition, finding ways to manage population decline for the better may also be a positive step
	The study of new welfare metrics and of the macroeconomics of population decline across affected countries, alongside debate over the merits of reduced production of less necessary consumption goods, may aid discussion on these issues
Shift selective necessary labour-intensive industries to labour-rich economies	Greater awareness of the EDM quadrant of each country (rich-old, rich-young, poor-old and poor-young) may help to foster dynamic factor-endowment congruent investment. In East Asia a process of gradual outsourcing by investors took place over decades. The same could take place across and between transition economies, as well as today's remaining "poor-young" developing countries

(*continued*)

Table 26.7 (continued)

Area	Prospective policy response details
Incentivise new industries	As the working-age population share falls, new, less-labour-intensive industries need to be sought by the market, especially where all related processes are unable to be automated. Similarly, given shifting dependency ratios, a shift in production away from unsustainable industries may be required. Such changes may need to be encouraged by government incentives
	Likewise, incentives that can tap into the greater spending power of the elderly cohort in most west European and north American economies may also pay dividends. A cold war tour for contemporary retirees starting at the location of John F. Kennedy's famous "Berliner" speech could be an example
Foster global economic & social dialogue on economic demography issues & lesson-sharing	This dialogue, started by Japan under its 2019 G20 presidency, should see enhanced understanding of how each country's unique economic demography transition affects its economy and politics. This could be accompanied by the sharing of lessons for cost-saving and improvements in living standards. It could also include macroeconomic lesson-sharing—on the implications for monetary and fiscal policy, for example
	It must also prioritise the welfare of the young, whose voices and lifespan interests may be lesser-weighted amid rapid ageing. The different national approaches to ageing should also be studied, including China's, since China began to focus on how the economy might be affected by demographic transition ahead of other countries; and Japan, which has the most intensified ageing circumstances among high-income countries that have experienced population ageing after reaching an advanced stage of economic development. That is, those that got old after getting rich

7 The EDT of Transition Economies in the Twenty-First Century

Economic demography lumps have historically been associated either with a large youth bulge producing a Malthusian stagnation, where per capita gains become impossible, or with a demographic dividend. In 2018, however, the world was for the first time home to more people over the age of 64 than those under 5. Some 85% of global GDP is now produced in countries that have rapidly ageing populations for the first time.

Following Slovenia's turning point—it being the first economy to "get rich after getting old"—the economic demography of transition economies puts them on the frontier of the transition from "getting old after getting rich" to "getting rich after getting old". This presents both challenges and opportunities, both structural and for global policymaking.

For ageing transition and non-transition economies alike, it is imperative to understand the ensuing economic and social effects, and to respond strategically in policy terms. For today's "young" populations, as minorities in ageing population countries or as majorities in poorer economies (such as Azerbaijan, Mongolia, Kyrgyzstan, Tajikistan, Turkmenistan or Uzbekistan), endogenising those lessons across time by adopting a continuous economic demography transition approach to policymaking may be increasingly fruitful. China offers a frontier reference point for this approach.

Most counties that develop later, including not just "young" transition economies but also most of those of South Asia and Africa, are likely to get old before becoming rich (see Johnston 2020, forthcoming). This means that understanding how best to manage their respective economic demography transition over the coming decades will be helped if lessons can be drawn from the successes and failings of todays "poor-old" and "rich-old" transition economies. Transition economies may provide a new development road map, or at least more reference points.

In the meantime, for any ageing population economy it is essential to avoid the late demographic transition phase Johnston Trap. In that case, ageing populations can progressively, or even exponentially, diminish per capita productivity and hence to serve to relatively stagnate the economy and society also. Table 26.7 offered some nascent suggestions for individual countries and groupings of countries, as well as a global effort, towards avoiding that fate.

Policy suggestions offered here include a continuous, economic demography-weighted, approach to reviewing tax policy. For example, where the working-age population share is falling, depending on the economic characteristics of those in the latter stages of their lives, it may be less efficient simply to increase income taxes on the smaller working-age population share and instead shift the tax base towards consumption, wealth or inheritance taxes. Similarly, the older a population becomes, if it moves home less often, property taxes may need to shift from point-of-sale towards value-based taxation. That is, the fiscal system is just one area that should be continuously adjusted to account for demographic change. A broader policy debate on these topics is required.

References

Becker, G. S., & Lewis, H. G. (1973). On the Interaction between the Quantity and Quality of Children. *Journal of political Economy, 81*(2, Part 2), S279–S288.

Bloom, D. E., Canning, D., & Lubet, A. (2015). Global Population Aging: Facts, Challenges, Solutions & Perspectives. *Daedalus, 144*(2), 80–92.

Cai, F. (2004). Demographic Transition. Demographic Dividend, and the Sustainability of Economic Growth. *Population Research, 128*(12), 2–9. (Chinese).

Cai, F. (2010). Demographic Transition, Demographic Dividend, and Lewis Turning Point in China. *China Economic Journal, 3*(2), 107–119.

Cai, F., & Wang, M. (2006). Challenge Facing China's Economic Growth in Its Aging But Not Affluent Era. *China & World Economy, 14*, 20–31.

Cai, F., Garnaut, R., & Song, L. (2018). 1. 40 Years of China's Reform and Development: How Reform Captured China's Demographic Dividend. *China's 40 Years of Reform and Development*, 5–25. ANU Press.

EU Observer. (2018, July 2). *EU Now Officially a High-Income Country*. EU Observer. Retrieved from https://euobserver.com/tickers/142247.

Feng, W., Cai, Y., & Gu, B. (2013). Population, Policy, and Politics: How Will History Judge China's One-Child Policy? *Population and Development Review, 38*, 115–129.

Garnaut, R., Johnston, L., & Song, L. (2017). Where Is the Chinese Economy Going? A Forum on Contemporary Policy and Performance. *Australian Economic Review, 50*(4), 441–449.

Gov.cn. (2009). 共和国的足迹——1979 年:创办经济特区. Retrieved from http://www.gov.cn/test/2009-09/07/content_1410916.htm.

Gov.cn. (2019a). 国务院办公厅关于推进养老服务发展的意见。 Retrieved from http://www.gov.cn/zhengce/content/2019-04/16/content_5383270.htm.

Gov.cn. (2019b). '国家积极应对人口老龄化中长期规划'应对老龄化上升为国家战略。 Retrieved from http://www.gov.cn/zhengce/2019-11/23/content_5454778.htm.

Gov.cn. (2020). '关于促进老年用品产也发展的指导意见'解读. Retrieved from http://www.gov.cn/zhengce/2020-01/22/content_5471545.htm.

He, L. (2019, March 13). China Transfers US$4.7 Billion of PICC Shares to State Pension Fund, Part of a Programme to Shift Assets to Make Up for Shortfall. *Shortfall China Morning Post*. Retrieved from https://www.scmp.com/business/china-business/article/3001402/china-transfers-us47-billion-picc-shares-state-pension-fund.

Hewitt, P. S. (2003). The Demographic Dilemma: Japan's Aging Society. *Asia Program Special Report, 107*, 1–24.

Huang, Y. (2016). Understanding China's Belt & Road Initiative: Motivation, Framework and Assessment. *China Economic Review, 40*, 314–321.

Jiang, Q., Li, S., & Feldman, M. W. (2013). China's Population Policy at the Crossroads: Social Impacts and Prospects. *Asian journal of social science, 41*(2), 193–218.

Jiang, S., Liu, X., Yang, M., & Zhang, X. (2018). 先老后福:全球北京下的中国人口与经济动态转型.中国经济增长的新源泉(第1卷):改革、资源能源与气候变化.社会科学文献出版社. Retrieved from http://press-files.anu.edu.au/downloads/press/n4153/pdf/ch10.pdf.

Johnson, P., & Zimmermann, K. F. (2008). *Labour Markets in an Ageing Europe.* Cambridge: Cambridge University Press.

Johnston, L. (2012, December 22). Getting old after getting rich: Comparing China with Japan. In *East Asia Forum* (Vol. 22). Retrieved from https://www.eastasiaforum.org/2012/12/22/getting-old-after-getting-rich-comparing-china-with-japan/.

Johnston, L. (2018). Harvesting from 'Poor Old' China to Harness 'Poor Young' Africa's Demographic Dividend. *Bridges Africa, 7*(5), 5. International Centre for Trade and Sustainable Development. Retrieved from http://www.ictsd.org/bridges-news/bridges-africa/news/harvesting-from-%E2%80%9Cpoor-old%E2%80%9D-china-to-harness-%E2%80%9Cpoor-young%E2%80%9D-africa%E2%80%99s.

Johnston, L. A. (2019a). The Economic Demography Transition: Is China's 'Not Rich, First Old' Circumstance a Barrier to Growth? *Australian Economic Review, 52*(4), 406–426.

Johnston, L. A. (2019b). The Belt and Road Initiative: What is in it for China? *Asia & the Pacific Policy Studies, 6*(1), 40–58.

Johnston, L. A. (2019c). *A Timely Economic Demography Lesson from China for the G20.* Institute for Global Dialogue (South Africa) Occasional Paper No. 75. Retrieved from https://www.africaportal.org/publications/timely-economic-demography-lesson-china-g20/.

Johnston, L. A. (2020, September). *Youth-Rich Africa is Demographic Dividend-Poor: The Case for a Global Economic Demography Transition Approach.* Murdoch University Africa Commission (forthcoming).

Johnston, L., Liu, X., Yang, M., & Zhang, X. (2016). Getting Rich After Getting Old: China's Demographic and Economic Transition in Dynamic International Context. *China's New Sources of Economic Growth, 1*, 215–246.

Lewis, W. A. (1954). Economic Development with Unlimited Supplies of Labour. *The Manchester School, 22*(2), 139–191.

Liang, Z. (1999). Foreign Investment, Economic Growth, and Temporary Migration: The Case of Shenzhen Special Economic Zone, China. *Development and Society, 28*, 115–137.

Lin, J. Y., & Wang, Y. (2014). *China-Africa Co-Operation in Structural Transformation: Ideas, Opportunities, and Finances* (No. 2014/046). WIDER Working Paper.

Lutz, W., Sanderson, W., & Scherbov, S. (2008). The Coming Acceleration of Global Population Ageing. *Nature, 451*(7179), 716–719.

Mason, A., Lee, R., Abrigo, M., & Lee, S. H. (2017). *Support Ratios and Demographic Dividends: Estimates for the World.* New York (NY): Population Division, United Nations.

Rankin, J.. (2020). Dubravka Šuica: The Woman Tasked with Solving EU's Demographic Crisis. *The* Guardian. Retrieved from https://www.theguardian.com/world/2020/mar/02/dubravka-suica-woman-tasked-solving-eu-demographic-crisis.

Rosenstein-Rodan, P. N. (1943). Problems of Industrialisation of Eastern and South-Eastern Europe. *The Economic Journal, 53*(210/211), 202–211.

Szakacs, G. (2019, February 10). Orbàn Offers Financial Incentives to Boost Hungary's Birth Rate. *Reuters*. Retrieved February 10, 2019, from https://www.reuters.com/article/us-hungary-Orb%C3%A0n-benefits/Orb%C3%A0n-offers-financial-incentives-to-boost-hungarys-birth-rate-idUSKCN1PZ0I0.

Szczepanikova, A., & Van Criekinge, T. (2018). The Future of Migration in the European Union. Retrieved from https://publications.jrc.ec.europa.eu/repository/bitstream/JRC111774/kjnd29060enn.pdf.

Tung, S., & Cho, S. (2000). The Impact of Tax Incentives on Foreign Direct Investment in China. *Journal of International Accounting, Auditing and Taxation, 9*(2), 105–135.

United Nations. (2019). *World Population Prospects: The 2019 Revision*. Retrieved from https://population.un.org/wpp/.

WHO. (2019). The Global Health Observatory. Retrieved from https://www.who.int/data/gho/data/indicators/indicator-details/GHO/total-fertility-rate-(per-woman).

World Bank. (2018). *New Country Classifications by Income Level: 2018–2019*. Retrieved from https://blogs.worldbank.org/opendata/new-country-classifications-income-level-2018-2019

World Bank. (2019a). *World Development Indicators Database*. Washington, DC: World Bank. Retrieved from https://datacatalog.worldbank.org/dataset/world-development-indicators.

World Bank. (2019b). *Demographic Dividend Operational Tool for Pre-Dividend Countries*. Retrieved from http://documents.worldbank.org/curated/en/781891550815372274/pdf/Demographic-Dividend-Operational-Tool-for-Pre-Dividend-Countries.pdf.

World Bank. (2020). *World Development Indicators*. Washington, DC. Retrieved from https://datacatalog.worldbank.org/dataset/world-development-indicators

Wu, C. (1980). The Objective Criterion to Measure the Adaptation of Population Development and Economic Development: The Economic Basis for Advocating a Couple to Have Only One Child at the Current Stage in China. *Population Research, 1*, 32–38.

Wu, C. (1986). *Population Ageing Discussion*. Shenyang: Liaoning People's Publishing House. (in Chinese).

Yang, D. L. (1991). China Adjusts to the World Economy: The Political Economy of China's Coastal Development Strategy. *Pacific Affairs, 64*,(1) (Spring, 1991), 42–64.

Zhou, J. (2019). China's 2019 Gov't Work Report Echoes NPC Deputies' Concern. *China Global Television Network*. Retrieved from https://news.cgtn.com/news/3d3d674d3255544d33457a6333566d54/index.html.

Part VI

Addressing New Issues by Comparative Analysis

27

Inequality and Well-Being in Transition: Linking Experience and Perception to Policy Preferences

Alexandru Cojocaru

1 Introduction

The 1990s inaugurated, in countries of Eastern Europe and the Former Soviet Union (FSU), a period of deep structural transformation across many dimensions of life and society—economic, political, social, and institutional. One of the characteristics typically associated with this period is an increasing level of economic inequality. Branko Milanovic, a leading scholar of economic inequality, associates the first 2 decades of transition with a "dramatic shift in the role of Eastern European/Former Soviet Union (FSU) countries from an 'inequality reducing' world middle class to an 'inequality increasing' downwardly mobile group" (Milanovic 2005, 44). While this chapter will present a more nuanced picture of inequality dynamics since the fall of the Berlin Wall, the 1990s have indeed heralded increased hardship, downward mobility, and even poverty for many (World Bank 2018), as well as considerable riches for some.

The increasing levels of economic inequality over the past 2 or 3 decades have been observed across a number of industrialized nations, notably in the United States (Atkinson 2015). These dynamics have sparked a renewed debate about the degree and implications of economic inequality both between and within countries. Against this background, this chapter has two

A. Cojocaru (✉)
Poverty Equity Global Practice, The World Bank, Washington, DC, USA
e-mail: acojocaru@worldbank.org

© The Author(s) 2021
E. Douarin, O. Havrylyshyn (eds.), *The Palgrave Handbook of Comparative Economics*,
https://doi.org/10.1007/978-3-030-50888-3_27

main goals. First, it aims to review the dynamics of economic inequality in the region starting with, data allowing, the beginning of transition, and tracing it until today, distinguishing between actual inequality dynamics and inequality perceptions. Second, the chapter aims to provide a review of the literature that tries to answer the question whether inequality (and increases thereof) matters for the well-being of people in the region, and for their policy preferences and choices, namely for their preferences for redistribution, which are connected to their tolerance of economic inequality. The chapter will conclude by pointing to some existing knowledge gaps and fruitful avenues for future research in this area.

2   Economic Inequality in Transition Economies: Magnitude and Dynamics Over the Past 3 Decades

In this section we will review the evolution of economic inequality both across the transition economies and for the region overall vis-à-vis other regions of the world. Before proceeding with this discussion, however, it is important to define the terms that the chapter will be referencing, and to clarify some of the assumptions and measurement issues involved in quantifying economic inequality.

2.1   Measuring Economic Inequality: Concepts, Data, and Methods

While global inequality is today at the forefront of public discourse, it is not always clear what "global inequality" refers to. When economists discuss economic inequality, they typically refer either to the distribution of wealth (or the distribution of ownership of assets, as in the above example from Forbes), or to the distribution of income, as measured by current income received by individuals. In some cases, income inequality may refer interchangeably to inequality in incomes and inequality in consumption, as measured by household expenditures recorded in household surveys. The choice is typically driven by the types of data household surveys collect.[1] These differences mat-

---

[1] In the countries of the European Union, income inequality typically refers to the distribution of disposable income, as recorded, for instance, in statistical instruments such as the European Union Statistics on Income and Living Conditions (EU-SILC). In many of the FSU countries, economic inequality statistics

ter, as inequality in the space of wealth tends to be greater than inequality in the space of incomes, which, in turn, tends to be greater than inequality in the space of consumption.[2] In this chapter, when discussing the evolution of economic inequality in transition economies, we will be referring to inequality measured with data from household surveys, either in the space of incomes, or that of consumption, depending on data availability.

Another important consideration, when discussing inequality at the regional, or global, level, is whether we are considering inequalities between countries or between individuals. Milanovic (2005) provides a useful typology of economic inequality, composed of three distinct concepts of inequality. Concept 1 inequality refers to unweighted international inequality, where comparisons are made between countries, represented by their income or GDP per capita, without taking account of their population sizes. Concept 2 inequality refers to population-weighted international inequality, where comparisons are the same as in Concept 1, except that now we acknowledge the fact that changes in per capita income in Russia, for instance, may have a greater impact on the region than changes in Armenia. In other words, Concept 2 inequality accounts for differences in population sizes, but still ignores inequality within each country—every individual from a given country is assigned that country's per capita income. Finally, Concept 3 inequality refers to inequality among all citizens of a given region (or the world), ranking all these individuals, as captured in representative household surveys, and ignoring which country they come from, to arrive at a measure of regional (or global) inequality.

The discussion here refers to inequality in the space of outcomes (wealth, or incomes, or expenditures). In recent years, the literature has also emphasized inequality in the space of opportunities, and not just outcomes. For instance, a number of studies have relied on pioneering work by John Roemer (Roemer 2000) that aims to distinguish between inequalities due to circumstances individuals have no control over (es gender, ethnicity, the socio-economic status of parents) and inequality due to differences in effort. This literature points out that not all inequalities are equally objectionable, from a normative point of view, and inequalities due to circumstances may have greater claims to be remedied than inequalities due to differences in effort (World Bank 2005; Ferreira et al. 2008). We will return to this discussion later in the chapter.

---

are derived from Household Budget Surveys, which provide a detailed record of household expenditures, but do not always collect information on household incomes.

[2] For a more detailed discussion, see Milanovic (2005) and Atkinson (2015).

Finally, the degree of inequality can be measured through different statistics. We will rely here on the most common measure: the Gini index, which measures how much the distribution of income departs from a situation when everyone has exactly the same income, that is, the Gini index would take on a value of zero. In the opposite extreme case, when all the income belongs to one person, and everyone else has zero, the Gini index would take on a value of 1 (or, using commonly used normalization—100). Other commonly used measures include various ratios, such as the 90/10 ratio, or the ration of the income of the richest 10 percent of the population to the poorest 10 percent of the population, or other measures such as the Theil Index, or the Atkinson Index.[3]

2.2   Dynamics of Economic Inequality in Transition Economies

The collapse of the socialist block has been associated with a significant economic contraction in the early 1990s. Output declined by some 40 percent in the Baltics, by more than 45 percent in Russia and by almost 65 percent in Ukraine (Svejnar 2002). While in some countries, particularly in Central and Eastern Europe, the economic contraction only lasted a few years, the recovery has been slow. By 1999, only Poland and Slovenia had reached the same level of GDP they had in 1989.

This has also translated into a rapid deterioration of household welfare and an increase in poverty in the region. According to Povcalnet data from the World Bank, the share of population of the Europe and Central Asia (ECA) region with incomes below the international $1.9/day poverty line increased from 2.9 percent in 1990 to 7.9 percent in 1999, while the share of population below the Upper Middle Income threshold of $5.5/day increased from roughly a quarter of the population to over 45 percent; during the same period, the share of the middle class population (defined here as having incomes in excess of $15/day) fell from 26 percent to 16 percent (Fig. 27.1).

The increase in poverty in transition economies was associated with a considerable increase in the degree of income inequality. This is the case both at the country and at the individual level. Consider first the Concept 1 inequality across countries in the region, according to the above nomenclature. In order to compute this measure of inequality across countries, we can take data on per capita GDP for each country, expressed, for comparability purposes, in

---

[3] For an accessible summary of the most commonly used inequality metrics, see UN (2015): https://www.un.org/en/development/desa/policy/wess/wess_dev_issues/dsp_policy_02.pdf.

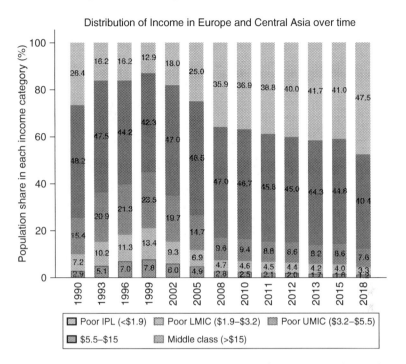

Fig. 27.1 Evolution of poverty in the ECA region. (Source: Povcalnet, The World Bank)

purchasing power parity (PPP) 2011 international dollars.[4] Only 18 transition economies in the World Development Indicators (WDI) database have GDP per capita estimates going all the way back to 1990, whereas for 2000 onward data is available for all 28 countries in the sample. For this reason, we present two series, the Gini index for the unbalanced sample for the 1990–2018 period, and a Gini index for a stable sample of 18 countries for which GDP estimates are available in every year (Fig. 27.2). It can be seen that the Concept 1 inequality Gini index increases from about 0.29 in 1990 to 0.40 in 1996, if we take the balanced sample, or 0.38 for the full sample in 1994 and then declines to about 0.29 by 2014, remaining roughly constant over the past 5 years.

At the regional level, the Gini index of inequality for the Europe and Central Asia (ECA) region (Concept 3 inequality in the above nomenclature) increased from about 25 in 1990 to 35 in 1995—a very large increase that resulted in ECA going from the region with the lowest level of inequality in

---

[4] Data from the World Bank's WDI database.

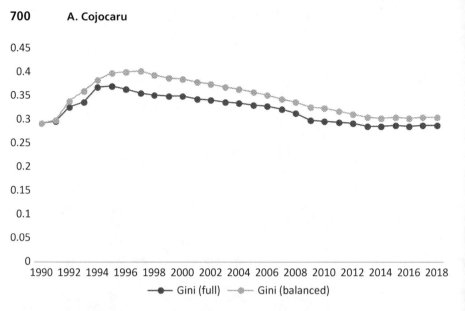

Fig. 27.2 Concept 1 inequality across transition economies. (Notes: Author's estimates based on data from the World Bank's WDI database. GDP per capita expressed in PPP 2011 international USD)

1990 to surpassing the level of inequality observed in industrialized nations, as well as in South Asia. It should be noted, that during the period 1990–1995 increasing inequality was a more general phenomenon, observed across all regions with the exception of Middle East and North Africa (MENA). Nevertheless, the magnitude of the increase in inequality in the ECA region stands out even against this secular trend.

As the transition economies stabilized around the mid-1990s, both poverty and inequality began to decline. Supported by strong economic growth throughout the 2000s, that was generally inclusive, as captured by the dynamics of indicators such as the shared prosperity premium, or the rate of income growth of the bottom 40 percent of the population in each country that is in excess of the average rate of income growth,[5] the overall level of inequality in transition economies declined by 2015 to a level that is again below the level of inequality observed in other regions in the world, or among industrialized economies (Fig. 27.3). The decline in the within-country inequality overtime was also associated with within-region convergence, as evidenced by the decline in Concept 1 inequality among transition economies (Fig. 27.2).

How does this picture of inequality dynamics look if we zoom in from the regional to the country level? Ferreira et al. (forthcoming) examine inequality

---

[5] See World Bank (2016).

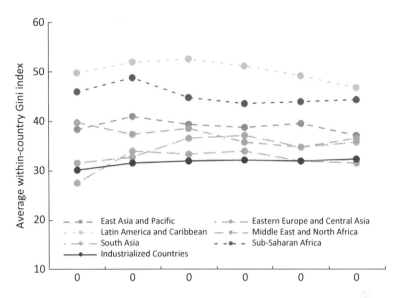

Fig. 27.3 Inequality across regions. (Source: Ferreira et al. forthcoming)

dynamics around the world during the 1990–2015 period. They find that for the Europe and Central Asia region, out of 5 countries for which comparable data is available for the 1990–2000 period, in 3 inequality went up, in 1 inequality went down, and in another county it remained stable. In the subsequent period (2000–2015) inequality increased in 3 out of 16 countries in the ECA region, and fell in 9 out of 16, remaining stable in 4 countries.

These trends of growing inequality within countries during the 1990–2000 period among transition economies appear to mirror inequality trends at the global level, with inequality increasing in more than half of the countries in the global sample in the first period, and falling in three-quarters of the global sample during the second period (2000–2015). Note that this is in stark contrast with inequality dynamics among industrialized nations, in which inequality at the national level appears to have risen throughout the entire 1990–2015 period (Table 27.1). If one takes a longer view, in the ECA region during 1990–2015 out of 9 countries inequality went up in 7 and fell in 2, whereas overall in the world, the Gini index increased in 32 countries by more than 1 point and fell in 23 countries.

If we abstract from the initial post-transition economic collapse of the early 1990s, and take the 20-year period of 1995–2015, inequality fell in 7 out of the 15 transition economies in the comparable sample, and rose in 4 as well as in Turkey, having remained within +/- 1 point in further 3 countries (Fig. 27.4). Among the FSU states, including in Ukraine, Moldova,

Table 27.1 Dynamics of country-level inequality around the world, 1990–2015

	1990–2000						2000–2015					
	Number of countries with:				Mean Gini		Number of countries with:				Mean Gini	
	↑	+/−1pp	↓	Total	1990	2000	↑	+/−1pp	↓	Total	2000	2015
E. Asia & Pacific	2	0	4	6	37.1	37.1	1	3	6	10	37.5	36.4
E. Europe & C. Asia	3	1	1	5	30.1	31.0	3	4	9	16	33.1	30.7
L. America & Caribbean	8	1	7	16	50.4	52.6	0	1	16	17	53.4	46.7
M. East & N. Africa	1	3	1	5	39.7	39.1	2	1	3	6	38.9	37.0
S. Asia	2	0	1	3	31.1	34.9	1	0	2	3	34.9	35.2
Sub-Saharan Africa	4	0	4	8	44.0	41.3	6	2	6	14	45.5	44.8
Industr. Countries	12	4	2	18	30.2	31.9	9	9	3	21	31.9	32.4
World	32	9	20	61	38.8	39.7	22	20	45	87	39.7	37.8

Source: Ferreira et al. (forthcoming)

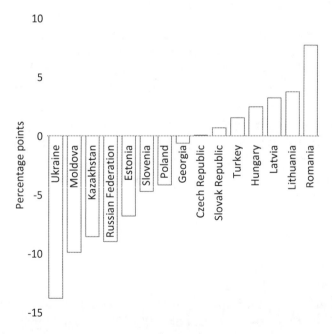

Fig. 27.4 Change in the Gini coefficient in transition economies, 1995–2015 (percentage points). (Source: Ferreira et al. forthcoming. Note: Inequality measures based on consumption data in Georgia, Kazakhstan, Moldova, Russian Federation, Turkey, and Ukraine, and on income data in all other countries)

Kazakhstan, and Russian Federation inequality fell after an initial increase during 1990–1995, and falling levels of inequality were also observed in Slovenia, Estonia, and Poland. At the same time, in a number of new EU member states such as Hungary, Latvia, Lithuania, and Romania, inequality rose during the same period. At the global level, inequality fell or remained stable in two-thirds of the countries and rose in one-third of the countries.

What can we conclude from these broad trends in inequality since 1990s? While the necessary data for a full comparison between inequality at the beginning of transition and today is clearly incomplete, available data show that the degree of inequality in transition economies (in the Europe and Central Asia region, as defined by the World Bank), has increased both in the sense of Concept 1 inequality and Concept 3 inequality (from a regional Gini of 27.5 in 1990 to 31.5 in 2015), and within-country inequality also increased in most countries. However, this is largely because of the considerable increase in inequality in the immediate aftermath of the collapse of the Soviet Union. Between 1995 and 2015, inequality in transition economies as a region (both across countries and across individuals) has been on the decline, and this is also the case for country-level inequality dynamics—in two-thirds of the available ECA countries the Gini index fell over this period. This decline is not unique to transition economies, and mirrors inequality trends over the same period across most regions and developing countries. Industrialized nations are an exception in this regard, having registered a rising level of inequality, both as a group, and among most individual countries.

This brings us to the current situation in the region, depicted in Fig. 27.5 using the most recently available data from World Development Indicators (WDI). While the overall level of inequality in Transition Economies may be low compared to other regions in the world, there is also quite a bit of heterogeneity across Transition Economies, with the Gini index ranging from 25 in Slovenia to almost 40 in Serbia. It is difficult to discern from looking at Fig. 27.5 any clear regional patterns; while a number of New EU member states have relatively lower Gini indices, this is not the case in Romania, Bulgaria, or the Baltic states, all of which are in the top 10 countries with the highest Gini indices. Likewise, in the Balkans, Serbia and North Macedonia have high levels of inequality, whereas in Kosovo it is relatively low; and within the Commonwealth of Independent States, the Gini indices range from very low in Belarus to very high in Russia.

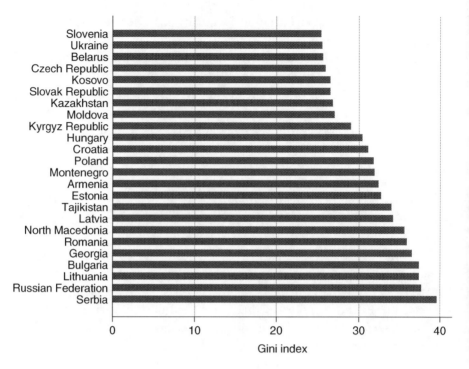

Fig. 27.5 Gini index of inequality across countries, circa 2015. (Source: Author's estimates based on WDI data)

2.3   Perceptions of Inequality Changes

The picture of falling inequality over the 1995–2015 period stands in contrast to the growing degree of concern, in the media, but also in academic and policy discourse, with the level of inequality in general, and with its consequences for individual and societal well-being. Given that much of the research on inequality and top incomes originates primarily in the United States, one could be led to conclude that concerns with respect to inequality, are primarily a problem of (or at least heavily weighted toward) industrialized nations, where inequality has indeed been on the rise over the past 25 years. Do the citizens of transition economies share the perceptions of increasing inequality in the region? Are they concerned about the degree of inequality in the region or in their countries? We turn to these questions now.

We thus investigate perceptions of inequality over time. One data source that does allow for such long comparisons is the International Social Survey Program (ISSP), which had questions trying to elicit the respondents' perceptions of inequality in their countries in the 1992, 1999, and 2009 survey rounds. Specifically, they were shown diagrams representing five different types of societies, with increasing levels of inequality, that roughly represent a span of the Gini index from 0.20 to 0.42 (Gimpelson and Treisman 2018). The respondents were asked to pick the diagram that best describes their country.

Bussolo et al. (2019) examine inequality perceptions over time in the ISSP sample, by constructing a "net equality perception" measure, which equals to the difference in the share of the population choosing the most equal society and the share of population choosing the most unequal society, such that positive values indicate a higher share of population reporting that they live in a very equal country vis-à-vis the share of population who think that they live in a very unequal country. They find that in transition economies there is a wide belief that societies are unequal, which persists throughout the entire period 1992–2009. For instance, in Bulgaria, where perceptions of inequality are highest, net inequality perception is minus 49 percentage points in 1992, becoming even more negative at minus 67 percentage points in 1999, before falling to minus 60 percentage points in 2009. In other countries in the ISSP sample (Czech Republic, Hungary, Poland, Russia, Slovak Republic, and Slovenia), the net equality perception is still negative, even if somewhat smaller in magnitude. Overtime, perceptions of inequality in transition economies appear to worsen between 1992 and 1999, subsequently improving between 1999 and 2009. In Western European countries, in the other hand, the net equality perception either hover around zero in countries like France, Germany and Spain), or tends to be positive (i.e. more people think they live in an equal society) in countries like Austria, Cyprus, Norway, and Sweden. For instance, in Sweden it increases from 24 to 31 between 1999 and 2009. Dynamically, inequality perceptions in Western European countries appear to worsen between 1999 and 2009, in contrast to the dynamics in Eastern Europe.

Another data source that allows us to look at inequality perceptions for a larger set of transition economies is the Life in Transition survey (LiTS), which has three waves of data collected in 2006, 2010, and 2016. In the LiTS, the respondents are asked whether they agree with the statement "the gap between the rich and the poor in this country should be reduced." This is somewhat different from the examination of inequality perceptions in the ISSP, because the question compounds the positive assessment of the perceived degree of inequality in a country with a normative assessment with respect to the need for reducing the perceived level of inequality. Figure 27.6 plots, for each country and wave of the LiTS, the share of adults who either agree or strongly agree with the statement that the gap between the rich and the poor should be reduced, for the 2006 and 2010 survey rounds, and

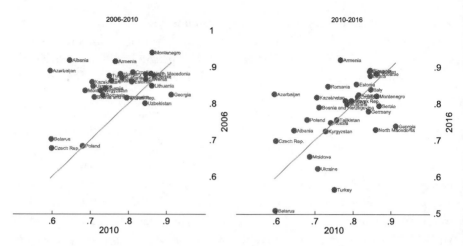

Fig. 27.6 Attitudes toward inequality across countries, 2006, 2010, and 2016. (Notes: The graphs show the share of adults in each country and each survey round who either agree or strongly agree with the statement "The gap between the rich and the poor should be reduced." The line in each panel is the 45-degree line. Source: Author's estimates based on LiTS data)

separately for the 2010 and 2016 rounds. Several conclusions can be drawn from this graph. First, in 2010, the share of adults who deem the gap between the rich and the poor in their country to be too large is substantial, according to the most recent data comprising of at least half of the population in all countries in the sample, and in 23 out of the 32 countries in the sample, more than three-quarters of adults would like to see a smaller gap between rich and poor. Second, the perception of inequality, as captured by this survey question, was even higher, on average, in 2006, having subsequently fallen in the 2010 survey round (left panel), and then having increased again slightly in 2016 (right panel). Third, the fall in the share or respondents who think that the gap between the rich and the poor should be reduced between 2006 and 2016 rounds of the survey is consistent with the observed decrease in the degree of economic inequality in the region. It is surprising, to some degree, to observe a lower preference for redistribution in 2010 in the aftermath of the financial crisis, although it is plausible that the effect of the financial crisis would have taken some time to translate into updated beliefs about inequality, and certainly the greater preference of redistribution in the latest 2016 round of the LiTS would be consistent with the very difficult and drawn out recovery and subdued growth in the aftermath of the crisis.

Inequality perceptions can also be compared to actual inequality statistics. Figure 27.7 plots the share of adults who either agree or strongly agree with the statement that the gap between the rich and the poor should be reduced

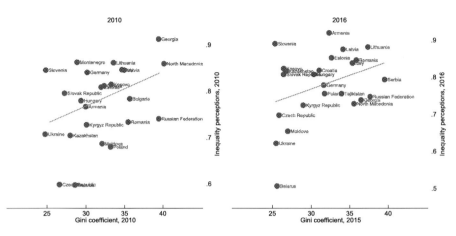

Fig. 27.7 Inequality perceptions and actual levels of inequality in transition economies in 2010 and 2016. (Notes: Inequality perceptions from the LiTS 2010 and 2016 survey rounds. Gini coefficients from the WDI database. Inequality perceptions based on the share of adults in each country and each survey round who either agree or strongly agree with the statement "The gap between the rich and the poor should be reduced.")

against the Gini index of inequality, separately for the 2010 round of the LiTS against inequality in 2010 (left panel) and from the latest round of the LiTS against the latest available inequality statistics from 2015 (right panel). Inequality perceptions and realized inequality are positively correlated, both in 2010 and in 2016, but this correlation is not very strong. A given level of income inequality, as measured by the Gini coefficient, can be associated with very different average perceptions of inequality across countries, and likewise, similar perceptions of inequality can be observed in countries with rather different values of Gini indices. Bussolo et al. (2019) similarly confirm that there exists a weak correlation between perceptions of inequality based on the ISSP Social Inequality dataset and actual Gini indices of inequality for the same country; they also find a weak correlation between inequality and preferences for redistribution based on the agreements or disagreements with the statement "it is the responsibility of the government to reduce income differences between people with high incomes and those with low incomes." At the same time, they find a strong correlation in the data between perceived levels of inequality and demands for redistribution.

Thus, for the region overall, there appears to be a discrepancy between widespread perceptions of inequality being very high, and empirical evidence suggesting that (i) the level of inequality in transition economies is not very high, on average, when compared to other regions of the world, and (ii) the level of inequality has been declining over the past 20 years after the initial increase during 1990–1995. However, these discrepancies between actual inequality and perceptions thereof are not specific to transition economies only. Gimpelson and Treisman (2018) find, across a number of datasets and countries that respondents predict poorly (slightly better than by chance) both the levels of inequality in their countries, as well as the trends in inequality, or other distributional statistics such as the top one percent's share of wealth, average salaries nationwide or for specific jobs, or the country's current poverty rate. When presented with diagrams representing different societies that differ by their degree of inequality, only 29 percent worldwide choose the diagram that most closely resembles the post-tax-and-transfers Gini of their countries. In a number of European countries (Estonia, Slovakia, Croatia, Hungary, and Ukraine) over 90 percent of respondents chose the wrong diagram as representative of their country (ibid.).

What may cause such misalignment between actual inequality and perceived inequality? Many factors could be at play. People may simply not know, and Gimpelson and Treisman (2018) present compelling evidence in favor of partial knowledge of inequality levels and dynamics. Other studies have similarly found perceptions of social mobility to differ from actual experience of social mobility (Alesina et al. 2018; Narayan et al. 2018). Alesina et al. (2018) find evidence that in the United States (in Europe) perceptions overestimate (underestimate) mobility vis-à-vis mobility measures that can be observed empirically from the data.

With actual inequality levels not readily observable, individuals can rely on a number of other macro and micro variables to infer the extent of inequality in their countries. Bussolo et al. (2018) find that macroeconomic variables such as the Gini coefficient, the unemployment rate, the poverty rate, and government expenditures on education together explain a quarter of the total variation in individual perceptions of inequality. In addition to these macro variables, individual circumstances such as employment status, also influence inequality perceptions. For instance, perceptions of inequality correlate with the level of education expenditures among the employed, but not among those who are unemployed; higher poverty rates correlate with inequality perceptions among the 24–34 years age group, but not among those who are 45 years of age or older; objective measures of inequality correlate with perceptions of inequality among those who experienced perceived downward mobility with respect to their fathers, but not among those who think that their job status is the same or better than that of their fathers (Bussolo et al. 2018).

Beyond partial knowledge, and especially when respondents are asked whether the degree of inequality is too high or needs to be reduced, their perceptions are also informed by some reference points that frame these comparative statements. In the case of Transition Economies, inequality increased following the collapse of the Soviet Union, and the perceived greater degree of equality pre-1989 may still loom large in respondent's minds. Indeed, studies have found that some 20 years after the beginning of transition, the pre-transition level of well-being is still an important determinant of subjective well-being today (Senik 2009; Cojocaru 2014a). It may also be the case that individuals make inferences on national-level inequality, which is hard to observe (Senik 2004), from local-level inequality. Frank and Levine (2007) argue that "the within-reference group level of inequality for an individual is likely to correspond more closely to the degree of inequality in the city in which [the person] lives than to the degree of inequality in his home country" (Frank and Levine 2007, 13). Cojocaru (2016) finds, based on data from several transition economies, that relative status perceptions are more salient for well-being at the local (city) level, when compared to regional, or national levels.

Another important consideration is with respect to the evaluative space in inequality perceptions. While inequality statistics presented in this chapter, or inequality perceptions that are usually queried in surveys, refer to (usually implicitly, rather than explicitly) inequality measured in the space of disposable incomes, this need not be the phenomenon that respondents have in mind when they answer. Individuals could be basing their perceptions, on, for instance, market income inequalities in the space of earnings, not accounting (partially or fully) for the redistributive effects of various taxes and transfers. To get an insight into this we can draw on a number of recently completed studies in the region that follow the so-called Commitment to Equity methodology (Lustig and Higgins 2013), which allows us to measure the degree of inequality across a number of income concepts, including: (i) *market income*, or household income before any tax-benefit interventions; (ii) *market income plus pensions*, which includes contributory pensions and exclude pension contributions; (iii) *disposable income*, which starts with market income plus pensions and then subtracts direct taxes and social insurance contribution and adds direct cash transfers; (iv) *consumable income*, or disposable income minus indirect taxes plus indirect subsidies; and finally (v) final income, which adds to the consumable income in-kind transfers such as public education and healthcare expenditures. The fiscal system does appear to have a significant redistributive effect in Transition Economies for which estimates are available. Contributory pensions alone reduce the Gini index by 10 percentage points

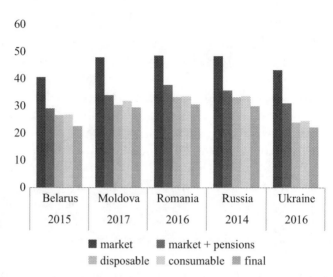

Fig. 27.8 Gini indices across income concepts. (Source: Cojocaru et al. 2019)

or more vis-à-vis the inequality in the space of market incomes (Fig. 27.8). Accounting for indirect taxes and transfers, and the imputed value of services such as publicly provided health and education reduces inequality even further (Cojocaru et al. 2019).

Yet, however large the differences between pre-fiscal and post-fiscal inequality may be, it's not clear how much these differences drive the discrepancy between actual and perceived inequality. In particular, Gimpelson and Treisman (2018) test whether respondents are good at estimating both pre-tax inequality and post-tax inequality in their countries, and find that their perceptions align well with neither of the two.

Another possibility is that they may not be thinking of inequality in the space of outcomes such as income (whether disposable or otherwise) at all; rather, they could be thinking of inequality of opportunity in some broad sense. Bussolo et al. (2018) show that while inequality in transition economies has been relatively stable in recent years, there is, at the same time, evidence of increasing concentration of wealth, increasing labor market polarization characterized by a hollowing out of the jobs in the middle of the distribution, with intensive and routine tasks, and an increasing generational divide, with young cohorts losing ground. In particular, they find that younger age cohorts are facing higher income inequality at every point of the life cycle relative to older generations. Narayan et al. (2018) similarly find intergenerational mobility in Europe and Central Asia to be worsening for the age cohorts growing up following the collapse of the Soviet Union. In other words, irrespective of the dynamics of income inequality as measured by national Gini indices or other statistics describing the distribution of incomes, perceptions of inequality may be driven more by these considerations of increasingly uneven opportunities for success in the region.

3   Inequality and Welfare

How relevant are these changes in inequality in the region, both actual and perceived, for individual well-being? Inequality measures such as the Gini coefficient, are merely statistical representations of the (usually, disposable) income distribution within a given population. Are high values of these inequality statistics intrinsically nefarious when it comes to individual welfare? Differences in outcomes (such as incomes) may be driven by many factors, and, when they are related to factors such as differences in effort across individuals, it is not clear whether such differences should be viewed as being detrimental to individual, or social, welfare. Indeed, the philosophical literature on inequality, has argued that inequalities that matter for justice should be inequalities in the space of resources (Rawls 1971; Dworkin 1981), opportunity for welfare (Arneson 1989), access to advantage (Cohen 1989), opportunities for a good life (Arneson 2000), capabilities (Sen 1980), or opportunities (Roemer 2000). These normatively-informed concepts of inequality are often-times difficult to measure, however, or disentangle from overall inequalities in outcomes. With these caveats in mind, the discussion of the links between inequality and well-being can be structured in terms of linkages at the macro level, and at the individual level. We turn our attention first to macro linkages.

3.1   Macro Linkages Between Inequality and Welfare

At the macro level, to look at the effect of inequality on economic outcomes and objective well-being, one needs to look first and foremost to the literature on economic inequality and growth, as economic growth is widely recognized as the key engine behind poverty reduction and improvements in living standards. Existing empirical evidence suggests that, on balance, higher inequality has a retardant effect on economic growth, although there a lot of heterogeneity in the literature, with both negative and positive associations between inequality and growth, depending on definitions, countries included in the sample and methods used (Boushey and Price 2014). De Dominicis et al. (2006), in an early meta-synthesis of the literature on inequality and growth find that among the various empirical estimates in the 22 studies they review, the correlation between inequality and growth was negative in roughly 40 percent of the values, close to zero in another 40 percent, and positive in about 20 percent of the estimates. The relationship between inequality and growth tends to be more negative in low income countries. Similarly, inequality at the bottom of the income distribution tend to be more pernicious for growth (Voitchovsky 2005). There is also some evidence that inequality in wealth is negatively associated with growth (Deininger and Squire 1997; Birdsall and Londono 1998). A number of studies also find higher levels of inequality to be associated with shorter duration of growth (Berg and Ostry 2011; Ostry et al. 2014), although there are methodological questions with respect to these findings (Kraay 2015).

It was noted earlier that some of the discrepancy between observed inequality and perceived inequality may be due to the latter being driven by dynamics of inequality of opportunity, more so than of inequality of outcomes. Some of the most recent literature on the links between inequality and growth also confirms this. Marrero and Rodriguez (2010), using state-level data from the United States, find that while there is no statistical relationship between growth and inequality of outcomes, there is a negative relationship between inequality of opportunity[6] and growth, and a positive relationship between inequality resulting from differences in effort and growth. Aiyar and Ebeke (2019) similarly find, in a cross-country setting, that the relationship between inequality and growth is more negative when intergenerational social mobility is lower, a situation that tends to be indicative of greater inequality of opportunity (Narayan et al. 2018).

In addition to having a retarding effect on growth, inequality has also been found to mediate the relationship between growth and poverty reduction. The ability of economic growth to reduce poverty, or the growth poverty elasticity, has been found to be higher when inequality is lower (Hanmer and Naschold 2000; Ravallion 2001). A recent World Bank study notes that the goal of eliminating extreme poverty by 2030 will not be reached with distributionally neutral growth, especially in a period of overall slowdown in economic growth. Reducing within-country inequality, especially in countries with large concentrations of the poor, is estimated to be essential in eliminating global poverty (World Bank 2016).

---

[6] Here inequality of opportunity is defined, following Van de Gaer (1993) and Van de Gaer et al. (2001), by a set of circumstances that an individual has no control over (here race and father's education), such that inequalities across groups defined by different circumstances is taken to indicate inequality of opportunity, and inequalities across individuals within a given circumstance type is indicative of inequality with respect to effort.

Inequality has also been found to be strongly correlated with socio-economic mobility, as shown in the now famous *Great Gatsby curve*, which shows a strong empirical association between higher levels of inequality and greater intergenerational immobility across high income countries (Corak 2017), but also across a much larger set of developing countries (Narayan et al. 2018). This means that high levels of inequality can lead to inequality traps: with children born to parents at the bottom of the income distribution being much more likely to remain at the bottom of the income distribution themselves as adults. While by international comparisons, the association between parent and children's outcomes (intergenerational persistence) in transition economies is relatively low, it is worrisome that for the latest two cohorts in the data (children born between 1970 and 1990), and thus the generations that grew up and reached adulthood in the aftermath of the collapse of the Soviet Union, the degree of persistence has increased and is currently almost on par with levels of mobility recorded in lower middle income countries, and much below the levels of intergenerational mobility in high income countries (Fig. 27.9). In other words, the transition period has been associated with a deterioration of social mobility in transition economies, when in other parts of the world the recent trends have been in the opposite

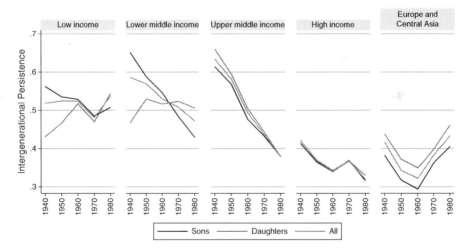

Fig. 27.9 Intergenerational mobility across 1940–1980 birth cohorts. (Source: Narayan et al. (2018) and author's estimates based on the Global Database of Intergenerational Mobility (GDIM) database. Notes: Intergenerational persistence measures the degree of association between the education of parents and children, using the coefficient from regressions of children's years of education on the education of their parents. Higher values of this regression coefficient indicate greater persistence across education, and hence lower relative mobility)

direction—that of generally improving mobility over time, with the exception of the 1970s cohort.

Fiscal policies play an important role in reducing inequality and promoting social mobility. For instance, transfers can aid low income families in ways that improves long-run outcomes of children. Likewise, taxation can influence the amount of resources that can be passed from one generation to the next (Narayan et al. 2018). The discussion in the previous section highlighted the fact that fiscal systems in Transition Economies can have an important redistributive effect—the degree of post-fiscal inequality can be much lower than pre-fiscal inequality. They also help reduce poverty—in countries like Belarus, Moldova, Russia, and Ukraine, the fiscal incidence analysis has shown the poverty rates based on the comparison of a given poverty line with a welfare aggregate based on disposable income to be considerably lower than if market income is used as a welfare aggregate (Cojocaru et al. 2019).

It is also widely understood that the mediating pathway from inequality of outcomes to socio-economic mobility is that of inequality of opportunity. Narayan et al. (2018) confirm empirically the importance of parental characteristics (other than education) for explaining income persistence across generations. (Brunori et al. 2013) argue that the reasons why higher inequality makes intergenerational mobility harder are likely related to the fact that "opportunities for economic advancement are more unequally distributed among children." Data from the latest round of the Life in Transition Survey (LiTS III) indeed show a positive association between overall income inequality in transition economies, and the extent of inequality of opportunity in these countries (EBRD 2016). Moreover, the data reveal that the extent of inequality of opportunity in transition economies is higher, on average, than in Western European countries like Germany or Italy; the extent of inequality of opportunity is also generally higher in countries of the Former Soviet Union, than in the new EU Member states or countries in the Western Balkans, although this is not universally so, with relatively high levels of inequality of opportunity in EU countries such as Bulgaria, Estonia, Latvia, and Romania. Roughly one-third of the overall income inequality is found to be attributable to inequality of opportunity, defined, following Roemer (2000), in terms of circumstance types based on characteristics such as urban/rural birthplace, parental education, gender, ethnic minority/majority status and parents' membership in the communist party. Among these circumstances, differences in parental background are the most prominent—this factor account for more than half of the overall inequality of opportunity in a third of the transition economies; gender is the second most important factor, accounting for between a quarter and half of overall inequality of opportunity in most countries (EBRD 2016).

These results should not lead one to conclude that inequality in transition economies is, for the most part, fair, on account of only one-third of it being attributed to unequal opportunities. The authors note that these estimates represent a lower bound because (i) the list of circumstances considered is not exhaustive, and if other circumstances were available in the data, the share of inequality of opportunity in overall inequality would likely be larger (in any case, no smaller), and (ii) estimates based on income underestimate true differences in opportunities because they exclude people who are out of the labor force (EBRD 2016). Indeed, the same data suggests that three-quarters of adults deem connections to be at least moderately important (more than half think them very important or essential) to get a good job in the government sector. More than two-thirds think connections are at least moderately important to get a good job in the private sector, and these perceptions of inequality of opportunity are associated with expectations of future socio-economic mobility (Cojocaru 2019).

3.2   Micro Linkages Between Inequality and Welfare

A number of experimental studies show that individuals have a preference for equity, in the sense of preferring equitable outcomes, engaging in cooperation and having strong other-regarding preferences (Thaler 1988; Camerer and Thaler 1995; Fehr and Gachter 2000; Fehr et al. 1997; Fehr and Schmidt 2006 and references therein). This aversion to inequality would imply that inequality would have a direct negative effect on individual's utility. This is what Clark and D'Ambrosio (2015) call the *normative view*, whereby individuals make judgments on inequality within a given reference group irrespective of their relative position in the reference group. Following this normative view, a growing literature takes subjective well-being, which is increasingly commonly reported in individual and household surveys, as a proxy for individual's utility to answer the question whether inequality has an impact—either positive or negative—on individual well-being. The benefit of this approach, when trying to examine the welfare effects of inequality, derives from the fact that it is difficult to answer this question by way of reliance on revealed choice analysis, as data on choices between environments with varying degrees of inequality are seldom available. On the other hand, it is relatively easy to ask the respondent directly about their attitudes about inequality, and about their individual well-being, and then use statistical techniques to probe the association between the two.

Several studies have investigated empirically the link between inequality and life satisfaction in transition economies. In one of the earliest papers, Sanfey and Teksoz (2007), relying on data from the World Values Survey from the first four survey rounds (covering the period 1981–2002) investigate the link between life satisfaction and inequality, conditional on other correlates of life satisfaction, separately for transition and non-transition countries, and find inequality (measured by the Gini index) to have a negative association with life satisfaction in transition economies, and a positive association in non-transition economies. The authors suggest that the negative correlation between inequality and well-being in Transition Economies is on account of the lingering dislike of inequality that was characteristic of the socialist systems.

Guriev and Zhuravskaya (2009), also based on data from the World Values Survey (waves 3 and 4), investigate the determinants of the "unhappiness gap", or the lower level of happiness reported by respondents from Transition economies relative to respondents from non-transition economies. They find that accounting for income inequality measured by the country's Gini coefficient reduces the gap between life satisfaction in transition and non-transition economies; in other words, inequality is one of the contributors, alongside income volatility, deterioration of public goods, and the depreciation of human capital, to lower levels of life satisfaction in transition economies, consistent with the findings of Sanfey and Teksoz (2007). In a subsequent study, Guriev and Melnikov (2018) find that this happiness gap, still present in the data in 2010, disappears by 2016, consistent with the predictions in Guriev and Zhuravskaya (2009), a result confirmed both by the Life in Transition Survey data and the Gallup World Poll data (see also Nikolova 2016). The follow-up study does not investigate the contribution of inequality to the closing of the happiness gap, but it should be noted that this gap closes during a period when inequality in transition economies is falling, in contrast to the inequality dynamics in industrialized countries, and some other regions of the world, although certainly this need not be the only, or even the main, difference between transition economies and other countries over the 2010–2016 time period.

Yet, not all studies find the relationship between inequality and individual well-being to be universally negative. Berg and Veenhoven (2010), in one of the largest cross-country studies of the relationship between inequality and life satisfaction across 119 nations find no statistically significant relationship between inequality and subjective well-being. A well-known study by Alesina et al. (2004) similarly find no relationship between inequality and reported well-being in the United States (across states), although they find a negative relationship in a sample of 12 European countries over the period 1975–1992, although Berg and Veenhoven (2010) claim that this negative relationship may be an artifact of the sample in Alesina et al. (2004). Clark and D'Ambrosio (2015) provide a comprehensive review of the literature on inequality and well-being, and find that among the 29 studies (either cross-country or single-country) that estimate the relationship between well-being and the Gini index of inequality (or some other statistical measure of inequality), 8 studies find no statistically significant association between inequality and well-being, 14 studies find a negative correlation, and 7 find a positive relationship.

Clark and D'Ambrosio (2015) conjecture that such a heterogeneity of estimates with respect to the relationship between inequality and well-being is due, in part, to methodological issues. In particular, not all studies that they examine in their review adequately control for relative income when estimating a conditional relationship between inequality and well-being, which compounds what they call the comparative view, or the perceived importance of one's own position in the income distribution relative to others, and the normative view, which reflects one's attitude toward inequality irrespective of one's position in the income distribution relative to others. Other methodological caveats include the fact that correlations between well-being inequality indices assume that (i) the degree of inequality as captured by the Gini index, for instance, is observable to the respondent; and (ii) the inequality measure used in the regressions is estimated over a relevant comparison group (which is unobserved). If either of these (largely untestable) assumptions are violated, it is not clear why one would expect to observe either a positive or a negative correlation between inequality and well-being, and even when one is observed in the data, how it may be interpreted. In this regard, it is not clear that national-level inequality is either observable to individuals, or is the relevant reference point. For instance, Kuhn et al. (2011) find shocks to relative status based on winning a lottery to be salient within very local postcode areas in the Netherlands (comprising roughly 20 households), and even then, restricted in large part to a household's nearest neighbors. Furthermore, since inequality indices such as the Gini index are constant within the groups for which they are estimated, a relationship between individual well-being and group inequality is, empirically, a relationship between mean satisfaction in a group, and that group's inequality. If an individual's utility function is concave in income, then there will be a negative relationship between mean well-being in a group and the group's inequality, even if inequality has no effect on well-being at the level of the individual (Atkinson 1970).

Several studies probe these implicit assumptions. Senik (2004), using data from the Russian Longitudinal Monitoring Survey (RLMS) for the period 1994–2000, find no relationship between national-level inequality and life satisfaction. To address the issues of observability, the authors also compute inequality indices at the regional level, and the Primary Sampling Unit (PSU), although these too are not significantly correlated with individual well-being. Cojocaru (2014a), using data from the 2006 round of the Life in Transition survey for all transition economies with the exception of Turkmenistan, finds that while there is no significant relationship between PSU-level inequality and individual well-being, this is a methodological artifact of trying to make inference on individual behavior from group outcomes. When an alternative specification, based on the Fehr and Schmidt (1999) specification of inequality-averse preferences is estimated, a significant and negative relationship between individual well-being and the Yitzhaki index of relative deprivation (Yitzhaki 1979) is found, conditional on own income and reference group income, which is indicative of aversion to inequality both in the New EU Member States, and in the non-EU countries in the LiTS sample.

Another strand of literature, described by Clark and D'Ambrosio (2015) as the *comparative view*, considers that individuals rely on their position in some reference group relative to others for purposes of self-appraisal. There is now a large literature (comprehensively reviewed by Clark and D'Ambrosio 2015) that shows that relative comparisons matter for self-evaluation. We do not review this literature here in part because relative status may be important to individuals in ways that need not relate directly to economic inequality in the sense described in this chapter; the implications of relative status considerations for individual well-being are a related but separate issue analytically. There are, however, two key areas of overlap where relative status concerns and inequality aversion are directly related. First, a number of studies investigate the importance of relative status concerns by relying on Yitzhaki's relative deprivation index (Yitzhaki 1979; Deaton 2001; Eibner and Evans 2005; D'Ambrosio and Frick 2007) and find a negative relationship between relative deprivation defined this way and individual well-being or health outcomes; Cojocaru (2014a) confirms this negative relationship in the case of Transition Economies as well. Hey and Lambert (1980) establish formally that if there are two distributions where one Lorenz dominates the other, such that the latter is more unequal, there will be more relative deprivation in the Yitzhaki sense at every level of income in the more unequal distribution. In other words, a negative well-being effect of relative deprivation can, although does not have to, be indicative of aversion to inequality and thus a negative relationship between the degree of inequality and individual well-being.

Second, relative status can serve as a mediator for the relationship between inequality and well-being. Delhey and Dragolov (2014), based on data from the European Quality of Life Survey, examine three mediating factors—generalized trust, status anxiety, and conflict—as mediating channels between inequality and well-being. They find that among Western European countries the main reasons why individuals dislike inequality is generalized distrust; neither status anxiety nor perceived conflicts among rich and poor or management and workers appear to mediate the effect of inequality on well-being. In transition economies, on the other hand, the key mediating pathway is status anxiety, with sufficient mediating power to reduce the contextual effect of inequality on well-being to statistical insignificance. Schneider (2019) similarly finds evidence of social status mediating the relationship between inequality and life satisfaction in a sample of mostly Western European countries—individuals in more equal societies report, on average, higher social status, and subjective social status fully explains the link between inequality and life satisfaction. Furthermore, Schneider (2019) also finds that inequality affects the strength of the link between status perceptions and well-being—in countries with higher levels of inequality social status is more important for life satisfaction.

The previous section has highlighted the important distinction between inequality of outcomes and inequality of opportunity, and that disparities driven by circumstance, effort and luck may warrant different normative judgments. The nature of the process that generates the distribution of income in a society will affect the link between inequality and well-being, in both the comparative and the normative views described above. For instance, Grosfeld and Senik (2010) find inequality to be positively associated with subjective evaluations of the economic situation in Poland in the early years of transition (1992–1996), the relationship between inequality and well-being turning negative in the second half of the transition period (1997–2005). They suggest that the evidence is consistent with the *Hirschman tunnel* effect (Hirschman and Rothschild 1973), whereby at the beginning of transition greater differentiation of incomes was perceived as a positive signal of greater opportunities, whereas over time, growing inequality amid unfulfilled reform expectations has led to disappointment and skepticism with respect to the legitimacy of the enrichment of reform winners, and economic inequality began to be perceived as being unfair. Senik (2009) uncovers systematic differences between "Old" Europe and "New" Europe, with inequality aversion being less prominent in transition economies (and in the United States) vis-à-vis Western European countries, which they interpret as being consistent with the evidence that reference group income is positively correlated with well-being in Transition Economies (in line with the Hirschman tunnel effect) and negatively correlated in western Europe. Like Grosfeld and Senik (2010), they interpret inequality in the 1990s in transition economies as a signal of opportunity, whereas in Western Europe inequality aversion is likely driven by perceptions of fairness.

Cojocaru (2014a) finds that inequality aversion in transition economies is not intrinsic, but rather driven by perceptions of fairness. In particular, inequality averse preferences are observed among those who think that need in society is due to injustice, but not among those who think that it is due to laziness. Similarly, those who think that effort and skills were key to success prior to 1989 whereas now success is driven by connections (and therefore would deem inequality to be unfair) are found to be averse to inequality, but not those who think that connections were key prior to 1989 but effort and skills are key to success now (and therefore would deem inequality to be fair) do not exhibit inequality averse preferences.

3.3   Inequality and Policy Preferences

If respondents hold inequality-averse preferences, or if status considerations play a role in determining one's well-being is a way that is being amplified by economic inequality, then we would expect inequality to be associated with demands to reduce income disparities, by way of redistributive policies or otherwise. Alesina and Angeletos (2005) show that in theory, when individuals are averse to unfair social outcomes, in societies with a greater degree of unfairness generating the income distribution, aggressive redistribution will be desirable, because anticipation of high taxes makes it optimal to exert low effort, making a high share of the heterogeneity in the income distribution the result of luck, which makes redistribution optimal *ex post*. Note that inequality can affect preferences for redistribution even when individuals are entirely self-regarding. In the canonical Meltzer and Richard (1981) model where redistribution policy consists of a flat tax and an equal lump sum transfer, the degree of redistribution preferred by the pivotal median voter will be a function of the degree of inequality, as measured by the distance between median and average income (see Bussolo et al. 2018 for a discussion), however, there is little empirical evidence to support the Meltzer-Richard model (see Alesina and Giuliano 2009 for a detailed discussion). Inequality is also not the only, or even the key, determinant of redistributive preferences, and a review of this literature is beyond the scope of this chapter (see Clark and D'Ambrosio 2015 for a review). We focus, instead, on the links between inequality and preferences for redistribution, and within this area, we restrict our attention to the studies focusing on transition economies.

Alesina and Giuliano (2009) provide a useful taxonomy for the various channels through which inequality can affect preferences for redistribution First, inequality can enter in the utility function indirectly, such that individuals do not care about inequality per se, but rather about its effect on their consumption flow. In particular, inequality could lead to sub-optimal education levels, or to higher crime rates, such that the affluent would support redistribution for the externalities that reducing inequality would produce. Second, inequality could enter directly individuals' utility functions; for instance, individuals could hold libertarian, or communist, or Rawlsian views with respect to "social justice," which would lead them to support different levels of redistribution. Finally, individuals' views about inequality can be intertwined with some sense of fairness, such that their demands for redistribution would be informed by the extent to which inequality may be perceived to be unfair or not.

It should be noted that the differences between actual inequality and perceived inequality in transition economies that were noted earlier will matter when it comes to preferences for redistribution. When the two diverge, it is perceptions of inequality that will determine one's beliefs and policy preferences, irrespective of the actual degree of inequality (or social mobility) even though perceptions are clearly informed by reality at least to some degree. The United States is a well-known example of a country where preferences for redistribution tend to be relatively low, on account of perceived high social mobility, even though empirical evidence shows that social mobility in practice is quite low, and lower than in many European countries where citizens prefer, on average, a higher degree of income redistribution. (Gimpelson and Treisman 2018) show that both within and across countries, the relationship between actual inequality and demands for redistribution was tenuous at best, whereas perceptions of inequality closely track demand for government redistribution and reported class conflict. Bussolo et al. (2019), based on ISSP data, similarly find that preferences for redistribution are not correlated with the actual Gini index of inequality, but are correlated with perceptions of inequality, where the perceptions are based on the net equality perception concept that was described above.

With this caveat in mind, several of these pathways appear to be borne out in the empirical data from post-socialist countries. For instance, Bussolo et al. (2019) finds support for redistribution concerns being driven by inequality entering directly into the utility function. Those on the left of the political spectrum are more insensitive to their perceptions of inequality when forming their demand for redistribution—they have a strong demand for redistribution regardless of the inequality level they perceive, whereas those who are right-leaning vary their demand for redistribution as their perceptions of inequality change. Cojocaru (2014b), using data from the 2010 round of the LiTS, finds evidence that fairness considerations (measured through perceptions of whether success is determined by informal connections, or need in society is determined by injustice) are important determinants of redistributive preferences in EU countries, but less so in non-EU transition economies, and conjectures that one possible explanation could be that outside of the European Union inequality of opportunity is more widespread, leading people to adapt to it, which in turn attenuates the link between perceptions of unfairness and preferences for redistribution. Cojocaru (2019) finds, on the other hand, that using the same data from the 2010 LITS, perceived inequality of opportunity[7] is an important determinant of preferences for redistribution; among those who perceive a greater degree of inequality of opportunity, not having connection is associated with greater demands for redistribution, and, among those without connections, perceptions of greater inequality of opportunity also heighted preferences for redistribution.[8]

4   Concluding Remarks

The end of 2019 marks the 30th anniversary of the fall of the Berlin Wall. The social, economic, and political transformation that has taken place over the past 30 years in countries of Eastern Europe and the Former Soviet Union has been monumental. One of the commonly invoked markers of the post-socialist transition is the considerable increase in the income inequality in the countries of this region. The evidence presented in this chapter paints a more nuanced picture. Inequality did increase considerably in the first half of the 1990s, but has since experienced a steady decline, such that by 2015 inequality in the ECA region was much lower than in 1995, and also lower than in all other regions in the world, including industrialized countries. Over the

---

[7] Perceived inequality of opportunity here is defined in terms of the beliefs with respect to the importance of connections for key opportunities in life (such as a good job or university education).

[8] A cross-tabulation of perceptions of inequality of opportunity (IO) and availability of connections generates 4 groups based on whether one perceives inequality of opportunity or not, and whether one has connections or not (IO, connections/IO, no connections/no IO, connections/no IO, no connections). Thus, two separate comparisons are made, varying one characteristic at a time: (i) between those who perceive IO and have connections, and those who perceive IO and do not have connections; and between two groups, both without connections, but one perceiving IO and the other one not.

past 15 years inequality has been declining in most countries in the region, for which the necessary survey data are available.

There is, at the same time, a stark difference between relatively low and declining levels of observed inequality in transition economies, and the widely held beliefs that the region has grown to be very unequal, and preferences for the level of inequality to be lower. Research has shown that this is due, in part, to the fact that individuals have very little knowledge of the actual level of inequality in their countries, as measured using data from household surveys. But this lack of knowledge is only a partial explanation. Recent literature also documents a growing degree of inequality of opportunity in transition economies, declining intergenerational mobility for the most recent birth cohorts, and a growing degree of polarization in the labor market. Younger cohorts are also being faced with higher levels of inequality through their life cycle compared to older cohorts. A large majority of adults believe that it is difficult to gain access to key opportunities in life, such as a good job or university education, without informal connections.

These perceptions matter. If opportunities are perceived to be unequally distributed, it can lead individuals at the bottom of the income distribution to under-invest in human capital and form lower aspirations for the future, thus perpetuating inequality traps across generations (see Narayan et al. 2018 and references therein for a detailed discussion). Bussolo et al. (2018) also document how the perceptions of the shrinking level of equity in the regions are putting fissures in the existing social contract in transition economies, through (i) a growing polarization in voting; and (ii) declining trust in institutions. Winkler (2019), using data from 25 European countries, including a number of transition economies, for the period 2002–2014, also finds that a 5-point increase in the Gini index of local inequality increases the likelihood of a voter supporting either a far-left or a far-right party by 4 percentage points.

There is also much that we still do not know about the relationship between inequality and welfare in this region. One key contribution to this literature would be to highlight to a much greater extent the heterogeneity across the countries in the region by undertaking comparative analysis. This chapter has reviewed, to the extent that the existing literature allows for it, the differences across transition economies, and in some cases between transition economies and western European countries, with respect to the extent of overall inequality, inequality of opportunity, and perceptions of inequality. There is also some evidence from the existing literature that different mechanisms may be mediating the link between inequality and well-being and between inequality and preferences for redistribution, in transition vs non-transition countries in Europe, or in New EU member states vs non-EU transition economies in the

Balkans and the FSU. However, most of the studies reviewed in this chapter are based on cross-sectional cross-country datasets, even in cases such as Grosfeld and Senik (2010) that look at within-country dynamics overtime, and as such, our ability to provide a high degree of differentiation from data of this kind is necessarily limited, as is our ability to adequately address issues pertaining to individual heterogeneity.

One of the main conclusions of this chapter is that people in the region perceive inequality to be too high, and would like income disparities to be lower, or perhaps more accurately, they would like opportunities to be distributed more equally. This knowledge was made possible by the increasing number of studies relying on subjective well-being data and allow us to make inference on the relationship between inequality and individual well-being. However, to better understand the implications of increasing inequality of opportunity, and falling intergenerational mobility in transition economies, and in order to help policymakers, we would need to move beyond subjective well-being data and obtain more direct evidence on the effects of inequality (and inequality of opportunity) on key decisions and actions that individuals make; such as (i) their investments in human capital, (ii) their engagement in the labor market, (iii) their policy preferences beyond a general preference for reducing the gap between rich and poor, in particular related to the current policy debates on issues such as the best ways to protect vulnerable households that lose out from the changing labor markets or which taxes to deploy to reduce inequality.

References

Aiyar, S., & Ebeke, C. (2019). *Inequality of Opportunity, Inequality of Income and Economic Growth.* IMF Working Paper 19/34.

Alesina, A., & Angeletos, G.-M. (2005). Fairness and Redistribution. *The American Economic Review, 95*(4), 960–980.

Alesina, A. F., & Giuliano, P. (2009). *Preferences for Redistribution.* NBER Working Papers No. 14825. Cambridge, MA: National Bureau of Economic Research.

Alesina, A. F., Di Tella, R., & MacCulloch, R. (2004). Inequality and Happiness: Are Europeans and Americans Different? *Journal of Public Economics, 88*(9–10), 2009–2042.

Alesina, A., Stantcheva, S., & Teso, E. (2018). Intergenerational Mobility and Support for Redistribution. *American Economic Review, 108*(2), 521–554.

Arneson, R. J. (1989). Equality and Equal Opportunity for Welfare. *Philosophical Studies, 56*(1), 77–93.

Arneson, R. J. (2000). Economic Analysis Meets Distributive Justice. *Social Theory and Practice: An International and Interdisciplinary Journal of Social Philosophy, 26*(2), 327–345.

Atkinson, A. B. (1970). On the Measurement of Inequality. *Journal of Economic Theory, 2*(3), 244–263.

Atkinson, A. B. (2015). *Inequality: What Can Be Done?* Cambridge, MA: Harvard University Press.

Berg, M., & Veenhoven, R. (2010). Income inequality and happiness in 119 nations In: Bent Greve (ed.) *Social Policy and Happiness in Europe*, Edgar Elgar, chapter 11, pp.174–194.

Berg, A., & Ostry, J. (2011). *Inequality and Unsustainable Growth*. Washington, DC: International Monetary Fund.

Birdsall, N., & Londono, J. L. (1998). No Tradeoff: Efficient Growth Via More Equal Human Capital in Latin America. In N. Birdsall, C. Graham, & R. Sabot (Eds.), *Beyond Tradeoffs: Market Reforms and Equitable Growth in Latin America*. Washington, DC: Brookings Institution Press and Inter-American Development Bank.

Boushey, H., & Price, C. C. (2014). *How Are Economic Inequality and Growth Connected? A Review of Recent Research*. Washington Center for Equitable Growth.

Brunori, P., Ferreira, F. H. G., & Peragine, V. (2013). *Inequality of Opportunity, Income Inequality and Economic Mobility: Some International Comparisons*. Policy Research Working Paper No. 6304. Washington, DC: World Bank.

Bussolo, M., Davalos, M. E., Peragine, V., & Sundaram, R. (2018). *Toward a New Social Contract: Taking on Distributional Tensions in Europe and Central Asia*. Europe and Central Asia Studies. Washington, DC: World Bank.

Bussolo, M., Ferrer-i-Carbonell, A., Giolbas, A. B., & Torre, I. (2019). *I Perceive Therefore I Demand: The Formation of Inequality Perceptions and Demand for Redistribution (English)*. Policy Research Working Paper No. WPS 8929. Washington, DC: World Bank Group.

Camerer, C. F., & Thaler, R. H. (1995). Ultimatums, Dictators and Manners. *Journal of Economic Perspectives, IX*, 209–219.

Clark, A. E., & D'Ambrosio, C. (2015). Chapter 13 – Attitudes to Income Inequality: Experimental and Survey Evidence. In A. B. Atkinson & F. Bourguignon (Eds.), *Handbook of Income Distribution* (Vol. 2, pp. 1147–1208). Elsevier.

Cohen, G. A. (1989). On the currency of egalitarian justice. *Ethics, 99*(4), 906–944.

Cojocaru, A. (2014a). Fairness and Inequality Tolerance: Evidence from the Life in Transition Survey. *Journal of Comparative Economics, 42*(3), 590–608.

Cojocaru, A. (2014b). Prospects of Upward Mobility and Preferences for Redistribution: Evidence from the Life in Transition Survey. *European Journal of Political Economy, 34*(C), 300–314.

Cojocaru, A. (2016). Does Relative Deprivation Matter in Developing Countries: Evidence from Six Transition Economies. *Social Indicators Research, 125*(3, February), 735–756.

Cojocaru, A. (2019). *Inequality of Access to Opportunities and Socioeconomic Mobility: Evidence from the Life in Transition Survey.* Policy Research Working Paper Series 8725. The World Bank.

Cojocaru, A., Matytsin, M., & Prohnitchi, V. (2019). *Fiscal Incidence in Moldova: A Commitment to Equity Analysis.* Policy Research Working Paper No. 9010. Washington, DC: The World Bank.

Corak, M. (2017). *Divided Landscapes of Economic Opportunity: The Canadian Geography of Intergenerational Income Mobility.* Working Papers 2017-043, Human Capital and Economic Opportunity Working Group, University of Chicago, Chicago, IL.

D'Ambrosio, C., & Frick, J. R. (2007). Income Satisfaction and Relative Deprivation: An Empirical Link. *Social Indicators Research, 81*(3), 497–519.

De Dominicis, Laura, Henri L.F. de Groot, and Raymond J.G.M. Florax. 2006, Growth and Inequality: A Meta-Analysis. Tinbergen Institute Discussion Paper TI 2006–064/3.

Deaton, A. (2001). *Relative Deprivation, Inequality, and Mortality.* NBER Working Paper 8099. National Bureau of Economic Research.

Deininger, K., & Squire, L. (1997). Economic Growth and Income Inequality: Reexamining the Links. *Finance & Development, 34*(March), 38–41.

Delhey, J., & Dragolov, G. (2014). Why Inequality Makes Europeans Less Happy: The Role of Distrust, Status Anxiety, and Perceived Conflict. *European Sociological Review, 30*, 151–165.

Dworkin, R. (1981). What Is Equality? Part 2: Equality of Resources. *Philosophy & Public Affairs, 10*(4), 283–345.

EBRD. (2016). *Chapter 3 – Inequality of Opportunity.* Transition Report 2016-207. London: EBRD.

Eibner, C., & Evans, W. N. (2005). Relative Deprivation, Poor Health Habits, and Mortality. *Journal of Human Resources, XL*(3), 591–620.

Fehr, E., & Gachter, S. (2000). Cooperation and Punishment in Public Goods Experiments. *The American Economic Review, 90*(4), 980–994.

Fehr, E., & Schmidt, K. M. (1999). A Theory of Fairness, Competition, and Cooperation. *The Quarterly Journal of Economics, 114*(3), 817–868.

Fehr, E., & Schmidt, K. M. (2006). The Economics of Fairness, Reciprocity and Altruism – Experimental Evidence and New Theories. In *Handbook on the Economics of Giving, Reciprocity and Altruism* (Vol. 1, pp. 615–691). Berlin: Elsevier.

Fehr, E., Gachter, S., & Kirchsteiger, G. (1997). Reciprocity as a Contract Enforcement Device: Experimental Evidence. *Econometrica, 65*(4), 833–860.

Ferreira, F. H. G., Molinas Vega, J. R., De Barros, R. P., & Chanduvi, J. S. (2008). *Measuring Inequality of Opportunities in Latin America and the Caribbean.* World Bank Publications.

Ferreira, Francisco H. G., Lakner, C., & Silwal, A. (forthcoming). *Inequality Increasing Everywhere? Conflicting Evidence from an Updated Global Database of Household Surveys.*

Frank, R. H., & Levine, A. S. (2007). *Expenditure Cascades.* Ithaca: Cornell University Mimeograph.

Gimpelson, V., & Treisman, D. (2018). Misperceiving Inequality. *Economics & Politics, 30*(1), 27–54.

Grosfeld, I., & Senik, C. (2010). The Emerging Aversion to Inequality. *The Economics of Transition, 18*(1), 1–26.

Guriev, S., & Melnikov, N. (2018). Happiness Convergence in Transition Countries. *Journal of Comparative Economics, 46*(3), 683–707.

Guriev, S., & Zhuravskaya, E. (2009). (Un) Happiness in Transition. *The Journal of Economic Perspectives, 23*(2), 143–168.

Hanmer, L., & Naschold, F. (2000). Attaining the International Development Targets: Will Growth be Enough? *Development Policy Review 18*, 11–36.

Hey, J. D., & Lambert, P. J. (1980). Relative Deprivation and the Gini Coefficient: Comment. *The Quarterly Journal of Economics, 95*(3), 567–573.

Hirschman, A., with Rothschild, M. (1973). The Changing Tolerance for Income Inequality in the Course of Economic Development. *Quarterly Journal of Economics, LXXXVII*(4), 544–566.

Kraay, A. C. (2015). *Weak Instruments in Growth Regressions: Implications for Recent Cross-Country Evidence on Inequality and Growth.* Policy Research Working Paper Series 7494. The World Bank.

Kuhn, P., Kooreman, P., Soetevent, A., & Kapteyn, A. (2011). The Effects of Lottery Prizes on Winners and Their Neighbors: Evidence from the Dutch Postcode Lottery. *American Economic Review, 101*(5), 2226–2247.

Lustig, N., & Higgins, S. (2013). *Commitment to Equity Assessment (CEQ): Estimating the Incidence of Social Spending, Subsidies and Taxes. Handbook.* CEQ Working Paper 1, Center for Inter-American Policy and Research and Department of Economics, Tulane University and Inter-American Dialogue.

Marrero, G. A., & Rodriguez, J. G. (2010). *Inequality of Opportunity and Growth.* ECINEQ Working Paper No. 2010–154.

Meltzer, A. H., & Richard, S. F. (1981). A rational theory of the size of government. *Journal of Political Economy, 89*, 914–927.

Milanovic, B. (2005). *Worlds Apart: Measuring International and Global Inequality.* Princeton University Press.

Narayan, A., Van der Weide, R., Cojocaru, A., Lakner, C., Redaelli, S., Mahler, D. G., Ramasubbaiah, R. G. N., & Thewissen, S. (2018). *Fair Progress?: Economic*

Mobility Across Generations Around the World. Equity and Development. Washington, DC: World Bank.

Nikolova, M. (2016). Minding the Happiness Gap: Political Institutions and Perceived Quality of Life in Transition. *European Journal of Political Economy, 45*(S), 129–148.

Ostry, J. D., Berg, A., & Tsangarides, C. G. (2014). *Redistribution, Inequality, and Growth.* IMF Staff Discussion Notes 14/02, International Monetary Fund.

Ravallion, M. (2001). Growth, Inequality and Poverty: Looking Beyond Averages. *World Development, 29,* 1803–1815.

Rawls, J. (1971). *A Theory of Justice.* Belknap Press.

Roemer, J. E. (2000). *Equality of Opportunity.* Harvard University Press.

Sanfey, P., & Teksoz, U. (2007). Does Transition Make You Happy? *Economics in Transition, 15,* 707–731.

Schneider, S. (2019). Why Income Inequality Is Dissatisfying – Perceptions of Social Status and the Inequality-Satisfaction Link in Europe. *European Sociological Review, 35*(3), 409–430.

Sen, A. (1980). Equality of What? In S. M. McMurrin (Ed.), *Tanner Lectures on Human Values.* Cambridge University Press.

Senik, C. (2004). When Information Dominates Comparison: Learning from Russian Subjective Panel Data. *Journal of Public Economics, 88*(9–10), 2099–2123.

Senik, C. (2009). Direct Evidence on Income Comparisons and Their Welfare Effects. *Journal of Economic Behavior & Organization, 72*(1), 408–424.

Svejnar, J. (2002). Transition Economies: Performance and Challenges. *Journal of Economic Perspectives, 16*(1), 3–28.

Thaler, R. (1988). The Ultimatum Game. *Journal of Economic Perspectives, 2*(4), 195–206.

UN. (2015). Retrieved from https://www.un.org/en/development/desa/policy/wess/wess_dev_issues/dsp_policy_02.pdf.

Van de Gaer, D. (1993). *Equality of Opportunity and Investment in Human Capital.* Catholic University of Leuven, Faculty of Economics, No. 92.

Van de Gaer, D., Schokkaert, E., & Martinez, M. (2001). Three Meanings of Intergenerational Mobility. *Economica, 68,* 519–538.

Voitchovsky, S. (2005). Does the Profile of Income Inequality Matter for Economic Growth? *Journal of Economic Growth, 10*(3), 273–296.

Winkler, H. (2019). The Effect of Income Inequality on Political Polarization: Evidence from European Regions, 2002–2014. *Economics & Politics, 31*(2), 137–162.

World Bank (Ed.). (2005). *World Development Report 2006: Equity and Development* (2006th ed.). World Bank Publications.

World Bank. (2016). *Poverty and Shared Prosperity 2016: Taking on Inequality*. Washington, DC: World Bank.

World Bank. (2018). *Poverty and Shared Prosperity 2018: Piecing Together the Poverty Puzzle*. Washington, DC: World Bank.

Yitzhaki, S. (1979). Relative Deprivation and the Gini Coefficient. *The Quarterly Journal of Economics, 93*(2), 321–324.

28

Authoritarian Populism in Comparative Perspective

Tomasz Mickiewicz

1   The Question

Between 1989 and 1991 the Soviet system imploded in Central and Eastern Europe. This, alongside democratisation and liberalisation processes in other parts of the world, led Fukuyama (1989) to argue that it was the 'end of history', in the Hegelian sense. The global scale of peaceful transformation witnessed was indeed unprecedented. It also transformed the European Union (EU), both with EU enlargement towards Central Europe and the Balkans, and through a drive towards more integration, which was perceived as necessary to keep the enlarged EU viable.

Yet at the time of writing, a generation after democratisation and liberalisation in Central Europe symbolised by leaders such as Lech Wałęsa and Vaclav Hável, we see Victor Orbán in Hungary proclaiming the new, pan-European transition to 'illiberal democracy', and Jarosław Kaczyński in Poland aiming to follow the same path. Moreover, elsewhere in the EU, the political order seems to be questioned by some other leaders.

I would like to express my gratitude for valuable comments I received from the editors of this volume, and from the participants of the conferences and seminars at the Polish Academy of Sciences, Warsaw; St. Antony's College, Oxford University; and Aston University, Birmingham.

T. Mickiewicz (✉)
Aston University, Birmingham, UK
e-mail: t.mickiewicz@aston.ac.uk

© The Author(s) 2021
E. Douarin, O. Havrylyshyn (eds.), *The Palgrave Handbook of Comparative Economics*,
https://doi.org/10.1007/978-3-030-50888-3_28

There has been a steady, long-term increase of electoral support for authoritarian populism, as documented by data from the Timbro Institute,[1] but the future direction of the process is not settled. While anti-systemic, populist movements in the EU gained local successes, they were also defeated by voters in a large number of countries, not only in the 'old' EU, but also in new member states, with Slovakia's and Croatia's presidential elections being recent examples. The question to be considered here is thus that of factors of success for authoritarian populism across Europe. This will be the subject of Sect. 5. Before we move to this, however, we will first describe the phenomenon of populism in Sect. 2, and discuss its features based on empirical examples, first of classic Latin American cases (Sect. 3), and then discussing the features of populism in Hungary and Poland (Sect. 4).

2   Populism

Müller (2017) points to two key elements of populist ideology: it is both 'anti-elitist' and 'anti-pluralist'. He argues that the anti-elitism, the criticism of elites, is a necessary but not a sufficient condition for a movement to be called 'populist', as it is a more widespread trait in political debates. Only when it is combined with the second element does it make the populist ideology complete, closed. This second element is anti-pluralism. That is to say the populist politicians make a distinctively moral claim to the exclusive representation of the people. Rosenblum (2010) describes this as 'holism', the notion that the polity should no longer be split and the idea that it is possible for the people to be one and for all of them to have one true representative. As further explained by Müller (2017), populism requires a 'pars pro toto' (a part taken for the whole) argument, and a claim to undivided representation, described in a moral, as opposed to an empirical sense. The populist party represents and therefore substitutes for the people, and the leader substitutes for the party. This is also reflected in the internal structures of populist parties, in which the role of the leader is particularly strong.[2] Populist programmes are thus implemented by fundamentally authoritarian parties. Politics is personalised and the 'will of the people' is seen as strongest when concentrated. In the words of Dahrendorf (2007): populism is simple, democracy is complex.

---

[1] https://populismindex.com/. I will refer to this data throughout the chapter.

[2] For example, the Law and Justice party in Poland has a statute that makes any initiative to change its leader next to impossible, including imposing supra-majority conditions across regional organisations as a requirement.

The assumed direct link to the people implies that populism has anti-systemic traits: a disregard for the constraints within the institutional system is not only justified, but necessary: breaking the constitutional limitations is required to implement 'the will of the people'. This is, for example, what Jarosław Kaczyński implies when he criticises 'legal impossibilism'.

This also explains the typical scenarios observed once these political parties are in power. First, the autonomy of the state administration is destroyed, as the administration becomes the tool of the ruling populist party, directly controlled by its nominees. Second, there is a drive towards centralisation, as the autonomy of the local authorities is presented as another institutional obstacle to implementing the 'will of the people'. Third, the independence of the judiciary comes under threat, as it represents a major constraint on power. Fourth, there are efforts to supress civil society and non-governmental organisations.[3] Fifth, 'those who represent the people' should also dominate the media, so that control over the media is expanded and independent outlets are taken over or marginalised. Of course, outcomes will always differ, at least somewhat, from these blueprints: in some countries populist leaders make little progress in destroying the constitutional order, when they encounter strong opposition. In other countries they advance further.

The anti-pluralism identified by Müller (2017) as a core populist trait has an old tradition in modern European thought. Some of these ideas can be traced back to Rousseau (2018 [1762]), who emphasised the unified 'general will' of the people, in contrast to De Montesquieu's (1989 [1748]) stress on the balance of powers. Similar views emerged later, both on the left and the right of the spectrum of political ideologies. Marx (2008 [1875]) is probably the most influential nineteenth century proponent of dictatorship, which he argued would be necessary, at least temporarily, to impose the will of the people, replacing liberal democracies that, in his view, are only a façade for capitalist interests. Since the early twentieth century, the ideas of Schmitt (1988 [1923]) remain influential, despite the fact that these were the same ideas that led him to support the Nazi takeover of power in Germany. Schmitt emphasised the notion of 'the people', a deep, existential phenomenon beyond all political forms and formations; and promoted a conceptual split between the 'substance' of the people on the one hand and the empirical outcomes of a democratic process. His ideal was a government based on identity with those governed (Müller 2017).[4]

---

[3] This is an effective policy if entrenching power becomes an objective. Boeri et al. (2018) demonstrate that individuals belonging to associations are less likely to vote for populist parties.

[4] Schmitt's ideas played a direct role in the ascent of populism in Central Europe. Jarosław Kaczyński's PhD from the University of Warsaw was gained under the supervision of Stanisław Ehrlich, who had

Needless to say, these ideas did not remain unanswered. Müller (2017) emphasises the arguments of Kelsen (2013 [1929]), for whom an unambiguous popular will is in fact impossible to discern, and the 'organic unity of the people', from which some policies could be interfered, amounts to 'metapolitical illusion'. As a consequence, democracy needs to be a pluralistic system, where people's ideas and interests should be mediated by multiple political parties. This corresponds to the view, expressed much earlier by Bagehot (1965 [1872]), that 'a parliamentary government is essentially a government by discussion'. Its modern counterpart is the argument developed by Sen (2009), who sees the core of democracy in the process of public reasoning and debate.

After this brief overview of populist ideas, we now turn to their implementation.

3   Classic Populism: Latin America

3.1   Context: Framework Conditions for Political Instability

According to the assessment of Freedom House 2019,[5] out of the seven largest Latin American countries, as defined by population, four are classified as politically free: Argentina, Brazil, Chile and Peru. Of those four, Chile has a very high score on the index, followed by Argentina, while both Brazil and Peru are borderline cases (i.e. just above the partially free threshold). The three other largest Latin American countries are not considered to be stable democracies: Colombia, Mexico and Venezuela. Colombia and Mexico are also borderline cases, but this time below the threshold separating partly free from politically free countries. Venezuela is an outlier, not only in this group, but in the Americas as a whole, and is seen at the time of writing as one of the most oppressive regimes in the world, as well as one characterised by exceptional economic failure. It is also probably the best-known recent exemplification of the populist cycle—a cycle that has yet to be broken, implying that the

---

significant influence on the intellectual formation of the future Polish populist leader. Ehrlich was a prominent Communist legal theorist, who in turn drew a lot of his ideas from Schmitt, whom he admired (Mazur 2016).

[5] See https://freedomhouse.org/report/freedom-world/freedom-world-2019/map, as accessed on the 7th of October 2019.

economy has still to run all the way down towards humanitarian disaster. The authoritarian military regime, supported by coercive know-how imported from Cuba, Russia and China, has become sufficiently entrenched, and the situation has been transformed into a state of permanent crisis, with no immediate solution in sight.

An influential account explaining the political economy of many Latin American countries is provided by Acemoglu and Robinson (2012). They point towards long-term history, and the specificity of colonial institutions that were organised around extraction of concentrated rents from natural resources. The core logic of this institutional setup was inherited from colonial times by the independent states that emerged in the region. Extractive institutions often lead to political instability. This is because huge concentrated rents imply that there are always significant gains from overthrowing a current regime. As a result, political change in the region has often taken a military form, with the opposition seizing power by violent means instead of via elections. In Latin America, military officers have played a significant role in governments across the political spectrum. The classic examples are Juan Perón in Argentina, Augusto Pinochet in Chile and, more recently, Hugo Chávez in Venezuela.

Thus, while international conflicts have been relatively infrequent in Latin America, compared to other parts of the world (Fukuyama 2015), weak political frameworks have often resulted in violent internal clashes, which have taken the place of rule-constrained political competition. In some countries, protracted civil wars have gone on for many years, often blending with criminal activities such as drug trafficking and kidnapping. Colombia until recently, and Peru in the past, are examples. Even where political frameworks are able to deliver a democratic vote, politicians who win elections often take advantage of the political power they gain to entrench their position by harassing opposition politicians, by controlling the media, and, if necessary, by failing to recognising the electoral outcome in the next round.

In some countries, such as Mexico, organised crime plays an important role, infecting politics. What often fuels organised crime is political instability that makes the government ineffective, and economic rents (e.g. drugs) that provide local mafia structures with resources. From that point of view, neighbouring the US may be less of a blessing and more of a curse, as the latter country, just across the border, is a large and lucrative market for narcotics.

3.2   Outcomes: Economics and Its Limitations; the Populist Cycle

Political instability may help to explain the short-term political horizons and political-economic cycles that became associated with populism, as argued by Dornbusch and Edwards (1989, 1990, 1991); see also Sachs (1989). I start with an account of a macroeconomic cycle of populist policies, which Dornbusch and Edwards (1989) based on their analysis of the economic policies of Salvador Allende and his government in Chile in 1970–1973, and those of the Alan García in Peru in 1985–1990. Figures 28.1 and 28.2 present the GDP paths of these two countries.

Dornbusch and Edwards' (1989) discussion of the cycle can be summarised in the following way. We start with the initial position, where typically growth and living standards are negatively affected by stabilisation implemented after some earlier macroeconomic crisis. Given the stagnant economy, there is public dissatisfaction. This creates political demand for a radically different set of economic policies. Meanwhile, the preceding stabilisation is improving both the budget and the external balance, and rebuilding foreign exchange reserves sufficiently to provide scope for a shift away from stabilisation policies. Yet, such a shift could proceed in more than one direction, and the classic populist programme has some distinctive features.

The first premise of the populist programme, as described by Dornbusch and Edwards (1989), is that there is idle capacity in the economy. The populists argue that this can provide room for expansion without inflation. Along this line of argument, the spare capacity and decreasing average costs curves, along which production may expand, imply that there will be no cost pressures. Furthermore, profit margins in 'big businesses' are argued to be excessive, and the chosen solution to the problem is to squeeze them by price controls, containing inflation. This way, the population is to gain at the expense of 'big capitalists'. Parallel to that, there is to be redistribution of income via wage increases. This is expected to stimulate demand, as workers spend more and save less, utilising an argument that can be traced back to Kalecki (1954). This change in domestic demand is also expected to result in a restructuring of production; sectors producing for workers are seen as more competitive, and likely to respond positively to stimulus, thereby increasing production. That in turn implies there is no need for additional imports to match higher demand, and could even lead to savings on foreign exchange. Furthermore, the risk of public deficit finance is dismissed as unfounded. Overall, it is expected that fast growth without inflation should follow. This constitutes a typical populist economic promise, on which they come to power.

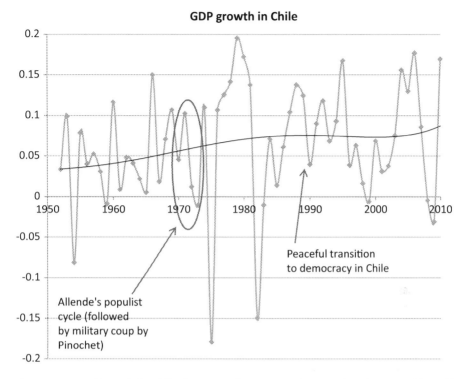

Fig. 28.1 Populist cycle in Chile. (Note: Real GDP growth rate taken from World Bank)

What follows initially from this programme is the first phase of the cycle, that of stimulus. An increase in wages comes with output and employment growth, confirming expectations. Demand and consumption expand. However, imposed price controls, combined with a fixed exchange rate, ensure that inflation does not emerge. Price controls imply that some shortages appear temporarily, but these are covered by imports, drawing from sufficient currency reserves, which therefore decrease. At the same time, the level of inventories in industry decreases as well.

During the second phase of the cycle, more serious bottlenecks emerge. Strong expansion in demand continues, but the low level of inventories now constrains domestic supply and, at the same time, the capacity to increase imports gradually becomes more restricted, as foreign exchange reserves dwindle.

Populist politicians respond to these challenges with specific policy tools. On the domestic market, controlled prices are realigned to eliminate some of the imbalance. To pre-empt a collapse in currency reserves, devaluation is introduced, now combined with exchange controls so that access to foreign

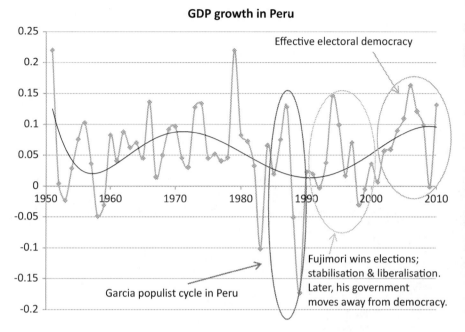

Fig. 28.2 Populist cycle in Peru. (Note: Real GDP growth rate taken from World Bank)

currency becomes rationed. Imports are discouraged by further protectionist measures. As a result of these policies, inflation increases, but wages are not controlled, in line with the core political promise, so that they keep rising. Ultimately, this leads to the emergence of a wage-price spiral. High wages, combined with price controls imposed on production, result in decreasing profitability. The latter is restored by targeted subsidies, which worsens the budget deficit.

At some point, this second stage of growing imbalance is transformed into the third stage of full-scale economic destabilisation. Now, the shortages under price controls become extensive, which results in widespread black markets. Internal disequilibrium is also associated with external disequilibrium. Both an overvalued currency and increasingly uncertain economic prospects lead to capital flight abroad. Inflation becomes so high that it results in the demonetisation of the economy: there is very little demand for the domestic currency. The latter is crowded out by widespread unofficial use of foreign currency in transactions. With no demand for domestic money, the seigniorage gains from printing money shrink as well. The budget deficit deteriorates rapidly. This is also due to the decline in tax collection and the increasing costs of subsidies. The government has an option to escalate fully into hyperinflation, or to slow down its emergence. In any case, the real value of government spending is decreasing; the question is whether this is done in a chaotic way or whether the government chooses to prioritise spending cuts. The government may decide to retain some control over the process by cutting subsidies that it considers less strategic, and to engage in real depreciation. Yet this implies that nominal wage increases no longer compensate for the nominal loss in the value of the domestic currency. In other words, there is a significant fall in real wages, either resulting from explicit decisions by the government, or from hyperinflation. Ultimately, the massive fall of real wages leads to destabilisation. The government is changed either by democratic or undemocratic means.

With this, the political-economic cycle enters its final phase. A new government enacts a stabilisation programme, typically supported by foreign assistance. Real wages decline further; as observed by Dornbusch and Edwards (1989), typically to a level that is lower than when the cycle began. The decline in real wages is likely to persist, as economic and political uncertainty leads to low investment and to capital flight, and there is no guarantee that the programme will succeed. It takes time for the economy to respond positively to stabilisation. The most striking outcome of the cycle is that while the initial populist policy objective was to redistribute towards workers, in the end the poor are hit hardest. The large scale of decline in incomes results from the fact that while capital is mobile across borders, labour is not, or at least less so than capital. Capital can and does flee from incompetent policies, but labour, and especially the poor, are trapped.

The way the political crisis that follows from these policies is resolved is of critical importance. In Chile, the populist government was overthrown by a military coup, and the human cost of the subsequent dictatorship far exceeded the cost of the misguided economic policies of Allende.[6] Peru is Chile's neighbour, and the human cost of the violent response to populism in Chile was not overlooked in the country. Thus, when García embarked on his own populist path in Peru, there was nobody willing to replace him with an oppressive dictatorship. As a result, the Peruvian economy continued into the spectacular free fall that can be detected on Fig. 28.2. Ultimately, political change was achieved by elections.

As the more recent case of Venezuela documents, however, these two scenarios are not the only ones possible. Two factors helped to entrench the populist regime in Venezuela, despite the collapse of the economy. One was that for some time it could draw on the rich oil sector, making the regime

---

[6] For an account of the Pinochet regime in Chile, see Spooner (1999).

immune to popular pressure. The second one was its strategy to import efficient coercive technology and expertise from nearby Cuba, and to a lesser extent from Russia and China. By the time its resources were depleted, the government's coercive technology was already successfully institutionalised, allowing the regime to survive.

Dornbusch and Edwards' (1989) classic account, as sketched above, suggests that what we face here cannot be modelled simply as a result of the interplay of interests of different social groups. Ideas matter as well, and misguided policies based on these ideas lead to suboptimal outcomes. Furthermore, their account of the populist cycle implicitly assumes some strong dose of either incompetence or irrationality. Yet in the sequence of events characterising developments after populists gain power, their projects may well have some rational interpretation, being more than just a bundle of misguided policies. We may think about it in the following way.

A political entrepreneur embarks on a project along which economic benefits are distributed to the population, securing social support. These policies may appear economically irrational, but their primary function is to gain time, and from that point of view, the account presented above by Dornbusch and Edwards (1989) is incomplete. Following the early economic results, support for populism initially increases (Goldberg 1975), and this is used to legitimise breaking the constitutional order and entrenching the new type of regime, where political competition from the opposition becomes increasingly difficult. When public dissatisfaction increases, the regime may be already entrenched (as in Venezuela). Such a programme may or may not succeed, but this risk-taking is not irrational for the political entrepreneurs: they gamble on gaining and securing power over an extended period of time.

If we adopt such a rational, economic model of populism, interpreted as a device to entrench political power, all that remains to be explained is the behaviour of the voters. Here, we can fall back on an assumption of widespread political ignorance (Somin 2016) that itself can be seen as an exemplification of the collective action problem. Alternatively, we could assume voters' decisions to be focused on the short term under conditions of uncertainty: the initial gains are real, and the initial redistribution is real. Those gains typically do not last for very long, but while they last, they are tangible.

My tentative conclusion from the discussion of classic Latin American populism is that the description of economic policies leaves us with more questions than answers. And if we are unwilling to assume myopic behaviour from political entrepreneurs, populism may be better conceptualised as a technique of gaining power, where initial economic policies are offered to buy support. These policies produce some temporary gains, and this gives populists sufficient time to entrench power. Adopting such a perspective will enable us to make the link between the Latin American and the Central Eastern European experience, to which I turn next.

4 Populism in Central Europe

The pattern of initial economic gains leading to increased support, where the latter is used to gain time and entrench political power by weakening or even demolishing democratic institutions, can be detected in Vladimir Putin's political project in Russia since 2000, or that of Viktor Orbán (who learned some techniques from Putin) in Hungary since 2010, and of Jarosław Kaczyński (who learned some techniques from Orbán) in Poland since 2015. However, the macroeconomics of these projects does not resemble that of classic Latin American cases just described. In particular, it is hard to identify the self-defeating pattern of a 'boom and a bust' cycle. Yet the microeconomic features of a power entrenchment scenario, something that Dornbusch and Edwards (1989) did not pay sufficient attention to, are shared, and so is clientelism. The main characteristics of the populist programmes in Hungary and Poland are explained below, based on the account presented by Bałtowski et al. (2020), who propose six major features of the populist political strategy in the two countries.

For Bałtowski et al. (2020), the analysis needs to start with an investigation of the populist project's beneficiaries. What is characteristic of those projects is not just the extent of government intervention, which can be fairly wide in stable democracies of developed economies as well, but the unsystematic character of the intervention, the fact that it is not rule-based, and has a clientelist flavour. In this sense, populism may be seen as a return to more primitive forms of modern political systems (Fukuyama 2015). This is also consistent with Ádám's (2019) analysis, in which he describes the phenomenon as 're-feudalising democracy'. The way that this perspective links with the conclusion to the Latin American section that I proposed above is as follows. If we accept populism to be a technique of gaining and entrenching power, the clientelist features of the populist policies can be explained by their functional role of locking in social support. Basically, the more arbitrary and selective the redistribution is, the more it depends for the recipients (clients) on the populists staying in power. This is a strong effect that locks in support.

Bałtowski et al. (2020) proceed to present the following six features of the economic aspects and the main beneficiaries of the populist programme in Central Eastern Europe.

First, a specificity of the post-Communist economies relates to the tangible size of the state sector and the overall degree of state involvement in firms' decisions, especially with respect to the largest companies. Indeed, for a number of these large companies, although the government has only minority stakes, legal provisions and corporate government arrangements place them under government control. While strengthening direct micro-level government control has been one defining feature of the populist programme since Allende (Goldberg 1975), in Central Eastern Europe the Communist heritage and unfinished privatisation programme left the state sector an especially attractive place for entrenching power. But there are also wider historical analogies. For example, Italy that after the Second World War emerged from another totalitarian project, this time fascist, from which it inherited a wide, concentrated state sector that continued to be used as a source of rents, corrupting politics (Aganin and Volpin 2005).

Compared to Hungary, the residual state sector is bigger in Poland. It implies that the politicisation of state firms also plays a more important role. The existing stock of state-owned companies is treated by government agents as a source of economic rents. Often, it boils down to appointing high-ranking state or party officials (as well as individuals chosen by them) to positions on the supervisory and management boards of state enterprises or offering them (well-paid) jobs in state-owned enterprises (SOEs). The politicisation of SOEs also involves state enterprises funding, through advertisement or sponsorship, of events and activities that improve the image of those in power, especially during elections.

Second, and specific to post-Communist countries, the state sector may be so strong in some cases that government policies are captured by the interests of specific firms or branches of industry. The coal mining sector in Poland is a prime example of such scenario. Well-organised employees of state enterprises, often hand in hand with their senior executives, exert pressure on politicians and the government in order to preserve the privileges held, or to arrest the necessary restructuring processes that would usually entail lay-offs. Politicians' susceptibility to pressure from SOEs is the cost—paid from the budget—of easing tensions or of buying specific voters' support.

Third, parallel to state firms, businesses outside the state sector may also be beneficiaries. Typically, 'crony' private entities are contracted, usually without a tendering procedure or after one that is a mere sham, to provide services and goods to the public sector. These include tasks such as legal and image-building services, the sale and distribution of products on a fee basis, general contractor services for public projects, construction, as well as facilitating selective access to loans granted by state banks.

Four, oligarchy represents a more consolidated form of cronyism. The difference between the two phenomena consists firstly of scale: not only are the benefits reaped greater, but there is also a more persistent pattern of reaping. While the beneficiaries of cronyism are private agents who are anonymous to the public, the enterprises controlled by oligarchs are among the largest private enterprises. Second, and most important, oligarchs display—unlike the beneficiaries of cronyism—close relations with the ruling elites, and have a real, direct influence on the shape of economic policies. In its full-fledged form, members of the ruling elite or individuals closely related to them (that is, family and friends) become indirectly or even directly such oligarchs. These phenomena are more visible in Orbàn's Hungary than in Poland at time of writing, possibly partly because the former regime is already more entrenched.

Fifth, clientelism also arises where wider groups of voters are beneficiaries of some type of government transfers. In contrast to the systemic, rules- and entitlement-based social policy, these transfers are constructed as specific channels of patronage, with ruling politicians handing out goods to their clients, expecting reciprocity by way of political support. For example, a paradoxical aspect of the populist project in Poland has been that the share of those living in extreme poverty has increased in 2017 and 2018 (Central Statistical Office), despite a massive increase in government transfers. This is because those transfers were not based on income criteria, but instead targeted typical conservative voters (families with more than one child).

SOEs may also serve to reward a well-identified group of voters, sometimes working in close association with politically affiliated trade unions, making the system close to the models of corporatism or Latin America's Peronism (Fukuyama 2015). This links back to the second feature of populism in Central Europe, as identified above.

Last but not least, economic nationalism occurs where the government exerts an impact on the economy with the declared objective of enhancing the state's political capacity, military power or 'international importance'. In this respect, the state administration itself may be treated as the major beneficiary. The role of SOEs, especially that of the so-called 'national champions', is again significant here: they are important tools for building power and 'national pride', and they are meant to 'protect' the national economy against 'exploitation' by foreign capital. Such a narrative corresponds to defending some specific local interest groups. This goes hand in hand with nationalisations. A characteristic feature of both Orbàn's and Kaczyński's programmes was that such nationalisations were not driven by a need for post-crisis bailouts, but by well-focused political objectives: following an earlier pattern established in Putin's Russia, the media sector was targeted, along with banks.

Economic nationalism often goes hand in hand with constructing cleavages based on 'us' and 'aliens', introducing forms of political clientelism that are based on ethnicity, declared ideological beliefs, or political party affiliation. Overall, for right-wing authoritarian populism, nationalism is an overarching phenomenon with multiple beneficiaries. It also suggests that it is important to look beyond the economy when considering factors of populism—the issue to which I will turn next.

5   Factors Behind Populism

Considering the factors behind populism, the first, consistent with the discussion so far, is the (narrowly defined) economic interpretation of the assent of populism, as articulated by Rodrik (2018), for example. 'It's the economy, stupid': there are some economic developments that people do not like, and therefore they turn to populists, prioritising the destruction of the 'political-economic' arrangement in place, and hoping that change will be for the better. In this account, while the economic effects appear with different strength in different countries, the common denominator relates to the processes of globalisation and technological change, which bring with them an unequal distribution of social costs. However, not everybody agrees on the impact of globalisation. For example, both Harrison et al. (2011) and Bjørnskov (2019) argue that the implications of international trade for the distribution of income are uncertain and conditional on a range of other factors; similarly, Dumas (2018) emphasises the impact of technological change over globalisation.

Consistent with the narrow economic approach, non-economic factors are of secondary importance. In particular, shared cultural identity matter only because it facilitates the collective action of populists (Rodrik 2018). Thus, in this interpretation, a combination of poor socio-economic outcomes and availability of effective means of mobilisation result in populism's success.

However, other economists take formal institutions more seriously. This leads to a second narrative explaining the emergence of populism. Here, some authors argue that there are long-term formal institutional traditions of doing things, of attitudes and of behaviour that are taken for granted. For example, Clague et al. (2001) show that common law legal origin makes democracy more likely in developing countries. More generally, the legal origin theory (La Porta et al. 2008) posits that the common law tradition is one of decentralised decision-making and adaptation, in contrast to the centralising features of the civil law tradition. It is in the latter environment, therefore, that authoritarian populism finds it easier to take root. This is the institutional economics approach to sources of populism.

Third, explaining the ascent of populism in some countries, we may need to reach even further beyond economics. In this interpretation, we may focus on informal institutions (social norms and values) that are often shaped, even if never entirely determined, by history. These shared norms are more than devices to facilitate social and political mobilisation based on shared socio-cultural identity: their content matters as well.

It is here that the Communist past may become a factor. It left a legacy of atomised societies, which were highly organised, but that organisation was imposed entirely from above, by a Soviet-type state. Sztompka (1996) labels this inherited social characteristics the 'bloc culture'. The capacity for self-organisation was weak, and remained so after the collapse of the Soviet system, given that social attitudes are persistent and are passed to the next generation via family structures. Applying a terminology of Guiso et al. (2010), we may say that these societies are characterised by weak civic capital. We argued above that populism is a centralising project, where 'the people' are claimed to be uniquely represented by the populists. Relatively atomised societies that can be shaped into new forms fit such a project well.

While a Communist past may play a role, there is more. The globalisation narrative, as discussed above, is typically limited to economic aspects, but culture may be important to many people alongside economic welfare. Recently, we have faced not only fast-paced economic change, but also rapid cultural change, and this may be deeply objectionable to a certain percentage of citizens (Müller 2017), generally to those who hold conservative values. Perception that one's identity is being endangered by pluralism (Fukuyama 2018) leads directly to support for populism, with its promise to replace pluralism with (traditional) cultural homogeneity, as discussed above.

These are themes in political conservatism; however, populism is by no means the only political path able to express them, and is actually alien to political conservatism—in so far as conservatism implies respect for the rule of law, in the tradition of Burke (1986 [1790]). Indeed, conservative leaders choose different strategies when confronted with the ascent of populists. As observed by Ziblatt (2017), the consolidation of democracies in Europe depended crucially on the choices of conservative elites. As further argued by Müller (2017), there is not a single case of a right-wing populist party that came to power without cooperation offered by local conservative elites.

But what shapes the attitudes and political strategies adopted by conservatives in different countries? Looking at differences between countries, one encounters cultural tradition as primarily represented by religion. Here,

Catholicism is seen by some as a hierarchical religion that could be associated with authoritarian traits, such as a 'social dominance orientation', for example Hiel and Mervielde (2002). Or is it?

The complicating issue is that the nature of Catholicism may differ across countries. For example, Maltese and Polish societies may be characterised by very similar values of social conservatism, yet may radically differ with respect to broad views on political order. In the second half of twentieth century, Western Catholicism undertook a radical transformation, in response to the tragedy of the Second World War inflicted by totalitarian regimes. It became far more appreciative of democracy, as originated in the work of Maritain (2012 [1942]) for example, one of the co-authors of the Universal Declaration of Human Rights of 1948. In contrast, in countries like Poland or Hungary, Catholicism had fewer chances to evolve in that direction under the Soviet-type regime. While some Western influences were present, and some Catholics from those countries, especially Poland, could even actively participate in global changes in Catholicism, at the same time the Central European local churches were subject to the strong influence of the environment they functioned in. In Poland right after the war, the Communist authorities found common language with the leader of the most extreme, totalitarian wing of the pre-war Polish Catholic movement (The National Radical Camp), for whom Western liberalism and 'the Jews' were more dangerous enemies than the Soviets. Saying that, this was not the line taken by the Polish church hierarchy, which actually played an important role giving shelter to democratic opposition, especially in the 1980s during the Martial Law period. Yet the radical, nationalist, totalitarian traits in Polish Catholicism remained visible.

The Soviet-type system had also more indirect impact on local churches, even if they actually resisted Communism. Under the Communist regime, Catholicism absorbed some features of the political environment. This is an exemplification of institutional isomorphism—that is, of organisations adjusting their features to the environment in which they operate (DiMaggio and Powell 1991). Compared to countries outside the Soviet block, these churches remained highly hierarchical, with a very limited role played by self-organisation of local parishioners, and cultivating a culture of distrust of the outside word. In other words, it was the Soviet-type regime that reinforced the hierarchical features of the Central European Catholicism, making it more receptive to populist logic.

This discussion leads to a three-dimensional framework that may be applied to explain support for populism. It comprises economic dimensions, formal institutions and informal institutions. I will now turn to an empirical illustration that applies it.

5.1   Factors of Populism in Europe: A Set-Theoretic Analysis

A measure of populism is illustrated by Fig. 28.3. It reproduces the shares of electoral support for authoritarian populist parties in the EU countries. These numbers were assembled by the Swedish Timbro Institute. They combine support for both right-wing and left-wing populist parties, albeit at present the former dominate over the latter in Europe, as the proportions between the two reversed around the beginning of the twenty-first century. More details can be found on https://populismindex.com/. Hungary, Greece and Poland are the three EU countries with the largest support for populist parties at time of writing.

The explanatory dimensions included will correspond to the factors discussed in the previous section. First, on the economic side, I will have the unemployment rate (from *Heritage/ Wall Street Journal* database). It was highlighted in recent work on factors of populism by Algan et al. (2017). To this I will add Gini coefficient to capture income inequality (from Eurostat); both dimensions represent potential economic sources of social discontent. However, they will be complemented by the proportion of government spending as a share of GDP (Heritage/Wall Street Journal) and the median income based on purchasing power parity (PPP; Eurostat), the latter corresponding to the level of economic development. Government spending and growth may act as moderating factors with respect to the two former dimensions (inequality, unemployment).

Second, as discussed above, legal origin is taken as a formal institutional dimension that makes some countries less susceptible to authoritarian populism. Accordingly, based on La Porta et al. (2008), countries are classified as either based on civil law or common law legal tradition. There are four

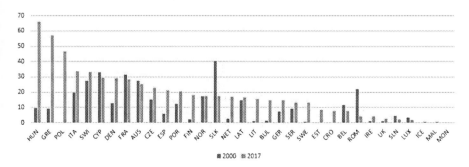

Fig. 28.3 Support for authoritarian populism in EU countries. (Source: Timbro Institute, Authoritarian Populism Index)

countries in the EU representing the second group: Cyprus, Ireland, Malta and the UK.

Third, informal institutions and the history that influences them are captured by two dimensions discussed above. We classify the countries as either having historical experience of Communism or not. This classification follows directly from the one presented by Douarin and Mickiewicz (2017). Last but not least, we include the percentage of population who are Catholic (from PEW Research Center), consistent with the discussion in the previous section.

All the data used in the analysis are presented in the Appendix, Table 28.2. Patterns revealed by this data will be simplified using set-theoretic analysis. For readers who are not familiar with this method, a brief explanation follows.

5.1.1   Method

I have data on 32 European countries, which are either EU member states or in the process of negotiation to join (excluding Turkey). Given the range of factors considered above, there is insufficient degree of freedom for the effective use of country-based regression analysis. However, we can move beyond case studies by applying set-theoretic analysis, and in this case its fuzzy set qualitative comparative analysis variant (fsQCA), where the adjective 'fuzzy' simply relates to the feature that partial set membership is allowed. In the set-theoretic approach there are no longer variables, as there is no assumption of stochasticity. Furthermore, performing the analysis based on set membership implies that the dimensions considered for analysis need to be transformed into the 0–1 range, where 1 implies full membership in a set defined by a given dimension.

The method relies on fuzzy set logic and is able to identify configurations of dimensions sufficient for a specific outcome to emerge (Ragin 2008). Any configuration of such dimensions is seen as sufficient for an outcome if fuzzy set membership in the outcome is higher or equal to the fuzzy set membership level for each of the dimensions that constitute this configuration (Schneider and Wagemann 2012).

It is not only data limitations that directs us towards fsQCA. The method has advantages over regression; an important one is that it is able to handle situations where more than one configuration of dimensions is associated with a given outcome (equifinality). In our case, the outcome relates to share of votes for authoritarian populist parties, and our previous discussion has identified seven explanatory dimensions, for which raw data (before transformation) are presented in Table 28.2.

As mentioned above, for each country, each dimension is defined as membership in a set representing a given characteristic, but this membership can be partial (fuzzy), therefore taking any value between 0 and 1. The share of the populist vote does not require any transformation, and likewise for both Post-Communism and common law legal origin; as the latter two are 0–1 indicators, or crisp sets in set-theoretic terminology. The other five explanatory dimensions either do not fit a zero-one range, or the distribution is skewed. For these reasons I have ranked-ordered all of these dimensions and standardized them between zero and one utilising the algorithm recommended by Longest and Vaisey (2008) in the context of fsQCA. That is, denoting X as an initial score of a case in a given dimension, the following formula was used for this transformation:

$$(\text{rank of } X - \text{min rank of } X) \, / \, (\text{max rank } X - \text{rank of } X) \qquad (28.1)$$

The data for all these dimensions after transformation is available on request. After the zero-one standardisation is applied, this data table, with rows representing cases and columns representing explanatory dimensions and the outcome, becomes what is called a *truth table* in set-theoretic terminology (Ragin 2008; Schneider and Wagemann 2012). It is utilised in this form in fsQCA, to which I turn next.

I performed fsQCA on the truth table, applying the *Fuzzy* module for Stata designed by Longest and Vaisey (2008). The module utilises fuzzy sets logic (Ragin 2008) to identify the alternative configurations of dimensions (solutions) consistent with the outcome (which in our case is defined by the share of electoral support for authoritarian populist parties). These solutions are next simplified. This is achieved by eliminating the dimensions that are spurious: when they appear both in a positive and in a negative form, then two particular solutions can be combined into a simpler one, eliminating the dimension for which all its range is allowed. The latter situation implies simply that they play no role in explaining the outcome.

Importantly, unlike the standard regression technique that is based on correlations and assumes symmetry (positive outcomes need to be associated with positive, and negative with negative), fsQCA does not have the symmetry restriction. Instead, fsQCA is consistent with the set-theory and the formal logic requirements, because it does not follow that if A implies B then *not A* implies *not B*. Thus, the standard regression technique is logically flawed wherever the zero point is meaningful and the range contains both positive and negative values; fsQCA is not, and the mid-point (0.5) in transformed data corresponds to the zero point and is called maximum ambiguity (or crossover) point, because there is evidence neither for a given set (dimension) membership nor for a lack of it (Schneider and Wagemann 2012).

The solutions (the simplified configurations of dimensions consistent with the outcome) should be interpreted as *sufficient conditions*[7] for the outcome (in the sense of the definition given above), and there may be many of them; that is, there may be many paths or configurations associated with a given outcome. This important feature is termed equifinality (Ragin 2008, 2014).

5.1.2 Results

The results are presented in Table 28.1, in a form that has become conventional in the applied literature; see Decker et al. (2020), for example. A black circle implies that a dimension is present as a sufficient condition for the outcome (the share of support for authoritarian populist parties), while a white circle implies that an absence of a dimension is a sufficient condition for the outcome. Empty space implies that the dimension plays no role in a given solution.

The configurations (solution sets) that I present in the rows of Table 28.1 are conservative. It is common in fsQCA to simplify the solutions further by utilising additional assumptions related to the counterfactual and possible outcomes of combinations not presented in the data (see Ragin 2008). However, these simplification methods are often questionable (Schneider and Wagemann 2012). Moreover, I did not feel that I had strong enough priors for any simplifications. Hence, the solutions are solely based on the information in the data and, as a result, they remain relatively complex. At the same time, without going beyond the results obtained in the analysis, we can still present some interesting lessons.

First, the results are consistent with empirical work coming from political science on the role of legal origin. Clague et al. (2001) estimate that common law legal origins increase the probability of democracy by 0.368 (ibid., p. 27). Consistent with this, all five of our solutions include civil law legal origin as associated with higher electoral support for populism.

Second, solutions 1 and 2 offer very clear economy-based paths to populism which explain patterns that can be found in Southern European countries (Greece, Italy, Portugal and Spain). For both of these solutions, we have high unemployment and high income inequality as two important dimensions.

---

[7] In fsQCA, it is also possible to perform the analysis in terms of necessary conditions. A condition is interpreted as necessary if set membership in it is either equal to or larger than each case membership in the outcome (Schneider and Wagemann 2012).

This is consistent with regression results obtained by Algan et al. (2017). Nonetheless, it is not a complete picture. These negative social outcomes need to be combined either with a low level of government redistribution or with low level median incomes to result in support for populism.

Third, Central Eastern European authoritarian populism is harder to explain with economic dimensions alone. One distinctive feature that characterises solutions 4 and 5 compared with solutions 1 and 2 is that a high share of Catholics emerges as an important condition. Thus, in the last two solutions of Table 28.1, we have a combination of post-Communism and Catholicism that proves fertile ground for the authoritarian populist projects

Table 28.1 The configurations of dimensions (solutions) associated with the share of support for authoritarian populist parties in Europe

Dimension	Solution				
	S1	S2	S3	S4	S5
Civil law origin	●	●	●	●	●
Post-Communist	○	○	○	●	●
High share of Catholics			○	●	●
High unemployment	●	●		○	○
Income inequality	●	●		●	●
Government spending	○			○	●
High median income		○	○	○	●
Best fit	Greece, Italy, Portugal	Greece, Portugal, Spain			
Consistency	0.871	0.910	0.901	0.806	0.818
Coverage, raw/ unique	0.329/0.048	0.291/0.007	0.238/0.031	0.085/0.023	0.081/0.019

Notes:

(1) Poland and Hungary are the closest fits in the data for solutions 4 and 5 correspondingly, but with the following differences. In both countries income inequality is in the medium rather than high range. Likewise, government spending has been in the medium range for Poland and Hungary, but higher for Hungary, and median income has been relatively low in both countries (all as of 2017). In other words, here the fit is driven more by institutional dimensions than economic factors

(2) Solution consistency indicates a better fit, where a perfect fit would imply a value of 1. A conventional benchmark for consistency to be considered acceptable is 0.75 (75%)

(3) Raw coverage shows how much of the outcome is covered by a given solution (with the upper limit being 1, or 100%). Unique coverage for a given solution is a part that is covered only by a given solution and not by others

in the region. This is the case of Hungary and Poland, the two clear-cut populist governments with authoritarian tendencies. Economic dimensions are
present, but there is not such a close match with country characteristics as in
Southern Europe. Rather, it is the culture-based theme, as discussed above: a
combination of the heritage of social atomisation inherited from Communism,
with stress on hierarchy and lack of respect for democratic values embedded
in local version of Catholicism.

Last but not least, there is a limit on what the fsQCA we applied could
explain. We offer an explanation of why populists gained strength in the
Eastern and Southern part of the EU, but from Fig. 28.3 we can see there are
also some Northern and Western countries that are not that far behind—for
example, Austria, Denmark or France. More work and thinking about a
different set of explanatory dimensions may be needed to explain these
additional cases.

5.1.3   A Further Empirical Illustration

Considering the economic dimensions, as confirmed above, we may now
focus on high income inequality combined with low government spending.
These economic dimensions are illustrated for all European countries in
Fig. 28.4. It corresponds to the factors highlighted by Solution 1.

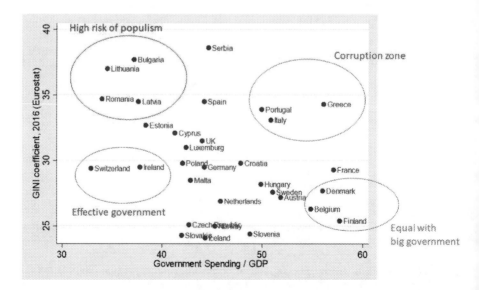

Fig. 28.4 Inequality and government spending in Europe, 2017

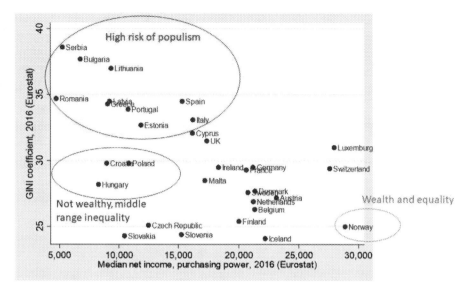

Fig. 28.5 Inequality and level of development in Europe, 2017

On Fig. 28.4, we may identify countries that are at risk of populism. These should be the countries with high income inequality and low level of government spending. We find four former Soviet blocks countries in this group: Bulgaria, Romania, Latvia and Lithuania.

However, we may follow the logic of Solution 2 instead, and emphasise high inequality combined with relatively low level of incomes (Fig. 28.5). Here, we are able to capture a larger number of both Southern European, and Eastern and Central European countries forming a group characterised by high risk of populism. Hungary and Poland are both in the group of European countries with a relatively low level of income. Yet, for both countries the level of income inequality is in the medium range. Thus, while they are now located close to the high risk group, they are still below it in terms of income inequality. It seems that to explain populism we need culture and history as well, as argued above.

6   Conclusions

The critical factor is that, so far, the populists in the EU and on its fringes are not engaged in politics of mass violence, even if in terms of rhetoric, they clearly borrow some themes from their more radical cousins, either Fascists or Bolsheviks. A policy common to all authoritarian populists, both on the right and the left, is the onslaught on the independence of courts and the free media. Whereas populists on the right are engaged in a nationalistic and xenophobic rhetoric of exclusion, those on the left define 'us vs. others' in terms of class warfare, even if anti-capitalist and anti-globalisation features position them as natural allies for their nationalist cousins. Thus, both share the same themes and sometimes find common ground. Both left-wing and right-wing populist parties aim to destroy the rule of law, to take over the state administration and the media, and to entrench themselves in power. To achieve this, the modern-day populist relies more on clientelism than on macro-economic cycles with a sequence of initial gains and later economic cost. Yet, they do not resort to mass violence, unlike populists in Latin America (Maduro in Venezuela, for example), which means it is an open question how stable these regimes will turn out to be. While peaceful exit from populism is difficult, it is not impossible in countries like Hungary and Poland, where populists have already scored some local defeats.

Support for authoritarian populist parties in Europe has been steadily growing since the global financial crisis of 2007–2008, according to the Timbro Institute, from an average of 15% to 23% per country in 2019. That would suggest that economic factors have played a role, consistent with the literature (e.g. Algan et al. 2017). Yet there is also a visible jump during the 2015 refugee crisis, which we could not capture in the cross-sectional list of factors above, as it influenced public opinion regardless of whether a given country was directly affected or not. Noticeably, since the refuge crisis, the increase in support for populism has been driven entirely by the growing strength of right-wing populism, which now dominates over the left wing (16.0% versus 6.7%), reversing the proportions observed in the 1980s and 1990s. At the same time, as illustrated by Fig. 28.3, Romania and Slovakia are the two countries that saw high support for populists in the early 1990s, yet in both cases it decreased significantly later. Thus, changes are not unidirectional.

The analysis I have presented above suggests that the growth of populism cannot be explained by economic factors alone, but that history and some cultural traits also play a role, especially for the Central European countries. Some other traits of collective memory and culture may also play in the opposite direction. Progress in the demolition of democratic institutions has been slowed down by social self-mobilisation in Poland, more so than in Hungary, thanks to the collective and individual memories of the Solidarity movement.

In these two countries, as elsewhere, external attitudes matter. The entrenchment of Orbàn in Hungary, turning his country into what he labels an 'illiberal democracy' and Freedom House describes as a politically partly free system, was facilitated by tolerance and some support of European conservatives who needed Orbàn in the European Parliament. Shouldn't European conservatives think wider? Isn't Europe connected?

It was Orbàn's strategy of weakening democratic institutions, the rule of law and independent media that Kaczyński aimed to copy in Poland, albeit with less success due to a lower level of support. These two political entrepreneurs were helped by the post-crisis recovery. Their resilience to less favourable economic circumstances, such as an economic crisis, has yet to be tested. Besides, the EU institutions now pay more attention to the ascent of authoritarian populism, and as long as these countries remain in the EU, they may be challenged in the future by decisions from the Court of Justice of the European Union and the European Commission. As long as the economic gains from EU membership are high, and there is support from the local population for the EU, it is a factor constraining the local candidates for autocrats, preventing them from adopting more violent political strategies, so distinguishing European populism from that in Latin America, and again making potential exit relatively easier.

More generally, while good economic policies that lead to development with widely shared gains is important in weakening support for populists in opposition, it is not the only dimension, and focusing policies on the economy alone may actually leave space for authoritarian populism to grow, as illustrated by the development in Poland before 2015. The key strength of populist movements is that they offer a sense of unifying purpose, while the democratic parties facing them too often descended into a competing plethora of claims based on identity politics (Lilla 2018). Ascending populists often face a fragmented opposition with little common ground.

Yet neither cultural traits nor even economic interests should be considered as given and in some way mechanically represented in the electoral process. As emphasised by Müller (2017), both ideas and interests are formed, modified and shaped by public debate, and by access to objective information. Ultimately, preserving and developing these two features, and the related social skills of reasoning and fact-based decision-making, will be critical for the success of the young democratic project of the last two hundred years of modernity.

Appendix

Table 28.2 Data used in the analysis (in the initial format)

Country	Populist vote in 2017 (Timbro)	Civil law origin (La Porta et al. 2008)	Post-Communist (Douarin and Mickiewicz 2017)	Share Catholic, 2017 (PEW)	Unemployment 2016 (Heritage/ WSJ)	GINI coefficient, 2016 (Eurostat)	Government Spending/ GDP (Heritage/WSJ)	Median net income, PPP, 2016 (Eurostat)
Austria	20–30%	1	0	74%	5.7	27.2	19.3	23,112
Belgium	0–10%	1	0	49%	8.7	26.3	9.6	21,313
Bulgaria	10–20%	1	1	1%	9.8	37.7	58.4	6746
Croatia	0–10%	1	1	84%	16.1	29.8	31.3	8982
Cyprus	20–30%	0	0	3%	15.6	32.1	48.8	16,178
Czech Rep.	20–30%	1	1	21%	5.2	25.1	45.3	12,476
Denmark	20–30%	1	0	4%	6.3	27.7	5.7	21,333
Estonia	0–10%	1	1	1%	5.9	32.7	55.8	11,870
Finland	10–20%	1	0	0%	9.6	25.4	0.0	19,995
France	20–30%	1	0	60%	10.6	29.3	2.0	20,624
Germany	10–20%	1	0	42%	4.6	29.5	41.4	21,179
Greece	50–60%	1	0	0%	24.9	34.3	5.4	9063
Hungary	50–60%	1	1	56%	7	28.2	25.3	8271
Iceland	0–10%	1	0	4%	4.4	24.1	41.1	22,182
Ireland	0–10%	0	0	75%	9.5	29.5	57.1	18,330
Italy	30–40%	1	0	78%	12.1	33.1	22.3	16,213
Latvia	10–20%	1	1	23%	9.8	34.5	57.4	9234
Lithuania	10–20%	1	1	75%	9.5	37.0	64.1	9360
Luxemburg	0–10%	1	0	67%	5.9	31.0	46.0	27,973
Malta	0–10%	1	0	89%	5.4	28.5	44.9	17,204
Netherlands	10–20%	1	0	20%	6.1	26.9	37.0	21,195

Norway	10–20%	1	0	1%	4.2	25.0	38.5	28,875
Poland	40–50%	1	1	87%	7.4	29.8	46.9	10,854
Portugal	20–30%	1	0	77%	12.1	33.9	25.1	10,799
Romania	0–10%	1	1	5%	6.9	34.7	65.3	4728
Serbia	10–20%	1	1	4%	19	38.6	40.3	5248
Slovakia	10–20%	1	1	66%	11.3	24.3	47.2	10,469
Slovenia	0–10%	1	0	74%	9.3	24.4	28.6	15,249
Spain	20–30%	1	0	60%	21.9	34.5	41.4	15,333
Sweden	10–20%	1	0	2%	7.4	27.6	21.7	20,752
Switzerland	30–40%	1	0	55%	4.3	29.4	67.5	27,602
UK	0–10%	0	0	17%	5.5	31.5	41.9	17,369

References

Acemoglu, D., & Robinson, J. A. (2012). *Why Nations Fail: The Origins of Power, Prosperity, and Poverty*. London: Profile Books.

Ádám, Z. (2019). Re-Feudalizing Democracy. An Approach to Authoritarian Populism Taken from Institutional Economics. *Journal of Institutional Economics*. Early View. https://doi.org/10.1017/S1744137419000304.

Aganin, A., & Volpin, P. (2005). The History of Corporate Ownership in Italy. In R. Morck (Ed.), *A History of Corporate Governance Around the World: Family Business Groups to Professional Managers* (pp. 325–366). Chicago: University of Chicago Press.

Algan, Y., Guriev, S., Papaioannou, E., & Passari, E. (2017). The European Trust Crisis and the Rise of Populism. *Brookings Papers on Economic Activity, 2*, 309–400.

Bagehot, W. (1965 [1872]). Physics and Politics. In N. S. John-Stevas (Ed.), *The Collected Works of Walter Bagehot*. Aylesbury: Hazell Watson and Viney Limited.

Bałtowski, M., Kozarzewski, P., & Mickiewicz, T. (2020). State Capitalism with Populist Characteristics. Poland and Hungary. In M. Wright, G. Wood, A. Cuervo-Cazurra, P. Sun, I. Okhmatovskiy, & A. Grosman (Eds.), *Oxford Handbook on State Capitalism and the Firm*. Oxford: Oxford University Press.

Bjørnskov, C. (2019). Populism: Three Approaches to an International Problem. *Economic Affairs, 39*(2), 273–281.

Boeri, M. T., Mishra, M. P., Papageorgiou, M. C., & Spilimbergo, M. A. (2018). *Populism and Civil Society*. Working Paper WP/18/245. International Monetary Fund.

Burke, E. (1986 [1790]). *Reflection on the Revolution in France*. London: Peguin.

Clague, C., Gleason, S., & Knack, S. (2001). Determinants of Lasting Democracy in Poor Countries: Culture, Development, and Institutions. *The Annals of the American Academy of Political and Social Science, 573*(1), 16–41.

Dahrendorf. (2007). Acht Anmerkungen zum Populismus. *Eurozine*. Retrieved from https://www.eurozine.com/acht-anmerkungen-zum-populismus/?pdf.

De Montesquieu, C. (1989 [1748]). *The Spirit of the Laws*. Cambridge: Cambridge University Press.

Decker, S., Estrin, S., & Mickiewicz, T. (2020). The Tangled Historical Roots of Entrepreneurial Growth Aspirations. *Strategic Management Journal*, early online.

DiMaggio, P. J., & Powell, W. W. (Eds.). (1991). *The New Institutionalism in Organizational Analysis*. Chicago: University of Chicago Press.

Dornbusch, R. & Edwards, S. (1989). The Macroeconomics of Populism in Latin America. World Bank Working Paper No. 316.

Dornbusch, R., & Edwards, S. (1990). Macroeconomic Populism. *Journal of Development Economics, 32*(2), 247–277.

Dornbusch, R., & Edwards, S. (Eds.). (1991). *The Macroeconomics of Populism in Latin America*. Chicago: University of Chicago Press.

Douarin, E., & Mickiewicz, T. (2017). *Economics of Institutional Change: Central and Eastern Europe Revisited*. Cham: Springer.

Dumas, C. (2018). *Populism and Economics*. London: Profile Books.

Fukuyama, F. (1989). The End of History? *The National Interest, 16*, 3–18.

Fukuyama, F. (2015). *Political Order and Political Decay: From the Industrial Revolution to the Globalization of Democracy*. London: Profile Books.

Fukuyama, F. (2018). *Identity: The Demand for Dignity and the Politics of Resentment*. New York: Farrar, Straus and Giroux.

Goldberg, P. A. (1975). The Politics of the Allende Overthrow in Chile. *Political Science Quarterly, 90*(1), 93–116.

Guiso, L., Sapienza, P., & Zingales, L. (2010). *Civic Capital as the Missing Link*. NBER Working Paper Series No. 15845. Cambridge, MA: National Bureau of Economic Research (NBER).

Harrison, A., McLaren, J., & McMillan, M. (2011). Recent Perspectives on Trade and Inequality. *Annual Review of Economics, 3*(1), 261–289.

Hiel, A. V., & Mervielde, I. (2002). Explaining Conservative Beliefs and Political Preferences: A Comparison of Social Dominance Orientation and Authoritarianism. *Journal of Applied Social Psychology, 32*(5), 965–976.

Kalecki, M. (1954). *Theory of Economic Dynamics. An Essay on Cyclical and Long-run Changes in Capitalist Economy*. London: Unwin Brothers Limited.

Kelsen, H. (2013 [1929]). *The Essence and Value of Democracy*. Lanham, MA: Rowman & Littlefield.

La Porta, R., Lopez-de-Silanes, F., & Shleifer, A. (2008). The Economic Consequences of Legal Origins. *Journal of Economic Literature, 46*(2), 285–332.

Lilla, M. (2018). *The Once and Future Liberal: After Identity Politics*. Oxford: Oxford University Press.

Longest, K. C., & Vaisey, S. (2008). Fuzzy: A Program for Performing Qualitative Comparative Analyses (QCA) in Stata. *Stata Journal, 8*(1), 79.

Maritain, J. (2012). *Christianity and Democracy, the Rights of Man and Natural Law*. San Francisco: Ignatius Press.

Marx, K. (2008 [1875]). *Critique of the Gotha Program*. Wildside Press LLC.

Mazur, K. (2016). *Jarosław Kaczyński – ostatni rewolucjonista III RP*. Kraków: Klub Jagielloński. Retrieved from https://klubjagiellonski.pl/2016/01/18/jaroslaw-kaczynski-ostatni-rewolucjonista-iii-rp/.

Müller, J. W. (2017). *What Is Populism?* London: Penguin.

Ragin, C. C. (2008). *Redesigning Social Inquiry: Fuzzy Sets and Beyond*. Chicago, IL: University of Chicago Press.

Ragin, C. C. (2014). *The Comparative Method: Moving Beyond Qualitative and Quantitative Strategies*. Oakland: University of California Press.

Rodrik, D. (2018). Populism and the Economics of Globalization. *Journal of International Business Policy, 1*(1–2), 12–33.

Rosenblum, N. L. (2010). *On the Side of the Angels: An Appreciation of Parties and Partisanship*. Princeton: Princeton University Press.

Rousseau, J. J. (2018 [1762]). *The Social Contract and Other Later Political Writings*. Cambridge: Cambridge University Press.

Sachs, J. D. (1989). *Social Conflict and Populist Policies in Latin America*. NBER Working Paper No. 2897.

Schmitt, C. (1988 [1923]). *The Crisis of Parliamentary Democracy*. Cambridge, MA: MIT Press.

Schneider, C. Q., & Wagemann, C. (2012). *Set-Theoretic Methods for the Social Sciences: A Guide to Qualitative Comparative Analysis*. Cambridge: Cambridge University Press.

Sen, A. K. (2009). *The Idea of Justice*. Cambridge, MA: Harvard University Press.

Somin, I. (2016). *Democracy and Political Ignorance: Why Smaller Government Is Smarter*. Stanford: Stanford University Press.

Spooner, M. H. (1999). *Soldiers in a Narrow Land: The Pinochet Regime in Chile*. Berkeley: University of California Press.

Sztompka, P. (1996). Looking Back: The Year 1989 as a Cultural and Civilizational Break. *Communist and Post-Communist Studies, 29*(2), 115–129.

Ziblatt, D. (2017). *Conservative Political Parties and the Birth of Modern Democracy in Europe*. Cambridge: Cambridge University Press.

29

Does Emigration Affect Political and Institutional Development in Migrants' Countries of Origin?

Artjoms Ivlevs

1   Introduction

On 10 August 2018, tens of thousands of people gathered in Romania's capital Bucharest for a major protest against the government and its plans to ease the fight against corruption. While initially conceived as a peaceful demonstration, the rally soon turned violent as protesters tried to enter the government building and clashed with the police. A remarkable feature about this anti-corruption, anti-government protest was that it was organised and promoted by the Romanian diaspora groups. Mobilised through social media under the motto 'Diaspora at Home', Romanians living and working abroad planned their holidays and took spontaneous flights to participate in the protest (Agerpres 2018; Balkaninsight 2018; Reuters 2018; The Guardian2018). Similarly to their non-migrant counterparts, migrants have been appalled and frustrated about the extent of corruption and low-quality governance in their home country. Many of the 3–5 million Romanians living abroad left the country because of the weak economy and poor governance, and many want to return—one day—to a place that is well functioning and focused on the well-being of citizens.

A. Ivlevs (✉)
Bristol Business School, UWE Bristol, Bristol, UK
e-mail: a.ivlevs@uwe.ac.uk

© The Author(s) 2021   **761**
E. Douarin, O. Havrylyshyn (eds.), *The Palgrave Handbook of Comparative Economics*,
https://doi.org/10.1007/978-3-030-50888-3_29

Well-functioning democratic institutions, manifested, among other things, by the rule of law, freedom of expression and control of corruption, are key for the prosperity and well-being of people. Corruption, for example, is recognised as one of the greatest obstacles to growth and development, and a great deal of policy effort is directed toward reducing it across the world. The organisation of the anti-corruption protest by Romania's diaspora groups and migrants' participation in it highlights that both non-migrants and migrants care about the political-institutional development of their home country. The Romanian migrants' 'Diaspora at Home' protest is probably one of the most direct ways in which emigrants may influence political processes and institutional development at home. There exist, however, a number of other, often less direct, channels through which migration may affect institutional quality back home. The objective of this chapter is to review the growing theoretical and empirical literature on this question. Does emigration affect the political and institutional development back home? What are the underlying mechanisms? Does money sent by migrants matter? What is the role of migrant characteristics?

The chapter starts with an overview of two major theoretical frameworks—Hirschman's 'Exit, Voice and Loyalty' and Levitt's 'Social Remittances'—as well as other conjectures, mainly related to migrants' monetary remittances, that scholars have used to explain the effects of emigration on political and institutional development back home. I then provide a summary of the growing empirical evidence on the question, paying particular attention to the issues of causality, and identify gaps and suggest areas for future research. This review aims explicitly at bringing together the knowledge produced by various disciplines within social science, for the most part economics, political science and sociology. These disciplines have often studied the question of political-institutional effects of emigration in parallel, but not always actively talked to each other; one of the aims of this chapter is to contribute to the dialogue across disciplines. In this work, I use a broad definition of migration (which encompasses, for example, student migration) and a broad range of outcomes to capture political-institutional development (e.g. indexes for democracy and institutional quality, electoral outcomes such as voter turnout and voting for particular parties, and attitudes to, and experience of, corruption).

Overall, this chapter aims to provide a comprehensive, up-to-date, critical review of the theoretical and empirical literature on the effects of emigration on home country political-institutional development. It is the first of its kind in a rapidly growing area of research[1] and, hopefully, it will inform and guide all those interested or willing to advance this field of enquiry.

2   Theoretical Perspectives

2.1   Hirshman's 'Exit, Voice and Loyalty'

Hirshman's model of 'Exit, Voice and Loyalty' posits that people dissatisfied with the quality of a service provided by any type of organisation can either 'exit', that is, seek a new service provider with a better-quality service, or 'voice', that is, communicate the dissatisfaction directly to the service provider in hope that latter will listen and improve its performance (Hirschman1970). One of the important insights of the framework is that, once 'exit' opportunities become available, it is usually the most 'vocal' people who exit, meaning that 'exit' reduces the amount of 'voice' remaining in a particular social environment and the quality of the service provided is likely to deteriorate further. This central idea of the Hirschman's model can be directly applied to study the links between emigration and political-institutional development at home. Migration here can be viewed as an 'exit' option for people dissatisfied with the political situation, institutions or governance at home. As the dissatisfied people also tend to be more activist and vocal, their 'exit' will result in less pressure and 'voice' exercised over the ruling authorities. So, emigration may lead to political-institutional drain, that is, weaker institutions and governance in the countries of origin. Furthermore, some governments may wish to be proactive in reducing 'voice' that threatens their existence and expel critics and dissidents abroad; emigration could thus be used as a safety valve to relieve political tension (Kapur2014).

However, migrants do not completely 'exit' their country of origin. Falling communication and transportation costs allow migrants to develop, and maintain, transnational spaces and communities, and participate in the social, economic and political life both at home and abroad. In this context, initial migrant 'exit' can strengthen 'loyalty'—emotional attachment to the home country—and empower 'voice', encouraging migrants to directly influence political and institutional processes in their country of origin (Burgess 2012; Kapur2014). Hoffmann (2010) argues that the externalised 'voice' of the

---

[1] I acknowledge an excellent policy brief by Lodigiani (2016). I expand on her work by considering contributions from a broader range of disciplines (in particular, political science) and a broader range of institutional outcomes (in particular, corruption).

diaspora returns to the home country in an internationalised form and has a stronger political impact. Indeed, migrant diasporas are known to have successfully influenced political processes in their countries of origin, at times playing major roles in processes of independence, statehood and democratic reform (Shain and Barth 2003; Hladnik 2009; Kapur2014). At a more local level, home town associations—host-country organisation of migrants from the same town or region—may not only provide economic support for their hometowns, but also get involved in local politics challenging the existing political power structures (de la Garza and Hazan2003).Furthermore, through their interaction with host-country governments, diasporas may influence the distribution of foreign aid (Lahiri and Raimondos-Møller 2000), which in turn could affect home country institutions (Jones and Tarp2016). Taken together, emigration has a potential to bring about political change and improvements in governance.

The ruling authorities may be well aware of the spectre of challenges to the status quo by the internationally empowered migrant 'voice' and design emigration policies accordingly. Taking a historical example, in the Kingdom of Serbs, Croats and Slovenes of the 1920s, an influential emigration policy proposal towards the pro-Bulgarian Macedonian minority (Bulgarophiles) was as follows: 'If the Bulgarophiles' organization is more vigorous in America than here, it is better to keep them at home and vice versa' (Miletic 2009, p. 110). Also, if governments want to keep their citizens in the country (e.g. because this assures a steady inflow of budget revenues), they may proactively improve governance and institutions. In this case the *prospect* of emigration would lead to better political-institutional outcomes.

Overall, looking through the lens of Hirshman's 'Exit, Voice and Loyalty' model, emigration could weaken domestic political-institutional environment if less 'voice' is left in the country or strengthen it if migrant 'voice' returns empowered to the country of origin. In addition, where migrant 'exit' options can be controlled, governments may encourage or discourage emigration of 'vocal' people to keep the quality of governance at the desired level. In this case, the quality of institutions would affect migration.

2.2   Levitt's 'Social Remittances'

In her seminal work, Levitt (1998) defines social remittances as 'ideas, practices, identities, and social capital that flow from receiving- to sending-country communities' (p. 927). The transmission of social remittances involves several stages. First, depending on the degree of social interaction among people in the host country, migrants become exposed to the norms and practices of the host society, challenge their original views and ultimately adopt new ideas and behaviours. Then, through correspondence, visits and return migration, these new or modified norms and practices are transferred from migrant host to home communities. While one would expect most exchanges to happen at the family level—arguably, family is the most important bridge linking migrants to their home countries—Levitt emphasises that the range of social remittance recipients goes well beyond the migrant household. Specifically, the diffusion of ideas, norms and practices can occur through local institutions, such as community centres and churches, as well as from migrant to non-migrant households.

Based on qualitative research conducted in Boston, US, and a village in the Dominican Republic, Levitt finds that migrants transfer notions of gender identity and intra-family responsibility, principles of community participation and norms about the work of clergy, judges and politicians. Several conditions need to be satisfied for the migration-driven transfer of political-institutional (and any other) norms and practices to happen. First, they must be different in the host and home countries. This is likely to be the case for the most common type of migration—from poorer to wealthier countries—as the societies of most high-income countries are typically characterised by better, more efficient, more transparent institutions and governance. It is, however, possible that migrants go to a country that is more developed economically but not institutionally. This implies that migrants can transfer both 'good' and 'bad' institutions—depending on their quality in migrants' host countries.

Second, migrants have to be exposed to the host country's political-institutional norms and practices, challenge their original views and adopt the new practices and ways of thinking about institutions. These processes will be easier if migrants are well integrated into the host society and more difficult if the contact with locals is limited. Third, there must be enough opportunities for information to be exchanged between the home and host communities— they include migrants visiting relatives back home, circular and return migration, friends and relatives visiting migrants in the host countries, calls, correspondence and so on. This condition is likely to be satisfied, as for some time migration has been viewed as a transnational phenomenon. Falling communication and travel costs make it easier to develop and maintain transnational spaces and communities (Vertovec2004) and participate in the social, economic and political life both at home and abroad.

Levitt (1998) also argues that not all migrants transmit norms and ideas in the same way. For example, migrants sending monetary remittances back home might be better able to influence the social behaviour of their family members. Following this line of reasoning, Ivlevs and King (2017) distinguish between *conditionality* effect, whereby monetary remittances senders may influence the behaviours and norms of those staying behind as the livelihoods of the latter depend on the money received from abroad, and *communication* effect, whereby monetary remittances imply closer links and more frequent communication between migrants and their family members back home, making value transfer more effective.

Taken together, Levitt's 'social remittances' framework suggests that migrants can influence political-institutional development at home through social learning and cross-border diffusion of values, norms and practices. It is important to emphasise however that depending on the level of institutional development at destination, both 'bad' and 'good' institutional practices can theoretically be transmitted, that is, emigration may contribute to worse institutional outcomes if this is what migrants are exposed to and absorb at destination. That this does occur in practice is suggested by Barsbai et al. (2017) on Moldovan emigration to Russia[2] and Karakoç et al. (2017) on Egyptian migration to Saudi Arabia, and it will be discussed later.

2.3   The Role of Monetary Remittances

Scholars have advanced several other channels through which emigration may affect the political-institutional development of home countries, and many of these channels are related to the receipt of remittances—money (or in-kind goods) that migrants send to family members staying in the countries of origin. For example, Pfutze (2012) develops an argument where the recipients of monetary remittances become less reliant on government clientelistic networks (ruling parties offering money or material goods in exchange for political support) and start voting for opposition parties. Specifically, monetary remittances increase household income and reduce the marginal utility of consumption, meaning that the ruling party has to offer compensation of greater value in exchange for political support. If governments' resources are limited, the clientelistic relationships will erode and remittance recipients may start voting for opposition parties and against prevailing political regimes. In a similar vein, Merino (2005) argues that the receipt of remittances reduces the importance of redistributional policies, making the remittance recipients more likely to vote according to ideological preferences. At the same time,

---

[2] The same effect might apply to the substantial migration into Russia from other former Soviet republics, but no empirical studies exist on that.

Goodman and Hiskey (2008) contend that remittance recipients disengage from formal political processes when they become less reliant on state as a provider of social services and public goods. However, Goodman and Hiskey (2008) also argue that those staying behind will develop a greater engagement in local civic groups that often serve as intermediaries in the emergent transnational communities.

The receipt of monetary remittances can also affect the extent of corruption in remittances receiving countries. Ivlevs and King (2017) outline several mechanisms through which remittance receipt may affect corruption experience of migrant family members staying behind. First, remittances may increase the demand for public services (e.g. if remittances are used to start a new business, buy property, enrol in education, undergo treatment in the hospital) and therefore the likelihood of paying bribes. In addition, once the contact with public officials has taken place, the probability of bribe payments may further increase if public officials consider remittance recipients as lucrative targets and solicit bribes or if remittance receivers are more willing and able to pay bribes to get higher-quality services quicker. The latter conjecture corroborates the prediction of the theoretical model of Höckel et al. (2018), where receiving monetary remittances enables people to afford informal payments to teachers in state schools, implying that remittances would lead to greater corruption in the public education sector.

At the same time, remittances may enable people to consume private sector alternatives to publicly provided goods, if such alternatives exist (e.g., private education or medical treatment). While the theoretical framework of Abdih et al. (2012) predicts that such shifts towards private goods will make authorities less accountable and eventually make corruption more widespread at the country level, the incidence of bribery for remittance-receiving households may instead go down. Tyburski (2012) argues that receiving remittances changes the balance of power between the state and citizens, with the latter becoming more willing to hold governments to account and corruption in this case will go down.

3   Migration and Political-Institutional Change: Evidence

Empirical evidence on the political-institutional effects of migration has grown rapidly over the last 10–15 years. There are several ways in which one could structure a summary of this evidence: according to discipline (economics, politics, sociology), type of analysis (qualitative, quantitative, causal, correlational), the world region/country type investigated (Latin America, post-Socialist countries, Africa, developing countries), type of migration (labour, refugee, student, high skilled, low skilled, return, accompanied by monetary remittances or not) and the level of influence (macro/country, local/community/region, micro/household). It is the latter categorisation that I consider most intuitive and clear and, therefore, adopt in this study. In what follows, I first summarise the evidence at the country level, then at the community/region level, and finally at the individual/household level. While looking at individual contributions, I will pay particular attention to whether the evidence provided can be considered causal or correlational.

3.1   Effects of Emigration on the Country-Level Political-Institutional Outcomes

In this section, I review empirical macro-level studies relating aggregate flows of migration or monetary remittances to outcomes such as the prevalence of democracy, democratic transitions and corruption.

Docquier et al. (2016) study the relationship between emigration and democracy at the country level. Using a sample of 104 developing countries in an unbalanced five-year-interval panel spanning the period between 1985 and 2010, Docquier et al. (2016) find that greater country-level emigration has a positive effect on three de facto indicators of country-level democracy/institutional quality (The Freedom House's 'Political Rights' and 'Civil Liberties' indicators, and the Simon Fraser Institute's Economic Freedom of the World Indicator) but not the de jure indicator (the 'Polity 2' Indicator of the Polity IV Project). This relationship holds for different types of migrants (high-skilled and low-skilled), different time periods and different country sub-samples (e.g. transition economies, sub-Saharan countries). In terms of magnitude, a 10 percentage point increase in the emigration rate increases the indicators of democratic and institutional quality by 5 percentage points in the short run and 15–20 percentage points in the long run. Finally, Docquier et al. (2016) find that the results are driven by emigration to the Organisation for Economic Co-operation and Development (OECD) countries, characterised by liberal democracies, rather than emigration to non-OECD countries. These results can be considered causal: to deal with endogeneity that could arise due to reverse causality (democracy driving emigration) or omitted variable bias (third factors driving both democracy and emigration), Docquier et al. (2016) use alternative instrumental variable estimations, whereby emigration is predicted by geography-related variables (such as distance between countries) interacted with time dummies (to reflect changing migration and communication costs), weather-based variables (natural disasters and temperature deviations) and internal instruments in a system GMM estimation, all of which yield consistent estimates of the effects of emigration on democracy back home.

Spilimbergo (2009) explores the relationship between the numbers of students going to study abroad and the level of democracy in home countries. Using the Freedom House Political Right index as an indicator of democracy in a five-year-interval panel for 183 countries spanning the period 1960–2005 in a system GMM estimation, that uses internal instruments to establish causality, Spilimbergo (2009) finds that students going abroad promote democracy in home countries, but only if foreign education is acquired in democratic countries. This result corroborates Docquier et al. (2016), pointing to the key role of host country characteristics in determining the political-institutional effects of migration. In a similar vein, Mercier (2016) studies the relationship between the migration experience of political leaders and the evolution of democracy during their leadership. Drawing on an original dataset on the characteristics of political leaders in 110 developing countries over the period 1960–2004, Mercier (2016) uncovers a positive link between leader's experience of staying abroad and the increase in the democracy score of the country (the Polity Score from the Polity IV project) in initially autocratic settings. The result is driven by studies (rather than exile, diplomatic or military stays) in high-income OECD countries, and of relatively long duration (more than two years). Mercier (2016) addresses the issue of potential reverse causality (future leaders returning because the country is becoming more democratic) by investigating whether democratisation is a factor affecting the likelihood that a leader studies abroad and finds that this is not the case. For the omitted variable bias, Mercier (2016) tests for the existence of several confounders—regional shocks, specific characteristics of leaders, dynastic political systems and intervention of foreign countries—potentially affecting both stays of leaders abroad and democratisation, and finds no evidence that these factors matter. Overall, these robustness checks reduce the likelihood that the reported effects are biased due to an omitted variable, although they do not guarantee a causal nature of the results.

Beine and Sekkat (2013) explore the link between bilateral migration and changes in four measures of institutional quality (the World Bank Governance Indicators: 'Voice and Accountability', 'Government Effectiveness', 'Regulatory Quality' and 'Control of Corruption') for all developing and developed countries, between 1994 and 2004. Implementing instrumental variable estimations, where emigration is predicted with country size, a dummy for low-income countries, a dummy for tropical countries and a dummy for countries having a British legal system, Beine and Sekkat (2013) find a positive effect of migration on all measures of institutional quality except 'Voice and accountability' where the effect is negative. The latter result is consistent with Hirschman's 'Exit and Voice' model, whereby migrants deplete the amount of 'voice' in left in a society and the associated capability to put pressure on governments. In addition, Beine and Sekkat (2013) also find the effects on institutional quality (negative for 'Voice and accountability' and positive for the remaining three outcomes) to be stronger for skilled migration and for developing countries. The analysis also allows for a direct test of the effects of quality of institutions in migrant receiving countries, which are found to be important (i.e. home countries benefit more if migrants go to countries with higher institutional quality), especially when skilled migration is considered. The causal nature of the results in Beine and Sekkat (2013) cannot be guaranteed as the authors do not provide a discussion regarding whether their instruments can be considered exogenous to the institutional quality outcomes. Instead, they rely on the overidentification (Sargan) test only. The evidence provided in this study should therefore be interpreted with caution.

Using the same measures of country-level institutional quality as Beine and Sekkat (2013), but focusing on migrant monetary remittances rather than migration in general, Abdih et al. (2012) perform a cross-sectional, instrumental variable analysis of 111 countries for 2000. The coastal area of a country is claimed to affect remittances (through higher migration) but not directly institutional quality and used as an instrument for remittances. Abdih et al. (2012) find that higher ratios of monetary remittances to GDP result in lower indices of control of corruption, government effectiveness and rule of law, that is, lower levels of institutional quality and governance. This finding supports the theoretical prediction that remittances allow households to substitute publicly provided goods with private alternatives, reducing incentives to hold governments to account. Berdiev et al. (2013) corroborate these results, drawing on a panel (1986–2010) estimation of 111 countries. They conclude that monetary remittances increase corruption at the country level (measured by the corruption index from the International Country Risk Guide), especially for non-OECD countries. The results of Berdiev et al. (2013) are estimated with a system of simultaneous equations in which remittances and corruption are both considered endogenous. While the authors claim that method addresses issues of endogeneity, this would be contested by some and causality cannot be guaranteed.

Escribà-Folch et al. (2015) study how migrant monetary remittances affect transition to democracy in autocratic settings. Drawing on data on 137 autocratic regimes in from 1975 to 2009, they find that greater levels of per capita remittances are associated with transitions to democracy and voting for opposition parties in a specific type of autocracy—dominant-party regimes (such as Mexico until 2000, Vietnam, China, Tunisia, Angola)—and not, for example, in personalist dictatorships (such as Azerbaijan, Russia, Tajikistan, Libya, Uganda).[3] Dominant-party regimes are some of the most common and resilient autocracies in the world, characterised by the dominant party exercising some power over the leader, distributing public services to large numbers of people in exchange of political support (clientelism), as well as holding elections allowing for opposition parties to participate. Escribà-Folch et al. (2015) argue that remittances allow severing clientelistic ties between the state and voters, and voting for opposition parties which, in turn, is more likely to lead to democratic transitions. To deal with potential endogeneity, Escribà-Folch et al. (2015) instrument remittances to autocratic regimes with the country's coastal and fertile soil areas, interacted with the trend of remittances sent to OECD countries, and argue that this composite instrument is exogenous to regime changes in autocracies. A broadly similar result, albeit based on correlational analysis, is obtained by Bastiaens and Tirone (2019), who find that the democratising effect of remittances is strong for mixed regime types and not present for countries that are highly autocratic.

Overall, the evidence presented so far is broadly consistent with theoretical models predicting a positive effect of migration on political-institutional outcomes and holds especially when migration is skilled and to countries with better institutional outcomes. The results on monetary remittances are more ambiguous, reflecting mixed theoretical expectations, and may depend on the type of political regime at home. Most contributions try to address the issues of potential endogeneity and, despite the fact that the usefulness of different techniques and instruments used to establish causality can often be assessed only subjectively, results presented so far go well beyond correlational evidence. I will return to the interpretation of these and other empirical results in Sect. 4 of this chapter, and now change to the overview of the local (regional and community)-level evidence.

---

[3] The classification of autocracies here follows Geddes et al. (2014).

3.2   Effects of Migration on the Local-Level (Regions/ Communities) Political-Institutional Outcomes

The analyses of the local-level political-institutional effects of migration have usually drawn on the local-level administrative data on electoral participation and voting for particular parties in a single country context. Most evidence to date comes from Mexico. For example, Goodman and Hiskey (2008) explore the relationship between the municipality-level intensity of migration (a summary measure used by CONAPO—the National Population Council of Mexico—to categorise Mexican municipalities according to their migration activity between 1995 and 2000) and voter turnout rates for the 2000 municipal elections. They find that greater local-level emigration intensity is associated with lower voter turnout, attributing the finding to the migration-driven 'political brain drain', as predicted by Hirshman's 'Exit and Voice' model. The results in Goodman and Hiskey (2008) are correlational, meaning that they could in fact be biased by endogeneity, and there is no guarantee that emigration has a causal effect on voter turnout. It is indeed possible that people emigrate from politically marginalised areas (reverse causality) or that other unaccounted-for local-level factors drive both emigration and political participation (omitted variable bias). Continuing with the case of Mexico, Pfutze (2012) studies the effect of the municipality-level share of migrant households (sourced from the 2000 Mexican Population Census) and the victories of the main state party (Institutional Revolutionary Party/PRI) and oppositional parties in Mexico municipal elections, conducted in 2000, 2001 and 2002. Using instrumental variable analysis, where local-level emigration intensity is predicted with historical (1924) region-level emigration rates and the distance to a major historical point of entry to the US (El Paso), Pfutze (2012) finds that more migrants at the municipality levels lead to a greater likelihood of victories by opposition parties. The results also reveal that greater migration intensity at the local level leads to an early opposition victory, that is, a greater probability that a municipality had a non-PRI majority by 1994/1997. In a series of additional analyses, Pfutze (2012) does not provide support for the hypothesis that the beneficial effects of migration on voting for opposition parties occur through social remittances ('social learning') and argues instead that migrant remittances may undermine the clientelistic relationship between the state and remittance receivers. Further meso-level evidence on Mexico is provided by Tyburski (2012), who finds that, in 2001–2007, the Mexican states receiving more remittances witnessed downward corruption trends (as measured by a survey-based index of bribe payments by citizens to officials providing public services). This evidence is correlational: while potential endogeneity is acknowledged, no convincing strategy to deal with it is provided. As for the conceptual framework behind the results, Tyburski, similarly to Pfutze (2012), argues that remittances reduce households' dependence on state programmes and clientelism. In turn, this encourages voting for opposition parties and increases government accountability.

Barsbai et al. (2017) focus on Moldova, one of the successor states of the Soviet Union to explore how emigration affected voting for the Communist and pro-democracy/pro-European parties at the municipal level. The analysis relies on what the authors argue is a quasi-natural experiment: a large and sudden outflow of Moldovans to Russia and Western European countries in the aftermath of the 1998 Russian Financial crisis. Although there were specific factors (ethnic networks and trading networks across the Moldovan-Romanian border) that affected migrants destination choice after the crisis hit, political preferences do not appear to be one of them. In particular, Barsbai et al. (2017) show that the size and direction (to Russia or the West) of the post-1998 emigration flows, as captured by the 2004 Moldovan Population Census, were not related to voting patterns for pro-Communist and pro-Western parties in the 1998 municipality elections (which took place before the crisis hit), meaning that there was no political self-selection of migrants. The authors then relate the intensity of the 2004 municipality-level emigration to Russia and Western countries to the municipality-level vote for the Communist party in 2009–2010. They find that the local-level emigration intensity to Western countries reduces voting for the Communist party, especially where migrants go to countries with the highest democratic standards (e.g. to Germany, France, the Netherlands, the UK and the US as opposed to Italy, Romania, Bulgaria and Poland). The effect of emigration to Russia on the vote for the Communist party tends to be positive but is not as robust as the effect of emigration to the West on anti-Communist vote, which among other things could be attributed to the fact that the Communist party is far from being the main political force in Russia. Overall, given that migrants in Moldova go to more democratic Western countries and less democratic Russia, Barsbai et al. (2017) attribute their results to 'cultural transmission and information diffusion' of political preferences, in other words 'social remittances'.

In one of the rare studies addressing the political-institutional effects of migration in sub-Saharan Africa, Chauvet and Mercier (2014) explore the local-level effects of return migration on political participation and electoral competitiveness. Relating the 1998–2009 commune-level change in return migration to the change in voter turnout rates, as well as two measures of electoral competitiveness—an index of fragmentation of votes given to different running lists, and the winning margin (the difference between the share of votes obtained by the winning and second lists)—Chauvet and Mercier (2014) find that voter turnout and political competitiveness increase with the intensity of local-level return migration. Similarly to Barsbai et al. (2017), Spilimbergo (2009), Docquier et al. (2016), Beine and Sekkat (2013) and Mercier (2016), the effects are driven by returnees from countries with more advanced democratic regimes (e.g. Western Europe), which lends further support for Levitt's 'social remittances' hypothesis. In addition, Chauvet and Mercier (2014) find that the impact of migration on electoral outcomes goes beyond returnees' own participation: returnees are shown to have a greater effect in areas where non-migrants are poorly educated; this further supports the conjecture that migrants transfer political norms from host to home countries and communities. All the results of Chauvet and Mercier (2014) are supported by instrumental variable estimations, where current local-level rates of return emigration are predicted with their 11-year lagged values.

Overall, the local/regional/community-level evidence supports the hypothesis that migration leads to an improvement in home country political outcomes, especially if migrants go to countries with better institutions. The evidence on the effect of monetary remittances is mixed again, and only one study in this area goes beyond correlational results. A broader discussion of these findings will follow in Sect.4, and now I turn to the household/individual-level evidence.

3.3 Effects of Migration on Individual/Household-Level Political-Institutional Outcomes

The studies looking at the individual-level effects of emigration on political-institutional outcomes (norms, attitudes, behaviours) of those staying behind have traditionally relied on household surveys, and more rarely experiments, administered in one or a group (of usually related) countries. In one of the early contributions, Batista and Vicente (2011) test for the effect of emigration on demand for government accountability in Cape Verde. Specifically, they administered an experiment where respondents were given a postcard and asked to mail it to a specified address. The respondents were informed that if more than 50% of the cards were posted, the results of the accompanying household survey on corruption would be published in national media; the costly action of mailing the postcard would capture the desire for better governance/government accountability. Batista and Vicente (2011) then relate the likelihood of sending the card to migration at the local level. They find that the demand for political accountability is higher in localities where migrants go to (and return from) countries with better governance, specifically the US as opposed to Portugal. These findings are confirmed by instrumental variable estimations, where emigration at the local level is predicted with the macroeconomic variables at destination weighted by five-year lagged local migration network indicators. It is therefore unlikely that omitted variables or reverse causality are driving the results.

Focusing on Morocco, Tuccio et al. (2019) study the relationship between respondents' social and political norms (based on questions such as 'Are you happy with how Morocco is administered?' and 'I think people should be more involved in the decision-making process') and the fact that a household has a return or current migrant. The authors use a multi-equation mixed system to address various selections: into emigration, into return migration and into specific destinations. They further address endogeneity by using foreign labour market attractiveness and conflicts/unfavourable changes in host-country legislation as exclusion restrictions for emigration and return migration, respectively. Tuccio et al. (2019) find that having a return migrant from a Western country increases household members' demand for social and political change (as measured by an index of social and political norms) while having a current migrant in a non-Western country reduces the demand for such change. These findings lend support for the Levitt's 'social remittances' hypothesis (Levitt1998), highlighting that the level of political-institutional development of destination countries matters and that both good and bad values and practices can be transmitted. Similarly, Karakoç et al. (2017) find that, in Egypt, emigration of household members to Gulf countries, and in particular Saudi Arabia (a destination of more than a third of Egyptian migrants), is associated with a greater likelihood of voting for Islamist parties. The authors claim that emigration from Egypt to Saudi Arabia has affected the religious orientation of those left behind, as well as their support for parties sceptical of democracy. The results presented in the paper are based on a correlational analysis of a cross-sectional survey and should therefore be treated with caution: reverse causality, whereby migrants from households with more radical religious views choose to go to the Gulf countries, may be driving the results.

Ivlevs and King (2017) explore the effects of household emigration on the experience of, and attitudes towards, bribery in six successor states of former Yugoslavia. It is a rare study addressing the effects of both household member migration and receiving monetary remittances. Ivlevs and King (2017) find that having relatives abroad reduces the probability of paying bribes to public officials, renders bribe-taking behaviour by public officials less acceptable and reduces the probability of being asked for bribes by public officials. In other words, emigration of household members has corruption-reducing effects among those staying behind, which the authors explain with Levitt's 'social remittances' (Levitt1998)—the migration-induced transfer of corruption norms and practices from host to home countries (most international migrants from former Yugoslavia go to industrialised Western countries, where corruption levels are lower than at home). Further findings suggest that receiving monetary remittances does not change the beneficial effects regarding bribe paying and attitudes towards corruption but counteracts the beneficial effect on bribe solicitations by public officials, suggesting that remittance recipient households become attractive bribe extortion targets for public officials. The effects of migration and monetary remittances can thus work in opposite directions. Höckel et al. (2018) corroborate the finding that emigration leads to less bribery in Moldova, showing, in particular, that parental migration leads to a reduction in informal payments to schoolteachers, which the authors attribute to the migration-induced change in corruption norms. Both Ivlevs and King (2017) and Höckel et al. (2018) address potential endogeneity by estimating instrumental variable models, where emigration of household members and receipts of monetary remittances are predicted with the *network-growth* instrument (an interaction between historical local-level migration networks and GDP growth at migrant destinations).

Ivlevs and King (2020) look at the relationship between emigration intentions, foreign work experience and having relatives abroad, on the one hand, and willingness to join the EU in the successor states of former Yugoslavia. The authors argue that joining a supranational institution, such as the EU, is likely to foster political and institutional development of migrants' origin countries. Ivlevs and King (2020) find that prospective and return migrants, as well as people with relatives abroad, are more likely to vote favourably in a hypothetical EU referendum, and people with relatives abroad are more likely to consider EU membership a good thing. The results are driven by migration to and from the EU. One of the conclusions of the study is that emigration is likely to contribute to the political and institutional development of the migrant countries of origin through raising support for joining the EU. While Ivlevs and King (2020) provide novel evidence on the links between emigration and willingness to join a supra-national institution, their results are correlational and should be treated with caution. For example, it cannot be excluded that migrants come from household characterised by the desire of institutional change or people choose to migrate to the EU because they come from more pro-European households—in those cases, reverse causality would bias the results upward, increasing the magnitude of the identified relationship.

Finally, Córdova and Hiskey (2015) use household survey data from six Latin American countries to delve into precise mechanisms through which migrants may affect political behaviours back home. They find that people with stronger international ties (as measured by frequency of communication with relatives in the US) are more likely to attend a local government meeting, identify with a political party and persuade others to vote for a party or candidate. Further analyses suggest that stronger cross-border social ties are a positive determinant of community involvement, political interest, political efficacy (greater sense of self-confidence in understanding political affairs) as well as Internet usage and knowledge of international political affairs, all of which feed into local political participation of those staying behind. Overall, Córdova and Hiskey (2015) highlight that not only the quality of institutions at destination but also frequency of communication between migrants and their family members back home are central for a transfer of cross-border norms and practices to take place. While the evidence provided by Córdova and Hiskey (2015) is correlational, the key role of communication is confirmed by the instrumental variable analysis of Batista et al. (2019). Using exposure to droughts as a source of exogenous variation for migration, they find that, in Mozambique, it is the chatting networks (chatting regularly to migrant household members) rather than kinship networks (having family links to migrant household members) that improve a range of measures of political attitudes and behaviours. Interestingly, as the vast majority of migrants from Mozambique go to South Africa (where the quality of political institutions is far from perfect but higher than in Mozambique), Batista et al. (2019) argue beneficial political effects of emigration are possible even in the case of South-South migration.

Taken together, the micro-level evidence supports the conjecture that emigration has a positive effect on home-country institutions, especially when migrants go to countries with higher quality of institutions. Communication between migrants and non-migrants appears to be an important factor in this relationship, giving further support to the 'social remittances' hypothesis. Only one study has explicitly addressed the effect (on corruption) of receiving monetary remittances and found that it counteracts the beneficial effect of emigration. Not all evidence reviewed in this sub-section can be considered causal and the results should therefore be interpreted with caution.

4   Discussion

There now exists a compelling theoretical base and solid, and growing, empirical evidence on the effects of emigration on the political-institutional development in migrant home countries. One of the most common findings that emerges analyses at all levels (country, local/regional, household) is that migrants going to countries with better governance are more likely to have a positive effect on the quality of institutions back home. This finding supports Levitt's 'social remittances' hypothesis (Levitt1998) that migrants transfer values, norms, behaviours and practices from migrant host to home countries. This should be good (or alarming) news for policymakers and authorities in many developing countries. In a typical case where migrants go to wealthier countries and wealthier countries have higher quality of institutions, emigration can be expected to contribute to a positive political-institutional change in the countries of origin. It should be remembered, however, that the political-institutional gains can be limited, or even reversed, if migrants go to countries that are wealthier but lag behind institutionally (e.g. Egyptians to Saudi Arabia); this type of findings again supports the prediction of the 'social remittances' framework that both good and bad practices can be transmitted—depending of what kind of institutions migrants are exposed to and absorb at destination.

There is much less evidence for the hypothesis that emigration reduces voice at home, which would be the basic prediction of Hisrchman's model of 'Exit and Voice' model. However, a prediction of an extended Hirschman's model—that migrant voice gets empowered abroad and returns home capable of affecting political landscape and institutions—is indirectly supported by various empirical studies showing that migration positively affects political-institutional development at home. From this point of view, the 'return of internationalised voice' à la Hirschman and 'the migration-driven cross-border diffusion of values, norms and practices' à la Levitt are not mutually exclusive, as in both cases migrants learn, absorb and transmit back home norms and practices of the destination.

A less clear picture—both theoretically and empirically—emerges when we consider the effect on home country institutions of migrant monetary remittances. In a widely accepted theoretical argument, monetary remittances reduce recipients' reliance on public services and government handouts, weakening clientelistic ties and changing the balance of power between the state and its constituents. This, however, could lead to both lower and greater incentives to hold governments to account and thus increase or decrease the level of political engagement of monetary remittance recipients. Interestingly, both predictions find at least some empirical support. Similarly, when the institutional outcome interest is corruption, especially at the household level, monetary remittances can be expected to have either good or bad repercussions. For example, it has been argued, and shown empirically, that recipients of monetary remittances can become bribe extortion targets for corrupt public officials, reversing institutional gains generated by the diffusion of corruption norms and practices (Ivlevs and King2017). Research on this front is, however, still in its infancy, and future work could focus more on disentangling the political-institutional effects of receiving monetary remittances from those of migration in general.

The individual-level determinants of absorption, adaptation and transfer of norms at destination are another less-well explored area in the debate. For example, in a theoretical extension of the 'social remittances' framework, Levitt and Lamba-Nieves (2011) argue that prospective migrants' experiences before migrating influence what they absorb at the destination and subsequently remit back home. Future research could provide more empirical evidence on this and several other related questions: Does the degree of migrant integration in the host countries and communities matter for transfer of norms and practices? Do migrants characteristics—gender, education, migration type (e.g. economic vs forced)—matter both for the absorption and transfer of norms? There is only limited evidence in this regard—see, for example, Chauvet et al. (2016) on the role of Malian migrants' personal attributes and living conditions for adoption of political norms in France and Cote d'Ivoire. More studies focusing on the political-institutional experiences of migrants in the host countries, rather than those staying behind in the countries of origin, will be beneficial for advancing the field.

Another question that has received relatively little attention in the broader enquiry on the political-institutional effects on migration is whether institutional environment at home drives emigration (e.g. see Cooray and Schneider (2016), Barsbai et al. (2017), Douarin and Radu (2020) and European Bank for Reconstruction and Development (2019) for some evidence). At a theoretical level, Hirschman's 'exit and voice' model predicts that it is people who are most dissatisfied with the quality of home institutions who will try to emigrate. Future research could provide more direct and systematic evidence of whether this is the case. Such evidence would not only offer validity to Hirschman's model's key prediction, but also help address the endogeneity-due-to-reverse-causality concerns commonly raised in the empirical studies on the political-institutional effects of emigration.

Potential endogeneity—due to either reverse causality (low-quality institutions pushing migrants to go abroad) or omitted factors driving both emigration and institutions—has been rightly seen as a major obstacle for determining causal effect of emigration on political-institutional development back home. Traditionally, scholars in economics have been explicitly trying to address endogeneity, often by using the instrumental variable approach. The commonly used instruments have included migration networks, often coupled with migration pull and push pull factors, such as macroeconomic conditions at destination and climatic factors at home. Finding a valid instrument is a notoriously difficult task and no formal statistical tests exist to assess instrument exogeneity, so ultimately a subjective judgement has to be made on whether instruments affect the outcome of interest directly. Compared to economists, scholars in political science and sociology have been preoccupied with endogeneity less, but tended to provide richer, more nuanced theoretical frameworks on how emigration might affect institutions back home. Probably because of the differences in appreciating causal evidence (much greater emphasis in economics),[4] the communication between the two camps has remained limited. Yet, they could talk more and learn from each other. Economists, for example, are still only tentatively—if at all—referring to Levitt's 'social remittances' framework when explaining the political-institutional effects of emigration, despite the wide acceptance and use of this model in other social sciences. On the other hand, sociologists and political scientists could be more cautious with using causal language and providing policy recommendations if the evidence is correlational.

Finally, I would like to highlight the variety of terms currently used to describe the political-institutional (and other social) effects of emigration: social, political, institutional, cultural, non-monetary remittances; social learning; diffusion, transmission of ideas, knowledge, practices; diaspora externalities. While such variety does not necessarily represent a problem, future research could pay more attention to the meaning of specific terms. For example, do the terms 'remittances' and 'transmission' imply migrant agency (i.e. migrants purposefully want to transfer norms and practices) while the terms 'externalities' and 'diffusion' do not (i.e. the norms and practices are transferred unintentionally and independently of migrants' will)?

To conclude, there is now considerable evidence that emigration affects the quality of institutions and political developments in the countries of origin; the effect is more likely to be positive if migrants go to countries with better governance. This evidence calls for a (re)consideration of broader, direct and

---

[4] The correlational evidence is also important as it reveals "stylised facts" that need to be explained.

indirect, impacts of emigration on the developing world. It can also help design national and international migration policies which provide political-institutional benefits to migrant-sending countries and communities and contribute to their development.

References

Abdih, Y., Chami, R., Dagher, J., & Montiel, P. (2012). Remittances and Institutions: Are Remittances a Curse? *World Development, 40*(4), 657–666.

Agerpres. (2018). Romanians from Abroad Gather in Bucharest; Rally in Piata Victoriei Announced on Social Media. Retrieved from https://www.agerpres.ro/english/2018/08/10/romanians-from-abroad-to-gather-in-bucharest-rally-in-piata-victoriei-announced-on-social-media%2D%2D158677

Balkaninsight. (2018). Thousands Join Romanian Diaspora Anti-corruption Protest. Retrieved from https://balkaninsight.com/2018/08/10/romanian-diaspora-rally-gathers-thousands-in-bucharest-08-10-2018/

Barsbai, T., Rapoport, H., Steinmayr, A., & Trebesch, C. (2017). The Effect of Labor Migration on the Diffusion of Democracy: Evidence from a Former Soviet Republic. *American Economic Journal: Applied Economics, 9*(3), 36–69.

Bastiaens, I., & Tirone, D. C. (2019). Remittances and Varieties of Democratization in Developing Countries. *Democratization, 26*(7), 1132–1153.

Batista, C., Seither, J., & Vicente, P. C. (2019). Do Migrant Social Networks Shape Political Attitudes and Behavior at Home? *World Development, 117*, 328–343.

Batista, C., & Vicente, P. C. (2011). Do Migrants Improve Governance at Home? *World Bank Economic Review, 25*(1), 77–104.

Beine, M., & Sekkat, K. (2013). Skilled Migration and the Transfer of Institutional Norms. *IZA Journal of Migration, 2*, 9.

Berdiev, A. N., Kim, Y., & Chang, C. P. (2013). Remittances and Corruption. *Economics Letters, 118*(1), 182–185.

Burgess, K. (2012). Migrants, Remittances and Politics: Loyalty and Voice after Exit. *Fletcher Forum of World Affairs, 36*(1), 43–55.

Chauvet, L., Gubert, F., & Mesplé-Somps, S. (2016). Do Migrants Adopt New Political Attitudes from Abroad? Evidence Using a Multi-sited Exit-Poll Survey During the 2013 Malian Elections. *Comparative Migration Studies, 4*(1), 1–31.

Chauvet, L., & Mercier, M. (2014). Do Return Migrants Transfer Political Norms to Their Origin Country? Evidence from Mali. *Journal of Comparative Economics, 42*(3), 630–651.

Cooray, A., & Schneider, F. (2016). Does Corruption Promote Emigration? An Empirical Examination. *Journal of Population Economics, 29*(1), 293–310.

Córdova, A., & Hiskey, J. (2015). Shaping Politics at Home: Cross-Border Social Ties and Local-Level Political Engagement. *Comparative Political Studies, 48*(11), 1454–1487.

De la Garza, R., & Hazan, M. (2003). *Looking Backward, Moving Forward: Mexican Organizations in the US as Agents of Incorporation and Dissociation.* The Tomas Rivera Policy Institute.

Docquier, F., Lodigiani, E., Rapoport, H., & Schiff, M. (2016). Emigration and Democracy. *Journal of Development Economics, 120*, 209–223.

Douarin, E.,&Radu, D. (2020). *Drivers of Political Participation: Are Prospective Migrants Different?* UCL Centre for Comparative Studies of Emerging Economies (CCSEE)—Working Paper Series.

Escribà-Folch, A., Meseguer, C., & Wright, J. (2015). Remittances and Democratization. *International Studies Quarterly, 59*(3), 571–586.

European Bank for Reconstruction and Development. (2019). *The Transition Report 2019–2020: Better Governance, Better Economies.* London: European Bank for Reconstruction and Development.

Geddes, B., Wright, J., & Frantz, E. (2014). Autocratic Breakdown and Regime Transitions: A New Data Set. *Perspectives on Politics, 12*(2), 313–331.

Goodman, G., & Hiskey, J. (2008). Exit Without Leaving: Political Disengagement in High Migration Municipalities in Mexico. *Comparative Politics, 40*(2), 169–188.

Hirschman, A. (1970). *Exit, Voice, Loyalty Responses to Decline in Firms, Organizations, and States.* Cambridge, MA: Harvard University Press.

Hladnik, M. (2009). From a Dollar Bill in an Envelope to a Petition to the White House: The Significance of Slovenian Migrants for Those Back Home. In U. Brunnbauer (Ed.), *Transnational Societies, Trans Territorial Politics. Migrations in the (Post-)Yugoslav Region, 19th–21st Century.* Munich: R. Oldenbourg Verlag.

Höckel, L. S., Santos Silva, M., & Stöhr, T. (2018). Can Parental Migration Reduce Petty Corruption in Education? *World Bank Economic Review, 32*(1), 109–126.

Hoffmann, B. (2010). Bringing Hirschman Back In: "Exit", "Voice", and "Loyalty" in the Politics of Transnational Migration. *The Latin Americanist, 54*(2), 57–73.

Ivlevs, A., & King, R. (2017). Does Emigration Reduce Corruption? *Public Choice, 171*(3–4), 389–408.

Ivlevs, A., & King, R. (2020). To Europe or Not to Europe? Migration and Public Support for Joining the European Union in the Western Balkans. *International Migration Review, 54*(2), 559–584.

Jones, S., & Tarp, F. (2016). Does Foreign aid Harm Political Institutions? *Journal of Development Economics, 118*, 266–281.

Kapur, D. (2014). Political Effects of International Migration. *Annual Review of Political Science, 17*, 479–502.

Karakoç, E., Köse, T., & Özcan, M. (2017). Emigration and the Diffusion of Political Salafism: Religious Remittances and Support for Salafi Parties in Egypt during the Arab Spring. *Party Politics, 23*(6), 731–745.

Lahiri, S., & Raimondos-Møller, P. (2000). Lobbying by Ethnic Groups and Aid Allocation. *The Economic Journal, 110*(462), C62–C79.

Levitt, P. (1998). Social Remittances: Migration Driven Local-Level Forms of Cultural Diffusion. *International Migration Review, 32*(4), 926–948.

Levitt, P. & Lamba-Nieves, D. (2011). Social Remittances Revisited. *Journal of Ethnic and Migration Studies, 37*(1), 1–22.

Lodigiani, E. (2016). The Effect of Emigration on Home-Country Political Institutions. *IZA World of Labor, 2016*, 307.

Mercier, M. (2016). The Return of the Prodigy Son: Do Return Migrants Make Better Leaders? *Journal of Development Economics, 122*, 76–91.

Merino, J.(2005). *Transition to Democracy Under a Clientelistic Autocracy: Remittances in the Making of Independent Citizens in Mexico*. Working Paper, APSA Annual Meeting 2005.

Miletic, A. (2009). (Extra-)Institutional Practices, Restrictions and Corruption. Emigration Policy in the Kingdom of Serbs, Croats, and Slovenes (1918–1928). In Brunnbauer, U. (Ed.), Transnational Societies, Transterritorial Politics. Migrations in the (Post-)Yugoslav Region, 19th–21st Century. Munich: R. OldenbourgVerlag.

Pfutze, T. (2012). Does Migration Promote Democratization? Evidence from the Mexican Transition. *Journal of Comparative Economics, 40*(2), 159–175.

Reuters. (2018). Anti-government Protest in Romania Turns Violent. Retrieved from https://www.reuters.com/article/us-romania-protests/anti-government-protest-in-romania-turns-violent-idUSKBN1KV1YO

Shain, Y., & Barth, A. (2003). Diasporas and International Relations Theory. *International Organization, 57*(3), 449–479.

Spilimbergo, A. (2009). Democracy and Foreign Education. *American Economic Review, 99*(1), 528–543.

The Guardian. (2018). Migrants Left for a Better Life. Now They Fight for a Better Romania. Retrieved from https://www.theguardian.com/commentisfree/2018/aug/22/romania-migrant-diaspora-protest-police-crackdown-corruption

Tuccio, M., Wahba, J., & Hamdouch, B. (2019). International Migration as a Driver of Political and Social Change: Evidence from Morocco. *Journal of Population Economics, 32*(4), 1171–1203.

Tyburski, M. D. (2012). The Resource Curse Reversed? Remittances and Corruption in Mexico. *International Studies Quarterly, 56*, 339–350.

Vertovec, S. (2004). Migrant Transnationalism and Modes of Transformation. *International Migration Review, 38*(3), 970–1001.

30

Understanding Tax Evasion: Combining the Public Choice and New Institutionalist Perspectives

Klarita Gërxhani and Ronald Wintrobe

1 Introduction

In the economic theory of tax evasion, individuals and corporations pay taxes only because they are forced to (i.e., because they believe that if they do not, they would be liable to prosecution by the state). If this were the case, it would be essential that the probability of being discovered for tax evading and the size of the penalty if caught and convicted are sufficiently large to deter evasion. One problem with this standard view is that for some taxes, such as self-reported income taxes, it is hard to believe that the probability of being caught for evasion is very large. In fact, all countries do encounter tax evasion, even those with the most sophisticated systems for gaining compliance. To illustrate, the United States Internal Revenue Service (IRS) estimates that the proportion of all individual tax returns that are audited was 0.5% in 2017 (down from 0.8% in 1990 and 4.75% in 1965). Civil penalties can add an additional 85% to the underpayment, depending on whether there is a specific misconduct such as negligence, substantial understatement, or substantial intentional wrongdoing. In very serious cases, criminal penalties may be

K. Gërxhani (✉)
Department of Political and Social Sciences, European University Institute,
San Domenico di Fiesole, Italy
e-mail: Klarita.Gerxhani@eui.eu

R. Wintrobe
Western University London, London, ON, Canada

© The Author(s) 2021
E. Douarin, O. Havrylyshyn (eds.), *The Palgrave Handbook of Comparative Economics*,
https://doi.org/10.1007/978-3-030-50888-3_30

applied. However, the penalties imposed are either small or infrequent (Alm 2019). Yet, the IRS estimates that, for the tax year 2015, 90.8% of income that should have been reported was in fact reported.[1]

Table 30.1 provides a comparison of the size of the shadow economy (total undeclared income), over the period 1991–2015, across developed, developing, and (former) transition countries. The table shows that shadow economy is particularly severe in developing countries. In Europe, countries from Central and Eastern Europe but especially those from the former Soviet Union appear to have the highest levels of shadow activities. Why is compliance lower in these countries? And why don't these countries simply raise the penalties for non-compliance and solve the problem that way?

An interesting literature has developed around these issues in recent years, centering around the idea that the willingness to pay taxes is culturally determined and differs across countries. Studies in this vein include Freidman et al. (2000), Alm and Torgler (2006), Frey and Torgler (2007), Gërxhani and Schram (2006), Hammar et al. (2009), Renooy et al. (2004), Torgler (2003), Torgler (2007), Torgler and Schneider (2009), Zhang et al. (2016), and Alm (2019). The willingness to pay taxes is sometimes viewed as a cultural norm or a product of values, which are specific to a particular country. This allows both estimates to be made of this variable (the willingness to pay taxes) and indirectly to get at the elusive and quasi-mystical concept of "culture" by providing a nice number quantifying at least one aspect of it—the propensity to pay taxes. Thus, Alm and Torgler (2006) suggest that the intrinsic motivation to pay taxes—their "tax morale"—differs across countries, and they provide evidence that this morale is much higher in the United States than in many European countries.

Table 30.1 The average size of the shadow economy, over the period 1991–2015, across developed, developing, and (former) transition countries

Countries/continents		Size as % of GDP
Developed	Old EU member states	16.1
(Former) Transition countries	Central and Eastern Europe	26.0
	Former Soviet Union	45.1
	Baltic States	23.7
Developing	Africa	39.2
	Latin America	38.9
	Asia	27.0

Source: Own calculations based on Medina and Schneider (2018, Table 18)

---

[1] All figures in this paragraph are from the Internal Revenue Service Data Book (2018).

Why these norms appear to differ so much is then a fundamental question. One idea is suggested by Kirchgässner (1999). He argues that in the northern states of Europe (in contrast to the south), state and religious authority were held by one person. Offenses against the state were therefore also religious offenses and consequently a sin. This "sinfulness" idea might explain why the propensity to pay taxes appears to be highest in the United States. Religiosity is much higher in the United States than in Europe. But this would be difficult to square with the fact that crime rates are also much higher in the United States. Also, in Canada, there is a similarly high propensity to pay taxes, but much lower levels of religiosity and crime.

Frey and Torgler (2007) view the payment of taxes as an example of "pro-social" behavior. They take a further step by suggesting that taxpayers are willing to pay their taxes conditionally, depending on the pro-social behavior of others. Put simply, people are more willing to pay taxes when they believe others are paying them. They develop an index of tax morale defined this way. Using survey data from a number of Western and Eastern European countries, they find a high (negative) correlation between perceived tax evasion and tax morale. They also relate tax morale to a number of variables, including political stability and the absence of violence, regulatory quality, and control of corruption.

In this approach, "trust" enters the picture because even if a government is expected to provide exactly what the citizen wants in the way of public programs, it is still usually rational for the individual to free ride and not pay her taxes if she expects she can get away with it. To put it differently, there is no way the "exchange" of taxes for services can be legally enforced at typical penalties for tax evasion, and raising penalties is not necessarily the right solution, as discussed later in the chapter. So trust in government, and in other citizens, that is, the belief that other citizens are going to pay their taxes, fills this gap. In this respect, our view can be linked to fiscal sociology and state capacity, which presents the development of the tax system and tax collection as the outcome of a continuous dialogue between the state and the wider population (see Moore 2004).[2] Moreover, our view can also be linked to new institutionalism, arguing that informal institutions, as captured in trust, determine the extent of tax compliance (Feige 1997). The importance of informal institutions is also stressed by Chhibber, for example: "Even when formal rules are similar, informal rules or social capital can in some situations explain a significant part of the reason why some societies progress faster than others"

---

[2] For a discussion of fiscal sociology applied to the transition region, see also Douarin and Mickiewicz (2017).

(Chhibber 2000, p. 297). We support this view by combining the public choice approach to the problem of tax evasion with a new foundation based on institutionalist insights such as those found in the literature on tax morale. The theoretical predictions we derive will be tested with a unique database for Albania where tax evasion and some informal institutions with respect to taxes are measured.

The chapter is organized as follows. The next section describes the economic theory of tax evasion. Section 3 describes the public choice approach. Section 4 takes us a step further in understanding the issue of tax evasion by introducing the concept of "trust-based political exchange", and providing precise definitions of trust and related variables like social capital. Section 5 tests two theoretical predictions established in the previous section. Concluding remarks and some policy implications follow in Sect. 6.

2   Economic Theory of Tax Evasion

The standard economic view of tax compliance in tax theory is that taxes are a "burden" or windfall harm. Individuals do not consider taxes in relation to the other side of the government ledger—expenditures. The chief problem in normative taxation theory is to devise taxes minimizing the "excess burden", that is, how to minimize the total burden of taxation.

In order to know more about this theory, let us have a look at the standard theoretical model (Allingham and Sandmo 1972; Yitzhaki 1974) in more detail. As is now common in the literature on tax evasion, the model visualizes an individual taxpayer facing a tax rate t on own income Y. If she chooses to evade taxes, she faces a punishment ftE, where E is the amount of unreported income and f is the size of the punishment (the fine rate) if caught. Thus, in one sense, the model adapts the standard crime model of Becker (1968) to the taxation case. In another sense, tax evasion is part of optimal portfolio choice: the individual who chooses to evade taxes in effect makes a risky bet that she will not be caught and convicted. However, the Yitzhaki (1974) model makes an odd prediction—namely, that an increase in the tax rate t actually leads to *less* tax evasion. This result holds in the model as long as individual absolute risk aversion decreases as income increases. This prediction is at variance with empirical evidence (e.g., Clotfelter 1983), the results of laboratory experiments (e.g., Friedland et al. 1978),[3] and, it would seem, even with com-

---

[3] In these experiments, the single most important factor resulting in evasion was the tax rate. On the other hand, raising the size of the penalty, even to exorbitant levels (e.g., from 3 to 15 times the amount

mon sense. However, the logic is simple once one realizes that in these models, tax evasion is treated as a risky gamble or a problem in optimal portfolio choice. The penalty if an individual is caught, ftE, is simply a constant multiple of the amount of tax evaded tE. As the individual is poorer as a result of the possibility of paying a higher penalty, this will make her take less risk and hence evade less at higher tax rates.

Of course, this relationship is derived from individual behavior and holds only at the individual level. The aggregate level of evasion may well move in a different direction as the level of tax also affects the *number* of taxpayers who choose to evade. One possible reason for this is that the "stigma" effect of tax evasion might be less at higher rates, as in effect rates are deemed to be so high by many that the stigma associated with avoidance is reduced (Benjamini and Maital (1985).

3 Public Choice Approach

The basic hypothesis of the field of economics known as "public choice" is that the citizens of democratic political jurisdictions perceive a connection between the taxes they pay and the government services they receive. In other words, citizens elect governments to provide them with goods and services and there is a certain sense in which every citizen must be aware that taxes must be paid to finance public services, whether they think their own burden is too high or low. This implies that every citizen knows that if taxes are reduced, a reduction in public services will follow.

One version of this approach is used by Cowell and Gordon (1988), who introduce public goods into the Yitzhaki model of tax evasion.[4] Their result is that if individuals display decreasing absolute risk aversion, the effect on tax evasion of an increase in the tax rate is positive or negative as public goods are under- or over-provided. Thus, if public goods are under-provided, an increase in tax rates means an increase in public goods as well. Individuals feel wealthier, and they wish to take more risk. Hence, they evade tax *more* when the increase in public goods and associated increase in tax rates makes them better off and *less* when it makes them worse off. However, this result remains at variance with the empirical evidence. The authors themselves find the result a bit counterintuitive and relate it to the fact that the relationship between

---

evaded), lowered the amount evaded and the probability of an under-declaration, but only marginally.

[4] Bordignon (1993) develops a "fairness" approach in which public goods are introduced as well. In this model, an increase in tax rates yields more evasion in accordance with the empirical evidence.

government and taxpayer has more dimensions than just the provision of public goods, something that their model does not capture (Gërxhani 2004a).

Note that in the public choice approach, it is still rational for each citizen to free ride, since whether she pays the taxes or not has little to do with the level of public services she receives. For example, suppose there are 1000 citizens in a jurisdiction and each one is supposed to pay taxes of $1000. Each citizen will reason that if she does not pay the taxes, *but everyone else does*, then her level of services will fall, but only by a tiny amount. This will hold if public services are constant cost and they are "pure" public goods, so that the non-tax paying citizen cannot be excluded from receiving services. Assuming services are shared equally, while an individual's own tax bill falls by 100%, her own level of services will fall by only 1/1000 = 0.1%. Consequently, it is rational for everyone to free ride and not pay the taxes independently of whether government services are delivered or not and whether other individuals pay or not.[5]

4   Introducing "Trust-Based Political Exchange"

It has become increasingly common to emphasize that social capital in general and trust in particular play an important role in the performance of an economy.[6] Several neo-institutionalists emphasize the importance of the relationship between informal institutions like trust (or rules of behavior, cultural norms) and formal institutions (i.e., laws, regulations). For example, Feige (1997) hypothesizes that more tax evasion will be observed when the two types of institutions are in conflict with each other. This hypothesis has found some empirical support (Gërxhani 2004b).

On this formulation, there is an exchange or an implicit contract between the citizenry and the government: the government provides goods and services to citizens in exchange for their support. In some versions of this type of model, the government tries to maximize this support, as in probabilistic voting models of the government sector.[7] In the aggregate, the government tries to maximize the sum of citizens' surpluses—value of public goods and services minus taxes—from the public sector. But how is this exchange between government and citizens enforced? That is where trust enters the picture.

---

[5] See Wittman (1995) for an explanation and description of the ways in which politicians can control free riding behavior.

[6] See Breton and Wintrobe (1982), Coleman (1990), North (1990), Fukuyama (1995), Knack and Keefer (1997), Putnam (1993, 2000), Chhibber (2000), Paldam and Svendsen (2000), and Frey (2002).

[7] See Mueller (1989), Chap. 11 for a good exposition of this type of model.

4.1 A Conceptual Discussion of Trust

To develop the argument in more detail, let us first give a more precise definition of trust. Trust arises between individuals in private transactions when there are difficulties of monitoring and enforcement and therefore always the possibility of cheating. One way that individuals solve this problem is through the accumulation of trust. Assume that $_aT_b^{1.00}$ represents the degree to which a person a trusts that another person, b, will not cheat him[8] on a transaction where the potential gain to b from cheating is \$1.00. We assume trust in this sense[9] has the following property:

$$0 < {_aT_b^{1.00}} < 1, that\, is, {_aT_b^{1.00}} \tag{30.1}$$

First, trust is measured in relative terms and ranges between zero and one. Note that this implies that trust between two persons is never zero (nonexistent) or one (perfect trust). Note also that the degree of trust is specified for a given opportunity to cheat (represented by the sum \$1.00). An individual may say in ordinary parlance that she trusts her grocer to always give her the correct change, but this does not mean she trusts him if the possible gain to the grocer is much larger than this (e.g., in a business deal worth millions). Presumably,

$$_aT_b^{1.00} >_a T_b^{2.00} \tag{30.2}$$

and so on for larger and larger opportunities for b to cheat. More generally,

$$_aT_b^y >_a T_b^x \text{ if } y < x \text{ where } x, y = \$.01, 1.00, 2.00,...\$\infty \tag{30.3}$$

For simplicity, in what follows, we assume that all the x's move up or down together, for example, if a believes that c is more likely to cheat her than b for a gain of \$5.00 ($_aT_b^{5.00} <_a T_c^{5.00}$), then she also thinks that c is more likely to cheat her when the gain is larger or smaller than this (e.g., $_aT_b^{\$100} <_a T_c^{\$100}$). Similarly, if something happens that raises a's trust in b when x is one value, say $x = \$5.00$, it raises it for all values of x. It is possible to think of exceptions to these ideas here, but if they were common, it is hard to know how people

---

[8] It is the trust a places in b; it is also b's trustworthiness according to a.

[9] "Trust" here is defined in the same way as first suggested in Breton and Wintrobe (1982). Some of the analytics here were introduced in Wintrobe (2006).

could use the word "I trust her" or "I trust him more than I do her" in every-day parlance as a shorthand for expressions like " $_aT_b^y$ " as we assume they do.

Despite the voluminous writings on trust in the last 20 years or so, there is still very little written on how trust may be accumulated. From the definitions here, it seems reasonable to suggest one way in which *the accumulation of trust* occurs between two persons (a *network*): when one party b has an opportunity to cheat another party a and doesn't take that opportunity. For example, if a and b trade with each other and transaction costs are non-zero, so there may be numerous opportunities for each of them to cheat one another, then this setting provides a natural opportunity for the two parties to accumulate trust. Thus, if b could have gained \$100 by taking an opportunity to cheat, then this is the amount she will have foregone by being honest, and therefore the amount invested in the trust relationship. The more opportunities that b fore-goes, the larger we can expect $_aT_b^x$ to be. Usually trust will be reciprocal: if a and b want to exchange, and they both have opportunities to cheat each other, they will both want to invest in a trust relationship. To the extent that they can build this relationship with each other, trust substitutes for legal contrac-tual enforcement. Trust is therefore a capital good, which permits trade to take place when enforcement and other transactions costs are high, or legal enforcement is simply unavailable.

Similar concepts of trust and processes of accumulation can be described for *general* trust, *social capital, social cohesion* or *solidarity, reciprocity,* and *con-ditional cooperation.* We discuss solidarity or social cohesion in the next sec-tion on political exchange. Here, we note that we can use the same notation for *generalized trust,* or *general social capital,* that is, the degree to which an individual trusts a stranger. This is the sense in which it is used by Fukuyama (1995) or Knack and Keefer (1997). This is just

$$_aT_j^x \ j = 1,...N, \ j \neq b, x = \$.01,1.00,2.00,...\$\infty \qquad (30.4)$$

where j represents any *stranger* rather than an individual b who is in a's net-work, or with whom a has a specific relationship. The community is repre-sented by members $j = 1, ... N, j \neq b$, and again the degree of trust is specified for a given opportunity to cheat (\$x). Of course, for people in a's network (the b's in Eq. (30.2) or (30.3)), the level of trust will be higher than this. But presumably if Eq. (30.4) and expressions like this for different members of the community were typically zero in a community, then it is hard to know how everyday activities like buying a dress or investing in a mutual fund could go on without a great deal of thought about how the contract will be enforced.

The level of trust will typically be higher in a network than it is for general-ized, impersonal contacts and contracts with other people whom a does not know. Indeed, a's *networks* may be defined precisely as all those people b for whom

$$_aT_b^x >_a T_j^x \; \text{ for any } x = \$.01, 1.00, 2.00, \ldots \$\infty \tag{30.5}$$

That is, a person may be said to be in another person (a's) *network* when a trusts her more than she does a stranger in the community.

Trust is also closely related to social capital. An individual a's stock of social capital is

$$\sum_b \left(_aT_b^x\right) + S_a^x \quad \text{where } j = 1, \ldots N, j \neq b \tag{30.6}$$

that is, the sum of her personal networks (the first term in Eq. (30.6)) and her degree of solidarity with the community (the same thing as the trust she extends toward strangers within the community).

The community's stock of social capital is

$$\sum_a \sum_b \left(_aT_b^x\right) + \sum_a {_aT_j^x} \tag{30.7}$$

that is, the sum of the networks of all of the individuals in the community plus the stocks of generalized trust within the community held by each indi-vidual. If, for simplicity, each person has the same level of generalized trust, then Eq. (30.7) may be simplified to

$$\sum_a \sum_b \left(_aT_b^x\right) + n_a T_j^x \tag{30.8}$$

It is immediately clear that the definition of social capital used by Coleman (1990) or Breton and Wintrobe (1982) neglects the second term, while the Fukuyama and Knack and Keefer type of definition excludes the first. And it is easy to imagine a society (Italy, Japan?) where individuals have strong per-sonal networks (the first term in Eq. (30.8) is high) but do not trust strangers (the second term is low). At the other extreme, one can imagine a society where individuals typically have a basic trust in strangers, but personal net-works are weak (the United States?). Indeed, if the formal institutions of a society (markets, courts, and governments) function efficiently, one might expect individuals to dispense to some extent with personal networks and rely on these institutions for many of their business activities. In that society, it would not be surprising if people exhibit a basic trust in strangers because the reputations of individuals are easily documented, redress can easily be had to well-functioning courts when one is cheated, governments support the possibility of individual formal transactions with infrastructure, and so forth. On the other hand, when these formal institutions do not work well, personal networks may be substituted for them. For example, Alesina and Giuliano (2010) argue that it has been documented that strong family ties have an important effect on many aspects of economic behavior, such as labor force participation. So it is not difficult to imagine that generalized trust and personal networks are sometimes inversely related because they are substitutes.

4.2   Adding Trust to Political Exchange

Now let us turn to the relationship between an individual taxpayer and the government. Let us first discuss the political exchange idea, which in fiscal sociology is known as "the exchange between taxation and representation (i.e., democratic rules and accountability)" (Moore 2004, p. 300). There is an exchange between citizens and government: Citizens pay their taxes and in exchange the government provides them with the goods and services they want. Thus, assume one public good S, for simplicity, is provided to the citizens of some jurisdiction. Since the good is public, all of the citizens in the jurisdiction must consume the same amount, whatever level the government desires to provide. Each citizen is assumed to be able to correctly calculate the tax price to her of a unit of the public good. At each tax price, each individual desires a particular level of the public good.

However, this "contract" is not enforceable. In particular, any government has numerous opportunities available for corruption, despite the safeguards involved if it is a democratic government and *a fortiori* if it is an authoritarian government. The solution which tends to be adopted here, we suggest, is the same as the solution in the private sector when contracts are not enforceable. A government which is in power for some time and proves to be honest can earn the trust of its citizens by foregoing opportunities to cheat them despite the infinite forms of corruption available to it. According to Easter (2002), the evolution of taxation in Poland in the early 1990s followed such a scenario. So we suggest that the process of accumulation of trust by a government with its citizens is similar to that in the private sector described above and results in a measure of trust by each citizen in their government:

$$_i T_g^y \quad \text{where } i = 1 \ldots n \tag{30.9}$$

where i indexes the n citizens in a particular jurisdiction, g is the government of that jurisdiction, and y indexes the size of the opportunity for that government to cheat, as before with a private citizen. Of course, different citizens will trust the government differently. The average level of trust by the n citizens in the government g for any *given* opportunity to cheat y is just

$$\sum_i \left(_i T_g \right) / n \tag{30.10}$$

Numerous measures of trust in governments as well as in other institutions and their pattern over time are presented in Putnam (2000) and the empirical literature which followed that work.

In the same way that citizens trust governments to a degree, governments also trust citizens to fulfill their part of the exchange, most basically by paying their taxes. This is

$$_g T_i^y$$

that is, the extent to which a government trusts a citizen i not to cheat for a given opportunity to evade taxes and profit by y. Average levels of tax compliance might provide a good measure of the extent to which government trusts its citizens in this sense. With sufficient trust between governments and citizens, they can "trade", that is, citizens can "signal" their preferences to the government, and the government can provide citizens with the goods and services they want, and citizens can support the government in exchange for that. So trust substitutes for legally enforceable contracts in the public sphere, just as it can in the private one.

The propositions described above for trust between persons all seem equally reasonable here: (1) trust between any two parties is never perfect, (2) it is always measured for a given opportunity to cheat on the exchange, and (3) one way it is accumulated is through foregoing opportunities to cheat. In addition, we would like to emphasize a new proposition in this context: (4) that if one party cheats, that motivates the other party to cheat in return.

Of course, (4) seems a reasonable possibility for private exchange as well. However, there is one particular difference which is relevant to the theory of tax evasion. If a private party cheats you (a citizen) on a private transaction, you have a number of alternatives, among which the most obvious is: never deal with that party again! You could also continue to have dealings with him or her, but you would become more suspicious, less trusting, and you might want to retaliate by cheating her in return. But when a person is dealing with a government that cheats her, she can exercise "voice" by not voting for that party in a democracy or "exit" by moving to a different jurisdiction,[10] but typically, the former option is ineffective and the latter option is very costly, and so there is a very high chance that the government will still be in power after the next election, and the citizen will have to deal with it again even though her trust in that government has fallen. Most citizens, most of the time, are stuck with the government they have got and their options for changing it are very limited.

Under such circumstances, we suggest that the individual who is cheated by a government through a corrupt act will tend to respond by cheating that government in return, by evading her taxes, as was the case in Russia in the early 1990s (Easter 2002). That is, the degree to which a government can trust an individual to pay her taxes depends on the extent to which an individual trusts the government to be honest and not corrupt.

$$_g T_i^y = h\left(_i T_g^y\right), h' > 0 \tag{30.11}$$

To illustrate, suppose that the government provides a *lower* level of public services *but still charges the same tax rate*, appropriating the extra revenue for itself or for a crony. As a consequence of this corruption, citizens are worse off. They feel cheated, and their trust in government falls. And they are more likely to evade tax or to evade to a greater degree than before. This *reciprocity* or *conditional cooperation* is the basic hypothesis of this chapter: government cheating or "corruption" or lack of trustworthiness stimulates tax evasion.

Thus, in our view, tax evasion and government corruption are related, and it might be difficult to address the first problem without doing something about the second one.

Finally, we suggest a fifth proposition with respect to the accumulation of trust: (5) each act of investment leads to a positive externality and an act of cheating to a negative one. To begin with private exchange, if *a* sacrifices an

---

[10] A discussion of the interplay between migration and institutional quality (including corruption) is beyond the scope of this chapter, but can be found in Ivlevs (Chap. 29) in this volume.

opportunity to cheat b in order to build trust with her, she also builds trust with other parties c... who witness or in some other way get information on that transaction. They will observe that a appears more "trustworthy" than before. So there is a spillover effect to the extent that the trust investments are public or observable by others, and a person can build a *reputation* (the average trust that other citizens have that a would not cheat them $\sum_i \left({}_i T_a^y \right)/n$) to this extent. Similarly, a party who cheats one person may find that this information becomes public and no one wants to deal with her after that.

These concepts are closely related to solidarity or social cohesion. In larger groups, such as firms, political parties, communities, or nations, the degree of *social cohesion* or *solidarity* can be expressed as follows. Let $S_a^{1.00}$ represent the probability that a will cooperate or make a sacrifice for the group—pay her taxes, give to charity, clean up after her dog, vote, work on weekends for the party or community, and so on—rather than cheat, free ride, or defect when the cost to her of cooperating would be $1.00. In general, S_a^x indicates the degree of solidarity a has with the community or group. Here, it seems reasonable to assume that

$$0 \le S_a^x \le 1 \tag{30.12}$$

These examples suggest that generalized trust is closely related to solidarity (or social cohesion). To see their relationship, let us make the following assumption, which seems reasonable: *An individual who will not cheat the community when the gain to her from doing so is $x also will not cheat an individual within that community in order to gain the same amount.*

With this assumption, *generalized trust is the same thing as solidarity*, that is,

$$_a T_j^x = S_a^x \tag{30.13}$$

The term on the left-hand side of Eq. (30.13), generalized trust, just specifies the probability that a will not cheat an individual in the community when she can gain $x by doing so. The term on the right, which represents solidarity, says that a will not cheat the community when she could gain the same amount by doing so. These two are the same by the assumption just made.

An individual act of tax evasion will not typically be observable by others, though the average level of evasion in a democratic jurisdiction tends to be widely reported and widely known. However, there is a substantial difference between tax evasion and cheating in private markets: unlike an act of private cheating, an act of tax evasion cheats everyone else in the community, who

will have to pay more taxes or get less government services because of the evasion. Similarly, an individual who pays her tax when she could possibly have
evaded doing so either reduces the tax others have to pay or raises the level of
goods and services that can be provided at any given tax rate. Again, therefore,
there is an externality. We suggest that once again there is *reciprocity or* conditional cooperation: the degree to which an individual pays or evades taxation
depends on her estimate of the number of others who are evading or paying,
or on the extent to which she trusts them, on average, to pay and not to cheat:

$$E_i = g(\sum_i \left({}_i T_j^y \right))/n \quad g' < 0 \tag{30.14}$$

where E_i is the extent to which individual i decides to evade taxes, and ${}_i T_j^y$ is
the extent to which she believes others are not cheating on their taxes.

This analysis can easily be carried forward along the lines of the ideas in
Benjamini and Maital (1985), Myles and Naylor (1996), or Frey and Torgler
(2007). In these papers, the utility of evasion to a taxpayer is positively related
to the number of others who evade, similar to Eq. (30.14) above. In the analysis of Benjamini and Naital, for example, an individual makes a binary decision either to pay or to evade taxes, and this decision is based on the number
of others who evade taxes. This dependence of individual decision-making on
the decisions of others leads to multiple equilibria, which can be broadly classified into two: one in which people assume that others are paying and so
most of them also pay, and in the other equilibrium, it is assumed that people
do not pay their taxes and do everything they can to evade. The theoretical
analysis in Benjamini and Maital (1985) or Myles and Naylor (1996) shows
that there is a tipping point, as is common in the analysis of group interde-
pendencies: when the number of tax evaders reaches a certain level, everyone
is better off evading and evasion becomes endemic. Consequently, a small
change in exogenous variables, for example, the tax rate or other variables that
precipitate a change in the number of evaders, can produce an epidemic of
evasion.

We will refer to the equilibrium in which it is assumed that people do not
pay their taxes as the *transition country* equilibrium, due to the well-known
problems these countries have with tax evasion.[11] In the latter group, the
Russian (Rose 2000; Easter 2002) or Albanian (Gërxhani 2002) equilibrium
can be considered amongst the worst. On the other hand, we will refer to the

---

[11] See Schneider and Enste (2002, 2013).

equilibrium in which most people pay their taxes the institutionally *advanced country* equilibrium.

To conclude, this discussion leads to two main hypotheses that a citizen will be more inclined to pay her tax bill: (1) the more she believes the government is honest and will provide the services promised in return and (2) the more she believes everyone else is paying. To put it differently, people are more willing to pay taxes when they have reason to believe the government is not corrupt, and it will also depend on the extent to which they believe that others are also going to pay their taxes.

4.3 Tax Evasion and Trust in Transition Countries

Given that the problem of tax evasion appears to be more substantial in institutionally less developed countries (i.e., transition countries), and since in this chapter we intend to look at the role of informal institutions on the decision to evade taxes, transition countries provide an excellent test bed for our ideas. About three decades ago, these countries went through an institutional shock, caused by the collapse of former communist regimes. The level of the institutional shock varied per country, depending on the type of regime. On the one hand, the communist regime was overorganized, where bureaucratic orders and ideological repression determined what individuals had to do. On the other hand, it was characterized by organizational failure, which motivated individuals to create and rely on informal networks. "Such a 'dual society' of formal versus informal networks [institutions] was far more developed in the Soviet Union, where it had been in place for more than 70 years, than in the Czech Republic [for example]" (Rose 2000, p. 166). In Eastern Europe, similar characteristics were observed in Albania, where the totalitarian regime lasted for more than 40 years. As a consequence, these societies experienced significant distrust in the government and formal institutions. The substitute was found in family—, friends—or local networks. After the collapse of communism, in countries where the "dual society" was dominant, and where in addition the new governments did not manage to function properly, trust has eroded even further, forcing people to invest and rely more on informal networks (see, e.g., Renooy et al. 2004).

Indeed, the level of trust in the Russian government appears to be extremely low based on survey data used in international comparisons (Hjolland and Svendsen 2001). A Russian scholar Anton Oleinik (n.d.) reports that only 3.4% of the respondents think that they can trust the state. Indeed, Oleinik suggests that it was the "non-reciprocal behavior of the state confirmed during the August 1998 crisis [which] led to a dramatic decline of the citizens' willingness to pay the taxes" (Oleinik n.d., p. 22).

Based on a survey run across several cities in Albania, De Soto et al. (2002) find that "people in all areas generally lack confidence in government". Only 25% of people appear to trust public institutions. The highest level of trust is expressed towards family members.

5   An Empirical Test

In this section, we provide an empirical test of the two hypotheses formulated above.[12] We do so based on data collected from a field survey conducted in the urban area of Tirana (the capital of Albania) in 2000.[13] The response rate was 89.3% out of a sample of 1500 households. This data set contains information on the informal institutions with respect to taxes, as well as sufficient information about income and taxes to derive estimates (where applicable) of the extent of personal income tax evasion per respondent. This gives us a unique opportunity to explore the relationship between tax evasion and informal institutions like trust and conditional cooperation.[14]

Due to sensitivity issues (i.e., respondents may be reluctant to confess noncompliance), various indirect questions were used to gather information and construct a variable measuring the evasion of personal income tax. For example, if the response to the question "Does your employer (state or private) deduct your personal income tax from your monthly salary" is "No", then this was considered as one indication of tax evasion, or if the response to the question "Please indicate who pays your tax on personal income" is "Nobody", this was another indication of tax evasion.[15] There were five such questions representing five (indirect) indications of tax evasion. For the group of respondents liable to personal income tax, the five indications were summarized to obtain our main variable on tax evasion: "the extent of personal income tax

---

[12] Some empirical support of these hypotheses for an institutionally advanced country, the United States, can be found in Scholz and Lubell (1998). As argued in the previous section, the focus here is on transition countries.

[13] See Gërxhani (2007) for more on the survey and the questionnaire.

[14] Note that the data set has no cross-sectional variation in formal institutions (i.e., tax and fine rate), which the standard economic theory of tax evasion suggest affects compliance. In addition, potential variation across individuals liable to different types of taxes is also taken care of since we focus on the extent of personal income tax only.

[15] The Albanian tax law is similar to that in most Western countries: individuals employed in the public or private sector are subject to tax on personal income.

Table 30.2   The extent of personal income tax evasion

	PITE (personal)	
	Number of cases	Percentages
No tax evasion at all	544	61.4
One indication of evasion	146	16.5
Two indications	76	8.6
Three indications	68	7.7
Four indications	43	4.9
Five indications	9	1.0
Total	*886*	*100*
At least one indication	342	38.6

evasion" (PITE).[16] The value of this variable gives the number of indications of tax evasion, with a minimum of 0 and maximum of 5. Table 30.2 summarizes the information.

To capture trust-based political exchange and trust in others, that is, beliefs in other citizens paying taxes, we considered two measures: (1) related to individual trust in government and (2) related to individual perception of others' compliance. For the former, we constructed a dummy variable *TrustGovernment* as follows. If a respondent strongly or mildly agrees with the statement "The Albanian Government deserves to be supported" *and* does not strongly agree with the statement that "Corruption in Albania is high", then we set *TrustGovernment* = 1, otherwise *TrustGovernment* = 0. We interpret a person who scores *TrustGovernment* = 1 as someone who believes in what the government is doing (the first statement) and who does not support the government for corrupt reasons, that is, because she is paid off to do so. So a person who scores *TrustGovernment* = 1 could be described as a person who genuinely supports the government and believes it to be honest. With this measure, 23.7% of the sample trusts the government. To capture an individual's trust or belief in others paying taxes, we use the variable *PerceivedComplianceOthers*, which on a scale from 1 to 5 measures the extent to which a respondent disagrees with the statement "The majority of people in Albania do not pay taxes".

Now that we have data on tax evasion, individuals' trust in government, and their belief in other individuals paying taxes, we can directly test our two main hypotheses. We do this by running a probit regression to determine the relationship between *TrustGovernment* and *PerceivedComplainceOthers* and the dummy dependent variable "Personal income tax evasion" (PITE). Note that this is a binary transformation of the variable "the extent of personal income tax evasion", which now takes the value 0 if there was no indication

---

[16] For a detailed description of the construction of this variable from the questionnaire, see the Appendix.

of tax evasion at all and the value 1 if there was at least one indication of personal income tax evasion (cf. Table 30.2). We also include background variables such as gender (a dummy with value 0 for males and 1 for females), family size, family income (divided by 10,000), age (divided by 100), and education level (distinguishing between four education levels, categorized from the lowest to the highest level) to control for individual differences. The highest absolute correlation coefficient between any two of these independent variables is 0.21.[17] The two main explanatory variables correlate with a (low) coefficient of 0.13 and the highest correlation coefficient (0.15) between either of the two main variables and any other variable is between trust in government and education. All of these correlations are low enough not to worry about multicollinearity issues.

Table 30.3 presents the estimated coefficients for various specifications of the model. The estimated marginal effects of the trust variables are given in Table 30.4.

The three models differ in the extent that they add respondents' characteristics as independent variables. Without correcting for these characteristics (Model 1), trust in the government and perceived compliance of others are both strongly and negatively correlated with the likelihood that a respondent will evade taxes. A switch from 0 to 1 in the *TrustGovernment* dummy decreases the likelihood of evading by 8.5% (see Table 30.4). A unitary increase in *PerceivedComplianceOthers* (which varies between 1 and 5) decreases the

Table 30.3 Explaining personal income tax evasion (PITE)

Variable	Model 1	Model 2	Model 3
Constant	−0.064 (0.101)	0.010 (0.293)	3.111 (0.474)***
TrustGovernment	−0.229 (0.111)**	−0.249 (0.112)**	−0.126 (0.117)
PerceivedComplianceOthers	−0.099 (0.043)**	−0.097 (0.044)**	−0.076 (0.045)*
Female	–	−0.243 (0.112)**	−0.221 (0.116)*
Family size	–	0.026 (0.034)	−0.017 (0.036)
Family income/10,000	–	−0.040 (0.014)***	−0.036 (0.015)**
Age/100	–	0.103 (0.494)	0.296 (0.511)
Education level	–	–	−0.701 (0.082)***
χ^2 (*p*-value)	11 (0.01)***	19 (0.00)***	97 (0.00)***

Standard errors are in parentheses. TrustGovernment = trust in government, PerceivedComplianceOthers = belief in others paying taxes. These variables together with the background variables are explained in the main text. The final row gives the χ^2 goodness-of-fit statistic for the regression as a whole and the corresponding *p*-value
Notes: The results show the estimated coefficients of probit regressions explaining whether or not an individual evades taxes
Statistically significant at the * 10% level, ** 5% level, *** 1% level

---

[17] Surprisingly, this highest correlation is between the variables age and gender. This may be an indication that in traditional families it is more likely that the elder man fills out the questionnaire.

Table 30.4 Marginal effects

Variable	Model 1	Model 2	Model 3
TrustGovernment	−0.085**	−0.092**	−0.047
PerceivedComplainceOthers	−0.037**	−0.037**	−0.028*

TrustGovernment = trust in government, PerceivedComplianceOthers = belief in others paying taxes. These variables together with the background variables are explained in the main text

Notes: The results show the marginal effects for the trust variables in the probit regressions of Table 30.1

Statistically significant at the * 10% level and ** 5% level

probability of evading by 3.7%. Clearly, the effect of trust in government is more important than the effect of one's perception of others' compliance. Very similar results are obtained in Model 2, where gender, family size, family income, and age are added as regressors. In Model 2, the negative marginal effect of trust in government on the likelihood of evasion is even larger than in Model 1. The results related to the explanatory variables confirm the existing findings that being a female and having a higher family income are significantly positively associated with higher tax compliance.

Things change slightly in Model 3, where we have added education. This reduces the marginal effects of both main explanatory variables on the probability that an individual will evade taxes. Apparently, some of the effects of trust are mitigated through education. To further investigate the relationship between education and trust in government, we ran a probit regression with TrustGovernment as the dependent variable and all of the personal characteristics of Table 30.1 as independent variables. Only education has a statistically significant effect on the trust an individual has in the government. The marginal effect is 0.113 with $p < 0.001$. This implies that the estimated difference between the lowest and highest education categories in the probability that they trust the government is over 45% points.[18]

The strong effect of education on trust explains the reduced effect of the latter variable in Model 3. Nevertheless, our results in Table 30.3 show the importance of individuals' trust in the government and their trust or belief in others paying taxes, when explaining the likelihood that an individual will evade taxes. These results are in line with existing findings on the role of the exchange between government and wider population (e.g., negative or positive perception of the government or trust in government) on compliance

---

[18] It is unlikely that the differences between Model 3 on the one side and Models 1 and 2 on the other is caused by an omitted variable (education) bias in the latter two models. Recall that the correlation coefficient between the two main variables (TrustGovernment and PerceivedComplainceOthers) and education is low (all below 0.15), while a high correlation is a necessary condition for such a bias to occur.

(e.g., Feld and Frey 2002; Wahl et al. 2010; Daude et al. 2012; Kastlunger et al. 2013; Kogler et al. 2013; Ferrer-i-Carbonell and Gërxhani 2016).[19]

To put these findings in a more comparative perspective, it is worthwhile to compare tax evasion levels in Albania with those in other countries. Some evidence on this point is presented by Schaffer and Turley (2002). Their methodology involves computing the E/S (effective/statutory) ratio, which measures "effective yields" versus statutory levels of taxation in transition economies. They develop indicators like this for value added taxes, payroll, and corporate income taxes in 25 transition economies where data was available. Statutory VAT tax rates in Albania were 12.5%, the lowest of the 25 countries, but rates there for payroll and corporate taxes were about average (42.5% and 30%, respectively). The E/S ratio for VAT in Albania was 0.42, while this figure is not available for the other two types of taxes in Albania. The ratio of 0.42 is not much lower than the E/S ratio for VAT for the 25 transition economies, which is 0.45. In general, they find that progress in transition and the effectiveness of tax collection are positively related. Albania has the lowest tax rate for VAT, but VAT evasion there is not far from the average.

6   Concluding Remarks and Policy Implications

There is an abundant amount of research trying to understand the phenomenon of tax evasion. Indeed, the fact that so many people in so many countries, perhaps most strikingly the United States, pay their taxes even when it seems likely they could get away with evasion might be elevated to a paradox on the level of the paradox of voting. Both the basic acts of a citizen in a democracy—voting and paying taxes—appear to be irrational!

Recently, this literature has become particularly interesting, as concepts like "tax morale", "pro-social behavior", and "conditional cooperation" have been increasingly used to explain some of the large residual leftover when only deterrence variables are employed to explain compliance. In this chapter, we build on these ideas, but we retain the basic idea of public choice: the citizen pays taxes because she expects to receive public goods and services in return. We suggest a "trust-based political exchange" approach. First, we provide a precise definition of trust and show the relationship between the different kinds of trust (e.g., general trust vs. networks of trust between individuals) and between trust and related concepts like social capital. By focusing on

---

[19] See Mascagni (2018) for an overview of experimental findings.

"trust-based political exchange", we argue that the level of compliance is related to the degree to which citizens trust the government to be honest and to provide services promised, and to the extent to which they trust or believe others pay their taxes. These hypotheses were tested using a unique data set from a household survey in Tirana, containing information on both tax evasion and the informal institutions with respect to taxes. The empirical test supports the hypotheses that when individuals trust the government and believe that other individuals pay taxes, they are more inclined to pay taxes themselves. The effect of trust in government in increasing compliance seems to be the strongest. This result remains even after controlling for background information like gender, family size, family income, age, and education, which also affect individuals' decision to evade taxes. A higher educational level in particular seems to contribute significantly to more trust in government and thus mitigates to some extent the relationship between trust in government and tax evasion.

Given the relevance of our findings to policy, we provide a few suggestions on what can be done. The framework outlined here suggests that one important avenue of solution to the problem of tax evasion is to develop and emphasize the logic of democracy, which is that there is an exchange relationship between the citizen and the government. This relationship can only be based on mutual trust, since a government cannot be sued if it does not deliver on its promises. Building trust implies de-emphasizing the relationship of coercion, implicit in economic models of taxation, which neglect the expenditure side of government. An alternative approach is to emphasize education, since more education has a positive effect on the propensity to pay taxes independently of its effect on trust-based political exchange. On both these findings, one implication of this approach is that the problem of tax evasion will not be solved by punitive measures and may in fact be worsened that way. This is in line with the work on criminal penalties which casts doubt on their effectiveness in solving the crime problem.[20]

One, obviously very difficult, line of reform is to take measures to increase trust in the government. Here, there is a distinction to be made between the rule of law and authoritarianism. Historically, the only strong governments Albania and Russia had have been authoritarian governments. These societies have not had experience with a government which is strong and implements the rule of law, both for itself and for its citizenry, but which is democratic. That is the only form of government which promotes voluntary tax compliance. Indeed, tax compliance will be promoted because the rule of law will be

---

[20] See Wintrobe (2006) for amplification of this point.

enforced, including appropriate penalties for tax evasion, but within the parameters of democracy, where citizens feel their relationship to the state to be one of exchange and not coercion.

Appendix: Construction of Tax Evasion Variable from the Questionnaire

Table 30.5 shows that given that a respondent is obliged to pay the personal income tax:

1. C.1. = 2 indicates evasion because if those respondents whose personal income tax is supposed to be deducted by their employers say that it is not, this means that they are working on an unofficial basis. In case of an "official" employment, the employer is obliged by law to deduct personal income tax from the monthly salary. Consequently, if it is not, the tax on personal income is evaded.

Table 30.5 Personal income tax evasion variable (PITE)

	Question(s)[a]	Indication of evasion	PITE
Deducted tax on personal income	C.1.	C.1. = 2	+
Gross minus net personal income	C.2., C.3.	C.2. − C.3. = 0	+
Household monthly expenses on personal income tax	C.6.	C.6. = a	+
Payment of personal income tax	D.2.2.	D.2.2. = 0	+
Who pays the personal income tax	D.3.4.	D.3.4. = 1	+

[a]Question C.1. "Does your employer (state or private) deduct your personal income tax from your monthly salary"; Question C.2. "Could you tell us your total personal income for the last month, BEFORE paying taxes on personal income (be these paid by you or your employer) or on small business; house rent; electricity; water or any other household expenses? Note that your total personal income should consist of the incomes from all your personal sources of income during the last month"; Question C.3. "Could you tell us your total personal income for the last month, AFTER paying taxes on personal income (be these paid by you or your employer) or on small business; house rent; electricity; water or any other household expenses? Note that your total personal income should consist of the incomes from all your personal sources of income during the last month"; Question C.6. "Could you indicate, on average, your household's monthly expenses during the last month?"; Question D.2.2. "Would you mind telling us which of the following monetary obligation do you and your household pay?"; Question D.3.4. "Please indicate who pays your tax on personal income or your tax on small business?"

2. C.2. – C.3. = 0 indicates noncompliance because if the reported gross and net incomes are equal, one potential explanation is the evasion of personal income tax.
3. C.6. = a indicates evasion because the selected respondents report that they do not spend any money on personal income tax. Although the question asks for the household's monthly expenses, we believe this to be an indication of PITE due to the fact that the respondent is the main income earner of the household.
4. D.2.2. = 0 indicates evasion because the selected respondents report that they do not pay their personal income tax.
5. D.3.4. = 1 indicates evasion when the payment of personal income tax is expected and the answer is that nobody pays it.

There are five indications of personal income tax evasion. The observed responses indicating evasion varied from 11.5% to 31.4%. An important reason for this discrepancy is that respondents are reluctant to admit that they evade. Moreover, some respondents might not know the answer to some questions. As a consequence, it is not possible to obtain precise information. We adopt the simple, but intuitively sensible assumption that more indications of tax evasion make it more likely that a respondent is evading taxes. Hence, we simply count the number of times (out of five) that a respondent fulfilled the criteria listed above.

References

Alesina, A., & Giuliano, P. (2010). The Power of the Family. *Journal of Economic Growth, 15*, 93–125.

Allingham, M. G., & Sandmo, A. (1972). Income Tax Evasion: A Theoretical Analysis. *Journal of Public Economics, 1*, 323–338.

Alm, J. (2019). What Motivates Tax Compliance? *Journal of Economic Surveys, 33*(2), 353–388.

Alm, J., & Torgler, B. (2006). Culture Differences and Tax Morale in the United States and in Europe. *Journal of Economic Psychology, 27*(2), 224–246.

Becker, G. S. (1968). Crime and Punishment: An Economic Approach. *Journal of Political Economy, 76*, 169–217.

Benjamini, Y., & Maital, S. (1985). Optimal Tax Evasion and Optimal Tax Evasion Policy: Behavioral Aspects. In W. Gaertner & A. Wenig (Eds.), *The Economics of the Shadow Economy* (pp. 245–264). Berlin: Springer-Verlag.

Bordignon, M. (1993). A Fairness Approach to Income Tax Evasion. *Journal of Public Economics, 52*, 345–362.

Breton, A., & Wintrobe, R. (1982). *The Logic of Bureaucratic Conduct.* New York: Cambridge University Press.

Chhibber, A. (2000). Social Capital, the State, and Development Outcomes. In P. Dasgupta & I. Serageldin (Eds.), *Social Capital: A Multifaceted Perspective* (pp. 296–310). Washington, DC: The World Bank.

Clotfelter, C. T. (1983). Tax Evasion and Tax Rates. *Review of Economics and Statistics, 65*, 363–373.

Coleman, J. (1990). *Foundations of Social Theory.* Cambridge, MA: Harvard University Press.

Cowell, F. A., & Gordon, J. P. F. (1988). Unwillingness to Pay. *Journal of Public Economics, 36*, 305–321.

Daude, C., Gutierrez, H., & Melguizo, A. (2012). *What Drives Tax Morale?* OECD. Development Centre. Working Paper #315.

De Soto, H., Gordon, P., Gedeshi, I., & Sinoimeri, Z. (2002). *Poverty in Albania—A Qualitative Assessment.* World Bank Technical Paper No. 520. The World Bank.

Douarin, E., & Mickiewicz, T. (2017). Public Finance. In E. Douarin & T. Mickiewicz (Eds.), *Economics of Institutional Change—Central and Eastern Europe Revisited.* Palgrave Macmillan, Chap. 10.

Easter, G. M. (2002). The Politics of Revenue Extraction in Post-communist States: Poland and Russia Compared. *Politics and Society, 30*(4), 599–627.

Feige, E. L. (1997). Underground Activity and Institutional Change: Productive, Protective and Predatory Behavior in Transition Economies. In J. M. Nelson, C. Tilley, & L. Walker (Eds.), *Transforming Post-communist Political Economies* (pp. 21–35). Washington, DC: National Academy Press.

Feld, L. P., & Frey, B. S. (2002). Trust Breeds Trust: How Taxpayers are Treated. *Economics of Governance, 3*(2), 87–99.

Ferrer-i-Carbonell, A., & Gërxhani, K. (2016). Tax Evasion and Well-being: A Study of the Social and Institutional Context in Central and Eastern Europe. *European Journal of Political Economy, 45*, 149–159.

Freidman, E., Johnson, S., Kaufman, D., & Zoido-Labaton, P. (2000). Dodging the Grabbing Hand: The Determinants of Unofficial Activity in 69 Countries. *Journal of Public Economics, 76*(3), 459–493.

Frey, B. S. (2002). *Direct Democracy for Transition Economies.* Budapest: The Collegium Budapest, Institute for Advanced Study.

Frey, B. S., & Torgler, B. (2007). Tax Morale and Conditional Cooperation. *Journal of Comparative Economics, 35*(1), 136–159.

Friedland, N., Maital, S., & Rutenberg, A. (1978). A Simulation Study of Income Tax Evasion. *Journal of Public Economics, 10*, 107–116.

Fukuyama, F. (1995). *Trust. The Social Virtues and the Creation of Prosperity.* New York: Free Press. Paperbacks.

Gërxhani, K. (2002). *The Informal Sector in Transition: Tax Evasion in an Institutional Vacuum* (Tinbergen Institute Research Series, no. 265). Amsterdam: University of Amsterdam.

Gërxhani, K. (2004a). The Informal Sector in Developed and Less Developed Countries: A Literature Survey. *Public Choice, 120*(3–4), 267–300.

Gërxhani, K. (2004b). Tax Evasion in Transition: Outcome of an Institutional Clash? Testing Feige's Conjecture in Albania. *European Economic Review, 48*, 729–745.

Gërxhani, K. (2007). "Did You Pay Your Taxes?" How (Not) to Conduct Tax Evasion Surveys in Transition Countries. *Social Indicators Research, 80*, 555–581.

Gërxhani, K., & Schram, A. (2006). Tax Evasion and Income Source: A Comparative Experimental Study. *Journal of Economic Psychology, 27*(3), 402–422.

Hammar, H., Jagers, S. C., & Nordblom, K. (2009). Perceived Tax Evasion and the Importance of Trust. *Journal of Socio-Economics, 38*, 238–245.

Hjolland, L., & Svendsen, T. G. (2001). *Standard Measurement of Social Capital: Preliminary Results from Russia*. The European Public Choice Society Meetings, Paris, April 2001.

Internal Revenue Service. (2018). *Internal Revenue Service Data Book* (Publication 55B). Washington, DC: Internal Revenue Service.

Kastlunger, B., Lozza, E., Kirchler, E., & Schabmann, A. (2013). Powerful Authorities and Trusting Citizens: The Slippery Slope Framework and Tax Compliance in Italy. *Journal of Economic Psychology, 34*(1), 36–54.

Kirchgässner, G. (1999). Schattenwirtschaft und moral: Anmerkungen aus ökonomischer perspektive. In S. Lamnek & J. Luedtke (Eds.), *Der sozialstaat zwischen "markt" und "hedonismus"?* (pp. 425–445). Opladen: Westdeutscher Verlag.

Knack, S., & Keefer, P. (1997). Does Social Capital Have an Economic Payoff? A Cross-country Investigation. *Quarterly Journal of Economics, 112*(4), 1251–1288.

Kogler, C., Batrancea, L., Nichita, A., Pantya, J., Belianin, A., & Kirchler, E. (2013). Trust and Power as Determinants of Tax Compliance: Testing the Assumptions of the Slippery Slope Framework in Austria, Hungary, Romania, and Russia. *Journal of Economic Psychology, 34*(1), 169–180.

Mascagni, G. (2018). From the Lab to the Field: A Review of Tax Experiments. *Journal of Economic Surveys, 32*(2), 273–301.

Medina, L., & Schneider, F. (2018). *Shadow Economies Around the World: What Did We Learn Over the Last 20 Years?* IMF Working Paper 18/17. International Monetary Fund.

Moore, M. (2004). Revenues, State Formation and the Quality of Governance in Developing Countries. *International Political Science Review, 25*(3), 297–319.

Mueller, D. (1989). *Public Choice II*. New York: Cambridge University Press.

Myles, G. D., & Naylor, R. (1996). A Model of Tax Evasion with Group Conformity and Social Customs. *Journal of Public Economics, 12*, 49–66.

North, D. C. (1990). *Institutions, Institutional Change and Economic Performance*. Cambridge: Cambridge University Press.

Oleinik, A. (n.d.). A Trustless Society: The Influence of the August 1998 Crisis on the Institutional Organization of the Russians' Everyday Life.

Paldam, M., & Svendsen, T. G. (2000). An Essay on Social Capital. Looking for the Fire Behind the Smoke. *European Journal of Political Economy, 16*(2), 339–366.

Putnam, R. (1993). *Making Democracy Work*. Princeton, NJ: Princeton University Press.

Putnam, R. (2000). *Bowling Alone*. New York: Simon and Schuster.

Renooy, P., Ivarsson, S., van der Wusten-Gritsai, O., & Meijer, R. (2004). *Undeclared Work in an Enlarged Union*. Technical Report May, European Commission, Directorate-General for Employment and Social Affairs.

Rose, R. (2000). Getting Things Done in an Anti-modern Society: Social Capital Networks in Russia. In P. Dasgupta & I. Serageldin (Eds.), *Social Capital: A Multifaceted Perspective* (pp. 147–172). Washington, DC: The World Bank.

Schaffer, M. E., & Turley, G. (2002). Effective versus Statutory Taxation: Measuring Effective Tax Administration in Transition Economies. In M. Cuddy & R. Gekker (Eds.), *Institutional Change in Transition Economies*. Ashgate.

Schneider, F., & Enste, D. H. (2002). *The Shadow Economy: Theoretical Approaches, Empirical Studies, and Political Implications* (1st ed.). Cambridge, UK: Cambridge University Press.

Schneider, F., & Enste, D. H. (2013). *The Shadow Economy: Theoretical Approaches, Empirical Studies, and Political Implications* (2nd ed.). Cambridge, UK: Cambridge University Press.

Scholz, J. T., & Lubell, M. (1998). Trust and Taxpaying: Testing the Heuristic Approach to Collective Action. *American Journal of Political Science, 42*(2), 398–417.

Torgler, B. (2003). Tax Morale, Rule Governed Behaviour and Trust. *Constitutional Political Economy, 14*, 119–140.

Torgler, B. (2007). *Tax Compliance and Tax Morale*. Edward Elgar.

Torgler, B., & Schneider, F. (2009). The Impact of Tax Morale and Institutional Quality on the Shadow Economy. *Journal of Economic Psychology, 30*(2), 228–245.

Wahl, I., Kastlunger, B., & Kirchler, E. (2010). Trust in Authorities and Power to Enforce Tax Compliance: An Empirical Analysis of the "Slippery Slope Framework". *Law & Policy, 32*(4), 383–406.

Wintrobe, R. (2006). *Rational Extremism: The Political Economy of Radicalism*. New York: Cambridge University Press.

Wittman, D. (1995). *The Myth of Democratic Failure*. Chicago, IL: University of Chicago Press.

Yitzhaki, S. (1974). Income Tax Evasion: A Theoretical Analysis. *Journal of Public Economics, 3*, 201–202.

Zhang, N., Andrighetto, G., Ottone, S., Ponzano, F., & Steinmo, S. (2016). Willing to Pay? Tax Compliance in Britain and Italy: An Experimental Analysis. *PLoS One, 11*(2).

31

The Rules of the Game in Transition: How Informal Institutions Work in South East Europe

Alena Ledeneva and Adnan Efendic

1   Introduction

Neoinstitutional theory defines institutions as rules of the game or 'the humanely devised constraints that structure political, economic and social interaction. They consist of *both* informal constraints (sanctions, taboos, customs, traditions, and codes of conduct), and formal rules (constitutions, laws, property rights)' (North 1991: 97). The effectiveness of such institutions is associated with their regulatory and enforcement capacity (Scott 2004). While the idea of formal and informal institutions is widely used in social sciences, and the effectiveness of formal institutions is monitored consistently, there are few empirical studies on the effects of informal institutions and little empirical data on the interaction between formal and informal institutions. With the exception of the INFORM project, namely, closing the gap between formal and informal institutions in the Balkans (2016–2019),[1] the quantitative data on informal institutions is rare and not integrated with the data on formal institutions.

---

[1] https://www.ucl.ac.uk/ssees/research/funded-research-projects/inform/en/.

A. Ledeneva (✉)
University College London, London, UK
e-mail: a.ledeneva@ucl.ac.uk

A. Efendic
University of Sarajevo, Sarajevo, Bosnia and Herzegovina
e-mail: adnan.efendic@efsa.unsa.ba

© The Author(s) 2021
E. Douarin, O. Havrylyshyn (eds.), *The Palgrave Handbook of Comparative Economics*,
https://doi.org/10.1007/978-3-030-50888-3_31

The idea of closing the gap between formal and informal institutions is especially relevant to societies in transition where legal rules change fast and are imposed top-down, often under the pressure of international organisations and donors. This often results in clashes with existing or local social norms. Such clashes put an enormous burden on people, asked to transform their behaviour, and on governments, required to implement changes in order to score well in international rankings. In SEE countries, the clash of the Europeanisation reforms with people's resistance to change has become associated with policy failures of 'over-regulation and under-enforcement', otherwise known as the 'policy implementation gap'. The respective roles of formal and informal institutions in closing the implementation gap are still to be addressed (Gordy and Efendic 2019).

It is widely recognised that a 'good institutional arrangement' is one where formal and informal institutions are not divergent or in conflict (De Soto 2000). In other words, legal norms are in harmony with social norms (Pejovich 1999), both are embedded in human behaviour, and their outcome is convergent (Helmke and Levitsky 2004). Views may differ on whether such convergence can be described as complementary or substitutive (North 1990; Brousseau and Glachant 2008; Furubotn and Richter 2005). The existing typologies of informal institutions that use such terminology presume that informal institutions are secondary to the operations of the formal institutions and residual, that is, everything that is not formal but passed the test of time is informal (Helmke and Levitsky 2004; Lauth 2007). The complexity of empirical data challenges such assumptions. It is convenient to presume that legal rules are enforced formally, by the state, organisations or formal hierarchies, while social norms are enforced informally, via families, peer circles and networks. Yet, in effect, these are hard to separate, as formal constraints tend to be enforced only if there is informal pressure to enforce them or can exist only on paper. The reverse is also true: informal pressure may only emerge because there is a formal constraint at work.

The INFORM[2] evidence from transition economies presents additional puzzles. Firstly, in SEE, for example, we witness multiple legislative changes that do not get implemented (Gordy and Efendic 2019). It raises questions on whether codified formal rules can qualify as 'formal institutions', if they are not enforced and do not constitute formal constraints as such (for examples of these, see Sakwa 2007; Ledeneva 2001; Ginsburg and Simpser 2013; Newton 2017).

---

[2] The project *INFORM: Closing the Gap between Formal and Informal Institutions in West Balkans* has received funding from the European Union's Horizon 2020 research and innovation programme under grant agreement. No 693537.

Secondly, the constraints posed by informal institutions need unpacking, as the enforcement of social norms, sometimes referred to as unwritten or informal rules, varies significantly and is context bound. 'Informal rules, then, are traditions, customs, moral values, religious beliefs and all the other norms of behaviour that have emerged spontaneously, survived the test of time and served to bind the generations' (Pejovich 2008:11).

Thirdly, in SEE and other transitional contexts, we witness practices and informal exchanges, deemed to be path dependent, traditional or linked to communism, while in fact they are temporal reactions to the post-communist reforms (Ledeneva 2006, 2008; Henig and Makovicky 2017). A common assumption about transitional societies has been that 'economies of favours', compensating for the 'economies of shortage,' defects in centralised planning and socialist systems of resource allocation and privileges, would become redundant once liberal reforms had opened markets and established democracies. However, the development of informal institutions in transition does not seem to follow this logic.

Fourthly, the role of networks in the enforcement of both formal rules and informal norms is not sufficiently integrated in the conceptualisation of the formal-informal interaction. The informal transaction costs associated with dense networks are often disregarded, and informal networks are not seen as effective for enforcing formal constraints. A more balanced analysis of the transaction costs associated with informal networking is needed (Efendic and Ledeneva 2020).

These four points need to be addressed to understand the formal-informal interaction in transition societies. Empirically, we need proxies for the degree of institutionalisation of both formal rules and informal norms and for the degree of their enforcement; a degree of independence of or derivativeness from the outcome of the reforms (norms and practices being a cause or a consequence); and a measure of sociability or instrumentality of networks. Conceptually, we need models accommodating such complexity and change (Andersson 2008; Brousseau and Glachant 2008; Ledeneva et al. 2018). The exiting literature on the interaction of formal and informal institutions is not balanced: the scholars either give the primacy to formal institutions and residual status to informal institutions, or informal institutions are studied without much consideration of their formal frameworks. Revisiting the conceptualisation of the formal-informal interaction is thus a necessary starting point.

This chapter starts with a discussion of the existing typologies of interaction between formal and informal institutions; it outlines key features of the institutional framework in SEE region, offers some empirical tests for the validity of claims about a dominant substitutive role of informal institutions and presents preliminary findings. We tackle the questions, 'what works when the formal institutions do not?' and 'to what extent changing formal institutions (operationalised as trust into formal rules and procedures) constitute real constraints in the societies with a strong hold of informal norms (operationalised as reliance on personal connections)?'

We rely on evidence from eight countries of South East Europe (SEE) and scrutinise the data quantitatively and qualitatively. The investigation is based on representative survey data collected among the general public (6000 respondents) and qualitative data collected among entrepreneurs in SEE (70 interviews), specifically in Albania, Bosnia and Herzegovina, Croatia, Kosovo, Montenegro, North Macedonia, Serbia and Slovenia. We conclude that both the general public and entrepreneurs invest much time and resources into informal networking to reduce the uncertainty and compensate for the inefficiency of formal institutions. The quantitative evidence suggests that maintaining informal networks is associated with substantial economic costs. The qualitative evidence emphasises the predominant role of particular relationships over universal rules, or reliance on 'trusted people and connections', without which it is not possible to model economic behaviour in particularistic contexts.

In the next section, we define 'informal institutions' and revisit the existing conceptualisations of formal-informal interaction by giving more explanatory power to informal institutions.

2   The Rules of the Game: Revisiting Formal and Informal Institutions

Institutions are 'perfectly analogous to the rules of the game in a competitive team sport. That is, they consist of formal written rules as well as typically unwritten codes of conduct that underline and supplement formal rules, such as not deliberately injuring a key player on the opposite team. And as this analogy would imply, the rules and informal codes are sometimes violated and punishment is enacted. Taken together, the formal and informal rules and the type and effectiveness of enforcement shape the whole character of the game' (North 1990: 4). Compressing this amalgamation of rules, codes, their interaction and their enforcement allowed North to revolutionise the notion of institution, now associated with neo-institutionalism.

The complexity of such conceptualisation that includes rules, enforcing mechanisms and players, however, does not lend itself easily to empirical research. Hence, the constituents of institutions—formal and informal constraints—have come to be considered apart from each other and from their interaction and enforcement. Informal institutions are regarded as 'conventions, norms of behaviour, and self-imposed codes of conduct' (North 1995: 23), which produce constraints to reduce uncertainty in human interaction, whereas formal constraints are associated with rules and specifications, statutes and common laws, and constitutions. However, '[the] difference between informal and formal constraints is one of degree. Envision a continuum of taboos, customs and traditions at one end to written constitutions at the other'. Instead of separate entities, North speaks of a continuum of constraints, which can be depicted as in Fig. 31.1 by a dotted line from formal rules to informal norms.

North (1995: 37) acknowledges the role of informal institutions in the functioning of formal institutions and presumes their amalgamation. Because of complexity, 'incompleteness of information' and the need to 'coordinate human interactions', informal institutions are necessary and include: '(1) extensions, elaborations and modifications of formal rules, (2) socially sanctioned norms of behaviour, (3) internally enforced standards of conduct' (North 1990: 40). Some well-known examples would include (1) the use of progress pushers to enable planned economies to reach their targets, (2) widely spread denunciation practices but also social norm of contempt for anonymous letters and whistle-blowers and (3) adhering to

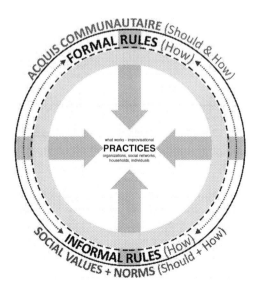

Fig. 31.1 The INFORM model of the interaction of formal and informal institutions—step 1

the notions of friendships and voluntary acceptance of obligations to help, to 'give away the last shirt' to a friend even where it involved formal rule-breaking.

The editors of *The International Handbook on Informal Governance* observe that various authors attach the adjective 'informal' to a wide range of conceptions: politics, arrangements, networks, institutions, organisations, norms, rules, activity or influence (Christiansen and Neuhold 2012). They distinguish at least three separate usages of it: first, the designation of the framework within which decisions are taken as being informal (institutions, organisations, networks); second, the identification of the process or procedure through which policies are made as being informal (politics, arrangements, activity); and, third, the classification of the outcome of any such process as being informal (rules, norms, influence). Adding the adjective 'informal' to a subject matter reveals some important dimensions of its analysis, but often conceals the intricacies of the formal-informal interaction. Thus, definitions of informal institutions, explicitly or implicitly, presume a certain perspective on the interaction between formal rules and informal norms, often determined by a particular disciplinary method. Four perspectives can be distinguished:

* Normative, top-down perspective: formal (legal, prescriptive) = good, informal (cultural, slow to change) = bad, participants are not given a voice. Prescriptions for formalisation and crusades against informality are taken for granted (see overview in Polese 2015).
* Residual perspective: formal and informal institutions are coexistent, but the priority, legitimacy and primacy are given to the formal. Types of informal institutions, for example, are determined by the (in)effectiveness of formal and convergence/divergence of outcomes of the formal and informal institutions (e.g. Helmke and Levitsky 2004).
* Symbiotic perspective: formal and informal institutions are co-dependent, presuming a balance between formal and informal institutions, as in the *yin/yang* approach (e.g. Fang 2012).
* Inductive, bottom-up perspective: informal institutions are given primacy, and formal institutions are seen as an outcome of a historical process of the institutionalisation of informal norms. 'Informal institutions can also serve as templates for formal institutions. Informal rules may generate precedents and prevalent practices that are then formalized for efficiency's sake, as with the rise of private property and the incorporation of capitalist entrepreneurs into the Communist Party in China' (Tsai 2006, cited in

Grzymala-Busse 2010; see also de Soto 1989). Participants are given voice and the formal institutions often shift out of the focus of inquiry, as in the majority of ethnographic studies of informal practices.

These perspectives are often implicit in disciplinary method or focus of inquiry. The limitations of each perspective create a niche for an interdisciplinary approach to grasp the complexity of the formal-informal interaction. However, in order to focus on the interaction of formal and informal institutions in the context of transition economies, we first need to resolve the four puzzles outlined in the introduction.

2.1 Differentiating Rules and Constraints: The 'Enforcement Belt'

North (1990) identifies formal institutions (formal rules) with formal constraints and informal institutions (informal norms) with informal constraints. However, for understanding communist, post-communist, authoritarian and transitional contexts, it is essential to envisage that both formal rules and informal norms do not always constitute real constraints, as many of them are meant to remain the façade of economic and political regimes or traditional practices. In other words, not all formally codified rules constitute formal constraints, and those which do might not necessarily do so with the consistency and predictability we associate with formal institutions. Moreover, relying on the record of codified rules would not produce sufficient data on the workings of an economy. Similarly, there can be informal rules, which never become constraints—this is how Bourdieu got the idea of strategies—he noticed that there are matrimonial rules in Algeria, which everybody knows, but only few follow. Both formal and informal rules can thus be 'empty shells' (Dimitrova 2010). As depicted in Fig. 31.2, the INFORM model differentiates between formal rules and formal constraints in order to point out the issue of the 'under-enforcement' of formal institutions in transition contexts, as well as between social norms and informal constraints in order to point out the context-bound nature of the social norms and their partial enforcement. The emphasis here is on the 'enforcement belt' that allows us to capture which rules and norms constitute actual constraints.

The main limitation of defining institutions as constraints is that North ignores the *enabling* aspects of institutions. 'Institutions do indeed forbid many activities, but they equally make possible an enormous range of activities that would be impossible-inconceivable-in their absence: that is, they are

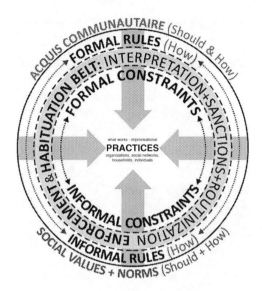

Fig. 31.2 INFORM model of the interaction of formal and informal institutions—step 2

always and everywhere liberating as well as limiting' (Neale 1993: 423). The ambivalent nature of constraints and their enabling power is essential for understanding the dual functionality of informal practices that both support and subvert the formal rules and informal norms that shape them (Ledeneva et al. 2018, Vol. 2: 3–5). Hodgson (2006) states that institutions both enable and constrain behaviour, whereas Searle (2005) suggests that the role of institutions is not to constrain people but to create new kinds of power relationships, which are enabling.

2.2   Enforcement of Formal Rules and Informal Norms: The Effectiveness of Constraints

Formal rules are enforced primarily by hierarchies: state organisations, like courts, legislatures and bureaucracies, and state-enforced rules, such as constitutions, laws and regulations. Informal norms include conventions, codes of behaviour, traditions, cultural norms, religious beliefs, moral norms and habits and are enforced by families, trust circles and networks or self-enforcement. These are passed from one generation to another through various transmission channels, such as imitation, oral tradition and teaching (Tonoyan et al. 2010), and represent an 'old ethos, the hand of the past or the carriers of history' (Pejovich 1999: 166), associated with the phenomenon of path dependency in transitions.

It is often presumed that formal rules are more important because the risks and penalties associated with their violation are more considerable. However, the enforcement of informal norms is sometimes more efficient as it is grounded in daily interactions, self-enforcement and subtle mechanisms that may not be visible. They are transferred from generations to generations (Pejovich 2008) and may be just as important determinant of socio-economic environment as formal institutions (Knowles and Weatherston 2006; Tabellini 2010). Hence, the presence of informal institutions is a strong determinant of development (Williamson 2009). This especially applies to co-coordinating activities where the costs of writing and enforcing contracts are high (Pollitt 2002), or where 'formal institutions exist on paper but are ineffective in practice' (Helmke and Levitsky 2004: 730). However, informal institutions can be also inefficient; informal institutional voids appear with inability of norms, values and beliefs to facilitate stable, efficient and effective transactions (Webb et al. 2019). Whereas formal institutions might resemble each other in different societies, the informal institutions in which people are socialised and that they learn to respect are seen as specific, cultural and emerging bottom-up.

2.3 Differentiating Informal Institutions from Other Informal Regularities: 'Trusted People and Connections' versus Informal Networking in SEE

Helmke and Levitsky define informal institutions as 'socially shared rules, usually unwritten, that are created, communicated, and enforced outside of officially sanctioned channels' (Helmke and Levitsky 2004, p. 727). An example from the Soviet Union, fitting this definition, is an effective and self-enforced set of norms associated with friendship, mutual help and social cooperation (us vs. them). In the SEE region, we establish a central role of the so-called 'trusted people and connections' for compensating or substituting the failure of formal institutions to operate effectively. According to a widely cited typology of informal institutions, both complementary and substitutive types are related to the convergent outcomes of formal and informal institutions (see Table 31.1), whereas the outcomes of formal and informal institutions in SEE are divergent (i.e. there is a gap between formal rules and informal

Table 31.1 Types of informal institutions

Outcomes	Effective formal institutions	Ineffective formal institutions
Convergent	Complementary	Substitutive
Divergent	Accommodating	Competing

norms). It is thus crucial to emphasise that our hypothesis that the informal norms act as *substitutes* for the failure of formal institutions does not imply the convergent outcomes of formal and informal institutions in SEE.

In order to qualify the SEE region case, we have to look deeper into the typology of informal institutions proposed by Helmke and Levitsky (2004). In the matrix above, informal institutions are perceived to be a dependent variable, with an independent variable—formal institutions and their effectiveness—given primacy. The convergent and divergent types of outcomes do not constitute an independent variable as they are intrinsically linked to the first one. Four types of informal institutions are then presented as accommodating, competing, complementary and substitutive relationships. This matrix is consistent with the focus of political science on formal institutions, which somewhat reverses the historical logic of their formation. An example of paving pathways in a park illustrates the point. If the pavements are laid beautifully but in a top-down fashion, without taking into account the bottom-up footpaths that had been in use for generations, the situation of convergence might never occur. Paving the existing footpaths will reduce the transaction costs for their users and the possibility of divergence.

* Complementary informal institutions mean that formal and informal institutions coexist, and informal institutions might serve as a foundation for effective formal institutions. This is clearly not the cases for the SEE.
* Substitutive informal institutions are compatible with formal institutions, but do not engage with them: they operate in environments where formal rules are not routinely enforced, such as local micro-credit schemes or rotational cooperation in rural areas (see Ledeneva et al. 2018). Substitutive institutions aim to achieve what formal institutions failed to achieve, but not by relying on informal contacts for getting things done or circumventing procedures within the remit of formal institutions.

When the outcomes of the informal and formal institutions (effective or ineffective) are divergent, which would primarily be the case of the SEE countries, the types of interaction are:

* Competing informal institutions coexist with ineffective formal institutions. These informal institutions are incompatible with the formal rules and are often found in post-colonial contexts in which formal institutions were imposed on indigenous rules and authority structures. This type would qualify to describe the situation in the SEE region, where external legal norms are imposed on traditional norms and customs.

* Accommodating informal institutions alter the substantive effects of formal rules, but without directly violating them. This, for example, includes *blat* in the Soviet Union, 'because strict adherence to the formal rules governing Soviet political and economic life did not allow enterprises to fulfil state targets or permit individuals to meet basic needs, a set of informal norms emerged in which individuals met these goals through personal networks' (from Ledeneva 1998 cited in Helmke and Levitsky 2004).

The Helmke-Levitsky typology is widely cited in the literature and rightly so. Despite the imbalance between formal and informal institutions it embodies, the typology points in the right direction for exploring the formal-informal interaction. In fact, their four types of informal institutions would work much better as four types of interaction, but the matrix should result from cross-tabulating types of formal institutions with types of informal institutions.

In order to focus on the interaction between formal and informal institutions specifically, we have devised a theoretical model that fits this empirical agenda much better. According to the INFORM model, both formal and informal institutions will only constitute constraints if they are effectively enforced. Needless to say, there will be formal rules that remain on paper and social norms that can be ignored without sanctions. In our study, however, we focus on informal institutions, which are effective (i.e. enforced, sanctioned and constitute informal constraints) and serve to deliver what formal institutions cannot (Webb et al. 2019). We operationalise these as relatively stable circles of 'trusted people and connections' that engage in problem-solving, perform economic functions and execute informal pressure on their members (Ledeneva 2008; Efendic et al. 2011; Efendic and Ledeneva 2020). These are different from socially shared norms, usually unwritten by the fact that they are enforced (actually make it through the 'enforcement belt') and thus constitute real informal constraints for economic behaviour (see Fig. 31.2).

2.4   Stability of Norms versus Temporality of Practices: Capturing Interactions between Formal and Informal Institutions

Neither formal nor informal institutions are static; they evolve and change over time (North 1990; Raiser 2001; Jutting 2003; Brousseau and Glachant 2008; Hinings and Malhotra 2008; Nelson 2008; Ebner 2008; Harriss 2008; Acemoglu and Robinson 2010; Efendic and Pugh 2015). The reasons for institutional changes are multiple: from incremental and hardly noticeable to geopolitical, such as the end of communism in central and eastern Europe, collapse of the Soviet Union and breakdown of former Yugoslavia. For example, existing organisations influence institutional change, political forces are very often invoked in the dynamics of institutional processes, economic reality sometimes provokes changes, outsiders can promote institutional changes and sometimes almost the whole institutional environment is changed as in the case of transition economies during their evolution from centrally planned systems towards market-oriented economies. Finally, revolutions or wars, that is, 'discontinuous institutional change' (North 1990: 89), may result in changes of institutional frameworks, which happened in some countries of SEE and to the biggest extent in Bosnia and Herzegovina (Efendic 2016). However, institutions should have durability as well, in order to be credible and acceptable to agents (Acemoglu 2009); accordingly, there is continuous tension between the need for persistence and the change in institutions (Andersson 2008; Acemoglu 2009).

A change in institutions may be caused by variations in formal rules and informal norms, as well as by changes in enforcement (North 1990), which implies that institutional change may be a very sophisticated process (Brousseau and Glachant 2008; Opper 2008). We probably still have a rather partial knowledge of how institutions change (Shirley 2008). However, the literature suggests that informal institutions are more stable than formal (North 1990; Williamson 2000; Pejovich 2008; Ebner 2008), though this does not mean that some social norms may not change very quickly. Since informal institutions change (generally) slowly, they are taken for granted in most institutional research (Williamson 2000; Andersson 2008) or focused upon in isolation from formal institutions as is the case with inductive, bottom-up approaches and ethnographic research. Because of difficulties in measurability, informal institutions have been a neglected dimension in empirical research (Raiser 2001; Harriss 2008) and treated as a 'residual category' conceptually (Helmke and Levitsky 2004: 727; Casson et al. 2010).

If we consider the potential causes and directions of changes, informal institutions tend to change gradually (driven by changes in social norms, customs, traditions, beliefs, habits and values, i.e. 'bottom-up'), while formal institutional change is determined by political forces in 'top-down' (Easterly 2008). The interaction of bottom-up and top-down forces is multidimensional and multilevel, which accounts for the complexity of institutional change. Since empirical studies cannot capture the complexity of institutional change, they have to be simplified and/or modified in various ways (Alston 1996; Williamson 2000; Fukuyama et al. 2007). Hence, a number of simplified institutional indicators and proxies are used in quantitative applied research. There are problems of measuring the quality or efficiency of formal institutions, but measuring informal institutions that relate to culture, mentalities, habits, trust, norms, conventions, codes and informal networks is additionally challenging. Proxies for informal institutions used in empirical research are easy to challenge conceptually: examples include variables capturing culture (Tabellini 2010; Williamson and Kerekes 2011), civil society (Moers 1999) and social capital (Jutting 2003).

Both formal and informal constraints shape human behaviour—they cannot be separated, as they are rooted in formal and informal institutions, which are intertwined and in continuous interaction with one another (Redmond 2005; Andersson 2008; Webb et al. 2019). The ideal types of such interaction are mostly seen as complementary or substitutive in their influence on socio-economic outputs (North 1990; Khan 1995; Eggertsson 1996; Raiser 2001; Jutting 2003; Furubotn and Richter 2005, Fukuyama et al. 2007; Aidis et al. 2008; Brousseau and Glachant 2008; Andersson 2008; Nye 2008; Efendic et al. 2011; Estrin and Prevezer 2011; Persson et al. 2013; Mungiu-Pippidi 2015). Some authors provide empirical evidence on the explanatory role of informal institutions in shaping formal institutions (e.g. Casson et al. 2010; Grzymala-Busse 2010; Williamson and Kerekes 2011), leading us to conclude that this interrelationship is very likely to be endogenous. This is an important point for empirical research. In our study, we operationalise the interaction of formal and informal institutions by looking into the workings of informal networks, which activate personal relationships (exercise informal constraints) in order to circumvent formal constraints in the SEE region.

The findings of the INFORM project indicate that informal norms in SEE tend to confront the top-down changes in formal institutions. The outcome of this clash results in the intense use of informal networking as an alternative mechanism of problem-solving and the rise of informal practices that point to the defects in workings of formal institutions. The willingness to engage into informal networking (i.e. invest time and money into socialising with the subsequent 'reliance on trusted people and connections') was found to be a common mechanism of problem-solving. However, informal networking cannot be associated exclusively with ineffective formal rules or with rational need for problem-solving. Informal institutions—social norms, cultural codes, customs and traditions—have some explanatory power for the predominance of informal networking (Alesina and Giuliano 2013, 2015; Cveticanin 2012; Grødeland 2013; Aliyev 2015; Stanojevic and Stokanic 2014).

3 Specifics of the Institutional Framework in the SEE Region: Transaction Costs of Informal Networks

Informal networks are used differently in different cultures and institutional frameworks. In some contexts, informal networks are oriented towards access to most basic needs and constitute strategies of survival, and in others they are associated with 'gaming the system' by elites (Ledeneva et al. 2018, Chap. 6). Trust-based networks can emerge in formal environments and even be generated top-down or initiated bottom-up in organisations (Granovetter 1985; Williamson 1993; Möllering 2014). For the purposes of our investigation, however, we focus on social networks that are biographical by-products of individuals ('trusted people and connections'). We refer to them as 'in-formal' because they are relationship-based, yet aimed at bending the formal rules for competitive advantage.

In a society that operates under *particularism*, the use of informal networks, or reliance on connections and exchange of favours, is the key mode of resource allocation. In general terms, societies of the SEE qualify as 'particularist', where relationships (and the pressure associated with them) mean more than rules and 'where individuals are treated differently according to particular ties or criteria' (Mungiu-Pippidi 2015: 14). They differ from societies of *ethical universalism*—'where equal treatment applies to everyone regardless of the group to which one belongs' (Ibid.). As Mungiu-Pippidi (2015) argues, a society must transform its dominant social order from *particularism* to *ethical universalism* in order to overcome the challenges of development and governance. Yet, instead of engaging in a collective battle to alter the rules of the game to ethical universalism, a highly particularistic society coerces individuals to seek access to the privileged group and reap the benefits under the current rules of the game. Such individual compliance with *particularism* can be reduced if the equilibrium of *opportunities* and *constraints* is changed—if one can build a 'critical mass' of individuals in favour of changing the rules of the game (Mungiu-Pippidi 2015: 183).

Effective formal institutions reduce risks and the cost of transactions; both households and entrepreneurs would rationalise their transaction costs and reduce their burden where possible. In the meantime, in the absence of effective formal institutions in SEE, informal networks serve a variety of purposes, from exchange of information, experience and ideas between agents to the provision of goods, services and favours, not freely accessible on the market. Maintaining such informal networks incurs costs (Efendic and Ledeneva 2019, 2020).

There seems to be a general consensus over the role of institutions in reducing transaction costs, even if definitions and calculations of transaction costs may vary significantly (Coase 1937). Transaction costs are presumed to go down once countries in transition have progressed further towards developed market economies, but for the time being monitoring the costs of informal networks can itself be a way of assessing the so-called 'implementation gap' (Blundo et al. 2013; Hudson and Marquette 2015; Mungiu-Pippidi 2015; Williams and Vorley 2015; Baez-Camargo and Ledeneva 2017). While the existing literature investigates predominantly the transaction costs of formal institutions or the benefits of social capital (e.g. Wallis and North 1986), the question of costs of sustaining informal networks—social networks used for getting things done—remains largely neglected.

Informal constraints and cultural norms are based on particularistic, rather than universalistic assumptions, and remain under-represented in the analyses of institutional frameworks. To reassess the balance, we associate the informal constraints with the costs they incur by using proxies of time and money (Efendic and Ledeneva 2020), but with important caveats about informal networks:

1. Whereas formal constraints are conceived to be universal and rational, informal networking serves to solve problems in particular contexts and tackle the complexity of social life.
2. Unlike social norms, informal networks are fluid and dynamic. Networks can change quickly and stay dormant until a particular problem arises.
3. Similarly to the formal hierarchies that grant access to resources, informal networks are just as valuable to their members. People care for, pay attention and invest time and money to establish and maintain them.
4. Just as formal organisations are perceived to enforce formal rules, informal networks are perceived to channel informal constraints, peer pressure and compliance with social norms. The potential of informal networks in channelling compliance with formal rules tends to be overlooked in policy-making.

4   Empirical Analysis of Formal-Informal Institutional Interaction in SEE

Now we move to the analysis of cross-country data and explore heterogeneity of formal and informal institutions in different countries by using representative micro data for individuals in the general public, supplemented with qualitative in-depth investigation of entrepreneurs.[3] Let us start with an outline of the existing assessments of the formal institutional environments in SEE (e.g. World Bank, 2018; Heritage Foundation, 2019). The region is characterised in most cases by institutional complexity, overlapping jurisdictions, government ineffectiveness and time-consuming processes, including some differences between the countries. In other words, there is room for further improvements in the formal institutional efficiency (see Table 31.2).

As for the workings of informal norms in the SEE region, we operationalise them as reliance on 'your trusted people and connections in important places' for problem-solving in particular contexts and assess their prevalence and functions (Efendic and Ledeneva 2020). The functioning of informal norms is not possible without enforcement (peer pressure) and supporting channels to access resources (informal networking). Hence, the operationalisation of reliance on 'trusted people and connections' (social networks, trust networks or social capital) is done through the use of informal networks. The emphasis

Table 31.2 Institutional environment in SEE looked through different institutional indices

Country	WB GE 2018	WB RQ 2018	WB RL 2018	WB CC 2018	IEF PP 2019	IEF JE 2019	IEF GI 2019
Albania	57.7	63.5	39.4	35.1	54.8	30.6	40.4
BiH	28.4	45.2	46.6	31.7	40.2	37.9	30.2
Croatia	69.2	68.3	63.0	60.1	66.0	42.9	38.6
Kosovo	38.0	41.4	40.4	35.6	57.2	53.5	44.7
N. Macedonia	55.8	71.6	43.8	42.3	65.1	60.7	44.7
Montenegro	58.2	65.9	57.7	58.2	55.4	51.8	39.5
Serbia	56.7	56.3	49.0	41.8	50.1	44.8	37.2
Slovenia	83.2	75.0	82.7	80.8	76.4	46.5	53.6

Sources: World Bank, 2018, https://info.worldbank.org/governance/wgi/; Heritage Foundation, 2019, https://www.heritage.org/index/ranking
Notes: *WB* refers to the World Bank Governance Indicators, the percentile rank (0 min to 100 max, indicates rank of country among all countries in the world), which includes: *GE* Government Effectiveness; *RQ* Regulatory Quality; *RL* Rule of Law; *CC* Control of Corruption; *IEF* refers to the Heritage Foundation Index of Economic Freedom (the scale is 0 min to 100 max), *PP* Property Rights; *JE* Judicial Effectiveness; *GI* Government Integrity

---

[3] Appendix 1 reports more details about the sample and how both types of data were collected.

is made on the use of networks, rather than on the network constitution. The strength of the informal institution of 'your trusted people and connections' is tested in the times of need and the data reveal the key importance of the instrumentality of informal networks in the SEE region.

And more generally, one could argue that informal networks are the best proxy for understanding channels and facilitation of interaction between formal and informal institutions: not only in the bottom-up direction, but also top-down. If one accepts that the formal rules are co-dependent with informal norms, then informal networks within formal organisations are just as essential for promoting top-down agendas: '(...) the discretionary zone in the interpretation and application of formal rules may itself be governed by a set of informal 'meta-rules' that tell civil servants when they can relax, suspend or modify rules, in respect of which persons, and in which circumstances' (Ledeneva et al. 2018: 474–475).

In terms of ideal types, in universalist cultures, where formal rules are enforced and followed more or less universally, the informal networks support or re-enhance these formal rules. In other words, informal networks are relationship based but not aimed at rule-bending, problem-solving or getting competitive advantage—they are conducive of the predominantly universalist values (in this case, informal norms and formal rules play a complementary role to each other). Institutional frameworks within which this is possible are characterised by a stage of development where resources are there to exclude predatory forms of exploitation and fierce competition over resources at the expense of the public good.

4.1   Informal Networking by General Public in SEE

The INFORM survey captures the informal practice of reliance on 'trusted people and connections' by asking the following: Q1. *In our society, if you want to get the job done, you always have to have your trusted people in important places and to have connections*—responses are in the range 1 not at all accurate to 10 completely accurate. Over 35% of respondents in SEE take the maximum value of 10 to indicate that having 'trusted people and connections' at different places in these societies is essentially important. Around 50% of respondents chose the value 8–10 (Fig. 31.3). This suggests that this type of informal norm is perceived as widespread and useful, with almost no difference between SEE countries. Similar responses are obtained for the question which asks to what extent is important to have large informal networks in this society (Q2. *On the scale from 1 to 10, please rate how important is to you to*

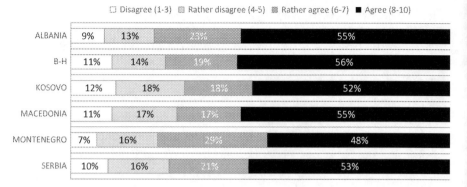

Fig. 31.3 'Trusted people and connections' in SEE countries. (Source: INFORM 2017)

have a large number of people that you can rely on—1 means not important at all, 10 means very important). Some 36% chose the maximum value of 10, while the mean value is 7.1, with slight variations between the countries.

When respondents reflect on their experience of formal institutions and trust in them (Q3. *Based on your own experience, what is your trust in state institutions in our country, like courts, police, governments, … —*1 no trust at all to 10 complete trust), their answers are almost the reverse. The most frequently given answer is the lowest level of trust—1 (22%), and the mean is 4.2. There are a bit more variations between SEE countries on this question, with the lowest trust recorded in Bosnia and Herzegovina (3.5). This suggests quite low level of trust in formal institutions and high incidence of reliance on personal networks and 'trusted people and connections' (Fig. 31.3). Thus, it would be important to know if personal trust is used as a solution to the lack of trust in formal institutions (Salinas et al. 2018). Consequently, to know whether the trust in state institutions (which we use as a proxy for efficiency of formal institutions, based on the experience of respondents with these institutions) is associated with the informal norm of relying on 'trusted people and connections', or with the use of 'informal networking' through which this informal norm is operationalised, we need a model that can enable us to investigate these complex relationships between formality and informality.

Following similar research by Efendic et al. (2011) on the link between confidence in formal and reliance on informal institutions in BiH, we assume that people's experience with formal institutions and reliance on connections and informal networking may differ. The difference can relate to both observable personal characteristics that we can control for—age, gender, marital status, education, economic performance, area of living and countries—and unobservable personal characteristics that we cannot control for directly (which might lead to the possibility of the omitted variable bias). In the context of SEE, possible candidates for unobserved factors are likely to be specific cross-cultural issues and influence of cultural diversity. The implication for our modelling strategy is that we need to control both: whether observable or not, both factors affect the informal-formal link that we investigate (inclusive of the immeasurable sociability skills and personal charm).

If there is an unobservable bias that has a systematic influence on the link formal-informal institutions, which is very likely due to the complexity discussed earlier, we hope to eliminate it by allowing the error term to be correlated between equations: that is, assuming (and testing) that this correlation will capture unobservable influence. A model possessing such properties is the 'system of regression equations' (Greene 2003), which in our case may be estimated as a seemingly unrelated bivariate probit model—SUPM. The SUPM is a system of equations in which the error terms are allowed to be correlated between equations (Gould et al. 2006), while common observed determinants are included in both regressions. The SUPM allows for a more complex (seemingly unrelated) pattern of joint determinations than simple simultaneity.

The relationship between efficiency of formal institutions and reliance on 'trusted people and connections' via informal networking is modelled implicitly through the unobserved correlations in the error terms (Heij et al. 2004). We expect that some culturally rooted factors, for example, 'Balkan mentality' that is mentioned by some of our informants (e.g. CRO_2[4] quote in the next section), might bias all regressions in our study, while this approach should capture it. In addition, we explicitly model the interaction by controlling for common observable variables in the system and use the conservative approach to estimate cluster robust model (with municipalities as clusters). The visual illustration of the model is shown in Fig. 31.4 and quantitative results are reported in Appendix 2, while we discuss the main findings on the type of formal-informal interaction.

Of particular interest for our interpretation is the likelihood ratio (LR) test, which provides a formal statistical check on the validity of the estimated model (or whether the model should be estimated with two independent binary probit equations). The LR tests the null hypothesis that the unobserved influences between the two equations are not associated in the manner

---

[4] Acronyms for countries are introduced in Appendix 1. CRO_4 means interview number 4 in Croatia. Other countries are Slovenia—SLO, Croatia—CRO, Bosnia and Herzegovina—BiH, Serbia—SRB, Montenegro—MNG, North Macedonia—MAC, Kosovo—KOS and Albania—ALB.

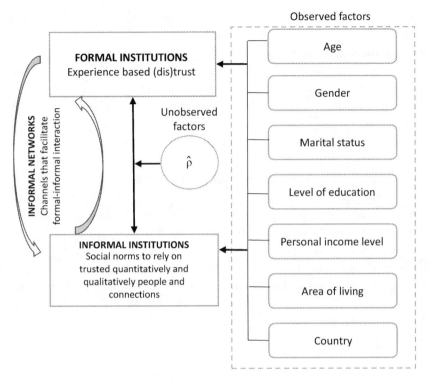

Fig. 31.4 Visual illustration of the formal-informal interaction model

suggested by our approach in Fig. 31.4. The outcome of LR test for the coefficient '$\hat{\rho}$' in Fig. 31.4 yields the p-value of 0.009. Thus, we reject the null hypothesis and conclude that this model is appropriately specified as a system.

The LR test is also informative to check whether formal institutions and informal norms are mutually exogenous (i.e. separate); or, if related endogenous (Fabbri et al. 2004), whether they act as substitute or complement to each other (Efendic et al. 2011). In our case, the test indicates a mutually endogenous relationship between the efficiency of formal institutions and the reliance on 'trusted people and connections' (Appendix 2, Table 31.4). According to the negative and significant *rho* coefficient ($\hat{\rho} = -0.09$), the two dependent variables are both determined by (unobserved) influences that are negatively correlated across the equations conditional on observed factors in the model. This means that unobserved (e.g. cultural) influences in the first equation, associated with lower trust in formal institutions, are associated with a greater reliance on 'trusted people and connections', enabled by 'informal networking'. The reverse also works: the higher the trust is into the workings of formal institutions, the lower the reliance on 'trusted people and connections'.

If we look at the influence of observable variables (Appendix 2), the effects of education, economic performance of individuals (measured through their personal income) and the country effects are mainly significant in both models that compose our system. The results indicate that more educated individuals and those with higher incomes report more trust towards formal institutions and less use of informal ones. Or more precisely, those individuals with education lower than the university degree and with lower level of incomes are less trusting towards formal institutions and rely more heavily on informal ones (if measured through the concept of 'trusted people and connections'). The country effects are also interesting as they report that respondents from all SEE countries in our sample have higher trust in their formal institutions in comparison to Bosnia and Herzegovina (BiH), which is the base category. This is not surprising, as the institutional set-up in BiH is well known for its complexity, on the one hand, and inability of political forces to agree on institutional reforms that would lead to institutional prosperity, on the other hand (Williams and Efendic 2019). However, there are no differences between countries in the use of 'trusted people and connections', which suggests that this informal norm is more persistent and less diverse in the region than perceptions regarding the efficiency of formal institutions.

Overall, in our survey, people's trust in formal institutions arises from their experience of constraints of formal institutions (see the related question) and, hence, corresponds to the actual enforcement and performance of formal institutions. Given the under-enforcement and overregulation features of formal institutions in the SEE region (Gordy and Efendic 2019), it is logical to presume that the substitutive role of informal institutions is essential and probably more persistent. It is often suggested in the literature that no society operates without trust. So if trust in formal institutions is low, the personalised trust would compensate for or substitute for it. On the basis of our data, we can offer further interpretation in that vein:

- First, the reliance on the informal norm of 'trusted people and connections' is empowered by the inefficiency of formal rules and procedures.
- Second, the instrumentality of 'informal networking' that channels pressure to circumvent formal rules and procedures grows together with the inefficiency of formal institutions.

Although not surprising in themselves, our findings confirm a substituting type of interaction between formal and informal institutions in SEE. Further tests are needed to be able to illustrate empirically that informal norms are more stable and more difficult to change (i.e. circles of trusted people and connections are fairly close and difficult to acquire).

4.2   Informal Networking by Entrepreneurs in SEE

Our qualitative in-depth analysis of informal networking among entrepreneurs seems to corroborate the possibility that while the general public is more compliant with the informal norms of reliance on 'trusted people and connections', the entrepreneurs are more dynamic in their attitudes: that develop more informal networks, invest in them, but also challenge their burden (Efendic and Ledeneva 2019). Indeed, the entrepreneurship literature reports that entrepreneurs tend to develop compensating mechanisms to operate their business when they need to address the challenges arising from emerging markets and imperfect institutional enforcements (Salinas et al. 2018; Ge et al. 2019). Entrepreneurial activity is thus affected by the formal and informal institutional voids and their interaction (Webb et al. 2019). However, they are also first to recognise the burden of doing so and other limitations associated with informal networking. Although networks might be more open, outreaching and give a better return on investment (supporting weak ties is more cost-effective than strong ties), they are also limited in what they can deliver. Our respondents believe that some problems can be solved only on the basis of strong bonds of reciprocity, so the informal norm of reliance on 'trusted people and connections' has been stressed as important also by entrepreneurs from all SEE countries:

> *In our society, there is still a system where you cannot make progress without some sort of informal connections*, BiH_1.[5] [Moreover, entrepreneurs believe that if they do not have a proactive position, nothing will change and they will face more challenges]: *If you do not have your own informal connections,… the doors will be closed*, SRB_3, and this is because: *There are segments in our society where you just have to have informal connections … you have to have the ear that listens to you in order to get what you need*, BiH_10.

What our respondents argue is that connections enable one to *'swim in muddy waters'*, MAC_3, and often help to offset political influences in their business. Some entrepreneurs see that *…corruption is everywhere*, SRB_3 and to get what they even deserve by the law, they *…would need informal*

---

[5] See the previous footnote for explanation and Appendix 1.

connections, BiH_4. This point of relying on informal forms to make the formal rules effective is of key importance to the understanding of the interaction of formal and informal institutions. For outsiders, informal networking may result in loose and open-ended associations, but these relationships have to become 'sealed' into tightly knit circle of trust, support and reciprocal obligations in order to be truly effective.

One of the entrepreneurs from Croatia, educated abroad, has explained the necessity to develop informal networking in order to get in touch with 'trusted people' but also for socialisation.

I was educated in the USA, so when I came back here and tried to do everything by the book, I did not fully understand informal networking and did not accept this environment, let's call it "Balkan mentality." This was the case until several years ago when I realized how our system is functioning, and that it was better for me to start socializing and networking more to find my 'trusted people'. I could not progress without them. (CRO_2)

What we find throughout the SEE region is that informal networking among entrepreneurs is commonly used, even if varied in scope and kind. On balance, it is the business interest that motivates entrepreneurs to participate in informal networking and much more so than adherence to an informal norm or cultural conformity (Efendic and Ledeneva 2020). Although some entrepreneurs acknowledge the necessity to accommodate the mentality of people in this region, their motivation seems proactive and driven by gaining access and creating opportunities, reducing risks and optimising costs. The majority of interviewees argue that informal networks are used primarily to compensate for the failures of formal institutional outcomes—informal networking is used as an efficient mode to cope with burdensome and unnecessary formal institutional challenges; they act as substitutes (BiH_1, BiH_3, BiH_4, BiH_6, BiH_7, BiH_8, KOS_3, KOS_5, ALB_1, ALB_2, MAC_1, MAC_3, MAC_6, SRB_1, SRB_3, SRB_6, SRB_8).

This investigation suggests that the functioning of informal norms is impossible without channels associated with informal networking. Although informal networks seem to be a biographical by-product, they are costly to establish, maintain and expand—it takes a lifetime of individual effort, time and resources. The costs of informal networking depend upon network size, which is limited, given the finite nature of individual time and monetary resources. The available literature reports that the density of networks has a significant influence on costs; higher density of informal networks lowers transaction costs (Henning et al. 2012). Moreover, the structure of networks might influence informal costs differently—network diversity based on race or ethnicity, for example, or networks based on family and friends or acquaintances (Marmaros and Sacerdote 2006; Silk 2003) all might have different effects on costs.

As for the costs of informal networking in SEE, individuals in the region invest considerable time and financial resources into informal networking (Efendic and Ledeneva 2020). The total informal networking cost, the costs of time and money (standardised by the PPP index to equalise prices between different countries), at the monthly level is estimated to be around 100 euros. This level of costs is not to be ignored considering that the average net monthly salary in Western Balkans region is less than 500 euros (exceptions are Croatia and Slovenia as EU countries in our sample). Our findings also suggest that the estimated (opportunity) costs of time are greater than the reported monetary costs and higher among entrepreneurs.

The complexity of conversion of informal networks into circles of trusted people and connections requires qualitative research, and this will help explain the interaction between formal institutions and informal institutions further, especially with respect of the pressure and enforcement that people of the circle are capable of imposing on each other. The importance of being networked, which can be estimated in quantitative terms, has to be coupled with the qualitative analysis of the grip that 'trusted people and connections' have over each other. Without understanding of this so-called lock-in effect, it is not possible to model economic behaviour in particularistic contexts.

5   Conclusion

In this chapter, we have reviewed the existing literature on formal and informal institutions and devised a model for conceptualising the formal-informal interaction and empirically testing the role of informal institutions in transition. We address the questions, 'what works when the formal institutions do not?' and 'to what extent do formal institutions (operationalised as trust in formal rules and procedures) constitute real constraints in SEE societies with a strong hold of personalised trust and reliance on personal connections.' We scrutinised the existing typologies of formal and informal institutions and suggested the INFORM model of the interaction between formal and informal institutions. We have established the advantages of the INFORM model for empirical testing as follows. Firstly, it works for transitional contexts where formal rules are often fast changing and might not necessarily constitute constraints. Secondly, it allows for variation in the pressure of constraints, both formal and informal, which is essential for accounting for the transaction costs. Thirdly, it distinguishes between informal institutions (informal norms) and other informal regularities (informal practices). Finally, it integrates informal networks as channels of interaction between formal and informal institutions. Although such theoretical adjustment in modelling might be of value in its own right, we have also undertaken to test it empirically with both quantitative and qualitative data.

To answer the questions on the role of informal institutions in transition, we rely on survey evidence from eight countries of South East Europe. When formal rules fail to be efficient, social norms of reliance on 'trusted people and connections' seem to predominate as a default (substitutive) option. Reliance on informal norms and investing time and money into facilitating channels, informal networking, to 'correct' the failure of formal institutions in the SEE region is so common that it makes us conclude on the predominantly substitutive role of informal institutions. Our findings hold for the general public, as well as for entrepreneurs, with entrepreneurs playing a more active role in informal networking. While these relationships are perceived to offset defects in the workings of formal institutions, and are used for instrumental purposes, they are also an enactment of trust and sociability in daily life, thus holding societies together vis-à-vis challenges of transition, crises or post-war development. The open question for policy-makers is how to reorient informal networks, make them more open and conducive of norms coherent with the formal rules and the universalist idea of the public good. We establish a further need to investigate the 'capabilities and functionings' of informal networks and their role in the workings of formal institutions.

Funding
This research has received funding from the European Union's Horizon 2020 research and innovation programme under grant agreement No 693537.

Appendix 1: Explanation of the SEE Sample and the Data

We analyse INFORM data collected in six South East European countries: Albania (ALB), Bosnia and Herzegovina (BiH), Kosovo (KOS), North Macedonia (MAC), Montenegro (MNG) and Serbia (SRB) over the period March–June 2017. A multi-stage random (probability) sampling methodology ensured representative samples in the data collection. In every household, the 'nearest birthday' rule was applied to select respondents for interviewing. Every subsequent address was determined by the standard 'random route' procedure. The survey was implemented by a professional research agency operating in all WB countries and implementing the survey simultaneously in all countries. The data set comprises 6040 respondents from six countries, with over 1000 observations per country. The survey covers a variety of topics related to formal institutions and informal norms in the WB countries.

Our qualitative investigation included the case of entrepreneurs from small- and medium-scale businesses in eight SEE countries (including Croatia—CRO and Slovenia—SLO, in this sample). Our point of entry—the entrepreneurs—enables us to explore the role of informal norms, as informal networking, in more detail, because entrepreneurs are the outsiders of the formal hierarchical structures, such as state or public services, but depend on them, so they have both an expertise and willingness to speak about using their contacts. The interviews were conducted by local INFORM researchers over the period November 2016–February 2017.[6] Majority of interviews were recorded with the consent of interviewees, anonymised, converted into transcripts and coded for the purposes of comparative analysis. Our sample includes 70 interviews,[7] which is not representative of the SME sector and puts certain limitations on the interpretation of results. However, the illuminating insights

---

[6] This research relies on the data collected in one point of time (2017); hence, we do not observe longitudinal or panel data. This approach makes limitation generally acknowledged for the most of cross-sectional research, as we are not able to uncover any dynamics or to be completely sure about the potential concern on causality.

[7] The questions were tested in five pilot interviews with entrepreneurs in BiH in September 2016 and modified accordingly. They covered five major topics: information about the main line of business, size and structure (density, centrality) of informal networks, costs of informal networks and general functioning of these networks. Overall, we did not have any major challenges in carrying out these interviews. The majority of respondents were willing to talk about these issues, although some were rather terse in their responses, while some started talking only after the recorder was turned off. INFORM researchers have conducted 5 interviews in ALB, 16 in BiH, 5 in CRO, 5 in KOS, 10 in MAC, 9 in SRB and 20 in SLO.

and research questions in this article provide valuable hypothesis for assessing the implications of informal networking in future research.

List of participants/interviewees from the business sector in SEE

Respondent	Type of business	Company age	Respondent age—category	Number of employees
BiH_1	Civil engineering construction	21–25	51–60	11–50
BiH_2	Automotive	0–5	31–40	0–10
BiH_3	Production of polymers	16–20	51–60	51–250
BiH_4	Land and real estate agency	0–5	21–30	0–10
BiH_5	Accounting agency	0–5	21–30	0–10
BiH_6	Business/start-up hub	0–5	21–30	11–50
BiH_7	Business/start-up hub	0–5	21–30	11–50
BiH_8	Association of entrepreneurs	16–20	51–60	0–10
BiH_9	Association of entrepreneurs	16–20	31–40	0–10
BiH_10	Civil engineering construction	36–40	51–60	0–10
BiH_11	Family winery	36–40	41–50	0–10
BiH_12	Wood instigators production	0–5	31–40	0–10
BiH_13	Catering industry	16–20	41–50	51–250
BiH_14	Catering industry	0–5	21–30	0–10
BiH_15	Private university	0–5	31–40	0–10
BiH_16	Mobile store and landscaping company	0–5	21–30	0–10
MAC_1	Healthy food stores	0–5	21–30	11–50
MAC_2	Hotel	11–15	31–40	11–50
MAC_3	Marketing agency	16–20	41–50	11–50
MAC_4	Accounting agency	21–25	61–70	0–10
MAC_5	Dairy factory	11–15	51–60	11–50
MAC_6	Catering industry	26–30	41–50	11–50
MAC_7	Online/web shopping company	0–5	31–40	11–50
MAC_8	Private high school	6–10	31–40	11–50
MAC_9	Drugs and medicine distribution	21–25	41–50	0–10
MAC_10	Metallurgy company	21–25	31–40	0–10
SLO_1	Service sector	0–5	31–40	0–10
SLO_2	Service sector—house maintenance	6–10	41–50	0–10
SLO_3	Service sector—mechanic	0–5	41–50	0–10
SLO_4	Restaurant	0–5	41–50	0–10
SLO_5	Service sector—electrician	21–25	51–60	0–10
SLO_6	Research institute	0–5	31–40	0–10
SLO_7	Catering industry	16–20	51–60	11–50
SLO_8	Restaurant	0–5	31–40	0–10
SLO_9	Marketing agency	6–10	31–40	0–10

(continued)

(continued)

Respondent	Type of business	Company age	Respondent age—category	Number of employees
SLO_10	Marketing agency	0–5	31–40	0–10
SLO_11	Computer shop	0–5	21–30	0–10
SLO_12	Service sector—hairdressing	26–30	41–50	0–10
SLO_13	Wood industry	26–30	51–60	0–10
SLO_14	Cosmetic industry	6–10	21–30	11–50
SLO_15	Service sector—hairdressing	0–5	21–30	0–10
SLO_16	Farming	11–15	11–20	0–10
SLO_17	Power distribution	6–10	41–50	11–50
SLO_18	Plastic industry for construction	16–20	51–60	0–10
SLO_19	Internet shop	16–20	41–50	11–50
SLO_20	Service sector—mechanic	0–5	31–40	0–10
SRB_1	Production of plastic derivate	6–10	31–40	11–50
SRB_2	Health industry—stomatology	6–10	31–40	0–10
SRB_3	Catering industry	6–10	31–40	0–10
SRB_4	Service sector—hairdressing	21–25	51–60	0–10
SRB_5	Private music school	0–5	41–50	0–10
SRB_6	Design agency	6–10	31–40	0–10
SRB_7	Cosmetic industry	11–15	51–60	0–10
SRB_8	Tectonics sector	11–15	51–60	0–10
SRB_9	Purchase and processing of milk	6–10	51–60	51–250
ALB_1	Private high school	0–5	41–50	51–250
ALB_2	Automotive	0–5	41–50	0–10
ALB_3	IT company	0–5	41–50	11–50
ALB_4	Trade, industrial materials	16–20	41–50	11–50
ALB_5	Printing house	11–15	41–50	11–50
CRO_1	Distribution of electric materials	0–5	41–50	0–10
CRO_2	Marketing agency	6–10	31–40	11–50
CRO_3	Hotel	0–5	51–60	11–50
CRO_4	IT company	21–25	41–50	11–50
CRO_5	Production of lighting solutions	6–10	41–50	11–50
KOS_1	Production of polymers	16–20	31–40	11–50
KOS_2	Trade company and production	6–10	41–50	11–50
KOS_3	Catering industry	26–30	51–60	11–50
KOS_4	Wood instigators production	11–15	41–50	0–10
KOS_5	Civil engineering construction	16–20	41–50	11–50

Table 31.3 Descriptive statistics of the main variables of interest

Variables	Description	No. of observations	Mean	Standard deviation
ownlinksd	Trusted people and connections 1-10; 0 is 1-5, 1 is 6-10	5943	0.74	0.44
insttrustd	Trust to institutions 1-10; 0 is 1-5, 1 is 6-10	5876	0.29	0.45
urban	Area of living; 1—urban, 0—other	6040	0.53	0.50
married	Marital status; 1—married; 0—other	5975	0.60	0.49
female	Gender; 1—female, 0—male	6040	0.55	0.50
age	Age in years	6040	46.53	17.64
hieduc	Education; 1—university or higher; 0—below university	6029	0.22	0.42
pincome	Personal income; 1—less than 100€; 2—101–200€; .... 9—over 1501€	4341	2.89	1.63
mac	Country; 1—North Macedonia, 0—other	6040	0.17	0.37
mng	Country; 1—Montenegro, 0—other	6040	0.13	0.34
kos	Country; 1—Kosovo, 0—other	6040	0.15	0.36
alb	Country; 1—Albania, 0—other	6040	0.15	0.36
srb	Country; 1—Serbia, 0—other	6040	0.19	0.39
*BiH**	Country; 1—Bosnia and Herzegovina, 0—other (*omitted category in the model)	6040	0.21	0.40

Table 31.4 SUPM formal-informal interaction model, cluster-robust estimates

	SUPM Model			
	Coefficient	P>|z|	Coefficient	P>|z|
Variables	*DEPENDENT VARIABLE 1—insttrustd*		*DEPENDENT VARIABLE 2—ownlinksd*	
urban	−0.02	0.774	0.07	0.290
married	−0.12	0.008	0.02	0.603
female	−0.05	0.302	−0.03	0.572
age	0.00	0.110	0.00	0.075
hieduc	0.17	0.004	−0.09	0.086
pincome	0.03	0.075	−0.03	0.040
mac	−0.14	0.169	0.02	0.819
mng	0.46	0.000	0.06	0.599
kos	0.21	0.052	−0.10	0.413
alb	0.47	0.000	0.08	0.533
srb	0.32	0.001	−0.03	0.766
constant	−0.88	0.000	0.86	0.000

Number of observations	4200
Cluster-robust estimate	Yes, clusters are municipalities
Coefficient of correlation in the residuals	$rho = -0.085$
Wald test of rho=0: chi²(1)	Prob > chi² = 0.0088
The Wald test for joint significance	Prob > chi² = 0.0000

Appendix 2

References

Acemoglu, D. (2009). *Persistence and Change in Institutions*. The Marshall Lectures 2008–09, Seminar at Cambridge University, 10–11th February.

Acemoglu, D., & Robinson, J. A. (2010). The Role of Institutions in Growth and Development. *Review of Economics and Institutions, 1*(2), 1–33.

Aidis, R., Estrin, S., & Mickiewicz, T. (2008). Institutions and Entrepreneurship Development in Russia: A Comparative Perspective. *Journal of Business Venturing, 23*(6), 656–672.

Alesina, A., & Giuliano, P. (2013). *Family Ties*. NBER Working Paper No. 18966, April.

Alesina, A., & Giuliano, P. (2015). Culture and Institutions. *Journal of Economic Literature, 53*(4), 898–944.

Aliyev, H. (2015). Post-Soviet Informality: Towards Theory-Building. *International Journal of Sociology and Social Policy, 35*(3/4), 182–198.

Alston, L. J. (1996). Empirical Work in Institutional Economics: An Overview. In L. J. Alston, T. Eggertsson, & D. C. North (Eds.), *Empirical Studies in Institutional Change*. Cambridge: Cambridge University Press.

Andersson, D. E. (2008). *Property Rights, Consumption and the Market Process—New Horizons in Institutional and Evolutionary Economics*. Cheltenham, UK and Northampton, MA: Edward Elgar.

Baez-Camargo, C., & Ledeneva, A. (2017). Where Does Informality Stop and Corruption Begin? Informal Governance and the Public/Private Crossover in Mexico, Russia and Tanzania. *The Slavonic and East European Review, 95*(1), 49–75.

Blundo, G., de Sardan, J. P. O., Arifari, N. B., & Alou, M. T. (2013). *Everyday Corruption and the State: Citizens and Public Officials in Africa* (1st ed.). J. P. O. de Sardan, Ed. Chicago: Zed Books.

Brousseau, E., & Glachant, J. M. (2008). *New Institutional Economics—A Guidebook*. Cambridge: Cambridge University Press.

Casson, M. C., Della Giusta, M., & Kambhampati, S. U. (2010). Formal and Informal Institutions and Development. *World Development, 38*(2), 137–141.

Christiansen, T., & Neuhold, C. (Eds.). (2012). *International Handbook on Informal Governance*. Chetlthenham: Edward Elgar Publishing Limited.

Coase, R. H. (1937). The Nature of the Firm. *Economica, 4*(16), 386–405.

Cveticanin, P. (Ed.). (2012). *Social and Cultural Capital in Serbia*. Nis: Centre for Empirical Cultural Studies of South-East Europe.

De Soto, H. (1989). *The Other Path: The Invisible Revolution of the Third World*. London: IB Tauris.

De Soto, H. (2000). *The Mystery of Capital: Why Capitalism Triumphs in the West and Fails Everywhere Else*. New York: Basic Books.

Dimitrova, A. L. (2010). The New Member States of the EU in the Aftermath of Enlargement. Do New European Rules Remain Empty Shells? *Journal of European Public Policy, 17*(1), 137–148.

Easterly, W. (2008). Design and Reform of Institutions in LDCS and Transition Economies. Institutions: Top Down or Bottom Up? *American Economic Review: Papers and Proceedings, 98*(2), 95–99.

Ebner, A. (2008). Institutional Evolution and the Political Economy of Governance. In A. Ebner & N. Beck (Eds.), *The Institutions of the Market—Organizations, Social Systems, and Governance*. Oxford: Oxford University Press.

Efendic, A. (2016). Emigration Intentions in a Post-Conflict Environment: Evidence from Bosnia and Herzegovina. *Post-Communist Economies, 28*(3), 335–352.

Efendic, A., & Ledeneva, A. (2019). The Cost of Informal Networking in the Western Balkans Region Matters! In E. Gordy & A. Efendic (Eds.), *Meaningful Reform in the Western Balkans—Between Formal Institutions and Informal Practices* (pp. 85–101). Peter Lang: Bern.

Efendic, A., & Ledeneva, A. (2020). The Importance of being Networked: The Costs of Informal Networking in the Western Balkans Region. *Economic Systems*. (Forthcoming).

Efendic, A., & Pugh, G. (2015). Institutional Effects on Economic Performance in Post-Socialist Transition: A Dynamic Panel Analysis. *Acta Oeconomica, 65*(4), 503–523.

Efendic, A., Pugh, G., & Adnett, N. (2011). Confidence in Formal Institutions and Reliance on Informal Institutions in Bosnia and Herzegovina—An Empirical Investigation Using Survey Data. *The Economics of Transition, 19*(3), 521–540.

Eggertsson, T. (1996). A Note on the Economics Institutions. In L. J. Alston, T. Eggertsson, & D. C. North (Eds.), *Empirical Studies in Institutional Change*. Cambridge: Cambridge University Press.

Estrin, S., & Prevezer, M. (2011). The Role of Informal Institutions in Corporate Governance: Brazil, Russia, India, and China Compared. *Asia Pacific Journal of Management, 28*(1), 41–67.

Fabbri, D., Monfardini, C., & Radice, R. (2004). *Testing Exogeneity in the Bivariate Probit Model: Monte Carlo Evidence and an Application to Health Economics*. Working Papers No. 514, Bologna: Dipartimento Scienze Economiche, Universita' di Bologna.

Fang, T. (2012). Yin Yang: A New Perspective on Culture. *Management and Organization Review, 8*(1), 25–50.

Fukuyama, F., Dinello, N., & Popov, V. (2007). Development and the Limits of Institutional Design. In *Political Institutions and Development: Failed Expectations and Renewed Hopes*. Northampton, MA: Edward Elgar.

Furubotn, E. G., & Richter, R. (2005). *Institutions & Economic Theory, The Contribution of the New Institutional Economics* (2nd ed.). Ann Arbor: The University of Michigan Press.

Ge, J., Carney, M., & Kellermanns, F. (2019). Who Fills Institutional Voids? Entrepreneurs' Utilization of Political and Family Ties in Emerging Markets. *Entrepreneurship Theory and Practice, 43*(6), 1124–1147.

Ginsburg, T., & Simpser, A. (Eds.). (2013). *Constitutions in Authoritarian Regimes.* Cambridge: Cambridge University Press.

Gordy, E., & Efendic, A. (2019). *Meaningful Reform in the Western Balkans—Between Formal Institutions and Informal Practices.* Bern: Peter Lang.

Gould, W., Pitblado, J. and Sribney, W. 2006. *Maximum Likelihood Estimation with Stata.*

Granovetter, M. (1985). Economic Action and Social Structure: The Problem of Embeddedness. *American Journal of Sociology, 91*(3), 481–510.

Greene, W. H. (2003). *Econometric Analysis* (5th ed.). Princeton, NJ: Prentice Hall.

Grødeland, Å. B. (2013). Public Perceptions of Corruption and Anti-Corruption Reform in the Western Balkans. *Slavonic & East European Review, 91*(3), 535–598.

Grzymala-Busse, A. (2010). The Best Laid Plans: The Impact of Informal Rules on Formal Institutions in Transitional Regimes. *Studies in Comparative International Development, 45*(3), 311–333.

Harriss, J. (2008). Explaining Economic Change: The Relations of Institutions, Politics, and Culture. In A. Ebner & N. Beck (Eds.), *The Institutions of the Market—Organizations, Social Systems, and Governance.* Oxford: Oxford University Press.

Heij, C., de Boer, P., Franses, P. H., Kloek, T., & van Dijk, H. K. (2004). *Econometric Methods with Applications in Business and Economics.* Oxford: Oxford University Press.

Helmke, G., & Levitsky, S. (2004). Informal Institutions and Comparative Politics: A Research Agenda. *Perspectives on Politics, 2*(4), 725–740.

Henig, D., & Makovicky, N. (2017). *Economies of Favours after Socialism: A Comparative Perspective.* Oxford: Oxford University Press.

Henning, C. H. C. A., Henningsen, G., & Henningsen, A. (2012). Networks and Transaction Costs. *American Journal of Agricultural Economics, 94*(2), 377–385.

Heritage Foundation (2019). https://www.heritage.org/index/ranking

Hinings, C. R., & Malhotra, N. (2008). Change in Institutional Fields. In A. Ebner & N. Beck (Eds.), *The Institutions of the Market—Organizations, Social Systems, and Governance.* Oxford: Oxford University Press.

Hodgson, G. M. (2006). What are Institutions? *Journal of Economic Issues, XL*(1), 1–25.

Hudson, D., & Marquette, H. (2015). Mind the Gaps: What's Missing in Political Economy Analysis and Why it Matters. In A. Whaites, E. Gonzalez, S. Fyson, & G. Teskey (Eds.), *A Governance Practitioner's Notebook* (pp. 67–82). OECD.

INFORM. (2017). https://www.ucl.ac.uk/ssees/research/funded-research-projects/inform

Jutting, J. (2003). *Institutions and Development: A Critical Review.* OECD Working Paper No. 210.

Khan, M. (1995). State Failure in Weak States: A Critique of New Institutionalists Explanations. In J. Harriss, J. Hunter, & C. M. Lewis (Eds.), *The New Institutional Economics and Third World Development*. London: Routledge.

Knowles, S., & Weatherston, C. R. (2006). *Informal Institutions and Cross-Country Income Differences*. Dunedin: University of Otago, Department of Economics.

Lauth, H. J. (2007). Informal Institutions and Democracy. *Democratization, 7*(4), 21–50.

Ledeneva, A. V. (1998). *Russia's Economy of Favours: Blat, Networking and Informal Exchange*. Cambridge: University Press.

Ledeneva, A. (2001). *Uwritten Rules: How Russia Really Works*. London: CER.

Ledeneva, A. (2006). *How Russia Really Works. Informal Practices in Politics and Business*. Cornell University Press.

Ledeneva, A. (2008). Informal Networks in Post-Communist Economies: A "Topographic Map". In T. Lahusen & P. H. Solomon Jr. (Eds.), *What is Soviet Now? Identities, Legacies, Memories* (pp. 101–134). Berlin: Lit Verlag.

Ledeneva, A., Bailey, A., Barron, S., Curro, C., & Teague, E. (Eds.). (2018). *The Global Encyclopaedia of Informality*. London: UCL Press.

Marmaros, D., & Sacerdote, B. (2006). How Do Friendships Form? *The Quarterly Journal of Economics, 121*(1), 79–119.

Moers, L. (1999). *How Important are Institutions for Growth in Transition Countries?* Tinbergen.

Möllering, G. (2014). Trust, Calculativeness, and Relationships: A Special Issue 20 Years after Williamson's Warning. *Journal of Trust, 4*(1), 1–21.

Mungiu-Pippidi, A. (2015). *The Quest for Good Governance: How Societies Develop Control of Corruption*. Cambridge: Cambridge University Press.

Nelson, R. R. (2008). Co-Evolution of Technologies and Institutions in Market Economies. In A. Ebner & N. Beck (Eds.), *The Institutions of the Market—Organizations, Social Systems, and Governance*. Oxford: Oxford University Press.

Newton, S. (2017). *The Constitutional Systems of the Independent Central Asian States: A Contextual Analysis*. Oxfrod: Hart.

North, D. C. (1990). *Institutions, Institutional Change and Economic Performance*. Cambridge: University press.

North, D. (1991). Institutions. *Journal of Economic Perspectives, 5*(1), 97–112.

North, D. C. (1995). *The New Institutional Economics and Third World Development*. In J. Harriss, J. Hunter, & C. M. Lewis (Eds.), *The New Institutional Economics and Third World Development* (pp. 17–26). New York: Routledge.

Nye, J. (2008). Institutions and the Institutional Environment. In E. Brousseau & G. Jean-Michel (Eds.), *New Institutional Economics—A Guidebook*. Cambridge: Cambridge University Press.

Opper, S. (2008). New Institutional Economics and its Application on Transition and Developing Economies. In E. Brousseau & G. Jean-Michel (Eds.), *New Institutional Economics—A Guidebook*. Cambridge: Cambridge University Press.

Pejovich, S. (1999). The Effects of Interaction of Formal and Informal Institutions on Social Stability and Economic Development. *Journal of Markets and Morality, 2*(2), 164–181.

Pejovich, S. (2008). *Law, Informal Rules and Economic Performance, the Case of Common Law*. Cheltenham, UK; Northampton, MA: Edward Elgar.

Persson, A., Rothstein, B., & Teorell, J. (2013). Why Anticorruption Reforms Fail—Systemic Corruption as a Collective Action Problem. *Governance, 26*(3), 449–471.

Polese, A. (2015). Informality Crusades: Why Informal Practices are Stigmatized, Fought and Allowed in Different Contexts According to an Apparently Understandable Logic. *Caucasus Social Science Review, 2*(1), 1–26.

Pollitt, M. (2002). The Economics of Trust, Norms, and Networks. *Business Ethics: A European Review, 11*(2), 119–128.

Raiser, M. (2001). Informal Institutions, Social Capital and Economic Transition: Reflections on a Neglected Dimension. In G. A. Cornia & V. Popov (Eds.), *Transition and Institutions: The Experience of Gradual and Late Reformers*. Oxford: Oxford University Press.

Redmond, W. H. (2005). Process of Gradual Institutional Drift. *Journal of Economic Issues, XXXIX*(2), 501–509.

Sakwa, R. (2007). Constitutionalism and Accountability in Contemporary Russia: The Problem of Displaced Sovereignty. In G. Smith & R. Sharlet (Eds.), *2007. Russia and its Constitution: Promise and Political Reality*. Martinus Nijhoff Publishers.

Salinas, A., Muffatto, M., & Alvarado, R. (2018). Informal Institutions and Informal Entrepreneurial Activity: New Panel Data Evidence from Latin American Countries. *Academy of Entrepreneurship Journal, 24*(4), 1–17.

Scott, R. (2004). Reflections on a Half-Century of Organizational Sociology. *Annual Review of Sociology, 30*, 1–21.

Searle, J. R. (2005). What is An Institution? *Journal of Institutional Economics, 1*(1), 1–22.

Shirley, M. M. (2008). *Institutions and Development*. Cheltenham, UK and Northampton, MA: Edward Elgar.

Silk, J. B. (2003). Cooperation Without Counting. In P. Hammerstein (Ed.), *Genetic and Cultural Evolution of Cooperation* (pp. 37–54). Boston: The MIT Press.

Stanojevic, D., & Stokanic, D. (2014). The Importance of Clientelism and Informal Practices for Employment among Political Party Members after 2000s—An Explorative Enquiry. In P. Cveticanin, I. Mangova, & N. Markovikj (Eds.), *A Life for Tomorrow—Social Transformations in South-East Europe*. Skopje: Institute for Democracy "Societas Civilis" Skopje.

Tabellini, G. (2010). Culture and Institutions: Economic Development in the Regions of Europe. *Journal of the European Economic Association, 8*(4), 677–716.

Tonoyan, V., Strohmeyer, R., Habib, M., & Perlitz, M. (2010). Corruption and Entrepreneurship: How Formal and Informal Institutions Shape Small Firm

Behaviour in Transition and Mature Markets. *Entrepreneurship Theory and Practice, 2010*, 803–832.

Tsai, K. S. (2006). Adaptive Informal Institutions and Endogenous Institutional Change in China. *World Politics, 59*(1), 116–141.

Wallis, J. J., & North, D. (1986). Measuring the Transaction Sector in the American Economy, 1870–1970. *Long-Term Factors in American Economic Growth*, 95–162. Retrieved from https://econpapers.repec.org/bookchap/nbrnberch/9679.htm.

Webb, J. W., Khoury, T. A., & Hitt, M. A. (2019). The Influence of Formal and Informal Institutional Voids on Entrepreneurship. *Entrepreneurship Theory and Practice, 2010*, 803–831.

Williams, N., & Efendic, A. (2019). Internal Displacement and External Migration in a Post-Conflict Economy: Perceptions of Institutions among Migrant Entrepreneurs. *Journal of International Entrepreneurship, 17*(4), 558–585.

Williams, N., & Vorley, T. (2015). Institutional Asymmetry: How Formal and Informal Institutions Affect Entrepreneurship in Bulgaria. *International Small Business Journal: Researching Entrepreneurship, 33*(8), 840–861.

Williamson, O. E. (1993). Calculativeness, Trust, and Economic Organization. *The Journal of Law and Economics, 36*, 453–486.

Williamson, O. E. (2000). The New Institutional Economics: Taking Stock, Looking Ahead. *Journal of Economic Literature, XXXVIII*, 595–613.

Williamson, C. R. (2009). Informal Institutions Rule: Institutional Arrangements and Economic Performance. *Public Choice, 139*, 371–387.

Williamson, C. R., & Kerekes, C. B. (2011). Securing Private Property: Formal Versus Informal Institutions. *Journal of Law and Economics, 54*(3), 537–572.

World Bank (2018). https://info.worldbank.org/governance/wgi/

32

Entrepreneurship in Comparative Economics Perspective

Slavo Radosevic and Esin Yoruk

1 Introduction

The conventional view of capitalism is rooted in the notion of entrepreneurship which operates best in conditions of unfettered markets. For example, Baumol (2002) ascribes entrepreneurial dynamism to 'the free-market growth process' or, more specifically, to competitive pressure that forces firms to create, seek out and promote innovation. The rise of neoliberalism as a political philosophy led to a research programme which considers entrepreneurship as a dominant individual level phenomenon. Within this research programme, it is individual-level characteristics, such as the aspirations and attitudes of individual entrepreneurs, that explain entrepreneurship at the national level. This methodological individualism rooted approach is the current prevailing perspective on entrepreneurship. Accordingly, from this conventional perspective, among the different types of capitalism, liberal market economies are perceived as the most conducive to entrepreneurship.

S. Radosevic (✉)
University College London, London, UK
e-mail: s.radosevic@ucl.ac.uk

E. Yoruk
Coventry University, Coventry, UK
e-mail: esin.yoruk@coventry.ac.uk

© The Author(s) 2021
E. Douarin, O. Havrylyshyn (eds.), *The Palgrave Handbook of Comparative Economics*,
https://doi.org/10.1007/978-3-030-50888-3_32

From a comparative economics perspective, we consider this conventional view to be unsatisfactory for the following two reasons. First, entrepreneurship is not just an individual level phenomenon it is also a system and a collective-specific phenomenon in which firm-level entrepreneurship also plays a role. Second, the reference institutional entrepreneurship context cannot be reduced to a 'free market machine' or a 'liberal market economy', but needs to consider different varieties of capitalism (VoC) and explore differences in their entrepreneurial propensities.

Capitalism is an entrepreneurial system (Baumol 2002), which takes a variety of forms (Amable 2003; Hall and Soskice 2001; Whitley 1999). However, the literature on entrepreneurial properties or the features of different variants of capitalism is sparse. In this chapter, we advance our understanding of this issue by adopting a comparative economics lens. We want to bridge the literature on VoC and entrepreneurship by focusing on institutional 'varieties of ERs'. This link is important since existing approaches to VoC are not designed to explore their entrepreneurial properties.

Our analysis builds on our proposed Entrepreneurial Propensity of Innovation Systems (EPIS) perspective. In Radosevic and Yoruk (2013), we show that, in the context of EU countries, knowledge intensive entrepreneurship (KIE) is an outcome of the interaction among three components of Entrepreneurial Opportunity: Technology Opportunities (TO), Market Opportunities (MO) and Institutional Opportunities (IO). We also demonstrate the conceptual and statistical robustness of these concepts and their empirical relevance. In this chapter, we develop a conceptual approach to exploring VoC from an entrepreneurial perspective. In line with much of the entrepreneurship literature, we consider the study of opportunities as central to entrepreneurship research. Our enquiry focuses on Schumpeterian or innovative as opposed to replicative entrepreneurship.

We take the view that different entrepreneurial opportunities (EO) are institutionalized in different ways, which assumes there is no one-to-one relationship between innovation system functions/activities and their organizational forms (Radosevic 1998). In other words, the same activities can be pursed via a range of institutional arrangements which can be represented as a continuum or as scale metrics.

To explore this, first, we review the literature on VoC from an entrepreneurship perspective and discuss the methodological issues involved in linking entrepreneurship to VoC. Second, we compare three conceptual and analytical approaches which are relevant for exploring the relationship between

VoC and entrepreneurship: the GEM[1]/GEDI[2] methodology (Acs et al. 2014), the RRN (Lazonick and Mazzucato 2013) and our proposed EPIS approach (Radosevic and Yoruk 2013). Third, by considering EO as central to entrepreneurship, we develop a conceptual framework to be used as the basis for research to measure the 'institutional varieties of ERs'. Our overall arguments are summarized in the conclusions.

2   Varieties of Capitalism and Entrepreneurship

VoC research assumes that varieties are not infinite and fall into a few generic types based on different criteria. Hall and Soskice (2001), the proponents of the VoC notion, distinguish between two modes of coordination based on liberal markets or strategic coordination governance of relations among companies. Amable (2003) developed an approach that focuses on 'social systems of production' and goes beyond the market/strategic coordination dichotomy. He uses several criteria to characterize his VoC typology: product markets (regulated/deregulated); labour markets (flexible, regulated); finance (stock markets, banks, property ownership); welfare (extent and type of welfare state) and education (extent and type public/private). Whitley (1999) proposed a national business systems approach, based on the degree (high or low) to which coordination occurs through ownership and non-ownership (e.g., networks or associations), respectively. Inspired by these three approaches, various contributors have applied a range of criteria to different country groupings with the differences in these approaches related to the significance of the different institutional domains. For example, Tridico (2011) uses the six institutional variables of the European Bank for Reconstruction and Development (EBRD) to classify VoC in the context of transition economies. These six institutional variables or dimensions are enterprise, market and competition, trade and openness, the financial sector, the wage nexus and social investment. He uses these dimensions to identify four socio-economic capitalism models: competitive, 'corporative dirigiste', hybrid and state. Knell and Srholec's (2007) taxonomy of VoC applied to the EU is effectively based on Hall and Soskice's (DATE) distinction between market and strategic coordination. Aiginger (2007) proposed an extension to the European Social Model typology, which differentiates between Anglo-Saxon, Nordic and Continental European, by adding Mediterranean and Catching-up or Central and Eastern Europe (CEE).

---

[1] https://www.gemconsortium.org/
[2] https://thegedi.org/global-entrepreneurship-and-development-index

Critical to the notion of VoC is the principle of complementarities. This captures the idea that the functional performance of one institution is affected by the presence/functioning of another institution. However, complementarities are not necessarily about compatibilities among similar types of institutions since specific types within a VoC typology are never found in their 'pure form'. Hodgson (1999) explains this by the notion of impurity. The 'impurity principle' contends that different kinds of subsystems are necessary for the system as a whole to function. He argues that 'every socio-economic system must rely on at least one structurally dissimilar subsystem to function' (Hodgson 1999: 1). Hence, a mixture of market and non-market elements is essential to VoC. For example, capitalism promotes market and profit-seeking activity, but relies on family and state, which are run on non-market principles (Hodgson 2015). Orthodox centrally planned systems also need informal network exchanges to survive (Ledeneva 1998).

Alongside the impurity principle, we recognize that, in reality, institutions are a mixture of functions, power relationships, path dependencies (isomorphism), evolution and social learning (Schmid 2004). The more institutions are perceived as a functionalist response to the changes affecting agents, the more we would expect a specific VoC typology to include coherent constellations of institutions. If we take a less functionalist approach, VoC taxonomies become much less robust. Thus, different understandings of institutions lead to differences in the interpretation of VoC as either tightly constructed networks or loosely coupled portfolios of institutional domains.

The issue is further complicated by the fact that VoC are not static entities. Rather, the reality is a continuous and on-going process of hybridization or transformation of VoC. Substantial functional change may be occurring, but it may, in some cases, be hidden behind formal institutional stability or the changes occurring in specific domains may not fit with the rest of the system (Hancke et al. 2007).

The problem has become more critical since the advent of globalization. There are no longer disparate sets of national varieties, but rather sets of variegated capitalisms or capitalism varieties based on the coupling between, asymmetries among and co-evolution of different accumulation regimes and modes of regulation (Jessop 2015). Within this perspective, national variations are structured and influenced by the dominant variant (e.g., by *Model Deutschland* in the EU) and its distinctive logic.

How the globalization process during the 1990s and early 2000s has affected VoC is a contested issue. For example, Jackson and Deeg (2006: 14) point out that Germany 'has undergone a major institutional change; in a sense, German firms have experienced an Anglo-Saxonization'. They suggest, also, that 'some national economies that have undergone sufficient institutional change no longer fit into the category or "type" of capitalism to which they were ascribed during the 1980s or 1990s. In some cases, this shift is quite radical (e.g. New Zealand, France), and a country can be convincingly moved to a different category of capitalism' (Jackson and Deeg 2006: 15). Finally, there may be processes of change which lead simply to less coherent national capitalist economies. This has been observed in the context of CEE and has been described as 'cocktail capitalism' (Cernat 2006), which refers to a highly incoherent variant that includes conflicts between the key domestic political actors and interest groups on the one hand, and external policy transfer processes, in particular, Europeanization and globalization.

As a result of the globalization process (at least up to 2008/2009), it might be that this trend towards 'cocktail capitalism' is a broader phenomenon making it difficult to differentiate VoC as stable and distinctive socio-economic, institutional formations. Also, it might be relevant to explore how events induced by the 2008/2009 global financial crisis and the subsequent Eurozone crisis have affected European VoC. Hall (2018) argues that the integration of Europe has yet to result in the disintegration of national variants. Grabner et al. (2019) argue that in response to the structural features of the Eurozone and globalization, four distinctive growth models gave emerged in Europe: core countries, peripheral countries, financial hubs and catching-up countries. These models emerged in response to increased trade and financial openness coupled with macroeconomic and other regulatory convergence. The issue is whether institutional convergence has produced an increase in variety as a response to similar constraints, but in structurally different economies, or if integration has undermined variety and led to institutional homogeneity.

The rationale for our enquiry is that none of these approaches considers institutional differences in entrepreneurial activities despite their being central to capitalism. The entrepreneurship literature recognizes the essential impact of institutions on entrepreneurship, but frames this within an 'institutional obstacles to entrepreneurship' perspective (Fogel et al. 2008; Harper 2003). There is a strand of work in the international entrepreneurship (IE) literature that explores international differences in entrepreneurship (see, e.g., Bowen and De Clercq 2008). These studies are concerned with how different institutional contexts affect entrepreneurship. However, they are focused strongly on individual entrepreneurship and how international institutional differences affect individual incentives and opportunities to engage in new activities. They do not take account of the broader institutional context and how it affects entrepreneurship.

Philosophically, the approach is rooted in the *Discovery, Evaluation and Exploitation* (DEE) framework (Shane and Venkataraman 2000), which, in an international context, is defined as 'the discovery, evaluation and exploitation of entrepreneurial opportunity in international markets' (Eckhardt and Shane 2003). Critiquing this approach, Baker et al. (2005: 36) argue that the DEE framework 'offers an unsuitable basis for promoting comparative international entrepreneurship research because it strongly de-emphasizes the role of social processes in creating and shaping the nexus of opportunities and individuals, while also holding constant, social and cultural phenomena that are central to comparative entrepreneurship research'. In response, Baker et al. (2005: 35) developed the *Comparative Discovery, Evaluation and Exploitation* (CDEE) framework, which 'explores how and why processes of opportunity discovery, evaluation and exploitation vary across and within nations, as well as the implications of these differences'. National institutional and cultural structures determine how EO are 'evaluated' while the amount and specificity of resources and supporting institutional infrastructure influences how and where favourably evaluated opportunities are 'exploited' (Baker et al. 2005). In this respect, the CDEE approach is aligned to the VoC research programme. However, its treatment of entrepreneurship is confined to individuals.

To our knowledge, the only paper that explicitly explores the relationship between VoC and entrepreneurship is Dilli et al. (2018). Their research is based on conceptual blocks (finance-related, labour-market, education and training and inter-firm institutions) common to the VoC literature, and proxies for entrepreneurship generally used in the literature. The most surprising result of their research is that these institutional blocks seen to match the institutional families identified in the 1990s VoC literature.[3] However, Dilli et al.'s (2018) findings show, also, that in liberal market economies perceived EO, which occur before entrepreneurship activities begin, are significantly less frequent than in supposedly rigid coordinated market economies. Also, low-tech venture birth rates are lower in liberal market economies than in any other group.

Given the heavy criticism expressed against the VoC approach and its decreasing relevance, these results are unexpected. They may reflect fewer varieties of entrepreneurship, but increasing divergences in economic growth

---

[3] Dilli et al.'s (2018) varieties of entrepreneurial capitalism are liberal market economies (Ireland, the UK, the USA), co-ordinated market economies (Continental and Northern European economies), mixed market economies (including France, Italy, Portugal and Spain), and the emerging market economies of Central and Eastern Europe. The variety of entrepreneurship most conducive to Schumpeterian forms of entrepreneurship is the Anglo-Saxon or liberal market economies with deregulated financial and labour markets, rapid investments and disinvestments and limited protection of dependent employment.

between different European macro-regions, including an increasing West–South divide. They may also reflect historically rooted specializations in various European countries with varying biases towards high tech and low-tech sectors. Also, the use of individual entrepreneurship as the outcome variable may reflect fewer structural differences among different variants and many more current growth opportunities.

Overall, with the exception of Dilli et al. (2018), VoC and international entrepreneurship have developed as two separate research streams. This may seem puzzling since entrepreneurship is deeply embedded institutionally and is the key to the differentiated dynamics in different VoC. Table 32.1 summarizes our conclusions so far.

Ultimately, the disconnect between VoC and entrepreneurship research is due to the way entrepreneurship is defined. From an international entrepreneurship (IE) perspective, entrepreneurship is an individual property and the issue is how different institutional contexts affect individual entrepreneurship. From a VoC perspective, entrepreneurship is considered both an individual and a social act. This requires the redefinition of entrepreneurship or its reconceptualization from a system perspective. In this view, entrepreneurship is a property of countries and their innovation systems. Hence, the issue is not only how different national institutional context affects the individual–opportunity nexus, that is, how individuals discover and exploit opportunities, but also the entrepreneurial propensity of different national settings.

Next, we discuss how VoC and entrepreneurship research programmes can be aligned.

Table 32.1 Key features of entrepreneurship and varieties of capitalism research programmes

Entrepreneurship		Varieties of capitalism
Institutional obstacles to entrepreneurship	**Empirical focus**	Modes of coordination
Entrepreneurship as an individual-level phenomenon	**Level of analysis**	Variety as a system-level property
Individual–opportunity nexus	**Methodological basis**	Impurity principle
Contextual factors shaping aspirations, attitudes and activities	**Key concern**	Complementarities and coherence

3   Three Analytical Approaches to Exploring the Relationship Between Varieties of Capitalism and Entrepreneurship

We find it useful to distinguish between three analytical approaches which link entrepreneurship and VoC: Acs, Autio and Szerb's (2014) Global Entrepreneurship Monitor/Global Entrepreneurship and Development Index (GEM/GEDI) method; Lazonick and Mazzucato's (2013) Risk-Reward Nexus (RNN) and the EPIS approach proposed in Radosevic and Yoruk (2013).[4] Common to all three approaches is the attempt to redefine the notion of entrepreneurship, which, as argued above, is the only way to connect VoC and the entrepreneurship research programme. The three approaches involve different, but complementary conceptions of entrepreneurship and separate but complementary views of EO.

In the GEM/GEDI approach, the individuals are entrepreneurs and the issue is whether the external environmental context is conducive to these individuals' entrepreneurial aspirations and attitudes. What distinguishes GEDI from mainstream approaches in the entrepreneurship literature is that it measures the mutual relationship between individual-level and contextual institutional factors. In the RNN approach, the major entrepreneur is the innovative enterprise interacting with its social conditions regarding its financial commitment, strategic control and organizational integration. In the EPIS approach, entrepreneurship is a system-level property or capacity to generate Knowledge-Intensive Entrepreneurship (KIE) based on Knowledge-Intensive Entrepreneurial Opportunities (KIEO).

The GEM/GEDI approach measures self-employment, business ownership rates, new venture creation, and Total Early-stage Entrepreneurship Activity Index (TEA), which refers to the percentage of the working-age population that is engaged in or willing to engage in entrepreneurial activity.[5] Its focus is on the individual rather than on new business registrations. The original GEM framework was adapted (Bosma et al. 2008, 2009) and considers entrepreneurship as shaped by entrepreneurial attitudes, entrepreneurial activity and entrepreneurial aspirations.

---

[4] The reader should note that Dilli et al. (2018) try to link VoC and entrepreneurship empirically, but leaving both notions conceptually intact. Of course, this approach is legitimate, but it ignores the epistemological and theoretical differences between two approaches, including differences in policy implications.

[5] A reader should not that conceptually and methodologically we consider the GEM/GEDI approach as very similar although they partly differ in the choice of indicators and construction of composite index.

The GEDI is part of an improved GEM approach which assumes that entrepreneurship depends on the mutual interplay of *individual-level and institutional variables* (Busenitz and Spencer 2000). The GEDI is a composite indicator of the health of the entrepreneurship ecosystem in a given country and measures the quality and quantity of business formation. The focus on entrepreneurial attitude, entrepreneurial activity and entrepreneurial aspirations aims to capture the contextual features of entrepreneurship.

GEDI measures quality differences across entrepreneurial activities, such as opportunity recognition, skills, creativity, innovation and growth, and differences in the efficiency and level of the institutional setup, which could have a significant influence on the quality of entrepreneurship.

This GEDI approach is entirely consistent with the revised GEM approach proposed by Bosma et al. (2008, 2009) as they both follow the same methodological individualism logic. The improvements which the GEDI has added to the original GEM approach is that it includes contextual factors related to individuals. GEM/GEDI defines entrepreneurship as 'a dynamic interaction of entrepreneurial attitudes, entrepreneurial activity, and entrepreneurial aspiration that vary across stages of economic development'.

In a theoretical work (Radosevic 2007, 2010) and some empirical studies (Radosevic and Yoruk 2012, 2013), we proposed a systemic perspective known as EPIS, which we define as the outcome of EO (technological, market and institutional) moulded by the complementarities and interactions among the different activities in the National Innovation System (NIS), including entrepreneurial experimentation. The EPIS is the capacity to generate and exploit entrepreneurial opportunities to create new Knowledge-Intensive Entrepreneurship (KIE), new technologies (innovations) and new knowledge (Radosevic 2007, 2010; Radosevic et al. 2010). The underlying idea is that KIE are a *systemic* feature of the innovation system and that new knowledge, innovation and new enterprises are integral to an entrepreneurial innovation system.

According to the GEM/GEDI approach, aspirations, attitudes and activities are individual not innovation system characteristics. However, they are influenced by crucial 'institutional factors', such as market size, education, riskiness of the economy, rate of internet use in the population and culture, which enter the indicator as interaction variables. The GEDI takes account of these institutional factors and explores how they *interact* with entrepreneurship variables. The methodological issues related to using GEDI are identifying which institutional variables relate to a particular entrepreneurship variable and how much weight to give each variable. The GEM/GEDI approach implicitly follows the theory of balanced growth by assuming that 'the performance of the system depends on the element that has the lowest value in the structure'. This introduces the notion of a *weakest link-type* variable, which is seen as a critical constraint to the performance of the whole system.

The EPIS approach recognizes the possibility of unbalanced growth and assumes that the entrepreneurial propensity depends on the existence or absence of complementarities and that these processes are non-linear, synergistic and unstable. It allows for the possibility of institutional compensatory mechanisms, although not necessarily substitutions in terms of the three types of opportunities we consider. This contrasts with the GEM/GEDI approach which assumes partial substitution amongst the elements in the system.

The EPIS approach assumes that entrepreneurship emerges from the interaction among Market Opportunities (MO), Technological Opportunities (TO) and Institutional Opportunities (IO). The GEM/GEDI approach assumes that individual attitudes, activities and aspirations interact and, 'if they are out of balance, entrepreneurship is inhibited'.

The RRN approach (Lazonick 2007, 2009, 2013; Lazonick and Mazzucatto 2012, 2013). identifies who are the risk-takers in contemporary capitalism. The mainstream 'maximizing shareholder value' perspective assumes that shareholders are the only contributors to the economy who do not have a guaranteed return and, hence, are residual claimants (Jensen 1986). The RRN approach argues that shareholders are not the only business enterprise participants who invest in productive resources without a guaranteed return (Lazonick 2009). Taxpayers via government agencies and workers via their employing firms also regularly make such risky investments. Thus, the state and labour are 'residual claimants'. The state makes infrastructural investments and subsidizes business enterprises' investments in innovation. Workers make investments in firm-specific human capital at one point in time, with the expectation, but no contractual guarantee, of reaping a returns on those investments throughout the course of their careers (Blair 1995). Public shareholders, on the other hand, are largely risk minimisers since they are able to diversify their financial holdings across several firms to minimise their risk.

This risk–reward nexus is crucial for understanding both the collective and cumulative process of innovation and the distribution of the gains that might result from it (Lazonick and Mazzucato 2012, 2013). The range of actors involved in the innovation process includes shareholders, managers, workers and financiers, who operate through the market allocation and intra-corporate allocation of their resources and have differing attitudes to investment and risk. The RRN differs across countries and can be seen as central to understanding the entrepreneurial propensities of different types of capitalism.

Similar to the EPIS approach, the RRN does not focus on individuals as entrepreneurs, but explores entrepreneurship from a system or organizational perspective. In the RRN approach, entrepreneurship is mainly about different variants of innovative enterprises. The primary agent of innovation is the innovative enterprise not the individual as in the GEM/GEDI approach. Lazonick (2007) considers innovation to be 'a social process, supported in particular times and places by what can be called the 'social conditions of innovative enterprise' (p.22), which can be loosely interpreted as the broad innovation system. The NIS represents the social conditions of the innovative enterprise and is composed of governance, employment and investment institutions (Lazonick, 2007).

This type of innovative firm emerges from differences across countries and who has strategic control of the innovative enterprise or who 'allocates the firm's resources to confront the technological, market, and competitive uncertainties that are inherent in the innovation processes' (Lazonick 2007: 25).

The role of the innovative enterprise is to generate collective learning. In this respect, it is not comprised of a 'stock of individuals' interacting freely with other institutions, as in the GEM/GEDI approach. Rather, it is the social conditions in which the innovative enterprise is operating that determine the country-specific risk–reward nexus. It is not individual aspirations and attitudes that matter, but how enterprises organize to achieve common objectives based on organizational learning. The entrepreneurship of innovative enterprises is driven by the risks and rewards (compensation system) for individuals engaging in cooperative learning. In this context, Lazonick (2007) consider the role of finance to be essential for sustaining collective learning. Most financing for innovation comes from retained earnings and own or venture capital, rather than from stock market which only provides liquidity for previous investments not new productive ventures.

In contrast to both the RRN and GEM/GEDI approaches, EPIS ignores the entrepreneur by taking a functional perspective on the innovation system. What matters is activities and how they complement each other, rather than specific actors—whether individuals interacting with institutions, or innovative enterprises. Institutional variety is considered secondary to functional variety, that is, the scale and existence of specific entrepreneurship-related activities.

Similar to the EPIS, the RRN assumes that it is not enough to look at business formation, that is, new enterprises and their growth. It is necessary, also, to look also at knowledge intensity and new technology as the infrastructure that, ultimately, determines how much risk innovative enterprise can accept. However, by focusing on activities and their outcomes, rather than on actors and inputs, EPIS ignores the organizational side of the entrepreneurship and innovation process. In that respect, RRN and EPIS can be considered complementary and as revealing different dimensions of entrepreneurship as a property of the innovation systems or as specific variants of capitalism.

From a GEM/GEDI perspective, the market is the preferred mode of governance for entrepreneurship. Hence, Liberal Market Economies (LME) are considered superior to Coordinated Market Economies (CME). However, in an RRN perspective, innovation is mainly an organizational not just a market process. The EPIS sees EO as shaped by various institutional arrangements, which include not only market and inter-organizational coordination but also inter-sectoral or inter-institutional matching among institutions that affect the market, technology and risks-rewards from KIE. This broad range of institutions may not necessarily overlap with the institutional domains measured by specific variant perspectives.

Table 32.2 presents a comparative analysis of the three perspectives on entrepreneurship. We next discuss the VoC perspective on entrepreneurship or, more specifically, EO. We draw on the idea of the 'institutional shaping of EO'. We assume that each type of the Entrepreneurial Opportunity (MO, TO, IO) is shaped differently in different countries or groups of countries. We are interested in whether there are coherent configurations of institutionally distinct varieties of EO.

4   Dimensions of Entrepreneurial Regimes: A Conceptual Approach

The VoC approach shows that there are different institutional configurations, all of which may be conducive to economic growth. Thus, there is no single best form of economic organization that is conducive to entrepreneurship.

In Radosevic and Yoruk (2013), we explore the EPIS from a functional perspective, that is, by looking at innovation systems through a series of activities that affect different components of EO. However, by definition, we ignore the institutional forms of these activities. In this chapter, we explore the variety of institutional arrangements that can facilitate EO. We start by assuming that each type of opportunity can be generated in different institutional constellations or *regimes*. We assume that there are various modes of institutional shaping of the discovery of TO or *Technological Regimes* (TR), of demand for new technologies and innovation or *Market Regime* (MR), and

Table 32.2 Comparative summary of three approaches

	GEDI	RRN	EPIS
	Global entrepreneurship and development index	Risk–Reward nexus	The entrepreneurial propensity of the innovation system
Analytical focus	Aspiration, attitudes, activities	Collective entrepreneurship	Interaction of innovation system activities
Level of analysis	Individuals	Enterprises	Innovation system
Type of entrepreneurship	Business formation (undifferentiated)	Innovative enterprise	Knowledge intensive entrepreneurship
Process issue	Individuals interacting with the institutional context	Enterprise interacting with social conditions	(Mis)matches among IS activities
Entrepreneurial opportunity as …	The outcome of the interaction of individual aspirations, attitudes and activities with the institutional context	The outcome of organisational integration of innovative enterprise	The outcome of interaction among technological, market and institutional opportunities
Risk-taking	Individuals as risk-takers	Each stakeholder is a risk-taker	Risk-taking is not considered
Key nexus	Individual–opportunity nexus	Risk–reward nexus	Nexus of innovation system activities
The dominant mode of interaction	Market mode	Organisational processes	System-level interactions
Constraints to entrepreneurship	The weakest link	Imbalances between risk-taking and rewards of various stakeholders	Low-level equilibrium due to lacking imbalances among different opportunities and IS activities
Policy focus	Improve the weakest link	Improve the social conditions of innovative enterprise	Nurture activities with the strongest linkage potential

institutional shaping of the risks and rewards from the innovation process or *Organizational Regime* (OR).

In essence, we build on Baumol's (1990) critical insight that institutions determine not only the level but also the type of entrepreneurship.[6] We extend his enquiry by exploring the variety of institutions shaping different components of EO. Institutions conducive to EO are usually perceived as those that encourage a 'free market'. However, this may be a reasonable assumption only if we define entrepreneurship as an individual-level and not a system-level phenomenon. At the system level, EO may be the outcome of a portfolio of institutional configurations, which are hybrid not 'pure' forms. In other words, they may involve institutions that encourage experimentation and open market opportunities, but also institutions that nurture technology accumulation as a collective rather than only an individual process. Institutional diversity can be expected since each of the significant components of EO—TO, MO, IO—may require a different portfolio of market/non-market institutions. TO may be nurtured through a combination of public and private activities which reflect not only the crucial role of entrepreneurs but also the critical role of the state as an entrepreneur (Mazzucato 2013). MO may be nurtured through trade liberalization and Foreign Direct Investment, but also government procurement by generating demand for new technologies (Edquist and Zabala-Iturriagagoitia 2012). Institutional opportunities may be nurtured through labour market liberalization and cooperative industrial relations conducive to the social conditions of the innovative enterprise (Lazonick 2013). This leads us to the core issue– the complementarity both within and between components of the ER.

The functional performance of one type and component of ER is affected by the presence or functioning of another type and component of the ER. Specifically, institutional forms of the MR may be complemented by institutional arrangements that differ in their risks and rewards (OR). As pointed out by Amable (2016), complementarity can work by reinforcing or weakening an existing institutional configuration. The argument in Radosevic and Yoruk (2013) is that the complementarities between the three components of ER are crucial to dynamic entrepreneurial economies.

---

[6] Our systemic view is not entirely structuralist. EO are generated by the structure of activities, but entrepreneurs also can change institutions What emerges as a systemic property is the outcome of interactions between agency (entrepreneurs) and structure (technologies and embedded institutions). So, institutional shaping may be conducted by the entrepreneurs themselves. However, here, we are less interested in who is conducting institutional change and more interested in the outcomes or social shaping of different components of the entrepreneurship regime For research on the drivers/agents of institutional change towards entrepreneurship see Henrekson and Tino (2011).

Complementarities do not necessarily mean synergies among similar types of institutions; they may derive from combinations of opposing institutional solutions (Streeck 1997; Crouch and Streeck 1997). Witt and Jackson (2016) define this as 'beneficial constraints' where 'an institutional logic of either market or coordinated exchange is counter-balanced by an opposing institutional logic'. Rigid labour markets may protect investments in core human resources, but need to be combined with internal flexibility to lead to technology capability building. For example, Filippo (2019) shows significant positive effects of more stringent labour laws in liberal market economies which 'may stimulate the workers to contribute to innovation by limiting the ability of shareholders to unduly retain all the rents generated by successful projects'. In a nutshell, the issue of complementarities and combination of opposing logics is essential to the VoC. Also, hybridization of institutional varieties of entrepreneurship can lead to loss of systemic coherence or loss of complementarities. The relevance of these issues can be determined only by further empirical analysis.

Table 32.3 presents our conceptual framework. Institutions that affect EO are grouped under the components of the ER technological, market—real and financial—and institutional. The left panel includes innovation systems activities and their binary institutional modes. We acknowledge that, in empirical research, it might not be possible to identify binary modes, but they are useful in the conceptual stage as starting hypotheses.

The TR is composed of three sub-components: knowledge development, competence building and knowledge networks. Knowledge development and competence building are undertaken respectively within public or business sector oriented R&D systems and within firms or public organizations. Knowledge networks may be dominantly market-driven or relational, that is, they may include a variety of market and non-market actors engaged in different alliances and cooperative linkages.

The MR consists of the 'real' market and financial market sub-components. The real MR includes generic demand-side activities, reflected in a variety of different market structures and institutional forms. These can be grouped into two generic types according to whether it is a highly regulated or liberal market environment. Financial market sub-components are demand-side factors, which, like TO articulate the demand for new technologies. It does not follow that finance automatically generates TO since this will depend on the orientation of the financial system. The financial market regime as a sub-component of the market regime can take a variety of institutional forms ranging between the banking driven to the stock market- driven financial system. These two represent core categories around which it is possible to associate a variety of

Table 32.3 Institutional varieties of EO: Activities in an entrepreneurial innovation system and their institutional modes

Activity in Entrepreneurial Innovation System	Institutional Modes
Technology regime (TR): institutional shaping of discovery of technological opportunities	
Knowledge development and diffusion (provision of R&D, creating new knowledge)	Public (extramural) vs business sector (intramural) orientation in funding and performing R&D
Competence building (provision of education and training, creation of human capital, production and reproduction of skills)	Firm vs public sector centred skills formation
Knowledge networks (R&D institutes and value chain partners)	Arm's length vs relational networks
Real market regime (MR): institutional shaping of demand for new technologies and innovation	
Demand-side activities (growth and structure of demand for new products and services; formation of new product markets; articulation of quality requirements)	Highly regulated vs. liberal market environment
Finance market regime (MR): institutional shaping of finance availability for new technologies and innovation	
Demand for funding of innovation and new technology	Bank-based vs. capital market-based financing systems
Organisational regime (OR): institutional shaping of risks and rewards from innovation process	
Institutions providing incentives to the innovative enterprise	Policy environment focused on direct vs. indirect support to the innovative enterprise
Institutions that influence the organization and behaviour of innovative enterprises	Cooperative vs. adversarial industrial relations

indicators which reflect these two orientations. The degree to which the economy moves towards venture capital will shape the EO.[7]

Entrepreneurship is a social activity and its risk and rewards are shaped by a variety of external institutions, such as laws, regulation, policies, etc., and by innovative enterprises, which, in turn are shaped by the specific national institutional set-up (Lazonick and Mazzucato 2013). The OR includes two groups of institutions. First, institutions that provide incentives to innovative enterprises. These include regulations which hinder or facilitate innovation, incubating activities, and the property rights. The policy environment can be focused on direct or indirect support for innovative enterprises. The second

---

[7] As Shane and Nicolau (2018) show, since the late 1990s there has been move away from traditional venture capital activity towards angel funding, business accelerators, micro venture capital funds and online equity crowdfunding platforms. Unfortunately, we do not have large scale international comparative data on these funding sources for EO.

group of institutions support cooperative or adversarial industrial relations. For example, weak or strong labour bargaining power, flexible labour market and industrial relationships, strong or weak pay-productivity link and flexible wage determination and management, all of which shape the organization and behaviour of innovative enterprises.

The framework in Table 32.3 indicates dichotomous institutional modes within which specific sub-components of entrepreneurial regime take place. These modes are relevant to explore institutional varieties from an entrepreneurship perspective. They are not varieties designed to explore dominant governance modes, such as strategic versus market coordination (*à la* Hall and Soskice 2001)m or whether countries are geared towards an open market economy (Tridico 2011) or the type of their social system of production (Amable, DATE). In contrast to these taxonomies, our framework is geared towards understanding national institutional varieties from an entrepreneurship perspective.[8]

We acknowledge that, in reality, institutional modes do not conform to pure institutional and, especially, dichotomous modes. More empirical research is needed to explore the degree to which different national systems conform to 'pure', 'hybrid' or 'cocktail' forms. Our ongoing work in this area (Radosevic and Yoruk 2020) suggests that individual country regimes are often an amalgamation of different institutional solutions, which is in line with Streeck (1997), Crouch and Streeck (1997) and Witt and Jackson (2016), who point to opposing institutional logics as core to dynamic capitalism. Our framework enables an exploration of the varieties of ERs ranging from pure institutional solutions to regimes with opposing institutional logics.

5 Conclusions

This chapter explored the EPIS from a VoC perspective. Existing VoC approaches are not designed to explore entrepreneurial properties. Also, the innovation systems literature is not focused on entrepreneurship as a systemic property of the innovation system. At the same time, research on international entrepreneurship is concerned mainly with how different institutional contexts affect individual entrepreneurship. Exploration of this issue requires a redefinition of entrepreneurship. From a VoC or systemic perspective, entrepreneurship is both an individual and a country and innovation system

---

[8] The reader might be tempted to refer to systems of entrepreneurship. However, we consider this a dubious notion since innovation systems, by definition, are entrepreneurial.

property. Hence, we need to understand both how different national institutional contexts affect the individual–opportunity nexus—how individuals discover and exploit opportunities—and the entrepreneurial propensity of different national settings.

We first outlined three analytical approaches, relevant for exploring the relationship between VoC and entrepreneurship: the GEM/GEDI approach, the RRN and the EPIS approach. These three perspectives represent different conceptions of entrepreneurship and different views of EO but they are also complementary rather than exclusive. In the GEM/GEDI approach, individuals are entrepreneurs and the issue is whether the external environment is conducive to individual entrepreneurial aspirations and attitudes. In the RNN approach, the entrepreneur is the innovative enterprise and its related financial commitment, strategic control and organizational integration. In the EPIS approach, entrepreneurship is a system-level property or the capacity to generate knowledge intensive entrepreneurship (KIE) based on KIEO. In the GEM/GEDI perspective, EO are about institutional obstacles or opportunities that can be exploited by risk-takers. In the RRN perspective, all stakeholders are involved in a risky innovation process in which distribution of risks and rewards is socially conditioned—that is, it is not objectively given. In the EPIS approach, EO is not about risks, but about the capacity of the system to generate knowledge intensive enterpreneuruship given (mis)matching MO, TO and IO.

We proposed a conceptual framework to explore the institutional varieties of entrepreneurial opportunities or the features of the TR, MR and OR. Each entrepreneurship regime can be generated in different institutional constellations, which we initially conceptualize as dichotomous. There are various modes of the technological regimes (institutional shaping of technological opportunities), of market regimes (demand for new technologies and innovation), and organisational regime (the risks and rewards from the innovation process).

This should be regarded as a preliminary investigation. It necessarily has some limitations. Our inquiry is initial and thus confined to conceptual issues. First, the validity of our framework is subject to availability of data on the variables and countries. Second, similar to the VoC literature, we assume that industries and firms are passive actors, while in reality they can 'escape' their institutional context. For example, EU integration and institutional differences among countries provide new opportunities for firms and industries to avoid the constraints of the dominant institutional form in their country of location, which limits this type of analysis. In the next stage of our research programme (see Radosevic and Yoruk 2020) we will explore the taxonomic features of entrepreneurial regimes. However, our ultimate aim is to explore the relationship between different types of entrepreneurship regime and growth or innovation-based growth, and whether divergence/convergence in individual regimes leads to divergence/convergence in terms of performance.

References

Acs, Z. J., Autio, E., & Szerb, L. (2014). National Systems of Entrepreneurship: Measurement Issues and Policy Implications. *Research Policy, 43*(3), 476–494.

Aiginger, K. (2007). Performance Differences in Europe: Tentative Hypotheses on the Role of Institutions, WIFO Working Papers, No. 304.

Amable, B. (2003). *The Diversity of Capitalism*. Oxford: Oxford University Press.

Amable, B. (2016). Institutional Complementarities in the Dynamic Comparative Analysis of Capitalism. *Journal of Institutional Economics, 12*(1), 79–103.

Baker, T., Gedajlovic, E., & Lubatkin, M. (2005). A Framework for Comparing Entrepreneurship Processes Across Nations. *Journal of International Business Studies, 36*(5), 492–504.

Baumol, W. J. (1990). Entrepreneurship: Productive, Unproductive, and Destructive. *Journal of Political Economy, 98*(5), Part 1 (Oct), 893–921.

Baumol, W. J. (2002). *The Free-Market Innovation Machine: Analyzing the Growth Miracle of Capitalism*. Princeton: Princeton University Press.

Blair, M. M. (1995). *Ownership and Control: Rethinking Corporate Governance for the Twenty-first Century*. Washington D.C: Brookings Institutions.

Bosma, N., Acs, Z., Autio, E., Coduras, A., & Levie, J. (2008). Global Entrepreneurship Monitor 2008 Executive Report. Global Entrepreneurship Research Association (GERA)

Bosma, N., Acs, Z., Autio, E., Coduras, A., & Levie, J. (2009). Global Entrepreneurship Monitor 2008, Executive Report. Babson Park, MA: Babson College, Santiago, Chile: Universidad del Desarollo and London, UK: London Business School.

Bowen, H. P., & De Clercq, D. (2008). Institutional Context and the Allocation of Entrepreneurial Effort. *Journal of International Business Studies, 39*, 747–767.

Busenitz, L., & Spencer, J. W. (2000). Country Institutional Profiles: Unlocking Entrepreneurial Phenomena. *Academy of Management Journal, 43*(5), 994–1003.

Cernat, L. (2006). *Europeanization, Varieties of Capitalism and Economic Performance in Central and Eastern Europe*. London: Macmillan.

Crouch, C., & Streeck, W. (1997). *Political Economy of Modern Capitalism: Mapping Convergence and Diversity*. London: Sage.

Dilli, S., Elert, N., & Herrmann, A. M. (2018). Varieties of Entrepreneurship: Exploring the Institutional Foundations of Different Entrepreneurship Types Through 'Varieties-of-Capitalism' Arguments. *Small Business Economics, 51*, 293–320. https://doi.org/10.1007/s11187-018-0002-z.

Eckhardt, J. T., & Shane, S. A. (2003). Opportunities and Entrepreneurship. *Journal of Management, 29*(3), 333–349.

Edquist, C., & Zabala-Iturriagagoitia, J. M. (2012). Public Procurement for Innovation as Mission-Oriented Innovation Policy. *Research Policy, 41*(10), 1757–1769.

Filippo, B. (2019). Institutional Complementarities Between Labour Laws and Innovation. *Journal of Institutional Economics, 15*(2), 235–258. https://doi.org/10.1017/S1744137418000139.

Fogel, K., Hawk, A., Morck, R., & Yeung, B. (2008). Institutional Obstacles to Entrepreneurship. In A. Basu, M. Casson, N. Wadeson, & B. Yeung (Eds.), *The Oxford Handbook of Entrepreneurship*. Oxford: Oxford University Press.

Grabner C., Heimberger, P., Kapeller, J., & Schutz, B. (2019). Structural Change in Time of Increasing Openness: Assessing Path Dependency in European Economic Integration, *Journal of Evolutionary Economics*, https://doi.org/10.1007/s00191-019-00639-6.

Hall, P. A. (2018). Varieties of Capitalism in Light f the Euro Crisis. *Journal of European Public Policy, 25*(1), 7–30.

Hall, P. A., & Soskice, D. (2001). Varieties of Capitalism, The Institutional Foundations of Comparative Advantage.

Hancké, B., Rhodes, M., & Thatcher, M. (2007). Introduction: Beyond Varieties of Capitalism, In Beyond Varieties of Capitalism: Conflict, Contradictions, and Complementarities in the European Economy, Edited by B. Hancké, M. Rhodes and M. Thatcher

Harper, D. A. (2003). *Foundations of Entrepreneurship and Economic Development*. London: Routledge.

Henrekson, M., & Tino, S. (2011). The Interaction of Entrepreneurship and Institutions. *Journal of Institutional Economics, 7*(1), 47–75. https://doi.org/10.1017/S1744137410000342.

Hodgson, G. M. (1999). *Economics and Utopia*. New York: Routledge.

Hodgson, G. M. (2015). *Conceptualizing Capitalism: Institutions, Evolution, Future*. Chicago: University of Chicago Press.

Jackson, G., & Deeg, R. (2006). How Many Varieties of Capitalism? Comparing the Comparative Institutional Analyses of Capitalist Diversity, MPIfG Discussion Paper 06/2.

Jensen, M. (1986). Agency Costs of Free Cash Flow, Corporate Finance, and Takeovers. *American Economic Review, 76*(2), 323–329.

Jessop, B. (2015). Variegated Capitalism and the Political Economy of Austerity. In R. Westra, D. Badeen, & R. Albritton (Eds.), *The Future of Capitalism After the Financial Crisis. The Varieties of Capitalism Debate in the Age of Austerity*. London: Routledge.

Knell, M., & Srholec, M. (2007). Diverging Pathways in Central and Eastern Europe. In D. Lane & M. Myant (Eds.), *Varieties of Capitalism in Post-Communist Countries*. London: Palgrave Macmillan.

Lazonick, W. (2007). Varieties of Capitalism and Innovative Enterprise. *Comparative Social Research, 24*(2007), 21–69.

Lazonick, W. (2009). The New Economy Business Model and the Crisis of US Capitalism. *Capitalism and Society, 4*, 2.

Lazonick, W. (2013). The Theory of Innovative Enterprise: A Foundation of Economic Analysis, AIR Working Paper 13-05/01, The Academic-Industry Research Network, February 2013.

Lazonick, W., & Mazzucato, M. (2012). The Risk-Reward Nexus in the Innovation-Inequality Relationship. Who Takes the Risks? Who Gets the Rewards?, University of Massachusetts and SPRU, University of Sussex, March 2012, FP7-SSH-2007-1.2.3-217466-FINNOV-D2.11

Lazonick, W., & Mazzucato, M. (2013). The Risk-Reward Nexus in the Innovation-Inequality Relationship. Who Takes the Risks? Who Gets the Rewards? *Industrial and Corporate Change, 22*(4), 1093–1128.

Ledeneva, A. (1998). *Russia's Economy of Favours. Blat, Networking and Informal Exchange.* Cambridge: Cambridge University Press.

Mazzucato, M. (2013). *The Entrepreneurial State: Debunking Public vs Private Sector Myths.* London: Anthem Press.

Radosevic, S. (1998). Defining Systems of Innovation: A Methodological Discussion. *Technology in Society, 20*(1), 75–86.

Radosevic, S. (2007). National Systems of Innovation and Entrepreneurship: In Search of a Missing Link. Economics Working Paper No. 73. UCL-SSEES, Centre for the Study of Economic and Social Change in Europe. https://discovery.ucl.ac.uk/id/eprint/17479/1/17479.pdf.

Radosevic, S. (2010). What Makes Entrepreneurship Systemic? In F. Malerba (Ed.), *Knowledge-Intensive Entrepreneurship and Innovation Systems* (pp. 52–76). London: Routledge.

Radosevic, S., & Yoruk, E. (2012). Entrepreneurial Propensity of Innovation Systems. Economics Working Paper No.117, University College London, School of Slavonic and East European Studies, January 2012. Paper available at http://www.ssees.ucl.ac.uk/publications/working_papers/wp117.pdf.

Radosevic, S., & Yoruk, E. (2013). Entrepreneurial Propensity of Innovation Systems: Theory, Methodology and Evidence. *Research Policy, 42*, 1015–1038.

Radosevic, S., & Yoruk, E. (2020). Entrepreneurship and Varieties of Capitalism in Europe: Empirical Exploration, UCL Centre for Comparative Studies of Emerging Economies, UCL Centre for Comparative Studies of Emerging Economies Working Papers 2020/1) (forthcoming).

Radosevic, S., Yoruk, E., Edquist, C., & Zabala, J. M. (2010). Innovation systems and knowledge-intensive entrepreneurship: Analytical framework and guidelines for case study research. Deliverable 2.2.1 for Project AEGIS – Advancing Knowledge-Intensive Entrepreneurship and Innovation for Economic Growth and Social Well-being in Europe, EU FP7 Large Scale integrated Research project, December 2010. Paper available at http://www4.lu.se/upload/CIRCLE/reportseries/201202_Radosevic_Yoruk_Edquist_Zabala.pdf.

Schmid, A. (2004). *Conflict and Cooperation. Institutional and Behaviour Economics.* Malden: Blackwell Publishing.

Shane, S., & Nicolaou, N. (2018). Exploring the Changing Institutions of Early-stage Finance. *Journal of Institutional Economics, 14*(6), 1121–1137.

Shane, S., & Venkataraman, S. (2000). The Promise of Entrepreneurship as a Field of Research. *Academy of Management Review, 25*(1), 217–226.

Streeck, W. (1997). Beneficial Constraints: On the Economic Limits of Rational Voluntarism. In J. R. Hollingsworth & R. Boyer (Eds.), *Contemporary Capitalism: The Embeddedness of Institutions* (pp. 197–219). Cambridge: Cambridge University Press.

Tridico, P. (2011). *Institutions, Human Development and Economic Growth in Transition Economies.* London: Palgrave Macmillan.

Whitley, R. (1999). *Divergent Capitalisms: The Social Structuring and Change of Business Systems.* Oxford: Oxford University Press.

Witt, M. A., & Jackson, G. (2016). Varieties of Capitalism and Institutional Comparative Advantage: A Test and Reinterpretation. *Journal of International Business Studies, 47*, 778–806.

Part VII

Methodologies for Comparative Analysis

33

Taxonomies and Typologies: Starting to Reframe Economic Systems

Randolph Luca Bruno and Saul Estrin

1 Introduction

In its heyday during the 1950s to 1980s, the field of comparative economic systems primarily focused on two economic systems, capitalist and socialist.[1] The former was characterised as being based on resource allocation through decentralised markets and the latter using a centralised resource allocation mechanism, planning, in order for the political authorities to determine the allocative and distributive outcome. The prime examples of these systems were the United States and Soviet Union, respectively, though other economies, mainly European but also some developing countries such as China,

Some of the ideas for this chapter have been developed in previous papers written with Michael Carney, Daniel Shapiro and Zhixiang Liang. These are referred to in the chapter and the discussions are gratefully acknowledged here. We have also received very helpful comments from the editors of this volume and Slavo Radosevic. Any remaining errors are our own.

[1] See, for example, the textbooks by Montias (1976), Wiles (1977), Gardner (1997) and Gregory and Stuart (1999).

R. L. Bruno (✉)
University College London, London, UK

Rodolfo DeBenedetti Foundation, Milano, Italy

IZA-Bonn, Bonn, Germany
e-mail: randolph.bruno@ucl.ac.uk

S. Estrin
London School of Economics, London, UK
e-mail: s.estrin@lse.ac.uk

© The Author(s) 2021
E. Douarin, O. Havrylyshyn (eds.), *The Palgrave Handbook of Comparative Economics*,
https://doi.org/10.1007/978-3-030-50888-3_33

871

were sometimes also considered. There was also allowance for some variation within each economic system. Thus, "market socialism" was put forward as an alternative to systems of Soviet-type planning (Brus and Laski 1991; Kornai 1992), and, when combined with workers' self-management of firms, was treated virtually as an economic system in its own right, represented by Yugoslavia under Marshall Tito (Estrin 1984). Some distinction was also made between red-blooded US-type capitalism and the more welfare-oriented version operating in, for example, Sweden (Montias 1976).

The relative performance of capitalism against socialism was the main subject of analysis in comparative economic systems; would one system consistently outperform the other or could they achieve comparable outcomes. Measures of performance used in this debate included static technical efficiency and allocative efficiency (Pareto efficiency); growth; and indicators of welfare, such as the distribution of income and wealth (Wiles 1977). At a theoretical level, Marxists believed that the capitalist market economy was fundamentally flawed and subject to intermittent and ever deepening crises (Marx 2007). In contrast, for critics of socialism such as von Hayek (1944), the market economy provided the only resource allocation mechanism capable of providing economic efficiency. From the 1920s, much of the debate was therefore about whether a socialist system could be designed that would outperform the capitalist system (Levy and Pert 2008). At its heart was the question of whether two fundamentally different economic systems could perform equally well; that is, whether there could be *equifinality* of economic outcomes. The tenor of the argument in the literature for the most part did not support the notion of equifinality (Kornai 1992), though Lange (1936) posited that a planned economy could replicate the outcomes of a market economy. But the bulk of the Western literature was focused towards identifying in theory and in practice the shortcomings of the socialist system (Wiles 1977; Ellman 2014; Brus and Laski 1991; Kornai 1992; Gregory and Stuart 1999). Perhaps more importantly, the actual outcome appeared to refute the possibility of equifinality because the Soviet and Eastern European models of socialist systems, in all their variants, abruptly collapsed between 1989 and 1990, a cataclysmic system failure associated with long-term poor economic performance (Lavigne 1995; Blanchard 1997; Sachs and Warner 1995). Though several economies remained under communist rule, notably but not exclusively China, the perceived failure of socialism as an economic system was interpreted by many as "proof" that one economic system—capitalism—was superior in terms of performance and would therefore predominate globally, referred to by Fukuyama (1989) as the end of history!

The economic superiority of a single system is obviously an existential threat to the field of comparative economic systems. In the face of that, recent literature has made several attempts to reposition the subject, for example, moving from an analysis of mechanisms of allocating resources and the flows of information along the lines of Montias (1976) or Koopmans (1957) towards institutional economics by building on the work of North (1990, 1994) and Ostrom (2009). Thus, Djankov et al. (2003) proposed that comparative systems as a field should align itself with the ideas of the New Institutional Economics (Williamson 2000).

However, such realignment has proven difficult. First, the notion of an economic system itself was often surprisingly underdeveloped in the comparative systems literature. As we have seen, the emphasis was on the identification of typologies of the economic system, defining socialism and capitalism at a theoretical level (Friedman 1962) and exploring whether these systems were equifinal across economic outcomes. By typology, we refer to the classification of the economic system based on theoretical or conceptual differences, for example, state versus private ownership of the means of production (Nuti 2018), while taxonomies refer to configurations based on empirical classification (Hotho 2014). Therefore, despite the huge cross-country heterogeneity in history, culture, geographical factors, institutional arrangements and economic performance, economic systems have not, for the most part, been empirically determined taxonomies: groupings of countries that share close historical and institutional similarities. In this chapter, we make a preliminary investigation into the potential of developing the latter approach in terms of its ability to explain observed performance outcomes.

The move from considering economic systems as taxonomies rather than typologies could represent an important research development. For example, it could improve our understanding of emerging and understudied economies in comparison with more advanced ones. We have recently seen the emergence and sustained growth of many countries with economic systems that cannot be fitted easily into the coarse bilateral distinction between capitalism and socialism, yet whose behaviours can be grouped into categories that are distinct from each other. Some models already exist to distinguish between different forms of capitalist economies, most notably the Varieties of Capitalism (VOC) framework (Hall and Soskice 2001) that focuses on the patterns of coordination between firms and other major economic actors on labour and capital markets. This framework identifies two broad forms of coordination—through the market, namely liberal market economies (LME) and through centralised organisations, whether voluntary or the state, notably coordinated market mechanisms (CME). The categorisation has been shown to provide significant taxonomic content, in that similar actors behave very differently in these different institutional contexts (Hall and Gingerich 2009; Hancke 2009; Schneider and Paunescu 2012), and, importantly, the system-level analysis is equifinal; there is no presumption about the superiority of one system over another, nor is there convincing evidence to that effect (Hancke 2009). However, the VOC approach has remained largely Eurocentric, primarily focused to understand how supportive labour and capital market institutions have permitted the development of a flourishing social capitalism in, for example, Germany.

However, the world economy has changed fundamentally since the 1960s, when the United States and Soviet were the world's two economic as well as political superpowers (O'Neill 2011). Take the example of China, a country that fits uncomfortably into a crude capitalist-socialist framework, yet whose economic successes derive from the long-term enactment of economic policies based around a combination of the market economy, entrepreneurship, state-led innovation and state ownership (Chow 2017), sometimes termed "state capitalism". Equally, it is unclear how to fit rising countries like Indonesia, forecast to be fourth largest economy in the world by 2050 (PWC, 2019), into traditional framing around state versus private ownership of firms or planning versus markets as resource allocation mechanisms. More generally, while many of the recently emerging economies of the past 20 years do not fit into the category of socialist, they are also clearly not capitalist in the traditional sense. For example, the ownership structures and governance arrangements of their firms are different in relying on Business Group or state ownership (see Aguilera and Crespi-Cladera 2016; Carney et al. 2018; Khanna and Palepu 2000a, 2000b; Khanna and Yafeh 2007).

We therefore provide in this chapter some preliminary evidence in support of the idea that research in comparative economic systems might begin to cover a wider variety of countries and be more empirically based, a shift from typologies to taxonomies. Thus, we suggest to extend the field of analysis beyond the traditional focus on North America and Europe to begin considering in a systematic way the large number of developing, emerging and transition economies. As noted by Estrin et al. (2019), an important but hitherto underexplored characteristic of developing and emerging economies is their heterogeneity in terms of political economy, institutions and resource endowments. Furthermore, we provide preliminary evidence of the research value of a new approach to comparative economic systems in which the standard typological framework defining "systems" through underlying concepts, such as resource allocation mechanism or ownership of firms, is replaced by a taxonomy in which countries are put into groupings based on empirical observations.

The research value of comparing economic systems is based on the notion that the system itself will exercise a systematic influence on the behaviour of individuals and firms within it. Thus, in the traditional typological approach, it was posited that enterprise behaviour would be fundamentally different when firm motivation was plan targets rather than profitability and resource allocation was through markets as against via plans (Wiles 1977; Ellman 2014). In this chapter, we argue that it is an important ongoing research agenda to devise a new classification of economic systems based on empirical observation rather than abstract reasoning, and then subject this to the test of empirical validity by exploring whether this taxonomy explains observed behaviour. However, we do not attempt in this chapter the massive task of developing an empirically based and new classification of economic systems. We are fortunate in that a group of researchers has already started work on that task. Fainshmidt et al. (2018) employed a wide variety of institutional data on many emerging, developing and transition economies, using expert panel input to obtain institutional profiles on 68 economies, as a basis for two-step cluster analysis (Ronen and Shenkar 2013) to identify nine groupings (configurations) of countries. Their taxonomy, the Varieties of Institutional Systems (VIS) configuration system, is the basis for our empirical work.

Our objective in this chapter is therefore quite narrow; we report the first attempt to *validate* a typology of economic systems empirically on a large number of understudied economies, using the system of configurations devised by Fainshmidt et al. (2018). Our research question is therefore whether, holding country-specific institutional factors, sector-specific technological characteristics and ownership-specific firm-level attributes constant, enterprise performance is contingent on the economic system, or configuration, as identified by Fainshmidt et al. (2018). To explore this issue, we develop a dataset that combines the seven VIS configurations in the developing world with firm-level data from the World Bank Enterprise Survey (WBES), resulting in a sample of around 30,000 firms from 57 countries.

We find that the taxonomy of countries does indeed provide an independent and statistically significant explanation of firm-level performance, even when controlling for standard national, sectoral and firm-level characteristics. We also find some evidence for equifinality, at least among some of the systems. While this is only a preliminary study, this finding provides some support for the view that a shift from a typological to a taxonomic approach represents a potentially valuable way forward for the field of comparative economic systems.

In the following section, we discuss the development of the Fainshmidt et al. (2018) configuration. We present the data and methods in the third section and the results in the fourth. Finally, we draw our conclusions.

2   A New Approach to Classifying Economic Systems

National institutional systems provide the formal and informal rules of the game to which domestic and foreign firms must adapt their governance and ownership structures (North 1994). However, why should differences in institutional systems explain firm performance (Aguilera and Crespi-Cladera 2016)? The VOC literature (Hall and Soskice 2001) proposes two mechanisms linking firm performance and institutional system. The first concerns institutional complementarity (Amable 2016). An economy has several institutional spheres, notably the financial sector, the labour, the industrial relations regime, the educational and skills training systems and so on. Institutional variation arises from the way different national institutional systems combine to form different patterns of coordination and to achieve cohesion. These institutional complementarities within countries can co-evolve with those of other countries to produce distinct governance configurations. The VOC model identifies two systems (Jackson and Deeg 2008), the first of which is the Coordinated Market Economies (CME), a social democratic economic model of capitalism in which coordination occurs through local or national state activity in collaboration with institutions representing the main actors in each sphere. This contrasts with the standard Liberal Market Economies (LME), in which coordination occurs market by market through the process of competition. The CME is viewed as a viable alternative architecture of national competitiveness to the LME; thus, CME and LME are potentially equifinal.

The second key concept is isomorphism. Each variety of capitalism is said to produce an "emblematic firm" (Boyer, 2005), an organisational form particularly well adapted to its national institutional system. The emblematic firm in the Liberal Market Economy (LME) is the managerially controlled firm (Estrin et al. 2009). Coordination between the conflicting ambitions of owners and managers and the asymmetry in the information they control is achieved by market disciplines: for example, from capital markets through the market for corporate control, or from managerial markets and incentive payments. In contrast, the CME emblematic firm is characterised by a dual board system, whereby strategic shareholders coordinate directly to address the agency problems, with capital and often labour also directly represented at the board level. The institutional system, therefore, supplies firms with "institutional capital" so that firms fit, or become isomorphic with, prevailing modes of institutional functioning. Thus, as firms strive to access resources in their local environment, they are likely to develop similar practices adapted to their institutional configuration (Hall and Soskice 2001).

This implies that economic systems and the firms within them will perform differently depending on the institutional arrangements within each country, and one can, in principle, identify empirically groups of countries with distinct economic systems. For example, the VOC literature distinguished between country-specific factors and systemic or configuration wide factors influencing firm-level competitive advantage in capitalist economies in Europe and North America. Authors have also raised questions about the relevance of complementarity amongst the institutional contradictions and frictions of less developed economies and in the cases of dysfunctional varieties of capitalism (Hancké et al. 2007; Peck and Zhang 2013). Once we widen the geographic lens to include the increasingly significant economies of Asia, Latin America and Africa, we observe that most countries are formally capitalist, in the sense that private ownership of firms usually predominates, and markets are the main mechanism for allocating resources. However, in these economies, an even more variegated range of capitalisms can be identified than across Europe, including dynamic "rising powers", some with significant state direction like China (Sinkovics et al. 2014), slower growing capitalist economies mired in a middle-income trap and low skill equilibria (Schneider, 2009), and even outright failures (Wood and Frynas 2005).

Given the large number of possible relevant historical, cultural and institutional characteristics, Fainshmidt et al. (2018) used empirical methods to identify from an institutionally and culturally heterogeneous set of countries a small number of economic systems. They employed a two-stage method. First, they developed a cross-country qualitative dataset, based on the role of five institutional dimensions of economic activity stressed previously in the VOC framework as defining the economic system. These are: (1) the state's role in the economy, (2) financial markets, (3) human capital, (4) social capital and (5) corporate governance institutions. They collected detailed country-level data on each dimension and used experts' qualitative inputs to construct a qualitative evaluation of each dimension. They then used a generalisation model to transform qualitative data into categorical data for quantitative analysis (e.g. Putnam and Jones 1982). Thus, the institutional profiles were subjected to a two-step cluster analysis in order to uncover natural groupings in the data. The Bayesian Information Criterion (BIC) is first calculated for each potential cluster, with cases grouped into pre-clusters. In the second step, the pre-clusters are used as input for a hierarchical clustering algorithm, which reduces the range of solutions based on the BIC (Rundle-Thiele et al. 2015). This method creates a set of nine configurations of the economic system for the understudied institutional contexts of Asia, Africa, Latin America, Middle East and Eastern Europe.

The way that enterprises might resolve internal contradictions and internalise external effects might be very different, for example, in the emerging LME, where reliance is placed on the market, and in the state led, where the state retains high ownership or control of enterprises. Thus, the standard Western corporation probably represents the emblematic firms in the emerging LME and state-owned firms within the state led. Other VIS configurations may also have settled into a stable institutional equilibrium; for example, the family-led configuration may be dominated by powerful rent-seeking business groups, which resist institutional developments that challenge their rents. Our proposition is that firm performance will be influenced by the configuration to which a country belongs, in addition to standard performance effects at the firm, national and sectoral levels.

The full VIS classification of nine national configurations is presented in Fainshmidt et al. 2018 as Table A1 page 319 in their paper; the first two configurations can be clearly identified as the standard LME and CME economies, containing developed European and Anglo-Saxon economies. We do not consider these in our work, which focuses only on understudied economies and therefore considers only firms in some of the latter seven configurations. These are the so-called *state led*, *fragmented* with fragile state, *family led*, *emergent LME*, *collaborative agglomerations* and *hierarchically coordinated configurations*, respectively. We exclude the Fainshmidt et al. (2018) configuration of "centralised tribe" because we do not have any countries in this configuration in our dataset.

Our research question is basic: we only ask whether, holding country-specific institutional factors, sector-specific technological characteristics and ownership-specific firm-level attributes constant, enterprise performance is contingent on the configuration. Thus, our proposition will be supported if we find that the configuration to which a firm in a country belongs exercises an independent and significant effect on enterprise performance, even when a full set of firm, sector and country controls have been taken into account. The null hypothesis is that this taxonomy of economic systems does not matter for firm performance, in which case the coefficient on the VIS dummy variables will all be insignificant.

We do not at this early stage of this line of research have well-formed expectations as to the character of the differences between the VIS configurations. But there are some important issues that we are testing, nonetheless. If the coefficients on the VIS systems are all the same, then this taxonomy of economics systems does not affect firm performance outcomes, and hence we have complete equifinality. It seems more likely that some systems will be better than others, though there may also be some that support similar levels of firm-level performance. If two systems have the same level of efficiency, they are equifinal. As to which systems we might expect to perform better, for a sample of understudied countries it is hard to have strong priors without reverting to a typological approach. A large literature attests that particular institutional forms that would be inefficient in a developed market economy emerge as a functionalist response to ubiquitous market failures (Khanna and Yafeh 2007), so parallels from advanced economies may be misleading. The evidence indicates that both models based on free market logic (emergent LME) as well as state capitalist economies (state led) have done especially well in recent years, while systems allowing rent-seeking and cronyism (Acemoglu and Robinson (2012) may be less efficient (e.g. hierarchical, collaborative, family led).

3 Data and Methods

We use the World Bank Enterprise Survey (WBES),[2] an enterprise database collected by surveys of over 120,000 firms in more than 130 countries across Asia, Latin America, Eastern and Central Europe and Africa between 2006 and 2016 (https://www.enterprisesurveys.org/). The World Bank conducted the surveys at different dates (i.e. waves), with some countries having only one wave (e.g. Brazil and India), most having two waves and a few having three (e.g. Bulgaria and DR Congo). The dataset therefore covers a wide variety of firms, countries and time. The Varieties of Institutional Systems (VIS) taxonomy includes many of the countries surveyed by the WBES. For example, of the 68 countries in the VIS taxonomy, the WBES dataset covers a remarkable sample of 57 countries. Table 33.1 shows their classification into six VIS configurations, and it also provides information about the number of firms in

---

[2] http://data.worldbank.org/data-catalog/enterprise-surveys.

each country sample. Using these 57 countries gives us a sample of around 30,000 firms.[3]

3.1   Measuring Total Factor Productivity: Capital-Labour Substitution

Our empirical analysis focuses on the question whether membership of the VIS configuration to the country in which the firm is based significantly influences enterprise level efficiency, when we include a large variety of controls for country, sector and time, ownership and size category. We do this using total factor productivity (TFP) as our measure of company performance. However, TFP is measured as the residual in a production function and is therefore sensitive to specification of that function. This issue is of particular relevance when we are considering firm in economies where there has previously been little or no micro-economic analysis of enterprise performance. Choosing to impose standard specifications of the production function derived from developed economies may lead to errors in the calculation of the TFP residual, and these may be correlated with the characteristics of the economic system, thus leading to bias in our conclusions about the empirical validity of the taxonomic approach. This leads us to experiment with alternative specifications of technology in our empirical work.

We first derive estimates from the workhorse of firm-level analysis, the Cobb-Douglas (CD) production function (Solow 1957); in this specification, the log of output is a function of the logs of labour and capital input, and the constant (residual) indicates TFP. Note that the Cobb-Douglas function is homogeneous, and the specification allows for returns to scale not necessarily equal to unity: an important assumption in developing economies, which, because of factor synergies in the growth process, may display increasing returns. Thus, the sum of the coefficients on capital and labour, which indicate returns to scale, is not constrained to unity but does not vary with output; much more restrictive is the assumption concerning the elasticity of substitution. In the Cobb-Douglas function, this is always assumed to be equal to unity. This is an especially strong assumption for firms in developing economies where the possibilities for factor substitution may be substantially

---

[3] The stratified sample provided by the World Bank comprises 86,323 firms' data point in total for 57 countries worldwide. However, the coverage—non-missing values—of the variables of interest (e.g. labour fixed assets sales, etc.) for our empirical exercise reduces a number of observations around 30,000. The latter sample still includes firms for all 57 countries, both foreign and domestic, state and private, for all size categories, within 15 sectoral decomposition and 11-year time span in all our specifications.

Table 33.1 Summary statistics of countries' samples (following Carney et al. 2018)

Configuration 1			Configuration 2			Configuration 3			Configuration 5			Configuration 6			Configuration 7		
State Led			Fragmented/fragile			Family led			Emergent LME			Collaborative agglomerations			Hierarchically coordinated		
Country	Freq.	Percent	Country	Freq.	Percent	Country	Freq.	Percent	Country	Freq.	Percent	Country	Freq.	Percent	Country	Freq.	Percent
Argentina	986	8.09	Angola	242	4.89	Azerbaijan	92	1.3	Botswana	172	7.7	Czech Republic	115	13.63	Bulgaria	545	20.94
Bangladesh	1095	8.99	Cameroon	74	1.5	Brazil	1125	15.89	Chile	1104	49.44	Estonia	108	12.8	Georgia	124	4.76
Belarus	97	0.8	DR Congo	357	7.21	Colombia	1140	16.1	Israel	147	6.58	Hungary	101	11.97	Jordan	258	9.91
China	1344	11.03	Egypt	1498	30.27	Mexico	1887	26.66	Namibia	133	5.96	Latvia	66	7.82	Kazakhstan	153	5.88
India	2940	24.14	Ethiopia	332	6.71	Morocco	133	1.88	South Africa	677	30.32	Lithuania	119	14.1	Lebanon	125	4.8
Indonesia	1632	13.4	Ghana	506	10.22	Nigeria	1350	19.07				Poland	112	13.27	Romania	168	6.45
Malaysia	337	2.77	Kenya	664	13.42	Peru	842	11.89				Slovak Republic	79	9.36	Turkey	867	33.31
Mongolia	192	1.58	Rwanda	59	1.19	Tunisia	322	4.55				Slovenia	144	17.06	Ukraine	363	13.95
Pakistan	262	2.15	Senegal	353	7.13	Yemen	188	2.66									
Philippines	709	5.82	Sudan	10	0.2												
Russia	698	5.73	Tanzania	433	8.75												
Sri Lanka	258	2.12	Uganda	421	8.51												
Thailand	563	4.62															
Vietnam	1068	8.77															
Total	12,181		Total	4949		Total	7079		Total	2233		Total	844		Total	2603	

lower. Indeed, Weitzman (1970) in part explained the slowdown in economic growth in the Soviet Union by a low elasticity of substitution, so that high levels of capital accumulation did not contribute in the same way over time to continued growth. Therefore, in this chapter, we consider a more flexible functional form, namely, Kmenta's constant elasticity of substitution (CES) function (Kmenta 1967). In Kmenta's formulation, the Cobb-Douglas specification is nested within the CES function, so we can test between them.

What are the common approaches to estimate the substitution between capital and labour? Hicks (1932) defined the elasticity of factor substitution as a ratio of ratios: the percentage change of the ratio of the two production factors as a ratio of the percentage change of the ratio of their marginal products. Fully competitive factor and product markets entail that inputs are paid their respective marginal products. We can then proceed to build the elasticity of substitution as a ratio of ratios, namely:

$$\sigma = d\left(K/L\right)/\left(K/L\right)/d\left(k^r/l^w\right)/\left(k^r/l^w\right)$$

and exploiting the properties of the logarithmic function

$$\sigma = -d\log\left(K/L\right)/d\log\left(k^r/l^w\right)$$

K and L are capital and labour, respectively, and k^r and l^w are the former's rental price and the latter's wage rate. Suppose we have a quasi-concave production function; then the elasticity lies in the interval [0; 1]. On the one hand, if the elasticity of substitution happens to be exactly zero (absence of substitution), $\sigma = 0$, capital and labour are perfect complements or used in a fixed proportion. The Leontief production function has such a property. If the elasticity lies in the interval (0; 1), capital and labour are *gross* complements. On the other hand, if the elasticity of substitution is one (perfect substitutability), $\sigma = 1$, the relative change in quantity of factors is exactly proportional to the relative change in prices. As noted, the Cobb-Douglas (CD) has such property. Finally, if the elasticity lies in the interval (1; ∞), capital and labour are gross substitutes.

Empirical estimates of the constant elasticity of substitution (CES) production function were developed by Solow (Solow 1957) and diffused by Arrow et al. (1961). Let's see its structure:

$$Y_t = C \left[\pi \left(A^K_t K_t \right)^{(\sigma-1)/\sigma} + \left(1 - \pi \right) \left(A^L_t L_t \right)^{(\sigma-1)/\sigma} \right]^{\sigma/(1-\sigma)}$$

As before, σ is the elasticity of substitution, while C is "the" efficiency parameter, and π is a measure of how the inputs are distributed within the production function. $(\sigma-1)/\sigma$ is ρ, a transformation of the elasticity called the substitution parameter. A^K_t and A^L_t denote the level of inputs' efficiency. If they vary over time, they show capital- and labour-augmenting technological change.[4]

The nonlinearity of the CES production function curtails linearisation. This is why scholars have tended to resort to the simpler (but more rigid) Cobb-Douglas function, where there exists a simple analytical linearisation. How could the CES production function be estimated other than in its non-linear form? Kmenta (1967) suggested a linearised form that we follow. He introduced a logarithmic form version of CES production function with Hicks-neutral technological change:

$$\log Y_t = \log C + \sigma / \left(1-\sigma\right) \log \left[\pi K_t^{(\sigma-1)/\sigma} + \left(1-\pi\right) L_t^{(\sigma-1)/\sigma} \right]$$

This is still not linear. Next, Kmenta suggested a second-order Taylor series expansion to the term log [.] around the point $\sigma = 1$ in order to allow to estimate a fully fledged function linear in input factors:

$$\log Y_t = \log C + \pi \log K_t + \left(1-\pi\right)$$
$$\log L_t - \left(\sigma-1\right)\pi\left(1-\pi\right)/2\sigma \left(\log K_t - \log L_t \right)^2$$

(33.1)

We therefore test the efficiency of different configurations—the parameter C across groups of countries—by starting with the CD production function and then extending to Kmenta CES. Note that equation (33.1) collapses from CES to a CD function if $\sigma = 1$.

3.2 Empirical Model

We estimate the empirical model on a rich firm-level dataset, which covers many "understudied" countries. In Table 33.1, we report the firms' sample for

---

[4] Technological change can be Hicks-neutral, the condition to be satisfied being that $A^K t = A^L t$, so the marginal rate of substitution does not change when an innovation occurs.

each of the six available VIS configurations. For example, Chile and South Africa have the highest number of firms in the "Emergent Liberal Market Economies" configuration; China, India and Indonesia account for a good proportion of "State-led" one; Egypt, Ghana and Kenya are relatively more numerous in the "Fragmented Fragile state" configuration; Mexico, Colombia and Brazil firms represent about 50% of the "Family led" configuration; "Collaborative agglomerations" present a quite good spread of Central and East European Countries; and finally Bulgaria, Turkey and Ukraine cover around 65% of the firms in the "Hierarchically coordinated" configuration.

In order to tackle omitted variable bias, which may occur when working with a varied dataset across countries, sectors, sub-national locations, and survey years,[5] we employ an extensive and granular set of fixed effects:

* Sector within sub-national location fixed effects (location as city/town)
* Country fixed effects
* Sector fixed effects
* Year fixed effects
* Country-sector fixed effects
* Country-year fixed effects
* Sector-year fixed effects
* Country-sector-year fixed effects
* Size categories fixed effects
* Foreign ownership fixed effects
* State ownership fixed effects
* Size-categories-foreign ownership fixed effects
* Size-categories-state ownership fixed effects

We cannot include configurations fixed effects because they are perfectly collinear with the full set of the country dummies. However, we can predict their average value after running the regressions (Table 33.4) as averages of countries' linear prediction values. Therefore, the empirical model is based on the following estimated equation[6] (note that $\alpha = \log C$):

---

[5] We do not have any panel component in this dataset, though.

[6] We omit the subscript of sub-national location city/town for simplicity.

$$\log Y_{icst} = \alpha + \beta_1 \log K_{icst} + \beta_2 \log L_{icst} + \beta_3 \left(\log K_{icst} - \log L_{icst}\right)^2$$
$$+\beta_4 \log Age_{icst} + \sum\sum D^{Sector} D^{Location(sub-national)} + \sum D^{Country} + \sum D^{Sector}$$
$$+\sum D^{Year} + \sum\sum D^{Country} D^{Year}. + \sum\sum D^{Country} D^{Sector}. + \sum\sum D^{Sector} D^{Year} \quad (33.2)$$
$$+\sum\sum\sum D^{Country} D^{Sector} D^{Year} + \sum D^{size\_cat} + \sum D^{foreign} + \sum D^{state}$$
$$+\sum\sum D^{size\_cat} D^{foreign}. + \sum\sum D^{size-cat} D^{state}. + \varepsilon_{icst}$$

Log Y_{tics} is the dependent variable expressed as log deflated sales in constant 2010 prices[7] for firm "i" in country "c", in sector "s" at time "t". We denote α the efficiency parameter on which "equifinality" will be tested; $\beta_1 = \pi$, parameter of capital (expressed as net deflated cost of repurchase of the entire fixed assets of a company at constant 2010 prices) on which the distribution of capital is measured; $\beta_2 = (1 - \pi)$ parameter of labour (expressed as full-time employees) on which the distribution of labour is measured. The more general functional form entails the existence of further "functional form" parameter, $\beta_3 = -(\sigma-1)\pi(1-\pi)/2\sigma$, also known as the Kmenta correction parameter that is assumed to be zero when estimating the CD production function; finally, β_4 is the elasticity of sales to the age of the firm and ε_{icst} is the idiosyncratic error term.

4 Results

In Table 33.2, we report the results of equation (33.2) for both the CD and CES specifications, where the sample is for all countries. The first two columns (left panel) report the traditional Cobb-Douglas function, with no Kmenta "correction", whereas the latter two columns (right panel) show the Kmenta CES production function. In turn, columns 1 and 3 look at the whole sample of firms for CD and CES, respectively (we call it full sample), whilst columns 2 and 4 are estimates based on a sub-sample of firms (we call it reduced sample) that excludes all small firms with less than 20 employees, as well as all state-owned and foreign-owned firms (regardless their size). In other words, the reduced sample includes firms with more than 20 employees that are only privately-owned domestic firms. This is to ensure that the results are not driven by potential outliers: small firms, very large ones or foreign-owned firms with much higher productivity. The comparison within

---

[7] Deflators from the World Development Indicators linked-adjusted time series.

Table 33.2 Estimating productivity in Cobb-Douglas and Kmenta specifications (1967)

	(1)	(2)	(3)	(4)
	Cobb-Douglas full sample	Cobb-Douglas reduced sample	Kmenta (1967) full sample	Kmenta (1967) reduced Sample
Log(Labour)	0.790***	0.792***	0.941***	0.905***
	(0.015)	(0.019)	(0.029)	(0.039)
Log(Fixed Assets)	0.251***	0.250***	0.099***	0.135***
	(0.007)	(0.009)	(0.025)	(0.036)
[Log(Fixed Assets)-Log(Labour)]^2	Not applicable	Not applicable	0.007***	0.005***
			(0.001)	(0.001)
Log(Age)	0.017*	0.036**	0.015	0.035**
	(0.010)	(0.014)	(0.010)	(0.014)
Test Const. Ret. Scale	$\alpha^k + \alpha^l = 1$	$\alpha^k + \alpha^l = 1$	$\alpha^k + \alpha^l = 1$	$\alpha^k + \alpha^l = 1$
F (Prob > F)	9.26	6.45 (0.0111)**	8.71	6.16
	(0.0024)***		(0.0032)***	(0.0131)**
Test Implied Elasticity of Substitution	1 (Assumed)	1 (Assumed)	0.87	0.92
Chi (Prob > Chi)			0.01 (0.9290)	0.01 (0.9064)
Observations	29111	16195	29111	16195
Adjusted R-squared	0.88	0.87	0.89	0.88
Country FE	YES	YES	YES	YES
Sector FE	YES	YES	YES	YES
Year FE	YES	YES	YES	YES
Country-sector FE	YES	YES	YES	YES
Country-year FE	YES	YES	YES	YES
Sector-year FE	YES	YES	YES	YES
Country-sector-year FE	YES	YES	YES	YES
State firms FE	YES	YES	YES	YES
Foreign firms FE	YES	YES	YES	YES
Size Category FE	YES	YES	YES	YES
Size Category-State FE	YES	YES	YES	YES
Size Category-Foreign FE	YES	YES	YES	YES

Robust standard errors in parentheses. *** $p < 0.01$, ** $p < 0.05$, * $p < 0.1$

panels—column 1 versus 2 and column 3 versus 4—indicates the impact of different samples of firms on the estimation of efficiency, keeping the production functional form constant. The comparison between panels—column 1 versus 3 and column 2 versus 4—indicates the impact of different functional forms on the estimation of firm-level efficiency, keeping the firms' sample of firms. Within the CES functional form, if the Kmenta correction coefficient—$\beta_3 = -(\sigma - 1) \pi (1 - \pi)/2\sigma$—is significantly different from zero, then the elasticity of substitution is statistically different (less than) 1. In our case, the Kmenta CES is preferred to the CD functional form.

The functional form of the CD versus the CES function is relevant for the estimated coefficients. When we allow for elasticity of substitution to be different from unity (CES), we notice a change in the labour and capital coefficients: the former increases and the latter decreases if the CES is adopted. This signals a key role played by the labour inputs in "understudied" countries, where capital is relatively less abundant. The Kmenta methodology allow us to flag this finding. However, in the CD regressions, returns to scale are estimated to be slightly above unity, implying increasing returns to scale. However, CD is not the preferred specification of technology: Kmenta correction coefficient is clearly significant (at 1% level), leading us to reject the CD specification and indicating the need for a more complex specification of the relationship between labour and capital inputs.

From its theoretical foundation, we know that $\beta_3 = -(\sigma - 1) \pi (1 - \pi)/2\sigma$, so we can compute the *implied* elasticity of substitution in our regressions: it oscillates between 0.87 and 0.92, clearly and statistically[8] less than one. The conclusion is therefore that the estimated elasticity of substitution for the production function of a large sample of firms in understudied countries is less than 1. The gross complementarity we identify between capital and labour in these understudied economies may be a consequence of the rigidity in functioning of factor markets. Incidentally, this result cannot be driven by an embedded technological feature (e.g. k/l ratio) since the regressions control for sector and sector-time dummies. Suppose that one sector has intrinsically a high K/L ratio, then the sector dummies will capture that; furthermore, suppose that the K/L ratio has been changing over time (e.g. robotisation in some manufacturing sectors), then the sector-year dummy would capture that too. In other words, the sector and sector-time dummies variables allow for a control of the Hicks-neutrality assumption.

Next we note that TFP is not much related to the age of the firm, at least in the "Kmenta" regressions with all firms (column 3). The age variable only plays a marginal role in the reduced sample (excluding small, state and foreign companies), indicating that the "attribute of time" might impinge differently

---

[8] The null hypothesis that the elasticity of substitution is equal to 0.87 (column 3) or 0.92 (column 4) is not rejected, see table.

(possibly in different directions) on different categories of firms (e.g. a state firm might not "suffer" by being too young if subsidised).

Finally, in Tables 33.3 and 33.4, we test our hypothesis by considering the independent effect of configurations. To do this, we calculate for each configuration an *efficiency parameter*, which we construct by taking the average of the relevant individual country's efficiency values within each of the six configurations. Thus, after the estimation of the equations in Table 33.2, we predict the level of efficiency in each country given the estimated coefficients, using Angola as the reference point (see Table 33.3). On this basis, we calculate the average efficiency of each configuration given the country groupings, with the LME configuration as the reference point (see Table 33.4).[9] On this basis, we find clear support for our hypothesis: we identify a significant and independent effect from the VIS of the country in which the firm is located. Hence, our results indicate that this taxonomy of economic systems does influence economic outcomes.

As noted, we do not have strong priors about the rank order of configurations in terms of TFP; it is precisely to this question that an analysis of system taxonomy could be devoted. But, we identify equifinality between several of the systems. Thus, as expected, the most market-oriented economic system, the Emergent Liberal Market Economy configuration, is found to outperform most of the others in terms of efficiency. Unsurprisingly, the state capitalist (state-led) economies, where growth has been so pronounced in recent years, also perform very well. Indeed, these two systems are equifinal, belatedly suggesting a modicum of empirical support for Lange's view of effectively run socialist systems! Also, as expected, all the other systems are much less efficient than these two, though rather similar to each other. Each of the four is not significantly different from the one below or above, though there is a small significant difference between the top and bottom configuration. The hierarchically coordinated configuration is found to be the least efficient one. This is consistent with the traditional argument in comparative economic systems that while coordinated economies (e.g. Ukraine, Kazakhstan) may be very effective at marshalling resources—labour and capital—they perform less well when one considers the total factor productivity (Wiles 1977; Ellman 2014).

We conclude that when estimating TFP for developing and emerging markets, it is important to relax the standard assumption-common in work on developed economies-that the elasticity of substitution between capital and

---

[9] The conditional expected values of the dependent variable (log sales) of Table 33.2 are averaged across countries (Table 33.3) and, in turn, are averaged across configurations (Table 33.4). All 57 countries in the sample are used for the prediction and their averages.

Table 33.3 Linear prediction of countries' efficiency parameter

	Cobb-Douglas full sample	Cobb-Douglas reduced sample	Kmenta full sample	Kmenta VIS reduced sample
Angola (omitted)	16.315***	17.538***	16.282***	17.518***
	(0.098)	(0.199)	(0.098)	(0.200)
Argentina	0.714***	0.112	0.696***	0.095
	(0.109)	(0.206)	(0.110)	(0.206)
Azerbaijan	−0.005	−0.775**	0.03	−0.746**
	(0.192)	(0.316)	(0.193)	(0.317)
Bangladesh	1.248***	0.785***	1.232***	0.768***
	(0.108)	(0.204)	(0.109)	(0.204)
Belarus	1.750***	1.190***	1.852***	1.258***
	(0.193)	(0.292)	(0.194)	(0.293)
Botswana	0.332**	0.017	0.316**	−0.001
	(0.152)	(0.267)	(0.152)	(0.267)
Brazil	0.351***	−0.173	0.375***	−0.161
	(0.108)	(0.205)	(0.109)	(0.205)
Bulgaria	0.079	−0.503**	0.096	−0.492**
	(0.118)	(0.212)	(0.119)	(0.212)
Cameroon	1.641***	0.990***	1.699***	1.029***
	(0.205)	(0.282)	(0.205)	(0.282)
Chile	1.932***	1.273***	2.029***	1.340***
	(0.108)	(0.205)	(0.109)	(0.205)
China	1.439***	0.544***	1.425***	0.530***
	(0.107)	(0.203)	(0.107)	(0.203)
Colombia	1.680***	1.315***	1.816***	1.411***
	(0.108)	(0.205)	(0.108)	(0.206)
Czech Republic	1.092***	0.29	1.086***	0.274
	(0.184)	(0.268)	(0.184)	(0.268)
DR Congo	0.426***	0.314	0.461***	0.351
	(0.127)	(0.259)	(0.128)	(0.259)
Egypt	0.300***	0.003	0.301***	−0.006
	(0.106)	(0.204)	(0.106)	(0.204)
Estonia	0.553***	0.367	0.568***	0.363
	(0.183)	(0.295)	(0.184)	(0.295)
Ethiopia	0.656***	0.359	0.645***	0.341
	(0.131)	(0.221)	(0.131)	(0.222)
Georgia	−0.365**	−0.533**	−0.327*	−0.517*
	(0.179)	(0.270)	(0.180)	(0.271)
Ghana	0.193	0.333	0.316***	0.416*
	(0.120)	(0.226)	(0.120)	(0.226)
Hungary	1.659***	0.788***	1.684***	0.794***
	(0.190)	(0.278)	(0.191)	(0.279)
India	0.879***	0.223	0.864***	0.208
	(0.102)	(0.201)	(0.102)	(0.201)
Indonesia	1.799***	1.641***	1.920***	1.739***
	(0.105)	(0.203)	(0.105)	(0.204)

(*continued*)

Table 33.3 (continued)

	Cobb-Douglas full sample	Cobb-Douglas reduced sample	Kmenta full sample	Kmenta VIS reduced sample
Israel	0.366**	−0.056	0.355**	−0.076
	(0.163)	(0.250)	(0.164)	(0.250)
Jordan	0.246*	−0.224	0.287**	−0.201
	(0.137)	(0.226)	(0.138)	(0.226)
Kazakhstan	1.571***	0.984***	1.600***	1.002***
	(0.159)	(0.237)	(0.160)	(0.238)
Kenya	1.488***	0.927***	1.498***	0.929***
	(0.115)	(0.209)	(0.115)	(0.209)
Latvia	0.34	-0.569*	0.376	-0.527
	(0.230)	(0.345)	(0.231)	(0.346)
Lebanon	1.607***	1.350***	1.805***	1.516***
	(0.178)	(0.267)	(0.179)	(0.267)
Lithuania	0.272	0.055	0.273	0.046
	(0.178)	(0.270)	(0.179)	(0.271)
Malaysia	0.717***	0.076	0.741***	0.094
	(0.129)	(0.215)	(0.129)	(0.215)
Mexico	0.674***	0.442**	0.662***	0.428**
	(0.104)	(0.203)	(0.105)	(0.203)
Mongolia	1.749***	1.106***	1.858***	1.179***
	(0.148)	(0.231)	(0.149)	(0.232)
Morocco	1.042***	0.268	1.086***	0.311
	(0.166)	(0.237)	(0.167)	(0.238)
Namibia	0.153	0.102	0.139	0.081
	(0.168)	(0.288)	(0.168)	(0.288)
Nigeria	−0.319***	−0.296	−0.290***	−0.28
	(0.107)	(0.209)	(0.107)	(0.210)
Pakistan	0.231*	−0.052	0.251*	−0.033
	(0.137)	(0.226)	(0.137)	(0.226)
Peru	0.532***	0.05	0.533***	0.046
	(0.111)	(0.207)	(0.112)	(0.207)
Philippines	1.009***	0.258	1.006***	0.252
	(0.114)	(0.209)	(0.114)	(0.210)
Poland	−0.008	−0.024	−0.02	−0.032
	(0.181)	(0.282)	(0.182)	(0.282)
Romania	0.223	−0.129	0.227	−0.131
	(0.167)	(0.264)	(0.168)	(0.265)
Russia	1.155***	0.699***	1.155***	0.694***
	(0.116)	(0.209)	(0.116)	(0.209)
Rwanda	1.288***	0.475	1.359***	0.527*
	(0.226)	(0.300)	(0.227)	(0.300)
Senegal	0.409***	0.528**	0.440***	0.556**
	(0.128)	(0.243)	(0.128)	(0.243)
Slovak Republic	0.825***	0.326	0.829***	0.318
	(0.212)	(0.303)	(0.213)	(0.303)

(*continued*)

Table 33.3 (continued)

	Cobb-Douglas full sample	Cobb-Douglas reduced sample	Kmenta full sample	Kmenta VIS reduced sample
Slovenia	0.23	−0.092	0.235	−0.086
	(0.163)	(0.257)	(0.164)	(0.258)
South Africa	0.813***	0.252	0.798***	0.237
	(0.114)	(0.209)	(0.115)	(0.209)
Sri Lanka	0.455***	0.631***	0.445***	0.615***
	(0.138)	(0.233)	(0.139)	(0.233)
Sudan	−0.669	−1.841**	−0.305	−1.570*
	(1.075)	(0.891)	(1.079)	(0.892)
Tanzania	1.164***	1.209***	1.252***	1.289***
	(0.123)	(0.222)	(0.124)	(0.223)
Thailand	0.824***	0.264	0.823***	0.26
	(0.117)	(0.209)	(0.118)	(0.209)
Tunisia	0.872***	0.12	0.897***	0.139
	(0.130)	(0.216)	(0.131)	(0.217)
Turkey	0.703***	0.121	0.712***	0.127
	(0.111)	(0.205)	(0.111)	(0.206)
Uganda	1.009***	0.893***	1.109***	0.972***
	(0.124)	(0.232)	(0.124)	(0.232)
Ukraine	0.317**	0.149	0.314**	0.142
	(0.127)	(0.220)	(0.127)	(0.220)
Vietnam	3.092***	2.126***	3.385***	2.335***
	(0.109)	(0.205)	(0.109)	(0.205)
Yemen	0.215	0.723***	0.231	0.748***
	(0.150)	(0.269)	(0.150)	(0.270)

Standard errors in parentheses. *** $p < 0.01$, ** $p < 0.05$, * $p < 0.1$. Angola as reference value for all other estimated dummies interpretation.

Table 33.4 Linear prediction of configuration groupings efficiency

		Cobb-Douglas full sample	Cobb-Douglas reduced sample	Kmenta full Sample	Kmenta reduced Sample
Constant (LME)	1st	**17.585***	**18.331***	**17.592***	**18.341***
		(0.035)	(0.039)	(0.035)	(0.039)
State led	1st/2nd	0.024	−0.103**	0.02	−0.110***
		(0.038)	(0.042)	(0.038)	(0.042)
Fragmented	3rd	−0.630***	−0.372***	−0.635***	−0.387***
		(0.042)	(0.049)	(0.043)	(0.050)
Family led	4th/5th	−0.689***	−0.481***	−0.699***	−0.492***
		(0.040)	(0.045)	(0.041)	(0.046)
Collaborative	5th/4th	−0.683***	−0.623***	−0.718***	−0.655***
		(0.070)	(0.086)	(0.071)	(0.088)
Hierarchically	6th	−0.780***	−0.760***	−0.800***	−0.777***
		(0.048)	(0.053)	(0.049)	(0.054)

Standard errors in parentheses. *** $p < 0.01$, ** $p < 0.05$, * $p < 0.1$. Reference liberal market economies

labour is unitary; in fact, rigidities in these systems mean that it is estimated to be below one, suggesting that there is gross complementarity between inputs. Our estimates therefore provide well-specified and robust indicators of the average firm-level TFP in each of our understudied countries. Even with a variety of fixed effects and controls, we are still able to identify significant effects from our empirically determined taxonomy of countries, following a logic that is perhaps consistent with priors about the advantages of market economies in efficiency terms.

5   Conclusions

We have argued in this chapter for a new approach to comparative economic systems in which the traditional typological approach is replaced by a taxonomic one and in which empirical analysis of characteristics is used to place countries into configurations. We have also called for an extension of the field of study to include the heterogeneous group of developing, emerging and transition economies.

This is a preliminary piece of work and subject to several important limitations. Most significantly, we did not propose our own classification of economic systems; rather we used a pre-existing typology developed for a different purpose. This has made some of our results, notably the rankings of different systems in terms of efficiency, difficult to interpret. It has also limited the scope of our research question as to whether the VIS taxonomy of the major new emerging economies has explanatory power over firm-level economic behaviour. Nonetheless, our empirical work, based on estimating Cobb-Douglas and Kmenta Constant Elasticity of Substitution production functions across around 30,000 firms in 57 countries, finds that this taxonomy of understudied economies does explain average firm-level performance, even when a granular set of national, sectoral, temporal and country-level fixed effects are taken into account. We also find evidence for some degree of equifinality, both between the top two systems and among the bottom four. While tentative, the result of equifinality between Emergent Liberal Market and State-Capitalist economies might be interpreted as supporting mildly Lange's view that socialist regimes can be effective—an indicator of the promise of this approach. Even so, future work might consider additional indicators of firm performance, for example, growth, employment creation or internationalisation. These are important items for future work.

Our empirical work allows us to tentatively conclude that a shift from a typological to a taxonomic approach represents a potentially valuable way forward for the field of comparative economic systems. This opens quite a large research agenda. In the first place, there is a need for further research to begin to establish a more robust and defensible configuration system from the perspective of comparative economic systems. While the Fainshmidt et al. (2018) approach represented a valiant first step, the set of institutional variables they used was perhaps more restricted, and the underlying methodology more qualitative, than comparative economic systems scholar might prefer. Thus, one might wish to base the identification of appropriate institutional parameters on the work of North (1990) and Williamson (2000) and to identify taxonomies using small sample empirical methods such as fuzzy set analysis (Ragin 2008). One might also wish to extend the reach of the work to cover developed as well as developing economies to provide a global classification of economic systems. Once such a taxonomy has been created, the real work can begin—identifying empirically the areas of strength and weakness of different systems, and the institutional arrangements supportive of key organisational forms in each configuration.

References

Acemoglu, D., & Robinson, J. (2012). *Why Nations Fail.* New York: Profile Books.

Aguilera, R. V., & Crespi-Cladera, R. (2016). Global Corporate Governance: On the Relevance of Firms' Ownership Structure. *Journal of World Business, 51*(1), 50–57.

Amable, B. (2016). Institutional Complementarities in the Dynamic Comparative Analysis of Capitalism. *Journal of Institutional Economics, 12*(1), 79–103.

Arrow, K. J., Chenery, H. B., Minhas, B. S., & Solow, R. M. (1961). Capital-Labor Substitution and Economic Efficiency. *The Review of Economics and Statistics, 43*(3), 225–250.

Blanchard, O. (1997). *The Economics of Post-Communist Transition.* Oxford: Clarendon press.

Boyer, R. (2005). *How and why capitalisms differ, Economy and Society, 34*(4), 509–557. https://doi.org/10.1080/03085140500277070

Brus, W., & Laski, K. (1991). *From Marx to the Market: Socialism in Search of an Economic System.* Oxford: Oxford University Press.

Carney, M., Estrin, S., van Essen, M., & Shapiro, D. (2018). Business Groups Reconsidered: Beyond Paragons and Parasites. *Academy of Management Perspectives, 32*(4), 2.

Chow, G. C. (2017). *Capital formation and economic growth in China.* Boston: Brill.

Djankov, S., Glaeser, E., LaPorta, R., Lopez-de-Silanes, F., & Shleifer, A. (2003). The New Comparative Economics. *Journal of Comparative Economics, 31*(4), 595–619.

Ellman, M. (2014). *Socialist Planning.* Cambridge: Cambridge University Press.

Estrin, S. (1984). *Self-management: Economic Theory and Yugoslav Practice*. Cambridge: Cambridge University Press.

Estrin, S., Hanousek, J., Kočenda, E., & Svejnar, J. (2009). The Effects of Privatization and Ownership in Transition Economies. *Journal of Economic Literature, 47*(3), 699–728.

Estrin, S., Mickiewicz, T., Stephan, U., & Wright, M. (2019). Entrepreneurship in Emerging Economies. In R. Grosse & K. Meyer (Eds.), *Oxford Handbook on Management in Emerging Markets*. Oxford: Oxford University Press.

Fainshmidt, S., Judge, W. Q., Aguilera, R. V., & Smith, A. (2018). Varieties of Institutional Systems: A Contextual Taxonomy of Understudied Countries. *Journal of World Business, 53*(3), 307–322.

Friedman, M. (1962). *Capitalism and Freedom*. Chicago: University of Chicago Press.

Fukuyama, F. (1989). The End of History. *The National Interest, 16*, 3–18.

Gardner, S. H. (1997). *Comparative Economic Systems*. Stamford: Cengage.

Gregory, P., & Stuart, R. (1999). *Comparative Economic Systems*. Boston: Houghton Mifflin.

Hall, P. A., & Gingerich, D. W. (2009). Varieties of Capitalism and Institutional Complementarities in the Political Economy: An Empirical Analysis. *British Journal of Political Science, 39*(3), 449–482.

Hall, P. A., & Soskice, D. W. (2001). *Varieties of Capitalism: The Institutional Foundations of Comparative Advantage*. Oxford: Oxford University Press.

Hancké, B., Rhodes, M., & Thatcher, M. (2007). *Beyond Varieties of Capitalism: Conflict, Contradictions, and Complementarities in the European Economy*. Oxford, UK: Oxford University Press.

Hancke, R. (2009). *Debating Varieties of Capitalism*. Oxford: Oxford University Press.

Hayek, F. A. (1944). *The Road to Serfdom*. London: Routledge.

Hicks, J. (1932). *The Theory of Wages*. London, Macmillan.

Hotho, J. J. (2014). From Typology to Taxonomy: A Configurational Analysis of National Business Systems and Their Explanatory Power. *Organization Studies, 35*(5), 671–702.

Jackson, G., & Deeg, R. (2008). Comparing Capitalisms: Understanding Institutional Diversity and Its Implications for International Business. *Journal of International Business Studies, 39*(4), 540–561.

Khanna, T., & Palepu, K. (2000a). Is Group Affiliation Profitable in Emerging Markets? An Analysis of Diversified Indian Business Groups, *Journal of Finance*, 867–891.

Khanna, T., & Palepu, K. (2000b). The Future of Business Groups in Emerging Markets: Long Run Evidence from Chile. *Academy of Management Journal, 43*, 268–285.

Khanna, T., & Yafeh, Y. (2007). Business Groups in Emerging Markets: Paragons or Parasites. *Journal of Economic Literature, XLV*, 331–372.

Kmenta, J. (1967). On Estimation of the CES Production Function. *International Economic Review, 8*, 180–189.

Koopmans, T. C. (1957). Three Essays on the State of Economic Science, McGraw-Hill Book Company, Inc.

Kornai, J. (1992). *The Socialist System: The Political Economy of Communism*. Oxford: Oxford University Press.

Lange, O. (1936). On the Economic Theory of Socialism: Part One. *Review of Economic Studies, 4*(1), 53–71.

Lavigne, M. (1995). *Economics of Transition*. London: Palgrave Macmillan.

Levy, D., & Pert, S. (2008). Socialist Calculation Debate, from Durlauf, S. and Blume, L.E. (2008) *The New Palgrave Dictionary of Economics*, Second Edition, 2008

Marx, K. (2007). *Das Kapital* (Vol. 1). Washington D.C: Regnery Publishing.

Montias, M. (1976). *The Structure of Economic Systems*. Yale: Yale University Press.

North, D. C. (1990). Institutions, Institutional Change and Economic Performance. In J. Alt & D. North (Eds.), *Political Economy of Institutions and Decisions*. Cambridge: Cambridge University Press.

North, D. C. (1994). Economic Performance Through Time. *American Economic Review, 84*, 359–368.

Nuti, D. M. (2018). *The Rise, Fall and Future of Socialism*, EACES Conference 2018 Keynote Address

O'Neill, J. (2011). *The Growth Map*. London: Penguin.

Ostrom, E. (2009). A General Framework for Analyzing Sustainability of Social-ecological Systems. *Science, 325*(5939), 419–422.

Peck, J., & Zhang, J. (2013). A Variety of Capitalism… with Chinese Characteristics? *Journal of Economic Geography, 13*(3), 357–396.

Putnam, L., & Jones, T. S. (1982). Reciprocity in Negotiations: An Analysis of Bargaining Interaction. *Communication Monographs, 49*(3), 171–191.

Ragin, C. C. (2008). *Redesigning Social Inquiry: Fuzzy Sets and Beyond*. Chicago, IL: University of Chicago Press.

Ronen, O., & Shenkar, R. (2013). Mapping World Cultures: Cluster Formation, Sources and Implications. *Journal of International Business Studies, 44*(9), 867–897.

Rundle-Thiele, S., Kubacki, K., Tkaczynski, A., & Parkinson, J. (2015). Using Two-step Cluster Analysis to Identify Homogeneous Physical Activity Groups. *Marketing Intelligence & Planning, 33*(4), 23.

Sachs, J., & Warner, A. (1995). Economic Reform and the Process of Global Integration, *Brookings Papers on Economic Activity*.

Schneider, B. R. (2009). Hierarchical market economies and varieties of capitalism in Latin America. *Journal of Latin American Studies, 41*(3), 553–575.

Schneider, M., & Paunescu, M. (2012). Changing Varieties of Capitalism and Revealed Comparative Advantages from 1990 to 2005: A Test of the Hall and Soskice Claims. *Socio-Economic Review, 10*(4), 731–753.

Sinkovics, R. R., Yamin, M., Nadvi, K., & Zhang, Y. (2014). Rising Powers from Emerging Markets? The Changing Face of International Business. *International Business Review, 23*(4), 675–679.

Solow, R. (1957). Technical Change and the Aggregate Production Function. *Review of Economics and Statistics, 39*(3), 312–320.

Weitzman, M. (1970). Soviet Postwar Economic Growth and Capital-Labor Substitution. *American Economic Review, 60*(4), 676–692.

Wiles, P. (1977). *Economic Institutions Compared.* London: Halsted Press.

Williamson, O. (2000). New Institutional Economics. *Journal of Economic Literature, 38*, 595–613.

Wood, G., & Frynas, J. G. (2005). The Institutional Basis of Economic Failure: Anatomy of the Segmented Business System. *Socio-Economic Review, 4*(2), 239–277.

34

Institutional Complementarities in Comparative Capitalism: A Bibliometric Account

Francesca Gagliardi

1   Introduction

The notion of institutional complementarities has gained a prominent role in the academic discourse that looks at the link between institutions and economic change in a comparative perspective. It has become particularly important in debates that seek to explain how interdependence among institutions not only accounts for the institutional diversity that can be observed across and within socio-economic systems but also affects economic performance. As such, the concept invites researchers to go beyond the widely accepted but fairly vague claim that "institutions matter". The focus has thus shifted to how different combinations of institutions generate a given performance outcome, and to what policy-makers can do to develop those institutions which, when working together, support economic performance.

Initially formulated in economics (Aoki 1994; Pagano 1992; Pagano and Rowthorn 1994), the concept of institutional complementarities was adopted in a number of disciplines, including political science, management, sociology, law and international business. Interdisciplinary analytical frameworks relying in one way or another on the concept have been developed by scholars of comparative capitalism. The most significant are comparative institutional analysis, (French) regulation theory, varieties of capitalism, comparative

F. Gagliardi (✉)
Hertfordshire Business School, University of Hertfordshire, Hertfordshire, UK
e-mail: f.gagliardi@herts.ac.uk

© The Author(s) 2021
E. Douarin, O. Havrylyshyn (eds.), *The Palgrave Handbook of Comparative Economics*,
https://doi.org/10.1007/978-3-030-50888-3_34

political economy and national business systems. The concept has been mobilized in analyses across a wide range of domains at the micro, meso and macro levels, including firm governance and performance (Aguilera and Jackson 2003; Gagliardi 2009a, b) industrial relations (Harvey 2009), legal institutions (Siems and Deakin 2010), economic policy (Thelen 2010) and political economy (Hall and Gingerich 2009).

This chapter presents the results of a bibliometric review of the journal literature that looks at institutional complementarities in comparative capitalism. Conducted on 177 journal articles published during the 20-year period 2000–2019, the study aims to map this field of inquiry through a comprehensive assessment of the research themes covered and the methods used, as well as the key authors and the main outlets in which the discussion takes place. The underpinning motivation for this state-of-the-art review is to offer insights into the evolution of the field that may help scholars working in this area of inquiry shape future research priorities and dissemination strategies.

2   Methodology and Data

The term bibliometrics was first used by Pritchard (1969) to describe the method of counting and analyzing relationships among various facets of specialized professional publications, such as scientific papers or patents, in order to "shed light on the processes of written communication and of the nature and course of development in a discipline" (ibid.: p. 350). For Donohue (1972), bibliometrics consists in the quantitative analysis of gross bibliographical units such as journal articles and books, while Boyce and Kraft (1985) define bibliometrics as the quantitative study of written communication through its physical realization.

Bibliometric methods improve the understanding of the evolution of a scientific research field by helping to identify the relevant body of work and classify it according to certain criteria such that an objective assessment of the seminal contributions and contributors may be carried out (Du and Teixeira 2012; Teixeira 2014). Bibliometric work represents a form of meta-review of the literature (Kim and McMillan 2008) and can involve counting citations in publications and using these counts to build co-citation maps of key researchers or research institutes (Culnan 1986; Willett 2007). Another use is to establish publication trends for authors, journals and patterns of research (Cruz and Teixeira 2010; McElwee and Atherton 2005; Silva and Teixeira 2009). This sheds a useful light on how the topics addressed and the types of methodologies used in a research area of interest have changed over time

(Cruz and Teixeira 2010; Silva and Teixeira 2008, 2009). This is the approach adopted in the present study, which aims to analyze the evolution of the journal literature that uses the notion of institutional complementarities within a comparative capitalism framework in order to provide insights that may help the formulation of future research trajectories.

The literature of interest was collected in Scopus and the Web of Science Social Science Citation Index (SSCI). Specifically, the corpus was built following a two-step search procedure. In a first step, the terms "institutional complementarities", "organizational equilibrium" and their derivatives were used.[1] The search procedure did not cover a pre-determined time period and was unrestricted in the sense that the search engine searched not only by subject and keyword but also by title, abstract and main text of the articles.[2] To cover only articles, books, book reviews, notes and editorials were excluded from the search criteria.[3] This procedure returned a total of 1292 records (1156 in Scopus and 136 in SSCI) for the period 1992–2019, with two gaps in 1993 and 1995 where no publications were found.

The records thus gathered cover the entire journal literature on institutional complementarities. The focus of the present study, however, is only the literature that uses the notion of institutional complementarities to study comparative capitalism. Hence in addition to the exclusion of duplicates (i.e. identical records included in both bibliographic databases), in a second step the search was refined so as to exclude articles on topics other than comparative capitalism. Records which did not include at least one of the following terms within the title, abstract or keywords were deleted: comparative capitalism; models of capitalism; varieties of capitalism; business systems; comparative systems; convergence; divergence.

The remaining articles were analyzed on a one-by-one basis, scrutinizing their abstract, main text and reference list, to check their actual relevance regarding the search terms. This labor-intensive procedure identified a number of articles that did not include any of the search keywords anywhere or included them only in the reference list. After deleting these records, the final

---

[1] As Aoki (2001) argues, the notion of organizational equilibrium as in Pagano (1992) and Pagano and Rowthorn (1994) is conceptually equivalent to that of institutional complementarities. In the searches that used the string "organizational equilibrium", spelling variations in British and American English have been accounted for.

[2] The search covered only articles written in English.

[3] This automated method was complemented by visual inspection of the export files obtained from each bibliographic database. This revealed additional records that were not journal articles and have therefore been excluded manually.

dataset included 177 journal articles (13.7% of the initial 1292 records)[4] spanning the years 2000–2019, with one gap in 2001 where no journal articles were found, and including two articles which as of 31 December 2019 had an "early access" publication status. The data gathered from the bibliographic databases used were not entirely accurate. The names of books, journals and authors were sometimes misspelled or not uniformly coded. The data were corrected manually.

The articles included in the corpus were first analyzed to gather information on trends in terms of the distribution of publications over time, the outlets in which they were published, and their contributing authors. The corpus was then examined in terms of types of articles, based on the methodology used, and main topics of research. All articles were carefully read. This led to the identification of 17 research themes covered in the literature: conceptual frameworks; development, growth and inequality; education systems; financial and sustainability reporting; financial crises: causes and responses; financial systems and institutions, monetary institutions; firm performance and governance; industrial and employment relations, human resource management (HRM, henceforth), unionism; industry and sector studies; innovation, science and technology; institutional change; internationalization, multinational corporations (MNCs, henceforth), globalization; legal and political institutions; macroeconomic policy; mapping models of capitalism; microeconomic policy; other.

The classification of articles by type of methodology used followed the distinction between formal and appreciative theorizing, first introduced by Nelson and Winter (1982) and later developed in Silva and Teixeira (2008, 2009), aimed at distinguishing theoretical explanations that are expressed through mathematical modeling from theoretical work in which mathematical constructs are absent. Following this logic, this study classified as "formal" all articles that develop analytical models and express theoretical explanations through mathematical modeling or simulation. Articles which are formal and also include data testing are classified as "formal and empirical". "Appreciative" articles are those which include theoretical arguments, critiques, judgments or appraisals not based on mathematical models. "Appreciative and empirical" is a category used for articles that are classified as appreciative and include appreciations or comments based on empirical data. A further category of articles is "empirical" and includes works involving the use of case studies, econometrics, statistical analysis or other qualitative and quantitative empirical

---

[4] The substantial number of records that were dropped out reveals that the concept of institutional complementarities has been largely used to examine topics other than comparative capitalism.

methods. Lastly, the category "survey" covers articles that provide literature reviews.

3   Results

The analysis of the corpus reveals a number of interesting trends. One is that the literature has developed in four distinct phases, each with its own distinctive set of key topics and specific mix of methods. Another is that although the concept of institutional complementarities was formulated by economists, it has been mobilized primarily outside economics.

3.1   Main Trends in the Journal Literature

Within the comparative capitalism journal literature, the first article that uses the notion of institutional complementarities was published in 2000. However, as Fig. 34.1 shows, it was not until 2005 that the use of this notion started to become more frequent within this line of research. Between 2000 and 2004, only eight articles were published; then from 2005, journal outputs increased significantly, albeit with yearly fluctuations, reaching a peak of 25 articles in 2009. From 2016 onwards, the yearly output decreased steadily, with only four articles published in 2019, the last year covered in the dataset. Looking ahead, at least two articles will be published in 2020, as two early access articles are captured in the dataset.

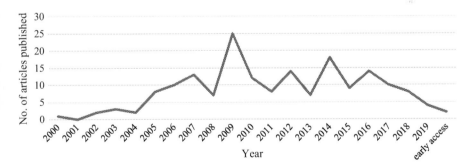

Fig. 34.1 Articles by year, 2000–2019. Note: The 177 articles have been obtained from SciVerse Scopus and SSCI using a battery of search terms chosen so as to capture research in comparative capitalism that uses the notion of institutional complementarities. The search was unrestricted but limited to journal articles

The findings of the bibliometric exercise reveal that in its early years the literature tended to focus closely on the issue of convergence and divergence of socio-economic systems. The first article published in the series depicted in Fig. 34.1 is Bruno Amable's "Institutional Complementarity and Diversity of Social Systems of Innovation and Production", published in 2000 in the *Review of International Political Economy*.[5] Amable (2000) proposes an institutional analysis of modern capitalist economies by resorting to the concepts of institutional complementarity and hierarchy. The main idea is that the institutional dimension is critical in explaining why convergence toward the same economic model cannot be expected. An analytical classification of developed economies is proposed.

In 2002, only two articles were published. The first was "The Effects of Convergence: Internationalization and the Changing Distribution of Net Value Added in Large German Firms", published in *Economy and Society* by Jürgen Beyer and Anke Hassel. The notion of institutional complementarities here appears in the context of firm internationalization and clarifies changes occurring in the corporate governance system. The discussion finds that the emerging convergence of German corporate governance practices toward Anglo-American standards has had a weak, but significant, impact on the distribution of net value added (Beyer and Hassel 2002). The other was "European Style of Corporate Governance at the Crossroads: The Role of Worker Involvement" by Antoine Rebérioux, which appeared in the *Journal of Common Market Studies*. Rebérioux (2002) examines the evolution of the continental European style of corporate governance in the context of the globalization of financial markets and, drawing on the notion of institutional complementarities, rejects the claim that national models are converging.

The year 2005 marks a significant change in terms of volume of published outputs. Four out of the eight articles included in the corpus for this year featured in an issue of the *Socio-Economic Review* that ran a "Symposium on Institutional Complementarity and Political Economy". Special issues seem to have played an important role in the diffusion of research in the field given that the years which are associated with higher numbers of published articles coincide with the inclusion of special issues in several journals. For example: *Asia Pacific Journal of Human Resources*, *Asia Pacific Journal of Management*, *Economy and Society* and *Socio-Economic Review* in 2009 (this is the year with the highest number of outputs, 25 in total); *Journal of European Public Policy* and *Socio-Economic Review* in 2012; *Socio-Economic Review* in 2013; *Capital and Class* in 2014.

---

[5] The article featured in the last issue of that year.

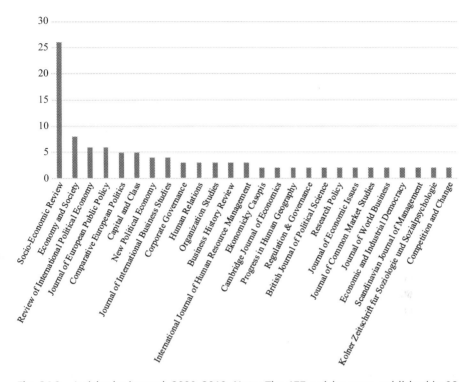

Fig. 34.2   Articles by journal, 2000–2019. Note: The 177 articles were published in 98 distinct journals. The 26 journals depicted here are those in which at least two articles were published. These journals account for 59% of total articles

The comparative capitalism journal literature relying on the notion of institutional complementarities is spread among a large number of outlets. The 177 articles were published in 98 journals. The most important in terms of numbers of articles published is *Socio-Economic Review* with 14% (i.e. 25 articles) of the total publications included in the dataset (Fig. 34.2). This is followed by *Economy and Society* with 4.5% (i.e. eight outputs), and *Review of International Political Economy* and *Journal of European Public Policy* at 3.4% each (i.e. 6 articles). *Comparative European Politics* and *Capital and Class* each account for 2.9% (i.e. five articles), while *New Political Economy* and *Journal of International Business Studies* are at 2.8% each (i.e. four articles). The top 4 journals account for 25.3% of total articles, while this figure is 59% for the top 26 journals (depicted in Fig. 34.2). The figures presented here indicate that *Socio-Economic Review* is the main outlet for research produced in this

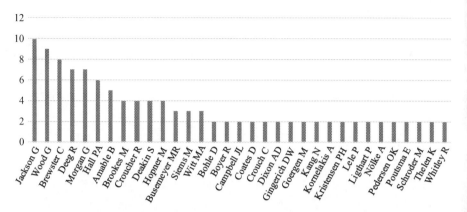

Fig. 34.3 Articles by author, 2000–2019. Note: A total of 223 authors are named on the 177 articles covering the period 2000–2019

line of inquiry. Multidisciplinary in scope and interdisciplinary in approach (Jackson 2012), the journal spans sociology, management, political science and economics.

Looking now at authorship, about 54% articles are singled authored, while nearly 46% are co-authored. The corpus included in the database features a total of 223 authors. Among them, 33 authors (i.e. about 15%) have at least two outputs. Overall, as indicated in Fig. 34.3, with 10 published (single or co-authored) articles Gregory Jackson is the most prolific contributor, followed by Geoffrey Wood (9 articles), Chris Brewster (8 articles), Richard Deeg and Glenn Morgan (7 articles each), Peter Hall (6 articles) and Bruno Amable (5 articles). An examination of the disciplinary background of the most prolific authors reveals that political scientists are the most represented group (38%), followed by management scholars (21%), sociologists (17%), economists (14%) and law scholars (10%).[6]

These insights regarding key researchers, coupled with the information revealed in relation to core publication outlets, seem to suggest that institutional complementarities research focused on comparative capitalism is disseminated in a rather wide spectrum of academic journals (177 articles published across 98 journals) and receives the interest of quite a number of scholars (177 articles authored by 223 scholars). However, the figures also reveal that this body of work is heavily published in a small number of

---

[6] Information on authors' disciplinary background was collected from their institutional and/or personal webpages. This information was not accessible for 4 out of the 33 top authors, here defined as having at least two journal publications included in the corpus under analysis.

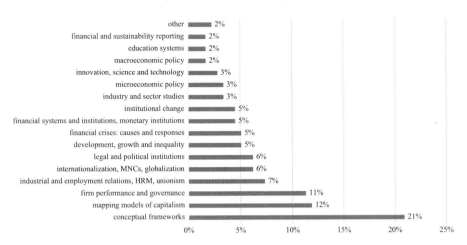

Fig. 34.4 Articles by theme, 2000–2019. Note: The 177 articles have been obtained from Scopus and SSCI using as search keywords "institutional complementarities", "organizational equilibrium" and their variations, on one hand, and "comparative capitalism", "models of capitalism", "varieties of capitalism", "business systems", "comparative systems", "convergence" and "divergence", on the other hand. The search was unrestricted but limited to journal articles

journals and has at its forefront a relatively small group of contributors. The flagship journal, *Socio-Economic Review*, is the official journal of the Society for the Advancement of Socio-Economics (SASE). A number of the most prolific authors have or have had links with *Socio-Economic Review* and/or SASE. This appears to indicate that over the years this group of scholars have been working as a relatively closely knit scientific community seeking to advance and promote the field.

It is of interest to note that few economists feature among the most prolific authors, and that even fewer economics journals, as illustrated in Fig. 34.2, are among the most popular outlets for this line of inquiry. Taken together, these two observations are in line with Gagliardi (2019) who in a work mapping the entire journal literature on institutional complementarities—a much broader scope than the present study—found that although research within the economic theory of the firm pioneered the early journal literature on institutional complementarities (Aoki 1994; Pagano 1992; Pagano and Rowthorn 1994), subsequent research largely moved away from the theory of the firm, hence from economics, and spread across sociology, political science, management, international business and political economy, as the concept of institutional complementarities gained traction in other research areas.

3.2   Themes

Over the entire period covered in the corpus, the most discussed topic is "conceptual frameworks", with 21% of all articles (Fig. 34.4). This is followed by the themes "mapping models of capitalism" and "firm performance and governance" (with 12% and 11%, respectively). The theme "industrial and employment relations, HRM unionism" has a share of 7%, while "internationalization, MNCs, globalization" and "legal and political institutions" each account for 6% of the journal literature. Articles focused on the theme "institutional change" occupy a relatively minor place within this journal literature, despite its centrality for discussions on models of capitalism and institutional complementarities.

The results show that changes in the yearly publication trend (see Fig. 34.1) have been accompanied by changes in the themes explored (Table 34.1). While "conceptual frameworks" is the most popular theme over the entire period studied, its share has varied over time, passing from 13% in 2000–2004 to 27% in 2005–2009 and 26% in 2010–2014 to 8% in 2015–2019. A possible explanation for this changing trend is that in the first few years after the publication in 2001 of Peter Hall and David Soskice's seminal *Varieties of Capitalism: The Institutional Foundations of Comparative Advantage*, scholars tended by and large to resort to the conceptual framework outlined in that volume. Subsequently the research agenda shifted toward further developments of Hall and Soskice's analytical framework, which was criticized particularly from 2003 (see, e.g. Blyth 2003; Goodin 2003; Watson 2003—all featured in a special issue of *Journal of Comparative European Politics*, which included a response from Hall and Soskice 2003).

"Firm performance and governance" as well as "internationalization, MNCs, globalization" were the two most covered themes in 2000–2004 (with 38% and 25% respectively), possibly a result of the focus that early studies on institutional complementarities had in the area of theory of the firm. These two themes then saw a steady decrease in popularity over the remaining years. Somewhat similarly, while "mapping models of capitalism", the fourth and last theme covered in this journal literature since its very beginning, accounted for 25% of total articles in 2000–2004 and remained very popular in 2005–2009, with 18%, a progressive decline in the coverage it received can be observed from 2010 onwards.

Table 34.1 Articles by theme, 2000–2019

	2000–2004 (%)	2005–2009 (%)	2010–2014 (%)	2015–2019 (%)
Firm performance and governance	38	11	10	8
Mapping models of capitalism	25	18	10	4
Internationalization, MNCs, globalization	25	6	2	8
Conceptual frameworks	13	27	26	8
Legal and political institutions	–	8	9	2
Industrial and employment relations, HRM, unionism	–	8	5	8
Institutional change	–	8	3	2
Financial systems and institutions, monetary institutions	–	3	5	6
Development, growth and inequality	–	3	3	10
Microeconomic policy	–	3	7	–
Innovation, science and technology	–	2	5	2
Industry and sector studies	–	2	2	8
Financial crises: causes and responses	–	–	5	13
Financial and sustainability reporting	–	–	3	2
Education systems	–	–	2	4
Macroeconomic policy	–	–	–	6
Other	–	–	2	6

Note: The 177 articles have been obtained from Scopus and SSCI using as search keywords "institutional complementarities", "organizational equilibrium" and their variations, on one hand, and "comparative capitalism", "models of capitalism", "varieties of capitalism", "business systems", "comparative systems", "convergence" and "divergence", on the other hand. The search was unrestricted but limited to journal articles

Starting from 2005, a large number of new themes started to be examined in this literature. These have included, among others, "development, growth and inequality" and "financial crises: causes and responses", both of which became rather prominent in the most recent years, as well as "financial systems and institutions, monetary institutions", "industrial and employment relations, HRM, unionism", "legal and political institutions" and "innovation, science and technology". The emergence of these new themes could be interpreted as a sign of maturity of the field, indicating that a wider range of questions is investigated because the concept of institutional complementarities is better accepted and understood, and is therefore applied more broadly.

3.3   Methods

Overall, the literature examined here is mostly empirically oriented. "Empirical" articles account for 50% of total journal output over 2000–2019, while "appreciative" pieces amount to 37%, and articles which are both "appreciative and empirical" represent 10% of the corpus. No "formal" paper has been published, while only 1% of the articles combines "formal and empirical" methods. Finally, "surveys" account for 2% of the journal production (Fig. 34.5).

"Empirical" articles accounted for only 25% of the journal publications in the initial 2000–2004 period (Table 34.2). This finding is not surprising,

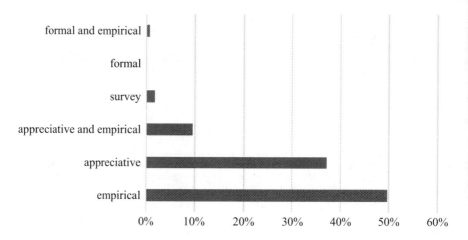

Fig. 34.5 Articles by type, 2000–2019. Note: The 177 articles included in the corpus have been classified by type using the distinction between formal and appreciative theorizing initially proposed by Nelson and Winter (1982)

Table 34.2 Methods by year

	2000–2004 (%)	2005–2009 (%)	2010–2014 (%)	2015–2019 (%)
Appreciative	50	46	36	30
Appreciative and empirical	25	13	8	4
Empirical	25	40	53	64
Formal	0	0	0	0
Formal and empirical	0	0	0	2
Survey	0	2	3	0

Note: The 177 articles included in the corpus have been classified by type using the distinction between formal and appreciative theorizing initially proposed by Nelson and Winter (1982)

given that these were the years during which the publication of Hall and Soskice (2001) sparked a body of work focused on conceptual applications of their analysis of comparative capitalism. Articles of an "appreciative" type were indeed the predominant type of articles in the initial periods, that is, in 2000–2004 and 2005–2009, with 50% and 46%, respectively. However, their popularity decreased significantly in later years (36% in 2010–2014 and 30% in 2015–2019) as a result of the steady growth of empirical research, which increased from 40% of total articles in 2005–2009 to 53% in 2010–2014 and to 64% in 2015–2019. "Appreciative and empirical" papers also dropped in popularity over time, a finding which is consistent with the pattern displayed by solely appreciative inquiry.

Given the prominence of empirical papers within this literature, it is interesting to see how the methodologies employed in empirical investigations have changed over time (Table 34.3). This analysis reveals that econometrics, which in the period 2000–2004 was employed in 50% of the empirical literature (the other 50% being articles that carried out only descriptive data analysis), has gradually lost its predominance as the empirical method of choice. Case studies and comparative case studies, on the other hand, were the main

Table 34.3 Articles by empirical method

2000–2004 (%)		2000–2004 (%)	2005–2009 (%)	2010–2014 (%)	2015–2019 (%)
0	Econometrics	50	28	16	45
0	Descriptive data analysis	50	–	5	3
0	Comparative case studies	–	25	22	18
0	Case studies	–	22	27	3
0	Statistical analysis	–	16	11	12
200	Construction of indicators/indices	–	6	–	–
200	Leximetric analysis	–	3	3	–
0	Mixed methods	–	–	5	3
0	Fuzzy-set qualitative comparative analysis	–	–	5	9
0	Historical analysis	–	–	3	–
0	Network analysis	–	–	3	–
0	Content analysis	–	–	–	3
0	Interviews	–	–	–	3

Note: The 177 articles included in the corpus have been classified by type using the distinction between formal and appreciative theorizing initially proposed by Nelson and Winter (1982)

empirical methods used in 2005–2009 as well as in 2010–2014, with a combined weight of 47% and 49%, respectively.

A number of other empirical research methods started to be used in the most recent years. Among them are leximetric analysis, network analysis, historical analysis, interviews and fuzzy-set qualitative comparative analysis. Developed by Charles Ragin (1987, 2000), fuzzy-set qualitative comparative analysis uses Boolean algebra to implement comparisons of cases as configurations and provide a means to portray their patterns of similarities and variations (Cárdenas 2012).[7] Whether fuzzy-set qualitative comparative analysis will become an established research method for scholars working on institutional complementarities and comparative capitalism remains to be seen.

4   Discussion and Conclusions

This chapter has proposed a bibliometric review of the structure and evolution of the journal literature devoted to the study of comparative capitalism using the notion of institutional complementarities published between 2000 and 2019. An assessment of general trends, such as changes in the volume of published research, as well as outlets that scholars choose for publishing their work on this topic, has been provided. The evolution of themes and methods used has also been discussed. Results have shown that the publication of articles has followed four distinct phases. The first, from 2000 to 2004, was characterized by low output levels. The second, going from 2005 to 2009, saw a rapid expansion of the research published in journals. The third phase, from 2010 to 2016, saw a fluctuating trend. There has been a steady decrease in the number of publications since 2016, perhaps revealing some exhaustion of interest in the matter of institutional complementarities in comparative capitalism.

During the period under study, there has been a change in the relative importance given to the various topics explored in the literature. Certain

---

[7] Used by scholars engaged in the qualitative study of macro social phenomena, fuzzy-set qualitative comparative analysis has also been applied in studies seeking to identify the complex institutional configurations of both sufficient and necessary causes of various outcomes (Boyer 2004; Jackson 2005; Pajunen 2008; Schneider et al. 2009). It has been claimed that the method can help shed light on the issue of institutional complementarities and variety of capitalism (Crouch 2005). Witt and Jackson (2016) summarize the advantages of the method: it is able to capture conjunctural types of causation that underlie theories of complementarities; it can identify how different combinations of independent variables can lead to the same outcome; it appraises set-theoretical relationships, rather than correlations among various factors, hence allowing for asymmetrical relationships in which high and low values of the outcomes are determined by different causal conditions.

topics are in decline (conceptual frameworks; firm performance and governance; mapping models of capitalism). Others have gained in popularity (financial crises: causes and responses; industry and sector studies; development, growth and inequality). New themes have also emerged in recent years (macroeconomic policy; education systems; financial sustainability and reporting). These changes have correlated with a growing trend toward empiricism, at the expenses of work of an appreciative type. Formal methods, narrowly defined as mathematical models in the context of this study, have hardly ever been employed in the field examined. In applied work, methodologies such as content analysis, fuzzy-set qualitative comparative analysis and leximetric analysis seem to be gaining traction since 2010, and some have gained significant ground recently.

Journals with a multidisciplinary reach are very important for this line of research. *Socio-Economic Review* is the undisputed leader in terms of number of articles and special issues devoted to institutional complementarities and comparative capitalism. Economics journals, including multidisciplinary ones such as *Journal of Institutional Economics*, have instead played a rather marginal role. The disciplinary background of the most prolific contributors is a further testimony to the marginal role occupied by economics in this field of research, which at first glance may be surprising, given that the concept of institutional complementarity originated in economics.

One possible explanation is that the main topics that have gained in prominence were developed by non-economists. For example, the analysis of corporate governance in comparative capitalism from a management perspective has received significant attention. A similar comment applies to the work of legal scholars in the field of comparative law, possibly initiated as a reaction against the legal origin theory. Another potential explanation for the relatively limited presence of economists and economics journals could be related to the fact that economists tend to express the concept of institutional complementarity in terms of utility functions and supermodularity. This is not the language used by scholars with other disciplinary backgrounds.

A clear gap in the journal literature examined in this chapter is the absence of links with studies on national systems of innovation, evolutionary economics and the Schumpeterian approach to innovation (or the Austrian approach to entrepreneurship more generally).[8] Future research should aim to build bridges across these gaps. Bridges should also be built to expand our understanding of how institutional complementarities in the context of

---

[8] See Radosevic and Yoruk in this volume for an attempt along these lines.

comparative capitalism explain processes of institutional change. While this theme is present in the literature analyzed, it has received fairly marginal coverage to date. This is somewhat unexpected, given that institutional change is generally taken to be central in the comparative capitalism literature. Finally, from a methodological point of view, fuzzy-set qualitative comparative analysis seems to be a method worthy of further attention in the future.

It is difficult to make predictions on where, given current trends, this field of inquiry is likely to go. Drawing on the results of this bibliometric review, one can nonetheless offer some speculations. The emphasis on empirical work is likely to be maintained. Themes that may continue to gain ground include macroeconomic policy; financial crises: causes and responses; development, growth and inequality. The resurgence of research activity following the decline in number of published outputs that occurred since 2016 would be aided by enhancing the opportunities for a larger number of scholars from different disciplinary backgrounds to work together. Scholarly networks such as SASE and WINIR (World Interdisciplinary Network for Institutional Research) can play a key role in this respect.

References

Aguilera, R. V., & Jackson, G. (2003). The Cross-National Diversity of Corporate Governance: Dimensions and Determinants. *Academy of Management Review, 28*(3), 447–465.

Amable, B. (2000). Institutional Complementarity and Diversity of Social Systems of Innovation and Production. *Review of International Political Economy, 7*(4), 645–687.

Aoki, M. (1994). The Contingent Governance of Teams: Analysis of Institutional Complementarity. *International Economic Review, 35*(3), 657–676.

Aoki, M. (2001). *Toward a Comparative Institutional Analysis*. Cambridge, MA: MIT Press.

Beyer, J., & Hassel, A. (2002). The Effects of Convergence: Internationalization and the Changing Distribution of Net Value Added in Large German Firms. *Economy and Society, 31*(3), 309–332.

Blyth, M. (2003). Same as It Never Was: Temporality and Typology in the Varieties of Capitalism. *Comparative European Politics, 1*(2), 215–225.

Boyce, B. R., & Kraft, D. H. (1985). Principles and Theories Information Science. *Annual Review of Information Science and Technology, 20*, 153–178.

Boyer, R. (2004). New Growth Regimes, But Still Institutional Diversity. *Socio-Economic Review, 2*(1), 1–32.

Cárdenas, J. (2012). Varieties of Corporate Networks: Network Analysis and fsQCA. *International Journal of Comparative Sociology, 53*(4), 298–322.

Crouch, C. (2005). *Capitalist Diversity and Change: Recombinant Governance and Institutional Entrepreneurs.* Oxford: Oxford University Press.

Cruz, S., & Teixeira, A. A. C. (2010). The Evolution of the Cluster Literature: Shedding Light on the Regional Science —Regional Studies Debate. *Regional Studies, 44*(9), 1263–1288.

Culnan, M. J. (1986). The Intellectual Development of Management Information Systems, 1972–1982: A Co-Citation Analysis. *Management Science, 32*(2), 156–172.

Donohue, J. C. (1972). A Bibliometric Analysis of Certain Information Science Literature. *Journal of the American Society for Information Science, 23,* 313–317.

Du, K., & Teixeira, A. A. C. (2012). A Bibliometric Account of Chinese Economics Research through the Lens of the China Economic Review. *China Economic Review, 23,* 743–762.

Gagliardi, F. (2009a). Financial Development and the Growth of Cooperative Firms. *Small Business Economics, 32*(4), 439–364.

Gagliardi, F. (2009b). Banking Market Structure, Creation and Activity of Firms: Early Evidence for Coperatives in the Italian Case. *Annals of Public and Cooperative Economics, 80*(4), 605–640.

Gagliardi, F. (2019). *A Bibliometric Analysis of the Journal Literature on Institutional Complementarities.* mimeo.

Goodin, R. E. (2003). Choose Your Capitalism? *Comparative European Politics, 1*(2), 203–213.

Hall, P. A., & Gingerich, D. W. (2009). Varieties of Capitalism and Institutional Complementarities in the Political Economy: An Empirical Analysis. *British Journal of Political Science, 39*(3), 449–482.

Hall, P. A., & Soskice, D. (Eds.). (2001). *Varieties of Capitalism. The Institutional Foundations of Comparative Advantages.* Oxford: Oxford University Press.

Hall, P. A., & Soskice, D. (2003). Varieties of Capitalism and Institutional Change: A Response to Three Critics. *Comparative European Politics, 1*(2), 241–250.

Harvey, G. (2009). Employment Relations in Liberal Market Economy Airlines. *Employee Relations, 31*(2), 168–181.

Jackson, G. (2005). Employee Representation in the Board Compared: A Fuzzy Sets Analysis of Corporate Governance, Unionism and Political Institutions. *Industrielle Beziehungen, 12*(3), 252–279.

Jackson, G. (2012). Editorial: Looking Backwards and Looking Forwards. *Socio-Economic Review, 11*(1), 1–4.

Kim, J., & McMillan, S. (2008). Evaluation of Internet Advertising Research: A Bibliometric Analysis of Citations from Key Sources. *Journal of Advertising, 37*(1), 99–112.

McElwee, G., & Atherton, A. (2005). Publication Trends and Patterns in Entrepreneurship: The Case of the International Journal of Entrepreneurship and Innovation. *Journal of Small Business and Enterprise Development, 12*(1), 92–103.

Nelson, R., & Winter, S. (1982). *An Evolutionary Theory of Economic Change.* Cambridge: Harvard University Press.

Pagano, U. (1992). Organizational Equilibria and Production Efficiency. *Metroeconomica, 43*(1–2), 227–246.

Pagano, U., & Rowthorn, R. (1994). Ownership, Technology and Institutional Stability. *Structural Change and Economic Dynamics, 5*(2), 221–243.

Pajunen, K. (2008). Institutions and Inflows of Foreign Direct Investment: A Fuzzy-Set Analysis. *Journal of International Business Studies, 39*(4), 652–669.

Pritchard, A. (1969). Statistical Bibliography or Bibliometrics. *Journal of Documentation, 25*(4), 348–349.

Ragin, C. C. (1987). *The Comparative Method: Moving beyond Qualitative and Quantitative Strategies.* Berkeley: University of California Press.

Ragin, C. C. (2000). *Fuzzy-Set Social Science.* Chicago: Chicago University Press.

Rebérioux, A. (2002). European Style of Corporate Governance at the Crossroads: The Role of Worker Involvement. *Journal of Common Market Studies, 40*(1), 111–134.

Schneider, M. R., Schulze-Bentrop, C., & Paunescu, M. (2009). Mapping the Institutional Capital Of High-Tech Firms: A Fuzzy-Set Analysis of Capitalist Variety and Export Performance. *Journal of International Business Studies, 41*(2), 246–266.

Siems, M., & Deakin, S. (2010). Comparative Law and Finance: Past, Present, and Future. *Journal of Institutional and Theoretical Economics, 166*(1), 120–140.

Silva, E. G., & Teixeira, A. A. C. (2008). Surveying structural change: seminal contributions and a bibliometric account. *Structural Change and Economic Dynamics, 19*(4), 273–300.

Silva, S. T., & Teixeira, A. A. C. (2009). On the Divergence of Evolutionary Research Paths in the Past Fifty Years: A Comprehensive Bibliometric Account. *Journal of Evolutionary Economics, 19*(5), 605–642.

Teixeira, A. A. C. (2011). Mapping the (In)Visible College(s) in the Field of Entrepreneurship. *Scientometrics, 89*(1), 1–36.

Teixeira, A. A. C. (2014). Evolution, Roots and Influence of the Literature on National Systems of Innovation: A Bibliometric Account. *Cambridge Journal of Economics, 38*(1), 181–214.

Thelen, K. (2010). SASE Annual Meeting 2009, Paris, France: Economic Regulation and Social Solidarity: Conceptual and Analytic Innovations in the Study of Advanced Capitalism. *Socio-Economic Review, 8*(1), 187–207.

Watson, M. (2003). Ricardian Political Economy and the 'Varieties of Capitalism' Approach: Specialization, Trade and Comparative Institutional Advantage. *Comparative European Politics, 1*(2), 227–240.

Willett, P. (2007). A Bibliometric Analysis of the Journal of Molecular Graphics and Modelling. *Journal of Molecular Graphics and Modelling, 26*(3), 602–606.

Witt, M. A., & Jackson, G. (2016). Varieties of Capitalism and Institutional Comparative Advantage: A Test and Reinterpretation. *Journal of International Business Studies, 47*, 778–806.

35

The Challenge of Identification and the Value of Descriptive Evidence

Ron P. Smith

1 Introduction

This chapter reviews a number of issues of measurement and methodology issues that arise in empirical economics and, in particular, their relevance for comparative economics, both macroeconomic and microeconomic. Section 2 provides some motivation, introducing some of the difficult issues that are involved in making causal statements, in particular the inability to observe the counterfactual. But even if one cannot make causal statements, it is natural to want to compare the various institutional experiments that nations have indulged in. Any such comparison must begin with a description of the differences in the economic systems and in the economic outcomes in the countries considered. Description involves a number of linked but distinct steps. The first step is to construct the data. Often innovative economic analysis is a response to new data sets. For instance, the availability of the Penn World Tables led to a transformation of the empirical and theoretical growth

I am grateful to the editors for inviting me to write this piece and for many helpful comments on earlier versions.

R. P. Smith (✉)
Department of Economics, Mathematics and Statistics, Birkbeck, University of London, London, UK
e-mail: r.smith@bbk.ac.uk

© The Author(s) 2021
E. Douarin, O. Havrylyshyn (eds.), *The Palgrave Handbook of Comparative Economics*,
https://doi.org/10.1007/978-3-030-50888-3_35

literature. Section 3 discusses the role of data improvements in the development of comparative economics.

The next step is to summarise the main features of the data which are relevant to the analysis. This is often done in the form of "stylised facts" that the theory needs to explain and Sect. 4 discusses such summaries. One of the stylised facts is the classification of the economic and political systems in terms of frameworks such as capitalist or communist, democratic or authoritarian.

An important form of descriptive summary comes from an examination of the associations between variables. Section 5 considers the use of such non-causal correlations and regressions. These are often criticised by those who argue that the role of social scientists is to follow the hypothetico-deductive method, attempting to falsify theoretical predictions about unknown outcomes. We examine the difficulties such testing procedures face.

Section 6 considers the difficult identification problems involved in measuring the causal effect of types of economic system, including mechanisms and institutions, on economic outcomes. Many of the strategies for identifying causal effects, such as difference in differences and regression discontinuity design, were developed at a micro-econometric level. After reviewing these, the section reviews some data-driven approaches, motivated by micro-econometric analogies, that have been used to provide macroeconomic counterfactuals. They include the synthetic control method and the panel data approach, which have been used to examine the effect of major systemic changes such as the reunification of Germany and of Hong Kong with China.

Section 7 draws some conclusions. Academic economists are prone to methodological dogmatism, asserting that there is only a single route to truth. This is also the case with different empirical strategies and within econometrics there have been heated disputes between the proponents of different methodologies; disputes that were well aired in two 2010 special issues on which I draw: the symposium on "taking the con out of econometrics" in the *Journal of Economic Perspectives* and the special issue of the *Journal of Economic Literature* on the local average treatment effect. In contrast, I suggest that there is no single road to truth and that there are great advantages in methodological pluralism, approaching a question in many different ways. In addition, I argue that telling a persuasive story remains central to economic analysis.

2   Motivation

Let us begin with the challenge of identifying causal effects. Statisticians are inclined to believe that the data can only reveal correlations, not causal effects, whereas many economists are inclined to believe that they can identify causal effects. Angrist and Pischke (2009, p. 3) say, "In the beginning we should ask, *What is the causal relationship of interest?* Although purely descriptive research has an important role to play, we believe that the most interesting research in social science is about questions of cause and effect".

To illustrate the issues, suppose that all the data, description and classification issues that are discussed in more detail below have been solved and the objective is to measure the causal effect of a "treatment" on an "outcome". For instance, suppose that the treatment is a political institution, say democracy, and the outcome is a measure of economic performance, say log GDP per capita. We consider a single unit, say country 1, with outcome in period t, of y_{1t}. The effect of the treatment is

$$\delta_{1t} = y_{1t}^1 - y_{1t}^0$$

the difference between the two potential outcomes: the outcome with treatment, y_{1t}^1, (being democratic) and the outcome without treatment, y_{1t}^0, (not being democratic). However, it is impossible to observe both y_{1t}^1, and y_{1t}^0, in period t. Country 1 is either democratic at that time or not democratic, but it cannot be both. If we define $d = 1$ if treated and $d = 0$ if not, then what we observe is

$$y_{1t} = dy_{1t}^1 + (1-d)y_{1t}^0$$

Since only one of the potential outcomes can be observed, one needs an estimated "counterfactual", a prediction of what would have happened in the unobserved case. Whether all causal statements involve counterfactuals is a matter of philosophical debate. What is meant by causality is also debated and Pearl (2009) is an interesting approach developed in computer science. Imbens (2019) compares the Pearl approach with the potential outcome approach, set out above, which is commonly used in economics.

Comparing GDP in democratic and undemocratic countries is unlikely to measure a causal effect because of "selection into treatment": those treated differ from those not treated. In addition, institutions and outcomes are both likely to be endogenous: jointly determined by deeper historical forces. If we observe an empirical association between them, we do not know whether democracy causes GDP; GDP causes democracy; they determine each other; or some other factors cause both. If we have data on a number of countries, y_{it}, some of which are democratic and some of which are not, we then have a problem of determining which features of the evolution of outcome are due to their democratic status. Acemoglu et al. (2019, pp. 48–49) note that the estimation of the causal effect of democracy (or democratisation) on GDP faces several challenges. Democracy measures are subject to measurement error. Democracies differ from non-democracies in unobserved cultural and institutional characteristics that have an effect on GDP. Democratisations are, on average, preceded by a temporary dip in GDP that violates the parallel trends assumption made in difference in differences-based measures of the causal effects, which we discuss below. Thus Acemoglu et al. argue that allowing for the dynamics of GDP is essential. Finally, democratisations could be related to expectations of future economic conditions biasing the results.

They use various strategies to control for these challenges including modelling the selection into democracy and using the fact that democratisations often come in regional waves. How effective these strategies are is a matter of dispute; the democracy and growth dispute is an old one. But before returning to these methodological difficulties, we consider the data and descriptions.

3   Data

Comparative economics uses both macro and micro data, and we begin with macro data. Although the quality of the data varies, there has been a massive increase in the quantity and type of data available that can be used to describe and compare countries. The computing power needed to process the data has also increased. There has also been more interest in issues of measurement often prompted by theoretical concerns such as an increased awareness of the limitations of GDP as a measure of welfare. The capability approach of Sen (1985) prompted the construction of the Human Development Index, which combined life expectancy, education and per-capita income in a relatively ad hoc way. Not only do theoretical concerns prompt the development of data, the data themselves are heavily theory-laden. National accounts measures like GDP are rooted in a particular economic theory and different systems have different accounting systems, like the Soviet Net Material Product system. Jones and Klenow (2016) construct a theory-based summary statistic for the economic well-being of a country. This incorporates not only consumption, which is a component of GDP, but also leisure, mortality and inequality, which are not reflected in GDP. These are combined in a theoretically consistent framework based on a utility function. Although this welfare measure correlates with GDP, the ranking of countries by it can be very different from the ranking by GDP.

Some of the data acquisition reflects completely new sources that can improve the accuracy of traditional measures. Nightlight data collected by satellite is an indication of development and can be used to supplement traditional GDP measures, providing more accurate comparisons of standards of living and local development. Satellite data are particularly useful in conflict areas where more traditional forms of data collection are not feasible. Online daily data on prices have been used by Alberto Cavallo and his colleagues, for example, Cavallo et al. (2018), to measure high-frequency price dynamics even when the official data on inflation have been regarded as suspect, as in Argentina and Venezuela.

Within political science many comparative databases have been developed. For instance, data on wars are provided in the long-standing correlates of war, COW, project and the more recent Upsalla Conflict Data Program, UCDP. Operationalising these concepts is often difficult, the definition of a war often involves arbitrary elements, such as a threshold number of battle deaths or the involvement of a state. The well-known Democratic Peace hypothesis—that democracies, while prone to war, do not fight other democracies—requires a specific definition of both democracy and of war. The hypothesis faces difficulties not only with the direction of causation between peace and democracy, but also with the correlation of democracy with other institutional features, such as market capitalism, which are as well, or better, correlated with peace. Freedman (2017, Chap. 10–12) discusses both the quantification of war and the democratic peace. He expresses an historian's scepticism about the value of quantification given all the issues involved in determining what should be measured and what could be measured and all the features that are lost in turning a complicated historical account into a number. As we will emphasise below, in practice, it is crucial to supplement the quantitative analysis with more qualitative analysis using case studies, field work and archival research. It is only by combining those elements into a coherent narrative that one can build a persuasive story.

At the micro level, large and repeated cross-country data sets make the creation of comparative indicators and analyses possible, which can extend the comparison beyond the standard economic variables. These data sets include the European Social Survey, ESS: the EBRD life in transition survey, LITS; the World Bank, Living Standards Measurement Surveys, LSMS and the World Values Surveys, among others. For instance, there has been a large growth in the collection and use of self-reported life-satisfaction data, which has also been used for comparative studies to try to determine which nations are the happiest and why. There have been controversies about the extent to which growing incomes are associated with growing happiness and about the characteristics of countries and cultures that explain different levels of happiness.[1]

Measuring democracy or war is difficult but, as Voigt (2018) discusses, it is even more difficult to measure informal institutions: commonly known rules that structure recurrent interactions but are not formally recorded. He quotes Elinor Ostrom "These rules may be almost invisible to outsiders, especially when they are well accepted by participants who do not even see them as noteworthy". Thus informal may imply unobservable. He illustrates his point by discussing the measurement of the overlapping concepts of trust and social capital. Different authors may regard these as aspects of either culture or informal institutions. They are often measured using World Values Survey responses, but the survey measures beliefs and these may be different from both behaviour and institutions. He discusses the use of experiments, which can capture aspects of behaviour respondents cannot articulate, but recognises that it can be difficult to design experiments in such a way that they have external validity.

Given the limitations of surveys in capturing how people really behave. Google Search data have also been used to supplement surveys and, in a number of cases, what people search for suggests that people are not always honest in their answers to surveys (Stevens-Davidowitz 2017).

The development of analysis and understanding requires clarifying the relevant theoretical concepts and providing operational measures of those concepts as was done with national accounting in the first half of the twentieth century. Dismissing data collection and construction as a purely descriptive activity, of second order of importance, underestimates its crucial role in providing the foundations for any empirical economic analysis.

4   Stylised Facts

One way of summarising the data is as a set of "stylised facts" that any theory must try to explain or at least be consistent with. Again we will start with the macro and then move to the micro. The classic macro stylised facts are that

---

[1] See in this volume Sanfey (Chap. 24) for a review of the literature on the dynamics of life satisfaction in Central and Eastern Europe and the former Soviet Union countries, and Morgan and Wang (Chap. 25) for a discussion of life satisfaction and economic growth in rural and urban China.

certain economic variables, typically ratios, are approximately constant over the long run. This is a long-standing belief. Klein and Kosobud (1961) labelled them Great Ratios and Kaldor (1957, 1961) described them as Stylized Facts. Kaldor's term has stuck, though it has generated a wider methodological literature about the process of abstraction and the nature of facts in economics.

Kaldor (1957, p. 591) said, "A satisfactory model concerning the nature of the growth process in a capitalist economy must also account for the remarkable historical constancies revealed by recent empirical investigations".

Before giving the list of constancies, Kaldor (1961, p. 178) added a qualification. "Since facts, as recorded by statisticians, are always subject to numerous snags and qualifications, and for that reason are incapable of being accurately summarized, the theorist, in my view, should be free to start off with a 'stylized' view of the facts—i.e. concentrate on broad tendencies, ignoring individual detail, and proceed on the 'as if' method, i.e. construct a hypothesis that could account for these 'stylized' facts, without necessarily committing himself on the historical accuracy, or sufficiency, of the facts or tendencies thus summarized".

Since some of the stylised facts are implied by others, they can be presented in different ways. The most cited list from Kaldor (1961) is as follows:

1. "The continued growth in the aggregate volume of production and in the productivity of labour at a steady trend rate; no recorded tendency for a falling rate of growth of productivity.
2. A continued increase in the amount of capital per worker, whatever statistical measure of 'capital' is chosen in this connection.
3. A steady rate of profit on capital, at least in the 'developed' capitalist societies; this rate of profit being substantially higher than the 'pure' long-term rate of interest as shown by the yield of gilt-edged bonds.
4. Steady capital-output ratios over long periods; at least there are no clear long-term trends either rising or falling, if the differences in the degree of utilization of capacity are allowed for. This implies, or reflects, the near identity in the percentage rates of growth of production and of capital stock—that is, that for the economy as a whole, and over longer periods, income and capital tend to grow at the same rate.
5. A high correlation between the share of profits in income and the share of investment in output; a steady share of profits (and of wages) in societies and/or periods in which the investment coefficient (the share of investment in output) is constant. ... The steadiness in the share of wages implies, of course, a rate of increase in real wages that is proportionate to the rate of growth of (average) productivity.

6. Finally, there are appreciable differences in the rate of growth of labour productivity and of total output in different societies, the range of variation (in the fast growing economies) being of the order of 2–5 per cent. ..."

He then goes on to say. "None of these 'facts' can be plausibly 'explained' by the theoretical constructions of neo-classical theory. On the basis of the marginal productivity theory of Bohm-Bawerk and followers, one would expect a continued fall in the rate of profit with capital accumulation, and not a steady rate of profit. (In this respect classical and neo-classical theory, arguing on different grounds, come to the same conclusion—Adam Smith, Ricardo, Marx, alike with Bohm-Bawerk and Wicksell, predicted a steady fall in the rate of profit with economic progress.)"

Solow (1970, p. 2) commented on Kaldor's list that there "is no doubt that they are stylized, though it is possible to question whether they are facts". Whether facts or not, Kaldor's list has certainly been influential. Jones and Romer (2010, p. 225), in a paper called "The New Kaldor facts", take the old ones for granted. They say: "Redoing this exercise nearly 50 years later shows just how much progress we have made. Kaldor's first five facts have moved from research papers to textbooks. There is no longer any interesting debate about the features that a model must contain to explain them. These features are embodied in one of the great successes of growth theory in the 1950s and 1960s, the neoclassical growth model. Today, researchers are grappling with Kaldor's sixth fact and have moved on to several others that we list below". Their new facts relate to ideas, institutions, population and human capital. It is ironic that they regard Kaldor's facts as being embodied in the neo-classical growth model, whereas Kaldor regarded them as being inconsistent with that model.

It is noteworthy that the empirical basis for modern growth theory rests on a set of verbal descriptions, not on an estimated causal relationship nor a hypothesis test. Jones and Romer regard Kaldor's stylised facts as consistent with standard theory, but there are many cases where the stylised facts are inconsistent with standard theory. These are characterised as "puzzles" that prompt theoretical innovation to resolve them. Summers (1991) argues that what has contributed most to thinking about substantive issues is pragmatic empirical work, using a variety of different types of evidence, producing stylised facts, of the Kaldor type, that theory can try to explain. He cites as an example of persuasive and influential empirical work the equity premium puzzle of Mehra and Prescott (1985). They argued that the spread between the returns on stocks and bonds was inconsistent with standard theory, implying an implausibly high degree of risk aversion. This observation has proved to be a major stimulus to theory, reviewed in Cochrane (2017). Summers also argued that formal econometric work, where elaborate technique is used to apply theory to data or isolate the direction of causal relationships, when they are not obvious a priori, virtually always fails. Summers also notes that the absence of replication in econometrics indicates that most of the econometric results are not important enough to be worth replicating. *The Replication Network* is trying to remedy this lack; see https://replicationnetwork.com/.

Similarly there is a role for development of stylised facts at the micro level also and two papers on populism, Guiso et al. (2017) and Inglehart and Norris (2016), provide examples. The latter uses a very wide variety of data sources including the European Social Survey to compare the economic insecurity and cultural backlash hypotheses for the rise of populism finding that the latter are more important. This prompted an extensive literature on the relative contribution of economic and cultural threats to the rise of populism. Autor et al. (2016). "Importing political polarization? The electoral consequences of rising trade exposure" consider 5 US elections detect an ideological realignment that commences prior to the divisive 2016 US presidential election. They regard their results as supporting the argument that adverse economic conditions are associated with support for nativist or extreme politicians.

The puzzles that prompt theoretical developments and the influential stylised facts are often correlations or regression coefficients and it is to these that we now turn.

5   Non-causal Interpretation of Association

One can give non-causal interpretations to the quantitative associations expressed in correlations and regressions and one can ask whether these relationships are consistent with particular theories. For instance, the Feldstein and Horioka (1980) puzzle is that the high cross-country correlation between shares of savings and investment seems to imply a very low degree of capital mobility. Their regression, of shares of investment in GDP on shares of savings, is clearly neither a structural nor a reduced form equation, since both are endogenous, but it has prompted a large and continuing literature.

Regressions that are neither structural nor reduced form relationships can also be interpreted as conditional predictions: observing X and Z allow one to predict that Y is likely. The lack of causal relationship does not make such regressions useless. There is no causal relationship between weight and height; both are driven by third factors. But comparing actual weight to predicted weight given height is useful to judge malnutrition or obesity, it is the basis of the body mass index.

The regressions used in comparative economics may be estimated on a cross section of countries, on time-series relationships for many countries, or on panels which combine both dimensions. Looking at the question in different ways is usually valuable and there are often differences between time-series and cross-sectional associations. Investigating the differences can be revealing. The permanent income theory of Friedman (1957) arose from the need to reconcile time-series and cross-sectional results on the relationship between consumption and income. The cross-sectional relationship showed consumption roughly proportional to income, and the time-series relationship showed a much lower marginal propensity to consume and a large intercept. Friedman interpreted this in terms of the classical errors in variables model. The time series measure of income was dominated by transitory variations, to which consumption did not respond, biasing the coefficient of income towards zero. This reflected a folk wisdom among econometricians that time series estimates tended to pick up short-run effects and cross-sections long-run effects.

When a new area of economics, such as cultural economics, develops, the first stage is to look at the associations and try to develop stylised facts often using very simple statistical procedures. With respect to culture and institutions, Alesina and Giuliano (2015, p. 899) comment, after noting a particular relationship may not be causal, "Yet the complex interaction between culture and institutions is interesting, regardless of the 'ultimate' causes". They recognise the data issues associated with the arduous task of defining culture, with its complicated combination of values and belief. But as we saw above, questions of definition, classification and association are a precondition for any empirical analysis including causal analysis. The broad definition of culture as customary beliefs and values that transmit fairly unchanged from generation to generation leaves a lot of scope for definitional differences. But more specific aspects such as the willingness to trust others can be investigated. There is a further possible confusion since sometimes cultural economics is treated as the economics of the cultural industries, museums theatres and so on.

The study by Djankov and Hauck (2016), in the divergent post-communist paths to democracy and economic freedom, looks at the long-term impact of religion and empires on economic and political liberalization and is based solely on correlations. There is an assumption that the chronological order is bringing interesting insights in the relationship between "culture" broadly defined and institutional quality. It considers 29 post-communist countries and finds that the economic transition has been more successful than the political transition. One might hope that temporal sequence may give some indication of causation, though there is the *post hoc ergo propter hoc* fallacy. While the present cannot influence the past, there may be a common factor that shapes present and past and behaviour in the past may be influenced by expectations of present events. Consumption predicts income, not because consumption causes income, but because consumption reflects expectations of future income.

Critics of such descriptive associations argue that the role of social science is to make theoretical predictions that can be tested on new data, allowing the theory to be falsified. This does not seem possible in economics. Despite the prevalence of testing, many argue that no economic theory has even been falsified. Keuzenkamp and Magnus (1995), in a special issue of the *Journal of Econometrics* on testing, challenge readers to suggest any economic theory that has been falsified. Cochrane (2017, p. 977), surveying macro-finance similarly, says, "formal testing of economic models has pretty much disappeared, and rightly so". On p. 949, he says, "In explaining which models become popular throughout economics, tractability, elegance and parsimony matter more than probability values of test statistics. Economics needs simple tractable models that help to capture the bewildering number of mechanisms people like to talk about. Elegance matters. Economic models are quantitative parables. Elegant parables are more convincing than black boxes". Subsequently he says, "Economics lives in the world of McCloskey (1983)", the famous article on the rhetoric of economics, and to persuade his readers, Cochrane tells stories rather than presents tests. It should be noted that Cochrane, past President of the American Finance Association and author of the standard text on asset pricing, is no post-modern, heterodox economist.

Not only is hypothesis testing not persuasive in economics, it also faces both social difficulties and more fundamental philosophical difficulties. The social difficulty is that few hypothesis-testers understand the statistical basis of the Neyman-Pearson framework that they use and those that understand it cannot explain it. The widespread misconceptions and misuse of this framework prompted the American Statistical Association to issue a statement in 2016 on p values and significance testing which is mainly a list of things that they are not.[2] I should also plead guilty on this. ASA captured my position: "Q: Why do so many colleges and grad schools teach $p = 0.05$? A: Because that's still what the scientific community and journal editors use. Q: Why do so many people still use $p = 0.05$? A: Because that's what they were taught in college or grad school". It should be noted that this is a frequentist problem; Bayesian statisticians do not do hypothesis testing.

---

[2] https://www.amstat.org/asa/files/pdfs/P-ValueStatement.pdf.

The more fundamental difficulty with hypothesis testing is known as the Duhem-Quine problem. One cannot test a scientific hypothesis in isolation, all tests are of joint hypotheses. They involve both the substantive hypothesis of interest, for instance, that some ratio is constant, and a set of auxiliary assumptions about such things as measurement, estimation and treatment of probabilities. Thus, one does not know what has been rejected, the substantive hypothesis or the auxiliary choices that are required to make the substantive hypothesis operational. For instance, the rejection may result from the lack of a sufficiently long sample for long-run tendencies to manifest themselves. Thus, a failure to find a constant ratio may not prompt a reconsideration of the validity of the theory that suggests that the ratio should be constant. Instead, it may prompt a reconsideration of how the ratio is measured, how stability is tested or any other aspect of the procedures that indicate the ratio is not stable.

As noted above, the Acemoglu et al. (2019) test of whether democracy has a significant effect on growth will be conditional on specification. The specification choices include how to measure the variables (is democracy a zero-one variable or a continuous variable like Polity IV?), the functional form, the other control variables included, treatment of dynamics (how many lags of GDP?) and sample used. Specification is a particular problem in panel data studies where there are many dimensions of choice including about the degree of heterogeneity (is the effect of democracy on growth the same in every country?), whether the coefficients are treated as random or fixed and the treatment of cross-sectional dependence and spatial effects.

If testing is difficult, identifying causal effects is even more so and it is to that we now turn.

6   Identification Strategies

Again we will consider the issues from both micro and macro perspectives. From a micro-econometric perspective, Angrist and Pischke (2010) argue that causal questions can be answered with credible research designs based on the use of instrumental variables, difference in difference analysis, regression discontinuities or randomised controlled trials (RCTs). Each of these will be examined discussing the advantages and limitations. Most of these strategies have developed in a micro-econometric context and Sims (2010, p. 59) says that what Angrist and Pischke (2010) say about macroeconomics is mainly nonsense. Even in a micro context, the answers to questions that have been investigated for many years, like the effect of class size on pupil attainment or education on earnings, remain disputed.

Comparative economics, comparing different countries, is inherently macroeconomic, though not usually about the macroeconomics of business cycle fluctuations that are the stuff of macro textbooks, rather they are about systemic differences or changes. Recently, methods such as synthetic controls and the panel data approach have been suggested ways to measure causal effects with macro data using the comparative method. At a macroeconomic level many of the ways recently adopted to measure the effect of "treatments" adopt an explicitly comparative approach. Measuring the effect of an event, treatment, X on Y involves an implicit counterfactual; for instance, what would have happened to Y if X had not happened? This can be for individual countries. What would have happened to Hong Kong had it not been reunited with China? Hsiao et al. (2012). What would have happened to Germany had it not re-unified? Abadie et al. (2015). Or, it can be for many countries. What would have happened had there not been a Civil War? Bove et al. (2017).

After reviewing the micro methods, we will contrast the micro and macro methods and review these recent macro methods.

6.1 Micro Methods

One procedure to deal with endogeneity of X in a regression of Y on X, and measure causal effects, is instrumental variables, IV. The central idea of IV is to find a variable W that influences X but does not influence Y directly. Then changes in Y driven by changes in X caused by changes in W are not contaminated by feedbacks from Y to X or variations in omitted variables. While the theory is correct, the difficulty is that one can never know that W does influence X but does not influence Y. This just-identifying assumption is untestable from the observed correlations. Many statisticians are sceptical about IV, because the causal claims depend on untestable just identifying assumptions. Over-identifying assumptions can be tested with a Hansen-Sargan type test, conditional on the just identifying assumptions; and endogeneity can be tested, conditional on the just identifying assumptions, with a Wu-Hausman test. But the just identifying assumptions themselves cannot be tested. A suitable instrument needs to be correlated with the variable of interest X, which can be tested, and uncorrelated with any unobservable omitted variables explaining Y, which cannot because you do not observe the omitted variable.

While the statistician would question how one can ever be sure that any observable is not correlated with some unobservable; the econometrician would use non-statistical arguments to make the case that some assumptions are more persuasive on the basis of theory or qualitative evidence. The untestable assumption is often justified as being credible or probable using a narrative argument based on case studies or analogies. Angrist and Pischke (2009) make this very clear by often using the term story, as in pp. 119–120: "Because an individual's date of birth is probably unrelated to his or her innate ability, motivation or family connections, it seems credible to assert that the only reason for the up and down quarter-of-birth pattern in earnings is the up and down quarter of birth pattern in schooling. This is the critical assumption that drives the quarter-of-birth IV story".

Angrist and Pischke are very careful, often econometricians do not even bother to provide a persuasive story and instead use the justification that someone else used this instrument.

Another procedure used to identify causal effects is regression discontinuity design. This relies on observations being very close on many dimensions but differ with respect to the treatment. Borders can be illuminating in this respect. Acemoglu and Robinson (2012) begin their book with a comparison of Nogales Arizona and Nogales Sonora, almost identical in geography, culture and history: Nogales Arizona was in Mexico until 1853. The part of the town on the US side of the fence has a per capita income three times that of the part of the town in Mexico, despite Nogales Sonora being a relatively rich Mexican town. Similarly it is interesting to compare Detroit US with Windsor Canada, just across the river, both car towns with similar socio-economic backgrounds but very different histories.

Two recent papers try to explain the current level of corruption in a cross section of countries using past events. Becker et al. (2016) use a regression discontinuity design to examine the link between the same variables (corruption and past empire). Their discontinuity is the former border of the Habsburg empire. They investigate whether a historical Habsburg affiliation increases current trust and reduces corruption in courts and police. They argue that the Habsburg Empire was known for its well-functioning bureaucracy, compared to the Russian or Ottoman empire, and the Habsburg boundary cuts through five countries today, so it is hoped that one can separate country effects from Habsburg effects. A difficulty is that the errors in these types of regression tend to show spatial correlations, which makes conventional standard errors misleading.

Uberti (2018) uses data from 64 countries in Eastern Europe and Middle East and North Africa to study the long-run effects of Ottoman and socialist rule on the incidence of corruption. It notes that Acemoglu and Robinson (2012, p. 56) claim that it is the institutional legacy of the empire that keeps the Middle East poor today. While the long-run historical determinants of corruption have explanatory power, it is less than the short-run determinant, current per-capita income. The paper concludes that although history matters the data are consistent with an interpretation of corruption as a manifestation of persistent economic underdevelopment. The paper uses as instruments coastal proximity and export orientation for income and distance from Istanbul, which is negatively correlated with length of Ottoman rule.

For some the Gold Standard for causal investigation is a randomised controlled trials (RCTs), but at the macroeconomic level of comparative economics these are not feasible. At the micro level even these have limitations particularly with respect to external validity: can the results be extended to other contexts? Even pharmaceutical drug trials have this problem. For instance, since drug trials are not carried out on children, one is never sure how the drugs will work on them.

Deaton (2010) notes that given the scepticism about the ability of econometric analysis to resolve development issues, there is increasing use in development economics of RCTs to accumulate credible knowledge of what works, without overreliance on questionable theory or statistical methods. Deaton and Cartwright (2018) have a detailed discussion of RCTs. They emphasise that the results from RCTs are often not robust to a variety of problems including the treatment of outliers. How one trims the data was an issue in the replication of a classic study. The authors respond to the replication of their study in Crepon et al. (2019). They note that "although conceptually straightforward in practice, RCTs are complex projects undertaken over many years, and they involve many decisions and many lines of code".

When RCTs are not possible, the proponents of these methods advocate quasi-randomisation through IV techniques or natural experiments. Deaton (2010) argues that many of these applications are unlikely to recover quantities that are useful for policy or understanding: two key issues are the misunderstanding of exogeneity and the handling of heterogeneity. He illustrates the issues from the literature on aid and growth. He argues that actual randomisation faces similar problems as does quasi-randomisation, and that experiments have no special ability to produce more credible knowledge than other methods, and that actual experiments are frequently subject to practical problems that undermine any claims to statistical or epistemic superiority.

Nonetheless, the hope is that one can exploit natural experiments or natural randomisation. Jones and Olken (2009) use the fact that whether assassination attempts succeed or fail is largely random, it was luck that President Reagan survived being shot, to estimate the effect of successful assassinations.

The classic micro-econometric method is difference in differences. If $\bar{y}_{C0}$ is the average over the units in the control group, C, in period 0 before treatment and $\bar{y}_{C1}$, in period 1, and similarly the treated group, A, averages are $\bar{y}_{A0}$ and $\bar{y}_{A1}$, then the difference in difference, DiD estimator is

$$\delta = \left(\bar{y}_{A1} - \bar{y}_{A0}\right) - \left(\bar{y}_{C1} - \bar{y}_{C0}\right) \tag{DiD}$$

The first term measures the change in the averages for the treated group, and the second term controls for any general trends, assuming that the trends in the control group are parallel to those for the treated group. Defining a dummy for group A, D_A, and a dummy for period 1, D_1, using the original observations it can be written as a two-way fixed-effect model plus a treatment effect:

$$y_{it} = \alpha + \alpha_A D_A + \alpha_1 D_1 + \delta D_A D_1 + \varepsilon_{it}$$

where the four parameters in the panel model are functions of the four means in DiD. In more general cases, where one has, for instance, more time periods, covariates or endogenous treatment, the panel representation is particularly useful.

The panel representation is particularly appropriate where we have comparative data for countries and regions with data on y_{it}, $i = 1,2,\ldots, N$ and $t = 1,2,\ldots, T$, where N and T are large. The panel potentially provides untreated control groups which can be used to construct the counterfactual, allowing the estimation of the effect of a policy intervention, treatment, on a treated group, and an evaluation of the policy. A lot of these approaches have developed from the micro-econometric potential outcome approach.

6.2   Micro-Macro Comparisons

While we can learn from the micro-econometric literature, the micro and macro issues are rather different. First, in micro cases N is large, T is small, often only $T = 2$, as in (DiD) above. In the macro examples we often have quite long time-series. In the micro literature, there are major problems associated with endogenous selection into treatment. The endogeneity and sample selection biases that arise in the micro case from heterogeneity correlated with treatment, across the units, are not problems in the macro case. There the focus is on a single unit, and the "policy on/policy off" comparisons are done over time rather than across units. In micro terminology, the parameter of interest in the macro case is the effect of "treatment on the treated", not the average treatment effect over individuals. Because it is primarily a time series problem, the rules for assignment to treatment are not an issue. It makes no sense to consider either the effect of Hong Kong being integrated with West Germany or of East Germany being integrated with China. In addition, macro panels tend to exhibit cross-sectional dependence that results from strong factors driving all units. This means that other units can be used to construct controls that can be used to specify the counterfactual in the analysis of a treatment effect or the evaluation of a policy intervention. Unlike difference in differences, the parallel trends assumption is not required.

Secondly, a multi-horizon effect is estimated for each period for the unit. There is no assumption that the effect is constant over time. One can average the effects over time to get an average treatment effect, ATE: but this ATE is quite different from the micro case, which compares the average over treated units with the average over untreated units. Tests on the effects in individual time periods are likely to be sensitive to the distributional assumption of the model, whereas tests on the averages over time can rely on the central limit theorem if H is large to obtain a distribution and may be more robust.

Thirdly, the Lucas critique, which refers *to ex ante* policy evaluation, is not a problem. Ex ante policy evaluations compare two predictions, one with the policy and one without and face the problem that the intervention may change the parameters. In *ex post* evaluation of a policy intervention, time series data are available before and after the policy change and the comparison is based on the difference between the realisations of the outcome variable of interest and counterfactuals obtained assuming no policy change. The counterfactuals, based on estimates using pre-intervention data, will embody pre-intervention parameters while the realised post-intervention outcomes will embody the effect of the change in the policy parameters and any consequent change in expectations.

Finally, whatever we use to predict the counterfactual in the absence of treatment, $\hat{y}_{1t}^0$, must not be influenced by the policy intervention or treatment itself. For major changes, with spillover effects, this can be a very strong requirement: a change in one country, like the re-unification of West Germany, can affect many other countries. Similarly, there must be no large change in the control units that would not have affected the treated units.

6.3   Macro Methods

The two main procedures used to construct counterfactuals are the synthetic control method, SCM, and the panel data approach, PDA, which we discuss in more detail below. In constructing the estimated counterfactuals, we may use (i) observations on the outcome variables in other units, (ii) observations on a vector of covariates in the treated or untreated units and (iii) lagged values in dynamic models. The models may be data driven (atheoretical or non-parametric), just based on correlations or similarity, or the models may be more theoretical parametric models.

Suppose that there are N-1 controls not subject to the intervention and not affected by the intervention in unit 1. The estimated counterfactual is a weighted average of the outcomes in these control or predictor units. In a static model the effect of the intervention is measured as

$$\delta_{1,T_0+h} = y_{1,T_0+h} - \sum_{i=2}^{N} w_i y_{i,T_0+h} \quad ; h = 1,2,\ldots,T_1 \qquad \text{(effect)}$$

The issue is how to choose controls and weights. SCM and PDA differ in how this is done.

The SCM was introduced by Abadie and Gardeazabal (2003) to measure the costs of Basque terrorism, and it was subsequently applied by Abadie et al. (2015) to German reunification. Since the package Synth became available in Matlab, R and Stata, SCM has been widely used. Campos et al. (2019) use synthetic controls to construct counterfactual countries for countries that joined the European Union from 1973 to 2004. Except for Greece the effects are positive and on average, for those that benefitted, per capita incomes would have been about 10% lower had they not joined the EU.[3]

SCM uses the analogy with micro-econometric treatment effect studies, where one chooses controls that are similar in characteristics to those that are treated. One would match patients treated with a drug to untreated controls with similar covariates such as age, sex and health and compare the outcomes in the two groups. Similarity is usually measured by propensity score, the probability of being treated conditional on the covariates.

To determine the SCM weights w_i let $\mathbf{x}_{1kt}$ be a set of $k = 1,2,\ldots,K$ covariates or predictor variables for y_{1t}, with the corresponding variables in the other units given by $\mathbf{x}_{jkt}$, $j = 2,3,\ldots,N$. These variables are averaged over the pre-intervention period to get $\bar{\mathbf{x}}_{1k}^{T_0}$ and $\bar{\mathbf{X}}_k^{T_0}$ the N-1 × 1 vector of predictor k in the control group. Then the N-1 × 1 vector of weights $W = (w_2, w_3, \ldots, w_N)'$ are chosen to minimise

---

[3] In a related exercise, Akhmadieva and Smith (2019) look for structural breaks associated with the adoption of the euro.

$$\sum_{k=1}^{K} v_k \left(\overline{\mathbf{x}}_{1k}^{T_0} - \mathbf{W}' \overline{\mathbf{X}}_k^{T_0} \right)^2$$

subject to $\sum_{i}^{N} w_i = 1$, $w_i \geq 0$, where v_k is a weight that reflects the relative importance of variable k. Call the SCM weights $\tilde{w}_i$, many of them will be zero, for countries not included in the synthetic control.

SCM chooses the comparison units to be as similar as possible to the target along the dimensions included in $\mathbf{x}_{ikt}$. The v_k are often chosen by cross-validation, which may be problematic for potentially non-stationary time-series samples. The pre-intervention outcome variable may be included in $\mathbf{x}_{ikt}$; it is argued that matching on the pre-intervention outcomes helps control for the unobserved factors affecting the outcome of interest.

In the case of German Reunification, Abadie et al. (2015) use controls and weights w_i of Austria, 0.42, US, 0.22, Japan 0.16, Switzerland 0.11 and the Netherlands, 0.09. The synthetic West Germany is similar to the real West Germany in pre-1990 per capita GDP, trade openness, schooling, investment rate and industry share. As they note, there may be spillover effects. Since Austria, Switzerland and the Netherlands share borders with Germany, there is a distinct possibility that their post-1990 values may be influenced by German reunification. Those that are geographically the most similar are most likely to show spillover effects.

Given the way the SCM estimate is constructed, inference, testing whether the effect of the intervention is significant, is not straightforward.

The PDA was introduced by Hsiao et al. (2012), to measure the benefits of political and economic integration of Hong Kong with mainland China. They use the same measure of effect given above, using a weighted average as a counterfactual, but choose the weights by regression of y_{1t}, growth in Hong Kong, on y_{jt}, $j = 2,3,\ldots, N$, growth in the control countries during the pre-intervention period. Then using the pre-intervention estimates, they predict the post-intervention counterfactual as

$$\hat{y}_{1,T_0+h}^0 = \hat{\beta}_1^{T_0} + \sum_{i=2}^{N} \hat{\beta}_i^{T_0} y_{i,T_0+h}$$

Because the counterfactual is a forecast from a standard regression, inference is easier and they use robust standard errors to allow for serial correlation. The coefficients for most countries will be zero, only a subset of other countries is used to predict Hong Kong. The subset is chosen by a model selection procedure, but other procedures have been used. They emphasise that Hong Kong is too small for the effects of integration with China to influence any of the control countries. The control group, weights chosen by AIC for the period 1993:Q1–1997:Q2, are Japan -0.69, Korea -0.38, US 0.81, Philippines -0.16 and Taiwan 0.62. They find that the political integration had little effect on the growth rate, but that the subsequent economic integration did; an example of the issues in choosing when the treatment happened.

The motivation for the approach is that the outcome in a unit is determined by a vector of common factors, which have different effects on different countries. In a macroeconometric context, it is natural to think of very different countries driven by the same common trends: the 2008 crisis hit most countries, though to different degrees. They include the US in the controls, not because the US is like Hong Kong, the justification in the SCM procedure, but because US growth is a good predictor of Hong Kong growth. Factors are said to be strong if they influence almost every unit and weak if they only influence a subset of units.

Both SCM and PDA equations can be interpreted as regressions, but the SCM regression is constrained, it has no intercept and the weights are non-negative and sum to 1. The PDA regression is unconstrained. SCM, just matching on covariates, can be estimated with fewer pre-treatment observations than PDA, which requires the pre-intervention sample to be large enough to estimate a regression. SCM treats the other outcomes as providing controls, PDA treats them as providing predictors, and both are data-driven. SCM proponents criticise the fact that regression methods can give negative weights to controls. But this is to be expected if one interprets the procedure as involving prediction using common factors. Suppose Hong Kong before integration is largely driven by global factor A, the US by factors A and B, and Japan largely by factor B; then the US minus Japan provides an estimate of factor A, which drives Hong Kong.

Bove et al. (2017) use both SCM and PDA to measure the effect on GDP of Civil Wars. They find that the results from the two methods are similar, perhaps because they both tend to weight the same countries. What makes a large difference is whether the outcome measure modelled is log GDP or the change in log GDP, the growth rate. These give very different results for the costs of civil war to a country. The sensitivity of results to specification is always an issue.

The fact that the counterfactual is a prediction, means that we can learn from the forecasting literature about good ways to construct it. For instance, it is well known that averaging over forecasts improves performance and Hsiao and Zhou (2019) suggest averaging over counterfactuals produced by different procedures. Pesaran and Smith (2016) point out that simple parsimonious models tend to forecast better than ones with more parameters, so there are arguments for using simple models to generate the counterfactuals.

Counterfactuals differ from a conventional forecasts in that they tend to be about the past rather than the future and while eventually an actual will be revealed with which the forecast can be compared, with the counterfactual there will never be an actual to compare with the counterfactual. This presents a major difficulty for the evaluation of the different methods of generating counterfactuals. Because we never observe the truth, we cannot say which method gets us closest to the truth. To get around this problem, evaluation is often based on simulations, where by construction we do know the truth. But the results are then dependent on the choice of data-generating process, DGP, in the simulation. Gardeazabal and Vega-Bayo (2016) and Wan et al. (2018) differ on the appropriate way to define the DGP in simulations used to compare the SCM and PDA. The fundamental difficulty, that we cannot observe the counterfactual, cannot be avoided.

7   Conclusion

The questions confronted by comparative economics are inherently hard, thus it seems sensible to use all the tools that are available: employ a wide range of methods and evidence to investigate an issue. Diversification works in research as it does in finance, thus there are definite benefits from methodological pluralism. While there are also benefits from an academic division of labour, no particular technique should be regarded as particularly privileged. Data collection, descriptive statistics, summaries in the form of stylised facts and statistical models which are neither structural nor reduced form, all have their role to play alongside more formal theoretical and econometric techniques. In particular, it is crucial to supplement quantitative methods with more qualitative analysis using case studies, field work and archival research. The comparative method plays a central role in techniques like synthetic control which are used to provide counterfactuals to evaluate systemic changes like the unification of East and West Germany or of Hong Kong and China. If one is able to triangulate one's conclusions: show that the narrative history, other qualitative evidence, the relevant theories and the statistical analysis all point in the same direction, those conclusions are likely to be more persuasive.

The need to bring multiple pieces of evidence to bear also applies to econometricians using instrumental variables and other techniques to obtain causal estimates. Since any identification strategy depends on assumptions that are non-testable, such as just-identifying restrictions, the researcher must use other considerations than the data, to persuade the reader of the validity of the assumptions. Typically the researcher tries to construct a qualitative persuasive story to justify those assumptions as in the example given above from Angrist and Pischke (2009).

The importance of persuasive narratives in economics has long been recognised and is discussed by McCloskey (1983), writing on the rhetoric of economics, and more recently by Shiller (2019), writing on narrative economics and how stories become contagious and go viral. However, the certainties of methodological dogmatism may make it a more infectious story than the ambiguities of methodological pluralism, making dogmatism more likely to go viral.

References

Abadie, A., & Gardeazabal, J. (2003). The Economic Costs of Conflict: A Case Study of the Basque Country. *American Economic Review, 93*(1), 113–132.

Abadie, A., Diamond, A., & Hainmueller, J. (2015). Comparative Politics and the Synthetic Control Method. *American Journal of Political Science, 59*(2), 495–510.

Acemoglu, D., & Robinson, J. A. (2012). *Why Nations Fail: The Origins of Power, Prosperity and Poverty*. Profile: Books.

Acemoglu, D., Naidu, S., Restrepo, P., & Robinson, J. A. (2019). Democracy Does Cause Growth. *Journal of Political Economy, 127*(1), 47–100.

Akhmadieva, V., & Smith, R. P. (2019). *The Macroeconomic Impact of the Euro*. BCAM Working Paper, 1903. Birkbeck, University of London.

Alesina, A., & Giuliano, P. (2015). Culture and Institutions. *Journal of Economic Literature, 53*(4), 898–944.

Angrist, J. D., & Pischke, J.-S. (2009). *Mostly Harmless Econometrics: An Empiricists Companion*. Princeton University Press.

Angrist, J. D., & Pischke, J.-S. (2010). The Credibility Revolution in Empirical Economics: How Better Research Design Is Taking the Con Out of Econometrics. *Journal of Economic Perspectives, 24*(2), 3–30.

Autor, D., Dorn, D., Hanson, G., & Majlesi, K. (2016). *Importing Political Polarization? The Electoral Consequences of Rising Trade Exposure*. NBER Working Paper 22637.

Becker, S., Boeckh, K., Hainz, C., & Woessmann, L. (2016). The Empire Is Dead, Long Live the Empire! Long-Run Persistence of Trust and Corruption in the Bureaucracy. *The Economic Journal, 126*(Feb), 40–74.

Bove, V., Elia, L., & Smith, R. P. (2017). On the Heterogeneous Consequences of Civil War. *Oxford Economic Papers, 69*(3), 550–568.

Campos, N., Coricelli, F., & Moretti, L. (2019). Institutional Integration and Economic Growth in Europe. *Journal of Monetary Economics, 103*(May), 88–104.

Cavallo, A., Diewert, W. E., Feenstra, R. C., Inklaar, R., & Timmer, M. P. (2018). *Using Online Prices for Measuring Real Consumption Across Countries. AEA Papers and Proceedings, 108*(May), 483–487.

Cochrane, J. F. (2017). Macro-Finance. *Review of Finance, 21*, 945–985.

Crepon, B., Devoto, F., Duflo, E., & Pariente, W. (2019). *"Verifying the Internal Validity of a Flagship RCT: A Review of Crepon, Devoto, Duflo and Pariente": A Rejoinder.* Document de Travail DT/2019-07A.

Deaton, A. (2010). Instruments, Randomisation and Learning About Development. *Journal of Economic Literature, 48*(2), 424–455.

Deaton, A., & Cartwright, N. (2018). Understanding and Misunderstanding Randomized Controlled Trials. *Social Science & Medicine, 210*, 2–21.

Djankov, S., with Hauck, O. (2016). *The Divergent Postcommunist Paths to Democracy and Economic Freedom.* Working Paper 16-10 Peterson Institute for International Economics.

Feldstein, M., & Horioka, C. (1980). Domestic Saving and International Capital Flows. *Economic Journal, 90*(2), 314–329.

Freedman, L. (2017). *The Future of War: A History.* Allen Lane.

Friedman, M. (1957). *A Theory of the Consumption Function.* Princeton University Press.

Gardeazabal, J., & Vega-Bayo, A. (2016). An Empirical Comparison Between the Synthetic Control Method and Hsiao et al.'s Panel Data Approach to Program Evaluation. *Journal of Applied Econometrics, 32*(5), 983–1002.

Guiso, L., Herrera, H., Morelli, M., & Sonno, T. (2017). *Demand and Supply of Populism.* EIEF Working Papers Series 1703, Einaudi Institute for Economics and Finance (EIEF), revised Feb 2017.

Hsiao, C., & Zhou, Q. (2019). Panel Parametric, Semiparametric and Nonparametric Construction of Counterfactuals. *Journal of Applied Econometrics, 34*(4), 463–481.

Hsiao, C., Ching, H. S., & Shui, K. W. (2012). A Panel Data Approach for Program Evaluation: Measuring the Benefits of Political and Economic Integration of Hong Kong with Mainland China. *Journal of Applied Econometrics, 27*(5), 705–740.

Imbens, G. W. (2019). *Potential Outcome and Directed Acyclic Graph Approaches to Causality: Relevance for Empirical Practice in Economics.* NBER Working Paper 26104.

Inglehart, R. F., & Norris, P. (2016). *Trump Brexit and the Rise of Populism: Economic Have-Nots and Cultural Backlash.* Harvard Kennedy School RWP16-026.

Jones, C. I., & Klenow, P. J. (2016). Beyond GDP? Welfare Across Countries and Time. *American Economic Review, 106*(9), 2426–2457.

Jones, B. F., & Olken, B. A. (2009). Hit or Miss? The Effect of Assassinations on Institutions and War. *American Economic Journal: Macroeconomics, 1*(2), 55–87.

Jones, C. I., & Romer, P. M. (2010). The New Kaldor Facts: Ideas, Institutions, Population and Human Capital. *American Economic Journal: Macroeconomics, 2*(1), 224–245.

Kaldor, N. (1957). A Model of Economic Growth. *The Economic Journal, 67*(268, Dec), 591–624.

Kaldor, N. (1961). Capital Accumulation and Economic Growth. In F. A. Lutz & D. C. Hague (Eds.), *The Theory of Capital*. New York: St. Martin's Press.

Keuzenkamp, H. A., & Magnus, J. R. (1995). On Tests and Significance in Econometrics. *Journal of Econometrics, 67*(1), 5–24.

Klein, L. R., & Kosobud, R. F. (1961). Some Econometrics of Growth: Great Ratios of Economics. *The Quarterly Journal of Economics, 75*(2, May), 173–198.

McCloskey, D. N. (1983). The Rhetoric of Economics. *Journal of Economic Literature, 31*(2), 482–504.

Mehra, R., & Prescott, E. (1985). The Equity Premium: A Puzzle. *Journal of Monetary Economics, 15*(2), 145–162.

Pearl, J. (2009). *Causality: Models, Reasoning and Inference* (2nd ed.). Cambridge University Press.

Pesaran, M. H., & Smith, R. P. (2016). Counterfactual Analysis in Macroeconometrics: An Empirical Investigation into the Effects of Quantitative Easing. *Research in Economics, 70*(2), 262–280.

Sen, A. (1985). *Commodities and Capabilities*. North Holland.

Shiller, R. J. (2019). *Narrative Economics: How Stories Go Viral and Drive Major Economic Events*. Princeton University Press.

Sims, C. A. (2010). But Economics Is Not an Experimental Science. *Journal of Economic Perspectives, 24*(2), 59–68.

Solow, R. (1970). *Growth Theory: An Exposition*. Oxford University Press.

Stevens-Davidowitz, S. (2017). *Everybody Lies: Big Data, New Data and What the Internet Can Tell Us About Who We Really Are*. Harper Collins.

Summers, L. H. (1991). The Scientific Illusion in Empirical Macroeconomics. *Scandinavian Journal of Economics, 93*(2), 129–148.

Uberti, L. J. (2018). Corruption in Transition Economies: Socialist, Ottoman or Structural? *Economic Systems, 42*(4), 533–555.

Voigt, S. (2018). How to Measure Informal Institutions. *Journal of Institutional Economics, 14*(1), 1–22.

Wan, S.-K., Xie, Y., & Hsiao, C. (2018). Panel Data Approach vs Synthetic Control Method. *Economics Letters, 164*, 121–123.

36

Conclusion: So, What Is Comparative Economics Now?

Elodie Douarin and Oleh Havrylyshyn

1 Approaching a Conclusion

This handbook contains a very large number of different individual chapters addressing a wide variety of topics using a comparative analytical approach, as well as chapters which represent examples of what comparative economics is today and thus owe something to the parent field of Comparative Economic Systems (CES). There are many different ways one might approach providing a summary and conclusions for such a collection, and to cut through this extensive forest of research, we propose to take the following approach. First, in Sect. 2, we will summarize briefly the main findings of each contribution, and to maintain some systematic perspective, we will do so largely following the different themes designated by the seven parts of the handbook. Second, having thus given a succinct image of all the different trees in this forest, Sect. 3 will then step back to characterize the forest itself: what overarching

E. Douarin
School of Slavonic and East European Studies, University College London, London, UK
e-mail: e.douarin@ucl.ac.uk

O. Havrylyshyn (✉)
Carleton University, Ottawa, ON, Canada
e-mail: olehhavrylyshyn@cunet.carleton.ca

© The Author(s) 2021
E. Douarin, O. Havrylyshyn (eds.), *The Palgrave Handbook of Comparative Economics*,
https://doi.org/10.1007/978-3-030-50888-3_36

conclusions and implications can one draw from this diverse collection? Third and finally, Sect. 4 will turn back, full circle, to the genesis of this handbook, to finally address the question engendered by the dissolution of the communist regimes, that is, *if there are no more economic systems to compare, is there any comparative economics to be done—and what is it?*

Before moving on, however, an important qualifier is in order here. The conclusions summarized in this chapter for each individual chapter, as well as the broader common lessons, represent the interpretations and understandings of the editors. All authors have provided their own conclusions at the end of each chapter, and we have attempted to hew closely to those. However, in the belief that the whole is greater than the sum of the parts, we have drawn a picture of the interrelationships and commonalities, and any shortcomings of our interpretations are attributable to the editors alone.

2 The Main Findings of Individual Contributions

The four chapters in Part I describe the traditional field of Comparative Economic Systems (CES) and implicitly or explicitly debate whether it has continued relevance or is indeed best replaced by a focus on what now matters most, the quality of institutions. Brada's historiography of CES spans millennia from Plato, through the Middle Ages and philosophers like Ibn Khaldun[1] to late-twentieth-century textbooks comparing market capitalism and socialist central planning. He concludes that not only is the task of comparisons old standing, but it will also continue. With a neutral value-free approach, because any normative position is temporary with the coming and going of "fads", about whether the criterion of comparison should be efficiency as it was recently, or institutional quality as proposed now, Dallago and Casagrande offer a more moderated view on such "fads": after a thorough and in-depth reasoned critique of the claim by Djankov et al. (2003) that CES must now give way to a new comparative approach focused on institutions, they end up recommending a compromise: there are enough differences in systems (varieties of capitalism) to justify continued traditional comparison, but there should be no question that investigating the role of institutions is very valuable.

The chapter of Balcerowicz is broadly consistent with this compromise, as it emphasizes that there is an almost organic link between different political economy systems and institutions, and this then ties in to understanding why

---

[1] Who, Brada argues, presaged the neo-classical axioms of Adam Smith.

for example the Soviet system was a failure. His analysis incidentally points to the importance of both the economics and politics of regimes,[2] from which one should infer that there is often a need to integrate work of political science and economics to achieve useful comparisons. Gregory takes a much narrower approach, using post-1992 access to Soviet archival material to dispel a myth of CES that the leadership made decisions for the greatest good, aiming to maximize some inferred welfare function. In addition to revealing the self-interested inner workings among various Soviet agencies, his insights can be viewed through the political economy lens, noted by others, and confirming the methodological conclusion: a full understanding of how different regimes function and why their outcomes differ requires a multidisciplinary approach. The motivations, in particular, of different actors seem to rarely fit the typical assumptions made by economists.

With Part I having set the stage by debating the relative merits of the traditional economic systems comparisons and the newer institutional focus, the chapters of Part II take a very long look back at the history of different economic regimes, their institutions and their performance. Some chapters show how useful comparisons across polities in some earlier period can be to understand relative success in economic performance (Havrylyshyn, Roland); others investigate the long-term persistence of preceding cultural and institutional characteristics and their effect on current developments.

Thus, Havrylyshyn compiles a few proxies for institutional quality in Dalmatian city-states like Ragusa (today's Dubrovnik), Zadar or Split and shows that good institutions did indeed result in strong economic performance for Ragusa—but not the others. The reason may be that mighty Venice occupied the others and restricted their ability to trade freely, as a way to maintain its own monopoly. Ragusa, in contrast, remained independent and was thus able to leverage strong institutions into economic success. The conclusion? Institutions always mattered, but so too did forces of history—like military might. Roland first describes an enormous new data bank retrospectively rating institutions in polities of mediaeval period and even far back in antiquity (Egypt, China and others). A key and most relevant conclusion is that regimes fall into two clusters of institutions: statist, or market oriented—echoing to some extent the correspondence of institutions and systems noted by Balcerowicz, but also pointing to the fact that the twentieth-century comparisons of socialism and capitalism can be done fruitfully far back in time by economic history researchers. Roland's analysis, for example, demonstrates

---

[2] A theme reflected in many chapters throughout the book: including Roland, Novokmet, Djankov, Aslund, Guriev, Douarin, Fidrmuc, Cojocaru and Mickiewicz.

that specific geographical conditions can be used to explain the appearance of a given historical regime-type over the other, and that historical regime-types are associated, centuries later, to important differences in the values held by descendant populations.

The three other chapters use empirical analysis to demonstrate the very long-term persistence of historical forces—culture, institutions, policies—and their influence on specific outcomes even to the present day. Kung covers the longest period of analysis, from the imperial periods of China almost a millennium back to present-day phenomena, specifically educational attainments and entrepreneurship. He first describes the gradual introduction of meritocratic civil exams for officials over the sixth to tenth centuries to allow commoners equality of opportunity relative to elite members. Then, he undertakes some econometric analysis within municipalities of China, concluding that ancient success rates in such exams for a given family (surname) correlate positively and significantly with current levels of human capital and entrepreneurship. To be able to demonstrate that a cultural institution established a millennium ago still affects relevant phenomena today is at a minimum unique.

An analogous correlation, but over a "mere" 500 years or less, is presented by Djankov. In a cross-country analysis with change in economic liberalization and democratization indicators during the transition as dependent variables, he tests the hypothesis that historical and cultural forces—specifically religious affiliation and colonial status under imperial regimes of Ottoman Empire, Tsarist Russia or Austro-Hungary—still had a differential impact. The econometrics suggests differences in democratization are far more affected by history than economic reforms. Addressing a narrower but currently extremely important theme, inequality trends of post-communist countries, Novokmet comes to two interesting conclusions: first, over the period from the late nineteenth century, they all exhibit the same long-term U-shape with high inequality, then a narrowing, followed by a widening in recent decades—attributable to variations in policy; second, countries in Central Europe exhibit less inequality than Russia throughout. In doing so, Novokmet thus points toward an important, and sometimes neglected, dimension when one studies long-term trends in a specific outcome: the importance of ideology. Indeed, even market economies had lower levels of inequality when communism represented a credible alternative, as perhaps redistribution was ideologically better accepted, overall and everywhere, then.

One way of perceiving Part III is as the current-day pivot around which the handbook turns from forces of past history to the very diverse, multi-issue and multidisciplinary issue of where social science analysis is trending for the future. Of course, the chapters here also comprise a useful 30-year retrospective on the outcome of the very unique phenomenon of transition from planned communist regimes to market democracies. To set the stage, Havrylyshyn describes 30 years of transition in nearly 30 countries, presenting statistics for various socio-economic measures. From this a number of stylized facts are drawn, of which three main tendencies stand out. Almost all countries have experienced a transformation into market economies, though democratization was far from achieved in the FSU; a sharp decline in output in the nineties was followed by two decades of recovery, sometimes faster, sometimes slower, but overall enough that eventually all attained living standards well beyond Soviet ones. But the degree and pace of these changes were distinctly greater in Central Europe and the Baltics than in the rest of the Former Soviet Union. That these changes have been great enough to turn post-communist countries into "normal" developing countries is demonstrated in fine comparative detail by Wachtel. He indeed provides an extensive quantitative picture of the current states of these countries, arguing that they have by now ceased to transit away from central planning, and can simply be considered as typical developing countries or emerging economies, like any other countries at similar levels of development. One intriguing exception is noted however: this normalization has not yet been achieved in financial sectors. An important implication for research may thus be that issues of "how to do transition" are now firmly in the past. Current problems for policymakers in the region are therefore now much the same as in other emerging markets.

The chapters by Aslund and Guriev focus on the political economy of the transition process, illuminating the circular causation involved. Aslund argues, with many concrete illustrations, that strong commitment by leaders, including a willingness to risk political standing by moving rapidly, was an essential element in achieving an early and successful transition, which itself enhances the society's commitment. However, other circumstances are critical to facilitate strong leadership, such as a democratic breakthrough based on mass mobilization,[3] a strong civil society and national cohesion. Guriev also shows one cannot truly understand transition unless it is seen as the political economy interaction between underlying political structures and vested interests on one hand and the need for economic liberalization on the other hand. This is consistent with Aslund's descriptions, though Guriev gives greater emphasis to the socio-political consequences of incomplete reforms, the renowned "winners take all" phenomenon and the creation of an oligarch class, whose

---

[3] Later, Chap. 20 by Fidrmuc shows the econometric relation between democratization and transition reforms.

interests differ from that of society at large, and whose power prevents complete reforms.

While the above look inside transition countries to understand the process, the chapters of Campos and Tanzi, each in its own way, look from the outside. In Campos, one will find a rigorous econometric analysis confirming the widely held view that the quest for EU membership provided a strong incentive to undertake early and resolute reforms, both on the economic and political fronts. This "EU Anchor" resulted in a far more advanced development of institutions by Central European and Baltic country candidates than seen in the FSU. Tanzi's reflections on transition start by stepping back to review both the theory and practice of socialist central planning, to show why it failed and why the transition to market capitalism was essential. He then assesses the efforts of outside agencies in supporting/guiding the needed changes, with a special emphasis on the International Monetary Fund (IMF), elaborating on both the things that were done right and those that were not. Implicitly he attributes the errors to outsider's insufficient understanding of that history which led to the need for transition.

The chapter by Douarin takes a different tack—it draws some retrospective lessons from developments in the transition literature to suggest a broader future research agenda on understanding not only the role of institutions, but also the process of their evolution. She shows how the policy focus evolved from the too-simple view of transition as a natural experiment to the deeper concept of comprehensive institutional transformation. Delving into this then reveals one must better understand societal preferences, culture and history as key elements for future pluri-disciplinary research.

Part III thus takes stock of the experience of transition, as a momentous event in the development of comparative economics. It shows a progressive opening of the field, away from the narrow focus of the early years and toward a broadening of the outcomes and key drivers considered—thus reflecting the evolution described by Brada or Dallago and Casagrande in Part I. But looking beyond transition in Central and Eastern Europe, Parts IV, V and VI reinforce the importance and relevance of this evolution.

First, Part IV groups together chapters taking the precepts of New Comparative Economics seriously, by focusing on its central concern—the key role of institutions in economic growth—but also pushing this further to qualify the limitations and mechanisms through which institutions have an influence. Thus, Fidrmuc revisits the relationship between democratization and economic growth focusing on previously centrally planned economies (both in Central and Eastern Europe, and Southeast and East Asia) to emphasize the importance of institutional quality for growth. But more importantly, he demonstrates the role of "democratic capital" for growth: a cumulative effect associated with the length of time during which democratic institutions persist. However, he does not limit his analysis to the role of institutions, but also considers important policy changes (namely those associated with economic liberalization). In doing so, he goes beyond what some see as one of the key limitations of New Institutional Economics (e.g. Brada) in its relative disregard for policies. His results contrast with findings in worldwide studies—thus he argues for a more careful investigation into country-level heterogeneity, driven by geographical or historical legacies. Chapter 18 by Uberti and Knutsen also explicitly complements the institutional focus with an analysis of the simultaneous role of other policies. They present an extensive review of the literature linking institutional quality to growth, but exploring specifically how human capital nuances the picture. Institutions matter has now become common sense and more needs to be understood of why and how it matters. So, starting from an existing debate in the literature regarding the relative role played by human capital and institutional quality, they make use of a new very long-term data set to investigate the role of property rights protection and human capital in economic performance. They conclude that both have a direct effect on growth, but also that conditional on human capital, property rights institutions only appear to foster growth for middle-income and high-income countries.

Thus, if both contributions can be seen as emerging from the broad "New Institutional Economics" tradition, they offer qualifying conclusions, as far as the field as a whole is concerned: the first regards the role of policies in association with institutions—institutional quality might be important for growth, but countries with comparable institutions may still make widely different policy choices that might complement and enhance the benefits of good institutions, or not. Thus, these contributions echo the eclectic broadening of the field discussed in Part I, and illustrate that a too narrow focus on institutions might be insufficient. The second key contribution regards cross-country heterogeneity; both chapters do demonstrate that there is still a lot that we cannot control for in cross-section analysis, and ignoring that heterogeneity can be misleading. A narrower focus, supported by an understanding of the specificities of the subregions or subsamples investigated, can thus be fruitful.

And indeed, these can be illustrated with Chaps. 19 and 21, as they go further along these two directions. First, Chap. 19 makes a convincing argument for a more detailed analysis of policies, as constituents of an overall coherent (or not) effort to generate growth. Oliveira Martins and Rocha present the theoretical basis of their view and demonstrate through a careful review of recent econometric studies the importance of policy complementarities. Thus, not only policies matter, but also how and when they are implemented also matters.

Finally, in Chap. 21, Lin implicitly revisits the idea of system/policy complementarities, by arguing that policies can only be said to be appropriate or inappropriate with careful consideration for initial conditions, which he calls "endowment structure", and which encompass not only geographical conditions and natural resources endowment, but also the demographic characteristics of the population, human capital, availability of capital and so on. In a comprehensive approach aimed at guiding policy-making for economic development—the New Structural Economics—Lin thus argues not only for a detailed analysis of the starting point conditions, but also for a reflection on realistic stages of development, built through appropriate comparative analysis.

Overall, all these chapters thus recognize, implicitly or explicitly, the importance of institutions, but call for a more careful investigation of context—be it the policy context, or other country-specific characteristics. They therefore illustrate comparative economics as a discipline promoting "context-rich" economic analysis.

Part V then explores a broadening of the goals, beyond economic growth only. This, as suggested earlier by both Brada and Dallago and Casagrande, is in fact a partial return to the broader objectives advocated by researchers of Comparative Economic Systems, and a move that reflects both a recognition that transition economies are becoming "normal" emerging economies (as was argued by Wachtel) and thus a progressive evolution of comparative economics away from "transition economics" and maybe closer to "development economics" (reflecting partly the discussion in Douarin). Consistently, Chap. 22 by Kharas and MacArthur presents a rethinking of the goals of development, away from economic growth and toward more precisely defined goals, arguably, more country-specific goals, reflecting a need to consider the sustainability of development and the need to address some of the most unjust global and national disparities. Some of the recommendations they advance thus announce the discussions coming in Chaps. 23, 24, 25, and 26. Chapter 23 by Gerry focuses on health, as a key outcome to measure progress, rather than growth and brings a completely different picture on the well-being impact of growth—confirming Kharas and MacArthur's contention that growth does not, by itself, improve well-being and thus may not be the unique goal of development. In fact, Gerry concludes on a complex interplay between culture and history explaining how individual's perceived role and status impact on their outlook and thus their health more strongly than growth only. "Growth alone is not enough" is also a conclusion that can be derived from Sanfey's chapter. Indeed, he presents a retrospective of what has been learned from life satisfaction studies over 30 years in Eastern Europe. With a detailed review of the literature, he argues that we now have a better understanding of the ingredients of a good life, and they include a profit-driven private sector as well as socially oriented government policies. Impressive progress has been made throughout the transition region, but more work remains to get the balance right and create a sustainable and efficient system, promoting both growth and well-being. Finally, Johnston presents a demographic analysis of China's recent development path, to draw lessons for other emerging economies including in Central and Eastern Europe. Her argumentation implicitly refers to the political economy of reforms and the difficult balance to be made between convincing the population at large that reforms are worthwhile and keeping promises in check to limit disillusionment or inter-generational injustice. Overall, this part of the book firmly argues for a people-focused approach to development, balancing short-term objectives with sustainability and fairness in the longer run.

Part VI provides some further illustrations of ways through which comparative analysis has evolved in recent years to include insights from other disciplines and broaden the goals even further. The chapters by Cojocaru (Chap. 27), Gërxhani and Wintrobe (Chap. 30) and Radosevic and Yoruk (Chap. 32) introduce the issue of perception and values in the way people assess their expectation and views on success (Chap. 27) or how they respond to formal institutions (Chaps. 30 and 31). More specifically, in Chap. 27, Cojocaru discusses how inequality relates to life satisfaction. He provides convincing evidences that perception of inequality matters much more than inequality *per se*. In addition, these perceptions of inequality, especially inequality of opportunity and if they are seen as unfair, further impact on people's policy preferences. The evidence he presents thus hints toward a vicious circle situation where negative perception hinders support for further change, when this change could actually contribute to reduce inequality. In a similar way to Guriev in Part III, Cojocaru thus concludes that there may be a need to manage expectations when designing policy reforms.

In Chap. 30, Gërxhani and Wintrobe propose that citizens' interaction with the state can be presented as "trust-based" exchanges, in the logic of a repeated game where actors build trust over time. Their theoretical model contributes to explaining why both formal institutions (the states and its representants) and informal institutions (such as society-specific social norms) matter to understand the behavior of individual citizens. Using Albanian data, they then demonstrate that the prediction of the model is indeed confirmed for tax evasion. Following a similar logic, Ledeneva and Efendic (Chap.

31) investigate the interplay between formal and informal institutions implicitly through the decision to invest in an informal network of trusted people. They argue that individual's decision to invest in these relationships represents a response to both the quality of formal institutions, and the mechanisms available within society to substitute these formal institutions. They provide qualitative and quantitative evidence of this substitutive effect.

Then the chapters by Mickiewicz (Chap. 28) and Ivlevs (Chap. 29) investigate drivers of political institutional change; the former in the form of a populist takeover of power and the latter as potentially driven by migration. Mickiewicz investigates the drivers of populism in Europe in comparative perspective, first reviewing the literature and experiences in Latin America in particular. He then discusses the specificities of Eastern European populism and argues that the populist rise in the region cannot be explained by economic factors alone, and instead specific historical and cultural factors are at play. However, populist parties in Poland or Hungary have been hard at play dismantling the institutional setup—using in particular the tools of clientelism. The author questions how populism can be removed and points toward a possible peaceful end to populism in the region. In contrast, Ivlevs is interested in institutional change driven by citizens through the circulation of (imported) ideas that can possibly change views. Ivlevs proposes a detailed and critical review of the literature to illustrate the level of accumulated evidence on the role of migration for institutional change. In particular, he is interested in the degree to which people who have chosen to migrate away can "remit" ideas back home that then lead to democratization. He concludes that the evidence accumulated does indeed tend to show a link toward political institutional change back home especially when migrants have moved to more democratic settings. He also indicates that this result is often credibly causal. He then concludes from his review on a need for greater and closer collaboration across the disciplines, as social remittances have long been studied by sociologists and political scientists but have only recently been investigated by economists.

Finally, Radosevic and Yoruk argue for a greater need to understand institutions as systems, so as to recognize that a number of economic activities and outcomes, such as entrepreneurship, are in fact a societal product—at least to the extent that would-be entrepreneurs can only act with the infrastructure available, within the existing social rules and given their personal skills. Thus, entrepreneurship and possibly even innovation cannot be conceptualized as produced by a self-interested individual in isolation, instead it needs to be understood as caused by a large range of factors in complex systems. The chapter presents an organized review of the literature, presenting three strands of literature arguing for such a conceptualization of entrepreneurship, discussing their key advantages and drawbacks.

Overall, Part VI thus reflects chapters recognizing a greater degree of complexity in the way outcomes are reached. Indeed, for some, citizens make decisions based on their beliefs and perceptions rather than on objective facts, bringing in notions of identity, social norms, expectations or narratives. One fundamental dimension to understand thus becomes the human decision-making process, away from the simplistic assumption of selfish utility or profit maximization—or at least where the utility to be maximized is more complex than what is usually envisaged in economics textbooks. Then for others, the relevant concept is that of system—thus recognizing the joint effect of formal and informal institutions, reflecting the amalgamation of formal and informal institutions into an overall set of rules consistent with North (1995).

Finally, Part VII presents some interesting methodological innovations, but these chapters also contribute to a better understanding of what comparative economics is today by presenting findings of interests in their own rights. First, in Chap. 33, Bruno and Estrin reflect on important changes brought about by the switch from typology to taxonomy in the way systems are defined. They present a critical review of the terms and some illustrations of what they mean in practice. They subsequently develop an example, where, using an existing taxonomy, they demonstrate empirically its relevance to our understanding of the relative economic performance of firms in under-studied economies. They conclude arguing for a greater use of taxonomies to dig further into the definitions and assessments of systems, institutional complementarities and the possibilities of equifinality. In Chap. 34, Gagliardi also focuses on institutional complementarities, but this time by producing an exhaustive bibliometric account of the evolution of a subfield of research in comparative capitalism. In doing so, she presents a form of literature review, maybe less often used than meta-analysis, or narrative reviews, but providing unique insights into the place and evolution of a given field of investigation. Finally, Smith in Chap. 35 presents a detailed discussion of causal analyses, arguing for the value of descriptive evidence and cross-disciplinary collaborations to advance complex fields of research where much still remains to be learned. Smith follows the logical steps of an empirical analysis discussing how data availability, stylized facts and known associations are important to guide more advanced empirical work, relevant in their own rights. He then discusses different methodologies that can be used to demonstrate causality but warning explicitly about their limitations. Overall, in an argumentation also illustrated by Ivlevs' review, Smith calls for greater interdisciplinary dialogue, moving beyond divergent views on technicalities, to focus instead on mutual understanding and knowledge exchange.

3   The Big-Picture Lessons

When we step back from the details of the trees to see the big picture of this forest, a number of overarching lessons stand out from the collective findings of these contributions. To limit the discussion, we focus on three broad themes:

1. While study of institutions has not and will never completely replace comparisons of system characteristics, there can be no question that understanding the role and evolutionary process of institutional development must be part of any meaningful analysis of economic performance. However, while the early attempts at doing so were focused on simplifying the concept of "institutions", often narrowing it down to property rights protection, for example, recent literature embraces complexity to investigate the interplay between policies and institutions, between formal and informal institutions, and the possible complementarities between different institutions. In essence, institutions are increasingly seen as part and parcel of the entire system.

2. The collapse of the communist system and ensuing transition process, which had engendered the motivating question for this handbook, can now be said to be largely completed and out of the way—at least to the extent that transition economies can be considered to be "normal" emerging economies.[4] However, this unique 30-year "experiment" provides many useful lessons for development and socio-economic performance questions. In particular, they have highlighted that if common recipes might be applied to most when it comes to spurring economic development, it is still key to investigate in depth initial conditions and country-specific factors. Institutions matter, but so do policies, and so do their combinations, and so do historical and cultural legacies and so on.

3. Accordingly, beyond transition, there is no single silver bullet policy to achieve the goals of general well-being for all members of a society—no matter how one turns and finesses analysis of past performance, one finds that in some combination or other, short-term macro policies always matter, but so too do longer term refinements of institutions, and deeply

---

[4] Arguably, this might be a lowering of the objective of transition, which some have argued should have been to catch up with the standards of living of advanced western economies.

rooted historical forces (which are also less controllable by even the wisest of policy-makers).

We elaborate further on these three lessons.

3.1   Institutions and Varying Regime Characteristics Are Not Really Separable

High-quality institutions like rule of law, fair treatment for all citizens, equality of economic opportunity, protection of personal and property rights and so on are a necessary ingredient for all successful social arrangements, but these can come in different varieties and evolve at a different pace, with different combinations of statist and individualistic character. Thus, the best resolution to the trade-off between institutions and systems is a blending of the two. Comparative analysis of past performance—even very far back in history—and policy recommendations for the future are probably incomplete unless both elements are studied and their interplay considered. As several chapters in Parts II, III and IV have demonstrated, there is a symbiotic relationship between institutions and macro policies, they contain strong complementarities, the interplay of democracy and economic efficiency cannot be ignored—but at the same time, it is clear especially from Asian experience that narrower economic success is possible in a partially capitalist market economy. The broader goals of new approaches to development investigated in Part V, like health, life satisfaction, problems of aging as well as a variety of new issues of the day like inequality and populism, all require in-depth understanding of policies, institutions and the inertia of cultural norms rooted in history.

3.2   Transition May Be Over, but Its Unique Experiences Carry Many Lessons for Future Analysis of (Economic) Development

Perhaps the main development lesson from post-communist transition of Eurasian countries is that indeed incentives of properly competitive markets and private ownership result in superior economic performance—and this is not contradicted by the success of China and Vietnam as academics tend to agree that allowing private entrepreneurs to act in competitive markets, rather than improving efficiency of state enterprises, was the main factor behind their rapid growth and development.[5] However, achieving success is conditional on two points. First, one must ensure sufficiently high-quality institutions are developed in parallel, not only to have good property rights protection, but also to have fair rule of law that, for example, ensures competitive entry, generally maintains competition and guarantees fair treatment to all firms. Secondly, policies must be in place to avoid non-competitive aspects of markets such as insider privileges, rent-seeking activities, political dominance by large economic vested interests and so on. The latter problems—captured in the term "oligarchy"[6]—have two negative consequences: a suppression of small- and medium-sized businesses, which reduces overall growth performance, and sometimes extraordinary deterioration of income and wealth distributions (i.e. rising inequality). These are well known in the transition literature but have considerable relevance in other contexts, and may thus provide guidance for broader work in the field of comparative economics.

3.3   Policies, Institutions and Historical Forces All Matter in Some Combination

Many individual chapters show how policies combined with institutions do affect the attainment of specific societal goals; others show that history may play an important role by constraining or facilitating good policies; and some explicitly suggest that all three factors—policies, institutions, historical forces—function as a complex way to affect the overall result. In a word, they all matter. This may seem at first to be an unhelpful conclusion for understanding social and economic tendencies and inferring recommendations, but paradoxically it may to the contrary be very useful: to know that in different measures and in different times and circumstances, some combination of historical and current forces all play a role might be a salutary lesson for policymakers. Such a view of socio-economic dynamics may also help reconcile two apparently contradictory arguments concerning economic development. Some analysts contend all countries and societies face the same challenges in promoting high growth, and therefore the policies that should be pursued need to be more or less the same; the strategy implied in the Washington

---

[5] This is furthermore not inconsistent with the view of many observers that the very high growth rates until recently were also facilitated by their stage of development, that is, shifting the agricultural surplus into manufacturing and services.

[6] It is notable how the use of the word "oligarch" has spread from its nineties application in the former Soviet space to a wider global usage.

consensus epitomizes this position. Many analysts—especially with reference to their own country—frequently retort that: "our society is unique, it differs from others in its history, culture, values." These points of view may be reconciled as follows: the policies and minimal institutional requirements that will give the best outcomes are broadly similar for all countries, but the decisions made by political leaders and elites in each society on if, when and in what sequence to implement such policies are indeed unique and specific to each society, and generally depend on underlying historical forces.

4 Is There a Definition for the New Comparative Economics?

The main objective of scholarly analysis comparing different economies and different economic systems has always been *to seek and identify the socio-economic arrangements which lead to the best outcome for all members of the society*. In western societies of antiquity, the goal, as for example set out by Plato, was to have all citizens achieve justice and social virtue, material attainments being only a means to that end. In an analogous manner, Confucianism recognizes the satisfaction of basic needs, at least to reach a status of safety and relative comfort, as an important factor for well-being. However, much more weight is given to maintaining social ties, contributing to society and the pursuit of the common good. Eighteenth-century Enlightenment scholars like Jeremy Bentham and particularly Adam Smith defined the goal more narrowly, focusing on maximizing well-being or even more narrowly output and wealth—though such approaches had been presaged by some medieval scholars like Ibn Khaldun. The turn to self-interest of each (and all?) individual became the principal paradigm followed in economic analysis since then. However, as the chapters in Parts V and VI make clear, a new tendency to broaden societal goals is appearing. Looking at it this way, a very broad all-encompassing and timeless definition might be: *comparative economics comprise scholarly analysis searching for the optimal social arrangement*.

But this last definition is so broad that it covers not only comparative economics, but also any economics, and any social science research, either by comparing entities in a horse race to identify the characteristics of the best performers, or by assessing all against a specific goal. A little better may be a definition that is almost mechanical—*economic studies that try to understand important issues of the day by comparing how different countries, systems, deal with these issues*. The wide diversity of issues addressed and methodologies applied in the chapters of this handbook exemplify such a definition.[7] But if one insists on asking what defines the most recent forms of comparative economics, it is best to think of it, simply, as the use of comparative analysis to address *new* issues, or *new* goals, and recognize *new* knowledge at the frontiers of economics starting with the consensus that no serious analysis of optimal policy arrangements can ignore the critical role of institutions. Doing so, again as exemplified by the chapters of this handbook, does mean recognizing the benefits of pluri-disciplinary dialogue—at the very least it should today be clear that political and economic developments are closely intertwined, and economists have thus much to learn from political scientists. But at the same time, recent insights into the role of legacies, values, norms, identities and perceptions mean that sociologists, anthropologists, psychologists and also historians have much to contribute too. Overall, this implies an approach that recognizes important lessons from economic theory, and applies them in a context-rich analysis.

The above efforts to pin down a definition may strike the reader as flailing and raise the question whether a definition is needed at all. It is certainly not necessary to have a definition in order to go ahead and do good academic research, comparing countries or societies, and the 36 chapters attest to that: none of the authors, to the best of our knowledge, worried about a definition of what they were doing, whether it was new or traditional, and in what way comparative. Nevertheless given the genesis of this handbook as described in the introduction, that the demise of socialist central planning regimes of the Soviet type removed one half of the pair that was the basis of comparison in the field of Comparative Economic Systems, some sort of answer should be given to the question: *what is comparative economics now, and how new is it?* Without imposing a "pigeon-hole" upon the work of scholars making comparative analysis, our preferred wording would be the following one from above: *the use of (implicit or explicit) comparative analysis to address new issues, or new goals, and recognizing new knowledge as it evolves, including the critical role of institutions in its broader sense.*

---

[7] This is also more meaningful without slipping into the trite but true fallback definition: comparative economics is what comparative economists do.

Index[1]

---

[1] Note: Page numbers followed by 'n' refer to notes.

© The Author(s) 2021   **957**
E. Douarin, O. Havrylyshyn (eds.), *The Palgrave Handbook of Comparative Economics*,
https://doi.org/10.1007/978-3-030-50888-3